THEOLOGY FOR TODAY

THEOLOGY
FOR
TODAY

Elmer L. Towns

Harcourt College Publishers
Harcourt *Custom* Publishers

**Fort Worth Philadelphia San Diego New York Orlando Austin San Antonio
Toronto Montreal London Sydney Tokyo**

Editor: Joann Manos
Production Manager: Sue Dunaway
Production Coordinator: Lesley Kwan
Marketing Coordinator: Sara Hinckley

ISBN 0-15-516138-5

The Adaptable Courseware Program consists of products and additions to existing Custom Publishing products that are produced from camera-ready copy. Peer review, class testing, and accuracy are primarily the responsibility of the author(s).

TABLE OF CONTENTS

INTRODUCTION

They tell me theology is "out" because Baby Boomers did not want doctrine or theoretical teaching in the church. They want practical topics that will help them live for Christ. As a result, doctrine has taken a back seat in lay Bible study groups to such topics as "How to Parent" or "How to Manage Money" or "How to Overcome Depression." Even our seminaries are decreasing the required hours in theology, replacing doctrine in the curriculum with courses in counseling, strategies of leadership, and staff management. While these are all good and necessary, remember; theology is the foundation for our belief.

Sadly, many treat theology as something that is boring or irrelevant, but theology is at the core of allowing God and His plan into our lives. The Bible was not written as a theology book. At times it reads like a newspaper, or like the words of a song, or at other times like a message in a letter. The Bible is God's message communicated to every day people as only God would do it; i.e., accurately, consistently, and with authority. Because God is God, we can trust the Bible.

My love affair with theology began as a little boy sitting on the swing of the front porch of my mother's home where I would memorize the Children's Westminster Catechism. By the time I was in the third grade, mother made sure I could accurately answer all of the questions; and I am sure my catechism training gave me a high view of the sovereignty of God, His presence in my life, and the fact that my whole life should be lived in accountability to Him. As a little kid, we would stand in front of the Sunday school audience at Eastern Heights Presbyterian Church for a quiz, boys against girls.

"Children, you must answer the questions accurately, every word must be in place," pastor Lawrence Williams would tell us.

I always agonized because I was never the last boy standing. As a child I rationalized, "At least I am better than most of the boys . . ." You see Albert Freundt (who became professor of Church History, Reformed Presbyterian Seminary, Jackson, Mississippi) always got every question right . . . every word was right. I could get the answers right, it's just that once in a while I would get tripped up on a word. "Elmer, you missed a word and you will have to sit down," Lawrence Williams would smile at me as I took my seat with the other children. Then he would turn to one of the girls and repeat the question. The girls were good, but none of them were as perfect as Albert Freundt.

Because of the strong Calvinistic background, I developed a deep sense of the sovereignty

1

of God who directs, controls, and is present in every area of my life. When I entered Columbia Bible College, (now Columbia International University), I was a committed five-point Calvinist, and I enjoyed my study at CBC. As a matter of fact, I learned as much systematic theology in the shower room as I did in my doctrine classes at Columbia. I've often said that one of the best places to "hammer-out" your systematic theology is in the shower room. For there, you stand naked, as surely as we all are naked before God. It was at these times that we would argue eternal security, election, total depravity, limited atonement and the perseverance of the saints.

In the shower room, you can't rely on your Bible or your notes. You have nothing in your hand but soap or a towel. What you are theologically is what you are when you have no notes to help you.

And when you are hammering on someone else's alleged false doctrine, they hammer back. Call it arguing, dialogue or debating, but in reality it was just plain "hammering." We always pointed out the weaknesses in the other's system, but usually we were blind to the chinks in our own armor.

Shower room theology makes us stronger and more committed to our beliefs, and it forces us "to give an answer for the hope that is within us . . . ." But shower room theology also reinforces our bias and our limited view of life. For in these moments we reach out for any life preserver as in a storm, and we will say anything to win the argument; rather than being on a mutual quest for the truth of God.

When I transferred from Columbia Bible College to Northwestern College, Minneapolis, Minnesota, I did more than leave the south and go to a school in the north. I left the friendly confines of a college that was oriented towards the Presbyterian church and strong five-point Calvinism. Northwestern College grew out of First Baptist Church, Minneapolis, Minnesota, and there I was immersed into dispensationalism, a system that my Presbyterian pastors had taught me was wrong.

My senior seminar in Bible radically changed my thinking. We read and discussed Eric Sauer's book *The Dawn of World Redemption* (Eerdmans). This book was a theological survey of the Old Testament and convinced me dispensationalism was biblical.

I am not ashamed to be called a dispensationalist; however, read carefully what I say for I don't agree totally with many of those holding the historic position of dispensationalism, nor the present positions of progressive dispensationalism. The author is a Calvinist; however, I do not agree with the five major points of Calvinism. I feel hyper-Calvinists tend towards fatalism. Yet in the way the church understands the word Calvinism, I would be identified with that position because I believe in the over-arching sovereignty of God in the world, the depravity of man that he cannot save himself, and the security of the believer, that once a person is truly born-again, he cannot lose his salvation.

I am a Baptist; however, this does not mean I do not love and respect others in the body of Christ, i.e., Presbyterians, Pentecostals, and Holiness. Being a dispensationalist led to my becoming a Baptist. I arrived in the Baptist camp by conviction, not by birth. I was born Presbyterian and the great presuppositions I learned in a Presbyterian Sunday School will always stick with me. However, being a Baptist leads me to: (1) the priesthood of the believer, that every individual has the right and a responsibility to read, understand, and interpret the Word of God; (2) that the local church is governed by all believers, hence, I accept the old adage, "Let the minority have their say, let the majority have their way"; (3) that the purpose of the church is the missionary outreach of the Great Commission to (a) make disciples of all nations, i.e., by church planting, (b) to baptize all people, i.e., to identify them with the local church, and (c) to teach them to obey all that Jesus has commanded; (4) that each church is independent in its responsibility for its nurture, outreach, and self-support; yet, is inter-dependent in associated fellowship with other churches; (5) that all converts should be identified by immersion with the local body of Christ just as by the baptism of the Holy Spirit they have been identified with the universal body of Christ.

I do not take credit for this volume of systematic theology, I only take responsibility. Those teachers whose classes influenced me were J. Robertson McQuilkin, Ed Simpson, Philip Watson, Charles Ryrie and John Walvoord. However, as much as they influenced me, none would fully agree with all aspects of this volume.

I began to write this volume in the Fall of 1958, actually putting an outline together in the late hours of the night (or early hours of the morning) when I first became a professor at Mid-West Bible College, St. Louis, Missouri. I was assigned to the Department of Christian Education, but Mid-West was a small school with only eight faculty members, so we all filled in where necessary. During my first two years, I taught every course in systematic theology. d Not wanting to simply "parrot" the thinking of my seminary professors, I outlined extensively my own thinking in systematic theology. At that time, my ego (selfish desire for attention) probably controlled my life a lot more than it does today (I do not claim to have solved this drive, only some expressions of it). As a result, I did not go into a class unless I was totally prepared. While my motives were not always pure, i.e., to see that students received a good learning; many times my extensive preparation was to save embarrassment and to cause students to think well of me. Whatever the motivation, the notes were developed in the late 1950s, and then over a period of time at Winnipeg Bible College, Trinity Evangelical Divinity School, Baptist University of America, and finally at Liberty University. I polished these notes every time I taught the class in theology. This means that within certain places in the outline, a full-text would develop as I wrote out my reasons, including any new insight or research that I had done (I read more of Strong, Hodge and other classic theologians after graduating from seminary, than during).

During my early Church Growth conferences (the late 60s and early 70s) I would tell pastors that theoretical theology, and wrong theology, had contributed to church decline more than anything else. I promised them that one day I would write a systematic theology. I explained to these pastors that theology rightly expressed would produce evangelistic churches, holiness in individuals, and a personal responsibility for Christian service. The acid test is what the students do after they have been influenced by studying it. This book is the result of that promise.

The majority of the text was developed while I was Dean of Liberty Baptist Theological Seminary, 1979-1991. During this time I taught all of the courses in systematic theology, giving attention to writing out the outline that had been previously established. As a result many of my students now in ministry have manuscripts of varying lengths and varying stages of completion. While they do not have the now completed copy, they did help to develop the final product with their critiques, insights, and as only students will do, occasional rejections of what I said. As a result, I was able to view this book "through the eyes of my students" making it more systematic, defensible, and hopefully, more practical.

While at Liberty, I had several graduate assistants who helped in research, checking footnotes, and running down quotations. My graduate assistants were more than messenger boys. I discussed the issues with them, trying to defend my position so that they could understand it. I felt if they could not understand it, neither could anyone else. Therefore, these graduate assistants have made as much contribution to this manual as anyone else, and I salute them. My thanks go to Dr. Douglas Porter, who received both his seminary training and doctorate here at Liberty Baptist Theological Seminary and has been my friend and theological sounding board. When he first came to Liberty, he lived in our home and I introduced him to his wife Sharon. Other students who helped include John C. Thomas, Ron Holcomb, and Robert Knuteson.

Thanks also to Dr. Thomas A. Howe, Professor of Bible and Biblical Languages at Southern Evangelical Seminary for editing the manuscript and designing the page layouts in the Second Edition.

In preparing this Third Edition I want to especially thank the following: Dr. James Borland, Professor of Theology and New Testament at Liberty University for checking the footnotes, editing the manuscript and "fine tuning" the manuscript; Linda Elliott my editorial assistant who coordinated this project; also Jill Walker, student assistant; and my current graduate assistant, Matthew Chittum and his wife Charity, for formatting and designing the page displays. While so many have made a contribution to this volume, in the final analysis I must take responsibility for every word, thought, and mistake. For the cases where I have overstated a point, or understated a truth; I bear the full responsibility. And like all of us, I plead the grace of God to overlook all of the human finite contributions, and give all of the glory to the Lord Jesus Christ.

May God use this volume according to its purpose, and may it accomplish His glory.

Elmer L. Towns, Dean
School of Religion
Liberty University
July, 2001

CHAPTER I – PROLEGOMENA TO THEOLOGY

I. INTRODUCTION

To some people, *theology* is a queen that reigns over the sciences. To some people theology is the "words of God," or at least they respect it as man's thoughts about God. Other people reject the word *theology* because it means dead orthodoxy, and in some churches, theology has taken the place of Christ and the Bible. To others, theology is equated with liberalism. Still there are some who attack theology because they feel it will stifle their soul-winning zeal.

The great evangelist Dwight L. Moody often accused theology of being the sterile wrapper of Christianity. He once said, "Feeding on doctrine is like trying to live on dry husks." Then he went on to add, "I pity a person who has to be fed religion with a theological spoon."

"I don't like your theology!" a woman once said to Dwight L. Moody. He laughed, "Theology!" he said to the lady, "I didn't know that I had any theology." Even though Moody was reacting to dead theology, he had a living theology of his own. Anytime someone takes several Scripture verses and synthesizes them into one sermon or Sunday school lesson, he is constructing a theology. Therefore, when Moody took several references to Jesus Christ in Scriptures and gave his listeners a broad picture of the Son of God, he was theologizing. Moody understood the cohesive glue that held theology together, and he emphasized the ultimate aim of theology. He said, "A creed is a road or street. It is very good as far as it goes, but if it doesn't take us to Christ, it is worthless."[1]

This volume is an attempt to present in a systematic, comprehensive and complete form the doctrines of God and His works. But the aim is to go beyond a theological statement of belief. It is an attempt to give theology a heart, which is the Lord Jesus Christ.

Christianity begins with the statement, "In the beginning God . . . ." Since every finite thing has to begin somewhere, an excellent place to begin one's study is with God. But what about the preparations we must make before we get started? Just as there are many things to prepare before the driver starts his car on a race day, so there are attitudes, tools and assumptions that go before the study of theology. This preparation is called *prolegomena*, which means "things that are said before." Therefore, prolegomena is the introduction to the study of theology because it comes first and gives direction to the formation of one's belief. Prolegomena comes from the

Greek word πρo "before" and λεγω "to say." Just as the blueprints will determine the shape of the building to be constructed, so your attitude and principles of studying theology will determine your doctrinal position. Even the words and definitions you use to answer the question "What is theology?" will determine the way you express your faith and its content.

Prolegomena deals with your presuppositions, which are the attitude you bring to the question, "What is theology?" It is similar to people who say in the contemporary world, "I know where you are coming from." They are describing an approach to a topic.

Prolegomena begins with the presuppositions that there is a God, that truth exists, and that a person can know truth. Therefore, as we begin our study, we assume there is a God and that the truth exists with Him. We assume we can know the truth, hence we can know about God or even come to know Him directly. These presuppositions are not proof, nor are they evidence for truth. But as we continue our study, we will find evidence that verifies our presuppositions. Here it is important to make a distinction between the existence of our presuppositions and later demonstrating the validity of our presuppositions. In so doing, we are constructing theology.

A. WHAT IS THEOLOGY? In approaching the subject of theology, we must first define the word. Not everyone means the same thing by using the term *theology*.

1. *Greek etymology.* First, the term theology comes from the Greek compound theologia (θεολογια) derived from two roots, theos (θεoς—"God") and logos (λoγoς— "word" or "idea"). Theology originally meant an idea concerning God. The original term fell into two categories. Theology could be sayings about God, or the actual sayings, or discourses by God or the gods.

2. *Pagan usage.* Plato (427-347 B.C.) used the word *theology* in connection with *statements* that he found in the poems about the gods. His master teacher, Socrates— who was often criticized—apparently wanted the gods to be more godly. Aristotle (384-322 B.C.) used the word *theology* as a synonym of metaphysics or as a study of the realm beyond the physical. To him, theology was a rational explanation of all that concerned the Supreme Mind.

3. *Early Christian usage.* Christians were reluctant at first to use the term *theology* because of its pagan association. Their original discussion of theology, even though they did not use the term, revolved around the humanity of Jesus Christ or the doctrine of the Trinity. Christians examined the issues and arrived at conclusions about the object of their faith before they used the term *theology* to identify the method and content of their faith.

4. *Clergy.* During the fourth and fifth centuries, theology became a study of the content that every priest should know before he became pastor of a church. Chrysostom (A.D. 407) said a priest should not only be as virtuous as angels, but also proficient in knowledge of ordination to study both scriptural content and external scriptural tradition (that stemming from apostolic practice and teaching but was not grounded in Scripture). This study later became known as theology. Augustine, a contemporary of Chrysostom, wrote a book for ministers entitled *On Christian Doctrine.* In this volume he advocated not only the mastery of original biblical languages, but the techniques of reasoning and persuasion, and also mastery of subjects such as history, natural science, mechanical arts and numbers (mathematics).

These topics were all included in the study of theology, but its study was confined to the clergy. After the fifth century, the study of theology spread beyond the monastery to church members.

5. *Contemporary usage.* To answer the question "What is theology?" we must examine how theologians used the word, no matter how others define it. A theologian defines the term *theology* when he says, "I am going to use the term *theology* to mean . . . ." But this does not mean he is right. Different theologians will differ in their definition of the term. Also, these definitions will not necessarily relate to the historic uses of the term.

Strong and Fitzwater both define theology in their respective works in keeping with the etymology of the term. Strong writes, "Theology is the science of God and the relations between God and the universe."[2] Fitzwater's definition is similar, but more confining. He concludes, "Theology, therefore, is the science of God's essential being and His relationship to the universe as set forth in the Holy Scriptures."[3] Both writers take note of the fact that other theologians define theology as "the science of religion" or "the doctrines of the church."

6. *Catechism and theology.* Many have tried to answer the question "What is theology?" by setting theology within a scheme of questions and answers. As a result, throughout their discourses about theology, a person is given a question so that he may give a proper doctrinal answer. The study of theology, stimulated by a question, is thought to challenge the mind to explore an obvious answer. But there are problems with this method, known as the catechism. Over the years, the answers become catalogued, and neither the questions nor the answers are any longer spontaneous. That which was created to be a vehicle to challenge the mind, usually dulled the senses because the answer was memorized rather than analyzed.

7. *Theology and doctrine.* Blackwood defined doctrine as "an intellectual formulation of an experience."[4] But this is a limited definition. In one sense, doctrine

and theology are similar, but theology cannot be limited to doctrine. Doctrine is usually defined as the study of God that arises from the Bible. Theology is generally defined as the study of God from all sources. Doctrine is a New Testament term used as both a verb and a noun. The verb is usually translated *to teach* (Acts 5:42), whereas the noun, translated "doctrine" (Acts 2:42), refers to the actual content being taught. Teaching is the process—doctrine is the product. In contemporary usage, doctrine is, in fact, limited to teaching from special revelation (i.e., the Scriptures), whereas theology may draw its source, method or proof from any and all sources of truth (logic, arithmetic, biology, history, etc.), because all truth (both special revelation and general revelation) comes from God.

Writing in *The International Standard Bible Encyclopedia*, Thomas Rees identified the similarities that exist between doctrine and dogma in Greek theology.

> In Gr[eek] theology 'doctrine' and 'dogma' meant the same thing. Each had its origin in the opinion of some great teacher; each rested upon revelation and claimed its authority; each meant an exposition of a particular truth of the gospel, and of the whole of Christian truth, which the church adopted as the only right exposition.[5]

8. *Religion and theology.* The word *religion* comes from the Latin *religare* which means "to bind up." Whereas religion commonly refers to a set of beliefs, attitudes, and practices expressed in worship of God, theology usually deals with the systematic collection and arrangement of one's beliefs.

The study of religion is used in at least three different ways. First, the study of religion is the study of any person who has beliefs in, attitudes toward, or worship of any supreme being. Therefore, a pursuit of religion is an objective study of the existence of different religions of the world.

In the second sense, religion refers to the way a person expresses his beliefs. As such, the Bible speaks of true religion (James 1:27) and false religion (James 1:26). When a person is conscientious in his worship of God, the adjective "religious" is used. When the noun *religion* is used, we are discussing the end product of one's devotion. Therefore, a study of religion to a certain person is an inquiry that makes this person more devoted so he can receive the blessing he perceives to be available in his religion.

A third use of religion is synonymous with Christianity. This use indicates that a person has a right relationship with God through Jesus Christ and is therefore religious, and that the only true religion is Christianity. Therefore, a study of religion is the broad inquiry into the Scriptures and reason leading to faith.

But Christianity is different from religion. Because there are so many false religions in the world, we do not usually refer to Christianity as a religion. If we did, it would place Christ on a par with the many alleged deities. If this were true, it might allow a person a choice between religions. But Christianity is not a religion with similar types of practices and beliefs that characterize false religions. Christian beliefs and practices are empowered with life. Since Jesus Christ is the only way to God (John 14:6), Christianity is Jesus Christ. At the center of every Christian's belief and practice is a person, Jesus Christ. Jesus Christ makes Christianity unique and alive. Jesus Christ makes Christianity more than a religion.

After we embrace the dynamic life of Christianity, we then strive to understand the forces that work in our lives. We identify these principles, categorize them, see how they fit into a consistent pattern and how they relate to life. This is the role of theologizing. Hence, both religion and Christianity use theology in arriving at their beliefs, but Christian theology evolves out of an experience that is based on God's Word, and that is successfully reinforced by its correspondence to the realities of this world.

II. THE TASK OF THEOLOGIZING

Before we begin the task of formulating a theology, we must recognize the existence of at least two conditions. First, we must be aware of the presuppositions that are in our minds before we examine the first aspect of theology. Second, we must be aware of the method or principles by which we do the work of theology.

First, let us examine our presuppositions. A presupposition is a conclusion that is not arrived at on the basis of any reason, experience or demonstrated proof. In reality, a presupposition is a "self-evident truth." By this we mean that our presuppositions do not have a chronological beginning, but they are axiomatically accepted without verification. However, this does not mean that we as theologians, or others who are not Christians, should accept our presuppositions simply because we "feel" them or know they are true. A presupposition, if it is true, will and must be verified by the test of consistency, correspondence and scientific demonstration in that it is repeatable and reliable.

We accept the following presuppositions: (1) that there is a God and that He has revealed Himself, (2) that there are laws that are self-evident, (3) that man has the ability to know things to the degree to which he directly observes them, (4) that truth does not contradict itself, but is consistent and corresponds to reality, and (5) that the mind accepts that which is logical and rejects that which is illogical.

As a presuppositionalist, one must accept that there is a God who has revealed Himself in the Bible, and that God has used human words in His self-revelation by which He wants man to know Him. Further, we must believe that it is possible to have a knowledge of God that is not contradictory with the actual existence of God, but corresponds to the metaphysical world and to the world of reality.

The second task before us is to understand the method we will use in formulating our theology. Inasmuch as our procedure will determine the final theological product, our theologizing must be correct if our theology is to be accurate.

The terms *systematic* and *theology* are interrelated, so that one cannot think of theology without thinking in a systematic way. Our thinking (method) must consider all relevant data (content). The word *theology* could be used without the descriptive word *systematic* because theology has come to imply a system. But because of common usage, the combined phrase "systematic theology" is used and inferred.

According to Thiessen, "The human intellect is not content with a mere accumulation of facts: it invariably seeks for a unification and systematization of its knowledge."[6] This is one of the prime reasons for the development of systematic theology.

> *Systematic Theology* takes the material furnished by Biblical and Historical Theology, and with this material seeks to build up into an organic and consistent whole all our knowledge of God and of the relations between God and the universe, whether this knowledge be originally derived from nature or from the Scriptures.[7]

The following definition of theologizing takes into consideration the content (natural and supernatural revelation), the method (rational, scientific, faith) the person (spiritually and mentally perceptive) and the tools (words, communication, defense, etc.).

> Theologizing is the process whereby a person who has both experienced salvation and has grown in spiritual maturity, searches out all truth concerning God and His work, in both supernatural and natural revelation, using the rational process of inquiry, the resources of faith, and the scientific method of demonstrating, with a purpose of organizing the results of his study into a complete, comprehensive, and consistent expression that can be communicated, defended and admired.

Theologizing implies five steps for the student if he is to develop a comprehensive and adequate view of God and His world. These steps apply to every aspect of one's theology and to theology as a whole.

A. COLLECTING. The gathering of data is necessarily the first step to preparing one's theology. Theology demands the collection of all facts, not just the biblical facts. This means we must go outside of special revelation to that truth which God has revealed in natural or general revelation. Truth is that which is consistent with itself and corresponds to reality. There is truth in mathematics, nature and logic. To gain the most comprehensive understanding of God and His works, no source can be overlooked. Many of the false theologies stem from the neglect of this first premise—they have ignored or rejected some truth. Hence, these theologies are flawed.

B. SCIENTIFICALLY ARRANGING AND COMPARING. The next step is the scientific arrangement or integration of all the gathered facts into a coherent whole. The end product is a complete, comprehensive and consistent explanation of the topic under consideration. This is called a *systematic* way of thinking about truth. No doctrine is exhaustively treated by any biblical writer in a single verse. The theologian must find all the facts (or verses) that contain a fragment of the truth and fit them into a coherent pattern. Because truth will not contradict itself, we know we have arrived at an acceptable system when all our facts are consistently interrelated. Before adopting and teaching any theory as fact, we must apply certain tests.

1. *The test of consistency.* First ask, "Is the system consistent?" But consistency is not enough to guarantee that a system is true. Although truth is consistent with itself, it is possible for a system to be internally consistent yet not be true. To be true it must be consistent, but it may be consistent and still not be true.

2. *The test of correspondence.* The second question is "Does it correspond to reality or life?" A system of theology may be a consistent doctrinal system, but when the second test of correspondence is applied, its theory may not correspond with truth found in natural revelation. Christianity is not proved by pragmatism, but once embraced, it will reaffirm its credibility in the application of its message to the lives of its recipients. If Christianity is true, then its principles will work within the parameters of their intended objectives.

3. *The test of priority of data.* The third step in constructing a systematic theology is to discriminate between what is essential and what is irrelevant. The important data will become foremost in our theology, and that which is less important will fall to the rear of our thinking. Many times that which appears to be contradictory is usually irrelevant to the main understanding of a doctrine. This does not mean that truth is contradictory, but it does sometimes appear that way to man in his sinful, limited, understanding and interpretation of life. By way of illustration, if we are going to do a systematic study of Francis Bacon, his books, letters and diaries

are important to interpret his influence on the thoughts of men. But it is not as essential to know the color of his hair, nor his eating habits.

4. *The test of cohesiveness.* The fourth major concern of the theologian is to determine the cohesive nature of the data. It is said that theology has a firm center, but no hard-and-fast circumference which ultimately influences every area of life. The center of Christianity rests in the historical and supernatural revelation of Jesus Christ who lived, died and was buried in a tomb outside of Jerusalem. He arose again from the dead and His present life is the basis of Christianity for all who believe in Him. Jesus Christ is so uniquely revelatory of and related to the living God that He is the foundation of one's faith. The controlling test of all data is its relationship to Christ.

5. *The test of thoroughness.* The fifth concern of the theologian is a rigorous examination of any and all questions related to the topic. This is more than an examination of all data. It is an attempt to answer all inquiries regarding a system of belief. To ignore or omit any question regarding any subject matter is to have a theology that is not complete and comprehensive. Finally, a word has to be said about the areas of philosophy, sociology, logic, ethics, history, psychology, and other areas of concern which may seem to have little to do with theology, but each of which deals with matters relevant to one or more aspects of the total theological task. The person who raises the question "What is theology?" must be willing to be a student of all these areas. Because of this comprehensive, yet thorough overview, theology is called the Queen of the Sciences.

C. EXHIBITING. While the Bible is supernatural in origin, it was originally given to people in cultures far different from ours today. Every group in every age must have the gospel interpreted to their culture so that it is meaningful to them. The theologian must present his theological system in a comprehensive and understandable form. This is imperative for the fulfillment of the Great Commission, "teaching them to observe all things whatsoever I have commanded you" (Matt. 28:19).

D. DEFENDING. The final responsibility of the theologian is the defense of the theory or laws of his system. When the theologian first brings all his facts into a system, it is a theory that has not been tested or proven. However, after it has been verified by the test of truth, then his theories become accepted principles, an expression in accord with eternal law. These conclusions must be displayed to the world for all to see. Then, after his findings are publicized, he must defend them. Of course, if his interpretation of theology is based upon a correct understanding of Scripture, supported with rational thinking to demonstrate its consistency, and reaffirmed by repeatable and workable application in life, the task of defense is somewhat diminished. Martin Luther was allegedly asked if he would defend the Bible, he supposedly responded, "Defend the Bible? I would as soon defend a lion."[8]

III. EXPRESSIONS OF THEOLOGY

Depending upon one's starting point (presuppositions) and self-imposed limitations (method), theology will have varied expressions. It is possible in some schools of thought to study theology without ever making a close examination of the biblical material relating to a particular doctrine. In contrast, another extreme position might consider a biblical doctrine without considering the contributions of the historic creeds of Christendom.

A. BIBLICAL THEOLOGY. Biblical Theology not only involves a study of Bible content, but also an examination of the dynamics involved in forming the Bible. Biblical Theology involves a study of (1) the languages in which the Bible was written, (2) textual criticism to determine the best biblical text, (3) literary criticism to determine its date,

> Biblical Theology systematically examines one area of revelation limiting its concern to a writer or a period of time with a purpose of gathering, examining, classifying and placing the results into a correlated whole so that the reader may understand the purpose, motives, and contribution of the specific biblical author.

authorship, matter of composition, historical and sociological background by which the Bible is interpreted, (4) the problems of canon (the makeup of the Bible), and (5) the principles of exegesis by which the Bible is to be interpreted.

Various writers define Biblical Theology differently. Thiessen calls it "exegetical theology," noting, "EXEGETICAL THEOLOGY occupies itself directly with the study of the Sacred Text and such related subjects as help in the restoration, orientation, illustration and interpretation of that text."[9] Vos also recognizes a field of exegetical theology but notes, "Biblical Theology is that branch of Exegetical Theology which deals with the process of the self-revelation of God deposited in the Bible."[10] Fitzwater calls biblical theology "the historical exhibition of the redemptive purpose of God as progressively unfolded in the canonical Scriptures."[11] Strong's functional definition suggests,

> *Biblical Theology* aims to arrange and classify the facts of revelation, confining itself to the Scriptures for its material, and treating of doctrine only so far as it was developed at the close of the apostolic age.[12]

B. HISTORICAL THEOLOGY. Our Christian faith is organically linked to the New Testament by Christians who have lived before us. Church history is a study of the continuing influence of Christianity, so Historical Theology is a study of man's expression of his faith by each generation in different sociological and ecclesiastical settings. Church history is more than the accumulation of facts, it is an understanding of missionary outreach, the

> Historical Theology is the study of the expression of theology in each age with an examination of its expressed aim, emphasis, omissions and forces that change its expression from generation to generation since the closing of the canon.

form of worship, the nature of the church in all of its settings, the history of doctrine and the formulation of creeds in every age.

Concerning Historical Theology, Thiessen notes, "It deals with the origin, development, and spread of the true religion, and also with its doctrines, organizations and practices."[13] The emphasis of Historical Theology is normally focused on the developments of Christian doctrine after the closing of the canon.

C. DOGMATIC THEOLOGY. Dogmatic Theology is a study of the beliefs held by other groups throughout history. Some say Dogmatic Theology is the communication of one's dogma, while others say that it is technically the ecumenical study of what others have believed. The first purpose of Dogmatic Theology is to help

> Dogmatic Theology is the study of varied beliefs and creeds of the different religious sects and orders throughout church history with a view of producing a deeper understanding of Christianity in other generations and cultures and producing a deeper understanding of one's unique theology.

the student appreciate the problems and interpretations of other theologies, which become his private dogma. This involves analyzing, interpreting and communicating a creed or doctrinal statement.

Strong calls Dogmatic Theology "the systematizing of the doctrines as expressed in the symbols of the church, together with the grounding of these in the Scriptures, and the exhibition, so far as may be, of their rational necessity."[14] Phillip Schaff's *The Creeds of Christendom*[15] is normally considered a standard work for the student of Dogmatic Theology. A study of the historic creeds of Christianity will help the contemporary theological student avoid many common heretical tendencies. Often the importance of a doctrine is only fully understood when viewed in the context of the battle which led to its formulation.

D. PHILOSOPHICAL THEOLOGY. We do not arrive at our theology through philosophy but we make use of some philosophical or logical principles in arriving at theology. When a theologian articulates his Christian faith, he is making a clear statement of his understanding of God and the created universe. Hence, the theologian must

> Philosophical Theology is the collecting, scientifically arranging, comparing, exhibiting and defending of all data including logic, experience, reason, and facts from the natural world.

use the scientific method of inquiry to arrive at his theology, and he must use linguistic symbols to communicate the realities of God and his world. Philosophical studies raise questions which cannot be ignored. These are questions regarding the validity of Christianity and its truth-claims. The fact that Christianity is doubted by non-Christians on both scientific and philosophical grounds is a problem. Hence, Philosophical Theology evolves into apologetics. The word *apologetics* does not mean "to regret," but "to give an answer" to those who question Christianity. At one time, Philosophical Theology was called "Natural Theology."

E. CONTEMPORARY THEOLOGY. Contemporary Theology analyzes current thinking regarding Christianity. Inasmuch as Christianity must always be expressed in contemporary terms, the validity or non-validity of each person's expression of Christianity must be examined and verified. This would involve tracing modern beliefs such as neo-orthodoxy, neo-

> Contemporary Theology is a study of the men, movements, institutions, and trends found in the current theological world.

liberalism, post-modernism, process theology, liberation theology, feminist theology and open theism.

F. SYSTEMATIC THEOLOGY. Systematic Theology is an effort to draw truth from any and every source concerning God and His universe and to express this truth simply in a comprehensive and complete system. In this regard, an understanding of the above-mentioned expressions of theology are foundational to the preparation of one's personal systematic theology.

> Systematic Theology may be defined as the collecting, scientifically arranging, comparing, exhibiting and defending of all facts from any and every source concerning God and His works.[16]

G. PRACTICAL THEOLOGY.   The last and ultimate expression is Practical Theology. Practical Theology usually falls in the realm of how man worships God and how the work of God is carried out in the world.   Too often, Practical Theology has been disassociated from Systematic Theology.   When this happens, Practical Theology has appealed to pragmatism or contemporary educational methods.   In fact, Practical Theology should be based upon theological principles.   A theology that is in agreement with Scripture will successfully work in any culture or age.

In the broad field of theology, there are courses within the realm of all of these specializations.   Just as every branch of learning has become more and more the object of specialized attention, so a study of Systematic Theology in our contemporary society has become sharper in its understanding and specialization.

Most theologians recognize the importance of integrating their philosophy of ministry with their theology.   Strong suggests that Practical Theology "is the system of truth considered as a means of renewing and sanctifying men, or, in other words, theology in its publication and enforcement."[17]   To understand why a pastor leads a church the way he does, you must understand his ecclesiology.   Most Christian Education professors in conservative seminaries will begin a course by discussing the biblical and theological foundation of their subject.   The first lecture of a course in elementary education may be on what the Bible has to say about the education of children.

Thiessen suggests the ideal that,

> Practical Theology treats the application of theology in the regeneration, sanctification, edification, education and service of men.   It seeks to apply to practical. life the things contributed by the other three departments of theology.[18]

H. THE DIVISIONS OF THEOLOGY. Systematic Theology discusses the entire coverage of God and His Word. But it is divided into several particular areas, each one centered around a section of theology.

1. Theology begins with PROLEGOMENA, which is its introduction. *Pro* means "to go before" and *lego* means "to say or speak."

2. The theology of the SCRIPTURES is called BIBLIOLOGY. Bibliology comes from

> **THE USE OF REASON**
> 1. To recognize and receive truth
> 2. To interpret truth
> 3. To accept and confirm the evidence that supports truth
> 4. To correlate truth with other truth
> 5. To apply truth
> 6. To defend truth

biblion (book or Bible) and *logos,* (a word).

3. The theology of GOD is referred to as THEOLOGY PROPER. Theology comes from *theos,* which means "God," and *logos.*

4. The theology of JESUS CHRIST is called CHRISTOLOGY. Christology comes from *Christos* (Christ) and *logos.*

5. The theology of the HOLY SPIRIT is called PNEUMATOLOGY. Pneumatology comes from *pneuma* (Spirit) and *logos.*

6. The theology of MAN is called ANTHROPOLOGY. Anthropology is derived from *anthropos* (man) and *logos.*

7. The theology of SIN is called HAMARTIOLOGY. Harmartiology comes from *Hamartia,* which means "sin," and *logos.*

8. The theology of SALVATION is called SOTERIOLOGY. Soteriology comes from *soteria* (salvation) and *logos.*

9. The theology of ANGELS (including Satan and demons) is called ANGELOLOGY. Angelology comes from *angelos* (angel) and *logos.*

10. The theology of the CHURCH is called ECCLESIOLOGY. Ecclesiology comes from *ecclesia* (church) and *logos.*

11. The theology of LAST THINGS is called ESCHATOLOGY. Eschatology comes from *eschatos* (last) and *logos.*

IV. THE NECESSITY OF THEOLOGY

The possibility of theology itself is often cited as reason enough for the study of Systematic Theology. Thiessen identifies two concepts, the revelation of God and the endowments of man.[19] These are also enunciated by Strong, but a third is also given, "the existence of a God who has relations to the universe."[20] In all, there are at least five good reasons that demand the preparation of a systematized theology.

A. THE ORGANIZING INSTINCT OF MAN. It is natural for man to seek order. Man was created in the image and likeness of God (Gen. 1:26, 27), who is described as a God who sets all things in order (Deut. 1:8; Gen. 9:13). The Bible was not written as a theoretical book. Had the Bible been written as such, the initiative to understand God would have probably been taken from man.

The Bible is belief and life-oriented. God tests us in all areas of our life to determine how close we come to the truth. If theology were revealed in a doctrinal statement, men would have known everything about God, hence eliminating the need to study and apply oneself to Scripture. Man would not have had an opportunity for spiritual growth. God intended rather that theology should be a lifelong pilgrimage.

Even though some deny the influence of reason in the formulation of theology, there are several ways by which the theologian should use his God-given ability to reason when he is constructing his theology. Some reject the use of reason because they feel that man is totally depraved and unregenerate. They feel it is wasted effort to try to tell man the truth. They say that it is like trying to teach an imbecile or a mentally retarded child geometry. Also, they say the mind of man, unaided by the Spirit of God, cannot comprehend God. However, the mind can use its reasoning ability to accept facts as true simply because they are not internally contradictory nor in contradiction to other known facts. Therefore, man's ability to reason is not just tolerated in theologizing. It is necessary. The Christian is morally and intellectually bound to accept as truth that which is rationally consistent. To go a step farther, the Christian is morally bound not to believe anything that is contradictory. The false gospel is rejected because it is a contradiction to the gospel (Gal. 1:8-9). If a Christian does not use reason to reject that which is contradictory and to accept that which is consistent, then he is saying that belief to him is nothing at all.

B. CHARACTER OF UNBELIEF. Few people today desire to understand doctrine. Humanism and rationalism are inherently anti-supernatural and anti-theistic. No one comes into the world with an inborn system of doctrine. The pastor cannot assume his people will be taught good doctrine from culture, schools or sermons from liberal churches. He cannot assume that people will naturally understand doctrine or will seek out doctrine. The nature of unbelief demands that doctrine be constructed and taught.

C. CHARACTER OF SCRIPTURE. The Bible is a revelation of God that demands a response. Our duty is to study, understand, and obey the revelation that God has given. Since the different biblical authors contributed different discussions of various topics, the Christian must organize all contributions to understand the complete message of the Holy Spirit concerning a particular doctrine.

D. CHRISTIAN CHARACTER. Through the precepts and principles taught in the Scriptures, Christian character is established and strengthened. These principles may be gleaned from proverbs, songs, epistles or biographies. Again, the Christian must organize his theology so as to establish the strongest Christian character. This means the Christian life should be grounded on the whole Word of God, not just one book of the Bible or just one topic of doctrine.

E. CHRISTIAN SERVICE. Doctrine is important to successful Christian service. There is a perfect will of God related to a perfect truth that comes when a Christian has perfect understanding, a consistent life, diligent and successful service, plus the empowerment of the Holy Spirit. When a stone is thrown into a pond, the waves are highest near the center. The further from the center, the smaller the waves. So the closer we come to the center of God's truth and His will, the more God will bless us. While proper doctrine does not insure the blessing of God, it is a part of the total picture including yieldedness, hard work, prayer, and purity. The key to the blessing of God must include faith which is the only thing that is said to please God (Heb. 11:6). A person who expresses faith in God will grow as he learns more of the nature and attributes of God.

V. THE REQUIREMENTS FOR THEOLOGY

One must possess the proper methodology and tools to accurately arrange a systematic theology. The proper methodology was discussed earlier (see section II). The tools of theology are just as important.

A. INSPIRED REVELATION. The source of authority and the direction for our life and ministry is found in the Scriptures. They stand as the inerrant revelation of God to mankind. If God had not revealed Himself to mankind, theology would be impossible. "The secret things belong unto the Lord our God: but those things which are revealed belong unto us and to our children for ever, that we may do all the words of this law" (Deut. 29:29). The Bible is the foundational tool of theology in addition to being its source.

With the rise of secular humanism there is decreased recognition of the authority of God. The tendency is to deny the existence of absolutes and oppose or reinterpret that which claims for itself final authority. As a result, one of the major theological debates of our day is the inerrancy of Scripture. Some are broadening their view of revelation in an attempt to develop a "universal theology." Therefore, they are prepared to use the Koran and the Bible to learn about God. These "theologians" need to be reminded of the declaration of Strong that "God himself, in the last analysis, must be the only source of knowledge with regard to his own being and relations."[21] In a somewhat similar line of thought, Thiessen wrote,

> The Bible is to the theologian what nature is to the scientist,—a body of unorganized or only partly organized facts. God has not seen fit to write the Bible in the form of a systematic theology; it remains for us, therefore, to gather together the scattered facts and to build them up into a logical system.[22]

B. FAITH. The total meaning of the Scripture cannot be understood by the natural man (1 Cor. 2:14). There must be a personal faith in God on the part of the theologian. We cannot disassociate one's personal faith from the content of the doctrine which is also called *The Faith*. But the word "faith" (*pistis*) is used in a number of ways. It usually means what people want it to mean. Therefore, we must ask ourselves four questions regarding faith.

First, is the present-day Christian faith in harmony with, and growing out of, that continuous faith of Christians found in the New Testament? If contemporary faith is different from New Testament faith, then we can question whether it truly is Christian faith. Many people have confused the essentials of faith by reading into Christianity their preconceived ideas about the content and expression of faith.

The second question deals with the predictability of faith. If faith is a reality and is available to all, then the method of acquiring it and expressing it must be predictable; is your concept of faith available to all individuals? That implies that the faith of one person will be similar to the faith of others, hence there is an objectivity to the existence of faith.

The third question deals with private faith. The study of theology is public, because anyone can examine it. However, personal faith is private and not directly amenable to public examination. When a person has experienced faith, it becomes nonverbal (experiential) in personal acquisition. The credibility of one's faith is evidenced by one's internal confidence and assurance based on outward objectivity. Hence, when we study theology and faith, we are delving into the area of axiology (that which is assumed to be true) and mysticism (that which is felt to be true). Is private faith based on objective faith?

The fourth question about faith involves its symbols and expressions. To understand faith, one must describe it as well as define it. This description is seen in church symbols, word symbols, and its influence upon one's life. Hence, are the symbols of one's faith meaningful? A Baptist theologian who gives meaning to water baptism, but has never been baptized or is unconcerned about getting others baptized, has raised a question about the credibility of his faith.

C. LANGUAGE. The third tool of the theologian is a working knowledge of biblical languages. The Bible was originally written in Greek (New Testament), Hebrew and Syriac (Old Testament). The serious theologian will desire to analyze the Scriptures so that he will not have to depend solely on the work of others, no matter how accurate their work. He will want to read the Bible in the language in which it was written and attempt to come to a better understanding of the culture of the people to whom the prophets or apostles wrote. I must add, however, that most good English translations accurately reflect the original languages, so that those without such original language skills may still understand the Bible.

D. HISTORY. A fourth tool of the theologian is an understanding of history, particularly the history of Christendom. In years past, most of the major doctrines of the faith have been argued, defended and even distorted. The theologian who learns from history will not only learn the best expressions of theology in the past, but he will also be aware of natural heretical tendencies and so avoid them.

In conclusion, some would support additional prerequisites to the study of theology with varying degrees of importance. Additional suggestions by Strong include a disciplined mind, an intuition, an acquaintance with the various sciences, a holy affection toward God and the enlightening influence of the Holy Spirit.[23] However, even the most qualified and capable theologian must face certain limitations to his study.

VI. THE LIMITATIONS OF THEOLOGY

Perhaps the most discouraging reality the theologian must confront is the impossibility of ever arriving at a completely comprehensive and exact theology. Certain things exist beyond his control so his theology will always be limited. In other ways, the theologian himself may be the source of limitations on his theology. Here are some areas that tend to limit man's fuller knowledge of God.

A. HUMAN UNDERSTANDING. Isaiah correctly observed, "For my thoughts are not your thoughts, neither are your ways my ways, saith the LORD. For as the heavens are higher than the earth, so are my ways higher than your ways, and my thoughts than your thoughts" (Isa. 55:8-9). Whatever else may be true of man and his intellectual ability, it must be acknowledged that he knows less than God. God, who is infinite, cannot be fully comprehended by finite minds.

Because man does not know everything about God, about life, about science, or about the explorations in historical theology, he cannot have perfect understanding in theology. Not only is man's source of knowledge limited, but his reasoning processes are limited. Therefore, even when he has done his best, his theology will be limited.

B. LANGUAGE.[24] God has used words to communicate his revelation to mankind and thus the limitations of language will limit our understanding of God. Human words are symbols, only partially able to communicate ideas. While they are useful in most situations, they fall short of perfection. Someone identified this problem by saying, "I know what I think I heard, but I am not sure it is what you think you said."

Because words are used to represent only ideas, the idea of an infinite God is limited by the use of finite words. Therefore, even with the best of words, dictionaries and applications of language, we cannot fully or accurately communicate God, nor can we ever completely understand God. This is not saying God cannot be known, for all we need to know about God has been communicated and is available to us in the Bible. All that a person needs to obtain salvation and have a meaningful life can be understood and applied by any normal person.

C. IGNORANCE OF SCRIPTURE. The Psalmist prayed the prayer of the theologian. "Open thou mine eyes that I may behold . . ." (Psa. 119:18). The best interpretation of a verse of the Bible is learned only as we understand the context of the whole. The fact that we do not know everything in the Scriptures prevents us from a fuller understanding. This produces somewhat of a limitation in our theology. As our understanding of the Bible increases, this limitation will diminish, but it may never be totally eliminated.

D. THE SILENCE OF GOD. Because Christians recognize the application of biblical revelation to every area of life, God has some secrets He has sovereignly chosen not to

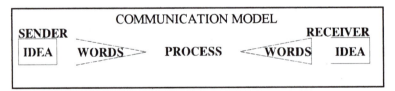

reveal (Deut. 29:29). This silence is evident in Scripture when God instructs writers not to write (i.e., Rev. 10:4). This serves as a further limitation to our understanding of theology.

E. THE NATURE OF SCIENCE. Part of the tools that develop systematic theology are based on the sciences which are neither complete nor absolutely accurate. Science is based upon observations, and often theories and interpretations are based upon *limited* observations or limited facts. Preliminary observations in the past have been overturned by the discovery of previously unknown facts. Hence, our ability to perfectly understand God is limited by the imperfect state of our developing sciences. We do not know everything, nor is all our knowledge accurate.

F. SPIRITUAL BLINDNESS. Sin in our lives will hinder our ability to understand the Bible. There are several kinds of blindness discussed in Scripture. Israel experiences a partial blindness as seen in their rejection of their Messiah (Rom. 11:25), but Gentiles have also been blinded by the god of this world (2 Cor. 4:3-6). Beyond this, the Christian will experience some blindness by allowing sin in his life. This spiritual inability to completely perceive God's pattern is a further limitation of systematic theology.

VII. TEACHING AND PREACHING THEOLOGY[25]

When most people think of preaching or teaching theology, they tend to think in terms of lectures on irrelevant interpretations of obscure texts that have little to do with life. Actually, the preaching of the Word of God is still the greatest enticement to get people into the house of God. Phillips Brooks told students of his day,

> The world has not heard its best preaching yet. If there is more of God's truth for men to know, and if it is possible for the men who utter it to become more pure and godly, then, with both of its elements more complete than they have ever been before, preaching must some day be a completer power.[26]

This type of doctrinal preaching is somewhat different from what most people consider when they think of theology. John Booth wisely noted that "doctrinal preaching is the arranging and setting forth of truth."[27] A more contemporary writer states, "*Doctrinal preaching* is preaching which aims at instructing the people methodically in the truths of the gospel."[28]

In contemporary Christianity very little emphasis is placed upon teaching theology outside the Christian college or seminary classroom. Little theology is communicated in the contemporary pulpit. This is in contrast to the obvious importance of teaching doctrine that is seen in God's working through historic revivals.

> In the past every evangelistic movement blessed of God has come largely through preaching doctrine. Evangelism has flourished, or languished, according to the amount and the fervor of such pulpit work.[29]

Because teaching doctrine is important, there are certain principles the pastor should consider as he prepares to teach or preach.

A. IMPORTANCE. Every pastor should recognize the importance of preaching doctrine. George Pepper in his Yale lectures on preaching, defined preaching as "the public use of speech with intent to reveal God to man."[30] Phillips Brooks called it "the communication of truth by man to men."[31] In one sense, then, doctrine determines the content of all preaching. As such, it also provides the aims and strategy of preaching. Powerful preaching is the preaching of doctrine. Brooks told the ministerial students at Yale,

> The truth is, no preaching ever had any strong power that was not the preaching of doctrine. The preachers that have moved and held men have always preached doctrine. No exhortation to a good life that does not put behind it some truth as deep as eternity can seize and hold the conscience. Preach doctrine, preach all the doctrine that you know, and learn forever more and more; but preach it always, not that men may believe it, but that men may be saved by believing it.[32]

B. ALLEGIANCE. The pastor who would teach his people a biblical theology must be certain of his loyalties. This may involve surrendering any denominational allegiance to the Lord. It is more important to teach what the Bible says than to teach Presbyterian or Baptist doctrine. Do not treat doctrines as sectarian issues. If the distinctives of your group are biblical, then teach them the Bible. If they are not, change them.

C. RELEVANCE. Too many pastors and teachers spend much of their time answering unimportant questions. We should study to answer critical questions. Powerful preaching does not merely describe doctrine; it applies religious faith to a specific human concern, and helps to bring out physical, mental, and spiritual health."[33]

Tozer's dissatisfaction with the biblical illiteracy in his day is evident in the following statement from one of his editorials in a denominational paper.

> One marked difference between the faith of our fathers as conceived by the fathers and the same faith as understood and lived by their children is that the fathers were concerned with the root of the matter, while their present-day descendants seem concerned only with fruit.[34]

In the generation since his death, if there has been a change in this condition, it has been for the worse. Gordon Lewis acknowledges,

> *Many Christians never leave the first principles of the gospel. Still spiritual infants, they must be bottle-fed the same formula. When confronted at the*

door by a representative of another sect, they are helpless to give a reason for the hope that is in them. On the basis of their faith they are speechless; yet on the reasons for their choice of a house or a car they can discourse at length. This sinful negligence by even one member of the church causes the whole body to suffer [italics in original].[35]

Often I remind my students when they study theology, be careful not to sharpen your pencil too sharp. When the pencil is too sharp, the point will break. So it is when we become so precise in our theology as to seemingly forget the limitations of this study, and begin to speak authoritatively out of our ignorance. It is at that moment we break the pencil and render it useless.

We must study theology. We must organize revelation in a systematic manner. We must seek to gather material to compile the fullest and most accurate and precise answer possible in the revelation of God. But we must also never forget, "The secret things belong unto the Lord our God" (Deut. 29:29).

ENDNOTES

1. This story about Moody has been quoted in classes of theology, but not documented. The author has heard it several places and has repeated it here.
2. Augustus Hopkins Strong, *Systematic Theology: A Compendium* (Old Tappan, NJ: Revell, 1970), 1.
3. P. B. Fitzwater, *Christian Theology: A Systematic Presentation* (Grand Rapids: Eerdmans, 1956), 19.
4. Andrew Watterson Blackwood, *Doctrinal Preaching for Today: Case Studies of Bible Teachings* (New York: Abingdon Press, 1956), 115.
5. Thomas Rees, "Dogma," *The International Standard Bible Encyclopedia* (Grand Rapids: Eerdmans, 1974), 2:868.
6. Henry Clarence Thiessen, *Introductory Lectures in Systematic Theology* (Grand Rapids: Eerdmans, 1949), 27.
7. Strong, *Systematic Theology*, 41.
8. Phillip Schaff, *Creeds of Christendom*, 3 Volumes (Grand Rapids: Baker, 1977).*
9. Thiessen, *Lectures in Theology*, 46.
10. Geerhardus Vos, *Biblical Theology: Old and New Testaments* (Grand Rapids: Eerdmans, 1948), 13.

11.   Fitzwater, *Christian Theology*, 20-21.
12.   Strong, *Systematic Theology*, 41.
13.   Thiessen, *Lectures in Theology*, 46.
14.   Strong, *Systematic Theology*, 41.
15.   Schaff, *Creeds of Christendom*.*
16.   Lewis Sperry Chafer, *Systematic Theology* (Dallas: Dallas Seminary Press, 1947), 1:6.
17.   Strong, *Systematic Theology*, 42.
18.   Thiessen, *Lectures in Theology*, 46.
19.   Ibid., 31.
20.   Strong, *Systematic Theology*, 2.
21.   Ibid., 25.
22.   Thiessen, *Lectures in Theology*, 28.
23.   Strong, *Systematic Theology*, 38-40.
24.   Marshall McLuhan, *The Medium is the Message* (New York:: Bantam Books, 1967).*   The "COMMUNICATION MODEL" diagram is based upon a model by his design.
25.   For a plan by which a pastor can teach a summary of biblical doctrine over the course of a year in his church, see Elmer L. Towns, *What the Faith Is All About* (Wheaton, IL: Tyndale House Publishers, 1983).
26.   Phillips Brooks, *Lectures on Preaching* (Grand Rapids: Zondervan, n.d.), 33.
27.   John Nicholls Booth, *The Quest for Preaching Power* (New York: MacMillan, 1943), 18.
28.   Lloyd M. Perry, *Biblical Preaching for Today's World* (Chicago: Moody Press, 1973), 126-27.
29.   Blackwood, *Doctrinal Preaching*, 51.
30.   Cited by Blackwood, *Doctrinal Preaching*, 17.
31.   Brooks, *Lectures on Preaching*, 5.
32.   Ibid., 129.
33.   Booth, *Preaching Power*, 23.
34.   A. W. Tozer, *The Root of the Righteous* (Harrisburg, PA: Christian Publications, 1955), 7.
35.   Gordon R. Lewis, *Decide for Yourself: A Theological Workbook* (Downers Grove, IL: InterVarsity, 1970), 9-10.

* Denotes page number(s) could not be verified.

CHAPTER II – BIBLIOLOGY

The Doctrine of the Bible

I. INTRODUCTION

The relationship that exists between the Bible and Christianity is undisputed among conservative theologians who hold to the historic view of inspiration and biblical authority. Harold Lindsell, who has represented evangelical Christianity as editor of *Christianity Today*, says, "The Bible is the starting point, or the source, of our religious knowledge."[1] In making that statement, he was identifying with past generations who held to a similar position on the importance of the Bible. Arthur W. Pink (1886-1952) wrote,

> Christianity is the religion of a Book. Christianity is based upon the impregnable rock of Holy Scripture. The starting point of all doctrinal discussion must be the Bible. Upon the foundation of the Divine inspiration of the Bible stands or falls the entire edifice of Christian truth. If the foundations be destroyed, what can the righteous do? (Ps. 11:3). Surrender the dogma of verbal inspiration and you are left like a rudderless ship on a stormy sea, at the mercy of every wind that blows.[2]

When Arthur Pink was born, the 1644 public statement by Baptists of their belief in the Bible [below] had been written for nearly two hundred and fifty years.

THE 1644 CONFESSION OF THE PARTICULAR BAPTISTS

Article 7. The Rule of this Knowledge, Faith and Obedience, concerning the worship and service of God, and all other Christian duties, is not man's inventions, opinions, devices, laws, constitutions, or traditions unwritten whatsoever, . . . but onely the Word of God contained in the Canonicall Scriptures [archaiac spelling in original].

Article 8. In this written Word God hath plainly revealed whatsoever he hath thought needfull for us to know, beleeve, and acknowledge, touching the Nature and Office of Christ, in whom all the promises are Yea and Amen to the praise of God.[3]

Christianity is as credible as its foundation which is the immutable rock of holy Scripture. But this Book is no natural book, for it claims to be a divine revelation, penned by human authors. As such, the Bible has dual authorship, written by men in their own language, yet the process was supernaturally guided by the Holy Spirit so that both words and messages are without error or mistake. The following rational argument that the Bible is the accurate Word of God is based on the presupposition that there is a God.

Since God is what He is—infinite, loving and the Redeemer—we can only expect that a loving and wise God would reveal a plan of redemption to man powerful enough to save him.

Since man is what he is—limited, sinful and needy—we can only conclude that he needs a message of help that will meet his need.

Therefore, we expect the message of redemption from God that is given to meet the needs of sinful man to be authoritative, accurate and reliable.

If the message of redemption were riddled with mistakes, man could not exercise faith in the message, and this would be counter-productive to revelation. If the message of redemption were not authoritative, man could have no confidence in its claim. Therefore, we can only conclude that the Bible is a revelation that is given in a manner that produces full confidence in both its content and its transmission to mankind.

---

1. Is the Bible the Word of God?
   A QUESTION OF REVELATION
2. Are the words of the Bible accurate and without error?
   A QUESTION OF INSPIRATION
3. Are the words of the Bible authoritative?
   A QUESTION OF INERRANCY
4. Do the present books in the Bible belong there?
   A QUESTION OF CANONICITY
5. Can we interpret the meaning of the Bible in today's language?
   A QUESTION OF HERMENEUTICS
6. Can we understand and apply the spiritual nature of the Bible to our lives?
   A QUESTION OF ILLUMINATION

The material in this chapter is presented in sequence. Note the order of the following questions. They begin with the authenticity of the content of the Word of God and end by asking if the Bible is meaningful in today's society.

A. REVELATION. The first section of this Bibliology deals with the doctrine of revelation which involves the content of God's message to us. Here we define and examine revelation, then give the proofs that God has disclosed Himself in the Bible.

Revelation is the act whereby God gives us knowledge about Himself which we could not otherwise know.

B. INSPIRATION. The second section is inspiration and bases its proofs on the previous argument that the Bible is a revelation from God. Since God has revealed Himself in the Bible, then we can only conclude that every word is accurate.

Inspiration is the supernatural guidance of the writers of Scripture by the Spirit of God whereby they wrote the divine Word of God, transcribed accurately and reliably.

C. INERRANCY. The third section of Bibliology demonstrates the authority and perpetuity of the inspired revelation. Not only are the words accurate, they are authoritative and without error of any kind.

Inerrancy recognizes that what God revealed and inspired is accurate, reliable, authoritative and without error.

D. CANON. The next section deals with how many books are in the Bible, and what is the basis upon which each one is included. There are only sixty-six books in the Bible. Other books will not be added, and none of the books in the present Bible will ever be proven false.

The Canon is the standard by which the sixty-six books in the Bible and their content were determined and the basis upon which they were included in Scripture.

E. INTERPRETATION. Once the content and the authority of the Bible is established, the next question involves the correct meaning of the content of Scripture. We do not force an external set of rules on the Bible by which to interpret its meaning. Within the Bible, God gave principles by which we should interpret its meaning.

Hermeneutics is the science of biblical interpretation.

F. ILLUMINATION. Once we learn the rules of interpreting the authoritative Bible, we must then realize that there is a second level of difficulty in understanding Scripture. This is the problem of spiritual blindness. Because the Bible was authored by God's Spirit, and its central theme involves a spiritual message, only those who are in proper relationship to the Holy Spirit can understand its message. Those who are not in proper relationship to God are unable to comprehend its spiritual message apart from spiritual illumination.

Illumination is the work of the Holy Spirit in helping the believer understand and apply the spiritual meaning of the Scriptures.

The study of Bibliology is not an attempt to make the Bible something it is not, nor is it an attempt by conservative theologians to make the Bible the Word of God. Rather, Bibliology attempts to recognize what the Bible claims for itself. The Bible claims to be the objective Word of God. Whether man understands it or not, whether he recognizes it or not, and whether he applies it to his life or not, it is still the Word of God.

II. GOD COMMUNICATING HIMSELF TO MAN

Revelation is the act of God whereby He gives knowledge of Himself which man could not otherwise know. Therefore, there is a great difference between the revelation of God and the discovery of God. Discovery implies that man, by exploration or research, has found God, who was unknown or had hidden Himself. Discovery further implies that God was inactive in the process and that man took the initiative in seeking after God. However, the opposite is true. God revealed Himself because man could not have found God by searching for Him. Man is spiritually limited, and man would not have sought for God, because a holy God condemns and punishes man, who is a sinner.

Dispensational theologian Charles Baker called revelation "the making known of truth to man which he could never learn through sense experience alone."[4] His reference to "sense experience" recognized man as incapable of knowing God through his emotions, although God may use the senses to reveal Himself to man. Buswell defined revelation as "the doctrine of God's making Himself, and relevant truths about Himself, known to man."[5] Here he emphasizes God as the source of revelation, which implies self-revelation.

The self-revelation of God teaches at least four things. First, God is the core of all revelation, for He has revealed Himself. Of course, revelation includes the works of God and the plan of God, but the essence of revelation is the self-disclosure by God. Second, we see that the ones to whom God revealed Himself did not seek after Him, implying they cannot perceive God without divine aid. In the third place we learn that the result of revelation is the communication of ideas or concepts. In the act of revelation, God revealed Himself to man. As the receiver of revelation, man had to interpret the stimulus/revelation he received. This reception process deals with ideas or concepts. The self-revelation of God was not made in vague feelings or ecstatic experiences. The self-revelation of God resulted in words and concepts that have meaning; the meaning of these words is objective, for they can be measured, repeated and interpreted. God did not reveal Himself in mysterious gobbledygook words. The self-revelation of God was an act that resulted in meaningful words. The fourth thing about revelation is that the message was written, which gives it perpetuity so that it can influence future generations. If the self-revelation of God was only oral, the receivers would have had no difficulty in understanding who God was. But there would have been problems as one generation sought to pass the message to a second generation. The self-revelation would have become corrupted if it were entrusted to the memory of man. But the self-revelation of God was encapsulated in a Book for man to read and pass on to others. Hence, God preserved its objectivity.

The primary motivation of revelation was not to give man doctrine, although the end product of revelation is doctrine. In the same manner, the primary motivation of revelation is not to communicate words, although these are the result of revelation. Revelation is not primarily given to communicate supernatural knowledge, nor is it given to stimulate man's ability to respond to God. Revelation is essentially an act whereby God unveils Himself to His people. This is more than a revelation of knowledge about Himself. Also, it is more than a revelation of information or doctrine of God. In the act of revelation, God revealed Himself— the living God disclosed Himself. This does not mean that the Bible is not a revelation of words, concepts, theology, or law, for it is all this and more. But the primary consideration of revelation is that the Bible reveals the Lord God Almighty who ultimately was made flesh in the incarnation and tabernacled among us. Baillie summarizes this point.

> . . . there appears a remarkable breadth of agreement in recent discussions about revelation. It is that what is fundamentally revealed is God Himself, not propositions about God. Equally remarkable, however, is the recent agreement on the second, which is this: That God reveals Himself *in action*—in the gracious activity by which He invades the field of human experience and human history which is otherwise but a vain show, empty and drained of meaning . . . The Bible is essentially a story of the acts of God . . . . Other sacred books are composed mainly of oracles which communicate what profess to be timeless truths about universal being or timeless prescriptions for the conduct of life and worship. But the Bible is mainly a record of what God has done.[6]

A. THE NATURE AND METHOD OF REVELATION. God used variety in revealing Himself to mankind. In both general and special revelation, God reveals Himself by revealing His names (Gen. 1:1; Exod. 3:12), His nature (Psa. 139), and His Creation (Gen. 1).

God revealed information about man (Gen. 2), angels (Heb. 1), demons (Rev. 12:4), sin (Rom. 3:10-23) and holiness (Lev. 19:2). Revelation was given in a variety of methods. God gave revelation to His prophets and apostles in visions (Isa. 6; Rev. 4:2-6), dreams (i.e., Joseph, Daniel), poetry (Exod. 15, Job and Psalms), biographical writings (Esth.), parables or stories (Luke 15), history (1 & 2 Kgs.), and sermons (Matt. 5-7, 24-25). God dictated (Rev. 2:1-3:22) and wrote on stone tablets (Exod. 34:1). God taught His spokesmen directly (Lev. 1:1), and led His prophets by an inner voice. God revealed Himself through circumstances and through angels. But the greatest self-revelation of God is through the incarnation of Jesus Christ who was the God-Man.

METHODS OF GOD'S SELF-REVELATION	
1. Visions—Isa. 6	8. Miracles—John 6
2. Dreams—Dan. 2	9. Parables—Luke15
3. Poetry—Psa. 139	10. Inner compulsion—Acts 21:10-13
4. Biography—Gospels	11. History—1 & 2 Chron.
5. Sermons—Matt. 5	12. Angels—Luke 1:26-38
6. Spoke face to face—Deut. 5:4	13. Historical Research—Luke 1:1-4
7. Wrote on Stone—Deut. 10:4	14. Jesus Christ—John 1:14

Divine revelation has not told everything there is to know about God. "The secret things belong unto the LORD our God: but those things which are revealed belong unto us and to our children for ever, that we may do all the words of this law" (Deut. 29:29). This does not mean the Bible is incomplete or the task of writing revelation was poorly done. It means God has not revealed everything there is to know about Himself, but everything that He intended to be revealed is found in the Bible. Therefore, the Bible is complete, yet, in its completed form, it is only a partial revelation of God. We do not know everything there is to know about God. We have what is necessary and adequate.

When John wrote the Revelation, he was prevented from recording something God had revealed to him (Rev. 10:4). Paul had a similar experience where "he was caught up into paradise, and heard unspeakable words, which it is not lawful for a man to utter" (2 Cor. 12:4). God has wisely seen fit not to reveal some things to us. There are things about God still hidden and unrevealed. Whatever these things involve, we can be certain that the revelation that God has given us is sufficient to accomplish His purpose in our lives.

The fact that revelation is partial does not mean it is incomplete, or not sufficient in what is revealed. Divine revelation is complete concerning the facts of redemption. There is nothing else we need to know to get saved. The Christian does not expect to find some new truth that he needs to do to gain merit with God. In fact, the final words of the closing chapter of the Bible make it clear that this is a completed Book. "For I testify unto every man that heareth the words of the prophecy of this book, if any man shall add unto these things, God shall add unto him the plagues that are written in the book" (Rev. 22:18). Even though these words were written for the book of Revelation, they apply to the total Bible.

God used all five senses when He gave a revelation to man. Sometimes men recorded what they saw, and at other times they communicated the message they heard. Some of the prophets spoke from their feelings, recognizing the burden of the Lord (Hab. 1:1). God called Ezekiel to eat a scroll to reveal to him truth through his sense of taste. There was even one occasion when the Son of God used the sense of smell in the process of His revelation (John 11:39). Through it all, the Holy Spirit was governing the human authors so that the end product they wrote was the very Word of God.

The purpose of revelation is the salvation of men (2 Tim. 3:15). Toward the end of the first century, Jude wrote, "that ye should earnestly contend for the faith which was once [*and for all*] delivered unto the saints" (Jude 3, emphasis added). Though partial, it is as complete as it needs to be.

> ### HOW GOD USED THE SENSES IN REVELATION
>
> 1. Sight—Rev. 1:19
> 2. Hearing—Rev. 1:10
> 3. Smell—John 11:39
> 4. Taste—Ezek. 3:3,4:9-17
> 5. Touch/feeling—1 John 1:11

Divine revelation is also progressive. God spoke both "in time past unto the fathers by the prophets" and "hath in these last days spoken unto us by his Son" (Heb. 1:1-2). Revelation was progressive not in the sense that prior facts (i.e., Old Testament) were false, but rather that they were incomplete. In Jesus Christ we know more about the person of God and His plan of salvation than was known in the Old Testament. Even those who wrote and recorded the Scriptures did not always fully understand what they wrote: "the prophets have inquired and searched diligently, who prophesied of the grace that should come unto you; searching what, or what manner of time the Spirit of Christ which was in them did signify, when it testified beforehand of the sufferings of Christ, and the glory that should follow" (1 Pet. 1:10-11). Even though Isaiah has given the most extensive contribution to Christology of any Old Testament book, it is highly unlikely that he had as thorough an understanding of the doctrine of Messiah as the average member in the church at Jerusalem being taught that doctrine by Peter and John.

The influence of revelation continues today as God enables men to gain knowledge about Himself based on the revelation that has already taken place in general and special revelation. But this does not mean that new insights or new facts about the nature of God may not be learned. The Bible is a continuing influence of revelation so men may continually learn something of the existence and nature of God that has already been revealed.

> Natural revelation is the self-revelation of God through His Creation and through the makeup of man.

Sometimes the terms "revelation" (content) and "inspiration" (the guarantee of the words) are confused. They may occur at the same time, but they are not synonymous. Revelation has to do with the content of God's message, while inspiration deals with the accuracy of the written words. While we speak of the Bible as the result of both the revelation of God and the inspiration of God, we are recognizing two separate works of God. When John wrote the final book of the Bible, God gave him truth (revelation) while the Holy Spirit guided his writing (inspiration) in such a way as to produce the very Word of God.   In that activity, two distinct processes were taking place simultaneously.

B. THE TWO AREAS OF REVELATION.   God's act of self-revelation can be divided into two areas. First, the self-revelation of God is evident in nature, or, as someone has observed, "the Creator is evident in His Creation." Second, God has revealed Himself through the Word of God and its central message, who is Jesus Christ. This second area is called special revelation.

General revelation is the self-revelation of God that can be objectively seen in nature (Rom. 1:12-20) and objectively perceived by man (Rom. 2:14, 15). Natural revelation is given to communicate the person of God and the power of God. This is sometimes called general revelation. Man does not need a special enablement of the Holy Spirit to perceive natural revelation; it is available to all men.

> Special revelation is the self-revelation of God through the Scriptures and finalized in Jesus Christ and relates to God's plan of salvation for man.

But some have rejected the testimony of natural revelation so often that it no longer communicates to them because they have rendered themselves immune to its credibility. Revelation is always an act of God, whether He uses natural or supernatural means to reveal Himself.

Supernatural revelation is also found in the Scriptures and ultimately in the person of Christ. This is sometimes called Special Revelation. It is special in the sense that it reveals God's unique plan of salvation. God's special revelation must be spiritually discerned. Those who perceive it must not only apply the general methods of literary interpretation, but must also be correctly related to the Holy Spirit to receive and understand His special revelation.

It is not coincidental that the last book of the Bible is called the Revelation of Jesus Christ, for it is the final and complete disclosure of the Lord Jesus Christ.

HOW GOD REVEALS HIMSELF	
General Revelation	Special Revelation
1. Nature (Psa. 19:1-6; Rom. 1:18-21)	1. Bible (Deut. 29:29; 2 Pet. 1:20-21)
2. Conscience (Rom. 2:14-16)	2. Christ (John 1:14, 18)
3. History (1 Cor. 10:1-6)	

III. GOD'S SELF-REVELATION FROM NATURE

As we examine the self-revelation of God in nature, remember that these are also arguments used to prove the existence of God. Although the mind intuitively accepts the idea of the existence of God before it faces these proofs, these arguments provide a logical reason why the mind has accepted God's existence. Actually, these arguments do not guarantee the existence of God, but show a degree of probability that He does exist. We intuitively know that God exists, but this is not proof. And in the same vein, the Bible does not attempt to prove God, but it accepts His existence as fact: "In the beginning God." Once we accept this presupposition, our proof is based on consistency with truth and correspondence with reality.

The rational arguments to prove God's existence and the results of general revelation are dealt with in this section because they have a cause-and-effect relationship to one another. The cause is the general, self—revelation of God—the result is the proof for His existence.

REVELATION FROM NATURE	
TITLE	PROOF
Cosmological	God is the Cause
Teleological	God is the Designer
Anthropological	God is a Person

This section uses logic or rational philosophy to prove its arguments. Here we can raise the question, "What is the relationship between revelation and reason?" Some theologians teach that God is revealed through man's reason, while other theologians leave no room for reason or philosophy. This conclusion is based upon a misinterpretation of Col. 2:8, "Beware lest any man spoil you through philosophy and vain deceit, after the tradition of men, after the rudiments of the world, and not after Christ." But this extreme position that rejects reason is answered by the clear statement, "Come now and let us reason together" (Isa. 1:18).

God does not reveal Himself through reason and we should never base a doctrine on reason. But correct doctrine is always reasonable, because it reflects the mind of God. God is perfect intellect, so His doctrine will always exemplify truth and never contradict itself. Since everything that God makes is an extension of His nature, then the mind of man and his ability to reason must be an avenue that man can use, just as God uses it.

Reason is the intellectual and moral faculties of man as exercised in the pursuit of truth apart from supernatural aid. Hence, reason is not a means of revelation, meaning God does not use it to reveal Himself. But God uses reason for man to understand His power and personal activity in nature (Rom. 1:18, 20). Reason can also perceive the message of God's special revelation in the Word of God, and when aided by the Holy Spirit, man can come to know God through His Word.

A. COSMOLOGICAL ARGUMENT: NATURE REVEALS GOD'S POWER AND GODHEAD. Paul declares that the facts of nature reveal the existence of God. "For the wrath of God is revealed from heaven against all ungodliness and unrighteousness of men, who hold the truth in unrighteousness; Because that which may be known of God is manifest in them; for God hath shewed it unto them" (Rom. 1:18, 19). The word "cosmological" comes from kosmas (world) and logos (word). It is a study of the world as it reveals God. Two things are known about God from the study of nature. First, "His eternal power" and, second, His "Godhead." This means a study of nature reveals the omnipotent power of God and the personhood of God. The cosmological argument is based upon the fact of causation, or that God is the First Cause. Because something (nature) cannot come from nothing, and something (Creation) does exist by itself, therefore there must have been a force more powerful than nature to create the world. Hence the existence of Creation implies a Creator.

Chafer explained, "The cosmological argument depends upon the validity of three contributing truths: (a) that every effect must have a cause; (b) that the effect is dependent upon its cause for its existence; and (c) that nature cannot produce itself."[7]

Major Premise:	The present world reflects an interrelated existence that is described as a cause-and-effect relationship.
Minor Premise:	Everything begun traces its existence back to an independent and all-powerful First Cause that had a prior existence.
Conclusion:	Therefore, the world must be the result of an omnipotent and eternal First Cause that exercises free will.

Hodge concludes this argument, "Hence the universe must have a cause exterior to itself, and the ultimate or absolute cause must be eternal, uncaused and unchangeable."[8] Strong, however, is not convinced that much can be concluded from this argument. He states the argument, "Everything begun, whether substance or phenomenon, owes its existence to some producing cause. The universe, at least so far as its present form is concerned, is a thing begun, and owes its existence to a cause which is equal to its production. This cause must be indefinitely great."[9] According to Strong, the cause of the universe must be greater than the universe, but not necessarily omnipotent or eternal.

First, let us examine the law of causation. The existence of cause is recognized. Every event must have a cause. Only in theoretical speculation do philosophers deny the possibility of cause. This world is a long chain of cause-and-effect relationships. Every time the mind encounters an effect, it logically traces the sequence back to a beginning cause. There must be a first cause, because the mind rejects a chain that hangs on nothing.

The world is constituted as a mass of interacting dependent causes. Everything in the universe has an influence on everything else. Whether we consider the balance in nature, the balance within the unsplit atom or the balance within the human body, we see that Creation has an infinite number of interacting parts in dependent relationship to one another. The chain that has no beginning or that hangs on nothing is impossible to conceive. Therefore, behind nature's chain of events the mind conceives of a larger force that causes its existence. The most logical explanation for this world is a "Free Cause" or an "Uncaused Cause," also called the "Prime Mover."

This argument states that a First Cause must be eternal. And if the First Cause is eternal, then how did it at a moment in time change its immutable existence to create a series of cause-and-effect relationships? The only answer is that the First Cause possessed free will. In summary, First Cause possesses two qualities. First, it has power to create the world, and second it has the quality of free will or personality. The First Cause must have possessed the ability to interpret its eternal existence and at a particular moment decide to begin the existence of the world as we now know it. Therefore, we come to the logical conclusion that the First Cause is a powerful person, who is God.

When scientists examine the world, they find physical minute cells of matter. These are called molecules, exactly equal and each interrelated to another, yet not possessing the features of eternal self-existence. Reason requires that they be explained by an external and omnipotent power that was uncaused, yet at the same time possessing free will or personality. This argument results in certainty, but stops short of demonstration because Creation cannot be recreated.

B. TELEOLOGICAL ARGUMENT: DESIGN IN THE UNIVERSE REVEALS A DESIGNER. The word "teleological" comes from τελος (*telos*, end) and λογος (*logos*, word), which is a study of God as He is revealed in the design or goal of His Creation. God is an intelligent Creator because of the design that is apparent in the animate and inanimate universe. Thus, the teleological argument implies a Creator because of the design that is apparent in the world.

Hodge notes the teleological argument "is ultimately based upon the recognition of the operations of an intelligent cause in nature."[10] Thiessen states the argument, "Order and useful arrangement in a system imply intelligence and purpose in the originating cause; the universe is characterized by order and useful arrangement; therefore the universe has an intelligent and free cause."[11] Thiessen cites Psa. 94:9 as a biblical example of the use of the teleological argument. Here the psalmist reminds us that someone "planted the ear" and "formed the eye." Baker goes as far as to state that the teleological argument demonstrates the personality of God, writing, "the various things and objects which make up the universe appear to have been made to fulfill a purpose, to accomplish a certain end. There seems to be some intelligence or mind behind the Creation, i.e., a Cause which is intelligent and purposeful, and therefore personal."[12] Some might question whether intelligence alone is enough to determine personality without an indication of emotion.

The psalmist states the teleological argument, "The heavens declare the glory of God; and the firmament sheweth his handywork" (Psa. 19:1). This bolsters Paul's thought that "the invisible things from the creation of the world are clearly seen, being understood by the things that are made" (Rom. 1:20).

This argument implies that the design in the universe leads to a designer. As with the cosmological argument, the teleological argument does not prove certainty, but only probability. It is impossible to prove conclusively that there is a design in the universe because we cannot examine all the relevant data. But there are substantial evidences of design from what we have observed. The argument is strengthened when we say the results of a design lead to a designer.

By design we imply three things. First, it means the First Cause had a blueprint or design before the process began. Second, the First Cause selected the proper means (laws, decision, interdependency of parts, etc.) to accomplish the results that were desired. And third, the First Cause used the means according to His independent and all powerful nature to accomplish the preconceived design.

By way of illustration, compare a pile of bricks to a brick wall. The pile of bricks may have been dumped from a truck with no thought of pattern. They fell haphazardly to the ground. In contrast, the brick wall was laid in a perpendicular angle, each brick held in place by mortar, each row level, and no brick out of pattern. It is not necessary to observe the truck dump the bricks to realize there is no pattern or logical arrangement to the whole. Nor is it necessary to see the brick mason lay each brick to realize he had a design in mind as he constructed the brick wall. First, the brick mason had a design or pattern in mind before he began laying bricks.

Major Premise:	The reflection of an orderly and harmonious universe in all its parts is accounted for by a design.
Minor Premise:	Design in the universe comes from a predetermination of design, a selection of proper means to accomplish the design and the ability to implement the design.
Conclusion:	The First Cause of the universe possesses intelligence.

Second, he had the proper means (tools, intellectual capacity, and physical ability) to finish the wall. And third, he had the free choice supported by his intellectual ability to carry out the project. From this illustration we imply there is a Creator who is free and powerful enough to create this world according to a design.

A denial of the order in the universe is a denial of the uniformity of nature and a denial of the existence of the laws or principles upon which science is based. Huxley noted, "The object of science is the discovery of the rational order which pervades the universe."[13]

C. Anthropological Argument: Human Nature Reveals a Personal God.   The anthropological argument is also called the moral or psychological argument because it reasons that the higher parts of human nature could never have come from non-intelligent matter. Man's intellect must come from the First Cause, and since the First Cause possesses qualities far higher and different than materialism (proved by cosmological and teleological arguments), then man must have come from God.

Strong considered the anthropological argument highly complex and divided it into three parts, including:

1. Man's intellectual and moral nature must have had for its author an intellectual and moral Being.
2. Man's moral nature proves the existence of a holy Lawgiver and Judge.
3. Man's emotional and voluntary nature proves the existence of a Being who can furnish in himself a satisfying object of human affection and an end which will call forth man's highest activities and ensure his highest progress.[14]

First, man's intellect must have an adequate explanation. It could not evolve from matter, and it could not come from anything that is described as non-intellect. Matter and intellect are essentially different in nature, i.e., matter is classified by its physical properties while mind is described by its non-material existence and is measured by its result. Since an effect cannot be greater than its cause, matter cannot be greater than mind. Since man with his mind can control matter, and man can modify the makeup of matter, while the reverse is not true, then mind is greater than matter. Therefore, mind cannot be the result of matter, and the existence of the mind (with memory, discernment, choice, and reason) leads us to accept the First Cause as possessing mind. And since man has similar rational facilities, then man must have received his mind from God.

Second, man's freedom must have an adequate explanation. Man possesses the conviction that he is free and cannot be alienated from his freedom. Man's freedom is exposed in his desires. And man's desire for freedom usually leads us to believe in his moral nature. Man is not like an inanimate object or similar to a rock that can only follow the laws of gravity and fall toward the center of the earth. Man has the power to perceive alternative choices and to follow alternative choices. Man's freedom is based on his mind. The First Cause was free to create the world, or begin the chain of cause-and-effect relationships. The freedom of man is evidence that he was caused by the First Cause who began all things.

Major Premise:	Man is a free and intelligent being.
Minor Premise:	Because matter does not have the properties of freedom and intelligence, it is not an adequate explanation for man.
Conclusion:	Therefore, man's freedom and intelligence are explained by God who is a person characterized by intellect and freedom.

D. ONTOLOGICAL ARGUMENT: OUR THOUGHTS OF GOD IMPLY THE EXISTENCE OF GOD. This is not one of the strongest arguments for the existence of God. But the probability of God's existence is established in the descending credibility of the previous three arguments. However, once God's existence is accepted and the aspects of His self-revelation are examined, the ontological argument illustrates His existence.

The word "ontological" comes from οντος (*ontos*, being) and λογος (*logos*, word). This is an argument to prove the existence of God from man's idea of a perfect being. It was originated by Anselm during the Middle Ages. He said man has the idea of a perfect being. Since a more perfect or greater being cannot be conceived, there must be a perfect being to correspond to the idea. Anselm implies actual existence is a necessary conclusion to actual thought of the most perfect being. He stated, "An ideal thing, however perfect in conception, cannot answer to the idea of the most perfect. Hence we must admit the actual existence; for only with this content can we have the idea of the most perfect being. This most perfect being is God Therefore God must exist."[15]

This argument does not reason from effect to cause as do the other arguments to prove God's existence. Whereas the others are inductive in nature, this is deductive, and as such does not lead to probability or certainty, but to logical certitude only if the premise is unchallenged. But the phenomenology of perception is greatly influenced by subjective desire, subconscious motives, and sociological conditioning. The rationalistic philosopher Descartes added an inductive aspect to this argument. He said the idea of a perfect and infinite Being cannot be derived from a finite and imperfect man. Therefore, there must be a perfect and infinite Being who put an idea of His being in man.

E. ARGUMENTS FROM CONGRUITY: THE EXISTENCE OF GOD IS IN HARMONY WITH THE FACTS. "Congruity" means agreement, harmony or correspondence. This is not a separate argument for the existence of God, nor does it add any content to the general self-revelation of God. The existence of God is in harmony (congruity) with all facts, whether those facts be connected with man's innate knowledge of God, the revelation of God in nature, or the knowledge of God that man can have through or as a result of his rational process. This argument states that since there is a lack of conflicting evidence that God does not exist, the rational mind can only accept the existence of God as revealed through general revelation.

Immanuel Kant describes the argument of congruity in reverse. He reasons that the "antinomies" or self-contradictions are rival alternatives to the proofs for the existence of

God. By this he means a person must believe in the cosmological argument for the existence of God, or he must believe that matter is eternal. He must believe that the design in nature points to God or he must believe everything was fashioned by random chance. The mind must reject the one while accepting the other. Therefore, he concludes that if a person cannot answer the arguments, he must accept them. If a man cannot disprove God, he must accept Him.

When the wise men came from the east seeking the baby Jesus (Matt. 2:1-11), they knew God existed, and they followed the star. That was general revelation in nature. Their knowledge of history might have told them of a time in the past when God had done something special with His people. Their conscience might have influenced them to seek to worship a God who was greater than themselves. Their examination of natural revelation led them to Jerusalem, where they encountered special revelation. There they heard a verse of Scripture (Mic. 5:2) that directed them to Bethlehem. In Bethlehem, they had their fullest revelation of God as they worshipped the baby King, the Word that became flesh (John 1:14). Finally, God warned them in a dream. This pattern can be followed in reaching lost people with the gospel. People should respond to natural revelation; but that will never save them. Natural revelation points them to special revelation where they learn of the Person of Jesus Christ and His salvation. Special revelation far surpasses history, conscience and nature. As we study the Bible, we will be constantly pointed to Christ. Someday Christ shall return and we shall know even as we are known (1 Cor. 13:12).

IV. GOD'S SELF REVELATION FROM WITHIN MAN

At the beginning of this section we said God has revealed Himself in three ways through general revelation. First through Creation, second, through man's conscience, and third, through the existence of laws in the world. This section deals with the general revelation of God through conscience and laws within the world.

GENERAL REVELATION WITHIN MAN	
1. Conscience	Rom. 2:15
2. Moral absolutes reflected in laws	Rom. 2:12

A. THE CONSCIENCE IS A REVELATION OF A MORAL GOD. One of the reasons that Paul gives for the judgment by God of all men is that they have an inner witness that reveals the existence of God to them. He states, "which shew the work of the law written in their hearts, their conscience also bearing witness" (Rom. 2:15). Just as God has revealed Himself as the Creator in His Creation, God also has revealed Himself as the lawgiver in that the law is written in the conscience of man.

The word "conscience" comes from "con" (with) and "science" (to know), meaning a person knows certain things innately with himself. It is built into our very nature. The conscience is an extension of the law of God that was placed in man at Creation. Because man was created in the image of God (and God is moral), then we expect that man would possess a moral nature. The conscience is based on the same standard as the Ten Commandments, which *is* an expression of the nature of God Himself. When man violates the standard of God or displeases the person of God, he must ultimately answer for his transgressions. Man's knowledge of breaking God's law is one of the bases for God's judgment. Paul says, "their thoughts the mean while accusing" (Rom. 2:15). The accusation will be brought "in the day when God shall judge the secrets of men" (Rom. 2:16). The Gentiles' conscience becomes "a law unto themselves" (Rom. 2:14).

James Stalker described conscience, noting, "when the will stands at the parting of the ways, seeing clearly before it the right course and the wrong, conscience commands to strike into the one and forbids to choose the other."[16]   S. S. Smalley suggests that conscience "implies more than simply 'consciousness' or 'awareness,' since it includes also judgment (in biblical terms a precisely moral judgment) upon a conscious act."[17]

Man has a conscience because he is the pinnacle of Creation.   And the highest relationship that the creature has with his Creator is in moral relationship.

B. LAWS IMPLY THE EXISTENCE OF A LAWGIVER. This aspect of the general revelation of God is debated by theologians. Some feel that the existence of laws in society or the existence of a moral law within the individual is evidence of God's self-revelation. They argue that, since laws are an extension of the nature of God, the presence of laws in society are our evidence that God has made man a social creature and placed within man a desire for law and order. Obviously they do not say civil law is meritorious, but that its existence reveals God the lawgiver. Also, they imply that man's inborn impulse to judge others who break the law is evidence of that law.

How can we know that a straight line is straight and not crooked if there is not a standard somewhere to judge the "Straightness" of the line? Thus all desire for justice and for a perfect law that is based on a "perfectly straight line" implies the existence of the perfect law.

Paul uses this as evidence that God will judge men. "Therefore thou art inexcusable, O man, whosoever thou art that judgest: for wherein thou judgest another, thou condemnest thyself; for thou that judgest doest the same things" (Rom. 2:1). Evidence that the inner man recognizes the law of God is found in the next verse. "But we are sure that the judgment of God is according to truth against them that commit such things" (Rom. 2:2).

The argument for the existence of God based on laws is another side of the teleological argument. The argument from design implies a "fixed standard," which is another way to say "law."

Other theologians do not see the existence of laws as a separate revelation of God, but a continuation of the revelation of God through man's conscience. Man is guilty of the things of which he accuses others, because man's inner conscience tells him that he does the same thing.

V. ARGUMENTS THAT THE BIBLE IS THE WORD OF GOD

The positive question "Is the Bible the Word of God?" can also be phrased negatively, "Does the Bible have mistakes?" Actually, this is a question concerning the credibility of revelation. It is not an attempt to prove that every word in the Bible is accurate. That is a question of inspiration which will be dealt with in the next section. Also, this section does not answer the question regarding the trustworthiness of the message in the manuscripts that we now possess. That will be dealt with in the section on inerrancy.

This section does not begin its arguments that the Bible is the Word of God because it says so. That would be arguing in a circle. That would be like saying, "Wood comes from a tree because it is made of wood." This section bases its claim upon the demonstration (1) that the Bible is consistent with itself, (2) that the Bible corresponds with reality, and (3) that the Bible's claims can be scientifically demonstrated. We shall examine the Bible's claim that it is the Word of God. Being presuppositionalists, we accept it as God's self-revelation—now we must demonstrate that: (1) its claims are consistent, (2) its claims correspond with reality, (3) its claims work in the life of the reader, and (4) its claims are in harmony with history, with archaeology and with all of nature. When we can successfully apply to the Bible all the methods of proving truth, we can accept its premise that it is the self-revelation of God.

THE BIBLE IS THE WORD OF GOD BECAUSE OF:

---

1. The unique revelation of Jesus Christ.
2. The extraordinary claims that the Bible is from God.
3. The empirical fulfillment of prophecy.
4. The convicting, convincing, converting power of the message.
5. The inexhaustible infinity of its message.
6. The unity of the message from diverse human sources.
7. The trans-cultural appeal of the message.
8. The unmistakable honesty of the Bible.
9. The immeasurable superiority to other literature.
10. The pragmatic test of experience.

This section will present ten proofs that the Bible is the Word of God. These arguments are not all equally convincing, but descend in order of importance.

A. THE BIBLE IS THE WORD OF GOD BECAUSE OF ITS UNIQUE REVELATION OF THE PERSON OF CHRIST. No other book except a book from God could have contained a convicting yet extraordinary message about the Son of God. Even if another book could have conceived such a message, it would not have done so. The first argument that the Bible is the Word of God is based on the person of Jesus Christ. The Bible teaches that the person of Christ existed before Creation, that He was the Creator, that He manifested Himself in the Old Testament through Christophanies, that He was born of a virgin and came into the world as the God-man. The Bible declares that Christ lived without sin and died as a substitute for the salvation of sinners. The Bible further declares that Jesus was buried and on the third day arose from the dead and ascended into Heaven where He makes intercession at the right hand of God the Father. Finally, the Bible teaches that Jesus Christ shall return to take those who believe in Him to be with Him forever. This unique revelation of the God-man demands an examination by any rational person who is seeking the truth. The claims of Jesus Christ are so radical that they cannot be ignored. The claims are so overwhelming that a person must fully accept them, or utterly reject them. If Jesus Christ is the Son of God, as He claimed, and if He died for all men, then everyone is obligated to believe in Him. If Jesus Christ is not what He claimed, then man must respond by rejecting His claim.

The claims of Jesus Christ are quite remarkable when examined thoroughly. Jesus Christ affirmed his deity: (1) He applied to Himself the statement of Jehovah, "I am" (John 8:24). This affirmation is taken from the root word for "Jehovah," "I am that I am" (Exod. 3:14-15; John 4:26, 18:5-6). The Jews did not misunderstand His claim. They knew that Jesus was claiming full deity, and they tried to stone Him (John 8:59). (2) Jesus claimed to be identical with the Father (John 14:9, 10:33). (3) He asserted His omnipresence (Matt. 18:20; John 3:13), omniscience (John 11:14), and omnipotence (Matt. 28:18; John 5:21-23, 6:19). (4) Jesus received and approved of human worship (Matt. 14:33; 28:9; John 20:28-29). (5) He forgave sins (Mark 2:5-7, Luke 7:48-50). (6) He made Jehovahistic statements, "I am"— i.e., bread, light, the door, the way, the truth and the life, resurrection and life,—hence identifying Himself with God (John 6:37, 8:12, 10:9, 11:25, 14:6). Obviously, Jesus took Himself extremely seriously. Why? Because He understood who He was. There is no doubt that Jesus claimed to be God and told others that He was God. C. S. Lewis has rightly stated his position.

I am trying here to prevent anyone saying the really foolish thing that people often say about Him: "I'm ready to accept Jesus as a great moral teacher, but I don't accept His claim to be God." That is the one thing we must not say. A man who was merely a man and said the sort of things Jesus said would not be a great moral teacher. He would either be a lunatic—on a level with the man who says he is a poached egg—or he would be the Devil of Hell. You must make your choice. Either this man was, and is, the Son of God: or else a madman or something worse.[18]

C. S. Lewis brings us to a dilemma. The claims of Jesus Christ must be accepted for what they are: "He was God" or "He must be rejected." Lewis adds,

You can shut Him up for a fool, you can spit at Him and kill Him as a demon; or you can fall at His feet and call Him Lord and God. But let us not come with any patronising nonsense about His being a great human teacher. He has not left that open to us. He did not intend to.[19]

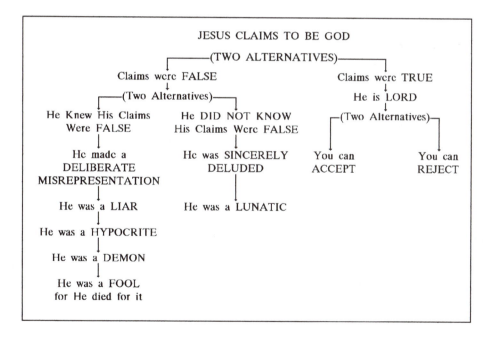

The remarkable teachings of Jesus Christ draw us to the following conclusions: that Jesus Christ is God, that Jesus Christ is the message of the Bible, and that the Bible is the

Word of God. Josh McDowell has given us the chart on the previous page to illustrate this claim.[20]

The claims of Jesus Christ are so all-encompassing that there is no alternative or middle road. Either a person must believe in the message of the Bible or reject it. If he believes, he will go to Heaven as Jesus promised, but if he rejects, he will be punished in Hell. The logical conclusions are so absurd that if accepted, man believes in Christ and hence accepts the Bible as the Word of God. However, the claims are so constructed that if man rejects, it is an automatic rejection, because the logic of rejection drives a man to deny its credibility.

Some claim that Jesus Christ is a journalistic or creative invention. If man invented Christ by journalistic fiction or by religious mysticism, then two questions face us. First, if man invented Christ, why has man not invented a greater god than Jesus Christ? And second, if man invented Christ, why has He not been able to improve on Christ over the years?

> If man invented Christ,
>   why has he not improved upon Him?
> If man invented Christ,
>   why has he not invented another?

Let us examine the first question. The fact that Jesus Christ is presented as the perfect God-man implies He has all the attributes that the average man would project onto deity. The Greeks had their concept of deity which is nothing more than an extension of the adoration of man. The Americans have invented Superman, Spiderman, Batman or some other super-hero. Again, all of these qualities are the amplification of man and his desires to live beyond his present human limitations. The gods created by man are an extension of the desires of man and not a personification of the infinite and eternal power that are usually inherent in deity. The fact that Christ possesses absolute powers suggests He must be God who has revealed Himself to man.

The second question follows the same nature as the first: if man journalistically created Christ out of fiction, why has he not been able to improve on the idea of Christ? Many men have tried to humanize Christ, making Him less than God. But no one has ever tried to improve on Jesus Christ to make Him more loving, more powerful or more eternal. The fact that He possesses absolute power implies He cannot be improved. Yet Jesus is perfectly human, and He is therefore the God-man who cannot be equaled or duplicated. Therefore, the absolute qualities of the person of Jesus Christ as revealed in Scripture give credence that the Bible was written by God, and not by man. This argument is not absolute proof, but is a strong suggestion that the Bible is a revelation from God.

Man would not write the Bible if he could, and man could not write the Bible if he would. By this we mean man would not write the Bible, for in doing so he has created a message of the perfect Son of God who condemns all men. Since God will judge sin, no rational man would write a book that would be self-condemning. Rather, the average man will write a book that reinforces the way he lives. Surely judgment in Hell would not be desired by any rational thinking man for himself or for others. In the second place, man could not write a Bible if he would. Because of the limitations of humanity, it is impossible for an imperfect human with limited rational ability to conceive of an unlimited God who is all-powerful and eternal in attributes.

Man could not have written the Bible if given the ability.
Man would not have written the Bible if given the opportunity.

Lewis S. Chafer, founder and former president of Dallas Theological Seminary, puts it this way: "It is not such a book as man would write if he *could*, or could write if he *would*."[21]

Jesus Christ has equal appeal to all nations, and very few readers consider Him a Jew born in Asia. In the nations of the earth, Jesus Christ is loved and revered by all people whether young or old, male or female. The universal appeal of Jesus Christ is not an argument that stands by itself, but it does contribute to the fact of the uniqueness of the self-revelation of God in the incarnation of His Son. The unique revelation as found in the Bible points to the fact that it is the Word of God.

Also consider the fact that Jesus Christ has all the ideal characteristics and qualities that are found in an exemplary person. Abraham was known for his faith, Job for his patience, Elijah for his boldness and Paul for his logical rationality. Luther was a reformer, Whitfield a preacher and Bill Bright is a soul winner. But Jesus Christ has all of these traits wrapped up in One Person. As a matter of fact, every exemplary quality found in an ideal person is present in Jesus Christ. The all-encompassing characteristics of Jesus Christ point to the uniqueness of His revelation, which in turn points to the Bible as being the Word of God.

B. THE EXTRAORDINARY CLAIMS THAT THE BIBLE IS FROM GOD. We cannot prove that the Bible is the Word of God merely by saying, "It claims to be the Word of God." This is a circular argument. Many false leaders have claimed to speak God's Word, but they were wrong. Therefore, how can we use this argument to prove the Bible's credibility? We do this by putting it to the test. Either the Bible is the Word of God (and it must be accepted as from God) or it is the greatest forgery every printed (and must be rejected). First, let us examine the claims that the Bible makes concerning the source of its message. Over 3,000 times in Scripture the authors claim their message is from God. Expressions like "thus saith the LORD" appear approximately 500 times in the Pentateuch and over 1,200 times in the prophets.

Old Testament prophets used expressions like "thus saith the LORD or "The word of the LORD came unto . . . ." These expressions are themselves among the strongest arguments for accepting the Bible. Concerning the expressions "Word of the Lord" (*debhar Yahweh*), B. B. Warfield writes that it "is at once the simplest and the most colorless designation of a Divine communication." He then goes on to note, "Both phrases ['Word of the Lord' and 'Law of the Lord'] are used for any Divine communication of whatever extent; and both came to be employed to express the entire body of Divine revelation, conceived as a unitary whole . . . and both passed into the NT with these implications."

We would expect that if God wrote a book, His truthfulness would demand that He claim to be its author. Therefore, when we find such phrases as "The word of the LORD came to me" or "The mouth of the LORD has spoken . . ." it is not unusual that God is claiming authorship of the Bible. Seldom do human authors not add their by-lines to their stories or their names to the front of their books. So that man could not mistake its source, God has placed His autograph throughout the Scriptures in thousands of places.

If we argue from the a priori arguments that there must be a message from God, and if we argue that Jesus Christ could not be invented by the human mind, then we must have a book with a unique message from God. Then, to argue a step farther, the uniqueness of the message demands a unique avenue of communication. Since the message demands credibility so it can be accepted, God must communicate the message in a way that guarantees its reliability. Therefore, God gives the message, and the human messengers tell everyone the message came from God.

The question of revelation does not concern the reliability of the human authors, but the authenticity of its divine author, God. Did God write the Bible? We must accept the Bible as the Word of God, or we must reject it as a hoax or a fraud. If it is a fraud, we should reject it completely for its lack of integrity and reliability. On the other hand, if the Bible is God's Book, we must accept its message and respond accordingly.

The world has attempted to minimize the Bible by stating, "It is a good book, but full of errors." Actually, this antithesis is difficult to believe, if not impossible. How can the Bible be a good book with errors? If it is a good book, meaning it has an acceptable message, then it should be accepted and believed. If it is a book with errors, then it cannot be trusted and should be rejected. Actually, "a good book with errors" is a fairy tale, cartoon, or fiction. These "good" books have a purpose to amuse us, or to allow us to escape reality, but we do not accept their message as authoritative. If a book is merely for our enjoyment, it surely does not compare with the Word of God. If it is written to deceive us, surely it could not be from God who claims to be the truth.

C. THE EMPIRICAL EVIDENCE OF THE FULFILLMENT OF PROPHECY. The strongest empirical argument that the Bible is the Word of God is based on its demonstrated ability to predict the future. Man does not have knowledge of the future. Only God claims to have that knowledge. Therefore, if one can accurately predict the future, He must be God, and we must accept the truthfulness of his message. Christianity is the only religion that gives fulfilled prophecy as one of its bases for credibility. When the writers of Scripture predict the future, and then their predictions are fulfilled, they have credibility for their claims that they speak for God. Note what Wilbur Smith said of fulfilled prophecy.

A man who has read several thousand books, concludes that whatever one may think of the authority of the message presented in the book we call the Bible, there is worldwide agreement that in more ways than one it is the most remarkable volume that has ever been produced in these some five thousand years of writing on the part of the human race.

Mohammedanism cannot point to any prophecies of the coming of Mohammed uttered hundreds of years before his birth. Neither can the founders of any cult in this country rightly identify any ancient text specifically foretelling their appearance.[23]

The enemies of Scripture usually do not attack the fact of fulfilled prophecy. They usually try to explain it away. First, they try to make fulfilled prophecy an historical event by moving the date of the prediction forward. They claim the Bible is not the Word of God and that the Bible is a human book. Giving their motives the benefit of the doubt, they are trying to make the Bible consistent in their own eyes, but it would be a deceitful way of writing history. They discredit the Bible. A second attempt to explain away prophecy is to "spiritualize" the prediction and fulfillment. They try to make words mean something other than what the authors originally wrote.

An English deist once said that a man named Jesus Christ read the Old Testament prophecies concerning the Messiah and then went out and attempted to fulfill them. If this man were correct, Jesus Christ was a lunatic for dying to prove predictions that He knew were not true.

Some say that certain Old Testament prophets wrote after the events happened. But the Septuagint and the Dead Sea Scrolls establish a historical date to indicate that these books were written before the events they predicted. The Septuagint was the Greek translation of the Old Testament (c. 285 BC) that indicates that Daniel correctly predicted the events of Jesus Christ before they transpired. The Dead Sea Scrolls indicate that the Hebrew text was written and collected before Christ was born.

1. *The prediction of names.* Cyrus was predicted by name (Isa. 44:26-28, and 45:1) one hundred years before he lived. Three hundred years before Josiah was born, an unnamed prophet predicted that Josiah would reign (1 Kgs. 13:2). Josiah became the sixteenth king of the Southern Kingdom and the fulfillment is recorded in 2 Kings 23:15-18..

2. *Predictions concerning Messiah.* The messianic prophecies related to Christ that have already been fulfilled are divided into four areas. The exact details of their fulfillment indicate the supernatural insight that the author had into the future and qualifies the Bible as the Word of God.

    a.   The prophecies of the birth of Christ
        1.) To be born of the lineage of David.
            (a) Abraham (Gen. 12:1-3)
            (b) Isaac (Gen. 17:19)
            (c) Jacob (Gen. 28:14)
            (d) Judah (Gen. 49:10)

        (e) David (2 Sam. 7:12-13)

    2.) Date of birth. According to Daniel 9:25, the Messiah was to be born before AD 30, or the expiration of the Daniel's 69 weeks of years (445 BC-AD 30).

    3.) Place of birth. Bethlehem (Mic. 5:2)

    4.) Supernatural of a virgin. (Isa. 7:14).

  b.   Prophecies of His life on earth

    1.) To be a Savior and Deliverer. (Gen. 3:15; John 19:23; Isa. 53:5-6, 12)

    2.) His deity. (Isa. 7:14; 9:6-7; Mic. 5:2; Isa. 11)

    3.) To be preceded by a messenger. (Mal. 3:la; cf. Isa. 40:3-5)

    4.) To be a prophet. (Deut. 18:15; cf. John 1:21; 4:29; 6:14; Acts 3:20-24; John 5:46; 8:28; 14:24)   52:13-53:12.

    5.) To be a priest. (1 Sam. 2:35; Psa. 11:4; Zech. 6:12)

    6.) To be a king. (Gen. 49:10; Num. 24:17; 2 Sam. 7:12-16; Psa. 2; Isa. 2:1-4; 4:1-6; 9:6-7; 11:1-12; 49:7; 52:15; Jer. 23:1-6; Zech. 9:9)

    7.) To be a corner stone and foundation. (Isa. 28:14-18; Gen. 49:24; 1 Kgs. 7:10-22; Psa. 118:22; Isa. 8:14; Zech. 4:7)

    8.) To be the obedient Servant of Jehovah. Important passages: Isa. 42:1-7; 49:1-7; 52:13-53:12

  c.   Prophecies of His death

    1.) Betrayed by a friend. (Psa. 41:9)

    2.) Falsely accused. (Psa. 35:11)

    3.) Spit upon. (Isa. 50:6)

    4.) Pierced. (Psa. 22:16-17)

    5.) Ridiculed. (Psa. 22:6-7)

    6.) Forsaken of God. (Psa. 22:1)

    7.) Bones not broken. (Psa. 34:20)

    8.) Silent before accusers. (Isa. 53:7)

    9.) To die with the wicked. (Isa. 53:9)

    10.) To be buried in a rich man's tomb. (Isa. 53:9)

    11.) To be a sacrifice for sin. (Isa. 53:5-6, 12)

    12.) New Testament Prophecies. (Matt. 16:21; Mark 8:31; Luke 9:22; John 12:32-33)

  d.   Prophecies of His Resurrection. (Psa. 16:10; cf. Psa. 22:22; 118:22-24; Matt. 12:38-40; 16:21; 17:9, 23; 20:19; 27:63; Mark 3:31; 9:9, 31; 10:34; 14:58; Luke 9:22; 18:33; John 2:19-22)

3. *Predictions concerning the nations.* Many predictions about nations were made concerning events unlikely to happen when the prophecy was made. Isaiah predicted that Babylon would fall and not be inhabited (Isa. 13:19-22). When this prediction was made, Babylon was the capital city of the most powerful nation on earth. This becomes an important

fact because this prophecy was fulfilled outside the Bible. Also, the downfall of Nineveh (Zeph. 2:13-15) was predicted when it ruled the world. Its collapse was unexpected, yet fulfilled. Tyre was a mighty city when God predicted it would be thrown into the Mediterranean Sea (Ezek. 26:3-6, 12:14); later, Nebuchadnezzar partly destroyed the city, and, in 330 BC, Alexander came and took pillars from the city and cast them into the sea to make a causeway to an island offshore where the people were fortified. Today, the pillars are used for a spreading of the nets exactly as God had predicted. Philistia was strong when God predicted its downfall (Zeph. 2:4-7) and by the time of the New Testament, the land of Gaza was called desert (Acts 8:26). Egypt was one of the primary kingdoms of the world during the time of the Bible, but God predicted, "It shall be the basest of the kingdoms; neither shall it exalt itself anymore above the nations: for I will diminish them and they shall no more rule over the nations" (Ezek. 29:15). Egypt has never again gained international superiority since God predicted its downfall. These are only a few of the then unfulfilled prophecies regarding the nations.

4. *Prophecies about Israel.* God has promised that He would bless Israel (Gen. 12:3) and that they would endure as a race. Most Jews are recognizable by physical characteristics. Every Jew that walks the face of the earth is a proof that God wrote the Bible and that His predictions came true. God promised to curse those who curse Israel. We have seen the nation of Israel prosper when her contemporaries have faded into the dust—i.e., the Hittites, Edomites, and Canaanites. But, on the other side, because of Israel's unbelief and rejection of God, He promised that the Jewish people would always endure suffering and affliction (Lev. 26:28-29; Deut. 28:25, 32, 37, 49, 53, 62, 64, 65, 68). This apparent contradiction is fulfilled by the continued, yet humanly unexplainable, persecution of the Jewish race. But, despite continued tribulation and recurring holocaust, the Jews continue as a race. Because God has predicted future blessings for them, they will continue as a people.

For all of the prophecies that have been complete, the most miraculous demonstration is yet to come. Some have estimated that approximately 75 percent of biblical prophecy has yet to be fulfilled. This involves the Second Coming of Christ, the Great Tribulation, the Millennium and the judgments by God. These prophecies cannot be used to prove the Bible is the Word of God, but the credibility of past fulfilled prophecy should warn us that the prophecy of future judgment will be fulfilled.

D. THE CONVICTING, CONVINCING, CONVERTING POWER OF THE MESSAGE. Even though the Bible tells us of sinful acts, it is not a popular book where sinful acts take place. Even though the Bible tells of adultery and sexual immorality, the Bible is not found in houses of prostitution or immorality. Even though the Bible tells of men getting drunk, the Bible is not found in taverns and nightclubs. The Bible is unique in its call to repentance, in its convicting power to unsettle those who sin, and in its power to convert and transform those who accept its message. The transformation in the life of those who receive the message of the Bible is another proof that it is a message of God.

The Bible has a transforming power to change the lives of individuals. This is an empirical argument that other books cannot claim. There are thousands of individuals who have rejected the existence of God, but began reading the Bible for various reasons. As they came in contact with the message of God's Word, they were brought under conviction and accepted its message concerning Jesus Christ. When they came to know Jesus Christ as their personal Savior, they were converted. These people usually do not come to a place where they intellectually accept the integrity of the Bible. They skipped the academic steps of logical persuasion and when they were converted, their attitude toward the Bible changed. They instantaneously accepted the testimony of the Bible, that God was its divine Author and that it was authoritative for their lives.

Harold Lindsell calls this "the pragmatic test" and suggests its validity is demonstrated in Scripture when God proved Himself with signs to men like Abraham. Concerning its validity to prove the supernatural nature of the Bible, Lindsell suggests,

There is the changed life that proves to the person whose life is changed, and to those outside who see the transformed life, that what the Bible promises it delivers.

The Bible is as powerful as...	Powerful to...
1. A hammer (Jer. 23:29)	Judge sin
2. A mirror (James 1:23)	Reveal sin
3. Water (Eph. 5:26)	Cleanse sin
4. A sword (Heb. 4:12)	Defeat Satan
5. A lamp & light (Psa. 119:105)	Guide
6. Honey & gold (Psa. 19:10)	Satisfy
7. Milk (1 Pet. 2:2)	Sustain & nourish
8. Bread (Matt. 4:4)	Sustain & nourish
9. Seed (Luke 8:11)	Produce growth

For two thousand years, the Church of Jesus Christ has manifested before the eyes of an unbelieving world that Jesus Christ does make a difference. Because of Him, thousands of people have lived noble lives. Tens of thousands of people have willingly suffered martyrdom by burning, by torture, and by the axe. Children and grandchildren have followed the faith of their fathers and continued their witness.[24]

Some who profess to be Christians have not had the victories that are promised in Scripture. Usually they have never experienced the saving power of the Word of God. And there are certain Christians who are born again, but they have had intellectual problems with

Scripture. Perhaps it is their ignorance of Scripture or some false doctrine in their lives that has given them problems with sin.

E. BY THE INEXHAUSTIBLE INFINITY OF REVELATION. In a casual reading, the Bible is a simple book. It can be understood by children in Sunday School with a minimal amount of teaching. When it is preached, it can be understood by those who are illiterate and without the ability to comprehend the written page. But on the other hand, there is such an infinity in the Word of God that no reader can ever exhaust the depths of the message of the Word of God. Whether a person is reading about the Trinity, the two natures of Christ, or the sovereignty of God, there is an inexhaustible mystery in every doctrine. As sincerely as finite man attempts to understand theology, he encounters the infinity of God—he cannot comprehend every part of its teaching.

At times the infinity of God is seen as a contradiction by those who have not read it carefully. Truth never contradicts itself, but truth transcends itself, especially when God introduces a higher authority, such as times when God supernaturally performs a miracle.

Arthur W. Pink suggested the infinity of spiritual resources as another reason to recognize the Bible as the Word of God. Not only is the Bible infinite in content, it is infinite in application.

> Although one may know, word for word, the entire contents of some chapter of Scripture, and although he may have taken the time to ponder thoughtfully every sentence therein, yet on every subsequent occasion, provided one comes to it again in the spirit of humble inquiry, each fresh reading will reveal new gems never seen there before, and new delights will be experienced never met with previously. The most familiar passages will yield as much refreshment at the thousandth perusal as they did at the first. The Bible has been likened to a fountain of living water: the fountain is ever the same, but the water is always fresh.[25]

The fact that the Bible is infinite and unfathomable implies that the Author is infinite in His nature and expression. Since the Bible is infinite, we can only conclude that an infinite God would have written it. Yet, because God desires to communicate His message to everyone, we can only conclude that He wrote a simple Bible for everyone to understand. Since God is infinite and compassionate, we have a Bible that is easy to be understood yet at the core of every doctrine is an infinity that reaches beyond man's comprehension.

F. THE UNITY OF THE MESSAGE FROM DIFFERENT HUMAN SOURCES. The unity of the message of Scripture is an internal argument that has its strongest appeal to those who are familiar with the Bible's content. As a person objectively reads the Bible, he finds a unified message that centers in Jesus Christ, a unified theme which is the redemption of God, a unified structure so that each part of the Bible contributes to the whole. And when a person is finished reading the Bible he realizes that the subtraction of any book takes away from the composition of the whole. Finally, there is a unity of literary emphasis, even though there are numerous authors, so that the reader gets the impression that there was one mind that guided the preparation of the entire Bible.

The unity of the Bible is contrary to what one would normally expect from a book that was written by authors in the circumstances in which they wrote. Pink observes,

> The manner in which the Bible has been produced argues against its unity. The Bible was penned on two continents, written in three languages, and its composition and compilation extended through the slow progress of sixteen centuries. The various parts of the Bible were written at different times and under the most varying circumstances. Parts of it were written in tents, deserts, cities, palaces, and dungeons, some parts in times of imminent danger and others in seasons of ecstatic joy. Among its writers were judges, kings, priests, prophets, patriarchs, prime ministers, herdsmen, scribes, soldiers, physicians, and fishermen. Yet, despite these varying circumstances, conditions, and workmen, the Bible is *one* Book; behind its many parts there is an unmistakable organic unity. It contains *one* system of doctrine, *one* code of ethics, *one* plan of salvation, and *one* rule of faith.[26]

The argument of unity is based on the dual authorship of Scripture. First, human authors wrote Scripture and each book of the Bible is reflective of that author's occupation, vocabulary, style, and his sociological background. But the Bible does not have a single author. Rather, it has dual authorship. Each book of the Bible was written by a human author as he was guided by the Holy Spirit. The human author used the literary tools available to him, such as vocabulary, ability to think rationally, poetical nature and historical observation, but the Holy Spirit guided the writing of Scripture so that each book was inspired of God and was written without error or mistake. As such, the Holy Spirit gives unity to the Scriptures, hence supplying a supernatural dimension that proves it is the Word of God.

There were at least 36 authors, perhaps 40, who wrote the 66 books of the Bible inasmuch as some men wrote more books than others (the apostle John wrote five books of Scripture). Yet in spite of the diversity of authors, there is unity in the Bible, reflecting its supernatural origin.

There were approximately 1600 years during which the various authors wrote the books of the Bible, from Moses, who began writing around 1440 BC to John who finished the last book of the Bible around AD 100. The Bible was written over 55 generations, yet there remains a singular unity. Only God who transcends all time could be its source.

There was also a great diversity of occupations of the writers of Scripture. Inasmuch as a man writes out of his background, the different occupations of the Bible writers should have produced different kinds of books. Yet there is no clash in their points of view. Rather than contradictions, there is a unity in the Bible pointing to God as its Author.

THE OCCUPATIONS OF THE WRITERS

Moses	Politician
David	Shepherd/King
Samuel	Prophet
Peter	Fisherman
Isaiah	Politician
Luke	Physician
Matthew	Tax-collector
Paul	Theologian
Amos	Herdsman
Joshua	General
Job	Businessman
Nehemiah	Butler/Cupbearer
Jeremiah	Prophet

The Bible was written in different locations stretching over 2000 miles. Ezekiel wrote in Babylon some 560 miles east of Jerusalem, while Paul composed his final prison epistle in Rome, approximately 1450 miles west of Jerusalem. Some prophets were sent to the ten northern tribes while other prophets wrote to the southern tribes. Yet the social background does not change the perspective nor destroy the unity.

An anthology, or compilation of authors, will sometimes detract from the unity of a book. However, in the Scriptures there is different subject matter, but their unity is obvious.

Considering that the Bible was written by approximately 40 different authors, over 1600 years, by men from a vast number of occupations, separated by as much as 2,000 miles and covering a vast number of subjects, its unity is evident in its theme, structure, literary emphasis and thrust. Any objective reader of the Scriptures should recognize that it is the Word of God.

1. History	Pentateuch/Historical books
2. Biography	Gospels
3. Hygiene/Holiness	Leviticus
4. Poetry	Psalms
5. Theology	Epistles
6. Prophecy	Daniel
7. Letters	Paul's epistles
8. Psychology	Ecclesiastes
9. Genealogy	Chronicles

G. THE TRANSCULTURAL APPEAL OF THE MESSAGE. The Bible has a universal appeal, whether people read it during the first century of the church or in the modern twenty-first century.

There seems to be a common spirit in receiving, interpreting, internalizing and applying the message of the Scripture. Although nearly 2,000 years old, the Bible always seems to be up to date and meets the needs of its readers.

The universal appeal extends to all races. Seldom does anyone take the attitude that Orientals wrote the Bible. As a matter of fact, many linguists have pointed out that the "translatableness" of the Bible is another demonstration that it is a unique book whose Author is God. No matter what language, the Bible's message comes through clearly when it is translated from one language to another.

The argument for the universal appeal applies to the rich as well as to the poor. The Bible is found in the bookcases of the rich, as well as on the coffee tables of the poor. And, finally, all ages love the Word of God, from children to the elderly. Because God wanted to communicate to all people, in all circumstances, at all periods of time, and at all levels of society, He supernaturally endowed the Bible with His Spirit so that it would have a universal appeal. While not a conclusive argument, it reaffirms the others when taken en masse.

H. THE UNMISTAKABLE HONESTY OF THE SCRIPTURES. When an objective reader is studying the Word of God, he does not get the impression that the writer is holding back on anything. When the authors talk about themselves, they are honest about their sins, their nations, and their exploits. They do not give in to their pride and cover up their mistakes, nor do they allow false humility to keep them from deserving their achievements.

The Bible is unmistakably honest in objective statements. If the Bible were "invented" by men, they would have been more respectful in omitting the sins of some of God's people. However, the sins of God's heroes are always included. Usually, these great men of God fell at their strongest point. Perhaps God wants us to take our eyes off men and put our eyes on Him. Also, God wants us to know that all men are mortal and fallible. When we see a flaw in our heroes, it makes us accept ourselves and our failures with a little more humility and perseverance.

Pink notes several illustrations in both the Old and New Testaments of this type of honesty in Scripture before concluding,

> Surely it is apparent to every impartial mind that the New Testament is no mere human invention. And surely it is evident from the honesty of its writers, in so faithfully portraying the enmity of the carnal mind against God, that their productions can be accounted for only on the ground that they spoke and wrote "not of themselves," but "as they were moved by the Holy Spirit" (2 Pet. 1:21).[27]

Noah	Drunkenness
Abraham	Lied about his wife
Moses	Pride
Eli	Undisciplined, wicked sons
David	Adultery
Solomon	300 wives, 700 concubines
Elijah	Ran from Jezebel

Peter	Denied the Lord
Thomas	Doubter
Paul	Paid a vow in the Temple

I. THE IMMEASURABLE SUPERIORITY OF THE BIBLE WHEN COMPARED TO OTHER LITERATURE. A comparison of the Bible to the other religions books of the world—*The Koran, Science and Health with Key to the Scriptures, The Book of Mormon*—will demonstrate the superiority of the Bible in most literary aspects. The same can be achieved when comparing the Bible to classics, such as the writings of William Shakespeare, Sir Walter Scott, Charles Dickens, or any of the modern authors.

When the Bible is compared to the religions of the world, they all teach that man must do something to please God. But the Bible teaches grace: i.e., that God has done everything for man. No other religion in the world offers a salvation that is free, complete, comprehensive, yet all man has to do is receive it. The religions of the world say, "Do this to live." Christianity says, "Done." When considering the superior message of the Bible, one can only conclude that it is the Word of God.

J. PRAGMATIC TEST OF EXPERIENCE. The world is quick to test any claim that is made by man, organizations, or especially by a new product. The Underwriters Laboratory tests the validity of new products before they place their seal of approval upon them. Perhaps the greatest test that the Bible is the Word of God is its pragmatic impact on the lives of those who test its conclusions. Those who have a personal experience with Jesus Christ know that the Bible is inspired by the Holy Spirit of God to produce new life in the believer. The child of God has come to know the Lord Jesus Christ through Scripture, therefore there is no doubt in his heart that the Bible is the Word of God. E. Y. Mullins agrees with this point:

> I have, for me at least, irrefutable evidence of the objective existence of the Person so moving me. When to this personal experience I add that of tens of thousands of living Christians, and an unbroken line of them back to Christ, and when I find in the New Testament a manifold record of like experiences, together with a clear account of the origin and cause of them all, my certainty becomes absolute. One of the most urgent of all duties resting upon modern Christians is to assert with earnest and vigor the certainties of Christian experience.[28]

But many people have claimed to have had some type of experience. What validity is there to the claim that the Bible is the Word of God because lives have been changed by its message? Could not someone claim that *The Koran* is the Word of God because it changed his life? Josh McDowell faced this question and replied,

For example, let's say a student comes into the room and says, "Guys, I have a stewed tomato in my right tennis shoe. This tomato has changed my life. It has given me a peace and love and joy that I never experienced before, not only that, but I can now run the 100-yard dash in 10 seconds flat."

It is hard to argue with a student like that if his life backs up what he says (especially if he runs circles around you on the track). A personal testimony is often a subjective argument for the reality of something.

Therefore, don't dismiss a subjective experience as being irrelevant.

There are two questions or tests I apply to a subjective experience. First, what is the objective reality for the subjective experience, and second, how many other people have had the same subjective experience from being related to the objective reality? Let me apply this to the student with the "stewed tomato" in his right tennis shoe.

To the first question he would reply: "A stewed tomato in my right tennis shoe." Then the second question would be put this way: "How many people in this classroom, in this university, in this country and on this continent, etc., have experienced the same love, peace, joy, and increased track speed as the result [of] a stewed tomato in their right tennis shoe?"

At this point, most of the history students laughed. I didn't blame them, for it was obvious that the answer to the second question was "No one!"

Now I had to apply these same two questions to my own subjective experience:

1. What is the objective reality or basis for my subjective experience—a changed life?

    Answer: the person of Christ and His resurrection.

2. How many others have had this same subjective experience from being related to the objective reality, Jesus Christ?

The evidence is overwhelming . . . that truly millions from all backgrounds, nationalities and professions have seen their lives elevated to new levels of peace and joy by turning their lives over to Christ. Indeed, the professor confirmed this when he said, "I have met scores of people around the world that have been transformed by Christ."[29]

The result of Josh McDowell's argument is that there is an objective reality back of the experience that is repeatable in various circumstances by many individuals.

On resurrection morning the angel invited the women to, "Come, see the place" (Matt. 28:6), telling them to put God on the spot and to determine if the tomb was not empty. They found by experience that their observations were correct. Jesus had been raised from the dead. In the same way the psalmist invites the reader, "O Taste and see that the LORD is good" (Psa. 34:8). Those who come to the Bible and read it, internalize its message and apply it by faith, find that God will keep His promises. Those who have doubts about the Word of God should respond to the words of the Lord Jesus, "If any man will [wills to] do his will, he shall know of the doctrine, whether it be of God, or whether I speak of myself" (John 7:17, translation by author).

Jesus is saying that the key to doubt is man's *will*, not his intellect. If a person will surrender his will to God, he will experience the new life that is promised in Scripture. The problem is that the "natural man understandeth not the things of the Spirit of God" (1 Cor. 2:14), since he is spiritually blind. He cannot understand the dual nature of its source, nor the spiritual impact of its message. But when a man comes to know Jesus Christ as his Savior, he experiences the message of salvation.

VI. INSPIRATION: GUARANTEEING THE WORD OF SCRIPTURE

Inspiration is the guidance or influence of the Holy Spirit on the human writers of Scripture so that God controlled them in such a way that what they wrote was exactly what God wanted them to write without error. There was no error in grammar, historical locations, sociological understanding, mathematics, geology, geometry, or geography. Inspiration is a supernatural guidance executed on the sacred writers by the Spirit of God, by which their own personal writings become the divine Word of God. The influence of inspiration is applied to the author's vocabulary, knowledge of grammar, ability to develop a logical thought, or to his poetic, homiletical or scientific ability to do historical research. While inspiration has used the limitation of the authors, it does guarantee that what they wrote was accurate. When authors transcribed material words unknown to them, the act of revelation was happening along with the influence of inspiration.

To say that God inspired every word of Scripture (2 Tim. 3:16) does not mean that every statement is true. It only means that they are accurate. Scripture accurately records that the serpent said, "You will not surely die" (Gen. 3:4). But it was a lie. The advice given to Job by his friends is wrong, yet the Bible is accurate in recording exactly what they said.

A. A DEFINITION OF INSPIRATION. The central focus of the doctrine of inspiration is based on a Greek word *theopneustos* (θεοπνευστος) used in 2 Timothy 3:16. Inspiration is based upon two words, (θεος, "God") and (πνευμα, "spirit"). It might be better translated "God breathed out," rather than the usual translation "in breathed." Inspiration comes from the same word that is translated "God is spirit," or "the breath of God." Since breath is life, when God put His Spirit into the words of Scripture, He was also putting His life in Scripture. Paul believed that the Scriptures are directly from God. Of his own writings Paul wrote "which things also we speak, not in the words which man's wisdom teacheth, but which the Holy Ghost teacheth" (1 Cor. 2:13). Note the following description of inspiration.

Inspiration Involves . . .
    a. Inspired guidance by the Holy Spirit
    b. Inspired personality of the authors
    c. Inspired words,
    d. Resulting in an inspired text.

1. *Inspired guidance.* Inspiration recognizes the supernatural influence of the Holy Spirit upon the writers. But everyone does not use inspiration with this meaning. Sometimes people use "inspiration" to describe the "enthusiasm" of a brilliant artist or musician. We define the word as it is used in its context in Scripture. The Bible says "Holy men of God spake as they were moved by the Holy Ghost" (2 Pet. 1:21). The moving by the Holy Spirit means "to be borne along." The Holy Spirit filled the human writers so that the process was not natural, but supernatural. These men were "moved" (picked up and borne along) as they wrote God's message. Therefore, inspiration means an author was guided to write (in his thinking or in his own written expression) what God wanted him to write, not what he chose.

2. *Inspired personality.* Inspiration also incorporates the personality of the writer into the final product. Some have argued in the past that God dictated to the writers, who simply recorded it, much as a secretary would type a letter that the boss had dictated. This is called the dictation theory. There are many places where the Scriptures were dictated directly by God (cf. Rev. 2:1-3:22); at other times, the style of the writing and the selection of words reflects the personality and background of the writer. This is especially evident when we read the four Gospels.

Matthew was a Jewish tax collector impressed with the fact he had found the King of the Jews. His Gospel begins with a royal genealogy and the arrival of kings from the east to worship Christ. Mark, a young disciple of Peter, seems to reflect Peter's "activism" in his Gospel. The key word "straightway" (or "immediately") makes it appear as though Jesus is always on the move, doing something as a servant. Luke's Gospel is more methodical, reflecting his historical investigation. Luke the medical doctor, reflects the humanity of Christ, and his key phrase is "the Son of man." The fourth Gospel, written by one "whom Jesus loved," seems to be obsessed with love for Jesus and His love for others. John's key word is "believe." Though each of the four Gospels reflects a different style of the writer and a different perspective on Jesus Christ, they do not contradict each other. They harmonize completely to give us the full inspired, accurate record of the life of Christ.

3. *Inspired words.* Inspiration means more than God guiding the thoughts, or God giving the authors a general impression. Inspiration means the words are placed there by God. Every word in the Bible is inspired equally, though some may have a greater influence on our lives than others. This is because the words describing the Person of Christ can influence our

lives in a greater way than the words describing a historical event in the Old Testament. The accuracy of the Holy Spirit's ministry extends to the words. "We have received, not the spirit of the world, but the spirit which is of God; that we might know the things that are freely given to us of God. Which things also we speak, not in the words which man's wisdom teacheth, but which the Holy Ghost teacheth" (1 Cor. 2:12-13).

When a man is sailing on a lake, he is dependent upon both the wind and his own skills in sailing a designated course. In the same way, God communicated His revelation to the world in an accurate and reliable Book. Every word was written by the moving of the Holy Spirit of God, yet every word was chosen and expressed through the personality of the human author.

4. Inspired results. Because the Bible is inspired by God, it is completely accurate and reliable in the original autographs. The Bible differs from other good books in its content, method of writing and the final result. Whereas some say God inspired the concepts of the writers, or God inspired the readers of Scripture, these terms are wrong. Inspiration affects the result of the writing process so that the total written revelation was accurate and guaranteed because it was written under the influence of inspiration.

We have already looked at the argument of revelation that proves the Bible to be the Word of God (the content of Scripture). The argument for inspiration that every word in the Bible is accurate and reliable is built on revelation. Since God has given us a message, it is only natural to expect that He will guarantee the accuracy of His message.

B. OTHER VIEWS OF INSPIRATION. Not every theologian would agree with our definition of inspiration. Throughout the years, various men have put forward alternative statements concerning the nature and extent of divine inspiration. Today, some variant views are held by those who identify themselves with such terms as "conservative" and "evangelical" and "fundamental." A more complete understanding of the biblical doctrine of inspiration can be achieved as one recognizes the limitations of certain false or incomplete views.

1. *Intuition theory.* The intuition theory of inspiration holds that all men have an intuitive knowledge of God and that those who wrote Scripture developed this ability to a higher degree than what was normally accomplished by men. In the words of J. D. Morell, "Inspiration is only a higher potency of what every man possesses in some degree."[30] The result of this logic makes it difficult to understand revelation as beginning with God. In fact, Frederic Palmer goes so far as to say, "We can draw no sharp distinction between the human mind discovering truth, and the divine mind imparting revelation."[31] This theory, then, is an essential denial of revelation or theistic involvement in inspiration.

2. *Conceptual inspiration.* A second alternative view suggests God inspired the ideas of Scripture, yet failed to direct the authors to record specific terms. Thus the ideas are inspired,

though the facts may be nonexistent. This view is reflected in the following statement by Clifton J. Allen.

> Let this principle of revelation be stressed. The treasure of inspired revelation, the truth of biblical revelation, has come to us in "earthen vessels." The writers were men. They were finite and fallible. They were human, and hence subject to limitations of knowledge and understanding. But they were persons through whom the transcendent power of God operated—quickening, illuminating, guiding, and enabling them to the media of the saving message of God in Christ. The Holy Scriptures have their essential character in their nature as the inspired revelation of God. Pointing to Christ and finding their meaning and unity in Christ, they are the Word of God.[32]

Allen makes the human author the authority, rather than their writings. He divorces inspiration of words from inspiration of the men who wrote the words. His only theological authority lies in the concepts and ideas of the authors. Calvin E. Stowe holds this position, stating, "It is not the words of the Bible that were inspired. It is not the thoughts of the Bible that were inspired. It was the men who wrote the Bible that were inspired."[33]

3. *Illumination/Inspiration.* A third deviation from the principle of verbal inspiration suggests the Bible becomes the Word of God (i.e., inspired) only as the Holy Spirit impresses truth upon the life of the reader, presumably through what is generally referred to as illumination. Further confusing the difference between biblical doctrines of revelation and illumination, E. G. Robinson claims, "The office of the Spirit in inspiration is not different from that which he performed for Christians at the time the Gospels were written . . . . When the prophets say: 'Thus saith the LORD,' they mean simply that they have divine authority for what they utter."[34] This view presents such a subjective test of inspiration, agreement could never be reached concerning the inspired text.

4. *Partial inspiration.* There are those who propose a vague suggestion that God did in fact inspire parts of Scripture, but failed to identify which part of Scripture was inspired. Their argument is usually based on an alternative translation of 2 Timothy 3:16 given in a footnote of the *Revised Standard Version of the Bible,* "Every Scripture inspired by God is also profitable." This wrong interpretation implies that there can be other Scripture which is not inspired. The verse is correctly translated, "All Scripture is given by inspiration." Hence no part of Scripture can be omitted from inspiration. This vagueness is reflected in the doctrinal statement of Fuller Theological Seminary which reads in part, "Scripture is an essential part and trustworthy record of this divine disclosure. All the books of the Old and New Testaments, given by divine inspiration, are the written Word of God, the only infallible rule of faith and practice."[35] One of the major problems with this statement is not what it says about divine inspiration, but what it leaves unsaid and therefore implies. It, like the RSV marginal rendering of 2 Timothy 3:16, implies that some of the Bible's parts are not given by inspiration.

5. *Limited inspiration.* Limited inspiration is similar to the above position in that it acknowledges only partial inspiration of the text of Scripture, but differs in that it identifies the inspired part of the text. Those holding to a view of limited inspiration argue the Scriptures are inspired and authoritative only in matters of religious dogma. Normally this takes the form of denying the importance of the accuracy of the Bible outside of theological issues. For instance, George Ladd suggests concerning verbal plenary inspiration, "This conclusion, as logical and persuasive as it may seem, does not square with the facts of God's Word; and it is the author's hope that the reader may be helped to understand that the authority of the Word of God is not dependent upon infallible certainty in all matters of history and criticism."[36] Pointing out this problem of limited inspiration, Dr. Henry Smith told the more conservative Presbytery of Cincinnati, "Now, I suppose it to be generally understood—the Committee certainly has no reason to be ignorant of it—that we stand on the common ground of the infallibility of the Scriptures as the church's rule of faith and practice. There is no difference between us, therefore, as to doctrine or precept. The sole question at issue is whether every statement on matters of fact, outside the sphere of doctrine and precept, is without error."[37]

6. *Plenary nonverbal inspiration.* A contemporary trend among those identifying with the neo-evangelical movement is to claim for themselves belief in plenary inspiration of Scripture without a commitment to the inspiration of the very words. This trend is noted by Boston University theologian, Harold DeWolf. He writes, "There is a noticeable, though indecisive change in the doctrine of biblical inspiration and authority. Some of the new evangelicals, unlike most of the fundamentalists, avoid teaching 'verbal' inspiration of the Bible, stressing rather plenary or full inspiration. This marks a movement to a more flexible position."[38]

Each of the above positions falls short of the essential implications of divine inspiration. Raymond Surburg notes, "A rational and authentic doctrine of biblical revelation and inspiration can under no circumstances be harmonized with the idea that God the Holy Spirit has caused men to be given a book that is replete with contradictions and misrepresentation of facts."[39] Any biblical view of inspiration must at least recognize the inspiration of words.

7. *Dictation.* Perhaps an overstatement of the issue is the position that God dictated the words of Scripture to the human authors much as a boss might dictate a letter to his secretary. This view omits the appearance of human personality in writing Scripture, such as word selection, expression, and the background of the author. A leading advocate of this position was the late John R. Rice. In his book on inspiration, Rice notes:

We would have to say that word-for-word inspiration, verbal inspiration, is necessarily divine dictation. We do not deny that God used men; we simply say that

God gave the men the words they wrote down and we say it because the Bible says it so plainly and so often that honest Bible believers must accept it.[40]

8. *Inspired translations.* Even more extreme than Rice's dictation theory is the position that certain translations of the Bible are inspired. This view is being popularized among a narrow group of fundamentalists by Peter S. Ruckman and his followers. His advocacy of the *King James Version* of the Bible is so extreme that he appears highly critical of anyone who advocates the use of any text outside of the KJV. In an article, Ruckman went so far as to suggest that the Greek text was a gimmick developed by Satan, stating, "Now the 'original Greek' is the greatest gimmick Satan ever invented in this century for covering up truth, overthrowing truth, perverting truth, magnifying flesh, and exalting humanism."[41] Ruckman goes even farther. He elevates the English text over the Greek. In a chapter entitled, "Correcting the Greek with English," he writes:

Mistakes in the A.V. 1611 are advanced revelation . . . . In exceptional cases, where the *majority of Greek manuscripts stand against the A.V. 1611, put them in file 13* . . . . Where the Greek says one thing and the A.V. says another, throw out the Greek.[42]

Such a statement is inconceivable to one who believes in the preservation of God's revelation to man. Also, it fails to recognize that the original *King James Version* of 1611 is not used today. The *King James Version* has been revised several times since its first printing. This can be seen by anyone who will read a contemporary KJV alongside a copy of an earlier edition. But Ruckman is apparently not interested in honesty and accurate scholarship in his efforts to criticize and destroy the ministries of other fundamentalists whom God is using. He has gathered a following of those who accept his oversimplifications and are unwilling or unable to face the real issues forced by the proliferation of Bible translations today.

C. THE INERRANCY DEBATE. The raging theological controversy of the 70s and 80s goes beyond the debate whether every word is inspired by God. The historic position holds that all Scripture is inspired and true, including the historical, geographical and scientific teachings. The new position is that the Bible's teaching on salvation and doctrine is true and is authoritative for faith and practice, but God intended the writers to use their limited knowledge, especially in scientific areas and hence make non-revelatory, or non-authoritative statements. This group is composed of those who hold to inspiration, but deny the inerrancy of the Scriptures.

This group apparently bases its arguments on two sources. First, they dismiss questionable passages because: (1) they are morally objectionable; (2) they are divergent accounts of the same "event"; (3) they cannot explain divergent numerics; and (4) "alleged" errors. William E. Hull, dean of the School of Theology at the Southern Baptist Theological Seminary attempted to solve these problems thus:

To apply the concept of infallibility to the Bible may do justice to the fact that it was inspired by a perfect God, but it does not do justice to the fact that this revelation was apprehended and written down by imperfect men. If the human writers were limited, as they themselves claimed, then their limitations belong also to a balanced doctrine of Scripture . . . .

We need not—and indeed do not—choose between these two positions [infallibility vs. fallibility] but should reconcile them.[43]

The second way the non-inerrantists solve their problem is by ridicule. They accuse the inerrantist of "bibliolatry"—worshipping the Bible. One critic ridiculed inerrantists for believing in a quadruple God: Father, Son, Holy Spirit, and Scripture. The critic asked, "Did the Bible die for your sins?" Dr. Robert Bratcher reflected this view when he spoke before the Christian Life Commission of the Southern Baptist Convention on the topic "Biblical Authority for the Church Today." In part, he stated,

Only willful ignorance or intellectual dishonesty can account for the claim that the Bible is inerrant and infallible. No truth-loving, God-respecting, Christ-honoring believer should be guilty of such heresy. To invest the Bible with qualities of inerrancy and infallibility is to idolatrize [sic] it, to transform it into a false God.[44]

John Wesley, Martin Luther, A. H. Strong and other conservative scholars have never had to face the problem of those who denied the inerrancy and inspiration of Scripture. But each generation has had to fight its own theological battles, meaning it examines the attacks upon the faith, looking at all sides of the arguments. Each attack has been faced and answered by the people of God. In later generations men may disagree, but they do not find pertinent new arguments or new positions. The church at large becomes settled on the issue. The battle of inerrancy is one of the current battles.

The attack against the inerrancy (the authority) of the Bible is involved in the issue of inspiration. At least, they are intertwined in the way critics are answered. When we prove the Words of the Bible are accurate, we also are answering the attack on the inerrancy of Scripture. Therefore, the answers to inerrancy and inspiration will be given together.

Inerrancy states that what is inspired is authoritative.[45]

D. ARGUMENTS FOR INSPIRATION/INERRANCY. Verbal plenary inspiration and its sister doctrine, inerrancy, is not a doctrine that is invented by theologians and forced on the church. Quite the contrary, the Bible reflects an attitude toward itself that every word was placed there by God. Hence, it is God's Book and has God's authority. The following proofs for verbal plenary inspiration and inerrancy arise from the Bible. These arguments are internal, based on the internal consistency of the Bible. Their credibility is based on the objective proofs that the Bible is a revelation of God. This was proved in the previous section.

1. *The Bible teaches that it is inspired/inerrant.* The content of the Bible teaches that it was given by the process of inspiration from God so that the words were God's Word and that they are accurate and reliable, hence they are authoritative. When Paul said, "All scripture is given by inspiration of God" (2 Tim. 3:16), he was dealing with one area—the Old Testament. Again, in reference to the Old Testament Peter wrote, "Holy men of God spake as they were moved [picked up and carried] along by the Holy Spirit" (2 Pet. 1:21). The Scriptures are equated with God's revelation in words (Matt. 19:4-5; Heb. 3:7; Acts 4:24-25; 13:34-35).

a. Moses. Moses did not attempt to hide the source of his writing, but readily acknowledged that it came from God. First he noted, "The secret things belong unto the LORD our God; but those things which are revealed belong unto us and to our children for ever, that we may do all the words of this law" (Deut. 29:29). At his trial, Stephen recognized that Moses wrote Scripture: "This is that Moses, which said to the children of Israel" (Acts 7:37). Here Stephen quotes Deuteronomy 18:15, then notes Israel rejected Moses, "to whom our fathers would not obey" (Acts 7:39). Yet God said, "Ye stiffnecked and uncircumcised in heart and ears, ye do always resist the Holy Ghost" (Acts 7:51). Resisting the words of Moses is equated with resisting the Holy Spirit. Just because Moses declared that he was recording the words of God did not make it a fact, but when supported by a New Testament writer, it reaffirms the co-authorship of Scripture by means of verbal inspiration.

Despite the claims of both Moses and others in the Scriptures concerning the Mosaic authorship of the Pentateuch, it is popular among higher critics today to suggest that the Pentateuch is the product of four or more writers and not written until the period of Josiah's reforms in Jerusalem. But a greater witness than Stephen or Moses claimed Mosaic authorship of the Law. The following statements attributed to Jesus all recognize this premise. Before the higher critic can achieve any credibility in the eyes of the Christian who recognizes the Lordship of Christ, the following verses must be explained.

Matt. 4:4, 7, 10; cf. Luke 4:4, 8, 12. Luke 4:16-27. Matt. 5:17, 18, 21-43. Matt. 6:29. Matt. 8:4; cf. Mark 1:44; Luke 5:14. Matt. 8:11; cf. Luke 13:28. Matt. 9:13. Luke 16:29-31. Matt. 10:15; cf. Mark 6:11. Matt. 11:10; cf. Luke 7:26, 27. Matt. 12:3-8; cf. Mark 2:24-28; Luke 6:3-5. Matt. 12:40-42; cf. Luke 11:29-32. Matt. 13:14, 15. Matt. 15:1-9; cf. Mark 7:8-12. Matt. 16:4. Matt. 17:11; cf. Mark 9:11-13. Matt. 19:3-9; cf. Mark 10:2-12. Matt. 19:18-19; cf. Mark 10:19; Luke 10:26-27; 18:20. Luke 18:31. Matt. 21:13-16; cf. Mark 11:17; Luke 19:46. Matt. 21:42; cf. Mark 12:10, 11; Luke 20:17. Matt. 22:28-33; cf. Mark 12:24-31; Luke 20:37-39, Matt. 22:36-40. Matt. 22:34, 44, 45; cf. Mark 12:35-57; Luke 20:41-44. Matt. 23:1-3, 23, 35; cf. Luke 11:51. Matt. 24:15-16; cf. Mark 13:14. Luke 17:26-31. Matt. 24:24, 31. Mark 14:21, 27. Luke 22:37. Matt. 26:53-56. Mark 14:49. Matt.

27:46; cf. Mark 15:34. Luke 23:46. Luke 24:25-32, 44-47. John 3:14; 5:39, 45-47; 6:32, 45; 7:19-23, 38, 39; 8:39-40, 44, 56-58; 10:33-36; 13:18, 26; 17:12, 17; 19:28.

b. David. Another major contributor to the Old Testament, David, experienced the same dual authorship of his manuscripts. Jesus said, "For David himself said by the Holy Ghost" (Mark 12:36). This introduction to an Old Testament quote by Jesus demonstrated the method of inspiration in Scripture. It recognizes that God permitted David the full use of his faculties and personality so that it is accurate to say, "David himself said." At the same time, he spoke "by the Holy Ghost." An understanding of inspiration must recognize that both are true without effecting a compromise upon the other. "For prophecy came not in old time by the will of man, but holy men of God spake as they were moved by the Holy Ghost" (2 Pet. 1:21). In another place this truth is again illustrated, "Men and brethren, this scripture must needs have been be fulfilled, which the Holy Ghost by the mouth of David spake" (Acts 1:16).

The process of inspiration at times will emphasize the human author and at times will emphasize the divine author. In his desire to have fellowship with God, David once prayed, "Cast me not away from thy presence; and take not thy holy spirit from me" (Psa. 51:11). As he wrote the Psalms, he was recording his feelings, but the Holy Spirit was guaranteeing the work that David wrote. The New Testament church also recognized divine emphasis in inspiration when they said, "Thou art God, which hast made heaven, and earth, and the sea, and all that in them is: who by the mouth of thy servant David hast said" (Acts 4:24-25). This powerful text shows that the people of the New Testament recognized that God the Creator spoke through human authors by inspiration.

c. The prophets. As you read the writings of the major and minor prophets you cannot help but be impressed with their reliance upon God for their message. Again and again you read "thus saith the LORD." Isaiah said, "The Spirit of the LORD GOD is upon me; because the LORD hath anointed me to preach good tidings unto the meek; he hath sent me to bind up the broken-hearted, to proclaim liberty to the captives, and the opening of the prison to those who are bound" (Isa. 61:1). God told Jeremiah, "Behold, I have put my words in thy mouth" (Jer. 1:9). Ezekiel dates his prophecy, acknowledging, "I saw visions of God" (Ezek. 1:1). Even the minor prophets acknowledged the word of God, "Not by might, nor by power, but by my spirit, saith the LORD of hosts" (Zech. 4:6). The prophets gave abundant witness to speaking God's Word.

That the Old Testament was considered inspired by the authors of the New Testament is evident in the following summary statement by Rene Pache.

At least 295 quotations or direct references to the Old Testament have been counted in the New, a total of one verse out of every 22. If we add to this the evident allusions (613, according to C. H. Toy), the proportion reaches to about 10 percent of the New Testament text. The discourses of Jesus and such books as Hebrews,

Romans and Revelation are literally saturated with expressions, allusions and actual texts drawn from the Old Testament. The exact quotations number 278, coming from every book of the Jewish canon except 6 (Judges-Ruth, the Song of Solomon, Ecclesiastes, Esther, Ezra-Nehemiah and the Chronicles); whereas the allusions go back to every book in the Old Testament without exception.[46]

d. Disciples. Jesus promised His disciples that the Holy Spirit would enable them to record the Word of God. "But the Comforter, which is the Holy Ghost, whom the Father will send in my name, he shall teach you all things, and bring all things to your remembrance, whatsoever I have said unto you" (John 14:26). While some misapply this text, applying it to the Holy Spirit's ministry of illumination, it more properly speaks of inspiration and revelation. Commenting on this verse, Edward J. Young states,

The Apostles were not to be left on their own. They would not need to depend upon their own fallible hearts and minds to tell them what to say. Rather, to them had been promised an infallible Teacher, even God and the Holy Ghost. It was thus that the Apostles themselves understood their own words.[47]

"Howbeit when he, the Spirit of truth, is come, he will guide you into all truth: for he shall not speak of himself; but whatsoever he shall hear, that shall he speak: and he will shew you things to come" (John 16:13). It is interesting in the light of this promise to see how one of these disciples began the final book of the Bible. "The Revelation of Jesus Christ, which God gave unto him, to shew unto his servants things which must shortly come to pass; and he sent and signified it by his angel unto his servant John" (Rev. 1:1). It should also be noted that John "was in the Spirit on the Lord's day" (Rev. 1:10) when he received this revelation; and at least seven times, Jesus says, "He that hath an ear, let him hear what the Spirit saith unto the churches" (Rev. 2:7, 11, 17, 29; 3:6, 13, 22). This promise, fulfilled in the ministry of John, was also fulfilled in the ministries of two other apostles, Peter and Matthew, as they recorded what the Holy Spirit revealed to them in their manuscripts.

e. Paul. The apostle Paul acknowledged God had given him a special revelation. He spoke of "my gospel, and the preaching of Jesus Christ, according to the revelation of the mystery, which was kept secret since the world began, but now is made manifest" (Rom. 16:25-26). Concerning his revelation, the apostle stated in another place, "But God hath revealed them unto us by his Spirit" (1 Cor. 2:10). Actually, Christ revealed Himself by vision or revelation to Paul on several occasions. It was during these experiences that Paul received the basic content he would later record.

The Revelation of Christ to Paul

1.) At his conversion (Acts 9:3-8, 17; 22:6-11, 14-15; 26:12-19; I Cor. 9:1; 15:8)
2.) Three years in the desert (Acts 9:23; Gal. 1:17-18)

3.) At Jerusalem (Acts 22:17-21)
4.) At Corinth (Acts 18:9-10)
5.) Later in Jerusalem (Acts 23:11)
6.) During prayer to remove his thorn in the flesh (2 Cor. 12:1-4)
7.) On board a ship (Acts 27:23)

The Holy Spirit had a ministry in the life of Paul to reveal the message of God to him so that he could teach it to others (1 Cor. 2:12-13). Very quickly in the early church, the epistles of Paul were collected and studied as equal to the Old Testament Scriptures, "even as our beloved brother Paul also according to the wisdom given unto him hath written unto you; as also in all his epistles, speaking in them of these things; in which are some things hard to be understood, which they that are unlearned and unstable wrest, as they do also the other scriptures, unto their own destruction" (2 Pet. 3:15-16). Notice that Peter equates Paul's epistles with Scripture. Peter equates the writings of Paul to "other Scriptures." Those who read the Scriptures recognized that Paul's writings were accepted on the same level as Moses and the writers of the Old Testament.

2. *Jesus affirmed inspiration/inerrancy.* Jesus recognized the authority and inerrancy of Scripture. He made constant appeal to it when tempted by Satan (Matt. 4:1-11) and used it often in his ministry to defend his actions (cf. Matt. 11:15-17, 26:54-56). This demonstrates the authority Jesus placed in the Scriptures, but we are not left to make assumptions on the basis of Jesus' actions alone. He, on at least four occasions, taught the Scriptures in such a way as to make clear His position on biblical inerrancy.

In a confrontation with the Sadducees over the doctrine of the resurrection which that group denied, Jesus silenced His opposition, arguing the entire resurrection belief on the tense of a simple verb, "to be" (Matt. 22:32). Jehovah had told Moses at the burning bush, "I am the God of Abraham," but as Jesus implied, Abraham had been dead 480 years when the statement was made. Arguing that God was the God of the living, not the dead, Jesus claimed life after death must be true. Jesus used the tense of a verb to prove Abraham was not simply physically dead, but was living in the presence of God. The fact that Jesus used a word and its tense demonstrates His deep confidence in inspiration and inerrancy. Commenting on this situation, Gaussen states,

> Listen to his reply to the Sadducees who denied the resurrection of the body. How does he refute them? By ONE SOLE WORD of an HISTORICAL passage of the Bible; by a single verb in the present tense, instead of that same verb in the past tense . . . . It is thus that he proves to them the doctrine of the resurrection.[48]

On another occasion Jesus claimed the "Scriptures cannot be broken" (John 10:34-35). The word broken means "annul or divorce." An annulment of a marriage is to act as if the marriage never happened. The Scriptures cannot be treated as if the event—its record or the concepts it teaches—never happened. On this text, Edward Young notes,

> If a man breaks a law, he is guilty and so liable to punishment. When he breaks the law, the lawbreaker treats the law as nonexistent, and in effect annuls it. The Scriptures, however, possess an authority so great that they cannot be broken. What they say will stand and cannot be annulled or set aside. If the Scripture speaks, the issue is settled once and for all; it cannot be broken. Since the Scriptures cannot be broken, so our Lord's argument runs, these particular words, which form a part of the Scriptures, likewise cannot be broken.[49]

The third statement of Jesus pertaining to inerrancy occurred during His Sermon on the Mount. In identifying His relationship to the Law, Jesus said, "For verily I say unto you, till heaven and earth pass, one jot or one tittle shall in no wise pass from the law, till all be fulfilled" (Matt. 5:18). Most scholars agree the reference to a jot and tittle referred to the *yod*, the smallest letter of the Hebrew alphabet, and a small *id* distinguishing several similar letters. Gaussen notes, "All the words of the Scriptures, accordingly, even to the smallest stroke of a letter, are no less than the words of JESUS CHRIST."[50] Young concludes on this text, "If, therefore, the inspiration of the Bible is plenary, it should be evident that it is one which extends to the very words."[51]

The fourth place where Jesus affirmed the inspiration and inerrancy of Scriptures was in Nazareth (Luke 4:18; Isa. 61:1-2). There he read half of a text and stopped in the middle of a sentence. In doing so, he separated the two comings of Messiah. The argument for the Second Coming involves the usage of verb tenses. If Jesus used the tenses of verbs to argue a point, so should we.

3. *Church fathers recognized inspiration/ inerrancy.* While fundamentalists are not bound by the teaching of church fathers, an understanding of their position will sometimes help clarify a position. A survey of the statements of the fathers on the subject of inerrancy reveals that inerrancy is not the recent discussion of more contemporary theologians. Clement of Rome (A.D. 80-100) suggested,

> You have looked closely into the Holy Scriptures, which are given through the Holy Spirit. You know that nothing unrighteous or falsified has been written in them.[52]

Later, Augustine wrote to Jerome (A.D. 394),

> It seems to me that most disastrous consequences must follow upon our believing anything false is found in the sacred books; that is to say, that the men by whom the Scriptures have been given to us, and committed in writing, did not put down in these books anything false.[53]

4. *Argument from the character of God.* God cannot lie. The nature of God is truth; therefore, what God has said cannot create a breach in His character. The unity, justice, and truthfulness of God is shown in the Old Testament. Therefore, what God says, He is; and what God proclaims Himself to be, He must be. Credibility is the key word. Note that the character of God and His word is the ultimate appeal in Scripture: Rom. 2:4; Heb. 6:18; Titus 1:2; John 17:17; Psa. 119:160. In this section we compare the nature of the Bible with the

	The Character of God	God	Bible
1.	Holiness	Isa. 6:3	Psa. 119:3, 9-11
2.	Truth	John 17:3	Psa. 119:43, 143
3.	Justice	1 John 1:9	Psa. 119:149
4.	Power	Nah. 1:2	Psa. 119:114, 116-120
5.	Love	1 John 4:8	Psa. 119:32
6.	Goodness	Psa. 119:68	Psa. 119:66
7.	Righteousness	Psa. 119:137	Psa. 119:138
8.	Purity	1 John 3:3	Psa. 119:140
9.	Wisdom	Jude 25	Psa. 119:98-100
10.	Life-giving	Isa. 40:31	Psa. 119:50
11.	Comforting	2 Cor. 1:3	Psa. 119:50, 76
12.	Mercy	Psa. 119:64	Psa. 119:58
13.	Faithfulness	Psa. 119:90	Psa. 119:86
14.	Immutability	Heb. 1:12	Psa. 119:89
15.	Joy-producing	Jude 24	Psa. 119:111
16.	Wonder	Isa. 9:6	Psa. 119:18, 129
17.	Eternity	Psa. 90:2	Psa. 119:89, 144

nature of God. Since the Bible comes from God, we expect that its nature would be similar to its Author.

5. *Argument from animation or the life-giving spirit of the Scriptures.* Since the process of inspiration is "in-breathing," God did more than breathe accurate content into the Bible. He breathed His Spirit into it. Since spirit is life, the Word of God is the life of God. This results in a unique supernatural blend of objective truth and spiritual life. Through the mystery of inspiration, human authors are joined to the divine Author. The result is a book with a dual nature.

The best illustration and parallel of the dual nature of the Bible is to compare it to the hypostatic union of God and man. Just as "The Word was made flesh" (John 1:14), so "The Word of God was spoken through human instruments." The Bible is the Word of God and Jesus Christ is the Word of God (John 1:1; Rev. 19:14). The Bible is inspired and Jesus is incarnate, both supernatural acts. The mystery of the incarnation demands a virgin birth where perfect divinity is joined to perfect human nature. The mystery of inspiration is the joining of human authors to the divine Author so that the Bible is a supernatural book.

Just as Christ was fully God at all times, so the Bible is accurately composed by the Holy Spirit and every word, thought, and idea is divine. But, while retaining His full deity, Jesus Christ was totally human in that He got tired and hungry and did not know the hour of His return. In the same manner, the Bible is a human book composed within the vocabulary, flow and journalistic style of human authors. Just as the human Jesus was perfect and did no sin, in the same manner the Bible is without error; it is a perfect Book. Therefore we conclude that the Bible is the divine-human book and, as such, is fully inerrant and authoritative.

God spoke to the world through His Son, the incarnate Word (Heb. 1:1-4). In a similar manner God speaks through the inspired Word. Just as Jesus was the final and full self-revelation of God, the Bible is the final vehicle of God's self-revelation. Therefore we conclude that the perfection of God demands a perfection extending to every word. For if one word were in error, there is the possibility of a flaw in God's self-revelation, hence leading to a flaw in our understanding of God. If an all-powerful God cannot control the vehicle of His self-revelation, then His power and nature can be questioned.

But the vehicle of self-revelation is more than an inanimate book. God revealed Himself in a Book that is an extension of Himself. The Bible is life and spirit (John 6:63). When we describe it as "the Word of God" we mean more than the fact that God's words are recorded therein. The Bible is God's Word, meaning the Bible belongs to Him as much as our words belong to us. The Bible is God's Word, meaning it reflects God, communicates God and symbolizes God just as our words come from our hearts, brains and feelings. Just as a man can say, "I am as good as my word," God can say the same thing, for the Bible is God's Word. When the Bible is raised to this level, it is as perfect as God, and its perfection extends to every word.

Written Word of God (1 Thess. 2:23)		Living Word of God Jesus Christ (John 1:1, 24)	
1.	Come from God (Matt. 22:31, 32)	1.	Come from God (Heb. 1:1; Gal. 4:4)
2.	Claim the same authority (Isa. 55:11)	2.	Claim the same authority (John 5:19-27)
3.	Complements Jesus (Luke 24:44)	3.	Complements the Bible (John 17:17, Matt. 5:18)
4.	Both include human element (2 Pet. 1:21)	4.	Both include human element (John 1:14, Luke 2:52)
5.	Never contradicts Jesus Christ	5.	Never contradicts written Word

I. PRESERVATION: INSURING THE AUTHENTICITY OF THE TEXT

God "in breathed" the writings of Scripture so that the writers wrote the Word of God, without error. God chose three languages for his self-revelation. First, the Old Testament is written in Hebrew, a language structure that reflected the Jew. Of all the semitic languages, it is simple, solitary and straightforward. Hebrew is beautiful in its descriptive words as it was ingenious in its idiomatic expressions. Some parts of Daniel were written in another semitic language, Chaldean. The New Testament was written in Greek, at one time falsely called "Holy Ghost language." This was because the Greek of the New Testament was different from the classical Greek of the philosophers. However, the archaeological excavations have uncovered thousands of parchments of "common language Greek," verifying that God chose the language of common people (*Koine* Greek) in which to communicate His revelation. God chose an expressive language to communicate the minute colors and interpretations of His doctrine. Still others feel God prepared Greeks with their intricate language, allowed them to conquer the world, used them to influence their tongue as the universal "trade language," then inspired Men of God to write in common Greek, the books of the New Testament. This made the Word of God immediately accessible to everyone. If the Bible were written in literary Greek or "a special language of the Holy Ghost," Christianity would have had a language barrier to cross to reach the common people.

We do not have the original manuscripts, called "autographs," of any book of the Bible. These were lost, mostly during the persecution of the early church. Roman emperors felt that if they could destroy the church's literature, they could eliminate Christianity. Others were lost due to "wear and tear." The fact that some early churches did not keep these autographs, but made copies and used them, demonstrates that they were more concerned with the message, than the vehicle of the message. God in His wisdom allowed the autographs to vanish. Like the relics from the Holy Land, they would have been venerated and worshipped. Surely "Bibliolatry" (worship of the Bible) would have replaced worship of God.

While some may have difficulty with the idea of not having an original manuscript, scholars who work with the non-biblical documents of antiquities usually do not have access to those originals. When considering the manuscript evidence, it should be remembered there are close to 5,000 Greek manuscripts and an additional 13,000 manuscript copies of portions of the New Testament. This does not include 8,000 copies of the Latin Vulgate and more than 1,000 copies of other early versions of the Bible. These figures take on even more significance when compared to the similar statistics of other early writings.[54]

AUTHOR	WHEN WRITTEN	EARLIEST COPY	TIME SPAN	NO. OF COPIES
Caesar	100-44 B.C.	900 A.D.	1,000 yrs.	10
Livy	59 B.C.-A.D. 17			20
Plato (*Tetralogies*)	427-347 B.C.	900 A.D.	1,200 yrs.	7
Tacitus (*Annals*) also minor works	100 A.D. 100 A.D.	1,100 A.D. 1,000 A.D.	1,000 yrs. 900 yrs.	20[*] 1
Pliny the Younger (*History*)	61-113 A.D.	850 A.D.	750 yrs.	7
Thucydides (*History*)	460-400 B.C.	900 A.D.	1,300 yrs.	8
Suetonius (*De Vita Caesarum*)	75-160 A.D.	950 A.D.	800 yrs.	8

AUTHOR	WHEN WRITTEN	EARLIEST COPY	TIME SPAN	NO. OF COPIES
Herodotus (*History*)	480-425 B.C.	900 A.D.	1,300 yrs.	8
Horace			900 yrs.	
Sophocles	496-406 B.C.	1,000 A.D.	1,400 yrs.	100
Lucretius	Died 55 or 53 B.C.		1,100 yrs.	2
Catullus	54 B.C.	1,550 A.D.	1,600 yrs.	3
Euripedes	480-406 B.C.	1,100 A.D.	1,500 yrs.	9
Demonsthenes	383-322 B.C.	1,100 A.D.	1,300 yrs.	200[*]
Aristotle	384-322 B.C.	1,100 A.D.	1,400 yrs.	5□
Aristophanes	450-385 B.C.	900 A.D.	1,200 yrs.	10

* All from one copy. □ Of any one work.

Some of the actual New Testament books were written on a prepared animal skin. We know this by other contemporary literature that has been uncovered. However, the expensive cost made it prohibitive for many copies to be made on skins, and probably some New Testament books were written on papyrus sheets. Papyrus was manufactured from a reed. 2 John 12 refers to paper, ζαρτης (chartēs), which was papyrus. The pen was a reed that was softened in the mouth and the ink was a mixture of soot from any fire and gum diluted with water. Papyrus was called *chartas* from which we get "charter." Several pages were sewed together and called *biblos* or little book. Later, *Ta Bibla* was a collection of little books, and from this we get the word Bible.

Some of the New Testament books were written by the author (Gal. 6:11) and others were dictated to an "amanuensis," a scribe (1 Pet. 5:12; Rom. 16:22). The author then signed the manuscript at the end to authenticate it (2 Thess. 3:17). An amanuensis was used to give the writer greater freedom and use of language.

The books of the New Testament remained in the possession of the addressee, unless they were written to more than one church (Col. 4:16). However, by the time Peter wrote 2 Peter 3:16, there was a collection of Paul's letters in one spot, and the church recognized them as Scripture equal to the New Testament.

Other churches wanted copies of the letters that were authoritative so they could have a complete set of the teaching of the apostles and those who were companions of the apostles. Churches were the first to have complete sets of apostolic writings. Later, wealthy men collected them.

The Bible was circulated in these forms. First, New Testament books were rolls of papyrus sheets. On the outside would be written, "The epistle of Paul to the Romans." Second, a Codex was used, which was a collection of papyrus sheets, sewn together, not rolled. This way, they could write on both sides of the sheets like our present-day books. Third, they used skins of young animals which made a durable and beautiful finish. This was known as vellum or parchment.

There were many reasons why the church collected the books into *Ta Bibla*. (1) The fact that the Old Testament had been collected into 39 books influenced the church to bring together a New Testament collection. Also, (2) since these books were immediately authoritative because they were written by apostles, or eyewitnesses to Christ, everyone wanted a copy. (3) The content of these books was about Jesus Christ, and every Christian wanted a copy because of their love for Him. (4) As the apostles began to die, everyone wanted a copy of their teaching. (5) The churches began using them in public worship (1 Thess. 5:27) and reading them in church services (Col. 4:16). As a matter of fact, churches exchanged copies to expand their collection (Rev. 3:1). (6) The growth of false doctrine and controversy motivated churches to expand their collection to answer all heresy. (7) The arrival of apocryphal books motivated church leaders to establish collections of biblical material and reject non-biblical material. With the church recognition of these books that were canonical, many wanted a complete set of canonical material. (8) The persecution by Dioclesion (303) when he ordered the destruction of all sacred books, forced Christians to catalogue their books, recognize what books were threatened, and hide them.

Between A.D. 70 and 170, the church was circulating many copies of Scripture. From 170 to 303, the books that were being circulated were gradually gathered into a collection and were separated from the rest of Christian literature. From 303 to 397, the unity and completeness of Scripture was recognized. We are talking about church recognition of the canon, not God's recognition. His books were authoritative even before the ink was dry. However, some books were not widely known, hence they were not accepted until later. They were inspired and authoritative the moment they were written. But in history, it took time for some books to gain recognition (canonization).

A study of the Bible text is called "textual criticism," but the word "criticism" does not mean "to find fault." Rather it is an investigation of the facts to determine the credibility of the text.   Criticism falls into two categories.   First, lower criticism, also called textual criticism, deals with the actual text with a view of determining the original manuscript.   The second is higher criticism, dealing with the area of authorship, sources, dates, and historical matters.   Both conservative and liberal theologians deal with lower and higher criticism. The presuppositions that a person brings to the Bible and his conclusions determine his theological persuasion.

The aim of textual criticism is to recover the actual words of the autograph.   Conservative scholars admit that in some cases we do not have the actual words, but the Bible is the best attested of all ancient books.   We have more manuscripts, with less interval between their original writing and the copies we possess.   Due to the science of textual criticism we can have confidence that we have the very words themselves.

While we do not have the originals, we have a better posture to determine the autographs for the New Testament than for any other ancient manuscripts.   We have more manuscripts that were copied from the original and we have better manuscripts for our study.   Whereas, we only have one manuscript of Sophocles since his death, yet we have 40,000 documents/manuscripts that are copies of the New Testament.

The 40,000 manuscripts from which textual criticism draws its source is spread among the following sources.   (1) The unical manuscripts are those codices of the New Testament written in capital letters that date back to A.D. 200; of all the texts in our possession, these are the best and most complete.   (2) The minuscule manuscripts were written in small letters beginning around 900.   (3) The early translations include approximately 8,000 copies of the Latin Vulgate dating back to the unicals.   While Latin is not as rich as Greek, because it has no aorist tense and no article, its early date helped establish the original from which it was translated.   Also, early Syrian and Coptic (Egyptian) versions have the same advantage.   (4) The patristic citations are quotations of Scriptures by the church fathers.   These were early and usable to locate and place a date on the various other texts.   Every verse in the New Testament has been quoted at least once by a church father, establishing credibility for the 27 book canon.   (5) The Lexionaries were books of early texts used for public reading of Scripture.   Over 2200 of them have been found, and they are helpful in that they insert parallel verses from other Gospels.   (6) There are other sources not counted in the 40,000 manuscripts.   These include a multitude of ostraca, which were broken pieces of pottery on which the poor wrote tax receipts, recipes, and other household messages.   Scripture quotations were abundant by Christians, and these account for all Scripture.   The ostraca take us to the heart of the people during the time the autographs were available, yet are hard to use because they were written in cursive style, with many abbreviations and quotations for memory.

These nontextual sources should not be thought of lightly.   Recognizing their importance to the reconstruction of the biblical text, Bruce Metzger states, "Indeed, so extensive are these citations that if all other sources for our knowledge of the text of the New Testament were destroyed, they would be sufficient alone for the reconstruction of practically the entire New

Testament."[55] Geisler and Nix suggest, "A brief inventory at this point will reveal that there were some 32,000 citations of the New Testament prior to the time of the Council of Nicea (325). These 32,000 quotations are by no means exhaustive, and they do not even include the fourth century writers. Just adding the number of references used by one other writer, Eusebius, who flourished prior to and contemporary to the Council at Nicea, will bring the total citations of the New Testament to over 36,000."[56]

Of course, the greater the number of copies of those original autographs, the greater the potentiality for error in transmissions. Such was not the case with the New Testament. After comparing the textual accuracy of the New Testament and the Iliad, Geisler and Nix conclude, "Only 40 lines (or 400 words) of the New Testament are in doubt, whereas 764 lines of the *Iliad* are questioned. This 5 percent textual corruption compares with one-half of 1 percent of similar emendations in the New Testament."[57]

These different readings have no impact on any major theological interpretation. Westcott and Hort suggest, "If comparative trivialities, such as changes of order, the insertion or omission of the article with proper names, and the like, are set aside, the words in our opinion still subject to doubt can hardly amount to more than a thousandth part of the New Testament."[58]

EARLY PATRISTIC QUOTATIONS OF THE NEW TESTAMENT						
WRITER	Gospels	Acts	Pauline Epistles	General Epistles	Revelation	Total
Justin Martyr	268	10	43	6	3 (266 allusions)	330
Irenaeus	1,038	194	499	23	65	1,819
Clement Alex.	1,017	44	1,127	207	11	2,406
Origen	9,231	349	7,778	399	165	17,922
Tertullian	3,822	502	2,609	120	205	7,258
Hippolytus	734	42	387	27	188	1,378
Eusebius	3,258	211	1,592	88	27	5,176

EARLY PATRISTIC QUOTATIONS OF THE NEW TESTAMENT					
WRITER	Gospels	Acts	Pauline Epistles	General Epistles	Revelation	Total
Totals	19,368	1,352	14,035	870	664	36,289

VIII. CANONICITY: THE STANDARD FOR INCLUDING BOOKS IN SCRIPTURE

Throughout history many cults have claimed to receive a revelation or a new message from God. Their revelation is found in the form of many books, such as *The Book of Mormon*, The Koran, and other forms of literature.

Some Christians mistakenly think there may be a "lost" book somewhere that will be added to the Bible in the future. Perhaps they dream there could be several books penned by Philip the Apostle or one of the women observers at the cross that could be added to the Bible.

Could there be 67 books in the Bible, or more?

The 66 books in the Holy Bible contain all that God has chosen to reveal about Himself and all man needs to know concerning God, His works and His salvation. The fact that salvation is limited to the self-revelation of God denies the necessity or possibility of additional books of Scripture that include any further revelation.

The title given to Scripture when referring to its completion is Canon. The word canon comes from the Greek root meaning "rod," which was used as a measuring reed and eventually became a standard. When applied to theology, the books that should be in the Bible, have had their contents applied to God's

---

THE BASIS FOR INCLUDING A BOOK IN SCRIPTURE

1. It must be prophetic (written by a prophet).
2. It must be authoritative (claims to be God's message . . . "thus saith the LORD").
3. It must be authentic (written by the person who claimed to be its author).
4. It had life-transforming power.
5. It was widely recognized as the Word of God.
6. It was reliable (the contents were consistent with the rest of Scripture, the data were accurate, and there were no inconsistencies in the book).

standard and as a result have been included therewith. Today, books in the canon are those that are officially recognized as the books of Scripture. Christianity accepted the 66 books of the Bible, 39 Old Testament books and 27 New Testament books. Remember, the church or a church council did not make the books of Scripture authoritative by their vote or recognition. Christians recognized that certain books had a spiritual ministry in their lives and were used by God to edify the church when they became the basis for preaching and teaching. Christians recognized that God spoke to them through certain books which had a certain innate spiritual power. They also recognized these books were written under the influence of God. They knew the human authors of these books and trusted their eyewitness reports, their spiritual counsel, or their testimony. When these authors claimed in their books that they were writing the message and actual words of God, the church accepted their testimony and recognized their books as Scripture.

A. OBVIOUS IDENTIFICATION. When the Scripture was written, there were few books being written and circulated as compared with today. To be accepted into the canon the quality of these books must appear to come from God. Hence, the public obviously recognized these books as being so inherently superior that they included them in the canon. Lewis S. Chafer says, "The same inherent divine character which inspiration secures had made these particularized books the Word of God in distinction from all other human writings."[59]

B. THE LOGICAL ARGUMENT. The a priori argument states that God would guard the gathering of the books into the canon because He had originally written each book. The argument is based on the following premise: (1) God had a message that He wanted to reveal to man. (2) God chose a multiple number of authors who would write the message for others to understand. (3) God knew that His message/revelation would be attacked from without. (4) God knew that the recipients of His revelation were not scholars, but average people in average circumstances. (5) Therefore, God could be expected to personally guarantee the contents (revelation), the accuracy of the words (inspiration), the compilation of the different messages from all His messengers into one coherent unit (canon), and that the message would be transmitted to future generations (inerrancy), so that there would be no corruption, alteration, deletion and/or addition to the Word of God.

C. IMPLICIT COMPLETENESS OF REVELATION. God implied in Scripture that the giving of revelation was complete. God's wisdom has anticipated the tendency towards corruption of His message, and He had issued warnings against those who "corrupt the word of God" (2 Cor. 2:17). The same warning was given to those who "pervert the gospel" (Gal. 1:7). Any tendency toward heresy was also condemned by God, apostasy being that which took away from God's message. God warned in the Old Testament not to add to His Word (Prov. 30:6). The New Testament ends with a warning of taking away or adding to the Word of God (Rev. 22:18-19). Since God has implied that there is a complete content of revelation to which man cannot add, nor from which he can take away, and God further recognizes and warns that some will try to add or take from revelation, then we should determine the completeness of revelation as a mandatory step to determining the makeup of the canon. Another implication of the completeness of revelation is James's speaking of the "perfect [complete] law of liberty" (Jas. 1:25).

D. THE ARGUMENT OF ORGANIC TERMINATION OF DOCTRINE. The Bible indicates that all doctrine that was revealed is complete and whole. From the very beginning God wanted a written revelation of His Word. The revelation began when "the LORD said unto Moses, Write this for a memorial in a book" (Exod. 17:14). The end of Scripture was noted by Jude who speaks of the faith (objective revelation) "once delivered" (Jude 3). This means that objective revelation is once and for all time delivered to the saints. It implies there will be no more revelation. There has been no revelation by God to men since the closing of the New Testament canon, hence we do not need additional books in the Bible because there is no additional message to communicate.

We believe that the next historical event in God's plan is the rapture, followed by the tribulation, the 1,000 years, the Great White Throne, followed by entrance into the new Heaven and the new earth. These events have already been graphically described to us in Revelation. Everything past and future has been described in a book. As far as we are concerned, God has given us a complete revelation of all that man needs to know about the nature and works of God in the world. Therefore, since the content of revelation is organically complete, we argue that the canon is structurally complete in 66 books.

E. THE PRESENCE OF MEN AND WOMEN WITH THE PROPHETIC OFFICE. When Paul says that the church was built upon the apostles and prophets (Eph. 2:20), he was indicating that these two offices were recipients of revelatory truth. They were to receive the divine revelation and pass it on to the people by preaching and teaching. The gift of a prophet was to receive a message from God and communicate it to people. Robert Saucy states,

> God's people accepted divinely inspired prophets who communicated God's revelation to them. Such leaders authenticated their message by miracles, by true predictions of the future, and by the dynamic nature of their message. A clear example is Moses to whom God gave the ability to work wonders to prove to the people that he was divinely commissioned . . . .[60]

There are four criteria to determine when a person is a biblical prophet and can receive the message of God and pass it on to his contemporaries or write it for succeeding generations—i.e., to record his message by inspiration to guarantee its accuracy. These four criteria are found in Deuteronomy 18:20-22 and 13:1-3.

First, the prophet must claim to have revelation and/or inspiration, i.e., he must claim that his message is from God. Moses set the standard: "When a prophet speaketh in the name of the LORD" (Deut. 18:22). He must be convinced that his message is from God. The second criteria of a prophet is the recognized predictability of his prophecies. The prophet who speaks in the name of the Lord must predict the future, and then it must come to pass. Moses noted, "If the thing follow not, nor come to pass, that is the thing which the LORD hath not spoken, but the prophet hath spoken it presumptuously: thou shalt not be afraid of him" (Deut. 18:22). Hence, the prophet is not from God if his predictions fail.

The third criteria is that his message must be in accord with the revealed will of God. When Moses gives the test of false prophets (Deut. 13:1-3) he commands, "For the LORD your God proveth you, to know whether ye love the LORD your God with all your heart and with all your soul" (v. 3). To love God was a written command (Deut. 6:5). Moses implies that some prophets may claim to be from God (criteria one) and even may produce miracles as did the magicians of Egypt (Ex. 7:11-12), which was criteria two. But if the message of the prophets contradicted Scripture, the people were to reject it. The people were to, "walk after the LORD your God, and fear him, and keep his commandments, and obey his voice" (vs. 4). The fourth criteria of judging a prophet is to determine if he leads the people away from God. Moses commanded the people, "That prophet, or that dreamer of dreams, shall be put to death; because he hath spoken to turn you away from the LORD your God" (vs. 5). The true role of the prophet was to point people to God, and when people were pulled from God by an alleged prophet, that man was not a prophet.

Today, we do not believe that there are prophets in the church, at least anyone who holds the office of the prophets. However, some may have the gift of prophecy, which seems to be preaching (1 Cor. 14:3). Do not confuse the two. Whereas men are given the gift of preaching (prophecy) to persuade and encourage and rebuke, no one is a prophet with the ability to receive a divine revelation and communicate it to the church today. Since there are no more prophets, there is no more revelation to be received and added to the canon.

F. A MESSAGE FROM GOD IS RECOGNIZED BY PEOPLE WHO HAVE HIS SPIRIT. One criterion that determined that the canon was closed in the past was the recognition and acceptance by the church. They were closer to the historical writings of Scripture and could determine the accuracy of what should be included in the canon.

The early church did not get together in a council and decide by vote which books should be included in the New Testament canon. They recognized how God was using certain books in the lives of individuals and in the life of the church. F. F. Bruce describes the acceptance they had in the life of Irenaeus.

> The importance of his evidence lies in his link with the apostolic age and in his ecumenical associations. Brought up in Asia Minor at the feet of Polycarp, the disciple of John, he became bishop of Lyons in Gall, A.D. 180. His writings attest the canonical recognition of the fourfold Gospel and Acts, of Rom. I and 2 Cor., Gal., Eph., Phil., Col., I and 2 Thess., I and 2 Tim., and Titus, of I Peter and I John, and of the Revelation.[61]

The early church recognized certain books as Scripture and used them in its preaching and teaching. Finally, to eliminate all doubt, a council recognized which books were used in the church. F. F. Bruce notes,

When at last a Church Council—The Synod of Hippo in A.D. 393—listed the twenty-seven books of the New Testament, it did not confer upon them any authority which they did not already possess, but simply recorded their previously established canonicity . . . . The ruling of the Synod of Hippo was re-promulgated four years later by the Third Synod of Carthage.[62]

We believe that the message of God is spiritually discerned and that only those who possess the Holy Spirit can recognize God's Spirit (1 Cor. 3:6-9). Jesus said, "My sheep hear my voice and . . . they follow me" (John 10:27). In essence His people will recognize His voice in the written page and obey His commandments. But at the same time, they will recognize that certain claims to inspiration are false claims. While this is a subjective argument and will not stand alone, it will support the other arguments for a closed canon.

Robert Saucy has put forth the following argument.

In the time of the Old Testament prophets, just as in Jesus' day, some people did not recognize the voice of God in the prophetic message and therefore an authoritative norm for their lives. Only through the influence of the Spirit of God were people compelled to accept the sacred writings as the authoritative Word of God.[63]

G. THE ACCEPTANCE OF THE OLD TESTAMENT. The canon of the Old Testament is now generally recognized as divided into three groups: The Law, The Prophets, and the *Kethubhim* (the Writings). The Law was composed of the five books of Moses or the Pentateuch; the Prophets were the books written by one who had the prophetic office—our major prophets, the twelve minor prophets, and some "former prophets," earlier writings such as Joshua and Judges. The Kethubhim includes the remaining books which are the poetical books, the *megilloth*, and the non-poetical books which are historical in nature.

There are three reasons for accepting the completion of the canon by the time of Ezra.

(1) The testimony of Josephus that the canon was completed . . . in the life-time of Ezra; (2) Ezra was especially concerned with the sacred books . . . and (3) the character of Ezra's time was such that the collection of the sacred book may appropriately have been made in it.[64]

One of the reasons for the establishment of the canon was the destruction of the Temple. Due to the dispersion, the Jews needed something to keep them together, although scattered. The Scripture was the standard by which they judged their lives and false religions. Hence, the books of Scripture were kept together for the Jews of the dispersion. When they returned after the exile they added Ezra, Nehemiah, Esther, Haggai, Zechariah and Malachi, and closed the canon.

Christ gave witness to the canonization of the Old Testament, saying "That all things must be fulfilled, which were written in the law of Moses, and in the prophets, and in the psalms, concerning me" (Luke 24:44). This broad, sweeping, inclusive statement of Jesus Christ supported the three divisions of the Old Testament. The Law was the Pentateuch, the prophets included the major and minor prophets, and the Psalms included some the historical and all the poetical books.

Additionally, 2 Timothy 3:16 recognizes and acknowledges the inspiration of the entire Old Testament that was commonly recognized during Paul's day. "All Scripture is given by inspiration of God and is profitable."

Finally, it should be noted that the Old Testament books are not recognized as canonical simply because Israel accepted them as such. They are recognized as canonical because of their divine origin, inspiration and preservation.

H. THE CANONICITY OF THE NEW TESTAMENT BOOKS. Most scholars believe that the New Testament canon was completed by A.D. 100. However, some feel it was completed earlier. Others (usually those who want to deny the supernatural predictions of some of the prophets) say it was not completed until 200 or later. The books of the New Testament were adopted on the basis of their own authority over all rivals for Scripture. And after their adoption there has been almost no debate concerning the issue. Year after year, men find other new books that date back to apostolic times, but on no occasion do they meet the standards for canonization.

Thiessen gives four basic principles to guide in the test of canonicity of the New Testament books.

---

(1) The authorship of the book by an apostle is necessary to be included in the canon. However, there were some books that were included because of the relationship of the author to an apostle that raised the book to the level of an apostolic book. Mark had fellowship with Peter, Luke had fellowship with Paul, and James was the brother of the Lord.

(2) The spiritual content of the book indicated it was revelation in nature, hence belonged in the canon.

(3) The universal acceptance of the book by the church indicated its canonicity. By the end of the second century all but seven books were accepted as Scripture, these being Hebrews, 2 and 3 John, 2 Peter, Jude, James and Revelation. Perhaps they were not accepted widely at the beginning because of their lack of distribution or their being written late in the apostolic period. However, as soon as they were exposed on a broad basis they were accepted into the canon.

(4) Was there evidence of divine inspiration? Whenever a book gave evidence to its being inspired by the Holy Spirit, it was included in the canon.[65]

There are a number of books that some have wanted to add to the New Testament. However, there has been no evidence of their canonicity by the Holy Spirit to be used in the lives of Christians and there has been no universal request by Christians that they be added to the canon.

1. *The indestructibility of the Canon.*   The fact that there has been little or no question concerning the 66 books in the Bible by consecrated Christians is an indication for their acceptability.   Some have claimed that Esther should not be in Scriptures because it does not contain the word God.   Martin Luther once claimed that James was a "strawy epistle." However, there has been no widespread movement among the people of God to take any books out of the canon.

I.   WHY REJECT THE APOCRYPHA?   There are collections of books known as the Old Testament and the New Testament Apocrypha.   The title "Apocrypha" means "hidden or concealed" and comes from the Greek word *apokruphos.*   The Apocrypha is not usually a collected unit of books, but are individual books written during or close to the time of the writing of Scripture.   Out of these Apocryphal books, fourteen were voted into the canon by the Roman Catholics at the Council of Trent in 1546.   These "hidden" books usually have isolated and varied support to be included in Scripture, but the vast majority of Christians

---

NEW TESTAMENT APOCRYPHA*

Epistle of Pseudo-Barnabas (c. A.D. 70-79)
Epistle to the Corinthians (c. A.D. 96)
Ancient Homily (Second Epistle of Clement) (c. A.D. 120-140)
Shepherd of Hermans (c. A.D. 115-140)
Didache (Teaching of the Twelve) (c. A.D. 100-120)
Apocalypse of Peter (c. A.D. 150)
Epistle of Polycarp to the Philippians (c. A.D. 108)
Epistle to the Laodiceans (c. A.D. 4th Century)
*This list is only suggestive.   There are other books which have been suggested for canonicity from time to time but none have been recognized.

---

have rejected any claim that they are Scripture.

The Apocrypha is included in many Bibles that are endorsed by the Roman Catholics. Also, some Bibles used by Protestants have included the Apocrypha; however, this practice is not as common today as in the past.   Because the Roman Catholics added the apocryphal books to the canon of Scripture at the Council of Trent, the modern-day believer must face the issue of the Apocrypha.

THE OLD TESTAMENT APOCRYPHA BOOKS[66]

I. Esdras	Baruch, with the Epistle of Jeremiah
II. Esdras	The Song of the Three Holy Children
Tobit	The History of Susanna
Judith	Bel and the Dragon
The Rest of Esther	The Prayer of Manasses
The Wisdom of Solomon	I. Maccabees
Ecclesiasticus	II. Maccabees

The main arguments against adding the Apocrypha to the canon are the ten previously listed reasons why the canon was closed after the apostolic fathers passed off the scene. Those arguments should be sufficient, but some claim that the books of the Old Testament Apocrypha date back past the actual New Testament. Therefore these additional arguments are added.

1. *The apocryphal books are generally weak in style and organization.* This argument does not stand by itself because there are some books of the Bible that are weak in organization such as 2 Peter. But the majority of the Apocrypha have so many major flaws in style and organization that they are identifiable as obvious human writing by authors unaided by the Holy Spirit.

2. *They contain historical and geographical errors.* Some apocryphal books have major historical and geographical errors. While it is not the purpose of this volume to demonstrate these problems, there are sources that will give additional data to the diligent scholars.

3. *They are Old Testament in nature but most were written in Greek.* The Old Testament was primarily written in Hebrew, the language of the people of God. The fact that the Apocrypha was written mostly in Greek raises a doubt in the mind of the Hebrew Old Testament scholar whether they should be included in the canon.

4. *The Apocrypha is not quoted by Christ or any of the New Testament writers.* This is not a conclusive argument because the New Testament quoted from all but three of the Old Testament books. If even one were quoted, there would be some credibility for the others being accepted. But the majority of evidence is against the Apocrypha, because not one of them is quoted.

5. *The plan of salvation runs through the Old Testament, but is not evident in the apocryphal books.* Obviously the word "salvation" is included in the Apocrypha, because the Jews of that period of time looked to God to save them. But the inherent qualities that give salvation to the reader are not evident in the Apocrypha as in the books of Scripture.

6. *There are no messianic prophecies mentioned in the Apocrypha.* Christ is the "warp and woof" of all Scripture. He is found throughout the Old Testament by type, prophecy, and implication, and His shadow is always evident. But He is the missing theme in the Apocryphal books.

7. *The Apocrypha makes no claim of divine Inspiration.* This is a strong argument against their validity. If they should have been included, there should have been evidence that the authors were giving the message of God, or they spoke for God or they were sent by God. There are no claims in the Apocrypha as "Thus saith the LORD," or "The word of the LORD came unto me . . . ." In addition to the lack of divine command there are no visions, dreams, or other means to validate their message.

8. *The Apocrypha were not included in the original Hebrew canon.* Since those who were closest to the original autographs omitted them from the canon, how can a council or individual who lived at a later time claim they should be included, especially when the claim is made hundreds of years later?

9. *Philo never referred to them.* When he referred to Scripture, Philo never included them. Even when quoting references outside Scripture he omitted them altogether in his writings. Philo was considered a scholar in his day, (20 B.C.-A.D. 40), and his omissions of any reference to the Apocrypha is another argument against recognizing them as Scripture.

10. *Jerome did not include the Apocrypha in Scripture.* He is regarded as a church father by the Roman Catholics and given a place of authority because he translated the Vulgate (the first recognized Roman Catholic Scripture). His omission of the Apocrypha from any books in the Vulgate should suggest to Roman Catholics that they are not canonical.

11. *The spiritual level is low in the Apocrypha.* Obviously this is a subjective argument, but most Christians feel the apocryphal books do not "feed the heart" as does Scripture. Since the Holy Ghost inspired Scripture and speaks through Scripture, He will not speak to the heart through false scriptures. The lack of the "inner voice of the spirit" (1 Cor. 2:13-16) is another reason to reject the Apocrypha.

12. *The Apocrypha implies doctrine contrary to Scripture.* Roman Catholics find proof for some of their doctrines in the Apocrypha, such as extreme unction, purgatory, and prayers for the dead. Many scholars hold that the Apocrypha was added to substantiate the growing non-biblical practices of the Roman Catholic church.

13. *The Apocrypha was not considered part of the canon until A.D. 1546 at the Council of Trent.* This late date would raise questions about the validity of the Apocrypha as fitting into the canon. Even when the Apocrypha was added, there was a split vote.

The Apocrypha is not currently recognized by many groups. Although the Catholic Church has indicated these books are Scripture, even today many Roman Catholics do not accept them with much authority.

IX. HERMENEUTICS: THE PRINCIPLES OF INTERPRETING SCRIPTURE

Directly related to the view of inspiration and inerrancy is an attitude and approach to biblical interpretation. All conservative interpreters of Scripture agree the Bible is its best interpreter. According to the Westminster Confession of Faith, "The infallible rule of interpretation of Scripture is the Scripture itself; and therefore, when there is a question about the true and full sense of any Scripture (which is not manifold, but one), it must be searched and known by other places that speak more plainly."[67] Still, there are some who claim to believe in inerrancy, but do so under the guise of "allegorical" and "cultural" interpretation. In effect they deny biblical inerrancy. Yet God has not made His revelation so difficult to understand that a normal grammatical literary method of interpretation cannot be used. When approaching the Bible, always interpret every word literally except when you come to figures of speech (i.e., similes, metaphors, etc.), then seek the literal meaning of the author. (The author rejects the rule that says the Bible should be interpreted literally except where a figure of speech allows a figurative interpretation. If we allow one exception then the entire view of literal interpretation crumbles). Note, the interpreter should seek the biblical author's literal meaning to every figure of speech. When this principle is followed, there is never the need to open the door to mystical or to "spiritual" forms of interpretation. Traditionally, believers have followed the historical grammatical interpretation which involves five basic elements.

A. INTERPRET THE BIBLE IN LIGHT OF ITS HISTORICAL BACKGROUND. Too often interpreters of the Bible appear to apply the message of Scripture to a modern context without first understanding the historical context in which revelation came. When we read a prophetic statement in Scripture, we are not to interpret that prophecy in terms of what we may see, but rather in the context of the historical background of the day in which it was written. Within that context, the message of the Bible becomes clear to the expositor.

Some overstep this principle and seek to explain difficult passages and apparent contradictions with an appeal to an "accommodation theory." In essence they acknowledge error in Scripture yet argue God was simply expressing the opinion of the day in allowing the statement to enter His revelation. Ramm approaches this position when he states,

When the religious liberal renounces much of the Bible because it is culturally conditioned he fails to understand that inspiration uses cultural terms and expressions to convey an infallible revelation. The mustard seed is not the smallest seed known to botanists, but among the Semites it was considered to be the smallest of seeds. Its phenomenal growth became the basis for an analogy for the growth of anything unusually small to something very large. For our Lord to have given the Latin terms of the smallest seed would have been grotesque.[68]

This concession by Ramm is not only inconsistent with inerrancy, it is unnecessary in the disputed text. The expression disputed was not a scientific statement but rather an idiomatic expression. Jesus did not say, "The mustard seed is the smallest seed" but he was saying, "The mustard seed is one of the smallest of seeds." There is never any need to culturally adapt the message of Scripture so that in effect inerrancy is denied.

B. INTERPRET THE BIBLE IN LIGHT OF THE AUTHOR'S PURPOSE AND PLAN. A second element of interpretation involves interpreting Scripture in light of the author's purpose and plan. Every book was written for a purpose, and that purpose gives direction to the primary interpretation of that book. One should not be so concerned with seeking mystical interpretations that he misses the clear message of the book. Most authors have stated their chief purpose so the reader is not misled. This is particularly true in the New Testament.

BOOK	REFERENCE	OBJECTIVE
John	20:31	To promote faith in Jesus as the Son of God.
1 Corinthians	1:10	To promote church unity in the church at Corinth
Galatians	1:6-9	To correct doctrinal heresy in the churches of Galatia.
1 Thessalonians	4:13	To correct false views concerning the return of Christ.
1 John	5:13	To provide a basis for Christian assurances.
Jude	3	To urge Christians not to waiver but to contend for the faith.
Revelation	1:1	To reveal Jesus Christ

C. INTERPRET BIBLE VERSES IN LIGHT OF THEIR CONTEXT. The context of a verse or chapter is a third important consideration when interpreting Scripture. This means we should seek to follow the author's thought which runs through a paragraph, rather than grabbing hold of some isolated thought in a verse. This is particularly important to consider when interpreting the wisdom literature of the Bible. Some men have quoted a text from Job only to be later embarrassed when, within the context of the quote, it is clear that the words are ascribed to the devil. Christians sometimes quote, "Touch not; taste not; handle not" (Col. 2:21) to justify their ethical position on a matter, when an analysis of the context demonstrates Paul is quoting and arguing against the position of a heretic. Be careful to check the context of a proof text before using it too widely.

D. INTERPRET THE BIBLE WITHIN THE AUTHOR'S MEANING OF WORDS. The basic building blocks of any language are words which are symbols that represent things. Careful consideration should be given to the meanings of words when interpreting Scripture. A literal grammatical interpretation of Scripture requires understanding three ways in which words may be interpreted.

Three steps should be taken before defining a word. First, check on the historical meaning of the word and its origins. Etymology is rarely the correct meaning but often helps to understand the word. Secondly, learn how the author normally uses the words, *Usus Loguendi*. This will involve searching a concordance for every use of the word, resulting in a comprehensive word study. This is foundational to all biblical theology and will help clarify the special meaning an author might attach to a word. Finally, check on the common use of the word within biblical times. This involves checking the idiomatic meaning of the word. Sometimes we may interpret a word in an expression which means other than what may first appear. When we say a man "flew down the road," no one assumes he had wings or was in an airplane. Rather, we recognize "flew" as part of an idiomatic expression referring to the speed with which a man drove his car. Similar expressions also appear in Scripture. Hodge reminds the interpreter,

The Interpretation of Words	
Etymology	Original meanings
Usus Loguendi	The use within the context
Koine	Common meaning

> The meaning of words is to be established by a study of their usage. A study of usage involves not only the usage of a particular author whose work may be under investigation, not only the usage of previous Scriptural writers, but the usage of the words under investigation in as wide a horizon as may be made possible by the available data. The Holy Spirit chose to use known human languages to convey to us the Word of God. The usage of the words in those languages, then, throws light on their meaning in the Scriptures.[69]

E. INTERPRET THE BIBLE ACCORDING TO GRAMMAR. Language is not a string of words, but a series of related words. Pay close attention to the rules of grammar when interpreting the Bible. This includes a consideration of verb tenses, the position of words and the relationship between words. The interpreter of the English Bible must first understand English before interpreting the Bible, and this will be sufficient for the average Christian. The one who will want to carefully interpret the Word of God will know and use the grammar of the original languages.

ENDNOTES

1.   Harold Lindsell, *God's Incomparable Word* (Wheaton, IL: Victor Books, 1977), 15.

2.   Arthur Walkington Pink, *The Divine Inspiration of the Bible* (Grand Rapids: Guardian Press, 1976), 5.

3.   Cited by L. Russ Bush and Tom J. Nettles, *Baptists and the Bible* (Chicago: Moody Press, 1980), 51.

4.   Charles F. Baker, *A Dispensational Theology* (Grand Rapids: Grace Bible College Publications, 1972), 30.

5.   James Oliver Buswell, *A Systematic Theology of the Christian Religion* (Grand Rapids: Zondervan, 1969), 1:183.

6.   John Baillie, *The Idea of Revelation and Recent Thought* (New York: Columbia University Press, 1956), 49-50.

7.   Lewis Sperry Chafer, *Systematic Theology* (Dallas: Dallas Seminary Press, 1957), 1:143.

8.   Archibald Alexander Hodge, *Outlines of Theology*, Rev. ed. (Grand Rapids: Zondervan; reprint of 1879 edition), 33.

9.   Augustus Hopkins Strong, *Systematic Theology: A Compendium Designed for the Use of Theological Students* (Old Tappan, NJ: Revell, 1976), 73.

10. Hodge, *Outlines of Theology*, 35.

11. Henry Clarence Thiessen, *Lectures in Systematic Theology* (Grand Rapids: Eerdmans, 1947), 59.

12. Baker, *Dispensational Theology*, 115.

13. Cited by Strong, *Systematic Theology*, 60.

14. Ibid., 81-83.

15. The Proslogion of Anselm is translated and reproduced in *Bibliotheca Sacra* and *American Biblical Repository* 8 (1851): 529-553.*

16. James Stalker, "Conscience," *The International Standard Bible Encyclopedia*, ed. James Orr (Grand Rapids: Eerdmans, 1939), 2:702.

17. S. S. Smalley, "Conscience," *New Bible Dictionary Revised*, ed. by J. D. Douglas (London: Lute Varsity Press, 1973), 248.

18. C. S. Lewis, *Mere Christianity* (New York: MacMillan Company, 1952), 40-41.

19. Ibid., 41.

20. Josh McDowell, *Evidence That Demands a Verdict* (San Bernardino, CA: Campus Crusade for Christ International, 1972), 108.

21. Chafer, *Systematic Theology*, 22.

22. Benjamin B. Warfield, "Revelation," *The International Standard Bible Encyclopedia*, ed. by James Orr (Grand Rapids: Eerdmans, 1939), 4:2581.

23. Wilbur Smith, *The Incomparable Book* (Minneapolis: Beacon Publications, 1961), 9-10.*

24. Lindsell, *God's Incomparable Word* (Wheaton, IL: Victor Books, 1977), 48.

25. Pink, *Divine Inspiration*, 18.

26. Ibid., 65.

27. Ibid., 28.

28. E. Y. Mullins, *Why Is Christianity True?* (Chicago: Christian Culture Press, 1905), 294-295.*

29. McDowell, *Evidence*, 339-340.

30. J. D. Morell, *Philosophy of Religion*, cited by Strong, 202.

31. Frederic Palmer, *Studies in Theological Definition*, cited by Strong, 203.

32. Clifton J. Allen, *The Broadman Bible Commentary* Vol. 1 revised (Nashville, TN: Broadman Press, 1969), 9.

33. Calvin E. Stowe, *History of Books of Bible*, 19, cited by Strong, 205.

34. E. G. Robinson, cited by Strong, 205.

35. Cited by Harold Lindsell, *The Battle for the Bible* (Grand Rapids: Zondervan, 1976), 116.

36. George Ladd, *The New Testament and Criticism* (Grand Rapids: Eerdmans, 1967), 17.

37. Cited by Benjamin B. Warfield, *Limited Inspiration* (Grand Rapids: Baker Book House, 1961), 9.

38. L. Harold De Wolf, *Present Trends in Christian Thought* (New York: Association Press, 1960), 44.

39. Raymond F. Surburg, *How Dependable Is the Bible?* (New York: Lippincott Company, 1972), 66.

40. John R. Rice, *Our God-breathed Book—the Bible* (Murfreesboro, TN: Sword of the Lord Publishers, 1969), 290-291.

41. Peter S. Ruckman, "Using 'Original' Greek to Prevent Young People From Learning Bible Truth," *Bible Believers' Bulletin* 4 (March 1982) 11:5.*

42. Idem, *The Christian's Handbook of Manuscript Evidence* (Pensacola, FL: Pensacola Bible Institute, 1976), 126, 130, 137.

43. William E. Hull, "Shall We Call the Bible Infallible?" *The Baptist Program* (December 1970): 17, 19.*

44. Robert Bratcher, "Biblical Authority for the Church Today," *Christianity Today*, (May 29, 1981).*

45.   James Montgomery Boice, *Does Inerrancy Matter?* (Wheaton, IL: Tyndale, 1979), 13.

46.   Rene Pache, *The Inspiration and Authority of Scripture* (Chicago: Moody, 1976), 97.

47.   E. J. Young, *Thy Word Is Truth* (Grand Rapids: Eerdmans, 1957), 44.

48.   L. Gaussen, *Theopneustia: The Plenary Inspiration of the Holy Scriptures*. Rev. ed. trans. By David Scott (Chicago: Bible Institute Colportage Ass'n., n.d.), 98.

49.   Young, *Thy Word Is Truth*, 27.

50.   Gaussen, *Theopneustia*, 102.

51.   Young, *Thy Word Is Truth*, 48-49.

52.   I Clement, XLV. 2. 3.

53.   Cited by James Oliver Buswell, *Outlines of Theology*, 24.*

54.   McDowell, *Evidence*, 48.

55.   Bruce M. Metzger, *The Test of the New Testament*, Second Edition (New York: Oxford University Press, 1968), 86.

56.   Norman L. Geisler and William E. Nix, *A General Introduction to the Bible* (Chicago: Moody Press, 1968), 353-354.

57.   Ibid., 367.

58.   Brooke Foss Westcott and Fenton John Anthony Hort, *The New Testament in The Original Greek* (Cambridge and London: MacMillan, 1889), 565. Exact data unknown.

59.   Chafer, *Systematic Theology*, 1:92.

60.   Robert L. Saucy, *The Bible: Breathed from God* (Wheaton, IL: Victor Books), 1978), 96.

61.   F. F. Bruce, *The Books and the Parchments*, Third Rev. ed. (Westwood, NJ: Revell Co., 1963), 109.

62.   Ibid., 113.

63.   Saucy, *The Bible*, 96.

64.   Henry C. Thiessen, *Introductory Lectures in Systematic Theology*, 103.

65.   Ibid., 104.

66.   Ralph Earle, *How We Got Our Bible* (Grand Rapids: Baker), 37-41. The author gives an excellent capsule of each of the Old Testament Apocryphal books.

67.   Cited from Chapter One, paragraph 9 by Buswell, *Theology*, 24.

68.   Bernard Ramm, *Protestant Biblical Interpretation* (Boston: W. A. Wilde, 1950), 192.*

69.   Buswell, *Theology*, 25. Exact data unknown.*

* Denotes page number(s) could not be verified.

THEOLOGY FOR TODAY

CHAPTER III – THEOLOGY PROPER

The Doctrine of God

I. INTRODUCTION

There are many reasons to study God, but perhaps we should start with the command, "Be still and know that I am God." There is no greater reason to study God than the fact that God invites us to know Him. But there are others, such as the fact that there can only be one God and we have an inner desire to know all things, including God. Also, since we are made in the image of God, we should understand Him in order to better know ourselves.

But there are some other reasons. The wror g view of God will always cause a multitude of problems in the daily life of a Christian. In contrast, the proper knowledge of God will give wholeness to our beliefs and ultimately to our lives. For if we properly understand God, the other doctrines concerning sin, salvation, angels, the church, and the last things will properly fall together. But when we misunderstand God, we automatically drift in our theology. And those who drift in their theology ultimately suffer in their practical life, because proper belief is the foundation for proper action. Therefore, the only way to regain lost ground is to go back to the core of our beliefs—return to God Himself. A. W. Tozer pointed out,

> The low view of God entertained almost universally among Christians is the cause of a hundred lesser evils everywhere among us. A whole new philosophy of the Christian life has resulted from this one basic error in our religious thinking.[1]

According to Tozer,

> A right conception of God is basic not only to systematic theology but to practical Christian living as well. It is to worship what the foundation is to the temple; where it is inadequate or out of plumb, the whole structure must sooner or later collapse. I believe there is scarcely an error in doctrine or a failure in applying Christian ethics that cannot he traced finally to imperfect and ignoble thoughts about God.[2]

Without qualification, the most important thing about any Christian is his thoughts about God. A study of civilization shows that no culture has ever risen above its religion, and no religion is greater than its view of God. Therefore, those who have the greatest view of God obviously will have the greatest civilization. Tozer suggested:

95

What comes into our minds when we think about God is the most important thing about us.

The history of mankind will probably show that no people has risen above its religion, and man's spiritual history will positively demonstrate that no religion has ever been greater than its idea of God. Worship is pure or base as the worshiper entertains high or low thoughts of God.[3]

The most revealing insight about a man is his idea about God. Those who will not kill, steal, or fornicate because of their fear of God reveal something about themselves through understanding their idea of God. On the other hand, those who give themselves over to sexual liberties in the name of religion also reveal something about their idea of God. Nor can we deny that the person who takes God's name in vain has told us his idea of God. But in the final analysis, those who are the most silent about God are the most revealing about themselves. Since man can never escape self-disclosure, the fact that he ignores God, reveals his attitude toward God. J. B. Phillips reminds us that our knowledge of God is constantly growing.

We can never have too big a conception of God, and the more scientific knowledge (in whatever field) . . . becomes our idea of His vast and complicated wisdom.[4]

It is not a coincidence that the Second Commandment excluded idolatry. Of all the things that God hates, he despises anything that slanders His character. The man that bows down to idols has an adulterous heart. He worships the extension of the thoughts of his mind. The fact that he makes God into an animal, bird, or a statue reveals his attitude toward God. He is a rebel against God and has exalted his estimation of himself. God hates idolatry because it is a monstrous lie, because it is intellectual snobbery, because it permits moral laxity, and because it leads other men astray. But the greatest reason that God hates idolatry is because man creates deity in his deceitful heart. Idolatry is terrible because man who is made in the image of God reverses his role. He makes God in his image.

The Bible teaches that man was made in the image of God. To this statement we cannot add that man is made in the exact image of God. That would make man a replica of God which is not accurate. But the closest likeness or appearance we have of God, is man.

Tozer, in his book on the attributes of God, asked, "What is God like?" and then commented, "This book is an attempt to answer that question. Yet at the outset one must acknowledge that it cannot be answered except to say that God is not like anything; that is, He is not exactly like anything or anybody."[5]

Some have suggested that by describing God, we rob Him of His infinitude. They go on to suggest that by describing God we make an idol, not with our hands, but with our thoughts. And the critics claim the idol of our minds is just as offensive to God as if it were a clay statue. But we are not making idols in our mind as though we are creating a fictional person. We are attempting to understand what the Bible teaches about God.

Zophar, the friend of Job asked the question, "Canst thou by searching find out God?" Canst thou find out the Almighty unto perfection?" (Job 11:7). This is a difficult question. The answer is NO! We can never perfectly describe God, for our language is limited, our minds are finite, and God has not completely revealed Himself. But on the other hand, the answer is YES! We can have a personal knowledge of God in our hearts/minds, and this desire of our hearts to know God was placed there by God Himself.

Of all the words in the English language, an understanding of the term God has both mystified and eluded mankind. Great creeds have attempted to define God. Even the beginners in Sunday school ask, "Who is God?" Philosophers, historians, and theologians have struggled to define the term God. Thousands of books have been written and millions of sermons have been preached on the topic, "God." But God is unknowable, the wholly Other One. Man in his greatest wisdom can never fully understand God, because man is limited in understanding. Human words can never adequately describe God. Even the best vocabulary can never approach an adequate description of God. God, who is the source of wisdom and definition, can never be defined by words, because God, the source of wisdom could only be perfectly understood by a mind as great as His.

Nicholas Cusa expressed something of the limitations that face the one desirous of knowing God when he stated. "The intellect knoweth that it is ignorant of Thee, because it knoweth Thou canst not be known, unless the unknowable could be known, and the invisible beheld, and the inaccessible attained."[6]

The only Book that can adequately tell the story of God is the Bible. That is because the Bible is inspired and life giving—the Bible is animated as the life of God and reveals the Person and work of God. Some read the Bible and judge it as a dusty history book. As a result, they miss seeing the self-revelation of God. Others see in the Bible what they feel are apparent inconsistencies. Others have concluded that the Bible is a forgery or that it contains unexplainable mysteries. Yet in spite of the critics, the Bible is the self-revelation of God—the only perfect story of God.

II. THE NATURE OF GOD

We begin our discussion of God by stating, "God is a being." This means God is a substantive entity, an eternal Person who exists in Spirit with certain absolute attributes. As a being, God has an existence that is real, measurable and, to a certain degree, knowable. This is the opposite of those who have denied the existence of God by redefining Him. Plato said God was eternal mind, the cause of all good in nature. Aristotle considered God to be the "the ground of all being." Spinoza, a pantheist, called God "the absolute universal substance." Hegel identified God as the absolute Spirit. God is also called "the First Cause" or "the Unmoved Mover." We object to the denial of His actual and literal existence as a being. God is an essence or a substance, not an idea.

Perhaps one of the best man-made statements of God is found in the Westminster Catechism in response to the question, What is God? "God is a spirit, infinite, eternal, and unchangeable in His being, wisdom, power, holiness, justice, goodness and truth."[7] As adequate as this statement is, it leaves out the Personhood of God and confuses the distinction between God's nature and His attributes.

The nature of God is His "essence" or His "substance." God's nature is what He is, and if we could take away God's nature, it would eliminate His existence. God's nature is His being and without it He would not be God.

The nature of God is singular, because God is one and has only one existence. In the next section we will discuss the attributes of God which are plural because God manifests Himself by many duties and relationships.

The nature of God defines his existence, whereas the attributes of God reflect His nature through attitudes, actions and points of relationship with His creation/creatures. Each attribute is an extension of the nature of God and becomes a focus by which God is revealed. Just as sunlight is a part of the sun and emanates from the sun, so the attributes of God are manifestations of the nature of God.

Any complete definition of God's nature must include these seven aspects, for these are the nature of God, without which He has no existence. The Scriptures define God as: (1) Spirit, (2) personhood, (3) life, (4) self-existent, (5) unchanging, (6) unlimited by time or space, and (7) unity, which means God is one God.

Every definition must have a definitive term that gives direction to the meaning it defines. The following chart gives seven definitive terms that give meaning to the nature of God. Notice that each contains a specific truth about God. All taken together, reveal a more complete picture of God's nature.

A. GOD IS SPIRIT. The first definitive term to help in the description of God is the word spirit. Some theologians use the term spirituality" in their description of God, but by today's definition it is misleading because spirituality describes personal piety. The term "spirit" when used in description of God means that He is immaterial, incorporeal, and invisible.

Russell Byrum points out that the spiritual motive of God is implied beyond biblical Christianity. He suggests,

GOD IS	WHO IS GOD
	Spirit
	Person
	Life
	A self-existent Being
	Unity (one God)
	Unchangeable
	Eternal and immense

The theistic conception of God implies spirituality. Even idolaters usually do not think of their image as their God, but rather as a symbol or abode of a spirit which they worship. In some of their images is an opening to a cavity into which the spirit is supposed to enter.[8]

God is spirit who is invisible and incorporeal; who is a divine Person that reveals Himself in perfect intellect, emotion, and will; who is the source and personification of all material and spiritual life; who is a self-existent Being; who is eternal in relation to time; who is unlimited in relation to the immensity of space; who is immutable in his nature; who is the unity of all existence, consistent within His being and corresponding, in reality, to the manifestations of His nature and attributes.

Jesus told the Samaritan woman, "God is a Spirit: and they that worship him must worship him in spirit and in truth" (John 4:24). Even though the King James Version uses the article "a" with Spirit, God should not be described as a Spirit, which means "one of many." The original language should be interpreted to read "God is spirit," (as NKJV, NASB and NIV), which describes His nature. As Spirit, God is not limited by a physical body. "Spirit" means incorporeal being; God is a real Being who does not exist in or through a physical body (Luke 24:39). Although God is said to have hands (Isa. 65:2), feet (Psa. 18:9), eyes (1 Kings 8:29) and fingers (Exod. 8:29), these are not to be understood as actual parts of God's physical body. These statements are "anthropomorphisms," whereby man projects onto God his own characteristics for the sake of understanding and expression.

According to Strong,

Those passages of Scripture which seem to ascribe to God the possession of bodily parts and organs, as eyes and hands, are to be regarded as anthropomorphic and symbolic. When God is spoken of as appearing to the patriarchs and walking with them, the passages are to be explained as referring to God's temporary manifestations of himself in human form—manifestations which prefigured the final tabernacling of the Son of God in human flesh.[9]

Hodge defines the term "anthropomorphism" as "a phrase employed to designate any view of God's nature which conceives of him possessing or exercising any attributes common to him with mankind."[10]

Anthropomorphisms are commonly expressed in the Bible as authors attempt to describe God in terms understandable to men. The following is a summary list of those statements as compiled by West.[11]

He has location: Gen. 4:16; Exod. 19:17-21; 20:21; 33:14-15.
He moves: Gen. 17:22; 18:33; Exod. 19:20; Num. 12:5; 23:4; Deut. 33:2; Judg. 5:4; 1 Sam. 4:7; Psa. 47:5; 68:7-8; Ezek. 11:23; Micah 1:2; Hab. 3:3; Zech. 2:13.
He uses vehicles: 2 Sam. 22:11; Psa. 18:10; 104:3; Hab. 3:8, 15; Zech. 9:14.
He is said to dwell on the earth: Exod. 25:8; 29:43,44; 1 Kings 6:13; 8:12-13; 2 Chr. 6:1-2; Psa. 132:14; Mic. 1:2-3.
He dwells with man: Exod. 29:45; Lev. 26:11-12; 2 Chr. 6:18; Zech. 2:10; Rev. 21:3.
He dwells in men: 1 Cor. 3:16-17; 6:19.

He has a face: Gen. 32:30; Exod. 33:11, 20; Deut. 5:4; 34:10; Rev. 20:11; eyes: 2 Chr. 16:9; Prov. 22:12; nostrils: 2 Sam. 22:9, 16; Psa. 18:15; mouth: Num. 12:8; Psa. 18:8; Lips and tongue: Isa. 30:27; breath: Isa. 30:28; shoulders: Deut. 33:12; hands and arms: Exod. 33:22-23; Psa. 21:8; 74:11; 89:13; 118:16; Isa. 52:10; Hab. 3:4; fingers: Psa. 8:3; back: Exod. 33:23, feet: Psa. 18:9; voice: Exod. 19:19; 20:22: Lev. 1:1; Num. 7:89; 12:4; 22:9; Deut. 4:12,36; 1 Kings 19:12-13. Psa. 29:3-9; 68:33; Jer. 25:30,31; Ezek. 43:6.

His voice is spoken of as dreaded: Exod. 20:19; Deut. 4:33: 5:24-26; Joel 2:11; 3:16; Amos 1:2; Heb. 12:19, 26.

He is said to exercise laughter: Psa. 2:4.

He appears to men: Gen. 35:9; 48:3; Exod. 3:2-6; 24:9-11; 1 Kings 9:2; Job 42:5-6; Amos 9:1.

His appearance is described: Exod. 24:10; Deut. 31:15; Isa. 6:1; Ezek. 8:1-2, 4; 43:2; Dan. 7:9-10; Rev. 4:5.

He has a human form: Gen. 18:1; Ezek 1:26-27: Rev. 4:2-3.

As spirit, God is a real Being not limited by a human body. God is much greater than any body. Even Jesus distinguished His resurrected body from a spirit; He noted, "A spirit hath not flesh and bones as ye see me have" (Luke 24:39). Therefore, we conclude that a spirit is a real being without body; however, on some occasions in Scripture, spirits possessed bodies and revealed themselves through physical form. Angels, demons, and even Satan himself are described as spirits. But remember, God is "the Father of spirits" (Heb. 12:9; Num. 16:22). Even though these spirits have the same "spirit" characteristics as God, they do not have moral attributes nor the nature of God. They are just similar in their existence.

A spirit is also invisible. Though God was in the pillar of fire that led Israel through the wilderness, He was never visible to the nation (Deut. 4:15. There are some passages in Scripture where it seems that men actually saw God (Gen. 32:30; Exod. 3:6; 24:9-10; Num. 12:6-8; Deut. 34:10: Isa. 6:1). Actually it would be more correct to say these men saw a reflection or a result of God, but did not see Him directly. The only ones who have seen God are those who saw Christ, "the image of the invisible God" (Col. 1:15). Because God is an invisible Spirit, no one has ever seen Him (John 1:18; 1 Tim. 1:18).

The First Commandment was a ban on the making of idols. The Second Commandment prevented the use of idols in religious service. God prohibited idols for many reasons, but one of them was because God is spirit.

When God is described as spirit (John 4:24; Deut. 4:15-16, 19; Psa. 147:5), it is implied that God is absolutely pure spirit. God is perfect in all. His being and spirit is the highest form of being; therefore, we say that God is absolutely pure in kind, quality, and quantity, and He is different from every being He has created, both in measure and in kind.

Even though God is without body and physical existence, God is still a Person. As such He has personality. As a spirit who is a person, God has existence in and of Himself.

Further, God is not limited by time or space, so His omnipresence is an attribute born out of His nature. According to Boyce, "To have an omnipresent and eternal mode of existence is possible for a spiritual nature, because spirit has not of necessity succession of time and specific limitation of location."[12]

B. GOD IS PERSON. Most of the religions of the world portray God as an impersonal Being or a force. The German philosopher Hegel said that God is an impersonal Being just as a picture on the wall or a plate on the table. Others have said that God is an idea. Paul Tillich made Him the ground of all being. These definitions fall short of the New Testament designation that God is a Person.

That God is "The Personal Spirit" is fundamental to Clarke's identification of God. According to him, "A personal spirit is a self-conscious and self-directing intelligence; and a

The Personality of God	
Self-awareness and self-determination	Exod. 3:13-14
The intellect of God	Gen. 18:19
The emotions of God	Gen. 6:6
The will of God	Gen. 3:15

personal God is a God who knows himself as himself, and consciously directs his own action."[13] Strong suggests, "The Scriptures represent God as a personal being. By personality we mean the power of self-consciousness and of self-determination."[14]

1. *As a Person, God has self-awareness and self-determination.* A basic characteristic of personality is self-awareness, the ability to know oneself. When God told Moses, "I AM THAT I AM" (Exod. 3:14), God was describing Himself according to His own perception. He existed in Himself and was aware of who He is.

God also has self-determination, which implies freedom. God is free to do whatever He chooses. Hence, being a person is equated with freedom. The contrary of freedom is determinism, and there is nothing that makes God do or be anything. God is free to follow the direction of His nature.

Self-determination involves accepting the responsibility for one's life. The self-determination of God is seen in that He exists by Himself and perpetuates Himself by His nature (Rom. 9:11; Heb. 6:17; Job 23:13).

Thiessen reminds us, "Self-determination is more than determination. The beast has determination, but it is mechanical; but man has the feeling of freedom and makes his choices from within in view of motives and ends."[15] Implied in self-determination is the power of freedom of choice in decision-making. Animals do not have personality; therefore, they do not choose, even though they appear to be self-directing. Animals act out of instinct, they do not make rational or volitional choices. As a Person, God makes choices determined by Himself.

2. As a Person, God has the power of intellect. God is said to know (Gen. 18:19; Exod. 3:7) and have known. The infinite wisdom and omniscience of God are clearly taught in the Bible (Acts 16:18). The Bible also pictures God remembering (Gen. 8:1; Exod. 2:24), which implies classifying that which He knows because He is a rational and orderly God (1 Cor. 14:40).

God's intelligence is necessary to understanding Him as a Being with personality and existence. The theory that God is not intelligent is not only absurd, it is against the rational understanding of personality. God is essentially intelligent in all of His being and works. The design in nature implies the rationality of God.

Since intelligence is essential to the nature of God, and He is infinite, then His intelligence is infinite. One of the reasons to believe this is that an infinite whole must have infinite parts. Therefore, since God is intelligent in all of His being, everything He does is intelligent.

Since there is no intelligence without a wise plan and design, the intelligence of God presupposes a plan that is as infinite as Himself. And if God is great, His plan and design for the universe is great and infinite.

Since the nature of God is unity, we can only expect that when God's intelligence conceives a comprehensive plan for all His creation, then God must be mighty enough to exhibit the plan and equally great in power to carry out the plan.

Therefore, considering God's intelligence, there is no such thing as God's having difficulty in design, decision, and ability to implement His plan in the world.

The Word of God is an extension of the wisdom and nature of God. God has declared that all the wicked shall be eternally punished. This decree is based on the immutable wisdom of God. If a man chooses unrighteousness, he will be damned for all eternity. This is according to the unchangeable wisdom of God. This does not mean that God decrees a person to Hell or Heaven. Such a choice would be inconsistent with the nature of God and man.

The unchangeable wisdom of God is reflected in the regularity and uniform laws of nature. The fact that God has fulfilled the promises of His Word, and ruled the world by the unalterable principles of cause and effect tells us that God is able to carry out His plans.

The Wisdom of God	
1. In Creation	Prov. 3:19
2. In Preservation	Neh. 9:6
3. In Providence	Eph. 1:11
4. In Redemption	Eph. 1:7

3. As a Person, God has the power of emotions. Some theologians do not use the word "emotion" relating to God, but the word "sensibility." Perhaps they see the instability of human emotions and are reluctant to project such frailties on God. However, to say that God has emotions is to describe God with both the capacity of feeling and the display of feelings. Since God is perfect, His feelings are pure in their source and perfect in their expression. It is man's emotions that are questionable, because man is influenced by the Fall, affecting both his judgment and response.

Note the feelings that are present in God: grief (Gen. 6:6); love (John 3:16); kindness (Psa. 103:8-13); empathy (Exod. 3:7-8); sorrow (John 11:35); anger (Psa. 7:11). Whereas some might think God's anger is an expression of evil, remember, God knows with perfect understanding and His emotional response is perfect in expression. Of all God's emotions, His power to love is best known. He loves freely, because nothing in God's nature compels Him to act. He loves perfectly, because God is perfect. He loves because it is His nature.

The Love of God	
1. Father loves the Son	Matt. 3:16
2. Son loves the Father	John 14:31
3. God loves the world	John 3:16
4. God loves His children	John 14:23
5. God loves Righteousness	Psa. 11:7
6. God loves Judgment	Isa. 61:8

4. *As a Person, God has the power of volition.* The ultimate act of personality is the power to make rational decisions that give self-direction to one's life. This power is more than instinct found in animals which react according to the stimulus they perceive. As such, animals can be trained to give physical response to an outward stimulus. True volition involves more than physical response. A person has volition. Volition comes from the power of existence and is one of the attributes of personality. At times, the influence of volition is more dominant in one's personality than is the influence of emotions or the mind. At other times, feelings or the mind will overly influence the person.

God has the power of volition. At times it is based on His intellect or knowledge of the situation at hand. At other times God acts out of his emotions of love or hatred. Also, God acts independently from the influence of his volitional nature. However, when viewing the unity of God, He acts as a unit. Therefore, the will of God is the natural extension of what God thinks, feels and expresses out of his unchanging nature.

1. God can do whatever He wills to do.
2. God does not necessarily will to do everything.
3. God limits His power by the free will of His rational creatures.
4. God's will is exercised over His power.
5. God's absolute power is exercised without intervention of secondary causes.

5. *Conclusion.* Perhaps the weakest link in the writing of some theologians is their small emphasis given to the personhood of God. Some might even ask, "Can a term like 'person' be

applied to God?" Clarke answers this objection, acknowledging, "The word may be inadequate to the nature of him who is great above all, and to apply it to him may be to open mysteries that we cannot solve; but when this word asserts that God is self-conscious and self-directing, it describes him rightly, and we have no better word to take its place."[16]   Granted, we must not project onto God the personality we find in man. At the same time, man was made in God's image, and the immaterial powers of man are a reflection of God. These powers only reinforce the personhood of God that is seen in Scripture.

C. GOD IS LIFE. The fact that God has existence and is a Person implies a third characteristic in His description: God is life. Since the nature of personhood is life, and God is a Person, we conclude that God is life. Constantly, the Bible calls Him "the living God" (Josh. 3:10; 1 Sam. 17:26; Psa. 84:2; Matt. 16:16). According to Strong, "life is rather *mental energy*, or energy of intellect, affection and will. God is the living God, as having in his own being a source of being and activity, both for himself and others."[17]

The Bible teaches that God is the source of all life (Psa. 36:9, John 5:26) and that all life in plants, animals, and humans comes from Him, since He created all things. Also, since God is the Sustainer of all living things, God sustains them by His life.

Life is a part of the nature of God, and when God gives life to something, He gives a part of His nature to it. When man was made in the image of God, man was given the principle of life which was a reflection of God's life. And since God is self-existing, life is self-existing. Man's life cannot cease, for life continues once it is begun. Therefore, man's physical life and spiritual life will never end. For those who are in a saving relationship with God, they shall have eternal life with God, and those who have rejected the salvation of God will live forever, but it will be in eternal punishment.

D. GOD IS SELF-EXISTENT. The self-existence of God is His infinity in relationship to being. God is unlimited in His existence. This means God has the ground of existence within Himself. He is not dependent upon another person for His existence, otherwise someone caused God and someone could terminate God. But God is the first cause.

Self-existence of God is not based on His will. If it were, God's will would have determined when He should begin. The self-existence of God is based on His nature. He is what He is by reason of His nature. God's being is not based on a decision that He made at some point in the past. That would mean that God caused Himself. If God could cause Himself, then He could annihilate Himself. Both

> He who exists by reason of His nature rather than his volition must always have existed and must continue to exist forever.

statements are inconsistent with the nature of God.

God has always existed, because His nature implies a Person without beginning and without ending. The only type person with that characteristic is a self-existent being, God.

The name Jehovah is translated LORD in the English Bible. It comes from the root of the verb "to be." Exodus 3:13-15 introduces us to Jehovah, whose name is based on the meaning "I am." It means "he who always exists," not he who has "present existence."

If someone asks God "What are you like?" He could not liken Himself to the mountain, or the oceans, or man; because God would have limited Himself. There is nothing to which God can compare Himself. God has to answer "What are you like?" with, "I am that I am." This answer compares God to Himself. LORD has no limitations. To the Jew, the name LORD implied the personality of their God. They always use the name LORD as a proper noun, giving him personality. The name implies He is the only God.

God is self-existent, which is foundational to the very nature of God. When we use the term "self-existent" we mean a perfect existence, because that which is imperfect cannot continue, for it will self-destruct. Perfect existence cannot be added to or subtracted from, nor can it change, because that which is perfect must by its very nature be eternal. Therefore to say God is self-existent is essentially to say God is unchangeable; also, it says God is eternal.

E. GOD IS IMMUTABLE. By definition, the immutability of God is His unchanging nature. All changes are for the better, or the worse. By definition, God is perfect and cannot become better. If he became less than perfect, He would not be God. God is therefore immutable; He cannot change. On the immutability of God, Hodge states,

> By his immutability we mean that it follows from the infinite perfection of God; that he cannot be changed by any thing from without himself; and that he will not change from any principle within himself. That as to his essence, his will, and his states of existence, he is the same from eternity to eternity.[18]

Specifically, the Bible identifies four areas in which God is unchangeable.

(a) They declare Him to be unchangeable in duration and life (Gen. 12:33; Deut. 32:39-40; Psa. 9:7; 55:10; 90:2; 102:12; Hab. 1:12; Rom. 16:26; 1 Tim. 1:17; 6:16).

(b) They affirm the unchangeableness of His nature (Psa. 104:31; Mal. 3:6; Rom. 1:23; Jas. 1:17).

(c) They also assert that His will is without change (Job 23:13; Psa. 33:11; Prov. 19:21).

(d) His character is also said to be immutable, as, for example, His justice: Gen. 18:25; Job 8:3; Rom. 2:2; His mercy: Exod. 34:7; Deut. 4:31; Psa. 107:1; Lam. 3:22-23; Mal. 3:6; His truth: Num. 23:19; 1 Sam. 15:29; Mic. 7:20; Rom. 3:3; 11:2, 29; 2 Tim. 2:13; Titus 1:2; His holiness: Job 34:10; Hab. 1:13; Jas. 1:13; and His knowledge: Isa. 40:13, 14, 27-28).

Since God exists uncaused, by His very nature He must exist as He has always existed in an unchangeable existence. The only thing that could change God could be that which caused God. But since God has no cause, it is concluded that God cannot be changed. Therefore, God is immutable.

The nature of God is immutable, He must always love because that is the extension of His nature, and He cannot change in nature. Also, God is justice. He must always judge that which is unrighteous. He cannot change His nature. The Bible teaches that the promises of God are immutable (Rom. 4:20-21). Because God's promises are an extension of His truth, He cannot go back on His Word. Taking the argument a step farther, the plan and purpose of God is immutable (Isa. 46:9-10). What God has planned must come into existence, because decisions and promises are an extension of His nature. God cannot allow His nature to be countermanded.

The Bible states, "God is not man, that he should lie; neither the son of man, that he should repent" (Num. 23:19). To deny the immutability of God, some have pointed to the biblical accounts of God's repenting. A close look at these accounts (Gen. 6:6; 1 Sam. 15:11) reveals that it was men, not God, who changed. When men sinned, God was consistent in His nature to judge sin. When men sought to live for God, God was still consistent in His nature to reward believers. The changing lifestyles of men caused the consistent behavior of God to appear to change, but the change was not in God. The change was in man.

However, to be immutable does not mean immobile. God can still act, think, create, and make decisions. God has the power of personality, yet at the same time He possesses the divine quality of immutability.

F. GOD IS UNLIMITED IN TIME AND SPACE. God is unlimited by time. The Bible describes Him as the one who "inhabiteth eternity" (Isa. 57:15). Paul called Him "immortal" (1 Tim. 1:17). Abraham recognized "the everlasting God" (Gen. 21:33). Moses observed "even from everlasting to everlasting, thou art God" (Psa. 90:2). The psalmist wrote, "But thou art the same, and thy years shall have no end" (Psa. 102:27).

Time is the measurement of events that appear in sequence. Since God created the world, He existed before the first event. As a matter of fact, God never had a beginning point; He always existed. And God will continue without a terminal point. This is why Christ is called the Beginning and the End, the Alpha and the Omega (Rev. 21:6, 22:13).

Neither is God limited by space. Space is all the area where there is physical reality and being. Space is the distance between objects. But God is greater than space and is independent of space. His existence goes beyond the furthest located object. The existence of God never ends. Paul told the Athenian philosophers that "God, that made the world and all things therein, seeing that he is LORD of heaven and earth, dwelleth not in temples made with hands" (Acts 17:24). Solomon observed "the heaven and heaven of heavens cannot contain him [God]" (2 Chr. 2:6).

Both time and space are results of God's creative act. But He Himself exists beyond time and space. God is infinite, while time and space are limited. God alone exists in the universe without limitations. If another God did exist, then God would not be the self-existent, all-powerful, unlimited God. It is axiomatic that two unlimited beings cannot occupy the same space. If another God did exist, then God could not be an unlimited God. The infinity and immensity of God are strong arguments for the sovereignty of God in the universe.

G. GOD IS ONE. "Here, O Israel: The LORD our God is one LORD " (Deut. 6:4). There can only be one God. To speak of more than only one supreme, absolute, perfect and almighty Being makes about as much sense as talking about a square circle. The meaning of words would become useless and truth would collapse. "Thus saith the LORD, the King of Israel, and his redeemer, the LORD of hosts: I am the first, and I am the last; and beside me there is no God." (Isa. 44:6).

The Unity of God is expressed throughout Scripture as demonstrated in the following chart.[19]

(1.) The passages which declare explicitly that God is one: Deut. 6:4; Mal. 2:10; "Hath not one God created us?" Mark 12:29, 32; 1 Tim. 2:5; Eph. 4:5, 6; Jas. 2:19.

(2.) Those that assert that there is none else or none beside him: Deut. 4:35, 39; 1 Sam. 2:2; 2 Sam. 7:22; 1 Kings 8:60; Isa. 44:6, 8; Isa. 45:5, 6, 21, 22; Isa. 46:9; Joel 2:27.

(3.) That there is none like him nor to be compared with him: Exod. 8:10; 9:14; 15:11; 2 Sam. 7:22; 1 Kings 8:23; 2 Chron. 6:14; Isa. 40:25; Isa. 46:5; Jer. 10:6.

(4.) That he alone is God: 2 Sam. 22:32; Neh. 9:6; Psa. 18: 31; 86:10; Isa. 37:16; 43:10, 12; 46:9; John 17:3; 1 Cor. 8:4-6.

(5.) That he alone is to be worshipped: Exod. 20:5; 34:14; 1 Sam. 7:3; 2 Kings 17:36; Matt. 4:10; Rom. 1:25; Rev. 19:10.

(6.) Those which forbid anyone else to be accepted as God: Exod. 20:3; Deut. 5:7; Isa. 42:8; Hosea 13:4.

(7.) Which proclaim Him as supreme over all so-called gods: Deut. 10:17; Josh. 22:22; Psa. 96:4, 5; Jer. 14:22; 1 Cor. 8:4-6.

(8.) Which declare him to be the true God: Jer. 10:10; 1 Thess. 1:9.

When we talk about the Trinity, we are still talking about one God, but three Persons.

In the nature of the one God there are three eternal distinctions which are represented to us under the figure of persons, and these three are equal . . . Reason shows us the Unity of God; only revelation shows us the Trinity of God, thus filling out the indefinite outline of this Unity and vivifying it.[20]

The idea of a "compound trinity" was common in Hebrew thought and is reflected in the very name of God, Elohim.

Polytheism teaches many gods, and it is a denial of the Being of God. Tritheism teaches three gods, and it is not true for the same reason. Dualism teaches two independent divine beings, and that also falls for lack of an axiology. The multiplication of gods is a self-contradiction. There can only be one supreme, absolute, perfect, and almighty being. To say that there are two or more gods, is to say that one means two or more. To do so defies logic, and rationality.

The Unity of God is not the same as saying God is a unit. The term unit means a single thing and is marked by mere singleness. A unit usually admits no interior distinctions, whereas the term "unity" implies diversity in unity. Or in other words, more than one makes up the total. The Unity of God implies His Trinity.

The Unity of God means He is before all things as their vital, sustaining, and intelligent First Cause. When we recognize such a truth, we accept an intelligent system of the world that explains all the phenomena of universal being. When we accept a First Cause, we explain the unity of God's plan in the world, that God is One, that He is the prototype and center of the entire universe. Finally, when we accept the First Cause, we accept the unity of God's design in providence that all things willing or unwilling, active or passive, work in concerted action for the accomplishment of His design.

H. ERRONEOUS VIEWS OF GOD. Over the centuries, various men and movements have suggested views of God that are different from the description of God found in the Bible. Because part of knowing God is knowing what God is not, the following summary of leading non-Christian world views is provided.

1. *Atheism.* Literally the term "atheist" designates a negation of deity. In one sense, all non-Christian religions are atheistic in that they deny the true God, yet Thiessen suggests there are three kinds of atheism: Practical Atheism is used to designate those who have been disappointed because of Christianity and thus overreacted by describing all religion as fake. Dogmatic Atheism is that view which espouses the nonexistence of God. The third type of atheism according to Thiessen is Virtual Atheism which holds to principles inconsistent with belief in God.[21] In conclusion, atheism is not an affirmative position, but a negative posture. As a result, when the author meets someone who claims to be an atheist, he usually asks, "What kind of god do you deny?" He further asks, "Do you deny the Christian God, Muslim god, or Shinto god?" The purpose is to show that the person is only reacting, not holding an affirmative view.

2. *Agnosticism.* To be a dogmatic atheist, one must profess virtual omniscience in all areas to be certain that God does not exist. Few people are so foolish to make such a claim for themselves. Those who choose to deny the existence of God will sometimes profess agnosticism. Thiessen uses this term to identify any doctrine that affirms the impossibility of any true knowledge holding that all knowledge is relative and, therefore, uncertain."[22] The agnostic, if he is consistent, is not only unsure of the existence of God, he is necessarily unsure of any knowledge.

3. *Materialism.* Strong defines materialism as "that method of thought which gives priority to matter, rather than to mind, in its explanations of the universe. Upon this view, material

atoms constitute the ultimate and fundamental reality of which all things, rational and irrational, are but combinations and phenomena. Force is regarded as a universal and inseparable property of matter."[23] This theory which recognizes matter as God vaguely defined as a force has been popularized in the "Star Wars" films. Essentially, it denies the personality of God and is a natural consequence of such a denial.

4. *Animism.* Animism is the term used in primitive religions to describe the existence of spiritual beings who "are held to affect or control the events of the material world, and man's life here and hereafter; and, it being considered that they hold intercourse with men, and receive pleasure or displeasure from human actions. The belief in their existence leads naturally, and it might almost be said inevitably, sooner or later, to active reverence and propitiation."[24] Animistic religions tend to emphasize human efforts to pacify deity and are based on fear rather than devotion. The worship of ancestors and fetishes is often a part of primitive animism.

5. *Polytheism.* Polytheism represents the worship and belief in a multiplicity of gods. This was the theistic view of both Greece and Rome at the writing of the New Testament. It was also the predominant view of Egypt at the writing of the Pentateuch. Often, polytheism is characterized by idolatry through the making of idols and is not necessarily implied in the view. There are several varieties of polytheism, but all agree in their denial of the essential unity of God.

6. *Henotheism.* One view of polytheism recognizes one of many gods supreme over others. Jastrow suggests, "The monotheistic tendency exists among all peoples after they have reached a certain level of culture. There is a difference in the degree in which this tendency is emphasized, but . . . there are distinct traces of a trend toward concentrating the varied manifestations of divine powers in a single source."[25] Henotheism, then, recognizes many gods, but places them in various ranks, identifying one as supreme above others.

7. *Tritheism.* Some have abused the doctrine of the Trinity to suggest the existence of three gods coequal in every respect, yet distinct deities and personalities. This charge is often made against Christians by Jews, Mormons and Jehovah's Witnesses, who claim the idea of Trinity denies the Unity of God.

8. *Dualism.* An additional abuse of the unity of God is held by the position known as dualism. According to Thiessen, "This theory assumes that there are two distinct and irreducible substances or principles. In epistemology these are idea and object; in metaphysics, mind and matter; in ethics, good and evil; in religion, good (God) and evil (Satan)."[26] The Christian, of course, cannot recognize Satan as God's equal. Nevertheless, many Christians

fall into the trap of equating God and Satan when they identify them as two opposing forces in constant struggle.

9. *Pantheism.* Robert Flint defines pantheism as "the theory which regards all finite things as merely aspects, modifications, or parts of one eternal and self-existent being; which views all material objects, and all particular minds, as necessarily derived from a single infinite substance."[27] Pantheism normally involves the recognition of gods or God in matter, but falls short of the denial of God as is the case with materialism.

10. *Idealism.* Idealism equates God with mental energy of the thinking process. According to George Patrick, Hegel thought of reality as "thought, reason. The world is a great thought process. It is, as we might say, God thinking. We have only to find out the laws of thought to know the laws of reality. What we call nature is thought externalized; it is the Absolute Reason revealing itself in outward form."[28] The view was popularized most recently in the hippy and drug cultures of the 1960s.

11. *Deism.* A final erroneous view of God is that of deism. "For deism God is present in creation only by His power, not in His very being and nature. He has endowed creation with invariable laws over which He exercises a mere general oversight; He has imparted to His creatures certain properties, placed them under His invariable laws, and left them to work out their destiny by their own powers. Deism denies a special revelation, miracles, and providence."[29] This view is sometimes described as an "absentee landlord" view of God. This erroneous view of God denies the basic attribute of God—love—which implies God involves Himself in the affairs of His creation.

III. THE ATTRIBUTES OF GOD

The attributes of God are those virtues or qualities which manifest His nature. In another way, an attribute of God is the extension of His nature. God's attributes are different from such words as strengths, characteristics, or qualities. These are words that identify the positive influence of a personality. But an attribute of God is more than the influence of God. An attribute has a distinct existence and can be separately identified, yet an attribute can never be separate from God, who is the source of each attribute.

According to Boyce, "THE Attributes of God are those peculiarities which mark or define the mode of his existence, or which constitute his character.

They are not separate nor separable from his essence or nature, and yet are not that essence, but simply have the ground or cause of their existence in it, and are at the same time the peculiarities which constitute the mode and character of his being."[30]

When we describe the attributes of God, we are not describing God as the sum of His many characteristics. A man may be the sum of his parts, but not God. Since God is Unity, God's entire nature is manifested into every part of His being. We cannot describe God as a perfect balance between His parts, because that implies that one of His parts can stand alone. If that is so, His attributes which are so different (such as love and justice) would be a contradiction of His nature. But God is a trinity and all of His attributes are unified in Himself.

God cannot suspend one attribute to exercise another, for God's nature is working in unity at any one time. God does not divide Himself to perform a work, nor does God divide Himself to think a thought. God does not divide Himself to act in any way.

The key to understanding the description of God is seen in His six attributes. Tozer defined an attribute as "something true of God,. . . something that we can *conceive* as being true of Him."[31] The attributes of God are those virtues or qualities which manifest His nature. (The previous chapter discussed the nature of God.) The *Westminster Shorter Catechism* lists four attributes (holiness, justice, goodness and truth) in its definition of God. "God is a spirit, infinite, eternal, and unchangeable, in His being, wisdom, power, holiness, justice, goodness and truth."

Even though we attempt to number God's attributes, we do not know exactly how many He has. Because God has only revealed part of His nature, we do not know all of His existence; therefore, we cannot arrive at an exact number of attributes. One theologian said, "God has a thousand attributes." Charles Wesley, the hymn writer, described God's attributes as "glorious all and numberless."

Some theologians describe God with communicable attributes which are those attributes that are communicated to man. Other theologians call some attributes moral attributes, those involving the moral exercise of God's nature. Also, some theologians describe the affirmative attributes which express His positive perfection while others are called negative attributes which note His reaction to everything outside His nature, such as the justice of God. Some theologians use the phrase relative attributes, to speak of those that relate to the created world. In contrast, they also describe absolute attributes which belong in and to God Himself. This is the distinction used in this text.

A. THE ABSOLUTE ATTRIBUTES OF GOD. God manifests Himself in divine attributes that reveal His nature as being holy, the expression of all that is right and pure; love, the sharing of His life with His created beings; and goodness, the embodiment of all ideal qualities and rewarding all that personifies the law of God.

THE ATTRIBUTES OF GOD	
Absolute	Comparative
1. Holiness	1. Omniscience
2. Love	2. Omnipresence
3. Goodness	3. Omnipotence

1. *Holiness.* Holiness is the first description that comes to our mind when we think of God. God is holy and apart from everything that is sinful. The root meaning of "holiness" is "to separate or to cut off." The primary meaning of holiness implies separation. As this

applies to our life, it includes both separation from sin and separation unto God. The holiness of God makes it impossible for God to commit sin or to even look upon sin with approval.

Stephen Charnock defined holiness as "a glorious perfection belonging to the nature of God."[32] Thiessen further elaborated, "By the holiness of God we mean that He is absolutely separate from and exalted above all His creatures, and that He is equally separate from moral evil and sin. In the first sense His holiness is not really an attribute that is coordinate with the other attributes, but is rather coextensive with them all. It denotes the perfection of God in all that He is."[33]

Holiness may be one of the most difficult of the attributes to completely understand and define. The presence of sin in the human race makes the thought of the nonexistence of sin totally incomprehensible. Tozer suggests, "We cannot grasp the true meaning of the divine holiness . . . It stands apart, unique, unapproachable, incomprehensible and unattainable. The natural man is blind to it. He may fear God's power and admire His wisdom, but His holiness he cannot even image."[34]

Holiness is usually defined with negative limitations, i.e. that which is entirely apart from all evil and from all which defiles. In a positive sense, God is the personification of all purity, which implies a separation from everything outside of God's nature and His creation (evil is an appendage to God's work, and sin is anything outside the nature of God).

Holiness is the perfection of God in all of His moral attributes. Therefore, God is a holy being before He wills holiness into action. This means God did not will Himself to be pure— He is pure. If God could decide to become pure (but this act could not happen) then holiness would be above God or outside the nature of God, which is not possible. That would make a dualism out of holiness and God, meaning both are co-eternal in their being. But the only eternal being is God Himself and holiness is intrinsic in His Being. God did not attain holiness, nor does He need to make an effort to retain it.

The holiness of God is both passive and active. The Bible talks about "God, who cannot lie" (Titus 1:2). Another way of saying the same thing about the active holiness of God is to recognize that He always speaks the truth (John 17:17; Rom. 3:4). The holiness of God is the primary motive in all God's action. It is that which God desires us to remember, and is the means by which He glorifies Himself. Holiness denotes the perfection of God in all His moral attributes.

The name "Holiness" is synonymous with God. David said, "He sent redemption unto his people: he hath commanded his covenant for ever; holy and reverend is his name" (Psa. 111:9). Isaiah wrote about "the high and lofty One that inhabiteth eternity, whose name is Holy" (Isa. 57:15). Jesus called the Father "Holy Father" (John 17:11) and instructed His disciples to pray, "Hallowed be thy name" (Matt. 6:9). The angels around the throne of God will eternally shout the chorus, "Holy, holy, holy, LORD God Almighty, who was and is and is to come" (Rev. 4:8 cf. Isa. 6:3).

It is important that we recognize the holiness of God because so much of our relationship with God is dependent upon it. When we realize God is too holy to look upon sin, we begin to understand God. When Jesus hung on the cross and cried out, "My God, my God, why hast thou forsaken me?" (Matt. 27:46), God was actually unable to look upon His own Son as He died bearing our sins. An understanding of the holiness of God reminds us of the degree to which God loves us. "For God so loved the world, that he gave his only begotten Son" (John 3:16).

God's attitude toward sin that demanded our salvation, also demands of us a holy life. The central theme of Leviticus is "Ye shall be holy: for I, the LORD God am holy" (Lev. 19:2). Isaiah observed that, although God can hear and answer prayer, "Your iniquities have separated between you and your God, and your sins have hid his face from you, that he will not hear" (Isa. 59:2). David said, "If I regard iniquity in my heart, the LORD will not hear me" (Psa. 66:18). The holiness of God also demands that God judge the continual practice of sin in the life of a Christian (cf. 1 Cor. 11:30-32).

Holiness is the most communicable of all God's attributes. Man can become holy because he is made in the image of God (Gen. 1:26ff). But man cannot become omniscient, omnipresent or omnipotent. Man can never be unlimited in space and time, nor can created man be an incorporeal and invisible spirit on earth. When man becomes holy, it is not in himself, but man becomes holy by identification with God who shares His nature with His children. Because God is holy and man was made in the image of God, man was made a holy being. However, in the fall, man lost his original holiness, becoming a sinner in act and nature. However, in Jesus Christ, the sinner takes the righteous nature of the Son of God (2 Cor. 5:21).

When we think of God expressing His holiness in his relationship with men, we think of the justice of God. According to Boyce, justice is "that rectitude of character which leads to the treatment of others in strict accordance with their deserts."[35] Tozer suggested, "Justice embodies the idea of moral equity, and iniquity is the exact opposite; it is *in*-equity, the absence of equality from human thoughts and acts. Judgment is the application of equity to moral situations and may be favorable or unfavorable according to whether the one under examination has been equitable or inequitable in heart and conduct."[36]

The justice of God is the active extension of the holiness of God. God's Justice implies that: (1) God has the authority and ability to set the standard for all relationships within the world which he created, and (2) that He will consistently relate to all obedience and disobedience of His creatures by applying rewards and punishments according to His equitable nature. God's justice is both legislative and distributive.

First, God's legislative justice refers to the setting up of government or His law. Since law flows from the nature of God, there is no beginning to the law. The law does not have eternal coexistence with God, but there always has been law, because it has flowed out of the nature of God. However, at a point in time, law was established so that beings could understand their requirements to God. Hence this was the establishment or introduction of law or government to the created world.

After created beings have run their course, there must be distributive justice. This also flows out of the nature of God. Distributive justice has two parts; remunerative justice deals with awards for compliance with the law, while punitive justice punishes those who violate the law. Rewards and punishment cannot be omitted, for that would deny the eternal nature of God.

There are several qualities about the justice of God. First, the justice of God is an extension of the Law of God to all situations. Second, the justice of God is an extension of His nature, because the law of God also is an extension of His nature. Third, since God is Unity, justice will be equally dispensed to all, giving no exceptions to those who obey or disobey by reason of intent or ability. Fourth, justice is consistent to everyone in all its expectations and consistently applied to everyone in all its punishments and rewards. Fifth, justice must be all-inclusive, since the law is an extension of the nature of God and since God is sovereign, everything must be subservient to God's authority. No one can be excluded. Sixth, God's justice must be impartial. The law cannot be administered by emotions, decision or conditions outside the law itself. Seventh, the justice of God must be decisive. Once it is administered, there can be no change. Justice, like the nature of God, is immutable. Eighth, the justice of God must be understandable by those to whom it applies, or else the one who creates and administers the law is not fair. Finally, justice, like truth, will be consistent with itself and will correspond in its application. Therefore, justice is the infallible application of the manifestation of the nature of God.

THE JUSTICE OF GOD IS
----
1. Consistent
2. With equality
3. All-inclusive
4. Impartial
5. Immutable
6. Systematic
7. Workable
8. Truthful

Sometimes people say, "Justice requires God to do this," indicating that God must do something outside of Himself. This is an error in thinking because it believes there is a principle outside of God that makes Him act in an equitable way. Of course, that can never happen. If so, the principle would be superior to God because it would compel God to act in justice. The actual truth is that nothing outside of the nature of God can make Him act or react. All of God's motivation comes from within His self-existing being. Nothing has ever moved God in the past, nothing can move Him now, and nothing will move God, for He is eternal and immutable. Actually "Justice" is the name we give to an attribute that describes God acting like Himself in a certain situation.

2. *Love.* Perhaps the most popular attribute of God that readily comes to mind is love. When children are asked to describe God, they most often respond by saying, "God is love" (1 John 4:8,16). Love is basically an attribute as expressed in an act that emanates from God its source. When God loves, it reflects His whole being.

Therefore, love is not just a virtue of God. It is God Himself. Also, love is not something God begins, nor does He extend His energy to maintain. The love of God is as eternal as the nature of God. Therefore, the love of God is self-existing.

Love is basically an attitude, as expressed in an act that emanates from its source. The concept of love as an attribute of God makes Christianity a unique religion in the world. Evans suggests, "Christianity is really the only religion that sets forth the Supreme Being as Love. The gods of the heathen are angry, hateful beings, and are in constant need of appeasing."[37]

A. H. Strong described love as "a rational and voluntary affection, grounded in perfect reason and deliberate choice."[38] Henry Thiessen called love "that perfection of divine nature by which He is eternally moved to communicate Himself."[39] Love is the attitude that seeks the highest good in the person who is loved.

It may be possible to give without loving, but it is impossible to love without giving. Therefore, love involves giving yourself to another. Jesus said, "Greater love hath no man than this, that a man lay down his life for his friends" (John 15:13). John later wrote that the greatest love expressed by God was to give His life as a propitiation (payment) for our sins (1 John 4:10).

The love chapter of the Bible, 1 Corinthians 13, describes love in terms of giving. The word love in this chapter is translated "charity." Charity meant giving time and money to a worthy cause—one expressed his love by giving to charity. Therefore, charity meant giving to those people whom we think are worthy. God expressed his love to us by giving us His Son.

Love is the opposite of selfishness. Perfect love is selfless. It gives itself in devoted sharing with the object of that love. Only those who are strong can love, because they must reach outside themselves to others. God who is the source of all strength is also the source of all love. He can give Himself and never empty Himself or divide Himself. He can love perfectly and continually. The Bible speaks of both "the God of love" (2 Cor. 13:11) and "the love of God" (2 Cor. 13:14).

Theologians tend to emphasize a particular attribute of God, depending upon their view of soteriology. As a result, those who teach orthodox theology tend to stress the holiness of God, reacting to the liberal emphasis and abuse of the love of God. Actually, these two attributes in God are not contradictory. Furness suggests, "The constancy of God's love and the perfection of His holiness alike find expression in covenant. Divine love is no chancy affair, but is made to depend upon an agreement which He makes with man . . . . God will be our God, and we are to be His people, but because Yahweh is holy, covenant demands obedience to His righteous law."[40]

Emphasizing love in the relationship between these two attributes, Jesus suggested that obedience to the law could be summed up in our love for God and for our neighbor (Matt. 22:40).

3. *Goodness.* When parents teach their children to pray, they often teach them to say before eating, "God is great, God is good . . . ." The goodness of God is another of the absolute attributes of God. In a broad sense, the goodness of God includes all the positive moral attributes of God.

Tozer wrote, "The goodness of God is that which disposes Him to be kind, cordial, benevolent, and full of good will toward men."[41] In his classic work on the attributes of God, Charnock notes,

God is good by and in himself, since all things are only good by him, and all that goodness which is in creatures is but the breathing of his own goodness upon them. They have all their loveliness from the same hand they have their being from. Though by creation God was declared good, yet he was not made good by any, or by all the creatures. He partakes of none, but all things partake of him. He is so good that he gives all, and receives nothing; only good, because nothing is good but by him; nothing hath a goodness but from him. [42]

Later Charnock added,

Pure and perfect goodness is only the royal prerogative of God; goodness is a choice perfection of the divine nature . . . He is good, he is goodness, good in himself, good in his essence, good in the highest degree, possessing whatsoever is comely, excellent, desirable; the highest good, because the first good; whatsoever is perfect goodness is God, whatsoever is truly goodness in any creature is a resemblance of God." [43]

When Jesus told the rich young ruler "There is none good but one, that is God" (Mark 10:18), he was relating a truth the young man already knew. When God told Moses His name, He said "The LORD, the LORD God, merciful and gracious, longsuffering, and abundant in goodness and truth, keeping mercy for thousands, forgiving iniquity and transgression and sin" (Exod. 34:6-7, emphasis added). Moses later told the nation, "He [God] will do thee good" (Deut. 30:5).

The goodness of God is an attribute reflected in various actions of God. The mercy of God is an expression of His goodness. Henry Thiessen described mercy as God's "goodness manifested towards those who are in misery or distress." [44] His mercy is eternal in quality, but expressed only at His choice.

God's mercy is available to a wide range of individuals. The Bible speaks of mercy to the church (2 Cor. 1:3), mercy to believers (Heb. 4:16), mercy to Israel (Isa. 54:7) and mercy to those who are called (Rom. 9:15,18).

The mercy of God is demonstrated according to the will of God. "I will make all my goodness pass before thee . . . and will shew mercy on whom I will shew mercy" (Exod. 33:19).

The grace of God is another expression of God's goodness. The grace of God, according to Thiessen, is "the goodness of God manifested toward the ill-deserving." [45] The

THE MERCIES OF GOD	
1. Mercy to church	2 Cor. 1:3
2. Mercy to believers	Heb. 4:16
3. Mercy to Israel	Isa. 54:7
4. Mercy to God's called	Rom. 9:15, 18

grace of God is the opposite of the justice of God. Grace is God giving to man the exact opposite of what he deserves. Man deserves condemnation, but he receives eternal life. Man deserved hell, but he received heaven.

God's grace is the basis of our salvation. The Bible teaches, "The grace of God that bringeth salvation hath appeared to all men" (Titus 2:11). Paul wrote, "For by grace are ye saved through faith" (Eph. 2:8). Early in the same epistle, he wrote, "In whom we have redemption through his blood, the forgiveness of sins, according to the riches of his grace" (Eph. 1:7).

A third aspect of the goodness of God is His benevolence. Thiessen says, "The benevolence of God is [the goodness of God], manifested in His care for the welfare, and is suited to the needs and capacities, of the creature."[46] Jesus taught the benevolence of God: "He maketh his sun to rise on the evil and on the good, and sendeth rain on the just and on the unjust" (Matt. 5:45). Paul and Barnabas pointed to God's benevolence as a witness of the gospel: "He left not himself without witness, in that he did good, and gave us rain from heaven, and fruitful seasons, filling our hearts with food and gladness" (Acts 14:17).

Finally, the longsuffering of God reflects God's goodness. The term "longsuffering" means "slow to become angry." God is described as longsuffering (Rom. 2:4) because He waits for men to repent and believe on Him. Longsuffering is the patience of God whereby His love overshadows His holiness. God exercises longsuffering, hoping that men will trust Him and turn to Him in salvation.

IV. THE COMPARATIVE ATTRIBUTES OF GOD

The absolute attributes of God are those things man cannot know apart from the revelation of God to him. If any man has holiness, love or goodness, he first recognized it in God and then received it from God. The comparative attributes of God contrast human abilities and the divine nature. Every man has a degree of power, but only God possesses omnipotence. Every man has presence, but only God is omnipresent. Every man has some knowledge, but there is only One who is omniscient. These three attributes of God may be defined by a comparison of degrees which God and man share. Psalm 139 lays a foundation for understanding the comparative attributes of God. The omniscience of God is seen in Psalm 139:1-6, the omnipresence of God is seen in Psalm 139:7-11, and the omnipotence of God is seen in Psalm 139:12-16.

A. OMNISCIENCE. When we say God is omniscient, we mean He possesses perfect knowledge of all things. The prefix "omni" means "all" and the word "science" comes from a Latin root meaning "knowledge." The omniscient God has all the knowledge in the world. God has never had to learn anything. He has never forgotten anything He ever knew. God knows everything possible. That means He knows and understands the sum total of all the world's knowledge and even those things mankind has yet to discover.

David wrote, "Great is our LORD, and of great power: his understanding is infinite" (Psa. 147:5). Jude identified God as "the only wise God" (Jude 25). Most Bible commentators agree that wisdom in the Proverbs is personified in Christ. As a Christian seeks guidance in the daily affairs of his life, it is good to realize that God guides him because He knows the answers to questions he has not yet fully comprehended.

Charnock summarized the biblical teaching on the knowledge of God with the statement, "God hath an infinite knowledge and understanding; all knowledge."[47] Tozer suggests, "To say that God is omniscient is to say that He possesses perfect knowledge and therefore has no need to learn. But it is more: it is to say that God has never learned and cannot learn."[48]

1. *God has not learned.* The Bible teaches that God has not learned anything from any person. "Who hath directed the Spirit of the LORD , or being His counselor hath taught him? With whom took he counsel, and who instructed him, and taught him in the path of judgment, and taught him knowledge, and shewed to him the way of understanding?" (Isa. 40:13-14). Since God has always known everything, He could not have learned it from anyone. And if we say that God received knowledge in any manner at any time, we admit that God did not possess or did not know at some time in the past. This would make Him imperfect and less than Himself. But God who is the maker of Heaven and earth did not learn from any person. Since God exists within Himself, He has all knowledge in Himself from all eternity.

2. *God accurately knows Himself.* If God knows all things, then he must know Himself. This knowledge comes out of His nature and is a part of His being. The doctrine of revelation is partly based on the premise that God must know Himself to reveal Himself. But, because revelation is only partial does not mean God's knowledge of Himself is partial. God has chosen what He will and what He will not reveal. The partial revelation by God of Himself is also governed by the limited understanding of man. But, since God is perfect in all His being, it is only natural that His knowledge of Himself is perfect in time, scope and implication.

3. *God knows everything possible.* If God knows all things, He knows all things that happened in the past, in addition to everything that will happen in the future. But also, God has knowledge of everything that could have existed in the future (Rom. 4:17). This frightening insight ought to drive man to faith in God because He knows the outcome of every alternative. God knows what would have happened if we had not married our mate, and what would have happened if we had not received His Son as Saviour. All potential knowledge is bound up in the omniscience of God.

4. *God knows without effort.* God does not need to act or exert effort in order to recall an incident of the past. God is eternal; there is no past, for God is without time. Therefore, there is no need to recall, for God knows all things perfectly at all times. God does not remember, forget, or in a literal sense, make an effort to memorize for future use. If we say that God had to make an effort to recall, we would say that at one moment God does not know about the facts until He recalls it to His mind. Therefore, that would be saying God is not perfect, but He was limited at that given time. Therefore, a self-existent and unlimited God demands that He be omniscient, knowing all things at all times without effort.

5. *God knows all things equally well.* The Bible teaches, "Neither is there any creature that is not manifest in his sight; but all things are naked and opened unto the eyes of him with whom we have to do" (Heb. 4:13). God knows everything about every person equally well, but more than people: "He telleth the number of the stars; he calleth them all by their names. Great is our LORD, and of great power: his understanding is infinite" (Psa. 147:4-5). For as man may know a few things about a broad area, or he may have in-depth knowledge about a few things, God is infinite in His knowledge of everything.

Whatever God's omniscient mind knows, only an omniscient mind can understand, for only an omniscient mind has omniscient understanding. That means that man cannot fully understand the omniscience of God. The omniscience of God as the basis of prophecy is not that God "reveals" the future in a mystical way, but that God knows the future because of His nature. God knows all things.

B. THE OMNIPRESENCE OF GOD. God is present everywhere at the same time. The prefix *omni* means "all" and the main root "presence" means "here, indwelling, or in the approximate location." Therefore, God is everywhere present. God is in all things and God is close to everything that has existence.

According to Hodge, "Omnipresence characterizes the relation of God to his creatures as they severally occupy their several positions in space."[49] Clarke further suggested, "When we speak of God's omnipresence, we mean that God is not conditioned or limited by space in his power of acting, but is able to put forth his entire power of action anywhere. The whole of his ability for action, of every kind, is available for exertion everywhere at any time, without any need that he move from place to place in order to reach the scene of action."[50]

1. *God's omnipresence is a manifestation of His immensity.* The nature of God knows no limits in space. That means He is everywhere. But the immensity of God goes beyond space. It extends to "no space." God exists even where there is no space. There is no existence beyond God's existence. One theologian implied, God is to space as the sea is to fish, meaning God is larger in His totality than space—everywhere there is space there is God, and He exists beyond space.

Therefore, we can say God is over all things, under all things, enclosed within all things, and never excluded from anything. He is completely above, beneath, within and is the Sustainer of all things.

2. *God's omnipresence implies His immensity.* The immensity of God says that He is everywhere present at the same time. That means the center of God is everywhere and His circumference is nowhere. Man's mind is baffled by the immensity of God and it defies proper explanation. Because God is everywhere present, He is close to His created world. The Bible teaches that man cannot escape from God. "Whither shall I go from thy spirit? or whither

shall I flee from thy presence? If I ascend up into heaven, thou art there: if I make my bed in hell, behold, thou art there. If I take the wings of the morning, and dwell in the uttermost parts of the sea; even there shall thy hand lead me, and thy right hand shall hold me" (Psa. 139:7-10). There is no contradiction when the Bible says, "Cain went out from the presence of the LORD" (Gen. 4:16). Cain went out from the face of the Lord, the word "presence" meaning "God's face." This was the position of blessing and usefulness. Adam and Eve could not escape from God in the garden, because God is omnipresent. But after their sin, they were driven from the localized presence of the Lord, the place of honor and fellowship.

3. *God's omnipresence allows for transcendence.* God's omnipresence teaches us that He exists within His created world, yet is distinct from it. This means that God is transcendent over the world, because He is supreme. God exists within every part of the world as the Sustainer, but he also exists apart from the world to be worshipped by the world and one day to judge the world.

4. *God's omnipresence teaches He will manifest Himself in some places more than in others.* The Bible teaches the localized presence of God. The Lord is in the heavens (Isa. 66:1), for His throne is there, as well as His presence from which He speaks. But God is also on the earth and near to His people (Rom. 8:10; Acts 17:27). Also, God is under the earth (Luke 16:23; Rev. 14:10). The institutional presence of God, was in the Holy of holies (Num. 7:89), and is in the midst of the churches (Rev. 2:5). Beyond this, there is the indwelling presence of the Trinity in every believer. First, the Father and Jesus Christ indwell them, (John 14:23). Next, the Holy Spirit indwells every believer (Rom. 8:9). The fact that the presence of God dwells more in the believer than the unbeliever reinforces the principle that God manifests Himself in some places more than in others, yet the presence of God is everywhere present.

5. *God's omnipresence implies His omnipotence and omniscience.* Since God is everywhere present, it is to be assumed that God knows all things. Since God is omnipotent in sustaining and controlling the world, it is only natural that He is omnipresent, meaning He is everywhere present to run the world. Finally, He must be omniscient, knowing all that is happening. Any one of the three attributes presupposes and demands the other two attributes.

6. *God's omnipresence.* The perfections of God demand that He exist everywhere at the same time. Since He is perfect in knowledge and power, and these are part of His nature, it only implies that God's presence must necessarily exist where He is exercising His wisdom and works.

The existence of a God who has created all things logically did not begin itself; therefore there must be a First Cause who was capable of being everywhere present to create the world. Since all things came into existence at the same time, God was everywhere present at the same time bringing the world into existence. God is omnipresent.

Throughout time people had assumed the existence of God. The psalmist said, "Thou art there" (Psa. 139:7-9). Hagar who languished in the desert, cried out, "Thou God seest me" (Gen. 16:13).

The fact that God *is* means that God is here and now. He comforts, guides, and protects the believer with His omnipresence. And the fact that God is here, implies that God is everywhere.

C. THE OMNIPOTENCE OF GOD. God can do everything that is in harmony with His nature and perfection. Of all of the attributes of God, God has limited His omnipotence by His will. He can do whatever He wills to do, but He does not necessarily will to do everything. On many occasions, God has limited His power by the free will of His rational creatures. By this God does not force people to become Christians; therefore, He limits His power by the rejection of their will. God could have exercised His power to keep sin out of the universe, but that would have been inconsistent with the nature of His created beings. Therefore, God limited His power to allow sin to enter the world.

God's will controls His power, otherwise, God's power would act out of necessity and He

---

THE LIMITS OF GOD'S OMNIPOTENCE

1. God cannot create a being or world to which His essential incommunicable attributes can be given.
2. He cannot create a being whose nature is sinful.
3. He cannot impose laws not accordant with righteousness and holiness.
4. He cannot deal with any of His creatures unjustly.
5. He cannot commit sin.
6. He cannot change His own nature.
7. He cannot change His decrees or purpose.
8. He cannot do impossibilities or absurdities.

---

would cease being a free being. Berkhof suggests, "Power in God may be called the effective energy of His nature, or *that perfection of His Being by which He is the absolute and highest causality.*"[51] By the term "omnipotence," Byrum means, "the almightiness or unlimited power of God, or that God has power to do all things which are objects of power."[52]

1. *God's power is potentially unlimited.* Not only can God do impossible things (such as raising the dead), God does improbable things (such as walking on the water, John 6:19). God has the potential to do anything He wills. The Bible teaches, "With God all things are possible" (Matt. 19:26).

But when we analyze the omnipotence of God, we realize at times that God is limited. He will not do those things which are contrary to His nature. God cannot look on sin (Hab. 1:13),

But when we analyze the omnipotence of God, we realize at times that God is limited. He will not do those things which are contrary to His nature. God cannot look on sin (Hab. 1:13), deny His existence (2 Tim. 2:13), lie (Heb. 6:18), nor be tempted to sin. These things are against His nature (Jas. 1:13). Even though God is all-powerful to do everything that is in harmony with His nature, He cannot go contrary to His nature nor deny His being. God cannot make a square circle, nor can He make a true myth.

2. *God's power is comprehensive.* It does not require any effort on God's part to act in any way. The idea of exertion or labor is unknown to God. He spoke and the worlds were created. He wills and it is carried out (Isa. 59:1-2).

3. *The power of God is discernable.* The Bible teaches that God's power can be seen in the created world; "For the invisible things of Him from the creation of the world are clearly seen, being understood by the things that are made, even his eternal power and Godhead; so that they are without excuse" (Rom. 1:20). The power of God was not withheld from the understanding of man, but is made evident in nature. This self-disclosure of God's omnipotence is that man might know God and turn to Him.

4. *God's power holds the world together.* The Bible teaches that God "upholdeth all things by the word of His power" (Heb. 1:3; cf. Col. 1:17). The power of God keeps the comets in their path and the planets in their orbit. The power of God keeps the atom from exploding into unlimited nuclear fission.
The omnipotent God preserves the world as He created it in the beginning and is the greatest evidence of the Person of God.

5. *God's sovereignty is a result of His omnipotence.* The one cannot exist without the other. If God is going to reign, then He must have power. And if God is going to reign sovereignly, He must have omnipotent power. When recognizing God's sovereignty, it includes all things seen and known, plus the spiritual world we do not see and experience. The sovereignty of God includes all people, all things and all potential situations (Matt. 11:26-27; Rom. 11:33-36).

V. THE NAMES OF GOD

The study of the doctrine of God includes a study of His names, for they reveal the nature and works of God. In the East where the Old Testament was written, names had great significance. Names were given to people, places and things for the significance they had or the significance desired by someone. The Bible teaches that the main significance of God's many names is that they further reveal Himself. According to Berkhof, the name of God:

> . . . stands for the whole manifestation of God in His relation to His people, or simply for the person, so that it becomes synonymous with God. This usage is due to the fact that in oriental thought a name was never regarded as a mere vocable, but as an

expression of the nature of the thing designated . . . . In the most general sense of the word, then, the name of God is His self-revelation.[53]

Concerning the significance of the name of God, Thomas Rees states,

The name (shēm) of God is the most comprehensive and frequent expression in the OT for His self-manifestation, for His person as it may be known to men. The name is something visible or audible which represents God to men, and which, therefore, may said to do His deeds, and to stand in His place, in relation to men. God reveals Himself by making known or proclaiming His name.[54]

The different names of God have been one target of the liberal critics of Scripture. They maintain that the Bible is folklore and that the different groups of people had different gods. One called God "Elohim," another called Him "Jehovah," and another "Adonai." When these names are emphasized in certain portions of Scripture, the liberal critics claim that later scribes gathered sections of religious literature together, and the different names of God remained in the manuscript. However, we are not talking about different gods, but one God. We are not talking about different views of God. We are talking about one God who has revealed Himself through His different names, and we are talking about one God who reveals His different relationships to man through His different names. Like a man's name, they will not be changed, nor will they be forgotten. "His name shall endure forever: his name shall be continued as long as the sun: and men shall be blessed in him: all nations shall call him blessed" (Psa. 72:17).

A. THE PRIMARY NAMES OF GOD. There are three primary names of God: Elohim (God), Jehovah (LORD), and Adonai (Lord). When referring to the strength of God, the name Elohim (God) is used. It occurs 31 times in Genesis 1 to reveal His creative power. When referring to God's existing nature or His relationship to man, the name Jehovah (LORD) is used. The title Adonai (Lord) is used when referring to God's authority, such as the relationship of Master to servant.

After examining the primary names of God, we shall look at the compound names of God. As might be expected, their complexity is a reflection of His absolute attributes.

THE NAMES OF GOD IN SCRIPTURE	
PRIMARY NAMES	
Elohim	The Strong and Faithful One
Jehovah	The Self-Existent One

THE NAMES OF GOD IN SCRIPTURE	
Adonai	Lord or Master
COMPOUND NAMES	
El-Shaddai	The Almighty God
El-Elyon	The Most High God
El-Olam	The Everlasting God
El-Gibbor	The Mighty God
El-Roi	The God who sees
Jehovah-Sabaoth	The LORD of hosts
Jehovah-Jireh	The LORD shall provide
Jehovah-Nissi	The LORD our banner
Jehovah-Rapha	The LORD that healeth
Jehovah-Shalom	The LORD our peace
Jehovah-Maccaddeshcem	The LORD our Sanctifier
Jehovah-Tiskena	The LORD our righteousness
Jehovah-Shammah	The LORD is there
Jehovah-Roah	The LORD our Shepherd
Jehovah-Naheh	The LORD that smiteth
Jehovah-Elohim	LORD God
Adonai-Jehovah	LORD God
Jehovah-El-Gemuwal	The LORD God of Recompense

1. *Elohim-God.* One of the common names used in the Scriptures is the most common designation for deity, "God." The Hebrew word for "God" is Elohim. "El" means "the Strong One" who manifests Himself by His Word, "Elohim" being the plural form. Hence, the attributes of faithfulness and omnipotence are manifest by this name. Elohim is used over 2,500 times in the Old Testament, often to remind the reader of the strength or faithfulness of God. Moses wrote, "From everlasting to everlasting thou art God (Elohim)" (Psa. 90:2). Elohim is the name first used of God in the Scripture. "In the beginning God (Elohim) created the heaven and the earth" (Gen. 1:1). The final reference to the word "God" in the New

Testament is the Greek equivalent *theos* (Rev. 22:19). Usually, the name God (Elohim) is used in connection with the unsaved or inanimate objects.

Elohim is a plural form used in connection with plural verbs and adjectives (Exod. 20:3; Deut. 6:4). We see the implication of the Trinity in this word. However, Jewish writers speak of the "plural majesty" as used in reference to kings.

2. *Jehovah-LORD*. An unusual problem confronts the study of this second name of God. We really are not sure how to pronounce it. Some scholars say "Yahweh," but others say "Jehovah." Usually it is translated LORD in our Bibles, and all four letters are capitalized. The reason we are not sure of its pronunciation stems from the reverence Jewish leaders gave to this name. No one would pronounce it out of fear of offending God. When some scribes came to the word "LORD" in copying the Scriptures, they would stop and bathe and put on clean clothes. Others would begin with new pen and ink before writing God's name. This concern for not dishonoring the name of God was also expressed in the reading of the Scriptures. When the reader came to this name for God, he would either pause and omit it or often substitute another name for God in its place. Also, the Hebrew language has no vowels in its written alphabet so pronunciation of words is learned orally. Because men did not speak the name, LORD, it was not long before others did not know how to pronounce it.

This word "LORD" means "the self-existent One," coming from the word "to be or become." It comes from the verb to be repeated twice. "LORD" means, "I am, which I am." Jehovah is the name that is used when the Creator relates to His people in an intelligent and responsive relationship. In this note, Jehovah does not occur until Genesis 2:4 (after the creation of man). Jehovah is the name with which God identified Himself at the burning bush (Exod. 3:14). This name speaks of both the self-existence of God and His eternity. God is the only One who can say "I am": i.e., "I exist by Myself, independent of any other." He can always say "I am" because He always was in the past and always will be in the future.

Jehovah is used 6,823 times in the Bible, usually in association with His people. It has been called "the covenant name of God," as it is often used to identify God in His covenants (cf. Gen. 2:15-17; 3:14-19; 4:15; 12:1-3).

3. *Adonai- LORD*. The third name used of God in Scripture is Adonai, usually translated "Lord" in our English Bible. (Only the first letter is capitalized with Adonai Lord, whereas all four letters are capitalized in Jehovah LORD). Adonai was first used by Abraham as he sought the will of God in adopting an heir (Gen. 15:2). The term, which means "Master," implies two things. First, it indicates the sovereignty of God. The master is the one who assumes control of a situation. It is reasonable to assume that the servants will do the master's will. Of all the names used of God, this one identifies Him with the qualities of an earthly master. Hence, it gives human characteristics to God.

Secondly, this term implies the possibility of knowing the will of the master. Abraham used the name as he sought to determine a course of action. If the responsibility of a servant is to do the will of his master, it is reasonable to assume the master will make that will known to his servant.

Today, Christians often talk about "the LORD" but show little of allowing Him to control their lives. If we recognize Him as Lord, then there is no longer any question of obeying His commandments. When God told Peter to kill and eat unclean animals, three times Peter replied, "Not so, LORD" (Acts 10:9-16). As soon as Peter said, "Not so," he was no longer recognizing God as his Lord. Someone put it this way: "If He is not Lord of all, He is not Lord at all."

B. THE COMPOUND NAMES OF ELOHIM.

1. *El Shaddai - The Almighty God.* The primary names of God are sometimes used with other names to identify a specific characteristic of God. The name El Shaddai, means "the Almighty God." This name speaks of God's all-sufficiency. When Abraham was ninety-nine years old and still without an heir, "the Almighty God" renewed His covenant with him (Gen. 17:1-2). This was the God who was able to overcome any obstacle to keep His promise.

The term Shaddai means "rest or nourisher." It comes from a root word that means "breast or strength given or sustainer." Though translated "the Almighty God," it also means "the All-sufficient God." Today, we can claim the psalmist's promise, "He that dwelleth in the secret place of the Most High shall abide under the shadow of the Almighty (El Shaddai)" (Psa. 91:1).

2. *El Elyon - The Most High God.* This name is used to identify God, particularly to polytheistic Gentiles. The idea in this name is that the true God of Israel was above all false gods of the Gentiles. This title is first used in the Scriptures to identify Melchizedek's priesthood as "the priest of the most high God" (Gen. 14:18). At that time, Melchizedek attributed Abraham's recent military victory to El Elyon (the Most High God). God is also said to be "the possessor of heaven and earth" (Gen. 14:22).

3. *El Olam - The Everlasting God.* In his experience with God, Abraham also came to know Him as "the everlasting God" (Gen. 21:33). This name indicates God is not limited by time. He is eternal. Moses wrote, "From everlasting to everlasting, thou art God" (Psa. 90:2). The name El Olam personifies all that is true about the eternity of God.

4. *El Gibbor - The Mighty God.* Isaiah uses this designation for God when identifying the birth of the Messiah prophetically. Translated "The Mighty God" (Isa. 9:6), this name of God lays emphasis upon the omnipotence or power of God. Christians have often been accused of limiting God by thinking of Him in a limited way. In contrast, God has revealed himself in His omnipotence.

5. *El Roi - The Seeing God.* This name of God literally means "the strong one who sees." The name appears only once in Scripture after the angel of the Lord appeared to Hagar as she

fled from Sarai. After realizing God was aware of her situation, she identified God with the words, "Thou God seest me" (Gen. 16:13).

C. THE COMPOUND NAMES OF JEHOVAH.

1. *Jehovah-Sabaoth - The LORD of Hosts.* This name emphasizes the power and glory of God. The word "hosts" is used in the Bible to refer to heavenly bodies (Gen. 2:1), angels (Luke 2:13), saints (Josh. 5:15) and sinners (Judg. 4:2). It implies the power of the heavenly beings who serve the Lord. As the Lord of hosts, God is working through all these "hosts" to fulfill His purposes. The Christian can be encouraged today as he claims the promise "The LORD of hosts is with us" (Psa. 46:7). In discussing the second coming of Christ, David asked and answered a very important question. "Who is this King of glory? The LORD of hosts, he is the King of glory" (Psa. 24:10). The expression "LORD of hosts" is used over 170 times in Scripture to identify the LORD.

2. *Jehovah-Jireh - The LORD will provide.* Probably the single greatest test of faith in the life of Abraham occurred when God called him to sacrifice his son. When Isaac asked his father about the sacrifice animal, Abraham responded, "God will provide himself a lamb for a burnt-offering" (Gen. 22:8). Later that same day, God honored the faith of Abraham and prevented the death of Isaac by providing a ram in his place. "Abraham called the name of that place Jehovah-Jireh (the LORD will provide)" (Gen. 22:14). In the New Testament, Paul may have been thinking of this name of God when he asked, "He that spared not his own Son, but delivered him up for us all, how shall he not with him also freely give us all things?" (Rom. 8:32).

3. *Jehovah-Rapha - The LORD that healeth.* God always wants the best for His people. When He brought Israel out of Egypt, He wanted His people to live full and healthy lives. "If thou wilt diligently hearken to the voice of the LORD thy God, and wilt do that which is right in his sight, and wilt give ear to his commandments, and keep all his statutes, I will put none of these diseases upon thee, which I have brought upon the Egyptians: for I am the LORD that healeth thee" (Exod. 15:26). This name of God emphasizes God's concern for our good health.

God is certainly able and does on occasion heal people miraculously, but that is only part of what this name teaches. The context of the revelation of this name is preventive medicine more than curing. No doctor has found a cure for the common cold, but the mother who bundles up her children with scarves, mittens, boots and snowsuits on a cold winter day has "cured" her children's cold by preventing it. Here God has promised to heal us from the diseases that plagued the Egyptians by providing the resources that are available to those who obey the LORD. Obedience will produce good health.

4. *Jehovah-Nissi - The LORD our banner.* When God gave Israel the victory over Amalek, "Moses built an altar, and called the name of it Jehovah-nissi" (Exod. 17:15). The name Jehovah-Nissi means "The LORD is my banner" or "The LORD that prevaileth." The emphasis of this name for Christians is that we are not in the battle alone. As soldiers, we march under the banner and colors of God. The battle itself belongs to God, and victory is already guaranteed. The Christian can therefore serve the Lord with complete confidence in the outcome.

5. *Jehovah-Shalom - The LORD our peace.* When God called Gideon to deliver Israel from the oppressive Midianites, "Gideon built an altar there unto the LORD, and called it Jehovah-Shalom" (Judg. 6:24). The name Jehovah-Shalom means "The LORD is our peace." The building of that altar before the gathering of an army or forming of a battle plan was an act of faith on Gideon's part. The only way one can know Jehovah-Shalom is by faith. "Therefore being justified by faith, we have peace with God through our LORD Jesus Christ" (Rom. 5:1). As we seek to live for God consistently, the Bible says, "The God of peace shall be with you" (Phil. 4:9).

6. *Jehovah-Tiskenu - The LORD our righteousness.* When the Lord returns to this world at the end of the age, many Jews will recognize their Messiah and turn to Him as Saviour. At that time they will know a name of God that every Christian knows experimentally, "The LORD our righteousness" (Jer. 23:6). Our admission into Heaven is not dependent upon our personal righteousness, but rather upon the righteousness of God applied to our account. Someday this will also be the experience of national Israel and "The LORD our righteousness" will be the prominent name of God in that day.

7. *Jehovah-Shammah - The LORD is there.* As Ezekiel concludes his discussion of the eternal city he records, "and the name of the city from that day shall be, the LORD is there" (Ezek. 48:35). This name of God emphasizes His presence. When God called Moses to lead Israel out of Egypt, he promised, "Certainly I will be with thee" (Exod. 3:12). As we are faithful today in presenting a greater deliverance to the lost by preaching and teaching the gospel, Jesus has promised, "Lo, I am with you alway, even unto the end of the world [age]" (Matt. 28:20). The LORD is present.

8. *Jehovah-Maccaddeshcem - The LORD our Sanctifier.* When God appointed the sabbath under the law, He identified Himself with the words "I am the LORD that doth sanctify you" (Exod. 31:13). The biblical concept of sanctification did not involve the eradication of the sin nature, but rather noted God's setting a person apart for some reason. Though under law, this often involved special signs such as the vow of the Nazarite; under grace, God still expects His people to live apart from the world. Paul's prayer for the Thessalonian Christians was that "the very God of peace sanctify you wholly" (1 Thess. 5:23).

9. *Jehovah-Roah - The LORD our Shepherd.* One of the most familiar passages of Scripture is the Twenty-third Psalm, where God is identified as "The LORD is my Shepherd"

(Psa. 23:1). In the New Testament, this title is ascribed to the second Person of the Trinity who is described as the good shepherd who gives Himself for His sheep (John 10:11), the great shepherd who leads and cares for His sheep (Heb. 13:20), and the chief shepherd who is coming in glory to reign and reward His undershepherds (1 Pet. 5:4).

10. *Jehovah-Naheh - The LORD that Smiteth.* Only once in Scripture, God says, "I am the LORD that smiteth" (Ezek. 7:9). God was telling the people through His prophet Ezekiel of the coming invasion by the Babylonians, but He wanted them to know it was not the Babylonians who were fighting them, but God Himself. Because of the persistent sin of His people, God had been forced to judge His people. The name occurs only once in Scripture, but the truth continues. As it was true in Israel, it is also true in the church (cf. Heb. 12:5-11).

11. *Jehovah-Elohim - LORD God.* From time to time, Jehovah and Elohim are used together to identify a name of God. In doing so, all that is true of these two names is implied in the giving of this compound name of God. It was Jehovah-Elohim who created man (Gen. 2:4), sought for man after sin (Gen. 3:9-13) and clothed Adam and Eve with animal skins (Gen. 3:21). This relationship between Jehovah-Elohim and Adam is often understood as typical of our relationship to Christ in salvation.

12. *Adonai-Jehovah - LORD GOD.* Jehovah also appears in Scripture related to Adonai and is normally translated "Lord GOD." Again, the appearance of both names together reveals all the characteristics of both primary names, but tends to emphasize the Adonai (Master) aspect of God. This name was first used in Scripture by Abraham at the confirmation of his covenant with God (Gen. 15:2).

13. *Jehovah- El-Gemuwal - The LORD God of Recompense.* Jeremiah alone uses this name of God in his prophecy against Babylon (Jer. 51:56). Although God used Babylon to judge Israel's sins, that did not justify Babylon's abuses directed against Israel. The prophet here identifies a God of justice who will give Babylon exactly what it deserves. Throughout the Scriptures, the right of judgment is possessed solely by God (cf. Deut. 32:35; Prov. 20:22; Rom. 12:17-21).

VI. THE LAW OF GOD

Generally speaking, the law is an expression of the will of the lawgiver. As such, it has five characteristics: (1) those who are subject to the law, (2) an expression of will (the standard of expectation), (3) punishment for deviation, (4) reward for compliance, and, of course, (5) it assumes a lawgiver.

Man appeals to many sources for law, such as the study of science or physics based on the law of nature, or the study of jurisprudence based on civil law. But all law is ultimately based on the Lawgiver, who is God. Law is an extension of the nature and will of God over all His creation. This includes both spiritual and physical laws.

According to Finney, law could be defined as "A RULE OF ACTION."[55] Physical laws would then be represented as "the order of sequence, in all the changes that occur under the law of necessity, whether in matter or mind."[56] Finney went on to define moral law as "a rule of moral action with sanctions."[57]

A. THE LAW IS THE EXTENSION OF GOD'S NATURE INTO HIS CREATION. Everything God makes is the offspring of His mind and bears the impression of His determinate nature. He created man an intelligent being. Because man was made in God's image, he has God's nature with certain limitations and modifications. He was not made in the exact image of God, but after His likeness. As such, man was created as an independent being with freedom and opportunity. Yet man's freedom introduced a moral problem into God's economy. How could man be independent yet accountable to his Creator? How could an omnipotent God control His universe, yet allow freedom in His creatures? The answer is in the law. All of God's created beings are unalterably related to their Creator by law. And by law men relate one to another and to God who is their Creator. There was no other way for God to create a moral being who would be accountable to his Creator.

1. *The law of God is an expression of the will of God, which is an extension of His nature.* Therefore, the law and God's nature are similar to the sun and its rays. The law of God is not arbitrary, for it arises out of a divine Person who is perfect in intellect, emotion, and will. God understands all He does, and He created the law out of His goodness. Also, God is the source of all wisdom and knowledge, and from Him comes the eternal understanding of His decree. The source of the law is the nature of God. Therefore, the law of God reflects the wisdom and understanding of God.

2. *The law must also be the extension of truth, which is a reflection of the nature of God.* The moral law of God is a representation of the moral nature of God, for truth is that which corresponds to itself. The law corresponds to the nature of God and is the moral veracity of His being. The law must be truth, for it must be an exact representation of the nature of God and must be consistent in its application to men. The law must be consistent in the nature of punishments upon the disobedient, and consistent in rewarding happiness for the obedient.

3. *The law is a unity, since God is One.* This means the law is always consistent in itself and in its application. It never differs for individuals—it is universal in its application and it is perpetual in its obligation. Every person is obligated to the law of God. For everyone that is accountable to God—and that is everyone—the law reaches to that limit.

The whole system of law involving God, man, and creation is symmetrically magnificent. There are no anomalies in the plan of God. Every law or principle is constitutionally adjusted and adapted to every other principle or law and fits perfectly into one giant unifying plan over which God is the supreme governing, sustaining, sovereign head. Man is a part of that system, being made by God, fitting into the Unity of God, and answerable to God.

4. *The law is eternal as God is eternal.* Since God is without beginning and ending, then the law is applicable to every being, every situation and every relationship for all eternity.

5. *The law is immutable.* Because the law is an extension of the nature of God, it is as immutable as His divine nature. It could not change unless God's nature can change. The idea of change with reference to God would destroy His perfection, and therefore destroy His existence.

God cannot repeal His law, nor can He give another system of law different from the present law without contradicting His own nature. As a result, if God repealed His law he would destroy Himself. But God "who cannot lie" affirms the law and every relationship it touches. The law prescribes duty for all of its subjects, hence everyone must obey the law.

B. THE LAW IS A REFLECTION OF GOD'S ATTRIBUTES. Every quality including the law comes from the nature of God which is the source of all things. But the law also personifies the attributes of God. Since attributes radiate from God's nature to magnify the Person, then each of those perfections logically requires the other; and combined together they form the infinite majesty of God. To understand God's moral law, we must see it in symmetrical relationship to God's attributes. The law for God's creatures is a moral law and of necessity is a picture of God's moral nature.

1. *The law is holy.* Since God is holy, it follows that His law must be holy. This means it must not require anything contradictory to the nature of God. The law must be in conformity to the holiness of the divine Person who created it.

2. *The law must be just.* As such, it must be an extension of God's impartiality. Justice is the negative side of God's positive holiness. The law must treat all beings as equal, demanding conformity by every person. Nonconformity to the law will bring punishment. Obedience will produce happiness. The attributes and law of God are a symmetrical embodiment of His infinite nature; holiness without a spot, justice without partiality, and infinite goodness without compromise.

3. *The law is also the embodiment of God's benevolence and kindness.* Where the law is kept, it elevates man—God's created beings—to the level of God's expectation. The man who keeps God's law is good and he is happy. Therefore, obedience to the law leads to happiness. God, in love, has given to His creatures the ability to be happy and enjoy life given to them by God.

C. THE RELATIONSHIP OF THE LAWGIVER TO THE LAWBREAKER. God created man, therefore man has an obligation for his existence. On the other hand, God is responsible for His creatures; He must be man's benefactor. Since God's whole system—including the laws governing nature, humans, and angels—is a unity, not one law of God can be changed, and not one offense can be condoned. When an angel or human being rebels against the law of God, he flies in the very face of God who has created him.

How can God save the system when there is rebellion? God must punish the rebel and everything affected by the rebellion. God's system must be restored and balanced. Again, it is impossible for the law to pardon the rebel or to accept rebellion.

The rebellious person must suffer the penalty. However, this does not mean that pardon is not available. Someone outside the system must enter and provide pardon. But first, He must compensate the system and satisfy the demands of the law.

If law could pardon, then law would destroy itself, for it would render itself null and void. For law to pardon an offense is to say that its existence is not essential. Even God, who is the extension of the law, cannot pardon the lawbreaker, because then God would encourage a rebellion to His law. The law is inexorable and unbending. The demands of the law must be satisfied. The holiness, justice, and goodness of God make the law unpardoning.

The gospel does not superintend a new law into the legal system of God. Nor does it make a "milder law" by which God can extend His pardon to man. Man was placed under a law that required perfect obedience.

Also, God cannot pardon by mere prerogative. Just because God desires to pardon the sinner does not mean that He can forgive the sin. God can create worlds, and make man in His image, but He has no prerogative to change His own nature.

Man is obligated to the spiritual law of God. Because both man and law are extensions of the nature of God, there is a reciprocal relationship between man and the laws which govern him. Man's personality, reflective of God's nature, constitutes the centrifugal force that drives him into an independent orbit away from God. God's compelling love is the centripetal force that draws man back into harmony with Him. Both forces were properly equalized before the Fall. The Bible describes the voice of the Lord walking in the garden in the cool of the day— man and God in fellowship. The axis of man was properly adjusted to the plane of his orbit; man's nature reflected the nature and character of God in whose image be was created. But at the Fall, man flew in rebellion away from the center of his life, which was God. To this day, man is not aware of his rebellion against God; man feels he is only following his individuality.

Just as God is Unity, so man was created in harmony with the laws of the physical and spiritual universe. As a spiritual being, man had broken the immutable spiritual laws of the universe. As a physical being, he was naturally excluded from the perfections of Eden.

When man obeys the physical laws, he subjects himself to the principles by which God rules the world. When man obeys the spiritual laws he subjects himself to God's spiritual principles by which He rules His spiritual kingdom. Man's obedience to one area when harmonized with his obedience to the other causes him to prosper.

We do not know what would have happened if man had continued his life, living in harmony with the laws of God. We would assume that the race would have multiplied, every individual would have lived in harmony with reverence for other individuals. We can only assume that all of civilization would have lived in harmony with the physical world.

After God made man, He breathed into him His spiritual life. The breath of God is actually the Hebrew word for wind. When God breathes into man's nostrils the breath of lives (the plural is used in the Hebrew), man becomes a living soul. It does not say that man was given a soul or a soul was contained within him. Man became a soul. The First Cause, God, originated man, who was an effect. Man was made in the image and likeness of His Creator. Because man was similar to his Creator, he was joined to Him in a spiritual bond. Such a bond is something common to the nature of both God and man. Just as God is an autonomous being, responsible for Himself, He created man an autonomous being, responsible for himself. God decided that man would not be controlled by wires as a puppet. Man was given a mind to rationally direct his life. He was also given feelings to give him quality of life and a will to direct his own life.

But how could God control this autonomous creature He had created? What would make man responsible to his Maker? God placed man under law, both spiritual and physical law. Man has the rationality to search out and know the laws of God. Man has the emotions to reinforce his obedience to the laws of God, and man was given volitional powers to direct himself in following the laws of God. The laws are the basis by which God controls His universe and by which He relates to man.

The laws of God are the centripetal forces that constantly draw a man into constant relationship to God. "Centripetal" literally means to seek the center as the centripetal force draws the planets. "Centrifugal" literally means to fly from the center as forces which revolve around the sun tend to fly away from the sun. The centrifugal forces are the autonomous and independent natures of man.

D. THE PENALTY FOR VIOLATING THE LAW. The nature of law implies a penalty for the violation of that law. This is the foundation of all government. As a matter of fact, the certainty of the penalty for violating any law depends upon the credibility of the one who enacts the law. Since there is a God, and He rules by His laws, He will penalize those who break His law. This is another way of saying that one has no power to rule unless he has power to enforce penalties.

The justice of God requires that He judge those who violate His law. God's justice also requires that He equally assign the appropriate criminality to the nature of the violation. Since God's rule is universal, (He knows all things and is everywhere at the same time), those who violate His law cannot escape judgment. Every person who has broken God's law and those who have not lived up to the standards of God's law will he weighed in God's scale of justice and will be punished according to the degree of criminality. This means that a degree of guilt will be attached to every sin or violation of God's law.

Judgment cannot be carried out during life because sin cannot be correctly estimated until the entire intention, violation, and influence of the violation are evaluated. Remember, man is part of God's universe which itself is a unity. Therefore, every thought, word and act of man will have an influence upon God's universe. Just as every man is tied to those who have gone before him and lives in a world that is the result of the influence of his fathers, so every man will pass his influence on to his children. Therefore, every man will be accountable for all his failures and violations of the law during his life and also for the influences he leaves behind after death.

Since God is equitable, He must judge every violation of His law, both the intent and the action. Therefore, no one can be judged while he is living because the influence of his violation of the law has not yet ceased. The existence of the law of God implies there is a future judgment.

The nature of law implies that man is in trial on earth. God expects him to live by the law, hence God is testing His creatures to see if they will live according to His standard. The fact that man's life is a trial, implies that judgment is in the future. And it is obvious that man cannot be punished for the violations committed while he is still on trial. He must wait until the time of trial is ended. Some consequences of breaking the law may be suffered while man is in his trial, but the moral punishment cannot be imposed until the trial is over.

Because of the love of God, Jesus Christ became the Substitute for those who violated the law. He took the punishment of each man, and satisfied the demands of the law in general, and the demands of the law specifically for each individual. Hence, it is possible for everyone to be saved. Faith in Jesus Christ is the sole condition for the sinner to be forgiven of his violation of the law. Therefore, a person can be saved because Christ has blotted "out the handwriting of ordinances that was against us, which was contrary to us, and took it out of the way, nailing it to his cross" (Col. 2:14).

E. DIFFERENT EXPRESSIONS OF LAW. All law has the same characteristics, but is expressed in different forms because it governs different areas of God's creation.

1. *The physical law of God.* This world is the product of the creative will of God. Its complexities are kept functioning orderly by God. The Bible says, "By him all things consist" (Col. 1:17). God has established the physical laws of the universe. "While the earth remaineth, seedtime and harvest, and cold and heat, and summer and winter, and day and night shall not cease" (Gen. 8:22). The laws of this universe were established by God and are maintained by God to carry out His plan in the world. When a scientist determines the course of a rocket that will arrive at another planet several years from now, he is able to do so after careful study of those laws upon which our universe functions. The laws of the universe reflect a rational, orderly and consistent God. And, by implication, the law implies a God of judgment when we disobey Him, because there are always consequences when a law is violated.

2. *The moral law of God.* Because God is a moral being, He expresses Himself through moral law in the immaterial issues of life. In a day of rampant amorality and situation ethics, it is not popular to proclaim, "Thus saith the Lord." But it is a message that needs to be enunciated. The Bible is also called "the perfect law of liberty" (Jas. 1:25), the standard for our spiritual life. It is given that "the man of God may be perfect, throughly furnished unto all good works" (2 Tim. 3:17). The apostle Paul strongly opposed those who wanted to live above the law. Some taught that Christians were free from the moral standards of the law of God

because they were now under grace. Paul asked these people, "What shall we say then? Shall we continue in sin that grace may abound? God forbid. How shall we that are dead to sin, live any longer therein?" (Rom. 6:1-2). Notice the things that are prohibited in this dispensation: lying (Eph. 4:25), theft (Eph. 4:28), gossip (Jas. 4:11), lust (Matt. 5:28) and without a cause and anger (Matt. 5:22).

3. *The social law of God.* The Jewish rabbis often talked about the two tables of the law. The first table related to a man's relationship with God and included the first four Commandments. The second table, which included the final six Commandments, deals with a man's relation with other men. James emphasized the keeping of this second table of the law in his brief epistle. "If ye fulfil the royal law according to the scripture, Thou shalt love thy neighbor as thyself, ye do well" (Jas. 2:8). Every Christian needs to recognize the place of the law of God in establishing good relations with others. Since we are all made in the image of God, the principles of how we relate to one another also come from God and are His sacred laws.

4. *The spiritual law of God.* The final aspect of the law of God is that part which deals with a man's relationship with God. When Jesus was challenged to identify the most important Commandment of the law, He immediately responded, "Thou shalt love the LORD thy God with all thy heart, and with all thy soul, and with all thy mind. This is the first and great commandment" (Matt. 22:37-38).

F. SUMMARY AND CONCLUSION. There is much that man could never know. "The secret things belong unto the LORD our God; but those things which are revealed belong unto us and to our children for ever, that we may do all the words of this law" (Deut. 29:29). Since man could not know God, He gave His law to Moses and Israel to teach us about Himself. The psalmist often refers to the Bible, God's revelation of Himself to mankind, as "the law of the Lord." As Moses instructed the people in the law, he consistently challenged them to "observe to do all that is written." When Moses died and Joshua was left to lead Israel, he was commanded to "observe to do according to all that is written therein" (Josh. 1:8). While keeping the law never implied salvation in any dispensation, it is the standard by which God judges faithfulness to Him.

Paul recognized the typical significance of the law (1 Cor. 10:11). John the Baptist drew upon the teaching of the law when he announced, "Behold the Lamb of God" (John 1:29). The writer of Hebrews went to great lengths to quote the law and apply it to Jewish Christians. With the record of the first advent of Jesus Christ available to us today, we are not ignorant of how the atonement of Christ fulfilled the law. But, prior to Calvary, the Jews were reminded with each sacrifice that the day was coming when God would "provide himself a lamb for a burnt-offering" (Gen. 22:8).

Comparatively few theologians talk at length about the law. Fitzwater lists four purposes which demonstrate that the purpose of the law did not change with the gospel.[58]

"For until the law sin was in the world: but sin is not imputed when there is no law" (Rom. 5:13). Knowledge of the law does not make us sinners; we are sinners because we break God's law, whether or not we know about the law we break. But the preaching of the law makes us realize we are sinners, and that includes everyone, "For all have sinned, and come short of the glory of God" (Rom. 3:23).

THE PURPOSE OF THE LAW

1. To show the oneness and sovereignty of God. (Exod. 20:2)
2. To place a restraint on the sinner. (Psa. 68:7-8)
3. To show the greatness and reality of sin. (Rom. 3:19-20)
4. To lead the sinner to Christ. (Gal. 3:24)

The chief desire in the heart of God is "all men to be saved, and to come unto the knowledge of the truth" (1 Tim. 2:4). The law is one of the tools God uses to accomplish this goal. "The law was our schoolmaster to bring us unto Christ, that we might be justified by faith" (Gal. 3:24). The law has never been able to save an individual, but it can bring a person to the place where he trusts Christ as his personal Saviour.

VII. THE DECREE OF GOD

The "decrees of God" is a controversial subject. When the topic is mentioned, some immediately think of extreme "Calvinism." They think the decrees are the same as fatalism. They think this indicates that God controls the universe by His decree as a child controls his toys. Berkhof, a Reformed theologian, defines "decree" from a Calvinist perspective,

> Reformed theology stresses the sovereignty of God in virtue of which He has sovereignly determined from all eternity whatsoever will come to pass, and works His sovereign will in His entire creation, both natural and spiritual, according to His pre-determined plan.[59]

The word "decree" comes from the biblical doctrine that God directs the world He has created. There are at least four different interpretations of how God decrees or controls His creation.

A. KINDS OF DECREES. Pantheism is one proposal. Pantheism teaches that God is an inanimate force within nature and controls all things through the laws of nature. God does not have personality or volition, and He cannot interrupt the affairs of life for His purpose.

In the second proposal, God is understood by the deist to be a powerful being who has created the world and has arranged for an orderly management of the world by the laws of nature. God is the Source of all things but is not personally involved in the present affairs of the world. God has finished His work in this world, like a man winding up a clock that will run down independently. The deists describe God as an absentee landlord who will return in the end of this age, but is not actively involved in controlling the day-to-day affairs of this life.

A third group teaches that God is the architect, engineer, and workman of this universe. They teach that God controls this world down to every small detail. His control is predetermined and, thus, man must fit into God's minute blueprint. At the same time, they teach that man is a free agent who operates according to his freedom and one day will be judged for the use of his freedom.

A fourth view teaches that God directs the affairs of this life by the laws He has created. God and man live by the limits of these laws, and man, made in the image of God, was also created with freedom to use the opportunities of life for the glory of God. One day man must give an account of his stewardship to God. In the meantime, God influences man by laws, by the Holy Spirit, by circumstances, by spiritual dynamics and by the means of grace. God is the divine chess player guiding the chess pieces through life. But this illustration is faulty because it likens people to chess pieces, inanimate objects. People have a free will. This view of the decree of God is similar to a director guiding actors who are chosen to perform in a play. The freedom and ability of the actors must be considered, along with the ability of the director, to set the stage, determine the plot, create the rules of production and guide the actors to the best performance possible.

B. DEFINITION OF GOD'S DECREE. The decree of God has been variously defined. According to Hodge,

> The decree of God is his eternal, unchangeable, holy, wise, and sovereign purpose, comprehending at once all things that ever were or will be in their causes, conditions, successions and relations, and determining their certain futurition. The several contents of this one eternal purpose are, because of the limitation of our faculties, necessarily conceived of by us in partial aspects, and in logical relations, and are therefore styled DECREES.[60]

Boyce suggested, "The decrees of God may be defined as that just, wise, and holy purpose or plan by which eternally, and within himself, he determines all things whatsoever that comes to pass."[61] Strong called the decree of God, "that eternal plan by which God has rendered certain all the events of the universe, past, present, and future."[62] Thiessen adds to the discussion,

> We believe that the decrees of God are His eternal purpose (in a real sense all things are embraced in one purpose) or purposes, based on His most wise and holy counsel,

whereby He freely and unchangeably, for His own glory, ordained, either efficaciously or permissively, all that comes to pass.[63]

Chafer suggests, "The term *decree* betokens the plan by which God has proceeded in all His acts of creation and continuation."[64]

The decree of God is His plan by which He creates, directs, sustains and takes responsibility for His creation and His creatures, including their salvation, nurturing, reward or punishment within the predetermined limits of His nature. According to the decree of God, everything brings glory to Him, nothing goes contrary to His plan. This does not mean everything goes exactly as God would choose, for within His decree, God allows the freedom of man to be exercised, sometimes in rebellion to God. But God has decreed that ultimately all things will be judged by Him, for all things are accountable to Him.

Since God is all-wise, His decree is completely wise and perfect. No one can later second guess the decree of God, nor can anyone say God was not good in the way He planned this universe.

Since God is eternal, His decree is without end. Therefore, God's plan for this world did not gradually emerge from the conference table of eternal strategy. God has always had this plan and it will extend throughout the coming ages. God's decree is as eternal as His nature.

Since God is immutable, His decisions are irreversible or unchangeable. God will not get part way through His plan and then change the rules, nor will He change the ultimate destination of His plan. The immutability of God's nature makes His decree unchangeable and eternal.

Some theologians describe "decrees" in the plural, as though God has many decrees. The only sense in which there is more than one decree is in man's comprehension. Man sees God's plan in salvation, creation and providence with disconnected avenues. There may be sequences by which the decree is executed but God decreed simultaneously, and since God is eternal, the decree is eternal.

The decree of God is God's plan for man and the universe. It begins with the will of God. The phrase "the will of God" is sometimes used by Christians to mean that God has a predetermined blueprint for each life that extends to the minutest detail. When God is described as controlling the smallest "interconnecting" phase of life, then man becomes a puppet and he surrenders to a "fatalistic" view of life. This view of a predetermined blueprint with its fatalistic implications is not a biblical picture of the will of God.

God's will is used here in the primary sense of definition; it is the volition or inclination of personality. The will of God is the decision of God, based on His nature.

God has decided that He will control the creation and creature in certain predetermined ways. God's control of the world is consistent with His nature. He will not, nor is He able to, devise a plan inconsistent with all that He is.

The fact that God allowed sin to enter the world reveals that God did not plan to be a dictator so that sin would not enter His plan. The fact that God allowed the free will of man reveals that He did not decree a totalitarian universe where free expression would be eliminated. The fact that God allowed the existence of Satan reveals that God did not decree to eradicate all opposition to His plan. God will punish within his plan; this is an expression of his decree.

The plan of God must take into consideration freedom, creativity, autonomy, and responsibility. As such, when God allowed freedom, He had to provide for punishment to those who rejected His plan.

God had to be sovereign over His plan, yet allow freedom within His plan. This involved a divine paradox: how could God remain an absolute Ruler of the universe, yet make man accountable to His plan? And even when man was given freedom, the plan of God had to bring glory to God, both in those who were rewarded for compliance with God's plan and in punishment of those who rebelled against His plan.

The decree of God is seen in the following. First, God decided to create a world that was good and beautiful. He decided that the universe would be stable and reflect the uniformity and regularity of laws that are the nature of His being. For it is through laws that God controls both man and the universe. Since laws are an extension of the nature of God, this is one way that God is everywhere present and makes everything accountable to Him. Next, God decided to create man in His image. God predetermined that man would have His nature, and man became the crowning act of creation. As such, man had freedom and autonomy, and in this wise decree, God decided to allow the freedom of His creatures to choose or reject His rule over them. Man could choose to live in harmony with God's eternal laws or rebel against them. God was glorified no matter what man decided, because when man worshipped his Creator, God was magnified; and when man rebelled, he suffered consequences of the unalterable laws of God, and God was vindicated. When all men sinned in Adam, God decided to provide a Saviour for all men. The Saviour came from without the universal system, since it was the only way to save all who had rebelled against God. The Saviour was the only begotten Son of God. God provided a plan for all men; the Son of God died for all men, and salvation is offered to all men.

The decree of God is that all people who believe and claim the righteousness of God shall be saved. By that same decree, God has determined that all those who will not believe on His Son shall be damned. The decree of God is not His predetermined choice of certain individuals for salvation or the exclusion of other individuals from the saving process. The decree of God is the plan of God whereby He offers salvation to mankind. If a man wills to be righteous He will be saved according to the immutable decree of God. If he wills to be wicked, he will be damned according to the immutable decree of God.

God's decree extends to certain other aspects of life, such as (1) the outward circumstances of nations, (2) the length of human life, (3) the mode of our death, (4) the continuation of senses, (5) the time when His Son shall return.

Finally, the decree of God includes His showing goodness to His creation in general and His specific decision to sustain those who obey Him. God promised that He will work all things together for their good (Rom. 8:28). In his discussion of this subject, Boyce notes,

The Scriptures recognize both the sovereignty of God, and the free agency, and accountability of man. Consciousness assures us of the latter. The nature of God, as has just been shown, proves the former. The Bible makes no attempt to reconcile the two . . . . The two facts are plainly revealed . . . . That we cannot point out the harmony between them is a proof, only of our ignorance, and limited capacity, and not that both are not true.[65]

The real conflict between the doctrine of the decree of God and the free will of man involves the execution of that decree. Strong suggests,

Whatever may be the method of God's foreknowledge, and whether it be derived from motives or be intuitive, that foreknowledge presupposes God's decree to create, and so presupposes the making certain of the free acts that follow creation.

But this certainty is not necessity. In reconciling God's decrees with human freedom, we must not go to the other extreme, and reduce human freedom to mere determinism, or the power of the agent to act out his character in the circumstances which environ him. Human action is not simply the expression of previously dominant affections; else neither Satan nor Adam could have fallen, nor could the Christian ever sin.[66]

C. CALVINISTIC DECREE. *The Westminster Shorter Catechism* defines the decrees as, "his eternal purpose according to the counsel of his will, whereby for his own glory, he hath foreordained whatsoever comes to pass."[67] This definition is used because it is probably the best known to reflect the "Calvinist" theological position.

These implications grow out of the above definition. First, the decrees are controlled by the sovereignty of God. Second, the basis of the decrees are grounded in the nature of God, for they come out of God's will (this means the decrees are not influenced by circumstances). Third, the decrees are all-encompassing because they control everything that comes to pass. In essence, the above definition of "decrees" makes God the Author of all events, circumstances and results in the universe.

But serious questions can be raised with the definition. We can question if Scripture teaches that God has a constricted plan without latitude for man's freedom. Next, we can question if God has an absolute authoritarian plan, especially when we see many circumstances that cannot be attributed to Him. Then, we can question if the inflexible plan was conceived by or out of the nature of God. The nature of God is different from the implications of an autocratic plan that controls the universe. Finally, in view of the compelling urgency of the Great Commission to reach every person with the gospel, using all of our available resources, we can question such an inflexible view of God and the world.

D. BIBLICAL WORDS RELATING TO DECREE. The apostle Paul used several words to describe God's decree: "predestinate," "foreknowledge," "chosen," "call," "counsel," "will" and "good pleasure." A proper understanding of these words will help understand God's decrees in salvation. These words are used in Scripture in relation to God's programs, principles and plans. These words speak of the time before Creation and relate to God's plan for salvation, sanctification and God's ultimate glorification. The confusion comes when these words are applied to individual people, the implication that He chose a specific person for salvation and excluded others. We know that God has an eternal plan for the salvation of all men, and God will work through the means of grace to confront all men with salvation. But does God specifically choose one person to salvation and exclude another from His plan? The only way to solve this questions is to look at each word in the New Testament and examine each Scripture. A careful study of the biblical teaching will aid in the understanding of God's decree in salvation.

One of these words is "predestinate" (*pro-orizwi*) (Eph. 1:5, 11; Rom. 8:29; Acts 4:28, translated "determine"). This word means "to mark off, bound beforehand, to draw a circle and include something." To "predestinate" means "to choose." The question is what does God choose or, more specifically, whom does God choose? Does the word "predestinate" mean that God specifically chose some for salvation before the foundation of the earth? We must be careful not to allow someone to "read" this meaning into biblical words. The word "predestinate" means God has a plan of salvation and extends it to everyone who would respond in faith. The apostle wrote of God's predestined plan, by which He has drawn a circle around the world because He loves all men (John 3:16). Then He died for all (John 1:29), and calls everyone to partake in that plan. Therefore, predestination deals primarily with what is God's plan, not the specific "who."

"Foreknowledge" - (*proginosko, prognosis*)—extends God's sovereignty into the future (Acts 2:23, 26:5; Rom. 8:29, 11:2; 1 Pet. 1:2, 20; 2 Pet. 3:17). Because God is omniscient, He possesses a full knowledge of events before they happen. He knows who will respond to His call and be a part of His plan (1 Pet. 1:2). God can have foreknowledge because He is eternal. He is not limited to time, but is always present in the future. On the day of Pentecost, the apostle Peter vividly illustrated the harmony that exists between the sovereignty of God and man's personal responsibility. Even though the cross was in the eternal plan of God and a part of His sovereign will, it was a rebellious act of their will. God had predetermined the plan, of which Peter said, "Him, being delivered by the determinate counsel and foreknowledge of God, ye have taken, and by wicked hands have crucified and slain" (Acts 2:23).

Paul used the word chosen (eklego), to describe the kind of people God will save (1 Cor. 1:27-28; Eph. 1:4). *Eklectos* and ekloge are also translated "elect" (Col. 3:12; Rom. 11:7; 1 Thess. 1:4). Those who responded to God's call were part of the plan that God had chosen for their salvation. God chose because he wanted to choose; the decision relates to His volition and is not restricted to certain recipients.

The word "call," (Kletos, Klesis), originates out of His sovereignty (Rom. 1:1, 6; 1 Cor. 1:26, 7:20; Eph. 1:18; 4:1). God called people for three reasons. He called people for (1) service, and (2) for sanctification and (3) to salvation. This word "call" was used to identify His plan. At times, God calls the Christian (Rom. 1:6; 1 Cor. 1:9), at times God calls to sanctification (1 Thess. 4:7), and at other times God is calling the world to Himself (Heb. 3:7;

Matt. 11:28-30). To say God calls only a few persons, or calls only those who respond; is to miss the total plan of God.

Paul used the verb "purpose," (*proistemi*), in terms of His overall plans (Rom. 1:13; 3:25; 8:28; 9:11; Eph. 1:9). The other word "will," (*boule*), also carries the same meaning (Acts 13:26; 20:27; Eph. 1:11). These words relate to the volitional nature of God, that He can translate His desires into an organized program relating to His Creation. Yet God's will is related to His knowledge. A final expression used by Paul that we will examine is "good pleasure" (Eph. 1:5, 9). Here the word (*eudokia*), relates to sovereignty. These words of sovereignty describe the initiative God has taken in salvation, but they never deny the free will of man or his moral responsibility before God. The basis of God's acts of sovereignty is His nature, "For it is God which worketh in you both to will and to do his good pleasure" (Phil. 2:13).

At times God calls, expecting man to answer, and at other times God punishes so man will respond by his free will. On other occasions, God sovereignly directs through inner direction, such as giving a "burden" to men (Isa. 21:1, 11, 13). The Christian can be led by circumstances (Acts 21:14). Whether God carries out His plan directly or indirectly, by leading or pushing, by enticement or by compulsion, "God works all things to His glory." But in free will, man can sin and miss God's best road, or man can reject God and go to Hell. And in the final analysis, God's sovereignty cannot be man's defense at the judgment. Because man was created in the image of God, each man is responsible for his free choice.

E. THE CONTENT OF THE DECREE OF GOD. God is at work in three specific areas of our lives— the physical, social and spiritual. Physical: Psa. 33:6-11; Isa. 45:18; Psa. 119:90-91; Gen. 8:22; Isa. 45:18; Job 14:5; Deut. 32:8; Acts 17:26. Social: Gen. 9:5-6; Rom. 13:11-12; Deut. 4:34-35; Matt. 19:3-10; Gen. 1:27-28; Psa. 127:3-5. Spiritual: Gen. 50:20; Psa. 33:10-11; Psa. 76:10; Dan. 3:19-30; Phil. 1:19-20; 1 Tim. 2:3-4; 1 John 2:2.

1. *The physical work of God.* All about us, we can see the work of God in the physical universe. The world in which we live was created by God and is sustained by God. The atmosphere, seasonal changes, heat and rain are all "acts of God." Sometimes we call a terrible storm an "act of God." While this is true, it is also an act of God when the sun rises on a clear summer day and when it hides behind a cloud during a refreshing spring shower. Our physical bodies are one of many amazing creations that exist in this world to remind us of the work of God. When we consider the intricacies of the body we begin to recognize the immense wisdom and creativity of God.

God does His work in other areas of our physical world. He has established the boundaries of the nations and the general course of human history. Many scholars of Bible prophecy believe God is at work today in the internal and international affairs of many nations as He prepares all nations for the end time.

2. *The social work of God.* God has established three institutions upon which our society rests: the home, government and church. These are the foundation of society. God accomplishes His work through these institutions. Each institution has a role to play in

carrying out the work of God in our society. As each functions under the authority of God, together they will work harmoniously to accomplish God's purpose. We need to recognize the divine authority of these institutions in determining the will of God in a particular situation in our lives.

3. *The spiritual work of God.* God is Spirit, so all He does is spiritual, yet we tend to distinguish the spiritual work of God as that which directly relates to the salvation of mankind. God has made the world and gives us a plan for society. But this aspect of the work of God deals with the salvation and spiritual growth of men. God permitted sin to enter the world, but He also provides for man's salvation. Lewis S. Chafer observed, "God determines not to hinder the course of actions which His creatures pursue; but He does determine to regulate and control the bounds and results of such actions."[68]

God's provision for man's salvation is twofold. First, He provided the means of salvation in the blood of Christ. Man is unable to save himself. Jesus alone was a suitable sacrifice to effect the forgiveness of sins. Secondly, God provides the messengers of salvation. God calls individuals into the ministry of proclaiming the gospel. Beyond that, He has directed that every Christian should be a soul-winner, actively involved in the bringing of the message of salvation to every creature.

F. THE STRATEGY OF THE DECREE OF GOD.

1. *God works through the laws of nature.* God the Creator of this universe has established the natural order of the universe. "While the earth remaineth, seedtime and harvest, and cold and heat, and summer and winter, and day and night shall not cease" (Gen. 8:22). When God works, He will normally work within the laws of nature.

2. *God works through the laws of human personality.* God made us the way we are. Our nature is a product of His work, and we should allow Him to work through the strengths and limitations of our personalities. When God works, He uses people to accomplish His work. In doing so, He considers the laws of human personality. God will use us to accomplish that for which we are best suited. "The king's heart is in the hand of the LORD, as the rivers of water: he turneth it whithersoever he will" (Prov. 21:1). The word "heart" often represents the seat of intellect, emotions, and will in an individual, the real person. Today, we define "personality" - as the sum total of all we are. Our personalities rest in the hand of God to be directed and used by Him in His work according to His will.

3. *God works through circumstances.* God is sovereign in all affairs of life. Because He is in control, He can direct our circumstances to accomplish His work. Paul told the Corinthians that " a great door and effectual is opened unto me" (1 Cor. 16:9). At other times God led in

the life of Paul by closing doors of opportunity (Acts 16:6-7). Back of circumstances we know that "All things work together for good to them that love God" (Rom. 8:28).

4. *God works through His revelation.* God always reserves the right to work beyond His natural laws within the boundaries of His supernatural laws. The important thing to realize is that all of His laws are a unit, and God will never work contrary to His laws. The Bible is God's revelation of Himself. As such, God would never contradict His nature by working inconsistently with biblical revelation. Jeremiah experienced the way God used the Word of God in his life to accomplish the work of God in his life (Jer. 20:9).

5. *God works both passively and actively.* Sometimes the work of God is active. This occurs when God causes things to happen to us according to His plan for our lives. Understanding what we need and what is best for us, God will sometimes direct the circumstances around us to provide experiences, opportunities and provisions to aid us in our lives.

At other times, the work of God is passive. The classic example of this is found in the life of Job. God allowed the devil to hinder the life of Job, but not the purpose of God. When the devil was permitted on two occasions to test Job, on both occasions divine limits were set on that testing. God used the devil to accomplish something in the life of Job, while God remained passive in the actual work. Today, when God allows the same to be accomplished in our lives, we have the promise of divine limits set by a God who knows us better than we know ourselves. "God is faithful, who will not suffer you to be tempted above that ye are able; but will with the temptation also make a way to escape, that ye may be able to bear it" (1 Cor. 10:13).

6. *God works all things to His glory.* God has "created all things, and for thy pleasure they are and were created" (Rev. 4:11). The psalmist wrote, "The heavens declare the glory of God" (Psa. 19:1). Paul informed the Romans of their responsibility to "make known the riches of his glory" (Rom. 9:23) and told the Ephesians that their conversion was "to the praise of the glory of his grace" (Eph. 1:6). The purpose of God's work is to bring glory to Himself. This is the responsibility of all creation—to glorify God. If in our lives and conversation we bring dishonor to God, we have failed to do the will of God. When we do what God desires, we will naturally glorify God and direct honor to Him.

VIII. THE TRINITY

One of the most difficult and yet most important things to understand about God is that He is Triune. God is referred to as three distinct Persons in Scripture, yet at the same time we are taught there is only one God. The teaching of one God in three Persons has baffled Christians for centuries as they have sought to understand the complete teaching of the Persons of God in Scripture. The Trinity has been compared to water: it exists as a solid in ice, as a liquid in water and as a gas in the atmosphere.

The Father, Son and Holy Spirit are each distinguishable from the other, yet everything that is true about "God" is true about the Father, the Son and the Holy Spirit. Ignoring this simple doctrine can lead to error. When understood, the doctrine of the Trinity forms a foundation to all doctrine we believe.

A. THE DEFINITION OF THE TRINITY. The Trinity is the designation of God in unity yet existing in three eternal Persons. The members of the Trinity are equal in nature, distinct in Person, and subordinate in duties. As Son, Jesus is eternally begotten by the Father. So Jesus is submissive to do the work of the Father, yet equal in nature to Him. "The LORD hath said unto me, Thou art my Son; this day have I begotten thee" (Psa. 2:7). Then the Son sends the Holy Spirit: "The Comforter whom I will send unto you from the Father" (John 15:26). Later Jesus prayed to the Father, saying, "I have finished the work which thou gavest me to do" (John 17:4). The Father is the source of authority, the Son is the channel, and the Holy Spirit is the agent whereby authority is exercised.

The oldest existing identification of the Trinity is the *Athanasian Creed* written about A.D. 250. "We worship one God, in Trinity, and Trinity in unity, neither confounding the persons, nor dividing the substance." Nearly two centuries ago, John Dick put the same truth this way: "While there is only one divine nature, there are three subsistences, or persons, called the Father, the Son, and the Holy Ghost, who possess, not a similar, but the same numerical essence, and the distinction between them is not merely nominal, but real."[69]

The word "Trinity" is not found in Scripture, but the idea and doctrine are its foundation. Many heretical groups have gone off into their doctrinal error by denying the existence of the Trinity or explaining the Trinity wrongly. Part of understanding what the Trinity is, is knowing what it is not.

1. *The Trinity is not three Gods.* The Trinity does not teach the existence of three distinct Gods, which is called "tritheism." Often evangelical Christians are charged by Jehovah's Witnesses and Jews with believing in three Gods. This charge is founded upon their misunderstanding of what is meant by the term "Trinity."

Christians are monotheists, meaning they believe in one God. "Hear, O Israel: The LORD our God is one LORD" (Deut. 6:4). When we acknowledge that the Father, Son and Holy Spirit are each part of the Triune God, we still hold to the unity of God. The Bible teaches the existence of only one God in three Persons.

2. *The Trinity is not three manifestations of God.* One of the heretical groups in the early church taught what was known as Sabellianism or Modalism. They held that the Trinity was three different manifestations of the same God. They explained "Person" to mean a representation of God, just as man could be father, husband and brother at one time. According to this view, there was only one God, but He revealed Himself as the Father and the Creator in the Old Testament. Next, they taught that the same person revealed Himself as

Redeemer. Finally, the same God reveals Himself as the Holy Spirit. "The unchanging God is differently revealed on account of the world's different perceptions of Him."

The basic error of Modalism is that it denies the eternity and distinctiveness of the three Persons of the Trinity. As we will see later, the Father, Son and Holy Spirit were all involved in the work of creation. All three have existed and worked together since before time began. All three, however, coexist separately in the Godhead.

3. *The Trinity does not teach that the Father created the Son or Holy Spirit.* One of the hottest doctrinal controversies of the early church was Arianism. Arius taught that only the Father was eternally God from the beginning. He taught that both the Son and the Holy Spirit were created out of nothing by God before anything else. Because they were created Beings, they could not be considered divine or possessing the attributes of divinity.

The Bible, of course, does not teach the creation of the Son or Holy Spirit, but recognizes the work of both in the creation of all things (cf. John 1:3; Col. 1:16-17; cf. Gen. 1:2). Historically, Christians have recognized the error or Arianism and taught the biblical doctrines of Christ and the Holy Spirit.

4. *The Trinity does not teach that Christ or the Holy Spirit was a power or attribute of God.* A fourth wrong view of the Trinity teaches that the deity of Christ was a mere power or influence of God. According to monarchianism, Christ had a personality as a historic Person, but sacrificed His essential deity after death. This error misunderstands the truth that Jesus is God. The Bible teaches, "The Word [Jesus] was God" (John 1:1). Then, in the same context, we are told, "the Word was made flesh, and dwelt among us, (and we beheld his glory, the glory as of the only begotten of the Father)" (John 1:14). John described the return of Christ when he "saw heaven opened, and behold, a white horse; and he that sat upon him was called . . . The Word of God" (Rev. 19:11, 13).

This erroneous view of the Trinity continues to persist in theology to this present date. Clarke argues, "God the eternal heart of love, Christ the rational expression of the eternal heart, and the Spirit the accomplisher of the work of both, make up the Godhead."[70] Barth concludes his discussion, "Thus, to the same God who in unimpaired unity is Revealer, Revelation, and Revealedness, is also ascribed in unimpaired variety in Himself precisely this threefold mode of being."[71]

B. THE OLD TESTAMENT POINTS TO THE TRINITY. There is an element of mystery in every Old Testament doctrine, particularly before it is more completely revealed in the New Testament. The Trinity is most clearly taught in the New Testament, yet throughout the Old Testament there are continuous signposts that point to the existence of the Trinity. These are seen in the names of God, the worship of God and the distinctions made within the Godhead.

1. *The Names of God imply the Trinity.* God reveals His nature in part through His names. The first name of God used in Scripture is Elohim. Even in the first verse of the Bible, a hint of the Trinity is given; the word "Elohim" is plural. Even though it identifies one God, it is a plural unity. This plurality of God is further manifested in the use of plural personal pronouns

for God. (Following emphasis by author:) "And God said, let us make man in our image, after our likeness" (Gen. 1:26). When man gained a knowledge of good and evil, God said, "The man is become as one of us" (Gen. 3:22). Before God judged at Babel, He said, "Let us go down" (Gen. 11:7). Isaiah "heard the voice of the LORD saying, Whom shall I send, and who will go for us?" (Isa. 6:8). Commenting on the term Elohim, Andrew Jukes notes the implications of this name.

> He is One, but in Him also, as His name declares, there is plurality; and in this plurality He has certain relationships, both in and with Himself, which, because He is God, can never be dissolved or broken. Thus, as Parkhurst says, this name contains the mystery of the Trinity. For the perfect revelation of this great mystery man had indeed to wait until it was declared by the Only-begotten of the Father, and even then only after His resurrection from the dead, to those whom He had called to be His disciples.[72]

Isaiah records a second name of God which is plural. The name Maker (Isa. 54:5) is plural in the Hebrew language. This verse then names three who are God. "For thy Maker is thine husband; the LORD of hosts is his name; and thy Redeemer the Holy One of Israel; the God of the whole earth shall he be called" (Isa. 54:5). These plural names of God suggest what is known as a "plural unity."

2. *The worship of God by use of a trinitarian formula.* A second indication of the Trinity is seen in the worship of God. Isaiah's vision of God included the threefold designation, "Holy, holy, holy" (Isa. 6:3). When Jacob blessed his son Joseph in the name of God, three times he identified God differently (Gen. 48:15-16). The Aaronic benediction given by God for recitation by Israel's first priest was also threefold in nature: "The LORD bless thee, and keep thee; The LORD make his face shine upon thee, and be gracious unto thee; The LORD lift up his countenance upon thee, and give thee peace" (Num. 6:24-26). While these are not conclusive in themselves, most biblical theologians agree this threefold emphases in the worship of God reflect the Triune nature of God.

3. *All three Persons are distinguished as God.* A third inference of the Trinity in the Old Testament is the practice of distinguishing between God and God. The judgment of the Lord on Sodom and Gomorrah distinguishes between the Lord who judged with fire and brimstone and the Lord who sent it from heaven (Gen. 19:24). More specifically, the Old Testament teaches Jehovah has a Son (Psa. 2:7) who is called God (Isa. 9:6). The Spirit of God is also distinguished in the Old Testament from God (Gen. 1:2; 6:3).

4. *A clear statement points to the Trinity.* Probably the clearest statement on the Trinity in the Old Testament is Isaiah 48:16, because it demonstrates an Old Testament belief in the three

personalities of the Trinity. God the Son is speaking in this verse. He identifies the Father (Lord God) and "his Spirit" as having sent Him. In the next verse the Son is more clearly identified as God. Therefore, this verse identifies three who are God, yet it does not deny monotheism. Missionaries to the Jews often use this verse when challenged by Jews that Christians believe in "three Gods." Christians believe in one God in three Persons, just as the Old Testament teaches.

C. DIRECT TEACHING OF THE NEW TESTAMENT. What was hidden in the Old Testament is clearly revealed in the New. The doctrine of the Trinity is clearly taught in the New Testament.

1. *Trinity revealed at the baptism of Jesus.* The early church fathers used to say, "If you want to see the Trinity, go to the wilderness beyond the Jordan." By this they meant one of the clearest revelations of the Triune God is recorded in the account of Jesus' baptism. The most vivid illustration of the Trinity occurs at the beginning of the earthly ministry of Jesus, when He was baptized by John the Baptist in the Jordan River (Matt. 3:16-17). As God the Son was raised from the water, they saw God the Holy Spirit "descending like a dove." The Bible also records the voice of God the Father breaking the silence of heaven to acknowledge His delight in His Son.

2. *Jesus taught the truth of the Trinity* (John 14:16-17). Jesus believed in and taught His disciples the doctrine of the Trinity. When attempting to prepare them for their life of service after His resurrection, He told them He had asked the Father to send the Comforter, which is God the Holy Spirit. By this point in His ministry, the disciples were well aware that Jesus was God the Son. In His instruction concerning the coming of the Holy Spirit, He taught in a way that assumes they understood the doctrine of the Trinity.

Later the same evening, Jesus made the same allusion to the Trinity to the same group. "But when the Comforter [God the Holy Spirit] is come, whom I [God the Son] will send unto you from [God] the Father . . ." (John 15:26). Jesus would have had only to say something once to make it true, but the repetition of this teaching in this context suggests not only was the teaching true, but the learners (disciples) could relate to that truth. They were familiar enough with the doctrine of the Trinity to be able to learn new truth built upon old truth.

3. *The New Testament church recognized the Trinity* (2 Cor. 13:14). The doctrine of the Trinity was taught in the early church. Two practices of the church revealed that the first Christians were trinitarians. The first is seen in the practice of greetings and benedictions. Christians often greeted one another in the name of the Lord. Even today some Christians will comment, "God bless you" as they part company. When the apostle Paul pronounced his final benediction upon the Corinthian church, he did so in the name of the three Persons of the Trinity. "The grace of the Lord Jesus Christ, and the love of God, and the communion of the Holy Ghost, be with you all" (2 Cor. 13:14).

A second practice in the New Testament church that recognized the Trinity was baptism. Jesus instructed His disciples to baptize converts, "in the name of the Father, and of the Son, and of the Holy Ghost" (Matt. 28:19) in obedience to Christ's commandment, hence in "the name of Christ."

4. *The distinct work of each Person of the Trinity points to the Trinity.* Much of the work of God is attributed to all members of the Trinity. Hebrews 9:14 illustrates the cooperative efforts of each member of the Trinity in the atonement: God the Son offered His blood through God the Holy Spirit to God the Father for our atonement. In this way, an understanding of the Trinity is foundational to an understanding of the atonement. The author of Hebrews felt this was important when reminding Hebrew Christians in Jerusalem of what God had done for them.

D. THE ATTRIBUTES OF THE TRINITY. One of the strongest proofs of the Triune nature of God is that the Bible reveals that each member of the Trinity possesses the same attributes of God.

In the corporate identification of God, the Trinity is called holy. The Father is called holy (Isa. 41:14; John 17:11), the Son is called holy (Acts 3:14) and so is the Holy Spirit (Eph. 4:30). The following chart reinforces the doctrine of the Trinity by showing that each Person of the Godhead is equal in attributes.

THE ATTRIBUTES OF THE TRINITY			
ATTRIBUTES	FATHER	SON	HOLY SPIRIT
Omnipresence	Jer. 23:24	Matt. 28:20	Psa. 139:7-12
Omnipotence	Rom. 1:16	Matt. 28:28	Rom. 15:19
Omniscience	Rom. 11:33	John 21:17	John 14:26
Immutability	Mal. 3:6	Heb. 13:8	Hag. 2:5
Eternality	Psa. 90:2	John 1:1	Heb. 9:14
Holiness	Lev. 19:2	Heb. 4:15	name "Holy"
Love	1 John 3:1	Mark. 10:21	name "Comforter"

E. THE WORK OF THE TRINITY. The above chart shows the Trinity equal in attributes, and, since the attributes are absolute, the Persons of the Godhead are equal. Two absolute forces would conflict with each other if in fact they were not a unified whole. The chart below shows that all three Persons of divinity are involved in works that only God can do.

THE WORK OF THE TRINITY			
WORK	FATHER	SON	HOLY SPIRIT
Creation of the world	Psa. 102:25	John 1:3	Gen. 1:2
Creation of man	Gen. 2:7	Col. 1:16	Job 33:4
Death of Christ	Isa. 53:10	John 10:18	Heb. 9:24
Resurrection of Christ	Acts 2:32	John 2:19	1 Pet. 3:18
Inspiration	Heb. 1:1-2	1 Pet. 1:10-11	2 Pet. 1:21
Indwelling believers	Eph. 4:6	Col. 1:7	1 Cor. 6:19
Authority of ministry	2 Cor. 3:4-6	1 Tim. 1:12	Acts 20:28
Security of believer	John 10:29	Phil. 1:6	Eph. 1:13-14

IX. THE FATHER

The concept of fatherhood comes from the First Person of the Trinity, who is addressed as "Our Father which art in heaven" (Matt. 6:9). The Bible teaches we have a heavenly Father. While the doctrine of the Trinity is foundational to biblical Christianity, the three Persons of the Godhead do not receive equal emphasis in the experience of the average Christian. Certainly the emphasis of teaching in contemporary pulpits is on the Son, though many also spend time to teach concerning the Holy Spirit. But the Fatherhood of God remains a vastly neglected doctrine. Willmington doubts the average Christian could list more than a half dozen statements concerning the first Person of the Trinity.[73] Fitzwater observes,

Careful thought and observation reveal a surpassing lack of reference to God as Father in the speech and prayers of Christians today, while there is constant reference to Jesus Christ as the Saviour. Saviourhood is much emphasized while the Fatherhood of God is given comparatively little attention. Few of our hymns are addressed to God or even describe Him as to His essential character and grace. It is sometimes painfully embarrassing to be unable to find a hymn setting forth the Fatherhood of God.[74]

A. THE FATHERHOOD OF GOD. Some teach that the Fatherhood of God means everyone is a child of God, hence everyone is going to heaven. This doctrine of "universalism" denies the basic fundamentals of the Word of God. It denies the necessity of the vicarious substitutionary atonement, implying there is no need of salvation. Because of the abuse of these humanistic teachings, many conservative Christians will not use the phrase "the Fatherhood of God." However, the Bible teaches that God is the Father of the universe and all its people, but that does not mean everyone is a Christian and that everyone will go to heaven (cf. Gal. 3:26).

1. *The Father of creation.* When the general public describes God the Father, they often use the phrase, "the universal Fatherhood of God." This phrase makes God the Father of all living things, including people, by virtue of the fact that He is their Creator. We prefer to use the phrase "The Father of Creation," because it identifies God with the reason that He is Father. The best verse to identify "the Father of Creation" is James. 1:17, "Every good gift and every perfect gift is from above, and cometh down from the Father of lights."

When we study the history of an organization or a nation, we find the term "founding fathers." The man who invents or develops some new product is often called the "father" of that product. We use the term "father" to identify its source. Since God is the Creator of all things, He is the Father of the universe.

2. *The national Father of Israel.* God has a unique relationship with the nation Israel; He is called its father. Although the doctrine of the Father is fully developed in the New Testament, we have noted that it exists in embryonic form in the Old Testament. Jeremiah put it this way: "I am a father to Israel, and Ephraim is my firstborn" (Jer. 31:9). Israel was a special son to God because He was its source; Israel was loved by Jehovah and He was their teacher, giving them the law to instruct them in the way they should live.

3. *The unique Father of Jesus Christ.* In an extremely unique way, God is the Father of Jesus Christ, His Son. Jesus was miraculously born of a virgin with no human father. Actually, He existed from before the beginning and simply became a man, while retaining His divinity at His birth. God claims to be the Father of Christ when He says, "Thou art my Son; this day have I begotten thee" (Psa. 2:7). This does not mean that Jesus Christ was begotten at a point in time. The phrase "this day" means God's eternal day, or a day without time. God was always in the process of being begotten by the Father—both Father and Son are eternal. At the baptism of Jesus, the Father Himself spoke. "This is my beloved Son, in whom I am well pleased" (Matt. 3:17). Jesus declared his sonship by telling the Jewish leaders, "My Father worketh hitherto, and I work" (John 5:17). This statement looks innocent to us because we do not see the implication of the original language. The Greek word for "my" is *idios*, by which Jesus meant, "My Father, of whom I am identical." When Jesus called God His Father, He also recognized Himself as equal in deity.

Paul related Jesus to God by saying "his dear Son" (Col. 1:13). John called Christ "his only begotten Son" (John 3:16). Jesus recognized His unique relationship with God. He used the title "Father" more than any other when referring to God. He distinguished between "my Father" and "your Father." Though He instructed His disciples to pray "*Our* Father," He never used the term. He recognized the uniqueness of His relationship with the Father.

4. *A protective Father.* "A father of the fatherless, and a judge of the widows, is God in his holy habitation" (Psa. 68:5). God is a father to those oppressed who need a father. This verse does not teach that all poor orphans and widows are saved, but rather that God is

concerned about those for whom no one else cares. Even among Christians there is a tendency to ignore "those who are less fortunate." But God is the Defender of those unable to defend themselves.

This aspect of the fatherhood of God was a major motivating factor in the life of George Mueller. As he considered renting a building for his first orphanage, God confirmed His leading in Mueller's life by speaking through Psalm 68:5. Mueller was prepared to believe God would provide as a father, if he were to gather the orphans. God honored Mueller's faith and proved himself to be "a father to the fatherless."

5. *Redemptive Father*. The major emphasis in New Testament doctrine is the Father's relationship to redemption. All who are saved, are born "of God" (John 1:13). God becomes our Father when we trust Christ as our Saviour and gain admittance into the family of God (John 1:12). We immediately, upon salvation, have an intimate relationship with God "whereby we cry, Abba, Father" (Rom. 8:15). We cannot know God as our redemptive Father until we are known by Him as His redeemed children.

ENDNOTES

1.   A. W. Tozer, *The Knowledge of the Holy: The Attributes of God: Their Meaning in the Christian Life* (San Francisco: Harper & Row, 1961), vii.
2.   Ibid., 2.
3.   Ibid., 1.
4.   J. B. Phillips, *Your God Is Too Small* (New York: The MacMillan Company, 1972), 120-121.*
5.   Tozer, *Knowledge*, 6.
6.   Nicholas of Cusa, *The Vision of God*, trans. by Emma G. Salter (New York: E. P. Dutton & Sons, 1928), 60.
7.   *Westminster Shorter Catechism*, Question One.*
8.   Russell R. Byrum, *Christian Theology* (Anderson, Indiana: Warner Press, 1976), 184.*
9.   Augustus Hopkins Strong, *Systematic Theology* (Old Tappan, NJ: Fleming H. Revell Company, 1970), 250.
10.   Archibald Alexander Hodge, *Outlines of Theology* (London: Thomas Nelson, 1896), 131.
11.   *West's Analysis*, pp. 17-19, cited by James Petigru Boyce, *Abstract of Systematic Theology* (Philadelphia: American Baptist Publication Society, 1887), 63-64.
12.   Ibid., 62.
13.   William Newton Clarke, *An Outline of Christian Theology* (New York: Charles Scribner's Sons, 1898), 67.
14.   Strong, *Systematic Theology*, 252.
15.   Henry Clarence Thiessen, *Introductory Lectures in Systematic Theology* (Grand Rapids:

Eerdmans, 1951), 121.
16. Clarke, *Christian Theology*, 67.
17. Strong, *Systematic Theology*, 252.
18. Hodge, *Outlines of Theology*, 143.
19. Boyce, *Abstract*, 58.
20. Strong, *Systematic Theology*, 304.
21. Thiessen, *Introductory Lectures*, 64-66.
22. Ibid., 66-67.
23. Strong, *Systematic Theology*, 90.
24. Edward Burnett Tylor, *Religion in Primitive Culture* (New York: Putnam, 1920), 426-427.*
25. Morris Jastrow, Jr., *The Study of Religion* (London: Walter Scott, Ltd., 1902), 76.
26. Thiessen, *Introductory Lectures*, 73.
27. Robert Flint, *Anti-Theistic Theories*, 4th ed. (Edinburgh and London: Wm. Blackwood and Sons, 1899), 336.
28. George T. W. Patrick, *Introduction to Philosophy*, Revised ed. (New York: Houghton Mifflin, 1952), 221.
29. Thiessen, *Lectures*, 74.
30. Boyce, *Abstract*, 65.
31. Tozer, *Knowledge*, 13.
32. Stephen Charnock, *The Existence and Attributes of God* (Minneapolis, MN: Klock & Klock, 1977), 448.
33. Thiessen, *Introductory Lectures*, 128.
34. Tozer, *Knowledge*, 104.
35. Boyce, *Abstract*, 99.
36. Tozer, *Knowledge*, 87.
37. William Evans, *The Great Doctrines of the Bible* (Chicago, Moody Press, 1912), 46.
38. Strong, *Systematic Theology*, 264.
39. Thiessen, *Introductory Lectures*, 130.
40. Malcolm Furness, *Vital Doctrines of the Faith* (Grand Rapids: Eerdmans, 1974), 9.
41. Tozer, *Knowledge*, 82.
42. Charnock, *Attributes*, 534-535.
43. Ibid., 538.
44. Thiessen, *Introductory Lectures*, 131.
45. Ibid., 132.
46. Ibid., 131.
47. Charnock, *Attributes*, 183.
48. Tozer, *Knowledge*, 55.

49.   Hodge, *Outlines of Theology*, 141.

50.   Clarke, *Christian Theology*, 79.

51.   Louis Berkhof, *Systematic Theology* (Grand Rapids: Eerdmans, 1981), 79.

52.   Byrum, *Christian Theology*, 47.

53.   Berkhof, *Systematic Theology*, 47.

54.   T. Rees, "God", in *The International Standard Bible Encyclopedia* (Grand Rapids: Eerdmans, 1974), 1253.

55.   Charles Grandson Finney, *Finney's Systematic Theology*, ed. And abridged by J. H. Fairchild (Minneapolis, MN: Bethany Fellowship, Inc. 1976), 1.

56.   Ibid.

57.   Ibid.

58.   Fitzwater, *Christian Theology*, 357-58.

59.   Berkhof, *Systematic Theology*, 100.

60.   Hodge, *Outlines of Theology*, 200.

61.   Boyce, *Abstract*, 115.

62.   Strong, *Systematic Theology*, 353.

63.   Thiessen, *Introductory Lectures*, 147.

64.   Chafer, *Systematic Theology*, 1:225.

65.   Boyce, *Abstract*, 118.

66.   Strong, *Systematic Theology*, 362.

67.   Westminster Shorter Catechism.*

68.   Chafer, *Systematic Theology*, 1:236.

69.   Robert Dick, *Lectures on Theology*, cited in Chafer, *Systematic Theology*, 1:283.

70.   Clarke, *Christian Theology*, 177.

71.   Karl Barth, *The Doctrine of the Word of God* (New York: 1936), 344.

72.   Andrew Jukes, *The Names of God in Holy Scripture* (Grand Rapids: Kregel Publications, 1967; reprint of 1888 edition), 19.

73.   H. L. Willmington, *The Doctrine of the Father* (Lynchburg, VA: By the author, 1977), 1.

74.   Fitzwater, *Christian Theology*, 90.

* Denotes page number(s) could not be verified.

CHAPTER IV – CHRISTOLOGY

The Doctrine of Christ

I. THE DEITY OF JESUS CHRIST

Jesus Christ, the second Person of the Trinity, is equal with the Father in nature, yet the Father sent Him to die for the sins of the world so that Christ is submissive to the Father in duties. Jesus Christ possessed all the divine attributes of the Father, and was one with the Father, yet was separate in person. Christ effected redemption for men because in Him was united both the human and divine natures. In humanity, Christ was totally human; in deity, Jesus was unalterably God. Yet in Jesus Christ was a single, undivided personality in whom these two natures are vitally and undividedly united, so that Jesus Christ is not God and man, but the God-man. For all these reasons and more, Christ is God. The following reasons help classify and demonstrate His deity. Yet these points are only suggestive, for all the doctrines of Christianity point to the deity of Christ.

A. THE NATURE OF THE CLAIMS OF JESUS CHRIST ATTEST HIS DEITY. Simply because Jesus Christ claims to be God does not make His claim true. On the other hand, it is assumed that if God would reveal Himself, He would also identify Himself by a claim that He is God. The self-revelation and claim to deity is the basis for our consideration of Jesus Christ. The one who claims to be God would have to demonstrate God-like moral attributes of holiness, love and goodness, or those qualities that are associated with deity. This person would also have to back up His claim with demonstrations of power, vast knowledge and omnipresence. Finally, His teachings must be consistent within themselves and correspond to the wisdom of God. Some liberals say that Jesus did not claim to be God, yet the biblical account of Christ records ample evidence that Jesus did make this claim.

There are eight aspects to Jesus' claim to deity. (1) In the Gospel of John He used the Jehovistic I AM, that identified him with deity. (I am the way . . . I am the resurrection . . . I am the door . . . etc.). Also, the Jehovistic I AM is used without the figures of speech (John 8:25, 56-59; 18:6, 8 the pronoun "he" is not in the Greek). (2) Jesus claimed to be the Old Testament Adonai (Matt. 22:42-45). (3) Jesus identifies Himself with God in the baptismal formula (Matt. 28:19). (4) Jesus claims to be one with the Father (John 10:30) and that the person who saw Him was seeing the Father (John 14:9). (5) When Jesus claimed to forgive sins (Mark 2:5-7), He was assuming a prerogative that belonged to God. (6) When Jesus allowed people to worship Him, He was asserting Himself as deity, for He was approving an act

155

that belonged to Deity (Matt. 14:33; 28:9; John 20:28, 29). (7) Finally, Jesus claimed the comparative attributes of omnipresence, omniscience and omnipotence. Jesus claimed to be in Heaven (John 3:13). Jesus claimed omnipotence (Matt. 28:18), that the dead would respond to His authority (Luke 7:14) and that nature would obey His word (Mark 4:39). (8) Finally, Jesus claimed to have a special relationship to the heavenly Father by addressing Him, "My Father" (John 5:18). This is a common expression today, and many Christians say "My Father" when speaking of God. But when Jesus said, "My Father," the Jewish leaders recognized that He claimed deity for Himself and they responded accordingly. "Therefore, the Jews sought the more to kill him [Jesus], because he not only had broken the sabbath, but said also that God was his Father, making himself equal with God" (John 5:18). On another visit to Jerusalem, Jesus was asked for a clear statement concerning His claim. He responded, "I and my Father are one" (John 10:30). The Jews understood He was saying, "I am the Son of God" (John 10:36). On several occasions they attempted to kill Jesus for claiming to be God. When the religious leaders finally brought Jesus to Pilate for crucifixion, it was because of His claims. They accused Him of blasphemy. "The Jews answered him, We have a law, and by our law he ought to die, because he made himself the Son of God" (John 19:7). Conservative theologians have always noted and emphasized the fact that Christ claimed to be God. When Jesus claimed deity in John 5:18, Tenney suggests,

> His enemies understood what He meant, for they sought to kill Him because he had assumed the prerogatives of deity in calling God "his own Father." The term *his own* meant peculiarly his, in a way that could not be applied to anyone else.[1]

Commenting on John 10:31 following a claim of oneness with the Father by Jesus, Arthur Pink notes:

> This is quite sufficient to settle the meaning of the previous verse. These Jews had no difficulty in perceiving the force of what our Lord had just said to them. They instantly recognized that He had claimed absolute equality with the Father, and to their ears this was blasphemy. Instead of saying anything to correct their error, if error it was, Christ went on to say that which must have confirmed it.[2]

On this passage even Barclay must admit the obvious.

> To the Jews Jesus' statement that He and the Father were one was blasphemy, insult against God. It was the invasion by a man of the place which belonged to God alone. It was a human being claiming equality with God.[3]

Discussing these claims of Christ, Thomas Schultz notes,

> Not one recognized religious leader—not Moses, Paul, Buddha, Mohammed, Confucius, etc.—has ever claimed to be God; that is with the exception of Jesus

Christ. Christ is the only religious leader who has ever claimed to be deity and the only individual ever who has convinced a great portion of the world that He is God.[4]

William Robinson further notes,

> However, if one takes a historically objective approach to the question, it is found that even secular history affirms that Jesus lived on earth and was worshipped as God. He founded a church, which has worshipped Him for 1900 years. He changed the course of the world's history.[5]

B. THE TEACHING OF THE BIBLE. Jesus recognized His claim was not enough to make Him God. "If I bear witness of myself, my witness is not true" (John 5:31). Jesus was pointing out that any claim, true or false, could be assumed false if unsubstantiated. To His critics Jesus cited another authority: "Search the scriptures; for in them ye think ye have eternal life: and they are they which testify of me" (John 5:39).

The Bible records many statements concerning the deity of Christ. John says, "the Word was God" (John 1:1). Writing hundreds of years before His birth, Isaiah called Him "The Mighty God" (Isa. 9:6). Paul was "looking for that blessed hope, and the glorious appearing of the great God and our Saviour Jesus Christ" (Titus 2:13). Paul quotes an early church doctrinal statement, "God was manifest in the flesh, justified in the Spirit, seen of angels, preached unto the Gentiles, believed on in the world, received up into glory" (1 Tim. 3:16). Since the Bible was demonstrated to be the inspired and authoritative Word of God in our section on Bibliology, we can accept the claims of Scripture about the deity of Christ. The following chart illustrates how many titles for Jehovah are applied to Jesus.[6]

JESUS IS JEHOVAH		
OF JEHOVAH	MUTUAL TITLE OR ACT	OF JESUS
Isa. 40:28	Creator	John 1:3
Isa. 45:22; 43:11	Savior	John 4:42
1 Sam. 2:6	Raise the dead	John 5:21, 25
Joel 3:12	Judge	John 5:27, cf. Matt. 25:31
Isa. 60:19-20	Light	John 8:12
Exod. 3:14	I Am	John 8:58, cf. John 18:5-6
Psa. 23:1	Shepherd	John 10:11

Isa. 42:8; cf. 48:11	Glory of God	John 17:1, 5
Isa. 41:4; 44:6	First and Last	Rev. 1:17; 2:8
Hosea 13:14	Redeemer	Rev. 5:9
Isa. 62:5; Hosea 2:16	Bridegroom	Rev. 21:2, cf. Matt. 25:1-13
Psa. 18:2	Rock	1 Cor. 10:4
Jer. 31:34	Forgiver of Sins	Mark 2:7,10
Psa. 148:2	Worshipped by Angels	Heb. 1:6
Through the Old Testament	Addressed in Prayer	Acts 7:59
Psa. 148:5	Creator of Angels	Col. 1:16
Isa. 45:23	Confessed as Lord	Phil. 2:11

C. THE PRE-EXISTENCE AND ETERNALITY OF JESUS CHRIST ATTEST HIS DEITY. The Bible teaches that Jesus Christ is the second Person of the Trinity. As such He is equal with God the Father in attributes and nature. Since God is eternal, then any proof that demonstrates that Jesus Christ lived before His birth points to His deity. The term "pre-existence" means that Christ existed in the Old Testament. To this, Jesus Christ testified, "Before Abraham was, I am" (John 8:58). The Jews understood He was claiming deity so they took stones to kill Him for blasphemy (John 8:59). Paul adds to the proofs of His pre-existence; "He is before all things" (Col. 1:17). The proofs that Christ appeared to people in the Old Testament in Christophanies also lay the foundation for His deity, (See Section III). The term "eternality" means Jesus Christ is not limited by time, but that He has no beginning or end. To this testifies the writer to the Hebrews, "Jesus Christ the same yesterday, and today, and forever" (Heb. 13:8). The same writer also states of Christ, "They [the heavens and earth] shall perish; but thou remainest" (Heb. 1:11). To make the eternality of Christ emphatic, he adds, "Thy years shall not fail" (Heb. 1:12).

D. THE TRIUNE NATURE OF GOD. God is one God in three Persons: Father, Son, and Holy Spirit. Each member of the Trinity is completely God. As part of the Trinity, Jesus Christ, who is God the Son, is deity. The deity of the Trinity has been recognized from the beginning. Isaiah recorded the predictive words of Jesus, "Come ye near unto me, hear ye this; I have not spoken in secret from the beginning; from the time that it was, there am I: and now the LORD GOD, and his Spirit, hath sent me" (Isa. 48:16). When Christians are baptized, they are baptized "in the name of the Father, and of the Son, and of the Holy Ghost" (Matt. 28:19). The very act which God has prescribed for every believer as he begins the Christian life, recognizes the place of Jesus Christ as the Son of God. Everything that is true about God is true of every member of the Trinity of God. Since God has existed from eternity past (Psa. 90:2), then every member of the Trinity has existed equally as long. (See section on Trinity).

E. THE HEAVENLY ORIGIN OF CHRIST. In one sense one cannot talk about the origin of Christ— He is eternal. The writer of Hebrews describes his eternity, comparing Melchizedek to Christ, "without father, without mother, without descent, having neither beginning of days, nor end of life; but made like unto the Son of God" (Heb. 7:3). But in a second sense, when we think of the earthly life of Christ, we recognize that He had come from Heaven. John the Baptist said, "He that cometh from above is above all: he that is of the earth is earthly, and speaketh of the earth: he that cometh from heaven is above all" (John 3:31). Because of this, John could accept the growing popularity of Jesus at his expense. Jesus told the people of His home region, "I came down from heaven, not to do mine own will, but the will of him that sent me" (John 6:38).

F. THE NEW TESTAMENT AUTHORS ASCRIBE THE WORK OF CREATION TO CHRIST. Another proof for the deity of Jesus Christ is the description of His works. John sets Him forth as Creator: "All things were made by him and without him was not anything made that was made" (John 1:3). Paul noted, "For by him were all things created, that are in heaven, and that are in earth, visible and invisible, whether they be thrones, or dominions, or principalities, or powers: all things were created by him, and for him" (Col. 1:16).

G. THE NEW TESTAMENT AUTHORS ASCRIBE DIVINE ATTRIBUTES TO CHRIST. John attributed omniscience to Christ, "But Jesus did not commit himself unto them, because he knew all men, and needed not that any should testify of man: for he knew what was in man" (John 2:24-25). The writer of Hebrews attributed to Christ the power to hold the world together: "Upholding all things by the word of his power" (Heb. 1:3). Later in the same chapter he claims Christ is immutable, "Thou art the same, and thy years change not" (Heb. 1:12). Again the same writer notes, "Jesus Christ the same yesterday, and today, and forever" (Heb. 13:8). John describes the eternality of Christ when he attributes to Him the following quote: "I am he that liveth, and was dead; and, behold, I am alive for evermore" (Rev. 1:18).

H. THE FACT THAT WORSHIP WAS GIVEN TO AND ACCEPTED BY CHRIST DEMONSTRATES HIS DEITY. Only God is worthy of and can rightly be worshipped. The fact that Jesus allowed people to worship Him shows that He conceived of Himself as deity (Matt. 14:33; 28:9; John 20:28-29). But others also taught that Jesus Christ should be worshipped, implying they ascribed deity to Him (Acts 7:59-60; 1 Cor. 1:2; 2 Cor. 13:14; Phil. 2:9-10; Heb. 1:6; Rev. 1:5-6; 5:12-13).

I. THE NEW TESTAMENT WRITERS GIVE DIVINE TITLES TO CHRIST. A person reveals his attitude about Jesus Christ by the names/titles that he gives Him. The New Testament writers attributed the highest praise and devotion possible to Jesus Christ as evidenced in the names attributed to Him. Both the vast number of names (see next section for listing of 365 names) and the quality of the names (Christ is ascribed equality with the Father) demonstrates His deity. (See Section II for a full discussion.)

II. THE NAMES OF CHRIST

As the names of God are given in Scripture to reveal the nature of God, so the names of Christ reveal truth concerning Jesus Christ. These names, however, refer to various aspects of the second Person of the Trinity, sometimes emphasizing His deity, at other times emphasizing His humanity. Some of these names reflect His character, while others emphasize various aspects of His work.

Scholars disagree concerning the number of names of Christ which the Scriptures contain. Perhaps more of these names appear in the first chapter of John than in any other chapter of Scripture. The assigning of names with meaning is particularly characteristic of Hebrew writing, and much of the Gospel of John is Hebraic in style. As John began his treatise to demonstrate the deity of the Saviour (John 20:31), he began by reminding the reader of the names of Christ.

THE NAMES OR TITLES OF CHRIST IN JOHN 1		
Word	Life	Flesh
God	Light	Only Begotten of the Father
Light of Men	True Light	Jesus Christ
Only Begotten Son	Lord	Jesus
Lamb of God	Son of God	Rabbi
Master	Messiah	Christ
Jesus of Nazareth	The Son of Joseph	King of Israel
Son of Man	Him	He

A. JEHOVAH. Perhaps the most honored of all names of God in Scripture was that of Jehovah. Yet as was illustrated earlier in this chapter, Jesus is equated with Jehovah throughout the Scriptures. The name is derived from the Hebrew verb "to be" and was the name God used most often when relating to man, especially in covenant. Scotchmen suggests, "The identification of our Lord Jesus Christ with the Lord of the Old Testament results in an explicit doctrine of His deity."[7] Particularly in the Gospel of John, Jesus reveals Himself as the "I AM" of the Old Testament.

THE GREAT I AM's		
1.	I am the bread of life	John 6:35
2.	I am the light of the world	John 8:12
3.	I am the door	John 10:9
4.	I am the good shepherd	John 10:11
5.	I am the resurrection and the life	John 11:25
6.	I am the way, the truth, and the life	John 14:6
7.	I am the vine	John 15:5
+1	I am . . . I am (Exod. 3:14)	John 4:26; 8:58; 18:5, 6, 8

B. SON OF GOD. Another name of Jesus Christ in the New Testament is "Son of God," which is used by Christ in referring to His deity. In the Old Testament the reference to the Sonship of Christ is, "I will declare the decree: The Lord hath said unto me, Thou art my Son; this day have I begotten thee" (Psa. 2:7). This verse reveals a conversation between God the Father and God the Son. The Father calls the second Person of the Trinity by the name "Son" and says, "I have begotten thee." Again the Bible teaches "A son is given" (Isa. 9:6).

When the expression "Son of God" is used by and of Christ, it is obviously a reference to His divine relationship to God the Father. Christians are the "sons of God" (not capitalized), and they call God their Father. But Jesus identifies a special relationship to His Father, as Felder notes,

> *As often* as Jesus speaks of his relations with his Father he uses constantly and without exception the expression "My Father"; and as often as he calls the attention of the disciples to their childlike relation to God, there is the equally definite characterization, "Your Father." Never does he associate himself with the disciples and with men by the natural form of speech, "Our Father." . . . Even on those occasions in which Jesus unites himself with the disciples before God, and when therefore it would be certainly expected that he would use the collective expression, "Our Father," there stands, on the contrary, "My Father" . . . Thus and similarly does Jesus distinguish unequivocally between his divine Sonship and that of the disciples and men in general.[8]

Further discussing the Sonship of Christ, Stevenson explains the relationship between Christians being called "sons of God," and Christ the "Son of God."

It is true that the term "sons of God" is used of men (Hosea 1:10) and of angels in the Old Testament (Gen. 6:2; Job 1:6; 38:7). But in the New Testament, the title 'Son of God' is used of, and by, our Lord in quite a different way. In every instance the term implies that He is the one, only-begotten Son; coequal, co-eternal with the Father.[9]

Some Bible interpreters raise a question as to when Jesus became the Son of God. The first theory teaches that Jesus became the Son of God at the incarnation. To prove this, they use the prediction to Mary by the angel, "He shall be called the Son of God" (Luke 1:35). In the second place, others say He became the Son of God at His baptism. It was there God broke the silence of Heaven to announce, "This is my beloved Son, in whom I am well pleased" (Matt. 3:17). A third view is that Jesus became the Son of God at His resurrection, because Paul said, "Declared to be the Son of God with power, according to the Spirit of holiness, by the resurrection from the dead" (Rom. 1:4). Yet another group cites Hebrews 1:1-4, arguing that Jesus became the Son of God by "appointment" at His ascension. A fifth false view concerning when Jesus became the Son of God suggests that in eternity past the Father and Son agreed and entered into some type of covenant relationship resulting in Jesus becoming the Son of God. The Holy Spirit is then said to have agreed to be the agent to carry out the plan. Advocates of this view are unable to provide any scriptural support for their idea, and the Bible reminds us our "eternal life" was "promised before the world began" (Titus 1:2). While this does not prohibit the establishing of a covenant prior to the promise, it does make it highly improbable.

All of these views fail to recognize the teaching of one of the Bible's best-known verses: "For God so loved the world, that he gave his only begotten Son, that whosoever believeth in him should not perish, but have everlasting life" (John 3:16). Jesus always has been the Son of God. Jesus was recognized as the Son of God before He came to earth to provide eternal salvation. Jesus was the Son of God even before the proto-evangelium or first giving of the gospel in Genesis 3:15, "And I will put enmity between thee and the woman, and between thy seed and her seed; he shall bruise thy head, and thou shalt bruise his heel." This verse predicted the coming of the seed of the woman to bruise the head of the serpent.

The key to understanding when Jesus became the Son of God is to understand the meaning of the word "day" in Psalm 2:7. The word "day" does not refer to a twenty-four-hour period in time. God lives beyond time. This word means an eternal day. Technically, the Sonship of Jesus Christ is called "Eternal Generation." Jesus did not become the Son of God at a point of time. He has eternally been in the process of being generated as the Son in God's eternal day. The conclusion is that there never was a time that Christ was not the Son of God.

C. ONLY BEGOTTEN SON. The Bible identifies angels, Jews and Christians at various times as sons of God, but the relationship that exists between God the Father and Jesus Christ is different. Jesus is the "only begotten Son of God." The term "only begotten" is used to describe the unique relationship between the Father and Jesus (John 1:14, 18; 3:16; 1 John 4:9). Though any individual who trusts Christ personally for salvation will become a child of God (John 1:12), there is only one "only begotten Son of God." Because of His relationship to the Father, Christ expresses the nature of God, just as a son possesses the nature of his father. The son of a human has a human nature. The only begotten Son of God is just like His heavenly Father, for He is God.

D. SON OF MAN. Jesus used the term "Son of man" when discussing His earthly ministry (Matt. 8:20; 9:6; 11:19; 16:13; Luke 19:10; 22:48), when foretelling his passion (Matt. 12:40; 17:9, 22; 20:18), and in teaching regarding His return in power and great glory (Matt. 13:41; 24:27, 30; 25:31; Luke 18:8; 21:36). The Jew who heard this title would immediately think "Messiah." Montefiore argues, "If Jesus said these words we can hardly think that he distinguished between himself, the Son of man, and the Messiah. The Son of man must be the Messiah, and both must be himself.[10] Kreyssler and Scheffrahn write, "Jesus clearly believed Himself to be the fulfillment of the Old Testament prophecies of the Messiah. In referring to Himself, He continually used the title 'The Son of man' from David's vision."[11] Concerning this name of Christ, Stevenson notes,

> This was the designation which our Lord habitually used concerning Himself. It is not found in the New Testament on any other lips than His own—except when His questioners quoted His words (John 12:34), and in the one instance of Stephen's ecstatic exclamation in the moment of his martyrdom, "Behold, I see the heavens opened, and the Son of man standing on the right hand of God" (Acts 7:56). It was clearly a Messianic title, as the Jews recognized (John 12:34).[12]

E. WORD. One of the most important titles of Christ is "the Word." Pink suggested that "a word is (1) *a medium of manifestation*;" (2) "*a means of communication,*" (3) "*and a method of revelation.*"[13] In his commentary on the Fourth Gospel, Tenney suggests,

> The term LOGOS, which occurs four times, includes more than its English translation, "word." A word is an idea expressed through a combination of sounds or of letters. Without the idea or concept behind it, the medium would be meaningless. KXBZ might represent a radio station; but as a combination of letters and or sounds, if it could be pronounced, it has no meaning whatsoever because no concept is attached to it. Just so the term LOGOS implies the intelligence behind the idea, the idea itself, and the transmissible expression of it. The term was used technically in the Greek philosophy of this period, particularly by the Stoics, to devote the controlling Reason of the universe, the all-pervasive Mind which ruled and gave meaning to all things. LOGOS was one of the purest and most general concepts of that ultimate Intelligence, Reason, or Will that is called God.[14]

Scholars debate whether John borrowed the term "word" from the Greeks or the Jews. If the term is Greek, there may be numerous philosophical implications. If the term is Hebrew, he may be making reference to wisdom in Proverbs 5-8. Probably Jesus is called the Word of God because this phrase is used over 1200 times in the Old Testament to refer to the revelation or message of God, as in the phrase "the Word of God came to" a certain prophet. Jesus Christ was also the message, meaning, or communication from God to men. Jesus was everything the written and spoken Word of the Lord was in the Old Testament. Jesus is therefore the expression, revelation and communication of the Lord. He is both the incarnate and inspired Word.

	TEN CONCLUSIONS ABOUT THE WORD IN JOHN 1:1-18
1.	The phrase "In the beginning" is not a reference to a point in time, but a reference to eternity past.
2.	The personality of the Word is evident in that it is capable of individualizing Himself.
3.	The Word has active and personal communication with God.
4.	There are two centers of consciousness in that the Word was God yet also was "face to face" with God.
5.	The Word has the essence of deity.
6.	The Father and the Word are one.
7.	The Word was the avenue by which God expressed or revealed Himself.
8.	The incarnate Word is the continuity of the preincarnate Word.
9.	As God lived in a tent, spoke in a tent and revealed Himself in the Old Testament tabernacle, so the Word tabernacled among us.
10.	The incarnation of the Word is the unique revelation of God.

F. ADDITIONAL NAMES OF CHRIST. There are many additional names of Christ, which reveal truth concerning the second Person of the Trinity. The following list was compiled by T. C. Horton and Charles E. Hurlburt.[15]

NAMES OF CHRIST IN SCRIPTURE

The Seed of the Woman
The Stone of Israel
Wall of Fire

The Branch
The Messenger of the Covenant
The Sun of Righteousness
Son of Abraham
A Governor
Friend of Sinners
A Sower
My Beloved Son
The Bridegroom
Good Master
One Son, His Well Beloved
The Son of the Highest
The Highest
The Babe
The Salvation of God
A Sign
Lord of Sabaoth
A Certain Samaritan
A Light to Lighten the Gentiles
A Certain Nobleman
The Word
The Only Begotten of the Father
A Prophet Mighty in Deed and Word
Rabbi
The Gift of God
The True Bread from Heaven
The Living Bread
The Resurrection
Master
The Life
Our Keeper
My Lord and My God
The Holy One and Just
A Prince and a Savior
Lord of All
Jesus of Nazareth
His Own Son
The Man Whom He Hath Ordained
The First Born among Many Brethren
Minister of the Circumcision
Righteousness
The Last Adam

The Image of God
The Angel of Jehovah
The Peace Offering
The Captain of the Host of the Lord
Tender Grass
The Lifter Up of Mine Head
My Shepherd
Jehovah, Mighty in Battle
My Rock and My Fortress
A Stranger and an Alien
Showers Upon the Earth
My High Tower
Understanding
Bundle of Myrrh
The Lily of the Valley
Altogether Lovely
The Child
Wonderful
The Everlasting Father
A Rod Out of the Stem of Jesse
The Ensign of the People
A Glorious Throne to His Father's House
A Refuge From the Storm
A Diadem of Beauty
A Tired Stone
Shadow of a Great Rock in a Weary Land
Our Lawgiver
The Everlasting God
The Polished Staff
A Man of Sorrows
The God of the Whole Earth
The King in His Beauty
Mine Elect
A Leader
The Redeemer
The Angel of His Presence
My Physician
A Righteous Branch
The Shepherd of Israel
A Stone Cut Without Hands
The Hope of His People
A Star

The Rock of my Salvation
The Daysman
Fortress
Restorer
King of Glory
The Rock that is Higher than I
The King's Son
My First-Born
Wisdom
A Friend that Sticketh Closer than a Brother
Cluster of Camphire
Him Whom My Soul Loveth
The Branch of the Lord
A Sanctuary
Counsellor
The Prince of Peace
A Branch Out of His Roots
My Strength and My Song
Strength to the Poor and Needy
The Rock of Ages
The Foundation
A Cover from the Tempest
As Rivers of Water in a Dry Place
Jehovah
The Light of the Gentiles
The Holy One of Israel
My Righteous Servant
A Witness to the People
The Lord Jehovah
A Root Out of Dry Ground
Thine Everlasting Light
Balm of Gilead
My Portion
David, Their King Feeder
Ancient of Days
Manna
My Servant, the Branch
The Meat (Meal.)
Offering
My Glory
A Worm and No Man
The Strong and Mighty Jehovah

My Strong Rock
A Strong Tower
Rain Upon Mown Grass
The Head Stone of the Corner
Ointment Poured Forth
Excellent
A Rose of Sharon
The Chiefest Among Ten Thousand
Jehovah of Hosts
A Great Light
The Mighty God
The Light of Israel
The Root of Jesse
A Nail Fastened in a Sure Place
A Shadow from the Heat
A Crown of Glory
A Sure Foundation
As a Hiding Place from the Wind
My Maker
A Commander
Our Potter
The Hope of Israel
Resting Place
A Plant of Renown
Stronghold
A Ruler
The Prince of Princes
King over All the Earth
The King
The Light of the City
Purifier
The Son of David
Emmanuel
A Nazarene
My Beloved
Jesus the Christ Master
Our Brother
Jehovah, My God
Refiner
Jesus Christ
Jesus
The Young Child

The Servant of Jehovah
The Christ
The Prophet of Nazareth
The Carpenter
Thou Son of the Most High God
Christ, the Son of the Blessed
God My Savior
The Dayspring from on High
The Consolation of Israel
The Child Jesus
A Great Prophet
The Master of the House
The Chosen of God
The Light of Man
The Lamb of God
The King of Israel
Messiah
The Bread of God
His-Only Begotten Son
The Bread of Life
I Am
One Shepherd
A Grain of Wheat
The Truth
The Way
The Vine
The Overcomer
The Man
The Head of Every Man
The Lord from Heaven
The Wisdom of God
Lord Both of the Dead and the Living
Our Passover
That Spiritual Rock
A Quickening Spirit
The Head
Head over All Things
Shiloh (Peacemaker)
A Scepter
The Son of Mary
A Ransom
Son of Man

The King of the Jews
Horn of Salvation
Christ, the Lord
The Lord's Christ
The Glory of the People Israel
The Holy One of God
Physician
The Christ of God
A Guest
The True Light
The Son of God
The Light of the World
The Good Shepherd
The Christ, the Savior of the World
The Door of the Sheep
The Christ, the Son of God
The Sent of the Father
A Man Approved of God
The Prince of Life
The Just One
Judge of Quick and Dead
Jesus Christ our Lord
God Blessed Forever
The Deliverer
The Power of God
Sanctification
The Foundation
Thine Holy One
The Holy Child Jesus
Lord Jesus
Redemption
Lord Over All
The Lord of Glory
The Unspeakable Gift
He That Filleth All in All
Christ
Our Peace
The First-Fruits of Them That Sleep
One Lord
A Sacrifice to God
The Lord Jesus Christ
The First-Born of Every Creation

The Beginning
Christ our life
Lord of Peace
The Mediator
Blessed and Only Potentate
The Great God
Brightness of His Glory
The Upholder of All Things
The Captain of Our Salvation
The Builder
King of Righteousness
The Minister of the Sanctuary
Mediator of a Better Covenant
Mediator of the New Covenant
The Great Shepherd of the Sheep
A Lamb Without Blemish or Spot
The Bishop of Souls
The Day Star
That Eternal Life
The Propitiation
The True God
Jesus Christ
The Savior of the World
The Prince of the Kings of the Earth
The First and the Last
The Hidden Manna
The Beginning of the Creation of God
The Lamb Slain
The Lamb in the Midst of the Throne
A Sweet Smelling Savor
His Dear Son
Creator of all Things
The First-Born from the Dead
All and in All
Our Hope
The Man Christ Jesus
The Judge of Quick and Dead
God our Savior
God
The Apostle
The Great High Priest
The Forerunner

The Surety
Author of Eternal Salvation
Higher than the Heavens
He That Shall Come
The Author of Faith
A Priest Forever
My Helper
That Worthy Name
A Living Stone
A Stone of Stumbling
A Rock of Offense
A Chief Corner Stone
Lord and Savior Jesus Christ
The Advocate
Jesus Christ the Righteous
The Son of the Father
The Faithful Witness
The First Begotten of the Dead
He that Liveth
The Lion of the Tribe of Judah
King of Saints
Lord God Omnipotent
Faithful and True
The Bright and Morning Star
An Offering
The Image of the Invisible God
The Head of the Body
Hope of Glory
The Lord Christ
Christ Jesus
God Manifest in the Flesh
The Righteous Judge
Heir of All Things
The Sin Purger
The Express Image of His Person
The Seed of Abraham
The High Priest
King of Peace
Our Intercessor
Separate from Sinners
The Testator
A Rewarder

The Finisher of Faith
Jesus Christ the Same
The Word of Life
The Just
An Elect Stone
A Precious Stone
The Chief Shepherd
The Son
Eternal Life
The Almighty
The Morning Star
The Alpha and Omega
The Amen
The Faithful and True Witness
Lord of Lords
King of Kings
The Testifier
The Temple
The Offspring of David
Word of God

III. THE CHRISTOPHANIES

The pre-existence of Christ is further substantiated by the many recorded Christophanies in the Bible. A Christophany is the manifestation of God in visible and bodily form before the incarnation. Some call them theophanies, but Christophanies is a better term since it was an appearance of Christ. Often the Bible identifies these appearances as "the angel of the Lord." A closer look at the references of these events will demonstrate that this angel was more than just another angel—He was God. At other times these Christophanies were an appearance of Jesus in physical form, but not identified as the Angel of the Lord.

The older theologians often referred to these phenomena as theophanies, but the term was used broadly to identify more than the appearances of Christ. The term was used in Greek culture when Christian writers adopted it for their own use. Bernard Pick explains,

> The ancient Greeks were accustomed, during a certain festival named $T\alpha$ $\theta\varepsilon o\varphi\acute{\alpha}v\iota\alpha$, to display at Delphos before the public gaze the images of all their gods. $\theta\varepsilon o\varphi\acute{\alpha}v\iota\alpha$ denoted the apparition of one or more gods.

> The term thus understood was applied by ancient Christian writers to the manifestations of God under the Old Covenant and to the incarnation of Christ.[16]

The term "Christophany" is used by many contemporary writers to identify certain appearances of Christ. In his work on the subject, James Borland explains,

> The term Christophany in this work will denote those unsought, intermittent and temporary, visible and audible manifestations of God the Son in human form, by which God communicated something to certain conscious human beings on earth prior to the birth of Jesus Christ.[17]

A. THE ANGEL OF THE LORD. By far the most common appearance of Jesus Christ in the Old Testament is that of the Angel of the LORD. There can be no question but that He is God. When He appeared, it was usually to an individual who was commissioned to do a special work for God. The Angel of the LORD took the time personally to enlist that individual in His service.

THE ANGEL OF THE LORD		
Reference	Occasion	Called of God
Gen. 16:7-13	To Hagar	Gen. 16:13
Gen. 22:11-14	Sacrifice of Isaac	Gen. 22:14
Exod. 3:2-4:17	Burning Bush	Exod. 3:10
Judg. 6:11-24	To Gideon	Judg. 6:22
Judg. 13:2-23	To Samson's Mother	Judg. 13:18, 22

The term "angel of the Lord" is used generally to identify any angel or messenger of God, but also to identify a specific angel of the LORD. On several occasions, the angel of Jehovah is distinguished from Jehovah (Zech. 1:12-13; Gen. 24:7; Exod. 23:20; 32:34; Isa. 63:9; Judg. 2:1-5). Yet, as J. Barton Payne notes, the angel of Jehovah is more than another angel. He writes,

> *Malakh Yahwe* may refer to any of God's angels (I Kings 19:7; cf. v.5). But at certain points, though the Angel of Yahweh may seem initially to be no more than any other angel (as Judges 6:11), He soon transcends the angelic category and is described in terms that are suitable only to a distinct Person of the Godhead (Judges 6:12, 14).[18]

The best way to reconcile these two apparent contradictions is to recognize the angel of the Lord as a distinct angel related to Christ, as specific angels are related to people today. This angel has both corporeal and incorporeal existence and represented Christ in His work. At times when Christ chose to appear to man before His incarnation, He chose to use the body of the angel of the Lord. This explains why at times the angel of the Lord is "just an angel" and at other times he appears to be God. That He is God is stated in the text as illustrated in the chart above. That He is the second Person of the Trinity is based on the four reasons listed below.

WHY THE ANGEL OF THE LORD IS CHRIST	
1.	Both the angel of Jehovah and Christ are visible.
2.	The angel of Jehovah never appears after the incarnation.
3.	Both the angel of Jehovah and Christ are sent by the Father.
4.	Both the angel of Jehovah and Christ execute judgment for God.

B. A MAN (GEN. 18:1-33; 32:24-32; DAN. 3:23-29). On at least three occasions, Jesus appeared in a Christophany as a human before the incarnation. On these occasions, he appeared among men as a man. Three men appeared to Abraham and Sarah to confirm God's provision of a son and to inform Abraham of the coming destruction of Sodom and Gomorrah. One of these men is identified as "the LORD" (Gen. 18:1, 13, 17, 20, 26-27, 30-33) and is also called "the Judge of all the earth" (Gen. 18:15). This man must have been Jesus Christ because, "No man hath seen God at any time; the only begotten Son, which is in the bosom of the Father, he hath declared him" (John 1:18). Since Christ is the only one of the three Persons of the Trinity to be seen, we are left to believe this man on this occasion and the angel of the Lord who is called God was in fact the second Person of the Trinity, Jesus Christ. Jesus is the only member of the Trinity to have taken on a physical body at any time (besides the Holy Spirit's brief coming in the from of a dove).

At a later time, Christ appeared to Jacob and wrestled with him during the night. Jacob recognized the next morning he had met with God. "And Jacob named the place Peniel; for I have seen God face to face, and my life is preserved" (Gen. 32:30). On a third occasion, Jesus joined the three young Hebrews in Nebuchadnezzar's furnace. Though assured that Nebuchadnezzar had thrown only three men into the furnace, "He answered and said, Lo I see four men loose, walking in the midst of the fire, and they have no hurt; and the form of the fourth is like the Son of God" (Dan. 3:25).

IV. MESSIANIC PROPHECIES

Before the incarnation of Christ, a great deal concerning his life and ministry had been recorded prophetically. These prophecies were all fulfilled literally in Christ's first advent, which assures us those prophecies relating to his second advent will also be literally fulfilled. Some of these are recorded in obscure or figurative language (cf. Gen. 49:10; Isa. 11:1). Even though predictive in nature, these prophecies were normally written in the past tense. Because prophecies are horizontal and not vertical in nature, often they may include aspects of Christ's first and second advent (cf. Isa. 61:1-2).

When interpreting messianic prophecies, two principles should be remembered. The first is that of time element. One prediction may be fulfilled at two intervals. When Christ read from Isaiah 61:1-2, He stopped in the middle of verse 2 because the next part referred to His second advent. The second principle is that of double fulfillment, that a prophecy may be fulfilled more than once in some cases (cf. Joel 2:28-32; Acts 2:16). Though not comprehensive, the following chart summarizes some of the major prophecies concerning Christ.

Prophecy	Old Testament	New Testament
1. Born of the Seed of Woman	Genesis 3:15	Galatians 4:4
2. Born of a Virgin	Isaiah 7:14	Matthew 1:23
3. Son of God	Psalm 2:7	Matthew 3:17
4. Seed of Abraham	Genesis 32:18	Galatians 3:16
5. Son of Isaac	Genesis 21:12	Luke 3:23, 34
6. Son of Jacob	Numbers 24:17	Luke 3:23, 34
7. Tribe of Judah	Genesis 49:10	Hebrews 7:14
8. Family line of Jesse	Isaiah 11:1	Matthew 1:6
9. Through David	2 Samuel 7:12	Matthew 1:1
10. Born at Bethlehem	Micah 5:2	Matthew 2:1
11. Time of His Birth	Daniel 9:25	Galatians 4:4
12. Presented with Gifts	Psalm 72:10	Matthew 2:11
13. Herod kills the Children	Jeremiah 31:15	Matthew 2:16
14. His preexistence	Micah 5:2	Col. 1:17
15. Descent to Egypt	Hosea 11:1	Matthew 2:14-15
16. He shall be called Lord	Psalm 110:1	Luke 2:11
17. Shall be Immanuel	Isaiah 7:14	Matthew 1:23
18. Shall be a Prophet	Deut. 18:18	Matthew 21:11
19. Priest	1 Sam. 2:35	Hebrews 3:1
20. King	Numbers 24:17	Matthew 27:37
21. Judge	Isaiah 33:22	John 5:30
22. Special anointing of Holy Spirit	Isaiah 61:1-2	Luke 4:15-21
23. Preceded by a Messenger	Isaiah 40:3,5	John 1:23
24. Called a Nazarene	Isaiah 11:1	Matthew 2:23
25. Zealous for God	Psalm 69:9	John 2:15-17
26. Ministry to begin in Galilee	Isaiah 9:1	Matthew 4:12, 13, 17
27. Ministry of miracles	Isaiah 35:5-6	Matthew 9:35
28. Teacher of parables	Psalm 78:2	Matthew 13:34
29. He was to enter the Temple	Malachi 3:1	Matthew 21:12

30.	He was to enter Jerusalem on a donkey	Zech. 9:9	Matthew 21:6-11
31.	Stone of stumbling to the Jews	Psalm 118:22	1 Peter 2:7
32.	Light to the Gentiles	Isaiah 60:3	Acts 13:47-48
33.	Resurrection	Psalm 61:10	Acts 2:31
34.	Ascension	Psalm 68:18	Acts 1:9
35.	Seated at right hand of God	Psalm 110:1	Hebrews 1:3
36.	Betrayed by a Friend	Psalm 41:9	Matthew 10:4
37.	Sold for 30 pieces of Silver	Zech. 11:12	Matthew 26:15
38.	Money thrown in God's House	Zech. 11:13	Matthew 27:5
39.	Price given for Potter's Field	Zech. 11:13	Matthew 27:7
40.	Forsaken by disciples	Zech. 13:7	Mark 14:50
41.	Accused by false witnesses	Psalm 35:11	Matthew 20:59-61
42.	Wounded and bruised	Isaiah 53:5	Matthew 27:26
43.	Dumb before His accusers	Isaiah 53:7	Matthew 27:12-19
44.	Smitten	Isaiah 50:6	Matthew 26:67
45.	Mocked	Psalm 27:7-8	Matthew 27:31
46.	Fell under the Cross	Psalm 109:24-25	Matthew 27:31, 32
47.	Hands and feet pierced	Psalm 22:16	Luke 23:33
48.	Crucified with thieves	Isaiah 53:12	Matthew 27:38
49.	Prayed for His persecutors	Isaiah 53:12	Luke 23:34
50.	Rejected by His own people	Isaiah 53:3	John 7:5, 48
51.	Hated without cause	Psalm 69:4	John 15:25
52.	Friends stood far off	Psalm 38:11	Luke 23:49
53.	People shook their Heads	Psalm 109:25	Matthew 27:39
54.	Stared Upon	Psalm 22:17	Luke 23:35
55.	Garments parted and lots cast	Psalm 22:18	John 19:23,24
56.	Suffered Thirst	Psalm 69:21	John 19:28
57.	Gall and vinegar offered Him	Psalm 69:21	John 19:28-29
58.	Forsaken by God	Psalm 21:1	Matthew 27:46
59.	Committed Himself to God	Psalm 31:5	Luke 23:46
60.	Bones not broken	Psalm 34:20	John 19:33
61.	Heart broken	Psalm 22:14	John 19:34
62.	Side pierced	Zech. 12:10	John 19:34
63.	Darkness over land	Amos 8:9	Matthew 27:45
64.	Buried in rich man's tomb	Isaiah 53:9	Matthew 27:57-60
65.	Voluntary death	Psalm 40:6-8	
66.	Vicarious suffering	Isaiah 53:4-6	
67.	Ridiculed	Psalm 22:6,7	
68.	Spit upon	Isaiah 50:6	Matthew 27:67

V. THE TYPES OF JESUS CHRIST

One of the more disputed aspects of Christology is that of types. Unfortunately, there have been those who have abused types by making all or many pictures into types. Other Christians are reluctant to acknowledge the existence of any types. Essentially, there are four positions on typology among Christians today. First is the exclusionary view that claims there are no types in Scripture and concludes the study at that point. The next position held by some Christians is the declarative view that types occur, but only as they are so declared in the Bible. The third is the analogy view held by some who are desirous of finding types wherever they can find an obvious parallel between the Old and New Testament. A common example of this is probably the recognition of Eliezer, the servant of Abraham, as a type of the Holy Spirit and also Joseph as a type of Christ. The fourth view is the hidden or mystical view which holds that all of Scripture contains types because the Bible is a supernatural Book. In the minds of these Bible students, because the cross is referred to as a tree in the New Testament, the occurrence of most trees in the Old Testament is a type of the coming Cross.

William Moorehead defines the idea of a type claiming, "Types are pictures, object-lessons, by which God taught His people concerning His grace and saving power."[19] *The New Scofield Reference Bible* suggests, "A type . . . is a divinely purposed illustration of some truth. It may be: (1) a person (Rom. 5:14); (2) an event (1 Cor. 10:11); (3) a thing (Heb. 10:19-20); (4) an institution (Heb. 9:11-12); or (5) a ceremonial (1 Cor. 5:7)."[20] While the Bible contains typical teaching about many subjects, the largest number of types relate to the purpose and

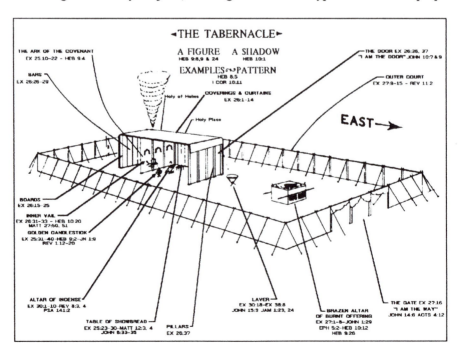

work of Christ and are therefore part of the study of Christology.

A type shows the preexistence of Jesus Christ, although it does not provide a cause-and-effect argument. If the Old Testament types are predicting Christ who is to come, then God must have inspired the writing of that type. The divine writer must have had a prior knowledge of events or persons that would come into existence, therefore types imply preknowledge that was not based on prediction, but knowledge of actual events.

One of the most generally accepted types in Scripture is that of the tabernacle. While some writers have attempted to find meaning in the pattern of threads and the number of boards, Sumner Wemp has taken a more sane approach to the subject. According to Wemp, "The most important thing is not to inform people with truth but to transform them with great truth. The tabernacle is filled with transforming truth."[21] The diagram on the previous page illustrates the plan of the tabernacle and notes its major truths.[22]

The religion of the Jews was in part to point them to Christ who is the fulfillment of the Law. It is only natural, then, to expect the various feasts of the Jewish calendar to be typical of Christ. The following chart illustrates how Jesus fulfilled the major feasts in the Jewish years as recorded in Leviticus 23.[23]

THE FEAST (Leviticus 23)	THE FULFILLMENT IN CHRIST
Passover (April)	Death of Christ (1 Cor. 5:7)
Unleavened Bread (April)	Holy Walk for Christ (1 Cor. 5:8)
Firstfruits (April)	Resurrection of Christ (1 Cor. 15:23)
Pentecost (June)	Outpouring of the Spirit of Christ (Acts 1:5, 2:4)
Trumpets (September)	Israel's Regathering by Christ (Matt. 24:31)
Atonement (September)	Cleansing by Christ (Rom. 11:26)
Tabernacles (September)	Rest and Reunion with Christ Zech. 14:16-18)

The study of types should be governed by several guiding principles. First, it should be recognized that every type had a historical reality. To argue that an event has a typical significance is not to deny its historicity or to remove any meaning from that context. The primary purpose of a type is not to be a type—but to accomplish its historic purpose. In accomplishing that aim, the type formed an analogy.

Not only does a type speak of an historic reality, but it also identifies a spiritual reality. It is a likeness that was ordained by God. That which exists in the Old Testament is similar to some other truth in the New Testament. Although it appears that most types are in the Pentateuch, they are scattered throughout the Scriptures.

The controlling point in typology is the Word of God. A type is a valid biblical type when it is designated or interpreted in the New Testament. A type is not a type unless it is said in Scripture to be a type. Without this control, we would do great disservice to the Word of God, having no standard by which it is to be interpreted. Those who push the interpretation of types too far call into question their commitment to historical grammatical interpretation. Also, although much truth can be learned from the study of types, no doctrine should be based on a typical interpretation.

VI. THE ANOINTED OFFICES OF CHRIST

Christ fills the threefold anointed offices of prophet, priest and king. The first reason why these are called anointed offices is that a person was inducted into the three offices when he was anointed: as prophet (1 Kgs. 19:16), as priest (Exod. 29:4-7; Lev. 8:12), and as king (1 Sam. 10:1; 16:13; 1 Kgs. 19:15). Apparently, oil was used to anoint a person into office, symbolic of the Holy Spirit who would give His wisdom and power. *The New Scofield Reference Bible* notes that Jesus was now to receive His anointing with the Holy Spirit (Matt. 3:16) into His threefold office of prophet, priest and king. In the Levitical order (Exod. 29:4-7), the high priest was first washed then anointed, while Christ's priestly work did not begin till He "offered Himself without spot to God" (Heb. 9:14), and His full manifestation as King-Priest after the order of Melchizedek awaits the Kingdom (Gen. 14:18 note), yet He was then anointed once for all.[24]

The second reason these are called "anointed offices" is that the term "Christ," a Greek word (its Hebrew equivalent, "Messiah") is translated "the anointed One." This title recognizes three anointed offices belonging to Christ: (1) Prophet (Deut. 18:15-19), (2) Priest (Heb. 4:14-16), and King (Acts 17:7).

The idea that these three anointed offices applied to the Messiah in Jewish literature is generally accepted. But in the performance of these offices, Jesus actually fulfilled them beyond the success of any previous person. L. D. Bevan notes,

Jesus as the Offerer of Himself perfected the function of the priest, as He became the Lamb of God who taketh away the sins of the world. He thus completed the threefold ministry of the Messiah as the Prophet who reveals, the Priest who offers and intercedes, the King who rules. In Him, the offices are commingled. He rules by His sacrifice and His teaching; He reveals by His kingship and His offering.[25]

Strong adds,

> Although these terms are derived from concrete human relations, they express
> perfectly distinct ideas. The prophet, the priest, and the king, of the Old Testament
> were detached but designed prefigurations of him who should combine all these . . . in
> himself, and should furnish the ideal reality, of which they were the imperfect
> symbols.[26]

A. THE PROPHETIC OFFICE OF CHRIST. When Israel was preparing to enter the Promised Land,
God instructed them not to learn and practice the false religions of Canaan. Rather than have
them to be satisfied with these illegitimate means of gaining spiritual insight, God promised to
give the nation prophets who would speak for Him. Though each prophet had a message from
God for the people, their presence would also serve as a reminder of another promise God
made. "The LORD thy God will raise up unto thee a Prophet from the midst of thee, of thy
brethren, like unto me; unto him ye shall hearken" (Deut. 18:15). This "Prophet" was none
other than Jesus Christ Himself.

The prophets of God were often unpopular among their own people. This was often due to
their message of judgment. Many times the people would rebel against God's message that
judged their sin. The prophet was simply doing his job. He represented God before the people
and gave them God's message. Prophecy was not only foretelling but also forthtelling and for
telling. Strong warns against making too narrow a definition of the prophet, stating,

> Here we must avoid the narrow interpretation which would make the prophet a mere
> foreteller of future events. He was rather an inspired interpreter or revealer of the
> divine will, a medium of communication between God and men.[27]

1. *Spokesman for God—"For teller."* If God had a message to give to this world, how
could He do it? The answers to that question are unlimited, for God could do anything. The
problem is that God has chosen to limit Himself to a strategy of using people who know the
message to tell others who do not know. In the Old Testament, God revealed a message to His
prophets and they in turn gave the message to the nation. Some of these men described this
revelation in terms of visions (Isa. 1:1; Ezek. 1:1). Others simply acknowledged the coming of
the Word of the Lord (Jer. 1:4; John 1:1). Commonly, these men simply announced with
authority, "Thus saith the LORD" (Obad. 1:1). Nahum and Habakkuk described their message
in terms of a "burden" (Nah. 1:1; Hab. 1:1). These prophets knew they were speaking on
behalf of God.

Jesus preached the message of God, and so fulfilled the office of prophet. Everything Jesus
said was the Word of God. In fact, "His name is the called The Word of God" (Rev. 19:13).
Jesus consciously said and did the will of the Father while here on earth. He told the religions
leaders of His day, "The Son can do nothing of himself, but what he seeth the Father do: for
what things soever he doeth, these also doeth the Son likewise" (John 5:19). Later in the same
conversation Jesus said, "I can of mine own self do nothing: as I hear, I judge: and my

judgment is just; because I seek not mine own will, but the will of the Father which hath sent me" (John 5:30).

2. *Prediction—"Foreteller."* When we think of prophecy, our first thought is normally that of predicting future events. In the role as foreteller, Jesus made several prophecies. He told His disciples about the coming of the Holy Spirit (John 14:26) which was fulfilled at Pentecost (Acts 2:1-4). Further, He described the ministry of the Holy Spirit in this age (John 16:16-17). He also described His death, burial and resurrection to His disciples (Matt. 16:21) and told them He would come again (John 14:2-3). Additional prophecies made by Christ dealt with the church age (Matt. 13) and the existence of the church itself (Matt. 16:18).

One of the tests of the true prophet in the Old Testament was that his prophecies came to pass as predicted (Deut. 18:22). Jesus had been clearly demonstrated to be a genuine predictive prophet in the Old Testament tradition. The accuracy with which his prophecies were fulfilled gives the Christian greater confidence in the accuracy of what is currently unfulfilled prophecy, i.e., the return of Christ.

3. *A Preacher to People—"Forth-teller."* In His wisdom, God has always "sought for a man among them" (Ezek. 22:30) whenever He chose to communicate His message. Missionaries have discovered today that national workers are more effective in reaching their own people than are international workers. When people can identify with the messenger, they will respond to the message. This is one of the reasons why Jesus came as a man. "And the Word was made flesh, and dwelt among us, (and we beheld his glory, the glory as of the only begotten of the Father,) full of grace and truth" (John 1:14). Jesus became a man so men could effectively communicate with Him and His message.

Jesus taught the people the things concerning God. Nicodemus, a Pharisee and ruler of the Jews, acknowledged, "Rabbi, we know that thou art a teacher come from God: for no man can do these miracles that thou doest, except God be with him" (John 3:2). When Jesus taught, "the people were astonished at his doctrine: for he taught them as one having authority" (Matt. 7:28-29). Speaking for God, Jesus spoke with authority. Several extended discourses of Jesus are recorded in Scripture, including the Sermon on the Mount (Matt. 5-7), the seven parables of the Kingdom (Matt. 13), the Olivet Discourse (Matt. 24-25), and the Upper Room discourse (John 13-16).

B. THE PRIESTHOOD OF CHRIST. A second anointed office appointed by God in the Old Testament was that of the priest. His main function was to represent man before God. The job of Israel's high priest was to appear before God to make intercession for the people. The priest was the one who offered the sacrifice upon the altar. Because God is a just but forgiving God, the priest could always tell the Jews that he was representing God who would forgive them if they met His conditions. The priest was usually a channel of forgiveness while the prophet was usually a channel of judgment. The people would have chosen to see a priest over a prophet any day.

According to Strong, "The priest was a person divinely appointed to transact with God on man's behalf. He fulfilled his office, first by offering sacrifice, and secondly by making intercession. In both these respects Christ is priest."[28]

Jesus is our great high priest. The Bible teaches, "He is able to save them to the uttermost that come unto God by him, seeing he ever liveth to make intercession for them" (Heb. 7:25). As our high priest, Jesus is constantly interceding for us. He understands the problems we encounter in life, having experienced the same when He lived on earth. "For we have not an high priest who cannot be touched with the feeling of our infirmities, but was in all points tempted like as we are, yet without sin" (Heb. 4:15). When we discuss the priesthood of Christ, we must rely heavily on the Epistle to the Hebrews, as Bevan demonstrates.

The chief source of the priestly conception of Our LORD is the Epistle to the He[brews]. Christ is declared to have by Himself purged our sins (He **1** 3); to taste of death for every man (He **2** 9); that He might be a merciful and faithful High Priest to make reconciliation for the sins of people (He **2** 17; cf He **3** 1); the community of sacrifice (He **3** 14); our great High Priest has passed into the heavens (He **4** 14); His pitifulness (**4** 15); the authority and power of Christ's priesthood fully set forth (He **5**). Christ was made a High Priest after the order of Melchizedek (He **5** 6). The priesthood of Christ being of the order of Melchizedek is more excellent than the Aaronic priesthood (He **7**). Christ's priesthood being eternal, that of the Aaronic is abolished (He **8**). Christ's high-priesthood is made effectual by His own blood; and He entered once for all into the holy place, and has become the Mediator of a New Covenant (He **9** 11-15). Christ is forever the representative of man in heaven (He **9** 24-28). Christ by the sacrifice of Himself forever takes away sin, and has consecrated the new and living way to God (He **10**). He is the Mediator of the New Covenant (He **12** 24). The entire Epistle is steeped in the conception of Christ's priesthood.[29]

The priesthood of Jesus is superior in that other priests have died, whereas Christ "ever liveth" (Heb. 7:25). His priesthood is more secure in that God swore with an oath concerning it (Heb. 7:21). The Old Testament priests could only offer sacrifices that pointed to a complete offering for sin yet future. As Jesus hanged on Calvary, He offered the final sacrifice for sin. "We are sanctified through the offering of the body of Jesus Christ once for all" (Heb. 10:10).

C. THE KINGSHIP OF CHRIST. God appeared reluctant to give Israel a king like the Gentile nations because He was their king. But when God finally allowed Israel to have a king, the earthly sovereign was made responsible to represent Him. The king was the leader of the nation and filled the third "anointed" office. In this manner, Christ so fills the anointed office of King. In application of this doctrine, Christians were persecuted in the first century when they taught the kingship of Christ (Acts 7:7). They recognized that Jesus alone must be the single supreme Ruler in their life. This was offensive to Rome, who believed their Caesar was both god and king.

Strong suggests,

Christ's kingship is the sovereignty of the divine-human Redeemer, which belonged to him of right from the moment of his birth, but which was fully exercised only from the time of his entrance upon the state of exaltation. By virtue of this kingly office, Christ rules all things in heaven and earth, for the glory of God and the execution of God's purpose of salvation.[30]

1. *Jesus is King.* The kingship of Christ is seen in His deity. Because he is God, he is also King. Paul gave praise "Unto the King eternal, immortal, invisible, the only wise God, be honor and glory forever and ever" (1 Tim. 1:17). In heaven "they sing the song of Moses the servant of God, and the song of the Lamb, saying, Great and marvelous are thy works, Lord God Almighty; just and true are thy ways, thou King of saints" (Rev. 15:3). The Romans considered their Caesar to be a god. Christians, on the other hand, recognized Jesus alone to be their King. The idea of calling Jesus "King" implied a claim to His deity.

2. *Jesus has a kingdom.* Every king has a domain over which he rules. Jesus is no exception. Jesus said, "My kingdom is not of this world" (John 18:36), but He never denied He had a kingdom. It was the custom of the Romans to identify the crime of a condemned man on the cross upon which he died. Jesus was executed as "The King of the Jews" (John 19:19). When He returns to this earth, He will do so to establish His kingdom. Revelation 20 describes His future kingdom as a thousand-year reign of peace on the earth. Theologians call this the Millennial Kingdom, and it is discussed more fully later in this book.

3. *Jesus has subjects.* Christ is now a ruler to those who submit their lives to Him. Someday, "At the name of Jesus every knee shall bow, of things in heaven, and things in earth and things under the earth; and . . . every tongue should confess that Jesus Christ is LORD" (Phil. 2:10-11). Today, those who receive Christ as Lord and Savior recognize the kingship of Christ in their life. Jesus told a parable equating the Christian with a servant. He concluded, "So likewise ye, when ye shall have done all those things which are commanded you, say, We are unprofitable servants: we have done that which was our duty to do" (Luke 17:10). One of the unique differences between the Christians of the New Testament and those of today is their attitude toward their relation with Christ. They saw Him as a supreme ruler and themselves as slaves in comparison. Perhaps if we had a similar biblical conviction today we would see similar biblical results.

VII. THE VIRGIN BIRTH OF CHRIST

At the beginning of this century, liberal theologians were greatly influenced by the humanistic attitude to Christianity that manifested itself in an anti-supernatural approach to doctrine. Fundamental doctrines were denied, such as the verbal inspiration of Scriptures, the substitutionary atonement, the physical resurrection and the bodily return of Jesus

Christ at the end of this age. Of the fundamentals, the virgin birth was usually the first to be denied. Liberal theologians tried to maintain that belief in the virgin birth was not necessary, hence it could be denied.

The virgin birth of Christ is not an independent doctrine, which we can receive or reject without affecting our Christianity. It is one of the foundation stones of Christianity. Our faith will crumble if it is removed. This doctrine is tied to inerrancy, Christ's sinless character, the atonement and other key doctrines of the Bible. If Jesus was not born of a virgin, He would be unable to save Himself, because He would not be a sinless Savior. If we cannot accept the virgin birth of Christ, very little credibility remains in the Bible. Therefore, we must understand the virgin birth if we are going to understand our faith.

In discussing the importance of the doctrine of the virgin birth of Christ, Louis Sweet notes,

> It involves in general the question, never more vital than at the present time, of the trustworthiness of the gospel tradition. This particular fact, i.e., the virgin-birth has been a favorite, because apparently a vulnerable, point of attack. But the presuppositions of the attack and the method according to which it has been conducted involve a general and radical undermining of confidence in the testimony of the gospel witnesses.[31]

Sweet's contention has long been that of fundamentalists. The doctrine of the virgin birth of Christ has become a sort of test case for Christians. As early as January 1924, Clinton Howard warned,

> Some say that belief in the virgin birth is not important. But it is. If this attack upon His cradle is allowed to go unchallenged, they will attack his tomb next, and end their attack upon His cross. If they are allowed to deny the miracle of His birth and we keep silent, they will attack the miracle of His resurrection and the miracle of His incarnation; and we will soon be without any Christ.[32]

A. THE VIRGIN BIRTH IN PROPHECY. As many as seven biblical authors believed and wrote of the virgin birth of Christ. Together, these men wrote 29 or 30 books of the Bible. If we choose to deny this doctrine, we would raise the issue of the credibility of some of the most prominent and prolific Bible writers. This is true in both the Old and New Testament. Three of these seven authors spoke prophetically of the virgin birth, the others wrote after the fact.

1. *Moses.* When Moses quoted the words of God in Gen. 3:15, he became the first biblical writer to imply the virgin birth. After Adam and Eve sinned in the Garden of Eden, God had to immediately judge their sin. Even in judgment, however, God demonstrated Himself as a merciful God. He told the serpent, "I will put enmity between thee and the woman, and between thy seed and her seed; it shall bruise thy head, and thou shalt bruise his heel" (Gen. 3:15). When God introduces a theological subject in Scripture, usually He speaks

embryonically (called the Law of First Reference). This means that the doctrine is there in "seed" form. When God introduced the prospect of salvation to Adam and Eve and the whole race, the implication of the virgin birth was present. This first mention of salvation in Scripture alludes to the virgin birth when it speaks or "her seed." If the coming Messiah was to have a normal physical birth, the "seed" would also have come from Adam or another man. Certainly, God who created the world in six days knew the biological nature of the human being. God knew the man produced the "seed" which is joined to the woman's "egg," thus conceiving a new life. But God made this reference to a woman's "seed" because He knew His Son would not have a human father. God would be the Father of His only begotten Son, and a virgin would give birth to "her seed."

Commenting on this verse, Keil and Delitzsch note,

> If then the promise culminates in Christ, the fact that the victory over the serpent is promised to the posterity of the woman, not of the man, acquires this deeper significance, that as it was through the woman that the craft of the devil brought sin and death into the world, so it is also through the woman that the grace of God will give to the fallen human race the conqueror of sin, of death, and of the devil. And even if the words had reference first of all to the fact that the woman had been led astray by the serpent, yet in the fact that the destroyer of the serpent was born of a woman (without a human father) they were fulfilled in a way which showed that the promise must have proceeded from that Being, who secured its fulfillment not only in its essential force, but even in its apparently casual form.[33]

2. *Isaiah.* Probably the best known Old Testament verse teaching the virgin birth is found in Isaiah. God had instructed Isaiah to allow King Ahaz to ask God to perform a miracle. Ahaz, apparently apathetic to God and the divine message, refused to ask God for a sign. The Lord chose to give a sign to the king who had rejected it: "Therefore the LORD himself shall give you a sign; Behold, a virgin shall conceive, and bear a son, and shall call his name Immanuel" (Isa. 7:14). Some have commented this was an unfair sign because it was impossible for Ahaz to witness the virgin birth that occurred many years after his death. It must be remembered, however, that Ahaz had already rejected the sign before it was identified.

Some also argue that when he wrote this verse Isaiah did not mean a "virgin" but rather a "young maid." Actually, the Hebrew word "*almah*" can be translated either way. In defining the term "*almah*," Lawlor notes,

> It has been shown in the preceding brief consideration of *almah* in the eight other passages where it occurs (Gen. 24:43; Exod. 2:8; 1 Chron. 15:20; Psa. 46:1; 65:25; Prov. 30:19; Song of Solomon 1:3; 6:8), that it is impossible for anyone to prove in any of these occurrences that the word *almah* means anything else than "virgin."[34]

But the context suggests Isaiah was talking about a virgin. A non-virgin having a child would not be an extraordinary event, but would be expected. The introduction of a miraculous sign implies the use of "virgin" rather than "young woman." Also, today there can be a big difference between a young lady ready for marriage and a virgin. That was not likely in the Old Testament. Under Mosaic law, a young woman could be stoned if she was found pregnant out of wedlock. Contemporary birth control methods and therapeutic abortions were not available to cover one's promiscuity in Bible times. Also, the threat of death by stoning and the moral standards of the day prevented the loose morality so common today. Even if Isaiah was referring to a young woman ready for marriage, it is reasonable to assume she had not known a man. When the Septuagint version of the Old Testament was translated, they used the Greek word that could only mean "virgin." These Jewish translators felt this was the best understanding of what the prophet was saying. Until comparatively recent times, it was generally assumed by translators that Isaiah here refers to a woman who had not known a man.

One of the reasons given by critics for rejecting the idea of a virgin birth is that another Hebrew word, *bethulah*, could have been used to more clearly identify a virgin. But as Lawlor observes,

> The difference between the two words, *almah* and *bethulah*, seems to be that *bethulah* suggests the state of a maiden who is living with her parents, and whose marriage is not yet impending. *Almah* indicates a maid who has been withheld from intimacy with a man, but who is approaching readiness to engage in marriage.[35]

Not only are there cultural and traditional reasons for accepting the translation of the word "virgin," there is a biblical mandate. When Matthew wrote under the inspiration of the Holy Spirit, he cited this verse to demonstrate that Christ's birth was fulfilling Bible prophecy. In doing so, he followed the LXX translation and used a Greek word which could only be translated "virgin." If he had so desired, he could have used another Greek word to identify a young woman, but this is not the word chosen by the Holy Spirit. Matthew notes, "Now all this was done, that it might be fulfilled which was spoken of the LORD by the prophet, saying, Behold a virgin shall be with child, and shall bring forth a son, and they shall call his name Emmanuel, which being interpreted is, God with us" (Matt. 1:22-23).

3. *Jeremiah.* The third Old Testament writer to speak prophetically of the virgin birth was also a major prophet. "How long wilt thou go about, O thou backsliding daughter? for the LORD hath created a new thing in the earth, A woman shall compass a man" (Jer. 31:22). Most of the early fundamentalist writers pointed to this verse to show that even the weeping prophet believed in and taught the virgin birth. Though women have given birth to men since the birth of Eve's first son, the emphasis here is that God is performing a new thing. This requires a unique event, different from just the birth of another baby boy. Jeremiah's use of the word "create" in this verse implies the Lord will use His divine power to accomplish the task. Most older commentaries agreed that the word "man" could be a reference to the God-man (Isa. 9:6).

B. THE VIRGIN BIRTH IN HISTORY.   As three Old Testament writers wrote prophetically of the virgin birth, four New Testament writers wrote historically of the virgin birth.

1. *Matthew.*   Just as the virgin birth was implied at the beginning of the Old Testament, so it is fully revealed at the beginning of the New Testament.   Matthew clearly believed Mary was a virgin until the birth of Christ.   He cites Isaiah 7:14, identifying the birth of Christ as the fulfillment of Isaiah's prophecy (Matt. 1:22-23).   On two occasions, Matthew identifies the Holy Spirit as the source of Mary's son (Matt. 1:18, 20).   In listing the genealogical data concerning Christ, Joseph is listed as the husband of Mary, but not the father of Jesus.   Even though this is an argument from silence, its omission is not accidental.   Matthew records that Joseph married Mary knowing her condition.   Then he clearly states, "And knew her not till she had brought forth her firstborn son; and called his name Jesus" (Matt. 1:25).   Even in announcing the birth of Jesus, it was the birth of "her son" (vs. 25), not "his son" or even "their son."

In Matthew's account of the birth of Christ, there are at least seven direct or indirect statements suggesting Jesus was born of a virgin.   Since Matthew was one of the original twelve apostles, it is reasonable to assume that the doctrine of the virgin birth of Christ was one of the original parts of "the apostles' doctrine" taught to the members of the Jerusalem church (Acts 2:42).

2. *Luke.*   Matthew's Gospel was written by a Jew primarily to a Jewish audience.   The only other Gospel writer to emphasize the virgin birth of Christ was a Gentile writing primarily to a Gentile audience.   It is particularly significant that Luke, a medical doctor, should be among the men that the Holy Spirit chose to comment on the doctrine of the virgin birth.   Luke twice calls Mary a virgin.   He tells of an angel sent by God "to a virgin espoused to a man whose name was Joseph, of the house of David; and the virgin's name was Mary" (Luke 1:27).   When she learned she was to become a mother, "Then said Mary unto the angel, How shall this be, seeing I know not a man?" (Luke 1:34).   Later, Luke listed the family tree of Mary, not Joseph.   Here he identified Jesus as "being (as was supposed) the son of Joseph" (Luke 3:23).

Luke also teaches the virgin birth by his careful phrases.   He calls Jesus "the Son of the Highest" (Luke 1:32) and "the Son of God" (Luke 1:35), but never clearly identifies Him as the son of Joseph.

Luke was both a medical doctor and historian concerned with accuracy "to write unto thee in order . . . that thou mightest know the certainty of those things, wherein thou hast been instructed" (Luke 1:3-4).   The virgin birth was not simply a rumor, but rather an event that was investigated by a historian who was also a physician.   Because a woman trusted her doctor, Mary probably told Dr. Luke more of the details of the virgin birth than she would tell others.   He then wrote under the inspiration of the Holy Spirit the events of which he was sure.

3. *John.* John records the events of Jesus arguing His divine origin with the Jewish leaders. Jesus told them He came from the heavenly Father (John 8:38). The Jews answered Jesus that their father was Abraham (v. 39). Then in retaliation, the Jews cast a "veiled accusation" at Jesus. They said "we be not born of fornication" (John 8:41). In this they imply that Jesus was born out of wedlock. From this, we gather that news of Mary's pregnancy before the wedding to Joseph was public knowledge. This gives added historical credibility to the virgin birth.

4. *Paul.* The fourth New Testament writer to teach the virgin birth was the apostle Paul. Writing to the churches in the province of Galatia, he said, "But when the fullness of the time was come, God sent forth His Son, made of a woman, made under the law" (Gal. 4:4). The readers of Galatians were concerned with Old Testament law, so they would have been careful to list the genealogies from father to
son. But Paul recognized the uniqueness of this birth. Jesus was "made of a woman." This means more than a simple acknowledgement that Jesus had a mother. It suggests that Jesus

FOUR STATEMENTS OF CHRIST'S SINLESSNESS	
SCRIPTURE	TRUTH
2 Cor. 5:2	Christ knew no sin
Heb. 4:15	Christ was without sin
1 Pet. 2:22	Christ did no sin
1 John 3:5	In Christ is no sin

had only a mother. This is a reasonable assumption when we realize that both Paul and Luke were closely related in the ministry, and both accepted the virgin birth.

C. THE VIRGIN BIRTH IN THEOLOGY. At stake in the controversy surrounding the doctrine of the virgin birth of Christ are a number of other doctrines. If Jesus had a human father, he would have inherited a sin nature. In that case, he would be unable to save Himself, let alone be the sinless substitute for the sins of the world. With human parents, it would be impossible for Him to be the Son of God.

1. *Sinless character of Christ.* If Jesus had a human father, He would have inherited the sin nature of Adam, the head of the human race. "Wherefore as by one man sin entered into the world, and death by sin, so death passed upon all men, for all have sinned" (Rom. 5:12). It would only have taken one sin to make Jesus a sinner. The only way Jesus could be a man without a sin nature was to have parents without a sin nature. Jesus is the only begotten Son of

the heavenly Father and was born of a virgin, being conceived by the Holy Spirit. Hence He became flesh.

2. *Word of salvation.* When Paul implied the virgin birth of Christ, he also identified a purpose in His coming, "to redeem them that were under the law, that we might receive the adoption of sons" (Gal. 4:5). God required a lamb "without blemish or spot" as a sacrifice for sin (Exod. 12:5). Jesus was unblemished in that He did not have a sin nature, and unspotted in that He lived a sinless life. Because of this, Paul can say, "For he [God] hath made him [Christ] to be sin for us, who knew no sin" (2 Cor. 5:21).

3. *Son of God.* A man can only be the son of his father. This universal principle also applies to the Son of God. Jesus is called "the Son of the Highest" (Luke 1:32) and the "Son of God" (Luke 1:35). This could only have been true if Mary was a virgin when she conceived and gave birth to her son.

4. *Inerrancy.* A key battle among theologians today is over the question of inerrancy. If the doctrine of the virgin birth is false, then we can have no confidence in the accuracy of anything else in Scripture. The following chart illustrates what books we would question in our Bible if we denied the virgin birth.

THE VIRGIN BIRTH AND INERRANCY			
	Virgin Birth Taught	Author	Writings
1.	Gen. 3:15	Moses	Genesis Exodus Leviticus Numbers Deuteronomy
2.	Isa. 7:14	Isaiah	Isaiah
3.	Jer. 31:22	Jeremiah	Jeremiah Lamentations
4.	Matt. 1	Matthew	Matthew
5.	Luke 1:3	Luke	Luke Acts (Hebrews?)
6.	John 1:13	John	John 1, 2, & 3 John Revelation

7.	Gal. 4:4	Paul	Romans 1 & 2 Corinthians Galatians Ephesians Philippians Colossians 1 & 2 Thessalonians 1 & 2 Timothy Titus Philemon (Hebrews?)
If the virgin birth is an unreliable fact, then 24 or 25 of the 66 books of the Bible are also unreliable.			

5. *Supernatural power of God.* When Mary was confronted with the announcement that she would give birth to the Son of God, she asked, "How shall this be, seeing I know not a man?" (Luke 1:34). She learned the answer to her question when the angel observed, "For with God nothing shall be impossible" (Luke 1:37). If the truth were known, the real reason some theologians deny the virgin birth of Christ is their unwillingness to recognize a supernatural God.

VIII. THE KENOSIS

The incarnation of Jesus Christ is central to all Christian doctrine. "The Word became flesh and dwelt among us" (John 1:14). The earthly life, ministry, and passion of our Savior are predicated upon the fact that He was God in human flesh. The Scripture passage which has aroused most controversy concerning the Lord's incarnation is Philippians 2:6-7. These verses comprise what has been called the "kenosis passage."

A. CHRIST EMPTIED HIMSELF.

1. *Definition.* The term "*kenosis*" is derived from a Greek word used in Philippians 2:7 that describes what happened when Christ became a man. The term is translated in the King James Bible "made himself of no reputation." It is translated "He emptied himself" in the New American Standard Version. This one word has perhaps motivated more investigation than any other in the New Testament. For ages theologians have faced the dilemma of interpreting this one word, "*kenosis*." They cannot deny that "Christ emptied Himself," but "What was poured out?" Can Christ give away part of His deity and remain God? Can God be less than God? The solution to the kenosis problem is found in a threefold explanation. "Christ emptied Himself" by: (1) veiling His glory, (2) accepting the limitations of human nature, and (3)

voluntarily giving up the independent use of His comparative attributes.   John Walvoord comments on the third aspect of *kenosis*.

> The act of kenosis as stated in Philippians 2 may therefore be properly understood to mean that Christ surrendered no attribute of Deity, but that He did voluntarily restrict their independent use in keeping with His purpose of living among men and their limitations.[36]

When Jesus came to live among men over two thousand years ago, people did not recognize the One they met. Jesus is God—always was and always will be. Yet it was God in the form of a man that was symbolically rejected by the innkeeper, and later to be rejected, hated, and even crucified. Yet, He was no ordinary man. When Jesus became a man, He remained God. He was truly God during His earthly ministry. Hodge describes the unique person.

> The whole immutable divine essence continued to subsist as the same eternal person. That divine person now embraced a perfect human nature, exalted by, yet dependent upon, the divine nature, to which it is united.[37]

A few conservative scholars hold a different interpretation of Philippians 2:7. Paul K. Jewett cites B. B. Warfield in support of his position that, "An expression such as this must be understood as a figurative and dramatic way of expressing the marvelous condescension of our Lord."[38]   To interpret the word "*kenosis*" in a figurative way is not consistent with grammatical-historical hermeneutics, nor does it satisfy grammatical demands of the text. For Christ, who was God before time began, to take on "the form of a servant" was indeed a humiliating experience, but Philippians 2:7 is a bold doctrinal declaration in the midst of an otherwise instructional passage. The subject of the passage is a literal, historical event, the incarnation of Jesus Christ.

2. False theories of the Kenosis. Among the false theories of the *kenosis* which have been proposed are those of Gess, Beecher, Ebrard, Martensen, and Thomasius.[39] W. F. Gess and H. W. Beecher both argue that Jesus was not God during His life on earth. In explaining the *kenosis*, they say Jesus gave up all His comparative and moral attributes.[40] If Jesus gave up His attributes, that would make Him less than God. Ebrard claims He gave up the right to be worshipped, by emptying Himself of "the glows of the attributes." Ebrard maintains that Christ still possessed divine attributes while on earth, but "only in the time-form appropriate to a human mode of existence."[41] In other words, His attributes were hidden. A third argument by Hans L. Martensen is that Jesus gave up the divine self-consciousness, meaning He had the attributes of God, but did not know it. "Martensen postulated the existence of a double life in the incarnate Logos from two non-communicating life-centers."[42] If Jesus were God, but did not know it, then we have an obligation to question the omniscience and truthfulness of God. Still others such as Thomasius will argue that Jesus   abandoned   only   the   absolute,   or comparative, attributes of God while His essential attributes of holiness, love, truth, etc., were retained and revealed in His life on earth.[43] *The International Standard Bible Encyclopedia* writer, Burton S. Easton, has been somewhat influenced by this view because he defines "*kenosis*" as a term which "in recent years has acquired a still more technical sense, i.e., of the Son's emptying Himself of certain attributes, esp. of omniscience."[44] A problem exists if we say that Jesus could have given up any attributes. If He had, He would have ceased to be God.

In refutation of these false theories, it must be noted that all of them contain common or similar errors. To rob God of any attributes would be to rob God of deity. It would mean that God is no longer immutable (unchanging), and therefore causes Him to be less than God (cf. Psa. 90:2). If one class of attributes is not essential to deity, then another class of attributes is not essential. What standard could be used to determine what attribute is essential? The occurrence of the word "*kenosis*" has given theologians a problem, but at some point undiminished deity must touch limited humanity. God chose the word "*kenosis*" to be the point in contact. We cannot change the word "*kenosis*," nor can we change the nature of God. In our human finite understanding we must struggle to see how the two fit together. And as they interface, we see that God has chosen the best term to help us understand a difficult topic. And out of this difficulty we have a better view of Christ than could otherwise be attained.

We disagree with those who have arrived at a false view of the *kenosis*. But, in the following passage Jesus reveals that He retained the comparative attributes: (1) omniscience— John 2:24-25; "Jesus knew all men . . . knew what was in man; John 18:4, "Jesus, knowing all things that should come upon him." (2) Omnipotence—John 14:11; 5:36; 10:25, "the works that I do in my Father's name; they bear witness of me." (3) Omnipresence—John 1:48; 3:13, "And no man hath ascended up to heaven, but he that came down from heaven, even the Son of man which is in heaven." (emphasis added)

One of the chief purposes of the Gospel of John was to illustrate the deity of Christ. "But these are written, that ye might believe that Jesus is the Christ, the son of God; and that believing ye might have life through his name" (John 20:31). John's use of the term "Son of God" refers to deity. Jesus was "the only begotten Son of God," which means He possessed the nature and character of His Father while on earth. John begins His Gospel by arguing, "In the beginning was the Word, and the Word was with God, and the Word was God" (John 1:1). Describing Jesus when He became a man, John wrote, "And the Word was made flesh, and dwelt among us (and we beheld his glory, the glory as of the only begotten of the Father), full of grace and truth" (John 1:4). "God in becoming man did not diminish His deity, but added a human nature to the divine nature."[45] Therefore, the *kenosis* was a self-emptying, not a self-extinction on the part of Christ. In support of the fact that Christ continued to be God during His life on earth, Buswell notes,

If Paul had thought that Jesus in His self-emptying had deprived Himself of any of the essential divine attributes, he could never have spoken of Him in the exalted terms which he constantly used. See for example his statement (Colossians 2:9) that "in Him dwells all the fullness of deity in bodily form." Paul's thought is certainly not that the Second Person of the Trinity deprived himself of certain characteristics.[46]

THE KENOSIS: CHRIST EMPTIED HIMSELF	
1.	Christ veiled His divine glory.
2.	Christ subjected Himself to human limitation.
3.	Christ voluntarily gave up the independent use of comparative attributes.

B. WHAT IS THE SELF-EMPTYING?

1. *Veiling His glory.* J. B. Lightfoot in his commentary on Philippians defined *kenosis*, "stripped Himself of the insignia of majesty."[47]   Wisely, Jesus hid His glory when He became a man. No one could see God, yet man must know what God is like. "No man hath seen God at any time; the only begotten Son, who is in the bosom of the Father, he hath declared Him" (John 1:18).   When Old Testament believers saw a Christophany, they were often fearful for their lives. They knew that sinful man could not look upon God and live. The glory of God was also the judgment of God; the unprotected person who saw it died.   When Moses spent forty days alone with God on Mount Sinai, it was necessary to cover his face when he came down because it reflected the glory of God. The people could not look upon him.

When John was on the Isle of Patmos, he too had a vision of Christ. When John saw Jesus in the full glory that was His from the beginning, John wrote, "And when I saw him, I fell at his feet as dead" (Rev. 1:17). When Paul had a similar vision of Christ, he was blinded with light from heaven (Acts 9:3). Later he wrote of being "caught up into paradise, and heard unspeakable words, which it is not lawful for man to utter" (2 Cor. 12:4). When Isaiah saw the Lord in the Temple, he cried out, "woe is me" (Isa. 6:1-8).

The apostle John clearly declares that both the glory and the nature of God dwelled in the body of Jesus Christ. "And the Word was made flesh and dwelt among us, (and we beheld his glory, the glory as of the only begotten of the Father), full of grace and truth" (John 1:14). Leon Morris calls this verse "the most concise statement of the incarnation."[48]   The verb "dwelt" is the Greek word *eskenosen* which literally means "to tabernacle" or "to pitch one's tent." It is derived from the same root as the noun *skene* which means "tent" or "tabernacle."[49] Jesus was God as He "tabernacled" among men in a body of human flesh. Just as God lived among men in the tabernacle in the wilderness, now God has a different tent. God dwells among men in the human tent, the body that was born in Bethlehem. Just as the tabernacle was the place of redemption in the Old Testament, so the human tent/body of Jesus Christ will be the place of redemption in the new. Vincent notes,

The tabernacle was the dwelling-place of Jehovah; the meeting-place of God and Israel. So the Word came to men in the person of Jesus. As Jehovah adopted for His habitation a dwelling like that of the people in the wilderness, so the Word assumed a community of nature with mankind, an embodiment like that of humanity at large, and became flesh.[50]

R. V. Tasker observes:

> The Greek word *eskenosen* implies 'dwelt as in a tent' or 'tabernacled.' Its use here
> might be to emphasize that the incarnate life of the Word was but a temporary
> sojourning. More probably, it means that the divine presence, which it was believed
> was especially 'located' in the tabernacle and later in the temple, now came to dwell
> in the man Jesus.[51]

On the mount of transfiguration, Christ briefly allowed the fullness of His glory to be
witnessed by Peter, James and John. That brief manifestation stands in sharp contrast against
the manner in which Jesus was viewed daily by those around Him. The transfiguration
illustrates that Jesus possessed glory, that which was not revealed during His life on earth.

If Jesus had not veiled His pre-incarnate glory He could not have accomplished what He
came to earth to do. Christ had to hide His glory temporarily as He sought to redeem the souls
of men. Hodge accurately states,

> If Christ is not in the same person both God and man, he either could not die, or his
> death could not avail. If he be not man, his whole history is a myth; if he be not God,
> to worship him is idolatry, yet not to worship him is to disobey the Father. - John V.,
> 23.[52]

After the work of atonement was done, Jesus could pray, "And now, O Father, glorify thou
me with thine own self with the glory which I had with thee before the world was" (John 17:5).

2. Submitting to the limitations of humanity. As a result of the incarnation, Jesus became
the God-man. He was at all times both God and man as He lived on earth. When Jesus
became flesh, He voluntarily subjected Himself to human limitations. Before His birth, Heaven
was His throne and He traveled the universe at will. Now in the flesh, Jesus was limited to the
distance that a man could walk on the paths of Galilee. The Son of God who created water,
voluntarily lived in a body that got thirsty.

Strong has described five stages in which Christ "emptied Himself" or "made himself of
no reputation." The kenosis is the ultimate act of emptying oneself.[53]

Jesus was born into this world as other humans. His was a normal, physical birth (Luke
2:1-20), even though His conception was supernatural. As a child, He developed as every
human must. Jesus grew in mental, physical, spiritual and social areas of life (Luke 2:52). He
had the essential elements of human nature. He was body (Heb. 10:5), soul (John 12:27), and
spirit (Mark 2:8). Jesus became hungry when He did not eat (Matt. 4:2). He became tired and
asked the woman at the well for water to drink (John 4:6). Throughout His life on earth, Jesus
was just as human as any of us, subject to experiencing the same emotions sorrows, pains and
hurts any man experiences. G. C. Berkouwer correctly observed,

. . . Scripture speaks of Jesus Christ as truly God and truly man. He is one of us, like us in all things. our brother. sharing *our* flesh and *our* blood . . . He entered into the reality of our world and life. having assumed the form of a servant.[54]

The willingness of Jesus to limit Himself to becoming a man gives us confidence that He understands the events of our life. "For we have not an high priest who cannot be touched with the feelings of our infirmities. but was in all points tempted like as we are, yet without sin" (Heb. 4:15). Because He has experientially known the frustrations of humanity, we have a "God of all comfort" (2 Cor. 1:3) upon whom we can depend.

3. *He surrendered the independent use of His comparative attributes.* The third aspect of his self-emptying took place by the voluntary non-use of His comparative attributes.

THE COMPARATIVE ATTRIBUTES OF GOD	
OMNISCIENCE	Mark 13:32
OMNIPRESENCE	John 1:14
OMNIPOTENCE	John 11:41-42

Perhaps the best expression of omnipotence is the performing of the miracles by Christ. Even though Jesus was known as a miracle worker, He performed those miracles through the power of the Holy Spirit (Matt. 12:28). He voluntarily gave up the independent exercise of His omnipotence and He ministered in the power of the Holy Spirit or the Father (Luke 4:1, 14, 18). On various occasions He made it clearly known that He was doing the work of His Father. "Then answered Jesus, and said unto them, 'Verily, verily, I say unto you, The Son can do nothing of himself, but what he seeth the Father do; for whatever things he doeth, these also doeth the Son likewise'" (John 5:19).

During His earthly life and ministry, Jesus did not apparently exercise the independent use of His comparative attributes. The nature of His humanity and the purpose of His mission demanded that He live and minister in the power of the Father and Holy Spirit. He was omniscient, but did not know the time of the Second Coming (Mark 13:32). He was omnipresent, but when He became flesh, He limited Himself to being in one place at one time. He was omnipotent, yet He prayed to God to perform the raising of Lazarus from the dead. Jesus had not lost these attributes of God, but rather, in the process of emptying Himself, He voluntarily engaged in the non-use of His comparative attributes. Theissen supports this view with the following statement.

Thus, though he did not surrender his divine attributes, he willingly submitted to not exercising certain attributes of deity so that he could identify with man.[55]

IX. The Hypostatic Union

A. UNDERSTANDING THE PERFECTION OF CHRIST. A most difficult doctrine to understand concerning Christ is the relationship of His divine and human nature. The Bible affirms that Jesus is both God and man. But does this mean He is half God and half man, or does it maintain He is God sometimes and man at other times? The answer seems to imply a contradiction, for Christ is completely God at all times and completely man at the same time. Is it possible for two different capacities and natures to occupy the same space and identical existence at the same time? Would such a union make Christ less than God or more than man? Would such a union of the divine and human result in a hybrid being whose nature was a mixture of deity and humanity?

Christianity has generally affirmed that Jesus is the God-man. The term is hyphenated to reflect that Jesus is totally God and totally human at the same time. Both sides of the second Person of the Trinity are seen in the titles that describe Him. In the Gospel of John, Jesus is often called the Son of God, which implies His deity, while in Luke He is often called the son of man, which implies humanity. He is at all times 100 percent God in His nature, words and actions. Yet at the same time He is not diminished in His humanity. He is 100 percent man. He left footprints in the sand as He walked on the shore of the Sea of Galilee. He needed rest when He was tired and nourishment when He hungered; but the winds and waves obeyed Him because He was God. He was at all times and in every way the God-man, totally God and totally man. This union of divine and human is one of the most difficult doctrines to understand, yet one which is foundational to understand the person of Christ. And if Christ is not properly perceived, then Christianity is not properly understood.

The difficulties become less severe when the central issues are clarified. The doctrine involves questions concerning the union of two natures and not the union of two persons.

Before analyzing the hypostatic union, it is necessary to define the term. First, a clear distinction must be made between the person of Christ and the natures of Christ. The confusion or misunderstanding of these two terms easily results in heresy.

"Nature" is defined by Webster as "the inherent character or basic constitution of a person or thing." John Walvoord speaks of "nature" as being "the real essence, the inward properties which underlie all outward manifestation."[56]

Louis Berkhof says "nature" is that which,

denotes the sum-total of all the essential qualities of a thing, that which makes it what it is. A nature is a substance possessed in common with all the essential qualities of such a substance.[57]

From the above quotations a definition of nature must include its properties and its function. These two are included in the following definition; "that intrinsic make-up of being, without which being would cease to exist (spirit, personality, volition, ability, etc.)." Therefore the human nature of Christ refers to His intrinsic humanity without which the incarnate person of Jesus Christ could not have existed as man. The divine nature of Christ refers to His intrinsic deity without which Christ could not have existed in either His preincarnate or incarnate states, i.e., without which He could not be God.

The next word to define is "person." Berkhof distinguishes it as,

> A complete substance endowed with reason, and, consequently, a responsible subject of its own actions. Personality is not an essential and integral part of a nature, but is, as it were, the terminus to which it tends. A person is a nature with something added, namely, independent subsistence, individuality.[58]

As seen earlier in discussing the nature of God, the term "person" involves intellect, emotion, will and self-perception that includes a moral identity. A person is larger than a personality, although it is surely included in the definition. In discussing the hypostatic union it is important to stress that it is the union of two distinct natures in one person, Jesus Christ the God-man. Christ has two natures, but He is one person.

B. THE INCARNATION. The most familiar thing that people usually remember is His birth celebrated at Christmas. Many who have a basic acquaintance with the events surrounding that birth fail to understand that it represented the merging of God and man into one human body. John summarizes this miracle in one statement. "And the Word was made flesh, and dwelt among us" (John 1:14). When we use the term "incarnation," we are speaking of the miracle of God becoming man, yet remaining God.

1. *The Eternal Word.* The title "Word," used only by the apostle John, implies the deity of Jesus Christ. The usual meaning of the term "Word" is a medium of communication. When John called Jesus the Word, he was implying that God communicated Himself to man through Jesus Christ. Vincent observes,

> The Logos of John is the real, personal God (i. 1), the Word, who *was* originally before the creation with God, and *was* God, one in essence and nature, yet personally distinct (i. 1, 18); the revealer and interpreter of the hidden being of God; the reflection and visible image of God, and the organ of all His manifestations to the world.[59]

The Word was the embodiment of a Person—showing to people what God was and what God revealed to them.

The theologian William G. T. Shedd interprets the term "Word" to mean the eternal Son of God before His incarnation. Even though it is a correct understanding of the preincarnate Christ, one gets the impression in reading Shedd that the eternal Word is distinct from Jesus Christ because a human nature was joined at the virgin birth—incarnation.

Previous to the assumption of a human nature, the Logos could not experience a human feeling because he had no human heart, but after this assumption he could; previous to the incarnation, he could not have a finite perception because he had no finite intellect, but after this event he could; previous to the incarnation, the self-consciousness of the Logos was eternal only, that is, without succession, but subsequent to the incarnation it was both eternal and temporal, with and without succession.[60]

This trinitarian person was not complex, but simple; God the Son, but not God-man; the un-incarnate Logos (Λογος ασαρκος), not the incarnate (Λογος ενσαρκος). Jesus Christ is not the proper name of the unincarnate second person of the trinity, but of the second person incarnate.[61]

Again, the knowledge of the God-man depended upon the divine nature for its amount, and this proves that the divinity is dominant in his person. The human mind of Jesus Christ stood in a somewhat similar relation to the Logos, that the mind of a prophet does to God. Though not the same in all respects, because the Logos and the human mind in the instance of Jesus Christ constitute one person, while the Holy Spirit and the inspired prophet are two persons, yet in respect to the point of dependence for knowledge, there is an exact similarity.[62]

The divine-human person, Jesus Christ, was produced by the union of the divine nature of the Logos with a human nature derived from a human mother. Before this union was accomplished, there was no theanthropic person. There was the divine person of the Logos existing in the Trinity before this union, and there was the unindividualized substance of Christ's human nature existing in the virgin Mary before this union; but until the two were united at the instant of the miraculous conception, there was no God-man. The trinitarian personality of the Son of God did not begin at the incarnation, but the *theanthropic* personality of Jesus Christ did.[63]

Some New Testament scholars claim John got the title Word for Jesus from Greek philosophy. Others argue he was thinking of the Hebrew idea of wisdom, as the personification of wisdom described in Proverbs 5-8. But this author's conviction is that John was using the term "Word" as it was used literally in the Old Testament "The Word of God." As such John is meaning that Jesus Christ is the human revelation of God to men, just as in the Old Testament the Word of God was the vocal revelation of God to man. Since the term "Word" means expression or communication, John probably called Jesus the Word of God to remind his readers how God spoke over 1200 times in the Old Testament. The Word of the Lord, whether communicated audibly or through an agent, was the message from God to men. Since Jesus was the personification of the written and spoken Word of the Lord, He is the revelation of the Lord. He is the incarnate Word of the Lord, just as the Bible is the inspired Word of the Lord. Chafer notes:

(*Logos* – 'Word') is used in the New Testament about two hundred times to indicate God's Word written, and seven times to indicate the Son of God—the Living Word of God (John 1:1, 14; 1 John 1:1; 5:7; Rev. 19:13); and it is important to recognize that in either of these forms of the *Logos* both the divine and human elements appear in supernatural union.[64]

Jesus is the perfect, ultimate revelation of God. The first eighteen verses of the Gospel of John provide our fullest description of the Word. "In the beginning was the Word" (John 1:1) refers to the eternal origin of Christ. He did not begin at a specific point in time. Secondly, we are told through the use of "became" that at a point in time He became incarnate or assumed humanity. "The Word became flesh and dwelt among us" (John 1:14). Thirdly, the Word was engaged in active personal communion with God. This is seen where "The Word was with God" (John 1:1). The term "with" means Jesus was face to face with God. The fact that the Word and God are identified separately suggesting the plurality of the God-head, both are considered deity. Also, the deity of Christ is clearly asserted in the statement, "the Word was God" (John 1:1). Yet this verse cannot be translated "God was the Word," or "the Word was a God" as some religious cults suggest. To do so would ignore the rules of Greek grammar.[65] Groups like the Jehovah's Witnesses are unable to find a single reputable Greek scholar to acknowledge the possibility of translating the verse "The Word was a God" or "God was the Word," because that would be a violation of grammatical rules and would also deny the distinction between the Person of God the Father, and the Person of Christ. Even though Christ and the Father are separate, note the fourth observation: this passage concerns the unity of the Father and Son. They are one together, two consciousnesses, yet one essence. "There is nothing which is said to be true of God which is not said to be true of Christ and to the same degree of infinite perfection."[66]

John also points out that the Word was the avenue by which God expressed or revealed Himself. "No man hath seen God at any time; the only begotten Son, who is in the bosom of the Father, he had declared him" (John 1:18). The incarnate Word which is the continuation of the pre-incarnate Word, is the avenue whereby God showed to men what He was like.

A final and crucial observation concerning the Word may be made in this passage. "The Word was made flesh and dwelt among us" (John 1:14). The word "dwelt" means "to tabernacle." In the Old Testament, God's glory dwelt in the tabernacle. As Israel set up their tents in the wilderness around the tabernacle, the Shekinah glory of God descended on the holy of holies. This meant God's presence dwelt with Israel. In the New Testament, God comes to live with man in the human form, and God does not choose a tent to live with man in the human form, but dwells in a human body, a human tent. Just as God dwelt with Israel by His glory cloud in the Old Testament, so God dwells in a human tabernacle with His people in the New Testament. The body of Jesus Christ is likened to a tent that was called glorious. The idea of God dwelling among His people is prominent throughout Scripture. "What had been hinted at and even realized in a dim, imperfect fashion earlier was perfectly fulfilled in the Word made flesh."[67]

The Synoptic Gospel writers record the glorification of Jesus on the mount of transfiguration where His earthly body was transformed. But John describes a more glorious scene that is void of shining lights and changed countenances. It is simply the Son of God in sinless humanity. "And we beheld his glory, the glory as of the only begotten of the Father" (John 1:14).

JESUS THE WORD IN JOHN 1:18

1. Jesus is eternal
2. He is a person
3. He is face to face with God
4. He is deity
5. He is distinct from God
6. He is one with the Father
7. He is the expression of the Father
8. He is a continuation of the pre-incarnate Word
9. The glory of God is tabernacled in His body

---

2. *Jesus in human flesh.* Not only was Jesus God, but He was at the same time flesh. The term "flesh" speaks of His humanity. In the effort to combat the liberal denial of Christ's deity, conservative Christians have sometimes neglected His humanity. Dr. William G. T. Shedd seems to stress the deity of Christ to the point of de-emphasizing His humanity. Observe the following quotations taken from Shedd's *Dogmatic Theology.*

If the human nature and not the divine had been the root and base of a Christ's person, he would have been a man-God and not a God-man.[68]

The knowledge of the God-man depended upon the divine nature for its amount, and this proves that the divinity is dominant in his person.[69]

That the divinity is the dominant factor in Christ's complex person, is proved by the fact that the degree of his happiness was determined by it. The human nature had no more enjoyment than the divine permitted.[70]

Although Shedd's position on the deity and the humanity of Christ agrees basically with the historic orthodox beliefs of other conservatives, it appears that he has overreacted to the liberal views of such men as Gess and Dorner who have so humanized Jesus Christ that they take away from His deity.

When we say "virgin birth," we are really meaning a supernatural conception without the aid of man. Like any other child, Christ inherited His nature from His human parent. He had the divine nature of God, but His mother was human. Consequently, He has a human nature also. (Jesus did not possess a sin nature because it was not a part of the original nature of man.) Jesus identified with man in everything but sin. "For we have not an high priest who cannot be touched with the feeling of our infirmities, but was in all points tempted like as we are, yet without sin" (Heb. 4:15).

Jesus grew as a normal child would grow (Luke 2:52) and experienced the common development of a growing child. He had the limitations of human nature. There were times when Jesus got hungry (Matt. 4:2), and, on at least one occasion, He had to stop His journey to rest (John 4:6).

C. THE UNION OF NATURES. When we think of the dual nature of Christ, we must somehow not divide Him into two parts as though He had a schizophrenic personality or was two persons in one body. Rather we must think of Him in unity; He is the God-man. This union has been described a number of ways. Shedd publishes the clearest accounts of the statement from the Council of Chalcedon in A. D. 451.

> We teach that Jesus Christ is perfect as respects godhood, and perfect as respects manhood; that he is truly God, and truly a man consisting of a rational soul and a body; that he is consubstantial (ὁμοὐσιον) with the Father as to his divinity, and consubstantial (ὁμοὐσιον) with us as to his humanity, and like us in all respects sin excepted. He was begotten of the Father, before creation (πρὸ αἰώνων), as to his deity; but in these last days he was born of Mary the mother of God (θεοτόχος) as to his humanity. He is one Christ, existing in two natures without mixture (ἀσυγχύτως), without change (ἀτρέπτως), without division ἀδιαιρέτως without separation (ἀχωρίστως),—the diversity of the two natures not being at all destroyed by their union in the person, but the peculiar properties (ἰδιοτης) of each nature being preserved, and concurring to one person (πρόσωπον), and one subsistence (ὑπόστασιν).[71]

To summarize the Chalcedon creed, "Conservative doctrine forbids us either to divide the person or to confound the natures."

When the council said it could not "divide the person" it meant that Christ did not have two personalities (persons), but one. He did not have a perfect divine mind and a limited human mind—Christ had one mind. As humans we cannot understand it, but we can see it in the Gospels. As a person, Christ had one mind, one set of emotions as well as one volitional will.

Commenting again on this union, Shedd wrote: "The two natures, or substances . . . constitute one personal subsistence. . . . A common illustration employed by the Chalcedon and later fathers is, the union of the human soul and body in one person, and the union of heat and iron, neither of which loses its own properties."[72]

RESULT OF THE HYPOSTATIC UNION

1. The union of Christ's two natures into one Person.
2. The union of Christ's two natures was complete.
3. The union of Christ's two natures was constant.
4. The union of Christ's two natures is eternal.

---

1. *The union of two natures in one Person.* This union of the two natures of Christ into one person means they merged into the Person of Christ. Common man is both material and nonmaterial, body and soul. Man's personality exists in his immaterial nature or intrinsic being. Jesus possessed both a divine nature and a human nature, but the result is one Person. He had one intellect, one set of emotions and one volitional ability to make decisions. He did not vacillate between His previous experience as God and His human experience learned on earth. Christ had one coherent personality. He was one Person.

The two natures are bound together . . . by a bond unique and inscrutable, which constitutes them one person with a single consciousness and will—this consciousness and will including within their possible range both the human nature and the divine.[73]

2. *The union of two natures was complete.* Jesus did not act as God on some occasions and man at other times. We do not say that He performed miracles as God and suffered on the cross as a man. What Jesus did, he did as a unity. He was at all times and in all ways the God-man .

Christ uniformly speaks of himself, and is spoken of, as a single person. There is no interchange of 'I' and 'thou' between the human and the divine natures, such as we find between the persons of the Trinity (John 17:23) . . . The attributes and powers of both natures are ascribed to the one Christ, and conversely the works and dignities of the one Christ are ascribed to either of the natures, in a way inexplicable, except upon the principle that these two natures are organically and indissolubly united in a single person.[74]

3. *The union of two natures was constant.* Some have tried to understand the God-man by recognizing His work as God at times and His work as man at other times. The hypostatic union guarantees the constant presence of both the divine and human natures of Christ at all times.

4. *The union of His two natures is eternal.* When Christ took on human flesh in the incarnation, he did not give it up when he ascended back into Heaven. Today we worship a Person who is both God and man. The physical body that was born in Bethlehem is now seated at the right hand of the throne of God. The Hebrews were told of Jesus, "But this man, because

he continueth ever, hath an unchangeable priesthood" (Heb. 7:24). Jesus is the Man seated in glory. Paul reminded Timothy, "There is one God, and one mediator between God and man, the man, Christ Jesus" (1 Tim. 2:5). He reminded the Romans that their salvation was dependent upon the work of a man who had overcome the failings of the first man (Rom. 5:12-21). Strong agrees, "The union of humanity with deity in the person of Christ is indissoluble and eternal."[75]

In the following sections, three outlines have been used which come from Dr. John F. Walvoord's book *Jesus Christ Our Lord*. These outlines are being used because they provide the most complete, comprehensive overview of several factors related to the hypostatic union. These outlines also present concisely many of the most profound truths regarding this vital doctrine.

"THE RELATION OF THE TWO NATURES"[76]	
1.	The two natures were inseparably united in such a way that there was no mixture or loss of their separate identity.
2.	The two natures of Christ cannot lose or transfer a single attribute.
3.	The two natures of Christ are not only united without affecting the respective attributes of the two natures, they are combined in one Person.
4.	The attributes of both natures are properly attributed to His person.

1. *"The two natures were inseparably united in such a way that there was no mixture or loss of their separate identity."*[77] In the union of Christ's two natures, both natures remained distinct. The human and divine natures did not mingle or merge together into a third nature with a different expression. The idea that Christ's two natures merged into a third nature would imply their loss of separate identities. This is called the Monophysite heresy of the Eutychians. Eutychus was condemned in A. D. 451 by the Council of Chalcedon.

2. *"The two natures of Christ cannot lose or transfer a single attribute."*[78] The deity of Christ demands that His divine nature remain unchanged. The loss of any attribute would change His nature. Since attributes are the manifestation of the nature, it would be impossible for any nature to manifest attributes it does not possess. In the person of Christ, the attributes of both His natures may be found, but never does the human nature reflect divine attributes nor does the divine nature reflect human attributes. Each attribute finds its source in its respective nature within Christ's person. "It is emphatically said that the one nature does not change into the other. Each nature retains its properties and the properties of the one can never become the properties of the other."[79]

3. *"The two natures of Christ are not only united without affecting the respective attributes of the two natures, they are combined in one Person."*[80] Jesus Christ was not two persons in one body, but rather He was one person with two natures. His personality was never divided. He was not God and a man living together in one body. He was the unique Person, the God-man.

4. *"The attributes of both natures are properly attributed to His person."*[81] Although the attributes of both the divine and human natures remain intrinsic to their respective natures, they are all intrinsic to the person of Christ. Since the person of Christ includes two distinct natures, whatever attributes are characteristic of either nature, will be characteristic of Christ's person. It must be re-emphasized at this point that sin is not an essential element in human nature. It became a parasite attached to human nature at Adam's fall.

A SEVENFOLD CLASSIFICATION OF THE PERSON OF CHRIST[82]	
1.	Some attributes are true of His whole person.
2.	Some attributes are true only of Deity, but the whole person is the subject.
3.	Some attributes are true only of humanity, but the whole person is the subject.
4.	The person may be described according to divine nature, but description is predicated by the human nature.
5.	The person may be described according to human nature, but the description is predicated on the divine nature.
6.	The person may be described according to the divine nature, but the description is predicated on both natures.
7.	The person may be described according to human nature, but the description is predicated on both natures.

5. *Some attributes are true of His whole person.* There is only one Person, and as such, Christ possessed characteristics that would be true of His whole person. Christ must be God and He must be man. This is essential. In order for Christ to be the Mediator (1 Tim. 2:5) between God and man, He possessed human and divine attributes. But the point must be re-emphasized. They belonged to the incarnate Christ.

6. *Some attributes are true only of Deity, but the whole person is the subject.* Christ possessed characteristics true only of Deity, but the whole person is subject to Deity. When Christ spoke in John 8:58, "Before Abraham was, I am," He spoke as a united person, but what He said was true only of His divine nature. The same type of statement is found in John 17:5

where Christ declares His existence with the Father before the incarnation. The whole person of Christ is speaking, but only His divine nature was preexistent.

7. *Some attributes are true only of humanity, but the whole person is the subject.* Christ has characteristics of humanity, but His whole person is subject to humanity. In John 4:6, Jesus is said to have been "wearied" (tired). Matthew 4:2 speaks of Jesus as being hungry. These verses show that the person of Christ experienced conditions which are characteristic only of humanity. Deity does not become fatigued or hungry, but humanity needs food and rest. In these particular circumstances, the God-man was subjected to His human nature.

8. *The person may be described according to divine nature, but description is predicated by the human nature.* For the purpose of this discussion, "predicate" should be understood as "to take from or add to." In Matthew 9:1-8, Christ is questioned because He exhibited His divine prerogative by telling a palsy-stricken man, "Thy sins be forgiven thee." The verbal attack from the scribes came because they failed to recognize the deity of Christ as presupposed in His declaration that He could forgive sins. Then Christ healed the palsy victim to reveal his divine nature which they had not recognized. Even after the miracle, the multitude did not view Him according to His divine nature, but according to His human nature. Verse 8 says they "glorified God, which had given such power unto men."

9. *The person may be described according to human nature, but description is predicated on the divine nature.* In John 8:40, Jesus called Himself a man whom the unbelieving Jews sought to kill. The context of this declaration of His humanity also includes a declaration of His deity in verse 58. In verse 42, Christ states that His rejection by these Jews is due to the fact that he proceeded from God the Father, while these men were not children of God. These verses describe Christ as a man, but also show He was God.

10. *The person may be described according to the divine nature, but the description is predicated on both natures.* John 18:4 says that when Judas and the soldiers went to the garden to take Jesus captive, "Jesus therefore, knowing all things that should come upon him, went forth, and said unto them, 'Whom seek ye?'" Christ is shown to possess divine knowledge of the forthcoming events, yet the subsequent verses tell of His voluntary submission to His captors. In verse 11, He rebukes Peter's attempt to free Him and rhetorically asks, "The cup which my Father hath given me, shall I not drink it?" These verses describe Christ's divine nature, yet they also show Him voluntarily submitting to the torture and death which His human body must undergo to provide redemption for mankind.

11. *The person may be described according to human nature, but the description is predicated on both natures.* John 19:30 relates the closing scenes of Christ's crucifixion, "When Jesus therefore had received the vinegar, he said, it is finished: and he bowed his bead, and gave up the ghost." Again the human nature of Christ is portrayed as experiencing thirst, but more importantly the person of Christ is viewed as He died. The euphemistic

phrase "gave up the ghost" tells us of Christ's death. Death is an experience which is almost always associated with only the human nature of Christ. However, when Christ died on the cross, His divine nature as well as human nature died. Death is not cessation of life, but is equivalent to separation. The Father was separated from the sin that was on His Son. Although God, being omnipresent, could not be separated, in a sense, their fellowship was broken. There was not a real breach in the Trinity—God is immutable. If you sin and your fellowship with God is broken, you, in a sense, are forsaken by God—His fellowship is taken from you. This does not mean that God is not there. God of necessity is everywhere. God is in Hell because He is omnipresent. Christ's divine nature, in a sense, died in that He was separated from God. There is a serious problem here that has never been resolved. How could there be a breach in the Trinity? Luther said, "How could God, be forsaken being God?"

The most important results of the hypostatic union have been summarized well by Walvoord and appear in the following chart.

IMPORTANT RESULTS OF THE UNION OF THE TWO NATURES IN CHRIST[83]	
1.	The union of the two natures in Christ is related vitally to His acts as an incarnate Person.
2.	The eternal priesthood of Christ is also based on the hypostatic union.
3.	The prophetic office of Christ is related to the act of incarnation.
4.	The kingly office of Christ was dependent upon both the divine and human natures, and would have been impossible apart from the incarnation.
5.	The incarnate person of Christ is worshipped as the sovereign God.
6.	In the ascension of the incarnate Christ to heaven, not only was the divine nature restored to its previous place of infinite glory, but the human nature was also exalted.
7.	The union of the two natures in Christ, while not affecting any essential attribute of either nature, did necessarily require certain unique features to be manifested such as the absence of the sin nature, freedom from any act of sin, and lack of a human father.

X. THE TEMPTATION OF CHRIST

Understanding the doctrine of the temptation of Christ is foundational to understanding the doctrine of the hypostatic union. Since Christ's deity and humanity are asserted, then God must allow the relationship of the divine nature to the human nature of Jesus Christ to be empirically tested. As a result, a believer can have confidence that Christ has demonstrated that He is the God-man, and he can trust the claims of Christ.

There is no doubt that Christ successfully endured the test regarding His character. The Bible witnesses that He did not give in to temptation, nor violate the moral standards of God, nor was He inconsistent with the nature of His character, (2 Cor. 5:21; Heb. 4:15; 1 Pet. 2:22; 1 John 3:5). The first observation of the temptation of Christ was that the Holy Son of God demonstrated His sinless character—that He did not sin when given the opportunity. The second is that no one can say His character or nature was unchallenged, because Christ was actually tempted.

The temptation of Christ was not an accident where Satan just happened to catch up with Christ and, taking advantage of the circumstance, tried to get Him to violate His mission on earth or deny His nature. The temptation was instigated by Satan to carry out his evil desire. Satan attacked Christ because of his explicit desire to destroy Christ, just as he had destroyed his own lofty position with God before Creation. Even though the temptation was initiated by Satan, God would not have allowed His Son to be humiliated by the temptation if the ultimate results did not fit into God's fulfilled puzzle. God used Satan to demonstrate the sterling character of His Son, that, when faced with an alternate choice, Christ was not only able "not to sin, but He was not able to sin."[84]

Two problems arise out of the historical event of the temptation of Christ. First, was the temptation of Christ real? And, second, if the temptation was real, then was it possible for Christ to have sinned? The answer to these questions helps to explain the nature of the temptation and how it demonstrates the credibility of His deity.

These two questions are embolden in two words: "temptability" and "impeccability." Barnes defines "temptability" as "Generally understood as the enticement of a person to commit sin by offering some seeming enticement." Because of this definition, Barnes concludes, "In this sense our sinless Redeemer was absolutely untemptable and impeccable." Barnes uses the usual definition, but in this study "temptability" is defined to mean "to have an appeal." The internal desire to temptation and the external object of temptation are not included in the definition. Because Christ is different, temptability must be defined in light of His nature.[85]

In addition to understanding the nature of temptation, it is imperative to be aware of the nature of the temptee. Scriptures reveal the existence of four different groups and records their responses when subjected to temptation. The first group is the unregenerate. This group will invariably succumb to many temptations placed before them, simply because there is an absence of a restraining element within them. They are forced to rely upon their own character and stamina to resist temptation (but they desire evil). The second group is comprised of regenerated people. When the believer is confronted with temptation, a struggle emerges within him (Rom. 7:13-20), because the restraining element (the new nature) and the Holy Spirit, resist the temptation. At the same time his human sinful nature seeks self-indulgence. The believer's response to temptation is determined by his degree of submission to the Holy Spirit (1 John 4:4). The third group is represented by Adam and Eve. Apart from their communion with God, Adam and Eve did not possess a new nature or the assistance of the

Holy Spirit as available to believers today; also they did not have an innately evil nature. Rather, they had an innocent disposition to do good (unconfirmed holiness). Yet, as we learn from the original temptation, man in and of himself will eventually submit to the desires of the flesh. The fourth group is personified in the person of Jesus Christ. Not only was Christ equipped with a disposition to do good (due to the presence of deity and the ramifications of the hypostatic union), but He also was strengthened by the Spirit (Luke 4:24; Acts 10:38), and when these two elements are welded together with the immutable aspect of deity, they make it impossible for Christ to desire evil or to commit sin. However, this does not mean He is not susceptible to temptation. Even an invincible city with a powerful army is susceptible to a furtive attack.

Feinberg gives five stages of temptation, and states that sin does not occur until step four. His paradigm is built on the presupposition that man is attracted by sin. Jesus was attracted by that which was offered to Him, but probably did not go beyond step one. He desired but did not intend to satisfy himself at Satan's band.

FIVE STEPS TO SIN
1. Desire for something
2. Intention to have the object
3. Plan to get the object
4. Willingness to have the object, to put the plan into action
5. Bodily movement towards the object[86]

"Impeccability" means Christ could not sin and did not sin. Shedd gives meaning to this word. "An impeccable will is one that is so mighty in its self-determination to good that it cannot be conquered by any temptation to evil, however great."[87]

On a superficial examination, two verses seem to contradict each other. One verse says God cannot be tempted. The other says Christ was tempted. "God cannot be tempted" (Jas. 1:13). "He . . . was in all points tempted like as we are . . ." (Heb. 4:15). If Christ were God, (and He is God), does this mean He could not be tempted? It would seem inconsistent that God could or would desire sin in any form. Yet, on the other hand, if Christ were a true man (and He was true man), then He must have been capable of sinning.

We cannot say Christ was tempted in His human nature, but not tempted in His divine nature. The hypostatic union teaches that Christ is one person, which means he has one mind, one will and one set of emotions (the intellect, emotions and will are all involved in temptation to sin). Chafer examines the hypostatic union of Christ in light of the temptation and concludes,

> The human element in Christ certainly was never separated from the divine; still, the divine proved ever the dominant factor in His theanthropic being. He was not a man, then, to whom the divine nature had been added. He rather was God, who took upon Him by incarnation the form of a man. He became thereafter an indivisible Person. Whatever either nature did, His whole being did. No other such person ever existed and there will never be another. Because of the presence of His divine nature with manhood, then, He is incomparable. He could not be rendered peccable by the presence of His human nature: instead He was an impeccable, theanthropic Person. Had His humanity sinned, God would have sinned. A wire may be bent when alone, but not after it is welded into an unbendable bar of steel. His humanity could not contradict or dishonor His deity.[88]

Since Christ acted as a unit, He could not have desired sin as a human and at the same time rejected sin as God. Whatever temptation Christ faced, it did not confront Him in the form of lust or evil desire, as a human is confronted with temptation by a sinful nature. No evil nature (lust) could arise in Christ to mix with an outward enticement to sin.

> Temptations from evil desire have a different moral quality than those presented through innocent desire. The former are δι᾽ ἁμαρτίας, or ἐξ ἁμαρτίας not χωρις ἁμαρτίας. A temptation from pride, envy, or malice, is plainly different in its nature from the temptation from hunger experienced by our Lord in the wilderness; or from the desire to be acknowledged as the Messiah; or from the dread of suffering experienced by him in the garden of Gethsemane. "'When a temptation comes from without,' says Owen (Indwelling Sin, VI.), it is unto the soul an indifferent thing, neither good or evil, unless it be consented to. But the very proposal from *within*, it being the soul's own act, is its sin.'"[89]

When the Bible states that "God cannot be tempted with evil" (Jas. 1:13), a hyphen can be placed between "God" and "with evil." In other words, Christ as God cannot be tempted with evil, but this does not mean the Christ cannot be tempted. Christ was tempted, but not from a sinful nature. The nature of temptation must be defined. Therefore, the question can be asked, "What was Christ tempted to do?"

The nature of Christ's temptation was that He was asked to do the things He could do and the things He wanted: the results of which would have come from doing what Satan asked. The nature of His temptation was not with inherent evil, but with the fact that He, as God, was tempted to do the things He could do. The things Christ is asked to do are not inherently evil, but appear to be valid requests.

Christ had no sinful lust of any sort. This is taught in Christ's own words: "The prince of this world cometh, and hath nothing in me," John 14:30. It is also taught in Heb. 4:15, "We have a high priest who was in all points tempted like as we are, yet without sin." This text teaches that the temptations of Christ were "without sin" in their *source* and *nature*, and not merely, as the passage is sometimes explained, that they were "without sin" in their *result*. The meaning is not, that our Lord was tempted in every respect exactly as fallen man is—by inward lust, as well as by other temptations—only he did not outwardly yield to any temptation; but that he was tempted in every way that man is, excepting by that class of temptations that are sinful because originating in evil and forbidden desire.[90]

His temptation was to do things Christ could have done, but if He had succumbed to the tempter, it would have meant Christ had stepped outside the plan of God and Christ would have been inconsistent with the nature of the *kenosis*.

The nature of God is to do the miraculous or supernatural. Therefore, if Christ had done what Satan asked, He would have done what He had been accustomed to do and what He desired to do.

The word "desire," *epithumia*, is translated "lust and desire." "The essential point in $\dot{\epsilon}\pi\iota\theta\upsilon\mu\iota\alpha$ is that it is desire as impulse, as a motive of the will."[91] Hence, it is pure in its nature, but when tied to sinful man it is sin. When tied to the sinless Son of God, desire is direction of the will (Gal. 5:16). A desire in normal circumstances does not mean evil until it is directed at the wrong thing; then it becomes lust. (However, when desire comes from the sinful heart of man it is lust and is sin.) Christ desired to do the miraculous and to glorify Himself, which was the thing that Satan asked. Hence, when Christ was tempted, it was not with inherent evil, nor did it involve evil desires within Him. He wanted to do the things suggested by Satan, but to do them was outside the plan of God. He had the ability to do what He was asked, and He desired to do what was suggested, hence Christ was tempted. But He was not tempted with evil or tempted by evil desire, but if He had yielded, the act would have been sin.

The nature of God is to reveal Himself and His work. Christ wanted to manifest His deity with an act such as having angels bear HIM in the sight of the multitude. He wanted the worlds to fall down in adoration and worship Him. But if He had submitted to Satan, He would have violated the nature of the *kenosis* and He would have abdicated His purpose in coming into the world. In the *kenosis*, He had given up the independent exercise of His omnipotence. In the temptation He was asked to violate that contract. To do so would be inconsistent with His character. In the hypostatic union, He had united flesh with eternal deity. In the temptation He was asked to exercise half of His nature independent of the other half.

The validity of temptation is seen in the comparative light of the person actually doing it. It would not be a temptation for a man to turn stones into bread, because no human could do it. But Christ could do the things He was asked to do, therefore the temptation was real. But the temptations were not evil in themselves, nor did they hinge on, or imply, an evil nature in Christ. Some popular sermons suggest that there were three aspects to the temptation of

Christ: i.e., the lust of the flesh, the lust of the eyes and the pride of life (cf. 1 John 2:15-17). However, Christ was not tempted by these desires/lusts.

When the Bible teaches that "He was tempted in all points like as we are" (Heb. 4:15), it does not mean He faced a temptation to curse, express anger, or engage in illicit sex. It meant Christ was tempted in all points of His being, or in every aspect of His personality. He was so completely tempted that there were no aspect of His inner being that was untouched.

Since Christ was sinless, He was far more sensitive to hunger and abuse than the common man. One of the characteristics of God is unity, and Christ as God was perfect unity, which implies perfect self-understanding. When He was tempted in all points, it implies He was tempted in all His thinking, desires (emotions) and decision-making ability. Christ was tempted in every part of His being as a person is tempted in every part of human nature. The primary meaning of the phrase "every part of His being" refers to His desire. Christ wanted to do the things requested of Him. So, when a man is tempted with evil, he wants to do those things because man has an evil nature. (Christ was not tempted with every kind of evil, nor every kind of temptation.) But Christ was tempted just as we are, to work apart from the divine plan and purpose.

Perhaps the greatest temptation of Christ was not in the wilderness (Matt. 4:1-11), but when He was interceding in the Garden of Gethsemane. It was a temptation to recoil from drinking the cup of the judgment of God from taking the sin of the world upon Himself.

> The divine nature, at the very moment of this agony and passion, was sustaining the human nature so that it should not sinfully yield to what was the most powerful temptation ever addressed to a human nature: namely, the temptation to flee from and escape the immense atoning agony, which the God-man had covenanted with the Father to undergo. This is implied in Christ's words, "If it be possible, let this cup pass; nevertheless, not my will but thine be done. The cup that my Father giveth me, shall I not drink it?"[92]

No one can understand the temptation of a holy person to avoid becoming the judgment for the sins of the world.

> Christ had more temptations from Satan and the world than ever had any of the sons of men; and yet in all of them he had to do with that which came from without. But let a temptation be proposed to a man, and immediately he hath not only to do with the temptation as outwardly proposed, but also with his own heart about it.[93]

CONCLUSION. The word "temptability" means Christ was tempted, but He was not tempted with evil, nor was He tempted by evil desires. Therefore, the temptability of Christ complements the hypostatic union and demonstrates the perfection of deity. The word "impeccability" retains its historic meaning that Christ could not have sinned. Christ is immutable (Heb. 13:8; Heb. 1:12). Therefore, he could not sin.

A will may be positively holy and able to overcome temptation, and yet not be so omnipotent in its holy energy that it cannot be overcome. The angels who fell could have repelled temptation with that degree of power given them by creation, and so might Adam. But in neither case was it infallibly certain that they would repel it. Though they were holy, there were not impeccable. Their will could be overcome, because it was not omnipotent, and their perseverance was left to themselves and not made sure by extraordinary grace. The case of Jesus Christ, the second Adam, was different, in that he was not only able to resist temptation, but it was infallibly certain that he would resist it . . . .

. . . .

The success of temptation depends, in part, upon deceiving the person tempted. "Adam was not deceived, but the woman being deceived was in the transgression," 1 Tim. 2:14. A finite intelligence may be deceived, but an infinite intelligence cannot be. Therefore, the omniscience which characterizes the God-man made his apostasy from good impossible.[94]

Christ is omnipotent (since the argument of peccability implies weakness), therefore, Christ could not sin because He had no weakness. Christ is omniscient (sin frequently appeals to ignorance), therefore Christ could not sin because He knew all things. Christ is omnipresent (His presence in Heaven at the time of the temptation disallows sin), therefore, Christ could not sin for He lived a perfect life in Heaven at the moment of the temptation. "Christ was not only able not to sin, but He was not able to sin."

XI. THE DEATH OF CHRIST

One of the greatest questions of the ages involves the death of the Son of God who was love incarnate. How could anyone desire to murder Him, or even to harm Him? Was He not the Creator of all humanity and the personification of goodness to everyone? Yet He was tortured and killed. The symbolic hatred of mankind was vented against Him.

The early apostles seem to be guilt-ridden over their responsibility for His death. After all, Peter had denied Christ and with the others had fled. One of their own, Judas, had betrayed Him to the enemy. When assessing responsibility for Christ's death, who was responsible?

A. THE FATHER WAS RESPONSIBLE. (Isa. 53:6; 53:10; Psa. 22:15; 2 Cor. 5:21; Acts 2:28; Rom. 3:25; 1 John 4:10.) All of the above Scriptures evidence the fact that God the Father was actively involved in the death of Christ. The Father "laid on Him the iniquity of us all" and exacted upon Him the penalty for such iniquity. God was "pleased" to bruise Christ as an offering for our sins. Only the Father could have the authority to accept and command (decree) the substitutionary work of Christ's being made to be sin for us (2 Cor. 5:21). Before any Roman soldier ever touched the body of our Lord, He had already been "delivered by the determinate counsel and foreknowledge of God." Indeed, He is "the Lamb slain from the foundation of the world," the propitiation for our sins set forth by God the Father. "It is quite alien to biblical thought to overlook the agency of God the Father in the provisions of redemption and it is perversion to represent the Father as won over to the exercise of grace and mercy by the intervention of Christ's propitiatory accomplishment."[95]

B. THE SON WAS RESPONSIBLE. (John 10:17-18; Gal. 2:20; Matt. 20:28; Heb. 9:14-15; 1 Tim. 2:5-6.) Jesus foretold His death in John 10:17-18, where He clearly stated that no man could take His life, but rather he Himself would lay it down, knowing that He also had "power to take it again." In teaching His disciples the value of willing servitude, Jesus referred to the purpose of His earthly ministry as being "to minister, and to give His life a ransom for many." Paul speaks of Christ as the One "who gave Himself a ransom for all" (1 Tim. 2:6), and also as the One "who loved me and gave Himself for me" (Gal. 2:20). The giving of Christ's self refers not merely to His life of humble, willing service to others, but to His giving His life to provide for man's salvation. The evidence of Christ's willingness to die for us is further substantiated by Hebrews 9:14-15, where the Savior is presented as both the High Priest and the Holy Sacrifice who offered Himself (His life) to God on our behalf.

C. HUMAN RESPONSIBILITY. (Acts 4:27-28.) Although Christ's death was decreed by the Father and accomplished by the Son, it was also implemented by the hands of mortal men. In Acts 4:27-28 the death of Christ is partially attributed to "Herod, and Pontius Pilate, with the Gentiles, and the people of Israel." Luke 23:6-12 gives the account of Herod's involvement. Matthew 27:11-26 and John 18:28-19:16 narrate both Pilate's interrogations and the sentencing of Jesus to the cross. The conspiracy and wicked intent of the Jewish leaders to put Christ to death is exposed in Matthew 26:57-68. Matthew also records the treacherous bargain of Judas Iscariot (26:14-16), his betraying kiss (26:47-50), and his suicide that resulted from his guilt (27:3-10).

D. SATANIC RESPONSIBILITY. The instigator of enmity against Christ is Satan. John explicitly records that Satan entered into Judas at the Last Supper (John 13:27). The fact that Satan has long sought the destruction and overthrow of Christ is verified through Scripture (Isa. 14:12-15; Rev. 12:7-9; Col. 2:15; Eph. 6:12). The first recorded promises of our Savior's triumph (Gen. 3:15) includes a prophecy of Satan's involvement in Christ's death.

In one sense, every person who is born will ultimately die, but the birth of Christ was different from other men for many reasons, primarily because Christ came into the world for a purposeful, predicted and productive death. His death was not simply the termination of His life, because His death was purposefully for others; because His death was predictive, for Christ was the Lamb slain before the foundation of the earth; and because His death was productive in bringing eternal life to many. Just as the life of Jesus Christ changed mankind, so His death changed the makeup of eternity and Heaven.

In modern life, a medical officer usually includes the cause or reasons for death on a death certificate. Sometimes it is due to disease, accident, murder, suicide or just natural causes. Christ suffered a violent death, with several contributors or causal factors that brought on His sufferings and demise.

D. PURPOSE OF CHRIST'S DEATH. There are many reasons for the death of Christ. It is true that Christ's death was a result of His loyalty to what He believed; it was an expression of God's love, and it removed the stain from God's honor, that is, it demonstrated the righteousness, holiness and justice of God. These are but partial explanations of Christ's death and secondary insignificance in comparison with the main idea of His death. This section shall deal with the meaning and extent of the atonement of Christ.

In discussing the purpose of Christ's death, there are at least 11 reasons accomplishments.

Eleven Results/Accomplishments of the Death of Christ	
1.	The substitutionary work of Christ
2.	Redemption by blood
3.	Propitiation
4.	The demands of the law are satisfied
5.	Reconciliation
6.	Judgment of the sin nature
7.	Basis for daily cleansing
8.	The basis of forgiving sins committed before the Cross
9.	The basis of the national salvation of Israel
10.	Judging Satan
11.	The purification of things in heaven

1. *The substitutionary work of Christ.* The substitutionary work of Christ involves the fact that Christ is a substitute for sin and explores the heart of the text declaring the meaning of Christ's death—"When Thou shalt make His soul an offering for sin" (Isa. 53:10).

Included in the substitutionary work of Christ is the vicarious nature of His death. Hodge notes, "Vicarious suffering is suffering endured by one person in the stead of another," i.e., in his place. It necessarily supposes the exemption of the party in whose place the suffering is endured. A vicar is a substitute, one who takes the place of another and acts in his stead.[96] Since Christ was without sin, it is evident that He did not die for His own sin (John 8:46; 1 Pet. 2:22; Heb. 4:15). Christ died for the sins of others: He died in our place.

    a. Isa. 53:6: "Jehovah . . . laid on him the iniquity of us all."

    b. 1 Cor. 15:3: "Christ died for our sins" (cf. Rom. 5:8; 2 Cor. 5:21).

    c. 1 Pet. 2:24: "who His own self bore our sins in His own body" (cf. 1 Pet. 3:18).

d. Mark 10:45; John 10:11: "layeth down his life for the sheep."
e. Exod. 12; 1 Cor. 5:7: the true passover Lamb.
f. Isa. 53:10: the true sin offering (cf. Lev. 6:24-30; Heb. 10:1-4).

It is overwhelmingly evident that Christ died in our stead. There are, however, some objections to this interpretation.

The first objection to the idea of a substitutionary atonement is a lexical objection. This objection is based on the usage of two prepositions found in the Greek: *anti* and *huper*. The argument is that *anti* can only be translated "instead of." The second preposition, *huper*, is nearly always used when the sufferings and death of Christ are the subject. *Huper* means "in behalf of," "with a view to the benefit of." *Anti* is used as "instead of" (Matt. 5:28; 20:28; Mark 10:45; Luke 11:11; Rom. 12:17; 1 Thess. 5:15; 1 Pet. 3:9; and Heb. 12:16).

The first objection differentiates between *huper* and *anti*. Its purpose is to explain away Christ's substitutionary work. Shedd has exposed the error of such a lexical objection by pointing out that the two words are often used with the same purpose. "The preposition ὑπὲρ, [*huper*], like the English preposition "for," has two significations. It may denote advantage or benefit, or it may mean substitution. . . . The sense of "for" in these two prepositions must be determined by the context, and the different circumstances in each instance."[97]

The following Scriptures also show that *huper* is equivalent to *anti*; (Rom. 13; 2 Cor. 5:14; John 10:11, 15).

Another enlightening dimension of the usage of the prepositions *huper* and *anti* is discussed by Shedd as he notes:

The latter preposition [*anti*] excludes the idea of benefit or advantage, and specifies only the idea of substitution. The former [*huper*] may include both ideas. Whenever, therefore, the sacred writer would express both together and at once, he selects the preposition ὑπὲρ, [*huper*]. In so doing, he teaches both that Christ died in the sinner's place, and for the sinner's benefit.[98]

In several Scriptures a usage of *huper* occurs regarding Christ's death in our behalf: 1 Corinthians 15:3; Galatians 2:20; John 10:11,15; Titus 2:14; Galatians 3:13; Romans 5:8; and 2 Corinthians 5:21.

Apart from the refuted "lexical" objections, the major objection to the substitutionary death of Christ is that it is immoral for God to punish an innocent one, i.e., Christ. This "moral" objection errs severely in assuming that God and Christ are two beings as different from each other as two individual men. Such an objection fails to realize that Christ died, not of compulsion, but voluntarily (John 10:17,18; Matt. 20:28; Gal. 2:20). It is not immoral for the judge to pay the penalty Himself—if He chooses.

Another slightly different, moral objection says that satisfaction and forgiveness are mutually exclusive. This objection holds that if a substitute pays the debt that we owe, God cannot collect the debt for us also, but He is morally bound to let us go free; that is, on this theory, God does not exercise mercy in forgiving us, but merely does His duty.

The primary error of this second "moral" objection is that it overlooked the fact that the one who pays the debt is not a third party, but the Judge Himself. Forgiveness is, therefore, still optional with Him and may be offered upon terms agreeable to Himself. As Dr. D. James Kennedy once preached, "We shall be judged by the 'hanging judge,' that is, the Judge who Himself hanged upon a tree to pay the penalty for our offenses." On the cross of Calvary, God placed our sin upon Christ and accepted Him in our place as He provided for our atonement. "For He hath made Him to be sin for us, Who knew no sin, that we might be made the righteousness of God in Him" (2 Cor. 5:21). Paul reminded the Romans "that, while we were yet sinners, Christ died for us" (Rom. 5:8). The Bible teaches that Christ was the Christians' willing substitute at Calvary. Twenty-one verses say Christ died for us. Even though one verse should be enough to convince, when looking at them all, there can be no doubt about the substitutionary nature of Christ's death: (1. Matt. 20:28; 2. Luke 22:6, 20; 3. John 6:51; 4. John 10:11; 5. John 10:15; 6. John 10:18; 7. John 15:12; 8. John 15:13; 9. Rom. 5:6-8; 10. Rom. 8:32; 11. 2 Cor. 5:14; 12. 2 Cor. 5:21; 13. Gal. 2:20; 14. Gal. 3:13; 15. Eph. 5:2; 16. Eph. 5:25; 17. 1 Thess. 5:9,10; 18. 1Tim. 2:5-6; 19. Titus 2:13-14; Heb. 2:4; 20. 1 Pet. 3:18; 21. 1 John 3:16).

2. Redemption by blood. Since the law is eternal, unchangeable and applicable to every man, no man can escape the demands of the law. Since a degree of criminality is attached to every violation of the law and God will punish according to the degree of criminality (Luke 10:10-15; 12:47-48), every violation of the law will be punished according to a predetermined standard. Since every man has violated the law and will suffer its consequences, then there is no hope for those who have violated the law. Nothing in man can help him escape the criminality of his actions. Nor can God treat the violation as if it never occurred, neither can God forgive any violation arbitrarily. Since the law was an extension of the Person of God, then breaking the law is offending God, and God must be compensated before the person is saved.

God has two opposing, yet eternal, desires within His nature. First, God wants to let man go free, hence, God is satisfying His desire to be good or loving. On the other hand, God must punish every violation of a crime to the degree of its criminality, to satisfy His justice. Both desires in God were satisfied when He found another person to suffer the punishment of criminality, allowing man to go free (Gen. 22:8). To carry out this transaction, God's Son, Jesus Christ, satisfied man's violation of God's law. Christ was born without sin, lived a perfect life, neither breaking the Law or deserving its criminality. Christ took upon Himself criminality that had been accumulated by every man. Christ suffered in the place of man. Since punishment must be eternal and complete, Christ suffered ultimately for all criminality. This act, called the vicarious substitutionary atonement, means that Christ suffered in the place of the sinner (vicarious), and the death of Christ was both the substitute for our sin and the satisfaction of the law.

The symbol of this transaction was the actual blood of Jesus Christ which is a symbol of His substitutionary death. "It is *shed* blood which has always been required for deliverance, and thus it was in the type and the antitype, Christ in His crucifixion."[99] Yet, the symbol of the blood was not introduced at the time of the cross of Jesus Christ. It goes back into the pages of the Old Testament.

> The truth of God's requiring a blood sacrifice as the righteous ground for the remission of sin was established beyond all dispute in Old Testament times . . . from Abel's lamb to the day of Christ's death, is the only interpretation which fully and rightly construes all that the Bible presents on this its central theme of salvation.[100]

When Adam and Eve sinned, the Bible says, "And the eyes of them both were opened, and they knew that they were naked; and they sewed fig leaves together, and made themselves aprons" (Gen. 3:7). Adam and Eve experienced guilt that came from breaking the law of God. God did not punish them on the spot, for that would mean eternal death and separation from God. God knew that one day His Son would die for all men, including Adam and Eve. "The Lamb slain from the foundation of the world" (Rev. 13:8). Peter also tells us that the symbolic price of this transaction was "with the precious blood of Christ, as of a lamb without blemish and without spot" (1 Pet. 1:19). Therefore, God chose an animal, most likely a sheep, for later God's Son would be called the "Lamb of God that taketh away the sin of the world" (John 1:29). Although the account in the Garden of Eden does not include the word blood, the skins of the animals were given as a symbolic covering for their nakedness (Gen. 3:21). Because of their criminality, they deserved the wrath of God. Yet, they watched God put to death an animal, shedding innocent blood. As such, God was providing His sovereign grace to point them to Calvary where the Lamb of God would die for their sins. Adam and Eve left the garden realizing that "Without shedding of blood there is no remission" (Heb. 9:22). This was a type of salvation without works. Nothing that Adam and Eve did deserved salvation. The animal had shed its blood in Eden to provide a covering for their nakedness; even so the blood of Jesus Christ, the Lamb of God, covers the criminality of all who believe in Him, and robes them in His righteousness (Rom. 3:24-25).

Cain and Abel, sons of Adam and Eve, brought their sacrifices to God. Both brothers recognized the existence and the demands of God over their lives. Both brothers brought an offering to God, but only one offering was acceptable to God. Cain brought the fruit of the field, representing what he had done in the raising of food. It was a symbolic gift of hard work. Cain's offering was rejected. It was not as though Cain rejected God, nor did he refuse to bring something to God. Cain actually attempted to satisfy God by bringing the results of his work; he rejected the use of a blood sacrifice. Throughout Scripture, Cain is represented as a type of salvation by works. No matter how hard man works to save himself, it is not acceptable to God. The Bible calls the religion of good works "a form of godliness but denying the power thereof" (2 Tim. 3:5). Man is always saved by grace through faith, not of works (Eph. 2:8-9).

In contrast, Abel brought an animal sacrifice which was predictive of the blood of Jesus Christ which would be offered in the future. "By faith Abel offered unto God a more excellent sacrifice than Cain, by which he obtained witness that he was righteous" (Heb. 11:4).

When God's people were in bondage in Egypt, God brought a series of plagues upon the nation to motivate Pharaoh to free them. After nine plagues, the Lord finally said to Moses, "Yet will I bring one plague more upon Pharaoh and upon Egypt" (Exod. 11:1). The last plague was the death of the firstborn of each family. God told His people in Egypt that they were to take a lamb and kill it; hereby God instituted the first Passover. The New Testament calls Jesus Christ our Passover Lamb (1 Cor. 5:7). Moses instructed Israel to choose a lamb "without blemish, a male of the first year" (Exod. 11:5). This was a type of Jesus Christ "who knew no sin" (2 Cor. 5:21), hence, Jesus Christ fulfilled the type of being without blemish. The Jews were instructed to separate the Passover lamb from the rest of the flock to make certain it was without blemish. In type, Jesus Christ was "holy, harmless, undefiled, separate from sinners, and made high in the heavens" (Heb. 7:25-28).

The Passover lamb was killed and its blood was sprinkled on the sides and top of the door. God commanded, "The blood shall be to you for a token upon the houses where ye are: and when I see the blood, I will pass over you" (Ex. 12:13). When the death angel came to Egypt to punish every home, he passed over the home that was protected by the blood. From then on, Israel was to celebrate the Passover each year by the slaying of a lamb as a type of Jesus Christ.

Israel also recognized the blood atonement on the tenth day of the seventh month each year. The high priest took the blood of a slain goat and went into the Holy of holies to offer atonement. This was repeated once each year for the sins of the nation. This included any sins that were committed intentionally or in ignorance (Lev. 4:1 35). The high priest went into the Holy of holies and sprinkled the blood of the sacrificial animal on the mercy seat to atone for the sins of the people (Lev. 16:14-19).

The argument, therefore, is that the Scriptures expressly declare that these sacrifices were made for the expiation of sin. This idea is expressed by the word כָּפַר *to cover*, to hide from view, to blot out, to expiate. Hence, the substantive כֹּפֶר means that which delivers from punishment or evil. It is the common word for an atonement, but it also is used for a ransom, because it is rendered to secure deliverance.[101]

This is a type of Christ, our High Priest who "entered into Heaven" after His death on the cross. The high priest, also a type of Jesus Christ, was the mediator between God and man. Christ fulfilled that priestly office, "He is the mediator of the New Testament, that by means of death" (Heb. 9:15). At another place Paul tells us, "For there is one God and one mediator between God and man, the man Christ Jesus" (1 Tim. 2:5).

The word "redemption" comes from a word which means "to buy back." Christ gave His blood a ransom for sin, hence redeeming the lost (1 Pet. 1:18-20). In the context of soteriology, the price of redemption is blood which is paid for the remission of sins (Heb. 9:12, 22). The Greek words for "redeemed" are applied to purchasing servants in the ancient slave market. The biblical use of the terms reveals the extent of redemption to all men.

First, the Bible teaches that Christ purchased the sinner in the marketplace. *Agorazo* is the verb which means to go to the marketplace (*agora*) and pay the price for the slave. The verb "is common in deeds of sale"[102] and generally meant the paying of a price for a group of slaves. Those who were "sold under sin" are redeemed (Gal. 3:10). In each of the following Scriptures the term *"agorazo"* is used: Revelation 14:3-4 speaks of the 144,000 as those redeemed from the earth. Revelation 5:9 notes that Christ's blood was the price paid for redemption; and 2 Peter 2:1 shows that Christ redeemed (paid the price for) not only the saved, but also the false Christians. *Agorazo* speaks of the aspect of redemption which is simply paying the purchase price—the purchase price is the blood.

The next word used of redemption in the Bible is *exagorazo* (*ek* out; to buy out from). This term refers to the fact that Christ paid the price with His blood and bought the slave "out of the marketplace" (*exagorazo*). The slave was never again exposed to sale (Gal. 3:13). Galatians 4:5 also shows that when Christ took man out from under the Law, He placed them in a different relationship with God by providing for them the opportunity to become the adopted sons of God. *Exagorazo* emphasizes the removal of the curse of the Law.

The third word which refers to redemption is *lutrao*. This word means to pay the price for the slave and release him. It emphasizes the freedom that Christ makes available to those He redeemed. In Titus 2:14, the use of *lutrao* (redeemed) shows that Christ wants to completely separate us from all sin. In Luke 24:21 *lutrao* is used of redeeming Israel from Roman domination.

NEW TESTAMENT WORDS
FOR REDEMPTION

AGORAZO—Purchased   —2 Peter 2:1
EXAGORAZO—Removed   —Gal. 3:13
LUTRAO—Given Freedom   —Titus 2:14

A consideration of each of these terms and the verses in which they appear clearly demonstrates that Jesus Christ has provided redemption for all people, including false teachers (2 Pet. 2:1), by the shedding of His own blood (Heb. 9:12).

3. *Propitiation.* "Propitiation properly signifies the turning away of wrath by an offering. In the NT this idea is conveyed by the use of *hilaskomai* (Heb. 2:17), *hilasterion* (Rom. 3:25), and *hilasmos* (1 John 2:2; 4:10)."[103] The biblical terms for propitiation denote the fact that satisfaction was made for the sins of the world by Christ's death. The justice of God had been offended by the sin of mankind. The sin could not be retracted and the nature of God could not forgive the sinner without a payment of satisfaction. The price of satisfaction was the blood of Jesus Christ, and the act of satisfaction is propitiation. The Bible teaches that Jesus is the propitiation for the world. "He is the propitiation for our sin, and not for our's only but also for the sins of the whole world" (1 John 2:2, cf. 1 John 4:10; Heb. 9:5; Luke 18:13; Rom. 3:25).

Redemption contemplates our bondage and is the provision of grace to release us from that bondage. Propitiation contemplates our liability to the wrath of God and is the provision of grace whereby we may be freed from that wrath.[104]

The concept of propitiation involves the satisfying of God's just wrath against sin—by the holiness of Jesus Christ's death. Romans 3:25-26 declare the mercy, forbearance, and righteous justice of God in His setting forth of Christ to be our propitiation. God gave His Son for our sin. Christ did more than die for us; He turned around and gave Himself up for God's wrath. This is the ultimate in love in that Christ, being God, went against His nature for us.

The necessity of propitiation is found in the holiness of God and the sinfulness of man. A holy God cannot look on sin. Neither can sin stand in the presence of God. "Our God is a consuming fire" Heb. 12:29. The death of Jesus Christ satisfies the justice of God that must be poured upon sin. The coordinate reason for propitiation is the love of God as proclaimed in 1 John 4:10. A holy God could justly consign all sinful men to hopeless condemnation, but because of His love He provided a propitiation.

Hebrews 9:2-5 describe briefly the Old Testament tabernacle and its furnishings. Verse 5 speaks of the "mercy seat" which was a lid on the ark of the covenant. The term "mercy seat" (*hilasterion*) and "propitiation" are synonymous. (Other verses which amplify this doctrine are Rom. 3:25; 1 John 2:2; and 1 John 4:10.) In Luke 18:13 the praying publican realized that the law could never satisfy the demands of a holy God. Therefore, he prayed "God, be merciful to me a sinner." The term "merciful" is *hilastheti* and the verse may properly be translated "God be propitious (satisfied) to me a sinner." Today we would pray the publican's prayer: "Lord, look upon me as You would look upon the mercy seat of Christ's death, and be satisfied."

4. *The demands of the law are satisfied.* God's moral nature was offended when man broke His law and partook of the fruit of the garden. Everyone sinned in Adam, the head of the human race, and was guilty before God. The law not only condemned Adam, but every man who sinned, and would continue condemning because of the demands of the law. The law could not be abrogated because it was a reflection of God's holy character. The law demanded a penalty for every transgression. The law was a unit, and to break one law was to break all of the laws (Jas. 2:10). Hence, the demand of all of the law was upon every person who broke any of it.

One aspect of the "good news" is that Jesus has satisfied all the demands of the law against all persons. He even satisfied the demands of the law against those who reject Him. Jesus nailed the demands of the law to the cross and made an end of the law (Col. 2:14-15; Eph. 2:15-16). The law is no longer in effect as a moral judge to condemn mankind. Christ lifted the law from all (including the unsaved). This does not mean all will go to heaven. A person is no longer condemned for breaking the law, he is condemned for rejecting Jesus Christ.

Matthew 5:17 is one of the strongest New Testament statements which attests that Christ has satisfied all the demands of the law. In this verse, Jesus states, "Think not that I am come to destroy the law or the prophets: I am not come to destroy but to fulfill." The Greek word translated "to fulfill" is an aorist infinitive of *pleroo* and denotes the idea of "carrying out" and "completion."

The goal of the mission of Jesus is fulfilment (Matt. 5:17b); according to Mt. 5:17a this is primarily fulfilment of the Law and the prophets, i.e., of the whole of the O.T. (IV, 1058, 15). . . . He has come in order that God's Word may be completely fulfiled, in order that the full measure appointed by God Himself may be reached in Him. His work is an act of obedience also and specifically in the fact that He fulfills God's promise, cf. Matt. 3:15. He actualises the divine will stated in the OT from the standpoint of both promise and demand.[105]

The demands of the law include total obedience and absolute righteousness (Jas. 2:10; 1 Pet. 1:15-16; Lev. 11:44). Rom. 10:4 declares, "For Christ is the end of the law for righteousness to everyone that believeth." In regard to this verse, F. F. Bruce notes:

> The word "end" (telos) has a double sense; it may mean "goal" or "termination." On the other band, Christ is the goal at which the law aimed in that He is the embodiment of perfect righteousness, having 'magnified the law and made it honorable' (cf. Is. xlii. 21); . . . On the other hand (and this is the primary force of Paul's words), Christ is the termination of the law in the sense that with Him the old order, of which the law formed part, has been done away, to be replaced by the new order of the Spirit. In this new order, life and righteousness are available through faith in Christ; therefore, no one need attempt any more to win these blessings by means of the law.[106]

It should be noted that in satisfying the demands of the law, Christ did not "destroy" (Matt. 5:17) nor abolish the law. The law has a use today. Gal. 3:19-25 says that the law serves as a School-master to show us we are sinners. 1 Tim. 1:8-10 also speaks of the law as good because it shows sinners their sin.

Two abuses of the law are (1) its use as a means of salvation and (2) its use as a means of achieving spirituality. The law was never intended to give salvation, only to show the need for God's grace. And people who think they are going to become spiritual by keeping the law are Pharisees. Spirituality is of the Holy Spirit and one cannot become spiritual apart from the Holy Spirit.

5. *Reconciliation.* The word "reconciliation" is not found in the Hebrew text of the Old Testament, but is found in the English text in such places as, "Poured the blood at the bottom of the altar, and sanctified it, to make reconciliation upon it" (Lev. 8:15), and "seventy weeks are determined upon thy people . . . to make reconciliation for iniquity" (Dan. 9:24). The word "*kaphar*" is used in these Old Testament references, translated as the word "atonement." Here, the translators are substituting the word "reconciliation" for a specific aspect of the atonement. Brown, Driver, and Briggs correctly define *kaphar* to mean to cover, to wash away, to pacify, to obliterate."[107]

In the New Testament, Paul's use of the word for reconciliation, *katallage*, has the concept of God taking men up again into fellowship with Himself."[108] Paul notes this meaning: "You, that were sometime alienated and enemies in your mind by wicked works, yet now hath he reconciled" (Col. 1:21). Therefore in the act of reconciliation, man is reunited with God. The implication is that man who was once in favor with God (in the garden) is now reunited to fellowship with God in the death of Jesus Christ. Again Paul says, "That he might reconcile both unto God in one body" (Eph. 2:16). Whereas the rebellious sinner was previously disapproved and dispatched from a positive relationship with God, he is now rendered "no longer disapproved." Now man is in a favorable position with God because of reconciliation. This does not imply man is saved. Man is placed in a saveable position, but man must choose to be saved. One must guard against assuming that those after the cross are in a better position than those who preceded the cross. God is able to look at the Old Testament saint in anticipation of Christ's death as easily as He sees the New Testament saint in the shadow of the cross.

In the act of salvation, God looks at the blood of His Son (redemption); God's wrath is satisfied (propitiation); the broken law no longer accuses the offender; therefore God no longer views man as an alien and rebel. The result of this is the act of reconciliation. Man is now saveable because he is in a savable position to God. However, the act of reconciliation does not make man a child of God, which implies (regeneration), for that would be universalism (all saved because of the death of Christ), but all can now come to the Father through Jesus Christ (John 14:6) by accepting Jesus Christ (John 1:12).

The Bible never teaches that God is reconciled. In the famous hymn *And Can It Be*, Charles Wesley uses the phrase, "My God is reconciled," when in reality man is reconciled when God is propitiated. John Murray in his book *Redemption Accomplished and Applied* has aptly stated:

> Reconciliation presupposes disrupted relations between God and men. It implies enmity and alienation. This alienation is two-fold, our alienation from God and God's alienation from us. The cause of the alienation is, of course, our sin, but the alienation consists not only in our unholy enmity against God but also God's holy alienation from us.[109]

With the death of Christ, God's holy enmity toward man was terminated. Man was positionally reconciled to God. However, actual reconciliation occurs when the sinner applies the atoning blood of Christ to his life. The doctrine of reconciliation is not an experiential doctrine that works out into man's lifestyle, but reconciliation is a change in relationship that is enacted in Heaven.

The object of reconciliation is the world, for Paul writes, "That God was in Christ, reconciling the world unto himself" (2 Cor. 5:19). There is a double transference associated with the act of reconciliation. First, our sins were imputed to Jesus Christ, "For he hath made him to be sin for us" (2 Cor. 5:21). The second act of imputation is, "that we might be made the righteousness of God in him" (2 Cor. 5:21). In the act of salvation, the righteousness of Jesus Christ was placed on the account of the sinner, and, in reverse, the sins of sinners were assumed by Jesus Christ when He died for the sins of the world. It is noteworthy to realize that the tense of the verb "reconciled" suggests that this work is specifically a work of God and is completed. Therefore unregenerate man today is not guilty of sin under the Old Testament law. Rather, man's guilt and punishment stems from a rejection of Christ as personal Savior and Lord.

A sinner may feel that God does not love him or that God is not close to him. However, the sinner cannot determine God's perspective on him solely by his feeling. He is as close to God as Jesus Christ. When Adam sinned in the garden, man turned his back on God and God turned His back on man. However, in the death of Jesus Christ, God turned around (propitiation) and now no longer has anger toward man. Reconciliation means God has favor and mercy toward man, and man is in a position to be saved. However, men must call upon - the Lord and be converted.

6. *Judgment of the sin nature.* The judgment of the sin nature is a positional result where Jesus Christ in His death paid the penalty for sin and dealt judicially with the believer's old nature.

Every person is a sinner on three (3) accounts: First, every person is guilty of personal sin (1 John 1:10). Personal sin is an act of rebellion against God in thought and deed. It includes sins of omission or commission. Individuals are fully responsible for these sins. The penalty for personal sins is separation from God. The consequences of personal sins include both earthly results and also eternal punishment. The remedy for personal sin is the substitutionary death of Jesus. By faith in Christ, men are forgiven and thus redeemed.

Second, a person is a sinner because of imputed sin. This has to do with his standing in heaven. Adam sinned, therefore death came (Rom. 5:12). The penalty for imputed sin is physical death. There are two ways that imputed sin is transmitted, either the Federal headship or the Seminal headship. The Federal headship view states that the transmission of imputed sin is from Adam directly to me. The Seminal headship view states that the transmission of imputed sin was from Adam, to my successive ancestors, and through them to me. The remedy for imputed sin is Jesus' righteousness imputed to us.

Third, a person is a sinner because of his sin nature. Every individual is born with a sin nature inherited from his parents (1 John 1:8; Psa. 51:5). This sin nature is the tendency to do evil. The penalty for the sin nature is spiritual and physical death. The sin nature is transmitted through the father to the child. The remedy for the sin nature is that it was judged at the cross. The key verse is Romans 6:6 in which it is evident that the sin nature already has been judged. "Knowing this, that our old man [the sin nature] is crucified with him, that the body of sin might be destroyed, that henceforth we should not serve sin" (Rom. 6:6).

Although the desire and ability to sin will remain in the Christian as long as he dwells here on earth in a mortal body, Christ's death effected the legal pronouncement that the old (sin) nature is dead. Romans 6:1-16 describes the death of the sin nature and also prescribes the course of action for each Christian to take when faced with his own sin nature:

The judgment of the sin nature is a judicial view by which God enables believers to accomplish practical holiness in their lives (1 Pet. 1:14-15) by realizing that their old (sin) nature was "crucified with Christ" (Rom. 6:6; Gal. 2:20; 2 Cor. 5:17; Rom. 8:1).

Romans 6:1-16

Know—verse 9

Reckon—verse 11

Yield—verse 13

Obey—verse 16

7. *Basis for daily cleansing.* When Christ died for the sin of the world, He dealt with the legal and judicial obligation to God. This was not a limited act, but Christ dealt with all sin of all mankind of all ages. When the believer accepts Jesus Christ as his Savior, the moral implications of the transaction are applied to his account. He is justified, (non-experiential) and given a new nature (experiential). But what about the sins that are committed by the Christian after he becomes saved?

There is a difference between judicial and personal guilt. Judicial guilt is the non-experiential condition of the sinner who stands guilty before God. He was born in sin, he has a sin nature and he personally commits sin. At Calvary, his relationship to God has changed, and he no longer is guilty. However, personal guilt is experiential in nature and becomes a means by which a sinner is convicted of his sins. When the Christian consciously sins, he will experience personal guilt (if he has not hardened his conscience), but will not have judicial guilt again. The Christian is expected to "walk in the light" (1 John 1:5), which is attempting to know the truth and apply it to one's life. This is more than being sincere and attempting to do the best one can. "Walking in the light" is applying the spiritual dynamics of Scripture and the Holy Spirit so that the Christian is allowing the new nature to control him. He is living triumphantly over sin (not without sin). When one walks in the light, that does not mean he sees everything that is illuminated by the light, nor does it mean he will spontaneously travel where there is light, nor does it mean he will never walk in darkness again. It means that he is taking advantage of the light so he does not stumble or make mistakes, and that he is influenced by the light.

Those walking in the light are not perfect, for they walk at different speeds, with different confidence and for different reasons. The apostle John reminds the Christian to walk in the light (v. 5), then reminds them, "If we say that we have no sin, we deceive ourselves, and the truth is not in us" (1 John 1:8). Here the Christian is reminded that he has a sin nature, for sin (ἁμαρτιαν, *hamartian*) is singular, which refers to the source of sin in one's life.

Next, the apostle John reminds the Christian he cannot live without committing an act of sin (1 John 1:10). He uses the plural (ἁμαρτιας, *hamartias*), "sins." Some may think they do not sin. Perhaps they are deceived concerning sinless perfection, thinking if they live without conscious intention to break God's law they are perfect. Buswell offers an excellent refutation of perfectionism simply by describing the true aspirations of believers.

> If it is true that born again people will by the continuous work of the Holy Spirit, and by the agencies employed by the Spirit, grow in holy living, it is equally true that while we live in this life in the flesh here upon earth, we do not attain sinless perfection. Perfection is the standard which God has set before us and which we shall reach when we see our Lord face to face (1 John 3:2). To use a mathematical expression, we approach sinless perfection asymptotically.[110]

Others have wrongly interpreted the doctrine of sin, not realizing how far the depravity of man has deviated from the standard of God. Sin is more than a conscious act or volitional disobedience. Man is a sinner because he does not attain to the perfection of the law. A failure to comprehend this truth stems from a failure to understand the role of the law. Paul makes it abundantly clear that the law serves as a schoolmaster (Gal. 3:24-25) to point men to Christ and away from their own ability to reach and maintain God's standard of holiness.

After salvation, the Christian's sins do not affect his position in Christ. Once a person receives eternal life and becomes a son of God, nothing can abrogate his position in God. But his fellowship with God is affected. The sins of a Christian adversely affect the Christian's walk with God. His ability to pray (John 15:7; 1 John 3:24), be filled with the Spirit (Eph. 1:14; 4:28; 5:17) or have fellowship with God (1 John 2:15) is greatly thwarted.

The hindrance in fellowship has a twofold influence. First it affects the Father and, second, the Christian. The blood of Jesus Christ is the basis for the continual cleansing of any and all sins committed by a Christian. The historical act of Jesus Christ satisfied the demands of the law and judgment of God. When the Christian commits a sin in the course of time, there is no judicial decree by God to forgive the sin. God has already acted to forgive that sin at a point in history. However, God views the sinning Christian through the blood of Christ and is able to restore him.

The obstructed fellowship is also experienced by the Christian. If he has consciously sinned, then he needs to consciously ask for forgiveness and to empirically enjoy forgiveness (1 John 1:9). The word "confess" means "to agree with God concerning the sin." Since Christianity is a confessional religion, the Christian must, (1) admit the sin, (2) forsake it, (3) ask for cleansing, and (4) re-enter into fellowship with Christ.

But Christians are guilty of many sins that violate the law of God, many of which are committed ignorantly or unconsciously. Also, Christians can never fulfill all that God expects of them in a positive way. They do not have any righteousness in themselves. Does the Christian lose fellowship for every sin he commits ignorantly, and as soon as he articulates confession, get forgiven and restored? Probably not. The apostle John reminds us "If we walk in the light as he is in the light, we have fellowship with one another, and the blood of Jesus Christ his Son cleanseth us from all sin" (1 John 1:7). Three facts are noted from this verse. First, the Christian should live as conscientiously near to Christ as possible. This does not imply human perfection, but human obedience to what he feels God expects of him. This is abiding in Christ (John 15:5). Second, the Christian is constantly covered by the effects of the blood sacrifice of Christ. He does not have to ask for God's forgiveness. He is constantly forgiven. But, third. when the Christian consciously breaks fellowship with Christ by an act of disobedience, then he must actively confess his sin to be restored to fellowship with Christ. The basis of his daily cleansing and his confessional cleansing is the blood of Jesus Christ.

The question often arises, "How broad should our confession be?" Confession of sin may extend into at least three areas: (1) private, (2) personal, and (3) public. All sins must be confessed privately and sincerely to God. Some sins should be confessed to another individual if that person is directly involved (Matt. 5:23). In some instances there are sins which should be confessed publicly, to the church. Public confession should be undertaken if God tells you to do so. At least three questions should serve as guidelines in determining if public confession is necessary: (1) Will this confession edify the body of Christ? (2) Will it hurt another person? (3) Will it hinder my future usefulness in God's service? Public confession is never permanent. Between private confession and public confession, you could lose your fellowship again. You cannot undo the course of history by confession; what has been done cannot be undone. God forgives our sin, but the effects of it remain.

8. *The basis of forgiving sins committed before the cross.* Many Christians have wrongly thought that the blood of lambs sacrificed in the Old Testament was the basis for forgiving sin. Some are just as wrong in thinking that when a Jew attempted to keep the law, it was the basis of his sanctification. In every dispensation, a person was saved by faith through grace. He kept the law as an expression of his obedience and fellowship to God, and on the same basis he offered the blood sacrifice to God. It is not possible that "the blood of bulls and goats could take away sins" (Heb. 10:4).

The blood sacrifice of a lamb was a type that pictured the coming "lamb of God that taketh away the sin of the world" (John 1:20). As a prefigure, it portrayed the coming sacrifice that atoned for the sin of the world. In one aspect the sin was covered (the O.T. meaning for atonement was to cover, *kaphar*) until Christ "took away sin" (John 1:29).

Paul reminds us, "Whom God hath set forth to be a propitiation through faith in his blood, to declare his righteousness for the remission of sins that are past" (Rom. 3:25). In this sense, Christ dealt with the sin that was committed before Calvary. The etymological aspect, of *kaphar* has been aptly stated by Chafer, when he writes:

> The Hebrew word *kaphar* expresses with divine accuracy precisely what took place on the Godward side of the transaction. The sin was *covered*, but not "taken away," pending the foreseen death of Christ. To translate *kaphar* by 'atonement,' which etymologically may mean at-one-ment, could truthfully convey no more than that the offender was at one with God by a transaction which rested only on a symbolism. On the human side, the offender was pardoned; but on the divine side the transaction was lacking the one and only act which could make it conform to the requirements of infinite holiness.[111]

A famous evangelist tells the story of taking a light tan suit on an ocean cruise. He planned to preach in the suit each evening. He spilled food on the suit the first night and the spot wouldn't come out. His wife used her talcum powder to cover the spot so he could wear the suit, but the powder came out. Each night he had to re-cover the spot, with talcum powder. In the same way, the blood atonement covered the Old Testament sin, and, since the sacrifice was not permanent, the saint had to continually bring a blood sacrifice. But Christ "was once offered to bear the sins of many: and unto them that look for him shall he appear the second time without sin unto salvation" (Heb. 9:28).

9. *The basis of the national salvation of Israel.* God is not finished with the Jewish people, but has a wonderful plan for the future of the nation. Their future is based on past unconditional agreements that God made with the Jewish people. In the Abrahamic covenant, God agreed that he would bless the Jews, give them the land of Israel, and provide a Saviour through them (Gen. 12:1-3,7; 13:3,14:17). In the Davidic covenant, God promised that He would raise up a King to rule Israel from the lineage of David (2 Sam. 7:8-16). In the New Covenant, God promised that after their dispersion around the world they would be spiritually renewed and they would be the source of blessing to all people (Jer. 31:31-34; Heb. 8:6-13).

God made a sweeping promise, "All Israel shall be saved" (Rom. 11:26). The basis for their salvation is the blood of Jesus Christ (Matt. 26:28), which is the basis for any and all forgiveness of any and all sin. The night of his death, Jesus stated, "For this is my blood of the New Testament, which is shed for many for the remission of sin" (Matt. 26:28).

The phrase "All Israel shall be saved" needs examination. First the statement "All Israel" could refer to: (1) each Jew, implying salvation of the nation was on an individual basis, (2) national salvation, or (3) to every Jew who responds in faith to Jesus Christ. Since the context is referring to national Israel, most would think that salvation is national in character and scope. Charles Hodge strongly supports a nationalistic interpretation.

> Israel, here, from the context, must mean the Jewish people, and *all Israel*, the whole nation. The Jews, as a people, are now rejected; as a people, they are to be restored. As their rejection, although national, did not include the rejection of every individual; so their restoration, although in like manner national, need not be assumed to include the salvation of every individual Jew. . . . [All Israel] is not therefore to be here understood to mean, all the true people of God, as Augustin, Calvin, and many others explain it; nor all the elect Jews, *i.e.*, all that part of the nation which constitute "the remnant according to the election of grace;" but the whole nation, as a nation.[112]

Perhaps the answer lies in the interpretation of the word "shall." Is the future of Israel nationalistic or individualistic? When Israel "shall be all saved" is this the nation entering into the millennial kingdom,—to nationalistic salvation? Others think this is an individualistic salvation, when the person (each Jew) calls on Christ and is given eternal life.

The final questions involve the word "saved." Is this (1) God delivering Israel from the Tribulation, a nationalistic deliverance, or (2) is God regenerating those who ask for the forgiveness of sins, i.e., individualistic regeneration?

The context refers to the nation; therefore it is primarily a national salvation. At the same time, the reference to the dry bones (Ezek. 37:1-14) implies that the nation (collectively and individually) have new life when the Holy Spirit breathes life into them (Ezek. 37:5). Each Jew shall look upon Him whom the nation pierced (Zech. 12:10) and confess that Jesus Christ is his Savior. As Jews are saved individually, the nation corporately turns to Christ, and "All Israel is saved." The basis of their individual salvation is the blood of Christ. As such, the Jewish conversion is the basis of the New Covenant (Matt. 26:28). Ryrie has correctly stated this idea in his book *The Basis of the Premillennial Faith.*

The one new covenant has two aspects, one which applies to Israel, and one which applies to the church. These have been called the realistic and spiritual aspects of the covenant, but both aspects comprise essentially one covenant based on the sacrifice of the Lord Jesus Christ.[113]

10. *Judging Satan.*   Christ delivered a mortal wound to Satan at Calvary.   This devastating act to Satan's authority and power was predicted along with the first promise of the Savior. "And I will put enmity between thee and the woman, and between thy seed and her seed; it shall bruise thy head, and thou shalt bruise his heel" (Gen. 3:15). The head wound is considered a fatal blow and was inflicted to Satan when Christ died. The heel infliction was a temporary irritation and was fulfilled when Satan dealt Jesus his death. It is called a temporary irritation, because Christ arose on the third day.

But obviously Satan is alive and has influence in today's world. How can we say that Satan received a fatal blow? Jesus predicted Satan would be judged: "Now is the judgment of this world: now the ruler of this world will be cast out" (John 12:31). This reference to his death (v. 32-33) portrays it as a judgment. Again Jesus revealed that Satan was judged at the cross, "of judgment because the ruler of this world is judged" (John 16:11). When a person stands before the judge to receive his verdict, the sentence is not usually carried out immediately. When a person hears, "You shall be hanged by the neck," there is usually a period of time before he is executed. Satan received the verdict (was judged) by the death of Christ, but he still has limited power until the sentence is executed. Hell is prepared for Satan (Matt. 25:41), and one day he shall be cast into the lake of fire (Rev. 20:10).

To avoid minimizing the power and authority of Satan over mankind we need to be reminded of the words of Chafer concerning the Old Testament personalities.

They were without God and without hope, because they were without Christ, in the world. No way of approach either for them to God or for God to them having yet been provided, Satan evidently assumed the rule over them which he could do on the ground of the fact that he had wrestled the scepter of authority from Adam. During that extended period, had God approached one of these souls without a righteous provision having been either promised through animal sacrifices or made actual by the blood of His Son, Satan, it is probable, could have challenged the Almighty, charging Him with unrighteousness. Thus on the ground of man's sinfulness Satan held his prisoners bound. But since Christ died for all men, and as He certainly did, there remains no barrier between God and man other than a lack of faith on the part of man in the Saviour. The prisoners who otherwise would be "without hope" are now confronted with the gospel of divine grace—"Whosoever will may come."[114]

The ultimate power of Satan was death, but in the cross of Christ, Satan lost his control and ability to exercise death. "Through death He might destroy him who had the power of death, that is, the devil" (Heb. 2:14). When a ruler such as Satan loses his ultimate control, he begins to lose influence. His kingdom may not collapse immediately, but the seeds of destruction are there. When Christ took away Satan's control of death, He delivered the judicial verdict that is the basis for Satan's defeat.

With the judgment of Satan, the same legal decision was rendered to the demons who are the servants of Satan. Paul describes the result, "Having disarmed principalities and powers, He made a public spectacle of them, triumphing over them in it" (Col. 2:15). The word disarm implies the legal results of Calvary. Satan and his demons have power, only if the Christian allows them to have it. In the name of Jesus Christ, and through the blood of Jesus Christ, the Christian can overcome the influence of demons.

11. *The purification of things in heaven.* Heaven is a perfect place because it is the centralized abode of God. However, the Bible tells us that Satan has easy access into heaven (Job 1:6). Because of this, the Bible teaches that Heaven was purified. The writer of Hebrews declares, "with His own blood He entered into the Most Holy Place once for all to having obtained eternal redemption" (Heb. 9:12). Even though he does not call it Heaven, the most holy place is the presence of God. The primary purpose was to propitiate the wrath of God and pay the price of redemption. But, also as the earthly high priest took the blood of bulls and goats to cleanse the Holy of holies (Heb. 9:19-22), so Christ the eternal high priest entered Heaven to purify it. "It was therefore necessary that the patterns of things in the heavens should be purified with these; but the heavenly things themselves with better sacrifices than these" (Heb. 9:23).

Some have questioned whether Christ took the literal blood into Heaven, to literally sprinkle in Heaven, or whether God the Father saw the blood of His Son on Calvary and declared Heaven purified when Satan's authority was terminated, and in the future to be totally banned from Heaven (Rom. 12:9). Conservative scholars seem to be divided over the alternative interpretation. Those who insist that Christ took His literal blood to Heaven have little tolerance toward those who interpret it otherwise.

Those who insist the blood literally cleansed Heaven base their view on one verse, "by his own blood he entered in once into the holy place" (Heb. 9:12). Also, this is a recent interpretation and perhaps they are reacting to the liberal who denies the blood of Christ. Chafer supports the literal blood view when he states,

> Among the contrasts set up in Hebrews, chapters 8-10, between the typical ceremonials which foreshadowed Christ's death and that death itself, it is pointed out (Heb. 9:23) that, as the tabernacle on earth was purified by the blood of animals, so the heavenly "things" were purified on the ground of Christ's blood when He, as High Priest, entered the heavenly realms. We read: "But Christ being come an high priest of good things to come, by a greater and more perfect tabernacle, not made with hands, that is to say, not of this building [the old tabernacle]; neither by the blood of goats and calves, but by his own blood he entered in once into the holy place, having obtained eternal redemption for us" (9:11-12). And, referring to the service of the high priest of old in the earthly sanctuary, the writer adds: "Moreover he sprinkled

with blood both the tabernacle, and all the vessels of the ministry [things]. And almost all things are by the law purged with blood; and without shedding of blood is no remission" (9:21-22) . . . the old sanctuary was ceremonially cleansed by the blood of goats and calves, but by His own blood Christ entered into the holy place on high and on the ground of that blood the heavenly "things" were purified and by "better sacrifices" than that of the animals.[115]

They believed Jesus purified heaven after He ascended on Resurrection morning. When Jesus met Mary in the garden He told her, "Touch me not; for I am not yet ascended to my Father: but go to my brethren, and say to them, I ascend to my Father, and your Father; and to my God, and your God" (John 20:17). The first thing after resurrection was the obligation to ascend to God with the literal blood and purify Heaven.

Historically, scholars have interpreted the cleansing of Heaven to be the expelling of Satan from Heaven and terminating his access to it. To prove their point they note the phrase "by his blood" is a prepositional phrase in Greek that can be translated "through his blood." This means that because his blood completed the atonement, Christ entered Heaven. A second argument is that if Jesus literally purified Heaven, he did it on the third day—Resurrection day. However, the atonement was one act that took place three days earlier on Calvary. Jesus became the substitute for sin, and in the act of dying He atoned for the sin of the world. If Heaven were cleansed on Resurrection day, it wrongly separates propitiation into two acts. A third aspect of the issue implies the commercial aspect of the atonement: i.e., making the atonement quantitative rather than qualitative. The final argument is that "the pattern of things in the heavens should be purified" (Heb. 9:23), meaning the appearance of Heaven was cleansed, not the actual Heaven itself. Thus interpreted, when God saw the blood of His Son, He declared that Heaven, which is a pattern of the Holy of holies, was cleansed.

D. FALSE THEORIES CONCERNING THE ATONEMENT. Since the death of Christ, men have speculated on the exact purpose of his death. The motivation and intent behind those erroneous theories range from malicious perjury to well-intended but grossly misinformed accounts of the atonement. These theories will be dealt with in brevity in order to simply become acquainted with them:

1. *The Martyr or Accident Theory.* This theory contends that the death of Christ did not have soteriological purpose or value. Christ's death was an unforeseen incident that abrogated His plans upon the earth. Rather than controlling history, Christ is circumstantially caught in the political machinery and, through a series of unfortunate events, He wound up on the cross.

2. *The Recapitulation Theory.* Originated by Irenaeus, this view states that the entire life of Christ and His death constitute the atonement. In essence He achieved what the first Adam forfeited. Jesus is all that Adam was not.

3. *The Ransom-to-Satan Theory.* Endorsed by early apologists such as Origen and Augustine, and even contemporary authors C. S. Lewis, J. R. Tolkien, and the Seventh-day Adventists, simply stated this view contends that Christ's death was a ransom paid to Satan for the purpose of delivering mankind from any indebtedness to the devil. However, Satan, due to his lack of omniscience, was deceived by the apparent humanity of Christ. Upon His resurrection, Christ stripped Satan's authority over death and ascended to Heaven triumphant.

4. *The Commercial or Satisfaction Theory of Anselm.* Because man chose to rebel against God in the Garden of Eden, he must now be restored to God by either punishment or satisfaction. Motivated by compassion, God selected His Son as a substitute payment for man's disobedience. While living upon the earth, Christ kept the whole law (which was required), yet in order to secure man's salvation He had to take an additional step, namely the cross. Christ's death upon the cross supplied the additional merit (called superogation) which is transferable to unbelievers.

5. *Mystical Experience of Thomas Aquinas.* Demeaning the necessity of the atonement, this view states that God in a hypothetical fashion selected the cross for man's mode of redemption. The application of salvation is obtained through a mystical union (via the sacraments) with Christ and the church.

6. *Moral Influence of Abelard.* This theory refutes the death of Christ as having any substitutionary efficacy. Man is not reconciled to God through the blood of Christ, rather the moral and noble life of Christ should compel man to seek after God. After man voluntarily responds to God in loving obedience, God reciprocates and eagerly forgives.

7. *Governmental Theory of Grotius.* To demonstrate His hatred for sin, God commissioned His Son to die upon the cross. God is not able to simply forgive sins, but He must be appeased through a sacrifice (Isa. 53). For this reason, Christ died for our sins. Christ's death does not totally seal our salvation, but allows God to relax the demands of the law, and respond favorably to man.

8. *Mystical Experience Theory of Modern Liberal Theology.* Propagated by Schleiermacher, Ritschl, and Irving, this view—like the moral influence theory—envisions Christ's death as a positive influence upon man. The vehicle of communication between God and man is an existential relationship. Upon encountering Christ, man is enabled to achieve victory over the sinful nature and enjoy personal union with God.

XII. THE RESURRECTION OF CHRIST

There is a paradigm to history; it is not the uncontrolled flow of destiny. In past history God was moving events toward the cross and resurrection; then from this eternal watershed that gives meaning to life, everything flows away from these events. So great are these historical incidents that one proclaimed, "To a greater extent than it is anything else, Christianity—at least the Christianity of the New Testament—is a religion of resurrection."[116] So all-consuming are the scope of the cross and resurrection that without them there is no Christianity, and without belief in them there is no salvation.

Whereas many sculptors and painters have portrayed Christ on the cross, the catalyst of Christianity is the empty cross and the empty tomb. "He is not here," said the angel. "He is risen as he said" (Matt. 28:6).

A. HISTORY AND THE RESURRECTION.   Since the resurrection is the fundamental truth of Christianity (1 Cor. 15:14), if the critics can successfully raise questions, or can disprove its veracity, then they have successfully crippled the faith in general and destroyed a person's faith in particular. Hence, the main attack against the resurrection is an attack on Christ. The main onslaught is centered in the question, "Is the account of the resurrection an accurate historical account of what really happened?"

Now history is what has happened. No objective system of historical interpretation can reinterpret the past to say it did not happen or it happened differently than suggested by the data. The science of historical research is an attempt to gather, analyze, arrange and interpret the facts from the past. When this is done, the researcher arrives at historical objectivity.

Rudolf Bultman denies the resurrection by stating, "An historical fact which involves a resurrection from the dead is utterly inconceivable!"[117]   Bultmann is correct in stating that "the historical method includes the presupposition that history is a unity in the sense of a closed continuum of effects in which individual events are connected by the succession of cause and effect."[118] However, Bultmann's problem is that he has rejected, or reinterpreted evidence for supernatural occurrences, so that he cannot include a supernatural resurrection in his view of Christianity.

1. *Historical Theories Opposing the Resurrection.*   The first historical attack on Christianity is that the disciples stole the body. This view persisted in New Testament times. Matthew records that the priest bribed the guards to spread the tale, "His disciples came by night, and stole Him away while we were asleep" (Matt. 28:13).   An early church father, Origen, answers this charge that men do not risk their lives for a lie (Acts 7:60; 12:2). H. S. Reimarus who died in 1768, in his *The Goal of Jesus and His Disciples*, said the disciples stole His body and said He would soon return as the people's Messiah.[119]

The Swoon Theory was suggested by Paulas, a German, in 1828. He suggested that because of the short time on the cross, He was taken down in a death-like swoon (perceived as death by the soldiers). The cool grave revived Him, the earthquake rolled the stone away, and He stripped off His graveclothes and left them in the tomb. Dressed in a gardener's clothes (why Mary mistook Him) He went away to meet His disciples in the upper room.

Hugh Schonfield in *The Passover Plot* suggests a similar, but more sinister, plot.[120] He suggests that Jesus felt He was a prophet, studied the Old Testament and realized He must suffer for the sins of Israel. He provoked the Jews and prodded Judas to betray Him. He knew the body would not be left on the cross over the Passover, so He allowed Himself to be crucified. He had arranged for the code words, "I thirst," to signal someone to give Him a knockout drug that made it appear He was dead. Joseph of Arimathea was part of the plot and rushed to Pilate to get the body, but, unknown to them, a soldier pierced Jesus' side and He died by mistake. Jesus had planned His resurrection and told them to meet Him in Galilee. He was mistakenly placed in the wrong tomb, leaving the original tomb empty. The women and disciples came to the previously designated tomb, but He was not there. A young man (perhaps the gardener) at the tomb told them, "He is not here" and pointed to the correct tomb and said "Go." They misunderstood and thought he said "Go tell . . ." While this was a popular novel, and a different explanation of the resurrection, its interpretation is not consistent with historical data.

Kirsopp Lake earlier wrote *The Resurrection of Christ* in 1912, analyzing what he called "the facts behind the resurrection." He suggested there were several tombs in the place where Jesus was buried, so the women and disciples had gone to the wrong tomb.[121]

2. Naturalistic Theories Opposing the Resurrection. Modern theology has produced a group of views that accept the reality of the resurrection while denying its historical validity. Generally, they hold that the resurrection was not supernatural in past history, but its spiritual nature transcends history; therefore, the resurrection is real, whether or not it is history. It is not subject to proof, nor do they seemingly care if it is verified.

Walter Kunneth in *The Theology of the Resurrection* proposed, "The resurrection of Jesus is clearly rooted in history, although it is not in itself a historical fact."[122] He suggests a dual level for interpreting history: what may be nonsupernatural in this world is supernatural in another world. He states, "The reality of the resurrection of Jesus lies beyond our earthly categories."[123] When we question where this non-earthly resurrection took place, he says that the resurrection is a "primal miracle beyond the bounds of the immanent world."[124] Reginald Fuller suggests, "It was not a 'historical,' but an eschatological and meta-historical event, occurring precisely at the point where history ends, but leaving its mark on history negatively in the empty tomb ('He is not here') and positively in the appearances."[125] Therefore, we find the latest attack on the resurrection is that which denies its "historicity," but affirms its reality.

Spawning from the modern theological approach of the resurrection are three prominent naturalistic theories. The prominent and most favored is the Subjective Vision theory espoused by Rudolf Bultmann, who states, "The historian can perhaps to some extent account for that faith from the personal intimacy which the disciples had enjoyed with Jesus during his earthly life, and so reduce the resurrection appearances to a series of subjective visions."[126] George Hanson aptly describes this theory as referring to the apostles and witnesses as "well-meaning, perfectly honest men, but fanatics and visionaries, carried away with the exuberance of their own fancy, and that their visions of their Master after His death were simply 'externalized pictures of an excited imagination and had no reality outside their own expectant and highly sensitive minds.'[127] Yet, this view has many difficulties. How could such visions arise to a fearful and scared band of men who did not understand or expect the resurrection? How could these visions appear to the disciples while they were busy in their ordinary tasks and not given to prayer and meditation? Why was it that the subjective visions began on the third day and not on an earlier or later date?

A second theory is the Telegram or Objective Theory. Rooted within this theory is the concept that Christ, through mystical messages, conveyed to His disciples that all was well."[128] Alexander Thomson states this view which holds that it "was not the body of Christ risen from the grave, but the glorified spirit of Christ producing visions of Himself for the comfort of His disciples, as if sending telegrams from Heaven to let them know that all was well." However, Scripture does not describe Christ's entrance into Heaven in a lowly and meek fashion even as His entrance to Jerusalem on Palm Sunday riding upon a colt. Instead, Scripture makes it amply clear that Christ arose triumphant (Heb. 2:14-15; Col. 2:15).

The final theory is the Mystical Theory. According to this theory Christianity simply adopted resurrection concepts from other surrounding nations and implemented them into their religions program. Berkhof describes and denounces this view by stating,

A new mythical school has come into existence, which discards, or at least dispenses with, theories of vision and apparition, and seeks to account for the resurrection legend by the help of conceptions imported into Judaism from Babylonia and other oriental countries. This school claims not only that the mythology of the ancient oriental religions contains analogies of the resurrection story, but that this story was actually derived from pagan myths. This theory has been worked out in several forms, but is equally baseless in all its forms. It is characterized by great arbitrariness in bolstering up a connection of the gospel story with heathen myths, and has not succeeded in linking them together. Moreover, it reveals an extreme disregard of the facts as they are found in Scripture.[129]

Surely the resurrection was an event in Heaven that had reverberations in spiritual realms. Also, when Jesus arose from the dead, He was not restored to normal human life, but to a new sphere of life. These facts give some support to those who interpret the resurrection in a "non-historical" way. But the resurrection was both/and. It was a historical event on earth that happened in time and a metaphysical phenomenon. To deny the physical while affirming the spiritual is to (1) misinterpret the meaning of words, (2) deny objective principles of interpreting history, and (3) operate from a mistaken bias against the supernatural.

Clark Pinnock in his paper, "On the Third Day," says historicity is necessary when interpreting facts to build one's faith. "Faith in the risen Lord arises out of the work of the Spirit in the mind of a man considering the claims of the gospel. The Spirit acts through evidence to accredit the message. The evidence consists chiefly, as historical evidence does, of the personal testimony of those claims to this event."[130]

Since history is an analysis of historical causes and effects, the historical resurrection is the result of a historical cause. Tenney, who argues for "The Historicity of the Resurrection," bases his interpretation on cause and effect. "The existence of the church demands a historical cause for its origin.[131]   Actually there are a variety of empirical data that suggest the scholar accept the cause (the resurrection) to explain the varied effects. It is further suggested that the effects cannot be explained by any other cause than the resurrection of Jesus Christ from the dead. Denney captures the historical veracity of the resurrection in his remarks, "The real historical evidence for the resurrection is the fact that it was believed, preached, propagated, and produced its fruit and effect in the new phenomenon of the Christian Church, long before any of our Gospels were written."[132]

B. PROOFS OF THE RESURRECTION. (1) The phenomenon of the empty tomb, (2) the sudden transformation of frightened disciples into bold proponents of the resurrection,

> It is astonishing that a few simple and uneducated men should have been able to devise and execute a plan, which has eluded all search, and has obtained credit among the wise and learned, as well as among the vulgar, for the space of eighteen hundred years.[133]

(3) The rapid emergence of the church (a fellowship of like believers) which claimed to be the body of Christ in whose midst He lived and empowered for godliness and service; (4) the testimony of various individuals and groups of people who claimed they conversed with and had fellowship with the resurrected Christ; (5) the transformation of a Christ-hating persecutor like Paul into a fervent preacher of Jesus Christ; (6) the testimony by Paul and others that the resurrected Christ indwelt them in their physical life on earth; (7) a hermeneutical conviction by the emerging church that correlated the death, burial and resurrection of Christ with Old Testament references to the Jewish expected Messiah; (8) the production of a body of literature (New Testament) that comprehensively, completely and historically explains the purpose, cause and effect of the resurrection of Jesus Christ in a consistent system that corresponds to the rest of Scripture; (9) the inability of the Jewish leaders to disprove the resurrection in the very city in which Christ died and was buried; (10) the use of Sunday as the Christian day of worship instead of the sabbath. Dabney expresses this latter thought more fully.

> The change of the Sabbath is a perpetual monumental evidence of the resurrection. For 4,000 years it had been observed on the 7th day of the week. It is now universally observed on the 1st day by Christians. Whence the change? The Church has constantly asserted that it was made to commemorate the rise of its Redeemer from the dead. Now a public, monumental observance cannot be propagated among men to commemorate an imaginary event. The introduction of the observance would inevitably challenge remarks, and the imposture would have been instantly exposed.[134]

(11) The conversion of James, the brother of Christ, who was opposed to Christian teaching before the resurrection but later assumed an active role in the Jerusalem Church; (12) the testimony of Ignatius of Antioch; who was born around A.D. 30, later martyred by Emperor

Trajean (A. D. 97-117) when thrown to the beasts in the Flavian amphitheater in Rome. He wrote,

As for me, I know that even after His resurrection He was in the flesh, and I believe this to be true. For, when He came to those who were with Peter, He said to them: "Take hold on me and handle and see that I am not a spirit without a body." And, as soon as they touched Him and felt His flesh and pulse, they believed. It is for this reason that they despised death and even showed themselves superior to death. After His resurrection He ate and drank with them like anyone else with a body, although in His spirit He was one with the Father. (Ignatius of Antioch, Epistle to the Smyrnaeans, chapter 3, reprinted in Francis Glimm, *The Apostolic Fathers* (Washington: The Catholic University of America Press, 1962), p. 119).[135]

Therefore, the resurrection of Christ is the foundation of a world view that gives meaning to life on earth and life after death. Everett F. Harrison sums up well the immense significance of historical data.

The crucial importance of the resurrection for the demonstration of the divine origin and full authority of the Christian religion has long been recognized, both by friends and foes, perhaps by the latter even more than by the former, since they are on the alert to detect that portion of the foundation which will involve the collapse of the whole edifice in case it can be successfully removed. Though the method of attack has changed through the years and consequently, to a degree, the method of defense, yet the basic facts remain as they have from the very beginning, and to them we make our appeal. The three prominent lines of evidence for Jesus' resurrection are the empty tomb, His appearances to the disciples, and the transformation wrought in them by those appearances. In the background, but no less deserving of consideration as historical evidence, are the very existence of the church and the literature which emanated from it, our New Testament. Finally, though not lying properly within the category of evidence, there is a congruity between His resurrection and all else that we know about Him. The consistent supernaturalism that belongs to Him makes the resurrection a virtual necessity and creates in one who starts from the fact the increasing realization that it was inevitable.[136]

Now granted, historical verification cannot give one faith, even if it is an accurate verification of the resurrection. But one cannot have faith without an object that has credibility (biblical faith is not blind faith). Biblical faith cannot have as its object that which is untrue or that which has no reality (if an interpretation of an event such as the resurrection is inconsistent with the facts or does not correspond to the existing world, then it is not true). Since biblical faith involves an inner commitment to one's understanding of God, an honest person could not commit himself in faith to that which he inwardly knows is false or does not exist. Therefore, a person could not have biblical faith in an interpretation of a non-historical resurrection. The question is raised, "What good is this interpretation of the resurrection since it cannot produce faith?" It is apparently an explanation to satisfy those who reject the supernatural, but still desire to retain historical language.

C. TOWARD A DEFINITION. The disciples were apparently surprised at the resurrection of Christ on Easter Sunday morning, even though He both taught it and predicted it. They apparently forgot that they had previously discussed its meaning. At the mount of transfiguration, "He charged them to tell no man what things they had seen, until the Son of man should have risen from the dead" (Mark 9:9). They obeyed, "So they kept the matter to themselves, questioning what the rising from the dead meant" (Mark 9:10).

Previously Jesus taught them "the Son of man must suffer many things and be rejected by the elders and the chief priests and the scribes and be killed, and after three days rise again" (Mark 8:31). This was not a casual reference, for it occurs in Matthew 16:21; 17:23; 20:17-19; 26:12, 28, 31; Mark 9:30-32; 14:8, 24, 27; Luke 9:22, 44-45; 18:31-34; 22:20; John 2:19-21; 10:17-18; 12:7. Once Jesus had told the disciples, "I lay down my life, that I might take it again" (John 10:17).

Also, the disciples should have been "resurrection-oriented" from the Old Testament and their own past experience. The resurrection was believed by the patriarchs (Gen. 22:5; Heb. 11:19; Job 19:25-27) and taught by the prophets (2 Kgs. 4:25-35; 13:21); and the dead were raised by Jesus (Matt. 9:25; Luke 7:12-15; John 11:43, 44).

D. THE NATURE OF THE RESURRECTION. When the women arrived at the tomb on Easter morning, they discovered that the body of Jesus was missing. They expected to find His body and were discussing the problem of rolling away the stone. Obviously, the disciples now fully understood what had happened. Only a complete examination of the Scriptures will reveal what really happened. The physical body that had died was given life. The body and spirit that separated at death once again were reunited. Jesus had subjected the powers of death to Himself and made eternal life possible to all who would believe. Before His death, He was subjected to the limitation of humanity (*kenosis*), but in His resurrected body He once again enjoyed His previous privileges. In addition to a physical renewal, there was a quickening of His spirit, and all who believe in Him enjoy a new spiritual position. Finally, Christ received His glorified body at the resurrection; the glory that He had in eternity past (John 17:5) was now added to His physical body. Concerning Christ's restoration to life, Berkhof states,

> The resurrection of Christ did not consist in the mere fact that He came to life again, and that body and soul were re-united. If this were all that it involved, He could not be called "the first-fruits of them that slept," 1 Cor. 15:20, nor "the firstborn of the dead," Col. 1:18; Rev. 1:5, since others were restored to life before Him. It consisted rather in this that in Him human nature, both body and soul, was restored to its pristine strength and perfection and even raised to a higher level, while body and soul were re-united in a living organism. From the analogy of the change which, according to Scripture, takes place in the body of believers in the general

resurrection, we may gather something as to the transformation that must have occurred in Christ.[137]

1. *Resurrection—renewed life.* There can be no denying that Jesus died physically on the cross. The Romans were professionals; they understood when a man was dead. When they came to break the legs of those on the cross, they realized that Jesus was already dead: "When they came to Jesus, and saw that he was dead already, they broke not his legs" (John 19:33). Later when they pierced the side of Jesus, the blood and water had began to separate, indicating approaching death (John 19:34). There is not doubt concerning the physical death of Christ.

Jesus had predicted, "Destroy this temple, and in three days I will raise it up" (John 2:19). By this prophecy, He was predicting both his resurrection and attributing its source to Himself. Jesus was responsible for raising Himself from the dead, but it was not His power alone. At Pentecost, Peter reminded his listeners that God the Father was also responsible, "Whom God both raised up, having loosed the pains of death, because it was not possible that he should be holden of it" (Acts 2:24; cf. 13:30). Finally, the Scriptures also teach that the Holy Spirit was responsible for the resurrection. "For Christ also hath once suffered for sins, the just for the unjust, that he might bring us to God, being put to death in the flesh, but quickened by the Spirit (1 Pet. 3:18).

Those in the Old Testament and under the ministry of Jesus who had been returned to life, were technically not resurrected (which implies new life), but were resuscitated (the former life restored). Obviously the life of Jesus was restored to His original personality as before His death. He had the same body (not an identical body for His body was now glorified and had new capacities). When Jesus exited the grave, He had renewed the life that was terminated in death, but there was much more to His resurrection than taking up where He had left off three days earlier.

2. *Resurrection—reunion of body and spirit.* It was once thought that death occurs when a person's heart stops beating, but today medical technology has advanced to the point that a heart can sometimes be revived after it stops beating, as during a heart attack. Also, lack of brain activity or no bodily impulses are methods of determining death. Medically, the definition of death may fluctuate, but the biblical definition of death is always considered the separation of a person's body and spirit: "For as the body without the spirit is dead, so faith without works is dead also" (Jas. 2:20). When Jesus died, "He bowed His head, and gave up the ghost" (John 19:20). There was a separation of spirit and body. When Jesus died He did not cease to exist, His soul apparently went to Sheol where He announced His victory over death to the Old Testament saints, "By which also He went and preached unto the spirits in prison" (1 Pet. 3:19). The word "preach" is εκηρυξεν (ordinary proclamation) which does not mean to offer a second chance of salvation to those already dead. It means to announce, as He told those in captivity the good news of His victory. At the resurrection, the body and spirit of Christ were reunited.

3. *Resurrection—subjecting the power of death.* Death, never part of the original plan of God for man, became a part of the human experience after the Fall. "Wherefore, as by one man sin entered into the world, and death by sin; and so death passed upon all men, for that all have sinned" (Rom. 5:12). In death, Christ defeated the influence of death. The resurrection of Jesus is proof that those who believe in Him will also be raised after they die and are buried in the grave. In discussing the resurrection, Paul wrote, "Death is swallowed up in victory. O death, where is thy sting? O grave, where is thy victory?" (1 Cor. 15:54-55). The apostle recognized that Christ had gained for believers a victory over death in His resurrection to new life. "Behold, I shew you a mystery; We shall not all sleep, but we shall all be changed, in a moment, in the twinkling of an eye, at the last trump: for the trumpet shall sound, and the dead shall be raised incorruptible, and we shall be changed. For this corruptible must put on incorruption, and this mortal must put on immortality" (1 Cor. 15:51-53).

The devil thought he had gained a victory when he silenced the message of Jesus Christ, but a far greater victory emerged on the horizon when Christ arose triumphant. Satan wanted to destroy Christ (Gen. 3:15; Matt. 4:1-11). His part in "bruising the heal of Christ" (Gen. 3:15) was a necessary step to seal his fate and subject his power to Christ's authority. When Jesus conquered the power of the grave, He promised that all who would someday have to die physically would live again in the resurrection from the dead.

4. *Resurrection—a new glory.* When Jesus left Heaven in the *kenosis*, He voluntarily set aside some use of His comparative attributes, and assumed the limitations of a human body. As such, He submitted Himself to the plan and protection of the Father. He performed His miracles through the power of the Holy Spirit and did all His works through the Father and the Holy Spirit (Acts 10:38). Jesus told His disciples, "My meat is to do the will of him that sent me, and to finish his work" (John 4:34). When Jesus arose from the dead, he had finished the work that His father had sent Him to accomplish and was ready to receive His former glory (John 17:5) and add it to His physical life, to have a glorified body. Whereas during the years He spent as a man on earth He was led by the Holy Spirit and accomplished the purpose of the Father. After the resurrection Jesus was "the man" in the glory (1 Tim. 2:5).

Because of His resurrection, Jesus has new responsibilities. He is now our intercessor before the Father (Heb. 7:25) and our Advocate with the Father (1 John 2:1). Because of His resurrection, Jesus has received greater responsibilities than He possessed prior to the virgin birth. He did pray to receive "the glory which I had with thee before the world was" (John 17:5), but He also is the Lamb who is glorified in heaven (Rev. 5:6-14), and who serves as our High Priest in mediating our cause.

5. *Resurrection—spiritual life.* The apostle Paul identified his spiritual experience with the resurrection life of Christ, "I am crucified with Christ: nevertheless I live; yet not I, but Christ liveth in me: and the life which I now live in the flesh I live by the faith of the Son of God, who loved me, and gave himself for me" (Gal. 2:20). This was the co-crucifixion and co-resurrection life that Paul experienced with Jesus Christ. Being co-raised with Christ results in a change in the Christian's standing in the heavenlies, and should result in a change in

a change in the Christian's standing in the heavenlies, and should result in a change in his actions on earth. "Therefore, we are buried with him by baptism into death, that like as Christ was raised up from the dead by the glory of the Father, even so we also should walk in newness of life" (Rom. 6:4).

One of the obvious results of the resurrection of Christ is the sharing of spiritual life with believers. God works in the lives of Christians, "according to the working of His mighty power, which he wrought in Christ, when he raised him from the dead" (Eph. 1:19-20). The secret to the victorious Christian life is allowing Christ to live His resurrected life through you.

6. *Resurrection—a glorified body.* Jesus arose from the dead with a glorified body. This was the body He had on earth, but it was not the exact body, for it was now transformed. Shedd emphatically states that "the spiritual body is not wholly a new creation *ex nihilo*, as the Manichaeans asserted, but is the old body transformed.

The resurrection-body is an identical body. An identical body is one that is recognized by the person himself and by others."[138] The wounds of the nail prints in His hands and feet (Psa. 22:16) and the wounds in His side were still visible (John 20:25-29). His transformed body engaged in some of the same physical activity as He did in His previous state. He still breathed (John 20:22), talked (John 21:15), stood (John 21:4), ate (Luke 24:41-43) and walked (Luke 24:15). John Gill claims that Christ's glorified body is the same body He possessed prior to His death.

It was the same body that was raised that died, and was laid in the grave; it was a real body, consisting of flesh, blood, and bones; and was not only to be seen, but to be handled; and it was the same identical body, as appears from the print of the nails in his bands, and the mark in his side, made by the spear, Luke xxiv. 39, 40; John xx.25, 27.[139]

Yet, after His resurrection, the body of Jesus was also different. He was not always easily recognized by His disciples (Luke 24:31). When speaking of Christ's resurrection or exaltation it should be noted that only the human aspect of Christ was given life. Loraine Boettner underlines this teaching clearly by stating,

In the first place it must be apparent to all that the exaltation of Christ, as well as His humiliation, relates not to His Divine nature, which is and always has been infinitely blessed and glorious, but only to His human nature. His divine nature is immutable, and therefore not capable of either increase or diminution. His humiliation was temporary. It began with His birth and was completed with His burial, and it can never be repeated. His exaltation is permanent. It began with His resurrection and ascension. It continues now as He sits at the right hand of God the Father and directs the affairs of His advancing kingdom.[140]

He could pass through barred doors and appear or disappear. He traveled great distances (from Jerusalem to Galilee) apparently without being seen. There is no evidence that the resurrected body of Christ needed rest or sustenance to sustain itself. While He could eat, the Bible does not indicate that He had to do so. While this resurrection body of Jesus was the same as His pre-resurrection body, it was also uniquely transformed.

The resurrected body of Christ was immediately glorious in that it was new and eternal. It had triumphed over death and decay. But the "halo effect" of Christ's glorification was not evident until after the ascension. "Halo effect" means the shining and lustrous appearance. When on the Isle of Patmos John saw Christ, (Rev. 1:13), He was both glorified and transfigured as He probably appeared on the mount of transfiguration (Matt. 17:2). When John saw Christ, His head and hair were white (Rev. 1:14), His eyes were as a flame of fire (Rev. 1:14), His feet reflected as brass (Rev. 1:15), His countenance shined as the sun (Rev. 1:16).

But when Mary saw Him in the garden, she thought He was the gardener. When Cleophas and friend met Christ on the road to Emmaus, they thought He was just another fellow traveler. Obviously, Christ was not transfigured, for if He had been, they would have noticed the difference.

E. THE RESULTS OF THE RESURRECTION. Jesus accomplished a number of things in His resurrection that affect the Christian. Essentially, the resurrection of Christ enabled Him to apply the victories or accomplishments of the cross to the believer. But beyond the benefits of the cross that come through the resurrection, there are also its unique benefits that apply directly to the believer.

1. *Giving eternal life.* Every Christian has eternal life, which is the purpose of Jesus Christ's mission on earth (John 3:16). The basis for eternal life is the life that is supplied by the resurrection. Jesus said, "I am the resurrection and the life; he that believes in me, though he were dead, yet shall he live" (John 11:25). Paul stated, "The gift of God is eternal life through Jesus Christ our LORD" (Rom. 6:23). Eternal life is communicated to the believer by belief: "He that heareth my word, and believeth on him that sent me, hath everlasting life, and shall not come into condemnation, but is passed from death unto life" (John 5:24).

2. *Imparting power.* The Christian has power to overcome the devil, the world and the lust of the flesh. This ability comes through the resurrection. Paul prayed that the Ephesian Christians would understand "what is the exceeding greatness of his power to us-ward who believe, according to the working of his mighty power, which he wrought in Christ, when he raised him from the dead" (Eph. 1:19-20). When Christians understand and apply the power of the resurrection of Christ to their lives, it radically changes the work they do for God. Christians need not be defeated, because they are raised together with Christ (Rom. 6:4-5). They can have victory by reckoning themselves alive (Rom. 6:11), yielding (Rom. 6:13), and obeying (Rom. 6:17).

3. *Manifesting Justification.* The Christian is justified by the substitution of Jesus Christ for sinners on Calvary. Some Christians have mistakenly thought they were justified by the resurrection, basing their view on the verse that reads in the King James, "Who was delivered for our offences, and was raised again for our justification" (Rom. 4:25). The verse should be translated "raised because, or as a result of our justification." We are "Justified freely by his grace through the redemption that is in Christ Jesus" (Rom. 3:24). The substitution of Christ on Calvary was all that was needed for our justification, but that act is not accomplished in our life until a person puts his faith in Christ as Savior. This accomplishment of Calvary wins God's approval for us; the resurrection of Christ announces it to the world.

4. *Providing our future resurrection.* A major concern among Corinthian Christians was a misunderstanding of the resurrection. Some did not realize that they would be raised from the dead (1 Cor. 15:12). The fact that Jesus rose from the dead guarantees the future resurrection from the dead of every person who has died in Christ. His resurrection is a pattern and prediction of the believer's resurrection. "But now is Christ risen from the dead, and become the firstfruits of them that slept" (1 Cor. 15:20). Paul used this truth to comfort troubled Christians (1 Thess. 4:13-18). "For if we believe that Jesus died and rose again, even so them also which sleep in Jesus will God bring with him" (1 Thess. 4:14).

5. *Union with Christ.* On of the greatest privileges for a Christian is to experience identification with Christ in His death, burial and resurrection (Rom. 6:5-6). Paul uses the preposition συν (*syn*, with), in compound with 38 different words to reflect the believer's identification with Christ. Called the syn-compounds, Paul reminds Christians of their co-crucifixion, co-burial and co-resurrection. The word συν actually is translated "together" to mean complete identification between us and Christ. It fulfills the words of Jesus "you in me and I in you." Paul reminds us that He has "raised us up

THE BELIEVER'S BODY (1 Cor. 15:42-44)			
SOWN		**RAISED**	
1.	in corruption	1.	in incorruption
2.	in dishonor	2.	in glory
3.	in weakness	3.	in power
4.	a natural body	4.	a spiritual body

together and made us sit together with him in heavenly places" (Eph. 2:6). To fully understand all that happens to a Christian, we must fully understand all that happened to Christ in His resurrection.[141]

This new position is called the believer's standing in the heavenlies, as opposed to his state on earth. In Heaven the Christian is perfect, but in his state on earth he struggles with his sinful nature. In his heavenly standing he enjoys the position of being the son of God. In his earthly state, he experiences the limitations of finite life. His standing before

OUR UNION WITH CHRIST		
1.	Planted together	Romans 6:5
2.	Made alive together	Colossians 2:13 Ephesians 2:5
3.	Raised together	Ephesians 2:6
4.	Sit together	Ephesians 2:6
5.	Glorified together	Romans 8:17

God is non-experiential, but his union with Christ is his personal guarantee that one day he will enjoy all the blessings of the heavenlies that Christ now has. His state on earth remains experiential with its frustrations, temptations and despair; yet because the believer knows he is united with Christ, he experientially enjoys fellowship with the indwelling Christ, which is his assurance of the heavenly blessings to come.

> At the resurrection and ascension of Christ, the Christian received a new standing in the heavenlies. Because of the substitution of Christ for the sinner, he is identified with Christ in death, burial, and resurrection. This union is illustrated by the vine and the branches. When looking at a vine as it climbs toward the sun, it is hard to tell where the vine ends and the branches begin. So is the spiritual life of the child of God. It is not his life, but the life of Christ in him.

Chafer lists seven reasons for the resurrection and how they have a direct bearing upon His creation:

(1) Christ arose because of who He is, [Acts 2:24; John 5:26].
(2) Christ arose that He might fulfill the Davidic covenant, [2 Sam. 7:18-29; Psa. 89:20-27].
(3) Christ arose that He might become the source of resurrection life, [1 John 5:11-12; John 10:10-11].
(4) Christ arose that He might become the source of resurrection power, [Matt. 28:18; Eph. 1:19-23).
(5) Christ arose to be Head over all things to the Church, [Eph. 1:22].
(6) Christ arose on account of justification, [Rom. 4:25].
(7) Christ arose to the First-Fruits, [1 Cor. 15:20-23].[142]

Of course, there may exist some tension between one's standing and state. A believer possesses the life of Christ, but he does not always allow Christ to live through him. A Christian life is a continual growth toward becoming more Christlike here on earth. He attempts to bring his state into conformity with his standing. The moment he is saved, he receives perfection (Christ's righteousness) in Heaven, but in life he is to strive toward perfection. Like the apostle Paul, he must realize he has not "arrived" spiritually, but he is constantly pressing in the right direction (Phil. 3:11-14).

F. CONCLUSION. The witness of the resurrection of Jesus Christ from the dead begins in historical verification; i.e., He was "crucified under Pontius Pilate, dead and buried." This same Jesus Christ was reunited with His physical body and came back from the dead a spiritual body, subjecting the powers of death and Hell to God. He ended the kenosis, and made available all the spiritual resources to those who through faith were co-raised with Him. And as such, the resurrection is the indispensable foundation of Christianity.

> Blessed be the God and Father of our Lord Jesus Christ, which according to his abundant mercy hath begotten us again unto a lively hope by the resurrection of Jesus Christ from the dead. To an inheritance incorruptible, and undefiled, and that fadeth not away, reserved in heaven for you (1 Pet. 1:3-4).

XIII. THE ASCENSION

There is a dividing line between the Christ of history (birth, ministry, death and resurrection) and the Christ in Heaven who now ministers to Christians in spiritual experiences. That line is the ascension. Paul describes: "Even though we have known Christ according to the flesh, yet now we know Him thus no longer" (2 Cor. 5:16). After He ascended into Heaven, Christ was no less alive than on earth. His ministry is different and is based on all He accomplished while on earth.

The ascension involves two steps: (1) He was received up into Heaven, and (2) He sat down at the right hand of God. These are technically called His ascension and His session. Sometimes one aspect is mentioned, at other times both.

The Historical narrative of the ascension is barely mentioned in the Gospels (Mark 16:19; Luke 24:51), not because it is unimportant, but because it would have emphasized the importance of the termination of His earthly life. Obviously the emphasis is on the continuation of what Christ began on earth. The main reference to the ascension is given at the beginning of Acts, emphasizing it as the gateway to Pentecost and the point from which Christ sent the Spirit to the church.

The ascension is described by Luke, "until the day in which He was received up" (ανελήφθη, *anelephthen* "to be taken up," Acts 1:2). Next He describes the eleven, "as they were looking He was taken up (έπήρθη "to receive") and a cloud received Him out of their sight" (Acts 1:9). Then Luke describes the ascension, "The heavens must receive Him until the times of restoration of all things" (Acts 3:21). Stephen saw Christ "standing on the right hand of God (Acts 7:56), and Peter speaks of Jesus as having "gone into heaven" (1 Pet. 3:22). Paul adds, "He that descended is the same also that ascended up far above all heavens" (Eph. 4:10), and then He was "received up into glory" (1 Tim. 3:16). The writer of Hebrews also notes that Christ was "a great high priest that is passed into the heavens" (Heb. 4:14).

The ascension should not have come as a surprise to the disciples. Jesus had predicted, "What and if ye shall see the Son of man ascend up where he was before?" (John 6:62), and "I go to my Father and ye see me no more" (John 16:10), "I ascend unto my Father, and your Father, and to my God, and your God" (John 20:17).

After the resurrection, each time Jesus left His disciples He seemed to disappear instantaneously (Luke 24:31). However, at the ascension, He left them gradually. He was giving them a message that He would no more appear physically, nor would they relate to Him in the flesh. The ascension was gradual: "While they beheld" (Acts 1:9), He slowly ascended until He was "taken up" from them. The ascension puts an end to all physical contact with Christ. It was a once-and-for-all withdrawal by Christ from His earthly ministry.

The word "ascend" comes from the Latin word *ascendit*, which implies "the going up" of the Son of God. But the Scripture also notes, "He was taken up," as though the ascension was an assumption. The first implies Christ entering the presence of the Father in a triumphant display of power and majesty. The second emphasizes the Father's act in exalting His Son and putting Heaven's seal of approval on all that Christ did on earth. The first reveals Christ as the sinless man who is able to ascend into Heaven on His own righteousness (Psa. 24:3). The second is tied to the *kenosis* where the Son who is perfect, yields to the Father who exalts Him into Heaven.

When Jesus ascended He went beyond the earthly atmosphere. Paul notes the plural for heavens, He "that ascended up far above all heavens" (Eph. 4:10). The author of Hebrews observes that Christ "passed into the heavens" (Heb. 4:14), and, "made higher than the heavens" (Heb. 7:26). The eleven saw Him go into heaven, (singular) (Acts 1:11). Perhaps this is only describing the disciples' point of reference.

When Christ entered Heaven, He was the triumphant Son of God who now was given "the glory" which He had with the Father "before the world was" (John 17:5). But He was not simply the restored Son of God who was returning to take up where He left off when He came to earth. Christ returned as the eternal God-man, He was eternally joined to flesh. He was now a man in the glory (Heb. 7:24), with a new priestly ministry of intercession and advocacy.

Psalm 110:1 was fulfilled at the ascension: "The Lord said unto my Lord, sit thou at my right hand, until I make thine enemies thy footstool." Here is a conversation of Jehovah asking a person identified as "Lord," to sit at His right hand. Christ on earth understood this was a reference to Him because He told the High Priest, "ye shall see the Son of man sitting on the right hand of power" (Matt. 26:64). Psalm 110 describes the Person sitting at the Father's right hand as one given the duty of a priest. "The Lord has sworn and will not repent, Thou art a priest forever after the order of Melchizedek" (v. 4). After the ascension, Christ is a priest. The picture is complete. The One who entered the presence of the Father is seated at His right hand. He is the Priest who will hold this office forever. Jehovah further assures Christ that in the future He will have complete victory over His enemies. The author of Hebrews describes this scene, "We see Jesus . . . crowned with glory and honor . . . from henceforth expecting till his enemies be made his footstool" (Heb. 2:9; 10:13).

The picture of Christ sitting is one of rest and calm. Just as God rested after His six days of work in Creation (Gen. 2:2), the Son rested after His work on earth. There were no chairs or furniture on which the priest could sit in the Tabernacle, because he was to work, to carry out His work of atonement. On Calvary, Christ finished His work of atonement; now, as the prototype; He is seated in glory. To the overcomers, He promises, "I will give to him to sit down with me in my throne, as I also overcame, and sat down with my Father in His throne" (Rev. 3:21).

Hoeksema believes that when Christ sat in Heaven, it was only a figure of speech.

Now we all understand, of course, that the expression, "sitting on the right hand of God" is a figurative term. It is not to be understood in a local sense; nor is there a particular spot in heaven that is indicated by the phrase "at the right hand of God." The expression rather indicates a position of power and might, of authority and dominion, of majesty and glory, and that too, of universal and of the very highest power and authority and might and dominion. It denotes that Christ is Lord over all and is exalted over all created things in heaven and on earth and under the earth. It signifies that He is raised to the very pinnacle of all created things. In all the wide creation there is no creature over which Christ does not sway His scepter, which He does not hold in His power, and which He does not render subservient to His will and purpose.[143]

While there is figurative language in Scripture, this is not one of the references. Christ was actually seated at the right hand of the Father, which is called his localized presence. Yet Christ lives in believers, which is called his indwelling presence. He is in the church, which is called his institutional presence and He is everywhere present equally at all times, which is called His omnipresence. Strong explains that Christ can be at different places by making a distinction between Christ's soul and glorified body.

But this is not to say that Christ's human *body* is everywhere present. It would seem that body must exist in spatial relations, and be confined to place. We do not know that this is so with regard to soul. Heaven would seem to be a place, because Christ's body is there; and a spiritual body is not a body which is spirit, but a body which is suited to the uses of the spirit. But even though Christ may manifest himself in a glorified human body, only in heaven, his human soul, by virtue of its union with the divine nature, can at the same moment be with all his scattered people over the whole earth.[144]

While this explanation seems plausible, it may be too simplistic. Even though Christ has a glorified body, we know little of it, yet we affirm He is everywhere present, and that presence is more than just His soul.

A. THE NATURE OF THE ASCENSION. The disciples who witnessed the ascension of Christ probably did not completely understand what they were seeing, for it involved more than His physical return to Heaven. There are five different aspects of the ascension.

1. *The end of self-limitation.* Technically called the *kenosis*, this self-limitation of Christ ended at the ascension. Jesus Christ in the flesh was the omnipotent God who spoke the world into existence (John 1:3; Heb. 11:3); yet during His earthly life and ministry He chose not to exercise that power (John 18:36f; Acts 10:38). Jesus

---

NATURE OF THE ASCENSION

1. The end of self-limitation
2. The transfiguration of Christ
3. The exaltation of Christ
4. The entrance of humanity into heaven
5. The beginning of a new ministry

Christ in the flesh was the omniscient God who understood all the intricacies of our immense universe, yet during His earthly ministry there were some things He chose not to know (Mark 13:32). Jesus Christ in the flesh was omnipresent, meaning He was everywhere present in the vast universe, yet during His time on earth, He chose to limit Himself to the confines of a human body (John 1:14). At the ascension of Christ, these self-limitations were ended.

2. *The transfiguration of Christ.* That celestial glory that Jesus had from the beginning, was temporarily hidden during His earthly life. Even though John said, "We beheld His glory, the glory as of the only begotten of the Father" (John 1:14), John was not referring to the outward manifestation of light and the bright, shining appearance. The "glory of God" was that Deity condescended to become flesh and dwell with men. Perhaps the phrase "glory of God" was a reference to the Shekinah Glory that tabernacles in a tent in the Old Testament, but in the New Testament tabernacles in flesh. Only once during His life do we obviously see His shining glory when Jesus "was transfigured" (Matt. 17:2) on the mount. Others imply it was revealed in the garden and drove back these who would arrest Jesus (John 18:6). Some feel the earthly humanity was the perfect example of what every man should become, hence as a man Jesus glorified God.

As Jesus approached the cross, He prayed, "And now, O Father, glorify thou me with thine own self with the glory which I had with thee before the world was" (John 17:5). When Jesus hung on the cross, He looked forward to the glorification of Himself, "Thou shalt be with me in paradise." The glorification of Christ innately involves who He is and what He has accomplished. The glorification means to recognize Christ and worship Him, giving honor and worth to the Son of God. The transfiguration of Christ involves the celestial (shining, bright, illuminated) appearance that He gives.

At the ascension of Christ, Jesus was both glorified and transfigured. He was glorified: "Wherefore God also hath highly exalted him, and given him a name which is above every name" (Phil. 2:9). Where the previous glory of Christ in Heaven was dependent upon His Person, this added dimension of glory is based upon His completed work. He was transfigured, in that when John saw Christ on the isle of Patmos, His face shone, His feet were shining, etc. (Rev. 1:13-18).

It is interesting to contrast the post-resurrection appearances of Christ and the post-ascension revelations. In the former instances, Christ often veiled His glory to the point He was not recognized, such as when the disciples at Emmaus did not recognize Him (Luke 24:16, 31), or Mary Magdalene did not recognize Him (John 20:14). The post-ascension revelations involve His shining appearance. The difference between John's meeting with Christ in John 21 and Revelation 1 was, first, seeing the resurrected physical body and second, seeing the transformed and celestial body.

3. *The exaltation of Christ.* Closely related to His glorification was the exaltation of Christ to His new position of authority as the God-man. Peter quoted Psalm 110:1 in his message on the day of Pentecost, emphasizing Christ's resurrection. Then he concluded by pointing out the lordship of Jesus Christ, "Therefore let all the house of Israel know assuredly, that God hath made that same Jesus, whom ye have crucified, both Lord and Christ" (Acts 2:36). The apostle Paul also cited the ascension of Christ as the point of His exaltation. "Wherefore, God also hath highly exalted Him, and given him a name which is above every name" (Phil. 2:9). Jesus is the object of worship by those around His throne. They cry out, "Worthy is the Lamb" (Rev. 5:12).

4. *The entrance of humanity into heaven.* Jesus was the first man to enter Heaven. Actually the first to enter God's presence without dying were Enoch and Elijah (Gen. 5:24; 1 Kgs. 2:11, *Criswell Reference Bible*, p. 13). Yet some question if they entered Heaven, but rather Sheol/Abraham's bosom. Even if they entered heaven, Christ's entrance was first in priority because of its significance, rather than chronologically. Sheol was apparently divided, with no fellowship between the believers and unbelievers. But with the resurrection and ascension of Christ, the believers in Sheol went into Heaven with Christ. The Scriptures teach, "When he [Jesus] ascended up on high, He led captivity captive" (Eph. 4:8). Now a believer enters immediately into heaven upon death (Phil. 1:21-23). Paul noted, "To be absent from the body, and to be present with the Lord" (2 Cor. 5:8). This part of the believer's experience is only possible because the "forerunner is for us entered, even Jesus" (Heb. 6:20). Jesus was the first man to enter Heaven with a glorified body. At His ascension, He became a man in the glory.

5. *The beginning of a new ministry.* When Jesus ascended into Heaven, He did not cease from His labors. He has added a new ministry. On earth, Christ finished His task of dying for

the salvation of the world (John 3:17), but now He lives for the saved as their intercessor and advocate. As an intercessor, Jesus is continually interceding for Christians when they are tempted by sin (Heb. 7:25). He gives them grace to keep from sinning. If, on occasion, they should yield to temptation and sin, Jesus becomes their Advocate before God (1 John 2:1). As such, Christ forgives the sin, based on His sacrifice, and restores the Christian after he sins. (For a further discussion of the present ministry of Christ, see Christology, V).

While the doctrine of the ascension appears to be straightforward so that the average Christian could not mistake its meaning, there are those who interpret it wrongly. Berkhof has summarized the Lutheran view of the ascension. "They regard it, not as a local transition, but as a change of condition, whereby the human nature of Christ passed into the full enjoyment and exercise of the divine perfections, communicated to it at the incarnation, and thus became permanently omnipresent."[145]   In answer, Christ did not change His nature after the incarnation, but He was recognized for His accomplishments. Also He assumed the exercise of those attributes He had voluntarily given up at His birth.

Berkhof says that some have claimed that Heaven was a condition rather than a place, therefore the ascension was not a local event. They suggest that the lifting up of Christ in the sight of the eleven might have been momentary and symbolic of the lifting up of our humanity to be a new heightened spiritual order.[146]   But Heaven is a real place and should not be "spiritualized" away.

Finally, Lewis S. Chafer holds to the two ascensions or the many ascension theory.

> While it is probable that Christ was resident in heaven from the resurrection day onward and only visited the earth as contact with His followers dictated (cf. John 17:16)—in which case there were a number of ascensions.[147]

However, Chafer indicates on Easter morning that Christ ascended to cleanse Heaven. In John 20:17, Jesus said, "Touch me not; for I am not yet ascended to my Father: but go to my brethren, and say unto them, I ascend unto my Father, and your Father; and to my God and to your God." Then Chafer points out that Christ allows Himself to be handled that evening (Luke 24:38-40).

> The implication is clear that, since He could not be touched in the morning until He ascended and yet He could be "handled" at evening of the same day, He had ascended during the day. He ascended at once from the tomb and returned for such manifestations as were appointed for that day. "Go to my brethren, and say unto them, I ascend unto my Father" means that He was about to ascend. Had He made reference in this message to His final ascension, there was no need that Mary carry the message of that to His disciples, since He Himself had before Him the entire forty days in which to deliver the news Himself. Of the two recorded ascensions, that of the resurrection morn holds the greater doctrinal significance.[148]

This view takes away from the significance of the historical ascension. Also, if Christ went to Heaven on Easter morning, it was not the triumphant entrance that is associated with the ascension. Many question whether the cleansing of Heaven took place on resurrection morning, or actually occurred elsewhere.

B. The Results of the Ascension of Christ. Everything Jesus accomplished impacts the life of the believer. As a result of the ascension of Christ, Christians have a number of benefits for a fulfilled life and successful service. The following chart identifies some of the results of the ascension of Christ.

THE RESULTS OF THE ASCENSION OF CHRIST		
1.	The sending of the Holy Spirit	John 16:7
2.	The giving of spiritual gifts	Ephesians 4:8
3.	The imparting of spiritual power	Acts 1:8
4.	The preparation of a heavenly home	John 14:3
5.	The standing of the believer	Romans 8:29

1. *The sending of the Holy Spirit.* Christ ascended to Heaven, and provided the ministry of the Holy Spirit for the church. Jesus taught that both He (John 15:20) and the Father (John 14:26) would send the "Comforter." The ministry of the Holy Spirit is needed to fulfill the work that Christ accomplished on Calvary. Jesus promised, "Nevertheless, I tell you the truth; it is expedient for you that I go away: for if I go not away, the Comforter will not come unto you; but if I depart, I will send him unto you" (John 16:7). This promise was again repeated by Jesus on the last recorded meeting with His disciples on the day of His ascension (Acts 1:5). After they tarried in the upper room, the Holy Spirit came in mighty power upon the disciples (Acts 2:1-4). Today the Holy Spirit lives in every Christian (1 Cor. 6:19) giving him the ability to live for God (Gal. 5:25).

2. *The giving of spiritual gifts.* When a person is saved, he not only receives the Holy Spirit, he also receives his spiritual gift(s) (1 Cor. 12:11; 1 Pet. 4:10). Spiritual gifts were given initially by Christ. "When he ascended upon high, He led captivity captive, and gave gifts unto men" (Eph. 4:8). These spiritual abilities were given embryonically at either the resurrection or ascension, when the Holy Spirit was made available to the church in general and to believers in particular. The gift that is like a seed, must be discovered and developed by the believer.

3. *The imparting of spiritual power.* At the ascension of Christ, He promised spiritual power to His disciples. Jesus instructed His disciples to "tarry ye in the city of Jerusalem, until ye be endued with power from on high" (Luke 24:49). On the day of Pentecost, the disciples

received this spiritual power to witness. The power was continuously present in their lives as they continued to be filled with the Holy Spirit.

Some have developed a doctrine of "tarrying," whereby they plead and wait for spiritual power. Many go to the church altar to pray for spiritual power as the mourners' bench was used in former days. The Christian does not need to plead for the Holy Spirit because he is indwelt with the Holy Spirit. The Holy Spirit is available to those who yield (Eph. 5:18) and obey (Rom. 6:11-17). The Christian does not need more of the Holy Spirit; the reverse is true. The Holy Spirit needs more of the Christian. Christ's instruction to "tarry" was not a theological principle, but rather a geographical necessity until the day of Pentecost.

4. *The preparation of a heavenly home.* The ascension involves Christ's preparation of Heaven for Christians. Jesus said, "In my Father's house are many mansions; if it were no so, I would have told you. I go to prepare a place for you" (John 14:3). When Jesus ascended to His Father's house, we must assume He began preparing a heavenly home for those who believe in Him.

5. *The standing of the believer.* When Jesus ascended to His Father, Christians ascended with Him. God "hath raised us up together, and made us sit together in heavenly places in Christ Jesus" (Eph. 2:6). Because of their identification with Christ, the Christian is raised up and stands before God as co-partakers in the ascension of Christ.

C. CONCLUSION. Very little space is given in Scripture to the virgin birth and ascension— entrance and exit from the world. While only one reference is needed to verify their truthfulness and importance for theology, the little space given to these two doctrines confirms God's priority towards truth. It is not His entrance and exit that is efficacious, but His death on Calvary. However, if these two doctrines were not mentioned at all, many questions would linger. Is Christ still limiting His relative attributes today, or does He fully manifest His omniscience, omnipresence and omnipotence? Was the atonement fully acceptable to the Father, or does the sinner still need to do good works to please the Father? What will happen to the Christian at death? Where are those today who have died in Christ? But these and other questions are answered by the ascension and present session of Jesus Christ in Glory.

ENDNOTES

1.   Merrill C. Tenney, *John: The Gospel of Belief* (Grand Rapids: Eerdmans, 1948), 106.

2.   Arthur Walkington Pink, *Exposition of the Gospel of John* (Grand Rapids: Zondervan, 1974), 2:146.

3. William Barclay, *The Gospel of John* (Philadelphia: Westminster Press, 1956), 2:88.
4. Thomas Schultz, "The Doctrine of the Person of Christ with an Emphasis upon the Hypostatic Union" (Dallas: Dallas Theological Seminary, May 1962), 209.
5. William Robinson, *Our Lord* (Grand Rapids: Eerdmans, 1949), 29.*
6. Norman L. Geisler, *Christ: The Theme of the Bible* (Chicago: Moody Press, 1969), 48-49.
7. Cited by Robinson, *Our Lord*, 115.*
8. Hilarin, Felder, *Christ and the Critics*, trans. by John L. Stoddard (London: Burns Oates and Washburn Ltd., 1924), 1:268-269.
9. Herbert F. Stevenson, *Titles of the Triune God* (Westwood, NJ: Fleming H. Revell Co., 1956), 123.*
10. C. F. Montefiore, *The Synoptic Gospels* (London: MacMillan and Co., Ltd., 1909), 1:361.
11. Karl Scheffrahn and Henry Kreyssler, *Jesus of Nazareth: Who Did He Claim to Be?* (Dallas: Pat Booth, 1968), 9-10.*
12. Stevenson, *Titles*, 120.*
13. Pink, *Gospel of John*, 1:21.
14. Tenney, *Gospel of Belief*, 62.
15. T. C. Horton and Charles E. Hurlburt, *The Wonderful Names of Our Wonderful Lord* (Los Angeles: Grant Publishing House, 1925). There are 365 names and titles of Christ covered on pp. 1-183.
16. Bernard Pick, "Theophany," *Cyclopedia of Biblical, Theological, and Ecclesiastical Literature*, ed. John McClintock and James Strong (Grand Rapids: Baker Book House, 1970), 10:332.
17. James A. Borland, *Christ in the Old Testament* (Chicago: Ross-shire: Christian Focus, 1999), 17.
18. J. Barton Payne, *The Theology of the Older Testament* (Grand Rapids: Zondervan, 1962), 167.
19. William G. Moorehead, "Type," *The International Standard Bible Encyclopedia*, ed. by James Orr (Grand Rapids: Eerdmans, 1939), 5:3029.
20. *New Scofield Reference Bible*, 6. ftnt. 1.
21. C. Sumner Wemp, *Teaching from the Tabernacle* (Chicago: Moody Press, 1976), 11.
22. Ibid., 12.
23. Geisler, *Christ*, 41.
24. *New Scofield Reference Bible*, p. 995, ftnt. 3.
25. L. D. Bevan, "Offices of Christ," *The International Standard Bible Encyclopedia*, 1:621.

26. Augustus Hopkins Strong, *Systematic Theology*, 710.
27. Ibid.
28. Ibid., 713.
29. Bevan, "Offices of Christ," 1:620.
30. Strong, 775.
31. Louis Matthews Sweet, "Virgin Birth of Jesus Christ," *The International Standard Bible Encyclopedia*, 3056.
32. Clinton N. Howard, "Jesus—Son of Joseph or Son of God?" *The Sword of the Lord* 48 (December 25, 1981), 52:7.*
33. C. F. Keil and F. Delitzsch, *Commentary on the Old Testament* (Grand Rapids: Eerdmans, 1975), 102.
34. George L. Lawlor, *Almah—Virgin or Young Woman?* (Des Planes, Illinois: Regular Baptist Press, 1973), 26-27.*
35. Ibid., 30.*
36. John F. Walvoord, *Jesus Christ Our Lord* (Chicago: Moody, 1969), 144.
37. Archibald Alexander Hodge, *Outlines of Theology* (New York: Robert Carter and Brothers, 1867), 285.*
38. Paul K. Jewett, "Kenosis," *Wycliffe Bible Encyclopedia* (Chicago: Moody 1975), 2:988.
39. Alex. B. Bruce, *The Humiliation of Christ* (Grand Rapids: Eerdmans, 1955), 133-191. See this volume for a thorough discussion of the various erroneous views of the *kenosis*.
40. Louis Berkhof, *Systematic Theology* (Grand Rapids: Baker, 1951), 327.
41. Bruce, 153.
42. Berkhof, 328.
43. Bruce, 143.
44. Burton Scott Easton, "Kenosis," *The International Standard Bible Encyclopedia* (Grand Rapids: Eerdmans, 1939), 3:1792.
45. Walvoord, 138.
46. James Oliver Buswell, Jr., *A Systematic Theology of the Christian Religion* (Grand Rapids: Zondervan, 1963), 2:24.
47. J. B. Lightfoot, *St. Paul's Epistle to the Philippians* (London: Macmillan and Co., 1869), 110.
48. Leon Morris, *The Gospel According to John*, ed. F. F. Bruce, *The New International Commentary on the New Testament* (Grand Rapids: Eerdmans, 1971), 102.
49. Marvin R. Vincent, *Word Studies in the New Testament* (Grand Rapids: Eerdmans, 1973), 2:51.
50. Ibid.

51.   R. V. G. Tasker, *The Gospel According to St. John*, ed. R. V. G. Tasker, *The Tyndale New Testament Commentaries* (Grand Rapids: Eerdmans, 1960), 48.

52.   Hodge, 288.*

53.   Strong, *Systematic Theology*, 704.

54.   G. Cornelius Berkouwer, *The Person of Christ* (Grand Rapids: Eerdmans, 1954), 224.

55.   Henry C. Thiessen, *Lectures in Systematic Theology*, rev. Vernon D. Doerksen (Grand Rapids: Eerdmans, 1979), 216.

56.   Walvoord, 114.

57.   Louis Berkhof, 321.

58.   Ibid.

59.   Marvin R. Vincent, *Word Studies in the New Testament*, 3 vols. (Grand Rapids: Eerdmans, 1946), 2:32.

60.   William G. T. Shedd, *Dogmatic Theology*, 3 vols. (Nashville: Thomas Nelson, 1980), 2:267.

61.   Ibid., 2:279.

62.   Ibid., 2:272-73.

63.   Ibid., 2:268-69.

64.   Lewis Sperry Chafer, *Systematic Theology*, 8 vols, (Dallas: Dallas Seminary Press, 1948), 1:72.

65.   See H. E. Dana and Julius R. Mantey, *A Manual Grammar of the Greek New Testament* (Toronto: The Macmillan Company, 1955), 149, "Sometimes with a noun which the context proves to be definite the article is not used. This places stress upon the qualitative aspect of the noun rather than its mere identity." In other words, John 1:1 declares that the Word was of the same nature as God; He was Deity; also see A. T. Robertson and W. Davis, *A New Short Grammar of the Greek Testament* (New York: Harper and Brothers, 1933), 279,* "As a rule when the article is used with the one and not with the other means that the particular noun is the subject . . . in John 1:1 the meaning has to be 'the Logos was God,' not 'God was the Logos.'"

66.   Chafer, *Systematic Theology*, 5:8.

67.   Leon Morris, *The Gospel According to John*, in *The New International Commentary on The New Testament* (Grand Rapids: Eerdmans, 1971), 104.

68.   Shedd, 2:269.

69.   Ibid., 2:272.

70.   Ibid., 2:278.

71.   William G. T. Shedd, *A History of Christian Doctrine*, 2 vols. (New York: Charles Scribner & Co., 1868), 1:399-400.

72. Shedd, *Dogmatic Theology*, 2:327-28.

73. Strong, 684.

74. Ibid.

75. Ibid., 698.

76. Walvoord, *Jesus Christ Our Lord*, 114-116.

77. Ibid., 114-115.

78. Ibid., 115.

79. G. C. Berkouwer, *The Person of Christ* (Grand Rapids: Eerdmans Publishing Co., 1954), 276.

80. Walvoord, *Jesus Christ Our Lord*, 116.

81. Ibid.

82. Ibid., 117-118. In the outline Walvoord uses the definite article "the" before the word "predicate." However, the seven points aforementioned are explained by the author from his perspective.

83. Ibid., 120-22.

84. Shedd, *Dogmatic Theology*, 311-349.*

85. Charles Randall Barnes, *The People's Bible Encyclopedia* (Chicago: People's Publication Society, 1913), 2:1691-92.*

86. John S. Feinberg, *Theology of Man, Sin, and Angels* THEO 625 (class lecture, Liberty Baptist Seminary, Spring 1983).

87. Shedd, *Dogmatic Theology*, 2:330.

88. Lewis Sperry Chafer, *Systematic Theology* (Dallas: Dallas Seminary Press, 1962), 3:302.*

89. Shedd, 2:344.

90. Ibid., 2:343.

91. Friedrich Büchsel, *"Theology Dictionary of the New Testament*, ed. G. Kittel (Grand Rapids: Eerdmans, 1974), 3:171.

92. Shedd, *Dogmatic Theology*, 2:335.

93. Ibid., 2:344.

94. Ibid., 2:330-31.

95. John Murray, *The Epistles to the Romans*, in *The New International Commentary on the New Testament* (Grand Rapids: Eerdmans, 1973), 117-118.

96. Charles Hodge, *Systematic Theology* (Grand Rapids: Eerdmans, 1975), 2:475.

97. Shedd, *Dogmatic Theology*, 2:379.

98. Ibid., 2:382.

99. Chafer, 7:53.

100. Ibid.

101. Hodge, 2:502.

102. James Hope Moulton and George Milligan, *The Vocabulary of the Greek Testament* (Grand Rapids: Eerdmans, 1972), 6.

103. Leon Morris, "Propitiation," *Baker's Dictionary of Theology,* ed. Everett F. Harrison (Grand Rapids: Baker Book House), 424-25.

104. Murray, 116.

105. Gerhard Delling, *Theological Dictionary of the New Testament,* ed. G. Friedrich (Grand Rapids: Eerdmans, 1975), 6:294.

106. F. F. Bruce, *The Epistle of Paul to the Romans* (Grand Rapids: Eerdmans, 1963), 203.*

107. Francis Brown, S. R. Driver, and Charles A. Briggs, *A Hebrew and English Lexicon of the Old Testament* (Oxford: Clarendon Press, 1977), 497.

108. Büchsel, *Theological Dictionary of the New Testament* (Grand Rapids: Eerdmans, 1972), 1:258.

109. John Murray, *Redemption Accomplished and Applied* (Grand Rapids: Eerdmans, 1982), 33.*

110. James O. Buswell, Jr., *A Systematic Theology of the Christian Religion* (Grand Rapids: Zondervan, 1962), 2:202. Buswell explains asymptotically as meaning "two lines which constantly approach one another but do not actually meet."

111. Chafer, 3:103-104.

112. Charles Hodge, *A Commentary on Romans* (London: The Banner of Truth Trust, 1972), 374.

113. Charles Caldwell Ryrie, *The Basis of the Premillennial Faith* (New Jersey: Loizeaux Brothers, 1981), 107.

114. Chafer, 3:111.

115. Ibid., 3:113-114.

116. Christopher F. Evans, *Resurrection and the New Testament* (Naperville: Allenson, 1970), 1.

117. Rudolph Bultmann, *Kerygma and Myth: A Theological Debate* (London: S.P.C.K., 1953), 39.

118. Rudolph Bultmann, *Existence and Faith: Shorter Writings of Rudolf Bultmann,* ed. And trans. by Schubert M. Ogden (New York: Meridan Books, 1960), 291.

119. Herman Samuel Reimarus, *The Goal of Jesus and His Disciples,* trans. by G. W. Buchanan (Leiden: Brill, 1970), 108-110.

120. Hugh Schonfield, *The Passover Plot* (New York: Bernard Gels, 1965). The theory did not come out of the academic community, but was a popular novel that was successfully promoted by TV appearances, autograph parties and other sales devices.

121. Kirsopp Lake, *The Resurrection of Jesus Christ* (London: Williams and Norgate, 1912).*

122.   Walter Kunneth, *The Theology of the Resurrection* (London: S.C.M., 1965), 60.

123.   Ibid., 78.

124.   Ibid., 80.

125.   Reginald H. Fuller, *The Formation of the Resurrection Narratives* (New York: Macmillan and Co., 1971), 48.

126.   Bultmann, *Kerygma and Myth*, 42.

127.   George Hanson, *The Resurrection and the Life* (New York: Fleming H. Revell, 1911), 27.

128.   Alexander Thomson, *Did Jesus Rise From the Dead?* (Grand Rapids: Zondervan, 1940), 24.

129.   Louis Berkhof, *Systematic Theology* (Grand Rapids: Eerdmans, 1972), 349.

130.   Clark Pinnock, "On the Third Day," in *Jesus of Nazareth: Savior and Lord*, ed. by C. F. Henry (Grand Rapids: Eerdmans, 1966), 153.*

131.   Ibid., Merrill Tenney, "The Historicity of the Resurrection," 139.*

132.   James Denney, *Jesus and the Gospel* (London: Hodder and Stoughton, 1908), 111.*

133.   John Dick, *Lectures on Theology* (New York: Robert Carter and Brothers, 1878), 2:106.

134.   Robert Dabney, *Lectures in Systematic Theology* (Grand Rapids: Zondervan Publishing Co., 1975), 548.*

135.   Richard Riss, *The Evidence for the Resurrection of Jesus Christ* (Minnesota: Bethany Fellowship, 1977), 62.

136.   Everett F. Harrison, *The Christian Doctrine of the Resurrection*, unpublished manuscript, p. 56, cited by L. S. Chafer, *Systematic Theology*, 5:241-42.

137.   Berkhof, 346.

138.   Shedd, *Dogmatic Theology*, 2:653.

139.   John Gill, *A Body of Divinity* (Grand Rapids: Sovereign Grace Publishers, 1971), 413.

140.   Loraine Boettner, *Studies in Theology* (Philadelphia: Presbyterian and Reformed, 1970), 191.

141.   Carl B. Hoch, Jr., "The Significance of the *Syn*-Compounds for Jew-Gentile Relationships in the Body of Christ," *Journal of the Evangelical Theological Society*, 25:2 (June, 1982) 175-183.

142.   Chafer, 5:245.

143.   Herman Hoeksema, *Reformed Dogmatics* (Grand Rapids: Reformed Free Publishing Assoc., 1966), 429.

144.   Augustus Hopkins Strong, *Systematic Theology* (New Jersey: Fleming H. Revell Co., 1907), 709.

145.   Louis Berkhof, *Systematic Theology* (Grand Rapids: Eerdmans, 1932), 351.
146.   Ibid., 350.
147.   Chafer, 5:262.
148.   Ibid., 263.
* Denotes page number(s) could not be verified.

CHAPTER V - PNEUMATOLOGY

The Doctrine of the Holy Spirit

The historic neglect of the doctrine of the Holy Spirit has caused more than one Christian leader to refer to Him as "the forgotten member of the Trinity." Classical theologians rarely devote more than a single chapter to pneumatology in their systematic theology. Prior to the beginning of the twentieth century, comparatively little was addressed concerning the person and work of the third Person of the Trinity. In this present century, much of the pneumatological discussion has been introduced by two sources. First, the dispensationalists have called this the Age of the Holy Spirit. Second, the charismatics seem to make the Holy Spirit the apex of their Christian experience. Anglican Canon Michael Green is correct when he observes,

> The Christian Church has always had a good many professing members who know about as much about the Holy Spirit in their experience as those disciples at Ephesus who were asked by Paul, "Did you receive the Holy Spirit when you believed?" and who replied, "No, we have never even heard that there is a Holy Spirit" (Acts 19:2).[1]

Green is implying that the average Christian has little understanding of the Holy Spirit. A. W. Tozer agrees.

> The idea of the Spirit held by the average church member is so vague as to be nearly nonexistent. When he thinks of the matter at all he is very likely to try to imagine a nebulous substance like a wisp of invisible smoke which is said to be present in churches and to hover over good people when they are dying. Frankly he does not believe in any such thing, but he wants to believe something, and not feeling up to the task of examining the whole truth in the light of Scripture he compromises by holding belief in the Spirit as far out from the center of his life as possible, letting it make no difference in anything that touches him practically. This describes a surprisingly large number of earnest persons who are sincerely trying to be Christians.[2]

261

Certainly the apparent neglect and subsequent ignorance about the Holy Spirit demands a closer examination. Further, the presence and growing international influence of the charismatic movement means non-charismatic Christians need to review their pneumatology in light of this contemporary phenomenon and be certain their principles and practices in this area are indeed biblical. Also, he who desires a clearer understanding of God and His work cannot achieve this end without an understanding of the personality and work of the Holy Spirit. Finally, an understanding of the Holy Spirit will protect a Christian from error that would not only frustrate spiritual growth, and will insulate him from some cultic groups that might attempt to seriously disrupt social relationships, and in some cases, physically endanger him. The importance of pneumatology as an imperative part of one's systematic theology was stressed by the writer who observed, "I have come more and more to view that the real cause of many controversial issues is the implied doctrine of the Holy Spirit."[3]

Fortunately, this sadly neglected doctrine is not as neglected today. There are several reasons for the recent emphasis on the study of this doctrine. The study of the Holy Spirit has been highlighted by dispensationalists who have noted the differences between the Old and New Testaments, noting the special ministry of the Holy Spirit in this dispensation.

Secondly, present-day needs have made the study of the Holy Spirit imperative. The influence of evolutionary teaching during the past century has caused Christians to study the work of the Holy Spirit in creation. Also, the doctrine of inspiration has been consistently attacked by liberals. As a result, conservatives have again focused their attention on the major role of the Holy Spirit in inspiration. As the evangelical doctrine of regeneration has been clarified, the role of the Holy Spirit has again been studied.

A third major reason for the renewal of interest in the Holy Spirit is the contemporary charismatic movement and the emphasis of that movement on the miraculous sign gifts of the New Testament. Some choose to write off the entire movement as faddish enthusiasm, while others regard it as a satanic attempt to duplicate the temporary phenomena of the first century. Regardless of one's opinion of the movement, the fact is that the many opinions about the movement have caused others to study the doctrine of the Holy Spirit.

A restoration of apostolic Christianity requires a biblical pneumatology. According to C. K. Barrett, "No more certain statement can be made about the Christians of the first generation than this: They believed themselves to be living under the immediate government of the Spirit of God."[4] In apparent agreement, Vincent Taylor notes, "The most immediate and striking impression regarding the origin and progress of early Christianity which we gain from the New Testament is the strong consciousness of the first believers of the being and the power and direction of the Spirit of God."[5]

I. THE PERSONALITY OF THE HOLY SPIRIT

Much confusion exists today concerning the Person of the Holy Spirit. His personality is denied by both liberal theologians and extreme religious cults. Some liberals will acknowledge he is portrayed as a Person, but claim the Scripture is communicating a myth. Radical cults like the Jehovah's Witnesses deny His personality, referring to Him as simply an influence. Because of the comparatively little teaching about the Holy Spirit that has been done over the years, some good Christians do not realize that the Holy Spirit is a Person.

Contemporary denial of the personality of the Holy Spirit is not a recent trend. Historically, there have been several sects that have denied the personality of the Holy Spirit, claiming He is merely "energy of God." As Hodge notes,

> Those early heretical sects, generally styled Monarchians and Patripassians, all with subordinate distinctions taught that there was but one person as well as one essence in the Godhead, who, in different relations, is called Father, Son, or Holy Ghost. In the sixteenth century Socinus, who taught that Jesus Christ was a mere man, maintained that the term Holy Ghost is in Scripture used as a designation of God's energy, when exercised in a particular way. This is now the opinion of all modern Unitarians and Rationalists.[6]

Theologians who deny the personality of the Holy Spirit tend to use the term "Spirit" to refer to the involvement of God in the world or some aspect of the work of the Trinity, i.e., revelation or the enduement of power. Hendry reveals this bias when he attempts to define the Holy Spirit as a non-person. In two attempts at such a definition, he suggests,

> If the Holy Spirit means the Living action of God in the world (and we can accept this as a provisional definition), our formulations cannot hope to catch up with the reality . . . The Spirit, which is from God, or "proceeds" from God, makes God known to us, because the Spirit is God's knowledge of Himself, and we can know God only as he shares his self-knowledge with us.[7]

A correct understanding of the personality of the Holy Spirit is foundational to several areas of Christian experience. R. A. Torrey correctly emphasized His importance in three aspects.

1. It is of the highest importance from the standpoint of worship that we decide whether the Holy Spirit is a divine person worthy to receive our adoration, our faith and our love, or simply an influence emanating from God, or a power that God imparts to us. If the Holy Spirit is a Divine Person and we know it not, we are robbing a Divine Being of the love and adoration which are his due.

2. It is of the highest practical importance that we decide whether the Holy Spirit is a power that we in our weakness and ignorance are somehow to get hold of and use, or whether the Holy Spirit is a personal being infinitely wise, infinitely holy, infinitely tender, who is to get hold of and use us. The one conception is heathenish, the other Christian. The one conception leads to self-humiliation, self-emptying and self-renunciation; the other conception leads to self-exaltation.

3. It is of the highest experimental importance that we know the Holy Spirit as a person. Many can testify to the blessing that came into their lives when they came to know the Holy Spirit not merely as a gracious influence (emanating, it is true, from God), but as an ever-present loving-friend and helper.[8]

A. THE HOLY SPIRIT HAS THE ATTRIBUTES OF A PERSON. Since the Holy Spirit is the third Person of the Trinity, equal with the Father and Son in essence, then, since one major aspect of God's nature is that He is a Person, it follows that the Holy Spirit is a Person.

Personality implies the existence of certain attributes: intellect, emotion or sensibility, and volition or willpower. In clarifying what is meant by the personality of the Holy Spirit, Fitzwater suggests,

> By personality is meant separateness of being, individuality, mode of subsistence. The essential characteristics of personality are self-consciousness, emotion and self-will. All beings lacking these attributes are not persons.[9]

By this definition, it can be demonstrated from the Scriptures that the Holy Spirit is a Person, because He possesses the attributes of personality.

The Apostle Paul noted the intellectual ability of the Holy Spirit when he asked, "What man knoweth the things of a man, save the spirit of man which is in him? Even so the things of God knoweth no man, but the Spirit of God" (1 Cor. 2:11). Paul recognized that the rational capacity of the Holy Spirit included wisdom and communication when he prayed, "That the God of our Lord Jesus Christ, the Father of glory, may give unto you the spirit of wisdom and revelation in the knowledge of him" (Eph. 1:17).

The emotional ability of the Holy Spirit is evident in the word of the apostle, "the love of the Holy Spirit" (Rom. 15:30). One of the problems associated with emotions is the possibility of being grieved by someone who is loved. The Bible warns Christians, "Grieve not the holy Spirit of God" (Eph. 4:30). Isaiah cited an example of how Israel "rebelled, and vexed his holy Spirit" (Isa. 63:10). The Holy Spirit has the ability to respond emotionally to the ideas and experiences He encounters.

The Holy Spirit also has the faculty of will and the ability to exercise it. By His own choice, the Holy Spirit accomplishes a number of specific acts, such as giving spiritual gifts. "But all these worketh that one and the selfsame Spirit, dividing to every man severally as he will" (1 Cor. 12:11).

B. THE HOLY SPIRIT PERFORMS THE ACTIONS OF A PERSON. The Holy Spirit does a number of things only a person can do. It should be noted that the Holy Spirit is not a Person because He does those things attributable to personality, but rather does the actions of the personality because He is a Person. Consider the following chart to see how the Holy Spirit does those things which only a person can do.

C. THE HOLY SPIRIT WAS ADDRESSED AS A PERSON. The New Testament clearly shows the early Christians recognized and affirmed the Holy Spirit as a Person. Peter obeyed the Holy Spirit when he was commanded to go to Cornelius' household (Acts 10:19). Philip followed the leading of the Holy Spirit in his ministry (Acts 8:29-30). Against his better judgment, Ananias came to Saul, obeying what the Holy Spirit had revealed to him (Acts 9:10-17). Paul and Silas were constantly led by the Holy Spirit in their ministry (Acts 16:7-10).

The Bible also records the story of two disciples who attempted to lie to the Holy Spirit (Acts 5:3-4). At his trial, Stephen addressed the Sanhedrin, saying, "Ye stiff-necked and uncircumcised in heart and ears, ye do always resist the Holy Ghost: as your fathers did, so do ye" (Acts 7:51). Jesus also warned about blaspheming the Holy Spirit (Matt. 12:31), and the Bible also warns of the consequences of insulting the Holy Spirit. "Of how much sorer punishment, suppose ye, shall he be thought worthy, who hath trodden under foot the Son of God, and hath counted the blood of the covenant, wherewith he was sanctified, an unholy thing, and hath done despite unto the Spirit of grace?" (Heb. 10:29). Is it any wonder the writer concludes, "it is a fearful thing to fall into the hands of the living God" (Heb. 10:31)? This would not happen if we had a proper reverence for the Person of the Holy Spirit as did David (Psa. 51:11).

THE ACTS OF THE PERSON OF THE HOLY SPIRIT

1. He teaches .... John 14:26
2. He testifies...................... John 15:26
3. He guides........................ Rom. 8:14
4. He speaks .... 1 Cor. 2:13
5. He enlightens.................. John 16:13
6. He strives........................ Gen. 6:3
7. He commands................. Acts 8:29
8. He intercedes.................. Rom. 8:26
9. He sends workers............ Acts 13:4
10. He calls........................... Rev. 22:17
11. He comforts .... John 16:7
12. He works .... 1 Cor. 12:11

The above actions cannot be accomplished by a mere influence or force. Only a rational, emotional, and active person could do all that the Scriptures teach that the Holy Spirit accomplishes.

D. THE PERSONALITY OF THE HOLY SPIRIT IS ALSO IMPLIED BY THE APPLICATION OF MASCULINE PRONOUNS. The Holy Spirit is designated as "He." This is a significant argument, as the Greek language had not only a masculine and feminine gender, but also a neuter. As the word "spirit" is neuter in Greek, it would be natural to expect a neuter pronoun to be used in its place. In contrast, the masculine pronoun is used to refer to the Holy Spirit in John 14:17; 16:13 and in other places. Commenting on this use of the masculine pronoun, Thiessen notes, "in the last reference the neuter substantive *pneuma* is referred to by the masculine pronoun *ekeinos*, recognizing the Spirit's personality. The neuter 'itself' in Romans 8:16, 26, has in the A.S.V. been properly changed to 'himself.'"[10]

E. THE SPIRIT OF GOD CAN BE TREATED AS A PERSON. The Holy Spirit received the affirmations of personality, hence He is a Person. He can be obeyed (Acts 10:19), lied to (Acts 5:3), resisted (Acts 7:51), grieved (Eph. 4:30), reverenced (Psa. 51:11), blasphemed (Matt. 12:31), outraged (Heb. 10:29) and called (Ezek. 37:9). Because these things can only be accomplished in relation to persons, the personality of the Holy Spirit is implied by these activities directed toward Him.

An additional scriptural illustration of the Holy Spirit as a Person is seen in the references to the Trinity. Jesus commanded His disciples to "teach all nations, baptizing them in the name of the Father, and of the Son, and of the Holy Ghost" (Matt. 28:19). Jesus acknowledged three distinct Persons of the Trinity, but recognized their unity in a simple name. In our understanding of the Trinity, we realize that what is true of God as a whole, is true of each Person of the Trinity. God the Father is personally interested in us (John 3:16; 1 John 3:1). So the Holy Spirit has a personal interest in our lives (He baptizes, seals, indwells, fills, and leads us). If the teaching of Scripture were unclear concerning the personality of the Holy Spirit, there might be room to speculate about His personality. But His association with other members of the Trinity indicates that He too is a Person.

As noted above, some liberal theologians agree that the Scriptures portray the Holy Spirit as a Person, but deny that it necessarily implies the actual personality of the Holy Spirit. They argue that these biblical expressions represent a personification (as a simile, metaphor, or figure of speech), but not a distinct person. A closer look at the biblical text makes this assumption practically impossible. Strong countered this tendency.

> This ascription to the Spirit of a personal subsistence distinct from that of the Father and of the Son cannot be explained as personification; for: (a) This would be to interpret sober prose by the canons of poetry. Such sustained personification is contrary to the genius of even Hebrew poetry, in which Wisdom itself is most naturally interpreted as designating a personal existence. (b) Such an interpretation would render a multitude of passages either . . . meaningless, or absurd,—as can be easily seen by substituting for the name Holy Spirit the terms which are wrongfully held to be its equivalents; such as the power, or influence, or efflux, or attribute of God. (c) it is contradicted, moreover, by all those passages in which the Holy Spirit is distinguished from his own gifts.[11]

II. THE DEITY OF THE HOLY SPIRIT

Not only is the Holy Spirit a Person, but He is also God. As God, He is worthy of our worship and obedience. In his brief discussion of the Holy Spirit, Thiessen argues, "All these things prove that the Holy Spirit is a Person.

But He is a divine Person."[12] The Scriptures clearly teach the deity of the Holy Spirit, and those who accept the verbal authority of Scripture will concur. Still, this has not prevented some from teaching that the Holy Spirit is something less than God. Summarizing the history of those who taught the Holy Spirit as a created being, Hodge observes,

> The divinity of the Holy Ghost is so clearly revealed in Scripture that very few have dared to call it in question. The early controversies of the orthodox with the Arians precedent and consequent to the Council of Nice, A.D. 325, to such a degree absorbed the mind of both parties with the question of the divinity of the Son, that very little prominence was given in that age to

questions concerning the Holy Ghost. Arius, however, is said to have taught that as the Son is the first and greatest creature of the Father, so the Holy Ghost is the first and greatest creature of the Son; a κτίσμα κτίσματος, a creator of a creature . . .

Some of the disciples of Macedonius, bishop of Constantinople, A.D. 341-360, are said to have held that the Holy Ghost was not Supreme God. These were condemned by the second General Council, which met at Constantinople, A.D. 381.[13]

The ancient Arian heresy concerning both Christ and the Holy Spirit is today promoted by The Watch Tower Bible and Tract Society, more popularity known as Jehovah's Witnesses. The expression "deity of the Holy Spirit" when used by orthodox theologians means the Holy Spirit is in His essential nature and being God. To consider the Holy Spirit as anything less is to effectively deny He is the Spirit of God. Fitzwater suggests, "By the deity of the Holy Spirit is meant that He, in the essentiality of His being, possesses the attributes of God and that he is of the same substance as God."[14]

There is no shortage of biblical material to demonstrate the deity of the Holy Spirit. This material may be summarized under seven primary arguments. Strong identifies five of these in the following list.

(a) He is spoken of as God; (b) the attributes of God are ascribed to him, such as life, truth, love, holiness, eternity, omnipresence, omniscience, omnipotence; (c) he does the works of God, such as creation, regeneration, resurrection; (d) he receives honor due only to God; (e) he is associated with God on a footing of equality, both in the formula of baptism and in the apostolic benedictions.[15]

To this list can be added the sixth argument which is summarized by Thiessen that the words of the Holy Spirit are recognized as the words of God.[16] Also, the seventh proof is that the names of the Holy Spirit in Scripture imply His deity.

A. THE HOLY SPIRIT IS SPOKEN OF AS GOD. In the New Testament, both Peter and Paul refer to the Holy Spirit as God. They did this in a way that His deity was assumed true, and was not contested by other church leaders. Peter asked Ananias, "Why hath Satan filled thine heart to lie to the Holy Ghost?" (Acts 5:3) and charged, "Thou has not lied unto men, but unto God" (Acts 5:4). Later Peter charged Sapphira with involvement in the conspiracy "to tempt the Spirit of the Lord" (Acts 5:9). No one challenged Peter in his interchange of titles identifying the Holy Spirit as God.

Writing to the Corinthians, Paul also used the title "Lord" to designate the Holy Spirit. "Now the Lord is that Spirit: and where the Spirit of the Lord is, there is liberty" (2 Cor. 3:17). Within the same context, the apostle speaks of "the glory of the Lord," perhaps a reference to the Old Testament Shekinah glory present in the tabernacle and first Temple. It is probably that the rabbinically trained apostle here ascribes the name *YHWH* to the Holy Spirit and does it in a matter-of-fact way. He could assume his readers at Corinth would accept that statement and, therefore, makes no attempt to argue the point.

This practice of referring to the Holy Spirit as God is not exclusively a New Testament phenomenon. In his exhortation to Job, Elihu said, "The Spirit of God hath made me, and the breath of the Almighty hath given me life" (Job 33:4). It is significant that the name of God, Shaddai (Almighty), is the characteristic name of God used by the patriarchs and is used to identify God frequently (thirty-one times) in the Book of Job.

B. THE ABSOLUTE AND COMPARATIVE ATTRIBUTES OF GOD ARE POSSESSED BY THE HOLY SPIRIT. His holiness and justice are identified in His titles "Holy" (Psa. 51:11) and "Spirit of judgment" (Isa. 4:4). The apostle Paul spoke of "the love of the Spirit" (Rom. 15:30). The goodness of the Holy Spirit is seen in Psalm 143:10. Jesus identified the Holy Spirit as a good gift from God (Luke 11:13).

The comparative attributes of God--omniscience, omnipotence, and omnipresence—are also attributed to the Holy Spirit. His omnipotence is seen in His ability to accomplish what could not otherwise be accomplished. Zerubbabel recognized the work of God was done "Not by might, nor by power, but by my spirit, saith the Lord of hosts" (Zech. 4:6). David recognized the omnipresence of the Holy Spirit when he asked, "Whither shall I go from thy spirit? or whither shall I flee from thy presence?" (Psa. 139:7). Paul taught that the Scriptures could not be understood without the aid of the omniscient Spirit of God (1 Cor. 2:10-16). The degree of the omniscience of the Holy Spirit is seen in the statement "the foolishness of God is wiser than men" (1 Cor. 1:25).

When the authors of the *Westminster Confession of Faith* sought to define God, they did so by listing His attributes. The following chart shows how all the attributes of God as identified in the *Westminster Confession* are also ascribed to the Holy Spirit in the Scriptures.

C. THE HOLY SPIRIT ACCOMPLISHES THE WORK OF GOD. By doing the work that only God can do, the Holy Spirit demonstrates His deity. At creation, "The Spirit of God moved upon the face of the waters" (Gen. 1:2; also Job 26:13; 33:4; Psa. 104-30). The Holy Spirit is also active in the work of regeneration. "Jesus answered, Verily, verily I say unto thee, Except a man be born of water and of the Spirit, he cannot enter into the Kingdom of God" (John 3:5). Both Peter and Paul saw the Holy Spirit involved in the work of sanctification and spoke of the "sanctification of the Spirit" (I Pet. 1:2; 2 Thess. 2:13).

Sometimes theologians adopt a form of Modalism by describing the work of God in three distinct and sequential spheres of ministry done by each member of the Trinity respectively. For example, E. Stanley Jones expressed what he calls,

Attributes of God in the Westminster Confession of Faith	Biblical Teaching Regarding Attributes of the Holy Spirit
Spirit	1 Peter 4:14
Infinite	Isa. 40:12-18
Eternal	Heb. 9:14
Unchangeable in Being	Isa. 48:16
Wisdom	Isa. 11:2
Power	Rom. 15:13
Holiness	Eph. 4:30
Justice	Isa. 63:10
Goodness	Psalm 143:10
Truth	John 16:13

Three facts about God: (1) God for us, (2) God with us, (3) God in us. God for us, the divine intention, the Father; God with us, the divine invasion, the Son; God in us, the divine indwelling, the Holy Spirit. The divine intention becomes the divine indwelling. It is not enough to have redemptive intention and redemptive invasion. They are both outside of us, therefore inadequate, for our need is within us. There must be indwelling.[17]

What Jones has missed is that God the Trinity is at work in individuals at all times doing the work of God, even though certain persons of the Trinity perform certain functions assigned to His person. In a similar vein of thought, Fitch writes,

We must never confuse the offices of the Father, the Son, and the Holy Spirit. Equal in power and Godhead, each Person of the blessed Trinity has a specific ministry to fulfill. God the Father is the Father Almighty, Author of all. God the Son reveals the Father; in Him the perfect image of God is revealed, brought near to us, made manifest; He is the form of God and He fulfills the perfect will of God in the redemption of the world. God the Holy Spirit is the indwelling God, inhabiting the temple of our bodies when we believe in God through Jesus Christ. What the Father has purposed, and what the Son has procured, can be appropriated only through the activity and power of the Holy Spirit.[18]

The Scriptures present the Trinity working together and harmonious in all areas. Father, Son, and Holy Spirit are all recognized in Scripture for their creative role (Gen. 1:1-2; John 1:3). The atonement is likewise a work of God involving each member of the Trinity (Heb. 9:14). While most Christians are vaguely aware of the truth of the Spirit's indwelling (1 Cor. 6:19), many do not realize the Father and Son are also described as abiding (indwelling) in the believer (John 14:23).

An additional work of the Holy Spirit is His inspiration of the Scriptures. The Scriptures were written by "holy men of God [who] spake as they were moved by the Holy Ghost" (2 Pet. 1:21). As men wrote the Word of God, they did so as the Holy Spirit guided them and gave them the message from God, so there are no mistakes in what they wrote, the original autographs (John 16:13). The Holy Spirit who originally inspired Scripture, uses Scripture today to "reprove the world of sin, and of righteousness, and of judgment" (John 16:8). For the Christian, the Holy Spirit has a ministry of illumination whereby He helps them understand the Bible. "Now we have received, not the spirit of the world, but the spirit which is of God; that we might know the things that are freely given to us of God" (1 Cor. 2:12).

D. THE HOLY SPIRIT RECEIVES HONOR DUE ONLY TO GOD. When Paul used the term "temple" in the context of the Spirit of God indwelling the believer (1 Cor. 3:16), he was also implying the deity of the Holy Spirit because only deity can indwell a believer. Temple describes a place in which deity lives or is worshipped. Commenting on this verse, Strong notes, "He who inhabits the temple is the object of worship there."[19] As Pauline theology does not conceive of the legitimacy of other than God receiving worship, Paul, therefore, must have considered the Holy Spirit to be God.

E. THE HOLY SPIRIT IS ASSOCIATED WITH THE TITLES OF DEITY. When we speak of the Trinity, we are speaking of one God in three distinct persons, each being God. The Holy Spirit is a part of the Trinity and is therefore God. Some theologians err in their pneumatology when they use the term "spirit" to apply to the spirit nature of the Godhead and confuse their thinking by identifying the same term with the third person of the Godhead. Walters notes,

Since God is said to be Spirit (John iv. 24), the whole Trinity has been thought of by some in terms of Spirit. This has a tendency to cloud the distinction between the Spirit, the Father, and the Son. Moreover, to speak, as some do, of the Spirit as the relation of love between the Father and the Son, or further, to define the Spirit as the Living action of God in the world, while emphasizing a valuable, yet partial, truth, nevertheless tends to depersonalize the Spirit and to reduce Him to an influence or force, albeit a benign one.[20]

Even in the Old Testament, where the Trinity is not as clearly taught as in the New Testament, the Holy Spirit is identified as God. Jeremiah revealed that the new covenant came from the "LORD" (Jehovah) (Jer. 31:31), but the writer to the Hebrews identified the same as from "the Holy Ghost" (Heb. 10:15). Thus we see that the name Yahweh was used sometimes in the Old Testament to identify the Holy Spirit.

F. THE EARLY CHURCH RECOGNIZED THE DEITY OF THE HOLY SPIRIT IN THE EQUAL RECOGNITION GIVEN HIM IN THE BENEDICTION AND BAPTISMAL FORMULA. "The grace of the Lord Jesus Christ, and the love of God, and the communion of the Holy Ghost, be with you all" (2 Cor. 13:14). Jesus gave equal recognition to the Holy Spirit with the other two members of the Trinity in the baptismal formula of the New Testament (Matt. 28:19). The teaching of Jesus, Peter, and Paul formed the basis of the doctrine taught and believed in the early church, and each of these recognized the deity of the Holy Spirit.

G. THE WORDS OF GOD ARE ASCRIBED TO THE HOLY SPIRIT. Because of the murmuring of the Jews in the wilderness after they crossed the Red Sea, God miraculously provided manna for forty years as an example of His provision for the nation. As Moses records the announcement of this provision, he begins with the words, "Then said the LORD unto Moses . . ." (Exod. 16:4). Later, the Psalmist recalls those wilderness experiences of Israel using the names God and LORD and refers to "his voice" (Psa. 95:6-7). When the writer of Hebrews quotes this Psalm, he begins with the words, "Wherefore, as the Holy Ghost saith" (Heb. 3:7). Therefore, he is making the title LORD and God equal with the Holy Ghost. The same thing seems to have happened in Isaiah's life. Isaiah "heard the voice of the Lord" (Isa. 6:8). John identified the one on the throne as Christ (John 12:41), but Paul identified the voice as "the Holy Ghost" (Acts 28:25-27).

When God identifies His name in Scripture, it is not without meaning. The first mention of the Holy Spirit in Scripture identifies Him clearly as God. "And the Spirit of God moved upon the face of the waters" (Gen. 1:2). Early in the history of civilization, the rebellion of man grieved God. "And the Lord said, My Spirit shall not always strive with man" (Gen. 6:3). Strong argues that the name "Spirit of God" must imply the deity of the Holy Spirit, stating, "A spirit is nothing less than the inmost principle of life, and the spirit of man is man himself, so the spirit of God must be God."[21] This type of Hebraism is used in many titles of the Holy Spirit reflecting various attributes of deity. The most common name for the third Person of the Trinity is "Holy Spirit." While not a strong proof, this name associates Him with deity because holiness is a reflection of God's attributes, while "Spirit" is a reflection of His nature. His deity is also implied by the titles "Comforter" (John 16:7; 2 Cor. 1:3), "Spirit of Truth" (John 16:13), and "Holy One" (1 John 2:20). Most of the names ascribed to the Holy Spirit in Scripture either relate Him directly to deity, as "The Spirit of the Lord God" (Isa. 61:1), or to some attribute of God, such as "the eternal Spirit" (Heb. 9:14), or "The spirit of judgment and . . . the spirit of burning" (Isa. 4:4).

At least two verses in the Gospel of John appear to teach a lesser view of the Holy Spirit and have been misinterpreted by some concerning the deity of the Holy Spirit. Jesus said of the Holy Spirit, "For he shall not speak of himself, but whatever he shall hear, that shall he speak" (John 16:13). While this appears to teach the Holy Spirit lacks independence and sovereignty (something essential to deity), Hodge explains the context of the verse suggests this reference reflects on the office of the Holy Spirit and not on His essential nature.

This and other similar expressions are to be understood as referring to the official work of the Spirit; just as the Son is said in his official character to be sent by and to be subordinate to the Father. The object of the Holy Ghost, in his official work in the hearts of men, is not to reveal the relations of his own person to the other persons of the Godhead, but simply to reveal the mediatorial character and work of Christ.[22]

A second problem text is John 7:39. Here, in a footnote to the teaching of Jesus, John adds, "for the Holy Ghost was not yet given" (John 7:39). The word "given" is not supplied in the Greek and some have attempted to make the verse teach the Holy Spirit was at that time nonexistent. But, as David Brown observes,

Beyond all doubt the word 'given, or some similar word, is the right supplement here, if we are to insert any supplement at all. In ch. xvi. 7 the Holy Ghost is represented not only as the *gift of Christ*, but a Gift the communication of which was *dependent upon His own departure to the Father*. Now, as Christ was not yet gone, so the Holy Ghost was not yet given.[23]

On the same verse, Strong reinforces the view that "not yet given" refers to His duties and office, not His character.

This proof of the deity of the Holy Spirit is not invalidated by the limitatians [sic]of his work under the Old Testament dispensation. John 7:39—"for the Holy Spirit was not yet"—means simply that the Holy Spirit could not fulfill his peculiar office as Revealer of Christ until the atoning work of Christ should be accomplished.[24]

Paul told the Romans, "For as many as are led by the Spirit of God, they are the sons of God" (Rom. 8:24). A characteristic of a Christian's life should be his willingness to follow the leading of the Holy Spirit (Gal. 5:25). Because He is a Person, the Holy Spirit is able to lead, guide, and direct in our lives. Because He is God, He has a supernatural ability to help us overcome our temptations and successfully serve the Lord. Because He is a Person, the Holy Spirit can be followed. Because He is God, He must be followed.

III. THE PROCESSION OF THE HOLY SPIRIT

Historically, one of the most controversial aspects of pneumatology has been the topic identified as the procession of the Holy Spirit. The problem arises from the words of Jesus, "But when the Comforter is come, whom I will send unto you from the Father, even the Spirit of truth, which proceedeth from the Father" (John 15:26). The question is how can the Second Person of deity give direction to the Third Person of Deity, and they remain equal at the same time. It was not until A.D. 381 that the Council of Constantinople first issued the decree that recognized the Holy Spirit "who proceedeth from the Father." The subsequent discussion among early theologians concerned the relation of the Holy Spirit and the Second Person of the Trinity. At the third ecclesiastical assembly at Toledo in A.D. 589, the Latin term *"filoque,"* meaning "and the Son" was added to the statement formed at Constantinople. This fairly represented the theological position of the western church, but was strongly opposed by the eastern wing of Christianity. For a time, harmony between the two parties of the church was maintained through a compromise and statement recognizing "the Spirit proceeding from the Father through the Son," but eventually this statement was rejected by both parties. According to MacBeth,

The Eastern Church, however, though implicitly accepting the doctrine, resented any addition thus made to the Creed as sanctioned by the General Councils, and refused to accept the addition. This, together with other matters, such as the assumption of ecclesiastical jurisdiction by the Popes, led eventually (in 1053) to that schism between the Eastern and Western Churches which still exists.[25]

In light of the major historical schism surrounding this doctrine, it is perhaps surprising that a single verse of Scripture provides the full reference for the doctrine of eternal procession. The Bible recognizes three Persons in the Godhead, each equal in nature, separate in person, yet subservient in duties. According to John 15:26, Jesus Christ is the agent who will direct the Spirit from the Father to work in believers. Hence, the doctrine of procession deals with duties, and should not be confused with the nature of Persons of the Trinity.

The term "procession" is sometimes described by the term "spiration" to explain the relationship of duties and not relationship of nature in the Trinity. The word "proceedeth" means in the Greek "in the process" or "continually proceedeth." Hence, the title "Eternal Procession" is used to show that the Holy Spirit is eternally coming from the Father, not just at one time in history. According to Hodge,

> Theologians intended this phrase to designate the relation which the third person sustains to the first and second, wherein by an eternal and necessary, *i.e.,* not voluntary, act of the Father and the Son, their whole identical divine essence, without alienation, division, or change, is communicated to the Holy Ghost.[26]

Similarly, MacBeth explains,

> This was termed spiration by the schoolmen, who in vain attempted to explain the nature of the mysteries of the Divine Trinity. The word "procession," therefore, is only used as in some sense conveying an idea of the relation of the Spirit to Father and Son, in Scriptural language, without carrying with it a distinct conception of the nature of that relation, though indicating a distinct Personality."[27]

The Holy Spirit will continually proceed from beside, not out of, the Father. To some extent, conservative commentators disagree on the question concerning from whom the Holy Spirit proceeds. In apparent sympathy with the Eastern church's position, Godet argued the text was open to both interpretations and that only one's understanding of Johannine Christology could be depended upon to make a final decision. Commenting on John 15:26, Godet explains,

> It must be observed that the second verb differs entirely from the first; ἐκπορεύεσθαι, *to proceed from,* as a river from its source, is altogether different from *to be sent:* the παρά *out from,* which is added here to παρά, *from the presence of,* also marks a difference. But especially does the change of tense indicate the difference of idea: whom *I will send* and *who proceeds*

from. He whom Jesus will send (historically, at a given moment) is a divine being, who emanates (essentially, eternally) from the Father. An impartial exegesis cannot, as it seems to me, deny this sense.[28]

David Brown, also a conservative western theologian, was convinced the western position on the text was more in keeping with the teaching of the text. Commenting on the same verse, Brown suggests,

> That the *internal* or *essential* procession of the Holy Ghost is the thing here intended, has been the prevailing opinion of the orthodox Churches of the Reformation, and is that of good critics even in our day. But though we seem warranted in affirming—that the *economic* order follows the *essential* in the relations of the Divine Persons—in other words, that in the economy of Redemption the relations sustained by the Divine Person do but reflect their essential relations—it is very doubtful whether more is expressed here than the *historical* aspect of this mission and procession of the Spirit from the Father by the Agency of the Son.[29]

Just as in Eternal Generation (Psa. 2:7) the Son is eternally in the process of being "begotten" by the Father, so the Holy Spirit is eternally being sent by the Son from the Father. These are part of the nature of God. In his comparison of Eternal Generation and Eternal Procession, Hodge quotes Turretin who outlines three distinctions.

> They differ, 1st. *As to source*, the Son emanates from the Father only, but the Spirit from the Father and the Son at the same time. 2d. *As to mode.* The Son emanates in the way of generation, which affects not only personality, but similitude, on account of which the Son is called the image of the Father; and in consequence of which he receives the property of communicating the same essence to another person; but the Spirit, by the way of spiration, which effects only personality, and in consequence of which the person who proceeds does not receive the property of communicating the same essence to another person. 3d. *As to order.* The Son is second person, and the Spirit third, and though both are eternal, without beginning or succession, yet, in our mode of conception, generation precedes procession.[30]

IV. THE REPRESENTATIONS OF THE HOLY SPIRIT

One of the means by which truth is revealed is through symbolic representations. These include metaphor, simile, symbol, type, parable, allegory, and emblem. While these are similar in many respects, there is a slight technical difference in the definition of each term. This is illustrated by the definitions of each term on the following chart.[31]

TERM	DEFINITION
Metaphor	A figure of speech in which one object is made to stand for another.
Simile	Figurative language descriptive of one object in its likeness to another.
Symbol	Something which stands for something else.
Type	An object used to prefigure another object.
Parable	A truth illustrated by fact.
Allegory	A story which represents a fact, or illustrates a thing in parabolic language.
Emblem	A figurative representation of anything.

Conservatives disagree over the role that symbols play in revealing truth. Probably the safest way to use these representations is as supportive of illustrative material, rather than as a foundation for doctrine. Some would advocate a total disregard for types while others hold the opposite view, apparently seeing doctrinal significance in the woodgrains of the boards of the tabernacle or prophetic truth wrapped in the leaves on the cedars of Lebanon. Scofield represents one position, when in response to a question on the use of types, he answered,

> The absolutely safe rule is that nothing may be dogmatically asserted to be a type which is not so used in Scripture, e.g. , John 3:14; 6:31-33; 1 Corinthians 5:6,7 (Passover and leaven) Hebrews 9, etc. But we may safely look to the lives of typical persons, as also to events and institutions for spiritual analogies of great beauty and value.[32]

There are at least fifteen emblems of the Holy Spirit in the Bible. This is more than double those identified in a footnote in The New Scofield Reference Bible (1967).

The editors there note, "The symbols of the Spirit are: (1) oil (John 3:34; Heb. 1:9); (b) water (John 7:38-39); (c) wind (John 3:8; Acts 2:2); (d) fire (Acts 2:3); (e) a dove (Matt. 3:16); (f) a seal (Eph. 1:13; 4:30); and (g) an earnest, or pledge (Eph. 1:14)."[33] Perhaps the most exhaustive study of the representations of the Holy Spirit is the work by F. E. Marsh, which includes fourteen different emblems. The chart on the following page lists these emblems and Marsh's interpretation concerning their spiritual significance.[34]

EMBLEM	BIBLICAL REFERENCE	MEANING
Dove	Matt. 3:16; 10:16	The *Dove* speaks of the beauty and gentleness of the Spirit's character.
Seal	Song. 4:12 John 6:27 2 Cor. 1:22 Eph. 1:13; 4:30 2 Tim. 2:19 Rev. 7:3-8	The *Seal* indicates the security of the Spirit's grace and the proprietorship of His love.
The Holy Anointing Oil	Exod. 30:25-38 Lev. 21:10	*The Holy Anointing Oil* is emblematic of the Holy Spirit's character and claims as the Holy One.
The Act of Anointing	Lev. 21:10 2 Cor. 1:21 Heb. 1:9	*The Act of Anointing* is suggestive of the Spirit's consecrating grace and guidance.
Oil	Luke 4:18 Acts 10:38 2 Cor. 1:21 1 John 2:27	The *Oil* is typical of the Spirit's grace and the illumination of His teaching.
Fire	Exod. 3:2; 19:18 Mal. 3:2 Matt. 3:11 Acts 2:3 Heb. 12:29 Rev. 4:5	The *Fire* is an emblem of the purification and penetration of the Spirit's operations.

EMBLEM	BIBLICAL REFERENCE	MEANING
Rain	Deut. 32:2 Psa. 72:6; 84:6 Hosea 6:3 Jer. 5:24 Zech. 10:1	The *Rain* designates the abundance and grace of the Spirit's supply.
Atmosphere	Gal. 5:16-25 Eph. 5:18 R.V.M. Phil. 3:3 Rev. 1:10	The *Atmosphere* portrays the element and use of the Spirit's exclusiveness.
Wind	Isa. 40:7 Ezek. 37:9 John 3:8 Acts 2:2	The *Wind* proclaims the winnowing and searchingness of the Spirit's power.
Rivers	Psa. 1:3; 46:4 John 7:38	*Rivers* proclaim the abundance of the Spirit's supply and the plentitude of His grace.
Dew	Gen. 27:28 Deut. 32:2; 33:13, 28 Psa. 133:3 Job 29:19 Isa. 18:4 Hosea 14:5	The *Dew* shadows forth the refreshing and fertilization of the Spirit's presence.
Water	Psa. 65:9 Isa. 44:3 John 3:5; 4:14; 7:37, 38	The *Water* symbolizes the effectiveness and sufficiency of the Spirit's ministry.
Clothing	Judg. 6:34 R.V. Luke 24:49 R.V.	The *Clothing* depicts the equipment and strength of the Spirit's endowment.
Earnest	2 Cor. 1:22; 5:5 Eph. 1:14	The *Earnest* delineates the sample of the Spirit's promise of glory.

In addition to the above emblems, many suggest that Abraham's servant (Gen. 24) is a type or picture of the Holy Spirit. Although there is no particular designation in the New Testament of this servant as a type, several parallels have been drawn between the work of servant and the work of the Holy Spirit in this present age. (1) The servant is sent to secure a Gentile bride for the son. (2) The servant was to speak for his master much as the Holy Spirit is to speak for the Father. (3) Abraham gave the servant gifts which in turn were to be given to the bride; a picture of spiritual gifts which in turn are given to the church (cf. 1 Cor. 12:11-14). (4) The servant was to conduct the bride back to the son; a picture of the program of the Holy Spirit conducting the bride of Christ to heaven.

V. THE HOLY SPIRIT AND CREATION

Following the law of first reference, the first emblems of the Holy Spirit in Scripture directly ties the Holy Spirit to the creative process. According to A. B. Simpson,

> The first emblems under which we see the Holy Spirit in the New Testament is the dove descending upon the head of Jesus at His baptism on the banks of the Jordan. The first emblem under which the Holy Spirit is presented in the Old Testament is also a dove.[35]

The Old Testament reference is Genesis 1:2 where the Spirit of God "moved [lit. brooded] upon the face of the waters." The parallel of these two accounts is also noted by Sweet, who observes, "At the Baptism the New Creation took its rise out of the waters of the Jordan; the Spirit of God again moved upon the face of the waters, bringing forth an ordered life."[36]

The importance of the Holy Spirit in creation should not be minimized simply because of a limited number of specific references to His role in creation.[37] Neither should this doctrine be abandoned because of the particular terminology used in the creation references. While rejecting the conclusions of liberal theologians that the Holy Spirit had no creative role, Kuyper summarized their usual line of thought.

> It should be noticed that hardly any of these passages mention the Holy Spirit by *His own name*. It is not the *Holy* Spirit, but the "Spirit of His month," "His Spirit," "The Spirit of the Lord." On account of this, many hold that these passages do not refer to the Holy Spirit as the Third Person in the Holy Trinity, but speak of God as One, without personal distinction; and that the representation of God as creating anything by His hand, fingers, word,

breath, or Spirit is merely a human way of speaking, signifying only that God was thus engaged.[38]

Walters explains further the work of the Holy Spirit in creation.

The Spirit brooding over the primeval waters (Gn. i. 2) and creating man (Gn. ii. 7), the Spirit who garnishes the heavens (Jb. xxvi. 13), sustains animal life, and renews the face of the earth (Psa. civ. 30), is the *ruah* (breath, wind) of God, the outgoing divine energy and power. He is the principle of man's physical and psychological life. Man in every part of his nature—spirit, soul, and body—is meant to be open to the resources of the Spirit of God, learning to reflect God.[39]

The Scriptures give the Holy Spirit a major role in creation, and this activity is reflective of His continued ministry to individuals. Palmer observes, "The creative work of the Holy Spirit, then, is all-embracing, pertaining to both the physical and spiritual realms. It began in a special way at creation. It continues throughout today, including even the re-creation of man.[40] According to Kuyper,

This inward, invisible something is God's direct touch. There is in us and in every creature a point where the living God touches us to uphold us; for nothing exists without being *upheld* by Almighty God from moment to moment. In the elect this point is their spiritual life; in the rational creature his rational consciousness; and in all creatures, whether rational or not, their life-principle. And as the Holy Spirit is the Person in the Holy Trinity whose office it is to effect this direct touch and fellowship with the creature in his inmost being, it is He who *dwells* in the hearts of the elect; who *animates* every rational being; who sustains the *principle of life* in very creature.[41]

In the same Reformed tradition, Berkhof observes,

So intimate is the Spirit to man's life that we sometimes feel ourselves on the brink of pantheism. Job says that he has the Spirit of God in his nostrils. Nevertheless, in his immanence this Spirit remains strictly sovereign and transcendent. We cannot dispose of the Spirit within us. God gives His Spirit; he also takes him away, in which case man and nature die away. "If he should take back his spirit to himself, and gather to himself his breath, all flesh would perish together, and man would return to dust."[42]

Those Scriptures which make specific reference to the creative work of the Holy Spirit use a number of metaphors to identify both the sphere of creation and the means or degree of His creative work. Because another Scripture may ascribe the same creative function to another member of the Trinity, this does not minimize the role of the Third Person. It simply serves to illustrate the cooperative work of the Trinity in this particular work of God. The above chart illustrates the specific role of the Holy Spirit in creation.

THE HOLY SPIRIT IN CREATION	
Psa. 33:6	Creation of the World
Gen. 1:2	Moved upon the World (Lit. "brooding")
Job 26:13	Garnishing of the Heavens (i.e., solar bodies)
Psa. 104:30	Renewal of Earth (i.e., vegetation)
Job 33:4	Making of Human Personality
Psa. 104:29	Sustaining of Life

The role of the Holy Spirit in creation appears to be both passive and active. At times the Scriptures appear to portray the Holy Spirit as almost a spectator to the creative process, whereas on other occasions His active involvement is unquestionable. Commenting on Genesis 1:2, Kuyper argues,

> The Hebrew text shows that the work of the Holy Spirit moving upon the face of the waters was similar to that of the parent bird, which with outspread wings hovers over its young to cherish and cover them. The figure implies that not only the earth existed, but also the germs of life within it; and that the Holy Spirit impregnating these germs caused the life to come forth in order to lead it to its destiny.[43]

Some suggest this is an inferior role of the Holy Spirit and this has prompted Green to question whether the Holy Spirit should be considered as a Creator at all.[44] While the creation account of Genesis 1 does not specifically emphasize the active role of the Holy Spirit, neither does it specifically mention the role of the Second Person of the Trinity. But in the light of the biblical teaching covering the Trinity, it can be assumed that the God (Elohim) of Genesis 1 included Father, Son, and Holy Spirit. While some seek to explain the use of this term merely as a plural of majesty, the Hebrew verbs used with this name are also plural, something not common in the use of a plural of majesty. Basically, to the extent one would allow for a plurality of persons in the Old Testament concept of God (cf. Isaiah 48:16), to that extent is a plurality in creation recognized.

But the active role of the Holy Spirit in creation is not based only on the implications of trinitarianism. The active role of the Spirit is specifically mentioned in Job 33:4. Kuyper observes,

> Of himself, i.e., of a *man*, Job declares: "The Spirit of God hath made me, and the breath of the Almighty hath given me life." The Spirit of God hath made *me*. That which I am as a *human personality* is the work of The Holy Spirit. To Him I owe the human and personal that constitute me the being that I am. He adds: "The breath of the Almighty hath given me life"; which evidently echoes the words: "The Lord God breathed into His nostrils the breath of life."[45]

The Holy Spirit had an active role in the creative work of God. The result is the order, life, beauty and renewal properties of the created world that would not exist in the same degree without His activity. The following chart identifies these four results of the Holy Spirit in creation.

THE RESULTS OF THE HOLY SPIRIT IN CREATION

Isa. 40:12, 14; Gen. 1:2	Order
Job 33:4	Life
Job 26:13	Beauty
Psalm 104:29	Renewal

VI. THE WORK OF THE HOLY IN THE OLD TESTAMENT

There is a tendency among some Christians to minimize the work of the Holy Spirit in the Old Testament. Because there is not a great emphasis on His Person, some have erroneously assumed that He is absent from the pages of the Old Testament. Also, because some overemphasize the Holy Spirit in the New Testament, they have a tendency to develop two distinct doctrines of the Spirit of God. Actually, there is unity in the biblical doctrine of the Holy Spirit. He is the Third Person of the Trinity who has a consistent and unified ministry that adapts itself to the fluctuations of man in different dispensations. The teaching of the New Testament concerning the Holy Spirit is built upon the foundation of Old Testament doctrine. There is a distinct harmony between the past, present, and future ministries of the Holy Spirit. As Ridout points out,

> Before Christ, the Spirit's work, as well as all God's ways, was one of *preparation*; after the descent of the Spirit at Pentecost, and in connection with the Church it was a time of *realization*. All is now real. During the Millennium, when Christ will be displayed in glory as King of His people and over all the earth, it will be the time of *manifestation*.[46]

The work of the Holy Spirit is similar in the Old Testament to His present work in several respects. First, He enables individuals to become spiritual and serve God. Several expressions are used to describe these relationships, such as, the Holy Spirit is "in" men (Gen. 41:38; Num. 27:18; Dan. 4:8) and "upon" men (Judges 3:10; 6:34; 11:29; 1 Sam. 10:9-10; 16:13). Only during the building of the tabernacle are men said to be "filled" with the Holy Spirit (Exod. 31:3; 35:31).

Wisdom (Num. 27:18), physical skills (Exod. 28:3) and strength (Judg. 13:25) are among the benefits of the Spirit. But also included in the Spirit's enabling ministry was the ability to perform miracles (1 Kgs. 18:12). The Spirit of God is necessary for the accomplishment of miracles in both the Old and New Testaments.

A second similarity can be seen in the Spirit's restraining efforts. As He does presently, the Holy Spirit was involved in opposing unrighteousness (Gen. 6:3; cf. 2 Thess. 2:7). This ministry of restraint was also manifested through the prophetic ministry of Spirit-anointed men of God. As Mullins has observed,

> The most distinctive and important manifestation of the Spirit's activity in the OT was in the sphere of prophecy . . . The prophet was esp. distinguished from others as the man who possessed the Spirit of God (Hos. 9 7). The prophets ordinarily began their messages with the phrase, "Thus saith Jeh," or its equivalent. But they ascribed their messages directly also to the Spirit of God (Ezk. 8 3; 11 1.24; 13 3).[47]

As similar as the Old and New Testament ministries of the Holy Spirit are, there are also some significant differences. The Old Testament ministry was limited in its purpose, effect, and quality. Relatively few people prior to Pentecost had an awareness of the ministry of the Spirit of God to them. Those who did were not guaranteed of its continuity. Thus David on at least one occasion prayed, "Take not thy holy spirit from me" (Psa. 51:11). The limitation of the effect of the Spirit's work is implied in John 7:37-39. Prior to the cross, there was no baptism in the Holy Spirit (identification with the death of Christ) because it had not yet become reality. Today there is a greater quality in a Christian's relationship with the Holy Spirit. In the Old Testament, the Holy Spirit was "with" men; today He is "in" men (John 14:17).

As noted above, much of the work of the Holy Spirit was preparatory. According to Berkhof, "God's deepest meaning with Israel was that in his gracious covenant relation with Israel the nature of created and fallen manhood might be revealed in such a way that the necessity of the incarnation and atonement might become evident."[48] But the preparatory work of the Holy Spirit in the Old Testament involved more than messianic expectation. As the editors of the *New Scofield Reference Bible* observe,

> The OT contains predictions of a future pouring out of the Spirit upon Israel (Ezek. 37:14; 39:29), and upon "all flesh" (Joel 2:28-29). The expectation of Israel, therefore, was twofold—of the coming of Messiah-Immanuel, and of such a pouring out of the Spirit as the prophets described.[49]

VII. The Future Ministry Of The Holy Spirit

There are yet two future periods to follow this age, where the ministry of the Holy Spirit will differ from this age. In both the Tribulation and Millennium the Holy Spirit will not be completing the body of Christ, but will again be working with Israel. Admittedly, the Bible does not portray a complete picture of the Holy Spirit's work in these yet future periods, but what is presented is helpful to better understand God's future program.

Paul's teaching to the Thessalonians concerning the removal of "He that restrains" prior to the revelation of the man of sin (2 Thess. 2:6-7), has resulted in an area of controversy over the presence of the Holy Spirit in the Tribulation. Some prophetic teachers emphasize this verse to mean all of the ministries of the Holy Spirit and His Person are to be withdrawn at the rapture of the church. Do these verses in question refer at least in part to the Holy Spirit? The argument that the restrainer is the Holy Spirit need not necessarily mean the cessation of the Holy Spirit's ministry on earth. The comment on this verse in the Scofield Bible suggests,

> There are various views as to the identity of the restraining influence. The use of the masculine pronoun "he" indicates that it is a person. It seems evident that it is the Holy Spirit: (a) in the O.T. the Holy Spirit acts as a restrainer of iniquity (Gen. 6:3); (b) the restrainer is referred to by the use of both neuter and masculine genders ("*what*," v. 6; "*he*," v. 7), as in John 14:16-17; 16:12-13, concerning the coming of the Holy Spirit; and (c) it will be when the restrainer is "taken out of the way," that the man of sin will be revealed; this will be when the Church is translated and the Spirit's

restraining ministry through it will cease. Observe, however, that it is not said that the restrainer will be "taken away," but "taken out of the way" thus the Holy Spirit will continue a divine activity to the end-time, though not as a restrainer of evil through the Church.[50]

Pache observes that even when the Spirit's ministry of restraining is removed, the Holy Spirit still is present to perform His ministries.

If it is true that the Church, the temple of the Spirit and the salt of the earth, is taken up into the heavens at a given moment and that her departure is marked by a greatly increased spiritual decline, it remains nonetheless true that the Spirit will continue to act among men through perhaps in a different fashion.[51]

Perhaps it is easier to understand the ministry of the Holy Spirit in the Great Tribulation if it is realized the Tribulation is essentially an extension of the age of law. What the Holy Spirit did in the Old Testament, He will perform in the coming period when God reestablishes His work with the nation of Israel. According to Chafer,

Not only does the law dispensation require the yet future Tribulation period for the execution of those divine judgments which belong to it, but, by the recognition of the sequence connecting these two periods of time, the continuity of purpose is preserved wherein the Messianic, earthly kingdom, which follows the Tribulation, is seen to be both the legitimate expectation and logical consummation of the dispensation of the law. By so much it may be observed that the present unforeseen dispensation of grace is wholly parenthetical within the dispensation of the law.[52]

The ministry of the Holy Spirit will be very similar to that of the Spirit in the Old Testament with perhaps one notable exception. It appears that the prophetic utterances concerning the outpouring of the Spirit upon the nation Israel are yet to be fulfilled, probably in the latter half of the Tribulation years (Dan. 9:24; Zech. 12:9-10). While the Holy Spirit will not be restraining evil through the church, it is difficult to be dogmatic in the removal of the ministry of restraint completely. Commenting on Isaiah 59:19-20, Pache observes,

It would seem that reference is clearly made here to the last days. Moreover when shall the enemy most clearly resemble the rushing of a flood if it be not when the rising tide of Antichrist will threaten to overwhelm all? This text warrants the belief that the Spirit will, to the very end, contribute to Christ's triumph over the forces of evil.[53]

The most glorious of all dispensations is that of the thousand-year reign of Christ. During most of this period, the Satanic rule on earth will be non-existent. Children will be born and people will be saved during this period. Christ will rule with a rod of iron and the fullness of the Spirit will be manifest in His government (Isa. 11:2). Perhaps this age will have a greater manifestation of the Holy Spirit than even the church age which is called the age of the Holy Spirit. The Millennium will be characterized by a manifestation of righteousness, peace, worship, and spirituality, surely an outgrowth of the Holy Spirit. Ridout summarizes the role of the Holy Spirit in the millennium stating,

> The Millennium, then, will be marked by the outpouring of the Spirit upon all flesh in connection with a display of special prophetic gifts and judgments upon the enemies of Christ. You will note this is not baptism into one Body, nor Indwelling.[54]

VIII. THE HOLY SPIRIT IN THE LIFE OF CHRIST

The Holy Spirit was involved in the life and ministry of Christ on earth, especially in view of the *kenosis*. The Holy Spirit was involved in the virgin birth of Christ (Luke 1:35). The ministry of Christ began with the descent of the Holy Spirit upon Him (Matt. 3:16) and continued by the presence of the Holy Spirit on Him (Luke 4:14-15). Christ was "declared to be the Son of God with power, according to the spirit of holiness, by the resurrection from the dead" (Rom. 1:4). Even as Christ prays for us in heaven today (Heb. 7:25), so "the Spirit Himself makes intercession for us with groanings which cannot be uttered" (Rom. 8:26). So intimate was the

THE HOLY SPIRIT IN THE LIFE OF CHRIST	
Incarnation	Heb. 10:5
Birth	Matt. 1:18
Growth	Luke 2:40,52
Baptism	Luke 3:21-22
Temptation	Luke 4:14
Ministry	Luke 4:18-19
Miracles	Matt. 12:28
Death	Heb. 9:14
Resurrection	Rom. 8:11
Glorification	John 16:14

involvement of the Holy Spirit in the earthly life of Christ that Mullins concludes, "It is clear from the preceding that in the thought of the NT writers Jesus is completely endued with the power of the Holy Spirit."[55]

In the same article, he observes, "in the NT there is unusual symmetry and completeness of teaching as to the work of the Spirit of God in relation to the Messiah Himself . . . . "[56] This completeness of the work of the Holy Spirit is evident from the *kenosis* to the exaltation of Christ. As Strong observes, the humiliation consisted, partly,

> In the submission of the Logos to the control of the Holy Spirit and the limitations of his messianic mission, in his communication of the divine fullness of the human nature which he had taken into union with himself.[57]

During the life of Christ on earth, the main ministry of the Holy Spirit was not to glorify Himself (John 16:13) but to enhance the ministry of Christ to carry out the purpose of the Father. The Holy Spirit glorified the Son. Fitch notes,

> There is one sole objective in the Holy Spirit's activities, He is present to glorify Jesus. This means that whatever begins with the Holy Spirit always ends in Jesus Christ. This is the glorious communion of the blessed Trinity: the Father glorifies the Son even as the Son glorifies the Father, and it is the peculiar and exalted ministry of the Holy Spirit to exalt and glorify the Son.[58]

The side chart identifies a number of specific references to the role of the Holy Spirit in the life of Christ.

The birth of Christ of a virgin was a result of the ministry of the entire Trinity, but especially that of the Holy Spirit. The angel Gabriel announced that the Holy Spirit was the agent of the virgin birth (Luke 1:35). As Palmer has noted,

> Although the incarnation was an act of all three Persons of the Godhead, yet it was especially the work of the Holy Spirit. He, and not the Father nor the Son, was the efficient cause by which Mary was found with child. He was "the power of the Most High," as Luke puts it, that effected the conception of Jesus. As the Apostles' Creed confesses, Jesus was conceived not by the Father nor by himself, but by the Holy Spirit. Therefore, in this special sense, the Holy Spirit was the originator and efficient cause of the incarnation.[59]

The baptism of Jesus is included in the introductory chapters of each of the Gospels and each makes specific reference to the dove-like appearance of the Holy Spirit. In each Gospel, the baptism appears as an introduction to, or initiation into, His public ministry. On the basis of these accounts, Mullins concludes,

> We gather from these passages that at the baptism there was a new communication of the Spirit to Jesus in great fullness, as a special anointing for His Messianic vocation. The account declares that the dovelike appearance was seen by Jesus as well as John, which is scarcely compatible with a subjective experience merely.[60]

A harmony of the Synoptic Gospels reveals a uniquely thorough involvement of the Holy Spirit in the temptation of Christ. Matthew declares, "Then was Jesus led up by the Spirit into the wilderness to be tempted of the devil" (Matt. 4:1). In Mark, the language is somewhat more severe, making use of a verb used elsewhere to identify the practice of casting out demons, "And immediately the Spirit driveth [lit. "casteth out"] him into the wilderness" (Mark 1:12). Luke adds to this that Jesus was both "full of the Holy Ghost" and "led by the Spirit" during the wilderness temptations (Luke 4:1). It may be safely assumed that this intimate relationship with the Holy Spirit was also characteristic of Jesus in His later temptations (cf. Luke 22:28).

The New Testament reveals several dimensions of the relationship between Jesus and the Holy Spirit during his ministry. He was anointed by the Spirit (Luke 4:18; Acts 10:38; Heb. 1:9), filled with the Holy Spirit (Luke 4:1; John 3:34-35), empowered by the Holy Spirit (Matt. 12:22), led by the Spirit (Luke 4:1) and He rejoiced in the Spirit (Luke 10:21). The Holy Spirit was necessary for the accomplishment of miracles by Christ. Palmer notes,

> That the Holy Spirit also gave him special powers to perform miracles for his ministry is seen in one of his struggles with the Pharisees when he said: "If I by the Spirit of God cast out demons, then is the kingdom of God come unto you" (Matt. 12:28). He then lets the Jews know that by calling him Beelzebub, the prince of the devils, they are blaspheming chiefly against the Holy Spirit, since it was the Holy Spirit who was really the Author of those miracles, even if they were done through Jesus.[61]

More completely, Mullins speaks of the work of the Holy Spirit in the miracles of Jesus, noting,

> The miracles of Jesus were wrought through the power of the Holy Spirit. Occasionally He is seized as it were by a sense of the urgency of His work in

some way as to impress beholders with the presence of a strange power working within Him . . . One of the most impressive aspects of this activity of Jesus in the Spirit is its suppressed intensity. Nowhere is there lack of self-control. Nowhere is there evidence of a coldly didactic attitude, on the one hand, or of a loose rein upon the will, on the other. Jesus is always an intensely human Master wrapped in Divine power. The miracles contrast strikingly with the miracles of the apocryphal gospels. In the latter all sorts of capricious deeds of power are ascribed to Jesus as a boy. In our Gospels, on the contrary, no miracle is wrought until after His anointing with the Spirit at baptism.[62]

Part of the *kenosis* included submitting to the limitations of humanity. Though Jesus was still God during His life on earth, He was nevertheless dependent upon the Third Person of the Trinity to accomplish much of the work of God. While not denying the deity of Christ, this truth illustrates His humanity.

IX. THE PRESENT MINISTRY OF THE HOLY SPIRIT

The Holy Spirit is active in the world today. Though at times one may wonder if anything is going right and think the world is in total chaos, things are never as bad as they would be if the Holy Spirit were not at work in the world. The Holy Spirit is working to restrain sin in the world and to reprove sin in the unbeliever.

The moment a person is saved, a number of things take place in his life. He is born again by the Holy Spirit, indwelt by the Holy Spirit, baptized by the Holy Spirit into the body of Christ, sealed with the Spirit, and a host of other things almost too numerous to list. Many times a person will not be totally aware of all that takes place when he is saved until years later, but these things happen the moment he trusts Christ as personal Savior. The Agent of this regeneration is the Holy Spirit.

The ministry of the Holy Spirit in our lives does not end at conversion, but continues beyond. He fills Christians as they yield to Him and allow Him to control their lives. He leads them and sheds light on the Scripture, helping the Christian to learn better the things of God. He gives them the fruit of the Spirit for character and the gifts of the Holy Spirit for Christian service.

The best way to understand the ministry of the Spirit is to take the Scripture at face value. Yet many are confused regarding the ministry of the Holy Spirit. McConkey suggested the ministry of the Spirit could be summarized in His incoming (i.e. indwelling), fullness and constant manifestation.[63] H. Berkhof, commenting on one particular ministry of the Spirit, notes the inadequacy of a Reformed approach to the subject.

As we mentioned before, dogmatics traditionally speak about regeneration in a twofold way: justification and sanctification. This division has been challenged, however, since the Revivalist and Pentecostal movements began. These movements experienced still another blessing of the Holy Spirit in the life of the individual, which is now widely known as the "filling by the Holy Spirit" or "The baptism by the Holy Spirit." So these groups believe in a threefold work of the Spirit; justification, sanctification, and being filled by the Spirit.[64]

Oswald Smith, whom Berkhof might identify as a part of "the revivalist movement," suggests a sevenfold work of the Spirit.

There are seven words that describe the work of the Holy Spirit in the life of the believer. They are the Baptism, the Gift, the Indwelling, the Sealing, the Earnest, the Filling and Anointing of the Spirit.[65]

This section deals with the work of the Holy Spirit, in twelve general areas. Some of this is illustrated chronologically in the following chart. While the chart is not necessarily exhaustive, it does serve to identify the major ministries of the Holy Spirit in human experience.

THE HOLY SPIRIT AND YOU		
PRECONVERSION	CONVERSION	POSTCONVERSION
1. Reprove/Convict (John 16:7-10)	1. Regeneration (Titus 3:5)	1. Fullness (Eph. 5:18)
2. Restraint (2 Thess. 2:7)	2. Baptism (1 Cor. 12:13)	2. Sanctification (2 Cor. 3:18)
	3. Indwelling (1 Cor. 6:19)	3. Illumination (1 Cor. 2:12)
	4. Sealing (Eph. 4:30)	4. Prayer (Rom. 8:26-27)
		5. Fruit of the Spirit (Gal. 5:22-23)

		6. Gifts of the Spirit (Rom. 12:3-8; 1 Cor. 12:1-31; Eph. 4:7-11)

A. CONVICTION. The word conviction includes a number of biblical expressions in its meanings. Originally, the word comes from two Latin terms meaning "cause to see." Broadly speaking, reproof, conviction, and illumination are all part of this ministry of the Holy Spirit whereby He causes the individual to see (i.e., with understanding) truth. These terms speak of the work of the Holy Spirit in setting forth the truth and causing a person to see it as such. Jesus identified at least three areas in which the Holy Spirit could convict a person in the world. "And when he is come, he will reprove the world of sin, and of righteousness, and of judgment" (John 16:8). This does not necessarily mean a person will respond positively to the gospel and accept the truth, but that the Holy Spirit will cause a person to see the truth.

1. *The Holy Spirit will convict of sin.* The sin which keeps people out of heaven is unbelief. "He that believeth on him is not condemned: but he that believeth not is condemned already, because he hath not believed in the name of the only begotten Son of God" (John 3:18). Of course, all sin can be forgiven, but sin is not forgiven apart from faith. "But without faith it is impossible to please him; for he that cometh to God must believe that he is, and that he is a rewarder of them that diligently seek him" (Heb. 11:6). When a man refuses to believe God, he has attacked the character of God. The Holy Spirit convicts "of sin, because they believe not on me [Jesus]" (John 16:9).

2. *The Holy Spirit convicts concerning righteousness.* When Paul described the process in which an individual or society degenerates into gross immorality, he identified the starting point of the downward cycle as "unrighteousness of men, who hold the truth in unrighteousness" (Rom. 1:18). When Jesus spoke of righteousness, he was not referring to the good works or moral codes of men. He was speaking of the righteousness of God (i.e., the perfection of Jesus Christ).

When Jesus was among men, He stood as an example and reflection of the righteousness of God. His sinless life convicted men who saw their own unrighteousness. When the religions leaders of Jerusalem brought a woman caught in the act of adultery, Jesus responded, "He that is without sin among you, let him first cast a stone at her" (John 8:7). That statement brought conviction to the accusers (John 8:9).

Now that Jesus has returned to heaven, the Holy Spirit convicts of righteousness, because "I [Jesus] go to my Father, and ye see me no more" (John 16:10). It is the

Holy Spirit who today causes men to see themselves in relation to the righteousness of God. When that occurs, like Isaiah, we can say, "I am a man of unclean lips, and I dwell in the midst of a people of unclean lips; for mine eyes have seen the King, the Lord of hosts" (Isa. 6:5).

3. *The Holy Spirit convicts of judgment.* He convicts of "judgment, because the prince of this world is judged" (John 16:11). When Jesus died on the cross, one of His last statements was, "It is finished" (John 19:30). That victorious pronunciation marked the sealing of a victory in a battle which began in the Garden of Eden. At the Fall of man, God promised One who would win the battle over the serpent and his seed (Gen. 3:15). This struggle continued through the years and continues today. When Jesus was about to leave His disciples for the cross, He said, "Be of good cheer, I have overcome the world" (John 16:33). Though the struggle between God and the devil has continued since then, the victory is secure. The Holy Spirit causes men to see that the devil has been judged and their sin will also be judged if they continue in it.

Oftentimes it is our tendency to classify certain sins as more evil than other sins. Depending upon cultural values, some sins may be more acceptable than others in the world, but all sin is repulsive to God. The sins we may choose to identify in our soul-winning efforts may not be committed by all people. For example, not everyone lies, cheats, steals, or hates, but everyone apart from Christ is guilty of the sin of unbelief and unrighteousness. The Holy Spirit convicts men of the sins of which they are guilty and "causes them to see" that their sin already has been judged. In this way He shows men their need of a Savior and draws them to the place of salvation.

B. RESTRAINT. A major ministry of the Holy Spirit in the world today is that of restraint, The discouraging reports of increasing crime in the our cities may make it hard to believe, but things are not as bad today as they could be. The presence of the Holy Spirit prevents the complete corruption of the world. As bad as conditions may be in some places, they are not as bad as they someday will be. At the rapture of the church, the Holy Spirit—particularly in this ministry of restraint—will "be taken out of the way" (2 Thess. 2:7). Describing conditions on earth during the time following the removal of this restraint, Jesus said, "For then shall be great tribulation, such as was not since the beginning of the world to this time, no, nor ever shall be" (Matt. 24:21).

The Holy Spirit's work of restraint is often accomplished through the testimony of a Christian whose presence makes the unsaved feel guilty about his sin. When the Christian is not there, the non-Christian does not feel comfortable in his sin. As God can use the presence of godliness to restrain some in their sinful lifestyle, so the Holy

Spirit restrains the devil and the fallen angels of hell in their efforts to corrupt the world.

C. REGENERATION. The doctrine of regeneration is a work of the Holy Spirit which was emphasized by John Wesley (1703-1791) while soteriology was emphasized by Luther, whose primary concern was justification, (i.e., man's legal standing before God). Wesley was concerned more with the change in human nature that occurs at and following conversion or regeneration.

The Greek word translated "regeneration" is used only once in the Bible as it relates to this ministry of the Holy Spirit. "Not by works of righteousness which we have done, but according to his mercy he saved us, by the washing of regeneration, and renewing of the Holy Ghost" (Titus 3:5). Jesus told Nicodemus, "Except a man be born of water and of the Spirit, he cannot enter into the kingdom of God" (John 3:5). Regeneration is that work of the Spirit of God whereby men are given God's life and God's nature and made a part of the family of God. Occurring at the moment of conversion, it is the giving of eternal life to the individual (not quantity of life only— life without end, but quality of life—the life of God). Jesus said, "He that heareth my word, and believeth on him that sent me, hath everlasting life, and shall not come into condemnation, but is passed from death unto life" (John 5:24). This passing "from death unto life" is the initiation of regeneration.

Perhaps the chief area of controversy among theologians addressing the subject of regeneration deals with the conditions under which it occurs. Calvinism's view causes Reformed writers to deny any active role that man has in this experience. Thus Palmer declares,

> According to Scripture, faith does not precede and cause regeneration, but rather, regeneration precedes and causes faith. Regeneration is necessary before man can do a single thing that is spiritually good. In regeneration man is 100 percent passive, and the Holy Spirit is 100 percent active.[66]

This erroneous conclusion is often defended by an incorrect exegesis of Ephesians 2:8 that suggests saving faith is a gift of God. The chief difficulty with this interpretation is its total disregard for the grammar of the verse. Bruce observes,

> But the fact that the demonstrative pronoun "that" is neuter in Greek (tonto), whereas "faith" is a feminine noun (pistis), combines with other considerations to suggest that it is the whole concept of salvation by grace through faith that is described as the gift of God. This, incidentally, is Calvin's interpretation, although many of his followers have professed to take faith itself as a gift from God here.[67]

As Bruce acknowledges, this Calvinistic interpretation of the complete passivity of man in regeneration differs from Calvin's own understanding of the Scriptures. In a sermon on Ephesians 2:8, he declared,

> And when we receive by faith the grace offered us in the gospel, we confess thereby that we have need of Jesus Christ, because there is nothing but perdition in ourselves. Also, when he says in this text that it is by faith, he shows that if comparison is made between God and man, we must come, as it were, stark naked, and there must be nothing in us but shame and abashment until God has received us to mercy.[68]

> Moreover, let us note along with this that if we are to be partakers of the salvation that God offers us, we must bring nothing with us but faith alone. For (as I said in another place) faith takes no help from good works.[69]

Perhaps a more biblical response then to the conditions which effect regeneration must include a recognition of the necessity and ability of man to believe. In keeping with this, Pache writes,

> When does regeneration take place? At that very moment when the heart, under the Spirit's double conviction of sin and righteousness, accepts the Saviour, who is presented to him. On God's part it is an immediate act even though man may have taken years to reach the point of yielding and receiving salvation.[70]

D. BAPTISM OF THE SPIRIT. John the Baptist, after witnessing the descent of the Holy Spirit as a dove at the baptism of Jesus, recorded these words: "He that sent me to baptize with water, the same said unto me, Upon whom thou shalt see the Spirit descending, and remaining on him, the same is he which baptizeth with the Holy Ghost" (John 1:33).

Later Jesus promised His disciples, "Ye shall be baptized with the Holy Ghost not many days hence" (Acts 1:5). On the day of Pentecost, the disciples had a number of experiences involving the Holy Spirit, including the baptism of the Holy Spirit. Some Christians today have confused some of the facts recorded in Acts 2 and, as a result, they do not fully realize what the Holy Spirit did for them at their conversion. A key to clearing up this confusion is to understand the difference between the terms "baptism" and "fullness."

To baptize means to immerse or totally surround something. Fullness, on the other hand, refers to placing something within another. It can carry with it the idea of control. On the day of Pentecost, the group in the upper room were both baptized and filled with the Holy Spirit. At conversion the person is baptized or placed into Jesus Christ, "For by one Spirit are we all baptized into one body" (1 Cor. 12:13). Then there is the filling of the Spirit which Paul commands for Christians. "But be filled with the Spirit" (Eph. 5:18). The baptism of the Spirit is our new position in Jesus Christ (non-experiential), and the filling of the Spirit is His power working through us in Christian service (experiential).

The baptism of the Holy Spirit is an act whereby the individual is placed in the body of Christ. Even though it is realized at a believer's conversion, which is experiential, the baptism of the Spirit is non-experiential. That all the Christians at Corinth are said to have been baptized in the Spirit is evidence in itself that this does not involve an eradication of the sin nature (1 Cor. 12:13). This is contrary to the claims of some Holiness teachers.

One of the phenomena of the twentieth century has been the emergence and growth of Pentecostalism. From its humble beginnings in the first decade of the twentieth century, it has become a major influence in Christianity, not only in North America, but around the world. Many of the world's largest and fastest growing churches are affiliated with various Pentecostal denominations. One of the distinctives of this movement is its view of the baptism of the Holy Spirit. In an attempt to state the Pentecostal view of the baptism of the Holy Spirit, Hoekema writes,

> Though it is difficult to sum up the views of a great many people from various Christian denominations in a single statement, the following is an attempt to reproduce what is commonly held by Neo-Pentecostals about this matter: the baptism in the Holy Spirit is an experience distinct from and usually subsequent to conversion in which a person receives the totality of the Spirit into his life and is thereby fully empowered for witness and service.[71]

> Often the initial evidence of the spirit baptism is identified by charismatic Christians by the practice of speaking in tongues. Article 8 of the *Statement of Fundamental Truths of the Assemblies of God* states in part, "The Baptism of believers in the Holy Ghost is witnessed by the initial physical sign of speaking with other tongues . . ."[72]

The key to understanding the baptism of the Holy Spirit is a correct interpretation of 1 Corinthians 12:13. This is the central passage on this doctrine and it teaches that all Christians participate in this baptism. If the "one baptism" of Ephesians 4:5 is taken to mean the baptism of the Spirit, as it probably should be, this text constitutes added proof of the universality of this baptism among Christians. The implication of

Romans 6:3-5 is that this universal baptism of the Holy Spirit took place theologically in the historic death, burial, and resurrection of Christ and experientially at the

WHEN DID THE BAPTISM OF THE HOLY SPIRIT OCCUR?	
Theological Answer	In the death, burial and resurrection of Christ
Historical Answer	On the day of Pentecost, the embryonic church was baptized in the Spirit.
Experiential Answer	At the moment of my conversion, I was baptized in the Spirit.
Testimonial Answer	As I submitted to water baptism, I testified of my Spirit baptism.

moment of conversion. Historically, the baptism of the Holy Spirit occurred on the day of Pentecost (cf. Acts 1:5; 2:1-4, 11:15-16). When a Christian is baptized in a New Testament Church in water, he is giving public testimony to having been baptized by the Spirit into the body of Christ. In symbol, he is added to the local body by water baptism because he was added to Christ's body by Spirit baptism.

The baptism of the Holy Spirit is unique to this dispensation. Until Pentecost, all references to Spirit baptism were prophetic. This was one of the ministries which began at Pentecost. Since it began at Pentecost, it is probable that it will end at the rapture of the church. In Spirit baptism, a Christian is baptized into the body of Christ. The body of Christ is often used as a representation of the church in the Pauline epistles. It is through the baptism of the Spirit that each individual is brought into a union with Christ. Thus there is a twofold identification in this baptism, with Christ and with His body, the church. When the church is removed at the rapture, this latter aspect of identification is no longer possible. Therefore, the baptism of the Holy Spirit is limited to this dispensation.

On two occasions, references to the baptism with the Holy Spirit include the words "and fire" (Matt. 3:11; Luke 3:16). There are least three interpretations of this expression. Some see in this at least more than a reference to the tongues of fire that appeared on Pentecost. According to Leisegang, "Baptism with fire is nothing else than Baptism with the Spirit, which would, in Hellenistic circles of early Christianity, in reference to the Greek cultus of Dionysus, to magic and the mysteries, be thought of as bound up with an appearance of fire."[73] Others consider this statement to be a reference to divine judgment. Barrett suggests,

> Wellhausen and Bultmann are of the opinion that the original form of the saying was, "He will baptize you with fire", and that this simple eschatological doom saying was corrupted to its present forms by the Christian experience of the Spirit. It seems even more plausible to conjecture that the earliest form of the logion was, "He will baptize you with πνευμακτι και πυρι πνεύματι being taken to mean, not "spirit" but "wind" . . . Wind and fire are the instruments of judgement.[74]

The third view sees the expression as a general statement concerning the mission and ministry of the apostles. Rayan explains,

> This reference here is to mission of the apostles and the proclamation of the Word. The Spirit is the Communicator of the Word. The creative Spirit and the creative Word work together. Pentecost is the immediate equipping of the disciples for their mission. Their words are to be words of fire, fire that destroys and consumes what is worthless, fire that purifies and makes ready for a new creation, a creation of brightness, genuineness, beauty, authenticity, effectiveness. When we relate or proclaim the Word, our self-expression has to be genuine and truly authentic.[75]

E. INDWELLING. One of the purposes of God since the beginning was to dwell with man and enjoy fellowship with Him. In the Garden of Eden, God would come to walk with Adam and talk with him. After the Fall, God spoke with various men to enjoy their fellowship.   When men failed to live for God even after the Flood, God established a unique relation with the heads of the patriarchal families. Later on Mount Sinai, He gave Moses the plans for the tabernacle which served as "the dwelling place of God's glory." When the tabernacle was replaced with a temple, the glory of the Lord moved into that place where men could meet their God. During the life of Christ, God's desire to dwell with men was fulfilled when "the Word was made flesh, and dwelt among us" (John 1:14). Today, God dwells by His Holy Spirit in the bodies of those who have been redeemed.

"Know ye not that your body is the temple of the Holy Ghost which is in you, which ye have of God, and ye are not your own?" (1 Cor. 6:19). Our human bodies have become temples to house the Holy Spirit. A realization of this truth will assist us in our efforts to properly care for our physical bodies. It will also help to keep us spiritually pure and clean.   Within the context of the apostle's question, he is discussing morality. Even if a man had no concern about engaging in immoral activity, the thought of involving "the temple of God" in such a practice should help prevent the progress of sin. When we realize we are never alone, but that the Holy Spirit is always with us, even present inside, we will be more cautious in our efforts to live for God.

Jesus promises, "If any man thirst, let him come unto me and drink. He that believeth on me, as the scripture hath said, out of his belly shall flow rivers of living water" (John 7:37-38). The "living water" is the indwelling Holy Spirit. John adds the interpretation, "But this spake he of the Spirit, which they that believe on him should receive: for the Holy Ghost was not yet given; because that Jesus was not yet glorified" (John 7:39). This is a reference to the indwelling Holy Spirit. The Holy Spirit: (1) comes automatically when a person is saved, (2) is not an experiential act, but produces spiritual experiences, (3) remains permanently, (4) is the basis of all the other ministries of the Holy Spirit, and (5) is the new life of the believer.

Catholic theologians believe the sacraments are a means of grace and that this is the means by which the faithful are indwelt by the Spirit of God. Arguing this point, Leen states,

> The Holy Communion might in a wide sense be called a means to the indwelling of the Blessed Trinity in the human soul. It is true that at the moment of baptism the Three Divine Persons take up their abode in the soul of the infant. But baptism involves in a certain way a desire of the Eucharist, since of its nature it tends toward it. In baptism there is a *votum improprie dictum* of the Blessed Sacrament.[76]

Actually, the Spirit's indwelling begins at conversion and is one of the proofs of assurance that one is a child of God and is the basis of eternal security. Those who do not have the indwelling Holy Spirit are not saved. The Apostle Paul declared, "Now if any man have not the Spirit of Christ, he is none of his" (Rom. 8:9). The Holy Spirit within is the "earnest" of future blessing (2 Cor. 1:22; 5:5; Eph. 1:14). Even Christians living in sin are exhorted to righteousness in the New Testament on the basis of the indwelling Spirit (1 Cor. 6:19).

Several passages have been interpreted by some to teach that not all Christians are indwelt by the Spirit or that the Spirit may withdraw this ministry. These passages describe conditions prior to Pentecost (1 Sam. 16:14; Psa. 51:11; Luke 11:13) or unique features of the transition into this present dispensation (Acts 5:32; 8:14-20; 19:1-6). In Acts 19, twelve disciples of John the Baptist, who are engaged in an itinerate ministry, are confronted by Paul concerning their relation with the Holy Spirit. Later they receive the Holy Spirit and submit to Christian baptism. This is probably a group of men who were saved under Old Testament salvation, but had not yet experienced the New Testament ministry of the Holy Spirit. It would be unwise to use this passage against the many clear statements that all believers now have the Holy Spirit.[77]

F. SEALING. The Bible also teaches that Christians are sealed by the Holy Spirit. "Ye were sealed with that holy Spirit of promise, which is the earnest of our inheritance until the redemption of the purchased possession" (Eph. 1:13-14).

When a man and woman agree to marry, it is customary in our culture for the man to give the woman an engagement ring as a symbol of his commitment to her. Paul was drawing on a similar custom of the first century to explain this aspect of the ministry of the Holy Spirit in salvation. When an individual is born again, he immediately becomes an heir to all God has promised. The sealing of the Holy Spirit is not something God does to guarantee our salvation as a person might seal an envelope to guarantee its contents. The Holy Spirit is the seal. God gives the Holy Spirit as a down payment of His commitment to someday give all the other things He has promised. By way of application, it is important that we "grieve not the holy Spirit of God, whereby ye are sealed unto the day of redemption" (Eph. 4:30). Concerning the seal as an emblem of the sealing of the Holy Spirit, Marsh states,

> The Seal signifies the Holy Spirit. It is not some emotion or experience, but it is the presence of the Holy Spirit in the believer, witnessing to his full acceptance in Christ, telling us by the Word that as Christ is, so are we in this world (I. John iv. 17).[78]

G. FULLNESS. The doctrine of the fullness of the Spirit is vital to the living experience of the normal Christian life. By biblical standards, the average Christian life today is abnormal because so many Christians are not living Spirit-filled lives. Unlike other ministries of the Spirit, the fullness of the Spirit is experiential and is the power of all spiritual blessing in the life of the Christian.

The importance of this doctrine has not gone unnoticed by the spiritual giants of the past. In a sermon entitled "The Outpouring of the Holy Spirit," Spurgeon declared,

> Let the preacher always confess before he preaches that he relies upon the Holy Spirit. Let him burn his manuscript and depend upon the Holy Spirit. If the Spirit does not come to help him, let him be still and let the people go home and pray that the Spirit will help him next Sunday.[79]

Andrew Murray also sensed the importance of this doctrine when he wrote,

But one thing is needful. The Spirit did it all, on the day of Pentecost and afterwards. It was the Spirit who gave the boldness, the Spirit gave the wisdom, the Spirit gave the message, and the Spirit gave the converting power.[80]

Those who seek the filling of the Holy Spirit will receive power for Christian service. Dwight L. Moody had such an experience of the fullness of the Holy Spirit and saw God use him to accomplish more than he had previously done.

One day, in the city of New York—oh, what a day—I cannot describe it, I seldom refer to it; it is almost too sacred an experience to name . . . I can only say that God revealed Himself to me, and I had such an experience of His love that I had to ask Him to stay His hand. I went to preaching again. The sermons were not different. I did not present any new truths, and yet hundreds were converted. I would not now be placed back where I was before that blessed experience if you would give me all the world. . . ."[81]

We should study the biblical principles of how God works and examine the great men in our heritage so we can have the same power today. The Holy Spirit who used Peter on the day of Pentecost and Moody in the last century is the same Holy Spirit who will work in us today. God's will for us may not be as an evangelist like Dwight L. Moody. But for whatever task, and however mundane, God desires that we yield ourselves to Him (Rom. 6:13) so that He can use us fully.

Paul commanded the Ephesian Christians: "And be not drunk with wine, wherein is excess; but be filled with the Spirit" (Eph. 5:18). The word "filled" has the Greek meaning of "be continually filled" showing the filling could be a repeated experience for believers, whereas the baptism of the Spirit was a non-repeated act. The filling of the Spirit was for service, whereas the baptism of the Spirit and the indwelling of the Spirit were related to salvation. The context of Ephesians 5:18 refers to intoxication by alcohol. When a person is drunk, he is controlled by the spirits of the bottle; his walk, talk, and sight are controlled. So when a person is filled with the Spirit, his walk, talk, and sight are controlled by the Spirit. Rather than allowing alcohol to control the mind of the Christian, God desires that His Holy Spirit be in control. As we establish our fellowship with God through confession of sins (1 John 1:9) and yield to Him (Rom. 6:13) we can be filled with the Holy Spirit as commanded in Scripture. In light of Paul's command, no Christian can claim to be in the will of God who is not constantly being filled with the Holy Spirit.

Some sincere Christians today seek spectacular signs to accompany the fullness of the Holy Spirit in their lives. Actually, the Bible does not teach these should be expected today. The Holy Spirit's fullness within us is to produce the fruit of the

Spirit (Gal. 5:22-23). The evidence in the Book of Acts of the fullness of the Holy Spirit promised by Jesus was power to witness (Acts 1:8). On some occasions (but not every occasion) when Christians were filled with the Holy Spirit, sometimes the building shook (Acts 4:31), sometimes they spoke in tongues (Acts 10:44-46); but always the gospel was preached and people were saved. These occasional outward occurrences were often tools God used at that time to accomplish the main objective of witnessing. These outward signs were similar to the purpose that miracles had in the early church. They were an objective authority for the message of God. But when God provided the full revelation of the Word of God as the authoritative message, the outward signs or authorities passed off the scene.

H. SANCTIFICATION. The word "sanctification" means "to be set apart." The Holy Spirit is attempting to make the believer "holy" (lit. "to set apart") and "spiritual" (to reflect the character of God). There is a threefold sanctification. First, the believer was sanctified (forgiven and set apart to God in salvation). Second, the believer is constantly being set apart from sin as he utilizes the means of grace in his life. Third, he will be completely sanctified when he meets the Lord either in the rapture, or at death. At that time he will be without sin.

In the present process of sanctification, Paul reminded the Corinthians, "But we all, with open face beholding as in a glass the glory of the Lord, are changed into the same image from glory to glory, even as by the Spirit of the Lord!" (2 Cor. 3:18). This was not a special one-time experience with the Holy Spirit that instantaneously transforms carnal Christians into spiritual Christlike giants. To the Philippians, Paul wrote, "Being confident of this very thing, that he who hath begun a good work in you will perform it until the day of Jesus Christ" (Phil. 1:6). This is a practical growth in sanctification that is part of the will of God for every believer (1 Thess. 4:3). These changes into greater Christ-likeness cannot be accomplished apart from the Holy Spirit. Adams notes,

> The Holy Spirit is the source of all genuine personality changes that involve the sanctification of the believer, just as truly as He alone is the One that brings life to the dead sinner. It is time that Christian ministers and other counselors asked again, "Who has bewitched You . . .? Having begun in the Spirit, are you now being perfected in the flesh?" Why are Christians without peace turning to me who themselves know nothing of the peace of God that passes all understanding? How is it that Christian ministers refer parishioners to a psychiatrist who has never been able to discover the secret of control in his own life? Outwardly he may appear calm and assured, mature, patient and even suave. Can this be his actual condition if he does

not know Jesus Christ? Can he have the fruit of the Spirit apart from the Spirit?[82]

I. ILLUMINATION OF THE SPIRIT. Jesus promised, "When he, the Spirit of truth, is come, he will guide you into all truth" (John 16:13). While part of that promise relates primarily to the apostles who recorded Scripture by the inspiration of the Holy Spirit, it also has application to Christians today as the Holy Spirit illuminates Scripture today. The Holy Spirit has a present-day ministry in the life of a Christian, "that we might know the things that are freely given to us of God" (1 Cor. 2:12).

One of the expressions of Scripture to describe the work of the Spirit in illumination is the witness or testimony of the Holy Spirit. According to Ursinus,

> The most essential "evidence" of the "certainty of Scripture" is the testimony of the H. Spirit. "This testimony is unique, proper only to those reborn by the Spirit of Christ and known only to them. And it has such power that it not only attests and seals abundantly in our souls the truth of the prophetic and apostolic doctrine, but also effectually bends and moves our hearts to embrace and follow it.[83]

Apart from this illuminating ministry of the Holy Spirit, it would be impossible for man to know God. Tozer summarizes this truth.

> Man by reason cannot know God; he can only *know about God*. Through the light of reason certain important facts about God may be discovered. . . . Through the light of nature man's moral reason may be enlightened, but the deeper mysteries of God remain hidden to him until he has received illumination from above . . . When the Spirit illuminates the heart, then a part of the man sees which never saw before; part of him knows which never knew before, and that with a kind of knowing which the most acute thinker cannot imitate. He knows now in a deep and authoritative way, and what he knows needs no reasoned proof. His experience of knowing is above reason, immediate, perfectly convincing and inwardly satisfying.[84]

The importance of this "causing to see" ministry of the Holy Spirit is perhaps best understood in the historical context in which it was first clearly systematized. It is generally acknowledged that the witness of the Spirit was a doctrinal emphasis of all the reformers. Yet Calvin is credited with systematizing the doctrine of *Testimonium* as part of his prolegomena. The conditions of Europe at that time were significant in both motivating the development and clarifying the nature of the doctrine of illumination. Ramm suggests,

In developing his doctrine of the *testimonium* Calvin was faced with three alternative theories. Christian certainty was explained by Romanism as the gift of the infallible Church to the believing Catholic. The enthusiasts, or fanatics, found their certainty of faith in an immediate revelation of the Holy Spirit, a revelation which was not bound to the contents of Scripture. And some apologists were asserting that they could demonstrate the truthfulness of the Christian faith by purely rational evidences. Calvin was unhappy with all three theories, and developed his doctrine of the *testimonium* in opposition to each of them.[85]

The illumination of the Holy Spirit is directed toward believers so that they can understand Scripture. Palmer writes,

> The sum of the matter is, then, that the Holy Spirit comes into peoples' lives, he enlightens them, he gives them understanding, teaches them, open their eyes, removes the veil from their hearts, and softens their hearts so that they can know the things of the Spirit of God. Without him, man is blind to see the truth of revelation; but when there is a demonstration of the Spirit and of power, man knows all things.[86]

Recognizing that this work of the Spirit relates primarily to the removal of spiritual blindness helps explain why Christians may vary in their degree of spiritual insight and even disagree on the interpretation of a particular text or doctrine. When the Spirit illuminates the mind of a believer, it is essentially a ministry of subtraction not addition. We are "caused to see" by the removal of spiritual blindness. Illumination is not an internal communication of truth (content, insight, or principles) by direct intuitive communication. Illumination is the ministry of the Holy Spirit in taking away spiritual blindness so the believer can study and learn Scripture. The believer grows in spiritual insight when he obeys the biblical command to study (2 Tim. 2:15). The student who does not study cannot expect the Holy Spirit to reveal truth. The day of revelation is past; the Holy Spirit does not communicate new truth today. He illuminates that which is already revealed. The preacher who does not study in the preparation of a sermon can likewise not expect to communicate spiritual truth in the pulpit.

The Scriptures teach the existence of both general and special revelation. General revelation is evidenced in (1) nature and (2) the conscience of man. Hence, the Holy Spirit works through general revelation to illumine the heart of man to the demands of God upon his life. Thus an individual is responsible to God because the law of God is written on his heart (Rom. 2:14-15). Also, Paul holds the pagan world responsible because they rejected even the limited knowledge of God given them in nature (Rom. 1:21-23). Contemporary missiologists today interpret animistic religions as a corruption of a monotheistic concept of God universally found in natural revelation. In his book *The Go-Between God*, John Taylor attributes the various religions of the people of the world indirectly to this work of the Spirit. While coming dangerously close to formulating a doctrinal basis for syncretism, he observes,

> The eternal Spirit has been at work in all ages and all cultures making men aware and evoking their response, and always the one to whom he was pointing and bearing witness was the Logos, the Lamb slain before the foundation of the world. Every religion has been a tradition of response to him, however darkly it groped toward him, however anxiously it shied away from him.[87]

This does not mean missionaries should abandon their work of preaching the gospel to those in other religious traditions, but only that they may he assured of the ministry of the Holy Spirit in the lives of those they are trying to reach.

J. PRAYER. The Scriptures identify the Holy Spirit's prayer ministry (Rom. 8:26-27). When a Christian prays biblically, that prayer is normally directed to the Father through the Holy Spirit in the name of the Son. Because there are three Persons in the Trinity, it is not necessarily improper to address prayer to the Son or the Holy Spirit. But the majority of witness in Scripture exhorts the believer to pray to the Father. Still, those prayers must be "in the Spirit." Torrey states,

> . . . the only prayer that is acceptable to God is prayer in the Spirit, the only thanks that are acceptable to God, are thanks in the Spirit, and the only worship that is acceptable to God is worship in the Spirit. Would we worship aright our hearts must look up and cry, "Teach me, Holy Spirit, to worship"; and He will do it.[88]

Ironside adds to that by noting that just requesting the Spirit is not praying in the Spirit. Those who pray in the Spirit must pray according to the Word of God.

> The Word of God is the foundation on which we build. Prayer keeps the soul in touch with the power by which alone we build aright. Mere Bible knowledge may make one heady and doctrinal. Prayer alone, if unguided by Scripture, tends to fanaticism; but the Word and prayer together give a good, firm base on which to rear a sturdy Christian character.[89]

K. FRUIT OF THE SPIRIT. Another ministry of the Holy Spirit is the production of spiritual fruit in the life of the believer (Gal. 5:22-23) which relates to character. This is a ministry of the Spirit occurring after conversion and closely related to His work of sanctification. As the Holy Spirit is free to work in the believer's life, He begins to develop His character in the Christian. Fitch describes the result as,

> A loving, affectionate spirit, radiant with peculiar joy, and full of tranquility; it is very patient in disposition, even when provoked; it possesses unusual insights into the needs and wants of others, is generous in judgment and is utterly loyal; it is by nature very humble, forgets itself in the happiness of others, never allows itself to get out of control, and is always reliable because of its unusual adaptability and self-mastery.[90]

The fruit of the Holy Spirit is not converts gained as a result of ministry. That is the fruit of the Christian. The principle of "like begetting like" was established at the creation of the world (cf. Gen. 1). Because the most spiritual of Christians is still a sinner, it is impossible for any Christian to develop the character of God. Only the indwelling Holy Spirit can produce His character in the life of the believer. As Emery H. Bancroft notes,

> All real beauty of character, all real Christlikeness in us, is the Holy Spirit's work. He is to the Christian what the sap is to the tree,—the source of productive life and power.[91]

L. BESTOWAL OF SPIRITUAL GIFTS. A final aspect of the present ministry of the Holy Spirit here considered is the bestowal of gifts. The Bible teaches that every Christian has at least one gift, and perhaps more (1 Pet. 4:10; Rom. 12:6; 1 Cor. 12:11). In recent years, there has been an increased interest in spiritual gifts, but this has sometimes served to confuse rather than clarify this doctrine for many Christians. Before looking at the gifts themselves, it is first necessary to define just what a gift is. There is no shortage of opinion concerning the nature of spiritual gifts. Perhaps confusing gifts and fruit, Catholic theologian Lien suggests,

> The Gifts of the Holy Ghost are God's Divine inventions to remedy the native incapacity of the virtues to elevate man to the perfection to which he is called. The Gifts are necessary to man if he is to walk worthily of his vocation . . . Their function is to enable man to do righteously in a superhuman way to bring his actions into line with God's Own standard of conduct. The Gifts enable man to live his human life as God would live a human life.[92]

More accurately, Walvoord states, "Spiritual gifts are divinely given capacities to perform useful functions for God, especially in the area of spiritual service."[93]

The recent growth of Pentecostal denominations and widespread influence of the neo Pentecostal (charismatic) movement has popularized a view of some gifts that differ from the position of traditional conservative Christianity. The following are given to attempt to explain the biblical view of gifts.

Spiritual gifts are discussed primarily in three passages of Scripture, Romans 12:3-8; 1 Corinthians 12-14; Ephesians 4:7-11. These Scriptures suggest gifts deal with a spiritual ability or capacity to serve God. Spiritual gifts are given to men (1 Cor. 12:11) and these men are in turn given to the church (Eph. 4:11).

Lewis Sperry Chafer has given a broad understanding that gifts which are wrought by the Spirit are an expression of the Spirit's own ability rather than mere human ability.

1. *Sign Gifts*

As the gifts identified in the above passages are listed, it becomes apparent that there are two kinds of gifts, sign gifts and serving gifts.

The miraculous sign gifts were present in the first century to confirm apostolic revelation, but are no longer to be expected today. This concept is illustrated by the scaffolding principle. When constructing a building, it is necessary to erect a scaffolding to aid construction. When the building is built, the scaffolding is removed. The sign gifts were the spiritual scaffolding that God used as His authority to build the church. As such, sign gifts were temporary, given to serve a purpose. When the authority of the written Word of God was complete, God took the scaffolding down. There are several reasons sign gifts are not consistent with Christian experience today.

First, these gifts were first given as a sign to the Jews. As the church was made up primarily of Jews, signs were necessary to demonstrate that the Temple worship and sacrifice were no longer required. As the church entered an age of ministry primarily geared at Gentiles, signs became less important, "For the Jews require a sign and the Greeks seek after wisdom" (1 Cor. 1:22). Today, the church is founded on Christ, the wisdom of God as presented in the Word of God. Second, during the first century, the apostles were primarily communicating an oral tradition (2 Thess. 2:15). The word tradition is not a negative term here; it means the method by which the Word of God was communicated, i.e., word of mouth. As a result, sign gifts were necessary to give confidence to the church to discern who was speaking the Word of God and what was a message from a false apostle (Rev. 2:2). A third consideration concerning sign gifts is a recognition that the prophets and apostles were the foundation of the church (Eph. 2:20). These men were the channel of revelation in that they first received the Word of God, then wrote the revelation by inspiration. To give credibility to what they were saying and writing, God gave them signs and miracles (1 Cor. 12:11-12). When they passed off the scene, so did their signs. After the church was founded and the Scriptures were written, signs were no longer needed. By the end of the first century, it was physically impossible for living men to be qualified apostles (Acts 1:21-22). As an illustration, Paul taught tongues would cease (1 Cor. 13:8.), with the completion of the canon of Scripture (i.e., "that which is perfect" - 1 Cor. 13:10).

2. Serving Gifts

Today God is still giving His serving gifts to His disciples. These are part of the tools He has provided to help us accomplish the task of world evangelization. Also they are given for our ministry with other Christians that we can help build up the body of Christ.

a. Enabling Gifts. Among the gifts for today are the enabling gifts that all Christians seem to possess. This is more than the gift of salvation (Rom. 5:15-16; 6:23); these are general enabling abilities that are given to each Christian: (1) Faith (Rom. 1:11; 1 Cor. 12:9), (2) Knowledge (1 Cor. 12:8), (3) Wisdom (1 Cor. 12:8), and (4) Discernment (1 Cor. 12:10). These general gifts help the believer use his specific task gifts.

b. Task Gifts. These are special abilities that are given by the Holy Spirit for the believer to serve God. Not every believer has each of these task gifts and not every believer possessing a task gift has the same effectiveness in employing the gift. The following chart will help distinguish between spiritual gifts.

THE GIFTS OF THE SPIRIT	
SIGN GIFTS	SERVING GIFTS

	(Enabling gifts for all believers today)
Apostle, Eph. 4:11	1. Faith, 1 Cor. 12:9
Healing, 1 Cor. 12:9	2. Knowledge, 1 Cor. 12:8
Tongues, 1 Cor. 12:10	3. Wisdom, 1 Cor. 12:8
Miracles, 1 Cor. 12:10	4. Discernment, 1 Cor. 12:10
Interpretation of Tongues, 1 Cor. 12:10	
	(Task gifts for specific believers today)
	1. Prophecy, Rom. 12:6
	2. Teaching, Rom. 12:7
	3. Exhortation, Rom. 12:8
	4. Shepherding, (pastoring) Eph. 4:11
	5. Showing mercy, 1 Cor. 12:8
	6. Ministering, Rom. 12:7; 1 Cor. 12:28
	7. Giving, Rom. 12:8
	8. Governments, 1 Cor. 12:28; Rom. 12:8
	9. Evangelism (church planting), Eph. 4:11
	10. Government, 1 Cor. 1.2:28
	11. Evangelist (church planting), Eph. 4:11
	12. Hospitality, 1 Pet. 4:9
	13. Prophecy, Rom. 12:6

3. Definitions Of The Spiritual Gifts

Five terms are used interchangeably or explicitly in Scripture to identify spiritual gifts. These five terms occur in the introduction to the discussion of spiritual gifts in First Corinthians 12. An understanding of these terms will give insight into spiritual gifts and will lead to a workable definition; first, *pneumatikon* (plural) spirituals, (1 Cor. 12:1); second, *charismata* (plural) gifts (1 Cor. 12:4); third, *diakonia* ministry (1 Cor. 12:5); fourth, *energema* working (1 Cor. 12:6); and fifth, *phanerosis* manifest (1 Cor. 12:7).

a. Pneumatikon (spirituals). Paul advises the Christians in Corinth, "Now concerning spiritual gifts, brethren, I would not have you ignorant" (1 Cor. 12:1). The word "gifts" is not in the original text, but is supplied in the English translation, perhaps because the term appears in verse 4. Also the word "*pneumatika*" is found in 1 Cor. 14:1 and again the word "gifts" is added to spiritual, inferred from the context. Without the word "gift," the term simply means, "the spirituals."

Pneumatikon is an adjective, which gives meaning to the thing or person that possesses it. Hence, when the word "*pneumatikon*" is used, the author is emphasizing the spiritual nature of the gift. Therefore, the Holy Spirit who is the source of a

Christian's spirituality, who also dispenses the gift; make the gift spiritual. Walvoord argues,

> "the word *pneumatikon*, which with the article indicates the *things of the spirit*, i.e. spiritual gifts. The word directs attention to the *source*, the Holy Spirit, and the *realm* of these gifts.[94]

b. Charismata (gifts) is found in 1 Cor. 12:1 and is translated "spiritual gifts." The root of the word comes from *charis*, which is "grace." Of course, grace is given freely in salvation (Eph. 2:8-9), but when *charis* is used with spiritual gifts it implies a "gift" (freely and graciously given).[95] Hence, a spiritual gift is that which is not sought or earned by human initiative, but is bestowed by the Spirit.

c. Diakonia (ministry) is translated "ministries" or "administration," but is a reference to the spiritual gifts. "And there are differences of administrations, but the same Lord" (1 Cor. 12:5). Hence, a gift is a ministry that is given by the Lord. When the word "*diakonia*" is used in the context of spiritual gifts, it implies that spiritual gifts are in fact spiritual ministries. Therefore, gifts are for a purpose, i.e., to be used for ministry. The verb form *diakoneo* means to be a servant, to serve or wait upon another person, particularly to wait on tables by serving food to guests.[96] Hence, those who are given a spiritual gift should receive it with the purpose of serving other people. This implies a spiritual gift is not received to minister primarily to oneself, nor is a spiritual gift given to serve itself. A spiritual gift is given to serve others.

d. Energema (working) is translated "operations" in 1 Cor. 12:6. As such Paul teaches, "And there are diversities of operations, but it is the same God which worketh all in all" (1 Cor. 12:6). "Paul uses the word "*energema*" to denote spiritual gifts as the activity produced by God's enduements of men for service."[97] The word from *energeo*, where we get energy, implies the power or energy of God to activate or set something in motion. Hence, a spiritual gift is not the natural ability of the individual, but is a ministry empowered by God.

e. Phanerosis (manifest) is translated in 1 Cor. 12:7, to describe a spiritual gift, "But the manifestation of the Spirit is given to every man to profit withal." Hence, a spiritual gift is a manifestation of the Holy Spirit. The word "*phanerosis*" comes from the verb *phaneroo* which means "to make visible or make clear."[98] A spiritual gift is identified as residing in the believer. When a Christian exercises a spiritual gift, it should be an evident work of the Holy Spirit.

Therefore, a spiritual gift is spiritual in character (*pneumatikon*) , sovereignly given by God the Holy Spirit (*charismata*), to minister to others (*diakonia*), in the power of God (*energema*), with an evident manifestation of the Holy Spirit through the Christian as he serves God (*phanerosis*).

With this biblical description in mind, several definitions of spiritual gifts must be analyzed. First, a definition suggested by John R. W. Stott: "Spiritual gifts are certain capacities bestowed by God's grace and power, which fit people for specific and corresponding service."[99] Stott's definitive term is "capacity," which means a spiritual gift is a capacity. Howard A. Snyder amplifies the definition of a spiritual gift by adding the idea of ministry.

> Spiritual gifts are given not merely for personal enjoyment nor even primarily for an individual's own spiritual growth, although this, too, is important. Gifts are given for the common good, "that the church may be edified" (1 Cor. 14:5).[100]

The well-known book on spiritual gifts by Leslie B. Flynn devoted an entire chapter to define "What is a Gift?" He limits spiritual gifts to exercise in the church or the body of Christ. He also adds the designation that all believers have a gift.

> A gift has been described as a special qualification granted by the Spirit to every believer to empower him to serve within the framework of the body of Christ.[101]

Flynn provides a shorter working definition, "*A gift is a Spirit-given ability for Christian service.*"[102]

The Scofield Bible adds another dimension to the definition of gifts when they are identified first as an ability, and second as a person.

> . . . certain Spirit-endued men, viz. apostles, prophets, evangelists, pastors and teachers, are themselves the gifts whom the glorified Christ bestows upon His body the church. In Corinthians the gifts are spiritual enablements for specific service; in Ephesians the gifts are men who have such enablements.[103]

Out of an examination of biblical words for spiritual gifts and the contemporary definitions derived from these words, the following chart can be constructed to describe (not define) spiritual gifts.

1. Source: From the Holy Spirit
2. Bestowed: To all believers
3. Purpose: For Christian service

4. Nature: Spiritual ability
5. Discovery: Proper relationship to the Holy Spirit
6. Responsibility: To be exercised by believers
7. Number: Plural
8. Identification: Gifts are persons.

Spiritual gifts are the various abilities given sovereignly to believers by the Holy Spirit so that when they faithfully serve the Lord, there are spiritual results in the work of God and the believer grows in his effectiveness and/or develops other spiritual abilities of service.

4. Discovering And Developing Spiritual Gifts

a. *How many gifts may a person have?* We should not think of spiritual gifts in a singular capacity. One gift will be exercised in concert with other spiritual gifts. First, the church should be a body where many gifts are operative, hence, the term is plural (1 Cor. 12:4), and there are several lists of multiple gifts (Rom. 12:3-8; 1 Cor. 12:8-12, 28-29; and Eph. 4:11). Gene Getz suggests there is a plurality of gifts in the church. "God's plan is a multi-gifted body, a body made up of people who could contribute in a special way to the building up of the church."[104] Flynn notes, "Paul's opening remarks in the section on the gifts (1 Cor. 11:1-4) negates their singularity and emphasizes their plurality."[105] Flynn implies one person can have two or more gifts.

When Jesus related the parable of the talents, the first servant was given five talents, the next three and the final servant was given one. A talent in the parable is interpreted as a gift or ability, for in the parable Jesus explains, "to every man according to his several ability" (Matt. 25:15). Some of the servants represent multi-gifted individuals.

The word *talents* here is used to denote indefinitely *a large sum*, and is designed to refer to the endowments conferred on men. We have retained in our language the word talent as referring to the abilities or gifts of men. . . . He makes *distinctions* among men in regard to abilities, and in the powers and opportunities of usefulness, requiring them only to occupy those stations, and to discharge their duties there.[106]

But in the discussion of the multi-gifted person, what about the person who seems to be less gifted, as some may appear; or without a gift?[107] Even though the word for spiritual gifts appears in the plural (1 Cor. 12:4, 31), some people may have only one gift. The apostle Peter implies a person may have only a (singular) gift, "As every man hath received the gift, even so minister the same one to another" (1 Pet. 4:10). Therefore, it may be possible for some to have only one gift, while others are multi-gifted.

b. *What is the relationship of a spiritual gift and natural ability?* A spiritual gift is not the augmented natural ability of a Christian, nor is it innate talent. From the use of *phanerosis*, a spiritual gift is the evident and manifest work of the Holy Spirit through the Christian. Leslie B. Flynn explains,

> Talents instruct, inspire, or entertain on a natural level. Gifts relate to the building up of the saints (or to evangelization). Something supernatural happens in the one who is ministering when a gift is exercised. Nothing supernatural happens in one who is performing when a talent is displayed.[108]

c. *When does a person receive a spiritual gift?* Most contemporary authors are not sure when the Christian receives his spiritual gifts. Since every Christian has the Holy Spirit (Rom. 8:9) and he received the Holy Spirit at salvation, then it can be implied spiritual gifts came with the Holy Spirit. Also, since every Christian has a spiritual gift (1 Cor. 7:7; 1 Pet. 4:10), and the work of the Spirit regenerates a person at conversion (John 3:5; 1 Pet. 1:23), then spiritual gifts were probably given then. Spiritual gifts are probably bestowed at salvation. But Paul seems to imply that gifts were given earlier, "When he ascended up on high, he led captivity captive, and gave gifts unto men. (Now that he ascended, what is it but that he descended first into the lower parts of the earth? . . . that he might fill all things). And he gave [gifts to men]" (Eph. 4:8-11). Here Paul implies that gifts were given with the resurrection of Christ. Perhaps the answer is that God applies the benefits of resurrection to believers at conversion (Rom. 4:25; 6:4-5).

Some suggest that God gives His gifts without partiality and that every person has the potential of developing every spiritual gift. This is because every believer has the Holy Spirit and He is the spiritual ability. If this is so, then a believer has the responsibility to develop the gifts, and he can have as many gifts as he has taken the initiative to develop.

But, experience reveals that the spiritual gifts are usually manifested at

GIVING OF SPIRITUAL GIFTS	
1. Historically at the Ascension	Eph. 4:8-11
2. Embryonically at Conversion	Rom. 8:9; 1 Cor. 7:7
3. Actually Come to light later in experience	Rom 1:11 1 Cor. 12:31

a time later in life than conversion. The answer, though only suggested in Scripture, seems to indicate that God gave spiritual gifts at conversion, but they lie dormant (or latent as a seed in the soil) only to come to light at a later time. Paul was converted (Acts 9), but there was a gap in time until the church at Antioch sent him as a missionary church planter, "for the work whereunto I have called" (Acts 13:2).

Since human responsibility is connected with the development of gifts, perhaps some are called, but they do not immediately develop their spiritual gifts. When later they respond to God, then their spiritual gifts are manifested.

d. *Can a spiritual gift in one believer be greater than in some others?* There seems to be uneven manifestation of spiritual gifts. The spiritual gift of some appears to be stronger than in others. A spiritual gift is ministry, *diakonia* (1 Cor. 12:5), and faithfulness in ministry determines greater effectiveness (Matt. 25:23; Luke 19:17). Therefore, the person who ministers his gift with the greatest faithfulness should be more effective and will have greater results.

Paul exhorts, "Covet earnestly the best gifts" (1 Cor. 12:31), implying that *zeloute* (desire) results in a Christian receiving the best gifts *charismata*. At this place the word "gifts" is plural, suggesting a Christian can get more gifts. This implies that faithfulness in seeking and exercising a gift will lead to a greater number of gifts or a greater manifestation of one's gift. Whatever the interpretation of this "best gifts," (its identification is not germane to the argument) it is achieved by human responsibility. When properly exercised toward the proper goals, the Christian will grow in his number (quantity) of gifts and in the effectiveness (quality) of his gifts.

Many interpret 1 Corinthians 12:31 differently. Some believe Paul is speaking to the Corinthian *corpur* (the church), not to individual believers. To prove this, they refer to the context, "Now ye are the body of Christ" (1 Cor. 12:27) making this a reference to the church. Therefore, the interpretation is for the church to "covet earnestly" the higher gifts. In other words, the church should seek leadership gifts that will minister to the corporate life of the body. Even if this interpretation is accepted, it implies the growth of spiritual gifts, which is the original argument.

Jesus told the parable of the man with five talents, another with two talents, and the final man with only one talent (Matt. 25:14-30). The man with five was faithful. "He that had received five talents," implying gifts are sovereignly given by God. Yet, the same servant says, "I have gained beside them five talents more." Here human responsibility is evident and he was rewarded for his achievement. The man with two talents was faithful and received two other talents. The final servant had his talent taken away and given to the man with ten talents, thus making a total of eleven talents. The parable of the talents implies that the Christian who faithfully exercises his spiritual gift of faith will grow in his ability to accomplish bigger and greater things for God. This parable also implies that a person can lose the effectiveness of his spiritual gift through disuse or unfaithfulness. Some appear to even lose their spiritual gift altogether.

e. *Can one seek spiritual gifts?* The question of discovery and growth of spiritual gifts has no easy answer. First, the gifts are sovereignly given by the Holy Spirit (1 Cor. 12:11), yet Paul claims that he had part in communicating spiritual gifts to the Christians in Rome: "For I long to see you, that I may impart unto you some spiritual gift" (Rom. 1:11). Also, Paul challenged Timothy that he "Neglect not the gift that is in thee, which was given thee by prophecy, with the laying on of the hands" (1 Tim. 4:14). Paul notes, *edothe soi dia diapropheteias* (was given to thee by means of prophecy). The *dia* means "by means of," which is interpreted that prophecy was the instrument that communicated *charismatos*. Literally, the verse could be translated, "The in thee spiritual gift," implying Timothy's gift was embryonic, he had it before someone developed it by preaching. Also Paul notes, *"anazopurein to charisma tou theou,"* "stir up the gift of God" (2 Tim. 1:6). The word "stir up" literally means "fan the flame." The spiritual gift, like a flame, can burn more brightly, hence a gift can grow in effectiveness. The answer lies in the Holy Spirit's developing a spiritual gift in one person by using another faithful person as he ministers his gift. Timothy got his gift as he sat under the influence of the preaching of Paul. This has been called the "hot poker," meaning a young minister got his vision or compassion to win souls as he was associated with a man of God with these gifts.[109] As heat is transferred from the coals to the hot poker, so the young man becomes like those who influence him because they have the power of suggestibility to his ministry. Ryrie reinforces this view.

Although gifts are supernaturally bestowed, Paul indicates that they may be developed by the person to whom they are given. After listing some of the gifts in their order of importance, he says that believers should covet the best gifts (I Cor. 12:31). This means that an individual may be ambitious to exercise certain gifts, which ambition can only be fulfilled by study and work. Paul himself, even though he was reared on the Old Testament, needed three years in Arabia to develop his gift of teaching.

In Romans 1:11 Paul indicates that he hoped to have a part in the developing of the gifts in the churches in Rome (cf. I Tim. 4:14; II Tim. 1:6). Quite clearly others may have a part in bringing gifts to maturity and full use (cf. Eph. 4:7-12). Thus, gifts may be developed as one is ambitious in relation to self and attentive to others.[110]

f. *Does a person have a prominent gift?* Even though Christian leaders have the potential of being multi-gifted, the Bible seems to teach that every man has a prominent gift, i.e., a spiritual gift that identifies his ministry, and by which the person receives identification or self-awareness. Such was Agabus who was identified as a prophet (Acts 11:27-28; 21:20) or Philip who was called an evangelist (Acts 21:8). Paul seems to be referring to their prominent or unique gift by his own use of "proper," "Every man hath his proper gift of God" (1 Cor. 7:7).

> Every man has his own peculiar talent, or excellence. One man excels in one thing, and another in another. One may not have this particular virtue, but he may be distinguished for another virtue quite as valuable.[111]

g. *What is the relationship between a church office and a spiritual gift?* A spiritual gift is not the same as an office in the church. Most protestant churches recognize two offices: pastors and deacons (Phil. 1:1), but other groups recognize such church offices as prophets, teachers, and bishops. A spiritual gift is a supernatural endowment or ability given by the Holy Spirit, yet a man can desire more gifts (1 Cor. 12:31). Also a man can desire an office in the church, "If a man desire the office of a bishop" (1 Tim. 3:1). Men who seek the office should have certain qualifications (spiritual gifts) presumably so the congregation can recognize those who should be placed in the office.

There is a relationship between gift and office or between ability and position. The person who has the office of bishop/elder, (1 Tim. 3:1-10) should have the gift of pastor (Eph. 4:11). The one who holds the office of deacon (1 Tim. 3:11-14), should also possess the gift of serving or ministering (*diakonia*, we get the title deacon from the word for serving). In the same manner, those who believe in the office of the prophet (1 Cor. 12:10) and those who advocate the office of evangelist (Eph. 4:11) should require that the person who fills them have the gift of prophecy and evangelism. Flynn has summarized this view.

> Naturally, a person with an office should have the gift corresponding to that office; otherwise his office would be in name only.
> Summing up, a believer would not hold a divinely-appointed office without possessing the corresponding gift.[112]

However, the opposite may be true, that is a person may have the gift without the office related to it. Flynn also holds this view: "Many Christians possess a gift without appointment to that office."[113] This might be a person who has the gift of serving *diakinos*, without serving in the office of deacon. Also, a person may have the gift of, shepherding without being a pastor. The author teaches that a Sunday School teacher is the extension of the pastor's responsibilities into the Sunday school class, and that "Everything a pastor is to his congregation, the Sunday School teacher should be to his class."[114] Therefore, those who shepherd a Sunday school class are exercising a similar gift as those who shepherd a congregation.

h. *What is the relationship between ministries and spiritual gifts?* Flynn suggests that "gifts are not ministries."[115] He identified a ministry as "an outlet for employment of a gift."[116] A gift may be exercised to an age group such as adults or youth; it may be through media such as radio, television or Bible college; or it may be at home or on the foreign mission field. Flynn also identifies ministries as music, writing, or linguistics through which particular gifts may be used.[117] Ryrie explains that spiritual gifts are not ministries.

> Neither does Paul suggest that there are special gifts for specific age groups. There is no gift of young people's work, for all ages need teachers, pastors, helpers, etc. (cf. Titus 2:1-8). The gift is the ability, according to Paul's thinking, and, not the place or age group in which that ability is used.[118]

i. *What is the relationship between the fruit of the Spirit and spiritual gifts?* The word "faith" is listed both as a spiritual gift (Rom. 12:3, 6; 1 Cor. 12:9), and fruit of the Spirit (Gal. 5:22), but that does not mean they are the same.[119] A spiritual gift is an ability to be used in service, whereas spiritual fruit relates to a Christian's character. It is possible to have spiritual gifts to serve God, but be lacking in spiritual character. (The Corinthian church had numerous gifts, but was guilty of envy, divisions, and fleshly sins.) Also, it is possible to have spirituality, yet not have many or all spiritual gifts. "Are all apostles? Are all prophets? Are all teachers? Are all workers of miracles?" (1 Cor. 12:29). It is possible to have the gift of faith to move mountains, yet lack love (1 Cor. 13:2). Flynn describes this person, "Possession of gifts does not indicate godliness of life.[120]

This probably does not mean the person is ungodly, nor is he void of love; it means the gift of faith that moves mountains is not tied to the fruit of love. Three possible conclusions may be drawn. First, the person has not grown in love as he has grown in exercising his gift of faith. Second, the exercise of the two has different objects; faith is toward God, while love is toward others. Third, love is a manifestation of the Holy Spirit (1 Cor. 12:7).

Spiritual gifts and the fruit of the Spirit are not the same, even though they both probably came with the baptism of the Spirit (1 Cor. 12:13) and have their source from the Holy Spirit. But, obviously there is a congruence of gifts and fruit, even if there is no cause-and-effect relationship. Those who have a godly life (spiritual fruit) will be closer to God so they may trust Him more fully for answers to prayer. Those who are godly will probably have a greater desire to exercise their spiritual gift; also, they will have a clearer vision of what God wants to perform in a certain situation.

(Since sin will blind or dull the vision of the saint, those who are godly will see a greater potential that can be accomplished for God.) Then because of the spiritual fruit in their life, they can better exercise the spiritual gift of faith in conjunction with other spiritual gifts.

To summarize, spiritual fruit, (1) is given to all believers, (2) produces spiritual character, (3) is singular (fruit is singular, meaning one's character is a unit), (4) is permanent (1 Cor. 13:8-10), and (5) grows internally. To summarize spiritual gifts, note the contrast to the previous five points. They (1) are given to specific believers, (2) produce spiritual service, (3) are plural (Flynn lists 19, Wagner 27), (4) will cease, and (5) operate externally.

X. SINS AGAINST THE HOLY SPIRIT

While all sin is serious and to some degree represents a challenge of and an attack on the authority and character of God, six sins are described in Scripture with particular reference to the Holy Spirit. As the Spirit is a person, He may be sinned against. As He is also God, it is an extremely serious matter to be found guilty of sinning against the Holy Spirit. In the case of one such sin, Jesus identified it to be "unpardonable." The key to not sinning against the Holy Spirit is to: (1) be led by the Spirit, (2) be filled by the Spirit, and (3) to be illuminated by the Spirit. The following chart identifies the six sins against the Holy Spirit.

SINS AGAINST THE HOLY SPIRIT	
Blasphemy	Matt. 12:31-32; Luke 12:10
Lying to/Tempting	Acts 5:4, 9
Despising	Heb. 10:29
Resisting/Striving with	Gen. 6:3; Acts 7:51
Vexing/Grieving	Isa. 63:10; Eph. 4:30
Quenching	1 Thess. 5:19

Probably because of the severity with which Jesus commented on the first of these sins, it has drawn the attention of a great many students of the Bible. One of the chief difficulties with interpreting references to the unpardonable sin is the identification of the nature of "blasphemy against the Holy Spirit." At least four possible explanations have been proposed.

Some Armenian theologians consider blasphemy to be a sin so severe as to result in the loss of salvation. In this line of thinking, Barrett concludes, "Blasphemy against the Holy Spirit seems, then, to be sin committed within the Church, which, because it denies the root and spring of the Church's life, cannot rediscover the forgiveness by which the sinner first entered the community of the forgiven."[121] The chief problem with this view is the lack of biblical support. Also, this view is contrary to the biblical teaching regarding the security of the believer.

A second view of this sin sees it as a rejection of the convicting work of the Holy Spirit. In fairness to those who hold this view, it should be emphasized that this does not simply refer to the case of someone not responding to the gospel the first time he hears it. Rather, the rejection which constitutes blasphemy can only occur after a person has fully understood the gospel and been moved by the Spirit to accept it. As such, only a few commit the unpardonable sin; those who reject the gospel after it is continually presented to them. Commenting on this view, Calvin explained,

> The reason why blasphemy against the Spirit exceeds other sins is not that the Spirit is higher than Christ, but that those who rebel, after that the power of God has revealed, cannot be excused on the plea of ignorance. Besides, it must be observed that what is here said about blasphemy does not refer merely to the essence of the Spirit, but to the grace which he has bestowed upon us.[122]

Similarly, Procksch argues,

> In the υἱος τοῦ ἀνθρώπου God is present but concealed, so that the sin against the Son of man, since it is committed in a state of ignorance, can be forgiven. On the other hand, God reveals himself through Christ in the πνεύμα ἅγιου of the time after Pentecost, and whoever is convicted by the Holy Spirit, yet nevertheless revolts against his power, and blasphemes (βλασφημεί) him, commits an unforgivable sin. The possibility of this sin therefore first arose in the age after Pentecost, after the Holy Spirit has passed from Jesus to the disciples, and had become their possession.[123]

Strong seems to agree with this interpretation of the unpardonable sin.

> The sin against the Holy Spirit is not to be regarded simply as an isolated act, but also as the external symptom of a heart so radically and finally set against God that no power which God can consistently use will ever save it. The sin, therefore, can be only the culmination of a long course of self-hardening and self-depraving. He who has committed it must be either profoundly indifferent to his own condition, or actively and bitterly hostile to God; so that anxiety or fear on account of one's condition is evidence that it has not been committed. The sin against the Holy Spirit cannot be forgiven, simply

because the soul that has committed it has ceased to be receptive to divine influences, even when those influences are exerted in the utmost strength which God has seen fit to employ in his spiritual administration.[124]

Thirdly, some interpret the unpardonable sin as a national sin of Israel which by definition cannot be committed by people today. This is the common view held by most dispensationalists. Scofield states,

The unpardonable sin, referred to Matthew 12:24-32, and again in 1 John 5:16 as the "sin unto death," is ascribing to Satanic power, rather than to the Holy Spirit, the works of Christ.[125]

Clark further explains,

Therefore it is our conviction that the sin of blasphemy against the Holy Spirit has no relationship to individuals in this age, but was strictly a national sin which Israel committed under the influence of the religions leaders of that day.[126]

Fitzwater likewise endorses this interpretation noting,

The sin here is that of attributing to the devil the works of the Holy Spirit. The implication clearly is that those who accused Jesus of performing His mighty works in the power of Satan knew definitely who Jesus was, but because of their unwillingness to acknowledge Him, rejected Him and declared that His mighty works were done because He was in league with Satan.[127]

A fourth and final interpretation of the unpardonable sin is that it refers to the final rejection of Christ through unbelief. According to this view, the sin is unpardonable simply because pardon is never received by the sinner. This differs from the second view above in that it is not the single act of rejection so much as the attitude of continual rejection which constitutes the unpardonable sin. In essence, everyone who has died outside of Christ has committed the unpardonable sin.

Pache, emphasizing that this sin can only be committed in one's final rejection of Christ, writes,

Who can commit the sin against the Holy Spirit? By definition those who to the bitter end refuse to repent and accept the Saviour. But can it be that one of God's children, truly born again might commit such a sin? We believe that he cannot since he has already allowed himself to be convicted by the Holy Spirit who has entered into him.[128]

Further emphasizing that the responsibility for making this unpardonable rests with the sinner and not God, Sanders explains,

> Why is there no forgiveness for this sin? Because there is not sufficient virtue in the blood of Christ? Because God is capricious? Surely not! There must always be two parties to forgiveness—the forgiver and the one who is to be forgiven. "If the one who has sinned obstinately refuses to be forgiven, what more can God do? For His Spirit to continue to strive would only increase the sinner's responsibility to no purpose. The sin is unforgivable, because it rejects forgiveness, and for such sin there be no provision in the nature of the case. Let all who as yet have not yielded to the wooings of the Spirit, cease to gamble upon the grace God, and yield at once, lest they cross the fatal line.[129]

Before concluding this discussion on sins against the Holy Spirit, two questions should be briefly addressed. The first is, "Is it possible that I may have committed the unpardonable sin?" The second is very similar. "Is it possible that someone I know has committed this sin?" While these questions have been a source of great concern, there is really no reason for concern. Though theologians disagree on the nature of the unpardonable sin, they appear to be agreed that it is accompanied by a growing loss of conviction and/or concern for one's soul. The very fact that one is concerned about the matter is evidence of the Spirit's work of conviction. This does not minimize the seriousness of the sin, but rather emphasizes the fact that one can and should seek forgiveness for it.

In response to the second question, the safest answer is "probably not." Those holding to the third view identified above would respond "definitely not." The Bible gives us no justification for determining the "saveability" of any person. Whenever men attempt to do so, they are limiting God and are often surprised. When a group of women felt burdened to pray for the salvation of a particular young lawyer in their town, their pastor advised them against this course of action declaring, "I do not believe Finney will ever be converted." When Finney later came under conviction and was converted, news of his conversion spread rapidly through the town. When Finney preached his first sermon in the church of that pastor who thought Finney could not be saved, it was the beginning of Finney's ministry as one of New England's greatest revivalists.

There is a tendency among some Christians to simply assume the rest of the sins against the Holy Spirit are simply metaphors describing sin in general. As all sin is against the character of God, then in that sense, all sin is against the Holy Spirit. But the remaining five sins against the Holy Spirit are more than simply a variety of ways to speak generally about sin. In his classic work on the doctrine of the Holy Spirit, John Walvoord illustrates the distinction between quenching and grieving the Holy Spirit. In defining the quenching of the Holy Spirit, he writes,

> It is patently impossible to extinguish the Holy Spirit in the absolute sense, or to put Him out. His abiding presence is assured for all Christians. His person is indestructible. It is, therefore, quenching in the sense of resisting or opposing His will. Quenching the Spirit may be simply defined as being unyielded to Him, or saying, "No." The issue is, therefore, the question of willingness to do His will.[130]

The sin of grieving the Spirit is a much more serious sin. It is more than simply unyieldedness, but rather includes a continuous state of unyieldedness. According to Walvoord,

> Grieving the Holy Spirit involves several factors. It is a spiritual condition characterizing unyielded Christians. The first step may well be the quenching of the Spirit, i.e., refusing to follow His leading and resisting His will. It is not an issue of salvation, as this is settled once for all when regeneration took place. The persistent resistance of the leading of the Spirit results in further departure from the will of God. The Spirit can no longer direct and bless in fullness as His ministry has been denied. It is this condition which is designated in Scripture as grieving the Spirit.[131]

THE MINISTRY OF THE HOLY SPIRIT					
Work	Scripture	Significance	How to Receive	Necessity	Feature
Regeneration	John 3:3-8 2 Cor. 5:17 Titus 3:5	rebirth; sons of God	believing and receiving Christ	for eternal life	passes from death to life

Indwelling	John 14:10-17 John 7:37-39 1 Cor. 6:19,20 1 John 4:12-15	Christ abides with us forever	believing and receiving Christ	for Spirit to work in the believer's character	secures the believer as being a son of God
Filling	Gal. 5:16 Eph. 5:18	power for service and Christian character	seeking, yielding, and confession	for victorious Christian service	life of dedication, prayer, Bible study, confession
Sealing	2 Cor. 1:22 Eph. 1:13 Eph. 4:30	the Holy Spirit guarantees the "contents" of the one He seals	automatic at salvation	for eternal security	assurance of everlasting life
Illumination	John 16:13 1 Cor. 2:12 1 John 2:27	to know the things of God in Scripture	as the Holy Spirit removes the blindness of a believer	for understanding the Bible	guide us into all truth
Reproves	John 16:7-11	convicts the world of sin	Holy Spirit works upon Scripture to reveal sin, righteousness, and judgment	draws men to Christ	convicts sin, convinces of righteous-ness, judgment
Restraint	1 Thess. 2:3-10	works against sin in the world	God's mercy to people in this age	restrains the world from utter corr-uption	when restraint is removed so are the believers

ENDNOTES

1.   Michael Green, *I Believe In the Holy Spirit* (London: Hodder and
      Stoughton, 1980), 11.*
2.   A. W. Tozer, *The Divine Conquest* (Old Tappan, New Jersey: Fleming
      H. Revell Company, 1950), 66.
3.   George S. Hendry, *The Holy Spirit In Christian Theology* (Philadelphia:
      The Westminster Press, 1956), 9.*
4.   C. K. Barrett, *The Holy Spirit and the Gospel Tradition* (London: The
      Society for Promoting Christian Knowledge, 1947), 1.
5.   Vincent Taylor, *The Doctrine of the Holy Spirit*, np. nd, 41.*
6.   Archibald Alexander Hodge, *Outlines of Theology* (London: Thomas
      Nelson and Sons, 1883), 174.
7.   Hendry, *The Holy Spirit in Christian Theology*, 13, 33.*
8.   R. A. Torrey, *What the Bible Teaches* (New York: Fleming H. Revell,
      1933), 225.*
9.   P. B. Fitzwater, *Christian Theology: A Systematic Presentation* (Grand
      Rapids: Eerdmans, 1948), 185.
10.   Henry Clarence Thiessen, *Introductory Lectures in Systematic Theology*
      (Grand Rapids: Eerdmans, 1951), 144.
11.   Augustus Hopkins Strong, *Systematic Theology: A Compendium
      Designed for the Use of Theological Students* (Old Tappan, New Jersey:
      Fleming H. Revell Company, 1970), 325.
12.   Thiessen, *Systematic Theology*, 144.
13.   Hodge, *Outlines of Theology*, 173-74.
14.   Fitzwater, *Christian Theology*, 189.
15.   Strong, *Systematic Theology*, 315.
16.   Thiessen, *Systematic Theology*, 145.
17.   E. Stanley Jones, *The Way* (Nashville: Abingdon Press, 1946), 274.*
18.   William Fitch, *The Ministry of the Holy Spirit* (Grand Rapids:
      Zondervan, 1974), 176.*
19.   Strong, *Systematic Theology*, 316.
20.   G. Walters, "Holy Spirit," *The New Bible Dictionary Revised*, ed. J. D.
      Douglas, et. al. (Grand Rapids: Eerdmans, 1977), 531.
21.   Strong, *Systematic Theology*, 316.
22.   Hodge, *Outlines of Theology*, 176.

23.   David Brown, *The Four Gospels: A Commentary, Critical, Experimental and Practical* (London: Banner of Truth Trust, 1969), 397.

24.   Strong, *Systematic Theology*, 317.

25.   John MacBeth, *Notes on The Thirty-Nine Articles, Historical and Explanatory* (Dublin: Wm. McGee, 1894), 27.

26.   Hodge, *Outlines of Theology*, 189-90.

27.   MacBeth, *Notes on the Articles*, 28.

28.   Frederick Louis Godet, *Commentary on the Gospel of John with an Historical and Critical Introduction*, trans. Timothy Dwight (New York: Funk and Wagnalls Company, 1886), 2:305.

29.   Brown, *The Four Gospels*, 443.

30.   Hodge, *Outlines of Theology*, 190.

31.   These definitions are those of F. E. Marsh, *Emblems of the Holy Spirit* (London: Pickering & Inglis, 1923), vii-viii.

32.   Ella E. Pohle, comp., *Dr. C. I. Scofield's Question Box* (Chicago: Moody Press, n.d.), 157.*

33.   *The New Scofield Reference Bible* (NY: Oxford University Press, 1967), 1163.

34.   Marsh, *Emblems of the Holy Spirit*, viii-ix.

35.   A. B. Simpson, *The Holy Spirit or Power from on High: An Unfolding of the Doctrine of the Holy Spirit in the Old and New Testament* (Harrisburg, Pennsylvania: Christian Publications Inc., n.d.), 1:15.*

36.   Henry Barclay Swete, *The Holy Spirit in the New Testament: A Study of Primitive Christian Teaching* (London: MacMillan and Co., Limited, 1910), 366.

37.   The following verses compose the complete specific reference to the creative role of the Holy Spirit: Gen. 1:2; Job 26:13; 33:4; Psa. 33:6; 104:30; Isa. 40:12-13.

38.   Abraham Kuyper, *The Work of the Holy Spirit*, trans, Henri DeVries (New York: Funk & Wagnalls Company, 1900), 28.

39.   Walters, "Holy Spirit," 531.

40.   Edwin H. Palmer, *The Holy Spirit* (Grand Rapids: Baker Book House, 1958), 27.*

41.   Kuyper, *The Work of the Holy Spirit*, 26.

42.   Hendrikus Berkhof, "The Doctrine of the Holy Spirit," *The Annie Kinkead Warfield Lectures*, 1963-1964 (Richmond, Virginia: John Knox Press, 1964), 95.

43.   Kuyper, *The Work of the Holy Spirit*, 30.
44.   Green, *I Believe in the Holy Spirit.**
45.   Kuyper, *The Work of the Holy Spirit*, 33.
46.   Samuel Ridout, *The Person and Work of the Holy Spirit* (New York: Loizeaux Brothers, Bible Truth Depot, 1945), 30.
47.   E. Y. Mullins, "Holy Spirit" *The International Standard Bible Encyclopedia*, ed. James Orr (Grand Rapids: Eerdmans, 1939), 1408.
48.   Berkhof, *The Doctrine of the Holy Spirit*, 99.
49.   *The New Scofield Reference Bible* (1967), 975.
50.   Ibid., 1295.
51.   René Pache, *The Person and Work of the Holy Spirit*, trans. J. D. Emerson (Chicago: Moody Press, 1954), 216.
52.   Lewis Sperry Chafer, *Major Bible Themes* (Chicago: Moody Press, 1926), 100-101.
53.   Pache, *The Person and Work of the Holy Spirit*, 217.
54.   Ridout, *The Person and Work of the Holy Spirit*, 27.
55.   Mullins, "Holy Spirit," 1412.
56.   Ibid., 1410.
57.   Strong, *Systematic Theology*, 703.
58.   Fitch, *The Ministry of the Holy Spirit*, 22.*
59.   Palmer, *The Holy Spirit*, 65.*
60.   Mullins, "Holy Spirit," 1410.
61.   Palmer, *The Holy Spirit*, 65.*
62.   Mullins, "Holy Spirit," 1412.
63.   James H. McConkey, *The Three-fold Secret of the Holy Spirit* (Chicago: Moody Press, 1897).*
64.   H. Berkhof, *The Doctrine of the Holy Spirit*, 85.*
65.   Oswald J. Smith, *The Enduement of Power* (London: Marshall, Morgan & Scott, 1974), 89.*
66.   Palmer, *The Holy Spirit*, 84.*
67.   F. F. Bruce, *The Epistle to the Ephesians: A Verse-by-Verse Exposition* (Old Tappan, New Jersey: Fleming H. Revell Company, 1974), s.v.*
68.   John Calvin, *Sermons on the Epistle to the Ephesians*, trans. Arthur Golding (Edinburgh: Banner of Truth Trust, 1973), 156.
69.   Ibid., 159.
70.   Pache, *The Person and Work of the Holy Spirit*, 69.
71.   Anthony A. Hoekema, *Holy Spirit Baptism* (Grand Rapids: Eerdmans, 1972), 10.*

72.   *The Statement of Fundamental Truths of the Assemblies of God*, Article 8.*

73.   H. Leisegang, "Pneuma Hagion," *Studies in Early Christianity*, ed. S. J. Case, 76.*

74.   Barrett, *The Holy Spirit and the Gospel Tradition*, 126.

75.   Samuel Rayan, *Breath of Fire: The Holy Spirit: The Heart of the Christian Gospel* (London: Geoffrey Chapman, 1979), 13.*

76.   Edward Leen, *The Holy Ghost and His Work in Souls* (New York: Sheed & Ward, 1937), 136.

77.   The King James Version of Acts 19:2 is unfortunate. "Have ye received the Holy Ghost since ye believed?" should he more literally translated, "Did ye receive the Holy Spirit, having believed?" or "Did ye receive the Holy Spirit when ye believed?"

78.   Marsh, *Emblems of the Holy Spirit*, 28.

79.   Charles Haddon Spurgeon, *Twelve Sermons on the Holy Spirit*, (London: Marshall, Morgan & Scott, Ltd., n.d.), 51.*

80.   Andrew Murray, *Absolute Surrender* (London: Marshall, Morgan & Scott, Ltd., n.d.), 22.*

81.   Cited by William R. Moody, *The Life of Dwight L. Moody*, (Murfreesboro, TN: Sword of the Lord Publishers; reprinted from 1900 edition), 149.

82.   Jay E. Adams, *Competent to Counsel* (Grand Rapids: Baker Book House, 1979), 21.*

83.   Ursinus, *Loci,* cited by Heinrich Heppe, *Reformed Dogmatics: Set Out and Illustrated from the Sources,* trans. G. T. Thomson (London: George Allen and Uwin, 1950), 24.

84.   Tozer, *The Divine Conquest*, 77-78.

85.   Bernard Ramm, *The Witness of the Spirit: An Essay on the Contemporary Relevance of the Internal Witness of the Holy Spirit* (Grand Rapids: Eerdmans, 1959), 12.

86.   Palmer, *The Holy Spirit*, 58.*

87.   Cited by Green, *I Believe in the Holy Spirit*, 50.*

88.   Torrey, *What the Bible Teaches*, 476.

89.   H. A. Ironside, *Praying in the Holy Spirit* (New York: Loizeaux Brothers, 1946), 2.

90.   Fitch, *The Ministry of the Holy Spirit*, 29.*

91.   Emery H. Bancroft, *Elemental Theology: Doctrinal and Conservative* (Grand Rapids: Zondervan, 1960), 169.

92.   Leen, *The Holy Ghost and His Work in Souls*, 319.

93.   John F. Walvoord, *The Holy Spirit at Work Today* (Lincoln, Nebraska: Back to the Bible Broadcast, 1973), 38.*

94.   John F. Walvoord, *The Holy Spirit* (Wheaton: Van Kampen Press, 1954), 164.

95.   Walter Bauer, *A Greek-English Lexicon of the New Testament*, trans. by William F. Arndt and F. Wilbur Gingrich (Chicago: The University of Chicago Press, 1957), s.v., *charisma*.*

96.   Joseph Henry Thayer, *A Greek-English Lexicon of the New Testament*, translated, revised and Enlarged (New York: American Book Co., 1889), s.v., *charisma*; Colin Brown, *The New International Dictionary of New Testament Theology*, 3 vol. (Exeter, U.K.: Paternoster Press, Ltd., 1978), s.v., *diakonia*.*

97.   Ibid., s.v., *energema*.*

98.   Bauer, *A Greek-English Lexicon of the New Testament*, s.v., *phaneroo*.*

99.   John R. W. Scott, *Baptism and Fullness* (Downers Grove: InterVarsity Press, 1964), 87.*

100.   Howard A. Snyder, *The Problem of Wine Skins*: Church Structure in a Technological Age (Downers Grove: InterVarsity Press, 1976), 132.

101.   Leslie B. Flynn, *19 Gifts of the Spirit* (Wheaton: Victor Books, 1974), 20.

102.   Ibid., 21.

103.   C. I. Scofield, *The Scofield Reference Bible* (New York: Oxford University Press, 1945), 1253.

104.   Gene A. Getz, *Sharpening the Focus of the Church* (Chicago: Moody Press, 1974), 127.

105.   Flynn, *19 Gifts of the Spirit*, 21.

106.   Albert Barnes, *Notes on the New Testament, Matthew - Mark* (Grand Rapids: Baker Book House, 1949), 267.

107.   Charles C. Ryrie, *Biblical Theology of the New Testament* (Chicago: Moody Press, 1959), 196. In this volume, Ryrie implies that every Christian has a gift. As such each Christian has one gift. However, when the author took the course in Pauline Theology from Dr. Ryrie at Dallas Theological Seminary in 1956, Ryrie maintained every Christian had the gift of serving, giving, and encouraging.

108.   Flynn, *19 Gifts of the Spirit*, 22.

109. Elmer L. Towns and Jerry Falwell, *Church Aflame* (Nashville: Impact Books, 1971), Chapter 5. The phrase "hot poker" is also used in several articles on Church Growth by the author and is his unique term to indicate how spiritual gifts are communicated on the human level.

110. Ryrie, *Biblical Theology of the New Testament*, 196.

111. Albert Barnes, *Notes on the New Testament*, 1 Corinthians, (Grand Rapids: Baker Book House, 1949), 113.

112. Flynn, *19 Gifts of the Spirit*, 24.

113. Ibid.

114. Elmer Towns, *The Successful Sunday School and Teachers Guidebook* (Carol Stream, Illinois: Creation House, 1980), 177-178.

115. Flynn, *19 Gifts of the Spirit*, 24.

116. Ibid.

117. Ibid., 25.

118. Ryrie, *Biblical Theology of the New Testament*, 196.

119. Flynn, *19 Gifts of the Spirit*, 25.

120. Ibid., 25.

121. Barrett, *The Holy Spirit and the Gospel Tradition*, 107.

122. John Calvin, *Commentary on a Harmony of the Evangelists Matthew, Mark, and Luke* (Calvin Translation Society, 1845), 2:74.*

123. Procksch, *Theologische Worterbuch zum Neven Testament*, 1:105.*

124. Strong, *Systematic Theology*, 650-51.

125. Pohle, *Dr. C. I. Scofield's Question Box*, 152.*

126. Sterling Clark, *The Unpardonable Sin - What Is it?* (Waterford, Ontario: The Fundamental Baptist Mission, 1978), 69.*

127. Fitzwater, *Christian Theology*, 213.

128. Pache, *The Person and Work of the Holy Spirit*, 64.

129. Oswald Sanders, *Holy Spirit of Promise*, 136.*

130. John F. Walvoord, *The Holy Spirit: A Comprehensive Study of the Person and Work of the Holy Spirit* (Wheaton: Van Kampen Press, Inc., 1954), 197.*

131. Ibid., 200.*

* Denotes page number(s) could not be verified.

CHAPTER VI– ANGELOLOGY

The Doctrine of Angels

I. INTRODUCTION

In 1975 the publishing world was shocked when Dr. Billy Graham's book *Angels* became a runaway best seller. Who would have thought that the secular and human influence in America would allow any interest in the spirit world? Most would have thought that the average American would reject the doctrine of angels as a Freudian nightmare from the Dark Ages. Yet angels are predominant in Scripture, and those who would fully understand the plan of God must study the nature and work of angels.

Angels are created spirit beings, though they have power to become visible in the likeness of a human form. The word "angel" means "messenger" and is always used in the masculine gender, although sex in the human sense is never ascribed to them. Their power is inconceivable (2 Kgs. 19:35), but not omnipotent. Their wisdom is extensive (2 Sam. 14:20), but not omniscient. Their number is great (Heb. 12:22), but not limitless. Man is made "a little lower than the angels" (Heb. 2:7).

Scripture mentions the ministry and nature of angels approximately 108 times in the Old Testament and 165 times in the New Testament. However, as with the Trinity or the devil, the Bible does not seek to prove their existence, rather, it assumes their existence. Nonetheless there exists a chasm of skepticism about their existence and ministry. Confusion and uncertainty concerning angels has arisen primarily from two separate sources: (1) Scripture never clearly delineates a detailed description of angels. The reader must indirectly glean their characteristics from select passages. And (2) our sophisticated and enlightened generation has repudiated much of the worthless conjectures of the Middle Ages concerning angels. Augustus Strong describes in detail the nature of superstitious thoughts about angels debated by the scholastics.

The scholastics debated the questions, how many angels could stand at once on the point of a needle (relation of angels to space); whether an angel could be in two places at the same time; how great was the interval between the creation of angels and their fall; whether the sin of the first angel caused the sin of the rest; whether as many retained their integrity as fell; whether our atmosphere is the place of punishment for fallen angels; whether guardian-angels have charge of children from baptism, from birth, or while the infant is yet in the womb of the mother; even the excrements of angels were subjects of discussion, for if there was "angels' food" (Psa. 78:25), and if angels ate (Gen. 18:8), it was argued that we must take the logical consequences.

Dante makes the creation of angels simultaneous with that of the universe at large. "The fall of the rebel angels he considers to have taken place within twenty seconds of their creation, and to have originated in the pride which made Lucifer unwilling to await the time prefixed by his Maker for enlightening him with perfect knowledge"—see Rossetti, Shadow of Dante, 14, 15. Milton, unlike Dante, puts the creation of angels ages before the creation of man. He tells us that Satan's first name in heaven is now lost. . . .

In medieval times men's minds were weighted down by the terror of the spirit of evil. It was thought possible to sell one's soul to Satan, and such compacts were written with blood. The cathedrals cultivated and perpetuated this superstition, by the figures of malignant demons which grinned from the gargoyles of their roofs and the capitals of their columns, and popular preaching exalted Satan to the rank of a rival God—a god more feared than was the true and living God. Satan was pictured as having horns and hoofs— an image of the sensual and bestial—which led Cuvier to remark that the adversary could not devour, because horns and hoofs indicated not a carnivorous but a ruminant quadruped.[1]

The doctrine of angels cannot be ignored if we are to teach the whole counsel of God (Acts 20:27). A number of benefits can be derived in studying angels. First, when we realize they constantly observe our Christian lives (1 Cor. 4:9), we will improve our conduct. When we understand their protection of us, we will be encouraged by God's care for us (Heb. 1:7). As we consider the tremendous strength and authority of the angels, we will be encouraged. Finally, the example of their unceasing service ought to motivate us to more consistent service for God.

II. THE DESCRIPTION OF ANGELS

There are many terms used in the Bible to describe angels: host, creatures, thrones, dominions, principalities, powers, sons of God, beasts (KJV), and the angel of His presence. The phrase "the angel of the Lord" usually implies the presence of deity in angelic form (Gen. 16:1-13; 22:11-16; 31:11-13; Exod. 3:2-4; Judg. 6:12-16). Most interpret the phrase "the angel of the Lord" as Christ, and Borland calls this appearance a "Christophany."[2] However, the phrase in Luke 1:11 and Acts 12:7,23 is not a description of deity.

A. CREATED BEINGS. When were the angels created? Obviously they were created before the beginning of the earth, because angels watched the magnificent drama of creation. God asked the question, "Where wast thou when I laid the foundations of the earth?" (Job 38:4). The narrative goes on to indicate, "When the morning stars sang together, and all the sons of God shouted for joy" (Job 38:7). If "the sons of God" is a reference to angels, then the angels were rejoicing as God created the world.

In relation to the time of creation for angels, three major views have emerged. The first endorses the view that angels were created in eternity past, well before Genesis chapter one. The second view places their creation during the creative process. The third believes the angels were created with the first creation before the gap of time between Genesis 1:1 and Genesis 1:3. Lockyer, an advocate for the first view, states,

> Originally, God existed alone in all the perfection and glory of His majesty. Before the appearance of any worlds, He surrounded Himself with a vast angelic host, spiritual beings far superior to man. Being pure spirit, the angels are invisible and immortal, but not immutable. When created, they were endowed with intellect, will and beauty, and power far above the human level. They all worshipped God in the excellence of His holiness, until the fall of Satan.
>
> . . . .
>
> Angelic beings then, we confidently conclude, were created long before the formation of the earth. But just when in the mysterious revolutions of eternity they were called into existence is not a subject of Divine revelation. That the angels were created by God and for His glory is an unassailable fact of Holy Writ, Heb. 1:1-3.[3]

Support for the first view is found in three scriptural passages: (1) Job 38:4-7 presents the angels as rejoicing in the creative work of God, suggesting their existence prior to the creation of the world, (2) Ezekiel 28:12ff demands a certain amount of time for Satan to be in the presence of God, conceive sin in his heart and then fall, and, (3) the argument from silence indicates that in Gen. 1-2 there is no clear mention of the creation of angels.

The argument for the second view that angels were created during the six creative days are: (1) Ex. 20:11, "For in six days the Lord made heaven and earth, the sea, and all that in them is, and rested the seventh day: Wherefore the Lord blessed the Sabbath day, and hallowed it" (emphasis added). The word "is" (including the angels) indicates they were created during the six days of creation. (2) Support for the second view includes Job 38:4-7 and Ezekiel 28:12ff which do not demand a long time for Satan's fall, but only the lapse of some time after Satan's creation. (3) Col. 1:16 suggests that everything was created at once. Furthermore, this view does not militate against Satan's fall shortly after his creation, for some time is required to have elapsed between the creation and the fall of man (Gen. 1:1 to 3:5). Writing on this issue, Chafer states,

> It is assumed from Colossians 1:16-17 that all angels were created simultaneously. In like manner, it is assumed that the creation of angels was completed at that time and that none will be added to their number.[4]

The third view claims that the account of the creation of angels appears in the first verse of the Bible: "In the beginning God created the heaven[s] and the earth" (Gen. 1:1, heaven is plural in the original). In the Hebrew language, the plural form of "heavens" reveals that God created the whole of heaven, composed of all its innumerable separate parts. The heavens included not only the stars, but the present abode of God, plus angelic beings. During the "gap" between Genesis 1:1 and 1:3, "The earth was without form and void" (Gen. 1:2). The word "was" could be translated "became." Hence, the earth could have gone through a cataclysmic judgment. Attached to this judgment could be the fall of Satan (Isa. 14:9-14; Ezek. 28:12-15). Out of this is an explanation of the earth's apparent long age (Jer. 4:23-26; Isa. 24:1; 45:18). Angels were created beings during the first creation. They admired God's beauty, orderliness, and power in the re-creation (making) of the earth in Gen. 1:3-31. Since one task of angels is to give glory to God, they sang and shouted during the Creation.

Even though the Father and the Holy Spirit were active in the creation of angels, Jesus Christ is identified as their Creator. "For by him were all things created, that are in heaven, and that are in earth, visible and invisible, whether they be thrones, or dominions, or principalities, or powers: all things were created by him, and for him" (Col. 1:16). The words "thrones," "dominions," "principalities" and "powers" are all terms used in the Bible to describe angels. David urged the angels to praise the Lord because they were created (Psa. 148:2-5).

B. INCORPOREAL BEINGS. Though angels have appeared to men in physical form, they are essentially spirit beings. David recognized and blessed the Lord "Who maketh his angels spirits; and his ministers a flaming fire" (Psa. 104:4).

Even though angels are spirits, they have the ability to become visible in the semblance of a human body (Gen. 19:1; Mark 1:26; John 20:12). Angels are always referred to as being masculine, but without specific reference to gender.

David reflected on the nature of man and observed, "For thou hast made him a little lower than the angels, and hast crowned him with glory and honour" (Psa. 8:5). In the hierarchy of heaven, angels are above man, yet they are listed below Christ. "Being so much better than the angels, as he hath by inheritance obtained a more excellent name than they" (Heb. 1:4).

Commenting on the possible corporeality of angels, the author of Hebrews writes, "Be not forgetful to entertain strangers: for thereby some have entertained angels unawares" (13:2). Concerning this verse Gaebelein writes,

We learn from this that pious Hebrews in Old Testament times received strangers into their homes, entertained them, only to discover later that they were the messengers of God. We conclude, therefore, that they did not appear, as pictured in art, with wings and a halo about the head. They looked like as if they were common mortals. From other Scriptures we learn that their bodies sometimes possessed a marvelous glory. Their garments are described as shining, their faces like the lightning and their whole appearance in whiteness like the snow. How can this be reconciled with the assertion that they are only spirits? It is answered, that they possess the faculty of appearing in corporeal form at will; that they can pierce the universe at a speed even greater than the speed of light; that they can come and go unperceived by mortal sense, or appear visibly. There can be taken no exception to these statements. We also believe that these holy beings possess such a faculty of taking on bodily form and appear and disappear as they desire.[5]

C. HOLY BEINGS. All angels were originally created holy to praise God and to serve Him. Perhaps the best-known phrase that came from the mouth of angels is, "Holy, holy, holy, is the LORD of hosts" (Isa. 6:3). The word "hosts" means "angels," hence God is the Lord of the angels. Again, the angels are fulfilling their task when they sing, "Worthy is the Lamb" (Rev. 5:12). They were created holy because their message of praise is holy. But there was a group of "angels who kept not their first estate, but left their own habitation" (Jude 6). Some theologians believe that some of these fallen angels are demons who now serve Satan, while those who did not fall are holy angels who serve the Lord God. Even those demons were originally created in a state of holiness. Another group of the fallen angels are "chained under darkness," awaiting the judgment of God (2 Pet. 2:4; Jude 6). This view represents the traditional understanding of Jude 6 and 2 Pet. 2:4. However, an alternative view with greater hermeneutical support will be given in the study of demons (see Demons, Destiny of Demons). The holy angels that did not sin are in fellowship with God and can look upon him. Jesus warned His disciples not to abuse children because their angels are in the presence of God. "Take heed that ye despise not one of these little ones; for I say unto you, That in heaven their angels do always behold the face of my Father which is in heaven" (Matt. 18:10). The fact that angels are in fellowship with God and remain in His presence implies their holiness.

D. PERSONAL BEINGS. Angels are personal beings, which means they are similar to God and man in that they have a personality, which is intellect, emotion, and will. Having personality or being a person gives the angel the power of self-perception and self-direction. God created angels with intellectual ability, and they are identified as wise (2 Sam. 14:20). Also, angels are portrayed in the obedient service of God, thus demonstrating the exercise of a will. The angel who showed John the Revelation exercised his independent will by not allowing John to worship him. "Then saith he unto me, See thou do it not: for I am thy fellow servant, and of thy brethren the prophets, and of them which keep the sayings of this book: worship God" (Rev. 22:9).

Today, the will of angels to choose evil has apparently been preempted by God because they chose not to follow Satan. Their will is "frozen" to do only the will of God. Today, angels cannot choose evil. Finally angels appear to exercise their emotions when the Scriptures indicate that "the angels desire to look into" the glories of salvation (1 Pet. 1:12). This is an indication of their emotions and the interaction of their will—obviously a reflection of personality.

The personality of angels is further demonstrated in the ability to speak or communicate with God and men. On several occasions an angel was sent by God to an individual to communicate a special message from God. To accomplish that task, the angel carried on a conversation that involved choosing words to convey meaning, then interpreting any words that were directed back to them. Angels had to use memory and rational ability to form sentences. They have the ability to discern (used to answer questions), wisdom and basic knowledge regarding life on earth and the plan of God.

E. DEATHLESS BEINGS. When God created angels, he did not plan for their death or extinction. Jesus taught we would someday be "deathless" like angels. After humans are resurrected, "Neither can they die any more: for they are equal unto the angels" (Luke 20:36). Death is an experience of the human race because of the entrance of sin into the world (Rom. 5:12). Scripture always represents the death of humans not as the cessation of life, but rather as the separation of the physical and the spiritual. The incorporeality of angels does not allow for such a separation; thus they are deathless.

Angels were created in a state of holiness. When Satan rebelled against God, certain angels chose to follow God, therefore there is no reason for their punishment. Hell was created for those angels that rebelled against God and some day they will be eternally consigned there. John noted that "the devil that deceived them was cast into the lake of fire and brimstone" (Rev. 20:10). Jesus described it as "everlasting fire, prepared for the devil and his angels" (Matt. 25:41).

F. UNSEEN BEINGS. Angels are unseen by man until they choose to appear for some special purpose. They seemed to have manifested themselves at certain times or epochs in Bible history more than others. They were frequent visitors during the period from Abraham to Moses, then primarily around the life of Christ. They were said to be present when the world was created. They apparently appear when circumstances on earth were changing and God needed to give specific "messages" to his people about new covenants, dispensations, or different responsibilities. Because they don't appear frequently as persons in bright apparel does not mean they have no ministry today, for they constantly minister to "them who shall be heirs of salvation" (Heb. 1:14). In their work they are not seen with the naked eye as angels, but may work through people; or perhaps they appear as persons. "Be not forgetful to entertain strangers: for thereby some have entertained angels unawares" (Heb. 13:2).

Many have wondered why angels do not remain visible at all times if for no other reason but to substantiate the biblical claims to their existence and provide additional empirical proof to God's existence and unfolding program. One can only derive the reasons by conjecture, but two reasons possess a great deal of credibility: (1) to restrain man from seeking to worship them. On this subject Chafer writes,

> One reason angels are rendered invisible to human sight may be that, if they were seen, they would be worshiped. Man, who is so prone to idolatry as to worship the works of his own hands, would hardly be able to resist the worship of angels were they before his eyes.[6]

(2) If angels were always visible, man's faith in an invisible God would be greatly diminished. Undoubtedly men and women would develop a shallow and possibly less sincere faith in God—a type of faith that sharply differs from the requirements of New Testament faith.

G. ORDER. The description of angels suggests that they exist in orderly arrangement, perhaps with line and staff responsibility. Jesus told those who arrested Him, "Thinkest thou that I cannot now pray to my Father, and he shall presently give me more than twelve legions of angels?" (Matt. 26:53). The writer to the Hebrews called them "an innumerable company of angels" (Heb. 12:22). The apostle John counted in excess of about one hundred million angels in heaven (Rev. 5:11), but this would not include about one-third of the angels that fell when Satan was cast out of heaven.

Some have wondered how many angels there are in existence. There is an exact number for they are not numberless. If they were unlimited in number, they would not be a created order, but they would be an extension of the nature of God, for only God is limitless in nature and attributes. If there is a guardian angel for each person on earth (Matt. 18:10; Acts 12:15), then the number could exceed at least six or seven billion, but fewer if only saints have guardian angels (Heb. 1:14). A group this large could not function efficiently without an organization. Various groups of angels are identified in Scripture in relation to specific spheres of ministry. Michael the archangel is apparently the leader among the holy angels.

H. ELECT AND NON-ELECT ANGELS. While writing to Timothy, Paul admonished him to diligently do the work before him without demonstrating partiality to anyone (1 Tim. 5:21). To lay stress upon this command, Paul charges Timothy by three separate sources that include God the Father, the Lord Jesus Christ, and the elect angels. Normally we would expect the third Person to be the Holy Spirit. However, Paul uses a very unique structure for a definite purpose. Timothy possessed the Holy Spirit already. If Paul had charged Timothy by the Holy Spirit, he would have suggested a separation between Timothy and the indwelling Spirit, an unbiblical relationship.

Is it correct to employ the term elect to angels in the same manner in which we apply it to men? The answer is emphatically "Yes!" The elect angels are all those who continued following God when Satan rebelled against God, and part of the angels chose not to follow God, but to follow Satan. Obviously, these elect angels could not be called saved angels, for they were never lost. They are elect angels.

Angels can be elect, just as men are elect. Just as God knows (based upon His foreknowledge) that certain men will not be saved, likewise He foreknew that certain angels would seek to topple His kingdom in a rebellion. To argue otherwise is tantamount to denying the omniscience (past, present, and future) knowledge of God. Furthermore, it should be noted that God's foreknowledge did not prompt or hinder the decision by the angels to rebel against God, as in the fall of man, for God's justice would have been violated. To explain further, prior to the fall of Adam and Eve, God knew they would sin. Yet His foreknowledge did not in any manner serve as an inducement to their sin. The sin committed by Adam and Eve was freely accomplished with absolutely no positive or external coercive force. If Satan had forcibly made Adam and Eve commit sin, they would have been innocent and not subject to the pronounced judgment by God. But Adam and Eve did exercise their independent use of their free wills. They deserved punishment. However, if an external force convinces a person of the positive or negative advantages or disadvantages of making a certain decision, and that person acts upon those suggestions (whether positive or negative) by employing his own will, only then can he be charged with guilt.

An examination of God in relation to His angels yields two observations: (1) God's foreknowledge allows Him to discern the ultimate destiny of His creation, and (2) God does not impinge the ultimate results of His foreknowledge upon His creation. All act independently in order to justly receive condemnation or glorification.

Scripture is clear that redemption was provided solely for man and not angels. Strong suggests several possible reasons.

> If no redemption has been provided for them, it may be because: 1. Sin originated with them; 2. the sin which they committed was "an eternal sin" (*cf.* Mark 3:29); 3. they sinned with clearer intellect and fuller knowledge than ours (*cf.* Luke 23:34); 4. their incorporeal being aggravated their sin and made it analogous to our sinning against the Holy Spirit (*cf.* Mat. 12:31, 32); 5. this incorporeal being gave no opportunity for Christ to objectify His grace and visibly to join himself to them (*cf.* Heb. 2:16); 6. their persistence in evil, in spite of their growing knowledge of the character of God as exhibited in human history, has resulted in a hardening of heart which is not susceptible of salvation.[7]

It logically follows that since Christ did not join His nature to angels in order to function as a mediator, the destiny of non-elect angels is already determined and their current evil state is permanent, or, as one theologian writes, one of "absolute depravity."

> It may indeed be said that the fall in the world of angels is absolute, that is, that there is no salvation for them. The distinction between absolute and total depravity has in late years been applied to men in their fallen and corrupt state . . . For by total depravity is meant that man by nature in all his existence, with all his heart and mind and soul and strength, has become a servant of sin, and that he is entirely incapable of doing any good and inclined to all evil. And by absolute depravity must be meant that the matter is settled, that there is no salvation for the sinner, that he is fallen so deeply that he can never be saved. . . . Also in the world of angels election and reprobation are in force. God's counsel also there makes separation. The difference, however, is this, that while in the world of man all fell under sin, and, therefore, the elect must be saved, the elect angels never fell. The power of election causes them to remain standing. Part of them fell; and because they, even as the reprobate among men, fell without a mediator and saving head, all the devils are fallen absolutely; and their case is absolutely determined. Election and reprobation in the world of angels are finished while in the world of sinful men they are being realized in the course of history.[8]

In relation to the elect angels, it must be argued that their state of goodness is also permanent (this will be further discussed under the Attributes of Angels).

III. The Character Of Angels

MORE EXCELLENT NAME		
	NAME	MEANING
1.	Jesus ("Saviour")	He shall save His people from their sins (Matt. 1:21)
2.	Lucifer	"Bearer of Light"
3.	Gabriel	"Man of God"
4.	Michael	"Who is like the Lord?"

Most of what we know about God is a result of His self-revelation through His names. God also gave names to His angels to reveal something about their character. (The practice of assigning a prominent attribute to a person through the medium of their name is primarily an Eastern custom and not Western.) Only three angels are named in Scripture, but the Bible indicates the significance of those names in contrast with the name of Jesus. "He [Jesus] hath by inheritance obtained a more excellent name than they [angels] "

(Heb. 1:4). The chart demonstrates the superior meaning of the name Jesus over the angelic names.

A. LUCIFER. Lucifer is thought to be the original name for the devil, reflecting not the present character of Satan, but his original created purpose and character. Lucifer originally possessed a high place in heaven (Isa. 14:12), perhaps the highest above all angels. He was cast down because of his desire to rise above God (Isa. 14:14). His name means "bearer of light," reflecting his purpose, to bear the light of God. The name Lucifer comes from the Hebrew word *Heblel* which means "brilliant, magnificent, or splendid." By bearing light, angels are messengers of God. Hence, Lucifer should have been a "light-bearer" to Jesus Himself, who is "the true Light, which lighteth every man that cometh into the world" (John 1:9).

B. GABRIEL. Gabriel is the messenger angel of God. Gabriel was usually sent from God to man with a special message. The name Gabriel means "man of God." His character trait is strength. Again, the name of Jesus surpasses the name of

APPEARANCES OF GABRIEL		
Appearance	To Whom	Scripture
1st	Daniel	Dan. 8:16; 9:21, 26
2nd	Zacharias	Luke 1:11, 19
3rd	Mary	Luke 1:26, 27
4th	Joseph	Matt. 1:20
5th	Joseph again	Matt. 2:13, 19
6th	Jesus in Gethsemane	Luke 22:43
7th	The apostles in prison	Acts 5:19
8th	Philip	Acts 8:26
9th	Peter	Acts 12:7
10th	Herod	Acts 12:23
11th	Paul	Acts 27:23
12th	John	Rev. 22:8

Gabriel. Whereas Gabriel is the "man of God," Jesus is the "God-man."

C. MICHAEL. The third angel named in Scripture is the most powerful. Michael is usually related to Israel and the resurrection (Dan. 10:13; 12:1, 2; 1 Thess. 4:19). He is described as the archangel (Jude 9), meaning he is the highest in the order of angels. His name means "who is like the Lord?" The name Michael emphasizes his godly character. Once again this angelic name falls short of the Lord Jesus Christ.

APPEARANCES OF MICHAEL		
Appearance	To Whom	Scripture
1st	Daniel	Dan. 10:13, 21; 12:1
2nd	Satan on earth	Jude 9
3rd	Satan in heaven	Rev. 12:7

D. CHERUBIM. This special group of angels is attached to the throne of God to guard the holiness of God. The term "cherubim" means "to till" or "to plough," which is expressive of diligent service to God. After Adam and Eve sinned, a cherub guarded the gate to Eden. Two likenesses of these angels were placed on the ark of the covenant in the tabernacle (Exod. 25:18-22), and later in the Temple (1 Kgs. 6:23-29). These statues stood symbolically in protection of the presence of God. Finally, John describes four angels (living creatures) that guarded the throne of God in heaven. "And round about the throne, were four beasts [living creatures] full of eyes before and behind. And the first beast was like a lion, and the second beast like a calf, and the third beast had a face as a man, and the fourth beast was like a flying eagle. And the four beasts had each of them six wings about him; and they were full of eyes within; and they rest not day and night, saying, Holy, holy, holy, Lord God Almighty, which was, and is, and is to come" (Rev. 4:6-8).

The unique nature and scriptural description of cherubim have prompted several theologians to question the personal existence of such angels. Note the following explanation of cherubim.

> With regard to the cherubim of Genesis, Exodus, and Ezekiel . . . the most probable interpretation is that which regards them, not as actual beings of higher rank than man, but as symbolic appearances, intended to represent redeemed humanity, endowed with all the creature perfections lost by the Fall and made to be the dwelling-place of God. . . .
>
> . . . .
>
> The doctrine of the cherubim embraces the following points: 1. The cherubim are not personal beings, but are artificial, temporary, symbolic figures. 2. While they are not themselves personal existences, they are symbols of personal existence— symbols not of divine or angelic perfections but of human nature (Ex. 1:5)—"they had the likeness of a man. . . ." 3. They are emblems of human nature, not in its present stage of development, but possessed of all its original perfections; for this reason the

most perfect animal forms—the kinglike courage of the lion, the patient service of the ox, the soaring insight of the eagle—are combined with that of man. . . . 4. These cherubic forms represent, not merely material or earthly perfections, but human nature spiritualized and sanctified. They are "living creatures" and their life is a holy life of obedience to the divine will. . . . 5. They symbolize a human nature exalted to be the dwelling-place of God. Hence the inner curtains of the tabernacle were inwoven with cherubic figures, and God's glory was manifested on the mercy-seat between the cherubim (Ex. 37:6-9). While the flaming sword at the gates of Eden was the symbol of justice, the cherubim were symbols of mercy—keeping the "way of the tree of life" for man, until by sacrifice and renewal Paradise should be regained (Gen. 3:24).

In corroboration of this general view, note that angels and cherubim never go together; and that in the closing visions of the book of Revelation these symbolic forms are seen no longer. When redeemed humanity has entered heaven, the figures which typified that humanity, having served their purpose, finally disappear.

The variable form of the cherubim seems to prove that they are symbolic appearances rather than real beings.[9]

The scholarly work of Strong has always represented and employed sound principles of interpreting Scripture. However, we must reject his view of cherubim as being untenable. Three reasons support these conclusions: (1) When Ezekiel and John recorded their visions of cherubim, they described actual beings and not simply symbolic parallels of human virtues. (2) If it is argued that cherubim do not exist, what certainty do we have that seraphim or other classifications of angels actually exists? (3) The primary reason for personality being attached to cherubim is discovered in Ezekiel 28:14, "Thou art the anointed cherub that covereth" (a reference to Satan, whose existence is not easily dismissed).

E. SERAPHIM. Literally, the word "seraphim" means "burners." Like the cherubim, they are concerned with the holiness of God (Isa. 6:3). Inasmuch as the seraph in Isaiah's vision cleansed his lips with a live coal from the altar (Isa. 6:6-7), this order of angels probably relates to sacrifice and cleansing. In contrast, the cherubim deal with judgment.

Dealing with the nature of seraphim, Gaebelein offers some insight into Isaiah's vivid description of them.

The covering of their faces denotes their deep reverence. The higher a being is in creation the greater is the reverence given to the Creator-God. The Seraphim are nearest the throne hence their great reverence. And reverence, in its fullest expression, as it beholds the infinite One, is worship. They teach us reverence. . . .

The Seraphim also covered their feet. It means, symbolically, their humility. In covering their feet, they acknowledge their own unworthiness. The last mentioned is "with twain he did fly." This stands for service. They execute promptly and swiftly His commands. It is the very last, showing that service is not the first thing, God wants. Reverence and worship is what God delights in.[10]

F. Various names or titles assigned the angels. Additional insights into the nature and work of angels emerges as we examine some of their titles as given in Scripture.

gods	Psa. 97:7; Heb. 2:7
Sons of God	Job 38:7; Dan. 3:25
Sons of the Mighty	Psa. 29:1; 89:6-7; Isa. 13:13; Joel 3:11
Watchers	Dan. 4:13-14; Isa. 62:6
Holy Ones	Zech. 14:5; Matt. 25:31; Dan. 8:13
Princes	Dan. 10:13 20-21; 12:1
Thrones (rulership)	Col. 1:16
Dominions (exercise the power to rule)	Col. 1:16
Powers (authority)	Col. 1:16
Principalities (government)	Col. 1:16
Morning stars	Job 38:7
Beasts	Rev. 4:6-8; Ezek. 1:6-11
Elect	1 Tim. 5:21

IV. The Attributes Of Angels

Angels were especially created by God to serve Him. To adequately represent God, they were given great strength and superior intelligence. Since God requires "all things be done decently and in order" (1 Cor. 14:40), angels are a highly organized company. They are described as "a multitude of the heavenly host" (Luke 2:13).

The apostle John fell at the feet of one angel to worship him (Rev. 22:8). John was certainly aware the worship of angels was not permitted by Scripture, even though it was practiced by some early sects within Christianity (Col. 2:18). We are therefore led to believe that John was so overwhelmed with all the angel had done and shown him that for the moment he looked upon him as God, perhaps even an incarnation of Jesus.

A. Strength. The power of angels is so vast that humans cannot comprehend it. The angels were given great power, yet they are not omnipotent. The apostle Paul calls them "mighty angels" (2 Thess. 1:7). The power of a single angel was demonstrated in part on the resurrection morning. "And, behold, there was a great earthquake; for the angel of the Lord descended from heaven, and came and rolled back the stone from the door and sat upon it" (Matt. 28:2). First, in an act of authority, the angel broke the Roman seal which was an immediate challenge to the sixteen armed guards, at the tomb. But in an act of strength, the angel rolled a massive stone away from the tomb. In all probability, "a wheel of granite, eight feet in diameter and one foot thick, rolling in a groove, would weigh more than four tons."[11] Isaiah records an instance where God sent an angel to kill 185,000 Assyrian soldiers during a single night (Isa. 37:36).

As we consider these two accomplishments by single angels, we must observe with David, "his angels, that excel in strength, that do his commandments, hearkening unto the voice of his word" (Psa. 103:20). While we recognize that angels are powerful, we also realize that omnipotence is never ascribed to them. There can only be one omnipotent One, and that is God. If another omnipotent being existed in the universe, by definition God would not be God.

While examining the awesome strength exercised by angels, three eminent truths emerge as discussed by Hodge: (1) the power of angels (good and evil) is dependent and derived from God, (2) their strength must be employed in accordance with the laws of the spiritual and material world, (3) their interference "with the freedom and responsibility of men" is not allowed.[12]

In relation to God, angels are subordinate both positionally and qualitatively; however, what, if any, is the relationship between angels and man? In areas of strength, intelligence, and mobility, angels far excel the accomplishments of man. Yet a careful study of Scripture reveals several distinct areas in which men surpass angelic beings. Writing on this subject Martensen stated,

> Although the angel, in relation to man, is the more powerful spirit, man's spirit is nevertheless the richer and the more comprehensive. For the angel, in all his power, is only the expression of a single one of all those phases which man is in the inward nature of his soul, and the richness of his own individuality is intended to combine into a complete and perfect microcosm . . . It is precisely because the angels are only spirits, not souls, that they cannot possess the same rich existence as man, whose soul is the point of union in which spirit and nature meet.[13]

B. INTELLIGENCE. Earlier we saw how angels had rational ability as an aspect of their personality. Jesus predicted his return, but qualified those who knew the time: "But of that day and hour knoweth no man, no, not the angels of heaven, but my Father only" (Matt. 24:36). Obviously, Jesus was teaching that the intelligence of angels was limited. There definitely are some things angels do not know, so they do not possess the omniscience of God. In the phrase "no, not the angels," Jesus was teaching that the angels were more intelligent than man. Jesus is listing the priority of intelligence from man who is knowledgeable, to angels who are more knowledgeable, to God who is omniscient in all things. The intelligence of the angels lies somewhere between that of men and God. They were created intelligent beings. But their wisdom is not static. They have continued to learn since their creation (Eph. 3:10). It should also be remembered that the learning capacity of the elect angels has not been corrupted with sin as is the case with man (Rom. 1:21). The extent and nature of knowledge acquired by angels is debated by scholars. Berkhof, writing on this subject, says,

> While all the scholastics agreed that the knowledge of the angels is limited, the Thomists and Scotists differed considerably respecting the nature of this knowledge. It was admitted by all that the angels received infused knowledge at the time of their creation, but Thomas Aquinas denied, while Duns Scotus affirmed, that they could acquire new knowledge through their own intellectual activity. The former held that the knowledge of the angels is purely intuitive, but the latter asserted that it may also be discursive.[14]

Scripture supports the conclusion developed by Scotus, for we read in 1 Peter 1:12, "Unto whom it was revealed, that not unto themselves, but unto us they did minister the things, which are now reported unto you by them that have preached the gospel unto you with the Holy Ghost sent down from heaven, which things the angels desire to look into" (emphasis added). Issues related to salvation are not fully known by angels. As a result, they are described by Peter as seeking to gain additional insights through examining how men obtain salvation. We cannot be dogmatic about how much angels do or do not know; however, as stated earlier, they know more than men, but far less than God.

C. CONFIRMED HOLINESS. Prior to the fall of Satan and the angelic hosts that pursued after him, it appears from Scripture that all the angels were in a position of unconfirmed holiness. This suggests that any, all, or none of the angels could or could not have rebelled against God. However, with the fall, there are now two distinct and permanent groups of angels: the elect with confirmed holiness, and the evil with confirmed wickedness. Contrasting these two groups of angels, Buswell writes,

> We infer that the angels which sinned did so in full knowledge of all the issues involved. They chose self-corruption, knowing exactly what they were doing. They sinned without remedy, and there is no atonement for them (II Pet. 2:4; Jude 6). On the other hand, it seems that the holy angels, being faced with the same ethical choice and possessing the same God-given ability to choose, remained and are confirmed in their state of holiness. They have never known the experience of sin.[15]

With confirmed holiness, this suggests that those angels who constantly behold the face of God will never lead in a second rebellion in the future to overthrow the throne of God. Angels do not now have the capacity to exercise free will and rebel against God. As stated by Gill, heavenly angels will never seek to rebel against God.

> Now in this state of constant obedience and perfect holiness, they are immutably fixed by the will of God, and have from their creation continued in it, and ever will; as

appears by their enjoyment of the presence of God perpetually; they always behold the face of God in heaven; they never left their habitation, but have always resided in heaven, where they were first placed; hence called the angels of heaven, Matt. xviii., 10, and xxiv. 36, and by their constant and perfect obedience to the will of God and which is made the pattern of obedience to it in men.[16]

V. THE WORK OF ANGELS

Since their creation, godly angels have concerned themselves with the task of carrying out the will of God. As noted in the previous section, the very nature of angels allows them to manifest ceaseless efforts in serving God and combating evil. As we study the many duties ascribed to angels in light of the global population of believers, we are astonished with the awesome task placed before them.

In light of God's omnipotence, some have argued against the necessity of angelic works. But they fail to realize the nature of a messenger, which is the basic meaning of the word "angel." A messenger not only delivers a message, but he also validates the content of the message by who he is and what he does. Surely God could manifest Himself to man by entering and exiting from the stream of humanity every time He desired to convey a message to His servants. But it is far more practical to conceive that God simply discharges His responsibility by a loyal servant.

Understanding the works of angels is not just studying a collection of stories with no relevance to contemporary life. The constant work of angels affects in some capacity the daily experiences of each one of us. Their works should be studied and understood by every Christian, not just theologians in the seminaries.

A. THE GENERAL WORKS OF ANGELS. God has in the past used angels to accomplish a number of tasks. They were involved in delivering the revelation of the Word of God. At times, God has sent angels to protect His people. Men have been encouraged and motivated to greatness by angels. They have also been used of God both to free captured men and to strengthen men in their service for God. When God has had to judge sin, often He has sent His angels to execute His judgment. Beyond these specific duties, angels have been the messengers of God to men on a number of occasions.

1. *Angelic transportation at death.* The Bible teaches that "to be absent from the body" (is) "to be present with the Lord" (2 Cor. 5:8). Apparently we are taken instantaneously to heaven at death. God once used angels to transport the soul of a saved man to the presence of God. Luke recorded a story that Jesus told about the death of two men, one who went to a place of eternal paradise, the other to the place of eternal punishment. "And it came to pass, that the beggar died, and was carried by the angels into Abraham's bosom" (Luke 16:22). Though this is the only reference to this phase of the works of angels, there is no indication that anything beyond the norm happened here or that anything less than the norm can be expected today. Since every Christian has a guardian angel, it is assumed that such an angel

accomplishes his final duty, which is to deliver the soul of the departed saint into the presence of God.

2. *Angelic revelation.* God has used a variety of ways to make His revelation known to man (Heb. 1:1); angels are just one means of delivering His revelation. After recording the Revelation of Jesus Christ and seeing the new heavens and new earth, John spoke of "the angel which showed me these things" (Rev. 22:8). Ezekiel described his vision of the cherubim in the first chapter of his prophecy. Also, the angel of God was sent on three occasions surrounding the birth of Christ to reveal something that God was about to do. First he appeared to the priest Zacharias, to tell him of the coming birth of his son, John (Luke 1:11). About six months later, "Gabriel was sent from God unto a city of Galilee, named Nazareth, to a virgin espoused to a man whose name was Joseph, of the house of David; and the virgin's name was Mary" (Luke 1:26-27). It was probably about five or six months later, after announcing the birth of Christ to Mary, "the angel of the Lord appeared unto him in a dream, saying, Joseph, thou son of David, fear not to take unto thee Mary, thy wife: for that which is conceived in her is of the Holy Ghost" (Matt. 1:20).

Angelic revelation should never be confused with the revelation supplied by the Holy Spirit to the authors of the Scriptures. Angelic revelation was simply an external message conveyed from God through the angels to man. Whereas, revelation by the Holy Spirit consisted of messages imparted to men being borne along by the Spirit in order to produce an inspired product, the Bible.

3. *Angelic protection.* Before God destroyed the cities of Sodom and Gomorrah, He sent two angels to warn Lot and his family to flee the city (Gen. 19:12-13). During the evening, the safety of Lot's family and his guests was threatened by the men of the city. The two angelic visitors protected Lot and themselves when they "smote the men that were at the door of the house with blindness, both small and great: so that they wearied themselves to find the door" (Gen. 19:11). After Daniel had spent the night in a den of lions, he was able to report to the king, "My God hath sent his angel, and hath shut the lions' mouths, that they have not hurt me: forasmuch as before him innocency was found in me" (Dan. 6:22). David, too, had learned throughout his experience as both shepherd and soldier that "the angel of the Lord encampeth round about them that fear him, and delivereth them" (Psa. 34:7).

4. *Angelic emancipation.* Angels not only protect people from trouble, they also on occasion provide for their deliverance. Very early in the experience of the church in Jerusalem, the Sadducees arrested the apostles and threw them into prison. "But the angel of the Lord by night opened the prison doors, and brought them forth" (Acts 5:19). It must have infuriated the Sadducees, who denied the theological existence of angels, that God should send an angel to release their prisoners. On another occasion, while the church prayed for Peter, who was awaiting execution in prison, God sent an angel to release him from his cell (Acts 12:7). This was quite different from the occasion when Peter attempted to prevent the arrest of Jesus with a sword, and Jesus said, "Thinkest thou that I cannot now pray to my Father, and he shall presently give me more than twelve legions of angels?" (Matt. 26:53).

5. *Angelic influence.* In addition to the wooing of the Holy Spirit upon believers to pursue a godly lifestyle, angels also influence Christians to live godly lives. Angelic influences upon believers stem from two different methods; first, from their constant and unerring steadfastness to God. Their testimony serves as a stimulus to us that the godly life is attainable. Secondly, angels are able to exert positive external inducements which spur us on to holiness. Unlike the Holy Spirit who can influence believers' minds directly, angels are limited to external impulses. However, we would do well not to minimize the impact of their influence. Writing on this issue, Strong states,

> Unlike the Holy Spirit, who can influence the human mind directly, they [angels] can influence men only in ways analogous to those by which men influence each other. As evil angels may tempt men to sin, so it is probable that good angels may attract men to holiness.[17]

6. *Angelic provision.* When Elijah ran from Jezebel in fear of his life, he was discouraged and tired. God sent an angel to prepare a meal while he slept. Then he was encouraged to eat. The nature of this food provided by the angel was such that "He arose, and did eat and drink, and went in the strength of that meat forty days and forty nights unto Horeb, the mount of God" (1 Kgs. 19:8).

After Jesus had fasted forty days in the wilderness and the devil had failed in his attempts to cause Jesus to sin, "Then the devil leaveth him, and, behold, angels came and ministered unto him" (Matt. 4:11). Part of that ministry of angels to Jesus may have included providing nourishment and physical sustenance.

7. *Angelic encouragement.* God has sent angels to encourage servants of God who were discouraged. The Book of Revelation was written in part to encourage those being persecuted by the Roman authorities. The reader is reminded in the final book of the Bible that God is still on the throne, no matter how bad things may appear. When the angel of the Lord appeared to Gideon (Judg. 6:12), he was a discouraged young man. After the angel commissioned him, Gideon was used of God to remove the idols from his father's house and deliver Israel from the Midianites.

In John 5:1-9, we are given the account of the paralyzed man who believed the water in the pool at Bethesda possessed healing power shortly after an angel stirred the water. Some have erroneously conceived the idea that this scriptural account accurately describes the works of an angel whose task is to heal the hurting. They cite as proof for this view the failure of Christ to rebuke the paralyzed man for believing in the healing power of the water and the extreme earnest belief of the man for over thirty-eight years. However, Christ's failure to rebuke or endorse the man's belief is an argument from silence for He did neither; hence, it neither endorses or refutes anything. Sincerity of belief by the paralyzed man is also a weak argument. Men can be sincerely wrong, for when one is desperate, he will believe just about anything told to him.

A more accurate understanding of John 5, as supported by a majority of scholars, seeks to explain this belief as an erroneous tradition. The lame man was repeating tradition that probably never happened. There never was an angel who stirred the waters. If God, in fact, healed the first person in the water, it would imply a preference by God rather than the idea of faith. Also, it would give the miracle a "gimmick" or sensational atmosphere much like the atmosphere that surrounds some Roman Catholic claims of miracles. Furthermore, the nature of angelic works always gives glory to God. Yet it appears from this passage that God was not glorified or worshipped among those who waited for the stirring of the waters. God has never performed a miracle in a careless or undesignated manner, for when God moves there is a purpose and order.

8. *Angelic administration.* Because God is holy, His nature demands that He judge sin. On several occasions, God used His angels to administer justice, and one angel in particular to judge sin—the angel of death. When David numbered the people of Israel, God decided to judge it as sin. "So the Lord sent a pestilence upon Israel from the morning even to the time appointed: and there died of the people, from Dan even to Beer-sheba seventy thousand men. And when the angel stretched out his hand upon Jerusalem to destroy it, the LORD repented him of the evil, and said to the angel that destroyed the people, It is enough: stay now thine hand" (2 Sam. 24:15-16). In the life of Herod (Acts 12:21-23) we are given the account of the king receiving undue honor from the people, and God responded by discharging one of His angels to smite Herod with death. There is coming at least one more occasion when God will use angels to administer judgment. "The Son of Man shall send forth his angels, and they shall gather out of his kingdom all things that offend, and them who do iniquity, and shall cast them into a furnace of fire" (Matt. 13:41-42).

9. *Angelic appearances.* Each time angels are commissioned by God to confront man with a message or to provide encouragement; we as humans can sense the extreme love God has for His children. The angels' appearances always mark an important transition or significant event in the life of a saint. A careful examination of angelic appearances endorses the necessity of their ministry.

1. Moses received the law from the angels.
2. Abraham entertained and was restrained by angels.
3. Eliezer was guided by an angel.
4. Lot was delivered by angels.
5. Jacob was preserved by an angel.
6. Balaam was reproved by an angel.
7. Joshua was encouraged by an angel.
8. Gideon was commissioned by an angel.
9. Israel was chastised by angels.
10. Elijah was confronted and was translated by angels.
11. Elisha was defended by angels.
12. Assyrians were destroyed by an angel.

13. Daniel was ministered to by an angel.
14. Zachariah was enlightened by an angel.
15. John's birth was foretold by an angel.
16. Mary was assured of Christ's birth by an angel.
17. The shepherds were told by angels.
18. Joseph was warned by an angel.
19. The Marys at the tomb were comforted by angels.
20. Apostles were liberated from prison by angels.
21. Jesus was ministered to by angels.
22. Cornelius was instructed by an angel.
23. Philip was instructed to go to the desert by an angel.
24. Paul was sustained in a storm by an angel.
25. John was directed to write the book of Revelation by an angel.

ANGELS IN THE MINISTRY OF CHRIST

1. Predicted His birth—Luke 1:30-33
2. Announced His birth—Luke 2:10-14
3. Warned of Herod's plot—Matt. 2:19-20
4. Ministry after the temptation—Matt. 4:11
5. Ministry before the betrayal—Luke 22:43
6. On call at the arrest of Jesus—Matt. 26:53
7. Rolled back the stone from the tomb—Matt. 28:2
8. Announcement of the resurrection—Matt. 28:6
9. Ascension of Christ—Acts 1:11
10. Return of Christ—Matt. 25:31
11. Execute the judgment of Christ—Matt. 13:39-40

B. THE SPECIFIC WORKS OF ANGELS. The Bible describes more specifically some of the works of angels. Angels served God throughout the life of Christ, at times prepared to do more than they were called on to perform. In some aspects of their work in relation to the work of Christ, the angels were waiting for service. Currently, much of the work of angels in this age affects the church and various political states. Even the lost are not exempt from the work of angels today.

1. *Angels and God.* Regardless of what age we are in, the foremost responsibility of angels will always center around ministering and offering due adoration to God. Since their creation, angels have unceasingly communicated verbal praise and worship to God. Isaiah 6:1-7 and Revelation 4:6-9 provide us with sufficient insight into the nature of their worship which is apparently His awesome holiness. Their ministry to God includes a variety of duties ranging from comforting a hurting saint to assisting God in discharging global judgment upon mankind during the Tribulation period.

2. *Angels and Christ.* From the prediction of His birth through the judgments by Christ at His return, the angels are engaged in working with Jesus. Not only did they predict His birth to Mary (Luke 1:30) and Joseph (Matt. 1:20), they were on hand at that historic birth to announce it to the shepherds (Luke 2:10). When Herod heard about the Messiah's birth and

planned to destroy Jesus, God warned Joseph and Mary through an angel to go to Egypt (Matt. 2:19). The angels ministered to Jesus at the beginning of His public ministry in the wilderness (Matt. 4:11) and at the end in the garden of Gethsemane an angel appeared to Him (Luke 22:43). They were on hand to defend Jesus during His arrest if He should have asked for them (Matt. 26:53), and one was present to roll back the stone on the resurrection morning (Matt. 28:2). Two angels were the first to officially announce Jesus' resurrection to the world (Matt. 28:6). They were nearby at the ascension of Christ into heaven and predicted His Second Coming (Acts 1:11). Jesus taught He would return accompanied by His angels (Matt. 25:31). At the judgment of Christ, angels will be on hand to carry out the judgment pronounced by Christ (Matt. 13:39-40).

3. *Angels and the church.* Much of the general works of angels discussed in the first section of this chapter relates specifically to the church and its members. The Bible tells us that angels may attend the services of the church as spectators of church worship, order, and ministry. The angels are present to observe and presumably report to God concerning the order in our corporate worship (1 Cor. 11:10; Eph. 3:10; 1 Tim. 5:21). Some commentators suggest that the book of Hebrews may have referred to angels: "Wherefore seeing we also are compassed about with so great a cloud of witnesses, let us lay aside every weight, and the sin with doth so easily beset us" (Heb. 12:1). If the witnesses that observed the race of Christians were angels, Christians would he motivated by their observation.

In addition to angels functioning as witnesses to the success and failure of the church, their roles sometimes require them to become actively involved in ecclesiastical matters. Gaebelein describes the ministering responsibilities of angels as such.

> As we think on this truth, it appears perfectly logical that angels minister to those who belong to Christ. . . . The angels of God are ministering to prevent the success of the devil's attacks.

> But how do they minister? What kind of a ministry do they exercise? They cannot minister to believers in spiritual things. They cannot assist them in the study and in the understanding of the Word and the Truth of God. Believers have the unction from above, they are indwelt by the Holy Spirit. . . . Therefore, angels are beneath us in this respect and they cannot minister to us in spiritual things; God, the Holy Spirit, through the Word of God, of which He is the Author, ministers to the spiritual needs of the flock of God.

> In what, then, consist their ministries? In physical, temporal matters exclusively. In a world which is antagonistic to the children of God, which is controlled by the forces of evil, dangers and pitfalls abound on all sides.18

The nature of their physical ministry extends to three specific areas: they guide, comfort, and defend. During the life of the early church, the angel of the Lord provided guidance to Philip as he helped the Ethiopian eunuch. Several chapters later, in Acts 27:21-35, the angel of God assures Paul and his companions with the comforting words that no one will perish in the storm, but rather that all of them will reach the land safely. On two separate occasions (Acts 5:19; 12:7) the angel of the Lord interceded in behalf of the apostles in order to defend them against antagonistic persecutors. The benevolent works of the angels in relation to the church encompasses a variety of works; however, the church is no longer embryonic in form. It is a major force to contend with, and, as a result, angels are not called upon merely to physically manifest themselves to men in order to perform a certain deed.

4. *Angels and nature.* During the closing day of this dispensation, God will administer His judgment upon civilization on a global scale. This period of time has been correctly described as the period of the Great Tribulation, a time unequaled by any other event. As referred to in the general works of angels, angels will be employed to carry out God's judgment upon the earth. As we read the book of Revelation, we discover another responsibility of the angels which may engulf contemporary times. Revelation 7:1 describes angels as having control of nature: "And after these things I saw four angels standing on the four corners of the earth, holding the four winds of the earth, that the wind should not blow on the earth, nor on the sea, nor on any tree." It is apparent from this Scripture that angels are actively involved in controlling the jet stream and possibly other aspects of nature.

5. *Guardian angels.* Today, there are guardian angels to give physical protection to the people of God. Children are described as having "their angels" (Matt. 18:10), and the Christians described the knocking at their door by Peter, "It is his angel" (Acts 12:15). Protection begins early in life and continues throughout life. The guardian angels "do always behold the face of my Father which is in heaven" (Matt. 18:21), implying that God, who knows what danger faces us, can send our angel immediately to help us. This protection seems to extend primarily to physical help. Our spiritual help comes from the indwelling Christ and the Holy Spirit. We should avail ourselves of the filling of the Holy Spirit and the presence of Christ to keep us from temptation and sin. Even though it is an argument from silence, there is not one verse that suggests we should pray to angels for help. Apparently we pray to the Father, and He sends angels.

In light of Matthew 18:10, Acts 12:15, and the apocryphal Tobit 6:3-18, scholars such as Origen have stated, "We must say that every human soul is under the direction of an angel who is like a father."[19] St. Basil, who also supports the idea of guardian angels states, "An angel is put in charge of every believer, provided we do not drive him out by sin. He guards the soul like an army."[20]

In contrast to the claims of Origen and Basil, some theologians oppose the idea of angels assigned to every human being. A major weakness with supposing that angels are given charge over the physical welfare of every or some people for their entire life is simply the lack of clear scriptural support. Berkhof states,

> The idea that some of them [angels] serve as guardians of individual believers finds no support in Scripture. The statement in Matt. 18:10 is too general to prove the point, though it seems to indicate that there is a group of angels who are particularly

charged with the care of the little ones. Neither is it proved by Acts 12:15, for this passage merely goes to show that there were some even among the disciples of that early day who believed in guardian angels.[21]

In harmony with the conclusion reached by Berkhof, Hodge expresses his views as being such.

> Whether each individual believer has a guardian angel is not declared with any clearness in the Bible. The expression used in Matt. xviii. 10, in reference to the little children, "whose angels" are said to behold the face of God in heaven, is understood by many to favour this assumption. So also is the passage in Acts xii. 7, where Peter's angel is spoken of (verse 15). This latter passage, however, no more proves that Peter has a guardian angel than if the servant maid had said it was Peter's ghost it would prove the popular superstition on that subject. The language recorded is not of an inspired person, but of an uneducated servant, and can have no didactic authority. It only goes to prove that the Jews of that day believed in spiritual apparitions. The passage in Matthew has more pertinency. It does teach that children have guardian angels; that is, that angels watch over their welfare. But it does not prove that each child, or each believer, has his own guardian angel.[22]

From a technical standpoint, one could argue against the necessity of every believer possessing his own guardian angel. Are we not preserved in Christ and then held firmly in the hand of God (John 10:27-30)? Some have argued that God is primarily concerned with preserving the spiritual aspect of man, whereas the angels are given the task of protecting the physical part. However, such an argument fails to recognize that God is keenly interested, not only in the immaterial, but the material parts of man. Was it not God who provided manna, quail, and water for the Israelites? God is concerned with the physical and spiritual needs. No greater confidence comes to Christians than to know that their lives are preserved by God personally and not discharged to some angel. This is not to minimize the serving capacity of angels for they are considerably more powerful than any man. However, in the presence of Satan, many of the godly angels must submit their rebuke to a higher Authority (Jude 9).

6. *Angels and the nations.* The prophet Daniel wrote of a time when Michael the archangel would help protect the nation Israel. "And at that time shall Michael stand up, the great prince which standeth for the children of thy people: and there shall be a time of trouble, such as never was since there was a nation even to that same time: and at that time thy people shall be delivered, every one that shall be found written in the book" (Dan. 12:1). As Israel passes through the Great Tribulation, they will have a national guardian angel.

7. *Angels and the lost.* In many instances when angels appeared to men, one of the first things they said was, "Fear not." Obviously, the lost should fear angels because they are sometimes used as agents of judgment. God used an angel to kill Herod when he accepted the worship of the people. "And immediately the angel of the Lord smote him because he gave not

God the glory; and he was eaten of worms, and gave up the ghost" (Acts 12:23). God may also do the same thing today. He will use angels to warn of the judgment of the world at Armageddon (Rev. 19:17) as he did in Sodom (Gen. 18:12-13). They will also be involved in gathering and casting the lost into their assigned place of punishment at the end of the age (Matt. 13:39-40). Although godly angels stand in opposition to the lost, their hatred turns to rejoicing every time a sinner accepts the Lord as Saviour (Luke 15:10).

8. *Angels and the second advent.* Toward the end of the Great Tribulation period in which much of humanity has been decimated, Christ returns to the earth in order to establish His kingdom. The angels are again on the scene to assist Christ in four separate ways as described by Scripture. According to Matt. 24:31, holy angels will return with Christ, showing forth praise and glory to the holy Son of God. Secondly, angels will gather all surviving unbelievers for judgment (Matt. 25:31-32). Thirdly, all believers will be gathered by angels and allowed to enter into the millennial kingdom (Matt. 25:33-34). Finally, angels will assist in binding Satan and his demonic hosts and casting them into hades (Rev. 20:1-3). However, Satan will be allowed to stir up a rebellion towards the end of the millennial kingdom.

9. *Angels and the eternal state.* When time is no longer calculated and the awesome judgment of the Great White Throne is history, believers will enter into eternity present with God. Believers will continually worship God, and in turn God will perpetually provide for them an unfailing source of light and fellowship. But what of angels, and what role will they assume? Revelation 21-22 suggests that angels will serve in a subordinate position to God and to the believers. However, Gerhart firmly believes that angels will partake of some of the blessings given to the church, and, as a result, will receive a more exalted position than they currently possess.

Emphasis is put by the apostle on the fact that unto principalities God's wisdom is made known *through the Church.* The existence of the Church, and the preaching of the unsearchable riches by the Church, condition the growth of the angels in spiritual knowledge. How much more of Christian truth will not the "principalities" know when the Church, now imperfect, shall attain to perfection; now militant, warring against enemies both human and diabolical, shall become the Church triumphant? The final consummation at the Second Coming will affect not only the relative position and the spiritual knowledge of the angels, but Scripture suggests that the final consummation will likewise affect the *life* of the angels. Indirectly at least, they will participate in the spiritual benefits which come to the Church from the Son of Man. Paul teaches that God the Father made known unto us the mystery of His will, according to His good pleasure which He purposed in the Beloved unto a dispensation of the fullness of the times, to sum up all things in Christ, the things in the heavens, and the things upon the earth. Both the human race upon the earth and the angelic orders in the heavens are embraced in "all things" to be summed up in Christ. Angelic spirits will then bear a relation to the Head of the Church which they do not bear to Him now, and which they will not realize before "the fullness of the time." Of similar import is the prophetic vision of Paul in Eph. [correction:Colossians] i.20. It was the good pleasure of the Father through the Son to reconcile all things unto Himself, whether things upon the earth, or things in the heaven. Things visible and things invisible, whether thrones or dominions or principalities or powers; all things were created through the Son, and unto the Son. Accordingly all angelic orders exist for the Son; He is their *end*. In the Son these orders of spirits consist, hold together; He is the law by which are upheld and governed. Having made peace between God and men, between Gentiles and Jews through the blood of His cross, He becomes also for the angels a Mediator through whom their life passes from its present plane to a higher plane of spiritual perfection and glory. The kingdom of the Son of Man comprehends all orders of angelic spirits no less than all races of mankind. When the impending transcendent eon now in process of ripening shall supersede the current eon, angels as a consequence of the glorification of the body mystical will rise into more intimate fellowship with the fontal Source of life, of light, and love. But though as to their life and knowledge advanced to a higher status of spiritual perfection through the Church, yet in the final glory of the kingdom the position and office of the angels will be subordinate to the authority and office of the saints.[23]

ENDNOTES

1.   Augustus Strong, *Systematic Theology* (New Jersey: Fleming H. Revell Co., 1907), 443-444.

2.   James A. Borland, *Christ in the Old Testament*, revised (Ross-shire: Christian Focus, 1999).

3.   Herbert Lockyer, *The Mystery and Ministry of Angels* (Grand Rapids: Eerdmans, 1958), 14-15.

4.   Lewis Chafer, *Systematic Theology* (Dallas: Dallas Seminary Press, 1948), 2:11.

5.   Arno C. Gaebelein, *The Angels of God* (Grand Rapids: Baker Book House, 1969), 30.

6.   Chafer, 8.

7.   Strong, 463-64.

8.   Herman Hoeksema, *Reformed Dogmatics* (Grand Rapids: Reformed Free Pub. Assoc., 1966), 252-253.

9.   Strong, 449.

10.   Gaebelein, 45-46.

11.   Strong, 445.

12.   Charles Hodge, *Systematic Theology* (Grand Rapids: Eerdmans, 1975), 644.

13.   Quoted by Chafer, 10.*

14.   Louis Berkhof, *Systematic Theology* (Grand Rapids: Eerdmans, 1976), 142.

15.   J. O. Buswell, *A Systematic Theology of the Christian Religion* (Grand Rapids:

Zondervan, 1962), 134.

16.   John Gill, *A Body of Divinity* (Grand Rapids: Sovereign Grace Pub., 1971), 265.*

17.   Augustus Strong, *Systematic Theology* (New Jersey: Fleming Revell Co., 1975), 453.

18.   Gaebelein, 96-97.

19.   Jean Danielou, *The Angels and Their Mission: According to the Fathers of the Church* (New York: Newman Press, 1976), 69.

20.   Ibid., 69.

21.   Berkhof, 147-48.

22.   Hodge, 1:640.

23.   E. V. Gerhart, cited by L. S. Chafer, *Systematic Theology*, 2:25-26.

* Denotes page number(s) could not be verified.

CHAPTER VII – SATANOLOGY

The Doctrine of Satan

I. INTRODUCTION

A study of theology is not complete without an examination of the origin of evil (before the fall in the garden), the force behind evil and the personification of evil in the person of Satan. But even as a study of Satanology is attempted, it is difficult to arrive at objective conclusions. The problem is that we live in a culture filled with fairy tales or false information about the devil. If we were to ask a dozen different people what they thought about the devil, we might get a dozen different answers.

The primary source of correct information about Satan is Scripture, perhaps the only reliable source. In other areas of theology, it is possible to examine data in natural revelation: however, the very nature of Satan is to deceive concerning his identity and purpose. Therefore, any data from natural revelation that would help to give insight or to verify our insight is subject to falsification by Satan.

During the Middle Ages, people enjoyed religious plays for entertainment. In these, the devil was played by one dressed in a red suit with horns and a pitchfork. We see that character in cartoons today. Modern people generally think the devil is evil-looking. When portrayed in movies, he has a sinister appearance.

Because of the recent increased interest in the occult, Satan has become a box office attraction. Also, we see a growing cult of Satan worshippers. Some people are prepared to give Satan control over their lives to a greater or lesser degree. The interest and influence of Satan is growing from such simple things as a Ouija Board or an astrological chart, to witches' covens and places that sell artifacts related to Satanism.

Another group denies the existence of Satan completely. Someone noted that Christian Science takes the "d" out of devil making it evil. Also, certain factions of liberal Christianity deny the supernatural existence of the devil while others recognize the existence of Satan, but deny his power. Since secrecy is one of the characteristics of Satan, it is understandable why so many Christians are deceived concerning his nature and work. Satan has blinded them about it. He is most effective when he keeps himself hidden from public sight.

A more abominable view seeks to describe the notion of an evil devil as being tantamount to a religious facade that divorces a benevolent and omnipotent God from the presence of evil in this universe. This view states, "The idea of the devil was a welcomed expedient for the need of an advanced religious reflection to put God out of relation to the evil and badness of the world."[1]

Despite these attempts to discredit the validity of an actual evil personage, there remains a strong bulwark of empirical evidence supporting Satan's existence, as found in the testimony of the One instrumental in his creation. However, even Christ's unveiling revelation of Satan's existence and practices has not escaped scathing denunciations by adamant skeptics. As a result, three views have been advanced to explain Christ's apparent belief in a personal devil and attendant evil spirits.

1. Our Lord, living in a primitive and unscientific age, shared with those of His own day a superstitious belief in a personal devil, but both He and they were mistaken. He had been granted only that degree of knowledge essential to His mission to earth. In other matters He shared the errors and superstitious beliefs of His age.

2. Jesus did not share these mistaken beliefs, but He accommodated His speech and actions to what was generally believed in His day. His mission was to teach spiritual truths, not science, and He did this in the language of the people. This argument has been stated more subtly: There can be no doubt, it runs, that Jesus spoke as though Satan was a reality, but it is open to argument that He was simply using the thought forms of His age without making any pronouncement on their truth or otherwise.

3. He believed in the existence of a personal devil, and in this He was correct.[2]

The first explanation is rejected because it suggests that Christ was led astray by the superstition of His day. This view questions the omniscience required in divinity, hence denies the deity of Christ. The second view is rejected because it implies Christ led others astray. If He did that, we could question His statement, "I am . . . truth" (John 14:6). Christ would become the source of superstition.

Therefore, from an apologetic standpoint, to deny the existence of Satan is to suggest that Jesus Christ is not divine (even though He repeatedly claimed divinity), and that His ministry was comparable to the mission of a lunatic. Yet, Scripture is indeed the inerrant Word of God and the testimony of Jesus Christ is fully authoritative as to the person of Satan.

I. THE PERSONALITY OF SATAN

The devil is a real person. Originally, he was created in time as one of God's angels possessing all the attributes of angels. He was an incorporeal being with the power of personality. Even after his rebellion and fall, Satan remained a person. He is identified in

Scripture by personal pronouns, and he is involved in various activities belonging only to persons. Those who deny the existence of a devil with personality have no biblical basis for their conclusions.

God does not deny the personality of Satan. When Satan appeared with the angels, "The LORD said unto Satan, Hast thou considered my servant Job?" (Job 1:8). Later in the story, the Bible notes, "Satan came also among them to present himself before the LORD" (Job 2:1). In Zechariah's vision of the high priest's meeting with Satan, "The LORD said unto Satan, The LORD rebuke thee, O Satan; even the LORD that hath chosen Jerusalem rebuke thee" (Zech. 3:2). When tempted by Satan, Jesus six times used personal pronouns in His conversation with Satan (Matt. 4:7, 10).

Satan demonstrated intellectual ability, emotions, and an active will. His intelligence is reflected in his ability to memorize Scripture. When he tempted Jesus (Matt. 4:6), he cited an obscure verse out of context (Psa. 91:11-12) to give authority to his temptation. His superior intellect is further demonstrated by his ability to organize in excess of 100 million angels under him. The Bible also portrays the devil's temptations in terms like "wiles" (Eph. 6:11), "depths" (Rev. 2:24), and "devices" (2 Cor. 2:11).

Jesus warned Peter of the volitional side of Satan when he told him, "Satan hath desired to have you that he may sift you as wheat" (Luke 22:31). James identified fear as part of the emotional experience of all fallen angels (Jas. 2:19). They also have the sensation of pain, because they will someday "be tormented day and night for ever and ever" (Rev. 20:10).

It is the will of Satan that best characterizes him. Isaiah cited the fall of Satan coming as a result of his attempt to take the place of God in heaven. Satan revealed his selfish nature in the exclamation "I will" five times (Isa. 14:12-15). The apostle Paul also identified pride as the sin of Satan (1 Tim. 3:6).

Satan is also identified as performing acts normally ascribed to persons. He exercised the power of word selection as he tempted both Eve (Gen. 3:1-6) and Jesus (Matt. 4:1-11). He is currently accusing the brethren "before our God day and night" (Rev. 12:10). On at least two occasions, Satan engages in battle (Rev. 12:17; 20:8-9). When Moses appeared before Pharaoh, Satan demonstrated limited power to perform miracles when he turned the Egyptian magicians' rods into serpents (Exod. 7:12).

Satan has great power, but he is not omnipotent. Satan has great wisdom (much of it accumulated by experience), but he is not omniscient. Satan has his emissaries seemingly at every place, and his world system is ubiquitous, but he is not omnipresent.

Satan's driving motivation apparently focuses upon a total abrogation or a major hindering of the plan of God. On four separate occasions Scripture explores Satan's motivation. In Isaiah 14, Genesis 3, Luke 4, and 2 Thessalonians 2, a vivid picture unmasks Satan as he seeks to take by force an unlawful throne. Try as he might, Satan's most cunning plans will always fall short of their ultimate objective, for the creature is never able to excel beyond the Creator. As Christ is Lord of lords and King of kings, Satan must recognize and acknowledge that his existence is dependent upon the deity of Jesus Christ. Writing on this issue William Cooke states,

> The selfishness which engendered the first sin has, during the lapse of ages, produced and developed every malignant principle which now so darkly stains their condition. Hatred of God produced hatred of all good—of all good in itself, and of all beings that are good, and of envy at their happiness. From hatred and envy springs the desire to corrupt whatever is good, and destroy whatever is happy. This desire seeks its end by stratagem, deceit, and all available means within reach. The archfiend is called "Satan," which means an adversary: "The old serpent," because of his guile: "a liar from the beginning," "the father of lies," and, "when he speaketh a lie he speaketh of his own." He is called "Apollyon," which means Destroyer, because he delighteth in destroying the souls of men and "goeth about as a roaring lion seeking whom he may devour." Not only is he a destroyer, but a "murderer," a murderer of both bodies and souls; all his arts of seduction having murder as its ultimate object. All the sin and misery of our world for six thousand years, and all the sin and misery of its future history, and all the misery of hell, is not only the result of his agency and influence, but results in which he and his minions find their gratification.[3]

The saddest epitaph inscribed for any person is undoubtedly written upon the life of Satan; for in the death of Christ there was no provision made for Satan and his diabolical host. With no hope, Satan and his demons are given additional stimulus to deceive the naive and to pursue a life of sensual gratification.

II. THE ORIGIN OF SATAN

As one begins to study Satanology, the obvious question eventually emerges. Where did Satan come from? If God is indeed a benevolent God, and able to exercise complete authority and power, where did Satan's evil objectives come from, and, furthermore, why did God allow him to go as far as he did without attempting to stop him?

God could not have created anything evil. Originally, man was created in the image and likeness of God but fell into sin when Adam exercised his will in rebellion against God. Satan was also originally created as a being with power of personality and the freedom of choice. He was an angel with apparent honor and leadership in heaven. When Satan's pride blinded him and led him to exercise his will in rebellion against God, he was cast out of heaven (Isa. 14:12-15; cf. 2 Pet. 2:4; Jude 6).

Three prominent factors were present within Satan's mind as he sought to unlawfully ascend to the highest throne in the heavenlies.

THE FALL OF SATAN (Isa. 14:12-15)	
I will . . .	Take God's Place
Ascend into heaven	Acts 1:9-11
Exalt my throne	Rev. 22:1
Govern heaven	Isa. 2:1-4
Ascend above the heights	Phil. 2:9
Be like the Most High	Gen. 14:19-22

"YET THOU SHALT BE BROUGHT DOWN TO HELL TO THE SIDES OF THE PIT."

According to 1 Timothy 3:6 the first is pride: "Lest being lifted up with pride he fall into the condemnation of the devil." Satan's ambitious pride in his God-given splendor convinced him that he was worthy of God's throne and glory. Secondly, unbelief was also in the mind of Satan. As a result he failed to believe that God would really punish him if he committed a sin. Even as a small child will purposely test his parent's prohibitions in order to find out if they will really punish him, so Satan, deluded by his pride, did not seriously believe that God would punish him. Thirdly, thoughts of self-deception were undoubtedly entertained by Satan. He deceived himself into believing that he could actually wrestle the throne of God away from the Almighty. With blinded confidence Satan and his host moved upon the throne, only to be met with a barrage of divine judgments.

Concerning the problem of the first sin of the first angel, it may be observed that, under existing conditions, almost every avenue along which sin advances was wanting. Self-assertion against God was the only direction in which such a being could sin. On this patent truth Hooker has written: "It seemeth therefore that there was no other way for angels to sin, but by reflex of their understanding upon themselves, when being held with admiration of their own sublimity and honor, the memory of their subordination unto God and their dependency on Him was drowned in this conceit; whereupon their adoration, love and imitation of God could not choose but be also interrupted" (*Ecc. Pol.*, Book I, ch. iv. 2 cited by Gerhart, *ibid.*, 672). This conceit which assumed self-direction where the Creator proposed to be the authority and guide, is alluded to by the Apostle when he wrote of a "novice" in matters of church order: "lest being lifted up with pride he fall into the condemnation [crime] of the devil" (1 Tim. 3:6; cf. Isa. 14:12; Ezek. 28:17).[4]

Commenting on the motive behind Satan's rebellion, Chafer writes, "The essential evil character of sin here, as everywhere, is an unwillingness on the part of the creature to abide in the precise position in which he has been placed by the Creator.[5] Driven by an inner sense of false authority, Satan and his evil host embarked upon a fivefold series of "I will's."

A. ASCEND INTO HEAVEN. The ultimate desire of Satan was to take God's place. Lucifer's first attempt involved his ascent into the abode of God. The Bible identifies three heavens. The first heaven is the sky surrounding our planet, the atmosphere. The second heaven is the stellar heaven which is apparently the abode of angels. The third heaven is the dwelling place of God (2 Cor. 12:1-4). When Lucifer determined to ascend into heaven, he sought to move into the third heaven, the dwelling place of God. Satan wanted to ascend above the position and place where he was created and assume the place of his Creator.

B. EXALT HIS THRONE. Satan sought authority over the other angels. Satan wanted to be exalted above the stars. The term "star" is often used in the Bible to identify angels (Rev. 1:20; 12:4). Some commentators believe Satan ruled the angels as an archangel along with Michael and Gabriel. If this were the case, Satan then sought to expand his sphere of authority over Michael and Gabriel and those angels they ruled. If Satan could have accomplished this, he would be the ultimate authority in heaven, perhaps taking the place of God over the angels. If this trinity of archangels existed before the Fall, it may suggest why a third of the angels fell with Satan (Rev. 12:4).

Since Scripture is silent on the nature of Gabriel's position, a second view, as espoused by some theologians, suggests that, "As there is one archangel among angels that are holy, so there is one archangel among angels that are unholy.[6]

In regard to Satan's apparent successfulness in soliciting the loyalty of many thousands of angels, Ezekiel offers us some very helpful insight by the repeated usage of the word "merchandise" (28:5,16,18). It is also translated "traffick," which means "to go about," suggesting as Pember does, that Satan slandered God in an effort to attract others to join in his rebellion against God."[7]

C. GOVERN HEAVEN. Satan desired to "sit also upon the mount of the congregation, in the sides of the north" (Isa. 14:13). The phrase "mount of the congregation" is an expression relating to ruling in the kingdom of God (Isa. 2:1-4). Lucifer seemed to be saying, "I want a share in the kingdom." The problem was he wanted God's share. The "north side" is a term relating to God's presence in Scripture (Psa. 75:6-7). During the millennial reign of Christ, Christ will rule this earth from the north (Psa. 48:2).

D. ASCEND ABOVE THE HEIGHTS.   There can be no question that Satan was prepared to attempt a coup in heaven. His desire was not simply to get closer to God, but to surpass God. "I will ascend above the heights of the clouds" (Isa. 14:14). Clouds are often used to refer to the glory of God. In fact, 100 of the 150 uses of the word "cloud" in the King James Version have to do with divine glory.

As illustrated in these passages, "Jehovah appeared in the cloud (Ex. 16:10); the cloud was termed the cloud of Jehovah (Ex. 40:38); when Jehovah was present the cloud filled the house (1 Kings 8:10); Jehovah rideth upon a swift cloud (Ps. 104:3; Isa. 19:1); Christ is to come, as He went, upon the clouds of heaven (Matt. 24:30; Acts 1:9; Rev. 1:7); so the ransomed people appear (Israel, Isa. 60:8; and the Church, 1 Thess. 4:17)."[8]

Satan sought glory for himself that surpassed the glory of God. Paul revealed the ultimate desire of Satan when he wrote, "who opposeth and exalteth himself above all that is called God, or that is worshipped; so that he as God sitteth in the temple of God, shewing himself that he is God" (2 Thess. 2:4).

E. BE LIKE THE MOST HIGH.   When Abraham paid his tithes to Melchizedek, this priest "blessed him and said, Blessed be Abram of the most high God, possessor of heaven and earth" (Gen. 14:19). "The Most High" (El Elyon) means "the possessor of heaven and earth," one who exercises divine authority in both spheres.   When Jesus appeared to His disciples in Galilee after His death, he said, "All power is given unto me in heaven and in earth" (Matt. 28:18). Satan sought the authority of God for himself. By becoming most high, Satan would be the possessor of heaven and earth. By ascending into heaven he would rule angels and ultimately enjoy a messianic rule.

Since his fall, Satan has become a zealot for propagating evil and immorality among the human race. This thought leads one to seriously question the sanity of those who seek to exalt and worship a fallen and judged angel, who for all intents and purposes literally hates their existence. Commenting on his fall, Chafer writes,

The fall of this mighty angel was not a compromise between good and evil. He became the embodiment of evil and wholly void of good. The essential wickedness of this being could not be estimated by the finite mind. His wickedness, however, is constructive and in line with vast undertakings and ideas which are evil because of their opposition to God.[9]

Returning to Isaiah 14:12-17, it must be noted that no less than six views have been developed to explain the actual personalities in this passage.

The first three views cannot be accepted in light of verses 12-15, which strongly indicate a person who possesses much more power than a mere man. Furthermore, what human being has ever sought to ascend into the heavens and take by force the throne of God? The fourth view, likewise, has its

> Isaiah is referring to
>
> 1. Historical king of Babylon
> 2. Future king of Babylon
> 3. Sennacherib
> 4. Solely Satan
> 5. King in the time of Isaiah with Satan behind him
> 6. Future king and Satan behind him

difficulties, for the context suggests the presence of a human personality. In verse 10, two questions are asked of this fallen person, "Art thou also become as weak as we?" and "Art thou become like unto us?" Questions of this nature could never be directed against Satan in spite of the fact that he is a fallen creature. The fifth opinion is rejected by the opening verses of Isaiah 14, which speak of a futuristic time for Israel and not as a contemporary period to Isaiah's day. In verses 1-3, Israel is described as returning to their land, as ruling over those who had ruled over them, and as resting from their sorrows and fears. When has this ever occurred for Israel? In verse 4 the Jews take up a chant dealing with the fall of the king of Babylon, which continues to the end of the chapter.

It is possible that the passage refers to an earthly king prior to the millennial kingdom, where Satan is the energizing force behind the king. The idea of an energizing force behind a personality should be no surprise to us, for the Scripture describes several different instances of this occurring. For instance, during the earthly ministry of Christ, Satan moved in the mind of Peter in order to thwart Christ's going to the cross, yet realizing the source of Peter's words, Jesus goes beyond Peter and rebukes not only Peter but also Satan. In Revelation 13, we have another account of a man being empowered by a more powerful and salient force. However, the most tenable view is that Isaiah 14 refers to the fall of Satan.

In Ezekiel 28, a similar phenomenon to Isaiah 14 occurs. To argue that Ezekiel is referring only to an earthly king represents poor exegesis and gross oversight of phrases that extend well beyond the human realm.

In dealing with this passage of Scripture, Jennings writes,

> One single chapter (xxv) is enough to deal with the four nations; Ammon, Moab, Edom and Philistia; yet the next three chapters all refer, not even to a nation, but to the one city—why this disproportion? Seventeen verses to *four nations*, eighty-three verses to one city! Surely Tyre is not . . . . so overwhelmingly important or prominent.
> Does not this at once suggest a typical or shadowy character of this earth-city; and behind it and its rulers—princes and kings—must we not see, somewhat indistinct and dim perhaps, yet sufficiently clear suggestions as to be unmistakable, of unseen

spiritual verities, and these of transcendent importance? Yet whilst one may get such light as this apparent disproportion affords, we must not overlook the positive significance of this city being thus selected, and its king affording a type and more than a type, of the dread personality we are considering.[10]

In summary, five prominent arguments from Ezekiel 28 reveal that Ezekiel is looking beyond the King of Tyre to the Satanic force that controls him. The first argument is: (1) that no such lofty terminology by Jehovah should be directed to a mere fallen man. (2) No king of Tyre was ever in Eden, only Satan. (3) The person spoken of was created "perfectly." The only other option is Adam and he is not in view. (4) No man was set above all the other angels and created beings, only Satan. (5) The "stones of fire" (v. 14) may denote the first estate of this angel, which was one of walking in unbroken fellowship with divine holiness.

III. THE ORIGIN OF EVIL

Many theologians discuss the origin of evil in relation to Adam and Eve while in the Garden of Eden. However, the actual origin of evil was not initiated on an earthly scene, but within the glories of heaven. Man was tempted by an external force. Although this does not make him any less guilty, it does suggest to us that evil was present in the universe prior to Genesis. On the other hand, Satan's sin arose within his own heart, leading many to believe that this is why no salvation is possible for angels, yet available to mankind.

As put forth earlier, why did Satan choose to forfeit the glories of heaven for a chance to seize the throne of God? To answer this question with selfish ambitious pride is correct. Yet the heart of the matter goes much deeper and asks two additional questions, "How could an uninfluenced, unfallen angel sin?" and "How could a holy God permit any creature to fall?" The nature of these questions go beyond the origin of Satan, though not inherently separated from his actions, and seek to intelligently understand how evil came into existence. The complexity of the situation is referred to by Jennings when he writes,

> Some will perhaps ask, if he did not come from God, as the Devil, since God cannot produce evil, where *did* he come from, or how was he produced in that evil character? I have neither wish nor ability to go into matters too high, or too deep for plain people like myself, yet may we perhaps, even in a simple way, get some light on this problem. We have seen him presented to us in Scripture as the highest expression of creature perfection. Then let me ask, "Which is highest in the scale of creation, a tree or a stone?" You at once answer "a tree." "Why?" "Because it has more freedom in life and growth." "True. Which is highest, a tree or an ox?" "An ox." "Why?" "Because it has will and freedom of motion according to that will, which the tree lacks." "True again. Once more: Which is higher, an ox or a man?" "The man." "Why?" "Again because he is not controlled—narrowed—limited by the laws that

shut in the brute creation. By his spirit he is capable of recognizing his Creator; he becomes therefore a creature with a moral responsibility; but this predicates a greater *freedom of will*, and its powers of going in any direction.

Then do you not see how the highest of all creatures must, by that very fact, be launched from his Maker's hand, with no external clog of heavy flesh—a gross material body that forbids the free and full exercise of his desires—with no internal law compelling him ever to continue on certain prescribed moral lines whether good or bad; but with liberty and power of going in any direction. Indeed in such perfect equipoise as to leave him truly *free*.[11]

Jennings does not rule out the possibility of man's understanding the nature of Satan's fall, but we are admonished not to limit our reasoning to the physical sphere, especially in ethical and spiritual areas.   Those who have failed to draw a distinction have in some cases erroneously accused God of creating Satan's desires. They argue that if God had not given him so much liberty and external beauty, Satan would not have started an insurgence. Those who endorse this syllogism fail to understand the nature of free will in relation to a free moral creature. God did not give Satan too much or too little of what he needed to avert his fall, nor did God allow a place for sin in His eternal decree. As suggested by Chafer, sin is the product of choice, not inherent weakness.

The decree of God anticipated all that would ever be; yet sin originates, not in the divine decree, but in the free act of the sinner. Sin is not in the constitution of creatures as they came from the creative hand of God, else all would sin. Sin is not an inherent weakness of the creature, else all would have failed. Sin is not a concomitant with free moral agency, else all free moral agents must fall. Dr. Gerhart, writing of the first sin, says: "*Ego* asserts itself against its own fundamental law, a fact for which no reason is to be assigned other than this, that the possibility of false choosing is a prerogative of finite autonomous being."[12]

It was necessary that God create the angels with free will in order that they might offer true praise and worship to God. Prior to his fall, Satan had the power of choice, not between good and evil, but between following the will of God or his own will. Writing on this issue, Augustine states,

If we ask the cause of the misery of the bad angels it occurs to us, and not unreasonably, that they are miserable because they have forsaken Him who supremely is, and have turned to themselves who have no such essence . . . If the further question be asked, What was the efficient cause of the evil will? There is none. For what is it which makes the will bad, when it is the will itself which makes the action bad? And consequently the bad will is the cause of the bad action, but nothing is the efficient cause of the bad will. . . . When the will abandons what is above itself, and turns to what is lower, it becomes evil, not because that is evil to which it turns, but because the turning itself is wicked. Therefore, it is not an inferior thing which has made the will evil, but it is itself which has become so by wickedly desiring an inferior thing.[13]

Therefore, to answer the question of how an uninfluenced unfallen angel could fall, it is necessary to understand the function of free will and the desire to usurp that will over a much higher will. For God to react and stop Satan from his plans, while he was entertaining them for the first time, would have squelched his God-given privilege of free will.

IV. THE TIME OF SATAN'S FALL

Since Scripture never clearly mentioned a precise time of Satan's fall, it is necessary to use deductive reasoning to pinpoint this time without contradicting the revealed truth we possess:

A. THE FALL IN ETERNITY PAST. Some would argue that Satan's creation and fall must have occurred in eternity past, usually before creation. They cite for their proof-text Job 38:4-7, which suggests that angels were present and sang together as the world was being created. A second proof text used in Ezekiel 28:13-19, seems to suggest that sufficient time was needed for Satan to be created, to secretly plan his attempt to overthrow God, to rally the support of an angelic host, and move upon the throne of God. The first verse in the Bible is a summary statement of all creation and is not necessarily the first chronological step of creation. Therefore, the statement, "In the beginning God created the heaven(s)" allows the creation of angels long before the first day of earth's creation.

B. THE FALL IN THE GAP BETWEEN GENESIS 1:1 AND 1:2. Many believe that Satan was created in the same creative experience that is described, "In the beginning God created the heaven and the earth" (Gen. 1:1). The word heaven is plural in the Hebrew implying the three heavens were created in the original creative act. Actually, creation involves the whole of heaven and all its innumerable parts. When God created the heaven it probably included the creation of His throne (only God is eternal in His nature, not His throne), and those beings (angels) who worship God. Obviously, when the angels were created, Satan was included in that act.

Between the act of creation and God's pronouncement, "the earth was without form and void" (v. 2), there was destruction upon the original creation, including Satan, for his insurrection against God. Hence they deduce that Satan, who was beautiful and desirable in Ezekiel 28, but became subtle and dangerous in Genesis 3, must have fallen during the catastrophic judgment on the original creation.

C. The Fall After Creation. The creation of Satan occurred during the six days of creation, thus necessitating that Satan's fall occurred shortly after his creation. Supporters of this view would quote Exodus 20:11, "For in six days the LORD made heaven and earth, the sea, and all that in them is, and rested the seventh day: wherefore, the Lord blessed the sabbath day, and hallowed it" (emphasis added).

Some support can be rallied for this third view, which does not really demand a short period of time between Satan's creation and fall. According to Genesis 1:31, God clearly announced that everything that He made was very good (this could not be true if sin was already present in the universe). In between the end of the sixth day and the appearance of Satan (in his fallen state) in Genesis 3, we cannot be dogmatic about the exact amount of time, but it should be sufficient time for Satan to incite his rebellion against God. Writing on this subject, Buswell states:

> The Scripture does not indicate precisely at what time, with reference to the creation of the world and man, the angels were created. Satan, the leader of the angels who fell, makes his appearance as a creature already fallen, while man is still in the Garden of Eden. If the phrase, "everything which he had made," in Genesis 1:31 means everything without exception, then we must infer that the angels had been created before the end of the sixth day, but that the fall of Satan and the evil angels took place after God's pronouncement that "everything he had made" was "all very good" (Gen. 1:31). So far as the teaching of the Scripture is concerned, the creation of the angels may have taken place at any time prior to the end of the sixth day. The fall of Satan must have taken place between the end of the sixth day and the temptation of man in the Garden of Eden.[14]

V. The Character Of Satan

The Bible describes the character of Satan in three ways. First, certain names or titles are ascribed to him which reflect his true nature. Second, his subtle character describes his behavior. In the third place, Satan is described through his nature and his kingdom.

A. Names of Satan. Just as God uses His own names to reveal who he is and what is His nature, so God has revealed the nature of Satan through his name. Over thirty different names or titles are given to this sinful, fallen angel. Unlike Western practices of randomly selecting a name for a person, those in the Eastern lands place great stress upon the name, for it depicts specific characteristics of that person.

B. Satan's subtle character. The Bible makes no effort to hide the craftiness of Satan. When false teachers and false apostles appeared in the church at Corinth, Paul wrote,

"And no marvel; for Satan himself is transformed into an angel of light" (2 Cor. 11:14). The apostle acknowledged that one of his purposes in writing a second epistle to the Corinthians was "lest Satan should get an advantage of us; for we are not ignorant of his devices" (2 Cor. 2:11). He further recognized the cunning and subtle character of Satan when he advised the Ephesians to "put on the whole armour of God, that ye may be able to stand against the wiles of the devil" (Eph. 6:11).

THE NAMES AND TITLES OF SATAN			
1.	Satan - Job 1:6	16.	Wicked one – I John 3:12
2.	Devil - Rev. 12:7	17.	Prince of the power of the air - Eph. 2:2
3.	Apollyon - Rev. 9:11	18.	Prince of this world - John 14:30
4.	Beelzebub - Matt. 12:27	19.	God of this age - 2 Cor. 4:4
5.	Belial - 2 Cor. 6:15	20.	Dragon - Rev. 12:9
6.	Old Serpent - Rev. 20:2	21.	Beast out of the bottomless pit - Rev. 11:7
7.	Adversary - 1 Pet. 5:8	22.	Accuser of the brethren - Rev. 12:10
8.	Anointed cherub - Ezek. 28	23.	Angel of the bottomless pit – Rev. 9:11
9.	Deceiver of the whole world - Rev. 12:9	24.	Angel of light – 2 Cor. 11:14
10.	Evil one - John 17:15	25.	Enemy - Matt. 13:39
11.	Leviathan - Isa. 27:1	26.	Father of lies - John 8:44
12.	Lucifer – Isa. 14:12	27.	Liar - John 8:44
13.	Murderer - John 8:44	28.	Prince of demons - Matt. 9:34
14.	Roaring lion - 1 Pet. 5:8	29.	Man of sin - 2 Thess. 2:3
15.	Son of the morning - Isa. 14:12	30.	Thief - John 10:10

In stark contrast to Satan's original lofty and majestic position as protector of God's throne, he has now become the embodiment of evil. By employing for evil all the cunning and shrewd wisdom with which he was endowed, Satan is truly a formidable enemy to those who acknowledge Jesus Christ as their Lord. Addressing this subject, Lockyer writes,

> A fact that must not be lost sight of is that the Devil, although a fallen angelic being, is *still* an angel. True, he is a rebel angel, a prevaricator, but an angel created by God with and among the other celestial spirits. Even his fall and disgrace did not deprive him of the angelic nature that is the definition of his being. Satan retains the privileges of his unchanged nature and is still able to display his original grandeur, 2 Cor. 11:14. Although now the Angel of Darkness, the Devil subsists because in spite of everything he is still an angel. We do not know the breathless height of perfection from which Satan fell: we only know that he carried such perfection with him into darkness.
>
> By his angelic nature, the Devil enjoys that independence distinctively characteristic of a pure spirit. Because of his "angelic independence he is immune to pain, to injury, to sickness, to death, indeed, he is even immune to the human discomfort of being crowded! Like God, and unlike man, he has no body. There are in him, then, no parts to be dismembered, no possibilities of corruption and decay, no threat of a separation of parts that will result in death. He is incorruptible, immune to the vagaries, the pains, the limitations of the flesh, immortal. Only God, by His Almighty power, could destroy Satan, recalling the borrowed existence by which the Devil lives; and this God will not do." Angels are spirits as opposed to flesh and blood, Luke 24:39; Eph. 6:12.[15]

C. EVIL NATURE OF SATAN. It is the nature of a man that causes him to act as he does. The same principle exists as we try to better understand Satan. John identified the devil as the originator and chief practitioner of sin (1 John 3:8). He further describes Satan as "that wicked one" (1 John 5:18). Jesus called Satan a liar (John 8:44) and a thief (John 10:10). The evil acts of Satan are a natural expression of his evil nature. "The thief cometh not, but for to steal, and to kill, and to destroy" (John 10:10). The apostle Paul recognized the destructive nature of Satan when he wrote, "The god of this world hath blinded the minds of them which believe not, lest the light of the glorious gospel of Christ, who is the image of God, should shine unto them" (2 Cor. 4:4).

We should never underestimate the depraved and debauched levels to which Satan would stoop, simply to thwart the plan of God. The extreme actions of Satan have been well articulated by Lewis Sperry Chafer.

When meeting the last Adam in the wilderness, Satan did not say, as he did to the first Adam, Ye shall be as Elohim; for Satan knows with no uncertainty that Jesus Christ is *God*. However, his master passion to himself *like the most High* was expressed in the words, "Worship me." The wicked and presumptuous character of that request cannot be duplicated in the history of the universe, nor will it ever be duplicated in future ages. It is probably that at no place does the lie come into such manifestation of its false and wicked character as here, where it addresses itself directly to the One who is Truth. It was audacious beyond measure for Satan to solicit the cooperation of angels and man; but who will estimate the wickedness of the one who suggests that God the Creator become a suppliant at the feet of a creature of His own hand? Pride had evidently befogged the mind of this being to the point of angelic insanity, yet not an insanity which bespeaks irresponsibility. Out of and above all the experiences of the threefold temptation in the wilderness, the one truth is disclosed, namely, that Satan purposes to be *like the most High*.[16]

D. NATURE OF SATAN'S KINGDOM. In order to constitute a kingdom certain factors must be present. There must be a king (governmental structure), subjects to rule over, a designated geographical area to rule over, and a common, unifying goal that stimulates their existence. In Satan's kingdom it is blatantly obvious that Satan rules with an iron hand, demanding strict obedience from his demonic followers, lest his kingdom suffer internal divisions (Luke 11:18). The subjects of Satan's kingdom are twofold; those angels who fell during his rebellion, and the hearts of unregenerate men (Luke 8:44). The domain of his kingdom is not just the physical earth, but the world system that denies the supernatural and exalts the natural. Berkhof clarifies the issue.

He remains the leader of the angelic hosts which he carried with him in his fall, and employs them in desperate resistance to Christ and His Kingdom. He is also called repeatedly "the prince of this (not, "of the") world," John 12:31; 14:30; 16:11, and even "the god of this world." II Cor. 4:4. This does not mean that he is in control of the world, for God is in control, and He has given all authority to Christ, but it does convey the idea that he is in control of this evil world, the world in so far as it is ethically separated from God. This is clearly indicated in Eph. 2:2, where he is called "the prince of the powers of the air, of the spirit that now worketh in the sons of disobedience."[17]

Finally, the common and unifying goal of Satan's kingdom focuses upon hindering the plan of God and manipulating as many souls as possible to eternal separation from God.

VI. JUDGMENT OF SATAN AND HIS KINGDOM

Chronology of Satan's Judgment:		
A.	Record of Satan's fall (2nd heaven)	Isa. 14:12-17; Ezek. 28; Luke 10:18
B.	Indictment recorded	Gen. 3:16
C.	Judgment penalty displayed	Col. 2:14; Heb. 2:14-15; John 12:13; 16:11
D.	Confinement to earth (1st heaven)	Rev. 12:12-17
E.	Confinement during the Millennium	Isa. 24; Rev. 20
F.	Execution of judgment	Rev. 20:10

A. RECORD OF SATAN'S FALL.   In Isaiah 14, Ezekiel 28, and Luke 10:18 are separate testimonies of Satan's sin and removal from the presence of God's throne.   Although these testimonies emphasize different aspects of Satan's fall (Ezekiel deals with Satan's position prior to the fall; Isaiah focuses on his militant attempt to grasp the throne of God; and Christ describes the sudden and swift expulsion from heaven), they are internally consistent.

Some have argued that Luke 10:18 refers not to a past judgment, but to a futuristic judgment (Rev. 12).   The context is not explicit as to which event Christ was referring. However, the more probable interpretation is a reference to Satan's fall in Genesis. Support for this conclusion is found in the immediate context in which the excited apostles, while reporting to Jesus their successful confrontations with the demon world, cause Him to reflect back to the time Satan was cast down from the third heaven, and how Satan is even now being defeated by His apostles.

B. INDICTMENT RECORDED.   When a person commits a crime and reasonable suspicion attributes the crime to him, he is indicted with a particular charge. In Genesis 3, man and Satan are clearly charged by God with committing sin. As a result, God issued the various curses upon the guilty parties. With man, the indictment can possibly be rescinded. However, with Satan, no parole is possible.

C. JUDGMENT PENALTY DISPLAYED.   Through the death of Christ, Satan was judged and his works destroyed. Hebrews 2:14-15 says, "Forasmuch then as the children are partakers of flesh and blood, he also himself likewise took part of the same; that through death he might destroy him that had the power of death, that is, the devil; And deliver them who through fear of death were all their lifetime subject to bondage" (emphasis added). Even though Satan has been judged and openly humiliated, he has not yet actually received his punishment. In 1 Peter 5:8,

Satan is still actively destroying the receptivity of the souls of men to the gospel, but in Revelation 20:10 his judgment will be completed. Jennings compares the relationship between Saul and David to the kingdom of Satan and coming kingdom of Jesus Christ.

Thus you remember that God permitted Israel to choose their first King, and they chose Saul; as to whom we are told that *"from his shoulders and upward he was higher than any of the people."* Why are we told this? Have we exhausted its significance when we picture to ourselves the towering height of that human king? I am sure not; but rather would the Spirit of God, provide a perfect figure or type of him who, exactly in the same way, towered over *his* fellows: in other words was, as the other Scriptures we have glanced at show the most exalted of all created spiritual intelligences.

But Saul disobeys, or, to use language that shall suggest the parallel I desire to keep before us;—*"iniquity was found in him"*; see Ezek. xxviii:15; and he was set aside from his kingly office: the kingdom was rent from him (I Sam. xv:27, 28), and then God anointed another king of His own choice: A *shepherd king*, David! Now no one questions David being a type of the beloved Son of God; why should not Saul afford us also a type of His opponent? He surely does.

But,—and this is the point that must be carefully noted and weighed,—*Saul retains the throne of Israel, and is still recognized as the king long after he is divinely rejected*; the sentence is pronounced, but judgment is not at once executed, whilst David, the now true king, is "hunted like a partridge upon the mountains, or finds his refuge in the cave of Adullam"! God does not at once intervene by *power*, and take the dignities of the kingdom from Saul,—although he has lost all *title* to them—and put them in David's hand: the power is Saul's,—the title is David's. The latter is king *de jure*, and former *de facto*.

Do you not see the marvelous and clear analogy? Satan too, whilst he may have forfeited all *title* to the throne of the earth—we shall consider this more carefully directly—still cleaves as did Saul, to its power and dignity; claims, as did Saul, all power of its government; whilst the true David, to whom all belongs in *title*, is as it were, in the cave of Adullam, where a few "discontented" ones, those who are not satisfied with such a condition of things—have found their way to Him, and own Him, even the day of His rejection, as rightful Lord of all. Therefore whilst Satan is the prince of this world at the present time, we are led by the analogy of the inspired history, as by every clear Scripture, to regard Him as its *usurping* prince: a prince in *power*, but not in *title*.

Yet whilst now a usurper, as Saul was: still since he was, also as Saul, divinely anointed as king, the dignity of that anointing still lingers on him, so that Michael recognized that dignity—not speaking evil, but reverently (even as David spoke of Saul ever as "the Lord's Anointed") and saying *"the Lord* rebuke thee."[18]

D. CONFINEMENT TO THE EARTH. During the Great Tribulation, John the Beloved describes in Revelation 12, the casting down of Satan from heaven by Michael. Some have erroneously believed that John is simply describing Satan's original fall from heaven in Genesis or possibly the casting down related to the death of Christ. Yet a careful reading of Revelation 12:5-12 reveals a chronology of events, some of which have already transpired and some are still future, even to our time. In verse 5 John tells us of the birth of Christ and His ascension to Glory before Pentecost. From verse 5 to verse 6 a large span of history is quickly passed over, as John introduces us to the Great Tribulation, in which the woman (Israel) is forced to flee for her life into the wilderness for 1260 days. After Israel's flight, the battle rages in the second heaven, resulting in the expulsion of Satan and his demons to the first heaven, or the immediate earth. It is this future expulsion that so enrages Satan that he empowers the Beast (Rev. 13) to further vent his wrath upon God's chosen people.

E. CONFINEMENT DURING THE MILLENNIUM. At the end of the Great Tribulation, while the blood is still flowing from the battle of Armageddon, Satan will be bound and cast into the bottomless pit for a thousand years. According to Revelation 20:1-3, the earth will again enjoy the blessings of God, man will enjoy longevity of life, and there will be no satanic temptations.

F. EXECUTION OF JUDGMENT. Near the end of the millennial period, Satan is loosed and allowed to deceive many, forming a final rebellion against Christ who rules in Jerusalem. In Revelation 20:9-10, God intercedes, totally annihilates all opposition and casts the devil permanently into the lake of fire, never again to tempt men to evil.

VII. THE WORK OF SATAN

All of Satan's work is against God. At times he actively opposes the work or plan of God. On other occasions, he simply imitates God so as to draw men away from the simple plan of God. But in the final analysis, Satan is bound by his corrupted nature to destroy all that he can. These three points comprise the outline of this section.

The Threefold Work of Satan
1. Opposition to the will and work of God
2. Imitation of the work of God
3. Destruction of all that is good.

A. OPPOSITION TO GOD.   Jesus portrayed the devil in one of His parables as the enemy of God (Matt. 13:39).   As such, the devil is constantly opposing God and all God does.   Satan first appears in the garden of Eden to oppose the plan and work of God that He established in Paradise. That opposition betrayed itself continually in his attempt to destroy the messianic line. Then he sought to destroy the race God sought to redeem. When God chose a people of His own, the nation Israel, Satan unreservedly sought their destruction. Throughout the life of Christ, Satan sought to distract the Saviour from His mission. God works through the church today, so Satan is opposed to the work of God there. According to Chafer, Satan is actively opposing the program of God in no less than twenty-four different areas, and as the last days draw nearer we can expect an increase in Satan's work (2 Tim. 3:1-9).

(1) He repudiated God in the beginning (Isa. 14:12-14).

(2) He drew a third part of the stars of heaven after him (Rev. 12:4).

(3) He sinned from the beginning (1 John 3:8).

(4) He is a liar from the beginning (John 8:44).

(5) In the Garden of Eden he belittled God and advised the first parents to repudiate God (Gen. 3:1-5).

(6) He insinuated to Jehovah that Job loved and served Him only as he was hired to do so (Job 1:9). No greater insult could be addressed to Jehovah than that He is not really to be loved on the ground of His own worthiness, but, being rich, is able to hire men like Job to *pretend* that they love Him.

(7) When permitted to act his own part, Satan brought five terrible calamities on Job (Job 1:13-2:7).

(8) He stood up against Israel (1 Chron. 21:2; Ps. 109:6; Zech. 3:1-2).

(9) He weakened the nations (Isa. 14:2).

(10) He made the earth to tremble (Isa. 14:16).

(11) He did shake kingdoms (Isa. 14:16).

(12) He makes the world a wilderness (Isa. 14:17).

(13) He destroys the cities thereof (Isa. 14:17).

(14) He opened not the house of his prisoners (Isa. 14:17).

(15) He causes war on earth with all its horrors; for when bound, war ceases, and when loosed, war is resumed (Rev. 20:2, 7-8).

(16) He tempted the Son of God forty days and then left Him but for a season. He proposed to Christ that He forsake His mission, that He distrust His Father's goodness, and that He worship the devil (Luke 4:1-13).

(17) He bound a daughter of Abraham eighteen years (Luke 13:16; cf. Acts 10:38).

(18) He entered Judas and prompted him to betray the Son of God (John 13:2).

(19) He blinds the minds of those who are lost (2 Cor. 4:3-4).

(20) He takes away the Word out of the hearts of the unsaved, lest they should believe and be saved (Luke 8:12).

(21) He deals with saints with wiles and snares (Eph. 6:11; 2 Tim. 2:26).

(22) He has exercised and abused the power of death (Heb 2:14; cf. Rev. 1:18).

(23) He, an adversary, as a roaring lion goeth about seeking whom he may devour (1 Pet. 5:8).

(24) He is opposed to God; is the persecutor of saints, the "father" of lies. Through his emissaries he dethrones reason, tortures human beings, and moves them to superstition and idolatry.[19]

To fully understand Satan's hatred of God's program, it is necessary to fully understand the evil nature of Satan. This is seen in the contrasting philosophies of the Spirit of Holiness and the spirit of evil. Strong delineates the differences.

> Contrasts between the Holy Spirit and the spirit of evil: 1. the dove, and the serpent; 2. the father of lies, and the Spirit of truth; 3. men possessed by dumb spirits, and men given wonderful utterance in diverse tongues; 4. the murderer from the beginning, and the life-giving Spirit, who regenerates the soul and quickens our mortal bodies; 5. the adversary, and the Helper; 6. the slanderer, and the Advocate; 7. Satan's sifting, and the Master's winnowing; 8. the organizing intelligence and malignity of the evil one, and the Holy Spirit's continuation of all the forces of matter and mind to build up the kingdom of God; 9. the strong man fully armed, and a stronger than he; 10. the evil one who works only evil, and the Holy One who is the author of holiness in the hearts of men.[20]

As a result of Satan's inherent evilness towards God, it is reasonable to assume that anything or any person who aligns himself with God immediately becomes the object of Satan's wrath. A quick examination of history, in which powerful movements for Christianity suddenly became nonexistent, effective preachers lapsed for a moment in their testimony and disqualified themselves for the ministry, or dynamic churches crumbled from internal divisions, reveals to us that Satan is not inactive, but alive and well.

> Christians are not exempt from this inability to understand where and how Satan is working. In fact, because his doctrine has been neglected for so long, they are sometimes the least discerning of all in understanding the world system. Young Christians are particularly vulnerable. As Francis Schaeffer has said, "We have left the next generation naked in the face of 20th century thought by which they are surrounded."
>
> Satan is not the man below, heaping coals into an eternal furnace. He's the original "jet-setter"; he's "right on" with the latest cause. When God asked Satan a direct question, his answer showed outrageous arrogance: "And the Lord said to Satan, From where do you come? And Satan—the adversary and the accuser—answered the Lord, From going to and fro on the earth, and from walking up and down on it" (Job 2:2, *Amplified Bible*).

What a picture! Satan trucking all over the earth, constantly doing his thing in every spot he can! He's working in our world system through governments, education, business, and culture. You name it — he'll tame it.

This modern "promoter" has had some help from his advance men who began planning his twentieth century campaign a few hundred years ago. Stand by for the shock waves from the nineteenth century thought-bombs that are threatening to bring the whole civilization into Armageddon.[21]

1. *Messianic line.* As soon as God in His righteousness judged the first sin in the garden, He also in His mercy promised a Redeemer. "And I will put enmity between thee and the woman, and between thy seed and her seed; it shall bruise thy head, and thou shalt bruise his heel" (Gen. 3:15). With the accuracy of His foreknowledge, God predicted Satan's opposition to the coming Redeemer. It did not take long to materialize. With the birth of Abel, the devil began his opposition. Satan worked in Cain to kill his brother, Abel. With Abel dead, the line would be broken and Messiah could never be born. But God replaced Abel with Seth (Gen. 4:25). Every attempt to destroy the godly line by extinction or by sexual contamination was an attempt by Satan to destroy the coming Messiah. Even in a small way, the danger to David, the shepherd boy, carried out Satan's plot. David twice tangled with wild beasts (1 Sam. 17:35). Satan may have felt David's great sin with Bathsheba would prevent God from using him in the line of Messiah, but in contrast, it was that very relationship God chose to use (Matt. 1:6).

At one point in Israel's history, the royal lineage was nearly destroyed when Athaliah sought to kill every person of royal birth. However, the protective action of Jehosheba preserved the life of Joash until he was able to assume the throne with the help of Jehoiada, the high priest (2 Kgs. 11:1-5).

2. *Human race.* God created man in His image and likeness to have fellowship with God and dominion over the earth. When Satan approached Eve in the garden, he promised Eve, not only that she would not die (Gen. 3:4), but that eating the fruit would lead to her experiencing life on a higher plane (Gen. 3:5). With the entrance of sin into the race, Satan knew God would have to judge them as He had judged him. Satan sought to contaminate the human race by leading them into grievous sins (Gen. 6:5). God did judge most of them for their sin, but eight—Noah and his family—were kept safe in the ark (Gen. 7:13).

In the parable of the sower (Matt. 13:4-19), Satan is seen actively removing the message of the gospel from the hearts of unbelievers. Satan doesn't necessarily have to steal the message of salvation from man's heart. He is equally effective in diluting the message with erroneous teaching, replacing it with a more appealing desire, or simply dismissing it as being a fanatical and old-fashioned perspective. Very few realize that Satan's temptations are both negative and positive; he takes away the seed sown and he sows tares.

3. *Israel.* From the time of the call of Abraham, the devil has been the enemy of the Jew. God had told Abraham, "Look now toward heaven, and tell [count] the stars, if thou be able to number them: and he said unto him, So shall thy seed be" (Gen. 15:5). After the nation went to Egypt and began to grow as God has promised, Satan moved Pharaoh to command the destruction of all male children (Exod. 1:16). Later, Satan used the personal animosity of Haman toward Mordecai to plan the first systematic genocide of the Jews. The book of Esther records this attempt and Haman's ultimate defeat (Esther 3:6; 7:9-10). Satan has continued to raise up anti-Semitic leaders who have unsuccessfully attempted to exterminate the Jews.

4. *Christ.* At the birth of Christ, Satan used Herod to plan the murder of all children Jesus' age in Bethlehem (Matt. 2:16). After forty days in the wilderness, Satan himself tempted Jesus trying to destroy the ministry of Christ before He could redeem the world (Matt. 4:1-11). On other occasions, Satan used Peter (Matt. 16:23) and Judas (John 13:27) to attempt to thwart Christ from His purpose. Even in the final hours before His death, Satan attempted to convince Christ to bypass the cross. After Christ died and was buried, Satan inspired the Jewish leaders to appoint guards and seal the tomb in a feeble effort to prevent the resurrection.

5. *Church.* Jesus said, "I will build my church; and the gates of hell shall not prevail against it" (Matt. 16:18). From the first mention of the church in Scripture, Jesus taught that it would be in opposition to Satan. The picture of gates is not that of a church struggling to hold out against the incredible opposition of the near overwhelming forces of hell, but rather that of an aggressive church smashing down the strongholds of the devil as he feebly attempts to keep the dynamic church from winning people to Christ.

As we read the book of Acts we see this principle at work. Opposition toward the church stimulated the church to more aggressive outreach. Throughout history, Satan has actively opposed the work of God by torturing and killing saints. But, the martyrs have been the seed of the church. Under the most severe opposition, God has worked to glorify Himself. His church has not only survived the opposition of the devil, it has survived it victoriously.

6. *Scripture.* History is replete with examples of evil men seeking to undermine man's confidence in the Bible. The Roman Emperor Diocletian ratified an edict which would secure the death of all those possessing a copy of the New Testament Scriptures. The Spanish inquisition saw the destruction of many Bibles. The rise of modern science introduced a new method of examining traditional values and absolutes, which gave birth to German rationalization. The Catholic Church sought to keep the Scriptures from the masses, suggesting that only the Church had the authority to interpret the Scriptures. Voltaire publicly boasted that the Bible would be obsolete within several decades and his work would replace it. More recently attempts have been made to exclude "meaningless or less profitable passages" from Scripture, or to neutralize the Scripture in order to rid it of its prejudices. Although the motive behind these alterations may or may not be overtly evil, they nonetheless fail to honor

the warning in Revelation 22:18-19, which strongly advises against removing from or adding to the Scripture.

7. *Accomplishes God's will.* In spite of themselves and their opposition to God, Satan and his demons execute God's plans of punishing the ungodly or chastening the good. In relation to the ungodly, Psalm 78:49 states, "He cast upon them the fierceness of his anger, wrath, and indignation and trouble, by sending evil angels among them." This verse suggests that God employs Satan and his demon host to keep the evil acts of the ungodly in check. Initially, the idea of God using Satan to control in part the world's evil sounds paradoxical. However, one must understand that every man is the object of Satan's hatred, and as long as man (even the most ungodly) is allowed to breathe, there exists the possibility that he might accept Christ as his Lord and Saviour. Satan is also used by God to chasten the good. In the Corinthian Church an immoral problem developed and the leadership failed to actively deal with it. When Paul learned of it, his counsel was firm, yet gracious, "Deliver such an one unto Satan for the destruction of the flesh, that the spirit may be saved in the day of the Lord Jesus" (1 Cor. 5:5). Eventually the fallen brother was restored to fellowship, yet it would likely not have occurred if he had not been excommunicated from the church and subjected to sifting by Satan. A similar situation occurred with Hymenaeus and Alexander, in which Paul in 1 Timothy 1:20 states, "Hymenaeus and Alexander, whom I delivered unto Satan, that they may learn not to blaspheme." Through excommunication Paul had hoped to alter their conduct; however, the greater fear experienced by these men was not the alienation of fellowship, but the subjection to Satan's authority. Finally, Satan is used by God to develop specific circumstances to carry out the will of God. When Satan moved upon the mind of Herod to slaughter the male children in Bethlehem, it was in fulfillment of God's prophecy. The working of Satan in the heart of Ananias and Sapphira and their ultimate death became the catalyst for a sudden surge in church growth. In the future, Satan will be used of God to draw the nations together for the Battle of Armageddon, the outcome of which is already recorded. Nonetheless, blinded by self-deception and the rejection of God's Word, Satan will be instrumental in producing the proper setting for Christ's return to the earth.

B. THE IMITATOR. One of Satan's desires is to be like the Most High (Isa. 14:14), if not to be God. But Satan is not God, nor is his nature anything like God. To accomplish his desire, Satan imitates God and carries out much of his work by counterfeit righteousness, rather than a manifestation of his wicked nature. The following chart contrasts the works of God and the devil's attempts to reproduce them.

THE COUNTERFEITS OF SATAN			
1.	Jesus is the Son of God - Psa. 2:1	1.	Satan is the god of this world - Eph. 2:2

2.	Trinity – Matt. 28:20	2.	Tri-unity - Rev. 20:10
3.	Mystery of godliness - 1 Tim. 3:16	3.	Mystery of iniquity - 2 Thess. 2:7
4.	Children of God - John 1:12	4.	Children of Satan - John 8:44
5.	God's mark on His servants - Rev. 7:3	5.	Satan's mark of the beast - Rev. 13:16
6.	Miracles of Christ - Matt. 4:23	6.	Miracles of Satan - 2 Thess. 2:9
7.	Christ the true Light - John 1 :7	7.	Angel of Light - 2 Cor. 11:14
8.	Christ appoints apostles - Matt. 10:1	8.	Satan's counterfeit apostles – 2 Cor. 11:13

1. *Imitation.* From the very beginning, it has been Satan's desire to be like God (Isa. 14:14). In his present work, Satan is attempting to duplicate the works of God. Almost everything God has established, Satan has duplicated. There even exists today a satanic "bible" and a church of Satan. When Moses stood before the Egyptian Pharaoh, delivered his message and validated it with the miracles that God gave to him, undoubtedly Pharaoh was not impressed for he had seen his own priests on occasions perform similar feats. Satan's inability to create or be original, offers us some insight into the mental capacity of Satan.

During the Tribulation, Satan's agents, the Antichrist and the False Prophet, along with Satan himself, will substitute tri-unity for the Triune Godhead. Antichrist will perform miracles to prove his credibility as a substitute Christ. The Antichrist will actually be killed and raised again from the dead, or will have an apparent death wound that will give the illusion that he has been raised from the dead. In either case, the attempt is to substitute as messiah and take the place of Christ.

Today, Satan is attempting to substitute an apostate church for the true church. His ministers (2 Cor. 11:15), are those who are humanitarian and outwardly commendable, yet inwardly enemies of the true gospel. His work of imitation is similar to the next section where Satan attempts to infiltrate the church.

2. *Infiltration.* "Satan transforms himself into an angel of light" (2 Cor. 11:14) so he can infiltrate among the people of Christ and affect the work of God. Jesus claimed that some who called themselves Christians would not be permitted entrance into heaven because they do not truly know Him (Matt. 7:23). By the end of the first century, Satan was clearly trying to control the church of Jesus Christ from both the outside (Rev. 2:13) and the inside (Jude 4). The apostle Paul warned the Ephesian pastors that Satan would attempt to destroy the church by sending into the church evil men who would attempt to corrupt good men (Acts 20:29-30).

The destructiveness of infiltration was apparent during the fourth century when Constantine amalgamated the church and state. Prior to the union, the church surged in growth despite the flame of persecution that snuffed out hundreds of Christian lives. With his appointment as the new leader in A.D. 312, Constantine eventually made Christianity simply one of the official religions of the empire. Many might have thought that with the absence of persecution, the true church would greatly increase and eventually usher in the Millennium. Yet, as history records, this was not the case. The true church mingled with the false church. The fervor it once possessed began to mellow into lofty cathedrals and cold orthodoxy.

C. DESTRUCTION. A third aspect of the work of Satan is to corrupt all that God has created. The nature of Satan is opposite to the nature of God. When Satan cannot imitate God's work and he is unable to infiltrate, he will do all he possibly can to destroy it. "The thief cometh not, but for to steal, and to kill, and to destroy: I am come that they might have life, and that they might have it more abundantly" (John 10:10). His destruction is carried out in several ways.

1. *Deceiving the nations.* Some of Satan's destructive energies are directed against the nations of this world. When Jesus returns, Satan will then be sealed in a pit "that he should deceive the nations no more" (Rev. 20:3). This happens during the millennial rule of Christ. Currently, though, Satan has freedom to perform his deceptive work among the nations.

The extent of Satan's domain among the nations is hinted at by Daniel (10:12-14). In response to Daniel's prayer, God sent a heavenly messenger to deliver His message to Daniel. However, the angel was hindered in his journey for twenty-one days by the prince of the Kingdom of Persia. This passage of Scripture suggests that a powerful angel is assigned to a specific geographical location to hinder in every possible respect the work of God. The strength of the evil angel excelled for a time.

2. *Deceiving the unsaved.* Satan is aggressively keeping the unsaved from understanding the gospel. Paul explained to the Corinthians, "The god of this world hath blinded the minds of them which believe not, lest the light of the glorious gospel of Christ, who is the image of God, should shine unto them" (2 Cor. 4:4). Not content with blinding the unsaved so they cannot understand the gospel, he also has another strategy. "Then cometh the devil, and taketh away the word out of their hearts, lest they should believe and be saved" (Luke 8:12). The book of Acts records one account after another where the devil used men to oppose the progress of the gospel. Satan's strategy is simple. If he can prevent men from hearing the gospel and understanding what Christ offers them, then men will be content to go their own way.

In regard to salvation, it has been stated that it is hard for an individual to go to hell, simply because God places so many road blocks in his pathway that point to salvation. Yet, this statement overlooks in part the blinded condition of the unsaved who stumble over God's invitations to salvation. This does not suggest that Satan is more powerful than God in human affairs (1 John 4:4). It does describe the extreme similarities between God and Satan, in their respective positive and negative external influence upon the human mind. Although, God, unlike Satan, can examine and know man's inner motivation, Satan and his demonic host nonetheless can examine man's actions and conversation to receive a fairly clear grasp of each individual's inner purpose. This means Satan cannot read the thoughts of men, but he can predict their thoughts and actions based on his knowledge of their sinful nature. With this information Satan is able to strike at man's weakest point and destroy him. In relation to the unsaved, Satan employs at least five separate methods to hinder the reception of God's Word and the internalizing of the truth. As outlined by Sanders:

> He *snatches the good seed of the Word.* "When anyone hears the word of the kingdom, and *does not understand it,* the evil *one* comes and snatches away what has been sown in his heart" (Matt. 13:4, 19, italics added). The picture is, of course, of birds swooping down and picking up the grain fallen from the sower's hand on the hard-beaten path. Even so, the devil snatches away good seed of the Word before it can sink into the understanding and be received by faith. This is the activity of the devil whenever the Word is preached. It underlines the fact we should pray *after* the preaching as well as *before,* for this subtle stratagem is all too often successful. How frequently the solemn impression of a powerful sermon is dissipated by idle chatter after a service. The good seed is snatched away.

> He *lulls the unbeliever into a false sense of peace.* "When a strong man fully armed guards his own homestead, his possessions are undisturbed" (Luke 11:21). The context makes it clear Satan is the strong man who drugs the senses of his victims, assures them there is nothing in God to fear, and no judgment to anticipate. He deflects the shafts of conviction which the Holy Spirit directs at their hearts, and says, "Peace, peace, when there is no peace."

> He *lays snares for the unwary.* "If perhaps God may grant them repentance leading to the knowledge of the truth, and they may come to their senses and escape from the snare of the devil, having been held captive by him to do his will" (2 Tim. 2:25-26). The devil is a master of subtlety, and adept at concealing his snares. He is too wise a hunter to lay snares in the sight of his victims.

> He gains advantage over men by concealing his true and sinister purpose, *by masquerading as an angel of light.* "For such men are false apostles, deceitful workers, disguising themselves as apostles of Christ. And no wonder, for even Satan disguises himself as an angel of light" (2 Co. 11:13-14). He is much more likely to succeed when he tempts certain people by appearing in the guise of a benefactor than as a foul fiend or a roaring lion.

> He *deceives those whose minds are not subject to the Word of truth.* "The serpent of old who is called the Devil and Satan, who deceives the whole world" (Rev 12:9). He was successful in deceiving Eve. "The woman being quite deceived, fell into transgression" (1 Ti 2:14), because she entertained doubts the devil injected into her

mind concerning the truth of God's Word, instead of immediately rejecting the disloyal suggestion. He is still active unceasingly in deceiving men about the integrity and authority of God's Word. This is the focal point of the great theological controversies of our day.

He *mixes truth with error.* "While men were sleeping, his enemy came and sowed tares among the wheat . . . and he [the landowner] said to them, an enemy has done this!" (Mt 13:15, 28). His strategy is to include enough truth in his teaching to make error appear both credible and palatable—the great appeal and hidden danger of many cults in vogue today. So much seems good and true that injection of error is not obvious. To achieve his end, Satan will quote or misquote Scripture as best suits his purpose. He is ingenious. He employs orthodox language, while giving the old words used a new and heterodox content. This is especially true in theological circles, where theological double talk confuses the issues and conceals the error.[22]

3. *Defeating the saved.* To merely defeat a Christian temporarily must be the most frustrating aspect of Satan's work, for he cannot destroy the child of God. He will use the lust of the flesh, the lust of the eyes, and the pride of life to attack Christians (1 John 2:15-16). Satan will attack them directly or indirectly. If Satan cannot get a Christian to fall into the pollution of sin, he will push the believer beyond the will of God into legalism or fanaticism. On occasion a Christian may stumble, but the Bible teaches, "A just man falleth seven times, and riseth up again" (Prov. 24:16). The Christian is not able to defeat the devil in himself, but is victorious only as he allows the power of Christ to live in him. "Ye are of God, little children, and have overcome them: because greater is he that is in you, than he that is in the world" (1 John 4:4). But remember, the fact that Satan cannot ultimately destroy us does not mean he will not tempt us.

Satan has successfully tempted Christians to lie to God in the past (Acts 5:3). He is called the "accuser of the brethren" (Rev. 12:10). He seeks to hinder Christians in their work for God (1 Thess. 2:18) and to defeat them in their Christian walk (Eph. 6:12). Satan tempted one Christian to engage in immorality in Corinth (1 Cor. 5:1). He attempted to destroy the Corinthian church, by sowing tares of dissension (Matt. 13:38-39) among the believers (1 Cor. 3:1-7). Also, Satan will attempt to destroy the church by sending in unsaved members and leaders (2 Cor. 11:5, 13-15). If internal opposition falls, Satan will attack the church through external persecution (Rev. 2:10). However, none of Satan's attempts to destroy the Christian need be successful; we have been promised victory over Satan (2 Cor. 2:14).

VIII. How To Overcome Satan

It should be more natural for us to defeat Satan than to be defeated by him. God has revealed certain principles in His Word that can protect the Christian against defeat. But more than insulating against evil, these principles should make the Christian victorious. The Bible clearly states, "There hath no temptation taken you but such as is common to man: but God is faithful, who will not suffer you to be tempted above that ye are able; but will with the temptation also make a way to escape, that ye may be able to bear it" (1 Cor. 10:13). The "way to escape" is found by applying biblical principles to each temptation.

A. THE PRINCIPLE OF RESPECT. Too often Christians rely on fleshly strength for victory. Though Jesus is greater than the devil (1 John 4:4), we must still have a healthy respect for our enemy. A good football team, if they become overconfident, may lose to a lesser team. Overconfidence will cause a team to play carelessly, allowing the opposition to do things they could not otherwise accomplish. So if a Christian does not realize that Satan possesses the ability to defeat him, he will allow Satan to gain victories where he could not otherwise do so. Even Michael, the archangel, was not prepared to confront Satan except in the name of the Lord (Jude 9).

B. THE PRINCIPLES OF REMOVAL. It has often been said that one bad apple will spoil the whole barrel. The leaven principle means that evil will spread surely and purposefully through the good. A wise Christian should evaluate his life and avoid those areas where he is more likely to be tempted. Paul reminds us to "Abstain from all appearance of evil" (1 Thess. 5:22). When Joseph found himself tempted by Potiphar's wife, "he left his garment in her hand, and fled, and got him out" (Gen. 39:12). Paul also applied this principle in reverse to false teachers, meaning that not only should we remove ourselves from evil, we should remove its influence from our lives. "A man that is an heretick after the first and second admonition reject" (Titus 3:10). By separating ourselves from the source of the temptation both morally and geographically, we can gain a temporary victory over the devil. The word "temporary" is used because no one is ever immune to temptation till death.

C. THE PRINCIPLE OF RESISTANCE. The principle of resistance possesses both a positive and negative aspect. It is positive in the sense of submitting to God. Vincent defines submission as "to place or arrange under." Christians should place themselves under the biblical principles and divine protection of Almighty God.[23] To live the Christian life apart from submission to God's authority and protection is tantamount to a haughty spirit of self-reliance, which is folly. The negative aspect demands resistance to the devil. "Submit yourselves therefore to God. Resist the devil, and he will flee from you" (Jas. 4:7). Vincent defines resist as meaning to "withstand," noting that "the verb means rather to be firm against onset, than to strive against it."[24] All of which compels us to believe that we are to actively engage in the spiritual battle with our spiritual instruments, with the purpose of not only stopping Satan's temptation, but advancing upon his kingdom. It is possible for the Christian to send the devil running in defeat by taking definite action. The apostle Peter advised the believer that he should not give in to Satan, but "resist steadfast in the faith" (1 Pet. 5:9). We would not be defeated if we would quote the name of Jesus Christ and refuse to listen to Satan's temptation.

When Jesus was tempted, He gained the victory by using the Scripture to resist the devil (Matt. 4:1-11).

D. THE PRINCIPLE OF READINESS. "Be prepared" is the watchword of the tempted Christian. "Watch ye and pray, lest ye enter into temptation" (Mark 14:38). Paul advised the Ephesians, "Put on the whole armour of God, that ye may be able to stand against the wiles of the devil" (Eph. 6:11). The prepared Christian will recognize his weak areas and strengthen them. David assured us that memorizing Scripture will help keep us from sin (Psa. 119:1, 11). One who is serious about gaining victory over some besetting sin should concentrate on memorizing several verses of Scripture that deal with the particular area of weakness in his life. Also, he should be certain he is fully equipped to meet the devil in battle.

PROTECTION AGAINST THE DEVIL Eph. 6:13-17
1. Girdle (belt) of truth
2. Breastplate of righteousness
3. Shoes of the preparation of the gospel
4. Shield of faith
5. Helmet of salvation
6. Sword of the Spirit
7. All prayer

1. *The belt of truth.* Prior to any exchange with the enemy the belt was the first piece of armor to be secured, simply because the breastplate and sword were attached to it. The belt was normally a thick leather strap that surrounded the waist of the warrior. In addition to holding up the other instruments of war, the warrior also bound up the lower portion of his garments and tucked them under the belt in order to free himself from tangling his feet while in pursuit thus having greater mobility. The significance of "the truth" indicates the unifying and strengthening factor in the life and experience of the Christian soldier. Since the Garden of Eden, Satan has sought to disqualify or dilute the nature of absolute truth with hypocrisy and half-truths. The Christian soldier who wishes to seriously confront his enemy must steadfastly bind up his mind in the great truths of God's holiness, love, power, and unfailing faithfulness.

2. *The breastplate.* The function of the breastplate, which covered the body of the soldier from neck to thigh, was to protect his vital organs. Righteousness here is not understood as an abstract quality of righteousness developed from moral achievements. It is the righteousness of Jesus Christ imputed to us. More specifically, it is His righteousness worked in us by the Holy Spirit. Sanctification or integrity of character gives us freedom over condemnation from our own hearts, and allows us to take great strides into the raging battle, without having to relive a struggle with past or current failures.

3. *The shoes.* Military officials place great emphasis upon the footwear of their soldiers, for improper shoes can hamper the mobility and readiness of the soldiers. Josephus records that the sandals of the Roman soldiers were thickly studded with nails to equip men for long, swift marches. The figure here, then, is readiness, the antithesis being lethargy and apathy. Willingness to capitalize upon a witnessing opportunity should characterize the mental prowess of every equipped and prepared Christian.

4. *The shield.* The typical Roman shield measured four feet in length and two and one-half feet in width. Each shield was made of brass, covered with several layers of leather. Prior to the battle, the shields would be dipped in water until the leather was completely saturated. The purpose of this exercise was to douse the fiery arrows that the enemy used. Arrows in ancient times were often dipped in pitch and set afire before shooting them. However, the oblong shield afforded the necessary protection to blunt the arrows and extinguish the fire. Just so, an unshakable trust in our God effectively stays the arrows and extinguishes their possible devastation. Believers who do not possess confidence in their Lord, vacillate. James tells us that such a one is unstable and destined for failure (Jas. 1:18).

5. *The helmet.* The helmet, normally constructed of leather and brass, has special reference to protecting the mind. An unguarded, undisciplined mind opens the believer to a barrage of attacks, ranging from thoughts of lust to doubting the existence of God. It has been stated that the idle mind is the devil's workshop; hence, the greater need to bring into captivity "every thought to the obedience of Christ" (2 Cor. 10:5). An examination of salvation produces a three dimensional spectrum: namely, the past, present, and future. In the past we have been saved from the guilt and condemnation of our sins—justification. In the present we are being saved from the influences of sin—sanctification. In the future we will be saved from the presence of sin and its effect upon us—glorification. In light of these observations, the helmet represents a valuable defensive implement in time of war.

6. *The sword.* So far the implements of war described were primarily defensive, but necessary for offensive attacks. With the sword, the emphasis is on the offensive attack. Furthermore, apart from putting on the different pieces of defensive armor, very little human involvement was necessary, but with the sword a greater demand is made upon human participation. The Roman sword was short, strong and sharp, and required close hand-to-hand confrontation with the enemy for use. The sword represents the skillful and practical application of scriptural truths and principles to our daily experiences. We are not to walk in our own efforts, but rather to seek the help of the Spirit of the living God (divine involvement), together with a submissive lifestyle to the biblical principles (human involvement).

7. *All prayer.* The last piece of armor we must appropriate is the lethal weapon of all-prayer. Unlike the other implements that have a specific location on the body, the weapon of

all-prayer should permeate all of them and give them a strong sense of unity and invulnerability. The admonition of Paul is to "pray without ceasing," (1 Thess. 5:17). The implication in this piece of armor is the vital role assumed by the Holy Spirit in taking our poor and inadequately expressed word and ushering them into the presence of God with "groanings which cannot be uttered" (Rom. 8:26-27).

[This armour] is not like those antiquated suits we are accustomed to look at with curiosity in the Tower of London, or elsewhere; it is for *present* use, and has never been improved upon. Modern weapons are out of date in a few years—this armour, never. God does not tell us to look at it, to admire it, but to put in on; for armour is not one atom of use until it is put on.[25]

IX. CONCLUSION

The Bible teaches the existence of a personal devil, the author of sin, who tries to destroy the work of God. When Christians see evidences of sin, all they need to think is soberly of their enemy, recognizing the existence of a person seeking their destruction. Peter warns us even today, "Be sober, be vigilant; because your adversary the devil, as a roaring lion, walketh about, seeking whom he may devour" (1 Pet. 5:8). Apart from total dependence upon God, we cannot win the victory over the devil.

ENDNOTES

1.   F. C. Jennings, *Satan: His Person, Work, Place and Destiny* (Neptune, NJ: Loizeaux Brothers, 1975), 9.*

2.   J. Oswald Sanders, *Satan Is No Myth* (Chicago: Moody Press, 1975), 14.

3.   William Cooke, *Christian Theology*, pp. 631-32, as quoted in Lewis Sperry Chafer, *Systematic Theology* (Dallas: Dallas Seminary Press, 1974), 74-75.

4.   Lewis Sperry Chafer, *Systematic Theology* (Dallas: Dallas Seminary Press, 1947), 30.

5.   Ibid., 49.

6.   Ibid., 33.

7.   G. H. Pember, *Earth's Earliest Ages* (Grand Rapids: Kregel Publishers, 1975), 62.

8.   Chafer, 49.

9.   Ibid., 35.

10.   Jennings, 32.

11.   Ibid., 64-65.

12.   Chafer, 31.
13.   Augustine, *City of God*, Book XII, vi, as quoted by Chafer, 31-32.
14.   J. O. Buswell, *A Systematic Theology of The Christian Religion* (Grand Rapids: Zondervan, 1962), 131.
15.   Herbert Lockyer, *The Mystery and Ministry of Angels* (Grand Rapids: Eerdmans, 1958), 43.
16.   Chafer, 95.
17.   Louis Berkhof, *Systematic Theology* (Grand Rapids: Eerdmans, 1976), 149.
18.   Jennings, 25-27.
19.   Chafer, 73-74.
20.   Augustus H. Strong, *Systematic Theology* (New Jersey: Fleming H. Revell Co., 1907), 2154.*
21.   Hal Lindsey, *Satan Is Alive and Well on Planet Earth* (Grand Rapids: Zondervan, 1972), 83.
22.   Sanders, 73-75.
23.   Marvin Vincent, *Word Studies in the New Testament* (New York: Charles Scribner's Sons, 1907), 1:756.
24.   Ibid., 1:670.
25.   Jennings, 152-153.

* Denotes page number(s) could not be verified.

CHAPTER VIII – DEMONOLOGY

The Doctrine of Demons

I. INTRODUCTION

The existence of a personal devil and demons is less and less considered a fairy tale or a superstition. Our society does not ridicule demons as it did in the recent past. Some even worship demons, while others engage regularly in occult practices relating to demon activity. Popular music and songs have been increasingly addressed to occult themes. As a result, the existence of evil and the accompanying demonic beings is not generally rejected by the common man in today's world.

Understanding demons is especially important for the Christian. The Bible makes it clear that we are engaged in a spiritual warfare (Eph. 6:12). As we seek to win the battle, it is to our best advantage to understand not only Satan, but his messengers. But a word of caution is in order. It is good to know about demons, but we should not be obsessed with learning about them.

The Bible is God's revelation to aid us as we search for truth and attempt to live for God (Deut. 9:29; 2 Tim. 3:15-17). It is our only reliable authority on the subject of demons. Some Christians affect their thinking negatively by engaging in excessive study of occult literature. Not only does this fail to provide accurate and reliable information about the devil and demons, it is a direct violation of the command of God (Deut. 18:9). The Bible contains all the "intelligence information" we need about demons to engage in battle with them and emerge successful.

II. THE ORIGIN OF DEMONS

Two Greek words are translated similarly in the New Testament but their meanings are slightly different. The word "*diabolos*" is translated "devil" and refers to the devil himself. Another word, *diamon*, is usually translated "devils" in the King James Version, but might be better translated "demons." The Bible makes a very real distinction between a single devil and many demons. Whenever we read of "devils" in the Bible, we are reading about demons. It appears most likely that demons are fallen angels who rebelled against God. According to Eastern thought, some have erroneously taught that evil (demons) have coexistence with God. This view of the existence of evil fails to consider the biblical account of Satan's fall with his diabolical host. Scripture makes it amply clear that God created all the angels, and some purposely chose to rebel, thus becoming an antagonistic force which God ultimately employs to glorify Himself.

As such, what things are true about the essence of good angels are also true of demons. When it comes to identifying demons, the question that should be asked is, "Where do demons come from?" At least four suggestions have been made to help explain the origin of demons.

A. SPIRITS OF THE DEAD. One contemporary idea relating to the origin of demons claims they are the spirits of the evil dead. This is the underlying assumption of much of all the popular occult literature. It is not a new idea at all, for it was the explanation of some Greek philosophers years before Christ. The early origin of this theory does not, however, make it any more believable. Josephus, the Jewish historian, was apparently persuaded of this view when he comments, "For the so-called demons—in other words, the spirits of wicked men which enter the living and kill them unless aid is forthcoming."[1] This view stands in direct conflict with biblical teaching. The Bible teaches that the souls of the evil dead go to "hades" (Luke 16:23). They will remain there until the end of the millennial reign of Christ on this earth. Only then are they brought before God to be judged (Rev. 20:11). Then they are cast into eternal punishment: "And death and hell [hades] were cast into the lake of fire. This is the second death" (Rev. 20:14).

B. CHILDREN OF ANGELS. Some have suggested that demons are the result of the union of angels and women as described in Gen 6:4: "There were giants in the earth in those days; and also after that, when the sons of God came in unto the daughters of men, and they bare children to them, the same became mighty men which were of old, men of renown." Some suggest that this verse describes sexual relations between angels and women, since the expression "sons of God" is used elsewhere in the Old Testament to identify angels. Even if this interpretation is correct, it is extremely unlikely that such a union produced demons. Before we can sensibly develop the idea that demons are the progenitors of sexual relationships between fallen angels and women, we must of necessity establish: (1) the differences, if any, between fallen angels and demons, (2) the feasibility of fallen angels impregnating human females, and (3) the possibility of a woman, who has had sexual intercourse with a fallen angel, giving birth to an invisible, morally perverted, eternal demonic being. The Bible does not describe any distinctive characteristics between fallen angels or demons, rather the writers of Scripture tend to treat them as a synonymous group, assigning expressions such as wicked spirits, evil spirits, unclean spirits, and lying spirits to those evil beings who choose by their own free will to rebel against God.

C. PRE-ADAMIC SPIRITS. The gap theory presupposes that the world is several million, or even billions of years old. According to it, God created a perfect world as recorded in the first verse of the Bible, but, for one reason or another, God had to destroy it before the status as described in Genesis 1:2. This theory allowed for a society which existed for millions of years, thus harmonizing the contemporary view of the age of the world with the Bible account of creation. The spirits of those who lived before Adam, still inhabit the earth as demons, according to those who hold this view.

But before we can conclude that demons are the disembodied spirits of a pre-Adamic race, we must first prove the existence of such a race. Once again, most biblical evidence is against such a theory, since Adam, for instance, was called the first man. Also, the New Testament claims in Romans 5:12-14 that Adam and not some other personality plunged the human race into sin. In payment for man's sin, the death of Christ extends back to the first Adam and no farther. Therefore, if there had been an existing race prior to Adam, they would not be "able" to participate in the atonement made by Christ. Contemporary scholars have for the most part rejected the possibility of the "gap theory" and its implications.

D. FALLEN ANGELS. Most conservative scholars believe that demons are fallen or evil angels. When Jesus described hell, he called it " everlasting fire, prepared for the devil and his angels" (Matt. 25:41). John described the fall of Satan in a highly symbolic fashion, noting that the devil took a third of the angels with him. "And his tail drew the third part of the stars of heaven, and did cast them to the earth: and the dragon stood before the woman which was ready to be delivered, for to devour her child as soon as it was born" (Rev. 12:4). This has led some to conclude that Satan was one of the three angels responsible, with Gabriel and Michael, to lead other angels. When Satan fell, a third of the angels over which he had supervision may have followed him in rebellion against God.

II. THE DESCRIPTION OF DEMONS

Demons are real beings, probably fallen angels. If this is true, whatever is known of the nature of angels is also true of demons. They are nonmaterial (incorporeal), because all angels are spirit beings. As good angels are the messengers of God to carry out His works, so demons are the emissaries of Satan to carry out his diabolical plans.

A. SPIRIT NATURE. Matthew describes them: "When the even was come, they brought unto him many that were possessed with devils, and he cast out the spirits with his word, and healed all that were sick" (Matt. 8:16). Even though they are incorporeal, there are times when these spirits can indwell a human. Demons can also take on other physical forms. John "saw three unclean spirits (demons) like frogs come out of the mouth of the dragon, and out of the mouth of the beast, and out of the mouth of the false prophet" (Rev. 16:13). Revelation 9 describes the release of many demons from the bottomless pit during the Great Tribulation. John described their physical form and appearance as distinct yet similar to that of locusts and scorpions.

B. LOYAL AND ORGANIZED UNDER SATAN. After Jesus cast out demons from the blind and dumb, the Pharisees accused Him of casting out demons in the power of Beelzebub (Matt. 12:24-26). Christ responded with, "Every kingdom divided against itself is brought to desolation; and every city or house divided against itself shall not stand. And if Satan cast out Satan, he is divided against himself; how shall then his kingdom stand?" Satan has an organized kingdom and at his disposal a loyal following of angelic spirits who seek to do his will. The demons are unified in their hatred toward God and desire nothing more than to totally annihilate God's plan for man (Luke 22:31). We are not told the scope of Satan's kingdom, yet we know that he, with his demons, is the prince of the power of the air (Eph. 2:2). Satan's demons possess differing responsibilities, ranging from controlling nations (Dan. 10:13) to tempting believers (Acts 5:3-5).

C. EMOTIONAL NATURE. During His Galilean ministry, Christ came to the demoniac of Gadara who was possessed with a legion of demons. After discovering their name, Christ commanded them to come out. Fearing they might be cast into the deep (hell), the Bible says (Luke 8:31) they besought (begged) Christ that He would not send them into the deep. Christ allowed them to leave, and they immediately departed to enter into a nearby herd of swine. From this dialogue we discover that fallen angels possess an emotional aspect that allows them to exhibit a genuine fear of punishment.

D. ESSENCE. As a result of the rebellion by angels, demons differ from the holy angels in their employments, moral qualities, and place of residency, but their essence remains unchanged. Essence deals with intrinsic being, such as immortal, invisible, and incorporeal. This point is aptly stated by Dick.

> With respect to their essence, they are still pure spirits, immortal, and possessed of great power and activity. But a change has taken place in regard to their qualities, intellectual and moral. Originally of a higher order of creatures than man, they retain their superiority in mental ability, although it cannot be doubted that it is greatly impaired . . . the intellectual powers of fallen angels have been blighted; that their understandings are obscured, and perverted by their passions; and that their wisdom, which has degenerated into cunning, often leads them astray, and involves them in perplexity and confusion.[2]

E. POWER. It would be a serious mistake to underestimate the power of demons. Because angels in general are called "mighty" (Rev. 10:1), we may assume demons are also mighty. The final book of the Bible describes demons performing many unusual feats during the Tribulation. Even a person possessed by demons in the New Testament was described as having tremendous strength (Mark 5:3-4). Actually it was the power of the demons working through him. The Christian that believes he can "wrestle" with demons without "taking on the whole armour of God" is seriously deluded (Eph. 6:10-18). The seven sons of Sceva (Acts 19:14-17) quickly discovered the power of a demon possessed man as they attempted to perform an exorcism. "The man in whom the evil spirit was leaped on them, and overcame them, and prevailed against them, so that they fled out of that house naked and wounded" (Acts 19:16).

When considering the power of demons in relation to the strength of believers, two truths need to be understood. First, the power of evil spirits over men is not independent of free will. Their power cannot be exercised without at least the original consent of the human will, and even then may be resisted and shaken off through prayer and faith in God. Secondly, demonic power is limited, both in time and in extent, by the permissive will of God. Describing the power of demons, Manton writes,

> Their power is great still, though limited, so that it cannot be exercised but when and where and as God will. They are able to raise tempests, to bring fire from heaven, as they did to ruin Job's house and children, Job i.; wrought by a divine power. Being of much sagacity and skill in the secrets of nature, they may poison the air, destroy the bodies of men, infest and trouble beasts and cattle; in short, do all that lieth within the compass of a natural cause where God permitteth. Again, they may possess the bodies of men, hinder the godly in the execution of their duty; overrule the spirits of wicked men, and act and stir them up to wrath, lust, filthiness, Eph. ii. 3, beset them with error, &c: It would require a distinct discourse to open this power to you. They cannot create new beings, nor raise dead bodies, nor compel the will of man; they can not do miracula.[3]

F. INTELLECTUAL NATURE. Many Christians live with the deluded idea that demons are ignorant servants of the devil. This is totally contrary to every biblical indication of their intellectual capabilities. Even if they had been created ignorant, today they would possess a great deal of knowledge because they have been observing and retaining knowledge since their creation. They were able to clearly identify the person and deity of Christ during His earthly ministry (Mark 1:24; 5:6-7). Also, they possess a limited understanding of some aspects of their future (Matt. 8:29). While they possess enough facts to believe intellectually in God, their moral state prohibits their possessing saving faith (Jas. 2:19). The apostle Paul credited demons with enough intellectual ability to design and propagate the various false doctrines of different religious sects (1 Tim. 4:1-3).

The extent of demonic intelligence is uncertain. Some have argued that demons have the ability to read our thoughts, while others have rejected this idea, claiming only the Holy Spirit is able to read the thoughts of men's hearts. The very nature of demons doesn't allow them to know our thoughts. However, our outward actions provide them excellent insight into what we are thinking. Manton describes demons' intellectual capacity.

> Their knowledge and cunning is great; they have much natural and experimental knowledge, so as they can discern hidden causes and virtues which escape the flight of man's reason and understanding; they know how to apply active to passive things, can guess notably at future events; but as for a certain knowledge of them, unless of such things as depend upon necessary causes, that is proper to God, and accordingly he challengeth it: Isa. xli. 23, 'Show the things that are to come, that we may know that ye are gods,' &c. Therefore the devil's oracles were either false or doubtful, as 1 Kings xxii. 16. Great skill in arts and tongues they have, as appeareth by their teaching those things with wonderful facility to those that have familiarity with them.

In divine things they know enough of God and his justice to feel a horror impressed upon themselves, James ii. 19; Luke iv. 34; Acts xix. 15. Besides they are of wonderful sagacity to judge of men's hearts by the gestures, the motion of the blood and spirits, and other such external signs, for directly they do not know the thoughts; that is the privilege of God.[4]

G. WILLFUL NATURE. In addition to possessing this other element of personality, demons are also able to exercise will (volition) so that they may make independent decisions. They express will through their persistent labors of hindering the purposes of God for humanity and extending the authority of Satan's kingdom. No repentance is possible for demons. Their destiny is already determined; for now, they await the bitter consummation of their evil deeds.

H. MORAL NATURE. The chief difference between angels of God and demons lies in their moral nature. Demons are reprobates and evil. Apparently they have no opportunity of repentance or salvation. They are perpetually immoral because of their rebellion against God. The sin was serious enough in the mind of God so that hell and everlasting fire were created for Satan and demons (Matt. 25:41). Their nature is described by the adjective "unclean" (Matt. 10:1; Mark 1:27; Acts 8:7). Peter described demons as "the angels that sinned" (2 Pet. 2:4). A major part of the work of demons today is to propagate evil, teach false doctrine, and recruit others to rebel against God. It is difficult for believers to comprehend the evil nature that demons possess. Demons far surpass in wickedness the vilest person we know. There exist cults who seek to exalt and offer praise to a being that bitterly hates them. Dick aptly describes the perverse moral nature of demons:

> Their moral qualities have undergone a total change. Of their original holiness, not a vestige remains. Sin is now so natural to them that it seems almost to be their essence; it is the element in which they live and move. Sin is the subject of their thoughts, and gives a character to all their actions. Evil is their only good. There is an important difference between them and men, which is worthy of particular attention. . . . Sin rages in them [demons] unrestrained; every malignant and furious passion boils within them: and if they experience any relief from their sufferings, it consists in wreaking their malice and cruelty upon man.[5]

I. NUMBER. We cannot be dogmatic as to how many angels fell, simply because Scripture does not provide us with this answer. The most popular view holds that Satan took one-third of the angels with him. According to Revelation 12:4, "And his tail drew the third part of the stars of heaven and did cast them to the earth." If indeed there are millions of holy angels, and Satan managed to align a third of them to follow him, his kingdom of demons is undoubtedly very large. Some have suggested that an equal number fell as remained loyal to God, some believe that the number of Satan's host is slightly smaller than God's host. John Gill provides as the reason for these differing views.

This question is sometimes put, What number of the angels fell? This cannot be said with any precision; some have thought that as many fell as stood; grounding it on a passage in Ezek. xli, 18. where it is said, that on the wall of the temple were carved, with cherubim and palm trees, a palm tree between a cherub and a cherub; by cherubim they understand angels, and by palm trees they understand good men, said to flourish like the palm tree; and who are supposed to fill up the places of fallen angels; and so conclude the same number fell as stood; but as such a sense of the text cannot easily be established, it is insufficient to build such a notion upon. Others have thought that not so many fell as stood, since evil angels are never said to be innumerable, as the good angels are, Heb. xii. 22. And which they also gather from the words of Elisha to his servant: Fear not; for they that be with us, are more than they that be with them; and the servant's eyes were presently opened, and he saw the mountain full of horses and chariots of fire round about; that is, angels in such forms, 2 Kings vi. 16,17. But then the comparison is not between good and bad angels; but between the good angels and the Syrian host. However, it is certain, that not a few of

the angels, but many of them, fell; even as many as to form a kingdom, with a prince at the head of it; and there were so many that possessed one man, as to be called a legion, which consisted of some hundreds; for when the devil in him was asked his name, he answered, My name is legion, for we are many.[6]

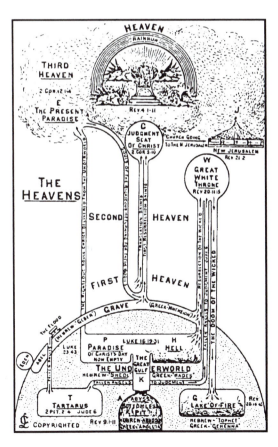

III. DESTINY OF DEMONS

When Jesus encountered a demon-possessed man, the demons asked, "Art thou come hither to torment us?" (Matt. 8:29). Demons understand something of their eternal destiny. The phrase "the time" could mean that they feared premature expulsion from the man, but it probably means premature judgment into hell. The destiny of demons can be summarized in three phases of confinement.

A. PRESENT CONFINEMENT. Apparently some demons have limited freedom while others are confined until the Tribulation. John described the release of some of these demons in Revelation 9 when they will come from the bottomless pit to afflict the people. Jude identified another group of demons whom God, "hath reserved in everlasting chains under darkness unto the judgment of the great day" (Jude 6). Peter referring to the same, confirmed, "God spared not the angels that sinned, but cast them down to hell and delivered them into chains of darkness, to be reserved unto judgment" (2 Pet. 2:4). Apparently the crime of these angels was so horrendous that they will never again experience any degree of liberty.

The chart by Clarence Larkin[7] is one interpretation of the chronology of these demons. Larkin pictures certain angels receiving special judgment (Jude 6; 2 Pet. 2:4) and bound in Tartarus under judgment because they cohabitated with women in Genesis 6:1-4. Satan and other angels roam about on the earth, and a third group of angels are bound in abyss (Rev. 9) until the Tribulation period.

Several Bible teachers believe that the "sons of God" (Gen. 6:2) which were angels, cohabitated with the "daughters of men" (Gen. 6:2), who were human women and produced giants (v. 4). God saw the wicked results, as well as potential ruin and destroyed the earth with a flood. The angels who were responsible were placed in Tartarus to wait for judgment at the Great White Throne judgment. Lawlor gives support for this view.

(1) The title "Sons of God" in Genesis 6:2, 4 is used in Job 1:6; 2:1; 38:7 to designate angels. Moreover, in the Septuagint the word "Sons" in these passages is the Greek ἄγγελοι "angels," and where the Authorized Version reads "Sons of God" in Geneses 6:2, 4 the Septuagint reads "angels of God." Nowhere in the Old Testament are God's people called "Sons of God," with one notable exception in Hosea 1:10, and the meaning there is obvious.

(2) The term "Sons of God" denotes beings brought into existence by the creative act of God. Such were the angels, and in the Old Testament the title refers to angels. Men are not "sons" until they are redeemed (Gal. 4:4, 5), born again in the New Testament sense (John 1:12, 13; 3:3-7).

(3) There was a strong Jewish stream of tradition with regard to Genesis 6:1-4 as being the description of a terrible sin committed by angels attracted by the beauty of mortal women, and who forsook their proper habitation in order to live on earth with the daughters of men.

(4) The early church held that Jude's statement in vs. 6 refers to Genesis 6:1-4. It was not until the latter part of the 4th century that any other view was suggested.

(5) The language of the text is foreign to the view that the "Sons of God" are the sons of Seth, while the "daughters of men" are the offspring of Cain. If the "Sons of God" are the sons of Seth, and the "daughters of men" are the offspring of Cain, then at the time of the amalgamation God's true people were limited to the male sex, for the

"Sons of God" were the ones who married the "daughters of men." And if the "Sons of God" were believers, they perished in the Flood, yet Peter states that it was the ungodly who received that judgment (II Pet. 2:5).

(6) The "daughters of men" can surely be held to include the daughters of Seth as well as the daughters of Cain, and this being so, then the "Sons of God" must refer to something entirely different from the human race.

(7) The progeny of the union between the "Sons of God" and the daughters of men" was of such a character as to indicate a super-human union. The word rendered "giants" in Genesis 6:4 is the same word as that found in Numbers 13:33, where it is used to describe the sons of Anak, seen by the spies, and who were gigantic in stature. The Hebrew word is

נְפִילִים from the verb נָפַל "to fall," hence designating these giants as "fallen ones." The result of this union was wickedness of such fearful character as to demand a new beginning of the human race (Gen. 6:5-7).

(8) This corruption of the human race by the "Sons of God" was in harmony with Satan's continued policy of trying to frustrate the plan and purpose of God, and thus answers the question of why these angels sinned. Herein is to be found the cause of their evil act. By influencing these angels to rebel, become insubordinate to God, to not keep their first estate, to leave their own habitation, and to come down into the realm of the daughters of men and seek them out for themselves, Satan aimed at the monstrous destruction of the human race (the channel through which the seed of the woman, Genesis 3:15, should come), and at its immediate perversion, by producing a race of frightful monstrosities. He almost succeeded. Genesis 6:12 says, "All flesh had corrupted his way upon the earth." Only one family remained by the grace of God: Noah's. Genesis 6:2, 4 shows that monstrosities *were* produced.

(9) The Scriptures reveal that angels fell, came down, and went after strange flesh (Jude 6, 7 with II Pet. 2:4), and the testimony strongly suggests that their sin was that of Genesis 6. The passage in Jude 6, 7 shows the awful sin of the people in Sodom and Gomorrah in comparison with the sin of the angels who fell.

(10) Matthew 22:30 is used in refutation of the "angels" view. But in this passage, the words "in heaven" make a great difference with the meaning. The angels *in heaven* do not marry, nor are given in marriage. But the "Sons of God" in Geneses 6:1-4 were no longer in heaven. They left their own place, forsook their habitation, and came seeking after strange flesh, hunting after unlawful alliance with the daughters of men.[8]

Initially those arguments appear conclusive. However, upon closer examination there is another side to the issue. The expression "sons of God" (argument #1) is not restrictive to angels in the Old Testament. Rather this phrase has been used to refer to the godly (Psa. 73:15), and the Israelites (Deut. 32:5, Hosea 1:10). Those who support the "angels cohabitate with women view" state that "the sons of God" has different usages, but in Genesis 6:1-7, as in Job 1:6, 2:1, 38:7, the expression clearly refers to angels.

To argue that the expression, "sons of God" denotes beings brought into existence by the creative act of God (argument #2), finds support within both views. Who could argue that God was not instrumental in creation? Granted, in a redemptive sense, the child of God stands in a closer relationship to God than unbelievers, but it would never be argued that we are not all part of God's wonderful creation.

The third argument states that Jewish tradition held that "Sons of God" were angels. But man is fallible, even in his interpretation of Scripture. Similar to the previous argument, the church's view should not receive undue credence (argument #4), for the church is composed of fallible men.

To argue that all the sons of God (Sethites) married the daughters of men (Cainites) clearly begs the question (argument #5). Are we to assume that there were no women in the godly line of Seth for the men of Seth to marry? Surely there were, for Noah found favor in God's sight, and he found a wife. Admittedly, very few of the male Sethites could have married into the godly line, but chose to materialize their fanciful lust with the immoral daughters of Cain.

The nature of the sixth argument confuses the intent of the passage. In writing this passage of Scripture, Moses is providing a cause for the Flood. Beginning with the genealogy of Cain (Gen. 4:16-24=ungodly line), and the genealogy of Seth (Gen. 4:25-5:32=godly line), Moses develops the cause of God's judgment upon the earth, namely the amalgamation of these two human lines, and the ensuing immorality of the remnant. Whenever the godly remnant becomes corrupted and unprofitable to God, He will purposely enter into the stream of humanity and purge out the leaven (as the destruction of Sodom and Gomorrah).

The term "giants" should not be restricted solely as a reference to physical stature or superhuman ability (argument #7). Giants can also refer to notoriety or renown, such as a notorious criminal or renowned speaker. If this is the case, then the expression in Genesis 6:4, "men of renown" could suggest that the depraved level of debauchery was manifestly low.

To suggest that Satan seeks to destroy man, and ultimately the promised Seed of the women is obvious and is endorsed by both views (argument #8). The "angel cobabitate with women view" fails to recognize the significance of God's sovereignty into the affairs of His creation. Scripture is abundantly clear that God uses the wicked devices of men and the evil nature of Satan to glorify Himself. Despite what many think, Satan is simply a pawn in God's overall plan. In the life of Job it is clearly evidenced that Satan needed to acquire permission from God before he could inflict any anguish upon Job. In light of God's sovereignty, it could be argued that angels (good and bad) are not able to develop physical manifestations apart from God's permission. Several obvious questions arise for those who support the "angels cohabitate with women view." "Why would God allow evil angels to develop physical bodies in order to destroy what God had created? Why would the object of God's anger in Genesis 6:6 be man and not man and fallen angels?" "And it repented the Lord that he had made man on the earth, and it grieved him at his heart."

If it can be shown from Jude 6 that they were angels who pursued after "strange flesh," then it is a strong argument for the "angels cohabitate with women view" (argument #9). However, if it can he shown from Jude 6 that it is not angels seeking "strange flesh," rather the people of Sodom and Gomorrah, the motive for God's judgment of fallen angels is no longer an argument.

Jude 6-8 could describe three examples of God's judgment poured out upon those who exhausted God's grace and patience. According to verse 16, the intent of those are "for an example." The three examples are the disbelieving Jews who fashioned a golden calf during Moses' absence on Mount Sinai, the angels who originally rebelled against God, and the ungodly men and women of Sodom and Gomorrah who submitted themselves to every imaginable sexual impurity. Notice the proximity of subject and verb. The subject for the verb "going after strange flesh" is the inhabitants of Sodom and Gomorrah. The use of the Greek word ἑτέρας suggests the idea that someone was pursuing "after other flesh" and not the idea of flesh that is a "different kind" from their own. According to Lenski ἑτέρας conveys this idea, "that these fornicators were not satisfied with their own people and ran after every stranger that came within their reach. A sample is given in Gen. 19:4)."[9] If Lenski is correct, then his view agrees with the Genesis account of Sodom and Gomorrah, a city that flagrantly engaged in homosexual relationships. In Sodom and Gomorrah men did indeed pursue after other flesh, namely men after men, a perverted deviation of God's standard.

Finally, to argue that fallen angels differ from holy angels (argument #10) negates what Scripture teaches (see description of demons). The Bible teaches that there are two classes of angels: holy and fallen. The differences in those groups include different moral qualities (holy angels possess confirmed holiness, and fallen angels are totally given over to evil, so much so that they do not even desire repentance), they have different employments (holy angels minister for God, fallen angels perpetually seek to thwart God's plan), and they have different places of residency (holy angels dwell in heaven primarily, fallen angels are restricted to the earthly atmosphere—see present confinement). Their differences do not extend to their essence or their being; fallen angels are still invisible and incorporeal, (see nature of angels). Therefore, if heavenly angels are "unable to marry, nor given in marriage," then it stands to reason that fallen angels are equally unable.

One further argument against "angels cohabitate with women view" is the expression "took them wives" in Genesis 6:2B. According to Keil and Delitzsch this expression can only refer to marriage established by God at the Creation. They write,

> . . . (to take a wife) is a standing expression throughout the whole of the Old Testament for the marriage relation established by God at the creation, and is never applied to πορνέια or the simple act of physical connection. This is quite sufficient

of itself to exclude any reference to angels. For Christ Himself distinctly states that the angels cannot marry (Matt. xxii. 30; Mark xii. 25; cf. Luke xx. 34 sqq.).[10]

The question of whether "the sons of God" speaks of fallen angels or of the godly line of Seth is not one of the most crucial issues in theology, but it is an issue in demonology. Therefore, a study of the issue must be made and allowance made for the possibility of demons in Genesis 6:1-7 or for the lineage of Seth and the daughters of Cain.

The judgment spoken of in Jude and 2 Peter probably refers, not to a second judgment upon fallen angels, but to the first judgment placed upon Satan and his host. Both Peter and Jude describe the threefold process of Satan's and the demons' demise.

	2 Peter 2:4		Jude 6
1.	Cast them down to hell	1.	Kept not their first estate
2.	Delivered them into chains of darkness	2.	Reserved in everlasting chains
3.	Reserved unto judgment	3.	Unto the judgment of that great day

The first stage of Satan's judgment came shortly after the rebellion in which he failed to keep his first estate (serving God in the heavenlies), and, as a result, God pronounced His judgment upon Satan and cast him out from heaven.

Following God's declarative act of judgment upon Satan and all his angels, Satan, with all his angels, remained free to roam the earth, bound only by the figurative chains of darkness, until the final execution of God's judgment. Just as there is a period of time between the reading of the judge's verdict and executing the judgment, so likewise there is a period of time between God's pronounced verdict upon Satan and His execution of that judgment shortly after the millennial kingdom (Rev. 20:10).

What is to be understood by the phrase "chains of darkness"? Some have sought to explain them as bonds which represent guilt of conscience, consistency in sinning, utter despair of deliverance, submission to God's power and eternal decree.[11] Both Peter and Jude are employing symbolic terms to explain their bondage. Therefore, the most likely understanding of the "chains of darkness" represents the atmosphere of the earth, which is surrounded by darkness. Satan and his demons are bound to the first level, and eventually in Revelation 12, his liberty will be further limited to activity upon the earth instead of in the air surrounding the earth. The consummation of their judgment is yet future, for both Peter and Jude clearly state that they are reserved unto the great judgment (which undoubtedly refers to the Great White Throne judgment) when they are thrown into the lake of fire. A picture would describe these verses as:

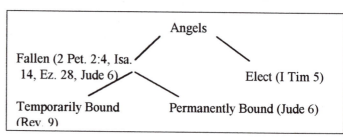

The demons who are currently bound in the abyss (Rev. 9), possibly represent those angels which were cast out by Christ and the apostles. During the Tribulation, they will be released to vent their fury upon those who do not possess the mark of God (Rev. 9:4).

B. MILLENNIAL CONFINEMENT. During the Great Tribulation there "are the spirits of devils, working miracles, which go forth unto the kings of the earth and of the whole world, to gather them to the battle of that great day of God Almighty" (Rev. 16:14). As demons are in part responsible for the battle of Armageddon, it is reasonable to expect they would be prevented from making war during the millennial reign of Christ. While their millennial destiny is not specifically identified in the Bible, most commentators would agree that they would be confined with Satan their leader in the bottomless pit (Rev. 20:3). They certainly are not active during Christ's reign on the earth.

C. ETERNAL CONFINEMENT. One of the key thoughts to keep in mind when attempting to understand hell is to remember that it was never the will of God that anyone should go there (1 Pet. 3:9). When confronted with that truth, the obvious question is, "Why did God create hell in the first place?" The answer to that question is found in Matthew 25:41. Hell was "prepared for the devil and his angels." A man will only go to hell by choice, his choice as expressed by his rejection of Christ. Demons are apparently aware that someday they will be eternally confined to the lake of fire (Matt. 8:29).

The second term to describe the destiny of demons is the word "Tartarus." Peter's usage of the term "Tartarus" is the only occurrence in the New Testament. To understand its significance we need to understand how it was used in classical Greek. Dick aptly describes its classical usage.

> The angels who sinned were expelled from heaven, as being unworthy to enjoy its felicity, and incapable of taking any part in its employments. "God spared not the angels that sinned, but cast them down to hell, and delivered them into chains of darkness, to be reserved unto judgment." He cast them into *Tartarus*, for Peter uses the word ταρταρωσας. Neither the verb, nor the substantive ταρταρος occurs in any other place of the New Testament, although frequently in Greek writers; and it is, therefore, from them, that we must learn its meaning on this occasion. Now by Tartarus, they understood the lowest of the infernal regions, the place of darkness and of punishment; in which those, who had been guilty of impiety towards the gods, and of great crimes against men, were confined and tormented. The word, as adopted by the Apostle, conveys the same general idea. Whatever mistakes the heathens committed with respect to the local situation of Tartarus, and the nature of its punishments, Peter, retaining the radical sense of the term, undoubtedly uses it in this passage as equivalent to hell. That is the region assigned to the apostate spirits: and

in the sentence of the last judgment, by which wicked men are also doomed to it, it is said to have been "prepared for the devil and his angels." It is represented as a region of darkness and sorrow. Darkness and light, when spoken of in relation to spirits, are metaphorically used; since, not having bodily senses, they are not affected, as we are, by the presence and absence of the sun. The darkness of Tartarus is therefore significant of the deprivation of all joy, and all hope. Having incurred the wrath of their Creator, the fallen angels can experience only evil, and must utterly despair of any favorable change. The positive misery of their state, is also described by figurative language. It is "everlasting fire," which is prepared for the devil and his angels; but spirits can no more be affected by fire than by light. But, as fire applied to the human body causes the most excruciating pain, this image has been chosen to awaken the idea of the most dreadful torment; and that the mind can suffer without the body, or while no injury is done to it, and there is no derangement of its parts, we all know by experience. The fallen angels are wretched as well as wicked.[12]

Therefore, Peter may not be referring to Tartarus as a separate place of punishment for demons. Rather he is using emphatic terms to describe the awesome judgment that Satan and his angels incurred.

IV. DEMON ACTIVITY

Several years ago, Hal Lindsey wrote a best-selling book dealing with the works of Satan and his demons. The book was heavily documented with evidence of demon activity in our contemporary society. One of the surprising facts brought out by the author was that demons are worshipped. Beyond that, it is evident that demons are at work today, not only in primitive and superstitious societies, but also among the upper echelons of highly civilized Western Europe and North America. From astrology to witches and their sciences, the author concluded *Satan Is Alive and Well on Planet Earth.*[13]

Everything God created performs a function. Even after sin has infected the creation of God, everything still has a purpose, so that God works His will indirectly. Not recognizing this principle, many Christians picture demons with their red suits, horns, and pitchforks sitting around a party table celebrating the progress of sin in the world. C. S. Lewis may have been more accurate in his fictional account *The Screwtape Letters,* as he described the efforts of one demon to hinder a person in his walk with God.[14]

Despite the clear instructions of the Word of God, some Christians may be engaged in occult practices. Oftentimes a person may not be fully aware of what he is doing. Unsaved individuals involved in such activities leave themselves open to the dangerous possibility of demon possession. Those who have studied the biblical doctrine of demons and are aware of contemporary trends in society share this conclusion.

The magnitude and power of Satan's kingdom comes directly from the ceaseless efforts of his dedicated followers. Equipped with myriads of demons, Satan is able to monitor and control the course of nature, the actions of men, and the outcome of major decisions. Writing on the vital role of demons in Satan's diabolic efforts, Chafer states,

Satan, though proposing to supersede the Almighty, is not omnipotent; but his power and the extent of his activity are immeasurably increased by the cooperation of his host of demons. Satan is not omniscient; yet his knowledge is greatly extended by the combined wisdom and the observation of his sympathetic subjects. Satan is not omnipresent; but he is able to maintain an unceasing activity in every locality by the loyal obedience of the satanic host.[15]

Quite often there is a tendency among those who read articles dealing with spiritual forces (good or bad) to attribute every mysterious event, unexplainable phenomenon, or bump in the dark to the presence of some spirit. It is the task of every mature believer to overlook these superstitious and silly beliefs of simpletons, which have done more harm than good to the doctrine of demonology. A Christian should base his life on a rational approach to the claims of Scripture concerning demonic activity. The admonition of Charles Hodge serves as an adequate preface to a serious study of demonic activity today.

Great evils, however, have arisen from exaggerated views of the agency of evil spirits. To them have been referred, not only all natural calamities, as storms, conflagrations, pestilences, etc., but what was far more lamentable, they have been regarded as entering into covenant with men. It was thought that any person could enter into a contract with Satan and be invested for a season with supernatural power upon condition that the person thus endowed yielded his soul to perdition. On this foundation rested the numerous prosecutions for witchcraft and sorcery which disgraced the annals of all Christian nations during the seventeenth and eighteenth centuries. The most enlightened men of Europe yielded themselves to this delusion, under which thousands of men and women, and even children, were put to the most cruel deaths. It is not necessary to go to the opposite extreme and deny all agency of evil spirits in nature or over the bodies and minds of men, in order to free ourselves from such evils. It is enough to adhere to the plain teaching of the Bible. These spirits can only act, as before stated, in accordance with the laws of nature and the free agency of man; and their influence and operations can no more be detected and judicially proved than the influence and operations of holy angels for good.[16]

The nature of all demonic activity centers around two ultimate objectives. The first deals with extending the kingdom of Satan. Secondly, demons greatly desire to destroy the plan of God. With these two objectives in mind, demons attempt to accomplish their objectives in the following ways.

A. PHYSICAL DISEASE. There are many reasons why a person may experience physical illness. Sometimes it is the result of God's judgment for sin (1 Cor. 11:30), breaking some health law, exposing oneself to germs or viruses, improper diet, or a number of other causes that result from breaking physical laws. On some occasions, demons may be the reason for physical suffering.

Several specific physical afflictions are attributed to demons in the Bible. Jesus cast a demon out of a dumb man who immediately began to speak (Matt. 9:32-33). On another occasion, a blind man and dumb man began to see and hear when the demon was cast out of him (Matt. 12:22). Job was afflicted physically with boils covering his body, the result of satanic activity (Job 2:1-10). Of course, afflictions are not always symptoms of demon activity, but demons are capable of causing, and do occasionally cause, physical pain and suffering.

B. ECCLESIASTICAL DIVISION. Since Christ launched the church in the first century, evil forces have successfully caused many divisions among the believers in the church. Many of these divisions later developed into church splits, which has greatly hindered the cause of Christ to unbelievers. Since false doctrines and falling from the faith are associated with demons (1 Tim. 4:1), it is only natural to conclude that their activity is associated with ecclesiastical divisions. However, not all church splits hinder the propagation of the gospel. When Martin Luther left the Roman Catholic Church for doctrinal reasons, his decision gave impetus to the birth of the Reformation.

Within the church of Corinth, discipline was administered to one of its members. After the erring brother repented and made restitution for his sins, Paul admonished the church to receive him back in order to avoid the threat of divisions within the Body of Christ by Satan's forces (2 Cor. 2:6-11). Paul warns that if the church did not handle the matter properly, "Satan should get an advantage of us: for we are not ignorant of his devices" (2 Cor. 2:11).

C. MENTAL DISEASE. Some manifestations of mental diseases can be related to demons. In at least two cases of demon possession treated by Jesus during His ministry, the demons had so affected the minds of the victims as to cause abnormal behavior. One man lived among tombs and created a disturbance day and night (Mark 5:4-5). A young boy possessed with a demon involuntarily went into an apparent convulsion when he encountered the presence of Jesus (Luke 9:37-42). In both instances, the victims engaged in some form of self-destruction and physical mutilation of the body. After the demon was cast out of the person, the apparent mental problem disappeared.

Not all mental diseases are caused by demonic influence, and apparently there is no certain type of disease caused only by demons. Their activity is manifested in and through mental disease that could be called common or that appears when there is no demon activity. At one time, people with epilepsy were considered demon-possessed, and exorcists were employed to remove the evil spirit. Sufficient is the warning that not all bizarre actions produced by people are demonic in origin. Scripture provides for us detailed characteristics of those who are demon possessed (see demon possession), and for anyone with abnormal behavior, a medical or psychiatric checkup may be advisable.

D. TEMPTATION. The primary task for demons lies in the area of tempting believers to pursue a lifestyle apart from God, thereby destroying the believer's testimony. Demons also influence the lost by binding them to some particular sin and convincing them that they are not worthy to become Christians. Writing on this subject, Dick states,

> Nothing is more plainly taught in the Scriptures, than that evil spirits are employed in tempting men to sin. The devil is called "the spirit that worketh in the children of disobedience;" the wicked are said to be "of their father the devil," and to do his works; and it is affirmed that "he who committeth sin is of the devil." It was Satan who tempted Judas to betray his Master, and put it into the heart of Ananias and Sapphira to agree together to lie to the Holy Ghost. His efforts are, in a particular manner, directed against the saints, who are the objects of his envy and hatred, because they have been restored to the favour of God, and are engaged in his service. Our Lord told his disciples, that Satan had desired to have them, that he might sift them as wheat. . . .
>
> These, and many other passages, fully prove that fallen angels are employed in endeavouring to draw men into sin, and justify us in believing their agency, although we cannot explain it. It would be endless to attempt to give a particular account of their temptations, which are greatly diversified, and adapted, we may presume, with consummate art, to the varieties in the tempers and circumstances of individuals. They solicit men to pride, to profaneness, to avarice, to sensuality, to malignity; to every evil, in a word, which will dishonour God, and bring ruin upon their souls.[17]

E. DISCOURAGING BELIEVERS. Through direct intervention and circumstances, demons possess the ability to discourage believers from accomplishing great things for God. Whether it is a young person who desires to go to a Christian college, yet holds back for lack of faith or a pastor who fails to challenge his people to evangelize the lost; both stem from doubting thoughts that may come from demonic influences. As long as believers allow evil forces to place skeptical thoughts in their minds, which leads them into a state of leisure and laxness, a believer will never experience the joy and satisfaction that comes from the life of faith.

F. FALSE DOCTRINE. Paul believed a principal work of demons "in the latter times," had to do with false doctrine. "Now the Spirit speaketh expressly, that in the latter times some shall depart from the faith, giving heed to seducing spirits, and doctrines of devils" (1 Tim. 4:1). Demons are the source of many organized doctrines of cults. Even in the early church, there were false apostles (Rev. 2:2) and false doctrines (Rev. 2:14). The Bible teaches the coming of an antichrist during the Great Tribulation. By the end of the first century, John wrote, "Little children, it is the last time: and as ye have heard that antichrist shall come, even now are there many antichrists; whereby we know that it is the last time" (1 John 2:18). The word "anti" had a twofold designation; first it meant "against" Christ, but the secondary meaning was the most evident which meant "in substitution for," or "instead of" Christ. The existence of "antichrist" leaders throughout the church age is the result of demon activity. Their chief activity is to foster a "substitute religion" in place of Christ and substitute the "doctrines of demons" for the Christian faith. Many have felt that secular humanism is a "substitute religion" endorsed by fallen angels; in that, like cults, it focuses man's attention on intellectual achievements and moral deeds. Demons convince man that he has found the truth. As a result of placing more emphasis upon the role of the creature than the Creator, man exalts himself to a more lofty position and instills in himself the final authority of life.

G. BLINDING THE MINDS OF UNBELIEVERS. Christ has energized the church with the power and authority to overcome Satan's kingdom, "And the gates of hell shall not prevail against it" (Matt. 16:18). Yet countless millions of unbelievers slip into eternity without Christ every year. Paul writes in 2 Corinthians 4:3-4 of the blinding work of Satan and his demons that keeps people from coming to Christ. "In whom the God of this world hath blinded the minds of them which believe not, lest the light of the glorious gospel of Christ, who is the image of God, should shine unto them." Despite the awesome force that confronts us, the church possesses a greater power (1 John 4:4), the convicting power of the Holy Spirit (to cause people to see their sin). Christ and the Holy Spirit, who acts upon Scripture, are God's plan to overcome spiritual blindness.

H. SPIRITUAL BATTLE. One of the chief difficulties of living for God today is the spiritual battle in which Christians are engaged. Our enemies are demons, "We wrestle not against flesh and blood, but against principalities, against powers, against the rulers of the darkness of this world, against spiritual wickedness in high places" (Eph. 6:12). The phrase "principalities . . . powers . . . rulers of darkness of this world, against spiritual wickedness" refers to demons and the power of the unseen world. Part of the work of demons, particularly as it relates to the Christian life, is struggling against Christians on the spiritual level. This condition is the reason behind the apostolic imperative, "Put on the whole armour of God, that ye may be able to stand against the wiles of the devil" (Eph. 6:11). Without spiritual help from God, the Christian is unable to win the battle against demons. Cyprian, the great church father, knew well the nature of this spiritual battle.

> For the rest, what else is waged daily in the world but a battle against the devil, but a struggle with continual onsets against his darts and weapons? With avarice, with lewdness, with anger, with ambition, we have a conflict; with the vices of the flesh, with the allurements of the world, we have a continual and stubborn fight. The mind of man besieged and surrounded on all sides by the assault of the devil with difficulty opposes these foes one by one, with difficulty resists them. If avarice is cast to the ground, lust springs up; if lust is put down, ambition takes its place; if ambition is disdained, anger provokes, pride puffs up, drunkenness invites, envy destroys harmony, jealousy severs friendships. You are forced to curse, which the divine law prohibits; you are compelled to swear, which is forbidden.[18]

I. THE WILL OF GOD. It must be frustrating to demons after they had accomplished some evil scheme to later find out that they were carrying out the will of God. Satan did not realize what

God wanted to do in Job's life when he caused him physical suffering. Also, God used "an evil spirit" to accomplish His will in the life of Saul, Israel's first king (1 Sam. 16:14). On another occasion, God used "a lying spirit" to deceive the false prophets of the evil king, Ahab (1 Kgs. 22:22-23). At the end of the Great Tribulation, demons will be used by God to gather the nations of the world to the battlefield of Armageddon (Rev. 9:16). God is able to use even demons to accomplish His will.

J. DEMON POSSESSION. The last activity of demons to be described is the work that has been popularly referred to as demon possession. However, this phrase does not occur in the original language; it is translated "demonized."

Demon possession, as we understand it, occurs when God permits demons to possess a person and control his mind or body. It is a culmination of a volitional rejection of God and a volitional acceptance of Satan and his demons.

Demon possession is the opposite of the filling of the Spirit. Just as some Christians are more effective when filled with the Holy Spirit, so some unbelievers have greater demonic power as a result of their demonic possession. The same word is used of the Holy Spirit's control in Ephesians 5:18 as Satan's control of Ananias and Sapphira (Acts 5:3). Demon possession and demon activity are more commonly recognized among heathen societies. However, there is increasing evidence of demonic activity in Western society because of its waning Christian influence. As this nation turns from God and more people worship Satan and demons, there will be more evidence of demon activity in our society.

Many have conjectured about whether or not demons can "possess" or "influence" believers. Although the Bible is silent concerning Christians being "possessed," this should not stop us from drawing theological principles from Scripture and developing a position on which to stand. A true child of God cannot be demonized because he is indwelt by the power of the Holy Spirit. Paul states in Ephesians 4:30, "And grieve not the Holy Spirit of God, whereby ye are sealed unto the day of redemption." The believer is sealed, or held in protective custody, by the Holy Spirit. If the Holy Spirit is infinitely more powerful than Satan, why would He permit one of His children to be snatched away by Satan? The Holy Spirit could easily destroy Satan and his entire ungodly horde, but He chooses not to, for the demons are part of God's master plan. The authority exercised by Satan is allowed by God, for he can do nothing without God's prior approval. Paul also describes the extent of the Holy Spirit's sealing. "Unto the day of redemption" is clearly a reference to when we finally arrive in heaven and are no longer subject to demonic attacks. However, a church member, who is simply a professing believer, is subject to demon possession. But a true possessor of salvation, according to 1 John, will not only obey Christ's commandments (1 John 2:4), but also walk in the ways of our Lord (1 John 1:6).

Therefore, when dealing with demon possession, the discussion must be limited to unbelievers only. This is not to suggest that believers are immune to demonic work. The Bible clearly reveals that believers can be externally harassed or influenced by demons. The difference between possession refers to internal control, whereas influence refers to external suggestions. An example of demonic harassment occurs in 1 Thess. 2:18, "Wherefore we would have come to you, even I Paul, once and again; but Satan hindered us." Through external circumstances, Satan was able to thwart the plans of Paul. Influence is more severe than harassment, for demonic influence affects the weaknesses of our Christian testimony (weaknesses which are readily learned by demons). Demons can influence the mind by placing certain objects or temptations before it.

To understand the extent of demon possession in the life of an unbeliever, we need to develop a concise definition and examine the reality, cause, characteristics, and stages of demon possession.

Charles Hodge, in his scholarly works, writes,

> By possession is meant the inhabitation of an evil spirit in such relation to the body and soul as to exert a controlling influence, producing violent agitations and great suffering, both mental and corporeal.[19]

The very nature of demon possession has led many skeptics to entirely repudiate the notion, suggesting that there exists a more plausible explanation for the bizarre behavior of people during the time of Christ. Merrill Unger and Charles Hodge supply us with four of the most prominent objections as given by skeptics.

1. *The Mythical Theory*. The basic idea of this hypothesis, advanced notably by David Friedrich Stauss and the mythical school, is that the whole narrative of Jesus' demon expulsions is merely symbolic, without actual foundation in fact. Demon possession, so-called, is but a vivid symbol of the prevalence of evil in the world, and the casting out of demons by our Lord, a corresponding figure of triumph over evil by His doctrine and life.

. . . .

2. *The Accommodation Theory*. The proponents of the accommodation theory say that our Lord and the Evangelists in making reference to demon possession, spoke only in accommodation to the prevalent ignorance and superstition of their auditors, without making any assertion as to the actual existence or nonexistence of the phenomena described, or the truth or falsity of current belief. It is concluded that, since the symptoms were often those of physical disease (as blindness and dumbness, Matt. 12:22; epilepsy, Mark 9:17-27), or those appearing in common dementia (as in Matt. 8:28; Mark 5:1-5), and since the phrase "to have a demon" was apparently used as equivalent "to be mad" (John 7:20; 8:48; 10:20), and since it is erroneously assumed that cases of demon possession are not now known to occur in our day, therefore, our Lord spoke, and the Evangelists wrote, in adjustment to the common convictions of the time and with a view to being clearly understood, especially by the patients themselves, but that the "demonized" were merely persons afflicted with uncommon diseases of body and mind.

3. *The Hallucination Theory.* Demon possession is explained, under the hypothesis of hallucination, as a mere psychological delusion on the part of the victim, who, diseased and distraught, becomes wrought up to such a high pitch of emotional frenzy or mental excitement that he imagines himself possessed and controlled by another and more powerful being. Under the suppression of human consciousness and the dethronement of reason, he speaks in the character of the fancied demon (Mark 5:7). The cure of this strange illusion is virtually the same as the ejection from him of a real demon. [20]

4. *The Nonexistent Today Theory.* It is objected that such cases of demonized people do not now occur. If indeed there exists the possibility of demon possession, science demands that it must exist today and be verifiable. Since demonized people do not exist today, it naturally leads to the conclusion reached by many secular psychologists that the possibility of demon possession is non-definitive theory, and probably never existed. [21]

If the claims as outlined in the first three objections are accepted, the character of Christ and the integrity of the Scriptures are questioned. When the Bible states that Jesus commanded an evil spirit to depart from a man, this individual possessed an evil spirit. To deny this truth is to deny the deity of Christ, for God cannot lie. When Jesus claimed to cast out demons from demonized people, He literally did it. The fourth objection is simply an argument from silence, which neither proves or refutes anything. The absence of a worldwide belief in demonic exorcisms today cannot regulate or be relegated to the period of time when Christ physically walked upon the planet earth.

In light of the fourth objection, we are faced with an interesting question. Does demon possession exist now? In highly civilized nations, demon possession is lightly treated or considered an issue of open ridicule. However, in primitive nations, missionaries frequently reveal the powerful belief in extraordinary achievements accomplished by those who are demonized. Some theologians respond to this question with an emphatic "No." Dabney describes the basis for their reasoning.

Do "possessions" now exist? Many reply, No; some, on the supposition of a progressive restriction of Satan's license; others, supposing that in the age of miracles, Providence made special allowance of this malice, . . . and show earnests of its overthrow. The latter is one object of Christ's victories over these "possessions." See Mark iii: 27; Luke xi: 20: x: 17-20, (where we have a separate proof of the spiritual nature of these possessions, as above shown). [22]

A major weakness with those who deny the possibility of demon possession today is a failure to realize that the victory accomplished by Christ on the cross extends solely to believers and not unbelievers. Jesus' statement concerning the lost is still relevant: "Ye are of your father the devil, and the lusts of your father ye will do" (John 8:44). If a person spends a great deal of his time seeking to communicate with the spirit world and desires to give himself over to the control of another being, then it is reasonable to conclude that he is able to become demonized. The restraining ministry of the Holy Spirit (2 Thess. 2:7) limits the forcible seizure of an unbeliever's mind and body by a demon. But if a person constantly and willingly gives himself over to demonic control, he probably will, in time, become demonized.

Having determined the possibility of demon possession, the next task is to discover the cause of demon possession. It is important to understand that when a person is possessed by a demon there is a struggle between the human soul and the demon. Just as the filling of the Spirit releases power according to the degree of yieldedness, so a person's yieldedness to evil and a demon will determine how much he is controlled by the demon. Demon possession is not an accident. A demon does not forcibly seize a person and possess him. The person has "willed" to become possessed by demons and has made a choice to allow the demon to come in, or asked the demon to come in. The more the person sells out to the demon, the more possessed he becomes. Hence, demon possession is a gradual phenomenon. Commenting on the causes of demon possession, Fred Dickson discloses two biblical reasons for the existence of demonized people:

> Causes for initiating the condition vary and are often complex. Probably "in the great majority of cases possession is doubtless to be traced to yielding voluntarily to temptation and to sin, initially weakening the human will, so that it is rendered susceptible to complete or partial eclipse and subjugation by the possessing spirit." In other cases, moral responsibility may be less, as in the case of the boy who suffered possession from childhood (Mark 9:21). It may be in such cases that the occult sins of the parents back to the third and fourth generation preceding have rendered children susceptible. The second commandment, forbidding idolatry, warns that God will recompense this iniquity of the fathers on the third and fourth generations of those who hate Him (Ex 20:4-5). Demons are the dynamic behind idolatry, and they may be allowed to lay claim to their devotees.[23]

As an unbeliever ventures deeper into the spiritual realm seeking for greater possession by demons, he will undoubtedly begin to emit certain characteristics that are manifested in demonized people. John Nevius, a Christian missionary for many years in China, recounts firsthand contacts with the rampant evil forces behind an ancient pagan culture. Through working with the Chinese, Nevius became acutely aware of demonic strongholds and predominant characteristics of demonized people. Nevius assigns the following characteristics to demon possessed individuals.[24]

a. The supposed demoniac at the time of "possession" passes into an abnormal state, the character of which varies indefinitely, being marked by depression and melancholy; or vacancy and stupidity amounting sometimes almost to idiocy, or it may be that he becomes ecstatic, or ferocious and malignant.

b. During transition from the normal to the abnormal state, the subject is often thrown into paroxysms, more or less violent, during which he sometimes falls on the ground senseless, or foams at the mouth, presenting symptoms similar to those of epilepsy or hysteria.

c. The intervals between these attacks vary indefinitely from hours to months, and during these intervals the physical and mental condition of the subject may be in every respect healthy and normal. The duration of the abnormal states varies from a few minutes to several days. The attacks are sometimes mild, and sometimes violent. If frequent and violent the physical health suffers.

d. During the transition period the subject often retains more or less of his normal consciousness. The violence of the paroxysms is increased if the subject struggles against, and endeavors to repress the abnormal symptoms. When he yields himself to them the violence of the paroxysms abates, or ceases altogether.

e. When normal consciousness is restored after one of these attacks, the subject is entirely ignorant of everything which has passed during that state.

f. The most striking characteristic of these cases is that the subject evidences another personality, and the normal personality, for the time being, is partially or wholly dormant.

g. The new personality presents traits of character utterly different from those which really belong to the subject in his normal state, and this change of character is with rare exceptions in the direction of moral obliquity and impurity.

h. A differentiating mark of demonomania, intimately connected with the assumption of the new personality is that with the change of personality there is a complete change of moral character.

i. Many persons while "demon-possessed" give evidence of knowledge which cannot be accounted for in ordinary ways. They often appear to know of the Lord Jesus Christ as a Divine Person, and show an aversion to, and fear of Him. They sometimes converse in foreign languages of which, in their normal states, they are entirely ignorant.

j. There are often heard, in connection with "demon-possessions," rappings and noises in places where no physical cause for them can be found; and tables, chairs, crockery, and the like are moved about without, so far as can be discovered, any application of physical force, exactly as we are told is the case among spiritualists.

Drawing from his experiences in China, Nevius was able to develop a system that categorized demonized people into one of four different stages. Based upon the nature and extent of the characteristics employed by a demon-possessed person, Nevius could determine how severely a person was possessed. Nevius concluded that no one suddenly became demonized. Rather demon possession represented a gradual process that was clearly marked by stages of development.

First, we have the initial stage of demon influence which may be called that of obsession. It is the stage of the first approach, and the introductory or tentative efforts of the demon. In this stage cases are often unpronounced in their character, leaving it difficult to determine whether they are to be classed with demon-possession, idiocy, lunacy, or epilepsy. In many cases of demon-possession, this stage is wanting, the second stage described below being the first.

Second. The stage marked by a struggle for possession, in which the unwilling subject resists and sometimes successfully, but generally pines away until he yields an involuntary subjection to the demon's will. This may be called the transition stage or the crisis. It is comparatively of short duration.

Third. This stage may be designated, with regard to the subject, as that of subjection and subserviency, and with regard to the demon, as that of training and development. The condition of the subject is most of the time healthy and normal. He is peaceful and quiet except in the paroxysm, which occurs in passing from the normal to the abnormal state. This stage may continue for years.

Fourth. In this stage the demonized subject has developed capabilities for use, and is willing to be used. He is the trained, accustomed, voluntary slave of the demon. He is called in China *Tu Shien,* "spirit in a body," or "Wu-po," "woman sorcerer;" in the language of the Old Testament, (according to the particular line of his development and use) a witch, or a "soothsayer", or a "necromancer;" in modern English phrase a "developed medium."[25]

V. THE WORSHIP OF DEMONS

When Israel finally prepared to enter the Promised Land, God gave definite instructions regarding their relationship to the occult religions of Canaan. "When thou art come into the land which the Lord thy God giveth thee, thou shalt not learn to do after the abominations of those nations" (Deut. 18:9). Paul reiterates the Old Testament command to abstain from demonic worship in equally strong language, "Let no man beguile you of your reward in a voluntary humility and worshipping of angels, intruding into those things which he hath not seen, vainly puffed up by his fleshly mind" (Col. 2:18).

A. DIVINATION. Divination was one of the specific practices named by Moses in his prohibition of occult worship (Deut. 19:10). Often this practice included the killing of a chicken or some small animal, and on occasion, observation of its liver to determine the state of affairs and direction of the immediate future (Ezek. 21:21). Essentially divination is an illegitimate means of trying to determine the will of God. This would apply to other variations of divination, including palmistry and tealeaf reading. The Christian desiring to know the will of God should consult the Scriptures, not the stars (Psa. 119:9).

B. NECROMANCY. A second occult practice banned by God, necromancy, is an effort to communicate with and interrogate the dead. As the Bible teaches the dead are unable to communicate with the living (Luke 16:27-31), it only stands to reason that those who claim to have this ability are lying or are themselves deceived. In either case, the necromancer was considered an abomination unto the Lord (Deut. 18:11-12).

C. MAGIC. The use of magic formulas and incantations was also forbidden. Today it is popular to distinguish between white and black magic, but leading biblical scholars agree that both forms of magic find their source and strength in demon power. Black magic describes people who employ evil spirits to bring forth calamity and sorrow upon another, whereas those who practice white magic are those who are "good people" who seem to do "good things" for people, usually for a "small price." White magicians would include healers who attempt to derive their power from "good forces," or witch doctors, who perform healing ceremonies upon sick people in which magical incantations are used.

White magic should not be confused with tricks that are simple illusions. Christian magicians have used tricks as object lessons in order to better communicate their lesson. These tricks should not be confused with white magic, for magic requires the intervention of a supernatural force, whereas tricks are devised by humans and performed by humans; no external force is called upon for assistance. Some biblical scholars have strongly denounced the practice of white magic as demonic in origin. Unger makes some pertinent observations concerning white magic.

White magic is black magic in pious masquerade. It uses, in a magic way, the name of God, Christ, and the Holy Spirit, along with Bible phrases and terminology, but is demonic in character. It is carried on in many so-called Christian circles, especially in areas of rampant cultism or where sound Bible teaching is lacking and the participants are not aware of its demonic nature (cf. 1 Timothy 4:1, 2; 1 John 4:1, 2). It is called "white" because it parades under the banner of light, in contrast to "black" magic that openly enlists the aid of the powers of darkness.

White magic furnishes a perfect illustration of the Apostle Paul's warning: "And no marvel; for Satan himself is transformed into an angel of light. Therefore, it is no great thing if his ministers also be transformed as the ministers of righteousness; whose end shall be according to their works" (2 Corinthians 11:14, 15).

White magic comes into play and alien spirits "not of God" (1 John 4:1) begin to operate when the truth of God is perverted. The Christian's only sure protection against deception by "spirits not of God" is found in Christ through the Bible, rightly understood, believed, and implicitly obeyed (1 John 4:1-3).

. . . .

In biblical faith, trust is placed solely in the Lord Jesus. In white magic it is deflected to someone else (the human agent) or to something else (one's own faith, etc.). In the biblical prayer of faith, the praying person subjects himself to the will of God. In white magic the help of God is demanded under the assumption that exercising such power is in accordance with God's will. In white magic the Christian markings are mere decorations that camouflage the magical means for knowledge or power.

The person who prays in true faith is under the Holy Spirit's inspiration. The white magician is inspired by spirits not of God.[26]

Those who practice magic are under certain limits as to what they can accomplish (Dan. 4:7). Even when it appears that magicians are able to duplicate the power of God, they still fall short of what God is able to accomplish (Exod. 7:11-12).

D. SORCERY. Closely related to magic is sorcery. Magic usually relates to accomplishing specific acts—such as rods becoming serpents—whereas sorcery relates more closely with calling upon demons to create situations around people. Thus the enchanter or sorcerer is one who uses incantations or omens. Their practices may have also included the use of mood-changing or psychedelic drugs. This has led some Bible scholars to denounce the use of such drugs because they are used as part of occult worship.

E. WITCHCRAFT. There exists a growing number of those who call themselves witches. Witchcraft is directly opposed to God (Deut. 18:10). When Saul became the first king of Israel, one of his acts was to ban the practice of witchcraft from the kingdom (1 Sam. 28:9). The witch is one who makes use of magic and sorcery to accomplish the will of demons.

A significant problem for any theologian to fully grasp occurs in 1 Samuel 28:7-20 in which the witch of Endor conjures up the spirit of Samuel. Several leading Bible scholars have rejected the possibility of Samuel, in spirit form, returning from the dead and communicating to the witch a message for Saul. In light of Deuteronomy 18, in which God strongly denounces the practice of necromancy (speaking with the dead) it is very unlikely that God would have permitted a witch to recall the spirit of Samuel.

On the other hand, some biblical scholars support the idea that Samuel's spirit did indeed appear to the witch. They attribute Samuel 's appearance not to the power of the witch, rather to the intervening power of God, who permitted Samuel to address the witch and answer Saul's question. Several reasons are given. First, the witch was surprised "when she saw Samuel." Apparently this was not the normal manner in which she communicated with her spirits. Secondly, the prophetic message of Samuel was so accurate that no demonic power could have possibly guessed that (1) Israel would fall to the Philistines the following day; (2) Saul would be killed and taken to the place where Samuel resided; (3) Saul's sons would also be killed and taken to where Samuel stayed, all of this occurring the very next day. Since demons cannot predict the future and only God can, then the accuracy of Samuel's message strongly supports the possibility that Samuel's spirit returned to speak to Saul. Agreeing with this position, Merrill Unger writes,

Saul asked that Samuel be brought up, because he knew there was none like the venerable prophet and judge who knew so well God's mind and future events. The woman doubtless began to make her customary preparations, expecting, as usual, to lapse into a trance-like state, and be used by her "control" or "divining demon," who would then proceed to impersonate the individual called for. The startling thing, however, was that the usual occult procedure was abruptly cut short by the sudden and totally unexpected appearance of the spirit of Samuel. The medium was consequently transfixed with terror, and screamed out with shock and fright, when she perceived that God had stepped in, and by His power and special permission, Samuel's actual spirit was presented to pronounce final doom upon Saul. The sight of Samuel was the proof of divine intervention, and was indubitable evidence that the man in disguise was Saul. The medium's terrified conduct and her complete loss of poise at the appearance of a real spirit of a deceased person, constitutes a complete and irrefutable Scriptural disclosure of the fraudulency all spiritistic mediumship.

The woman, to be sure, had the power to communicate with wicked spirits, as do modern mediums of spiritism and psychical research. These deceiving demons represent themselves to their mediums, and through them to their clients, as the spirits of the departed dead, but actually their messages do not emanate from the deceased at all, but from themselves as lying spirits, who cleverly impersonate the dead.

The return of Samuel from the spirit-world, though actual, is unique and exceptional, under any consideration. To begin, it is not the case of a medium bringing back the spirit of a deceased person. The woman's "divining demon" had nothing whatever to do with Samuel's sudden appearance. She and her spirit accomplice were completely sidetracked at the presence of Samuel, and had nothing more to do with the proceedings. Evil spirits may impersonate the dead, but they cannot produce them. Only God can do that, as He did in this case. Moreover, the incident is the only example in all Scripture where God permitted a deceased person to come back, as a spirit, to hold communication with the living. Others have come back from the dead, albeit not as spirits, but as raised persons, such as Jairus' daughter, the widow of Nain's son, and Lazarus of Bethany. They did not receive resurrection bodies, nor did they, we may confidently believe, retain any consciousness of the spirit-world, and they afterward died again. But Samuel's spirit was not re-embodied, and, therefore, he was not disqualified from relating information from the other world. The case of our Lord, and those who came "out of the tombs after his resurrection" and "appeared unto many" in Jerusalem (Matt. 27:52-53), were resurrected persons, not spirits (Luke 24:49), nor in any sense examples of spiritism.

The same is true of the appearance of Moses and Elijah on the Mount of Transfiguration. They, too, were present not as "spirits," but in their glorified bodies.

Samuel's return in spirit form from the realms of the dead is, then, altogether unparalleled and unprecedented, both in manner and purpose; in manner, because it was by special divine power and permission; in purpose, because it was for the unique intent of divine rebuke and warning to all who resort to occultism, and particularly, to pronounce immediate sentence on Saul for this, his final plunge into ruin (1 Chron. 10:13).[27]

F. ASTROLOGY. Perhaps the most popular form of the occult practiced today is astrology. Contemporary astrology is really a combination of astrological cults practiced in Babylon, Egypt, and Canaan. In Canaan, astrology centered around the bull. The worship of the golden calf, child sacrifices to Molech, and Baal worship were all part of Canaanite astrology. The Old Testament clearly prohibits God's people from involvement. In Egypt, God challenged the astrological gods of Egypt in sending ten plaques which directly attacked the authority of those gods. The highest of the Egyptian gods was Ra, the sun god. Three days of darkness was a direct indictment against the religion of Egypt.

VI. DELIVERANCE FROM DEMONS

The ability to cast out a demon from a person (exorcism), according to some theologians, is a spiritual gift that comes only from God. However, the Bible never supports this claim. Rather it supports the idea that any believer who is mature in the faith and knows the procedures of removing a demon from a person can perform the task. To deliver a person from a demon a person must have specific qualifications and a specific format. Writing on this subject, Dickason describes three qualifications expected of an exorcist.

1. *Spiritual.* The counselor must be born of the Spirit by trusting Christ, having the assurance of his right standing before God (Jn 1:12-13; 1 Jn 5:4-5, 18). He must have dedicated his life to God so that he does not participate in Satan's sin of independence (Ro 12:1-2). Only in this way can he resist the devil (Ja 4:6-8). He must allow the Holy Spirit of God to control his life (Gal 5:16-18, 25; Eph 5:18). Only in this way can he know God's power operating in his life to live for Christ and to help others.

2. *Scriptural.* The counselor must know God's Word. He must know what it says about the enemy, Satan and the demons, their power and methods (2 Co 2:11; 11:14). He must know God's armor and how to use it (Eph 6:10-18). He must know of Christ's victory over Satan and be convinced of his position of power in Christ (Col 2:15). He should be acquainted with the biblical accounts of Christ and the apostles in their dealings with demons.

3. *Special.* If possible, the counselor should have some medical qualifications and psychiatric training. Correct diagnosis is highly important and distinction between disease and demonic must be made. A mature Christian with experience in dealing with the demonic is preferred. There are definite symptoms of demon possession, but discernment is essential. The

wise counselor will seek advice and confer with other counselors for the oppressed when in doubt.[28]

In addition to the qualifications, a detailed format should be developed and closely followed. First, casting out demons is not something the exorcist does by his power; it is in the power of God. He must begin by recognizing the blood of Jesus Christ that cleanses from sin and is the only basis for helping anyone spiritually. The exorcist must be sure he has confessed all sin and is in fellowship with Christ. Secondly, there must be a choice by the patient (the demonized person) that he wants to be rid of the demon. Third, during the exorcism there must be an exposure of the demon as a demon. Most demon possession is hidden and observers do not perceive the person as demonized. In the fourth place, the patient has to decide whether he is going to follow God and be free of the demon, or if he is going to yield to the demon and remain in his possessed state. Just as God does not heal those who do not want to be healed, God will not cast out the demon for those who do not want the demon cast out. Fifth, the role of the exorcist is to share faith, strength, and wisdom with the person who needs help. The role of the exorcist is to witness what God can do in building up the faith of the person who is demon possessed. Then the demonized person can make a decision. Sixth, ultimate exorcism is not in the power of the person who is helping, nor is it in the power of the patient; but in the power of God who wrestles directly with Satan. The demon is cast out by the blood of Jesus Christ. Seventh, it is by faith that a person is free from the demon.

VII. CONCLUSION

There are many other forms of demon worship today. Those who are practicing in the occult need to follow the Ephesian example of denouncing their involvement with demons. Apparently, some Ephesian believers were "dabbling" in the occult until an attempted exorcism backfired in their town. Then "many that believed came," and confessed, and showed their deeds (Acts 19:18). The result of such action led to a revival in which many occult books were destroyed and the church experienced revival. Perhaps a similar abandonment of the occult will produce similar results today. In any case, every Christian needs to be properly equipped to do battle with demons.

ENDNOTES

1.   Flavius Josephus, *Wars of the Jews* (Massachusetts: Harvard University Press, 1976), 63.*

2.   John Dick, *Lectures on Theology* (New York: Robert Carter & Brothers, 1978),

399.

3.   Thomas Manton, *An Exposition of Jude* (Delaware: Sovereign Grace Publishers, 1972), 199.*.

4.   Ibid., 198.*

5.   Dick, 399.

6.   John Gill, *A Body of Divinity* (Grand Rapids: Sovereign Grace Publishers, 1971), 307-308.

7.   Clarence Larkin, *The Spirit World* (Philadelphia: Clarence Larkin Estate, 1921), 49.

8.   George Lawrence Lawlor, *The Epistle of Jude* (United States: Presbyterian and Reformed, 1972), 66-68.

9.   R. C. H. Lenski, *The Interpretation of The Epistles of St. Peter, St. John, and St. Jude* (Minneapolis: Augsburg, 1968), 624.

10.   C. F. Keil and F. Delitzsch, *Biblical Commentary on the Old Testament*, trans. James Martin (Grand Rapids: Eerdmans, 1951), 1:131.

11.   Manton, 202.*

12.   Dick, 400-401.

13.   Hal Lindsey, *Satan Is Alive and Well on Planet Earth* (Grand Rapids: Zondervan, 1972).

14.   C. S. Lewis, *The Screwtape Letters*.

15.   Lewis Chafer, *Systematic Theology* (Dallas: Dallas Seminary Press, 1948), 114.

16.   Charles Hodge, *Systematic Theology* (Grand Rapids: Eerdmans, 1975), 644-645.

17.   John Dick, *Lectures on Theology* (New York: Robert Carter and Brothers, 1878), 405.

18.   Cyprian, *Morality* quoted by Michael Scanlan & Randall J. Cirner, *Deliverance from Evil Spirits: A Weapon for Spiritual Warfare* (Ann Arbor: Servant Book Publications, 1980), 28.

19.   Hodge, 645.

20.   Merrill E. Unger, *Biblical Demonology* (Illinois: Scripture Press, 1963), 90-92.

21.   Hodge, 646-647.

22.   Robert Dabney, *Lectures in Systematic Theology* (Grand Rapids: Zondervan, 1975), 274.

23.   C. Fred Dickason, *Angels, Elect and Evil* (Chicago: Moody Press, 1975), 184.

24.   John Nevius, *Demon Possession* (Grand Rapids: Kregel, 1973), 142-145.

25.   Ibid., 285-286.

26.   Merrill E. Unger, *Demons in the World Today* (Wheaton: Tyndale House, 1971), 85-86.

27.   Merrill Unger, *Biblical Demonology*, 149-150.

28.   Dickason, 194-195.

* Denotes page number(s) could not be verified.

CHAPTER IX – SOTERIOLOGY

The Doctrine of Salvation

I. INTRODUCTION

The term "soteriology," identifying this section of theology, is a derivative of the two Greek words, *soteria* and *logos*, which literally means "a word, idea or study of salvation." Many works of theology include this division under Christology as a part of the work or atonement of Christ. Others deal with salvation only under the title of "Soteriology." This work has taken a combined approach. The atonement and direct results of the work of Christ are dealt with under Christology. This section (Soteriology) deals with the general aspects of salvation, including: election, salvation in the Old Testament, obtaining salvation, regeneration, sanctification, the believer's new position, and eternal security.

The first analysis of salvation was the historic work of Christ on the cross in saving man from sin, and the present section is on the saving work of Christ in the life of the believer. This distinction is evident in the preaching of Paul, as he defined "Christ crucified" (1 Cor. 1:23) as a historical fact, and "the power of God unto salvation to everyone that believeth" (Rom. 1:16) as a present experience. Paul did not preach different plans of salvation, but rather recognized two different aspects of the same gospel. Some ministers tend to dwell at length on the historical or theological aspects of salvation. Others tend to have an experience oriented approach to presenting salvation. Concerning the experience of salvation, Charles Hodge observed,

> The subjective change wrought in the soul by the grace of God, is variously designated in Scripture. It is called a new birth, a resurrection, a new life, a new creature, a renewing of the mind, a dying to sin and living to righteousness, a translation from darkness to light, etc. In theological language, it is called regeneration, renovation, conversion. These terms are often used interchangeably. They are also used sometimes for the whole process of spiritual renovation or restoration of the image of God, and sometimes for a particular stage of that process.[1]

Although people have been saved since Christ accomplished His work on the cross, only in time has there developed a distinction between salvation accomplished (justification) and salvation applied (sanctification). The historical and theological aspect of salvation includes the redemption by blood, the reconciliation of man to God, the propitiation of God's wrath, the fulfilling of the law and the forgiveness of sins. These great doctrines have always been the center of Christianity. The applied or evangelistic aspect of salvation includes evangelism, regeneration, sanctification and discipleship. Prior to the work of Martin Luther and other Protestant reformers, relatively little attention was given to putting the doctrine of salvation into systematic order. In his *History of Christian Doctrine*, Shedd observes,

> Taking the term atonement in its technical signification, to denote *the satisfaction of Divine justice for the sin of man, by the substituted penal sufferings of the Son of God*, we find a slower scientific unfolding of this great cardinal doctrine than of any other of the principal truths of Christianity. Our investigations in this branch of inquiry will disclose the fact that while the doctrines of Theology and Anthropology received a considerably full development during the Patristic and Scholastic periods, it was reserved for the Protestant church, and the Modern theological mind, to bring the doctrines of Soteriology to a correspondent degree of expansion.[2]

II. SALVATION

The term "salvation" is the most common biblical expression to identify the change wrought in the life of one who by faith obtains the benefits of the atonement of Christ. The term appears in both Old and New Testaments, implying the ideas of deliverance, safety, preservation, healing and soundness. American Evangelist Billy Sunday, in a sermon on Acts 16:31, said,

> *Salvation* means "to be brought from a state or condition not favorable to our welfare or happiness into a condition which is favorable." The salvation of the sick would mean their health, but the salvation mentioned here is from sin.[3]

Although the evangelist was not known as a systematic theologian, his simple definition of the term communicates the contemporary usage of the biblical expression. In a more technical definition of the biblical term, Walters observes,

> The English term used in AV is derived from Latin *salvare*, "to save" and *salus*, "health", "help", and translates Hebrew *yesúa* and cognates (breath, ease, safety) and GK. *soteria* and cognates (cure, recovery, redemption, remedy, rescue, welfare). It means the action or result of deliverance or preservation from danger or disease, implying safety, health, and prosperity.[4]

As with many other theological expressions, salvation has a more specialized meaning when brought from the exegetical to the contemporary theological arena. It "denotes the whole process by which man is delivered from all that would prevent his attaining to the highest good that God has prepared for him."[5] Chafer observes,

> According to its largest meaning as used in the Scriptures, the word *salvation* represents the whole work of God by which He rescues man from the eternal ruin and doom of sin and bestows on him the riches of His grace, even eternal life now and

eternal glory in Heaven. "Salvation is of the Lord" (Jonah 2:9). Therefore, it is in every aspect a work of God in behalf of man, and is in no sense a work of man in behalf of God.[6]

Salvation is both an instantaneous event and progressive experience in the life of the believer. The verb appears in Scripture in three tenses, past, present, and future. As noted in the *New Scofield Reference Bible*:

> Salvation is in three tenses: (1) the Christian *has been* saved from the guilt and penalty of sin (Lk. 7:50; 1 Cor. 1:18; 2 Cor. 2:15; Eph. 2:5,8; 2 Tim. 1:9) and is safe. (2) The Christian *is being* saved from the habit and dominion of sin (Rom. 6:14; 8:2; 2 Cor. 3:18; Gal. 2:19-20; Phil. 1:19; 2:12-13: 2 Th. 2:13). And (3) the Christian *will be* saved at the Lord's return, from all the bodily infirmities that are the result of sin and God's curse upon the sinful world (Rom. 8:18-23; 1 Cor. 15:42-44), and brought into entire conformity to Christ (Rom. 13:11; Heb. 10:36; 1 Pet. 1:5; 1 Jn. 3:2).[7]

The progressive nature of salvation does not in any way minimize the importance of an experience whereby the individual "is saved," but reveals what it means to be saved, including the understanding that that experience was the beginning, not the end, of the work of Christ in the life of the believer. As Easton notes,

> Salvation is both a present and future matter for us. The full realization of all that God has in store will not be ours until the end of human history (if, indeed, there will not be opened infinite possibilities of eternal growth), but the enjoyment of these blessings depends on conditions fulfilled in us and by us now.[8]

This future aspect of salvation does not by any means imply the possibility of an incomplete salvation. Those who hold that salvation in some way depends upon man's obedience of faithfulness, believe that those who do not "stick to it" will fail to acquire the benefits of their future salvation. But, as Chafer writes,

> The fact that some aspects of salvation are yet to be accomplished for the one who believes does not imply that there is ground for doubt as to its ultimate completion; for it is nowhere taught that any feature of salvation depends upon the faithfulness of man. God is faithful, and having begun a good work, He will perform it until the day of Jesus Christ (Phil. 1:6).[9]

Jesus only used the term "salvation" once (Luke 19:9), although He used many other expressions to identify the salvation experience. Perhaps John, more than any other biblical writer, was overwhelmed with the nature of this "so great salvation." He used the active word "believe" to communicate the relational aspect of salvation, showing that salvation is a dynamic quality of life, not just a passive point. In every chapter of his Gospel, John suggests this living aspect of salvation.

SALVATION IN THE GOSPEL OF JOHN[10]

1:12-13	Men are born sons of God by trusting in Christ.
2:5	Faith is doing "whatsoever he saith unto you."
3:5	New birth by the Spirit is essential for entering the kingdom.
4:22	Salvation is of the Jews and is a gift inwardly transforming and equipping men for worship.
5:24	Believers have already passed from death to life.
5:39	The Scriptures testify of life in the Son.
6:68	Jesus has the quickening words of eternal life.
7:39	Water symbolizes the saving life.
8:12	There is safety in the guidance of the Light.
8:32, 36	There is liberty through truth in the Son.
9:25, 37, 39	Salvation is spiritual sight.
10:10	Entrance into the safety and abundant life is through Christ.
11:25-26	Resurrection life belongs to the believer.
12:32	Christ lifted up in death draws men to Himself.
13:10	Initial washing signifies salvation.
14:6	Jesus is the true and living way to the Father's abode.
15:5	Abiding in Him is the secret of life's resources.
16:7-15	The Holy Spirit will convict to bring to salvation.
17:2-3, 12	Jesus keeps safely those who have knowledge of the true God and Himself.
18:28-38	Jesus witnessed a good confession before Pilate.
19:30	Salvation is accomplished.
20:21-23	Words of peace and pardon accompany His gift of the Spirit.
21:15-18	Healing love reinstils love in Peter and reinstates him for service.

III. SALVATION IN THE OLD TESTAMENT

The message of grace and salvation is clearly related to the atoning death of Christ. Repeatedly the apostles pointed to the cross as the event, which secured salvation. There is never any hint that salvation can be experienced apart from faith in the atoning death of Christ. This being so, the question naturally arises, "How were people saved before Christ died? What was the basis of their salvation?" The individuals of faith identified in Hebrews 11 lived before Christ. Who was the object of, and what was the content of their faith? Since Christ said, "No man cometh unto the Father, but by me" (John 14:6), it can be assumed that the Old Testament saints came to the Father by Christ. But how was this effected?

A dispensationalist believes that man is saved by grace through faith in every dispensation. Even so, one of the most oft-repeated charges against dispensationalists is that they teach more than one way of salvation. Dispensationalism is accused of having an approach to the Scriptures that requires more than one way of salvation. According to Broomall in his article on dispensationalism,

If any man is saved in any dispensation other than those of Promise and Grace, he is saved by works and not by faith! (The dispensationalist is clearly left with two methods of salvation on his hands—works for the majority of dispensations, faith for the rest—and we have . . . to deal with a fickle God who deals with man in various ways at various times.[11]

Voicing the same concern, Clarence Bass concludes,

Nevertheless, the presupposition of the difference between law and grace, between Israel and the church, between the different relations of God to men in the different dispensations, when carried to its logical conclusion will inevitably result in a multiple form of salvation — that men are not saved the same way in all ages.[12]

Lewis Sperry Chafer, founding president of Dallas Theological Seminary, was one of the early dispensationalists specifically named and charged with teaching more than one way of salvation. Chafer denied this charge in an article in *Bibliotheca Sacra*.

Are there two ways by which one may be saved? In reply to this question it may be stated that salvation of whatever specific character is always the work of God in behalf of man and never the work of man in behalf of God. This is to assert that God never saved any one person or group of persons on any ground than that righteous freedom to do so which the Cross of Christ secured. There is, therefore, but one way to be saved and that is by the power of God made possible through the sacrifice of Christ.[13]

Pettingill, another early dispensational Bible teacher writing on the subject of salvation, claimed,

Old Testament believers were saved exactly as New Testament believers are saved. . . . The Gospel of salvation by grace through faith is not a new thing contrary to the Old Testament and Scriptures, but is only a newly or more fully revealed thing.[14]

Actually, some statements made by covenant theologians appear to be more suggestive of two ways of salvation than the statements of dispensational writers. According to Allis, "The Law is a declaration of the will of God for man's *salvation*."[15] Berkhof notes, "Grace offers escape from the law only as a condition of salvation as it is in the covenant of works. . . ."[16] Again he says that the Scriptures refer to the law "as it functions in the covenant of works, in which the gift of eternal life was conditioned on its fulfilment.[17]

A more biblical approach to salvation in the Old Testament is to recognize the progressive nature of revelation as it relates to saving faith. As Ryrie notes, "The *basis* of salvation in every age is the death of Christ; the *requirement* for salvation in every age is faith; the *object* of faith in every age is God; the *content* of faith changes in the various dispensations."[18]

Prior to the Cross, salvation was acquired by faith in God as it is acquired today. Obviously, the content of their faith differed to some degree from that faith exercised today. This was due, not to a different Old Testament plan of salvation, but rather to the progressive nature of revelation. Thus Adam and Eve both expressed faith (Gen. 3:20; 4:1) prior to the revelation of God's Son. They did know that a Redeemer was coming, and they put their trust in Him. Easton, writing on salvation in the Old Testament, observes,

> Hence, of the human conditions, whole-hearted trust in God is the most important. (*Belief* in God is, of course, never argued in the Bible.) Inconsistent with such trust are, for instance, seeking aid from other nations (Isa. **30**:1-5), putting reliance in human skill (2 Ch. **16**:12), or forsaking Pal through fear (Jer. **42**). In Isa. **26**:20 entire passivity is demanded, and in 2 K **13**:19 lukewarmness in executing an apparently meaningless command is rebuked.[19]

In the Old Testament, men were saved as they are in the New Testament. They did not know as much as men know today, but they had to put their whole trust in what God revealed to them. They expressed their faith by bringing the blood sacrifice to God according to His instructions. They looked forward in faith to the coming Messiah and attempted to demonstrate their faith by obedience to the Old Testament law. The quality of their salvation was no different than that for those saved under grace; they simply expressed it differently according to the requirements of their dispensation.

IV. THE GRACE OF GOD IN SALVATION

Paul described "the grace of God that bringeth salvation" (Titus 2:11). That grace is the necessary basis and motivation that brings the experience of salvation to individuals. Then to reveal the progressive nature of salvation, the believer is expected to "grow in grace" as part of his experience of sanctification. As such, grace becomes an important part of the doctrine of salvation.

Formulating an all-inclusive definition of grace is difficult at best. Still, there are some basic ideas implied in the usage of this term in the New Testament. According to Easton,

> A rigid definition is hardly possible, but still a single conception is virtually present in almost every case where "grace" is found—the conception that all a Christian has or is, is centered exclusively in God and Christ, and depends utterly on God through Christ.[20]

The Greek word *charis* originally meant "to make a gift," including the idea of forgiving a debt or wrong. It came to include the forgiveness of sin. Commenting on this word as it occurs in Ephesians 2:8, Vaughan notes,

The phrase, "by grace," which has the place of emphasis in verse 8, expresses the means by which men are saved—not by weeping, not by their own willing, not through their own works or efforts, but by sovereign grace. But what is *grace*? The word is used more than one hundred fifty times in the New Testament (almost a hundred times by Paul alone) and with a wide variety of meanings. But its basic meaning is that of favor shown to the utterly undeserving. The words "by grace" assert that God was under no obligation to save man, that salvation is a bounty from God, not a reward for merit.[21]

The source of grace begins with God and is more than His response to man's request for salvation. Grace is an attribute of God which permits Him to save sinful mankind. Grace is an extension of the goodness of God toward humanity. According to Tozer,

Grace is the good pleasure of God that inclines Him to bestow benefits upon the undeserving. It is a self-existent principle inherent in the divine nature and appears to us as a self-caused propensity to pity the wretched, spare the guilty, welcome the outcast, and bring into favor those who were before under just disapprobation. Its use to us sinful men is to save us and make us sit together in heavenly places to demonstrate to the ages the exceeding riches of God's kindness to us in Christ Jesus.[22]

The concept of grace in the Scriptures is not limited exclusively to the New Testament. It is true that Jesus Christ is the Revealer of grace (John 1:17), but it is also true that grace characterized God and His actions in the Old Testament. The Hebrew word for grace is *hen*. Defining this Old Testament term, Stringer notes,

This is not a covenant word and not two-way. It is used of the action of a superior, human or divine, to an inferior. It speaks of undeserved favour, and it is translated grace (38) and favor (26). . . . No-one can show *hēn* to God (as one can show *hesed*), for no-one can do Him a favour.[23]

Salvation never has or will exist apart from the grace of God. Conservative Christians agree that salvation is all of grace and not of works. Most Christians would wholeheartedly agree with the following observation of Tozer.

No one was ever saved other than by grace, from Abel to the present moment. Since mankind was banished from the eastward Garden, none has ever returned to the divine favor except through the sheer goodness of God. And wherever grace found any man it was always by Jesus Christ. Grace indeed came by Jesus Christ, but it did not wait for His birth in the manger or His death on the cross before it became operative. Christ is the Lamb slain from the foundation of the world. The first man in human history to be reinstated in the fellowship of God came through faith in Christ. In olden times men looked forward to Christ's redeeming work; in later times they gaze back upon it, but always they come and they came by grace, through faith.[24]

V. Election And Salvation

Though Christians might agree that salvation is by grace alone, they disagree when it comes to specifically defining the implications of this grace. The question as to the origin of salvation, specifically as it relates to election and calling, is among the most controversial questions debated among conservative Christians today. While all conservative theological systems recognize the sovereignty of God in salvation, how and when sovereignty is exercised is a basic area of contention. Sooner or later, the debate usually involves what is commonly known as "Calvinism." Perhaps the best expression of Calvinism is seen in the acrostic TULIP. Those who use this rebus express Calvinism in five points and they apply these to their interpretation of Scripture.

T	Total depravity
U	Unconditional election — *unmerited favor*
L	Limited atonement
I	Irresistible grace
P	Perseverance of the saints

As such, those who hold this position believe that man is totally depraved, that he cannot even respond to God. As a result, God elected him for salvation on an unconditional basis; then Christ died for the elect and only the elect. Because God's sovereignty cannot be thwarted, the elect cannot resist the grace of God when it is presented, nor can the elect fall away nor lose salvation, but the elect will persevere to the end. Those who believe in the entire system as identified are "five-point Calvinists."

Some others claim to believe part of the system of Calvinism, but not all. As such, a person might call himself a "four-point Calvinist," or a "two-point Calvinist," depending on how many points agree with his position. The problem is that Calvinism is a system, and as such is a unity. Inasmuch as truth is consistent with itself, one cannot choose part of a system while rejecting other selections and hold to a coherent system. As such he must modify all aspects, hence creating a new system.

In fairness to John Calvin, it should be noted that there is some question as to whether so-called "Calvinism" accurately represents his real position. While the early editions of *The Institutes* appear to emphasize predestination, his later commentaries have a more biblical emphasis. An example of this is seen in his comments on 1 John 2:2.

> Christ suffered for the sins of the whole world, and in the goodness of God is offered unto all men without distinction, His blood being shed, not for a part of the world openly, but for the whole human race; for although in the world nothing is found worthy of the favor of God, yet He holds out the propitiation to the whole world, since without exception He summons all to the faith of Christ, which is nothing else than the door unto hope.[25]

In spite of the inherent weakness of Calvin, his contribution was scholarly and profound. Within the law of blessability, God blessed him greatly. His leadership in Geneva, Switzerland founded a theological movement that spread around the world. Its contributions for righteousness far outweigh the implied negative tendencies of fatalism and legalism.

The five points of Calvinism came into existence after Calvin's death. They grew out of a protest toward Arminianism through the teachings of Jacob Hermann, who lived from 1560 to 1609. He is best known by the Latin form of his last name—Arminius. In 1618, a national senate of the church of the Netherlands convened in Dort and examined the teaching of Arminius in light of Scripture. This council consisted of one hundred forty-four sessions stretched over at least seven months. They concluded that the points of Arminianism were heresy. At this conference in Dort, they reaffirmed the reformed teaching of John Calvin. They stated their conclusion in five points, expressing it in the form of the acrostic forming the word TULIP.

Some have narrowly divided Christianity into two camps, Calvinist and Arminian. As a result, some are identified as Calvinists because they were not Arminian in doctrine. These could be called Generic Calvinists because they believe in the sovereignty of God, salvation by grace and eternal security. They use this description to tell the world, "I am not an Arminian." (However, a person should not be forced to describe himself theologically by his affinity or proximity to any one church father.) A Definitional Calvinist usually identifies with the Reformed or Presbyterian Church and is committed to the major tenets of faith usually identified with John Calvin.

A. THE WEAKNESSES OF CALVINISM. The following section examines the weaknesses or inconsistencies of Calvinism. Careful attention should be given to the definition of terms. The way a person defines the terms will determine if he is a Calvinist or not. It will also determine whether or not the system is inconsistent.

1. *Total depravity.* Most Calvinists interpret total depravity to mean that any man in his natural state is incapable or unable to do anything to please or gain merit before God. He is totally depraved of any urging to seek after God. Total depravity means that man is in complete rebellion against God, and by his "free will" he cannot and will never make a decision for Christ. When man is totally depraved, he cannot discern the truth of the gospel or understand it when it is presented to him. The Calvinist qualifies the meaning of "free will," indicating that man is not totally free, but is able to respond to God because of election and irresistible grace.

However, the Bible teaches that man is made in the image and likeness of God. Since God is Person (personality), man reflects the personhood of God through his human personality, made up of intellect, emotion, will, and moral awareness. Because man's will is reflective of God's will, man has the duty and ability to make moral choices based on his understanding and motivations. Man is given an opportunity to make a moral choice for God—as reflected in repenting, turning, believing, and receiving salvation—and is condemned if he rejects. God, in the integrity of His nature, could not ask man to do what he was incapable of doing nor could He hold man responsible for all choices, whether good or evil, if the choices were not indigenous to man. Since man will be judged by God for his decision, it would be immoral for God to punish man for his lack of response to that which he could not do.

There are illustrations of men in Scripture who have made decisions against the purpose of God (Pharaoh, Esau, Lot, and Balaam). Also, there are some who have made difficult decisions, and God honored them (Abraham, Elijah, and those mentioned in Hebrews 11). Accountability follows responsibility.

2. *Unconditional election.* The second principle held by the Calvinist is based on the doctrine of predestination. Calvinists believe a man obtains salvation because God began the process by choosing him without any outside influence.

> Those of mankind who are predestinated unto Life, God, before the foundation of the world was laid, according to His eternal and immutable Purpose, and the secret counsel and good pleasure of His will, hath chosen in Christ to everlasting glory, out of His mere free grace and love, without any other thing in the creature as a condition or cause moving Him thereunto.[26]

The Calvinist bases election upon the divine plan (according to God's purpose), so that the ground of election is in God himself, which is to say salvation begins in God's will and purpose and not in an act of faith or some other condition in the responder. As a result, man has no part in it. Calvinists teach that God never elects anyone to salvation because of his goodness or potential merit. The choice is from Himself; hence, election is unconditional.

Conservative theologians appear to have some degree of disagreement among themselves as to the nature of this election. Some, like Strong, define "election" exclusively in terms of an independent decision of God. He claims,

> Election is that eternal act of God, by which in his sovereign pleasure, and on account of no foreseen merit in them, he chooses certain out of the number of sinful men to be the recipients of the special grace of his Spirit, and so to be made voluntary partakers of Christ's salvation.[27]

Others, like Thiessen, tend to modify the severity of this election by introducing such things as the foreknowledge of God. His attempt at defining election suggests, "By election we mean that sovereign act of God in grace whereby He chose in Christ Jesus for salvation all those whom He foreknew would accept Him."[28] Both of the above noted theologians would probably define themselves to some degree as Calvinists.

The Bible uses such phrases as "chosen in Him," and "predestinated us unto the adoption of children," and "elect according to the foreknowledge of God." But because these phrases are used by the Calvinist does not mean the terms reinforce the Calvinists position to the exclusion of another position. These are Bible terms that must be carefully interpreted.

First, election in the Bible is applied broadly. Election must always be interpreted within its context. The term "elect" is related to the church or to all believers, or those who have already accepted Christ. It is not applied to an unsaved, even if he is a candidate for salvation. As such, it relates to God's plan of salvation, because He has elected salvation and those in salvation are identified as elect. When taken in light of the nature of salvation, we understand that Jesus Christ made atonement for all. Those who respond to His plan of salvation are characterized as elect.

Second, to say that God has chosen some and passed over others is to breach the nature of God. God is One, which means He is Unity and acts in perfect harmony with His nature. Every part of God influences every other attribute of God. One attribute can never act in isolation from the others, hence God cannot be guilty of acting ignorantly or with a double mind. The nature of God expresses His love, as well as His justice. The Bible teaches that God so loves the world, hence this emotion is constant to all creatures at all times. Unconditional election implies that God chooses some out of His nature, but since others are not chosen, then the unity of God is breached. Also the love of God is breached because He is not able to love all equally. If God chooses (elects) some, it must proceed out of pure motives from His total Person. But the election of some and passing over of others divides the unity of God, implying duplicity, ignorance, or partiality in God.

3. *Limited atonement.* Calvinists indicate that this aspect of their system is the most difficult of their five points to communicate. They teach that if man is totally depraved so that he cannot respond, and God is sovereign in His unconditional choice, then when Jesus died, He died for those that were chosen by God. To keep their system intact, they must deny that Christ died for anyone else, for if He had, then they must also be saved. Since they are not, atonement is limited.

> Atonement is for the Elect only, since Christ died only for those whom the Father gave Him to be His Bride. Only the saints or elect ones are ever said to be "beloved of God," for they alone are the objects of His saving grace. The Calvinist reasons that if Christ died for all, then all will be saved. If only the elect are to be saved, then Christ died for them, and them alone. Although it is true that the blood of Christ is surely *sufficient* in value to atone for all, still it is obviously *efficient* only for those who are saved by His unmerited favor.[29]

In contrast to Limited atonement, the Bible teaches that the death of Jesus Christ was for all people of all time. This does not mean that all the world will be saved. The New Testament teaches that only those who receive Jesus Christ will enter into eternal life. There are at least five arguments against limited atonement. These are argued from the accomplishments of Christ on Calvary.

The first argument against limited atonement is the doctrine of substitution. The Bible teaches that Christ has given Himself for the sins of the world (John 1:29; 1 Tim. 2:6; Titus 2:11), that Christ was the Substitute for the church (Eph. 5:25), and that He gave Himself for individual Christians (Gal. 2:20). The Calvinist only uses the last group of verses to prove limited atonement, but overlooks the verses that teach Christ was the Substitute for every man (Heb. 2:9).

The second argument against limited atonement is that redemption is adequate, for Christ gave His blood a ransom for sin, hence redeemed the lost (1 Pet. 1:18-20). The price of redemption is blood. The Greek words for redeemed are applied to purchasing servants in the ancient slave market. The illustration reveals the extent of redemption to all men. First, the Bible teaches that He purchased the sinner in the marketplace—*agorazo*—that those who were "sold under sin" are redeemed (Gal. 3:10). But *agorazo* also applies to false teachers (2 Pet. 2:1); he died for these who obviously were not saved. Second, Christ paid the price with His blood and bought the slave out of the market place—*ekagorazo*; this person was never again exposed to sale (Gal. 3:13). This refers to those who were saved. In the third place, *lutroo* means to pay the price for the slave and release him (Gal. 4:5). This probably refers to the Christian who has learned to walk in grace and was not living by the law.

The third argument against limited atonement is that propitiation, which means "satisfaction," was made for the sin penalty of the world. The justice of God had been offended by the sin of mankind. The sin penalty of death could not be retracted and the nature of God could not forgive the sinner without satisfaction. The price of satisfaction was the blood of Jesus Christ, and the act of satisfaction is propitiation. The Bible teaches that Jesus is the propitiation for the world. "He is the propitiation for our sin, and not for our's only, but also for the sins of the whole world" (1 John 2:2). Since Christ is the propitiation for the world, the atonement cannot be limited.

The fourth argument against limited atonement is the fact that Jesus has satisfied all the demands of the law by nailing it to His cross (Col. 2:14). God's moral nature was offended when man broke the law and partook of the fruit of the garden. Everyone sinned in Adam, the head of the human race, and was guilty before God. The law not only condemned Adam, but every man who sinned, and would continue condemning them because of the demands of the law. The law could not be abrogated because it was an extension of the nature of God. The law was a unit, and to break one law was to break all the law (Jas. 2:10). Like sin, which is the sin-principle, the law is the law-unit. God did not deal with sins or the law on a "commercial" basis, meaning if there were more individual sins, Christ would have had to suffer more. Rather Christ dealt with the sin-principle and satisfied the law-unit. He satisfied the law-unit for the saved and unsaved. Jesus nailed the demands of the law to the cross and made an end of the law (Col. 2:14-15; Eph. 2:15-16; Matt. 5:17). The end of the law does not mean Christ put the law out of existence just for the elect, but that the law is no longer in effect as a moral judge to condemn mankind. Christ satisfied the law-principle, for both saved and unsaved, hence denying limited atonement.

The fifth argument against limited atonement is the fact that Jesus Christ reconciled the world unto Himself by His death. Reconciliation is God making man savable by placing him in a favorable light of God's mercy. The Bible teaches, "God was in Christ, reconciling the world unto himself, not imputing their trespasses unto them;" (2 Cor. 5:19; Eph. 2:16). This does not mean the world is saved, but man is now in a place where he can be saved when he meets the conditions of God's plan of salvation. Since the world is reconciled, surely the atonement is not limited to the elect.

The arguments against limited atonement are also powerful arguments for evangelism. Since Christ was the Substitute for the lost, and since Christ has paid the redemption for them, and since Christ fulfilled the demands of the law against them, and since Christ is their satisfaction (propitiation), and since Christ has reconciled them to God, the lost have an obligation to accept salvation, and Christians have an obligation to tell them the "good news."

One of the chief problems with this teaching of a limited atonement is rooted in one's understanding of some basic theological terms. Calvinists argue the atonement is somehow deficient if any of those for whom Christ died are not finally saved. This basic presupposition results in the belief that those who deny a particular aspect of limited atonement must necessarily teach the salvation of all men. This attitude is evident in Murray's discussion of the extent of the atonement.

> The very nature of Christ's mission and accomplishment is involved in this
> question . . . Did he come to make men redeemable? Or did he come effectually and
> infallibly to redeem? The doctrine of the atonement must be radically revised if, as
> atonement, it applies to those who finally perish as well as to those who are the heirs
> of eternal life. If we universalize the extent we limit the efficacy. If some of those for
> whom atonement was made and redemption wrought perish eternally, then the
> atonement is not itself efficacious.[30]

A closer look at the biblical concepts of redemption, reconciliation, propitiation and substitution, however, demonstrate a wider view of the atoning death of Christ (see above). As Chafer notes,

> The question at issue between the limited redemptionists and unlimited
> redemptionists is as much a question of limited or unlimited reconciliation, and
> limited or unlimited propitiation, as it is one of limited or unlimited redemption.
> Having made a careful study of these three words and the group of words which must
> be included with each, one can hardly deny that there is a twofold application of the
> truth represented by each.[31]

The Calvinist has misunderstood the separation between the historic accomplishments of salvation and how an individual obtains salvation. First, to teach that Christ died for all does not mean all will be saved, nor does it mean God has failed if some are lost. This does not question the sovereignty of God (obviously none can be lost if they are saved), but it shows a misunderstanding of the purposes of God by those who hold to limited atonement. Since God's desire is that none be lost (2 Pet. 3:9), He created a plan that provided for all, He offered it to all, and He wants all to participate in it. To say that God did not provide a universal salvation is to question His attribute of love. To say God saved all apart from their appropriate discharge of human responsibility is to question His integrity. To say God elected some to salvation, but not all is to question His justice. The necessity of human response fulfills our understanding of God's relationship to His creatures.

4. *Irresistible grace.* Calvinists teach that the grace of God is as immutable as the power of God so that man cannot resist it. They teach that since God of His own free will has chosen (elected) man and Christ has died for him, then man cannot resist the power of God that brings him to salvation. Accordingly, the *Westminster Larger Catechism* asks and answers,

Q. 67. *What is effectual calling?*

A. Effectual calling is the work of God's almighty power and grace, whereby (out of his free and especial love to his elect, and from nothing in them moving him thereunto) he doth in his accepted time invite and draw them to Jesus Christ, by his word and Spirit: savingly enlightening their minds, renewing and powerfully determining their wills, so as they (although in themselves dead in sin) are hereby made willing and able, freely to answer his call, and to accept and embrace the grace offered and conveyed therein.[32]

Since the Calvinists teach that salvation is the gift of God and man can do nothing to get it, he also can do nothing to resist it. However, the Calvinists claim it is not a passive human agent who involuntarily receives Christ. They teach that humans find Christ irresistible, i.e., they want to receive Him. But if the human is unable to resist, then human responsibility is taken away and man is but a passive agent. They claim,

Since it is the will of God that those whom He gave to His dear Son in eternity past should be saved, He will surely act in sovereign grace in such a way that the elect will find Christ irresistible. God does not *force* the elect to trust in His Son but rather, gives them life. The *dead* human spirit finds the dead spirit of Satan irresistible, and all *living* human spirits find the God of the living irresistible. Regeneration (the work of God) must precede true repentance and faith.[33]

The Calvinistic doctrine of irresistible grace is built on a misunderstanding of the doctrine of man. First, irresistible grace takes away initiative from man. The doctrine of conversion stands against irresistible grace. Salvation provided by Christ is obtained by both regeneration and conversion. To deny any human role in salvation is to formulate a doctrine which denies a substantial part of the biblical teaching on this matter. As Hodge notes,

The question whether man is active or passive in regeneration and whether regeneration is effected by the mediate or immediate influence of the Spirit must be answered in one way if regeneration includes conversion, and in another way if it be taken in its restricted sense. In the Bible, the distinction is generally preserved; μετάνοια "repentance, change of mind, turning to God," *i.e.*, conversion, is what man is called upon to do; αναγέννησις, regeneration is the act of God. God regenerates; the soul is regenerated.[34]

The second argument against irresistible grace is a correct understanding of the means of obtaining salvation. The Bible is the instrument of Salvation and the Holy Spirit is the Agent of Salvation. Before a person comes to Jesus Christ, the Holy Spirit is the Agent who works in his heart first by "common grace." This means the Holy Spirit works in the heart of all men to give them an awareness of God. The Holy Spirit works through the conscience (Rom. 2:1) and through the revelation of God in nature (Rom. 1:18-28). When the sinner comes under the influence of the Word of God, the Holy Spirit is the Agent of "special grace." The Bible is the instrument that God uses to bring salvation to individuals. The Word of God is pictured as seed which is planted in the human heart. As the Word of God germinates, it enlightens him, and convicts him of his sin, righteousness, and judgment (John 16:8).

The work of the Holy Spirit upon the Word of God in the human heart produces faith. Faith is not a gift through unconditional election. It comes in response to, and is produced by, the Word of God as a soul-winner implants the Scriptures into the human heart. This instrument becomes the basis of conviction and the impartation of a new nature (2 Pet. 1:4). As faith germinates, the person is able to reach out in the act of belief and receive Jesus Christ as his Saviour; hence, the whole process is a gift of God (Eph. 2:8-9).

The third argument against irresistible grace is that it is inconsistent with the nature of a man as reflected from the image and likeness of God. God cannot deny Himself by going contrary to the human nature in man which He created. A consistent God will not force salvation on a man against his will.

The fact that some individuals in Scripture turned their back on Christ is the fourth argument against irresistible grace. Israel resisted and Paul wept for them (Rom. 9:1; 10:1). The rich young ruler turned his back on Jesus Christ, and the book of Acts is filled with illustrations of those who rejected. Perhaps the most heartbreaking scene is King Agrippa, who said, "Almost thou persuadest me to be a Christian" (Acts 26:28). The Calvinist would say he was not among the elect. Yet the child of God would examine his heart to find out how he could get such a one saved.

This does not mean that God does not call certain people to salvation, but only that man may, for whatever reason, choose to resist the invitation of the Holy Spirit. A more accurate definition of the call of God as it relates to salvation is that of Mullins. He suggests,

> Calling is the invitation of God to men to accept by faith the salvation in Christ. It is sent forth through the Bible, the preaching of the Gospel, and in many other ways. Nothing can be clearer from the teaching of Scripture than the fact that the call and invitation are universal and that there is a free offer of salvation to all who hear and repent and believe.[35]

5. *Perseverance of the saints.* Calvinists teach that the saints will persevere because their salvation is dependent upon God's irresistible grace which was granted to them because Christ died in atonement limited to the elect. They teach that since man has absolutely nothing to do with his salvation, he will "persevere" because the Saviour has declared that he has eternal life. As Spencer notes,

> The logical conclusion of Calvinism is that since "salvation is of the LORD" and absolutely no part of it is dependent upon any *condition* found in the elect, but is wholly dependent upon the God who has *willed to save those whom He gave to His dear Son*, salvation can never be lost. The saints of God will surely persevere because He has given them His promise that no creature can take them away from Him (including themselves). We shall persevere because He wills to persevere![36]

Most Bible believers who reject Calvinism claim to hold the fifth point which is the perseverance of the saints. They claim perseverance is eternal security. However, the doctrine of eternal security is not the same as the perseverance of the saints. Calvin implies in his doctrine that if one is saved, he will persevere because of the election of God. It is rooted in the nature of God.

The occasions of believers in Scripture who died outside of the fellowship of God questions the perseverance of the saints, i.e., they persevered until death. Ananias and Sapphira (Acts 5:1-11) died in a state of rebellion. Other Christians who came to the Lord's table in Corinth with sin are described as, "many sleep" (1 Cor. 11:30). Also, there was a "sin unto death" (1 John 5:17-18), where certain sins led to the premature death of saints. The death of these believers outside of fellowship with Christ certainly does not take away eternal security, but it does question perseverance.

The Bible teaches that when believers are given eternal life, they have it forever. Rather than calling the doctrine the "perseverance of the saints," it should be called the doctrine of "preservation" or eternal security."

B. THE WEAKNESSES OF ARMINIANISM. The study of the history of doctrinal controversies seems to indicate that many movements usually begin as the result of the overstatement of a case in opposition to another system. The biblical theologian would do well to learn this lesson and be careful not to go beyond biblical revelation in the affirmation of doctrinal truth. Also, he should recognize the tendency of many to think only in extremes of dialectics. Therefore, when one states opposition of Calvinism, he tends to be labeled "Arminian" or "Pelagian" or sometimes "Semi-Pelagian." In the minds of those who so label, these words all refer to the same doctrinal system known popularly as Arminianism. It is difficult for some to realize that one can seek a consistent biblical balance in his theology and in so doing oppose the extremes of both Calvinism and Arminianism. As Mullins notes,

> The sense of proportion in the emphasis upon truth may be easily lost in our admiration for the harmony and beauty of a systematic arrangement. A simple doctrine or conception, such as the sovereignty of God, or election, or human freedom, may be given a dominating position and all other truths modified to make them conform. Theological controversy may lead to one-sided systems. Thus Calvinism and Arminianism have sometimes taken on extreme forms and have led to unfortunate results.[37]

Arminianism is that theological system originated by Jacob Arminius (1560-1609), while he taught at the University of Leyden in South Holland. Arminius was later condemned by the Council of Dort for his perceived teaching of a modified form of Pelagianism. While Arminianism and Calvinism today stand as two opposing theological systems, it has been suggested this is due primarily to the extremes of their respective followers more than the essential doctrines of their founding teachers. Actually, there is a substantial agreement in the basics or fundamentals of the faith in the teachings of Arminius and Calvin. Perhaps the best-known American teachers in England were John Wesley and John Fletcher. In America, this doctrinal system was popularized by such men as Francis Asbury and Charles Grandison Finney. Most holiness and Pentecostal denominations tend to be Arminian in theology; however, only a few Baptist groups are so identified.

Perhaps no man has had a greater influence for God during his life and in the ensuing years than John Wesley. Also, God has used many holiness evangelists to do a great work in winning souls, establishing churches and schools, and sending out missionaries. While the author praises God for what has been accomplished by these men, he also recognizes that orthodoxy is not always determined by one's ministerial successes. Also, God has greatly used many Calvinists who have opposed many of the fundamental tenets of Arminianism. In the determination of the theological orthodoxy of any Bible teacher, it is best to follow the Berean example and evaluate their teaching in the light of Scripture (Acts 17:11). When this is done, there are several reasons why I must also decline the label "Arminian."

1. *Denial of original sin.* One of the major problems with Arminianism is its view of sin. Since they differ in their definition of sin, it is only natural they would view differently the work of Christ on Calvary, the sanctification of the believer (how to live above sin) and the security of the believer (the consequence of those who fall into sin). There is a tendency among Arminians to deny or so define original sin as to practically deny its existence. According to Alexander Hodge, Arminians "usually deny the imputation of the guilt of Adam's first sin."[38] Summarizing the teaching of Arminius on this doctrine, Strong notes,

> According to this theory, all men, as a divinely appointed sequence of Adam's transgression, are naturally destitute of original righteousness, and are exposed to misery and death. By virtue of the infirmity propagated from Adam to all his descendants, mankind are wholly unable without divine help perfectly to obey God or to attain eternal life. This inability, however, is physical and intellectual, but not voluntary. As a matter of justice, therefore, God bestows upon each individual from the first dawn of consciousness a special influence of the Holy Spirit, which is sufficient to counteract the effect of the inherited depravity and to make obedience possible, provided the human will coöperates, which it still has power to do.
>
> The evil tendency and state may be called sin; but they do not in themselves involve guilt or punishment; still less are mankind accounted guilty of Adam's sin. God imputes to each man his inborn tendencies to evil, only when he consciously and voluntarily appropriates and ratifies these in spite of the power to the contrary, which, in justice to man, God has specially communicated.[39]

While Arminians usually employ the correct vocabulary and speak of original sin, they have in practice so redefined original sin as to deny the biblical teaching concerning the imputation of Adam's sin upon the race which he heads (Rom. 5:12). While the Bible teaches sin is imputed to all men and all men are born with a sin nature (experiential), according to Arminius, a man becomes a sinner only when he consciously and voluntarily sins, thus appropriating the sin nature of Adam. Thus sin tends to be volitional only, not omission, nor a center for lust within the person. As a result, there is some divergence of opinion concerning the motive in God's bestowal of ability to cooperate with the Holy Spirit. As Hodge observes,

> We may add that Wesley made the bestowal upon our depraved nature of ability to cooperate with God to be a matter of grace, while Arminius regarded it as a matter of Justice, man without it not being accountable.[40]

2. *Limited definition of sin.* A second problem with Arminianism is the tendency to redefine sin in such narrow limits as to deny all sin except "voluntary transgression." As noted elsewhere in this book, several Hebrew and Greek terms are used to identify sin or particular sins or classes of sins. To use any of these terms as an exclusive definition of all sin is to ignore or repudiate the wider biblical teaching. Yet this appears to be the practice of some Arminians. John Wesley once wrote in a letter,

> Nothing is sin, strictly speaking, but a voluntary transgression of a known law of God. Therefore every voluntary breach in the law of love is sin; and nothing else, if we speak properly. To strain the matter farther is only to make way for Calvinism. There may be ten thousand wandering thoughts and forgetful intervals without any breach of love, though not without transgressing the Adamic law. But Calvinists would fain confound these together.[41]

Apparently, in his opposition to extreme Calvinism, Wesley made the mistake of overstating an opposing case. While the voluntary transgression of the known law of God is sin, a biblical definition of sin includes far more. Perhaps his view of sin was a necessary part of his apologetic for his view of perfectionism. For if a person believed that sin was "every voluntary breach in the law of love," then it would be possible to attain perfection. On the other hand, if a person believed he had a sinful nature and he could never fulfill the perfect standard of Jesus Christ (he omitted divine perfection in his life), he could never believe in or gain perfection in this life.

3. *View of the completed work of Christ.* The meaning of the sixth cry from the cross, "It is finished" (John 19:30), is practically questioned by Arminian theologians. Paul defines the work of Christ on the cross in terms of a reconciliation of God and man (2 Cor. 5:19) and concludes that nothing can separate the reconciled from the love of God which makes that reconciliation possible (Rom. 8:38-39). In contrast, toward the end of his life, Wesley concluded, "Two things are certain: the one, that it is possible to lose even the pure love of God; the other, that it is not necessary."[42]

One of the implications of the denial of the security of the believer is a redefinition of the completed work of Christ. The giving of eternal life was in the teaching of Christ a guarantee against condemnation or perishing (John 3:16; 5:24; 10:28). In His high priestly prayer, Jesus identified the preservation of believers as a part of His work which was completed (John 17:12). Since God has completed His work and since the believer has life that is eternal, how could God abdicate a completed agreement and take away salvation? Christ used the anthropomorphism of "the Father's hand" to emphasize the secure position of each and every believer, emphasizing they could not be removed from that place (John 10:29). It is clear that the provision of salvation by Christ on the cross implied—at least in the mind of Christ—the security of the believer.

The idea that Christ would save and then allow a convert to lose what he did not merit nor achieve in repentance, causes one to question not only His work, but also His character. This is particularly so in light of such things as the sin unto death, which was apparently committed by some in the New Testament Church (cf. 1 Cor. 11:30). As one Calvinist has observed,

> Let our opponents inform us why it is that in regard to those who become true Christians, but who as they allege, fall away, God does not take them out of the world while they are in the saved state. Surely they will not have the perversity to say that it was because He could not or because He did not foresee their future apostasy . . . There is scarcely an error more absurd than that which supposes that a sovereign God would permit His children to defeat His love and fall away.[43]

4. *Method of retaining salvation.* Again Arminians appear to conflict with the clear teaching of Scripture when they make some work on their part necessary to retain their salvation. Paul questioned the Galatians, "Having begun in the Spirit, are ye now made perfect by the flesh?" (Gal. 3:3). While in the context of his epistle, Paul assumes a negative answer, the Arminian answer is apparently, yes. If it is possible for an individual to somehow fall away from grace, it therefore stands that the same individual—if he does not fall away—must be somehow at least in part responsible for the retention of his salvation. By definition, therefore, salvation ceases to be a free gift (Eph. 2:8). While the author knows of no Arminian so bold as to teach a salvation-by-works doctrine, this is implied by the idea that apostasy is possible for the believer.

It should be noted that there is a divergence of opinion as to what causes one to lose his salvation. E. B. Pusey, one of the Oxford Tractarians, suggested,

> The six sins which are accounted of old to be forerunners of the sin against the Holy Ghost are: "presumption of God's mercy, obstinacy in sin, impenitence, despair of salvation, impugning known truth, and envy at another's grace."[44]

In his testimony concerning his various experiences of attaining perfection, John Fletcher seems to suggest an unwillingness to confess publicly that a particular blessing of God could result in some degree of apostasy. On August 24, 1781, Fletcher gave the following testimony in a Methodist Society in Leeds.

> I received this blessing four or five times before; but I lost it, by not observing the order of God . . . When I first received this grace, Satan bade me wait awhile, till I saw more of the *fruits*: I resolved to do so; but I soon began to doubt of the *witness*, which, before, I had felt in my heart; and, in a little time, I was sensible I had lost both. A second time, after receiving this salvation, I was kept from being a witness

for my Lord, by the suggestion, "Thou art a public character—the eyes of *all* are upon thee—and if, as before, by *any* means thou lose the blessing, it will be a dishonor to the doctrine of *heart-holiness*." I held my peace, and again forfeited the gift of God. At another time, I was prevailed upon to hide it, by reasoning, "How few, even of the *children of God*, will receive this testimony. . . ."[45]

The doctrine of the security of the believer is sometimes opposed by those who use hypothetical cases involving horrendous crimes such as murder, rape, or child molesting. Fletcher, who was fifty-one when giving the above testimony would never have been suspected of any such acts. His reputation was, in fact, widely known as a man of piety and holiness. The implication of his testimony and Pusey's argument suggest a view where salvation can be lost for what most Christians might consider hardly worthy to be called sin at all.

5. *Confusion of salvation and sanctification*. The idea of perfection and the corresponding view of sanctification as a post-conversion experience, characteristic of Arminianism, tends to confuse the biblical teaching of salvation and sanctification. This experience is known under various terms, including the second-blessing, the second work of grace, the baptism of the Holy Spirit, fullness of the Holy Spirit, eradication, perfection, or salvation from sin and sanctification. As these various terms are used by holiness writers to describe the same experience, it is difficult to identify a single writer who represents the variations. In an attempt to summarize this tenet of Arminianism, A. A. Hodge observes,

> It is possible for and obligatory upon all men in this life to attain to evangelical perfection—which is explained as being perfectly sincere—as being animated by perfect love—and a doing all that is required of us under the gospel dispensation.[46]

The doctrine of sanctification is discussed elsewhere in this study, and the holiness doctrine of perfection is more closely examined there. The point of interest here is the use of expressions of salvation to identify this apparently post-conversion experience. The baptism of the Holy Spirit is one of several things happening to the believer at the moment of conversion, and is nonexperimental. This is more a question of semantics. Holiness writers speak of experiencing the love of God in this second blessing, yet Paul suggests that it is the result of justification (Rom. 5:5). Contemporary charismatic and Pentecostal writers speak of "receiving the Holy Spirit," yet again, this is a part of the Pauline doctrine of the conversion experience (Rom. 8:9-14).

6. *View of regeneration*. In the history of doctrine, various theological concepts have been redefined in different ages. Beyond a doubt, the great contribution of John Wesley to the field of systematic theology was his refinement of the doctrine of regeneration. In one sense, every evangelical and fundamentalist Christian is indebted to Wesley in this area. Alexander Hodge observes that the Arminian denial of eternal security challenges the biblical doctrine of regeneration.

It is an inseparable part of the Arminian system, flowing necessarily from their views of election, of the design and effect of Christ's death, and of sufficient grace and free will, that those who were once justified and regenerated may, by neglecting grace and grieving the Holy Spirit, fall into such sins as are inconsistent with true justifying faith, and continuing and dying in the same, may consequently finally fall into perdition.[47]

The very nature of regeneration denies this possibility. Regeneration is a work of God, therefore no man has the ability to change his nature, nor its fundamental existence. Creating new life was the prerogative of God. Since God created the new nature and gave it eternal life, only God can eradicate its existence. Man's actions cannot erase it. As Boettner says,

> The nature of the change which occurs in regeneration is a sufficient guarantee that the life imparted shall be permanent. Regeneration is a radical and supernatural change of the inner nature, through which the soul is made spiritually alive, and the new life which is implanted is immortal. And since it is a change in the inner nature, it is in a sphere in which man does not have control. No creature is at liberty to change the fundamental principles of its nature, for that is the prerogative of God as Creator. Hence, nothing short of another act of God could reverse this change and cause the new life to be lost. The born-again Christian can no more lose his sonship to the Heavenly Father than an earthly son can lose his sonship to an earthly father.[48]

7. *Union with Christ.* The security of the believer is to a large extent due to the unique union of the believer with Christ. Arminians tend to define this union as "A merely moral union, or union of love and sympathy, like that between teacher and scholar, friend and friend."[49] Rather, the Bible seems to teach an organic union where believers are "in Christ" and "partakers of the divine nature" (2 Pet. 1:4). Because of the indissoluble nature of this bond between the believer and his Lord, this union implies eternal security as Strong observes.

> Once formed, the union is indissoluble. Many of the ties of earth are rudely broken,—not so with our union with Christ,—that endures forever.
> Since there is now an unchangeable and divine element in us, our salvation depends no longer upon our unstable wills, but upon Christ's purpose and power.[50]

8. *The Nature of grace.* The word "grace" as used in Scripture is unlike any other theme. It includes the limitless goodness and kindness that God shows to sinners. Sinners did not deserve God's benefits. As a matter of fact, they deserved the opposite, damnation and eternal punishment. In grace, (1) God dispelled every charge against a sinner, and (2) God dismissed every human responsibility to Himself. Grace is more than love for the sinner. It is absolutely free merit bestowed on the sinner. God has dealt with all sin. Grace means all the sinner has to do is to receive it.

Not only is the sinner saved by grace (Eph. 2:8-9), but also, "We have access by faith into this grace wherein we stand" (Rom. 5:2). To stand in grace is to recognize that the sinner stands perfect (his position or standing before God) while he is still a sinner on earth (his state or place on earth). Since human ability did not gain a standing before God, human ability cannot maintain such a standing either.

The continued exercise of divine grace toward a Christian is the only basis for his salvation and eternal security. Grace recognizes he did nothing to get it and can do nothing to continue it. The Arminian believes the sinner is saved by grace, but his continued salvation is dependent on his endurance in that salvation, which is conditioned on human merit or works. However, many Arminians who have been saved, have been kept from the moment of their salvation, not because they remained good, but because unmerited grace is given to everyone who is saved by grace. The grace of God anticipated the sin of Christians (1 John 1:7), and took care of their sin, but God was never willing to encourage or condemn their sin. He demanded confession (1 John 1:9), taught a perfect standard (1 John 1:8-10), and rebuked those who broke the standard (1 John 2:3-12).

9. *Conclusion.*   As noted before, God has seen fit to use many who hold to an Arminian system of theology. He has also used many Calvinists in the same way. According to the doctrine of blessability, God will bless a man's faith and faithfulness even if he may be off on minor doctrinal points. If we would be biblical in our view of soteriology, we will necessarily oppose the extremes of both Calvinism and Arminianism. The biblical teaching on this doctrine lies outside these two systems. As Mullins correctly notes,

> Now the New Testament avoids the pantheistic tendency of extreme Calvinism and the deistic tendency of extreme Arminianism. The New Testament teaching and Christian experience are completely one in keeping the divine and human aspects properly related to each other. In both, there is a clear recognition of God's initiative. The shepherd seeks the lost sheep. This is Jesus' declaration. The saved man knows he is found, laid hold of, apprehended by Christ. . . . Again, the lost is not merely found; he is more than a sheep. He is a prodigal in a far country who must repent. So the New Testament teaches.[51]

LAPSARIANISM

SUPRALAPSARIAN	INFRALAPSARIAN	SUBLAPSARIAN
1. Decree to elect 2. Decree to provide salvation 3. Fall of man 4. Actual salvation	1. Decree to elect and to provide salvation 2. Fall of man 3. Actual salvation	1. Fall of man 2. Decree to provide salvation 3. Actual salvation 4. God foreknew and elects those who respond

The classical theological texts relating to election and salvation usually make reference to the decree of God for salvation with the terms sublapsarian, infralapsarian, and supralapsarian. These terms are based on the Latin term *lapsus* meaning "failing or falling" and were used historically to identify one's views concerning the order of the decree of God in relation to salvation. The term "supralapsarian" means that God first decreed to save the elect, then He decreed that Christ would die and provide salvation for them. The term "supra" means "above," and the decree to elect is above the decree to provide

View	Proponents	Decree
EXTREME SUPRALAPSARIAN VIEW	Some Reformed Churches	The decree to save some and reprobate others
SUPRALAPSARIAN VIEW	Beza	The decree to save some and reprobate others
REFORMED INFRALAPSARI	Synod of Dort, Westminster Assembly	The decree to create man
MEDIEVAL INFRALAPSARIAN VIEW	Anselm	The decree to create man
SUBLAPSARIAN VIEW	Strong	The decree to create man
PLAN LAPSARIAN VIEW	Towns	The decree to create
SALMURIAN VIEW	Camero, Amyrant, et. al. (Theological professors at Saumur, France early 17th Century) Some Lutherans	The decree to create man
INIAN VIEW	Arminius, Dutch Remonstrants (17th Century), Some Lutherans	The decree to create man

Decree 1	Decree 2	Decree 3	Description	Atonement	Grace
The decree to create both those who are to be saved and those who are to be reprobated latter	The decree to secure the fall of both the former and the latter	The decree to provide salvation only for the former, i.e., the elect	God not only elects all men, some to salvation, others to damnation. He also takes steps to secure these ends. Election is logically foundational to other aspects of the decree of God	Limited Atonement	Irresistible Grace
The decree to create both those who are to be saved and those who are to be reprobated latter	The decree to permit the fall of both the former and the latter	The decree to provide salvation only for the former, i.e., the elect	Election applies to all man, some to salvation and others to damnation. Election is logically foundational to other aspects of the decree of God	Limited Atonement	Irresistible Grace
The decree to permit the fall	The decree to elect certain men out of the masses of the fallen	The decree to provide salvation for the elect	Election applies to certain persons and logically precedes the decree of redemption	Limited Atonement	Irresistible Grace
The decree to permit the fall	The decree to provide in Christ a salvation sufficient for the elect	The decree that a certain number should be saved, i.e. the decree of election	Election insures the salvation of all for whom Christ died	Limited Atonement	Irresistible Grace
The decree to permit the fall	The decree to provide a salvation in Christ sufficient for the needs of all	The decree to secure the actual acceptance of this salvation on the part of some, i.e. the decree of election	Election to insure the salvation of some	Unlimited Atonement	Irresistible Grace
The decree to permit the fall	The decree to provide a salvation in Christ sufficient for the needs of all	The decree to provide a plan of salvation to those who believe	Election refers to plan, not people. It is applied after the fact by those who have responded to God's plan of salvation	Unlimited Atonement	Irresistible Grace
The decree to permit the fall	The decree to provide, in the mediation of Christ, salvation for all	The decree of election based on foreknowledge	Election based on foreknowledge God	Unlimited Atonement	Grace can be resisted
The decree to permit the fall	The decree that all believers should be saved and all unbelievers should be reprobated for their sins	The decree of election based on foreknowledge	Election based on foreknowledge of God	Unlimited Atonement	Grace can be resisted and is by the unbelieving
The decree to provide a free salvation available to all men and sufficient means for the application of the same	The decree that all believers should be saved and all unbelievers should be reprobated for their sins	The decree of election based on foreknowledge	Election based on foreknowledge of God and saving faith of some	Unlimited Atonement	Grace can be resisted and is by the unbelieving

salvation. The term "sublapsarian" means the decree to save came after a person had sinned and after Christ had died for him. The term "infralapsarian" means God decreed who would be saved (the elect) and the act of salvation in the same decree.

Unfortunately, these terms were born and widely used in the heat of theological controversy and, as such, were sometimes misused or misapplied. There is a tendency of some theologians to view the issue as though everyone not accepting his particular position belonged to one or two of the remaining camps. Strong, who identifies himself as a sublapsarian, makes no reference to the term infralapsarian and apparently assumes all who hold to the decree of God in salvation disagree with his position; therefore they must be supralapsarian, which he also identifies by the label hyper-Calvinistic.[52] Thiessen is somewhat broader in his discussion, identifying groups under the three above headings, but then later alluding to two modified positions distinct from the above.[53] In his chapter on the decree, A. A. Hodge assumes only three views of the decree, including the views of the Socinians, the Arminians and the Calvinists, but in a later discussion relating to predestination identifies five distinct groups with differing teaching relating to the decree.[54]

A second problem one confronts in this area is the tendency to identify significant persons or events with particular views. This difficulty can be illustrated in comparing the statement of three writers on the subject of Calvin and the Synod of Dort. Concerning the same, MacBeth argues,

> On the other hand, John Calvin (1509-1564), the chief of the Swiss School of Reformers, followed out to their logical conclusion the doctrines of St. Augustine with a severity and completeness that have left an indelible mark on Continental Protestantism. He not only taught that God's decrees were arbitrary as to Predestination to life, but also the complementary of a certain fixed number to damnation; and that those elected to life would receive grace which could not be lost . . . (Arminianism was) condemned at the Synod of Dort (1618), and Calvinism became the accepted system of Continental Churches.[55]

This view is diametrically opposed to Strong's interpretation of Calvin. He cites work done by Richards, noting,

> Richards, Theology, 302-307, shows that Calvin, while in his early works, the Institutes, he avoided definite statements of his position with regard to the extent of the atonement, yet in his later works, the Commentaries, acceded to the theory of universal atonement. Supralapsarianism is therefore hyper-Calvinistic, rather than Calvinistic. Sublapsarianism was adopted by the Synod of Dort (1618, 1619).[56]

Yet a third view of this issue is proposed by A. A. Hodge who argues that true Calvinism is infralapsarian. Though making no specific mention of Calvin, he resorts to bold type and caps when identifying infralapsarianism as the true Reformed position.

> The infra-lapsarian (*infra lapsum*) theory of predestination, or the decree of predestination, viewed as subsequent in purpose to the decree permitting men to fall, represents man as created and fallen as the object of election . . . THIS IS THE COMMON VIEW OF THE REFORMED CHURCHES, CONFIRMED ALIKE BY THE SYNOD OF DORT AND THE WESTMINSTER ASSEMBLY.[57]

Although some writers use the term "decrees" (plural) in discussing this doctrine, the singular term is preferred as it more accurately recognizes the unity of the divine decree. When one discusses the order of the decrees, that order is logical rather than chronological. Strong defines this doctrine.

> By the decrees of God we mean that eternal plan by which God has rendered certain all the events of the universe, past, present, and future. Notice in explanation that: (a) The decrees are many only to our finite comprehension; in their own nature they are but one plan, which embraces not only effects but also causes, not only ends to be secured, but also the means needful to secure them.[58]

Further explaining the nature of the statement "the order of the decrees," A. A. Hodge adds,

> As we believe that the Decree of God is one single, eternal intention, there can not be an order of succession in his purposes either (a) in time, as if one purpose actually preceded the other, or (b) in distinct deliberation or option on the part of God. The whole is one choice. Yet in willing the entire system God, of course, comprehended all the parts of the system willed in their several successions and relations. . . . The question, therefore, as to the Order of the Decrees is *not* a question as to the order of acts in God decreeing, but it *is* a question as to the true relation sustained by the several parts of the system which he decrees to one another.[59]

A survey of the literature relating to the decree and predestination reveals at least eight major positions held by those who would fall somewhere under the umbrella of conservative Christianity. These are summarized in the chart accompanying this discussion. The names used to identify these groups are based to some degree on traditional usage, notwithstanding the difficulties mentioned above. After identifying representative teachers in each group, the suggested order of four divine decrees are then listed. Based upon this order of decrees, the natural conclusions concerning the doctrines of election, the extent of the atonement and the ability of man to resist grace are stated. It should be noted that these conclusions are working definitions of the writer rather than formal theological statements.

It will be noted that the name of John Calvin is not listed among the representative teachers of any particular view. The reason for this is alluded to above. According to various standard works on the subject, Calvin could be placed under any one of seven headings. The author is not aware of anyone who seriously argues Calvin held to the view here designated "Arminian." Although a similar problem exists with the Synod of Dort and the Westminster Assembly, there is also a great deal of consensus, particularly within Reformed denominations, that the view of these councils is represented by what this writer identifies as the Reformed infralapsarian view.

Not all who hold a particular view of the decree of God may agree with this writer's conclusions regarding their view of election. As emphasized above, these statements represent a working understanding of the doctrine and not a formal theological statement. The example of Thiessen (Modified Sublapsarian View) is a case in point. The name of this view and statement of the decrees and their order are taken from his *Lectures in Systematic Theology.* Yet Thiessen himself would argue,

> By election we mean that sovereign act of God in grace whereby He chose in Christ Jesus for salvation all those whom he foreknew would accept Him
>
> . . . .
>
> Furthermore, He chose those who He foreknew would accept Christ. The Scriptures definitely base God's election on His foreknowledge . . . Although we are nowhere told what it is in the foreknowledge of God that determines His choice, the repeated teaching of Scripture that man is responsible for accepting or rejecting salvation necessitates our postulating that it is man's reaction to the revelation God has made of Himself that is the basis of His election.[60]

These statements taken from Thiessen's own formal definition of election, would clearly identify him as Arminian by some observers. Yet in fairness it should be noted that Thiessen himself would have readily identified himself as a Calvinist if given the choice between the two. It is interesting to note that he argues for the sovereignty of God in election, but never specifically applies election to individuals without a reference to the foreknowledge of God. In this way his Calvinism differs from that of others holding Sublapsarian, Infralapsarian and Supralapsarian views. Also, the wording of the fourth decree appears to lay emphasis upon the means of salvation rather than the means whereby certain individuals are elected to salvation (i.e., foreknowledge). In this way he differs from both the Arminian and Salmurian views. Therefore, while foreknowledge was obviously a part of Thiessen's formal definition of election, the logical conclusion based on his understanding of the decree is to speak of an elect plan whereby people are saved, rather than an elect people.

VI. THE PLAN OF SALVATION

While salvation is of the Lord (Jon. 4:22) and therefore a supernatural work which only God can accomplish, this is not to deny a sense of human involvement and responsibility. When an individual is saved, it is the result of both human and divine actions. As Charles Hodge notes,

> In this latter sense of the word supernatural, the coöperation of secondary causes is not excluded. When Christ opened the eyes of the blind no second cause interposed between his volition and the effect. But men work out their own salvation, while it is God who worketh in them to will and to do, according to his own good pleasure. In the work of regeneration, the soul is passive. It cannot coöperate in the communication of spiritual life. But in conversion, repentance, faith, and growth in grace, all its powers are called into exercise.[61]

While theological discussions of this doctrine sometimes make salvation appear to be very complicated, salvation is really as simple as a relationship with Jesus; putting faith in Him. Charles Haddon Spurgeon was saved as he heard a Methodist layman preach on the text, "Look . . . and be ye saved" (Isa. 45:22). When looking to Him to answer the sin problem, the sinner gets eternal life. Obtaining salvation seems to be centered in four aspects. Each aspect seems to progress naturally and the unsaved person must understand and act in each step to obtain salvation.

A. KNOWLEDGE OF THE NEED OF SALVATION. People do not turn to God until they sense a need for Him. A person must be aware of God and of His obligation to God. When a man recognizes God's demands and his own inability to fulfill these demands, he has become aware of his need. Man who does not fulfill God's demands is said to be in sin. "For all have sinned, and come short of the glory of God" (Rom. 3:23). The word "all" includes every human of every age, for no one has fulfilled God's requirements. Sin in this verse has the idea of "missing the mark." Anything that falls short of God's holy standard of perfection is sin. Because no one can with any degree of honesty confess to being as pure, righteous and holy as God Himself, the truth of this verse is self-evident. Man is a sinner in desperate need of God's help.

B. KNOWLEDGE OF THE PENALTY OF SIN. Because man is a sinner, he must pay the penalty of sin (Rom. 6:23). "Wages" refers to that which is paid for one's work or labor. It is that which a person innately deserves. "The wages of sin is death" means that all persons will die (both the physical and spiritual death) because they are sinners. Some might object to such a high price to be paid for even one sin, but when sin is understood as a violation of the law of God (all law is an extension of the nature of God), one is guilty of breaking the law-principle. According to James, "For whosoever shall keep the whole law, and yet offend in one point, he is guilty of all" (Jas. 2:10). It takes only one sin to make one guilty as a sinner, but in actuality it is doubtful the man will ever live who is guilty of only a single sin.

The Bible contrasts the free gift of salvation with wages paid for sin (Rom. 6:23). When one works for sin, he automatically gets death. Yet in contrast, God gives life as a gift. The term "gift" implies something that is not deserved or expected. God has given eternal life through Jesus Christ.

C. KNOWLEDGE OF GOD'S PROVISION. The gospel is good news—Christ died for sinners. The sinner should have received the punishment, but Christ died in his place. This substitution is the proof of Christ's love. "But God commendeth his love toward us, in that, while we were yet sinners, Christ died for us" (Rom. 5:8). The word "commendeth" means "to demonstrate." God has given His Son to die for our sins as a demonstration of His love (John 3:16). This is the gospel or "good news."

D. MAN MUST RESPOND TO THE GOOD NEWS. Many people know and intellectually believe all of the above and still have not experienced personal salvation. Mere adherence to the doctrines of Scripture will not save (cf. Jas. 2:19). Man must respond positively to the gospel. The gospel has two aspects: propositional truth and personal truth. First, propositional truth reflects the truth in theoretical principles as written in our doctrinal statements. This is the gospel which is God's plan for salvation. Paul defined it: "I declare unto you the gospel which I preached unto you . . . that Christ died for our sins according to the Scriptures; and that he was buried, and that he rose again the third day according to the Scriptures" (1 Cor. 15:1-4). The gospel explains the death, burial and resurrection of Jesus Christ. He died for us.

But the gospel is more than just propositional truth. It is personal truth that exists in a person. The Lord Jesus Christ is truth (John 14:6). When one accepts this truth, he does more than give mental assent to the death, burial and resurrection. He accepts Christ as his Saviour. The gospel becomes personal when he invites Christ into his life. "But as many as received him [Christ], to them gave he power to become the sons of God" (John 1:12).

There are many biblical expressions relating to man's positive response to the gospel. The outward expression is not as important as the inner faith that motivates the response. Some people "receive Jesus" while others "confess the Lord." Others ask God to take them to heaven or to keep them from going to hell. Still others "pray the sinner's prayer." Apart from saving faith, these outward actions are meaningless. The person who believes Christ for salvation will express faith in some positive response. While most of those who might read a theology book of this nature have probably been saved for some time, there may be some who have not yet trusted in Christ. The reader would do well to pause here and consider his own life. If you have never personally appropriated this great salvation in your life, why not now?

VII. CONVERSION

The term conversion may be one of the most misunderstood religious terms in popular use today. Often the concepts of conversion and regeneration are used interchangeably. This is particularly prominent in the confusion the contemporary media make between the terms "born again" and "converted," i.e., becoming a Christian. This confusion of terms is unfortunate, but can easily be resolved in understanding the biblical doctrine of conversion and regeneration (cf. Section XI). Conversion is the human side of that experience and regeneration is the divine side. In one sense, both terms refer to the same experience, although each term is used by biblical writers to emphasize different aspects of the salvation experience.

A second more serious erroneous view of conversion is to define it exclusively in terms of "a stimulus-response psychological experience." The Russian scientist Pavlov demonstrated that dogs can be trained to respond in certain ways as the result of particular stimuli. Applying this to humans, Behaviorism has become one of the more prominent theories of contemporary psychologists. William Sargant specifically attempts to examine behavioral and religious experience in his book *Battle for the Mind*.

It must be emphasized that this book is not primarily concerned with any ethical or political system; its object is only to show how beliefs, whether good or bad, false or true, can be forcibly implanted in the human brain; and how people can be switched to arbitrary beliefs altogether opposed to those previously held.

. . . .

The conclusion reached is that simple physiological mechanisms of conversion do exist, and that we therefore have much still to learn from a study of brain function about matters that have hitherto been claimed as the province of psychology or metaphysics. The politico-religious struggle for the mind of man may well be won by whoever becomes most conversant with the normal and abnormal functions of the brain, and is readiest to make use of the knowledge gained.[62]

Sargant's conclusions are allegedly based upon research into religious revivals as well as insights gained from his work with patients during World War II. Unfortunately, his theories become suspect when one examines the accuracy of his historical research. After examining some of these inaccuracies in recording the histories of Pentecost, the conversion of Paul, the ministry of John Wesley and the Welsh Revival, Martyn Lloyd-Jones concluded,

To sum up, then, the fallacy which seems to run right through the book *Battle for the Mind*, is that the Person and work of the Holy Spirit are entirely overlooked. It is assumed throughout that the history of the church can be explained solely in terms of human activity. As we have seen, the very facts of church history utterly disprove the assertion. Nothing is so clear as the fact that if the church were but a human institution, she would long since have ceased to be. The persistence of the church is due solely to the mighty and exceptional outpouring of the Holy Spirit which God grants from time to time. He does this in such a manner as to indicate clearly that the power is always 'of God and not of man'.[63]

Admittedly, some religious leaders might use particular methods or exercise some degree of personal charisma to gather about themselves a following of converts. If individual and masses could be psychologically induced to follow a religious dogma—and it is doubtful that such can be accomplished—the result would still be less than biblical conversion.

What, then, is biblical conversion? The word "conversion" means a "turning to God from sin" on the part of the sinner. Mullins notes,

Conversion is the word employed in theology to designate the turning of a sinner from his sins unto Christ for his salvation. This includes both the forsaking of sin which we have defined as repentance, and the trust in Christ which we have defined as faith. The term conversion usually refers to the outward act of the changed man which is the manifestation of the inner change in his soul.[64]

Similarly, Strong defines the term as follows.

Conversion is that voluntary change in the mind of the sinner, in which he turns, on the one hand, from sin, and on the other hand, to Christ. The former or negative element in conversion, namely, the turning from sin, we denominate repentance. The latter or positive element in conversion, namely, the turning to Christ, we denominate faith.[65]

The Apostle Paul described the conversion experience when he wrote, "Ye have obeyed from the heart that form of doctrine which was delivered you" (Rom. 6:17). Conversion embraces the total person, relating to each of the three powers of man: the intellect, the emotions, and the will. A person must know certain things to experience conversion, but a knowledge of these facts alone will not save him. Conversion also involves the emotions, but it is far more that an emotional experience. Conversion is not completed until an act of the will has taken place, but even an act of our will is not enough to save if it is done apart from the instrument of Regeneration, i.e., the Word of God; and the Agent of Regeneration, i.e., the Holy Spirit.

A. INTELLECT. The conversion of a man to Christ is different from a conversion to another religion or commercial product. As noted above, conversion cannot be passed off as a mere psychological phenomenon. It is imperative to know both the content (doctrine) and the Person (Jesus Christ) of the gospel to be converted (See Section VI above). While an individual does not have to understand the whole Bible to be saved, he must believe what he does understand. As Charles Hodge notes,

> It is conceded that all Christians are bound to believe, and that all do believe everything taught in the Word of God, so far as the contents of the Scriptures are known to them. It is correct, therefore, to say that the object of faith is the whole revelation of God as contained in His Word. As the Bible is with Protestants the only infallible rule of faith and practice, nothing not expressly taught in Scripture, or deduced there from by necessary inference, can be imposed on the people of God as an article of faith.[66]

B. EMOTIONS. Some place too much emphasis on a person's emotional response and create what may be described as a "psychological conversion." In reaction, others have attempted to deny or ignore the emotional aspect of conversion completely. Neither extreme is correct. God created man with an emotional capacity. If kept in proper perspective, our emotions cannot be ignored in conversion. The abuse of emotions by some should not cause any to abandon that which is good. A person will be emotionally affected by his conversion by either a cause or an effect experience.

The apostle Paul explained "not that ye were made sorry, but that ye sorrowed to repentance: for ye were made sorry after a godly manner . . . For godly sorrow worketh repentance to salvation not to be repented of: but the sorrow of the world worketh death" (2 Cor. 7:9-10). Paul recognized there were two kinds of emotional reactions to the gospel: "godly sorrow" and "sorrow of the world." There is a place for "godly sorrow" that leads to further spiritual insight. The "sorrow of the world" is remorse for getting caught. It does not lead to conversion.

There are many purposes for guilt. Sometimes God will allow a person to experience guilt so he can understand and appreciate forgiveness of sins. At other times, guilt drives us to respond to the gospel. On other occasions, God will use our emotional reaction to better deal with us after salvation. When Philip preached the gospel in Samaria and many people were saved, the Bible records, "There was great joy in that city" (Acts 8:8). The apostle Paul expected his converts to continue to respond emotionally to God. He told the Philippians, "Rejoice in the Lord always and again I say, Rejoice" (Phil. 4:4). It is all right to get excited about our relationship with Christ.

Each person has a different way of expressing emotions, depending on age, sex, background, and a host of other unique experiences that make us who we are. Sometimes a person shouts to express joy, while another cries loudly. Others sit apparently oblivious to what is happening around them. A person is not more saved or less saved, depending on the volume of his emotional outbursts; but when he is converted, it will affect his emotions.

C. WILL. God created man with a will to choose or reject the work of God in his life. In order to be converted, a person must respond. This does not mean we save ourselves. "For by grace are ye saved through faith; and that not of yourselves: it is the gift of God: Not of works, lest any man should boast" (Eph. 2:8-9). The following list reflects several ways a person may express his will in response to the gospel.

THE WILL AND CONVERSIONS	
1. Trust in	Prov. 3:4
2. Repent	Acts 2:38
3. Believe	Acts 16:31
4. Receive	John 1:12
5. Be born again	John 3:7
6. Call	Rom. 10:13
7. Confess	Rom. 10:9

In the book of Acts, most converts to Christianity were adults, but there are also instances of "household" conversions which may or may not have involved young children (Acts 16:15, 33-34). As the church became established, parents would bring their children under the preaching of the Word of God, resulting in conversions among young children. Today, it is estimated that large numbers of Christians, perhaps 80 percent or more, are converted as children or adolescents. Hundreds of bus workers and Sunday school teachers today define their primary task as reaching young children with the gospel.

One question that rises out of the contemporary situation is, "When is a child old enough to be converted?" This question has been variously answered throughout the years, but generally the discussion hinges upon "the age of accountability." Noting that a Jewish boy becomes "a son of the covenant" on his twelfth birthday, some have suggested that this is the time when every child becomes accountable before God. More probably, the age should be much younger, i.e., four to six years old. When a child is old enough to recognize the existence of God and His claims upon his life and to know he is a sinner, the child is old enough to be saved. Some children might come to this realization younger than others, some later. A mentally retarded individual might be well into physical adulthood (but not mental development) before understanding the need to be saved.[67]

VIII. REPENTANCE

Some object to including repentance as part of the doctrine of salvation because they believe it suggests a doctrine of salvation by works. But repentance was part of that gospel preached by both Jesus and the apostles (Mark 1:15; Acts 2:38). Throughout the centuries the gospel message has always included a call to repentance. Commenting on the early history of Baptists in Maritime Canada, Barry M. Moody notes, "It was with the resounding phrase 'repent and believe', uttered in pulpits, private homes and even the open fields, that the Baptists built their church in Maritime Canada in the late eighteenth and early nineteenth centuries."[68]

Repentance is necessary for salvation, but repentance does not save one. Like the bus ticket that says, "This half good for passage, not good if detached," salvation is good for passage to heaven, but it is not effective if detached from repentance. The second half of the bus ticket reads, "Not good for passage; keep in your possession until arriving at destination." This ticket stub represents repentance: not good for passage to heaven; keep doing good works until you get to your destination.

Repentance means to change one's mind about sin in such a way as to eventually effect a change in action. Willmington defines repentance, noting, "It is a voluntary and sincere change in the mind of the sinner, causing him to turn from his sin. It should be noted here the reference is to sin and not sins. True repentance involves the turning from one specific sin, and that sin is his previous rejection of Christ!"[69] According to Strong, "Repentance is that voluntary change in the mind of the sinner in which he turns from sin. Being essentially a change of mind, it involves a change of view, a change of feeling, and a change of purpose."[70]

Repentance is the English translation of both a Hebrew and Greek word and is taught in both the Old and New Testaments. According to the editors of the *New Scofield Reference Bible*,

> In the O.T., "repentance" is the English word used to translate the Hebrew *nacham*, *to be eased* or *comforted*. It is used of both God and man. Notwithstanding the literal meaning of *nacham*, it is evident, from a study of all the passages, that the sacred writers use it in the sense of *metanoia* in the N.T., meaning a change of mind. . . . As in the N.T., such change of mind is often accompanied by contrition and self-judgment.[71]

As a part of conversion, it is perhaps to be expected that both repentance and faith also affect the three major areas of human personality, i.e., the intellect, the emotions, and the will. The biblical concept of repentance applies directly to each of these areas. As Mullins has observed,

> Repentance includes three elements:
> (1) First, there is an intellectual element. It is a change of thought. A man's view of sin and of God and his relation to God undergo a change when he repents. . . .

(2) There is also a change of feeling. A penitent man has genuine regret. But this regret is of a godly kind which leads to a real change (2 Cor. 7:9-10). It is to be distinguished from the form of regret which has no godly reference . . .

(3) There is also a voluntary element in genuine repentance. The will is changed. A new purpose is formed. As a consequence of the change of will and purpose there is an actual forsaking of sin and an actual turning to God. This is the most vital and fundamental element in repentance. No repentance is genuine without it.[72]

Two Greek words are translated "repentance." The most common of these two terms is *metanoia* meaning "a change of mind or thought." This is the intellectual aspect of repentance. The second word for repentance is *metamelomai*. According to Mullins. "This word expresses the emotional element in repentance. It means regret. But this regret may be a godly sort leading to genuine repentance, or it may be a regret which produces no moral change (See 2 Cor. 7:9, 10; Luke 18:23; Matt. 27:3)."[73]

Some writers emphasize that the intellect is the only legitimate point in which an appeal can be made to man regarding repentance. Speaking to a group of English ministers, Martyn Lloyd-Jones suggested,

> Another important principle is that in presenting the Christian gospel we must never, in the first place, make a *direct* approach to either the emotions or to the will. The emotions and the will should always be influenced through the mind. Truth is intended to come to the *mind*. The normal course is for the emotions and the will to be affected by the truth after it has first entered and gripped the mind. It seems to me that this is a principle of Holy Scripture.[74]

Charles Finney was generally opposed to emotional outbursts during his meetings. As a trained lawyer, his conservative nature revolted at the thought of individuals interrupting his sermons, crying out over the condition of their souls. As a result, Finney instituted "the anxious seat" in his campaigns. Rather than cry out, those under conviction of sin were to come and sit in the anxious seats until the conclusion of his message. Finney's sermons were more like a well-reasoned defense to a jury than what might otherwise be considered good homiletical method. Though accused by some of emphasizing emotionalism in his revivals, Finney reasoned,

> It is true, in general, that persons are affected by the subject of religion in proportion to their conviction of its truth. Inattention to religion is the great reason why so little is felt concerning it. No being can look at the great truths of religion, as truths, and not feel deeply concerning them. The devil cannot. He believes and trembles. Angels in heaven feel, in view of these things. God feels! An intellectual conviction of truth is always accompanied with feeling of some kind.[75]

To be complete, biblical repentance must affect more than the intellect and emotions, it must result in a lifestyle change. The Thessalonian Christians demonstrated the completeness of their repentance when they "turned to God from idols, to serve the living and true God" (1 Thess. 1:9). According to De Ment,

> The words employed in the Heb and Gr place chief emphasis on the will, the change of mind, or of purpose, because a complete and sincere turning to God involves both the apprehension of the nature of sin and the consciousness of personal guilt (Jer 25 5; Mk 1 15; Acts 2 38; 2 Cor. 7 9.10). The demand for repentance implies free will and individual responsibility. That men are called to repent there can be no doubt. . . .[76]

Likewise, Strong argues that repentance involves,

> A voluntary element,—change of purpose—inward turning from sin and disposition to seek pardon and cleansing (Ps. 51:5, 7, 10; Jer. 25:5). This includes and implies the two preceding elements, and is therefore the most important aspect of repentance. It is indicated in the Scripture term μετάνοια (Acts 2:38; Rom. 2:4).[77]

Some have argued that John and Paul differed on the importance of repentance in conversion. While it is true John never uses the word repent in any of his writings, except in Revelation 2-3, his use of the word believe demands active obedience to that which is held to be true, thus implying repentance. So while John does not use the term specifically, except when quoting Jesus, the idea of repentance is implied in his doctrine of believing.

Repentance exists when men begin to think God's thoughts about sin and their standing before God. On the means to repentance, Thiessen suggests,

> On the human side it is brought about by various things. Jesus teaches that miracles (Matt. 11:20, 21), even the coming of one from the dead (Luke 16:30, 31), are insufficient to produce repentance. But the Word of God (Luke 16:30, 31), the preaching of the gospel (Matt. 12:41; Luke 24:47; Acts 2:37, 38; 2 Tim. 2:25), the goodness of God toward His creatures (Rom. 2:4; 2 Pet. 3:9), the chastisement of the Lord (Rev. 3:19; Heb. 12:10, 11), belief of the truth (Jonah 3:5ff.), and a new vision of God (Job 42:5, 6) are definite means that God uses to produce repentance.[78]

It should be noted that these means do not guarantee repentance on the part of the individual; they only create the conditions under which one is likely to repent should he so decide. Ultimately, repentance is a decision that must be made personally. This is evident from the example of apostolic preaching in the early chapters of Acts. On the day of Pentecost, Peter, in the fullness of the Holy Spirit, preached concerning the resurrected Christ and 3,000 of his hearers followed his injunction to repent and be baptized. Later, Stephen, in the fullness of the Holy Spirit, preached the resurrected Christ and his hearers decided to stone him.

IX. FAITH

Repentance and faith are both necessary in conversion. If conversion were likened to a coin, repentance and faith would be the "heads and tails" of the coin. As repentance falls short of salvation without saving faith, so faith falls short of salvation if it is somehow divorced from repentance. According to T. T. Martin,

> Wherever repentance and faith are mentioned in God's Word without one exception, repentance comes before faith. There is a faith that comes before repentance; but it is pure historical faith, and does not result in salvation. . . . If, therefore, the faith that saves must come after repentance, then those who have no saving faith after repentance, have no salvation, are not really redeemed. Not only so, but if saving faith must come after repentance, then those who place the only faith they claim before repentance, do not understand what saving faith is.[79]

Martin's observation concerning the order of repentance and faith may be misleading if one fails to understand just how closely these two concepts are in reality. Biblical repentance is not repentance apart from faith. Likewise, faith assumes repentance as a part of saving faith. As Chafer notes,

> Repentance, according to the Bible, is a complete change of mind and, as such, is a vital element in saving faith; but it should not now be required, as a separate act, apart from saving faith. The Biblical emphasis upon Gentile repentance or any repentance in this age will be more evident when the full meaning of the word "*believe*" is understood.[80]

Saving faith is both simple and complex. Faith is as simple as a drowning man reaching for a rope, a child taking a step, or a sinner looking to Jesus Christ. Faith is simple belief. But on the other hand, saving faith is complex, setting in motion all the judicial machinery of heaven. The ultimate purpose of God is activated by faith. But eternal consequences are not gotten as easily as an impulsive purchase at the discount store. To be saved a person must have proper knowledge, a proper emotion, and a proper decision of the will. So not everything that is called faith is proper faith.

Faith is one of those common words so difficult to specifically define. Some have suggested the concept of faith is actually beyond the ability of any human being to define. But we can recognize certain aspects of faith which make the idea more understandable. Leon Morris suggests,

> Faith is clearly one of the most important concepts in the whole New Testament. Everywhere it is required and its importance insisted upon. Faith means abandoning all trust in one's own resources. Faith means casting oneself unreservedly on the mercy of God. Faith means laying hold on the promises of God in Christ, relying entirely on the finished work of Christ for salvation, and on the power of the

indwelling Holy Spirit of God for daily strength. Faith implies complete reliance on God and full obedience to God.[81]

The closest thing to a biblical definition of faith is "the substance of things hoped for, the evidence of things not seen" (Heb. 11:1). Its importance in the Christian experience is seen in that it is impossible to please God apart from faith (Heb. 11:6). Chafer is accurate when he emphasizes that faith is "the one condition of salvation." He states,

> This one word *"believe"* represents all a sinner can do and all a sinner must do to be saved. It is believing the record God has given of His Son. In this record it is stated that He has entered into all the needs of our lost condition and is alive from the dead to be a living Saviour to all who put their trust in Him. It is quite possible for any intelligent person to know whether he has placed such confidence in the Saviour. Saving faith is a matter of personal consciousness. "I know whom I have believed." To have deposited one's eternal welfare in the hands of another is a decision of the mind so definite that it can hardly be confused with anything else. On this deposit of oneself into His saving grace depends one's eternal destiny. To add, or subtract, anything from this sole condition of salvation is most perilous.[82]

Faith is part of man's response to God in the salvation experience. Some who have difficulty recognizing the human role in saving faith, tend to identify faith as the gift of God. The *Heidelberg Catechism* seems to suggest,

> (Faith) is not merely a certain knowledge, whereby I receive as true what God has revealed to us in His Word, but also a cordial trust, which the Holy Ghost works in me by the Gospel, that not only to others, but to me also, the forgiveness of sin, and everlasting righteousness and life are given by God out of pure grace, and only for the sake of Christ's merit.[83]

An error comes from not recognizing the role of Scripture in producing faith in the individual. There seem to be six different uses of the term "faith" in Scripture. First, when faith is used with an article, as in the faith, it is a reference to the Scriptures or doctrinal faith. This is the source of the individual's faith and ultimately of the individual's regeneration. Second, there is saving faith. Third, there is a non-experiential faith that is described as justifying faith (Rom. 3:27-31) which is imputed to the believer. The fourth is indwelling faith, which seems to be the active faith of Christ that indwells the believer and gives him the ability to trust in God (Mark 11:22; Gal. 2:16, 20). The fifth is the daily faith of the believer which is living by the principles of God's Word (2 Cor. 5:7). The sixth is the gift of faith which is a spiritual gift that the believer has to move obstacles that hinder the work of Christ (1 Cor. 12:9; 13:2).[84]

Faith begins by knowing God and His plan. Intellectual faith has never saved anyone, but intellectual knowledge is the foundation for saving faith. Intellectual faith is measured by what a man knows about the historical facts of Christianity. It is not a matter of the emotions or the will, but simply knowledge of God.

Intellectual faith is the basis for volitional faith. In the first step, the person believes in the existence of God, that the Bible is God's Word, that Jesus has shed His blood on the cross for the sins of mankind, and that God will save those who call upon Him. This knowledge is not ultimate faith, but is the beginning.

There is a place for man's intellect in faith. Someone once defined faith as "believing what ain't so." He was wrong. Saving faith is not a blind leap in the dark. It is based upon objective truth. As Morris notes,

> The verb *pisteuō* is often followed by 'that', indicating that faith is concerned with facts. This is important, as Jesus made clear to the Jews, 'for if ye believe not that I am he, ye shall die in your sins' (John viii. 24). But it is not all-important. James tells us that the devils believe 'that there is one God', but this 'faith' does not profit them (Jas. ii. 19).[85]

Faith also involves the feelings of man, as either a cause or effect. As quickly as mentioning the emotional aspect of faith, it should be added that faith is not an emotional feeling, nor does the intensity of our emotions make our faith efficacious. Yet emotions cannot be removed from the trust process which is a response to God. Jesus Christ wants complete, not partial, love from those who are joined to Him in salvation (Matt. 22:37-39).

Emotions are interwoven in faith, as good works are the natural outgrowth of faith. Just as a person's faith without works is dead, so a person's faith without the accompaniment of emotions is barren. Sometimes emotions drive people to the Word of God; in this sense emotions bring people to faith. Other times, emotions are stirred by the Word of God and grow out of Scripture. In this sense emotions are an integral part of faith. In Scripture, the emotions of joy and peace are both associated with faith (Rom. 15:13).

This emotional element of faith, though valid in its place, is often abused or overemphasized by evangelists apparently concerned with recording results. Thiessen warns of the importance of emotions in their proper place.

> We may define the emotional element of faith as the awakening of the soul to its personal needs and to the personal applicability of the redemption provided in Christ, together with an immediate assent to these truths. It is the type of faith that we find so frequently in revivals that lay undue stress on the emotions. There seems to be an immediate acceptance of Christ and a manifestation of the fruit of the new life; but as in the parable of the sower, "when tribulation or persecution ariseth because of the word, straightway he stumbleth" (Matt. 13:20-21). While the emotional element is certainly to be recognized as a constituent of faith, it must not be treated as if it were the sole characteristic of faith. Those who have an undue amount of emotion in their faith tend to backslide and to feel the need of being "saved" over and over again.[86]

There is an irony when one tries to combine the human will and faith. In one sense, the human will must act in faith. On the other hand, faith comes to those who cease self-effort. Some Christians emphasize the need to surrender or become passive. Others believe that their faith will move mountains if it is strong enough. The answer to this apparent contradiction is seen in a biblical understanding of faith. Morris examines the place for human will in the biblical idea of saving faith.

> The characteristic construction for saving faith is that wherein the verb *pisteuō* is followed by the preposition *eis*. Literally this means to believe 'into'. It denotes a faith which, so to speak, takes a man out of himself, and puts him into Christ (cf. the expression frequently used of Christians, being in Christ). This experience may also be referred to with the term faith-union with Christ. It denotes not simply a belief that carries a intellectual assent, but one wherein the believer cleaves to his Saviour with all his heart. The man who believes in this sense abides in Christ and Christ in him (John xv. 4). Faith is not accepting certain things as true, but trusting a Person, and that Person is Christ.[87]

When the Philippian jailor asked, "What must I do to be saved?" he was told, "Believe." Faith involves an act of the will on the part of the believer in that he surrenders to the will of God. In one sense, no man can ever fully surrender to Christ as Lord and Savior because he still has a sin nature. Yet if an individual consciously refuses to surrender some part of his will to Christ, he is not exercising faith.

X. JUSTIFICATION

One of the most important questions ever asked in the history of mankind is, "How can a man be justified with God?" (Job 9:2; 25:4). This question becomes more crucial as one seeks to understand his relationship to God. Justification is an act whereby our legal standing in heaven is changed and man is given a new standing before God. Being declared justified is similar to the act whereby a government declares that an alien is a citizen. The moment the person is pronounced a citizen, nothing happens to him physically. His thought processes remain the same, as does his personality and pattern of speech. The only actual change is his legal standing. But as he becomes aware of his new legal standing, he may shout, cry, or break out into a grin. The emotional reaction has no organic connection to his changed legal status, but there surely is a cognitive awareness of his new advantages. In the same way, justification changes our legal papers in heaven; we become children of God. In response to this new relationship we may cry, rejoice, or worship God in silent gratitude.

Justification is an act of God in the unique experience of salvation and has been so defined by religious writers throughout the years. According to the *Westminster Catechism*, justification is, "An act of God's free grace, wherein He pardoneth all our sins, and accepteth us as righteous in his sight, only for the righteousness of Christ imputed to us, and received by faith alone."[88] According to Strong,

By justification we mean that judicial act of God by which, on account of Christ, to whom the sinner is united by faith, he declares that sinner to be no longer exposed to the penalty of the law, but to be restored to his favor. Or, to give an alternative definition from which all metaphor is excluded: Justification is the reversal of God's attitude toward the sinner, because of the sinner's new relation to Christ. God did condemn; he now acquits. He did repel; he now admits to favor.[89]

Likewise, Mullins observes,

Justification is a judicial act of God in which he declares the sinner free from condemnation, and restores him to divine favor. It takes place when the sinner trusts in Christ and his merits for salvation. These two statements contain the essential elements of the New Testament doctrine of justification.[90]

Justification is the act whereby God declares a person righteous when that person accepts God's Word. Hence, justification teaches that a relationship between God and man can exist. Justification makes man perfect in God's sight. It is a declarative act of God. It is not that man has become perfect, only that God has declared him righteous and therefore he stands perfect in the sight of God.

That justification is a declarative act of God is evident in the meaning of the words translated "justify" and "justification" in the Scriptures. Commenting on the use of four Greek terms in the Septuagint and New Testament, Strong suggests,

(a) δικαιόω—uniformly, or with only a single exception, signifies, not to make righteous, but to declare just, or free from guilt and exposure to punishment. The only O.T. passage where this meaning is questionable is Dan. 12:3. But even here the proper translation is, in all probability, not they that turn many to righteousness, but they that justify many, cause many to be justified. . . .

(b) δικαίωσις—is the act, in process, of declaring a man just—that is, acquitted from guilt and restored to the divine favor (Rom. 4:25; 5:18). . . .

(c) δικαίωμα—is the act, as already accomplished, or declaring a man just—that is, no longer exposed to penalty, but restored to God's favor (Rom. 5:16, 18; cf. 1 Tim. 3:16). . . .

(d) δικαιοσύνη—is the state of one justified, or declared just (Rom. 8:10; 1 Cor. 1:30).[91]

Of the thirty-nine occurrences of the verb "justify" in the New Testament, twenty-nine are found in Pauline epistles or attributed to Paul. Also, Paul exclusively makes use of the noun *dikaioeis*. This being so, the Pauline doctrine of justification is an important part of the New Testament teaching on this doctrine. According to Packer,

Justification means to *Paul God's act of remitting the sins of guilty men, and accounting them righteous, freely, by His grace, through faith in Christ, on the ground, not of their own works, but of the representative law-keeping and redemptive blood-shedding of the Lord Jesus Christ on their behalf.*[92]

Abraham is the first person in the Bible described as having been justified by faith. This is not saying he was the first person to be a child of God, only that he is the first recorded individual of whom this expression is used and applied. "He [Abraham] believed in the LORD, and he [God] counted it to him [Abraham] for righteousness" [Gen. 15:6]. God made a promise to Abraham which he accepted as possible and trusted in God as though it were actual. The "believing" constituted an act of declaration by Abraham. In return, God made His declaration.

The justification of Abraham and every other individual was on the basis of faith and faith alone. There never has or ever will be any other means of justification. Faulkner is accurate when he notes,

The means or condition of justification is faith (Rom. **3** 22.25.26.28. etc.) which rests upon the pure grace of God and is itself, therefore, His gift (Eph. **2** 8). This making faith the only instrument of justification is not arbitrary, but because, being the receptive attitude of the soul, it is in the nature of the case the only avenue through which Divine blessing can come.[93]

Some have noted the apparent contradiction of Paul and James in writing on justification. As noted above, justification in Paul's view is clearly by faith without works. Yet in James 2:14-26, James appears to connect works to justification. Actually, this "contradiction" can be resolved when one understands the difference in what these two writers are trying to demonstrate. As Faulkner observes,

He [James] is not trying to show, as Paul, how men get rid of their guilt and become Christians, but how they prove the reality of their profession *after* they receive the faith. He is not only writing to Christians, as of course Paul was, but he was writing to them *as* Christians ("my brethren," ver 14), as already justified and standing on the "faith of our Lord Jesus Christ" (ver 1), whereas Paul was thinking of men, Gentile and Jew, shivering in their guilt before the Eternal Justice, and asking, "How can we get peace with God?"[94]

Actually, both Paul and James agree on the nature of justification. Paul, using the expression in its technical sense, emphasizes the means whereby God justifies. James, using the term in a more popular way, emphasizes the evidence that an individual has, in fact, been justified by faith. As Packer notes,

James quotes Gn. Xv. 6 for the same purpose as Paul does—to show that it was faith that secured Abraham's acceptance. But now, he argues, this statement was fulfilled (confirmed, shown to be true, and brought to its appointed completion by events) thirty years later, when Abraham (was) justified by works, in that he offered up Isaac (verse 21). By this his faith was made perfect, *i.e.*, brought to due expression in appropriate actions; thus he was shown to be a true believer.[95]

XI. REGENERATION

The term "regeneration" is used to describe that work of the Holy Spirit in the salvation experience which produces new life in the believer. It is used only once in Scripture where Paul speaks of "the washing of regeneration" (Titus 3:5). But the concept is communicated in Scripture through other expressions, particularly the idea of being "born again." According to Mullins,

> Regeneration may be defined as the change wrought by the Spirit of God, by the use of truth as a means, in which the moral disposition of the soul is renewed in the image of Christ. All definitions come short of reality. But the above contains the essential points. It is a change wrought by the Holy Spirit. It is accomplished through the instrumentality of the truth. It is a radical change of the moral and spiritual disposition. It is a change in which the soul is recreated in the image of Christ.[96]

Strong notes,

> Regeneration is that act of God by which the governing disposition of the soul is made holy, and by which, through the truth as a means, the first exercise of this disposition is secured.
> Regeneration, or the new birth, is the divine side of that change of heart which, viewed from the human side, we call conversion.[97]

Regeneration is the work of God through the Holy Spirit, of placing in one who has faith, a new nature capable of doing the will of God. Regeneration results in more than eternal life. It gives the believer new desires to do the will of God (new nature) and gives him the life of God. Also, it makes possible his sanctification. Though an act of God, man is not entirely passive in the results of regeneration. As Gordon states,

> The initiative in regeneration is ascribed to God (John i. 13); it is from above (John iii. 3, 7) and of the Spirit (John iii. 5, 8). The same idea occurs in Eph. ii. 4, 5; 1 John ii. 29; iv. 7; *etc.* This divine act is decisive and once for all. Aorists are used in Jn. i. 3, ii. 3, 5, 7. The use of perfects indicates that this single, initial act carries with it far-reaching effects as in 1 John ii. 29, iii. 9, iv. 7, v. 1, 4, 18. The abiding results given in these passages are doing righteousness, not committing sin, loving one another, believing that Jesus is the Christ, and overcoming the world. These

results indicate that in spiritual matters man is not altogether passive. He is passive in the new birth; God acts on him. But the result of such an act is far-reaching activity; he actively repents, believes in Christ, and henceforth walks in newness of life.[98]

Regeneration is an act of God. Only God can save a soul. Jonah recognized that "salvation is of the Lord" (Jonah 2:9). Salvation is called the "gift of God" (Rom. 6:23; Eph. 2:8). No one is able to forgive sin and save a soul, but God (Mark 2:7).

When a person is born again (John 1:12-13), the indwelling presence of Jesus Christ comes into his life. Christ is the spiritual life of the new believer. But regeneration is more than the presence of Christ. Christ promised the Father would also indwell the believer, "We will come unto him and make our abode with him" (John 14:23). Finally, the Holy Spirit also indwells the Christian, and His presence is the guarantee of new life, "by his Spirit that dwelleth in you" (Rom. 8:11). Hence, when a person is regenerated, he receives the life of God because he is indwelt with the Trinity.

When a person receives Jesus Christ he becomes a new creation, but this does not mean the sin nature is eliminated or is diminished in any way. While on earth a Christian will struggle with the desires of his old nature. But in regeneration he receives a new nature with new power and new attitudes. Strong emphasizes this truth.

Regeneration is not a physical change. There is no physical seed or germ implanted in man's nature. Regeneration does not add to, or subtract from, the number of man's intellectual, emotional or voluntary faculties. But regeneration is the giving of a new direction or tendency to powers of affection which man possessed before. Man had the faculty of love before, but his love was supremely set on self. In regeneration the direction of that faculty is changed, and his love is now set supremely upon God.[99]

A. THE AGENT OF REGENERATION. The Holy Spirit is the Person who grants eternal life to the repentant sinner. He is the divine Workman who regenerates the individual. He works in the heart to convict the sinner of sin, then He draws the sinner to the Saviour. Next, the Holy Spirit effects the work that Paul describes, "Put on the new man, which is renewed in knowledge after the image of him that created him" (Col. 3:10). Paul described it further: "the Spirit of God dwell[ing] in you" (Rom. 8:9). After the Spirit is in our hearts, He witnesses our conversion, "The Spirit itself beareth witness with our spirit that we are the children of God" (Rom. 8:14). Thiessen comments on the work of the Holy Spirit in regeneration, noting, "The real efficient Agent in regeneration is the Holy Spirit (John 3:5-6; Tit. 3:5). Truth does not itself constrain the will; besides, the unregenerate heart hates the truth until it is wrought upon by the Holy Spirit."[100]

B. The Instrument of Regeneration.

1. *Negatively: not baptism.* For many, baptism is believed to be somehow involved in the regeneration process; hence the importance in their minds to sprinkle new Christians, or, specifically, infants. According to Hodge,

> It is a wide-spread belief that when baptism is administered to new-born infants, they are regenerated inwardly by the Holy Spirit; they are so born again to become the children of God and heirs of his kingdom. The word, however, includes more than simply the renewing of the soul. Prior to baptism, according to the Catechism of the Church of England, infants are in a state of sin and the children of wrath; by baptism they are said to be made members of Christ, children of God, and inheritors of the kingdom of heaven. In other words, in baptism the blessings signified in that ordinance are conveyed to the soul of the infant. Those blessings are the cleansing from guilt by the blood of Christ, and purification from pollution by the renewing of the Holy Ghost.[101]

How much of "a widespread belief" this view of baptismal regeneration may or may not be, one thing is certain, it is foreign to the Scriptures. There is no biblical suggestion that baptism in any way secures one's salvation. It is generally believed this doctrine was unknown prior to Tertullian. According to Mullins,

> . . . Regeneration is not effected through the act of baptism. In a number of New Testament passages baptism is clearly associated with conversion, and nearly always with the beginnings of the Christian life. (See Acts 2:38; Rom. 6:3-4; Col. 2:12; 1 Pet. 3:21). But there is no conclusive evidence that in any of these passages baptism is regarded in the Catholic sense as an *opus operatum, i. e.,* an act which of itself regenerates without reference to the mind of the recipient. Nor do they sustain the view of the Disciples that baptism completes the act of regeneration.[102]

Baptists, who for their insistence upon the need for every believer to be baptized, have generally opposed any effort to teach a regenerating power in this ordinance of the church. In what is generally considered to be his most famous sermon, Charles Haddon Spurgeon made clear that no one could be regenerated apart from faith. Aware of the popularity of infant baptism in his native England, he added,

> There is the truth, and I have told it to you; and if there should be one among you, or if there should be one among the readers of this sermon when it is printed, who is resting on baptism, or resting upon ceremonies of any sort, I do beseech you, shake off this venomous faith into the fire as Paul did the viper which fastened on his hand. I pray you do not rest on baptism.

> "No outward forms can make you clean,
> The leprosy lies deep within."

I do beseech you to remember that you must have a new heart and a right spirit, and baptism cannot give you these. You must turn from your sins and follow after Christ; you must have such a faith as shall make your life holy and your speech devout, or else you have not the faith of God's elect, and into God's kingdom you shall never come. I pray you never rest upon this wretched and rotten foundation, this deceitful invention of antichrist.[103]

2. *Positively: Word of God.* The Bible is the instrument that God uses in an individual's regeneration. Just as a workman uses tools to get his job done, so God uses the Bible as a tool to deposit spiritual life in the believer.

THE BIBLE AS A TOOL OF GOD	
Hammer (Jer. 23:29) Mirror (Jas. 1:23)	Judges Sin Reveals Sin
Sword (Heb. 4:12) Lamp & Light (Psa. 119:105)	Defeats Satan Guides the Believer

We are "born again, not of corruptible seed, but of incorruptible, by the word of God, which liveth and abideth forever" (1 Pet. 1:23). The Bible convicts of sin (John 16:8-11), gives a new nature (2 Pet. 1:4), and becomes the basis of spiritual power to overcome sin (Psa. 119:9, 11). The Bible contains an interesting promise concerning its power: "So shall my word be that goeth forth out of my mouth; it shall not return unto me void, but it shall accomplish that which I please, and it shall prosper in the thing whereto I sent it" (Isa. 55:11). Several symbols in the Bible represent the Word of God as a tool that can be used by God to accomplish His work.

The Word of God is the revealed truth God uses to regenerate the soul. Strong notes,

The Scriptural view is that regeneration, so far as it secures an activity of man, is accomplished through the instrumentality of the truth . . . the Holy Spirit . . . illuminate[s] the mind, so that it can perceive the truth.[104]

One reason Reformed and Catholic churches baptize infants is to insure their regeneration in the event they should die prior to reaching the age of accountability. While abortions are not routinely performed in Catholic hospitals, it is customary for priests to baptize aborted babies or infants that die after birth. Obviously, this has no regenerative power, but it does raise the question regarding the spiritual state of those who die not only without Christ, but also without coming to the place where they can consider the claims of Christ.

While the death of young children is not common in America, in other places many children die within the first few years of their lives. Most Christians are assured that babies who die will be in heaven. This conviction is generally based on the belief of David that he would someday go to the place where his dead infant had gone (2 Sam. 12:23). How this is possible is completely open to speculation. Mullins suggests, "Infants dying in infancy are changed in so far as they inherit a natural bias toward sin. But how this change is wrought by the Spirit it is needless to inquire, since there is no light available on the subject beyond our speculations."[105] One possibility is suggested by Strong.

> Since there is no evidence that children dying in infancy are regenerated prior to death, either with or without the use of external means, it seems most probable that the work of regeneration may be performed by the Spirit in connection with the infant soul's first view of Christ in the other world. As the remains of natural depravity in the Christian are eradicated, not by death, but at death, through the sign of Christ and union with him, so the first moment of consciousness for the infant may be coincident with a view of Christ the Savior which accomplishes the entire sanctification of its nature.[106]

Christians generally have believed that those who die before the age of accountability are not saved in the sense of experiencing salvation as Christians do, but they are safe, meaning God has protected and will protect them according to his own nature. This means that God could not condemn, without an opportunity to respond, an unborn baby or a child who dies before the age of accountability, because that would be inconsistent with His nature.

XII. ADOPTION

Paul exclusively used the term "adoption" as an expression of salvation. Though used only a few times by the apostle, this expression emphasizes the important new standing a believer has in Christ. According to Thiessen,

> The doctrine of adoption is purely Pauline, and we give to it the last place. The other N.T. writers associate the blessings which Paul connects with adoption with the doctrines of regeneration and justification. The Greek word rendered adoption in our English versions (*huiothesia*), occurs, but five times in the Scriptures, and they are all in Paul's writings: Rom. 8:15, 23; 9:4; Gal. 4:5; Eph. 1:5. Once he applies the term to Israel as a nation (Rom. 9:4); once he refers the full realization of adoption to the future coming of Christ (Rom. 8:23); and three times he declares it to be a present fact in the life of the Christian.[107]

While the term is used exclusively by Paul, the concept of adoption is not entirely foreign to other writers. In the Old Testament, Israel is spoken of as the son of God (Exod. 4:22: Isa. 1:2f; Jer. 3:19; Hos. 11:1). In the New Testament, according to Palmer,

> Though adoption as a theological formula occurs only in Paul, it is implicit as a relationship of grace in John's teaching about 'becoming a son' (John i. 12; 1 John iii. 1f), in the prodigal's acceptance into full family rights (Luke xv. 19ff), and in Jesus' oft-repeated title of God as Father (Mt. v. 16, vi. 9: Luke xii. 32).[108]

To understand Paul's use, it is important to understand the adoption process in Roman law. Adoption was a common manner of appointing an heir either before or after death. In the latter case the plan of adoption would have had to be expressed in a will. Describing the cultural process of adoption in Rome, Rees notes,

> For the adoption of a person free from paternal authority (*sui juris*), the process and effect were practically the same in Rome as in Greece (*adrogatio*). In a more specific sense, adoption proper (*adoptio*) was the process by which a person was transferred from his natural father's power into that of his adoptive father, and it consisted in a fictitious sale of the son, and his surrender by the natural to the adoptive father.[109]

Adoption deals not so much with the nature or relation of the believer's experience as with his position as an adopted son of God. The editors of the *Scofield Bible* note,

> "Adoption" (Gk. huiothesia, meaning placing as a son) is not so much a word of relationship as of position. In regeneration a Christian receives the nature of a child of God; in adoption he receives the position of a son of God. Every Christian obtains the place of a child and the right to be called a son the moment he believes (Gal. 3:25-26; 4:6; 1 John 3:1,2). The indwelling Spirit gives the realization of this in the Christian's present experience (Gal. 4:6); but the full manifestation of his sonship awaits the resurrection, change, and translation of saints, which is called "the redemption of the body" (Rom. 8:23; Eph. 1:14; 1 Th. 4:14-17; 1 John 3:2).[110]

The rights of a son of God are applied personally by faith as there is no meritorious work that could be accomplished by sinful man which could result in being adopted into the family of God. Since a believer has a new legal standing, by faith he must accept this accomplished fact, and by faith he must live accordingly. Mullins stresses the importance of faith in adoption.

> Faith is the condition of sonship. Adoption is the method of God for introducing sons into his family. Adoption was an idea derived from Roman law. Paul borrows it to express the idea of the gospel. (See Rom. 8:15, 21, 23; Gal. 4:5, 6). By adoption a son was received into the Roman family with all rights of the true son. So also by adoption we are received into God's family by faith, with all the rights of the household.[111]

XIII. UNION WITH CHRIST

The unique nature of biblical Christianity, and particularly the experience of the "Deeper life" with Christ cannot be understood apart from understanding the doctrine of union with Christ. In the introduction to his initial translation and paraphrase of the Pauline epistles, J. B. Phillips noted,

The great difference between present-day Christianity and that of which we read in these letters is that to us it is primarily a performance; to them it was a real experience. We are apt to reduce the Christian religion to a code, or at best a rule of heart and life. To these men it is quite plainly the invasion of their lives by a new quality of life altogether. They do not hesitate to describe this as Christ "living in" \them. Mere moral reformation will hardly explain the transformation and the exuberant vitality of these men's lives—even if we could prove a motive for such reformation, and certainly the world around offered little encouragement to these early Christians. We are particularly driven to accept their own explanation, which is that their little human lives had through Christ, been linked up with the very life of God.[112]

According to Strong, this doctrine of Union with Christ is the logical source of virtually every aspect of the salvation experience. Specifically, he suggests neither regeneration or justification would be possible without this union. Concerning the importance of this belief in one's system of doctrine, he suggests,

Dr. J. W. Alexander well calls this doctrine of the Union of the Believer with Christ "the central truth of all theology and of all religion." Yet it receives little of formal recognition, either in dogmatic treatises or in common religious experience. . . . .

The majority of printed systems of doctrine, however, contain no chapter or section on Union with Christ, and the majority of Christians much more frequently think of Christ more as a Saviour outside of them, than as a Saviour who dwells within. This comparative neglect of the doctrine is doubtless a reaction from the exaggerations of a false mysticism. But there is great need of rescuing the doctrine from neglect. . . . The doctrine of Union with Christ, in like manner, is taught so variously and abundantly, that to deny it is to deny inspiration itself.[113]

This doctrine is taught both directly and indirectly in the Scriptures. One of the unique expressions of Paul is "in Christ." For Paul, the entire Christian experience could be defined in Christ. Mullins observes,

The phrase "in Christ" is a favorite one in the writings of Paul. There is scarcely any phase of the Christian life which the apostle does not express by means of this or an equivalent expression. There is no condemnation to those who are "in Christ" (Rom. 8:1). Christians are alive unto God "in Christ Jesus" (Rom. 6:11). If any man is "in Christ," he is a new creature. (2 Cor. 5:17.) Paul declared that he had been crucified and that Christ lived in him. (Gal. 2:20.) We are baptized "into Christ" (Gal. 3:27). Christ dwells in the heart by faith (Eph. 3:17.) We are created "in Christ Jesus unto good works" (Eph. 2:10).[114]

Another Pauline expression teaching the doctrine of union with Christ is the word "together," normally the translation of the Greek prefix *sun*. The most popular expression of this aspect of the doctrine has become known as "the seven togethers." According to Strong,

> A tract entitled "The Seven Togethers" sums up the Scripture testimony with regard to the Consequences of the Believer's Union with Christ: 1. Crucified together with Christ—Gal. 2:20—συνεσταύρωμαι. 2. Died together with Christ—Col. 2:20—ἀπεθάνετε. 3. Buried together with Christ—Rom. 6:4—συνετάφημεν. 4. Quickened together with Christ—Eph. 2:5—συνεζωοποίησεν 5. Raised together with Christ—Col. 3:1—συνηγέρθητε. 6. Sufferers together with Christ—Rom. 8: 17--συμπάσχομεν 7. Glorified together with Christ—Rom. 8:17—συνδοξασθωμεν. Union with Christ results in common sonship, relation to God, character, influence, and destiny.[115]

Indirectly, this doctrine is taught in Scripture by the use of five biblical illustrations of the relationship of the believer to Christ. First, the Bible speaks of a building and its foundation, identifying Christ as the foundation and cornerstone and believers as the construction materials (Eph. 2:20-22; 1 Pet. 2:4-5). Second, Paul teaches union with Christ through the illustration of the union of husband and wife (Eph. 5:31-32). Third, gave the illustration of the vine and the branches (John 15:1-10). Fourth, teaching union and communion of Christ and believers Paul used the illustration of the body of Christ. Christ is the head, and believers are members of the body (1 Cor. 6:15; 12:12). Fifth, the union of the human race and its source of life in Adam is an illustration of this union of the believer with the second Adam, Christ (Rom. 5:12-21).

The life of God living within the soul of man has historically been one of the great motivating doctrines of Scripture. Wesley, Whitefield, Spurgeon and scores of others identified this truth as having a profound influence upon their lives and ministry. The very essence of biblical Christianity is concerned with this truth. In a letter written in 1677 which has since become a devotional classic, Henry Scougal wrote,

> But certainly religion is quite another thing, and they who are acquainted with it will entertain far different thoughts and disdain all those shadows and false imitations of it. They know by experience that true religion is an union of the soul with God, a real participation of the divine nature, the very image of God drawn upon the soul, or, in the apostle's phrase, *it is Christ formed within us*. Briefly, I know not how the nature of religion can be more fully expressed than by calling it *a divine life*.[116]

A more contemporary evangelical writer shared these sentiments, noting,

> The apostle Paul gives us his own definition of the Christian life in Galatians 2.20. It is 'no longer I, but Christ'. Here he is not stating something special or peculiar—a high level of Christianity. He is, we believe, presenting God's normal for a Christian, which can be summarized in the words: I live no longer, but Christ lives His life in me.[117]

The nature of this union is unique and cannot be defined in a single expression. In one sense it is unlike any other union known to man yet at the same time it is similar in some respects to intimate relationships experienced between people, believers and unbelievers alike. (Hence, it is not a mystical trans-human or trans-worldly experience.) Our union with Christ involves the union of a finite being with the infinite God. Strong characterizes this union in a fivefold way.

(a) An organic union, —in which we become members of Christ and partakers of his humanity. . . .

(b) A vital union,—in which Christ's life becomes the dominating principle within us. . . .

(c) A spiritual union,—that is, a union whose source and author is the Holy Spirit. . . .

(d) An indissoluble union,—that is, a union which, consistently with Christ's promise and grace, can never be dissolved. . . .

(e) An inscrutable union,—mystical, however, only in the sense of surpassing in its intimacy and value any other union of the souls which we know.[118]

Although this union of the believer with Christ is true of every believer at the moment of salvation, experientially it is often delayed until the believer practically experiences the benefits of this union. This is due, not to any flaw in this union on the part of Christ, but largely to ignorance or a lack of discipline on the part of the believer. As Watchman Nee observes,

As we study chapters 6, 7 and 8 of Romans we shall discover that the conditions of living the normal Christian life are fourfold. They are: (a) Knowing, (b) Reckoning, (c) Presenting ourselves to God, and (d) Walking in the Spirit, and they are set forth in that order. If we would live that life we shall have to take all of these four steps; not one nor two nor three, but all four. As we study each of them we shall trust the Lord by His Holy Spirit to illumine our understanding; and we, shall seek His help now to take the first big step forward.[119]

A. KNOW. Three times Paul used the word "know" to remind these Christians of what they knew was true (Rom. 6:3, 6 ,9). He realized their actions were the result of certain attitudes, and new attitudes could only be produced when they were built on an accurate intellectual basis. The key truth Paul wanted the Romans to know was their identification with Christ. "Know ye not, that so many of us as were baptized into Jesus Christ were baptized into his death?" (Rom. 6:3). Because of his identification with Christ, a Christian should have victory over sin. "Knowing this, that our old man is [has been] crucified with him" (Rom. 6:6; emphasis added). If we know the old man has received the death penalty on the cross, then we should realize we do not have to allow Satan to tempt and condemn us. Knowledge of our co-crucifixion with Christ is the basis of our victory over sin.

B. RECKON. The second word Paul used is "reckon," which carries the idea of "counting on" or "relying upon." Paul tells the Christians, "Likewise reckon ye also yourselves to be dead indeed unto sin, but alive unto God through Jesus Christ our Lord" (Rom. 6:11). Part of the key to appropriating our new position in heaven is to rely upon what we know to be true and to act accordingly.

C. YIELD. The third important word used is "yield." Based on what we know and how we have reckoned, we should surrender our lives to Christ. "Yield yourselves unto God, as those that are alive from the dead, and your members as instruments of righteousness unto God" (Rom. 6:13). Yieldedness involves giving God the "right of way" to every aspect of our lives.

D. OBEY. Obedience is the natural outcome of recognizing the Lordship of Christ in our lives. The one who is the Lord of our lives is the one we obey (Rom. 6:16-17). When a Christian refuses to do the will of God, he denies the Lordship of Christ in that area of his life.

The moment we are saved, we are risen with Christ into a new position and a new standing with God. But we still have natures with sinful desires. Many times our walk with God will be inconsistent with our standing before God, yet as we begin applying these four verbs daily, those inconsistencies will begin vanishing. The deeper life is not an automatic acquisition, but a learned response.

XIV. THE SECURITY OF THE BELIEVER

The doctrine of eternal security teaches that God is able to complete that good work of salvation that He has begun in every believer (Phil. 1:6), and that He has power over all flesh (John 17:2). The arguments for eternal security are guaranteed by the person and work of God. If God were to take away eternal life from anyone, it would be a denial of His nature and work. God is true and just and cannot deny Himself. So anyone who has eternal life, has it forever. Beyond the nature of God, a Christian has the promise of God, that no one can separate a Christian from God (Rom. 8:33-39).

Some writers make the mistake of confusing the doctrine of the security of the believer with the "fifth point of Calvinism," the perseverance of the saints. Actually, the security of the believer is more a matter of the preservation in Jesus Christ than the perseverance of the saints (Jude 1). Still, many theologians confuse these terms when writing of the security of the believer. Thiessen, for instance, using the expression perseverance explains the essential elements of the security of the believer.

> The Scriptures teach that all who are by faith united to Christ, who have been justified by God's grace and regenerated by His Spirit, will never totally nor finally fall away from the state of grace, but certainly persevere therein to the end. This does not mean that every one who professes to be saved is eternally saved. Nor even does it mean that every one who manifests certain gifts in Christian service is necessarily eternally saved. The doctrine of eternal security is applicable only to those who have had a vital experience of salvation. Concerning such it affirms that they shall "never

totally nor finally fall away from the state of grace." This is not equivalent to saying that they shall never backslide, never fall into sin, and never fail to show forth the praises of Him Who has called them out of darkness into His marvelous light. It merely means that they will never *totally* fall away from the state of grace into which they have been brought, nor fail to return from their backsliding in the end.[120]

The problems with the doctrine of perseverance are addressed briefly above (Section V). Positively, the doctrine of eternal security is sometimes popularly expressed with the phrase "once saved, always safe." Essentially, this doctrine teaches that the Christian can be assured his salvation experience will certainly be concluded in the final redemption of the world. "Assurance is the Christian's full conviction that, through the work of Christ alone, received by faith, he is in possession of a salvation in which he will be eternally kept."[121] This assurance is grounded upon the revealed truth of Scripture.

Most Christians tend to base their assurance of salvation and security on a single verse of Scripture. One of the most popular of these proof-texts is perhaps John 5:24, the verse J. Wilbur Chapman pointed to as proof that he "hath everlasting life, and shall not come into condemnation, but is passed from death unto life." But, certain doctrinal themes, if properly understood, demand a belief in eternal security. Commenting on these, Chafer noted,

According to His Word, the true child of God is secure in the divine keeping for at least seven reasons:

I.   The Purpose, Power and Present Attitude of the Father
II.   The Substitutionary, Sacrificial Death of God the Son
III. The Sealing by God the Spirit
IV.   The Unconditional New Covenant Made in His Blood
V.   The Intercession and Advocacy of Christ
VI.   The Eternal Character of Salvation
VII. The Believer's Heavenly Perfection[122]

One key passage where this doctrine is taught is John 10:27-30. There Jesus speaks of believers as His sheep and claims they have eternal life, they will never perish and no one shall "snatch them" out of his hand. According to Erickson,

The key portion of the passage, however, is "they shall not perish." This expression deserves closer examination. John reported Jesus' sayings by using a double negative. While this is poor English usage, it is appropriately used in Greek to show an emphatic denial. John also used a verb tense which indicates the action is thought of as a single event, and the mood of possibility rather than actuality. To paraphrase his statement, it is as if he is saying: "They shall not—they shall not— perish at all, by any stretch of the imagination." It is hard to imagine a more emphatic way of making the point. If taken as an all-inclusive description of Jesus' followers, this certainly denies that any ever do fall away.[123]

A common objection to the doctrine of eternal security is that it leads to antinomianism, i.e., lawlessness. Specifically, it is argued that if someone is securely saved, he usually is not concerned with his moral and spiritual life, and therefore he is likely to lapse into sin. While this might sound like a plausible argument theoretically, it overlooks several important areas. First, it is never suggested in the New Testament that a Christian can presume upon or take advantage of his relationship with God. Further, nowhere is encouragement given to the backslider that since he was once saved he will always be saved. In practice, the witness of the Holy Spirit is one of His ministries that is hindered when a Christian backslides. As a result, backsliders tend to question their own salvation while rebelling against God. Finally, God will punish the backslider. As a heavenly Father, God faithfully administers discipline to sons who need it (Heb. 12:5-8).

The line of argument suggested above also fails to understand the nature of salvation itself. The believer has a change of nature and is uniquely united with Christ. Actually, it was this line of argumentation which Paul addressed in Romans 6 (see Section XIII). There he noted that such a suggestion is so contrary to the true nature of salvation, no one could actually believe he could lose his salvation. Nothing has changed in this regard since Paul wrote that epistle.

XV. SANCTIFICATION

The word "sanctification" is used in the Bible to identify a person, institution, act, or thing set apart by God as holy. The confusion over sanctification is that many groups have wrongly defined "sanctify" to mean "eradicate the sin nature," or "to gain a position where it is no longer possible to sin." Those who believe in eradication of the old nature usually call it "entire sanctification." In both the Old and New Testaments, the Hebrew and Greek words for both holy and sanctify mean "to set apart to God." When sanctification is used of things, it does not mean that a vessel or piece of furniture has moral qualities (only God is holy). It means they are set apart for God. Commenting on the meaning of terms in Scripture relating to sanctification, Ironside suggests,

> Freed from all theological accretions, the naked verb, "to sanctify" means *to set apart*, and the noun "sanctification" means, literally, *separation*. This simple key will unlock every verse we have been considering and bring all into harmony where discord seemed complete.[124]

Speaking more specifically to the New Testament usage of the term, Mullins notes,

> The word "sanctification," as employed in the New Testament, expresses both the new relation to God and the new character which corresponds. Sanctification means then the state of one who is set apart to the service of God, who belongs to God. It also means the inner transformation of one thus set apart, the actual realization of holy character.[125]

Those who teach what has been called "entire sanctification" or "the eradication of the sin nature" generally identify closely with the holiness movement. Perhaps the best known holiness preacher in that movement's history was John Wesley. Addressing what he called "Christian Perfection," Wesley said that it was "loving God with all our heart, mind, soul, and strength. This implies that no wrong temper, none contrary to love, remains in the soul; and that all the thoughts, words, and actions, are governed by pure love."[126] Although Wesley taught what is called a sinless perfection, it is doubtful if the experience he described differed much from what is today referred to as "the Keswick view of sanctification." Though he taught "perfection," he so redefined sin so as to deny the reality of such an experience. In the same account cited above, Wesley noted, "A person filled with the love of God is still liable to these involuntary transgressions. Such transgressions you may call sin, if you please, I do not."[127]

Another view of entire sanctification is that of Finney. While he began his ministry closely identified with the Calvinistic New England Congregationalists, he later began to emphasize the need for entire sanctification. In the official publication of his school, he clarified the meaning of this term.

> By entire sanctification, I understand the consecration of the whole being to God. In other words, it is the state of devotedness to God and his service required by the moral law. The law is perfect. It requires just what is right; all that is right, and nothing more. Nothing more or less can possibly be perfection or entire sanctification than obedience to the law, Obedience to the law of God in an infant, a man, an angel, and in God himself, is perfection in each of them. And nothing can possibly be perfection in any being short of this; nor can these possibly be anything above it.[128]

The first group to teach sinlessness were the Pelagians, who were condemned at the Council of Carthage in 418 because it was generally believed their teachings denied the accuracy and reality of several biblical statements. Hodge notes,

> In the Council of Carthage, A.D. 418, the Pelagians were condemned, among other things, for teaching, (1.) that the effect of grace was merely to render obedience more easy. (2.) That the declaration of the Apostle John, "If we say that we have no sin, we deceive ourselves, and the truth is not in us," is, as to some, a mere expression of humility. (3.) That the petition in the Lord's prayer, "Forgive us our trespasses," is not suited to the saints. They use it only as expressing the desire and necessity of others.[129]

Just because the doctrine of sinless perfection is not biblical should not discourage the desire of every child of God to become more like Jesus. As A. J. Gordon observed,

If we regard the doctrine of sinless perfection as a heresy, we regard contentment with sinful imperfection as a greater heresy. . . . Certainly it is not an edifying spectacle to see a Christian worldling throwing stones at a Christian perfectionist.[130]

Mullins suggests,

While ever conscious of our imperfection, we should believe in the possibility of great attainment in the Christian life, both in character and in power for service. Sometimes there are great acts of consecration involving a complete surrender of the will, a renewed filling of the Holy Spirit, so that in a moment we pass to a higher stage of spiritual victory and power. But this should not be taken as final, nor lead to self-deception. Steady, plodding labor and growth should succeed it, not contentment. We should, after the greatest blessings, still press on toward the mark of the high calling of God in Christ.[131]

Sanctification for the Christian is past, present, and future, or positional, progressive and prospective sanctification. Paul reminded the Philippians that "he which hath begun a good work in you will perform it until the day of Jesus Christ" (Phil. 1:6). Our practical sanctification is a continual process beginning with conversion and being finally accomplished at the coming of Christ.

A. POSITIONAL SANCTIFICATION. Positional sanctification is the relationship with God which we enter by faith in Jesus Christ. What God made holy by redemption, remains holy. Positional sanctification applies to our completed standing in heaven. The moment a person is saved, he becomes a "new creature" (2 Cor. 5:17). His position is changed from an alien (Eph. 2:12) to a citizen (Heb. 11:13-16). In the book of heaven he is set apart as holy, having obtained the righteousness of Christ (Rom. 3:22). The rest of his Christian life is an attempt to apply that truth to his practical level of living.

B. PROGRESSIVE SANCTIFICATION. This is called experiential or practical sanctification and it takes place in this present life. It involves the struggles of victory and defeat of the Christian. God continues to work in the life of every Christian (Phil. 1:6) to change him into the image of his Son (Rom. 8:29). The various circumstances and experiences we encounter in our lives are the results of God's work in us (Rom. 8:28). We need to cooperate with God in living under the discipline of the Word of God which is given for our direction and spiritual growth (2 Tim. 3:17). As we grow and mature "in Christ" it will become more natural for us to practice the godly habits God desires that we develop.

C. PROSPECTIVE SANCTIFICATION. This is consummational sanctification, for God will not complete the process until we either die or are raptured. Then our position and our walk will be harmonious. That day is coming when "we shall be like him [Jesus] for we shall see him as he is" (1 John 3:2). At the coming of Christ, all the limitations we now experience will be removed, allowing us instantly to be transformed into holiness (1 Cor. 13:10-12).

1. *Personal Separation.* The personal holiness of the believer is necessarily related to the concept of personal separation from sin. This separation is twofold. Holiness requires not only separation from sin, but also separation unto God who alone is the personification of holiness. If Christians were committed to this practice of holiness personally, there is some doubt as to whether they would be too concerned over how separated other Christians may or may not be. The controversy among some Christians today in the area of separation unfortunately tends to focus exclusively on the negative aspect of this biblical doctrine and suggests the possibility that the positive aspect of separation is being sadly neglected.

THREE STEPS OF SANCTIFICATION			
Position	Positional sanctification	I was sanctified	Heb. 3:1
Experience	Progressive sanctification	I am being sanctified	1 Thess. 5:23
Consummation	Prospective sanctification	I shall be sanctified	1 John 3:2

Some Christians have practiced separation with the wrong motivation and have been guilty of legalism, i.e., keeping the law for the sake of the law. Separation demands a proper attitude, which is: (1) living godly to please the Lord, (2) showing gratitude for redemption, (3) testifying to others, (4) fulfilling the love-principle, and (5) being prepared to meet the Lord in His soon coming.

Some Christians have a problem knowing what is correct behavior. It is not the obvious sin that troubles them. It is in the gray areas where there is debate concerning the appropriateness of an action or attitude. A questionable action or attitude is wrong if: (1) it goes against the clear teaching of Scripture, (2) it violates a scriptural principle, (3) it produces impure thoughts or actions (Matt. 5:28; 2 Cor. 11:3), (4) it is a stumbling block to others (1 Cor. 8:8-13), (5) it is contrary to the example of Christ (1 Pet. 2:21), (6) it offends the conscience (Jas. 4:17), (7) it will harm one's walk with Christ (2 Cor. 6:14-17), (8) it will harm a believer's body (1 Cor. 6:18-20), or (9) it will hurt his faith (Rom. 14:23).

2. *Ecclesiastical separation.* The Bible teaches Christians not to fellowship with those who deny the faith or with heretics (2 Tim. 3:1-5). Paul describes Jannes and Jambres who withstood Moses as "reprobate concerning the faith" (2 Tim. 3:8). The apostate is more than one who is in error or an ignorant Christian. The apostate has fallen into the snare of Satan (2 Tim. 2:25-26) and has departed from the true faith, but not outward Christianity (2 Tim. 3:5). They are described as, "They shall turn away their ears from the truth, and shall be turned unto fables" (2 Tim. 4:4). Timothy is exhorted to "watch thou in all things" (2 Tim. 4:5), and "from such turn away" (2 Tim. 3:5). Apostate teachers will be judged (2 Tim. 2:10-12; 2 Pet. 2:1, 21, Jude 11-15; Rev. 3:14-16).

First-degree separation. Some contemporary Christians have used the phrase "first-degree" or "primary separation" to imply that no believer should fellowship or cooperate with an apostate or heretical organization. This means they should not cooperate or be involved with a church or parachurch organization that is apostate (2 Cor. 6:14-17; 2 John 9-10; Eph. 5:11).

Second-degree separation. Some contemporary Christians use this term to mean that believers should not only separate from apostate churches or parachurch organizations, but should also separate from believers who are guilty of cooperating with them. First-degree separation is over primary relationships, and second-degree or secondary separation relates to the second level of cooperation. As an illustration, second-degree separation says a believer cannot be a member of a church that cooperates with an apostate denomination, or an apostate parachurch organization; or a church could not have a speaker who also speaks to apostate groups. Verses used to support this are Rom. 16:17; 2 Thess. 3:6, 14; Titus 3:10 and others.

There seems to be no question among Christians that first-degree separation is biblical. However, others disagree with second-degree separation because, (1) the law of primary reference indicates a person is responsible for his relationship to God, not that of another, (2) the law of practicality indicates no one could ever be sure of pure associations, and (3) the law of illustration implies Christ was equally distant to all the churches in Revelation 2 and 3, whether the churches had sin problems or doctrinal problems.

Biblical separation should be based upon the difference between the saved and the lost, the believer and the unbeliever. Because he is basically different, the Christian has no fundamental basis for establishing meaningful relationships or cooperative efforts with non-Christians. The man who has entered into a union with Christ cannot also have close ties with one who by nature is an enemy of Christ. Therefore, friendship with the world is enmity with God (Jas. 4:4). A Christian may still talk with the unsaved, but fellowship within the deeper meaning of the word is impossible unless the Christian voluntarily denies his union with Christ. When one understands this difference in natures, separation is nothing more than the logical conclusion of a spiritual reality.

But separation was never intended to be exclusively negative. The Christian is also separated to the gospel (Rom. 1:1), to the work of God (Acts 13:2) and to the law of God (Psa. 1:2). The primary issue in separation is not how far one should stay from the world, but rather how close one should get to God. When positive separation is being practiced consistently, the negative aspects of this doctrine will necessarily take care of themselves.

Obviously, the Christian as a part of this world cannot completely divorce himself from any contact or degree of affiliation with the world. The world, as creation, is of course, different from the evil world-system with its temptations to the Christian and its anti-Christian bias. The diagram below illustrates one approach which still recognizes the positive and negative principles of separation. The degree of affiliation narrows as a commitment to others becomes greater. In the chart, the circumference of dialogue is wider than the circumference of unity. First, one can unite only with those who are in substantial agreement with his life-purposes and nature. This would include matters of doctrine and practices. Second, there may be some with whom one could not unite (because of differences of purpose within a Christian context), but cooperation for evangelism, education or service might still be possible. The third area includes fellowship, which is a still wider circle of acquaintances. Unless there are particular extenuating circumstances, it is conceivably proper to have fellowship on earth with those who will be in heaven. This may include different doctrinal persuasions within the realm of conservative Christian belief and practice. Fourthly, when it comes to dialogue, where there is no commitment to another except to discuss ideas, such as in a talk show format or in debate, even though a Christian appears on the same platform or is listed on the same program, there is no public understanding of mutual belief, fellowship or cooperation in a common Christian endeavor. Hence, a Christian could dialogue with an unbeliever or an apostate because he is sharing his faith with a view to evangelize or help others understand his position.

DEGREES OF AFFILIATION

XVI. So Great Salvation

What, exactly, happens to the sinner the moment he trusts Jesus Christ as Lord and Saviour? This is the essential question behind the doctrine of soteriology. Because soteriology relates specifically to man's experience with God, in one sense it involves every area of theology. Hence, it is perhaps the most difficult doctrine to deal with in an exhaustive manner. There are many expressions in the Bible to describe this experience, so that an adequate discussion of each one would result in an encyclopedia of terms. Yet each expression or phrase apparently defines some aspect of what has been described as, "so great salvation," and, therefore, each expression is important. Some have attempted to catalogue these terms or phrases in various lists. Chafer identified 66 aspects of "the riches of grace in Christ Jesus." The following list has been taken from Chafer and Willmington and has also been expanded to suggest[132] aspects of this "so great salvation" (Heb. 2:3).

1.   Foreknown (Rom. 8:29; 1 Pet. 1:2)
2.   Elect (1 Thess. 1:4; Rom. 8:33; Col. 3:12)
3.   Predestinated (Eph. 1:11; Rom. 8:29-30; Eph. 1:5)
4.   Chosen (Matt. 22:14; 1 Pet. 2:4)
5.   Called (1 Thess. 5:24)
6.   Foreordained (1 Pet. 1:20)
7.   Reconciled by God (2 Cor. 5:18-19; Col. 1:20)
8.   Reconciled to God (Rom. 5:10; 2 Cor. 5:20)
9.   Made near (Eph. 2:13)

10. Given the ministry of reconciliation (2 Cor. 5:18)
11. Made an ambassador (2 Cor. 5:20)
12. Accepted by God (Eph. 1:6)
13. Access to God (Rom. 5:2)
14. Redeemed by God (Col. 1:14; 1 Pet. 1:18; Rom. 3:24)
15. Passed from death unto life (John 5:24)
16. Removed from place of condemnation (Rom. 8:1; 1 Cor. 11:32; John 3:18)
17. Given liberty (Gal. 5:1)
18. Delivered from Satan (Col. 1:13)
19. Delivered from self (Rom. 6)
20. Delivered from law (Rom. 6:14; Gal. 3:25; 2 Cor. 3:11)
21. Dead to the law (Rom. 7:4)
22. Application of the propitiation (1 John 2:2; Rom. 3:25-26)
23. Application of the atonement (covering of sins) (Gen. 22:8)
24. Conscience purged (Heb. 9:14)
25. Application of Christ our Sin-bearer (1 Pet. 2:24; Rom. 4:25)
26. Acceptance of Christ as our Substitute (Rom. 4:3-25)
27. Application of a ransom (Matt. 20:28)
28. Made a living stone (1 Pet. 2:5)
29. Become part of the bride of Christ (Eph. 5:25-27)
30. Engrafted into the Vine (John 15:1-8, 16)
31. Engrafted into the olive tree (Rom. 11:17)
32. Crucified with Christ (Gal. 2:20)
33. Dead with Christ (Rom. 6:4)
34. Planted together with Christ (Rom. 6:5)
35. Quickened together with Christ (Rom. 6:4; Col. 2:13)
36. Raised together with Christ (Rom. 6:4; Col. 3:1)
37. Set together with Christ (Eph. 2:6)
38. Workman together with Christ (1 Thess. 5:10)
39. Live together with Christ (1 Thess. 5:10)
40. Glorified together (Rom. 8:17, 30)
41. Dead to sin (1 Pet. 2:24)
42. Born again (John 3:7; 1:12)
43. Became actual sons of God (1 John 3:3)
44. Became adopted sons of God (Rom. 8:25)
45. Made a new creation (2 Cor. 5:17)
46. Regenerated (Titus 3:5)
47. Made servants (Rev. 22:2)
48. Made vessels of honor (2 Tim. 2:21)
49. Made vessels of mercy (Rom. 9:23)
50. Made a child of the resurrection (Luke 20:36)
51. Made a child of day (1 Thess. 5:5)
52. Made a child of Abraham (Gal. 3:7, 29)

53. Made a child of light (1 Thess. 5:5)
54. Made brethren (1 John 3:14-18)
55. Became an heir (Rom. 8:16-17)
56. Made a sheep in the Shepherd's fold (John 10:1-16; 27-28)
57. Made Salt (Matt. 5:13)
58. Made light (Eph. 5:8)
59. Became a part of a holy nation (1 Pet. 2:9)
60. Received citizenship in Heaven (Phil. 3:20)
61. Made righteous (Rom. 3:22)
62. Made acceptable (Eph. 1:6; 1 Pet. 2:5)
63. Sanctified positionally (1 Cor. 1:30; 6:11)
64. Perfected forever (Heb. 10:14)
65. Made fit to be partakers (Col. 1:12)
66. Justified (Rom. 5:1)
67. Received peace with God (Rom. 5:1)
68. Forgiven (Col. 1:14; 2:13; 3:13)
69. Became the object of grace (Rom. 5:1-6)
70. Righteousness of Christ imputed (Rom. 4:1-11)
71. Sins remitted (Matt. 26:28)
72. Delivered from the powers of darkness (Col. 1:13; 2:13-15)
73. Translated (Col. 1:13)
74. Placed on the Rock (1 Cor. 3:11)
75. Part of God's inheritance (Eph. 1:18)
76. Part of God's gift of Christ (John 17:6, 11-12, 20)
77. Circumcised in Christ (Col. 2:11; Phil. 3:3; Rom. 2:29)
78. Holy priesthood (1 Pet. 2:5)
79. Royal priesthood (Rev. 1:6)
80. Chosen Generation (1 Pet. 2:9)
81. A people of God's own (Titus 2:14)
82. Access to God (Eph. 2:18)
83. Washing/Cleansing (1 Cor. 6:11)
84. A new Advocate (1 John 2:1)
85. Objects of Christ's Prayers (Heb. 7:25)
86. God's Beloved (Eph. 2:4; Rom. 1:7)
87. Objects of grace of God for salvation (Eph. 2:8)
88. Objects of grace of God for keeping (Rom. 5:2)
89. Objects of grace of God for service (Eph. 2:7)
90. Objects of grace of God for instruction (Titus 2:12-13)
91. Objects of power of God (Eph. 1:9; Phil. 2:13)
92. Objects of the faithfulness of God (Heb. 13:5; Phil. 1:6)
93. Objects of His peace (Col. 3:15)
94. Part of the body of Christ (1 Cor. 12:27)
95. Objects of the consolation of the Father (2 Thess. 2:16)

96. Receive a new Heavenly Father (Matt. 6:19)
97. Guaranteed an inheritance (1 Pet. 1:4)
98. Christ becomes our life (Col. 3:4; 1 John 5:10, 12)
99. Betrothed to Christ (2 Cor. 11:2)
100. Part of the household of God (Eph. 2:19; 3:15; Gal. 6:10)
101. Made a saint (Rom. 1:7)
102. In God (1 Thess. 1:1)
103. In Christ (John 14:20)
104. In the Spirit (Rom. 8:9)
105. Declared an epistle of Christ (2 Cor. 3:3)
106. Made rich (Eph. 1:3)
107. Baptized with the Holy Spirit (1 Cor. 12:13)
108. Indwelt by the Holy Spirit (1 Cor. 6:19)
109. Sealed by the Spirit (Eph. 4:30)
110. Given spiritual gift (1 Cor. 12:7, 11)
111. Develops Fruit of the Spirit (Gal. 5:22-23)
112. Received another Comforter (John 14:16-17)
113. Completed in Christ (Col. 2:10)
114. Placed in the heavenlies (Eph. 1:3)
115. Given every spiritual blessing (Eph. 1:3)
116. Became a Christian (Acts 11:26)
117. Qualified for promises of God (2 Cor. 1:20; 2 Pet. 1:3-4)
118. Given eternal life (John 5:24)
119. Indwelling faith of God (1 Pet. 1:1)
120. Guaranteed secured (John 10:27-29)
121. Witness of the Spirit (Rom. 8:15)
122. Assurance of salvation (1 John 5:13)
123. Received the Spirit of adoption (Rom. 8:15)
124. Led by the Holy Spirit (Rom. 8:14)
125. Qualify for the discipline of the Father (Heb. 12:5-8)
126. Partakers of the divine nature (2 Pet. 1:4)
127. Christ becomes our wisdom (1 Cor. 1:30)
128. Converted (Rom. 6:17)
129. Received the Holy Spirit (Luke 11:13)
130. New understanding of scriptures (1 Cor. 2:13-15)
131. Saved (Rom. 10:13).

ENDNOTES

1. Charles Hodge, *Systematic Theology* (New York: Scribner, Armstrong, and Co., 1874), 3:3.
2. William Shedd, *A History of Christian Doctrine* (New York: Charles Scribner's Sons, 1889), 2:204.
3. William Ashley Sunday, *Wonderful And Other Sermons* (Grand Rapids: Zondervan, n.d.), 27.
4. G. Walters, "Salvation" *The New Bible Dictionary*, ed. J. D. Douglas (Grand Rapids: Eerdmans, 1977), 1126.
5. Burton Scott Easton, "Salvation" *The International Standard Bible Encyclopedia*, ed. James Orr (Grand Rapids: Eerdmans, 1974), 2665.
6. Lewis Sperry Chafer, *Major Bible Themes* (Chicago: Moody, 1926), 154.
7. C. I. Scofield, ed. *The New Scofield Reference Bible* (New York: Oxford, 1967), 1211, ftnt. 1.
8. Easton, 2670.
9. Chafer, *Major Bible Themes*, 155.
10. Walters, 1127, gives each of the points in the following chart, except for Chapter 18.
11. John Wick Broomall, "The Bible and Modern Religions: II, Dispensationalism" *Interpretation* 10 (April, 1956), 178.*
12. Clarence B. Bass, *Backgrounds to Dispensationalism: Its Historical Genesis and Ecclesiastical Implications* (Grand Rapids: Baker, 1978), 34.
13. Lewis Sperry Chafer, "Inventing Heretics Through Misunderstanding," *Bibliotheca Sacra*, 102 (January, 1945), 1.*
14. William L. Pettingill, *Bible Questions Answered* (Findlay, OH: Fundamental Truth Publishers, n.d.), 72.
15. Oswald T. Allis, *Prophecy and the Church* (Philadelphia: Presbyterian and Reformed Publishing Co., 1945), 39.
16. Louis Berkhof, *Systematic Theology* (Grand Rapids: Eerdmans, 1939), 291.
17. Berkhof, 614.
18. Charles Caldwell Ryrie, *Dispensationalism Today* (Chicago: Moody, 1965), 123.
19. Easton, 2666.
20. Easton, "Grace" *The International Standard Bible Encyclopedia*, ed. James Orr (Grand Rapids: Eerdmans, 1939), 1292.
21. W. Curtis Vaughan, *The Letter of the Ephesians* (Nashville, TN: Convention Press, 1963), 48-49.
22. Aiden Wilson Tozer, *The Knowledge of the Holy: The Attributes of God: Their Meaning in the Christian Life* (San Francisco: Harper, 1961), 93.
23. J. H. Stringer, "Grace" *The New Bible Dictionary*, ed. J. D. Douglas (Grand Rapids: Eerdmans, 1977), 491.
24. Tozer, 95.

25.   John Calvin, *Commentary on 1 John*, s. v.*

26.   Duane Edward Spencer, *TULIP: The Five Points of Calvinism in the Light of Scripture* (Grand Rapids: Baker, 1979), 59.

27.   Augustus Hopkins Strong, *Systematic Theology: A Compendium Designed for the Use of Theological Students* (Old Tappan, NJ: Fleming H. Revell Company, 1970), 779.

28.   Henry Clarence Thiessen, *Lectures in Systematic Theology* (Grand Rapids: Eerdmans, 1951), 344.

29.   Spencer, 71.

30.   John Murray, *Redemption Accomplished and Applied* (Grand Rapids: Eerdmans, 1951), 344.*

31.   Lewis Sperry Chafer, "For Whom Did Christ Die?" *Bibliotheca Sacra* 137:548 (October-December 1980), 312.

32.   *Westminster Larger Catechism*, Question 67 (Richmond, VA: John Knox Press, n.d.), 225-226.

33.   Spencer, 73.

34.   Hodge, *Systematic Theology*, 3: 4.

35.   Edgar Young Mullins, *The Christian Religion in Its Doctrinal Expression* (Philadelphia: Roger Williams Press, 1917), 365.

36.   Spencer, 75.

37.   Mullins, 5.

38.   Archibald Alexander Hodge, *Outlines of Theology* (London: Thomas Nelson and Sons, 1883), 108.

39.   Strong, 601.

40.   Hodge, *Systematic Theology*, 2:330.*

41.   *The Letters of John Wesley*, 5:322.*

42.   *The Letters of John Wesley*, 5:188-89.*

43.   Loraine Boettner, *The Reformed Doctrine of Predestination* (Grand Rapids: Eerdmans, 1932), 183.*

44.   Edward Bouverie Pusey, *What Is of Faith as to Everlasting Punishment?* 2nd Ed., (Oxford: J. Parker, 1880), 7.*

45.   Cited by John Leland Peters, *Christian Perfection and American Methodism* (New York: Abingdon Press, 1956), 216.

46.   A. A. Hodge, *Outlines of Theology*, 109.

47.   Ibid., 543.

48.   Boettner, 184.*

49.   Strong, 799.

50.   Ibid., 801.

51.   Mullins, 434.

52.   Strong, 777.

53. Thiessen, 343-44.

54. Hodge, *Outlines of Theology*, 201-202, 231-34.

55. John MacBeth, *Notes on the Thirty-Nine Articles.* Historical and Explanatory (Dublin: The Association for Promoting Christian Knowledge, 1906), 91-92.*

56. Strong, 777.

57. Hodge, *Outlines of Theology*, 231-32.

58. Strong, 353.

59. Hodge, *Outlines of Theology*, 230.

60. Thiessen, 344.

61. Hodge, *Systematic Theology*, 3:215.

62. William Sargant, *Battle for the Mind*, revised (Baltimore: Penguin, 1961) xxviii.

63. D. Martyn Lloyd-Jones, *Conversions Psychological and Spiritual* (London: InterVarsity Press, 1959), 31-32.

64. Mullins, 377.

65. Strong, 829.

66. Hodge, *Systematic Theology*, 3:95.

67. See the author's discussion of the age of accountability, Elmer L. Towns and Roberta L. Groff, *Successful Ministry to the Mentally Retarded* (Moody: Chicago, 1972), 38-46.

68. Barry M. Moody, *Repent and Believe: The Baptist Experience in Maritime Canada* (Hantsport, N.S.: Lancelot Press Limited, 1980), ix.

69. Harold Willmington, *Willmington's Guide to the Bible* (Wheaton: 1981), 729.

70. Strong, 832.

71. *The New Scofield Reference Bible* (1967), 970, ftnt. 4.

72. Mullins, 369-70.

73. Ibid., 369.

74. Lloyd-Jones, 39.

75. Charles Grandison Finney, *Lectures on Revivals of Religion* (Old Tappan, NJ: Fleming H. Revell Company, n.d.), 155.*

76. Byron DeMent, "Repentance" *The International Standard Bible Encyclopedia*, ed. James Orr (Grand Rapids: Eerdmans, 1939), 2559.

77. Strong, 833.

78. Thiessen, 354-55.

79. Thomas Theodore Martin, *God's Plan with Men* (Fincastle, VA: Scripture Truth, n.d.), 125-26.

80. Chafer, *Salvation* (New York: Charles C. Cook, 1917), 50-51.

81. Leon L. Morris, "Faith" *The New Bible Dictionary*, ed. J. D. Douglas (Grand Rapids: Eerdmans, 1962), 413.

82. Chafer, *Salvation*, 45.

83. *Heidelberg Catechism*, question #1.*

84. The various kinds of faith are discussed in greater detail in the author's *Say-It-Faith* (Wheaton, IL: Tyndale, 1983).
85. Morris, 411.
86. Thiessen, 358.
87. Morris, 411.
88. *Westminster Catechism*, Chapter 1.5.*
89. Strong, 849.
90. Mullins, 389.
91. Strong, 850-52.
92. J. I. Packer, "Justification" *The New Bible Dictionary*, ed. J. D. Douglas (Grand Rapids: Eerdmans, 1962), 683.
93. John Alfred Faulkner, "Justification" *The International Standard Bible Encyclopedia*, ed. James Orr (Grand Rapids: Eerdmans, 1939, 1783.
94. Faulkner, 1786.
95. Packer, 686.
96. Mullins, 378.
97. Strong, 809.
98. M. R. Gordon, "Regeneration" *The New Bible Dictionary*, ed. J. D. Douglas (Grand Rapids: Eerdmans, 1962), 1081.
99. Strong, 823.
100. Thiessen, 369.
101. Hodge, *Systematic Theology*, 3:591.
102. Mullins, 383.
103. Charles Haddon Spurgeon, *Baptismal Regeneration* (Pasadena, Texas: Pilgrim Publications, n.d.), 323.
104. Strong, 822.
105. Mullins, 383.
106. Strong, 663.
107. Thiessen, 373.
108. F. H. Palmer, "Adoption" *The New Bible Dictionary*, ed. J. D. Douglas (Grand Rapids: Eerdmans, 1962), 16.
109. Thomas Rees, "Adoption" *The International Standard Bible Encyclopedia*, ed. James Orr (Grand Rapids: Eerdmans, 1939), 58.
110. *The New Scofield Reference Bible* (1967), 1272, ftnt. 4.
111. Mullins, 407.
112. J. B. Phillips, *Letters to Young Churches* (London: MacMillan Company, n.d.), xiv.*
113. Strong, 795.
114. Mullins, 410.
115. Strong, 803.

116. Henry Scougal, *The Life of God in the Soul of Man* (Philadelphia: Westminster Press, 1948), 30.

117. Watchman Nee, *The Normal Christian Life* (Fort Washington, PA: Christian Literature Crusade, 1973), 9.

118. Strong, 800-801.

119. Nee, 35.

120. Thiessen, 385.

121. *The New Scofield Reference Bible* (1967), 1349, ftnt. 1.

122. Chafer, *Salvation*, 116-37.

123. Millard J. Erickson, *Salvation: God's Amazing Plan* (Wheaton, IL: Victor Books, 1978), 114.

124. H. A. Ironside, *Holiness: The False and the True* (New York: Loizeaux Brothers, Publishers, n.d.), 48.

125. Mullins, 417.

126. John Wesley, *A Plain Account of Christian Perfectionism*, ed. Thomas S. Kepler (NY: World Publishing, 1954), 54.

127. Ibid., 67.*

128. Charles Grandison Finney, *Oberlin Evangelist*, 2:1.

129. Hodge, *Systematic Theology*, 3:251.

130. Adoniram J. Gordon, *Ministry of the Spirit* (Valley Forge, PA: Judson Press, 1949), 116-17.

131. Mullins, 432.

132. Chafer, *Salvation*, 59-67.

* Denotes page number(s) could not be verified.

CHAPTER X – HAMARTIOLOGY

The Doctrine of Sin

I. INTRODUCTION

The study of sin is called "hamartiology." This word comes from the Greek word *hamartia*. When approaching this topic, some would minimize its importance or neglect its truth. The world does not like to identify its problems with sin, nor does it identify those who break the law as sinners. Whereas some would consider the concept of sin as an illusion or archaic dogma, or as weakness in human ability, a proper understanding of sin will explain, (1) the inevitability of physical death, (2) the enigma of suffering and sickness, (3) the inherent selfishness in babies (an unlearned desire), (4) the propensity of men to lie, (5) the motive of one person to harm another, and much more. A person first studies the doctrine of God to understand the causes of goodness and justice, then he studies the doctrine of sin to understand the causes of failure, evil, rebellion and pain. Because sin has permeated every aspect of man, society and the world, one cannot fully understand life nor live a purposeful life without a proper understanding of the doctrine of sin.

II. SIN AND THE LAW

Although Webster's dictionary does not have the final or full definition, it defines sin as: "a transgression of divine law." This is a jumping-off point to examine sin, for it positions sin as the opposite of God, or a breaking of God's law, or God's standard. Earlier the law was defined as "the reflection of God and an extension of His nature into His creation." But, sin is more than breaking the law, for that only involves a volitional act against a standard. Since the law is an extension of God, and sin is in juxtaposition to it, then sin is anything that is opposed to, or is not in keeping with the nature or will of God.

A. THE NATURE OF THE LAW. The law is simply an expression of the nature of God in the form of moral dictates of God's holiness and moral perfections. Man's best efforts to live according to this standard are futile.

The law is both external and internal in relation to man's heart. It is external in that the law is expressed in precepts, prohibitions or dictates. It is internal in that man is born with an innate knowledge of God, hence an innate knowledge of the law. For those who do not have explicit revelation of the law of God in the Ten Commandments or other precepts, God has revealed it in nature.

485

In unveiling the external nature of the Old Testament law, Paul in his epistle to the Galatians delineates the function of the law as a schoolmaster. "Wherefore the law was our schoolmaster to bring us unto Christ, that we might be justified by faith" (Gal. 3:24). Beyond the specific revelation, the law of God resides in His creation, sometimes called "general revelation." Those without access to the Scriptures due to geographical location or political restriction, nonetheless have the law of God inscribed in their hearts. In his epistle to the Romans, Paul deals severely with this issue: "For when the Gentiles which have not the law [Old Testament Scripture], do by nature [general revelation] the things contained in the law [Old Testament] those having not the law [Old Testament] are a law unto themselves: which shew the work of the law written in their hearts, their conscience also bearing unto themselves: which shew the work of the law written in their hearts, their conscience also bearing witness, and their thoughts the mean while accusing or else excusing one another" (Rom. 2:14-15).

In light of contemporary fanatical demonstrations of what some believe the law of God demands of humans, the need to understand the contents of the law becomes even more important. Strong, in his classical systematic work, enumerates these principles.

> Law is an expression of will. The essential idea of law is that of a general expression of will enforced by power. It implies: (a) A lawgiver, or authoritative will. (b) Subjects, or beings upon whom this will terminates. (c) A general command, or expression of this will. . . . (d) A power, enforcing the command. . . . (e) Duty or obligation to obey; and (f) Sanctions, or pains and penalties for disobedience.[1]

It is important to realize that the law of God is not exclusive. It includes all. Everyone endowed with the gift of life becomes, through no choice of his own, a subject of the law. Man was created for fellowship with God and, more importantly, to glorify Him. Condemnation is the inevitable result of breaking the law. But this was not the original purpose of God's plan as revealed in Scripture. Eternal condemnation was designated solely for Satan and his ungodly angels, not man. In response to man's dilemma, grace, forgiveness and mercy were introduced to man early in his creation.

B. THE LAW AND ADAM. Only in the case of Adam was the law given as an instrument to guide his life with God. This raises a controversial issue: Would Adam have inherited the glories of heaven had he and Eve obeyed God's law during their probationary period? With the absence of sin in the Garden of Eden, Adam and Eve possessed immortality, for only sin can cause death unto separation. However, they possessed a type of unconfirmed holiness or innocence. If they had not sinned, we can only reason that they would have earned the right to immortality, not in heaven, but upon the earth. Therefore, the best that keeping the law could ever do for man was to guarantee his external position upon the earth. Initially most would seize upon this opportunity and be content, but it would only be for a period of time. Who in their right mind would not seek to exchange their sinless, immortal, physical bodies, with limited access to God, for a glorified body with limitless potential and continual access to God? For the glories of heaven are not to be compared with the best that earth could provide. With the introduction of sin, the law no longer possesses the capability to insure immortality, it rather serves to condemn men who trespass against God.

II. AN EXAMINATION OF THE COVENANT OF WORKS

A study of the establishment of the covenant of works with Adam is necessary because it is the foundation to hamartiology for many. Even though it is inconsistent with the view of other covenants taught in Scripture, we need to examine the feasibility of such a covenant. Those who support the existence of such a covenant claim that God and Adam entered into a covenant in which, if Adam did not sin, he would be removed from the probationary period and receive a confirmed state of immortality. If Adam did fail, he would receive the full consequences of the promised penalty. Charles Hodge, a prominent spokesman for the existence of this covenant, writes the following in relation to the covenant of works.

This statement does not rest upon any express declaration of the Scriptures. It is, however, a concise and correct mode of asserting a plain Scriptural fact, namely, that God made to Adam a promise suspended upon a condition, and attached to disobedience a certain penalty. This is what in Scriptural language is meant by a covenant, and this is all that is meant by the term as here used. Although the word covenant is not used in Genesis, and does not elsewhere, in any clear passage, occur in reference to the transaction there recorded, yet inasmuch as the plan of salvation is constantly represented as a New Covenant, new, not merely in antithesis to that made at Sinai, but new in reference to all legal covenants whatever, it is plain that the Bible does represent the arrangement made with Adam as a truly federal transaction. The Scriptures know nothing of any other than two methods of attaining eternal life: the one that which demands perfect obedience, and the other that which demands faith. If the latter is called a covenant, the former is declared to be of the same nature.[2]

A. THE NATURE OF A COVENANT. In the construction of a covenant, five separate elements need to be present: (1) Wording that lends itself to a legal agreement, (2) a promise of reward for successful completion, (3) a condition of the requirements of the covenant, (4) a penalty for breaking the covenant and, finally, (5) at least two participants. Supporters of the covenant view readily admit the absence of the use of the word "covenant" in Genesis. However, they argue that language lends itself to the possible establishment of a covenant. The promise, they claim, is abundantly clear, leading to immortality and the removal from the probation. The condition was obedience to God's demands concerning the Tree of the Knowledge of Good and Evil. The penalty of death for the participants is equally clear.

Concerning the condition—or as some have chosen to call it, the test—supporters of the covenant stress the importance of the condition being tested. Because if a covenant is established and man's free will never has the chance to act upon it, then a covenant does not truly exist. The significance of Adam's test is summarized by Hodge.

> The specific command to Adam not to eat of a certain tree, was therefore not the only command he was required to obey. It was given simply to be the outward and visible test to determine whether he was willing to obey God in all things. Created holy, with all his affections pure, there was the more reason that the test of his obedience should be an outward and positive command; something wrong simply because it was forbidden, and not evil in its own nature. It would thus be seen that Adam obeyed for the sake of obeying. His obedience was more directly to God, and not to his own reason.[3]

Having given the basis for the covenant, and the severity for breaking the covenant, Hodge takes one further step and seeks to tie the covenant of works with the importance of Adam's sin. Discussing the role of the two participants, Hodge says,

> It lies in the nature of a covenant that there must be two or more parties. A covenant is not of one. The parties to the original covenant were God and Adam. Adam, however, acted not in his individual capacity but as the head and representative of his whole race. This is plain. (1.) Because everything said to him had as much reference to his posterity as to Adam himself. Everything granted to him was granted to them. Everything promised to him was promised to them. And everything threatened against him, in case of transgression, was threatened against them. God did not give the earth to Adam for him alone, but as the heritage of his race. The dominion over the lower animals with which he was invested belonged equally to his descendants. The promise of life embraced them as well as him; and the threatening of death concerned them as well as him. (2.) In the second place, it is an outstanding undeniable fact that the penalty Adam incurred has fallen upon his whole race. The earth is cursed to them as it was to him. They must earn their bread by the sweat of their brows. The pains of childbirth are the common heritage of all the daughters of Eve. All men are subject to disease and death. All are born in sin, destitute of the moral image of God. There is not an evil consequent on the sin of Adam which does not affect his race as much as it affected him. (3.) Not only did the ancient Jews infer the representative character of Adam from the record given in Genesis, but the inspired writers of the New Testament give this doctrine the sanction of divine authority. In Adam, says the Apostle, all died. The sentence of condemnation, he teaches us, passed on all men for one offence. By the offence of one, all were made sinners. (4.) This great fact is made the ground on which the whole plan of

redemption is founded. As we fell in Adam, we are saved in Christ. To deny the principle in the one case, is to deny it in the other; for the two are inseparably united in the representations of Scripture. (5.) The principle involved in the headship of Adam underlies all the religious institutions ever ordained by God for men: all His providential dealings with our race; and even the distributions of the saving influences of his Spirit. It is therefore one of the fundamental principles both of natural and of revealed religion. (6.) What is thus clearly revealed in the word and providence of God, finds a response in the very constitution of our nature. All men are led as it were instinctively to recognize the validity of this principle of representation. Rulers represent their people; parents their children; guardians their wards. All these considerations are in place here, when the nature of the covenant of works, and the parties to that covenant are under discussion, although of course they must come up again to be more fully examined, when we have to speak of the effects of Adam's sin upon his posterity. Men may dispute as to the grounds of the headship of Adam, but the fact itself can hardly be questioned by those who recognize the authority of the Scriptures. It has therefore entered into the faith of all Christian churches, and is more or less clearly presented in all their authorized symbols.[4]

Another equally zealous supporter of the idea of the covenant of works states that the covenant of works, like the covenant of grace (enacted after the fall), finds its basis within the realm of God's grace. Dabney writes,

God, therefore, moved by pure grace, condescended to establish a covenant with His holy creature. in virtue of which a temporary obedience might be graciously accepted as a ground ior God's communicating Himself to him, and assuring him ever after of holiness, happiness, and communion with God. Here then is the point of osculation between the covenant of works, and the covenant of grace, the law and the Gospel. Both offer a plan of free justification, by which as righteousness should be accepted, in covenant, to acquire for the creature more than he could strictly claim of God; and thus gain him everlasting life. In the covenant of grace, all is "ordained in the hand of a mediator," because man's sin had else excluded him from access to God's holiness. In the covenant of works, no mediator was required, because man was innocent, and God's purity did not forbid Him to condescend to him. But in both, there was free grace; in both a justification unto life; in both, a gracious bestowal of more than man had earned.[5]

The suggested covenant of works involves certain conditions that are spelled out in the *Irish Articles of Religion* (1615). These conditions are implicit, but in Scripture they are never explicit.

Man being at the beginning created according to the image of God (which consisted especially in the wisdom of his mind and the true holiness of his free will), had the covenant of the law ingrafted in his heart, whereby God did promise unto him everlasting life upon condition that he performed entire and perfect obedience unto his Commandments, according to that measure of strength wherewith he was endued in his creation, and threatened death unto him if he did not perform the same.[6]

In addition to the *Irish Articles*, the *Westminster Confession* (Chapter VII) includes the same set of conditions: "The first covenant made with man was a covenant of works, wherein life was promised to Adam, and in him to his posterity, upon condition of perfect and personal obedience."[7]

B. OBJECTIONS TO THE EXISTENCE OF A COVENANT OF WORKS. In spite of the material presented in support for the existence of a covenant of works, there are several important objections, all of which question the existence of such a covenant. These objections are not intended to destroy the Representative or Federal Leadership theory of imputation. That will be dealt with at a later time. The headship of Adam of the human race is biblical. Objections to the covenant of works include:

1. *The lack of explicit scriptural support.* Supporters of the theory employ the argument of "in principle" reasoning, but it is an erroneous approach. "In principle" reasoning suggests that what is true in one example is equally true when applied to a similar situation. Supporters of the covenant view have examined the elements found with other clearly supported covenants in scripture (i.e. Abrahamic, Davidic, and others) and have discovered similar elements between God and Adam and therefore argue for the presence of a covenant. It is quite obvious to the objective reader that such a reasoning process lacks a cause-and-effect relationship.

2. *In a covenant both parties must act in voluntary capacities.* They must consent to the demands of the covenant. Yet it appears from the Genesis account that Adam did not have the option to accept or reject the demands laid upon him by God. God's one-sided approach to Adam in regard to the keeping of the garden and abstinence from the Tree of Knowledge of Good and Evil destroys a vital element in the constitution of a covenant, namely free will

3. *A covenant must be clearly a covenant.* In the other covenants (Abrahamic, Sinaitic, and Davidic) the biblical text makes it abundantly clear that a covenant has been established. In such passages the word "covenant" is frequently used. Yet, as we study the Genesis account no such reference is made to the word "covenant." Not even a synonym is alluded to.

4. *An examination of Results.* An earlier quote by Dabney states that in both the covenants of grace and works, free grace was available. Grace is best understood as "unmerited favor."

A rigid command to keep the garden and abstain from the specified Tree points not to unmerited favor.

5. *An examination of rewards.* As pointed out by Hoeksema, another problem with the covenant of works approach is that of rewards. What would have happened if Adam had kept the "suggested" covenant?

> Suppose that Adam would have obeyed the commandment of God. Then, according to the idea of the covenant of works, he would have been glorified and raised to a heavenly plane of immortal life. The question arises: when would this have happened? The usual answer is that the matter would have been decided in a comparatively short time, perhaps soon after Adam and Eve had resisted the temptation of the devil. At any rate, it is usually supposed that this moment of Adam's reward would have come before there would have been descendants, because Adam stood in paradise as the representative of the whole human race. But what then? Adam and Eve would have been translated to a kind of immortal, heavenly glory. Would they have brought forth the human race in that state of glory? This seems quite impossible, for the propagation of the human race and the replenishing of the earth appears inseparably connected with the present earthly state of man in his physical body. In heaven they do not marry and bring forth children. And what of the earth and all the earthly creation? Would it also have been glorified? Or would Adam simply have been taken out of it?[8]

Supporters for the covenant of works have meticulously combed the Scriptures for legitimate proof of their view, but they have managed to blind themselves or knowingly step over several basic elements of covenant. Therefore, the notion of a valid covenant between God and Adam is rejected, and God created man and charged to him responsibility of keeping the garden, and of abstaining from the Tree of Knowledge of Good and Evil. This was not a two-sided covenant, but a unilateral command that God gave to Adam.

III. THE FALL OF MAN

One of the most tragic days in the history of the world was when sin was introduced to humanity. Before that day, creation was approved when God "saw every thing that he had made, and behold it was very good" (Gen. 1:31). God had prepared a beautiful garden and placed Adam and Eve as the sole human residents, who lived in harmonious community with God, nature, and each other.

Satan entered the garden to tempt man to rebel against the stipulations given by God. Satan did not appear as a sinister character but as something with which both Adam and Eve were familiar, a serpent. Satan conversed with Eve, causing her to compromise her loyalty to

God. He began by making God's demands sound extreme and then seeking to show Eve how harmless it was to eat the fruit. When she ate and shared it with Adam, the evil purpose of Satan had been accomplished.

Satan began by placing doubt in the woman's mind concerning the word of God and then bringing her to the point of outright disobedience. When Eve began to entertain the thought that perhaps God was somewhat extreme, and perhaps He did not understand what was best for her, she opened the door of her mind to the lie of Satan. That moment of weakness resulted in the fall of all mankind, with all its consequences.

The Westminster Catechism described the Utopia in Eden, which served as a backdrop where man fell in the first sin.

How did God create man? After God had made all other creatures, he created male and female; formed the body of the man of the dust of the ground, and the woman of the rib of the man, endued them with living, reasonable and immortal souls; made them after his own image, in knowledge, righteousness, and holiness; having the law of God written in their hearts, and power to fulfill it, with dominion over the creatures; yet subject to fall.

What was the providence of God toward man in the estate in which he was created? The providence of God toward man in the estate in which he was created was the placing him in paradise, appointing him to dress it, giving him liberty to eat of the fruit of the earth; putting the creatures under his dominion, and ordaining marriage for his help; affording him communion with himself; instituting the Sabbath; entering into a covenant of life with him, upon condition of personal, perfect, and perpetual obedience, of which the tree of life was a pledge; and forbidding to eat of the tree of the knowledge of good and evil, upon the pain of death.

Did man continue in that a state wherein God at first created him? Our first parents being left to the freedom of their own will, through the temptation of Satan, transgressed the commandment of God in eating the forbidden fruit; and thereby fell from the estate of innocency where they were created.[9]

It is difficult to discover a clear parallel to the unique position and sinless nature Adam and Eve enjoyed prior to their volitional act into sin. Adam and Eve, while enjoying direct communion with God, were limited in knowing what was God's unfolding plan through the ages. They possessed no Scripture and knew nothing of redemption or the inevitable coarse their free will would lead. It is not correct to assume God withheld vital information from them, which might have prevented their fall, for what God had revealed to them was abundantly sufficient to allow them to exercise their will in accordance with God's explicit demand.

Much debate among biblical scholars has arisen in the struggle to resolve what is meant by "the image of God." Sufficient for the moment, the phrase "the image of God" involves character likeness to God in the realm of reasoning, will, emotions, morality and spirituality. Under the study of anthropology, "the image of God" will be given greater attention.

Scripture does not tell us how long Adam and Eve enjoyed the bliss of Eden. Perhaps it was only a brief period of time, possibly only several days. Support for a brief period comes from the command to Adam and Eve to replenish the earth. In order to keep in accordance with God's will and not be guilty of disobedience, Adam should have begun the procreation process almost immediately. Obviously, Eve had not conceived before the Fall. Scripture clearly states that it was not until after the Fall that Eve eventually conceived and delivered her first child (Gen. 4:1). However, on the time issue one cannot be dogmatic, only speculative.

In line with the nature of God's law, man must honor his responsibility to his Creator. One prohibition was placed upon Adam and Eve, namely, to abstain from the Tree of the Knowledge of Good and Evil. With so much good readily available to them, one seriously questions why Adam and Eve would choose to knowingly forfeit their surroundings for some thing or some knowledge they lacked. Perhaps their lack of trust in the knowledge God had given them (unbelief) was the prime motive for the Fall. The problem of evil will be studied in greater detail under an examination of the causes of man's fall

The prohibition placed upon Adam possessed greater significance than simply his ability to abstain from the fruit of the Tree of the Knowledge of Good and Evil. Adam's response to God's command would demonstrate mankind's response to the law and expectations the Creator placed upon His creatures. Also, Adam's actions would affect not only himself, but all of mankind.

Some have sought to place an unwarranted and unscriptural interpretation on the role of the Tree of Life. Some have suggested that the fruit contained a "magical" or innate element that ensured immortality. However, the Tree should not be understood to possess any inherent qualities; it served as an instrument to test the motives of Adam, to reveal if he could demonstrate his virtue through obedience. If Adam had obeyed, he would have lived. Buswell aptly described the role of the Tree:

> An eternal life of fellowship with God was symbolized by partaking of the fruit of the tree of life; but since sin has come into the world, such direct access to God is now unavailable. In its place there is the sacrificial system, pointing forward to the Way, which God will prepare for the attainment of this eternal life. Just as literally as the passover lamb was sacrificed, and the unleavened bread and the bitter herbs were eaten, just as literally as the manna was provided in the wilderness, so the tree of life before man fell had been "also in the midst of the garden" (Gen. 2:9).
>
> It is my suggestion that we should understand the tree of life in Genesis and in Revelation as something definitely analogous to the sacrificial system of the patriarchal age, the Levitical system instituted by Moses, and the sacraments of

baptism and the Lord's Supper, which we observe today. All of these are visible, tangible sacraments whereby faith in God is symbolized and fellowship with God realized.[10]

The term "knowledge of good and evil" should not be understood as cognitive knowledge, but as knowledge that seeks understanding in experience. Cognitive knowledge (reasoning) leads us to know things, as when knowledge is gathered from an encyclopedia. However, experiential knowledge comes to those who have actually been involved in the process. When a person knows God, it is more than knowing about God; it is having faith in Him (John 17:3). While apparently viewing the Tree, Eve soon found herself engaged in a cunning conversation. Two questions immediately emerge. First, why was she not afraid of the serpent? Second, how can a serpent talk? We need to remember that this event occurred prior to the Fall, when man and animals lived in total harmony. Therefore, there was no need of fear. Answering the question of a serpent talking, Hoeksema writes,

> And that he [Satan] chose the serpent for his temptation was undoubtedly due to the fact that it was the most suitable instrument for his purpose, because, according to Scripture, the serpent was the most subtle of all animals. This indicates, no doubt, that the serpent was endowed with a high degree of animal intelligence. It is not impossible that it represented the animal world with man. Besides, we receive the impression that it possessed some form of speech,—not of human language, of course,— but nevertheless of a language that enabled him to communicate with man. For even though it is true that the subject speaking through the serpent in paradise to Eve was Satan, yet we must note, in the first place, that the devil could not give the serpent the power of speech; and, secondly, that the narrative leaves the impression that Eve did not consider it extraordinary that the serpent spoke to her. Besides, from the rest of the chapter we receive the impression that the serpent originally presented a different form from that of the serpent, which we know today. Undoubtedly the serpent was an animal that could form a sort of connecting link between the animal world and man. And for that reason Satan could find no more suitable instrument than that most subtle of animals for his temptation of Adam and Eve. At the same time, it is also very evident that the subject speaking through the serpent is Satan. This is plain from the contents of the speech, which suggests that it is a rational, moral subject, and besides, that it is a wicked subject, lying and slandering God. And the same may be concluded from the general observation that the Bible everywhere puts a connection between the devil and fallen humanity. He is the prince of this world, the old serpent.[11]

The words spoken between Eve and the serpent were apparently similar to those employed between Adam and Eve. All that can be gleaned from the narrative is that Eve was approached by Satan in the body of a snake. Due to her innocence and the harmonious conditions, she felt comfortable conversing with the snake and did not sense any threat to her life. Whether Adam and Eve had previously conversed with the serpent or other animals is only conjecture. Probably not. This was probably the first conversation they had with an animal (and the last), but she was not surprised because they were new in the garden and were still exploring its mysteries.

Some have inferred from the narrative that Adam was present during the entire dialogue. In Genesis 3:6, it says that the woman gave of the fruit of the tree to her husband who was "with her." The phrase "with her" could be interpreted two ways. Either he was a party to the whole conversation, or he later became involved in committing sin. However, Scripture states that the serpent addressed Eve; if the narrative is interpreted in a straightforward manner, it is concluded that only Eve was present.

The conversation was clearly riddled with half-truths and lies, focusing upon the finite limitations of Eve's nature. Genesis records the following dialogue.

> Now the serpent was more subtil than any beast of the field which the LORD God had made. And he said unto the woman, Yea, hath God said, Ye shall not eat of every tree of the garden?
>
> And the woman said unto the serpent, We may eat of the fruit of the trees of the garden: But of the fruit of the tree which is in the midst of the garden, God hath said, Ye shall not eat of it, neither shall ye touch it, lest ye die.
>
> And the serpent said unto the woman, Ye shall not surely die: For God doth know that in the day ye eat thereof, then your eyes shall be opened, and ye shall be as gods, knowing good and evil.
>
> And when the woman saw that the tree was good for food, and that it was pleasant to the eyes, and a tree to be desired to make one wise, she took of the fruit thereof, and did eat, and gave also unto her husband with her; and he did eat.
>
> And the eyes of them both were opened, and they knew that they were naked, and they sewed fig leaves together and made themselves aprons (Gen. 3:1-7).

Immediately the blissful state enjoyed by Eve crumbled. The things she valued became worthless. She undoubtedly felt defiled and naked, so she sought out her husband. Learning of her state, Adam (cf. 1 Tim. 2:8-15), knowingly took of the fruit, and shared the guilt and shame of his wife. Eve sinned due to deception, and Adam sinned knowingly.

IV. THE CAUSES OF THE FALL

When God began to question Adam and Eve concerning their sin (Gen. 3:11-13), they passed off the responsibility to someone else. Adam blamed Eve; she in turn blamed the serpent. But the Bible teaches that man sinned, fully aware of his actions. "Adam was not deceived" (1 Tim. 2:14). Thus the entire race fell because he deliberately chose by an act of his own will to disobey God and fulfill his own desires. Those desires were encouraged by the temptation of Satan, who provided the occasion for the entrance of sin into the world.

Satan's temptations followed certain patterns. John spoke of temptation in three categories when he wrote, "For all that is in the world, the lust of the flesh, and the lust of the eyes, and the pride of life, is not of the Father, but is of the world" (1 John 2:16). When Satan tempted Eve in the garden, he appealed through three avenues of temptation.

A. THE LUST OF THE FLESH. The word "lust" means desire, so the first area of temptation had to do with the desires of the body. Satan appealed to the lust of the flesh to cause Eve to partake of the forbidden fruit. It was not until "the woman saw that the tree was good for food" (Gen. 3:6), that she ate and gave to her husband. Satan took something good, that appeared to be harmless fruit, and used it to appeal to the human desire to eat. Neither the fruit nor the desire to eat was inherently evil. Adam and Eve sinned when they disobeyed the clear command of God. Our parents violated the one prohibition, "Thou shalt not eat of it" (Gen. 2:17).

B. THE LUST OF THE EYES. The second area of temptation that motivated Eve to eat the fruit was "that it was pleasant to the eyes" (Gen. 3:6). A second characteristic of humanity is to have dreams or desires. Man constantly seeks to improve his surroundings and himself. Man's desire for excellence and advancement is reflective of his Creator, in whose image he was created. Therefore, the appearance of the fruit appealed to Eve's desire to have something she did not possess. Just as the desires of the body are not evil in themselves, so it is not sinful to desire things. But sin entered the human race when man's desire was contrary to the command of God.

C. THE PRIDE OF LIFE. The third temptation was an appeal to the basic self-worth, self-acceptance, and self-preservation of man. Man was created as an independent/dependent being, separate from God, yet an autonomous being dependent on God. God in His wisdom gave man the ability to protect, preserve, and perpetuate himself. Satan appealed to the basic self-interest of humanity

HOW SATAN TEMPTED			
STRATEGY		EVE (Gen. 3:6)	
1.	Lust of the flesh	1.	Good for food
2.	Lust of the eyes	2.	Pleasant to the eyes
3.	Pride of life	3.	Desired to make one wise

by showing Eve a tree to be desired to make one wise. "She took of the fruit thereof, and did eat, and gave also unto her husband with her; and he did eat" (Gen. 3:6).

The stages of the temptation appear to have been as follows:

(a) An appeal on the part of Satan to innocent appetites, together with an implied suggestion that God was arbitrarily withholding the means of their gratification (Gen. 3:1). The first step was Eve's isolating herself and choosing to seek her own pleasure without regard to God's will. This initial selfishness led her to listen to the tempter instead of rebuking him or flying from him, and to exaggerate the divine command in her response (Gen. 3:3).

(b) A denial of the veracity of God, on the part of the tempter, with a charge against the Almighty of jealousy and fraud in keeping his creatures in a position of ignorance and dependence (Gen. 3:4-5). This was followed, on the part of the woman, by positive unbelief, and by a conscious and presumptuous cherishing of desire for the forbidden fruit, as a means of independence and knowledge. This unbelief, pride, and lust all sprang from the self-isolating, self-seeking spirit, and fastened upon the means of gratifying it (Gen. 3:6).

(c) The tempter needed no longer to urge his suit. Having poisoned the fountain, the stream would naturally be evil. Since the heart and its desires had become corrupt, the inward disposition manifested itself in act (Gen. 3:6—'did eat; and she gave also unto her husband with her'=who had been with her, and had shared her choice and longing). Thus man fell inwardly, before the outward act of eating the forbidden fruit,—fell in that one fundamental determination whereby he made supreme choice of self instead of God. This sin of the inmost nature gave rise to sins of the desires, and sins of the desires led to the outward act of transgression (James 1:15).[12]

A study of the fall of man would not be complete without mentioning two other personalities that indirectly had a bearing upon man's first sin. The tendency to attribute Adam's sin to the environment of controlling circumstances should be cautiously guarded. The guilt and responsibility falls directly upon his shoulders. Their act to consciously disobey God's one command clearly reveals their complete responsibility for disobedience. Nothing was withheld from them that would have prevented their obedience to God. They sinned because they freely desired to sin.

The first personality is none other than God. Although God can in no way be linked to the cause of man's sin, He foreknew it would happen and chose not to interfere with its development. Chafer calls it "The eternal anticipation of sin in the foreknowledge of God." Chafer continues the thought with these words.

While the truth that God foreknew the oncoming reality of sin does not constitute a beginning, in the sense that it presents no enactment of sin, His foreknowledge does enter largely into this phase of the doctrine of sin . . . suffice it to say that, while in the permissive will of God there has arisen a kingdom of darkness into which are gathered fallen angels and fallen human beings. . . .[13]

Foreknowing the inevitable course of man's free will and permitting it to happen does not constitute shared guilt. God judiciously endowed man with the ability to overcome sin. If God had interrupted the temptation process, man's free will would not have been exercised, making him little more than a mechanical robot, and more importantly the loyalty of man would not have been tested.

The second personality is Satan. Sealing his own eternal state through his rebellions act, Satan seeks to tempt others to share in his punishment. Satan's relentless attacks to thwart the plan of God, serve only to fulfill the plan of God. Satan's temptation cannot be regarded as sin, for temptation and sin are not equal. The true cause of our first parents' sin resides in their minds. This will be understood when we examine the nature of sin.

V. Views Of The Fall

Having studied the scriptural account of the Fall and its causes, it is necessary to examine the attacks levied against the historical account of the Fall. The first of two attacks treat the Genesis account as a myth. This view alleges that, like many Oriental nations, which have developed and passed to successive generations a mythical account of how man originated and progressed to his current state, the Hebrew people possess a similar mythical story. Those endorsing the mythical view usually doubt the inerrancy of not only the Genesis story, but the entire Bible.

A second attack seeks to assign an allegorical interpretation to Genesis. Berkhof describes their attacks.

> Frequent attempts have been made and are still being made to explain away the historical character of the fall. Some regard the whole narrative in Gen. 3 as an allegory, representing man's self-depravation and gradual change in a figurative way. . . . Others maintain that the serpent at least should not be regarded as a literal animal, but merely as a name or a symbol for covetousness, for sexual desire, for erring reason, or for Satan. Still others assert that, to say the least, the speaking of the serpent should be understood figuratively. But all these and similar interpretations are untenable in the light of Scripture. The passages preceding and following Gen. 3:1-7 are evidently intended as a plain historical narrative. . . . [This] can be proved by many cross-references. . . . and therefore we have no right to hold that these verses, which form an integral part of the narrative, should be interpreted figuratively. Moreover, the serpent is certainly counted among the animals in Gen. 3:1, and it would not yield good sense to substitute "serpent" for the word "Satan." The punishment in Gen. 3:14,15 presupposes a literal serpent, and Paul conceives of the serpent in no other way, II Cor. 11:3. And while it may be possible to conceive of the serpent as saying something in a figurative sense by means of certain cunning actions,

it does not seem possible to think of him as carrying on the conversation recorded in Gen. 3 in that way. The whole transaction, including the speaking of the serpent, undoubtedly finds its explanation in the operation of some superhuman power which is not mentioned in Gen. 3. Scripture clearly intimates that the serpent was but the instrument of Satan, and that Satan was the real tempter, who was working in and through the serpent, just as at a later time he worked in men and swine, John 8:44; Rom. 16:20; II Cor. 11:3; Rev. 12:9. The serpent was a fit instrument for Satan, for he is the personification of sin, and the serpent symbolizes sin (a) in its cunning and deceptive nature, and (b) in its poisonous sting by which it kills man.[14]

Despite these attempts to undermine the historical and literal view of man's fall, a literal view of the Genesis account is believed for the following reasons: (1) our Lord and the apostles refer to the Fall in a literal sense, (2) there is no internal evidence that would disclaim the veracity of the Genesis account, (3) and, finally, the Fall is essential to the doctrine of redemption. If God allowed the truth of the Fall to be written in error, then the truth of redemption cannot be trusted.

With the emergence of evolutionary concepts and humanistic teachings, many have begun to doubt the Fall and its effects upon man. Man, they claim, is becoming increasingly better, and to suggest that man is depraved and unrighteous fails to account for the many positive advances and moral deeds. These trends have affected just about every segment of our society, reaching into schools, controlling media, and even finding a stronghold in our churches.

Those who deny the existence of the Fall, do not have a correct understanding of righteousness. When measured by human standards, any kind act possesses some inherent virtue. However, in God's accounting, those seemingly kind acts fall far short of His expectations. They are as "dirty garments" (Isa. 64:6). A more detailed picture of man's condition from God's perspective is found in Romans 3:10-18 which states,

There is not a righteous man, Not even one.
　　There is no man who understands,
　　There is no man who seeks for God.
All have turned aside.
Together they have been made worthless.
　　There is not one who does good things.
　　There is not even one.
Their throat is an open tomb.
With their tongues they have deceived.
　　The poison of cobras is under their lips.
　　Their mouth is full of cursing and bitterness.
Swift are their feet to shed blood.
Destruction and wretchedness are in their ways.

The way of peace they have not known.
The fear of God is not before their eyes.

Initially one recoils from this harsh characterization of man, suggesting that it does not correctly describe all aspects of all humans. Admittedly, not every human has committed every sin. However, from God's perspective every man is totally depraved and cannot please God. The writer of James makes the claim, "For whosoever shall keep the whole law, and yet offend in one point, he is guilty of all" (Jas. 2:10). Although we are no longer under the Mosaic Law system, we are under the moral law of God, which places greater demands upon man.

Applying the principle of James 2:10 today, it is concluded that if man commits a sin, he is guilty of breaking the whole law. Even though one may actively commit only one sin, he is placed under the condition of sin, just as though he had committed every possible sin. Here, it is imperative to understand the difference between active and conditional sin. The former is manifested in a deliberate and willful act, the latter stems from active sin but describes man's general state in this life which is influenced by sin. Due to Adam's act of sin, all men are, first, born into a condition of sinfulness, and, second, are born sinners who will actively sin.

VI. THE ASSERTION OF MAN'S SINFULNESS

A. EARLY MANIFESTATION OF SIN WITHIN ALL MEN. As soon as a child is capable of moral discernment, he reveals his inherent moral character to rebel against standards. Those early innate desires of anger, pride, and selfishness all give evidence of an internal sin nature. The aforementioned desires, when permitted to exercise themselves, serve to motivate the child into a worldly disposition of corruption and evil. Scripture also attests to this claim. Psalm 58:3 states, "The wicked are estranged from the womb: they go astray as soon as they be born, speaking lies." To counter this influence, many have sought to raise their children in a favorable atmosphere with positive examples. Yet the parents' expectations were thwarted when their child naturally demonstrates responses contrary to his home environment.

B. UNIVERSALITY OF SIN. The effects and acts of sin are not isolated, but are universally present in every man, no matter where he chooses to dwell. This is undeniably stated in the doctrines of the Bible. 1 Kings 8:46 says, "There is no man that sinneth not." Ecclesiastes 7:20, "There is not a just man upon earth, that doeth good, and sinneth not." Romans 3:19, "The whole world may become guilty before God." Romans 3:23, "For all have sinned, and come short of the glory of God."

With the exception of Jesus Christ, no man has ever lived without sin. Even those who have sought a pious life within sheltered monasteries admit the presence of sinful desires within them. The universality of sin serves as a strong argument for the reality of sin.

C. CORRUPTION OF MAN'S ENTIRE NATURE. This issue deals with the extent of sin upon man's entire being. Does sin affect simply the will, emotions, or intellect? Or does it reach into every aspect of man's being and corrupt it equally? All of humanity, by their apostasy from God, are totally depraved. This does not suggest that all men are equally sinful, but it indicates that man's entire being is affected by the fall. Man's material and immaterial nature have all been perverted by sin. This leads to a discussion of total depravity.

What is "Total Depravity?" An understanding is gained by stating what it is not. It does not mean that every man is as outwardly evil as he can be. It does not suggest that man no longer possesses any conscience or inborn understanding of goodness and evil. It does not mean that man cannot perform morally good works in the sight of other men. Nor does it necessitate that men will indulge in every form of sin. What is implied by total depravity is twofold. First, the influence of sin (corruption) extends to every part of man's nature. Secondly, man can do no spiritual good toward his salvation from God's point of view. In contrast to the above definition of total depravity are the views of Calvin and Arminius. Calvin would argue that not only is man unable to perform any spiritual good, he is also incapable of mentally understanding anything. It is only through the grace of God that man can function rationally. Arminius sharply disagreed with Calvin and laid the foundation that would eventually lead to the view that man through reasoning can approach God. These views can be charted as such:

Arminius ◄——————————————————————————————————► Calvin

Man can reason himself to God fully developed in the enlightenment era.	Man can reason, but he can't obtain merit from God	Man cannot reason, except through the grace of God
Man is capable of doing spiritual good.	Man is unable to do spiritual works unless he is regenerated.	Man can do no spiritual good until salvation occurs.
Moral works can be performed.	Socially moral works can be accomplished by unbelievers.	No moral works can be performed.

Another phrase frequently employed when discussing the corruption of man's being is "total inability." Total depravity focuses on man's fallen condition and the evidence of it, whereas total inability examines the effects of the Fall upon man. In light of total depravity we learn that man's entire being is altered, and he is unable to accomplish any spiritual good. However, total inability explains the effects of the Fall. Total inability describes how much capability resides within the essence of man. To fully comprehend the implications of total inability, we first gain understanding of what is not meant by it. Total inability does not mean that man no longer has a will or that he cannot make voluntary decisions. Nor is it implied that man cannot perform civic deeds of goodness or external religious works, or manifest natural talents in the areas of music, arts, and literature. A proper understanding of total inability involves two separate issues: first, an unbeliever in his own power cannot do any act that fundamentally meets with God's approval. Morally good acts in the sight of God can only be performed by believers, in the power of the Holy Spirit. Secondly, total inability states that man is incapable of altering his fundamental disposition regarding sin and self. Man can do nothing to merit God's respect if he were given the opportunity, and would not if he were able. The corruption of man's entire being as disclosed by total depravity and total inability serves as a prominent argument for the existence of sin.

D. THE PERSONAL EXPERIENCES OF BELIEVERS. Believers in every age and in every part of the world can attest to the pragmatic evidence of sin. Recognizing his own inherent sinful nature prompted Isaiah to cry out, "Woe is me! For I am undone; because I am a man of unclean lips, and I dwell in the midst of a people of unclean lips" (Isa. 6:5). David frequently refers to his sinful inclinations in his many Penitential Psalms (25, 32, 38, 39, 51). Paul even recognized the powerful influence of sin within his own life, claiming he was the chief of sinners (1 Tim. 1:15). Believers of every age who have sought to deepen their relationship with God have universally experienced the hindering force of sin.

E. HUMANITY MANIFESTS ITSELF IN THE IMPENITENT RESPONSE OF THOSE WHOM CHRIST CAME TO SAVE. On his own free will, Christ voluntarily gave up the glories of heaven and entered into the stream of humanity, with one primary objective—to die for the sins of the world (John 1:29). Subjecting Himself to the mockery and foolishness of men, He, who gave authority and life, permitted the created beings to kill the Creator. However, the greatest humiliation came not from the hands of man, but rather when He accepted man's sin (2 Cor. 5:21). He who was holy and knew no sin, took sin upon Himself. Spurred by the motivation of love, Christ saw His love rejected repeatedly. He came to His own nation and they received Him not (John 1:11). The world rejected Him then, and still rejects Him today. Man's persistent unwillingness to recognize Him as his God and Saviour reveals an internal evidence of sin. The clearest proof of sin stems from man's refusal to enter into a restored fellowship with his Creator.

F. THE SCRIPTURES EXPRESSLY TEACH THE DOCTRINE OF SIN. Those who accept the Scriptures as God's inspired and inerrant revelation must accept the reality of sin. Employing direct and indirect means, Scriptures clearly assert the doctrine of sin. Direct claims to sin include, "For thy name's sake, O LORD, pardon mine iniquity; for it is great" (Psa. 25:11.). "Come now, and let us reason together, saith the LORD. Though your sins be as scarlet, they shall be as white as snow; though they be red like crimson, they shall be as wool" (Isa. 1:18). "The heart is deceitful above all things, and desperately wicked, who can know it?" (Jer. 17:9). We also "were by nature the children of wrath, even as others" (Eph. 2:3). Scripture also signifies the existence of sin through indirect means, such as developing parallel thoughts or synonyms for the concept of sin. One such parallel is the word "flesh" which refers to our fallen and corrupt nature.[15] Paul, in the eighth chapter of Romans, described the enmity between the Spirit and the flesh, "Because the carnal [fleshly] mind is enmity against God: for it is not subject to the law of God, neither indeed can be. So then they that are in the flesh cannot please God. But ye are not in the flesh, but in the Spirit, if so be that the Spirit of God dwell in you. Now if any man have not the Spirit of Christ, he is none of his. And if Christ be in you, the body is dead because of sin; but the Spirit is life because of righteousness" (Rom. 8:7-10). The use of flesh in this passage involves more than simply the skin or the physical body. It probes much deeper into the selfish and carnal desires that well up from our sinful nature.

G. THE NEED OF INDIVIDUAL REDEMPTION ON A GLOBAL SCALE. Christ clearly articulated that all need to go to heaven by belief in Himself. "I am the way the truth and the life; no man cometh unto the Father but by me" (John 14:6). The death of Christ was absolutely necessary for the unfolding plan of salvation (John 1:29). If conversion were possible any other way, the death of Christ was in vain (Gal 2:21; 3:21). Not only has the death of Christ opened the way for men to become legal heirs to the kingdom of God, it has also placed the burden of responsibility upon man to respond to His death by believing in it. If indeed redemption is absolutely necessary to enjoy the glories of heaven, what has God remedied in the life of man, which now makes him saveable? His sin. The need for redemption exposes the existence of sin within the unbeliever. To argue against the existence of sin is tantamount to arguing that redemption by the Cross is folly.

H. THE NECESSARY PROCESS OF REGENERATION RECOGNIZES SIN. Beyond the act of redemption lies the process of regeneration. Regeneration involves the renewing act of the Holy Spirit within the life of the believer. The effects and influence of the sinful nature within man are so powerful that it necessitates the help of the Holy Spirit. In regeneration, the Holy Spirit indwells the believer and creates (generates) a new nature, with new desires and new abilities. These new forces can counteract the old sinful nature within man. The old nature is not eradicated until death, but the new nature give's the believer the ability to serve God and gain victory over sin.

I. THE INEVITABILITY OF DEATH. A final argument for the existence of original sin arises from the decisive factor of death. Death for man is not solely the cessation of life. From God's perspective, physical death involves the separation of the soul from the body. Death, according to the Scriptures, came as a result of man's sin (Rom. 5:12). Prior to the Fall, man enjoyed the enviable position of not knowing the sorrow acquainted with death. Writing on this subject, Hodge declares,

The only way to evade this argument is to deny that death is a penal evil. This is the ground taken by those who reject the doctrine of original sin. They assert that it is a natural evil, flowing from the original constitution of our nature, and that it is therefore no more a proof that all men are sinners, than the death of brutes is a proof that they are sinners. In answer to this objection, it is obvious to remark that men are not brutes. That irrational animals, incapable of sin, are subject to death is therefore no evidence that moral creatures may be justly subject to the same evil, although free from sin. But, in the second place, what is of far more weight, the objection is in direct opposition to the declarations of the Word of God. According to the Bible, death in the case of man is a punishment. It was threatened against Adam as the penalty of transgression. If he had not sinned, neither had he died. The Apostle expressly declares that death is the wages (or punishment) of sin; and death is on account of sin. (Rom. vi. 23 and v. 12.) He not only asserts this as a fact, but assumes it as a principle, and makes it the foundation of his whole argument in Rom. v. 12-20. His doctrine as there stated is, where there is no law there is no sin. And where there is no sin there is no punishment. All men are punished, therefore all men are sinners. That all men are punished, he proves from the fact all men die. Death is punishment.[16]

VII. IMMEDIATE CONSEQUENCES OF THE FALL

The Fall of man represents far more than just the sin of one man and woman. When one throws a rock in a quiet pond, the initial splash is followed by a continuous sequence of ripples. Likewise, the Fall of man influenced the entire world and, in turn, affects all today. When Adam and Eve disobeyed, God judged their sin. They immediately experienced the full force of God's judgment. Because of the widespread involvement of various beings, many others were immediately judged. These included the serpent, man, woman, and the earth itself. This section does not deal with the universal consequences of imputation, but the immediate consequences to specific recipients.

A. THE SERPENT. When Satan tempted Eve, he was embodied in a serpent. He did not form himself into a serpent nor take on qualities of a serpent, but a serpent was used as a vehicle for the tempter. Satan used an actual serpent, so God cursed the serpent for his active (or passive) part in the temptation. "And the Lord God said unto the serpent, Because thou hast done this, thou art cursed above all cattle, and above every beast of the field; upon thy belly shalt thou go, and dust shalt thou eat all the days of thy life" (Gen. 3:14). The actual physical movements of the serpent were changed as a consequence of the Fall. (What the serpent was like before the Fall is not known.)

B. ADAM AND EVE. An immediate consequence for Adam was a new emotion—sorrow (Gen. 3:17). He was to continue to have dominion over the ground, but now he would till a cursed ground. His labor would be greater; he would work harder and produce less. Physical death also was introduced into the human experience. "In the sweat of thy face shalt thou eat bread till thou return unto the ground; for out of it wast thou taken: for dust thou art and unto dust shalt thou return" (Gen. 3:19). Apparently Adam also lost the complete dominion he earlier possessed over the animals (Rom. 8:18). Man would still rule the beasts of the earth, but with far more difficulty. Some animals would attack and kill man, other animals would resist him, and still other animals would be too dumb to heed man's direction.

Eve also was cursed for her part in the Fall: "Unto the woman he said, I will greatly multiply thy sorrow and thy conception; in sorrow thou shalt bring forth children; and thy desire shall be to thy husband, and he shall rule over thee" (Gen. 3:16). Eve in particular, and women in general, live with two results of the Fall: First, they have a natural inclination to their husband which in some occasions leads to conception. And, second, they have increased pain in childbirth.

C. THE EARTH. The earth also became the recipient of Divine judgment. Prior to the Fall, harmony existed in the animal kingdom. The earth never experienced upheavals of earthquakes and volcanoes, nor did man experience the seasonal changes that bring adverse conditions. The utopia enjoyed in the garden could be experienced on the entire earth. Since the Fall, earth's turmoils have increased drastically, and animals have become carnivorous rather, then vegetarian. Paul notes the conditions: "Because the creature itself also shall be delivered from the bondage of corruption into the glorious liberty of the children of God. For we know that the whole creation groaneth and travaileth in pain together until now" (Rom. 8:21-22).

D. SATAN. God promised that Satan's head would be crushed (not immediately) by the seed of the woman (Gen. 3:15). This happened at Calvary when Satan was judged (John 12:31; 16:11). Otherwise, there was no immediate consequence pronounced to Satan in the garden.

E. ALIENATION. Adam and Eve, suddenly experienced a new feeling, guilt and shame that they had not previously known. They sought refuge, not from each other, but from God. They experienced a change in their very constitution, which now separated them from God. Their entire nature was now affected in two ways—negatively, in that there was the removal of a positive inclination towards God (original righteousness or unconfirmed holiness). Second, they now had a depraved desire that drew them to sin. Commenting on the altered nature of man, Strong writes,

> Man no longer made God the end of his life, but chose self instead. While he retained
> the power of self-determination in subordinate things, he lost that freedom which

consisted in the power of choosing God as his ultimate aim, and became fettered by a fundamental inclination of his will toward evil. The intuitions of the reason were abnormally obscured, since these intuitions, so far as they are concerned with moral and religious truth, are conditioned upon a right state of the affections; and—as a necessary result of this obscuring of reason—conscience, which, as the normal judiciary of the soul, decides upon the basis of the law given to it by reason, became perverse in its deliverances. Yet this inability to judge or act aright, since it was a moral inability springing ultimately from will, was itself hateful and condemnable.[17]

Man's unhindered fellowship with God in the garden ceased. Access to the Tree of Life was no longer possible. Expulsion from the garden separated them from their only home. In short the sin of Adam and Eve represents the darkest day for humanity.

VIII. DIFFICULTIES CONNECTED WITH THE FALL

Those who have examined the Fall from the various perspectives of philosophy, history or religion conclude that there are several apparent lingering problems. The first of these difficulties deals with how Adam and Eve, endowed with original righteousness and no hindering force of sin, were easily seduced into committing sin. Strong offers his keen insights into this issue.

Here we must acknowledge that we cannot understand how the first unholy emotion could have found lodgment in a mind that was set supremely upon God, nor how temptation could have overcome a soul in which there were no unholy propensities to which it could appeal. The mere power of choice does not explain the fact of an unholy choice. The fact of natural desire for sensuous and intellectual gratification does not explain how this desire came to be inordinate. Nor does it throw light upon the matter, to resolve this fall into a deception of our first parents by Satan. Their yielding to such deception presupposes distrust of God and alienation from Him. Satan's fall, moreover, since it must have been uncaused by temptation from without, is more difficult to explain than Adam's fall.

. . . .

But sin is an existing fact. God cannot be its author, either by creating man's nature so that sin was a necessary incident of its development, or by withdrawing a supernatural grace which was necessary to keep man holy. Reason, therefore, has no other recourse than to accept the Scripture doctrine that sin originated in man's free act of revolt from God—the act of a will which, though inclined toward God, was not yet confirmed in virtue and was still capable of a contrary choice. The original possession of such power to the contrary seems to be the necessary condition of probation and moral development. Yet, the exercise of this power in a sinful direction can never be explained upon grounds of reason, since sin is essentially unreason. It is an act of wicked arbitrariness, the only motive of which is the desire to depart from God and to render self-supreme.[18]

The gravity of this issue should not be treated lightly; it is expedient that an attempt be made to bisect the imaginary line between the sovereignty of God and the free will of man. For many years theologians and philosophers alike have wrestled to construct an answer that would resolve the dilemma within the following diagram:

> God is omnipotent (all-powerful)
> God is benevolent (all-loving)
> Evil exists in a world created by such a God.

All three statements, examined individually, present truth. However, when juxtaposed, several internal problems arise. If indeed God is all-powerful, and His motives solely benevolent, why did He allow sin to occur? Either He is not all-powerful, His motives not totally pure, or sin does not really exist. The answers are not direct, but are implied in a greater question, "What was God's purpose in allowing His creature to be tempted?" The answer to these questions are inherent in the answer to the second difficulty. It relates to God's allowing Satan to influence man to sin. God foreknew that Satan would seek to vent his anger toward him through the avenue of corrupting His creation, yet God chose not to hinder Satan's plan. Initially one would conclude that God was insensitive to man. However, upon closer examination, such a claim represents the absence of sufficient knowledge.

1. Temptation is never to be equated with sin. Adam's sin stems directly from his desire and act to have what God forbade him to have.
2. The nature of the prohibition was slight, yet sufficient to test the spirit of obedience.
3. God had endowed Adam and Eve with the ability to reject the temptation (1 Cor. 10:13).
4. Adam was commanded not to take of the Tree long before the temptation ever came. Adam fully understood what God expected of him.
5. If God had thwarted Satan from tempting man, man's loyalty would never have been determined—his infancy would have continued.
6. Withholding Satan from man would have greatly thwarted man's free will and the exercise of it, reducing him to nothing more than a puppet placed within a controlled environment.
7. The nature of the command was not arbitrary or insignificant. It was concrete and substantive in nature, posing no anxiety within Adam and Eve.

In light of the aforementioned fact, the temptation of man cannot be viewed as a calloused acquiescence of God.

A final difficulty related to the Fall centers on the severity of one sin. Should one act of disobedience lead to such harsh consequences as spiritual death, expulsion from the garden, the beginning of physical death, increased labor and birth pains, and loss of daily fellowship with God? These all appear to be too harsh for committing only one sin. In man's eyes, such a penalty may appear to be unjust. However, from God's perspective, sin demanded a terrible penalty, as evidence by the Cross, and not in the garden.

IX. THE NATURE OF ORIGINAL SIN

Sin is an exclusive topic. Attempting to restrict its meaning to a concise definition often leads to frustration. Philosophers and theologians have dedicated countless hours trying to write a universally acceptable definition of sin. Scripture affords the simplistic approach, describing all sin as lawlessness (1 John 3:4). However, even this definition does not totally explain the pervasive and internal nature of sin. Hoeksema offers some insight into why Scripture offers varied perspectives of sin.

> In Scripture many different terms are used to denote the reality which we call sin. This is not surprising: life is many-sided. The life of an individual comprises body and soul; and his spiritual soul includes his intellectual and volitional life. And the individual stands in manifold relationships in relation to God and man, as well as in relation to the whole world in which he has his existence and which he uses for the sustenance and development of his life. Small wonder, then, that we find in Holy Writ many different words for the concept of sin: for sin is as many-sided as life itself. It affects and corrupts the whole man in all his various relationships.[19]

It is not until all Scripture is considered that a feasible and workable definition of sin is developed. Yet it should be noted, that even when all Scripture is considered, a full understanding of all the implications involved in sin may not be grasped. Limitations related to our finite minds and the interpretation of the printed page are two primary hindrances. However, this should never discourage the student, but serve to compel him to objectively examine Scripture and draw conclusions.

Scripture employs the following terms to describe sin. Each term introduces something new, yet all serve to help affix a definition to sin.

1. Old Testament Words:
    a. צבד - transgress or overstep
    b. שגה - error through ignorance
    c. חטא - miss the mark, moral failure, fail,
    d. חעה - wander or stray, physical straying; also includes moral issues
    e. מאן - refusal to obey God's commandment

f. מרד - active revolt against God
g. פשע - to revolt, transgress, rebel
h. מעל - treacherous act, apostasy from God
i. חנף - profane, act apart from God
j. עול - perverse act
k. חמס - treat wrongfully
l. רעע - evil
m. עוה - conscious attempts to do wrong
n. רשע - guilty, condemnable

2. New Testament Words:
   a. ἁμαρτια   - miss the mark
   b. ἀγνοια   - error through ignorance
   c. παραπτωμα   - trespass
   d. ἀνομια   - lawlessness, attitude of anger
   e. παρακοη   - disobedience to God
   f. παρανομια   - wickedness, evil
   g. παραβασις   - to transgress the law
   h. παραβαινω   - go beyond a known principle
   i. ἀσεβεια   - godlessness
   j. πονηρια   - moral perversion
   k. ενοχος   - guilt for an act
   i. ὀφειλημα   - guilt and accompanied burden
   m. κακια -   moral and spiritual evil
   n. ἀδικια   - unrighteousness

The Old Testament gives a basic thrust of sin to include the idea of physically missing the mark or transgressing a known law or principle. As a result of the outward act, the sinner is inwardly immoral and wicked, therefore subject to guilt and condemnation.

The New Testament tends to reveal a deeper concept of sin by focusing not only on the outward acts of sin, but emphasizing the inner disposition and state of the soul. Sin is conceived more subjectively than objectively. When Christ connected sin with man's thought life, sin was no longer limited to outward acts, henceforth even the external righteousness of the Pharisees could in no way escape the examination of God's light.

The Westminster Shorter Catechism defines sin as "any want of conformity unto, or transgression of, the law of God."[20] Buswell defines sin as "Anything in the creature which does not express, or which is contrary to the holy character of the Creator." Strong defines sin as a "lack of conformity to the moral law of God, either in act, disposition, or in state." In his unpublished class notes, John Feinberg states, "Sin is the creature's willful and intentional decision to disobey God by refusing to obey His revealed precepts. As such, it involves the decision by the creature to place his own desires and person above those of the Creator."

The preceding definitions all represent good attempts to explain what we refer to as sin. Inherent within each definition are the following assumptions: (1) sin must necessarily come from a rational and voluntary agent—no coercion can be evident in sin; (2) there exists a moral law revealed to man that demands likeness in character to God in tendencies and overt activities; (3) sin is not limited solely to outward acts, but extends much deeper into a person's being, attesting his very nature and controlling his desires; (4) sin possesses no substantive aspect, but is an act, attitude or action; (5) sin is conceived when man exercises his will contrary to revealed law; and (6) a judicial sentence (as evidence of criminality) declares the act or attitude to be sin; and, (7) finally, God in no way can be chargeable with man's sin. God never withheld or placed too much upon man. Sin stems directly from man's wrong use of free will

It is appropriate to discuss not only the scriptural view of sin, as seen in the various words employed in Scripture, and to examine several definitions of sin, but it is also expedient that the power of sin and temptation is not overstated. Sin does affect man's entire being. It extends not only to his physical acts, but also engulfs his very being and his disposition. However, the power of sin has not reduced man to the level of the animals. The image of God, though greatly altered, has not been totally destroyed. More important than the salvaged image of God in man, is the interceding power of Christ over sin. Strong offers the following insight that needs to be considered whenever sin is discussed.

In adducing our scriptural and rational proof of the definition of sin as a state, we desire to obviate the objection that this view leaves the soul wholly given over to the power of evil while we maintain that this is true of man apart from God, we also insist that side by side with the evil bent of the human will there is always an immanent divine power which greatly counteracts the force of evil, and if not resisted leads the individual soul—even when resisted leads the race at large—toward truth and salvation. This immanent divine power is none other than Christ, the eternal Word, the Light, which lighteth every man (see John 1:4,9).[21]

X. INCORRECT VIEWS OF SIN

The nature of sin as defined in Scripture seems to be straightforward. However, attempts to understand and define sin have yielded a variety of conjectures. History is filled with serious attempts to define and classify the reality of sin. Beginning with the oldest popular known system, the following chart will work its way to contemporary schemes. (See next page)

A. DUALISTIC THEORY. The Gnostics, Marcionites, and Manicheans are credited with introducing this view of sin into the church. They recognized an eternal and omnipotent power of a benevolent Authority (God). However, this view was juxtaposed with the reality of eternal sin. Dualism is a scheme that allows for the continuous existence of both good and evil. Commenting on their beliefs, Hodge states,

> These two principles are in perpetual conflict. In the actual world they are intermingled. Both enter into the constitution of man. He has a spirit $(\pi v \varepsilon \hat{v} \mu \alpha)$ derived from the kingdom of light; and a body with its animal life $(\sigma \hat{\omega} \mu \alpha$ and $\psi v \chi \acute{\eta})$ derived from the kingdom of darkness. Sin is thus a physical evil; the defilement of the spirit by its union with a material body; and is to be overcome, by physical means, i.e., by means adapted to destroy the influence of the body on the soul. Hence the efficacy of abstinence and austerities.[22]

According to the advocates of this view, the eternal principle of evil assumed several different states. Some conceived evil as an eternal substance that God was unable to control or destroy. The more popular view considered evil as an eternal personal being equal to good, neither of which could destroy the other. Therefore they served to keep each other in check. Yet, in accordance with the perspectives of theism, (a) the dualistic theory obviously alters the nature of sin as a moral evil and assigns it a substantive nature. In addition to man's physical and immaterial aspects, dualists falsely assume man also possesses substance composed of evil matter. (b) Through impregnating man's constitution with an evil substance (something that would surely seal his sinful acts) the human responsibility for sin is destroyed. Therefore sin becomes a moral necessity, and not the wrong use of freewill. (c) More serious than the preceding objections to the teachings of dualism is the inference that God's infinite Being and absolute sovereign control of the universe no longer exist. If evil, as a substance or personality has always existed, then God's very identification as an absolute Being is destroyed. Absolute sovereignty demands total control.

The dualistic theory is thoroughly anti-Christian. This teaching has never received the endorsement of the church. Although the name dualism is no longer used, the teachings do exist under the contemporary term of "pantheism."

INSUFFICIENT VIEWS	DEFINITIONS		SUPPORTERS & ENSUING PROGRESSION	
Dualistic	Stresses the co-existence of evil and spirit within the universe (sin is a necessary element)	1.	Gnostics	Second century heresy led by Marcion
		2.	Marconites	Embraced initially by Augustine
		3.	Manicheans	Gave support for the view that sin exists as a necessary antagonism to good
Human Creation	Sin is linked to man's design due to some inherent privation or weakness - pragmatic - God is usually chargeable (sin is a necessary element)	1.	Spinoza	Sin is regarded as a mere limitation of man's being
		2.	Libnitz	Sin stems from some privation in man's being
Human nature	Sin is linked to human nature. Wrong exercise of free will - philosophical - God is not chargeable for our sin (Sin stems from a wrong use of freewill)	1.	Pride - Calvin	Followed by Niebuhr, *The Nature and Destiny of Man* "Biblical and Christian thought has maintained with a fair degree of consistency that pride is more basic than sensuality and that the latter is, in some way, derived from the former" (p. 198) Pursued by Barth, who viewed sin as developing from: Pride, Sloth, Falsehood
		2.	Sensuousness - Schleiermacher	"Sin is traced to the connection of the soul with the physical organism."
		3.	Selfish ness 1. Augustine 2. Aquinas 3. Edwards 4. Strong	
		4.	Natural Life - Scholten	"Life which is not yet extinct, the animal part in man which becomes sin only through the awakening of moral freedom."

B. SIN CONNECTED WITH THE LIMITATION OF MAN'S BEING. Conceived within the mind of the scholastic teachings of Spinoza and Professor Bauer of Tubingen, is the view that sin is a necessary cause that stems from our finite being. God, as the absolute substance, is good. However, man, not an absolute substance, is finite. His limitation of being is evil, or sinful. The lack of total virtue and being implies a limitation of being or inherent weakness, thus sin.

> Evil is what is finite; for the finite is negative; the negation of the infinite. Everything finite is relatively nothing a negativity which, in the constant distinction of plus and minus of reality, appears in different forms. Again, if freedom from sin is the removal of all limitation, so is it clear, that only an endless series of gradations can bring us to the point where sin is reduced to a vanished minimum. If this minimum should entirely disappear, then the being, thus entirely free from sin, becomes one with God, for God only is absolutely sinless. But if other beings than God are to exist, there must be in them, so far as they are not infinite as God is, for that very reason, a minimum of evil.[23]

According to this view, sin does not assume a quality role. Rather, sin stems directly from a quantity of being. Absolute being is absolute good. Anything less than absolute is evil

Objections to this view are as follows: (a) The salient indictment to this view centers on the One who is ultimately responsible for man's sin, God. This view teaches that God is necessarily responsible for sin, simply because He did not create man differently. If a mother leaves her newborn child to the elements of nature, expecting it to survive, but it dies, the person ultimately responsible and justly chargeable is the insensitive mother. Even so, according to this view, God is ultimately chargeable for placing man in the Garden of Eden, where he would be tempted and sin. (b) Taken to its logical extreme, this view would condemn Christ as a sinner. The limitations linked with the results of the hypostatic union (i.e. "I thirst," "tiring," and "he slept") would constitute Him as a sinner. Yet, this assumption stands in stark opposition to the scriptural truth that Christ was sinless. (c) This view also ignores the difference between moral and physical existence. Men commit sins with their physical bodies, but the desire to sin may stem from the intellect, emotions, or will, residing in the heart. Determining the difference between right and wrong deeds is not a metaphysical issue, it is a moral issue. The barometer for recognizing sin is not human ability, but the revealed moral law of God. Permitting the notion that ability is good to expand to its logical end, then mere strength and power are morally right. Hodge correctly traces the obvious weakness with this thinking.

> It not only teaches that all that is, is right; that everything that exists or happens has a right to be, but that the only standard of virtue is power. The strongest is the best. As Cousin says, the victor is always right; the victim is always wrong. The conqueror is always more moral than the vanquished. Virtue and prosperity, misfortune and vice,

he says, are in necessary harmony. Feebleness is a vice (*i.e.*, sin), and therefore is always punished and beaten. This principle is adopted by all such writers as Carlyle, who in their hero worship, make the strong always the good; and represent the murderer, the pirate, and the persecutor, as always more moral and more worthy of admiration than their victims. Satan is far more worthy of homage than the best of men, as in him there is more of being and power, and he is the seducer of angels and the destroyer of men. A more thoroughly demoniacal system than this, the mind of man has never conceived. Yet this system has not only its philosophical advocates, and its practical disciples, but it percolates through much of the popular literature [thought] both of Europe and America.[24]

The recognized "Father of the Theory of Evolution," Charles Darwin strongly endorsed this view and stated it as "the survival of the fittest." Based upon the preceding objection, this view should also be considered as an anti-Christian attempt to explain the existence and nature of sin.

C. LEIBNITZ'S THEORY OF PRIVATION. Closely related to the previous theory, Leibnitz, as a theist, sought to amalgamate the scholastic ideas of Spinoza with his theistic perception. Leibnitz rejected the notion that God was ultimately responsible for man's sin, yet at the same time he accepted the presence of evil as a necessary element. To vindicate God, he taught that man (endowed with finite characteristics) was placed in the best possible world, afforded with the best possible physical conditions, yet eventually sinned because of a simple negation of being, an offense for which no efficient cause was needed, it just happened. The origin of evil thus lies in the will, and the will of necessity led to error (indirectly and not directly) by the limitations linked to the nature of the creature. Hence the existence of sin as a necessary cause is explained and God is not directly charged with man's sin.

Objections to Leibnitz's view in addition to the arguments employed to refute Spinoza's view are twofold. (a) To argue that sin is a necessary element to man's being greatly minimizes the role of man's free will and reduces the significance of sin. If sin had to happen (necessity), then just how free is man's will to accept or reject sin? Also, if sin is necessary, it lessens our sense of evil and ensuing guilt, suggesting that sin is a mere misfortune of our physical infirmities. (b) A second weakness is succinctly stated by Strong.

Not all sins are negative sins of ignorance and infirmity; there are acts of positive malignity, conscious transgressions, wilful and presumptuous choices of evil. Increased knowledge of the nature of sin does not of itself give strength to overcome it; but, on the contrary, repeated acts of conscious transgression harden the heart in evil. Men of greatest mental powers are not of necessity the greatest saints, nor are the greatest sinners men of least strength of will and understanding.[25]

These theories of sin all claim that evil is a necessary cause in our world, ultimately charging God with the guilt of sin. The following four views do not recognize sin as a necessary result. Rather, they attribute sin to the improper use of man's free will in light of a revealed law. Each of the following views, as proposed by a dominant personality, is not totally incorrect, simply insufficient to explain the precise nature and origin of evil or sin.

D. SENSUOUS THEORY. In brief, this theory assigns the origin and nature of sin to the sensuous nature of man. Sin arises when the soul is placed in connection to the physical organism. The soul is viewed as the spiritual and pure aspect of man's being. On the other hand, the body and the will are understood to possess inordinate desires that, when permitted to satisfy themselves, are contrary to the holy desires of the soul. This theory, though highly endorsed by Schleiermacher, has existed for many years. The ascetics, who frequently practiced flagellation, sought to bring the sensuous desires of the flesh under the dominion of their inner soul. They took Paul's statement "I beat my body" as indicating that they should literally subject their body to physical pain and hardships. However, Paul does not suggest literal subjugation of the body; instead he seeks to admonish his readers to cautiously guard against the sinful desires of their mind and avoid gratifying them.

Whether the advocates for the sensuous theory teach that the body represents the lower part of man and the soul the higher part of man, or restrict the role of the soul to the spiritual and the body to denote the carnal, or evil, side of man, both views imply a schism in the dichotomy of man. This view suggests an internal struggle that frequently allows one side to temporarily take dominion, only to be later subdued. Life tends to be a struggle or a process of checks and balances. Frequently those who espouse this view appeal to the illustration of the white and black dogs. Whichever dog they fed with their activities that dog became the stronger and defeated the other one.

Inherent within this theory are several objections. (1) It erroneously implies that matter possesses a degree of evil substance. Paul's reference to flesh in Romans 7:18 does not only refer to man's literal flesh (skin or physical body); the scope is larger and suggests man's immaterial being or his sinful nature. Repeatedly, Scripture distinctly affirms the seat of sin as residing in the immaterial aspect of man and not in his physical organism. (2) This view fails to properly understand the nature of sin. Sin is more than a state or an act of the sensuous nature, although it may be so expressed. Satan and his demonic hosts, who possess no sensuous nature due to the absence of physical bodies, entertained and actively involved themselves in the sin process. (3) This view does not account for heinous sins that are, by their nature, distinctly separated from "fleshly" sins. Sins of pride, malice, avarice, envy, ambition, cruelty, revenge, self-righteousness, enmity and unbelief toward God have nothing to do with the physical organism of man. If we are to limit the origin of sin to the sensuous nature, then sin committed outside the senses would have to either be considered something other than sin (which is absurd) or sins of the mind (man's immaterial aspect) as simply an internal inconsistent dilemma. Either choice presents grave problems for those who support this view.

(4) The sensuous theory also places undue contempt upon other physical or sensuous desires that are not sinful in their nature. Physical desires of sleep and hunger, when not permitted to function to excess, are natural desires completely void of sinful properties. Advocates of this view claim the body to be the seat and source of sin, therefore any rigid and disciplined control of the body renders it more pure and virtuous. Yet, history and the confrontations of Christ with the Pharisees have taught us that strictness of living and perpetual fastings (attempts toward external righteousness) have served to draw men farther away from the kingdom of heaven than toward it.

It is imperative to understand that sin frequently employs the senses of man to commit an evil act. However, it is not the senses alone that compel man to act in an evil manner. Rigid subjugation of the senses serves only to sever man farther from the world, instead of allowing the Spirit of God to help man to overcome it (1 John 4:4). Asceticism and legalism are not Christian lifestyles. Christians are to be overcomers, not recluses.

E. SIN AS PRIDE. Theologians such as Calvin, Barth and Niebuhr trace sin's origin to pride in man. According to 1 Timothy 3:6, it was pride that motivated Satan to rebel against God, "Not a novice, lest being lifted up with pride he fall into the condemnation of the devil." Niebuhr states his position as follows: "Biblical and Christian thought has maintained with a fair degree of consistency that pride is more basic than sensuality and that the latter is, in some way, derived from the former."[26] Pride represents any attempt by man to usurp God's prescribed place in his life. God has clearly claimed that He created the heavens and the earth, yet man, filled with pride, has chosen to reject this simplistic explanation of creation and develop a naturalistic scheme. Pride has prompted men to engage in many forms of sin. However, pride does not originate sin. Something else must precede pride, to stimulate the feelings of pride. Furthermore, all sins are not linked to pride, and pride cannot always be regarded as sinful. It is not sinful for an artist to sense a degree of pride and satisfaction for a job well done. Francis Schaeffer bears this truth out in his book *Art and Literature*, in which he claims that regeneration redeems man's spirit, and that arts and literature serve to heighten man's physical being.

Pride undoubtedly functions as one of the elements or expressions of sin, but to assert that all sin stems directly from pride is incorrect assumption.

F. SIN AS NATURAL LIFE. This view is not widely held by many. J. H. Scholten, called by some the "father of modernism," claims that sin is merely natural life, "life which is not, yet ethical"; the animal part in man becomes sin only through the awakening of moral freedom. Once man's moral powers are awakened and he is able to discern the difference between right and wrong, then he becomes guilty of sin. In essence, the standard for right and wrong is determined by society's standard. But sin is a violation of God's law, and this definition reveals the weakness of this view. Even though some different societies may endorse through indirect means God's law, no one society properly endorses and enforces all of God's laws.

Furthermore, while society may alter its judicial code, with God's laws there is no room for deviation.

The natural life theory properly recognizes that sin is an infraction of a known standard. Through the improper use of the free will, man commits a sin. However, the weakness in this view forces us to reject it as an unfeasible theory for the origin of sin. Society's standard is susceptible to changes. Furthermore, society may establish rules and regulations that are not sinful from God's perspective.

G. SIN AS SELFISHNESS. Augustine, Aquinas, Edwards, and Strong support this view. Of the various views given to explain the essential origin and nature of sin, this view has broad recognition and many advocates. Selfishness is not to be confused with self-love. The latter is a natural element of all creatures, a part essential to man's self-preservation. Selfishness represents an undue preference for one's happiness, as opposed to the happiness or welfare of our fellowman. Strong states the view thus:

> By selfishness we mean not simply the exaggerated self-love which constitutes the antithesis of benevolence, but that choice of self as the supreme end which constitutes the antithesis of supreme love to God. That selfishness is the essence of sin may be shown as follows:
>
> A. Love to God is the essence of all virtue. The opposite to this, the choice of self as the supreme end, must therefore be the essence of sin.
>
> We are to remember, however, that the love to God in which virtue consists is love for that which is most characteristic and fundamental in God, namely, his holiness. It is not to be confounded with supreme regard for God's interests or for the good of being in general. Not mere benevolence, but love for God as holy, is the principle and source of holiness in man. Since the love of God required by the law is of this sort, it not only does not imply that love, in the sense of benevolence, is the essence of holiness in God,—it implies rather that holiness, or self-loving and self-affirming purity, is fundamental in the divine nature. From this self-loving and self-affirming purity, love properly so-called, or the self-communicating attribute, is to be carefully distinguished.
>
> . . . .
>
> B. All the different forms of sin can be shown to have their root in selfishness, while selfishness itself, considered as the choice of self as a supreme end, cannot be resolved into any simpler elements.
>
> (a) Selfishness may reveal itself in the elevation to supreme dominion of any one of man's natural appetites, desires, or affections. Sensuality is selfishness in the form of inordinate appetite. Selfish desire takes the forms respectively of avarice, ambition, vanity, pride, according as it is set upon property, power, esteem, independence.

Selfish affection is falsehood or malice, according as it hopes to make others its voluntary servants, or regards them as standing in its way; it is unbelief or enmity to God, according as it simply turns away from the truth and love of God, or conceives of God's holiness as positively resisting and punishing it.

. . . .

(b) Even in the nobler forms of unregenerate life the principle of selfishness is to be regarded as manifesting itself in the preference of lower ends to that of God's proposing.   Others are loved with idolatrous affection because these others are regarded as a part of self. That the selfish element is present even here, is evident upon considering that such affection does not seek the highest interest of its object, that it often ceases when unreturned, and that it sacrifices to its own gratification the claims of God and his law.[27]

Jonathan Edwards, a strong supporter of the Selfishness theory, recognized the importance of Christ's declaration that love to God is the first and great command, on which the whole law depends. Accordingly, sin must be the antithesis of righteousness. and it follows that sin must be the love of self over the love of God. Regardless of the sin, Edwards says, it can be traced eventually to selfishness within the individual.

Dabney, another advocate for the Selfishness theory states the view as follows:

> This theory states that the essence of sin is selfishness; and the term selfishness is not used here in the parlance of the street: that of love for self counteracting a tendency for benevolence. By selfishness is meant the choice of self instead of God as the supreme end. Since love to God is the acme of all virtue, love of self must be the essence of all sin. Therefore sin is the result of the choice of free, intelligent beings.
>
> All varieties of sin can be shown ultimately to have their root in selfishness. Murder is committed because of a selfish aim. Men steal because of selfishness. Men envy because other selves have arisen higher than their own selves.   Adultery is committed because the passions of the self must be satiated. The self is the *supreme end*; therefore all sin is an endeavor to please or satisfy the self. Augustine and Aquinas held that the essence of sin is pride, while Luther and Calvin held it to be unbelief. But it is maintained that selfishness is the root sin, for both pride and unbelief can be thrown back to selfishness. Paul, prior to his conversion, loved and worked for "righteousness"; but it was a "righteousness" that would result from his own will and achievement, thus bringing honor to himself. It was a case of the ego above God.[28]

Objections to this theory are as follows. It is not denied that selfishness in its various forms represents a large class of sin with which men are justly charged. However, to assign the essence of all sins to selfishness cannot be done. (1) The assumption is suggested that love in its extreme end, when not directed toward God, is sin, i.e., to love self is sin. The problem centers on the degree of love implied in this view. Shortly after Christ gave the command to "love the Lord thy God with all your heart, this is the first commandment," he went on to add a second commandment, "Love thy neighbor as thyself." Within this second command, Christ recognized the relevance of self-love, a love that compels one to attend carefully to the needs of his body. According to the Selfishness theory, is self-love sinful? Or does it become sinful only when allowed to usurp one's love for God? If the latter is true, sin no longer has a concrete basis, but now becomes an issue of degree. Permitting man to demonstrate a level of self-love, and then ceasing the love, raises the question of degree. Then it makes sin relative. Sin and holiness would differ only in degree. Does this scheme propose a dividing line?

(2) Strong suggests that love to God or to the welfare of others is the essence of all virtue. If this love is offered to any with a notion or desire that does not purely seek the "highest interest of its object," then this love is justly deemed "idolatrous affection." Is this not a rather lofty estimate of love? Are we to understand that when love is demonstrated in its purest sense, a husband should not expect appreciation from his wife when he purchases her a gift? Is God guilty of sin when expecting or desiring a response by man to accept the gift of salvation He provided to man through Christ's death? Scripture repeatedly refers to God's love for man as an agape type of love—a self-sacrificing love. However, agape love, though expressed in pure motives, nonetheless expects a response—either acceptance or rejection. To argue that love is given with absolutely no response needed is utterly foolish.

Those who have sought to understand the essence of sin from the perspective of selfishness have achieved a greater understanding of sin than those who would define sin as an expression of physical deprivation, or a necessary result of dualism. Nonetheless, to argue the essence of sin stems from selfishness presents serious problems.

XI. THE ESSENTIAL ELEMENT OF SIN

Having discovered the weakness within the other views, it is now necessary to present a view of sin which best states the issues and provides a systematic testimony of Scripture. Charles Hodge summarizes the essential nature of sin.

> (1.) That sin is a specific evil, differing from all other forms of evil. (2). That sin stands related to law. The two are correlative, so that where there is no law, there can be no sin. (3). That the law to which sin is thus related, is not merely the law of reason, or of conscience, or of expediency, but the law of God. (4). That sin consists essentially in the want of conformity on the part of a rational creature, to the nature or law of God. (5). That it includes guilt and moral pollution.[29]

1. Desire
2. Intention to have the object
3. Development of a plan to obtain the object
4. Willingness to put the plan into action and acquire the object
5. Physical movement to possess the object
6. Gratifying the desires through possessing the object.

The first three points enumerated by Hodge have received sufficient attention in the early remarks of hamartiology. Therefore the fourth and fifth points shall receive the greatest attention.

A. ACTUAL AND CONDITIONAL SIN. Two types of sin exist: Actual sin, which refers to an actual act of man who conscientiously chooses to violate a known law of God. Conditional sin describes the state in which man is born. The former occurs through man's conscious activities, usually resulting from the effects of Adam's sin upon his posterity. Both types will be discussed in more detail under the imputation of sin.

Defining sin, whether actual or conditional, from the viewpoint of Hodge leads to the following conclusion. (1) Man's best efforts toward internal and external righteousness will always fall short of God's ideal. Perfection professed by self-acclaimed saints or religious groups simply does not exist. (2) Man, apart from Christ, can do nothing that qualifies as a work to gain salvation. Man cannot do works of supererogation, those meritorious works performed by men whereby God, on the basis of justice, is indebted to man and must reward him. (3) On the basis of conditional sin or actual sin, man as a sinner stands guilty in God's sight. Unless God acts to resolve man's dilemma, judgment is inevitable. Yet, Scripture reveals God's consistent salvation for the problem of sin. The message of the cross provides man with hope and salvation, if only man avails himself of it.

B. THE NATURE OF TEMPTATION. Every sin has certain stages or a particular pattern that eventually leads to its manifestation. Whether or not man is conscious of these steps, they nonetheless exist. For many in whom sin is a perpetual lifestyle, there is no remorse. These stages occur very quickly with no deliberation. However, to those who sense the destructive force of sin, the steps to sin and temptation become even more overt. The normal steps to sin and temptation are as follows:

Within these six steps, a person moves from an innocent unconscious position to a state of conscious guilt. Two important truths need to be stated: (1) God does not tempt us to sin (Jas. 1:13), and (2) temptation is not to be equated with sin. Christ was tempted (Matt. 4) yet He never sinned (Heb. 4:15). At what point in these stages does temptation become a sin? Steps 1-4 refer to the internal aspect of temptation. Steps 5-6 are the visible and observable aspects.

Scripture supports the idea that sin is conceived in the internal stages of temptation and manifests itself in the external aspects. Those who limit sin to external acts must resolve several problems: (1) According to Matthew 5:21-22, 27-28, Christ clearly stated that sin could be committed even by wrongly desiring something in the heart, without actually doing the deed (see also 2 Cor. 10:3-5). If this is true, then King David, while looking upon Bathsheba, was not guilty of outward adultery while he merely desired her, yet he was as guilty of adultery as if he committed the act. (2) If sin is to be limited to physical deeds, it would be impossible to commit sins in your thought life. A paralyzed man could never sin. More importantly, the focus of sin would be upon the resulting act and not upon the heart that motivated the act. In keeping with the teaching of Scripture, sin apparently occurs in the internal stages of temptation.

James provides several important insights into sin. In James 1:13-15 all sins begin within the desires of man. Every person is tempted by his own desires, not by God or Satan. God or Satan may place man in a particular situation or place certain things before him, but it is man who acts upon these objects. Therefore, neither God nor Satan is responsible for man's sin. God allows man to be placed in certain positions in order to test him, with the ultimate goal of maturing him. However, Satan's motives are just the opposite. He seeks to draw man into sin and destroy him.

Within the four steps of the internal aspect of sin, overt sin may not be committed in the first step. Simply desiring an object cannot be overt sin. But, there are occasions when the desire is sin. (1) A person desiring an obviously prohibited goal commits sin. (2) A person desiring an object he does not realize is prohibited, but is in fact prohibited, has committed the sin of ignorance. (3) A person desiring a proper object for the wrong reason commits the sin of ignorance. While sin has been defined as "overt sin" because man is consciously aware of his actions, this sin is committed in ignorance. Then when man is tempted, but exercises no desire to sin, he still has a sinful nature and is in the condition of sin (because he is living in a sinful world).

The following step, the intention to have the object, likewise may not be considered overt sin. Intent is stronger than desire. Man can control or direct his intent. When man only desires the object, he has not committed overt sin. He is experiencing lust, but has not given himself to it, hence has not committed overt sin.

Overt sin is apparent when man acts upon the plan he has developed; the will is set in motion, and man seeks to materialize his desire. The natural lust that comes from his sin nature is acted upon. Now he is guilty of overt sin.

As mentioned before, all sins begin with human desires (Jas. 1:13-15). Desires lead to intent, then become a developed plan, and eventually an activated will to do evil, which is sin. Due to man's depravity, or sinful nature, there are several elements in man's being that seem to form a natural disposition for him to sin. These elements in man that lead him to sin are pride, selfishness, natural disbelief, ignorance, disobedience, and self-deception. These elements grow out of the depraved human nature and encourage the temptation process. These elements may not be sinful when not directed toward a biblical standard. The essence of sin is always understood in relation to the law of God, for it is the law that sets the parameters for sin. Some may argue that the above-mentioned elements represent the essence of sin. However, this can be debated. Satan and Adam possessed a positive disposition to do right.

They had no evil nature as we do today with feelings of disbelief, pride, and disobedience, yet they still sinned. This is not to say that Satan wasn't motivated by pride, for Scripture states that pride motivated him to desire something that was not his (1 Tim. 3:6). Nor does it imply that Adam did not entertain feelings of self-deception, deceiving himself into believing that God would not kill him. These feelings of pride, self-deception, disobedience, disbelief, ignorance, and selfishness are feelings that stem not only from man's sinful nature but, more specifically from an improper use of free will. Free will is not the cause of sin, rather it is man's improper use of his free will in seeking after his desires that leads men to decide in their will to do something contrary to the law of God. Unlike Satan and Adam, men today not only wrestle with properly controlling the desires of free will, but also the evil disposition of the nature that draws them to engage in sin.

The steps of temptation that lead to sin usually follow a predictable sequence. Upon sensing the desire to have something, recognizing the benefits of having it, and developing a plan to acquire it, man—prior to energizing his will—allows himself: (1) to be deceived or purposely deceives himself into believing that what he desires is more important than God's standard, (2) man, stirred by pride and selfishness, assumes that he knows better than God, (3) man naturally begins to disbelieve what God has said, and trusts his own ability, and (4) finally, having turned from God, man acts contrary to God's law, and sin is conceived.

The entire process that describes the many issues of the essence of sin can be shown in the following diagram:

1.	That sin is a specific evil, differing from all other forms of evil			a.	Desire for something				
2.	That sin stands related to the law of God			b.	Intent to have the object			(1)	Deception or self-deception
3.	That the law to which sin is not merely the law of reason, or of conscience, or of expediency, but the law of God.			c.	Development of a plan to have the object			(2)	Pride and selfishness

4.	That sin consists essentially in the want of conformity on the part of a rational creature, to the nature or law of God			d.	Willing to put the plan into action and acquire the object			(3)	Disbelief in God's law
5.	That it includes guilt and moral pollution			e.	Physical movement to possess the object			(4)	Overt disobedience to God's law
				f.	Gratifying the desire through possessing the object				

1. *Presumption.* The first and most prominent kind of sin is presumption. This sin represents a willful, premeditated and rebellious act by man to purposely deny and disobey God's clear command. God forbids the taking of His name in vain; when men openly abuse His name, they are committing a sin of presumption. Presumptuous sins are very serious, and have prompted God to intercede and bring about a premature judgment upon either believers or unbelievers who commit them.

2. *Ignorance.* Sins of ignorance are those things that are done, yet the person is not conscious of the fact that he is doing it. This does not imply that the will is unexercised, it simply indicates that the person is not conscious of the biblical standard of the effects of his actions. Sins of ignorance are not nearly as severe as sins of presumption. As a result, the intent and punishment greatly differ (Rom. 15:24-31 and 1 Tim. 1:12-14). The penalty for sins of ignorance is far less than the penalty for sins of presumption. Despite their difference, both are sins and are subject to punishment.

3. *Commission.* Unlike the sin of presumption in which there is a definite intent to purposely do evil, the sin of commission does not possess such an insolent attitude. Both sins of commission and presumption represent an individual doing something contrary to the law of God.

4. *Omission.* Sins of omission are those intentional acts where man fails to do something he should do. With sins of ignorance, a person is unaware he is doing something wrong. However, with the sin of omission, a person deliberately withholds something: i.e., he intentionally does not do right. Stevens describes sins of omission.

> But many times to omit is just as sinful; simply to do nothing is direct rebellion against God. The children of Israel asked Samuel at a certain time to pray for them, to which he replied, "Far be it from me that I should sin against Jehovah in ceasing to pray for you" (I Sam. 12:23). Not to pray for them would have been a sin of great reality. The New Testament presents the same teaching. "Then shall he answer them, saying, Verily I say unto you, Inasmuch as ye did it not unto one of these least, ye did it not unto me. And these shall go away into eternal punishment" (Matt. 25:45, 46). The sin of these people, for which they received eternal punishment, was simply doing nothing. "But whoso hath the world's goods, and beholdeth his brother in need, and shutteth up his compassion from him, how doth the love of God abide in him?" (1 John 3:17). "If a brother or sister be naked and in lack of daily food, and one of you say unto them, Go in peace, be ye warned and filled; and yet ye give them not the things needful to the body; what doth if profit?" (Jas. 2:15, 16). One of the strongest statements relative to the idea of sins of omission is found in this same epistle of James. "To him therefore that knoweth to do good, and doeth it not, to him it is sin" (4:17).[30]

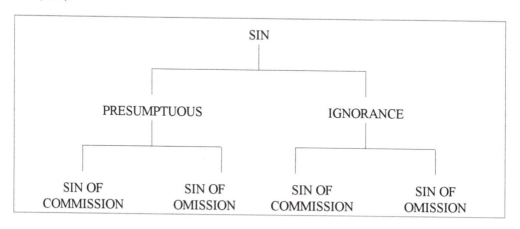

1. Presumptuous (sin of commission) - Purposely and intentionally rebelling against God's law, for the simple purpose of disobeying God (i.e., purposely killing another human).
2. Presumptuous (sin of omission) - Intentionally failing to do something (i.e., failing to tithe or help your brother).

3. Ignorance (sin of commission) - Exercising the will to do something, but unconscious of the evil effects (i.e., driving 60 mph in a 45-mph zone).
4. Ignorance (sin of omission) - Unintentionally failing to do something that you should have done (i.e., failing to pay back a debt you had forgotten about).

XIII. SPIRITUAL CONSEQUENCES OF SIN

The physical consequences of Adam and Eve's voluntary decision to disobey God were difficulty in growing crops, hard work, pain associated with childbirth, the serpent's lowered position, and the earth's global curse. Far more severe than the physical consequences of their sin—which simply made life's circumstances more difficult are the spiritual consequences of sin that strike deep into the heart and continue until today. The bliss of the creature enjoying the fellowship with the Creator was suddenly shattered. Never again in their physical life would they enjoy the blessedness experienced prior to the Fall. Man must wait until he receives his glorified body to enjoy unhindered fellowship with God. Inherent within God's pronounced judgment are other consequences on man: (1) Loss of original righteousness, (2) original guilt, (3) original pollution or a sinful nature, (4) altered image of God in man, and (5) spiritual death.

A. LOSS OF ORIGINAL RIGHTEOUSNESS. Prior to the Fall, Adam and Eve experienced and enjoyed a positive disposition to do deeds of righteousness. Although the potential to do evil existed, they initially chose to do good. This could be equated with the innocence of a child; however, Adam and Eve were mature adults. They did not possess an experiential or cognitive knowledge of sin. Today, a child will naturally rebel and refuse to obey, due to his sinful nature. However, with Adam and Eve there was no evil nature. Not only were they innocent, but Adam and Eve by their very nature had a bent to righteousness. After their sin, they were no longer innocent. Their positive disposition to do good was gone. Now they possessed a disposition to evil. Never once were they in a state of neutrality. The desire to do good was altered to a desire to do evil (original pollution or sinful nature).

B. ORIGINAL GUILT. With the loss of original righteousness, the verdict of God included original guilt. Original guilt now focuses upon man's condition at birth. Due to the imputation of Adam's sin (next section) man is accounted as guilty for Adam's sin. The guilt Adam experienced is shared by all of mankind; henceforth all men are guilty of breaking God's law and, as a result, stand to suffer for that action. The guilt for Adam's sin can be removed in one of two ways: (1) through satisfying completely the demands of the law (which no one can do except Christ), or (2) through the vicarious act of One who can satisfy the demands of God. It should be noted that even when One meets the demands of God and vicariously takes upon Himself the guilt that was originally man's, it does not indicate that man's sinful acts are no longer sinful, nor does it mean that man is no longer a sinner. It suggests rather that man is forgiven. Man is a forgiven sinner.

Hodge explains in detail the constitution of original guilt.

> There are, however, two things included in guilt. The one we express by the words criminality, demerit, and blameworthiness; the other is the obligation to suffer the punishment due to our offenses. These are evidently distinct, although expressed by the same word. The guilt of our sins is said to have been laid upon Christ, that is, the obligation to satisfy the demands of justice on account of them. But He did not assume the criminality, the demerit, or blameworthiness of our transgressions. When the believer is justified, his guilt, but not his demerit, is removed. He remains in fact, and in his own eyes, the same unworthy, hell-deserving creature, in himself considered, that he was before. A man condemned at a human tribunal for any offence against the community, when he has endured the penalty which the law prescribes, is no less unworthy, his demerit as much exists as it did from the beginning; but his liability to justice or obligation to the penalty of the law, in other words, his guilt in that sense of the word, is removed. It would be unjust to punish him a second time for that offence.[31]

Berkhof continues the thought of guilt by examining the potential guilt with the actual guilt and how it is removed.

> The word "guilt" expresses the relation, which sin bears to justice or, as the older theologians put it, to the penalty of the law. He who is guilty stands in a penal relation to the law. We can speak of guilt in a twofold sense, namely, as *reatus culpae* and as *reatus poenae*. The former, which Turretin calls "potential guilt," is the intrinsic moral ill-desert of an act or state. This is of the essence of sin and is an inseparable part of its sinfulness. It attaches only to those who have themselves committed sinful deeds, and attaches to them permanently. It cannot be removed by forgiveness, and is not removed by justification on the basis of the merits of Jesus Christ, and much less by mere pardon. Man's sins are inherently ill-deserving even after he is justified. Guilt in this sense cannot be transferred from one person to another. The usual sense, however, in which we speak of guilt in theology, is that of *reatus poenae*. By this is meant desert of punishment, or obligation to render satisfaction to God's justice for self-determined violation of the law. Guilt in this sense is not of the essence of sin, but is rather a relation to the penal sanction of the law. If there had been no sanction attached to the disregard of moral relations, every departure from the law would have been sin, but would not have involved liability to punishment. Guilt in this sense may be removed by the satisfaction of justice, either

personally or vicariously. It may be transferred from one person to another, or assumed by one person for another. It is removed from believers by justification, so that their sins, though inherently ill-deserving, do not make them liable to punishment.[32]

C. SINFUL NATURE. In addition to original guilt, Adam and Eve also experienced original pollution, meaning they received a sinful nature. Due to the absence of original righteousness (disposition to do right) Adam and Eve after the Fall discovered a change in their nature—there now existed a desire to do evil. Original guilt focuses on the effect of sin; original pollution (sinful nature) focuses on the cause of sin.

Many have misunderstood the sin nature within man. Berkhof enumerates these incorrect views calling the sinful nature, "original pollution."

(1) That original pollution is not merely a disease, as some of the Greek fathers and the Arminians present it, but sin in the real sense of the word. Guilt attaches to it; he who denies this does not have a Biblical conception of original corruption. (2) That this pollution is not to be regarded as a substance infused into the human soul, nor as a change of substance in the metaphysical sense of the word. This was the error of the Manichaeans and of Flacius Illyricus in the days of the Reformation. If the substance of the soul were sinful, it would have to be replaced by a new substance in regeneration; but this does not take place. (3) That it is not merely a privation. In his polemic with the Manichaeans, Augustine not merely denied that sin was a substance, but also asserted that it was merely a privation. He called it a *privatio boni*. But original sin is not merely negative; it is also an inherent positive disposition toward sin.[33]

Original pollution, or the sinful nature, consists essentially in a governing drive within man to do evil. The penalty for original guilt can be satisfied in justification, whereas for original pollution, the remedy is regeneration, i.e., a new nature to counteract the old nature. Within the regeneration process, man receives the enablement to do righteousness. Although the effect of the sinful nature is still within man, there now exists a greater force that assists him in overcoming sin and temptation. The chart on the following page reveals the type of sin and the divine remedy.

D. IMAGE OF GOD ALTERED. A fourth spiritual consequence of the fall of Adam and Eve centers on the altering of the image of God in man. Under the study of anthropology, this issue will be given greater attention. For the moment, the altered image of God shall broadly deal with the personality of man (physical) and his spiritual discernment.

E. PHYSICAL DEATH. The fifth consequence of Adam's sin is spiritual death. This is not the cessation of the existence of something, rather the separation of something from something else. From a biblical perspective, animals die and no longer exist; however, man in the accurate sense of the word never ceases to exist. At death, man merely passes from a temporary and finite state of existence to an eternal state. Man's reaction to the message of the cross determines where he will spend his eternal state.

Shortly after the fall, Adam and Eve experienced an immediate form of death. Again, the reference is not to their physical bodies, although they did begin to die physically. They felt the loss of close fellowship with God. The horror experienced by Adam and Eve of losing earthly fellowship with God was temporary (during the remainder of their physical life). However, far greater than the temporary death is the eternal spiritual death that fell to the human race. All those who die without faith in Christ will be cast into the lake of fire. The true agony is not so much in the tortures of the flames, although this will be grievous. The true dread lies in the knowledge that there is no more hope, for God has withdrawn Himself from them eternally.

	KIND OF SIN	FACT OF SIN	STATE OF SIN	PENALTY	TRANSMISSION	REMEDY
1.	Original Guilt Imputation	Rom. 5:12 Eph. 2:3 1 Cor. 15:22	Man's condition before God (non-experiential)	Physical and spiritual death	From Adam to us	Justification
2.	Original Pollution Sin Nature	Psa. 51:5 Rom. 1:21 Eph. 4:14 Titus 1:5 Jer. 17:9 Rom. 8:7	Experiential-man is born with a sin nature and it drives him to sin.	Physical and spiritual death	From parents to me	Regeneration
3.	Personal Sin Individual act	Rom. 3:23	Results of man's sinful condition	For believers, severance of fellowship with God.	None	Sanctification

KIND OF SIN	FACT OF SIN	STATE OF SIN	PENALTY	TRANSMISSION	REMEDY
			For unbelievers, further condemnation in the day of the Great White Throne Judgment		Justification

XIV. IMPUTATION OF ADAM'S SIN

The mainstream of theologians universally agree on the adverse affects of the fall, the destructive nature of sin, and the origin of sin due to man's improper use of his free will. However, they do not generally agree on the issue of how Adam's sin is transmitted to the human race. Much of the confusion exists in the inability of man to clearly understand just how Adam's sin is passed to each succeeding generation.

To discover the best possible explanation for the imputation of Adam's sin, it is expedient that a study of the incorrect views precede the formulation of a theory that provides complete accord with Scripture and the justice of God. Three basic issues are involved in the imputation: (1) How was Adam's sin imputed to the race?, (2) Why is Adam's sin imputed to the human race?, and (3) What is the nature of the imputed sin?

Prior to answering these questions, an understanding of the scriptural usage of "imputation" needs to be dealt with in a detailed manner.

In the original languages, the Hebrew word חָשַׁב and two Greek words ελλογέω and λογίζομαι are employed to disclose the judicial sense of attributing or reckoning something to someone else's account. All three of these words strongly suggest judicial transactions in much the way that the words "acquittal" and "pardon" convey legal significance. In the judicial and theological sense, to impute is simply to attribute anything, which initially belonged to someone else to a person or to a group of people, upon adequate ground. The substance for imputation can either possess inherent evilness or goodness.

Scripture presents three major imputations; (1) imputation of Adam's sin to the human race, (2) imputation of the sins of men to Christ, and (3) imputation of the righteousness of Christ to the believer.

Within the definition of "imputation" three extremely important points emerge, as recorded by Hodge.

1. To impute is to reckon to, or to lay to one's account. So far as the meaning of the word is concerned, it makes no difference whether the thing imputed be sin or righteousness; whether it is our own personally, or the sin or righteousness of another.

2. To impute sin, in Scriptural and theological language, is to impute the guilt of sin. And by guilt is meant not criminality or moral ill-desert, or demerit, much less moral pollution, but the judicial obligation to satisfy justice. Hence the evil consequence of the imputation is not an arbitrary infliction; not merely a misfortune or calamity; not a chastisement in the proper sense of that word, but a punishment: *i.e.*, an evil inflicted in execution of the penalty of law and for the satisfaction of justice.

3. A third remark in elucidation of what is meant by the imputation of Adam's sin is that by all theologians, Reformed and Lutheran, it is admitted, that in the imputation of Adam's sin to us, of our sins to Christ, and of Christ's righteousness to believers, the nature of imputation is the same, so that the one case illustrates the others. . . . And when it is said that the sin of Adam is imputed to his posterity, it is not meant that they committed his sin, or were the agents of his act, nor is it meant that they are morally criminal for his transgression; that it is for them the ground of remorse and self-approach; but simply that in virtue of the union between him and his descendants, his sin is the judicial ground of the condemnation of his race, precisely as the righteousness of Christ is the judicial ground of the justification of his people.[34]

A crucial issue in imputation is that Adam's sin is charged to the human race similarly to the imputation of Christ's righteousness to believers. This is not to suggest that Adam's imputation and Christ's imputation are identical in methodology. Several major differences exist. In relation to Adam's sin, man takes on the guilt of Adam simply by physical birth into the human race. But to partake of Christ's righteousness a man makes an objective act of repentance and exercises faith in Christ. The similarity in Adam's and Christ's imputations occurs in the legal realm. The consequences of Adam's sin is legally transmitted to the human race, just as the righteousness of Christ is legally transmitted to the believers.

How can God in light of His eternal justice, legally transmit the sinful acts of Adam to his entire posterity? In a legal sense, imputation requires a justifiable connection in order to reckon the deeds of the one to the many. When Christ through the incarnation became our Kinsman-Redeemer, He became one of us, thus providing a connection with the human race. Through this connection, the righteousness of Christ can be imputed to man. Scriptures never speak of the imputation of the sins of angels to either men or to Christ, or of Christ's righteousness to them. Why? There is no relation or connection between men and angels, or between angels and Christ. The connection of Adam to the human race is not to be confused with the method of the imputation, rather the connection provides the basis for God to legally declare sinful the human race as one organic whole. The deeds of the one (the head) affect the status of the many.

Adam, as the first human, is the national head (or fountainhead) of the human race, starting an unbroken union between him and men today. From God's perspective, all mankind constitutes one organic whole—a kind that begets a similar kind. When Adam sinned, the consequences of his deed affected the entire organic whole. The whole human race shared in his fallen and depraved state. Just as the sins of the father affect the lives of the children, the effects of Adam's sin extend to the entire human race.

Now the question arises, how is Adam's sin imputed to the race? Differences exist as to how this happened. Two prominent views have emerged, "mediate" and "immediate" imputation.

A. MEDIATE IMPUTATION. The theory of mediate imputation "was first maintained by Placeus (1605-1655), professor of theology at Saumur in France. Placeus originally denied that Adam's sin was in any sense imputed to his posterity, but after his doctrine was condemned by the Synod of the French Reformed Church at Charenton in 1644, he published the view which now bears his name.[35] His altered view gave birth to the mediate imputation theory which teaches Adam's original sin (involving both original guilt and original pollution) had only a partial effect upon his posterity. The guilt of Adam's sin (original guilt) was not passed to the human race; rather, only original pollution was transmitted to all men. Through natural generation man receives only the corrupted nature of Adam, and as a result eventually he will commit sin, thus becoming guilty of sin. Mediate imputation can be illustrated as such:

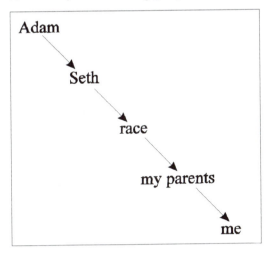

Berkhof declares that the race receives a sinful nature from Adam (from father to son). This is not a legal transmission, but a biological transmission.

This theory denies that the guilt of Adam's sin is *directly* imputed to his descendants, and represents the matter as follows: Adam's descendants derive their innate corruption from him by the process of natural generation, and on the basis of that inherent depravity which they share with him they are also considered guilty of his apostasy. They are not born corrupt because they are guilty in Adam, but they are considered guilty because they are corrupt. Their condition is not based on the legal status, but their legal status on their condition.[36]

Strong adds further insight to the mediate theory. He clearly identifies it as transmitted by physical procreation, not as a legal action.

> According to this view, all men are born physically and morally depraved; this native depravity is the source of all actual sin, and is itself sin; in strictness of speech, it is this native depravity, and this only, which God imputes to men. So far as man's physical nature is concerned, this inborn sinfulness has descended by natural laws of propagation from Adam to all his posterity. The soul is immediately created by God, but it becomes actively corrupt so soon as it is united to the body. Inborn sinfulness is the consequence, though not the penalty, of Adam's transgression.[37]

Through the medium of natural human propagation, Adam's sinful nature (original pollution) is passed from generation to generation. Placeus' view is not totally unique. It simply represents a much older view of Arminianism. It should be noted that Placeus is correct in asserting that man's sinful nature (original pollution) is indeed passed to all men through natural propagation.

However, to deny the absence of original guilt raises several serious objections. (1) The teaching of mediate imputation contradicts what Scripture claims: namely, that condemnation has passed upon all due to the sin of one man (Rom. 5:12). This condemnation is not inherent depravity transmitted through natural processes. Scripture repeatedly affirms that all men are partakers of Adam's sin, and that the guilt and corruption of that sin is equally imputed to all men.

(2) The doctrine of mediate imputation expressly denies the legal character of Adam's imputed sin, as stated and summarized in the judicial proclamation of "death to all men." Placeus would have to necessarily urge that people die as a result of personal sin and not due to the sin of Adam. A major weakness with this position arises when the death of an innocent child occurs. But death represents a penal infliction. However, a child, according to Placeus, is under no condemnation, but only possesses a morally polluted nature. A morally polluted nature is not sufficient cause for a legal infliction. Yet, children die everyday. Placeus' denial of imputed guilt is incorrect and lacks consistency.

(3) To assert, as Placeus, that the soul is created immediately (pure) and placed in the body which is morally polluted and destined to sin, questions the justice of God. Why would God confine a holy and righteous soul to a morally polluted body? To preserve His justice, it is necessary to urge that both are subject to condemnation or both are created righteous. The latter position is assumed by Pelagius, and has been strongly denounced and rejected by the Christian church. The former position discovers greater harmony and support with the Scripture.

(4) The most serious objection to mediate imputation is answered by Hodge. Placeus argues that man cannot be justly punished for the evil deeds of another man. Hodge answers his argument.

Perhaps, however, the most serious objection against the doctrine of mediate imputation is drawn from the principle on which it rests, and the arguments of its advocates in its support. The great principle insisted upon in support of this doctrine is that one man cannot justly be punished for the sin of another. If this be so then it is unjust in God to visit the iniquities of the fathers upon their children. Then it was unjust in Christ to declare that the blood of the prophets slain from the beginning should come upon the men of his generation. Then it is unjust that the Jews of the present day, and ever since the crucifixion of our Lord, should be scattered and peeled, according to the predictions of the prophets, for the rejection of the Messiah. Then, also, were the deluge sent in wrath upon the world, and the destruction of Sodom and Gomorrah, and the extermination of the Canaanites, in which thousands of children perished innocent of the offenses for which those judgments were inflicted, all acts of stupendous injustice. If this principle be sound, then the administration of the divine government over the world, God's dealings with nations and with the Church, admit of no defence. He has from the beginning and through all time held children responsible for the conduct of parents, included them without their consent in the covenants made with their fathers, and visited upon them the consequences of the violations of such covenants of which they were not personally guilty, as well as bestowed upon them rich blessings secured by the fidelity of their progenitors without anything meritorious on their part. Moreover, if the principle in question be valid, then the whole Scriptural doctrine of sacrifice and expiation is a delusion. And then, also, we must adopt the Socinian theory which makes the death of Christ instead of a penal satisfaction for sin, a mere symbolical inculcation of a truth—a didactic and not an expiatory service . . . . It is very clear that if no such constitution can be righteously established between men, even by God, that one man may justly bear the iniquity of another, then the Bible and Providence become alike unintelligible, and the great doctrines of the Christian faith are overthrown.[38]

B. IMMEDIATE IMPUTATION. In contrast to the mediate imputation theory is the immediate imputation theory, which receives the greater support of the church. This view teaches that guilt was immediately imputed to each individual. Adam's sin is credited to each man's account directly due to his relation to Adam. Immediate imputation can be demonstrated as,

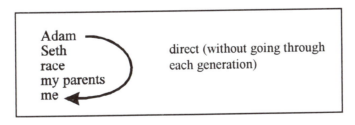

Unlike the sin nature, which is transmitted through human propagation, original guilt stems directly from Adam to each individual. From God's perspective, man represents a single generic unity, an organic whole in which the deeds of the one affect all.

The theory of immediate imputation is not without its objections. (1) Those who object to the theory of immediate imputation appeal to the passage of Scripture is Ezekiel 18:1-23, in which God states, "The soul that sinneth, it shall die" (v. 20). From this passage it is suggested that only those who actually sin receive penal infliction, an infliction which does not extend to innocent parties. However, this passage does not state that the judgment is limited solely to the active sinner. It could also involve others. What the passage does state is that the one who does sin will receive punishment; whether it involves others is not the issue at hand. (2) A second objection is that an improper parallel is made of Romans 5 between Adam and Christ. Those who advocate immediate imputation usually appeal to the imputation of our sins to Christ to illustrate the imputation of Adam's sin to mankind. However several important arguments against immediate imputation are made by Dabney.

> But it is argued, that since the imputation of our guilt to Christ is an immediate imputation of *peccatum alienum*, grounded in His community of nature with His people, the parallelism of the two doctrines shuts us up to a similar imputation of Adam's guilt to us. . . . Does any one suppose, for instance, that God would have condemned holy Gabriel for Satan's sin, without any assent, complicity or knowledge, on the part of the former? But we shall find that the cases of Adam and Christ are conditioned differently in two important respects. First: Christ's bearing our imputed guilt was conditioned on His own previous, voluntary consent. See Jno. x:18. All theologians, so far as I know, regard this as essential to a just imputation of *peccatum alienum* directly to Him. . . . If a man were to hold that the Father would have made this imputation of another's guilt upon His Son, in spite of the Son's exercising His legitimate autocracy to refuse and decline it, I should consider that man past reasoning with. But Adam's infant children receive the imputation, when they are incapable of a rational option or assent about it. The other difference in the two cases, (which it seems amazing anyone can overlook,) is the one pointed out in Rom. v: 16-19, and vi: 23. For the judgment was by one to condemnation; but the free gift (verse 15, "gift by grace") is of many offenses unto justification." The imputation of Adam's sin was a transaction of strict, judicial righteousness; the other transaction was one of glorious, free grace. Now, can any righteous judge be imagined, who would allow himself equal latitude in his judicial convictions, which he claims in his acts of voluntary beneficence? Would not the righteous magistrate answer, that in condemning, he felt himself restricted by the exact merits of the parties; but that in giving, he felt himself free to transcend their merits, and bestow what his generous impulses prompted? It may be praiseworthy to dispense blessings above the deserts of the beneficiaries; it cannot be other than injustice to dispense penalties beyond the

deserts of the culprits. We thus find that the imputation to us from Adam, and from us to Christ, are unavoidably conditioned in different ways in part; in other respects they are analogous.[39]

In his attempt to point out the illegitimacy of the immediate imputation theory, Dabney commits the very error he charges against the immediate imputation view. Satan's sin and its effects should not be strictly compared to the imputation of Adam's sin or Christ's righteousness. Due to the nature of angels (inability to procreate, and the absence of a physical body), they stand individually accountable for their deeds. In contrast, the race comes from one seed, hence it is a single organic whole.

The mediate imputation view lacks solid scriptural support, and raises several problems. On the other hand, the immediate imputation allows for the transmission of the sin nature through the process of natural propagation, and insists that the guilt of Adam's sin is likewise extended to all men through legal imputation.

XV. Various Theories Of Imputation

A. The Pelagian Theory.   In the early part of the fifth century, Pelagius, Coelestius and Julian developed a new theory in relation to the nature of sin as initiated by Adam and affecting the entire human race. Their views, once fully understood, were strongly denounced by the council of Carthage in 418, despite the exemplary character of these men, Pelagius (a British monk), Coelestius (a teacher), and Julian (an Italian bishop). Their theory sharply deviated from the Augustinian view (the prominent view at that time), and more importantly from the truth of Scripture. In brief, Pelagius believed Adam's sin had absolutely no effect upon his posterity, apart from a bad example. Strong summarizes the Pelagian view.

> According to this theory, every human soul is immediately created by God, and created as innocent, as free from depraved tendencies, and as perfectly able to obey God, as Adam was at his creation. The only effect of Adam's sin upon his posterity is the effect of evil example; it has in no way corrupted human nature; the only corruption of human nature is that habit of sinning which each individual contracts by persistent transgression of known law.
>
> Adam's sin therefore injured only himself; the sin of Adam is imputed only to Adam,—it is imputed in no sense to his descendants; God imputes to each of Adam's descendants only those acts of sin which he has personally and consciously committed. Men can be saved by the law as well as by the gospel; and some have actually obeyed God perfectly, and have thus been saved. Physical death is therefore not the penalty of sin, but an original law of nature; Adam would have died whether he had sinned or not; in Rom. 5:12, "Death passed unto all men, for that all sinned" signifies: "all incurred eternal death by sinning after Adam's example."[40]

In light of the justice of God (who would not hold someone else to be accountable for the deeds of another) and the ability of man to direct his liberty, Pelagius challenged the thinkers of his day to accept the radical claim, "If I ought, I can." Spurred by the doctrine of free will, Pelagius deemed man as a self-determined agent who had at his disposal the ability to choose between good and evil, thus self-determining his position in eternity.   Acts outside the determining will of man possess no moral value, therefore the sin of Adam, or an act outside man's determining will, in no way morally affected the status of his posterity. Pelagianism presupposed the following principles: (a) The nature of sin consisted only in deliberate acts of evil, therefore dismissing original guilt as an erroneous condition of man's state.   Men therefore become sinners because they sin and not vice-a-versa. (b) With no original guilt, all men are born with the same nature as Adam prior to the fall. Pelagius strongly insisted on this issue, arguing that if man's nature was sinful, then God as the author of nature must be the author of sin. (c) Adam's sin injured only himself. Pelagius emphatically denied any causal relation between the sin of Adam and the sinfulness of the human race. In order to remain consistent, Pelagius argued that death was not a penal infliction. Rather, death results from the very constitution of his being: i.e., man was not designed to experience immortality upon the earth. (d) Having denied original guilt and original pollution, Pelagius argued that men could pursue a righteous life and acquire salvation apart from the gospel. The necessity of the supernatural work of the Holy Spirit and the truth of the gospel simply represented another method to acquire salvation (provided for those who unfortunately already sinned). Finally, (e) in relation to infants, Pelagius taught that at birth they were destitute of any moral character, therefore neither guilty nor righteous. Since death was not a penal infliction, Pelagius, to consider the grieving parents, allowed that both baptized and unbaptized children became partakers of eternal life, a principle that was eventually called *limbus infantum.*

In reaction to the Augustinian view, Pelagius' attempt to modify Augustine's view proved disastrous.   To achieve his goal, Pelagius had to develop several dogmas that stood in opposition to the teaching of Scripture. When Pelagius' assertions were carried to their logical end, the result was something vastly different from the teachings of Scripture. Arguments against the Pelagian theory are twofold, philosophical and scriptural. In relation to the philosophical weakness, Strong writes,

It rests upon false philosophical principles; as, for example: (a) that the human will is simply the faculty of volitions; whereas it is also, and chiefly, the faculty of self-determination to an ultimate end; (b) that the power of a contrary choice is essential to the existence of will; whereas the will fundamentally determined to self-gratification has this power only with respect to subordinate choices, and cannot by a single volition reverse its moral state; (c) that ability is the measure of obligation,—a principle which would diminish the sinner's responsibility, just in proportion to his progress in sin; (d) that law consists only in positive enactment; whereas it is the demand of perfect harmony with God, inwrought into man's moral nature; (e) that each human soul is immediately created by God, and holds no other relations to moral law than those which are individual; whereas all human souls are organically connected with each other, and together have a corporate relation to God law, by virtue of their derivation from one common stock.[41]

In light of scriptural objections, the Pelagians are not correct in their claims. (1) They claim that evil and sinful dispositions are not equally considered sin. If this is true, then there would be no moral character in feelings or emotions, whether one hates or love, thinks with benevolence or with malice. All are amoral (no moral value). However, this teaching stands in direct contradiction to the teaching of Scripture. (2) The death of Christ upon the cross for man's redemption serves only to provide another way to eternal life. However, this principle fails to account for the claim stated by Christ, "I am the Way, the Truth, and the Life, no man commeth unto the Father but by Me" (John 14:6). (3) Pelagius' claims that all men are born with no evil disposition contradict the truth presented by David (Psa. 51), and Paul (Eph. 2:3). Both recognized their evil disposition at birth. (4) In claiming that man's present state is not directly linked with Adam's transgression, they totally ignore Romans 5:12, which links man's evil disposition to Adam's sin. Finally, (5) Pelagius' system overlooks one of man's deepest and most universal desires, namely, the need to place our trust not in the limited devices of mere men, but in the omnipotent and eternal wisdom of God. By placing too much emphasis upon the liberty of man to determine his own state, man overlooks grace. Man is left to his own devices to wrestle with sin and the powers of darkness.

From the preceding philosophical and scriptural objections, the Pelagian view should be recognized as a radical deviation from the truth. It has not and never should receive the endorsement of the church. It should be recognized for what it is, a rationalistic attempt to undermine the absolute necessity of man to offer a full account of himself to God.

B. SEMI-PELAGIAN/ARMINIAN VIEW. Although nearly a thousand years elapsed between Pelagius in the fourth century and Arminius (1560-1609), their views are practically identical, with only slight deviations. The Semi-Pelagian view was developed by John Cassianus, an Eastern monk and disciple of John Chrysostom, Vicentius Lexinensis and Faustus Rhegium. Spurred by much the same compulsion as Pelagius, these men sought to soften and modify the doctrine of Augustine and at the same time incorporate several of the tenets pronounced by Pelagius.

Arminius (1590-1609), a professor in the University of Leyden in South Holland, sought to challenge the views of his contemporaries, Luther and Calvin, who endorsed largely the view of Augustine. Unlike Pelagius, who rejected original guilt and original pollution, the semi-Pelagians recognized the effects of Adam's sin upon the human race. They allowed for the existence of sin nature, but they objected to the teachings of original guilt. They asserted that man indeed was born with an evil disposition to sin. However, the justice of God (as they understood it) would not allow for all men to be guilty for the sin of Adam. The fact that man is born with a polluted moral nature suggests that he is not guilty of committing any sin, or that he is liable for any punishment. Their reasoning can be diagrammed in the following manner.

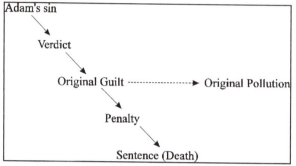

Since men (with the exception of Adam) were not directly involved in Adam's sin, it is unreasonable to conclude that all men must share his guilt. However, semi-Pelagians recognize that after Adam sinned, his moral constitution was altered. Man's altered moral character was transmitted through the agency of natural propagation.

It is not until a child (born without guilt) allows his corrupted disposition to lead him to commit a sin, that he becomes guilty and subject to penalty. Once the child sins, redemption is possible through the death of the cross. Semi-Pelagians would allow for the possibility of a child to mature to adulthood and eventually die, having never experienced the acts and results of sin. Although the possibility is actually attainable, they teach that few ever live a sinless life. Nevertheless, with the aid of the Holy Spirit, it is possible to live a sinless life. Commenting on the beliefs of the semi-Pelagians, Strong writes,

According to this theory, all men, as a divinely appointed sequence of Adam's transgression, are naturally destitute of original righteousness, and are exposed to misery and death. By virtue of the infirmity propagated from Adam to all his descendants, mankind are wholly unable without divine help perfectly to obey God or to attain eternal life. This inability, however, is physical and intellectual, but not voluntary. As a matter of justice, therefore, God bestows upon each individual from the first dawn of consciousness a special influence of the Holy Spirit, which is sufficient to counteract the effect of the inherited depravity and to make obedience possible, provided the human will coöperates, which it still has power to do.

The evil tendency and state may be called sin; but they do not in themselves involve guilt or punishment; still less are mankind accounted guilty of Adam's sin. God imputes to each man his inborn tendencies to evil, only when he consciously and voluntarily appropriates and ratifies these in spite of the power to the contrary, which, in justice to man, God has specially communicated in Rom. 5:12, "Death passed unto all men, for that all sinned," signifies that physical and spiritual death is inflicted upon all men, not as the penalty of a common sin in Adam, but because, by divine decree, all suffer the consequences of that sin, and because all personally consent to their inborn sinfulness by acts of transgression.[42]

Since the semi-Pelagians endorsed the thinking of Pelagius, many of the philosophical weaknesses discovered with the Pelagian theory apply equally to the semi-Pelagians. Two prominent philosophical weaknesses within the semi-Pelagian theory focus on why the law is restricted to solely volitional transgressions, and, secondly, the assertion that man possesses no organic or moral connection to Adam's sin. If only overt and volitional deeds are considered sin then what is the scriptural basis for claiming that lust, hatred, and malice are deemed sinful? Of course they are sin, but the semi-Pelagian fails to fully understand the precise nature of sin. Furthermore, to deny the moral connection embedded within the human race, fails to explain the repeated scriptural claim that the children for several generations share the condemnation of their father's injustice.

In addition to the philosophical argument, several scriptural problems exist within the semi-Pelagian theory. (1) Scripture claims in Romans 5 that death is a penalty directly linked to Adam's sin, since infants and mentally handicapped (both of whom are innocent in God's judgment) experience death. It is logical to conclude that their deaths (penalty) comes as a result of someone else's transgression. No penalty can be assessed if no guilt exists; however, if the guilt of another is passed to someone else, then that guilt can be justly punished. Whether it is justified to transmit guilt and punishment, will be discussed in further detail later. For the moment, innocent children die, death is a penal infliction connected with Adam's sin, therefore Adam's guilt must necessarily be passed to the entire human race. (2) Romans 5:16, 18 indicate that all men are condemned; however, condemnation never precedes guilt; guilt must of necessity precede condemnation. To argue otherwise, as the semi-Pelagians claim, contradicts Scripture. (3) Furthermore, Romans 5:19 clearly states that the sin of Adam constituted all men as sinners. Semi-Pelagians argue that man's individual sins constitute him as a sinner. Scripture never once suggests that a person becomes a sinner after having sinned. The opposite is true: men are born sinners, and a natural inclination of the depraved nature is to sin. (4) Semi-Pelagians imply the error of allowing good works to become another means of salvation, which is strongly denied in Scripture (Isa. 64:6). Finally, (5) because they maintain that inherited moral evil does not involve guilt, they have an inadequate understanding of what constitutes sin. A polluted nature stems from sin and does not precede it; they are naturally bonded together.

C. CLASSICAL PROTESTANT VIEWS. In contrast to the theories proposed by Pelagius and the semi-Pelagians, the two following views limit themselves to the truth of Scripture, as interpreted by their founders. A key similarity to the two Protestant views centers in the claim that both original guilt and the sin nature are transmitted to the human race. Slight variations to the Federal Headship and the Augustinian theory do exist; however, the crucial issues will be dealt with in considering the major arguments and weaknesses with each view.

1. *Federal headship or Representative view.* The Federal theory, or theory of the covenant theologian, gained acceptance and popularity when stated by Cocceius (1603-1669), a professor Leyden, yet the view received greater recognition through the careful works of Turretin (1623-1687). Within the Lutheran denomination, the Federal Headship theory has received broad support, and even greater attention in the writings of Charles Hodge.

The Latin noun *foedus*, from which the word "federal" comes, suggests treaty, or compact. The second picture of the Federal Covenant position, is the word "covenant," a word employed many times in the Hebrew text (*berith*) which refers to any arrangement more or less formally instituted between two or more parties. The arrangement may or may not involve a promise or specific condition, but more often than not a covenant usually involves a strict agreement that includes special conditions and some sort of reward or retribution.

According to this view, Adam was sovereignly appointed by God to act as the representative of the entire human race, in much the way representatives in legislature represent their respective districts. Inherent within the covenant established with Adam, prior to his fall, was the genuine promise that Adam and all his posterity would enjoy the blessings of God within the Garden of Eden if they remained obedient to God's command. If Adam and Eve were successful, then God would have removed them from their probationary period and endowed them with eternal life. On the other hand, if disobedience occurred, then the penalty of their deed would not only affect Adam and Eve, but all of humanity. Berkhof, former president of Calvin Seminary and supporter of the Federal Headship view, briefly summarizes the principles of this view.

This implies that Adam stood in a twofold relationship to his descendants, namely that of the natural head of all mankind, and that of *the representative head* of the entire human race in the covenant of works. (1) *The natural relationship.* In his natural relationship Adam was the father of all mankind. As he was created by God he was subject to change, and had no rightful claim to an unchangeable state. He was in duty bound to obey God, and this obedience did not entitle him to any reward. On the other hand, if he sinned, he would become subject to corruption and to punishment. . . . (2) *The covenant relationship.* To the natural relationship in which Adam stood to his descendants God graciously added a covenant relationship containing several positive elements: (a) *An element of representation.* God ordained that in this covenant Adam should not stand for himself only, but as the representative of all his descendants. Consequently he was the head of the race not only in a parental, but also in a federal sense. (b) *An element of probation.* While apart from this covenant Adam and his descendants would have been in a continual state of trial with a constant danger of sinning, the covenant guaranteed that persistent perseverance for a fixed period of time would be rewarded with the establishment of man in a permanent state of holiness and bliss. (c) *An element of reward or punishment.* According to the terms of the covenant Adam would obtain a rightful claim to eternal life, if he fulfilled the conditions of the covenant. And not only he, but all his descendants as well would have shared in this blessing. In its normal operation, therefore, the covenant arrangement would have been of incalculable benefit for mankind. But there was a possibility that man would disobey, thereby reversing the operation of the covenant, and in that case the results would naturally be correspondingly disastrous. Transgression of the covenant commandment would result in death. Adam chose the course of disobedience, corrupted himself by sin, became guilty in the sight of God, and as such subject to the sentence of death. And because he was the federal representative of the race, his disobedience affected all his descendants. In His righteous judgment God imputes the guilt of the first sin, committed by the head of the covenant, to all those that are federally related to him. And as a result they are born in a depraved and sinful condition, as well, and this inherent corruption also involves guilt. This doctrine explains why only the first sin of Adam, and not his following sin, nor the sins of our other forefathers, is imputed to us, and also safeguards the sinlessness of Jesus. . . . [43]

Principally, covenant theologians contend that two major covenants were established—one of works and the other of grace. The former occurred prior to the Fall, in which Adam entered into a covenant with God to tend the garden and abstain from the Tree of the Knowledge of Good and Evil. Since the responsibility was chiefly Adam's, this covenant placed a great deal of emphasis upon Adam's meritorious work. Meritorious in the sense that if he perfectly obeyed God, Adam and all his descendants would have earned the right to immortality upon the earth. The second covenant, that of Grace, began shortly after the Fall. The covenant of Grace moved the emphasis from Adam to God. God would now provide a means for man's salvation, initiated in the promise of a messiah (Gen. 3:15). Inherent within the covenant of grace, covenant theologians would argue, many secondary covenants have been established: i.e., Abrahamic, Noahic, Davidic, Palestinian, and the New Covenant.

Advocates for the Federal Headship Theory have successfully gathered a wealth of biblical data to support their claims. (a) Scripture repeatedly refers to Adam's relation to the human race in a twofold capacity, not only as man's natural head, but also the federal head. Even a casual reading of Genesis implies that God stated to Adam that any potential blessings or punishments would extend not only to him, but all his seed. The promise or command of dominion over the earth implied blessings to Adam that would be naturally enjoyed by men today. (b) In 1 Cor. 15:22, 45-49, Paul draws a parallel between the headship of Christ and the headship of Adam. According to verse 22, man's destiny is based upon his relationship to either personality. Such an analogy should only be interpreted in a representative sense, just as Christ is understood to represent the head of all believers. Conversely, Adam should be viewed as representing all mankind. The actions and ensuing consequences of both these men are juxtaposed in order to reveal the obvious distinctions. (c) The representative principle is frequently employed in Scripture. Hodge supplies a sample of this view,

This representative principle pervades the whole Scriptures. The imputation of Adam's sin to his posterity is not an isolated fact. It is only an illustration of a general principle which characterizes the dispensations of God from the beginning of the world. God declared himself to Moses to be, "The LORD, the LORD God, merciful and gracious, long-suffering, and abundant in goodness and truth, keeping mercy for thousands, forgiving iniquity and transgression, and sin, and that will by no means clear the guilty; visiting the iniquity of the fathers upon the children, and upon the children's children unto the third and to the fourth generation." (Ex. xxxiv. 6, 7.) Jeremiah says: "Thou showest loving-kindness unto thousands, and recompensest the iniquities of the fathers into the bosom of their children after them. The Great, the Mighty God, the LORD of Hosts, is his name." (Jer. xxxii. 18.) The curse pronounced on Canaan fell upon his posterity. Esau's selling his birthright, shut out his descendants from the covenant of promise. The children of Moab and Ammon were excluded from the congregation of the Lord forever, because their ancestors opposed the Israelites when they came out of Egypt. In the case of Dathan and Abiram, as in that of Achan, "their wives, and their sons, and their little children" perished for the sins of their parents. God said to Eli, that the iniquity of his house should not be purged with sacrifice and offering forever. To David it was said, "The sword shall never depart from thy house; because thou hast despised me, and hast taken the wife of Uriah the Hittite to be thy wife." To the disobedient Gehazi it was said: "The leprosy of Naaman shall cleave unto thee and unto thy seed forever." The sin of Jereboam and of the men of his generation determined the destiny of the ten tribes for all time. The imprecation of the Jews, when they demanded the crucifixion of Christ, "His blood be on us and on our children," still weighs down the scattered people of Israel. Our Lord himself said to the Jews of his generation that they built the sepulchers of the prophets whom their fathers had slain, and thus acknowledged themselves to be the children of murderers, and that therefore the blood of those prophets should be required at their hands. This principle runs through the whole Scriptures. When God entered into covenant with Abraham, it was not for himself only but also for his posterity. They were bound by all the stipulations of that covenant. They shared his promises and its threatenings, and in hundreds of cases the penalty of disobedience came upon those who had no personal part in the transgressions. Children suffered equally with adults in the judgments, whether famine, pestilence, or war, which came upon the people for their sins. In like manner, when God renewed and enlarged the Abrahamic covenant at Mount Sinai, it was made with the adults of that generation as representing their descendants to the remotest generations. And the Jews to this day are suffering the penalty of the sins of their fathers for their rejection of Him of whom Moses and the prophets spoke.[44]

(d) If there was only a seminal union between Adam and all men (the realistic or Augustine view), it is difficult to explain why all men are guilty of Adam's first sin and not all his sins. Such a truth suggests that the probation connected to the Tree of the Knowledge of Good and Evil involved a special relationship between God and Adam, with special attention applied to the first act of disobedience. (e) Paul refers in Romans 5:12-14 to the analogy between Adam and Christ to construct a type of syllogism in which he argues that punishment presupposes sin, sin presupposes a law, for sin is not imputed where there is no law. However, prior to the giving of the law to Moses, death (a penalty of sin) reigned (occurred) from Adam to Moses. Paul purposely selected this period of time simply because the law (of Moses) did not exist, yet men died. He suggested that it was not the evil deeds of men during this period that sealed their death (for no individual sin could be imputed with the absence of the law), rather their death stemmed from Adam's disobedience. Finally, (f) Covenant theologians appeal to Hosea 6:7 as proof that God established a covenant with Adam: "But they like men [Adam] have transgressed the covenant: there have they dealt treacherously against me." Since God makes covenants with individuals that directly affect the lives of a great host of people, Adam's selection as our representative should not appear as a surprise to any student of the Bible.

Despite the apparent truthfulness of the federal headship, several major objections reveal implied weakness. (a) The representative principle is operative within Scripture, but to infer (without solid and precise wording) that a covenant existed between God and Adam assumes the misnomer of framing an "in principle" argument (an argument that claims that when specific and similar actions and instances occur between two separate events, a similar principle can be assumed). For instance, if a person were standing outside on a windy day and suddenly a tree fell near him, he should not necessarily assign the falling of another tree on another occasion to the same cause, given similar conditions. In the first instance the wind may have been the cause; however, the second instance might have been soil erosion below the surface soil, undetected by the human eye. This type reasoning simply allows for the possibility of a covenant, not the proof of a covenant.

(b) The analogy principle as discovered between Adam and Christ in 1 Corinthians 15 and Romans 5 is not without its problems. According to Romans 5:14, "who is the figure of him that was to come," covenant theologians argue that a definite analogy exists; yet they differ in whether the analogy is a strict or a loose analogy. In a strict analogy there would be a one-to-one correspondence, requiring complete compatibility. On the other, if Romans 5 is a loose analogy, correspondence would only need to apply to major items and not to minor points. If it could be proven that Romans 5 is only a loose analogy, the representative principle would be destroyed, and the major support for the federal headship view would likewise collapse. To discover if Romans 5 represents a strict or loose analogy, a careful comparison is required. At the outset, five major contrasts exist, suggesting very strongly that Romans 5 is simply a loose analogy, and not a strict analogy as claimed by covenant theologians. (1) Romans 5:12 clearly states that, "all have sinned." Covenant theologians contend that because Adam was our representative, all men automatically at birth share his guilt. However, in applying this same imputation to Christ's righteousness, several major differences emerge. In one instance, man is active (in Christ); in the other instance (in Adam) man is not active. (2) The imputation of Adam's sin required no effort on man's part; however, to acquire salvation in Christ, man must demonstrate repentance and faith. (3) In one case imputation stems from justice; in the other, the basis rests upon grace. (4) A further contrast in this analogy reveals that in the imputation of Adam's sin, he did what all men could have accomplished; however, in relation to Christ's imputation of righteousness, it is discovered that He did what men could not do, and, more importantly, what needed to be done. (5) Romans 5:18, refers to benefactors of Adam's imputation and of Christ's imputation as "all men." The analogy breaks down, for these cannot be synonymous groups. Every man born has indeed experienced the imputation of Adam's sin; however, this same group cannot be equated with the "all men" who have internalized the righteousness of Christ. Covenant theologians usually explain this problem by suggesting that the "all" reflected to Adam represents all actual men; however, the "all" in relation to Christ refers to all those who have been saved. Hence, there is no strict analogy, but only a loose analogy.

Also, according to Romans 5:14, Adam is a figure of the one to come. Adam can represent a type of Christ, without having to be considered a representative of all men. The question to answer is, does Adam have to be a representative in order to function as a type? The answer is, no. Only a clear statement of Adam's representative function should provide the basis for the federal headship theory. However, such a statement does not exist. Through demonstrating the weakness of the existence of a covenant (argument one), and the role of a strict analogy (argument two), the federal headship does not have a strong basis.

(c) The third argument is more complex. The view of Adam as the representative head fails to provide an adequate response to why only Adam's first sin is chargeable to the human race. Admittedly the representative theory succeeds in providing a more plausible explanation, arguing that God established the covenant with only Adam's first sin. But the answer lies in the fact that the rest of Adam's sins are irrelevant, once man is judicially guilty. Hence, no additional guilt is necessary for God to assign a penalty.

(d) The statement made in Hosea 6:7 lacks solid hermeneutics when interpreted by theologians who argue that Hosea is describing a covenant of works that was established between God and Adam. Most covenant theologians recognize the illegitimacy of appealing to Hosea 6:7 for proof for the covenant of works. A better translation of Hosea 6:7 should read that man, not Adam, transgressed the covenant. The same Hebrew word that can be translated as "Adam," can also be translated "man," or even "red clay." In addition to these objections, Strong suggests several others.

It contradicts Scripture, in making the first result of Adam's sin to be God's *regarding and treating* the race as sinners. The Scripture, on the contrary, declares that Adam's offense *constituted* us sinners (Rom. 5:19). We are not sinners simply because God regards and treats us as such, but God regards us as sinners because we are sinners. Death is said to have "passed unto all men," not because we were regarded and treated as sinners, but "because all sinned" (Rom. 5:12). . . . That God holds men responsible for the violation of a covenant which they had no part in establishing. The assumed covenant is only a sovereign decree; the assumed justice, only arbitrary will.[45]

2. Augustinian or Seminal Head View. This view shares many similarities with the federal headship. Principally, both teach imputed guilt and the inheritance of a sinful nature. However, several major contrasts occur between the view of covenant theologians and that of Augustine. Whether one examines the federal headship theory or the Augustinian theory, careful attention should be given to the fact that both these views are merely theories, they are not scriptural dogma. Conceived within the rational ability of men, these views represent valid attempts by men to somehow understand from God's perspective the basis for the imputation of sin. Employing the same critical approach as applied to the federal-headship, it is equally expedient that the Augustinian view be allowed the opportunity to prove itself internally consistent and in agreement with the testimony of Scripture.

The Augustinian theory was developed and elaborated in the scholarly works of Augustine (354-430). This view, named after its major exponent, had been first expressed the works of Tertullian, Hilary, Ambrose. The Augustinian view is also called the seminal view and the realist view.

In brief, the Augustinian theory states that all humanity existed as a unity in Adam. All men were seminally in Adam and acted in Adam, hence all men were affected as was Adam. When Adam sinned, the very nature and constitution of his semen also sinned. Men today receive the guilt and sin nature of Adam justly, for they "sinned in Adam" (Rom. 5:12). Strong, a staunch supporter of the Augustinian view articulates with greater clarity the major premises of this view.

It holds that God imputes the sin of Adam immediately to all his posterity, in virtue of that organic unity of mankind by which the whole race at the time of Adam's transgression existed, not individually, but seminally, in him as its head. The total life of humanity was then in Adam; the race as yet had its being only in him. Its essence was not yet individualized; its forces were not yet distributed; the powers which now exist in separate men were then unified and localized in Adam; Adam's will was yet the will of the species. In Adam's free act, the will of the race revolted from God and the nature of the race corrupted itself. The nature which we now possess is the same nature that corrupted itself in Adam—"not the same in kind merely, but the same as flowing to us continuously from him."

Adam's sin is imputed to us immediately, therefore, not as something foreign to us, but because it is ours—we and all other men having existed as one moral person or one moral whole, in him, and, as the result of that transgression, possessing a nature destitute of love to God and prone to evil. In Rom. 5:12—"death passed unto all men, for that all sinned," signifies; "death physical, spiritual, and eternal passed unto all men, because all sinned in Adam their natural head."[46]

Augustine constructed the most widely accepted view for the imputation of sin. Support for this position is as follows: (a) It places the most natural interpretation upon Romans 5:12-21. Paul states, "death passed upon all men, for that all have sinned," referring to death, though not exclusively to physical death. This explains the occurrence of death in those who have no conscious or personal transgression, so as to justify the penalty of death. Through the single act, the "trespass of the one," death came to all men, because all (not "have sinned," but "sinned," *pantes hamarton*, aorist, with emphasis upon a particular past event). Although not all men actually and consciously sinned, yet in Adam their common nature, which existed seminally in Adam, did sin. (b) The issue of justice receives greater credence in the seminal view. The representative view claims that God selected a representative (Adam), and because he sinned, all men must share his guilt. This is injustice. To impute to innocent men the guilt of another, when the innocent did not actually participate in selecting their representative, fails to answer the issue of justice. The seminal view places universal guilt in the organic unity of the human race. (c) In relation to the nature of sin, Scriptures teach that one is personally accountable for personal sins committed, and not accountable for the sins of someone else. The representative principle implies that all men did not choose their representative, hence they did not actually sin, thus destroying the basis for their moral accountability. On the other hand, the seminal view provides some basis for moral accountability, i.e., the organic unity of the human race. (d) The seminal view allows for a more accurate understanding of Romans 5 and 1 Corinthians 15, suggesting that these passages do not point out the similarities of Adam and Christ (position taken by covenant theologians), but rather, they point out the dissimilarities.

Objections to the Augustinian Theory. (a) A major objection to the Augustinian theory rests in how man can bear guilt for sin which he did not personally or individually commit? Admittedly this is a serious problem for both views, for neither can clearly state all that is involved. However, greater problems exist within the representative view, which claims all men did not actually sin in Adam. The seminal view achieves a more plausible cause for the imputation, that all men in some sense were involved in Adam's sin. Paul makes it abundantly clear we "all sinned" (Rom. 5:12), which does seem to indicate some type of participation. (b) The seminal view must also answer the question, Are all men responsible for Adam's first sin, or for all his sins? Covenant theologians answer the question by claiming that the covenant of works applied only to the first sin, which is consistent if a covenant exists. On the other hand, the seminal takes the position described by Strong.

> We reply that the apostasy of human nature could occur but once. It occurred in Adam before the eating of the forbidden fruit, and revealed itself in that eating. The subsequent sins of Adam and of our immediate ancestors are no longer acts which determine or change the nature,—they only show what the nature is. Here is the truth and the limitation of the Scripture declaration that "the son shall not bear the iniquity of the father" (Ez. 18:20, cf. Luke 13:2, 3; John 9:2, 3). Man is not responsible for the specifically evil tendencies communicated to him from his immediate ancestors, as distinct from the nature he possesses; nor is he responsible for the sins of those ancestors which originated these tendencies. But he is responsible for that original apostasy which constituted the one and final revolt of the race from God, and for the personal depravity and disobedience which in his own case has resulted therefrom.[47]

(c) Covenant theologians object to the seminal claim that if sin and condemnation are transmitted by natural propagation, it stands to reason that righteousness and faith should be so propagated also. Yet, ordinary generation does not transmit personal guilt, but only that guilt which belongs to the whole human race. Men are born sinners, because they share the corrupted nature of Adam. Personal qualities, whether sin or righteousness, are not transmitted in propagation, they are individual in nature.

(d) Romans 5:14, "Death reigned . . . over them that had not sinned after the similitude of Adam's transgression." From this passage it appears initially that this verse denies the seminal view, which claims that everyone sinned individually in a single person, Adam. Those who lived from Adam to Moses did not sin according to the manner of Adam, suggesting that they did not sin in Adam as an organic unity. Upon closer examination, the context yields just the opposite. Paul purposely selected those who lived between Adam and Moses to illustrate the truth that they died not because of their individual sins committed after birth, but because they were guilty and deserving of judgment due to their sin in Adam. The distinction between Adam's sin and those of the group (from Adam to Moses) lies in that the former sinned against an explicit command. The latter did not, but all died because of Adam's sin, for all sinned in Adam.

In contrast to the Pelagian and semi-Pelagian views, which deny in part or totally the scriptural teaching of the imputed guilt and moral pollution, both the federal headship view and the Augustinian view support such teachings. Representing the historic Protestant view, both these views (federal headship and Augustinian) are not without their problems. The covenant theologians must provide adequate support for a covenant established between God and Adam, and, more importantly, supply a sufficient cause for imputing guilt to another, when the innocent party did not act in his own behalf. The Augustinian view fails to clearly answer the charge of how God could justly charge all mankind with guilt and punishment for an act of which he was not consciously aware, though directly involved in. A relatively new explanation of the imputation of sin, is suggested by Hoeksema. He suggests that the solution may be in combining the two.

We must remember that God created the human race not only an organism, with Adam as the root and first father, but also a legal corporation, with Adam as the representative head. Even from a legal viewpoint the human race is not a mere aggregate of individuals in which everyone stands and falls his own master, without being at all responsible for the whole. On the contrary, there is communal responsibility; and there is communal guilt and suffering in human life. This is evident in everyday life: individualism is condemned everywhere. Clearly this is illustrated in the life of a nation in relation to its government. Take the concrete instance of our nation as it goes to war with a foreign power. In that case it certainly is not every American citizen that declares war on that foreign power. And to be sure, for that act of the official declaration of war the government is responsible before God. The government is entrusted with the sword. It is the only God-ordained power that has the authority to handle the sword, also in declaring and waging war. The individual soldier who is called by the government and goes forth to battle does not commit murder and is not guilty of bloodshed if he kills the enemy on the battlefield. He merely handles the sword of the government, and that in the name of government. However, does that mean that there is no communal responsibility and suffering? What right-minded citizen would say that the government declared war and that therefore the government had better fight its own battles? When our government declares war, we are all very really in a state of war, and will have to suffer all the consequences implied in it. For even before God a nation is not an aggregate of individuals, but a legal body; and the government represents all its citizens. If the government in order to meet the expenses of a war accumulates a debt of many billions of dollars, we are all responsible for the payment of that debt; and even our children and our children's children will have to bear the burden of that responsibility. And thus it is in every department of life. It is true that there is individual responsibility and individual sin and guilt. It is also true that in this sense the children cannot be held responsible for the sins of the parents. It is, however, also true that there is a communal responsibility and communal guilt that runs into generations, and that God visits the iniquity of the fathers upon the children even in the third and fourth generation of them that hate Him. And thus God created the whole human race in Adam as a legal corporation, represented by our first father. And we cannot say that we are not responsible for his transgression: for we have all sinned in him, and his sin is imputed to us.[48]

As a possibility to the dilemma of imputation, Hoeksema's view appears initially as a fresh view. However, all the details to this have yet to surface. Inherent within the view, is the possibility of a specific claim that sharply contradicts Scripture. Time and additional research are the key elements to grasping a correct understanding of the imputation from God's perspective.

A brief summary of the various views of imputation are suggested by Strong:[49]

TABULAR VIEW OF THE VARIOUS THEORIES OF IMPUTATION			
NO CONDEMNATION INHERITED		CONDEMNATION INHERITED	
PELAGIAN	ARMINIAN	FEDERAL	AUGUSTINIAN
I. Origin of the soul	Immediate creation.	Immediate creation.	Immediate creation.	Mediate creation.
II. Man's state at birth.	Innocent, and able to obey god.	Depraved, but still able to co-operate with the Spirit.	Depraved, unable, and condemnable.	Depraved, unable, and condemnable.
III. Effects of Adam's sin.	Only upon himself.	To corrupt his posterity physically and intellectually. No guilt of Adam's sin imputed.	To insure condemnation of his fellows in covenant, and their creation as depraved.	Guilt of Adam's sin, corruption, and death.
IV. How did all sin?	By following Adam's example.	By consciously ratifying Adam's own deed, in spite of the Spirit's aid.	By being accounted sinners in Adam's sin.	By having part in the sin of Adam, as seminal head of the race.
V. What is corruption?	Only of evil habit, in each case.	Evil tendencies kept in spite of the Spirit.	Condemnable, evil disposition and state.	Condemnable, evil disposition and state.
VI. What is imputed?	Every man's own sins.	Only man's own sins and ratifying of this nature.	Adam's sin, man's own corruption, and man's own sins.	Adam's sin, our depravity, and our own sins.

VII. What is the death incurred?	Spiritual and eternal.	Physical and spiritual death by decree.	Physical, spiritual, and eternal.	Physical, spiritual, and eternal.
VIII. How are men saved?	By following Christ's example.	By co-operating with the Spirit given to all.	By being accounted righteous through the act of Christ.	By Christ's work, with whom we are one.

XVI. MISCELLANEOUS ISSUES RELATED TO SIN

A. SIN IN RELATION TO INFANTS. In light of the imputation of Adam's guilt and its accompanying death, different Christian groups have proposed several possible solutions to the problem of the death of children before the age of accountability. It is inconsistent with the justice and love of God to punish a child before he has been given an opportunity to exercise free will. During the Dark Ages, the ecclesiastical hierarchy suggested a solution to the death of children by teaching they went to a place called Limbo to await their acceptance into heaven. Limbo was a place outside the residence of hell in which there was no agony. However, this teaching lacks scriptural support and simply represents the creative work of fallible men. A second approach suggested salvation through infant baptism. Assuming that baptism possessed regenerative powers, infants were baptized by immersion, sprinkling or effusion. The major error with this view centers in the false teaching called "baptismal regeneration" (see Soteriology). Repentance and faith, not baptism, have always functioned as the foundation of salvation. Verses such as Matthew 18:3-4, 10, 14; 19:13-14 suggest that children through the grace of God are innocent until their age of accountability, a time that varies with the differing comprehensive abilities of children. A child's innocence should not be equated with the innocence experienced by Adam, for he did not possess a sinful nature, sin was not imputed to him, and he enjoyed a positive disposition to do good.

B. SIN UNTO DEATH IN RELATION TO BELIEVERS. "If anyone sees his brother sinning a sin which does not lead to death, he will ask, and He will give him life for those who commit sin not leading to death. There is sin leading to death. I do not say that he should pray about that" (1 John 5:16-17). The sin unto death as referred to in this passage should not be confused with the unpardonable sin which relates to unbelievers (Matt. 12:22-32). John relates the "sin unto death" to believers and not unbelievers. No believer can ever commit the unpardonable sin. The "sin unto death" usually results in a physical chastisement and not an eternal condemnation of both the body and the soul. However, spiritual punishment on earth (not in heaven) is a penalty for believers, but the outward manifestation is physical. Dr. A. C. Gabelein writes,

The brother [in this passage] is a believer. On account of sinning he is chastised. God permits sickness to come upon him, and the sinning, not having been unto death (physical death *only*), he is raised up. However, a believer may not go on *wilfully sinning* and remain there dishonoring Christ. He is to be taken away out of the land of the living, cut off by death. No request could be made for such a one. The question of death is not eternal condemnation but only physical death.[50]

Since this sin applies solely to believers, many have wondered what sin could believers commit in order to exhaust God's patience and prompt their physical sickness or death? Scripture supplies us with three separate illustrations. (1) Where a sin is so degraded in nature, God, in order to sustain a degree of purity in the church, may act to remove the one who committed such an act. A good example of this occurs in 1 Corinthians 5:1-5, in which a believer within the Corinthian church openly acknowledges that he was having sexual relationship with his mother or possibly with a woman that his father had married. The nature of this sin prompted Paul to direct the church to cast the man from their midst, to deliver him unto Satan for the destruction of the flesh (physical death). This man's sin was so reprehensible, that it was abhorred in the eyes of nonbelievers, therefore punishment had to be exercised. (2) The continued wicked practices that displease God lead to punishment. However, God does not always chasten his children for repeated acts of sin. He looks at the heart to determine an individual's attitude toward the sin. If a believer continually commits a sin, especially in direct rebellion to God, and demonstrates no remorse or ever seeks forgiveness, he stands in a position of judgment. An example is seen in the Corinthian church where believers who were dishonoring the Lord's Supper for an extended period of time were judged with sickness and even (physical death) (1 Cor. 11:29-31). Premature death for believers who repeatedly dishonored God apparently occurred more than once. This does not suggest that when a believer experiences a premature death in an accident or is struck down with a disease, he is judged by God. (3) The sin unto death may also occur to believers who commit a sin of such public notoriety, that discipline must be exercised to preserve the cause of Christ. Within the early church, such a sin occurred in Acts 5 where two believers made a promise to give to God the entire amount of money that they received from a business action. Having sold the property, Ananias and Sapphira withheld a portion of the money. When confronted by Peter with their deception, they lied, and divine judgment was executed.

The sin unto death should not be viewed solely as a dispensational truth, occurring only in the early church. God still reserves the right to exercise punishment upon any believer who flagrantly disregards the cause of Christ, and brings dishonor to the church.

XVII. SUMMARY

The doctrine of Hamartiology has utmost importance to the Christian. How he views sin will determine how he thinks and behaves. Sin is a transgression of the law, but it is more than stepping over the division between good and evil. Sin is also iniquity, an act that is inherently wrong. Sin is also a person's omission to do that which is right. As such sin can be an ignorant omission or commission. A person is born with a sinful nature that will motivate him to sin, and, even after he is converted, his sinful nature will still tempt him to sin. The sinful nature will not be eradicated with conversion; the convert will be tempted by his lust until death. At the resurrection, the believer will be given a glorified body which will not have a sinful nature. Sin was imputed to all people by Adam's sin, hence all are guilty and will die physically. Sin is a deed, thought or desire, and as such it can be defined as an attitude or an act. The person is born in a state of sin, with a sin nature and guilty because of imputation. Then he will commit acts of sin.

The Christian who properly understands the doctrine of sin realizes he is not perfect, nor will he have his sin nature eradicated. He should properly identify his lust and imperfections, and deal with them in a biblical manner. Yet, his sins should not make him pessimistic. Because he knows he can only get temporary victory over sin, he remains in contact with Christ, who is the source of victory.

A proper view of sin causes a Christian to grow toward maturity. He knows he cannot become a monk and run from sin, nor can he overcome sin through legalism or self flagellation. Sin is always with him, and as long as he lives. He will be tempted, and on occasions, he will fall. Yet, that thought does not destroy him. The promise of victory keeps him going. The desire to please God and grow in spiritual maturity is a constant challenge. Therefore, he lives to overcome sin, knowing in his struggle with sin he will become more mature.

ENDNOTES

1. Augustus Hopkins Strong, *Systematic Theology* (Valley Forge, PA: Judson Press, 1907), 533, 535.

2. Charles Hodge, *Systematic Theology* (Grand Rapids: Eerdmans, 1975), 2:117.

3. Ibid., 119.

4. Ibid., 121-122.

5. Robert L. Dabney, *Lectures in Systematic Theology* (Grand Rapids: Zondervan, 1975), 302.

6. Philip Schaff, *Creeds of Christendom*, (New York: Harper & Row, 1919), 3:530.

7. Ibid., 3:616-17.

8. Herman Hoeksema, *Reformed Dogmatics* (Grand Rapids: Reformed Free Publishing Association, 1966), 218-219.

9. *Lanser Catechism Westminster* (Confession of faith of the Presbyterian Church in the United States, 1965), 17, 20, 21.*

10. James Oliver Buswell, *A Systematic Theology of Christian Religion* (Grand Rapids: Zondervan, 1962), 274-75.
11. Hoeksema, 254.
12. Strong, 584-85.
13. Lewis Sperry Chafer, *Systematic Theology* (Dallas: Dallas Seminary Press, 1947), 2:236.
14. Louis Berkhof, *Systematic Theology* (Grand Rapids: Eerdmans, 1941), 223-24.
15. See Anthropology section for a study of the word "flesh." (1) The word "flesh" can mean the old nature, i.e. the sinful nature. It also means (2) skin, (3) physical body, (4) total inner man including the old and new nature, and (5) the total person including the physical and immaterial.
16. Hodge, 248.
17. Strong, 592.
18. Ibid., 585-87.
19. Hoeksema, 245.
20. Schaff, 3:678.
21. Strong, 146.
22. Hodge, 132.
23. Walter Bauer, *Orthodoxy and Heresy in Earliest Christianity*, ed. By Robert A. Kraft and Gerhard Krodel (Philadelphia: Fortress, 1934), 251.*
24. Hodge, 134.
25. Strong, 566.
26. Reinhold Niebuhr, *Nature and Destiny of Man* (New York: Charles Scribner's Sons, 1943), 1:186.
27. Strong, 567-70.
28. Dabney, 155-156.*
29. Hodge, 2:180-81.
30. William Wilson Stevens, *Doctrines of the Christian Religion* (Grand Rapids: Eerdmans, 1972), 153.
31. Hodge, 2:188-189.
32. Berkhof, 245-46.
33. Ibid., 246.
34. Hodge, 2:194-95.
35. Strong, 616-17.
36. Berkhof, 243.
37. Strong, 617.
38. Hodge, 2:213-14.
39. Dabney, 343-44.

40. Strong, 597.
41. Ibid., 600.
42. Ibid., 601-602.
43. Berkhof, 242-43.
44. Hodge, 198-199.
45. Strong, 614-15.
46. Ibid., 619-20.
47. Ibid., 630.
48. Hoeksema, 276-277.
49. Strong, 628.
50. A. C. Gaebelein, *The Gospel of Matthew* (Wheaton: Van Kampen Press, 1910), 250-51.

* Denotes page number(s) could not be verified.

CHAPTER XI - ANTHROPOLOGY

The Doctrine of Man

I. INTRODUCTION

Anthropology, from the Greek term *anthropos,* "man," indicates the study of man. This doctrine, like other theological doctrines, is pregnant with relevance and is essential in one's systematic understanding of Scripture. Even as the strength of a chain is determined by the cohesiveness of each link, likewise, the strength of one's theological system lies in the consistency and truthfulness of each doctrine.

One cannot view anthropology as a lesser doctrine, because that devalues the significance of God's crowning creation. As a matter of fact, the two anchor points of theology, like the two foundations of a cable bridge, are the doctrine of God and the doctrine of man. If these two areas are properly constructed, the theologian is building in the right direction.

Erickson summarizes the importance of anthropology with the following outline.[1]

(1) Anthropology interrelates to other major Christian doctrines, suggesting, of course, that anthropology complements other doctrines and, without it, the theologian cannot construct a consistent theological system.

(2) "The doctrine of man is important because it is a point where the biblical revelation and human concerns converge." Quoting Tillich, Erickson suggests that when witnessing to nonbelievers, a more practical approach may not be giving him propositional truths, but focusing on the empirical basis of man. While the author disagrees with giving this emphasis the primary focus of evangelism, he recognizes some contribution from it.

(3) Anthropology has achieved greater importance due to a great deal of attention given it by various intellectual disciplines. Whether one discusses sociology, psychology, ethics or any such disciplines, inevitably problems arise, such as absolutes, composition, and objectives. Such problems need to be addressed from a biblical perspective.

(4) "Because of the present crisis in man's self-understanding," the study of anthropology is important. As people struggle with the issue "What is man?" certain absolutes can be suggested in Scripture. Obviously, Scripture has not spoken in every area regarding man, nor has Scripture given all there is to know in each area. But its revelation cannot be ignored in attempting to understand man.

(5) One's perspective of anthropology will determine how he will minister to his fellow man. If man is viewed primarily from a physical perspective, then ministry will center on

human needs, usually via materialism. If man is considered a rational soul whose existence and purpose in life is found in God, then ministry will deal with man on a spiritual plane.

II. ORIGIN OF HUMANITY

As one deals with the origin of humanity, it is vital not to limit the study simply to the beginning of man upon the earth, rather consideration should also be given to the purpose of man's origin. Within the framework of purpose, the origin of man gives us a clearer and more complete description of his nature and mode of entrance upon the earth. (The ethical implications of Adam and Eve's placement in the Garden and the ensuing Fall, with all its moral overtones, will not be dealt with in this section. Rather, it is dealt with under the doctrine of Hamartiology.)

A. NATURALISM VERSUS SUPERNATURALISM. Two prominent and distinct views emerge in relation to the purpose of man's origin. Either there was a supernatural force(s), or there was simply a natural cause(s) to man's origination. Purpose denotes a force and an animating system. Within the theistic teaching, the force is God, and the animating system varies (various modes will be dealt with later). Atheists, who assign the origin of man to natural causes, argue that the force centers in the evolution of life from an initial cell to higher forms of life through survival of the fittest, and the life animating system of natural selection.

1. *Evolution*, according to atheists, provides the necessary principles to explain the origin of man upon the earth. The theory of evolution holds, not necessarily that man somehow descended from any kind of ape or monkey, but rather that probably he and they have arrived from a common ancestry. Man descended generally from the lower primates through natural processes, controlled entirely by inherent forces (a closed system).

However, several objections can be raised against the theory of evolution. (1) This theory of evolution, though often presented as an established fact, is up to the present time only an unverified hypothesis. Under the discipline of science, a theory must possess at least three essential properties to establish it as fact: data, observation and repeatability. Since evolution cannot demonstrate data linking evolution of one kind to another, or prove through data examination (such as fossils) a transition, then the evolutionary scheme remains a hypothesis. It should be noted that those who hold to the involvement of a supernatural force(s) in man's origin, also have only established a hypothesis, when examined in light of the prerequisites of science. (2) Science has utterly failed to discover any missing links between man and the supposed animals from which he originated. Despite the extensive excavation occurring around the world, there has at present been no conclusive data to link man's origin to the lower primates. (3) Furthermore, evolutionists argue that evolutionary trends occur through the processes of mutation. But this view fails to account for the increased complexity of man. Mutations are generally an inferior derivation, whereas man represents the apex of all living things. Man's ability to understand, comprehend and remember issues of morality, art, music, self-consciousness, and philosophy raises him above the primates. In addition, man can speak, interact with other men, enjoy and clearly create. All this distinguishes man from the lower primates. (4) Scientists have utterly failed to demonstrate or identify the origin of life (organic) from inorganic substances. Where did life begin? From a burning meteor? Perhaps from a pool of ooze? From hydrogen?

These observations are not intended to represent an exhaustive list of objections. Rather, the purpose is to reveal several major problems that must be answered, or the evolutionist has failed to adequately substantiate his hypothesis.

2. *Creation.* In contrast to natural explanations for man's origin, the theistic position assigns (in part or in total) the presence of man upon the earth to external factors (an open system). The theistic view engulfs nearly every religious system, for each system contains specific traditions or written dogma that in some manner accounts for man's origins. Due to the vastness of theories that explain the origin of man, it is necessary to limit this study to those views that deal with the Holy Scriptures.

a. Interpretation of the Genesis account of Creation. Despite the clarity with which Moses, under the power of the Holy Spirit, penned the creation account, there are those who strongly favor an historical approach to its interpretation. As one considers the many possible interpretations of Genesis 1 and 2, three prominent views emerge, while recognizing at the same time the presence of several minor differences. The first method of interpretation is summed up and captured in the works of Emil Brunner who interprets the Genesis account of man's creation as mythical. Brunner rejected an historical interpretation of Genesis, arguing that on external and internal grounds, it is best to understand the story of Adam and Eve in light of a parable. He does not believe in a literal Adam and Eve, saying this story has a mythical sense to pass on certain truths and principles. However, if one applies a mythical interpretation to Genesis, the questions arises as to why the author would include surnames and specific details? Why did the author of Genesis not simply use generic terms such as "a certain man."

Second, Cortis and (more recently) Karl Barth allow for the Genesis account to possess some historical importance. However, the real issue centers not on whether the serpent actually spoke, but what the serpent said. Using an allegorical approach to Genesis, Barth and others seek to extract more of a symbolic message, than an historical, grammatical, and literal interpretation. Cortis summarizes the allegorical method as "redemptive meaning," but in the final analysis, it is not historical.

The rib, the tree, the apple, the serpent, are a picturesque way of talking, that is all, and just the kind of language men would everywhere use had we dared to keep close to the glory of our childhood. That there may be no chance for misunderstanding, I will give an analytical statement of my full view: 1. This scriptural account of the creation and fall of man is a record of historic facts. 2. These facts are given in naïve dramatic form—"the primitive style of narration characteristic of the age in which it was written." 3. The account was handed down from the beginning as a world-tradition based upon an original revelation from God. 4. This world-tradition was, at last, under the inspiration of the Holy Spirit, *cleansed* (an examination of the traditions in the ethnic religions will show how necessary such a cleansing came to be), *cleansed* for a redemptional use. 5. As thus cleansed, this world-tradition was established in the canon by the Holy Spirit. 6. Thus, what we have is a world-tradition cleansed and endorsed by the Holy Spirit for its redemptional meaning.[2]

The third view is a literal or historical method of interpretation. It permits the Scriptures to speak for themselves. The context does not suggest the tree was anything but a tree. The serpent likewise is understood as a literal serpent; therefore a rigid interpretation is understood in light of the historical meaning in the mind of the author. The literal or normal approach affords an objective basis and greater harmony with Scripture and the testimony of other biblical writers. Any support for the literal approach should be considered as an inherent weakness with the other views. (1) The literal approach, from a hermeneutical viewpoint, achieves greater support. As indicated earlier, the context of Genesis does not employ symbolic language, nor suggests anything but a normal interpretation. (2) The apostle Paul on several occasions referred to Adam (Rom. 5; 1 Cor. 15) not as a mythical or symbolic personage, but rather as a definite historical person. Paul contrasted the introduction of sin by the first Adam with the introduction of righteousness by the Second Adam. If Adam is considered a mere symbol, how should we understand the Second Adam, namely Christ?

b. Possible methods of human origins. Within the context of Christianity four major views have been proposed to explain the method used by God to give life to man. These four are arrived at by having discarded all anti-supernatural theories, and by further limiting oneself to a literal interpretation of Scripture. However, as evidenced in other doctrinal controversies, whenever Scripture fails to offer a detailed description and explanation of occurring events, the speculative mind of man intervenes and attempts to fill in the possible gaps.

(1) Fiat Creationism. Typically conservative orthodoxy has tended to support this view. Basically, fiat creationism holds that God, by direct acts, brought into being virtually everything that exists. No previously existing material or biological mechanism has ever or will ever be employed by God to create matter. Virtually everything that exists, was created *ex-nihilo* (out of nothing).

It is apparent that those who believe in fiat creation have no difficulty in accepting the biblical account of creation in Genesis 1. The claim that God produced each animal and plant after its own kind has traditionally been interpreted as meaning that He created each species individually. One minor weakness with this view is apparent in the creation of man's material part. According to Scripture, God created mediately (not immediately—without any previous substance) the body of man from the earth. Furthermore, fiat creationists endorse a brief period of time for the creative process, hence the seven days of creation are considered seven twenty-four hour days.

(2) Deistic Evolution.   This view basically claims that God began the process of evolution within the context of created matter. Though God programmed the system, simple life forms were allowed to evolve into more complex life structures. During this entire process, God withdrew Himself from His creation, and allowed the ordained natural laws to guide the creative process. In this view, God is Creator of everything. As Creator emeritus, He is free of any direct creation since His initial act. In relationship to the evolutionary hypothesis, this view possesses no major difficulties. However, there is a definite conflict between the deistic view of an absentee God and the biblical picture of a God who has been involved in creative acts and the sustaining of His world. Through detaching God from His creation, this view appears to make God insensitive and uncaring for His creatures and tends to acquiesce to contemporary scientific objections to creationism. But most importantly, it overlooks the harmony of God's creative work with His redemptive plan.

(3) Theistic Evolution.   Similar in certain respects to deism, theistic evolution teaches that God began the creative process by bringing the first organism to life. He then discontinued His supernatural works, though He intervened to modify the process, and to insure the successful evolutionary trends. Unlike the deistic evolutionists who limit God's involvement to the initial life-giving force, the theistic evolutionists teach that God, as a necessary factor, has occasionally intervened to aid the evolutionary process. Through God's agency, major gaps that breach a specific kind or species are the direct result of His intervention. Any view that allows for macro-evolution (interkind development) as opposed to micro-evolution (intrakind development) fails to recognize the important data of mendelism (the science of genetics) which corroborates the Genesis record of "after their kind." Theistic evolutionism also overlooks the many complications associated with the evolutionary theory. Natural processes, except where personal intelligence intervenes, tend toward the simple and homogenous, rather than toward higher and more complex forms of life. Furthermore, the presence of evolutionary principles devalues the significance of man being created in the image of God. Finally, a literal interpretation of Scripture demands a direct creation of man by God, rather than allowing for evolutionary processes. The evolutionary scheme forces a symbolic approach to Scripture. Most theistic evolutionists misinterpret "dust," by which

man was created, to mean a lower form of life, rather than the fact that man was actually created from actual dirt.

(4) Progressive Creationism. This view combines the view of specific *de novo* (fresh or from nothing) creative acts with in-moment or processive operations of life. As outlined in Scripture, God at several times created *de novo* the heavens, the earth, the fish, the various kinds or species of animals, and man as the crown of His creation. There is no need to have any forms of macro-evolution. Each species is distinctly different from the other as ordained and created by God. Progressive creation also allows for limited degrees of evolution within a specific species. For instance, a great deal of debate arose over the ability of white moths in England to evolve into gray colored moths. Initially, the evolutionary scientists captured this observation and heralded it as definite proof of evolution (macro-evolution). Before the print dried on their scientific investigative reports, those rejecting evolution objected to their findings, arguing that this transformation of the moth's color does not prove macro-evolution, rather micro-evolution. What happened in England with the moth was primarily an environmental change. Prior to the industrial revolution, the white moths were able to camouflage themselves in the flowery scrubs. With the industrial revolution, there also came hundreds of smokestacks belching out soot which colored the landscape a dingy gray. In order to disguise themselves, the moths adapted (micro-evolution) to their surroundings. To assert, as those scientist did, that micro-evolution proves the validity of macro-evolution greatly prevents true scientific research.

From these four possibilities, the first (fiat creation) and the last (progressive creation) are in closer harmony with the testimony of Scripture. Both views agree in maintaining that the entirety of man's nature and the various species were specially created. They differ in regard to any development after the initial act of creation. Fiat creationism teaches that there has been no development whatsoever, whereas progressive creationism allows for limited developments within specific species. In relation to the Genesis account of creation, both views possess no difficulties, where Scripture is interpreted literally. Berkhof briefly sums up the different words used for the creation of man, and from an etymological vantage, the beliefs of the Christian are further substantiated.

> In the narrative of creation . . . three verbs are used, namely, *bará, asah,* and *yatsar,* and they are used interchangeably in Scripture, Gen. 1:26, 27; 2:7. The first word is the most important. Its original meaning is *to split, to cut, to divide;* but in addition to this it also means *to fashion, to create,* and in a more derivative sense, *to produce, to generate,* and *to regenerate.* The word itself does not convey the idea of bringing forth something out of nothing. . . . Yet it has a distinctive character: it is always used of divine and never of human production; and it never has an accusative of material. The word *asah* is more general, meaning *to do* or *to make,* and is therefore used in the general sense of *doing, making, manufacturing,* or *fashioning.* The word

yatsar has, more distinctively, the meaning of *fashioning out of pre-existent materials*, and is therefore used of the potter's fashioning vessels out of clay.[3]

Having established the most likely method of man's origin upon the earth, it is necessary to address the approximate time of man's origin from a scientific approach and from a biblical perspective.

III. TIME OF MAN'S ORIGIN

At first glance, this issue may appear somewhat irrelevant. Who cares if mankind is about 6,000 years old or perhaps several million? However, if conclusive evidence could be gathered to suggest a greater probability for a possible brief amount of time or a much longer period of time, it logically follows that the other view becomes suspect. To approach this issue, we will examine the methods employed by scientists to determine the antiquity of man, and what Scripture may offer concerning the age of man.

A. SCIENTIFIC APPROACH. The *Origin of the Species*, written in 1859 by Charles Darwin, became the catalyst for study and evaluation of various possibilities for man's origin. This is not to suggest that the biblical account of creation was the only view endorsed by man prior to Darwin. Rather, Darwin's book came at a time in history when rationalists were questioning the authenticity of Scripture, and science was being used in more areas for research and exploration. From a hundred-year vantage, the enlightenment and the effects of rationalistic skeptics had prepared the necessary environment for the evolutionary theory to gain rapid acceptance. During that time and in successive generations, the saints of God were so inundated with new finds, potential problems with Scripture, and significant advancements in science that many either rejected wholeheartedly the claims of science or accepted the theory of evolution. Many attempted to merge together the scientific discoveries with Scripture producing such views as theistic evolution, pictorial revelatory day (creation was revealed on seven days) and the six creative days theory (which suggests that the days were not literal twenty-four-hour days, but they were extended periods of time).

Now that much of the fervor attached to the evolutionary hypothesis has subsided, true scientific works have also discovered that the evolutionary theory has some basic inconsistencies and is unable to substantiate its claims.

In regards to the antiquity of man, evolutionists initially claimed that man was several million years old, and the earth was several billion years old, Yet as there is a closer examination of the scientific data for the antiquity of man, scientists are having to admit that their earlier estimates may have been somewhat exaggerated.

Several different methods have been advanced by the evolutionists to substantiate the longevity of man upon the earth. (1) The identification of human remains in fossil deposits help geologists assign an age to man that is consistent with fossil age. As one examines the data available, he soon discovers many problems.   Attempts by scientists to construct a prehistoric man from a mere bone is definitely suspect.   Recent discoveries of entire skeletons imbedded in limestone near Guadaloupe, in which the age is only about two hundred years old, have shown that it does not take millions of years for bones to fossilize. (2) Carbon 14 dating has been another method for determining the age of man.   However, the reliability of this test is uncertain.   If the object being tested by the Carbon 14 method maintained a consistent level of deterioration, then it is possible to substantiate a particular age.   Since no substance maintains a constant deterioration level, the Carbon 14 test is not always valid. Tests given by two separate scientists using the same substance have frequently yielded radically divergent dates.   Many other tests, such as the early separation of the races, the discoveries in ancient villages, the development of language, and the role of tool-making have all been used to determine the age of man.   In each instance the exact age of man is uncertain, suggesting that scientists cannot always supply all the answers, nor are their observations reliable.

B. BIBLICAL APPROACH.   Regarding the exact antiquity of man, it must be admitted that the Bible offers no exact age of man, even though some try to prove an exact date from internal Scriptural data.   When God created the world and man, He created them with an appearance of age.   The world was created with apparent age and man was not created as an infant.   It should be noted that the biblical data tends to support a shorter period of time for man's presence upon the earth, as opposed to the much longer period insisted on by evolutionists.

Many well-intended saints have attempted to allow their theological perspective to determine to some extent their understanding of the antiquity of man.   Employing the dates derived by Archbishop Usher (1581-1656), and the New Testament notion that "a day with the Lord is as a thousand years with man," some saints of God have determined not only the antiquity of man, but also provided suggestions for eschatology.   Their argument essentially rests upon the notion that seven is the number of completion.   According to Usher's chronology, man was created in 4004 B.C. (the Old Testament would represent four days), and since the time of Christ it has been nearly 2,000 years (the New Testament would represent two days).   After the return of Christ man will continue to live on the earth for 1,000 years (the seventh and final day), a very neat system that appears to support creation in 4004 B.C.

Usher's chronology was never intended to represent an absolute time, only a possible estimate.

Usher never intended his dates to be accepted as solidly based upon revealed information. For example, Usher disregarded Acts 7:4 in analyzing Genesis 11:26-14:2. He further disregarded the fact that the last verses of the eleventh chapter are in a transition between records which largely involve families or dynasties (chapters 10 and 11) and records which, in the large, clearly have to do with individuals (chapters 12 ff).

Though overlooking the possible distinctions between dynasties and individuals, the presence of gaps in the genealogies, certain omissions, various usages attached to the word son, and the exact meaning of "begat," one cannot seriously consider Usher's estimate as being even remotely accurate. B. B. Warfield, a more outspoken opponent to Usher's timetable, remarks,

In a word, the Scriptural data leave us wholly without guidance in estimating time which elapsed between the creation of the world and the deluge and between the deluge and the call of Abraham. So far as the Scripture assertions are concerned, we may suppose any length of time to have intervened between these events which may otherwise appear reasonable.[4]

According to Buswell, an accurate understanding of the genealogies of Genesis must include a recognition of two principle truths.

In other words, I believe the most reasonable interpretation of the genealogies of Genesis 5 and 11 requires us to recognize (1) that the names are selected without any indication of gaps or absence of gaps, and (2) that most of the names, if not all, are names of families or dynasties, as well as individuals.[5]

W. H. Green also rejects Usher's chronology.

It must not be forgotten that there is an element of uncertainty in a computation of time which rests upon genealogies as the sacred chronology so largely does. Who is to certify us that the antediluvian and ante-Abrahamic genealogies have not been condensed in the same manner as the post-Abrahamic. If Matthew omitted names from the ancestry of our Lord in order to equalize the three great periods over which he passes, may not Moses have done the same in order to bring out seven generations from Adam to Enoch, and ten from Adam to Noah? Our current chronology is based upon the *prima facie* impression of these genealogies. This we shall adhere to until we shall see good reason for giving it up. But if these recently discovered indications of the antiquity of man, over which scientific circles are now so excited, shall, when carefully inspected and thoroughly weighed, demonstrate all that any have imagined they might demonstrate, what then? They will simply show that the popular chronology is based upon a wrong interpretation, and that a select and partial register of ante-Abrahamic names has been mistaken for a complete one.[6]

IV. THEOLOGICAL SIGNIFICANCE OF MAN'S ORIGIN

Having connected the origin of man to God, an event which occurred sometime in the past (possibly 10,000 to 30,000 years ago), it is needful to examine the theological ramifications of this view. Erickson has developed eight important truths for our consideration, truths that should determine how we respond to God, our fellow man, and ourselves, in light of the fact that God created man.[7]

A. THAT MAN WAS CREATED MEANS THAT HE HAS NO INDEPENDENT EXISTENCE. He came into being because God willed that he should exist and acted to bring him into being. Man has received his life from God and continues to experience and enjoy life because of divine provision. There is nothing necessary about his existence. Man is a contingent being, not an indispensable part of reality. Nor does man ever come to the point where he is truly independent of God.

B. MAN IS PART OF THE CREATION. As different as man is from God's other created beings, he is not so sharply distinguished from the rest of them as to have no relationship to them. He is part of the sequence of creation, as are the other beings. He was brought into existence on one of the days of creation, as were the others.

C. MAN, HOWEVER, HAS A UNIQUE PLACE IN THE CREATION. There is an element which makes him unique, which sets him apart from the rest of the creatures. The rest of creation is said to be made "according to their kind." Man, on the other hand, is described as being made in the image and likeness of God. He is placed over the rest of the creation, to have dominion over it. He cannot in every respect be likened to the whole of creation. While subject to the laws governing created beings, he transcends those other beings and their status, for there is more to humanity than just creaturehood. Man cannot restrict his self-understanding to his creaturehood, or excuse his improper behavior by blaming instincts and drives. There is a higher level to his being, a level which sets him apart from the rest of the creation.

D. THERE IS A BROTHERHOOD AMONG MEN. The doctrine of creation and of the descent of the entire human race from one original pair means that we are all related to one another. In a sense, each of us is a distant cousin to everyone else on this earth. We are not totally unrelated. The negative side of our common descent is that in the natural state all persons are rebellious children of the heavenly Father, and thus are estranged from Him and from one another. We are all like the prodigal son.

E. MAN IS NOT THE HIGHEST OBJECT IN THE UNIVERSE. Man's value is great, for he is, with the exception of the angels, the highest of the creatures. This status is conferred upon him, however, by the highest Being, God. For all of the respect which we have for humanity, and the special recognition which we accord to humans of distinction or accomplishment, we must always remember that they, their lives, their abilities, their strengths, have been given by God. We must never elevate our respect for humans to the point of virtually worshiping them. Worship is to be given to God alone; when offered to any other person or object, it is idolatry. We must be careful to give the ultimate credit and glory to God.

F. THERE ARE DEFINITE LIMITATIONS UPON MAN. Man is a creature, not God, and has the limitations that go with being finite. Only the Creator is infinite. Man does not and cannot know everything. While we ought to seek to know all that we can, and ought to admire and esteem great knowledge wherever it is possessed and displayed, our finiteness means that our knowledge will always be incomplete and subject to error.

G. PROPER ADJUSTMENT IN LIFE. This can be achieved only on the basis of acceptance of one's own finiteness.

H. MAN IS, NONETHELESS, SOMETHING WONDERFUL. Although a creature, man is the highest among them, the only one made in the image of God. The fact that he has been made by the Lord of the entire universe simply adds to the grandeur of the human by giving him a trademark as it were. Man is not simply a chance production of a blind mechanism, or a byproduct or scraps thrown off in the process of making something better. He is an expressly designed product of God. (Erickson, pp. 487-493.)

V. UNITY OF HUMANITY

Another issue of contention between the scientific community and the claims of Scripture centers on the topic of man's inherent unity. Has all mankind had a common origin? Have all descended from a single pair, and do they constitute a single species? Is there a common element to man's nature? Questions of this nature strike deep into the very nature of man and his relation to others.

The Bible clearly asserts that all men have descended from a single pair. Evolutionists, on the other hand, argue that the many variations in man's anatomy, religion, and language might suggest several different species. The ancient Greeks taught the theory of autochthonism, a fallacious view which taught that man sprang from the earth by a sort of spontaneous generation. In 1655 Peyrerius developed the position that the different races stem from men who existed prior to Adam. Peyrerius' view, known as "Preadamites," strongly suggested that Adam was the first ancestor of the Jews, and not necessarily the head of the human race.

Louis Agassiz, a prominent objector to the idea of unity of the human race, argued that there were separate and distinct origins for the human race, all created equally by God. Agassiz, although openly opposed to evolution, was a devout theist. His theory, entitled "Coadamites," assumed there were various focuses of creation, and humanity did not come from a single catalyst, but many.

Attempts have been made to enumerate the number of possible species. The numbers vary greatly. However, most evidence suggests a single origin. In order to understand the nature of man's unity, it is necessary to examine the characteristics of a distinct species, possible definitions, and the arguments that endorse the notion that the race is a unity.

A. CHARACTERISTICS OF A SPECIES. Charles Hodge, in his treatise on anthropology, argues that there are three characteristics of every species which sets it apart from other species.

> (1.) Originality, i. e., they owe their existence and character to immediate creation. They are not produced by physical causes, nor are they ever derived from other genera or species. They are original forms. This is admitted by naturalists of all classes. Such is the doctrine of Cuvier, Agassiz, Dr. Morton, and of those who hold that the varieties of the human race are so many distinct species. They mean by this that they had different origins, and are not all derived from a common stock. Every species therefore, by general consent, has had a single origin. (2.) Universality, i. e., all the individuals and varieties belonging to the same species have all its essential characteristics. Wherever you find the teeth of a carnivorous animal, you find a stomach able to digest animal food, and claws adapted to seize and hold prey. Wherever you find fins to effect motion in water, you find a breathing apparatus suited to the same element. The species is transmitted whole and entire. It is the same in all individuals belonging to it, and in that sense universal. (3.) Immutability, or permanence. By this is meant first, that one species is never lost or merged in another; and secondly, that two or more species never combine so as to produce a third. The rose cannot be merged into the tulip; nor can the rose and tulip be made to produce a new species, which is neither the one nor the other. The only permanent transmissible forms of organic life, are such as constitute distinct species.[8]

B. DEFINITION OF A SPECIES. While maintaining the three distinct characteristics of a species (originality, universality, and immutability) a definition of a species is necessary. Frequently anthropologists have limited the concept of a species to external factors only, with little or no consideration to the immaterial aspect. If an animal looked and behaved differently from any other animal, it was deemed a unique and separate species. It is only when both the external and immaterial aspects are considered that a clearer definition of a species emerges. Louis Agassiz, in commenting on the significance of the immaterial aspect, writes,

> Besides the distinctions to be derived from the varied structure of organs, there are others less subject to rigid analysis, but no less decisive, to be drawn from the immaterial principle, with which every animal is endowed. It is this which determines the constancy of species from generation to generation, and which is the source of all the varied exhibitions of instinct and intelligence which we see displayed, from the simple impulse to receive the food which is brought within their reach, as observed in the polyps, through the higher manifestations, in the cunning fox, the sagacious elephant, the faithful dog, and the exalted intellect of man, which is capable of indefinite expansion.[9]

Therefore, a species can be properly defined as a form of life that demonstrates the characteristics of originality, universality, and immutability in regards to its entire being, or, more specifically to its material and immaterial aspects.

C. ARGUMENTS FOR THE UNITY OF MAN. Applying the characteristics and the definition of a species to man, it is no surprise that man clearly qualifies as a species. Five separate arguments demonstrate quite clearly the validity of man being a distinct unity.

1. *The historical argument.* Basically this argument contends that man has not, from an historical vantage, altered or evolved from a separate species to his current status, or is even now changing to a different species. Opponents would argue that sufficient time has not elapsed for man to detect any noticeable alterations. However, even when employing conservative figures for the number of years in which man has been upon the earth, there have been absolutely no changes. Commenting on this point, Hodge writes,

> (1.) The historical fact that all known species of plants and animals are now precisely what they were as far back as history reaches. The Bible and the records on the Egyptian monuments carry us back to a point thousands of years before the birth of Christ. During this whole period of five or six thousand years species have remained the same. (2.) If we are to receive the facts of geology as authenticated, it is clear that the same permanence has existed from the very beginning of life on our globe. As long as any species exists at all, it exists unchanged in all that is essential to it. (3.) There is an entire and acknowledged absence of all evidence of transmutation; none of the transition points or links of connection between one species and another is anywhere discoverable. (4.) If species were not thus immutable, the animal and vegetable world instead of presenting the beautiful order everywhere visible, would

exhibit a perfect chaos of all organic life. (5.) Notwithstanding the ingenious and long continued efforts to render hybrids prolific, such attempts have uniformly failed.[10]

2. *Physiological and organic argument.* Within the soma ("body") or the material aspect of man, there exists a structure totally unique to the human race. To this area of study belong all the intricate functions of the human body, such as the circulation of blood, nerve patterns, respiration, muscle control, propagation, and much more. Admittedly, there are some structural similarities between man and other species, but the focus is not upon the similarities, but upon the many distinctives which clearly separate man from all other species.

3. *Psychological argument.* From man's immaterial part, the principle of the uniqueness of the human soul in the human species surfaces. Commenting on this point, Hodge writes,

The ψυχή [psuche] is the immaterial principle which belongs to all animals, and is the same in kind in every distinct species. It is that in which the life resides; which is the seat of the instincts, and of that measure of intelligence, be it greater or less, which belongs to the animal. The ψυχή is the same in all the individuals of the same species, and it is permanent. The instincts and habits of the bee, the wasp, the ant, and the beaver; of the lion, tiger, wolf, fox, horse, dog, and ox; and of all the endless diversities of beasts, birds, fishes, and insects, are the same in all ages and in all parts of the world. This immaterial principle is of a higher order in some cases than in others, and admits of greater or lesser degrees of culture, as seen in the trained elephant or well-disciplined pointer. But the main thing is that each species has its own ψυχή and that this is a higher element and more decisive evidence of identity than the corporeal structure or even the φύσις, or animal nature. Where these three criteria concur, where the corporeal organization, in everything indicative of design, is the same; where the φύσις, and the ψυχή the physical and psychological natures, are the same, there, beyond all reasonable doubt, the species is the same. . . .

. . . .

There can be no reasonable doubt that the souls of all men are essentially the same. They not only have in common all the appetites, instincts, and passions, which belong to the souls of the lower animals, but they all share in those higher attributes which belong exclusively to man. They all are endowed with reason, conscience, and free agency. They all have the same constitutional principles and affections. They all stand in the same relation to God as spirits possessing a moral and religious nature.[11]

4. *Argument of propagation.* The ability of man as a race to maintain permanence

through the ability of indefinite propagation attests to his unity. Expounding upon this point, Hodge explains,

> We have seen that it is a law of nature, recognized by all naturalists (with a few recent exceptions), that animals of different species do not cohabit, and cannot propagate. Where the species are nearly allied, as the horse and the ass, they may produce offspring combining the peculiarities of both parents. But there the process stops. Mules cannot continue the mongrel race. It is however an admitted fact that men of every race, Caucasian, Mongolian, and African, can thus cohabit, and their offspring can be indefinitely propagated and combined.[12]

5. *Argument of philology.* Comparative philology (study of languages) points to an apparent common origin of all the more important languages, and further suggests that there is no evidence that the lesser important languages did not likewise stem from one language. By demonstrating that all languages are traceable to one dialect, this argument, though not conclusive, tends to illustrate the idea that there was only one initial pair, rather than several.

When juxtaposed, the arguments for the unity of man develop a formidable position, which strongly favors the biblical truth that humanity stems from a single pair and represents a distinct species.

VI. Universality Of Humanity

Designated as a specific species, human beings enjoy those properties of humanity uniquely ascribed to the human race. The ability of man to discern and know God serves as the fundamental trait distinguishing man from other forms of life. Despite the obvious simplicity of this claim, there are those who seek, whether in theory or practice, to segregate or take away the rights and privileges of various classes of society. It is necessary to combat these erroneous views about man. Special status is afforded to every human by God, and is indeed extended to every member of this human race.

A. ALL RACES. Every society seems to possess some inherent prejudices against at least one racial group. The principle object of prejudices in the U.S. has been the black race. Feelings of white supremacy have largely been responsible for the distorted concept about blacks in particular and humanity in general. In isolated examples, some clergy have suggested in part the superiority of the white race over the black race (*Is God a White Racist?* by William Jones).[13]

Those who argue for the existence of structured races (superior vs. inferior) have, in addition to employing anthropology, endorsed their views with Scripture. Their faulty reasoning is twofold, (1) slavery is not only taught in Scripture, but Scripture also establishes certain guidelines for masters in regard to their slaves, and slaves to their masters (Eph. 6:5-9).

(2) Secondly, they wrongly argue that Ham, as Noah's son, was cursed by God. The curse not only included the darkening of his skin, they argue, but also the burden of servitude. There have been some attempts to deny that blacks have souls or that they are a different species from man, or that Adam is the father of only the white race. These distorted views reveal the blinded or evil intents of men to pervert God's creative works.

Several problems occur within the preceding arguments which are used to deny the universality of humanity: (1) Scripture never once teaches that races possess differing levels of humanity. All men are positionally equal in the sight of God. (2) If we were to accept the idea that one's function determined the level of his humanity, then there are no complete humans, for every race, at one time or another or in one area or another, excels in function.

B. BOTH SEXES. History reveals a rather bleak picture of the male's attitude toward the person and function of the woman. Determined unworthy to vote, incapable of managing political and military strategy, and at times deemed only slightly more valuable than the animals that roam the hills, woman has in many generations suffered a terrible perversion of God's original intention.

Even well-intended clergy have grossly misinterpreted passages of Scripture that deal exclusively with the functional distinctions between males and females, and have taught that women are inferior to their male counterparts.

However, as one reexamines the Genesis narrative, Eve assumed a place of equal footing in the garden with her husband, and was greatly extolled for her virtues as a helpmate and her ability of propagation. She was not inferior as a person, but was equal with her husband before God. Their only difference existed in the job-related duties. Eve, as a helpmate, lovingly served Adam within a domestic context. On the other hand, Adam served Eve through provision and protection. Through serving each other, they deepened their love for each other, developed mutual respect, and esteemed highly the other above self.

VII. ORIGINAL CREATION OF MAN IN THE IMAGE OF GOD

The sixth day of creation brought forth one of the clearest demonstrations of God's creative power, when God created man. Immediately following each day of creation God "saw that it was good." But after the creation of man, God saw that it was "very good" (Gen. 1:31).

Within the garden, Adam and Eve enjoyed themselves in nature's created beauty. Their sinless nature allowed them to enjoy and experience fully their surroundings. They had direct communication with God. The image of God was fully recognized in them, affording them certain abilities that man after the Fall cannot fully experience. In regard to the image of God in man, theologians, philosophers, rationalists, and laymen have all attempted to describe its nature and function. Many different views have been developed. If man is to understand to some extent what is the image of God, he must of necessity stand firmly and solely upon Scripture. The teaching of the *imago Dei* is strictly a biblical concept.

According to the Genesis account of the image of God, it is restricted to the immaterial nature of man. There are those who extend the image to the material aspect of man (views which will be dealt with later), but Scripture asserts otherwise. "And the LORD God formed man of the dust of the ground [material], and breathed into his nostrils the breath of life; and man became a living soul" (Gen. 2:7). "And God said, Let us make man in our image, after our likeness: and let them have dominion over the fish of the sea, and over the fowl of the air, and over the cattle, and over all the earth, and over every creeping thing that creepeth upon the earth. So God created man in his own image, in the image of God created he him; male and female created he them" (Gen, 1:26-27).

A. A USAGE OF TERMS FOR THE IMAGE OF GOD. In the Genesis account of man's creation, two separate words are used in connection with the image of God. The word *tselem* translated "image," and *demuth*, translated "likeness" are interpreted by some to be two different words with two different meanings. Others interpret the two words as Hebrew parallelism, where both words refer to the same thing. Berkhof examines the two words,

> The terms "image" and "likeness" have been distinguished in various ways. Some were of the opinion that "image" had reference to the body, and "likeness," to the soul. Augustine held that the former referred to the intellectual, and the latter, to the moral faculties of the soul. Bellarmin regarded "image" as a designation of the natural gifts of man, and "likeness" as a designation of that which was supernaturally added to man. Still others asserted that "image" denoted the inborn, and "likeness," the acquired conformity to God. It is far more likely, however, as was pointed out in the preceding, that both words express the same idea, and that "likeness" is merely an epexegetical addition to designate the image as most like or very similar.[14]

Commenting on this same issue, Stevens remarks,

> The Hebrew words "image" (*tselem*), and "likeness" (*demuth*) mean nothing more nor less in the context than their English equivalents. The LXX translates *tselem* with the corresponding Greek word *eikon*, and *demuth* with the corresponding word *homoisis*. Whereas there is literally a distinction between an image and a likeness, the latter word being a broader and more inclusive one, yet it is futile to attempt to make any precise distinctions between the two words as they are found in this context. Parallel words to give essentially the same thought are a familiar Hebrew mode of expression. The meaning of the passage obviously is that man is created to resemble God in some important ways.[15]

Whether one uses the word "image" or "likeness," the significant issue to bear in mind is that the image does not have any materialistic properties. The image of God is restricted to man's immaterial part. The truth can best be illustrated with a mirror. As one stares into the mirror a reflected image appears. The image is not physical, it is simply a reflection. Man is a reflection of God. Just as the mirror portrays a likeness of the one standing in front of it, man's immaterial nature is a reflection, or image, of God. Stevens, in quoting the *Westminster Confession of Faith*, writes,

> The Westminster Confession of Faith elaborates this doctrine in the following paragraph: "After God had made all other creatures, he created man, male and female, with reasonable and immortal souls, endued with knowledge, righteousness, and true holiness, after his own image, having the law of God written in their hearts, and power to fulfil it; and yet under a possibility of transgressing, being left to the liberty of their own will, which was subject unto change. Beside this law written in their hearts, they received a command not to eat of the tree of the knowledge of good and evil: which while they kept, they were happy in their communion with God, and had dominion over the creatures.[16]

B. RELATIONSHIP OF THE IMAGE OF GOD TO MAN'S IMMATERIAL NATURE.   Having established that the image of God is, (1) limited to man's immaterial nature, and (2) serves simply to reflect specific attributes of God, it is necessary to determine the interrelationship of man's immaterial nature to the image of God. Does the image of God comprise the entire immaterial nature of man, or does it represent just a part of his nature? First, the image of God is not synonymous with man's immaterial nature. Animals, angels, and man (as forms of life) share certain immaterial characteristics, yet only man is fashioned in God's image. If these universal immaterial characteristics are discovered in different types of life forms, it suggests that man, in addition to possessing the image of God, also possesses immaterial functions apart from the image of God. Yet, as we will examine later, the image of God is an essential part of man's immaterial nature, though not exclusively limited to it. Dabney, a Reformed theologian, argues that the image of God is not an essential part of man's nature.

> This image has been lost, in the fall, and regained, in redemption. Hence, it could not have consisted in anything absolutely essential to man's essence, because the loss of such an attribute would have destroyed man's nature.[17]

Dabney makes several errors. First, he presumes that the unregenerate person does not possess the image of God. However, as will be shown later, every man is fashioned in the image of God. It is an inseparable part of man's nature. Secondly, Dabney fails to discern the distinctions between the essential and nonessential elements in the image of God. Berkhof clarifies the issue.

In connection with the question of whether the image of God belongs to the very essence of man, Reformed theology does not hesitate to say that it constitutes the essence of man. It distinguishes however, between those elements in the image of God, which man cannot lose without ceasing to be man, consisting in the essential qualities and powers of the human soul; and those elements which man can lose and still remain man, namely, the good ethical qualities of the soul and its powers. The image of God in this restricted sense is identical with what is called original righteousness.[18]

C. WHAT THE IMAGE OF GOD DOES NOT SEEM TO BE.

(1) It is not physical. There have been those who taught that the image of God possesses substantive properties, as discovered in man's body. Although this view has not received wide acceptance, it has nonetheless persisted. Applying a concrete sense to the word "image" they interpret it as "statue" or "form." The major proponents of this view from a contemporary vantage are the Mormons. In order to harmonize this view with their concept of God, the Mormons would have to necessarily argue that God has a body, a position they are willing to accept. Challenging this position, Stevens rejects the notion that God has a physical body.

> First of all we may say emphatically that the image of God in man does not in any sense consist of a physical resemblance of form. Since God is essentially an incorporeal Spirit, it would be a contradiction in terms to maintain that man's physical being in any way resembles the being of God. True, the Second Person of the Trinity "became flesh and dwelt among us" (Jn. 1:14). And the Father sent Him forth "in the likeness of sinful flesh" (Rom. 8:3), and as our Redeemer, He took to Himself our nature of flesh and blood and was made "in all points like to His brethren" (Heb. 2:14-18). Yet in all these references to the incarnation it is Christ who takes our likeness. Never is there a suggestion in the Scripture that our physical nature is in any way an aspect of the image of God in us.[19]

(2) It is not merely man's rational or moral abilities. The ancient Greeks are credited with interpreting the image of God as the natural gift of reason. This position was later supported by the Pelagians. Eventually it was refined by Schleiermacher, who extended the image of God to man's total personality, including will, emotions, and intellect (reason). Man's biological designation as a *homo sapiea* (thinking person) further supports this view. In response to this position, Strong offers a major objection.

> A likeness to God in mere personality, such as Satan also possesses, comes far short of answering the demands of the Scripture, in which the ethical conception of

the divine nature so overshadows the merely natural. The image of God must be, not simply ability to be like God, but actual likeness.[20]

(3) It is not man's ability to have dominion. According to the Socinians, the image of God consisted in man's dominion over the lower creation. Early in Genesis, the image of God is introduced, and almost immediately man is given dominion over creation and told to "subdue" it. Hence the connection between dominion and the image of God, as Stevens suggests.

> As the authors of the Westminster Shorter Catechism have noted, the context in Genesis chapters one and two in which the doctrine of the image of God is announced, implies that man was created to be like God in exercising dominion over the creation as God's vice-regent under the Divine Providence. Not only do we have this fact clearly stated in Genesis 1:26-28 quoted above, but the same fact is referred to in numerous other portions of Scripture. Before sin came into the world, God had said "Be fruitful and multiply and fill ye the earth and subdue it and have dominion. . . ." (Genesis 1:28), but long after sin had come into the world, after the judgment of the world by flood, the divinely intended dominion of man over the creation is re-asserted and re-emphasized as recorded in Gen. 8:15-9:17. See especially 9:1,2. Man's position in the creation is stated again in connection with the doctrine of the image of God in him. "Whoso sheddeth man's blood, by man shall his blood he shed; for in the image of God made He man. And you be fruitful and multiply. Bring forth abundantly in the earth and multiply therein" (Gen. 9:6,7). The dominion which man is intended to exercise is magnificently brought out in the eighth Psalm, ... "Thou madest him to have dominion over the works of thy hands; thou hast put all things under his feet" (Psa. 8:4-9).[21]

It is impossible to be dogmatic on this point; however, dominion generally appears to be a result of the image of God placed within man, but not necessarily part of the image. The ability to rule is a characteristic shared with the angels, yet, as seen in Scripture, the angels are not considered to possess an image of God. Furthermore, as Strong says, the image does not deal with "ability" (which would suggest exercising dominion), but the image of God suggests similarities in man's constitution to God's nature.

D. WHEN DOES ONE RECEIVE THE IMAGE OF GOD? No major debates have occurred over when a person actually receives the image of God implanted within man. Generally, the majority of discussions contend that a person receives/becomes an image of God at the point of conception or sometime during development in the womb. Some Anabaptists maintain that man is not born with the image of God; rather, the image occurs only in connection with man's regeneration. However, Scripture does not support this claim. God calls upon all men, regenerate and unregenerate, who are all made in the image of to exercise consistent and judicial governmental practices (Gen. 9:6). Every man possesses the image of God. Upon conversion, a regenerate person's image of God is quickened, causing a greater discernment of spiritual things.

E. WHAT IS THE IMAGE OF GOD IN MAN? Since Scripture does not explicitly describe the nature of the image of God, we can begin a description (not an explicit definition) by noting the terms within man's nature that bear a similarity or likeness to God. It should be noted that the image of God is not synonymous with man's entire immaterial nature. On the other hand, it is broader than individual items of man's immaterial nature (e.g. soul). It appears (merely speculation) that four separate elements exist in man's immaterial nature, two of which are shared with the brute, and two, unique within man. The common elements are soul (the life principle) and immaterial abilities (such as consciousness). Those elements exclusively discovered within man are the personality (intellect, emotions, will and moral awareness), and the image of God. This distinction presents a basis from which to begin a definition. The image of God as described within Scripture appears to have four separate aspects. If one of the items were removed, the image would cease to be the image of God.

1. *The image of God includes a rational aspect, though not limited to rationality.* Within this rational aspect, man is able to perform those functions that are uniquely characteristic of him. (a) Man is able to comprehend his own existence. No animal has self awareness. This is not to suggest that animals are not conscious, for they are conscious of their existence and what is occurring around them. But they do not have a personality to be aware of, nor are they able to reason that they exist. (b) Man has self-determination. Unlike the brute who responds by instinct or through learned responses to certain stimulants, man is able to exercise powers of deliberation and will. (c) Man is able to reason. Unlike the conditional nature of response made by animals, man can discern the nature of events, determine his motivation and implement his will to do his predetermined task. (d) Carl F. H. Henry attached one other rational characteristic to man, namely, the power of language and communication. Some have challenged this issue, citing proof that animals are able to communicate with one another. Such a claim can be neither disproved nor proved. Allowing for the possibility of some type of primitive communication in the animal kingdom, their type of communication cannot be compared to the intricate forms of communication demonstrated by man.

Commenting on the excellent knowledge with which Adam was endowed, Richard Watson writes,

He has been supposed to be the inventor of language, but history shows that he was never without language. He was from the first able to converse with God; and we may, therefore, infer that language was in him a supernatural and miraculous endowment. That his understanding was, as to its capacity, deep and large beyond any of his posterity, must follow from the perfection in which he was created, and his acquisitions of knowledge would, therefore, be rapid and easy. It was, however, in moral and religions truth, as being of the first concern to him, that we are to suppose the excellency of his knowledge to have consisted. "His reason would be clear, his judgment uncorrupted, and his conscience upright and sensible" (Watts). The best knowledge would, in him, be placed first, and that of every other kind be made subservient to it, according to its relation to that. The apostle adds to knowledge, "righteousness and true holiness," terms which express not merely freedom from sin, but positive and active virtues.[22]

2. *The image of God in man includes a moral aspect, though not exclusively.* The unperverted image of God within Adam also endowed him with the ability to properly discern between right and wrong. The ability to discern moral judgments is distinctly given to man. Even fallen man, with a perverted sense of right and wrong, still has a conscience (1 Cor. 8:1-13; 10:23-11:1; 1 Tim. 4:2; Gen. 9:6-7; Rom. 1-2; 9:1). Every man possesses an innate sense of right and wrong, or a moral law. Even the most primitive tribes have adopted and regulated specific laws simply to insure the rights and privileges of others. Despite the apparent dissimilarities of what man deems right or wrong, every man nonetheless recognizes a code of ethics. Isaac Watts describes Adam's moral points.

A rational creature thus made, must not only be innocent and free, but must be formed holy. His will must have an inward bias to virtue: he must have an inclination to please that God who made him; a supreme love to his Creator, a zeal to serve him, and a tender fear of offending him. For either the new created man loved God supremely or not. If he did not he was not innocent, since the law of nature requires a supreme love to God. If he did he stood ready for every act of obedience: and this is *true holiness of heart.* And, indeed, without this, how could a God of holiness love the work of his own hands? There must be also in this creature a regular subjection of the inferior powers to the superior sense, and appetite and passion must be subject to reason. The mind must have a power to govern these lower faculties, that he might not offend against the law of his creation. He must also have his heart inlaid with love to the creatures, especially those of his own species, if be should be placed among them: and with a principle of honesty and truth in dealing with them. And if many of those creatures were made at once, there would be no pride, malice, or envy, or falsehood, no brawls or contentions among them, but all harmony and love.[23]

3. *The image of God has a spiritual aspect, though not exclusively.* Inherent with the spiritual aspect are two separate issues. First, a true understanding or knowledge of God. In

light of Colossians 3:10, and Ephesians 4:24 which refer to the regenerate man receiving a renewed knowledge of God, it appears that Adam must have had a proper concept of God. With the introduction of sin, man's perception of God was distorted, only to be renewed in the regenerative act. Second, drawing from Ephesians 4:24, it is also inferred that the spiritual aspect included original righteousness. Adam had original or unconfirmed righteousness which involved both a judicial standing before God, and a nature that was not disposed to evil inclinations. It is important to realize that Adam's original righteousness was not the result of some meritorious deed, but rather a demonstration of God's grace. The image of God in man entailed a righteous position and correct knowledge of God.

As evidenced in the life of an unbeliever there is no desire to discern spiritual matters or to act in a spiritual way. The believer, on the other hand, has been renewed. Before regeneration, his nature was inclined continually to do evil; now he has the capacity to do evil or good, and with the enablement of the Holy Spirit he is amply able to be victorious over temptation and evil.

4. *The image of God includes immortality, though not exclusively.* According to Genesis 2:17, death was certainly not a part of man, nor is it a part of God. Despite the effects of sin (physical death), man will live eternally, either in a state of bliss or punishment.

Some would claim that immortality is not part of this image, contending that even animals possess immortality. However, if animals do possess immortality, there is no evidence in Scripture to either support or deny it. However, the destiny of immortal souls is determined by a response to the gospel, suggesting that it is unlikely that animals enjoy immortality, due to the absence of immaterial powers to respond to the gospel.

The image of God, as inclusive of rational, moral, spiritual and immortal elements, serves to differentiate him from the brute and the angels.

F. EFFECTS OF THE FALL UPON THE IMAGE OF GOD. A brief survey of the four elements in the image of God reveal the tremendous damage inflicted to man's immaterial nature by the Fall. (1) The rational nature has been maintained, but corrupted. Scripture repeatedly mentions man's inability to fully know God (Rom. 1; 1 Cor. 2). (2) The moral element has also been maintained, but greatly perverted. Despite the restraining element of the law (Rom. 2) written upon the hearts of all men, man nonetheless has the capacity to engage in some of the most heinous and debauched acts. (3) The spiritual image, including man's knowledge of God and original righteousness has been lost. Even though the act of regeneration practically restores man's knowledge of God and in justification he is declared righteous, it will not be fully restored until man receives his glorified body. (4) Finally, immortality was part of both Adam's material and immaterial nature. However, because of the effects of sin, man will suffer punishment. But with regeneration, he will experience immortality in paradise.

The Fall produced devastating effects upon the image of God, even more severe than the punishment of death upon the material part of Adam (Matt. 10:28). Yet we find in regeneration a partial restoration of the image, but it will be completely restored when man receives his glorified body.

VIII. Transmission Of Man's Immaterial Part

As evidenced in Scripture and indicated by theologians, man is undeniably composed of an immaterial and material nature. It is readily admitted by many that man's material part is passed from generation to generation through the biological act of propagation. However, it is extremely difficult to determine the manner in which man's immaterial part is transmitted. As discovered with other controversial issues in theology the cause for debate and speculation arises from the failure of Scripture to state explicitly how it is accomplished. Perhaps this issue can be clarified by examining implications in Scripture, and the conclusions of theologians, and then developing the most feasible and internally consistent view. There are primarily four views in regard to the transmission of man's immaterial part. The first two views have not received wide acceptance, therefore a brief description with the objections will be given. Greater attention will be given to the latter two views.

A. The Theory Of Preexistence. This view, taught notably by Origen, suggested that the souls of men existed in some previous state prior to the creation of man. In this former state, the soul somehow committed sin, became condemned, and was eventually placed in the human body. Charles Hodge, provides a succinct explanation.

> It supposes that the souls of men had a separate, conscious, personal existence in a previous state; that having sinned in that preëxistent state, they are condemned to be born into this world in a state of sin and in connection with a material body. This doctrine was connected Origen with his theory of an eternal creation. The present state of being is only one epoch in the existence of the human soul. It has passed through innumerable other epochs and forms of existence in the past, and is to go through other innumerable such epochs in the future.[24]

It has been argued by some that these preexistent sin(s) account for man's original sin, while others have suggested these sin(s) explain the disparity of abilities people have when they enter the world. The results are that every person has a natural desire to do evil at birth. Elaborating further, Shedd described the time and possible fashion of this pre-Adamic race.

The theory of preexistence teaches that all human souls were created at the beginning of creation—not that of this world simply, but of all worlds. All finite spirits were made simultaneously, and prior to the creation of matter. The intellectual universe precedes the sensible universe. The souls of men, consequently, existed before the creation of Adam. The preexistent life was pre-Adamite. Men were angelic spirits at first. Because of their apostasy in the angelic sphere, they were transferred, as a punishment for their sin, into material bodies in this mundane sphere, and are now passing through a disciplinary process, in order to be restored, all of them without exception, to their preexistent and angelic condition. These bodies, to which they are joined, come into existence by the ordinary course of physical propagation; so that the sensuous and material part of human nature has no existence previous to Adam. It is only the rational and spiritual principle of which a pre-Adamite life is asserted.[25]

Advocates of this view include Origen (185-254), Plato, Philo, Kant, Justin Martyr, Scotus Erigena, and Edward Beecher.

Objections to the preexistent theory. (1) The Bible never speaks of a creation of men prior to Adam, nor of any sinful acts prior to his birth. The assumption that all human souls were created simultaneously with Adam, and remain in a dormant, unconscious state until merged to the bodies has been adopted by so few as to hardly deserve any recognition by theological thinkers. (2) If indeed the immaterial part of man was conscious prior to its embodiment, is it not strange men have no awareness of this state? (3) If it is argued that the preexistent state was characterized by unconsciousness, the theory fails to demonstrate how an immoral act, with all its implications, could have been performed at all. (4) This view denies man's unity, for it assumes individual souls existed apart from the physical bodies, thus making it almost accidental to the person. This view is that the body is something that ought to be shed, for it is the inferior part of man. However, the body is valued in God's sight because it will be joined to the soul in resurrection. (5) This theory does not harmonize with the biblical notion of sin, since it contradicts the ideas that all men were really present in, and sinning in, Adam. (6) This view questions the justice of God. How could a holy God place a sinful soul in a holy body (position taught by those who teach that the preexistent sin is synonymous with original sin, which limits the sphere of sin to the immaterial and not inclusive of the material) knowing fully that the body would likewise sin, resulting in its condemnation?

The theory of preexistence is basically a rational approach that attempts to account for the origin of sin. Coupled with the idea of reincarnation, this view is pantheistic and anti-scriptural.

B. THE THEORY OF UNKNOWABILITY. According to Berkouwer, Scripture does not teach any ontological truth in relation to the origin of man's soul. Therefore, he rejects preexistence, creationism and traducianism as viable explanations. Such positions inevitably lead to fruitless debate. Berkouwer frequently points to Augustine's indecision on the current position (to be shown later) and concludes that if Augustine was not able to develop a solid position, then it is probably a mistake to even discuss it. Further, Berkouwer taught that any debate leads ultimately to a dualistic approach to man; the creationism view stresses man's vertical relation to God, whereas, the traducianist view pictures only man's horizontal relation to man. Berkouwer concludes, "there is no science, and no theology, which unveil for us the mystery of man."[26]

Objection to the theory of unknowability. Berkouwer makes the false presumption that Scripture does not teach any ontological truth of man, only relational truth. Ontology deals with man's being. In contrast, relational truth focuses on how man reacts with others. Due to Berkouwer's view of man's entire being, he refuses to permit any ontological statements of man to occur in Scripture. However, it will be shown later that Scripture does indeed teach ontological truths.

C. THE POSITION OF CREATIONISM. In contrast to the two former views, the creationist's and traducianist's positions are deeply rooted in the claims of Scripture and the theological writings of many excellent theologians. The primary distinction between creationism and traducianism exists in the manner in which the soul is originated. Creationism contends that the soul (man's immaterial aspect) is directly and immediately created by God and implanted with the foetus at either conception, birth, or at a period of time between these events. Traducianists, on the other hand, argue that both the material and immaterial parts of man are the result of God's indirect and mediate means of forming life through the agency of propagation. Initially it may be argued that it doesn't really matter; yet, as we shall discover later, this doctrine implicates the humanity of Christ as well as the whole field of truth relative to the transmission of original sin.

The creationist's position was generally accepted by the eastern church, whereas the traducianist's position had wide acceptance in the western churches. Such notables as Aristotle, Jerome, Pelagius, Calvin, Beza, and more recently Hodge, and Berkhof favor the creationist view. Supporters for the traducianist view include, Tertullian, Augustine, Milton, Gregory of Nyssa, and more recently Gerhard, Delitzch, Cremer, Strong, and Shedd.

1. *Arguments in favor of creationism.* Creationists argue that their view is in closer harmony to the testimony of Scripture for the following reasons:

a. Adam's immaterial part was a special creation by God, and the same pattern had been followed in regards to all other births, as evidenced in Ecclesiastes 12:7; Isaiah 42:5; Zechariah 12:1 and Hebrews 12:9. In these verses, the body is represented as a different substance from the immaterial, suggesting a different origin. Hodge states it in the following manner,

In the original account of the creation there is a marked distinction made between the body and the soul. The one is from the earth, the other from God. This distinction is kept up throughout the Bible. The body and soul are not only represented as different substances, but also as having different origins. The body shall return to dust, says the wise man, and the spirit to God who gave it. Here the origin of the soul is represented as different from and higher than that of the body. The former is from God in a sense in which the latter is not. In like manner God is said to form "the spirit of man within him" (Zech. xii. 1); to give "breath unto the people upon" the earth, "and spirit to them that walk therein." (Is. xlii. 5.) This language nearly agrees with the account of the original creation, in which God is said to have breathed into man the breath of life, to indicate that the soul is not earthy or material, but had its origin immediately from God. Hence He is called "God of the spirits of all flesh." (Num. xvi. 22.) It could not well be said that He is God of the bodies of all men. The relation in which the soul stands to God as its God and creator is very different from that in which the body stands to Him. And hence in Heb. xii. 9, it is said, "We have had fathers of our flesh which corrected us, and we gave them reverence: shall we not much rather be in subjection unto the Father of spirits, and live?" The obvious antithesis here presented is between those who are the fathers of our bodies and Him who is the Father of our spirits. Our bodies are derived from our earthly parents, our souls are derived from God. This is in accordance with the familiar use of the word flesh, where it is contrasted, either expressly or by implication, with the soul.[27]

b. The immaterial and thus indivisible nature of man's immaterial part is clearly recognized by creationists. The traducian theory must wrestle with the question of how the child derives its immaterial nature. Does it come from the mother, or perhaps the father, or possibly even both? Typically, those supporting the traducian theory teach that the immaterial part is derived from both parents, which only further complicates the issue. If the immaterial substance is derived from the parents, then it must be "divided off" or "split off" from the parents' immaterial part. But a person's immaterial substance is indivisible. Creationists do not have this difficulty, for God places the entire immaterial part within the bosom of man. Consider Hodge's insights,

> The latter doctrine, also, is clearly most consistent with the nature of the soul. The soul is admitted, among Christians, to be immaterial and spiritual. It is indivisible. The traducian doctrine denies this universally acknowledged truth. It asserts that the soul admits of "separation or division of essence." On the same ground that the Church universally rejected the Gnostic doctrine of emanation as inconsistent with the nature of God as a spirit, it has, with nearly the same unanimity, rejected the doctrine that the soul admits of division of substance.[28]

c. Finally, creationists teach that the immaterial nature of Christ was not, as the traducianists teach, derived from Adam. They teach that Christ did not have a sinful nature, and, in like pattern, other souls are created and placed in the human body. If the traducian theory is correct, then Christ must have derived His immaterial nature (soul) from human parentage and, given the link with Adam, Christ must have inherited a sinful nature. However, Scripture clearly asserts that Christ was sinless.

2. *Objections to the theory of creationism.* The creationist position is open to the following objections.

a. In regard to the scriptural passages employed to substantiate the creationist's position, it would appear upon closer examination that these verses could equally support the idea that God through an indirect agency originated the immaterial part of man. It is claimed alike by traducianists, that God is involved in the propagation of every person (both material and immaterial). The differences exists in the manner of God's involvement. For the creationists, human parents are instrumental in the material part of the child, and God immediately (without any intermediate agency) creates the immaterial part and places it in the child. The traducianists recognize God's involvement in the very process (through His agents—parents) for the development of the complete being (material and immaterial). Commenting on the verses used by creationists to support their position, Dabney writes,

It is replied, and the reply seems to me sufficient, that the language of these passages is sufficiently met, by recognizing the fact that God's power at first produced man's soul immediately out of nothing, and in His own image; that the continued propagation of these souls is under laws which His Providence sustains and directs; and that this agency of God is claimed as an especial honour, . . . because human souls are the most noble part of God's earthly kingdom, being intelligent, moral, and capable of apprehending His glory. That this is the true sense of Eccl. xii: 7, and that it should not be strained any higher, appears thus: if the language proves that the soul of a man of our generation came immediately from God's hand, like Adam's, the antithesis would equally prove that our bodies came equally from the dust, as immediately as Adam's. To all such passages as Is. lvii: 16; Zech. xii: 1, the above general considerations apply, and in addition, these facts: Our parents are often spoken of in Scripture as authors of our existence likewise; and that in general terms, inclusive of the spirit. Gen. xlvi : 26,27; Prov. xvii : 21; xxiii : 24; Is. xlv : 10. Surely, if one of these classes of texts may be so strained, the other may equally, and then we have texts directly contradicting texts. Again, God is called the Creator of the animals, Ps. civ : 30, and the adorner of the lilies, Matt. vi : 30; which are notoriously produced by propagation. In Heb. xii : 9, the pronoun in "Father of our spirits," is unauthorized. The meaning is simply the contrast between the general ideas of "earthly fathers," and "heavenly father." For if you make the latter clause, "Father of spirits" mean Creator of our souls, then, by antithesis, the former should be read, father of our bodies; but this neither the apostle's scope permits, nor the word σάρξ which does not usually mean, in his language, our bodies as opposed to our souls; but our natural, as opposed to our gracious condition of soul.[29]

Moreover in connection with the scriptural argument, it should be noted that in passages such as Psalm 139:13-14; John 1:5, there are clear references to God forming man's material part. Yet, creationists contend that Scripture suggests no teaching for the immediate creation of the material part of man.

b. Implied within the creationist's view is that God is guilty for the sin of man. The suggestion that God creates a pure soul and then places it in a depraved body . . . might mean that God is responsible for sin. Strong states, "This theory . . . makes God indirectly the author of moral evil, by teaching that he puts this pure soul into a body which will inevitably corrupt it."[30]

c. If the creationist's position is correct, then men are propagating mere bodies, not whole persons. Further, this theory does not account for the occurrence of mental, psychological and moral resemblances discovered between the parents and the children. Moreover, this theory ascribes to the beast nobler powers of propagation to man. The animal kingdom is endowed with the ability to produce after its kind, both the material and immaterial part, a privilege not extended in humans, as claimed by creationists. Dabney elaborates:

In Gen. v : 3, "Adam begat a son in his own likeness, after his image." How could this be, if Adam's parental agency did not produce the soul, in which alone this image inheres? Surely the image and likeness is in the same aspects. See also Ps. li : 5; Job. xiv : 4; Jno. iii : 6, &c. . . .
They also argue that popular opinion and common sense clearly regard the parents as parents of the whole person. The same thing is shown by the inheritance of mental peculiarities and family traits, which are often as marked as bodily. And this cannot be accounted for by education, because often seen where the parents did not live to rear the child; . . . But the chief arguments from reason are: if God creates souls, as immediately as He created Adam's or Gabriel, then they must have come from His hand morally pure, for God cannot create wickedness. How, then, can depravity be propagated? The Bible would be contradicted, which so clearly speaks of it as propagated; and reason, which says that the attachment of a holy soul to a body cannot defile it, because a mere body has no moral character. Creationists answer: the federal relation instituted between Adam and the race, justifies God in ordaining

it so that the connection of the young, immortal spirit with the body, and thus with a depraved race, shall be the occasion for its depravation, in consequence of imputed sin. But the reply is, first, it is impossible to explain the federal relation, if the soul of each child (the soul alone is the true moral agent) had an antecedent holy existence, independent of a human father. Why is not that soul as independent of Adam's fall, thus far, as Gabriel was; and why is not the arrangement, which implicates him in it, just as arbitrary as though Gabriel were tied to Adam's fate? Moreover, if God's act in plunging this pure spirit into an impure body is the immediate occasion of its becoming depraved, it comes very near to making God the author of its fall.[31]

d. The creationists theory, if correct, suggests that inherent evil lies with material substance. This implies that matter is evil. After all, creationists claim that a pure soul (created immediately by God) is placed within every person. Corruption must therefore arise from the material part of man. However, this is impossible; flesh does not possess ethical powers. Shedd provides an additional insight into the weakness of the creationist's view.

If I have my body from Adam, and not my soul from Adam but from God alone, since sin is in the soul and not in the body, how can I be said to have sinned in Adam? Adam sinned, and sin was in his soul alone, not in his body; but my soul, in which my sin is, I do not have from him. How then am I said to have sinned in him? If sin were in the body, I might rightly be said to have sinned in him because my body was in him; but as sin is not in the body, I cannot properly be said to have sinned in Adam.[32]

e. Further, creationism demands *ex nihilo* creation for each immaterial soul, but this does not seem to harmonize with the testimony of Scripture that indicates God performed all His created acts within the six days of creation. This is not to limit God from creating any new substances, but this objection stems from an overview of Scripture that implies new life forms are not continually being created. Moreover, the Genesis account implies that in creation, a completed act took place that includes a supreme design that would allow for the production of each "kind after its own kind."

f. As to the transfer of the essence, how does the child receive his immaterial part: from his father, or mother, or perhaps both? Candidly, neither the creationists or the traducianists can offer a feasible explanation for the merging or origination of man's immaterial and material parts, respectively. Since we are unable to know the manner in which the mind interacts with the body, it is difficult to fully understand its various implications. Creationists claim to have avoided this problem through claiming a distinct different origin of the material and the immaterial. Therefore, there is no need of somehow dividing the immaterial contribution of the parents. However, their avoidance of the frying pan is a leap into the fire. How is it possible to unite an immaterial substance (totally alien to both parents) to a material substance?

Given the philosophical and scientific inability to derive a feasible explanation to these sorts of questions, combined with the fact that Scripture does not answer them, perhaps the issue should not be employed for determining which view is correct. In other words, when both views are not able to resolve the difficulty, then the difficulty should not be the basis for deciding which view is correct. Dabney suggests, "With such difficulties besetting both sides, it will be best, perhaps, to leave the subject as an insoluble mystery. What an *opprobrium* to the pride of human philosophy, that it should be unable to answer the very first and nearest question as to its own origin!"[33]

g. Finally, with regard to the impact of these views upon Christ's nature, both views are forced to appeal to a miraculous intervention in order to preserve Christ's sinless position. Creationists contend that a miracle was performed in adding His sinless soul to His human body. Likewise, the traducianists argue that a miracle was necessary to prevent the passing of a sin nature into the immaterial parts of Christ's humanity. Stevens says neither has a bearing on Christ's birth.

In the birth of Jesus no new personal being came into existence. The eternal Son of God took to Himself a sinless body and a full and complete, but sinless, complex of human attributes. He, that is, His personal eternal being, His soul became a human person, a human soul, without in any way ceasing to be a divine Person, a divine Soul.

Considerable confusion is created by the unconscious assumption that human nature is a kind of substance, almost a material substance. In strict definition of our terms, we should hold that a nature is a complex of attributes, not a substance. Christ in the incarnation took to Himself a sinless body and a sinless complex of human attributes. When He was born, His personal identity did not begin to be.

Now if one holds to the traducian view of the origin of the soul one must hold that in the virgin birth of Christ a new personal identity simply was not brought into existence. If, on the other hand, one holds to the special creation view, then one must hold that in the birth of Christ a new personal entity was not created. In either case His personal identity is eternal, not derived nor created. On either theory of the origin of the soul of ordinary man, the eternal Son of God is the personal identity of Jesus. He had from eternity, fully and completely, the divine nature, and He took, fully and completely, the sinless human nature. His mind, spirit, soul, heart, etc. became a human mind, soul, heart, etc. without ceasing to be a divine mind, soul, heart, etc.

I suggest therefore that the sinless humanity of Christ in the incarnation does not in any way bear upon the question of traducianism or creationism. All that the Bible says on this subject can be consistently adhered to on either of these two theories.[34]

D. THE TRADUCIAN POSITION. According to the traducian position, the immaterial as well as the material part of man is propagated by human generation. Through God's design for each to reproduce after its kind, God has continued the human race mediately through human beings. All men were seminally in Adam, and each member is present in him totally, both materially and immaterially.

Arguments for the Traducian Theory. In conjunction with the objections to creationism, the following arguments support the traducian position.

1. *The arguments from Scripture.* (a) Only once does God breathe into the nostrils of man the breath of life. Thereafter, the species is to continue to produce itself "after its kind" (Gen. 1:24-25, 28; 2:7). (b) Eve was made a special creation (immaterial), coming from Adam as a body; and God did not need to create a soul/spirit to add to her. Eve was a complete person (Gen. 1:26-27; 2:22-23, 1 Cor. 11:8). (c) Having divinely created the universe, God set it in motion while sustaining its existence, but ceased in the creative acts (Gen. 2:2). (d) Descendants are in the loins of their fathers (Gen. 46:26; Heb. 7:9-10; John 3:6; Rom. 1:3; Acts 17:26). These passages suggest that the whole person and not just the material part, comes from the parents.

2. *Through the analogy of human and animal life.* In which the increase of numbers is seen not by immediate forms of creation, but from natural derivation from a parent stock (Psa. 104:30). Animals appear to have an immaterial part as well as a material part, but there is no indication that they are a result of a special creation in each instance.

3. *The traducian theory best accounts for the observed transmission, not merely of physical aspects, but also of mental or personality characteristics within family lineages.* The inheritance of mental and moral traits cannot be accounted for by education or example only. There are too many occasions when children reflect parents' traits when a death of the parent or separation takes place before environment can produce similarity. This apparent similarity suggests that the soul governs the body and not the reverse.

4. *Finally, the traducian theory offers the best basis for the explanation of man's inheritance of the moral depravity of Adam.* Moral pollution and depravity transmitted through the human race has affected both the material and immaterial part of man, not to the exclusion of either.

IX. THE CONSTITUTIONAL NATURE OF MAN'S IMMATERIAL PART

The terms used in Scripture for man have two separate and primary meanings, and failure to recognize these distinctions will inevitably lead to confusion. Scripture uses terms such as "mind," "spirit," "flesh," and "soul" in two senses, an ontological or a metaphysical sense, and a moral or ethical sense.

Ontology refers to the being of man, his functional capacities, and how they are related to one another. Ontology is a grocery list of what constitutes man's immaterial nature. The ethical sense deals with how the being relates to other individuals. Ethics employs the elements to perform an act, which may or may not have moral implications.

NATURE OF MAN	
Biblical Terms	
Ontological Sense	Ethical Sense

A. INTRODUCTION TO THE IMMATERIAL. One's philosophy of man's immaterial nature will determine ultimately how he views God. In addition to God, one's perspective can determine how he will deal with morality.

What is the immaterial? For many years the mind was considered immaterial, distinct from the brain. However, the past two centuries have witnessed the contributions of men such as Hume and Hobbs, who challenged the *status quo* and introduced the idea that the mind (immaterial) and the brain (material) are synonymous, a type of monism. If man is purely material, the existence of God and immortality for man is negated or, at least, highly questioned. Materialism claims that only things that actually exist (or that can be touched) are real; anything else is subjective or illusory. The more radical view of materialism, which denies God's existence, concludes that man is a complex machine, and any adjustment to man's behavior can be accomplished through manipulating the brain. Psychologists such as B. F. Skinner have advocated controlling human behavior through various physical stimuli. If man is purely material, why not attempt to control him by stimulants or chemicals? Of course, such a humanistic view equates man's mind or brain (synonymous) on the same level as a piece of flesh, a high estimate of an organism but a very low estimate of man as a soul made in the image of God.

B. BIBLICAL PERSPECTIVE OF MAN'S IMMATERIAL. In stark contrast to materialism, the Bible offers a higher description of man. There are those within Christian circles who would argue that the Bible does not attempt to teach anything about man's ontological structure. Instead, Scripture only pictures man in the world as he relates to God and other human beings. Therefore, they would argue it is wrong to ask any question about what man is. They contend God gave only a sociological description. On the other hand, there are those who rightly advocate that the Bible teaches not only how man should respond, but also what man is (ontology). Charles Hodge supports creationism, noting that:

This is evident, (1.) From the distinction everywhere made between soul and body. Thus, in the original account of the creation a clear distinction is made between the body as formed from the dust of the earth, and the soul or principle of life which was breathed into it from God. And in Gen. iii. 19, it is said, "Dust thou art, and unto dust shalt thou return." As it was only the body that was formed out of the dust, it is only the body that is to return to dust. In Eccles. xii. 7, it is said, "Then shall the dust return to the earth as it was, and the spirit shall return unto God who gave it." Is. x. 18, "Shall consume. . . . both soul and body." Daniel says (vii. 15), "I Daniel was grieved in my spirit in the midst of my body." Our Lord (Matt. vi. 25) commands his disciples to take no thought for the body; and, again (Matt. x. 28), "Fear not them which kill the body, but are not able to kill the soul: but rather fear him which is able to destroy both soul and body in hell." Such is the constant representation of the Scriptures. The body and soul are set forth as distinct substances, and the two together as constituting the whole man. (2.) There is a second class of passages equally decisive as to this point. It consists of those in which the body is represented as a garment which is to be laid aside; a tabernacle or house in which the soul dwells, which it may leave and return to. Paul, on a certain occasion, did not know whether he was in the body or out of the body. Peter says he thought it meet as long as he was in this tabernacle to put his brethren in remembrance of the truth, "knowing," as he adds, "that shortly I must put off this my tabernacle." Paul, in 2 Cor. 5 v. 1, says, "If our earthly house of this tabernacle were dissolved we have a building of God." In the same connection, he speaks of being unclothed and clothed upon with our house which is from heaven; and of being absent from the body and present with the Lord, knowing that while we are at home in the body we are absent from the Lord. To the Philippians (i. 23,24) he says, "I am in a strait betwixt two, having a desire to depart, and to be with Christ; which is far better: nevertheless, to abide in the flesh is more needful for you." (3.) It is the common belief of mankind, the clearly revealed doctrine of the Bible, and part of the faith of the Church universal, that the soul can and does exist and act after death. If this be so, then the body and soul are two distinct substances. The former may be disorganized, reduced to dust, dispersed, or even annihilated, and the latter retain its conscious life and activity. This doctrine was taught in the Old Testament, where the dead are represented as dwelling in Sheol, whence they occasionally reappeared, as Samuel did to Saul. Our Lord says that as God is not the God of the dead but of the living, his declaring himself to be the God of Abraham, Isaac, and Jacob, proves that Abraham, Isaac, and Jacob are now alive. Moses and Elijah conversed with Christ on the Mount. To the dying thief our Lord said, "To-day shalt thou" (that in which his personality resided) "be with me in Paradise." Paul, as we have just seen, desired to be absent from the body and present with the Lord. He knew that his conscious personal existence was to be continued after the dissolution of his body. It is unnecessary to dwell on this point, as the continued existence of the soul in full consciousness and activity out of the body and in the interval between death and the resurrection, is not denied by any Christian Church. But if this be so it clearly proves that the soul and body are two distinct substances, so that the former can exist independently of the latter.[35]

According to the teaching of Scripture, man is more than a mere physical being. He consists of parts. Three separate theories have been suggested that describe the constitutional aspects of man's immaterial nature.

C. THEORIES FOR MAN'S IMMATERIAL NATURE. Philosophers and theologians have wrestled with the nature of man's immaterial nature throughout church history. Much of the debate stems the vagueness of Scripture which centers around this issue.

1. *Trichotomy theory*. The trichotomy view traces its source to early Greek thought, and perhaps even earlier. Some have contended that the writers of the New Testament adopted this cultural teaching and inserted it into the Scripture, hence "Christianizing" it. This claim can neither be substantiated or denied, nor is it necessary, for the theory will be examined in light of its scriptural support.

Basically the trichotomy theory states that man is composed of three separate substances: body, soul, and spirit. Typically, trichotomists teach that body is the fleshly material substance, the spirit is the realm of the intellectual powers and the shrine of the Holy Spirit, and the soul serves as the region for affections and the emotional impulses. Erickson offers the following summation of the trichotomy theory.

A view rather popular in conservative Protestant circles has been termed the "trichotomist" view. Man is composed of three elements. The first element is the physical body. A physical nature is something man has in common with animals and plants. There is no difference in kind between man's body and that of animals and plants. The difference is one of degree, as man has a more complex physical structure. The second part of man is the soul. This is the psychological element, the basis of reason, of emotion, of social interrelatedness and the like. Animals are thought to have a rudimentary soul. Possession of a soul is what distinguishes man and animals from the plants. While the soul of man is much more involved and capable than that of the animals, their souls are similar in kind. What really distinguishes man from the animals is not that he has a more complex and advanced soul, but that he possesses a third element, namely, a spirit. This religious element enables the human to perceive spiritual matters and respond to spiritual stimuli. It is the seat of the spiritual qualities of the individual, whereas the personality traits reside in the soul.[36]

a. Arguments for trichotomism. (1) In both the Old Testament and the New Testament there exist separate words in the original language for soul and spirit. There is no conclusive evidence to reveal that these words are absolute synonyms, and to assume so is erroneous. (2) The trichotomy theory is endorsed through direct scriptural statements. Trichotomists usually appeal to the following verses: (a) 1 Thess. 5:23 - "And the very God of peace sanctify you wholly; and I pray God your whole spirit and soul and body be preserved blameless unto the coming of our lord Jesus Christ." In this verse, trichotomists argue that all three words are employed and are connected by the conjunction *kai* (and), which indicates three separate substances. Further, they argue that the presence of the word "whole" reveals that the writer is requesting that each substance be completely preserved. (b) Heb. 4:12 - "For the word of God is quick, and powerful, and sharper than any twoedged sword, piercing even to the dividing asunder of soul and spirit, and of the joints and marrow, and is a discerner of the thoughts and intents of the heart." From this verse, the trichotomist would contend that the soul and the spirit are separable, indicating that they are different substances, and distinguishable. (c) 1 Cor. 2:14-15 - "But the natural man receiveth not the things of the Spirit of God: for they are foolishness unto him: neither can he know them, because they are spiritually discerned. But he that is spiritual judgeth all things, yet he himself is judged of no man." The use of the two original words (*psuckikos* and *pneumatikos*) set forth strong distinctions in man's discerning ability, and suggest distinction in this spirit and the soul. (d) 1 Cor. 15:44 - "It is sown a natural body; it is raised a spiritual body. There is a natural body, and there is a spiritual body." Trichotomists conclude that Paul is showing the distinction between the physical and spiritual body, which serves to further support their contentions that they are different substances. (e) Phil. 1:27 - "Only let your conversation as it becometh the gospel of Christ: that whether I come and see you, or else be absent, I may hear of your affairs, that ye stand fast in one spirit, with one mind striving together for the faith of the gospel." In this passage, trichotomists stress the fact that Paul is appealing for unity in the Philippians' minds and spirits, two terms that cannot be equivalent, for Paul would be redundant. Instead, Paul is describing a distinction between the two functions, which again implies two substances.

b. Objections to trichotomism. (1) To say the usage of different words in the original language identifies three separate substances simply begs the issue. In reality there are many words used to describe the immaterial (mind, will, heart, soul and others). This does not assume there may be many parts to man's immaterial nature. However, the major weakness with trichotomy is that the terms for soul and spirit are used interchangeably, hence do not imply two different substances. Hodge described the different usages. He notes that *ruach* and *nephesh* in Hebrew, *psuche* and *pneuma* in Greek, and soul and spirit in English, are used in the Scriptures indiscriminately of:

Men and of irrational animals. If the Bible ascribed only a ψυχή [*psuche*] to brutes, and both ψυχή, [*psuche*] and πνεῦμα [*pneuma*] to man, there would be some ground for assuming that the two are essentially distinct. But such is not the case. The living principle in the brute is called both . . . [*nephesh* and *ruach*, and *psuche* and *pneuma*]. That principle in the brute creation is irrational and mortal; in man it is rational and immortal. "Who knoweth the spirit of man that goeth upward, and the spirit of the beast that goeth downward to the earth?" Eccles. iii. 21. The soul of the brute is the immaterial principle which constitutes its life, and which is endowed with sensibility, and that measure of intelligence which experience shows the lower animals to possess. The soul of man is a created spirit of a higher order, which has not only the attributes of sensibility, memory, and instinct, but also the higher powers which pertain to our intellectual, moral, and religious life. As in the brutes it is not one substance that feels and another that remembers; so it is not one substance in man that is the subject of sensations, and another substance which has intuitions of necessary truths, and which is endowed with conscience and with the knowledge of God.[37]

The following words are used by trichotomists to imply different substances, but note the following:

(1) Spirit, as well as soul, is used of the animals.
(2) Soul is ascribed to Jehovah.
(3) The disembodied dead are called souls.
(4) The highest exercises of religion are attributed to the soul, and are not limited to the spirit.
(5) To lose one's soul is to lose all.

(2) The usage of Scripture by the trichotomists will be examined for the purpose of seeing their faulty hermeneutics. (a) 1 Thess. 5:23—the context is not anthropological, that is, dealing with man. Rather, Paul is dealing with sanctification. The emphasis is upon each part being "wholly" sanctified, and not that the whole person (including the name of each part) be sanctified. Stevens notes, "The adverb "wholly" and the adjective "whole" show that Paul had no thought of parts of man, but rather of aspects of man as an entirety."[38] The word *holoteleis* relates to wholeness, not to parts. (b) Heb. 4:12 - Again the trichotomists have committed a serious hermeneutical error in attempting to use this passage to reveal the distinctiveness of the soul and the spirit. Stevens reveals the opposite is taught in this passage.

In answer it should be noted that this text does not indicate a division or separation of soul from spirit. That would have required some preposition such as *metaksu*, and a wording which suggests "dividing between soul and spirit." As a matter of fact, the objects of the participle "dividing" are a series of genitives, each one in itself naming something which is divided. We should more correctly read, "dividing asunder of soul and of spirit, of joints and of marrow." The Word is said to cleave the soul and to cleave the spirit by its piercing power, just as the joints are cleft and the marrow is cleft by the sword which slays the beast for sacrifice.

That no division between is indicated but rather a division . . . . is evident by the last part of the verse, "a discerner of the thoughts and intents of the heart." Obviously thoughts and intents cannot be regarded as separable, substantive entities. Actually, intents are a kind of thought. The Word is a discerner of thoughts and of intents. The meaning of Heb. 4:12 is reemphasized in verse 13, "Nothing is hidden but everything is open before the eyes of the Word with whom we have to do." We see, therefore, that Heb. 4:12 gives no support whatever to the trichotomous view that soul and spirit are separable or distinguishable, substantive entities They are no more separable than thoughts and intents are.[39]

Moreover, in Hebrews 4:12, trichotomists usually appeal to the usage of the conjunction *kai* to substantiate the idea of separate substances. However, if we were to apply this principle in Hebrews 4:12; Luke 10:27; Matthew 22:37; Mark 12:30, consistently, man's immaterial would be composed of not more than just two substances, but many. (c) 1 Corinthians 2:14-15 - Paul is not using the phrases "spiritual man" and "natural man" in an ontological sense (showing a difference in substance), instead he is focusing on the ethical distinctions. (d) 1 Corinthians 15:44 - The reference is not to two separate substances in man, but between our natural body and our glorified body. Hodge offers the following explanation:

> The Apostle there distinguishes between the σῶμα ψυχικόν [*soma psuchiton*], and the σῶμα πνευματικόν [*soma pneumiton*]; the former is that in which the ψυχή [*psuche*] is the animating principle; and the latter that in which the πνεῦμα [*pneuma*] is the principle of life. The one we have here, the other we are to have hereafter. This seems to imply that the ψυχή [*psuche*] exists in this life, but is not to exist hereafter, and therefore that the two are separable and distinct. In this explanation we might acquiesce if it did not contradict the general representations of the Scriptures. We are constrained, therefore, to seek another explanation which will harmonize with other portions of the word of God. The general meaning of the Apostle is plain. We have now gross, perishable, and dishonorable, or unsightly bodies. Hereafter we are to have glorious bodies, adapted to a higher state of existence. The only question is, why does he call the one psychical, and the other pneumatic? Because the word ψυχή [*psuche*], although often used for the soul as

rational and immortal, is also used for the lower form of life which belongs to irrational animals. Our future bodies are not to be adapted to those principles of our nature which we have in common with the brutes, but to those which are peculiar to us as men, created in the image of God. The same individual human soul has certain susceptibilities and powers which adapt it to the present state of existence, and to the earthly house in which it now dwells. It has animal appetites and necessities. It can hunger and thirst. It needs sleep and rest. But the same soul has higher powers. The earthly body is suited to its earthly state; the heavenly body to its heavenly state. There are not two substances ψυχή [*psuche*] and πνεῦμα [*pneuma*], there is but one and the same substance with different susceptibilities and powers. In this same connection Paul says, Flesh and blood cannot inherit the kingdom of heaven. Yet our bodies are to inherit that kingdom, and our bodies are flesh and blood. The same material substance now constituted as flesh and blood is to be so changed as to be like Christ's glorious body. As this representation does not prove a substantial difference between the body which now is and that which is to be hereafter, so neither does what the Apostle says of the σῶμα ψυχικόν [*soma psuchiton*] and the σῶμα πνευματικόν [*soma pneumiaton*] prove that the ψυχή [*psuche*] and πνεῦμα [*pneuma*] are distinct substances.[40]

(e) Phil 1:27 - Paul is not dealing with different substances, rather he is speaking of a unified attitude or mind.

The doctrine of a threefold constitution of man was adopted and popularized by Plato, and eventually introduced into the early church. Although it went through slight variants, it was endorsed by Clement of Alexandria, Origen and Gregory of Nyssa. The gnostics seized upon it and incorporated it into their system. Apollinarius adapted it to Christ, claiming Christ had only a human body and soul, but not a human spirit. Immediately Apollinarius and his view were condemned as being heretical. Apart from recent endorsements by those reading the Scofield Reference Bible, it has not had a scholarly following, only a popular following.

2. *Monism.* Monism has not received wide acceptance. Its primary advocates are those who apparently deny the spiritual realm and attempt to explain everything from a materialistic interpretation of life. Nonetheless, there are also those who would argue from a Christian perspective that Scripture tends to refer to people as a unity, rather than as different substances. Two views will be considered, the first as substantial monism, and the second, relational monism.

a. Substantial monism. According to this view, man is a substance, and only one substance. Those who hold this view reject the idea of an immaterial substance in man. Critics have regarded the immaterial as "the ghost in the machine." There are various forms of materialism in regard to the brain; the more radical forms demand that the mind is the brain in the strictest sense. Man as a unity is an isolated being; all that he is, and thinks, and acts is contained within his material existence.

b. Relational monism. According to this view the Bible does not assume an ontological approach to man in an attempt to explain his metaphysical components. Rather, the thrust of Scripture presents man as a whole person, and characterizes him in his relation to God and others. It is argued that terms such as "soul," "mind," and "spirit" do not imply something. In Scripture these words are used interchangeably to refer to the person and the "supposed" immaterial part. Relational monists suggest that both the material and immaterial man are the same. Erickson describes monism.

> Monism insists that man is not to be thought of as in any sense composed of parts or separate entities, but rather as a radical unity. In the monistic understanding, the Bible does not view man as body, soul, and spirit, but simply as a self. The terms sometimes used to distinguish parts of man are actually to be taken as basically synonymous. Man is never treated in the Bible as a dualistic being.[41]

c. Objections to substantial and relational monism. Several major weaknesses appear within the monistic argument: (1) It can be demonstrated that the writers of Scripture never intended to present a scientific or ontological description of man, but that does not prove that in the process of writing about man they did not give us statements which can be used to construct an ontology of man. If ontological proofs can be constructed, then man is more than a mere material being, and those theories which teach that man is a purely materialistic man, logically collapse. As has been demonstrated already, the Scripture presents an ontology of man. (2) The interchangability of terms does not necessitate that monism is correct. Functionally, the same term may be used in the material and immaterial sense. To insist that it teaches monism begs the question. (3) Further, monism is rejected on the basis of an intermediate state. A monist cannot explain how a person can exist outside his body, yet, according to Scripture there is a period of time in which people will exist without their material or glorified bodies (2 Cor. 5:8). Erickson pinpoints the problem.

> According to monism, to be human is to be or have a body. The idea that a human can somehow exist apart from a body is unthinkable. Consequently, there is no possibility of postdeath existence in a disembodied state. Immortality of the soul is quite untenable. Not only, then, is there no possibility of a future life apart from bodily resurrection, but any sort of intermediate state between death and resurrection is ruled out as well.[42]

Monism probably arose as a reaction to the difficulties related to the dichotomy and trichotomy positions, and as a reaction to the idea of the immortality of the soul. However, the difficulties associated with the monistic view do not present a viable alternative and serve only to further complicate the issues; therefore, it should be rejected.

3. *Dichotomy theory*. Probably the most widely held view through most of the history of Christian thought has been the view that man is composed of two elements, a material aspect (the body) and an immaterial component (the soul and/or spirit). Dichotomy is based on the argument that there are only two substances, one material and the other immaterial. This view does not absolutely necessitate that the soul and the spirit are strictly synonymous; however, it recognizes similar origin and substance (within the immaterial), characterized by different functions. Man is to be seen ontologically as a combination of two substances. Words like "spirit" and "soul" are not the name of the immaterial substance, any more than words like "flesh" and "bones," are the name of the material part of man. Words like "spirit," "mind," "will" in their ontological sense designate various functional descriptions of the immaterial substance. Even as the body has various operations (digestion, respiration), likewise the immaterial substance possesses certain functions, i.e, emotional, spiritual, intellectual and volitional functions.

a. Support for the dichotomy theory. (1) The Genesis account of creation supports the teaching that a material body was energized by the breath of God, and it became a living soul (Gen. 2:7). (2) the words "soul" and "spirit," are used interchangeably, suggesting similarity in origin (immaterial) yet a functional difference (Gen. 41:8; cf. Psa. 42:6; John 12:25 cf. John 13:21; Matt. 20:28; cf. 25:50; Heb. 12:23; cf. Rev. 6:9). (3) Scripture teaches the idea that the body and the soul (or spirit) constitute man's entire being (Matt. 10:28; 1 Cor. 5:3). (4) The terms "spirit" and "soul" are used in relation to animals, conveying the idea that there is no unique substance "spirit" within man (refutes trichotomy). (5) The word "soul" is used in relation to God (Isa. 42:1; Jer. 9:9; Heb. 10:38), but the Bible teaches, "God is Spirit" (John 4:24). If the trichotomists are right, the word "soul" would not be attached to God. (6) In relation to the various "understood" functions of the soul and the spirit, there are instances in Scripture that each word is used interchangeably (Mark 12:30; Luke 1:46; Heb. 6:18-19; Jas. 1:21), with special reference to the supposed function of the spirit. (7) All the arguments against trichotomy and monism are considered as supports for dichotomy.

X. THE MATERIAL AND IMMATERIAL ASPECTS OF MAN

A. THE FOLLOWING TERMS DESCRIBE THE VARIOUS ASPECTS OF MAN AND CATEGORIZE BOTH THE PHYSICAL AND IMMATERIAL FUNCTIONS.

1. *Basor, soma* - body. These words refer to the elementary fact that man has a material part. The New Testament word *soma* occurs many times (Matt. 6:22; 1 Cor. 15:44; Rom. 6:12; 1 Cor. 9:27) and describes the material part of man. The Old Testament word *basar*

refers to flesh and not directly to the body. (There really is no Old Testament word per se, for "body"), yet such passages as Ezek. 10:12; Isa. 10:18; Gen. 2:21, 23-24, clearly referred to the material body.)

2. *Sarx* - flesh. (a) *Sarx* is sometimes referred to as the tissue that covers the body, thereby contrasted with the blood and bones (1 Cor. 15:39; 2 Cor. 12:7; Col. 1:22). (b) *Sarx* is also used as a synonymous term for the entire body (Col. 2:5; 2 Cor. 4:10-11; 1 Cor. 6:16; Eph. 2:15; 5:28-31; Gal. 4:13). (c) *Sarx* can be used to describe man's origin, the basis for his origination to life (Rom. 1:3; 9:3; 1 Cor. 10:18). (d) *Sarx* is frequently used in an ethical sense, focusing primarily upon the depraved nature of the unregenerate man, though it is also used to describe the carnal believer as well. It is essential to understand that "flesh" used in the ethical sense does not suggest the idea of any intrinsic evil in matter or the material part of man. (Ethical usages include, Rom. 7:18; 8:8-9; Cor. 1:12; Gal. 5:17; 2 Col. 2:18.)

3. *Body of sin* (Rom. 6:6) refers to man's sin nature or to the body, the vehicle through which sin is manifested.

4. *Body of death* (Rom. 7:24) speaks of our mortality as a result of our sin.

5. *Body of humiliation* (Phil. 3:21) describes our current material body as contrasted to our future glorified body.

6. *Earthen vessel* (2 Cor. 4:7) highlights this inherent finiteness of our mortal bodies with no reference to moral ability.

7. *Natural body* (1 Cor. 15:44) is an ontological focus of our mortal bodies that has been adapted for life and propagation upon the earth.

8. *Spiritual bodies* (1 Cor. 15:44) is a reference to the glorified bodies into which our material bodies will be fashioned at the resurrection. It will be characterized as being incorruptible and immortal (denotes ontological emphasis).

B. SOUL—*nephesh, psuche.* (a) Descriptive of man's seat of appetites or desires, whether they are spiritual or material (Psa. 107:9; Prov. 25:25; Deut. 12:15, 20; 14:26). (b) Characteristic of the focal point of the emotions (Lev. 26:11; 2 Sam. 17:8). (c) Refers to the total person (Gen. 49:6; Gen. 12:5; Rom. 2:9; Rom. 13:1). (d) Descriptive of life (Rom. 11:3; Phil 2:30). (e) Principally, the idea centers on man as a living and active person in contrast to inanimate stone.

C. SPIRIT—*ruach, pneuma.* (a) Characteristic of the life-energizing force within man (Jas.

2:26; Luke 8:54-55). (b) A general description of man's immaterial nature (Gen. 41:8; Dan. 2:1, 3; Matt. 26:41). (c) Denotes an attitude (Rom. 11:8; 2 Cor. 12:18; Phil. 1:24). (d) Occasionally refers to one's intellect (Mark 2:8, 1 Cor. 2:11). (e) Primarily the idea of spirit speaks of that part of man that interacts with God in either establishing or rejecting a relationship with Him (Psa. 51:10; 2 Cor. 4:16; Rom. 8:16; 1 Cor. 14:14-15; Psa. 78:8).

D. HEART—*lebh, kardia*. (a) Employed to refer to the inner life of man as contrasted with his outward life (Rom. 2:29; 2 Thess. 2:17; 2 Cor. 5:12). (b) Used to describe the seat of emotions, both good and bad (Rom. 1:24; 10:1; 2 Cor. 2:4). (c) For man's intellectual activities, specifically to his intentions and purposes (Prov. 16:9; Rom. 1:21; Eph. 1:18; Gen. 6:5; Matt. 5:19-20). (d) Focal point of the will (Rom. 2:5; 6:17). (e) The source of religious experiences (2 Cor. 1:22; Rom. 5:5; Eph. 3:17; Col. 3:15). (f) The device within man to discern between good and evil (Rom. 1:21; 2:14). (g) The source of a person's self-awareness in a moral sense. (h) The physical organ, only in the Old Testament.

1. *Mind—notis*. Relates to the cognitive ability of the mind, to discern, reason and judge (Luke 24:45; 2 Thess. 2:13; Rom. 12:2; Eph. 4:23).

2. *Mind—phronema, phronesis*. Designates the nonmaterial part of man as a deep, reflective, and meditative thinker.

3. *Affections—rachamin, splangchna* - (bowels). The emotional and affectionate capacities of man with reference to the nonmaterial (Col. 3:12; Phlm. 7, 12, 20; Phil. 1:8; 2:1; 2 Cor. 6:12; 7:15; Gen. 43:30)

4. *Will—ratson, noule, and thalema*. Man's immaterial part that allows him to exercise choice in order to put forth effort and make decisions (Dan. 8:4; Luke 24:51; Heb. 2:4).

5. *Conscience—suneidesis*. The immaterial aspect of man that allows him to make ethical decisions and implies moral ability within all men (1 Cor. 8:1-13; 10:23-11:1; 2 Cor. 5:11; 1 Tim. 4:2; Rom. 9:1).

E. BIBLICAL PHRASES RELATING TO THE WHOLE PERSON

1. *Natural man—anthropos psuchokos*. This refers to the unregenerate man who fashions his activities and ethics according to his basic nature. He is natural because he has not been changed by regeneration (1 Cor. 2:14).

2. *Spiritual man—anthropos pneumatikos*. This is the believer who submits his thinking to the influence of the Holy Spirit. He is characterized by demonstrating the fruit of the Spirit.

3. Carnal man—anthropos sarkikos. This is a regenerated person who refuses to submit his life to the influence of the Holy Spirit, rather he pursues those tendencies and desires that are characteristic of the natural man. The word "carnal" means "fleshly," and this person is controlled by his flesh.

4. The Old Man—anthropos palaios. This describes the sinful nature of the unregenerate person. This is not the same as the unsaved or the rational man, because Christians have an old nature or "an old man."

XI. THE HEART AS CATALYST TO UNDERSTAND MAN

The various aspects of the immaterial nature of man are usually described with the following terms: "soul," "spirit," "heart," "mind," "conscience," "old man," "new man," "flesh," plus other minor references. However, "heart" is the primary term to describe the immaterial aspect of man and usually relates to, or is the catalyst for, the immaterial man. To understand the immaterial nature of man one must understand the heart of man. Chafer notes the importance of this word.

> The word *heart* occurs over 600 times in the Old Testament and at least 120 times in the New Testament. . . . The extensive use of the word *heart* in all its varied implications places it in a position of supreme importance in Biblical psychology.[43]

The heart is also important because of its bearing upon the spiritual life of the child of God. For a man to fully comprehend God's way of spiritual life, he must realize that the Lord (Mark 12) commands man to love God with all his heart. Then the heart is important in light of contemporary study in the psychological makeup of man. God has spoken on psychology, though the Bible is not a psychology handbook; but when the Word of God speaks on this subject, it is authoritative. Therefore, what the Bible has to say on "heart," the primary word to describe the psychological functions of man, is of utmost importance and will shed light on the immaterial man.

A. THE HEART IS THE SEAT OF THE ENTIRE INNER MAN. The term *kardia*, "heart," is never used in the New Testament to denote the whole physical man as used in the Old Testament in such places as Exodus 28:29; 1 Samuel 25:37; 2 Samuel 18:14; 2 Kings 9:24. It is used figuratively in the New Testament to denote the entire immaterial man or a function of the inner man, but never of the physical organ.

The Old Testament use of "heart" to denote the entire physical man grew out of the Hebrew use of it as the center of physical life. Since the physical heart is the center of the circulatory system that distributes the blood to the body, it was a natural transition for the Old

Testament writer to bring the term over into the spiritual realm. Fletcher witnesses to this fact.

> This way of regarding the heart as the focus and centre of man's conscious life arose from the very primitive and general belief that the life was in the blood. If the blood was shed, the life was lost with it. The Hebrews shared in this belief. "The life of the flesh is in the blood" (Lev. xvii. 11). Hence arose the prohibitions in the O.T. against eating blood, and the association of sacrificial efficacy with the ritual of blood-shedding. The blood diffused through every part of the body was the vehicle of the life of the organism, whether of animals or of men. Now, although it was only in modern times that Harvey discovered the circulation of the blood, yet the ancients were quite familiar with the fact that the heart was the receptacle of the blood and even the centre of its distribution. Hence if the life was in the blood, the centre of that vitality was the heart.[44]

1. *The heart in relationship to the entire inner man.* The heart is the center of the real person when used figuratively in the New Testament, and is the center of spiritual life. Oswald Chambers recognizes this in his following statement,

> The heart, then, is the centre of living, the true centre of all vital activities of body and soul and spirit. When the Apostle Paul says "with the heart man believeth" he means by the word 'heart' more than we are apt to mean. The Bible always means more than we are apt to mean. The term 'heart' in the Bible means the centre of everything. The human soul has the spirit in and above it and the body by and about it; but the vital centre of all is the heart. When we speak of the heart, figuratively or actually, we mean the midmost part of a person. The Bible teaching differs from that of science in that it makes the heart the soul centre and the spirit centre as well.[45]

To explain and illustrate the above-mentioned fact farther, Chambers writes more to the point.

> According to the Bible the heart is the centre: The centre of memory, the centre of mercy, the centre of damnation and of salvation, the centre of God's working and the centre of the devil's working, the centre from which every thing works which moulds the human mechanism.[46]

The term center (British spelling, centre) implies the entire immaterial man. When Paul speaks, "Doing the will of God from the heart" (Eph. 6:6), or when he says, "I have you in my heart" (Phil. 1:7), he is using the word heart as the center of man. Christ, in the parable of the sower, likened ground to the hearts of men (cf. Luke 8:12). When Jesus says, "So shall the

Son of Man be three days and three nights in the heart of the earth" (Matt. 12:40), He is making a Hebrew parallelism, linking the heart as the center of the individual to the heart as the center of the earth. (Note, this reference is the only place in the New Testament that heart is not used in reference to an individual.)

The heart physically is the center from which life is dispersed to the body, so the heart figuratively is the center from which spiritual vitality is dispatched. Note Chambers' link of the heart as center to the outward body.

> The heart is not merely the seat of the affections, it is the centre of everything. The heart is the central altar, and the body is the outer court. What we offer on the altar of the heart will tell ultimately through the extremities of the body.[47]

Then linking the heart figuratively to the immaterial parts of man, Chambers describes,

> We have used a purely mechanical term in order to picture what the heart is, viz., the centre that emits rays of light and heat in the physical frame, in the soul, and in the spirit. The heart physically is the centre of the body; the heart sentimentally is the centre of the soul; and the heart spiritually is the centre of the spirit.[48]

When the New Testament uses the term "heart," it can in almost every place be interpreted as the center or seat of the immaterial part man. When used in this way emphasis is seen as to the central seat of emotions, moral consciousness, thought and volition. Whether viewed in one aspect or as a whole the heart is still pictured as the fountainhead of life. Dickson observes these conclusions.

> In the great majority of passages, it is absolutely necessary to give to the term the wider meaning, which is obviously implied in the cardinal counsel of Prov. iv. 23: "Keep thy heart with all diligence [literally: above all that is kept—*prae omni re custodienda*] for out of it are the issues [or sources] of life." It is not merely the receptacle of impressions and the seat of emotion, but the laboratory of thought and the fountainhead of purpose. Sometimes it appears as pre-eminently the organ of intelligence, as at Rom. i. 21; "Their foolish (ἀσύνετος) heart was darkened"; 2 Corinthians iii 15: "a veil lieth upon their heart"; 2 Cor. iv. 6: "God . . . shined in our hearts"; Eph. i 18: "having the eyes of your heart enlightened".[49]

2. *The definition of heart.* Now that it has been established the heart is the central seat of the immaterial man, a definition is necessary. Chambers has a simplified definition: "The use of the Bible term 'heart' is best understood by simply saying 'me.'"[50] This could not be termed a definition, but a description and therefore does not give definitive directions. Dickson has offered the following definition: "The *central seat and organ* of the personal life

of man regarded in and by himself."[51] The term "personal life" is not narrow enough to give meaning. S. Lewis Johnson in his dissertation has set forth the following:

> The activities of the heart mentioned concern the whole inner life of the man. Thus, in simplification, the heart may be considered to be the inward, central seat and organ of man's conscious life.[52]

The definition of "heart" that will be examined in the next few pages is: the heart is the central seat and organ of man's conscious life in its moral, intellectual, volitional, and emotional aspects. Fletcher has come close to this perspective in defining "heart," although he has omitted the capacity of moral conscience. "The heart was the *one* organ of all thinking and of all willing as well as of all feeling."[53]

B. THE HEART IS THE SEAT OF THOUGHT AND REFLECTION. The word "heart" conveys the meaning that is applied to the brain in this modern era. The word brain is not found in the Bible, but its function of thought and reflection is found in the word heart. Chambers witnesses to this fact. "In the Bible the heart, and not the brain, is revealed to be the centre of thinking."[54] The brain is in the place (physical organ) where expression is given for the functions of the heart, that is, from the head of man. Delitzsch in his *Biblical Psychology* came to the same conclusion.

> The result of our investigation is pretty much this: that the Scripture, without excluding head and brain (as we may see on a glance at Dan. ii 28, etc.) from the psychico-spiritual activities and affections, attributes the central agency of these to the heart.[55]

If we place rational elements only in the brain—such as spiritual capacities of believing, rejecting, hardening and indwelling—these functions would have been limited to the mind. Scripture bears out these to be in the heart. Therefore, logically the immaterial functions of rationality must be assigned to the heart. Chambers comes to this conclusion as regarding relationships of spiritual and rational powers.

> Thinking takes place in the heart, not in the brain. The real spiritual powers of a man reside in the heart, which is the centre of the physical life, of the soul life, and of the spiritual life. The expression of thinking is referred to the brain and the lips, because through these organs thinking becomes articulate.[56]

Therefore we see that "heart" is the term used in Scripture to convey the immaterial function that is expressed through the physical organ of the brain.

1. *The heart is related to thinking.* The writer of Hebrews speaks of "the thoughts and intents of the heart" (4:12), showing that the heart is the immaterial instrument of mental action. The heart and mind are synonymous in Hebrews 8:10: "I will put my laws into their mind, and write them in their hearts." Mark 2:8 indicates reasoning functions through the heart, and in Luke 2:51 the heart is the storehouse of memory. The secrets of men are kept in the heart (1 Cor. 14:25). Fletcher, seeing this truth, has stated.

The one term used throughout the whole of the N.T. for the mind of man is 'heart.' Or rather, the heart was regarded as the one organ of the mental life and all its manifold activities.[57]

Thinking is the process whereby we speak with our self; it is also called "sub-vocal talking." The means of thinking is with words. When we speak within, we think. "If that evil servant shall say in his heart" (Matt. 24:48). "Say not in thine heart" (Rom. 10:6). Johnson comments in his dissertation that these words "are a Hebraism which means 'to think secretly.'"[58]

2. *The heart is related to perception.* Perception is the obtaining of knowledge through the senses and assimilating the data with a view to correlating or systematically arranging it so it can be viewed by the mind. This takes place in the heart of man. When Christ speaks of a person's inability to perceive spiritual things, it because of a darkened heart. "And seeing ye shall see, and shall not perceive; for this people's heart is waxed gross" (Matt. 13:14-15). Oswald Chambers places the capacity of perception within the heart.

Perception means the power to discern what we hear and see and read; the power to discern the history of the nations to which we belong, the power to discern in our personal lives. This power is also in the heart.[59]

Knowledge and stimuli of the outer world are perceived by the heart and assimilated by the immaterial man. The heart is the storehouse of knowledge, or the place of memory in the immaterial makeup of man. Since the heart is the place where thinking takes place, it is to be expected that the material for thinking (words, symbols, and numbers,) be stored in the heart. "And his mother [Mary] kept all these sayings in her heart" (Luke 2:51). "And all that heard them laid them up in their hearts" (Luke 1:66). "I will put my laws into their hearts, and in their minds will I write them" (Heb. 10:16). In this verse the heart and mind are used synonymously for the storehouse of knowledge, and especially for spiritual knowledge. Therefore the heart is the storehouse of knowledge as the seat of the memory.

C. THE HEART IS THE SEAT OF EMOTIONS. Man is an emotional being with diverse types of feelings and desires, and these are wrapped up in the heart. Scripture shows the emotions of man as resident in the heart. Chafer in his observations of the heart has noted: "Similarly, the heart is the organ that reacts to human emotions and is thus easily considered the center of sensibility."[60] There are many lists and divisions of emotions, and the purpose of the following section is not to suggest an accurate list, nor a complete list. The following list is reflective of some emotions, identified in Scripture.

1. *Anger could be described as "fury, vexation, irritation or revenge."* This type of emotion is pictured as coming out of the lusts of the heart. "But if ye have bitter envying and strife in your hearts" (Jas. 3:14). "For out of the heart proceed evil thoughts . . . blasphemies" (Matt. 15:19). The problem of evil in relationship to the heart will be considered later, but here we have a potential of unchecked emotions coming from the heart.

2. *Fear is a form of "dread, terror, anxiety, grief, or worry."* It is an emotion that grips or controls the heart. Jesus rightly associated fear and the heart when He said, "Let not your heart be troubled, neither let it be afraid (John 14:27). "Because I have spoken these things unto you, sorrow hath filled your heart" (John 16:6).

3. *Excitement is characterized as an emotion of "joy, love, or one of strong positive passions."* This emotion of excitement is definitely pictured as stemming from the heart. Jesus witnesses, "I will see you again and your heart shall rejoice" (John 16:22). "They ate their food with gladness and simplicity of heart" (Acts 2:46). Chambers agrees with this when he witnesses, "All degrees of joy reside in the heart."[61]

4. *Remorse could be pictured as "pity, sympathy, or sorrow."* Paul expresses this type of emotion when he speaks out of a broken heart, "I have great sorrow and continual grief in my heart" (Rom. 9:2). Also Paul speaks, "What you mean by weeping and breaking my heart?" (Acts 21:13).

5. *Sex could be described as "lust, desire, appetite, or embarrassment."* Today some think of sex with entirely an evil flavor. The evil side of sex is described as arising in the heart, as Jesus points out. "But I say unto you, that whosoever looketh on a woman to lust after her hath committed adultery with her already in his heart" (Matt. 5:28). "For out of the heart proceed evil thoughts . . . adulteries, fornications" (Matt. 15:19). The evil side of these emotions comes from the heart. But there is a positive side to the emotions of sex associated with love and stemming from the heart. Husbands are exhorted to love their wives (Eph. 5:25). Love, we see from Matthew 22:37, comes from the heart, "Love the Lord thy God, with all thy heart." Fletcher agrees with the placing of emotions in the heart.

More than any other Biblical writer Paul regards the "heart" as the seat of feeling. We shall see later that the Apostle takes over from the Greek certain psychological terms to express the mental and moral aspects of man's inner life, and so is free to develop in harmony with O.T. precedents, the emotional meaning of "heart."[62]

D. THE HEART IS THE SEAT OF MORAL CONSCIOUSNESS.

1. *The heart in relation to moral consciousness.* Deep within man there is an awakening to the Person and reality of a divine Being, an enlightenment to a divine standard. Whether men allow themselves to believe or force themselves to reject the voice of moral consciousness, it is still within man. Fletcher expands this truth.

> The "heart," being considered in Biblical psychology the organ of all possible states of consciousness, is pre-eminently the seat of moral consciousness or conscience. In it lies the fountain-head of the moral life of man. Hence in the N.T. the "heart" is the metaphorical term for the whole inner character and its ethical significance cannot be overrated.[63]

2. *The heart and the conscience.* Here Fletcher assigns moral consciousness and the conscience as the same capacity, and suggests they function in the heart. The Scriptures agree to this, for two verses place the conscience in the heart of man. "Which show the work of the law written in their hearts, their conscience bearing witness, and their thoughts the mean while another accusing or else excusing one another" (Rom. 2:15). In this verse we find the conscience in the heart acting as a moral regulator. Note the relationship between the conscience and thoughts, for the heart is the seat of thoughts, as well as the seat of the conscience. The other verse placing the conscience in the heart is Hebrews 10:22, "Let us draw near with a true heart in full assurance of faith, having our hearts sprinkled from an evil conscience." Since man has this moral consciousness or conscience in his heart, we cannot use the term without attempting to define it. "Conscience" comes from *suneidasis,* a "knowing with oneself." A modern definition from Emerson is that the conscience,

> is inherent in the human heart; the work of the law being written in their hearts which furnishes them with the point of contact with the demands of God and which is the basis of their moral nature.[64]

Conscience connects the standard of a knowledge of God with a person's self-awareness. As a person sees himself, he also sees God's requirement for his life. The functions of the heart are added to the definition of "conscience" by Delitzsch:

> The conscience, therefore, is the natural consciousness to man, as such, of the law in his heart; the religious-moral determination of his self-consciousness dwelling in the human spirit, and effectuating itself even against the will in all the forms of life of

man; the ethical side of the general sense of truth, (*sensus communis*). which remained in man even after his fall; the knowledge concerning what God will and will not have, manifesting itself progressively in the form of impulse, and judgment, and feeling.[65]

The Scriptures definitely place the conscience in the heart since it is the seat of thoughts, the storehouse of knowledge, the fountainhead of volition, all of which must operate in the function of the conscience. Since the heart is the place where God works in the individual (Rom. 5:5; Eph. 3:16; 2 Cor. 1:22; Col. 3:15) it is only natural to expect the heart to be the seat of moral consciousness. The heart is the immaterial organ in man which has the capacity to perceive God's expectation and receive a knowledge of His person.

E. THE HEART IS THE SEAT OF VOLITION. The seat of volition in man can be expressed as his power to choose or give self-direction. Both Scripture and experience tell us man has a will. The problem comes when we attempt to locate it in the immaterial makeup of man.

The Bible places the power to will and choose in the heart. "But God be thanked, that ye were the servants of sin, but ye have obeyed from the heart" (Rom. 6:17). To obey is to express one's freedom of choice. Johnson explains this verse, "This obedience is described as ἐκ καρδίαις. It seems evident that in this passage the heart is considered to be the seat of the will, the fountainhead of purpose."[66] Since man is a rational being with ability to think and rationalize, the heart which is the seat of thought is the logical place to locate the ability of volition. Choice is usually connected with thinking, emotions or instructions from the conscience. Chambers locates volition in the heart as he interprets Romans 6:17: "These passages [Rom. 6:17; Exod. 35:21] are typical of many which prove that the act of choice is in the heart, not in the brain."[67]

Another verse that places the will in the heart is 2 Corinthians 9:7, "Let each one give as he purposes in his heart." Here we see the act of choice taking place within the heart.

Willfulness is a volitional ability to reject and is called a "hardening of the heart" in Hebrews 3:8: "Harden not your hearts, as in the provocation." "To whom our fathers would not obey, but thrust him from them, and in their hearts turned back again into Egypt" (Acts 7:39). When the Scriptures speak of the heart in regard to "singleness," it means freedom from duplicity. "Be obedient to them that are your masters according to the flesh, with fear and trembling, in singleness of your heart" (Eph. 6:5).

In the above-mentioned Scriptures two aspects of will were manifested from the heart. First, that of choice—the response of our will to love God—was seen in Romans 6:17. Second, the will was exercised in planning, as observed in 2 Corinthians 9:7. Chambers follows this division of will. He notes that the Bible reveals that the power of choice springs from the heart, and there are two things to be looked at: Determination which means "to fix the form of our choice" and Design which means "planning in outline."[68]

Guard must be taken against separating the functions of the heart. The heart is a unity and functions as a unity. The will or choice as placed in the heart cannot be separated from influence by emotions, conscience or one's storehouse of knowledge. The heart must be thought of as a totality. The seat where thinking takes place as well as the home where emotions exist, is also the fountainhead of moral consciousness and volition. Within the heart these functions all interact. Therefore, the heart must be thought of as a unity.

XII. The Heart And The Soul And/Or Spirit

A. The relationship of spirit and soul. The Scriptures attribute both soul and spirit to man. Fletcher, in noting the connection of these two, has made the following remark: "The soul is that in each man which lives, the spirit is the power or principle by which he lives."[69] Both soul and spirit are immaterial, that is, the same in essence or nature. However, Fletcher separates their functions.

> The soul is life embodied, the spirit is life as coming from God. They are not different in essence. The one is life-human, the other is life God-given . . . God by the inbreathing of the spirit of life constituted man a "living soul." Two things are made clear in this narrative. The animating principle in creating man in the spirit from God. The animated result—is a living soul.[70]

In general, the soul in Scripture is connected with earthly life, while the spirit has a heavenly relationship. This is only a generality, as these two functions overlap many times. One distinction is made by *The International Standard Bible Encyclopedia*: "Man *is* not spirit, but he *has* it: he is *soul*."[71]

Guard against using the terms "spirit," "soul," and "heart" synonymously. Each is different and each has a different function in the inner man. Johnson in his views of Biblical psychology places the soul and spirit within the heart. It thus appears that the heart in this instance (John 14:1) is considered to be the seat and center of the individual man's personal life.

B. The heart as motivation of the soul-spirit. Essentially the soul-spirit is amoral, that is, it is neither good or bad, or has neither positive or negative motivations. The heart is the motivation of the soul-spirit and is the driving force to evil or to belief. All the capacities and functions of the heart are brought to influence and motivate the soul-spirit. It is the heart that is morally good or bad. In those few instances where the soul or spirit appear to have moral (evil or good) inclinations, it is because the heart is functioning through one or the other separately, or through both together.

Since the heart is the seat of volition, lust, and belief, it is not hard to see the heart as the motivation behind the soul-spirit. It is the power that drives men to evil or righteousness. Fletcher notes that the heart "is the starting point of all his activities."[72] The lust of a man's heart can motivate the soul-spirit (Matt. 15:18-19). The seat of volition which is centered in the soul, makes decisions which direct and guide the soul-spirit. The truth of 1 Peter 1:22 shows "the purifying of our souls" is the result of the motivation of the heart by obedience, which comes from the heart (Rom. 6:17).

Emotions arise in the heart and express themselves through the soul-spirit into or through the body. Scriptures which place the emotions in the heart imply that the heart is the motivating power behind the soul-spirit.

C. THE SOUL-SPIRIT FUNCTIONS THROUGH THE HEART. Since the heart is the motivation, the morality, and the force within man, the soul-spirit must be seen to function through the heart for it has no power of, and in itself. Chafer notes this in his observation of the heart: "It is to be seen that the term *heart* represents specific exercise of the realities of human life and may thus, to some extent, be distinguished from the soul and the spirit."[73] The heart is the center of man and, as such, all capacities flow from it, hence the soul-spirit must function through the heart. Cremer, in his *Biblico-Theological Lexicon*, puts forth this thesis.

> Altogether, indeed, the heart, as the point in which the entire personal life is concentrated, is specially . . . the point of concentration (focus and spring) of the religious life. This is its function, because it is the seat or organ of that which is the distinctive feature of man's personality, to wit the πνεῦμα, which ultimately and mainly must be regarded as the principle of the divine life, and therefore the principle of the God-related life.[74]

Some confusion remains concerning the relationship of the heart and the soul-spirit. Some functions have been identified with both the heart and soul-spirit, obscuring the definition of the heart as related to the soul-spirit. The spirit is identified as the focus of emotions in Mark 8:12. Volition is placed in the spirit by some Scriptures (Matt. 26:41; Mark 14:38; Acts 19:21; 20:22), but Fletcher notes the spirit functions through the heart, which is the seat of volition.

> The soul functioned through the heart and came thereby to itself in thought and purpose. So that while moderns speak of the mind as the organ of consciousness, the Biblical writers invariably regarded the heart as fulfilling that function.[75]

The heart is the organ in which one may receive knowledge of God (Rom. 5:5), yet 1 Corinthians 2:6-14 implies knowledge of God is received by the spirit of man. Fletcher implies the heart is where the spirit meets God.

The "heart," then, means the inmost and essential part of man whereby the human spirit functions in response to the presence of the Divine Spirit. "The love of God hath been shed abroad in our *hearts* through the Holy Spirit which was given unto us." The "heart" is the meeting-place of the human spirit and the Holy Spirit. Hence while it is true that "the Spirit himself beareth *witness with our spirit*, that we are the children of God," it is in *the heart* that the Spirit of adoption bears its witness to the spirit of man, "Because ye are sons, God sent forth the Spirit of His Son into our *hearts*, crying, Abba, Father."[76]

Therefore, the soul-spirit receives spiritual things through the heart. The heart of man believes, but the soul is saved. The heart expresses volition, but "the Spirit itself beareth witness with our spirit" (Rom. 8:16).

The heart contains the elements that make up personality. Yet most modern theological writers wrongly ascribe personality to soul. Fletcher follows this wrong identification by saying, "The soul in the Pauline psychology, is rather the bearer of the personality of the natural man."[77] In truth, the soul-spirit functions through the heart in that it receives and manifests spiritual principles and reality. Cremer supports this view,

> For as the personal life (of the soul) is conditioned by the spirit and mediated by the heart, the activity of the spirit must be *specially* sought in the heart. . . . As the spirit is specially the divine principle of life, and is therefore particularly employed where manifestations, utterances, states of the religious, God-related life come under consideration, we can understand why religions life and conduct pertain mainly to the heart.[78]

XIII. THE HEART AND THE MIND

The heart and mind are closely related in the New Testament, but are not synonymous. The two terms are named together in Mark 12:30, as heart and thoughts are used together in Philippians 4:7. The functions of mind are attributed to heart (Heb. 4:12; Rom. 10:6; Acts 2:26), so that the mind functions through the heart and because of this, one often appears to see the same function proceeding from both heart and mind. The New Testament makes a more noticeable distinction between the two, as Laidlaw notes,

> In the OT it by no means signifies mainly or only the emotional or volitional elements in human nature, but pre-eminently the intellectual. . . . It is only in the later Scriptures that the Greek habit of distinguishing the rational from the emotional finds place.[79]

A. THE MIND HAS AN ETHICAL SENSE IN THE NEW TESTAMENT. The mind is sometimes used in connection with sinful flesh, as in Colossians 2:18, "puffed up by his fleshly mind"; sometimes in direct contrast to it, as in Romans 7:25, "With the mind I serve the law of God;

but with the flesh the law of sin." In Titus 1:15 the mind functions parallel to the conscience, "Their mind and conscience is defiled." Conscience and mind apparently function through the heart and interact one upon the other. As man is corrupt to the center, which is the heart, the mind is subject to corruption because it functions through the heart. Phrases like "a reprobate mind" (Rom. 1:28) and "corrupt minds" (1 Tim. 6:5), show this connection. The result is that the mind operates through an unconverted heart, "the understanding darkened" (Eph. 4:18). Also note the parallel function of the mind with the flesh, "The desires of the flesh and of the mind" (Eph. 2:3). Hence, the depravity of man is linked with the heart and mind in Luke 1:51.

The renewal or regeneration of man takes place in the mind, as well as other parts of the immaterial man. Paul, speaking in Romans 12:2, mentions, "Be ye transformed by the renewing of your mind." Also the product of our transformed mind is seen in 1 John 5:20, ". . . hath given us an understanding, that we may know him that is true."

B. THE MIND AND ITS FUNCTION. The mind is conscious of the outer world, to perceive its stimuli, reflect in memory, consider the desires, respond to the will, and form opinions or direct one's life. This mental activity takes place in the mind, which functions through the heart. Hastings observes how Christ's mind was conscious to the outer world, "Perhaps the first characteristic to notice is the way in which the mind of the Lord Jesus was always so thoroughly *alive to everything around Him.*"[80] As the heart and mind are conscious to the world around, they are also conscious to the self, which means it has the ability of self-perception. Chafer, notes, "In this manner the Word of God relates the term *heart* to natural self-knowledge."[81] The mind also perceives stimuli from the outer world. Most people usually place the storehouse of knowledge or memory in the mind, but Scriptures place it in the heart, "Mary kept all these sayings, pondering them in her heart" (Luke 2:19). Fletcher has seen this distinction when he notes: "It [the heart] was regarded as the storehouse into which all sensations were received and the workshop from which all acts proceeded."[82] The heart then is seen as the center through which functions the mind and its activities. Fletcher supports this point: "The heart was the one organ of all thinking and of all willing as well as all feeling. It was the meeting place of all man's powers of mind."[83]

XIV. THE HEART AND THE CONSCIENCE

The conscience is a moral ability of the inner man received at birth to discern certain aspects of the moral law of God. As seen before, the heart is the seat of moral consciousness and as such contains the conscience. The conscience is part of the original nature given man by God. It has survived the Fall and is part of man's perpetual endowment. The conscience is not the communication of God directly to His creatures by His Spirit. Emerson notes this. "Conscience is definitely not, as some would have it, the voice of God's Holy Spirit speaking to us."[84] The conscience is a witness to man of a divine standard and the existence of God. Delitzsch, in his view of biblical psychology, bears this out. "If we ask about the nature of the conscience, it is everywhere found that it is not God who gives witness to the conscience, but the conscience that gives witness to man."[85]

A. THE CONSCIENCE WORKS IN LIGHT OF KNOWLEDGE. The heart is the seat of intellect and reflection, forming a close interaction between the heart and conscience. The ability to discern is based on knowledge that comes in the mind of man. Paul in 2 Corinthians 4:2 implies the relationship of knowledge and conscience, "By the manifestation of the truth commending ourselves to every man's conscience." To this could be added the substantiation by Delitzsch, "Why, then, ought not man's knowledge about his relation to God from the beginning to be called conscience . . . ?"[86] Thinking, memory and perception functions in the heart of man. These all come to action in the operation of the conscience. In a given situation, man must first perceive all stimuli and transfer them to the heart. Here man's memory produces facts and places them at the disposal of the mind. The conscience then discerns the moral worth of the issue.

B. THE CONSCIENCE ENLIGHTENS THE HEART TO MOTIVATION. After the conscience has functioned in its ability to discern, the heart motivates the outer life to the issue at hand. The conscience has no power to motivate the life. It is only a moral regulator. The only ability the conscience possesses is to discern, not to motivate, as noted in Hebrews 9:14; 13:18; 1 Peter 2:19; Romans 9:1. The heart, not the conscience, is the motivating power of life.

C. THE CONSCIENCE IS DEVELOPED BY RIGHT DOING. The conscience is not a static form placed in a person at birth, never to change. The conscience can grow in its ability and thus become a fair guide to the heart. Paul, by doing what is morally and religiously expected, could say, "I exercise myself to have always a conscience void of offence toward God, and toward men" (Acts 24:16). The development of the conscience is implied in 1 Corinthians 8:12, where it is called "weak." Here the weak brother is given opportunity to grow, so also was his conscience. Also the Christian is challenged to have a "good conscience" (1 Tim. 1:19), thereby implying that it can improve. One would generalize that when we grow in the Lord, it is our capacity that grows, so also our conscience grows. There is no growth of the heart mentioned in the Scriptures.

D. THE CONSCIENCE IS WEAKENED BY ITS SUPPRESSION. The heart is the seat of volition, also of lust. When the conscience discerns moral issues (i.e., knowing what is good), but the entire man acts evil, the heart has willed to ignore the conscience in moral issues. The will and emotions of the heart should interact with the moral direction of the conscience. By continual rejection of the light of the conscience, it loses its effectiveness to discern.

"Having their conscience seared with a hot iron" (1 Tim. 4:2). These have fallen away from the faith (vs. 1) and have made their conscience useless to discern. In Titus 1:15 one finds a worse case when, "Their mind and conscience is defiled." Here the conscience had degenerated; not only is it useless to discern good or evil, but by being defiled, what was thought to be wrong becomes right in its regulations.

XV. THE HEART AND THE OLD MAN OR FLESH

The heart has been shown as the motivating power in man; also, the heart was seen to contain the seat of lust in the individual (Matt. 15:18 -19). These facts relate the heart to the flesh and/or old man within the immaterial aspects of man. To use the terms "flesh" and "old man" call for a definition. Hastings, in his dictionary, gives the definition. "The flesh is the present abode of sin, which requires an obedient subject to execute its beliefs."[87] Although "flesh" is also used to describe the physical makeup of the human body, it is used here to refer to sin in the individual. In defining "old man," *The International Standard Bible Encyclopedia* identified it with flesh.

> A term thrice used by Paul (Rom. 6 6; Eph. 4 22; Col. 3 9) to signify the unrenewed man, the natural man in the corruption of sin, i.e., sinful human nature before conversion and regeneration. It is theologically synonymous with "flesh" (Rom. 8 3-9), which stands, not for bodily organism, but for the whole nature of man. . . .[88]

The flesh and/or old man therefore are seen to exist in the same realm where the abode of sin exists in the individual. The flesh and/or old man appear both in the regenerate and unregenerate man. Paul's design was to set forth not the origin of sin from the flesh, but the power of sin in the flesh. The origin of sin is from the heart.

A. THE HEART AND LUST. The heart is the motivating power of man. The power forcing man to evil is called lust or strong desire in Scripture. Paul in Romans 1:24 says lust proceeds from the heart, "God also gave them up to uncleanness through the lusts of their own hearts." Ephesians 2:3 speaks of "the lusts of our flesh." This might seem contradictory, if flesh is viewed only as the physical body, but "flesh" is another title for the old nature, or old man, and is pictured as functioning through the heart. Johnson places lust in the heart.

> The heart is spoken of as that which lusts or possesses lust. Of course, the word ἐπιθυμία is neutral in itself and it may refer to a good desire as well as an evil desire . . . it is used here (Rom. 1:24) to indicate evil lusts as the context and the following phrase proves. Thus in the passage under consideration the heart is seen to be the seat of lust.[89]

With the old man and/or flesh having its capacity or function in the heart, it is easy to understand lust as proceeding from it. We cannot equate the two, that is, calling heart and flesh the same, or identifying old man and the heart as one. They are different capacities of the immaterial man and must be treated as such. Their interaction is complex, the flesh and/or old man having its existence or function through the heart.

B. THE HEART AND TOTAL DEPRAVITY. Lust is the function of sin, and depravity the focus of sin in the individual. Depravity is man's inability to satisfy God by doing good and gain merit toward righteousness. In Adam's rebellion he became depraved, and sin as a principle spread to the center of man, that is, to the heart. Therefore, total depravity (not a biblical phrase, but a biblical principle) affects the heart of man. The principle of depravity has penetrated to every part of man's existence. Laidlaw has made a good summary of this.

> In the heart lies the moral and religious condition of man. Only what centers the heart forms a possession of moral worth, and only what comes from the heart is a moral production. On the one hand, therefore, the Bible places human depravity in the heart, because sin is a principle which has penetrated to the centre, and thence corrupts the whole circuit of life.[90]

The heart issues lust because it is the seat of the flesh and/or old man. Because the heart is depraved, the whole inner man is corrupt. The entire inner man is affected by sin, "Became vain in their imaginations and their foolish heart was darkened" (Rom. 1:21). Depravity as a principle affects intellect and reflection because its seat is in the heart of man. Liddon, writing on this verse, has noted: "The [heart] . . . is darkened, because the empty speculations had rendered it . . . i.e., incapable of understanding what is true and right.[91] Therefore, the corruption of the heart affects all capacities of the immaterial makeup of man.

C. THE HEART MOTIVATED BY SIN. Man is described as essentially evil because his heart is evil. While man can do many good deeds and have positive beautiful thoughts and creative moments, he also can be motivated by evil desires that harm others and himself, as well as rebel against God. For out of man arise evil thoughts, desires and a tendency toward sin. The Scriptures indicate this black side of man's personality resides in the heart.

> But the things which proceed out of the mouth come forth out of the heart; and they defile the man. For out of the heart come forth evil thoughts, murders, adulteries, fornications, thefts, false witness, railings: these are the things which defile the man; but to eat with unwashen hands defileth not the man (Matt. 15:18-20 ASV).

The heart is the problem to both the Christian and non-Christian in their relationship to sin. Man cannot do good apart from a new nature given him at the time of his regeneration. Not only is sin the motivating principle of the unsaved man, it is so of both the outwardly immoral person and the individual who regards himself as moral. Fletcher comments on this.

It is possible for one, whose outward behaviour may be irreproachable, by giving way to unholy imagination and desire to "commit adultery in his heart" in the region of moral choice and purpose.[92]

Sin is an act of volition, influenced by the intellect and emotion, but motivated by lust. The will of man, which has its seat in the heart, is a primary cause of sin. Emerson notices this. "Will is the basic fact in both sin and righteousness.[93]

D. THE HEART DECEIVED BY SIN. Sin as a principle motivating from the heart has so hindered the heart and its capacity to understand spiritual things that the heart is spoken of as having eyes that are blind to spiritual truth (2 Cor. 4:3-4). To understand spiritual truth, a believer must have "the eyes of your understanding being enlightened" (Eph. 1:18). Sin has affected the heart so that the inner man is incapable of receiving spiritual truth. "The god of this world hath blinded the minds of them which believe not" (2 Cor. 4:4). Two verses later Paul proclaims, "God . . . hath shined in our hearts" (2 Cor. 4:6), teaching the heart can be enlightened. Both deception and illumination take place in the heart. Notice Romans 16:18 teaches that it is possible to "deceive the hearts of the simple." Johnson refers to this act of beguiling.

The verb ἀξαπατάω as well as ἀπατάω always refers to a deception which reaches the inner man. The former word is used in two places, 2 Timothy 2:14 and 2 Corinthians 11:3, of the deception of Eve by the Serpent. In fact in the passage in 2 Corinthians the implication is that the deception of Eve took place in the thoughts of her mind. Thus, in this verse the memory is the same as in the other occurrence of the word, namely, the central seat and organ of man's conscious life in its moral and intellectual aspects. The activities of the heart as the central seat and organ of man's conscious life is here seen to be in the sphere of thought and reflection.[94]

Both heart and mind are beguiled because the mind functions through the heart, which is the seat of sin. Because of evil, man cannot perceive God in any way apart from a divine intervention. When the Holy Spirit convicts a man of sin, of righteousness and of judgment (John 16:8-11) the basic work is when the Holy Spirit enables a man to perceive these things.

The heart of both the saved and unsaved is capable of being deceived by sin. Of the unsaved Chafer says, "Satan's veiling of the minds of the unsaved relative to the gospel by which they may be saved."[95] Regarding the saved person's blindness he goes on to say, "The carnal Christian's blindness and limitation when attempting to understand Scriptures are described in 1 Corinthians 3:1."[96] The cure for blindness in the unsaved is when the Holy Spirit first causes him to see his sin, which establishes a need, and second when the Holy Spirit causes him to see the Gospel which can save. Then salvation begins in the heart (Rom. 10:9-10). The cure for carnal blindness is when the Christian completely yields to

Christ and is illuminated by the Holy Spirit to see truth. This also takes place in the heart since the heart is the seat of volition. After the heart is no longer deceived and blinded, that is, the cure has been effected in the heart, the individual perceives moral knowledge of spiritual things. Fletcher notes the results of an enlightened heart.

> Knowledge of divine truth, argues the Apostle, brings a feeling of certainty to the mind, and the free exercise of God-given power gives a sense of mastery and serenity to the moral life. The result is peace. The intellectual processes of the "heart" find satisfaction in reaching Truth, the moral functions of "heart" are harmonized in attaining Goodness, and the emotional states of the "heart" are fulfilled in Love.[97]

E. THE HEART HARDENED BY SIN. The starting point of faith and spiritual growth is in the heart; as it as also the starting point of belief in man. If the heart is inclined to faith, but sin and lust force the heart to unbelief continually, the heart is said to become hardened. This can happen in both the saved and unsaved man. The Lord warns His disciples of unbelief, "He upbraided them with their unbelief and hardness of heart, because they believed not" (Mark 16:34). Here the unbelief is said to be accompanied by hardness of heart. The unsaved man's heart can also be hardened as in Romans 2:5, "but after thy hardness and impenitent heart."

In the original language, hardness comes from *ametanontos*, which literally means "without change of mind." It comes from *menanoeo* "to change one's mind." The *alpha* privative, meaning a prefix of the letter "a," is added to the adjective to give the negative meaning. Therefore, this gives the meaning of thought and reflection which takes place in the heart when it is hardened. Fletcher says of this word, "It is the use of the heart devoid of feelings."[98] The modern evangelist might be in sympathy with him, but the original language gives it a different shade of meaning.

To picture more precisely the work of God in the hardening of a heart, Romans 1:24 gives this view. "Wherefore God also gave them up to uncleanness through the lusts of their own hearts." Man's part would be to choose sin that comes from his lust, hence man hardens his heart. God's part would be giving them up because of their choice based on reflection and intellect. Johnson says of this verse," παρέδωκεν does not signify that God impelled to evil, nor even that He permitted evil but rather that He positively withdrew His restraining hand."[99] Hence we see sin hardening the heart, making it incapable of belief and faith.

F. THE SPHERE OF DOUBT. At times the Christian finds himself in the state of doubt. This is the opposite condition to faith. Sin motivating the heart and trying to rule the Christian's life, is in most cases the cause of doubt. Doubt comes from the heart as seen in Mark 11:23, "And shall not doubt in his heart," because the spiritual center of man is the heart. Since faith comes from the heart, it is only logical that its antithesis comes from the heart. Christ places them so, "If ye have faith, and doubt not" (Matt. 21:21). Also obedience was noted as stemming from the heart. Note the comparison of absence of doubt with obedience in Acts 10:20, "Get thee down, and go with them, doubting nothing."

With motivation of sin and righteousness coming from the heart, doubt cannot be called an absolute quality. In Matthew 14:31, Christ, speaking to Peter, said, "O thou of little faith, wherefore didst thou doubt?" Faith and doubt, both coming from the heart, are mixed here. Faith is not completely absent nor is doubt. Gray notes here, "'Doubt' does not indicate a lack of faith, but rather 'a state of *qualified* faith': its weakness, but not its absence."[100]

XVI. The Immaterial Man And Salvation

A. THE AGENT OF FAITH. There are many expressions of faith, but in general, faith is a confidence in God built upon some knowledge of Him, put into action by a decision of the will, resulting in the expression of love or some other positive emotion. Therefore, all the functions of the heart are put into operation when the heart expresses faith. Scripture shows the heart as the agent of faith. "And Philip said, 'If thou believest with all thy heart'" (Acts 8:37). When speaking of one who had not believed, Peter said, "Thy heart is not right before God" (Acts. 8:21). A central passage teaches that belief takes place in the heart. ". . . and shalt believe in thine heart . . . for with the heart man believeth unto righteousness" (Rom. 10:9-10). Johnson says of this, "In the following verse the heart is seen as the seat of faith. . . . Thus, it becomes clear that . . . the activity of the heart is seen in the sphere of thought and reflection."[101] Therefore saving faith is believing with the heart, that is, putting all the functions of the heart into operation. Torrey says,

> In order to be saved we must believe with the heart. In the Bible the heart stands for the thought, feelings and will. A heart-faith, then, is a faith that rules the thought, the feelings and the will. The manifestation of heart-faith is action in the direction of that which is believed.[102]

The gospel message, "The word of faith, which we preach" says the apostle, "is nigh thee, even in thy mouth, and in thy heart" (Rom. 10:8). It not only finds a lodgement in the heart, as the intellect or reason, it meets also with a response from the heart, as the organ of spiritual consciousness. Our heart, which has "the love of God shed abroad" (Rom. 5:5), and the enlightenment of the Holy Spirit, has responded by an expression of faith.

The heart is the instrument of faith and is the recipient of the Holy Spirit given in justification, but this is only the first installment of a divine influence yet to be experienced. The believer can experience daily faith by obedience out of the heart (Rom. 6:17). The believer is indwelt in his heart by the Holy Spirit as Paul taught, "Who hath sealed us, and given the earnest [or first fruits] of the Spirit in our hearts" (2 Cor. 1:22).

In speaking of the daily faith coming from the heart, Fletcher gives the following:

The divine influence is conceived by Paul in the beginning of his ministry as moral energy intended to "stablish your *hearts* unblamable in holiness before our God" (1 Thess. iii. 13), "to comfort your *hearts*, and stablish them in every good work and word" (2 Thess. ii. 17). . . . But a growing experience of the work of God within all the processes of "the heart," as intellect, will and feeling, shows him that the final result is knowledge, power and peace.[103]

B. THE SEAT OF REGENERATION. When a person believes the gospel he becomes a child of God, a process called "regeneration." In the Old Testament the heart and regeneration were closely linked together in such verses as, "A new heart also will I give you, and a new spirit will I put within you" (Ezek. 36:26), and "Create in me a clean heart, O God; and renew a right spirit within me" (Psa. 51:10). In the New Testament the Holy Spirit operates within the heart, and since the Holy Spirit cannot be separated from the action of regeneration, it is implied that the heart and regeneration are vitally linked. When Luke described Lydia, "whose heart the Lord opened," (Acts 16:14) he is speaking of her regeneration. As noted before, the old man has its operation and function through the heart, so it is only logical to expect that the new man, a product of regeneration, has its function through the heart. Regeneration does not mean that a new personality is put within man, nor does it mean man loses his old heart. Fletcher notes, "That the saving process begins with a new heart means that not another self or personality is substituted, but that new principles of action are introduced."[104]

When man receives a new heart, it does not mean he loses his motivation to sin, nor does it mean he has a new volition, intellect, or emotions. Man retains these after salvation, but there is a creation within the heart, that is, a new function or capacity which is called "a new man." The capacities and functions which once were used for sin are now used for righteousness after regeneration. These capacities to sin or to perform righteousness take place in the heart. Note Chafer's observation of the new heart and regeneration.

> Into the whole "natural man" a new divine nature is imparted when the individual is saved. Salvation is more than a *change of heart*. It is more than a transformation of the old. It is a regeneration or creation of something wholly new which is possessed in conjunction with the old nature, so long as the child of God is in this body. The presence of two opposing natures (not two personalities) in one individual results in conflict.[105]

As seen in Chafer and before noted, the individual is not given another heart, but the addition as a "new creation" (2 Cor. 5:17). What then can be said of the heart? The Scriptures speak of the cleansing of the heart. "Out of a pure heart" (1 Tim. 1:5), "having our hearts sprinkled from an evil conscience" (Heb. 10:22). Note the act of salvation by faith comes from the heart, and purifies the heart, "purifying their hearts by faith" (Acts 15:9).

C. INDWELT BY THE HOLY SPIRIT. God the Holy Spirit dwells in the saved man. "The love of God is shed abroad in our hearts by the Holy Ghost" (Rom. 5:5). "God hath sent forth the Spirit of his Son into your hearts" (Gal. 4:6). "Who hath . . . given us the earnest of the Spirit in our hearts" (2 Cor. 1:22). Dickson notes this indwelling,

> The καρδία in this sense is accordingly set forth with special frequency as the recipient of the divine πνεῦμα as at Gal. iv. 6 . . . Rom. v. 5 . . . 2 Cor. i. 22 . . . It [the heart] is the sphere of the Spirit's various operations and influences, so as to be thereby comforted.[106]

The Holy Spirit in functioning in the heart first enables it to perceive or understand spiritual things. As before seen, the heart is darkened by sin, so the Holy Spirit must indwell and cause the heart to understand, since the seat of thought and reflection are centered there. Also the Holy Spirit puts into operation the entire spiritual life in man, seen in the act of regeneration, "born of the Spirit" (John 3:6). Also by the act of indwelling, the Holy Spirit insures a believer's final arrival in heaven (Eph. 1:13-14; 2 Cor. 1:22). Then too, the Spirit abides in the heart to help the weaknesses of the saint as he struggles against sin. "The Spirit also helpeth our infirmities for we know not what we should pray for as we ought . . . and he that searcheth the hearts knoweth what is the mind of the Spirit" (Rom. 8:26-27). Johnson comments on these verses as follows:

> God is described as the One who searches τὰς καρδίας. Two things may be noted here. In the first place, the human heart is again seen to be the place of the activity of the Holy Spirit, as it was in 5:5. By searching the heart, the Father hears the groanings of the Spirit. . . . Thus, the activity of the Holy Spirit is seen to be in the heart. In the second place, the verse is in agreement with the definition of heart just given. The words τὰς καρδίας are linked up in thought with the subject of the verbs προσευξωμεθα and οἴδαμεν and it seems clear that καρδία is used here as the central seat and organ of man's conscious life in its moral and intellectual aspects.[107]

D. INDWELT BY THE SON. Jesus Christ, the second Person of the Godhead indwells the Christian. Salvation is pictured as receiving the Son of God (John 1:12). As a result, Christ is said to dwell in the heart and is never pictured as indwelling other parts of the immaterial man. Paul prays of the Ephesians, "That Christ may dwell in your hearts by faith" (Eph. 3:17). This is an act of faith because it also is centered in the heart. Peter exhorts, "But sanctify the Lord God in your hearts" (1 Pet. 3:15). Paul identified the believer as participating in the substitutionary death of Christ, and as a result, Christ indwells the believer, "I am crucified with Christ: nevertheless I live; yet not I, but Christ liveth in me" (Gal. 2:20). Although here the heart is not pointed out as the sphere of indwelling, we can infer it, on the ground of the truth in the above-mentioned verses. In Galatians 2:20 the function of the indwelling gives the believer the strength or ability to live the Christian life.

E. INDWELT BY THE FATHER. The Scripture describes the Father as living in the individual believer, but does not mention specifically His indwelling the heart. By inference, we conclude He indwells the heart, or at least the immaterial aspect of man. Christ speaks of both Father and Son indwelling the Christian, "And my Father will love him and we will come unto him, and make our abode with him" (John 14:23). Paul speaks of this truth, "Ye are the temple of the living God; as God hath said, I will dwell in them" (2 Cor. 6:16). John writes of the Father's indwelling by stating it negatively, "Whosoever denieth the Son, the same hath not the Father" (1 John 2:23), to which he adds, "Let that therefore abide in you" (v. 24).

F. LOVE FROM THE HEART. Christ mentions the heart is required to love God, because our emotions come from the heart. Also knowing the inner struggle of the heart to lust and/or love, Christ mentions the heart must love God. "All thy heart," should leave no place for the lust-motivation of the heart toward sin. The soul and mind are mentioned here, because these have their functions through the heart, therefore the entire inner man must be given over to God in love. Of these three aspects of the inner person, Lenski adds interesting observations.

> Yet the heart is mentioned first, the soul properly next, and the mind last. . . . In the Biblical conception the *leb*, καρδία, "heart," is the very center of our personality; here also dwells the ψυχή, "the life" or "soul"; and here functions the διάνοια, "the mind" or power to think. The *nephesh* or ψυχή is the life that animates the body, the consciousness of which is in the "heart"; and the διάνοια is the reason together with all its functions, namely its thoughts, ideas, convictions, according to which the heart or personality acts.[108]

ENDNOTES

1.   Millard J. Erickson, *Christian Theology* (Grand Rapids: Baker Book House, 1984), 456-462.

2.   Olin Alfred Curtis, *The Christian Faith* (Grand Rapids: Kregel Publishing Company, 1905, reprinted 1971), 192.

3. Louis Berkhof, *Systematic Theology* (Grand Rapids: Eerdmans, 1932), 171-172.

4. B. B. Warfield, *Studies in Theology* (New York: Oxford University Press, 1932), 244.

5. J. Oliver Buswell, *A Systematic Theology of the Christian Religion* (Grand Rapids: Zondervan, 1962), 1:342.

6. W. H. Green, *Pentateuch Vindicated*, cited by A. A. Hodge, *Outlines of Theology* (London: Thomas Nelson, 1879), 297.

7. Erickson, 487-493.

8. Charles Hodge, *Systematic Theology* (Grand Rapids: Eerdmans, 1972), 1:78.

9. Louis Agassiz, cited by Charles Hodge, *Systematic Theology* (Grand Rapids: Eerdmans, 1972), 1:81.

10. Hodge, 1:79.

11. Ibid., 1:85, 87.

12. Ibid., 1:87.

13. William Jones, *Is God A White Racist?* (Garden City, NJ: Anchor/Doubleday Books, 1973).* This volume deals with the racial issues referred to in this paragraph.

14. Berkhof, 191.

15. William Wilson Stevens, *Doctrines of the Christian Religion* (Grand Rapids: Eerdmans, 1967).*

16. *Westminster Confession of Faith*, cited by William Cutson Stevens, *Doctrines of the Christian Religion* (Grand Rapids: Eerdmans, 1972).*

17. Robert Dabney, *Lectures in Systematic Theology* (Grand Rapids: Zondervan, 1975), 293.

18. Berkhof, 207.

19. Stevens, 207.*

20. Augustus Hopkins Strong, *Systematic Theology* (Valley Forge, PA: Judson Press, 1907), 520.

21. Stevens, 233-234.*

22. Richard Watson, *Theological Institutes*, II, 14-1115, cited by Lewis Sperry Chafer, *Systematic Theology* (Dallas: Dallas Seminary Press, 1975), 2:163.

23. Isaac Watts, cited by Richard Watson in Lewis Sperry Chafer, *Systematic Theology* (Dallas: Dallas Seminary Press, 1975) 2:163.

24. Hodge, 2:66.

25. William G. T. Shedd, *Dogmatic Theology* (Nashville: Thomas Nelson, 1980), 174.*

26. Gerrit Cornelius Berkouwer, *Sin* (Grand Rapids: Eerdmans, 1971), 309.*

27. Hodge, 2:70-71.

28. Ibid., 2:71.
29. Dabney, 319-320.
30. Strong, 493.
31. Dabney, 8-19.
32. Shedd, 255.*
33. Dabney, 320.
34. Stevens, 251-252.*
35. Hodge, 2:43-44.
36. Erickson, 520.
37. Hodge, 49.
38. Stevens, 245.*
39. Ibid., 243-244.*
40. Hodge, 50-51.
41. Erickson, 524.
42. Ibid., 525.
43. Lewis Sperry Chafer, *Systematic Theology* (Dallas: Dallas Theological Seminary Press, 1975), 2:187-188.
44. M. Scott Fletcher, *The Psychology of the New Testament* (London: Hodder and Stoughton, 1912), 76-77.
45. Oswald Chambers, *Biblical Psychology* (London: Simpkin Marshall Ltd., 1912), 99.
46. Ibid., 100.
47. Ibid., 99.
48. Ibid., 106-107.
49. William P. Dickson, *St. Paul's Use of the Terms Flesh and Spirit* (Glasgow: James Maclehose & Sons, 1883), 200-201.
50. Chambers, 99.
51. Dickson, 199.
52. Samuel Lewis Johnson, Jr., "A Survey of Biblical Psychology in the Epistle to the Romans" (unpublished Doctoral dissertation, Dallas Theological Seminary, Dallas, Texas, 1949), 103.
53. Fletcher, 76.
54. Chambers, 97.
55. Franz Delitzsch, *A System of Biblical Psychology* (Edinburgh: T. & T. Clark & Sons, 1879), 302.
56. Chambers, 124-125.
57. Fletcher, 74.
58. Johnson, 107.
59. Chambers, 110-111.

60. Chafer, 187.
61. Chambers, 115.
62. Fletcher, 79.
63. Ibid., 80.
64. Wallace Emerson, *Outline of Psychology* (Wheaton: Van Kampen Press, 1953), 434.
65. Delitzsch, 164.
66. Johnson, 102.
67. Chambers, 107.
68. Chambers, 107-108.
69. Fletcher, 50.
70. Ibid., 51.
71. J. I. Marais, "Soul," in *The International Standard Bible Encyclopedia* (Grand Rapids: Eerdmans, 1939), 5:2838.
72. Fletcher, 76.
73. Chafer, 2:187.
74. Herman Cremer, *Biblico-Theological Lexicon of New Testament Greek*, trans. Wm. Urwick (Edinburgh: T. & T. Clark, 1895), 349.
75. Fletcher, 77.
76. Ibid., 87.
77. Ibid., 45.
78. Cremer, 347.
79. J. Laidlaw, "Heart," *A Dictionary of the Bible*, ed. James Hastings (NY: Charles Scribner's Sons, 1909), 2:318.
80. E. P. Boys-Smith, "Mental Characteristics," *A Dictionary of Christ and the Gospels*, ed James Hastings (New York: Charles Scribner & Sons, 1906), 2:161.
81. Chafer, 2:187.
82. Fletcher, 76.*
83. Ibid.*
84. Emerson, 435.*
85. Delitzsch, 160-161.*
86. Ibid., 167.*
87. Hastings, 2:600.*
88. Dwight M. Pratt, "Old Man," in *The International Standard Bible Encyclopedia*, 4:2183 (page number could not be verified).
89. Johnson, 93.*
90. Laidlaw, 122.*

91.   H. P. Liddon, *Explanatory Analysis of St. Paul's Epistle to the Romans* (Minneapolis: James & Klock, 1899, reprinted 1977), 28.*
92.   Fletcher, 81.*
93.   Emerson, 444.*
94.   Johnson, 109.*
95.   Chafer, 2:51.*
96.   Ibid., 52.*
97.   Fletcher, 89.
98.   Ibid. 78.*
99.   Johnson, 93.
100.   James M. Gray, "Doubt," in *The International Standard Bible Encyclopedia*, James Orr, general editor, (Grand Rapids: Eerdmans, 1939), 2:871.
101.   Johnson, 108.
102.   R. A. Torrey, *What the Bible Teaches* (New York: Revell Publishing Company, 1898), 365-366.
103.   Fletcher, 90.
104.   Ibid., 83.
105.   Chafer, 2:347.
106.   Dickson, 201-202.
107.   Johnson, 104.
108.   R. C. H. Lenski, *The Interpretation of St. Matthew's Gospel* (Ohio: Wartburg Press, 1943), 880.

* Denotes page number(s) could not be verified.

CHAPTER XII -ECCLESIOLOGY

The Doctrine Of The Church

I. INTRODUCTION

American society seems to be growing more secular as humanism is becoming more influential in determining the attitudes and presuppositions toward institutions and life in general. The average person interprets society in general, and the church in particular, with less biblical perspective than in previous generations. This diversity, from a basic Christian orientation of life to a multifaceted interpretation of life, is called pluralism.

With the growth of pluralism in the secular community, there has grown an ecumenical pluralism in the church community. There are many expressions of Christianity: the different denominations, the different systems of theology, the different modes of worship, the different types of church polity, the different schools of evangelism and the different architectural expressions of church buildings. Along with this diverse expression of Christianity is the influence of the interdenominational movement, the charismatic movement, the electric church, the Bible college movement, the Christian school movement and the many expressions of evangelical media (Christian magazines, books, radio stations, television stations, film companies). Out of this milieu comes an ever-growing chorus of voices that attempts to either speak for the Christian church or to interpret it to the world. With the many expressions of Christianity and many models of the church, the question remains, What is the biblical church?

We live in a church age of sociological research where many people base their church ministry on the findings of surveys, median scores and case studies. These findings have their place. But this section assumes the only true model for the church is found on the pages of the New Testament. The student must study the New Testament to determine, first, the nature of the church, and second, the principles of ministry. After an ecclesiology is grounded in the Word of God, then the findings of sociological research can be applied to these principles for the outworking of ministry.

This section assumes the church has life and spirit because it is the body of Jesus Christ (1 Cor. 12:27; Eph. 4:15,16), and that its founder and head is Jesus Christ, who gives it authority and vitality. As such, the church is an organism and an organization. The church is an organism which elevates it above the business and social organizations of our day. But, the church is also an organization and, as such, must carry out its ministry in an age of business management and administration.

The media seem to have little respect for the contemporary church, portraying it as weak and anemic. The young person who watches a church service in the movies or reads about a religious ceremony in the newspaper gets the impression the church is filled with either the elderly or hypocrites. The problem is that the young people who are either "anti-church" or have rejected the church do not see it as a dynamic organization that is responsible for changing society and lives. The average young person usually hears of the hypocrisy of those who call themselves Christians or of the bureaucracy of those who serve in the church for the wrong reasons. As a result, many young people reject the church, not without some justification. Many churches are guilty of the abuse hurled at it by today's youth.

Young people who reject the contemporary church would like its founder, Jesus Christ. He was as anti-bureaucratic as they are. He condemned the religious sham of his age as young people condemn the religious sham of their day. Jesus was anti-bureaucratic in both His teachings and His life. In every sense of the word, Jesus was a revolutionary. But the problem is, the revolution that Jesus began against the dead religion of His day ultimately becomes the standard for the spiritual institutions of our day.

Christianity began with the man Jesus Christ. Jesus, the eternal Word of God, became flesh. It was in a physical body that Jesus at times was hungry, worked and became tired, and as all other humans, grew to full manhood. While in this physical body, Jesus was limited by its humanity. But on the other side, Jesus was also God and as such had the power of deity and possessed all of God's attributes. As the Son of God, Jesus did not sin, but the threat of death awaited him as all other humans. In his unique physical body, that was both divine and human, Jesus died, was buried, and on the third day his physical body arose from the dead. Finally, the physical body of Jesus Christ ascended into heaven, and today He is at the right hand of God the Father.

The physical body of Jesus Christ is the same one with which every Christian is identified on Calvary. In the Baptism of the Holy Spirit, the believer is baptized (placed into) Jesus Christ (1 Cor. 12:13). This action is also called the vicarious substitutionary death of Jesus Christ. In this body we died with Him, were buried with Him, and were raised again on the third day (Rom. 6:4-5).

Now the church is called His body (1 Cor. 12:27), sometimes called the local church, and is reflective of His human body. As such, the visible church is subject to the limitations of humanity, but is very much divine in its supernatural authority and spiritual power. Just as Jesus Christ in the human body was the God-man, so the church is both an organism and an organization.

The church of Jesus Christ should be anti-institutional, anti-establishment and revolutionary. That is because the church is God's institution to challenge the sinful ways of man, especially those which represent man's attempts to substitute for the provision of God. As such, the church should be those Christians who, on the cutting edge of society, form a more righteous way of life; but the church, as an institution established by God, is sometimes institutional and bureaucratic; it is the establishment that fights the progress of righteousness.

The fact that our youth misunderstand the church is reflective of the problem that the church faces today. The outward church is a misunderstood institution. It is diverse in appearance, conflicting in purpose, and often ineffective in ministry.

The Sunday morning church service varies from street to street and town to town. One church reminds you of an eighteenth-century ritual, while across town you enter a "mod" church service that is free-wheeling and contemporary.

Some churches meet in humble frame buildings on dirt streets. Others are cathedrals with soaring spires and magnificent stained-glass windows. Some churches are the "do it yourself" variety, with lay preachers and simple religious forms. Other churches are traditional, American main line Protestant churches. Some emerging groups emphasize "body life" and *koinonia* [sharing] fellowship.

Religious intensity varies from apathy in the traditional mainline denominational churches to the revivalistic fervor in some fundamentalist churches. The not-so-traditional ethnic sect (Mennonite) has family tradition, and the ritualistic, liturgical cathedral demands reverence from its worshippers. Those who worship in unstructured, loose-knit living room churches center their religious expression around *Koinonia*, while the emotional Pentecostal churches involve their members in charismatic worship. The mystical Eastern churches demand meditation and reflective worship. The only thing we know for sure is that churches are different from one another.

American churches give many images to the worshippers. Some churches appear to follow the New England Puritan tradition: a few hymns, some praying, and finally a sermon. Other churches resemble a schoolroom. The sermon-lecture is filled with references to the original text; many in the congregation take notes while the pastor--teacher may use an overhead projector to help deliver the sermon. Moving on to the next church, we may find the sermon sounding like a black-racist at an anti-white rally in Harlem. The next church visited may give the atmosphere of a group dynamics therapy session where the minister is the psychiatrist. The American church has a vast number of expressions. The differences in churches are deeper than doctrinal distinctives of denominations. There are cultural and social differences that affect the way that people worship God. There is such a varied expression in churches and denominations that we need to ask, What is the church? Where did it begin?

What is its biblical objective? and What are the New Testament distinctives of a church?

Each past generation has fought its own theological battle. This means that a theological issue was many times accepted as fact until it was carefully examined by society. This usually happened when culture changed and a doctrine was wrongly interpreted by some. Then there was a pressing need to determine what God's Word said on that doctrine. But once an issue became the focus of controversy, good men examined it carefully, disagreed passionately and finally exhausted every shade of meaning. Thereafter, the issue may still divide good men, but at least the implications of the doctrine were understood. Today's theological battle concerns the battle of the church: What is the *eccelesia*?

II. FIRST REFERENCE OF THE WORD "CHURCH"

The church is a New Testament doctrine not found in the Old Testament, although lessons and principles of the church that became revealed in the New are concealed in the Old. This present dispensation is called the "times of the Gentiles" and the inclusion of the Gentiles into God's plan is different than God's dealing with non-Jews in the Old Testament. To understand the church we must understand the relationship of the Testaments to one another.

There are basic distinctions between the Old and New Testaments. First, in the Old Testament we find the people of God are Jews, (i.e., a national ethnic entity), while in the New Testament the people of God are gathered from every ethnic background into a sociological community—Jews and Gentiles—into the church.

In the Old Testament we find the emphasis was on being born a Jew, a physical descendant of Abraham. The sign was a physical sign, circumcision. The New Testament assembly involves being born again, a spiritual birth.

In the Old Testament the symbols of redemption were located in the tabernacle (temple), priesthood and offerings; all were located at one place—Jerusalem. The New Testament symbols in the church–the Lord's Table and Baptism—could be administered any place the church gathered.

A. THE MEANING OF THE WORD "CHURCH." Since the church is a New Testament doctrine, the use of the term "church" is extremely crucial to an understanding of ecclesiology. The law of first reference concerning the church gives insight into ecclesiology (i.e., the first reference to any doctrine in Scripture usually contains the embryonic truth of its development. God introduces a subject in microscopic form and explains it fuller at a later time). "And I say also unto thee, That thou art Peter, and upon this rock I will build my church; and the gates of hell shall not prevail against it" (Matt. 16:18). Note the following from the first mention of the church.

1. *The church is built upon Divine Revelation.* In Matthew 16-17 Jesus told Peter that his insight concerning Christ as the Son of the living God came from the Father. Peter did not think up his ideas about Christ. "And Jesus answered and said unto him, Blessed art thou, Simon Barjona: for flesh and blood hath not revealed it unto thee, but my Father which is in heaven" (Matt. 16:17).

2. *The church was initiated by Jesus Christ.* When Jesus said he would build the church, it was in response to Peter's declaration of the deity of Christ. Since Christ is now properly recognized, the topic of the church can be introduced, for this is the vehicle for HIS future manifestation.

3. *The church when introduced was predicated as future.* Jesus stated, "I will" (future tense) "build," lit. Gk. "be building" my church.

4. *The church belongs to Christ.* He said, "I will build my church." It would be owned by Christ as a peculiar possession.

If one is puzzled over the use of "building" with the word *ekklēsia* it will be helpful to turn to I Pet. 2:5. Peter, the very one to whom Jesus is here speaking, writing to the Christians in the five Roman provinces in Asia (I Pet. 1:1), says: "You are built a spiritual house". . . . It is difficult to resist the impression that Peter recalls the words of Jesus to him on this memorable occasion. Further, on (2:9), he speaks of them as an elect race, a royal priesthood, a holy nation, showing beyond controversy that Peter's use of building a spiritual house is general, not local. This is undoubtedly the picture in the mind of Christ here in 16:18.[1]

5. *The church (ecclesia) is a group of "called out ones."* The word *ecclesia* comes from the Greek preposition "out" and the Greek verb "to call." Hence, the church is made up of those who are called out. This has a twofold meaning: (1) they are called out from the world and their previous ungodly life-style, (2) they are called together for a purpose. This purpose is to carry out the Great Commission.

The word "church" in this reference has four different interpretations. The term "church," *ecclesia,* appears in the singular in Matthew 16:18 and raises some difficulty in interpretation. (a). Christ was referring to one church (i.e., the Roman Catholic church and its system). (b). Christ was referring to the universal church, composed of all true believers. In essence, He would build up that assembly composed of every true believer in the entire age to come regardless of church affiliation. (c). Christ was referring to a church (i.e., He would build up one local church at a time, each one separate from the others, implying the independent nature of local churches). Christ would build a church in one area, then another. Those who hold this view are rejecting the Roman Catholic and the universal church view. (d). Christ was emphasizing "my church" indicating that He would build His kind of an assembly as opposed to other kinds of churches which were false.

Technically, "our English word 'church' like the German *kirche* . . . stems from the Byzantine [Greek] form *Kurike*, meaning "belonging to the Lord."[2] These words come from the Greek word *ekklesia* which means "to assemble."

The first mention of "church" introduces the embryonic teaching that will be elaborated throughout the New Testament. The church is uniquely the possession of the Savior. He will build it through His Word as He calls individuals into His fellowship. Once a person is incorporated into the church, he belongs to Jesus Christ. The church can never be disassociated from the deity of Jesus Christ, and when its members are responsive to Him, it will be victorious.

B. THE MEANING OF THE WORD "ROCK." "On this rock I will build my church" (Matt. 16:18). Much has been written concerning the meaning of the word "rock." Christ called Peter a rock, *Petros*, and said His church would be built upon this *petra*. Many modern scholars deny any significance to their similarity, yet there is a distinction in meaning of the two words for rock in the Greek language (one a smaller stone, the other a large shelf of rock). Some say there would have been no difference between the two words if Christ spoke in Aramaic. However, even if it were so, there would still be at least a play on words between the Aramaic *kephas* (Peter) and *kepha* (rock). It seems obvious, by virtue of the close proximity of the words, that Jesus intended there to be some distinction between Peter, the man, and the church. To identify the foundation as being Peter would do much to establish the Roman Catholic position regarding the primacy of the pope. But, this is neither necessitated by the immediate context nor borne out by the rest of the New Testament. Note the following interpretations of the word "rock."

1. *The word "rock" refers to the man in the sense of his ministry.* The phrase "upon this rock" means upon this man, whose ministry is soul winning, the church is established.

2. *The word "rock" refers only to the content of the message.* In this case, the rock is the revelation to man that Jesus is the Son of God as implied in v. 16, "Thou art the Christ, the Son of the living God." Hence, the church is built upon the preaching of the message that Jesus is the Son of God.

3. *The phrase "Upon this rock," has a dual meaning applying to both Peter, the man, and to his message.* Peter has just confessed that Jesus is the Son of God, which

is equivalent to confessing that the great truth revealed about Christ is His deity. A comparison of Matthew 16:16-19 with Ephesians 2:20 and 1 Corinthians 3:10-11 shows the human foundation of the church.

> And I say also unto thee, That thou art Peter, and upon this rock I will build my church; and the gates of hell shall not prevail against it (Matt. 16:18). . . . and are built upon the foundation of the apostles and prophets, Christ Jesus himself being the chief corner stone (Eph. 2:20).
>
> According to the grace of God which was given unto me, as a wise masterbuilder I have laid the foundation; and another buildeth thereon. But let every man take heed how he buildeth thereon. For other foundation can no man lay than that is laid, which is Jesus Christ (1 Cor. 3:10-11).

All three passages make important statements about the foundation of the church. First, Christ is the rock—foundation, upon which the church is founded. He becomes the foundation of the local church (1 Cor. 3) when He is preached and believed upon. Second, the apostles and prophets became the foundation when they received the revelatory message of the church from Christ and then went out as the human agents who correctly laid foundational truth (the Scripture) upon which all succeeding local churches would be built. In their preaching they were the human founders of the church, and in their writing of Scripture, they were the human instruments of divine inspiration, the message upon which the church is established. The primary function of the apostles and prophets was to set forth the inspired gospel message concerning Christ as the Son of God, the Redeemer.

Therefore, a twofold identity exists between Christ and Peter, *petros* and *petra*. As a believer in Christ, Peter was identified with the Savior. As an apostle, he was an inspired recipient of foundation truth; Peter was identified with the foundation of the church.

Here in Matthew 16:18 we find the ultimate law of church growth—"I will build my church." Church growth originates with the Lord. Because of this, church growth will always contain an element of mystery that defies our human penetration, analysis, and definition. We are cast back on the Head of the church in prayer, trustful waiting, and patient labor (2 Cor. 3:6-8).

The apostles were not prepared for such a drastic pronouncement. Apparently the imminent appearing of the church and its implications was new in their thinking and/or direction (Matt. 16:22). The apostles were still ignorant of the Cross and its foundation to the church that was yet to be introduced. Because of its radical innovation, the church is in no way an extension of the kingdom from the Old Testament. The entire context of Matthew indicates a newness—"I will (future) build my church."

C. THE MEANING OF THE WORD "KEYS." The next major problem involves the identification of the keys in Matthew 16:19. "I will give unto thee the keys of the kingdom of heaven: and whatsoever thou shalt bind on earth shall be bound in heaven; and whatsoever thou shalt loose on earth shall be loosed in heaven" (Matt. 16:19). Note the following problems:

1. *The word "keys" is plural, implying more than one key.* Is there more than one door to heaven, mandated by the suggestion of more than one key?

2. *The reference is to the "kingdom of heaven," usually referred to as the millennial kingdom.* Is the reference here to an earthly reward rather than to eternal life?

3. *The reference to "binding" could imply that what Peter bound on earth would determine whether the person or thing enjoyed eternal life.* Does Peter, a human instrument, have the power, actively or passively, to control anyone's destiny? The following are suggestive answers.

(a) The keys refer to Peter's role to forgive sins. This view reinforces the Roman Catholic's position or the human role to mediate salvation to individuals. (b) The keys refer to a ministry or to the involvement of a Christian as he exercises his spiritual assets. The most often used concept in this category is the ministry of soul winning. When the keys are used and a person is led to Christ, that soul-winner unlocks the door of salvation. (c) The keys refer to the content of the message to be delivered (i.e., the gospel). This view expands the previous one in that if Peter and other prophets had not received revelatory truth, sinners would have remained bound in sin. By being human instruments in writing Scripture, preaching to establish the church and general ministry of the Word of God, individuals could be free from the darkness of sin. (d) The keys are geographical expansions of salvation. For example, Peter first opened the door of salvation to the Jews on Pentecost and second to the Gentiles in the house of Cornelius. (e) The keys are predictions of Peter's role as preacher on the Day of Pentecost. Those who accepted salvation were given the freedom of eternal life.

Any time the Good News of Christ as the Son of God-Savior is proclaimed, the message opens the way into the kingdom for those who hear and believe; they thereby enter the kingdom. "The imagery of the keys is taken from the ancient practice of having a gate-keeper who would open a walled city or another large area to those entering."[3] This was not a special authority given to Peter establishing some kind of supremacy for him over the church or giving personal power to bestow salvation. Since the rock of verse 18 refers to the foundation of revelatory truth for the church, the keys probably continue this analogy and are a reference to the message of salvation that will free any who believe in its truth (John 8:32; 14:6).

D. THE MEANING OF THE WORDS "BINDING" AND "LOOSING." The fourth problematic phrase is "binding and loosing" (Matt. 16:19). This truth is also repeated in Matthew 18:18, "Whatsoever ye shall bind on earth shall he bound in heaven: and whatsoever ye shall loose on earth shall be loosed in heaven." There are at least four different interpretations to this phrase.

1. *Binding and loosing means apostolic authority.* Under the Roman Catholic system, the Pope (priest) has authority on earth and heaven with regard to the forgiveness of sins. They indicate that both Matthew 16:19 and Matthew 18:18 relate to the authority given to Peter at the foundation of the church. Hence, Peter and those who follow in papal succession have the authority to bind and loose on earth with a result that their decisions will determine who will enter heaven. This is not the place to refute papal authority, but the book of Hebrews teaches that, (1) salvation has been secured by Christ, (2) that grace is the means to obtain it, and (3) that each individual is a priest to God.

2. *Binding and loosing refers to soul-winning or to the ministry that results in bringing people to know Christ.* When a person accepts Christ, it means to bind Satan in relationship to eternal destiny while loosing involves freeing from sin. Those who follow the example of Peter can win people to Christ, hence loosing them from their sins. This ministry is available to all.

3. *Binding and loosing may refer to church discipline.* Those who hold this view claim that Matthew 18:18 interprets Matthew 16:19. Obviously Matthew 18:18 is a reference to church discipline. When brothers disagree, the offended brother goes to the one offending him, next takes a witness, and finally brings the matter before the church (Matt. 18:15-17). The church applies corporate wisdom to determine God's will. The church announces the results of what God has done. The church does not bind the person in heaven. It announces what will be bound in heaven because God is the One who has already made the judgment.

4. *Binding and loosing may refer to foundational truth that is revelatory in nature.* The church is built on the Scripture (Eph. 2:20; 1 Cor. 3:10) and Jesus Christ who revealed His truth to the apostles who preached it. To bind in rabbinical language means "to forbid;" to loose means "to permit." Jesus is announcing that Peter would be like a rabbi who communicates the law of God. The binding and loosing is repeated by Jesus to all the disciples (18:18). He (Peter) is simply first

among equals because on this occasion he was spokesman for the faith of all.[4] Christ purposed that the apostles be inspired by the Holy Spirit to establish the writings of the New Testament. By so doing, the "bound," ruled out error, and at the same time "loosed," permitted or established truth. The foundation of the church is revealed truth. Those who hold this view believe that Matthew 16:19 and Matthew 18:18 are references to two different actions. The first refers to Peter and other apostles in the role of establishing revelatory truth. The second refers to church disciples.

III. A BRIDGE INTO THE CHURCH

A. DISPENSATIONAL BRIDGE. To properly understand the church, one must realize its existence in the dispensation known as the church age. The word "dispensation" is a biblical term. Paul reminded the Ephesians when he introduced the topic of the church in Ephesians 3:2, "If ye have heard of the dispensation of the grace of God which is given me to youward." Here Paul implies the "dispensation of the grace of God" is new, something that they had not previously known. This new dispensation implies there was a former dispensation. C. I. Scofield teaches there are seven dispensations; the ultra-dispensationalists say at least eight, while others say there are fewer. This section is not trying to identify the number of dispensations, but the nature of a dispensation. The term "dispensation" means "stewardship;" hence, it is described as a period of time when men are given a stewardship of responsibility. In each dispensation, God deals differently with people who demonstrate their faithfulness to different criteria. Hence, the church dispensation has a different way for the Christian to express his faith than the Jew under the dispensation of the law. Remember, there is only one means of salvation. All men of all dispensations are saved by God's grace based on the blood sacrifice of His Son. Men of each dispensation are saved on the same basis, but they have different criteria by which to express their worship, love, and obedience to God.

B. MATTHEW BRIDGE. Of all the Gospels, Matthew is the most Jewish, and yet it is the only one of the Gospels to use the word "church." Even though the concept of the church is found embryonically in the other Gospels, the word "church" appears only in this one (Matt. 16:18; 18:17). Matthew is a bridge from the Old Testament dispensation of the law into the age of grace and God's new instrument, the church.

To understand Matthew, one must interpret his key phrase which is "kingdom of heaven." The kingdom of heaven is a reference to the kingdom of this earth, a phrase which does not occur in the other books of the New Testament. Since every word of the Bible is literally inspired, this phrase cannot be ignored, nor stretched to include a spiritual interpretation. A proper understanding of the church cannot be gained without separating it from an understanding of the kingdom of heaven.

C. THE SYNAGOGUE BRIDGE. The Old Testament tabernacle, and later the temple, was set up by God. The synagogue was not. The use and structure of the synagogue developed between the Testaments, hence, it is not seen on the pages of the Old Testament. But in the New Testament, it is fully developed. It was developed by Jews in the dispersion who were unable to travel regularly to Jerusalem to the temple (Deut. 16:16). Some used the synagogue because they did not want to travel to the Temple. This does not imply that men were wrong in setting up and using the synagogue. It was the place of teaching and the instrument to perpetuate Jewish religious culture.

Some have wrongly taught that the synagogue was the blueprint for the church. To imply this seems to deny that the church came by revelation, or that God used a tool that was available. Rather, the Jews originated the idea of the synagogue and followed natural social organizational patterns. Hesselgrave notes some correspondences between the church and the synagogue.

> Briefly look at the synagogue pattern. In order to organize a synagogue or hold meetings, it was necessary to have at least ten men. The elders of the congregation selected a ruler (or possibly several of them). The ruler was responsible for synagogue services and properties. He often designated others to conduct the expressions of praise, prayers, reading of the Law and prophets, and the giving of exhortations. Several assistants carried out menial duties, inflicted corporal punishment or otherwise disciplined members, and dispensed alms received from the members.
> New Testament believers, therefore, had a model for church leadership and organization. It is not to be inferred that they followed this synagogue pattern rigidly, however. The point is that the early believers were aware of basic ways and means for conducting corporate spiritual life and business.[5]

But the church belongs to Jesus while the synagogue belonged to the Jews. Jesus clearly said, "I will build my church." No such statement is made of the Jewish synagogue. "We can thus understand also how the Christian community in the midst of Israel could be simply designated $\dot{\epsilon}$ κκλησια [ekklesia], without being confounded with the Jewish community, the συναγωγή [synagogue] (Acts ii. 47, etc.).[6]

The church is a symbol of victory; the gates of hell could not stand against it. The synagogue was a symbol of defeat. The church is pictured by Christ on the offensive, not the defensive. Even from the Jewish perspective, the synagogue reveals no sacrifices or Levites—the essentials of the Jewish faith were not present.

The synagogue was primarily a place of learning. Later, the synagogue furnished a meeting place for the church (Acts 19). Basically, the synagogue was like a religious civic center owned by the Jews and open to all Jews. In no way is the church a continuation of the synagogue.

IV. NON-TECHNICAL DEFINITIONS OF THE CHURCH

The word "church" has many popular or generic meanings. When the word "church" is used, a reference may be made to a building or an incorporation—recognized legally as an organization. The term "church" also means an abstract institution (a general term that stands for religion). It may be an organized local group of people or a denominational structure which stands for all churches in that denomination. Another meaning is the Catholic church—the universal church. The word "church" can mean a denominational family such as "the Baptist Church," or when a person says "my church is Baptist" without reference to a particular local church.

When the word "church" was introduced by Christ, it took on a specific Christian context so that the *ekklesia* of Jesus was quite different from the *ekklesia* of the Jews or the secular *ekklesia*. Further, in the development of the word it came to be used in a technical sense to mean a Christian assembly—both physical and spiritual unity. Radmacher notes, "Concerning this development it has been observed that the meanings do not shade off into one another in abrupt, sudden changes, but in gradual, almost imperceptible growth."[7]

The word "church" can be used in a general, nontechnical way in Scripture. It can mean an assembly of people which is a gathering of folks—"The Assembly" (Acts 19:32). This was simply a gathering or an assembly of people. The term "church" also refers to the nation Israel because they were gathered as a church is gathered. It does not mean they have the same doctrine (Acts 7:38; Heb. 2:12). As Kuen relates,

The word *ekklesia* had a political meaning, never a religious meaning in Greece. In Athens, for example, the *ekklesia* was the regularly summoned assembly of all the citizens of the city, that is, of those who had the freedom of the city. All the inhabitants of the city did not have this right; full citizens formed only a small minority.

At the call of a herald, the citizens came out of their homes, separated themselves from the rest of the inhabitants of the city, and assembled in a place agreed upon (the *Pnyx)* to discuss city affairs, such as the nomination of magistrates, officers, governors of the city, military operations, etc. Each convocation began with prayer and a sacrifice. The word *ekklesia* is used by Luke in this sense: "in the legal assembly" (Acts 19:39).[8]

When a general word is used in a special way, it becomes technical. As such, the word "church" is used in a technical way in the Scripture. The word "church" was a deliberate choice by Christ. He chose the common word for assembly and gave it special content or theological meaning. "The Assembly" to which He referred was to be His assembly. Because the New Testament writers were verbally inspired, they initially used the word "assembly" without an explanation, then Paul later began to define it with new meaning and purpose. He gave it the interpretation that came to him by revelation.

V. THE TECHNICAL USE OF THE WORD CHURCH

A. THE CHURCH IS HIS BODY. The word body is sometimes used to refer to the physical body of Christ that died on Calvary. But as referred to later, the body is also a

---

1. Christ is walking in center (midst) of the churches. He was as close to one as another. This raises the question of when is a dying church no longer recognized as a church by Jesus Christ?

2. Even though these corporate assemblies did not meet New Testament criteria, there may have been believers in them, so Christ was still concerned about them.

3. Even if unbelievers are in a church, that does not disqualify it as a church. (See 2 Cor. 13:5-7)

---

reference to a local church (1 Cor. 12:27-28). This is a reference to those in heaven who are identified as dwelling "in Him." The reference to the church carries a two-fold meaning, revealing that the church is an organism with divine-like properties. This implies the church is more than an organization similar to worldly organizations even though made up of the saved. The spiritual application is reflected by the phrase "in Christ" (Eph. 1:22; 5:23, 29; Col. 1:24; 2:19; 1 Cor. 12:12ff). The body of Christ represents Paul's maturest reflections on the subject. The body concept is applied by Paul to the church with great effort and sheds much light on the nature of the church as he understood it.

B. THE CHURCH IS AN UNASSEMBLED ASSEMBLY. This is a reference to those in a local assembly when they are not meeting together. In Acts 8:3, Paul did not enter into the assembly while it was meeting, but into houses of Christians who belonged to the assembly (Cf. Acts 9:31; 14:17).

C. THE CHURCH IS AN ASSEMBLED ASSEMBLY. Technically, when the saved assembled, they were a unique assembly in God's sight. Note Matthew 18:17 and especially 1 Corinthians 14:4, 23.

D. THE CHURCH MAY REFER TO AN ASSEMBLY THAT DOES NOT BELONG TO JESUS CHRIST. This means an assembly that is not recognized by Jesus Christ because its aims, nature, and catalyst do not fit the New Testament criteria. In Revelation 3:14-19, Christ does not repudiate the term "church" although this group of people had denied the foundational makeup of a church. Note the following observations of non-church gatherings of people.

E. THE WORD "CHURCH" REFERS TO MORE THAN ONE CHURCH. The plural use of *ecclesia* in Acts 9:31 obviously refers to many local churches. It is also used in Galatians 1:2 to refer to several local churches in Galatia.

To properly understand the theological meaning of "church," we must look at both definition and description. A definition is explicit and is usually based on word meanings. That has been the basis thus far. Next the church is described by an implicit approach. The next section gives seven figures or descriptions of the church. These will give flesh to the skeleton thus established.

VI. DESCRIPTIONS OF THE CHURCH

In previous sections the word "church" has been defined by analysis. This section describes the church by seven images or pictures, each teaching some eternal truths about its nature, purpose, and function. These pictures were not haphazardly included by human authors as purely idiomatic expressions of the culture of the day, but were divinely included to represent important issues. Each image speaks to a different way that life is found in the church and each image portrays the church from a different perspective.

A. THE BODY OF CHRIST. The picture of the body is the most used analogy of the church. The Bible presents Christ as the head, and the church as the body. The members of His body are to grow up in all aspects into Him who is the head (Eph. 4:15). In the husband-wife relationship, Christ is the head of the church, the Savior of the body (Eph. 5:23). Christ is to be placed first in all things because He is the head of the body, the church (Col. 1:18). Paul's sufferings for the Colossian Christians were done on behalf of Christ's body which is the church (Col. 1:24). Christ is also the source and supplier of all growth to the body (Col. 2:19). Christians are a part of the body and part of one another (Rom. 12:5; 1 Cor. 12:12-31).

PICTURE	CENTRAL TRUTH
Body	Unity
Building	Indwelling
Bride	Intimacy
Flock	Provision
Garden (vine)	Union
Family	Identity
Priesthood	Service

Biologically, a body comes into existence when the seed or sperm joins the egg and forms a cell. In that embryonic cell are the components that will fashion the body as it is fully developed. The sex, color of hair, and thousands of other features are inherent in that first cell. The body grows by the division of cells, and when two cells emerge, it is impossible to determine which was the original.

When a local church is formed, believers are joined together into one unified body that should function in harmony. The Bible uses the analogy of a body for the church to reveal the inherent life with a church and its intended unity.

Saucy gives six aspects or principles of how the head (Christ) relates to the body (church): (1) unity, (2) diversity, (3) mutuality, (4) sovereign leadership, (5) the source of life, and (6) the sustenance of life.[9]

Every church and every Christian should give Christ first place in everything! The reason for His priority is: (1) He produced all things for Himself (Col. 1:16), (2) He preceded all things (Col. 1:17), (3) He preserves all things (Col. 1:17b), and (4) He purposes to be first in all things (Col. 1:18).

As the head controls our bodies, so Christ must be given preeminence. The head always gives direction to the body, so Christians must be willing to receive His orders. Both quantitative and qualitative growth in the church comes from obedience to the head, Jesus Christ.

The church in Corinth did not follow Christ. Christians were no longer a body united, but members divided! But if each member of His body, beginning with pastors, would acknowledge the Lordship of Christ and depend upon His presence, the resulting unity would produce growth. Robert Saucy explains the results of unity.

> The apostle [Paul] begins his discussion of gifts with the Corinthian church by placing all of the pneumatic gifts under one Lord and Spirit (1 Co 12:3-5). Therefore, there must be no schism in the body (12:25 ff.) caused by a disorderly display of gifts (1 Co 14:33). All of the gifted members are under the same Head and are part of the same body, and such members in a normal body do not oppose each other, thus tearing the body apart.[10]

If a body is healthy, all of its parts will function properly. Disease and sickness often strike the areas of greatest weakness, and when that happens the entire body is disabled (1 Cor. 12:26). Disease could be overt or covert sin by the members or by the body acting as a whole. But just as disease comes from without the body, so there are problems that weaken or destroy the body from sociological or internal problems.

In his reference to Colossians 2:19 and Ephesians 4:15-16, Saucy remarks, "The body grows through the supply of energy distributed to each part through the Head. As each member, receiving his gift of grace, contributes to the whole, the body grows."[11] Gary Inrig supports this view.

> The truth is that the Body of Christ is designed to teach us that we need one another and that we must care for one another. To the world we must show ourselves one in Christ, united in love and a shared life. Such a unity is not uniformity or conformity. It is rather a Spirit-given sense of our mutual needs and the recognition that our diversity is both God-given and essential to maturity and health. "Unity, diversity, interdependence." This is not to be just the motto of the local congregation, but its experience under God.[12]

When the Word of God uses the term "the body of Christ," it is important to realize whether it means a figure of speech or if it uses the term literally. First, if the church is actually the body of Christ, it makes the local assembly equal to Christ. This raises the question of Roman Catholicism, for the Roman church makes their church equal with Christ Himself. Saucy notes, "The heart of the Roman Catholic doctrine of a salutary and authoritative church rests upon the literal interpretation which identifies the church as the body of Christ with Christ Himself."[13] The figurative view implies the local church is only similar to Christ's body with no organic connection. A third view might be suggested. Just as Christ indwells the believer, so He indwells His church. And just as the life of the church depends upon the indwelling Christ, so the church is an organism (in addition to being an organization) because Christ indwells His church. This might be titled a mystical indwelling, not in the sense of a sixth-sense mysticism, but rather a biblical mysticism that is based on objective revelation—the Word of God.

In the mystical sense, each church is a body of Christ because Christ dwells in His church. No church is spoken of as a finger or eye, nor do we speak of a church as part of the body of Christ (members of the body are always individuals, not churches). Nor is there any reference in Scripture that one body (a denomination) is made up of many local churches. The Bible implies that the body is Christ, and that a body is a church.

In summarizing the church as the body of Christ, Radmacher brings the purpose of the body into clear perspective. "It is clear that the *source* of all—both unity and nourishment—is Christ Himself. The *channels* of the communication, however, are the different members of the body of Christ, in their relation one to another."[14]

B. THE TEMPLE OF GOD. The phrase "the temple of God" or "the building of God" is a word picture that presents the church as a place for the dwelling of God. Our bodies are also referred to as buildings and houses (2 Cor. 5:1) in which God dwells (1 Cor. 3:16).

Today, God's building is the church, which is also pictured as a growing edifice (Eph. 2:21). The illustration of the church as a growing building is similar to the analogy of the growing body, which is "built up" with spiritual gifts (1 Cor. 14:12; Eph. 4:12, 16). Some have seen spiritual gifts as mortar which joins the "living stones" (1 Pet. 2:5) together in the building. These bricks or living stones are carefully "fitted together" by the Holy Spirit (Eph. 2:21).

The building exalts Christ as His indwelling presence is seen in the individual believer and through the corporate building (the church). Paul warned the Corinthians that their individual bodies were the temple of God (1 Cor. 6:19-20). Kent writes,

> Each convert, whether he be Jew or Gentile, adds to the growth of the structure. And this structure is no less a holy temple, for God dwells within it. If the Jewish temple at Jerusalem suggested Paul's figure, it is important to note that he chose the word that denoted the sanctuary proper, rather than one that described the outer courts and buildings. It was this inner sanctuary which was regarded as God's dwelling place.[15]

A building is constructed to house a tenant, and the analogy suggests the building houses the Lord! Chafer writes, "Israel *had* a building in which God was pleased to dwell: the Church is a building in which God is pleased to dwell."[16]

There are three sections to a building: first, the foundation, second, the cornerstone, and third the building blocks or stones. Every building begins with the foundation. The foundation must be Jesus Christ alone (1 Cor. 3:11). Paul had determined that he would preach "Jesus Christ, and him crucified" (1 Cor. 2:2) who is the foundation.

Another important biblical issue concerning the building is the role of the human builder and how they built. In Ephesians 2:20, Paul indicates the apostles and prophets were builders of the church. This text refers to the apostles and prophets as laying the original foundation for the church, but how did they do it?

The apostles and prophets did establish many local churches, but is this what is meant? Their church planting activity was probably an application of Ephesians 2:20, but more was meant. They were the human instruments to establish the church in general. Paul was the church planter at Corinth: "as a wise masterbuilder, I have laid the foundation" (1 Cor. 3:10). Saucy explains that "the apostle has laid the foundation by teaching the doctrines of Christ and bringing men into a relationship with Him who is the only foundation that is laid. The church is not built upon a man or creed but upon the person of the living Christ."[17] But there is a greater sense of being the foundation to the church.

The apostles and prophets were the foundation in the sense that they established the faith in the basic tenets of Christian doctrine, of course, not on their own. They received revelatory truth, (1) direct from Christ, (2) by the Holy Spirit (John 14:26), (3) were the human instruments in inspiration (2 Pet. 1:21), and (4) swere the leaders of the church where doctrine and policy were received and recognized.

In addition to the apostles who laid the original foundation, there is need for many contemporary builders. In 1 Corinthians 3:10-15 Paul indicates that many builders are involved: "But let every man take heed how he buildeth thereupon . . ."; "Now if any man build upon the foundation . . ."; and the phrase repeated four times, "every man's work . . ." Everyone who is a "living stone" in the building can also be a builder of the building.

Paul urged the Corinthians to build a permanent church and to do it right. After the foundation is firmly settled, the rows of bricks or stones are then laid. The foundation determines the rest of the building. The Lord Jesus Christ is also the cornerstone. Lenski affirms the importance of this stone which is,

> . . . set at the corner of a wall so that its outer angle becomes important. This importance is ideal; we may say symbolic: the angle of the cornerstone governs all the lines and all the other angles of the building. This one stone is thus laid with special, sometimes with elaborate ceremonies. It supports the building no more than does any other stone. Its entire significance is to be found in its one outer angle. Its size is immaterial and certainly need not be immense. It is thus also placed at the most important corner, in or on the top tier of the foundation, so as to be seen by all.[18]

As the entire building is determined by the cornerstone, so the building is set by Christ, the stone "set at nought of you builders, which is become the head of the corner" (Acts 4:11).

The building material for the local church referred to by Paul in 1 Corinthians 3:12 includes gold, silver, precious stones, or wood, hay, and stubble. This material is none other than believers. If they properly allow the cornerstone to set the course for their lifestyles, the result is quality. In 1 Corinthians 3:9 Paul refers to a building of God. Boyer explains.

> Certainly the context makes the primary application to *people*. They [the materials] represent persons being built into the church. This is not to be understood, however, as a mere adding of another brick to the wall by getting

another convert to Christ. Remember, these people are "living stones." They themselves grow, so that the temple grows and is edified as its people grow. Thus, the minister's work is twofold: He builds (1) by getting new people into the building, and (2) by getting those in the building to increase in stature and maturity. And since both of these tasks are accomplished by a ministry of teaching, there is some truth to the interpretation often encountered in the commentaries that the works here refer to the *doctrines* of the church leaders. Doctrine, however, is involved only secondarily, as it affects persons.[19]

The people are the work (1 Cor. 9:1), and the building of God has no value unless it centers in people. Since believers are the building, then it is not biblical to use people to build a church, but rather to use the church to build believers. When the main concern of the building is quality people, it will bring glory to God. Getz summarizes,

> "Be careful how you build!" warned Paul. A church can be weak and immature—constructed of wood, hay, and stubble. Or it can be strong and mature—composed of gold, silver and precious stones (1 Co 3:10-15). If it is immature, it reflects impatience, jealousy, strife, divisions, pride, arrogance and unbecoming behavior. If it is mature, it reflects a growing love, a unity of faith, and a steadfast hope.[20]

C. THE BRIDE OF CHRIST. The church is described, "Come hither, I will shew thee the bride, the Lamb's wife" (Rev. 21:9); "For I am jealous over you with godly jealously; for I have espoused you to one husband, that I may present you as a chaste virgin to Christ" (2 Cor. 11:2; Eph. 5:23-32). Radmacher describes those who make up the bride of Christ, "the church, the bride of Christ, includes all those who have put their faith in Christ in this age of grace which had its beginning at Pentecost and will continue until the Bridegroom comes to receive His bride unto himself to consummate the marriage."[21]

It is said, "we are unable to love someone else until we first realize that someone loves us." Paul illustrates the love of Christ for His church by using an illustration of a husband's love for a wife. Christ loves His church first and far more than anything known in human relationships.

The major teaching of the picture of the bride and groom is its demonstration of Christ's limitless love. When Christians who are His church fail to live by His standards and thereby fail to show our love to Him, it is concluded that we do not love Him. But the root problem is that we fail to realize how much He loves us. The Scripture is clear: Christ loves Christians in spite of themselves, and not because of what they do, or how they show their love to Him. Because Christ is God, He is love (John 3:16).

For Christians to believe and accept His love requires faith. Accordingly, Christ loves us and, in the process, cleanses and perfects us. Like Paul prayed for the Ephesian church, so we should pray for others that they "may be able to comprehend with all saints what is the breadth, and length, and depth, and height; and to know the love of Christ which passeth knowledge" (Eph. 3:18-19).

The apostle John reinforces this principle: "we love him, because he first loved us" (1 John 4:19). People usually respond to those who refuse to stop loving them. However, the issue is the kind of love we will show to Him. Christ our Lord desires subjection to Him in every area. Since the church is totally dependent upon Him for life and purpose, so every believer should be totally dependent upon Him for the same reasons. Saucy reinforces this: "The life of the church in each member is to be arranged under the headship of Christ. Their authority and leadership are found in Him. His thoughts and attributes must be theirs."[22]

As human marriage involves intimacy, so the heavenly picture reflects an intimate relationship between Christ and His church. Paul notes, "Members of his body, of his flesh, and of his bones" (Eph. 5:30).

D. THE FLOCK OF GOD. The flock of God is one of the most practical illustrations of Christ and the church. Paul told the Ephesian church elders, "Take heed therefore unto yourselves, and to all the flock, over the which the Holy Ghost hath made you overseers, to feed the church of God, which he hath purchased with his own blood" (Acts 20:28). Peter used the picture when he instructed the elders to "Feed the flock of God which is among you, taking the oversight thereof, not by constraint, but willingly; not for filthy lucre, but of a ready mind; Neither as being lords over God's heritage, but being examples to the flock" (1 Pet. 5:2-3).

Jesus used the flock and the shepherd to illustrate the relationship between Himself and His followers. He observed, "Other sheep I have, which are not of this fold: them also I must bring, and they shall hear my voice; and there shall be one fold [flock] and one shepherd" (John 10:16). The King James fails to distinguish between flock and fold yet this is the distinction between Old and New Testament that reflects the relationship between God and His people. Saucy notes,

> It is important to note the distinction between "fold" and "flock" which is blurred in the Authorized Version. "Fold" denotes an outward organization and refers to Israel, some of whom were Christ's sheep but some who were not because they did not believe. "Flock" speaks of the inner unity of the sheep, "created in and by Jesus" (C. K. Barrett, *The Gospel According to St. John*, pp. 312-13).[23]

Christ is the Chief Shepherd who will reward his faithful undershepherds when He appears (1 Pet. 5:4). The human undershepherds of the flock are the pastors. Christ told Peter to "Feed My sheep" (John 21:16, author's emphasis). The church or sheep belong to Christ. Pastors work for Him and in place of Him, and will someday answer to Him concerning the sheep given to their care (Heb. 13:17).

The illustration of people as sheep may not be flattering, but true. The Word of God consistently refers to the church as a flock of sheep who need food, protection, and direction. Radmacher notes that "long lists of specific items could doubtless be listed at this point, but it seems that they could all be summarized under provision, particularly the provision of spiritual food."[24]

Before feeding or providing for the flock, the undershepherd must find lost sheep. This is the role of evangelism or church growth.

> God wants countable lost persons found. The shepherd with ninety-nine lost sheep who finds one and stays at home feeding or caring for it should not expect commendation. God will not be pleased by the excuse that His servant is doing something "more spiritual" than searching for strayed sheep. Nothing is more spiritual than the actual reconciliation of the lost to God.[25]

The Great Commission is fulfilled by finding sheep (making disciples), folding sheep (baptizing), and feeding sheep (teaching). (1) Finding results is bringing the lost one into the flock. No one can deny that when lost sheep are added to the flock, there is church growth (Luke 15:1-7). (2) Folding is following the scriptural example of the church in Acts by adding to the body. "Then they that gladly received his word were baptized: and the same day there were added unto them about three thousand souls" (Acts 2:41). (3) Feeding results in qualitative teaching of the sheep. Paul reminded the Ephesian elders, "For I have not shunned to declare unto you all the counsel of God" (Acts 20:27). He urged them to protect the flock as he had done to them: "Therefore watch, and remember, that by the space of three years I ceased not to warn every one night and day with tears" (Acts 20:31). Finally, he commended His sheep to God and "to the word of his grace, which is able to build you up, and to give you an inheritance among all them which are sanctified" (Acts 20:32). The undershepherd must know where to find the food, regularly supply it for his flock, or lead them to where it is located, causing His sheep to grow.

The shepherd's role of protection and discipline is also important. The rod and the staff were used by the shepherd to protect his flock (Psa. 23:4).

> The staff was a long, crooked stick used for pulling back straying sheep, while the rod was a stout piece of wood about three feet long with a lump on

one end; it was used as a weapon against wild beasts and robbers. It was also the practice of some shepherds to lay down across the opening of the fold during the night so that their bodies became literally the protecting door.[26]

The shepherd is no longer armed with the staff or the rod, but with the Faithful Word which is "profitable for reproof, for correction, for instruction in righteousness" (2 Tim. 3:16).

Peter writes, "For ye were as sheep going astray; but are now returned unto the Shepherd and Bishop of your souls" (1 Pet. 2:25). Isaiah also says, "All we like sheep have gone astray; we have turned every one to his own way" (Isa. 53:6).

For the sheep to know the shepherd's provision and protection, yet not follow, is to disobey Scripture. The illustration of the sheep and shepherd tell us that every Christian should be involved in a church and follow the undershepherd. Saucy notes,

Essentially, the sheep can provide nothing for itself and can only prosper as it follows the direction of the shepherd. Its only obligation is to submit to his leading and authority. Thus the church is directed as the flock of God to submit to His authority and that of the chief Shepherd. Because this direction is communicated through the Word and the ministry of the undershepherds which God has placed in the church, the members are exhorted to "obey them that have the rule over [literally, lead] you, and submit yourselves" (Heb 13:17). As even the leaders of the church are sheep, they also are obligated to submit ultimately to the chief Shepherd.[27]

E. THE GARDEN OF GOD is a collective phrase of several organic illustrations found in the New Testament: i.e., vine (John 15:1-7), planting (1 Cor. 3:6-8), husbandry (1 Cor. 3:9). Tippett notes, "The teaching of Jesus was charged with expectation of growth."[28] He classifies them into various types of imagery and refers to fields "white already to harvest" (John 4:35) and the mustard seed parable (Matt. 13:31-32) as well as other examples.[29]

A garden is a cultivated plot of ground where weeds and rocks are removed, seed is sown, and crops are harvested. In 1 Corinthians 3:6-9, the church is described as a cultivated field. In John 15, the Christians are pictured as branches, and Christ is portrayed as the life-giving vine.

In the church at Corinth, there was a schism in its leadership. To answer this problem, Paul taught that ministers are servants, co-laborers, and fellow workers with God. According to Paul, each laborer had his own special ministry, but God was the One giving life (1 Cor. 3:6). When two or more "farmers" or pastors are working in a garden, one planting and the other watering, they should be viewed as a team, although each will be rewarded individually. "Now he that planteth and he that watereth are one: and every man shall receive his own reward according to his own labour" (1 Cor. 3:8). All farmers are working together for one purpose—the harvest.

The Scriptures teach the Christian's dependence upon Christ, who is his only source of life and growth and is pictured by the vine and the branches given in John 15. There are two central issues to be considered. One is the cause of growth, and the other is the product or fruit of growth.

Jesus commanded Christians to abide in Him because it is impossible for them to produce fruit apart from Him. "Abide in me, and I in you. As the branch cannot bear fruit of itself, except it abides in the vine; no more can ye, except ye abide in me" (John 15:4). Scofield explains abiding,

> To abide in Christ is, on the one hand, to have no known sin unjudged and unconfessed, no interest into which He is not brought, no life which He cannot share. On the other hand, the abiding one takes all burdens to Him, and draws all wisdom, life and strength from Him. It is not unceasing *consciousness* of these things, and of Him, but that nothing is allowed in the life which separates from Him.[30]

To abide in Christ is to act on His indwelling presence, experiencing a vital faith-walk with Jesus day by day, and to faithfully obey the word of God. When the Christian abides in Christ, the resulting productivity of the vine's potential is reduced from what it could be.

The best way to know whether one is abiding in Christ is to obey His words (John 15:7). John explains that abiding in His love is keeping His commandments (John 15:10). In order to produce fruit, a healthy church must demonstrate love one to another which is another result of abiding in Him (John 15:12).

While both the vine (Christ) and branches (Christians) make up the church and are intimately related, the fruit-producing power flows only one way, from the vine to the branches. Chafer summarizes the results of abiding in Christ as "pruning (vs. 2), prayer effectual (vs. 7), joy celestial (vs. 11), and fruit perpetual (vs . 16)."[31]

The purpose of the garden of God is fruit bearing. Christ reminded His disciples, "Ye have not chosen me, but I have chosen you, and ordained you, that ye should go and bring forth fruit, and that your fruit should remain" (John 15:16). The central purpose of every Christian's life is to produce fruit because a fruitless branch denies the purpose of its existence.

What is the fruit? First, it is winning souls. Christians should be active in evangelism. But there is a second meaning: this fruit (singular) is best described by the fruit (singular) which the Holy Spirit produces (Gal. 5:22-23). Basically it is the life of Christ flowing through the branches, producing the nine qualities (fruit of the Spirit) cited by Paul in Galatians 5:22-23. This union is life, it is "Christ in you, the hope of glory" (Col. 1:27). Fruitbearing of Christian character in and through the branches causes others to be drawn to the Savior. In reality, (love, joy, peace, patience, kindness, goodness, faithfulness, gentleness, and self-control) it will attract others to Christ. Then the fruit of the Spirit will produce fruit in soul winning.

After referring to His Father as the vinedresser, Christ explained that the Father prunes the branches that they may bear more fruit (John 15:2). The word "prune" means "cleanse," signifying a purging process of anything that may reduce or prevent additional fruit. Every fruit-bearing Christian can expand his field of effectiveness and become more fruitful. Saucy remarks,

> Again the pertinency of this particular metaphor is seen in the fact that no tree requires such extensive pruning as that of the vine, and yet it is the characteristic of the vine, that even though it is severely cut back, it does not die but grows again.[32]
> Donald Grey Barnhouse cites an amazing example of this lasting potential fruitfulness.
> In Hampton Court near London, there is a grapevine under glass; it is about 1,000 years old and has but one root which is at least two feet thick. Some of the branches are 200 feet long. Because of skillful cutting and pruning, the vine produces several tons of grapes each year. Even though some of the smaller branches are 200 feet from the main stem, they bear much fruit because they are joined to the vine and allow the life of the vine to flow through them.[33]

Pruning, cleansing, or discipline in a believer's life is loving discipline from the Father (Prov. 3:11-12) and ultimately leads to additional fruit-bearing. "For they [earthly fathers] disciplined us for a short time as seemed best to them, but He disciplines us for our good, that we may share His holiness. All discipline for the moment seems not to be joyful, but sorrowful; yet to those who have been trained by it, afterwards it yields the peaceful fruit of righteousness" (Heb. 12:10-11, NASB).

The Father (the vinedresser) does the pruning. Hollis Green urges churchmen to think of the church as a living organism similar to a tree or a vine. While pruning primarily refers to the life of Christians, Green applies the principle of pruning to policies, programs, and organizational structures of the church that may be diseased or not as productive as they should be.

> Fruit-bearing always takes place on new growth. It is this aspect of administration that should be the primary concern of churchmen. The fruit bearing apparatus must be kept in operation. New growth in the fruit bearing area also produces foliage. Foliage has a direct relationship to the food

supply and the healing of wounds caused by pruning. In horticulture it is suggested that the pruning should take place as close to the main branch as possible so the growth tissue surrounding the wound may form new tissues to heal the wound. Since food moves down through the stems and comes from leaves above the wound, the wound must be in position near this food supply if healing is to occur. The implication here is one of distance. Pruning must be done close to the foliage and food-moving mechanism if the plant is to survive.

Arbitrary and indiscriminate pruning at a distance from the main branch leaves a stump because the healing of the wound cannot occur. When church leaders prune or tamper with the fruit-bearing mechanism of the church, it must be done with due caution and careful planning. The ultimate objective of repairing the wound and nurturing the whole body into a productive unit must be considered.

Where churchmen do not have the courage to prune, disease gnaws at the fruit bearing areas, and the process of strangulation cuts off the flow of life to the superstructure. Without the courage to prune, it is only a matter of time until fruit bearing stops and the slow but sure process of death destroys the foliage, the superstructure and even the roots. The tree may stand but it is dead. There is no shade for the weary traveler and no fruit for the hungry. The structure is there, the organization is there, but the life is gone. This is the sad plight of many churches.[34]

F. THE FAMILY OF GOD. This picture of the church incorporates several phrases or terms that depict it as saints, sanctified ones, elect, members of Christ, believers, disciples, Christians, and the term which closely reflects the family, i.e., brethren and children. To the Ephesian Christians, Paul emphasized that both Jews and Gentiles became a part of God's family (household—Eph. 2:19). In fact, Christians experience an entirely new family relationship different from anything previous. "For he is our peace, who hath made both one, and hath broken down the middle wall of partition between us; Having abolished in his flesh the enmity, even the law of commandments contained in ordinances; for to make in himself of twain one new man, so making peace; And that he might reconcile both unto God in one body by the cross, having slain the enmity thereby" (Eph. 2:14-16).

John describes believers as sons: "But as many as received him, to them gave he power to become the sons of God, even to them that believe on his name" (John 1:12). Because of this family relationship, Paul said, "God hath sent forth the Spirit of his Son into your hearts crying, Abba, Father" (Gal. 4:6). Vine states that according to the Gemara (a Rabbinical commentary),

Slaves were forbidden to address the head of the family by this title. . . . "Abba" is the word framed by the lips of infants, and betokens unreasoning trust; "father" expresses an intelligent apprehension of the relationship. The two together express the love and intelligent confidence of the child.[35]

As a result of believing in Jesus Christ, Jews and Gentiles enter the family of God. People who had no relationship to each other were now members of a household, the church. They were brothers and sisters, loving, helping, encouraging, teaching, and sharing with one another. Just as the human family demands order and direction, unity and oneness, so the church has the same demands. Every believer, once he becomes a part of the household of God, has full family privileges.

Paul indicated man must manage his family as a qualification for New Testament church leadership (1 Tim. 3:4-5, 12). Paul's main intent is not programs nor concern for the house-building itself, but giving leadership to the family so each person would grow and fulfill God's plan for his life.

G. THE PRIESTHOOD. In the Old Testament, a man was set aside to the office of priesthood. In the New Testament, all believers are priests, and they need no one to mediate to God for them. Every believer has access to Christ who mediates for him (1 Tim. 2:5). Peter notes that Christians are, "a royal priesthood" (1 Pet. 2:9).

In the Old Testament only the high priest could stand in the Holy of Holies. (The word for priest was *cohen*, which meant "to stand.") The thick veil that separated people from God was broken down by Christ so the believers could enter the "holy place" through Christ (Heb. 10:19-21).

The priest performed three functions: (1) sacrifice, (2) witness, and (3) intercession. The New Testament believer carries out these three functions. First, he does not sacrifice animals on an altar, because Christ has ended the ritualistic sacrifice. Rather, the believer sacrifices himself a "living sacrifice" (Rom. 12:1) by his holy life and service. Paul implied this when he said he was poured out "a drink offering" (Phil. 2:17). Then the Christian is obliged to, "offer the sacrifice of praise to God continually, that is, the fruit of our lips giving thanks to his name" (Heb. 13:15).

Second, the Old Testament priest was called the "messenger of the Lord" because the people were told to hear the law of God from him (Mal. 2:7; Deut. 33:10). When Christians share the gospel, they are carrying out this role of the priest. The third function of the priest was intercession. Granted, Christ is the intercessor for the church, but believers are also to intercede based on, (1) the example of Christians interceding in the New Testament, (2) the exhortation to Christians to pray, and (3) the nature of the church as a channel between God and the lost.

Remember, the emphasis is not on individual priests, but each Christian as a member of a priesthood with position and authority. This comes because they are in Jesus Christ, members of His body, and "bone of His bone."

CONCLUSION

The implications of understanding the pictures and metaphors of the church are important. In each case, the church is illustrated as a living organism. Even in the example of the building, the church is made up of "living stones." These pictures remind us that the church is not a building occasionally inhabited by people. Rather, the church is a gathering of believers who have the living Christ indwelling them individually and corporately. These illustrations reveal that the church has life in relationship to its Lord (organism) and the outgrowth of that life is seen in its practices (organization).

VII. THEOLOGICAL DEFINITION OF A CHURCH

A. A CHURCH IS AN ASSEMBLY OF PROFESSING BELIEVERS. The first criterion for a New Testament church is an assembly of those who have their faith in Jesus Christ (Rom. 10:9).

Not all who make an outward confession of faith, in fact, actually possess eternal life. There will be some in the church who are not saved, as was the case in New Testament times (Acts 8:13-23). However, all should be accepted into the church upon their profession of faith. The church is an assembly of professing believers. It seems, no matter how carefully the church examines individuals (Jude 4, 1 Pet. 2:1), some gain access into their fellowship, only to be questioned at a later time.

B. THE UNIQUE PRESENCE OF JESUS CHRIST DWELLS IN A CHURCH. Christ is the light of the world (John 8:12), and the primary purpose of the church is to hold up the light in a dark world (Phil. 2:15-16). The church does more than possess a light; it is a light, expressly a corporate group of lights; "ye are lights" (Phil. 2:15). Therefore, the church is an organism and its light and life is Jesus Christ. He dwells in the midst of His people. "For where two or three are gathered together in my name, there am I in the midst of them" (Matt. 18:20). But Christ does more than indwell a church; He is the church. It is His body and He is its life.

Christ walked through the seven churches in the book of Revelation. He commended them for their good works (Rev. 2:3) and rebuked them for their sin and false doctrine. When Christ rebuked the churches in the book of Revelation, He threatened to take away their candlestick (Rev. 2:5), which would have been removing His presence from the people. When Christ is removed from a New Testament church, it is similar to the shekinah glory cloud leaving the Old Testament temple. If a group of people do not have Jesus Christ dwelling in their midst, they are no longer a New Testament church, no matter what name they have over their door.

C. A CHURCH IS UNDER THE DISCIPLINE OF THE WORD OF GOD. One of the first religious exercises of the New Testament church after the day of Pentecost was that "they continued steadfastly in the apostles' doctrine" (Acts 2:42). Doctrinal purity is essential for a New Testament church. There is a unique union between Christ and the Bible, for both are the Word of God.

When an organizational problem came up in the early church, the apostles realized that they had to place priority on their time. They had to give themselves to the Word of God (Acts 6:4). A local church must place itself under the authority of God by placing itself under the discipline of the Word of God.

When the minister gives positive discipline with a positive proclamation of the Word of God, this leads to correct life and belief. When the minister rebukes a congregation for their sin, this is a negative discipline, just as a parent rebukes a child for going too near the fire. The purpose of discipline by the Word of God is the positive and negative correction of the New Testament church. When an assembly of people removed themselves from under the authority of the Word of God, they no longer met the criteria of being a New Testament church.

D. A CHURCH IS ORGANIZED TO CARRY OUT THE GREAT COMMISSION. In the early church they "ceased not to teach and preach Jesus Christ" (Acts 5:42). Since everyone is lost, the church believed that everyone must be presented with the gospel. The persecutors could say, "Ye have filled Jerusalem with your doctrine" (Acts 5:28). The early disciples were carrying out the Great Commission.

E. A CHURCH ADMINISTERS THE ORDINANCES. Two ordinances are given to the church—baptism and the Lord's Table. These are to be celebrated by the church as it assembles together. Even though the ordinances are given for personal edification and testimony, an individual does not partake of these apart from the church.

Baptism became more than in initiatory rite into a local church. It is a symbol portraying the ultimate meaning of the Lord's death. The church is the body of Christ (Eph. 1:22-23). When He hanged on Calvary, sinners were placed into the body of Christ, and when Christ suffered vicariously, the penalty of their sins was propitiated because they were in Jesus Christ. Individuals were identified with Christ in His death, burial, and resurrection (Rom. 6:4-6). And as a result, when Christ died, we died with Him: "I am crucified with Christ: nevertheless I live; yet not I, but Christ liveth in me" (Gal. 2:20). Since we were identified with Christ's body at salvation, the symbolism should be carried out when one enters the church. He is placed into a pool of water as a symbol of being placed in the grave, identified with Christ in His death, burial, and resurrection.

The Lord's Supper is a means of edification, fellowship, and personal introspection. A believer is to examine himself before partaking. God provided the Lord's Table to keep His church pure and separated from the world.

F. A CHURCH REFLECTS THE SPIRITUAL GIFTS. Not every group of Christians is destined to grow into a church. However, if it becomes a New Testament church, spiritual gifts will emerge. This process begins when God raises up leadership to bring the church into existence. These leaders minister through their "spiritual gifts" (1 Cor. 12; Rom. 12; Eph. 4). God gives gifted men to a church, and when the leaders appear, it is an indication that God wants the people to organize into a New Testament church. "God hath set some in the church, first apostles, secondarily prophets, thirdly teachers" (1 Cor. 12:28). "And he gave some apostles, and some prophets, and some evangelists, and some pastors and teachers" (Eph. 4:11). Paul wrote the church at Corinth to "covet earnestly the best gifts" (1 Cor. 12:31). The word "covet" is plural implying that a church must desire spiritual gifts. Hence, if there are no spiritual gifts, we can imply it is not a church or has not obeyed the admonition to seek gifted leaders to carry out its aim.

VIII. NON-CHURCH ASSEMBLIES

It is obvious from history that many New Testament churches have gone out of existence. The powerful church in Jerusalem passed into oblivion with the destruction of Jerusalem in A.D. 70. The missionary church in Antioch lost its spiritual dynamic, but probably not through the city being conquered or destroyed. Perhaps it was internal forces that destroyed its vitality. Can we assume that just as a physical body deteriorates into senility and ultimately death, so all churches will ultimately die? Are there causes that weaken a church, and if believers are aware of them, can they keep a church healthy and functioning? By understanding the nature of a church, we understand that, when aspects of a church deny its nature, there are causes for its internal destruction.

A question that needs to be asked is, "When does a church cease being a church?" In other words, when does a biblical church become a non biblical church?

A. WHEN A CHURCH CEASES TO CARRY OUT THE NATURE AND FUNCTION OF A CHURCH:

1. *The church ignores soul winning and its ministry of evangelism.*

2. *The church ceases its basic ministry.*

3. *The church ignores church discipline.* This may refer to negative discipline or positive discipline, including ignoring giving instruction from God's Word.

4. *The church ceases having fellowship within the assembly.*

5. *The church no longer baptizes new converts or serves the Lord's Table.*

B. WHEN A CHURCH STOPS BEING A CHURCH DOCTRINALLY:

1. *The church changes its beliefs.* A church should not be quick to weaken its doctrinal statement.

2. *The church ignores its beliefs.* In other words, when the church fails in its teaching ministry, it will suffer doctrinally and eventually become a non-church.

3. *The church allows the entrance of false teaching.* If false doctrine enters into the church, it is in danger of becoming a non-church doctrinally.

C. WHEN A CHURCH CEASES BEING A CHURCH ORGANIZATIONALLY:

1. *The church's authority is split.* Perhaps the church will not respond to the authority of the pastor or the pastor will not respond to the authority of the congregation.

2. *The pastor will not fulfill the biblical role required of him.*

3. *There is a complacent attitude.* This means there is a decision to do nothing.

4. *There is a failure to replace poor leaders, or retention of unbiblical church leaders.* When steps of discipline are not taken to remove an officer who should be replaced, or someone is not retained who should have been, this is an indication that the church is not functioning organizationally. Therefore, it could be in danger of becoming a non-church in this area.

There is a word of caution to those who are too quick to go "witch-hunting," which is condemning church leaders. Also, be careful of labeling a church a non-church. The church belongs to Jesus Christ; let Him be responsible for its closures.

Remember, Jesus called to the "church in Pergamos" (Rev. 2:12) and described it as, "I have a few things against thee, because thou hast there them that hold the doctrine of Balaam" (v. 14). Here was a church with false teaching, but Christ was equal-distance to it, as to the other churches. (He was walking in the midst (meaning middle) of the seven churches, Rev. 1:13; 2:1). Again, Jesus called it the church of Thyatira (Rev. 2:18), even though they were guilty of permitting Jezebel to commit fornication (Rev. 2:20). Here was a church that allowed outward sin, yet was called a church.

Two things must be noted. First, these churches were warned of their sin, so churches today must be aware of the message given by Christ to them. But second, Christ called them a church, not because of their degree of sin and heresy or lack of sin and false doctrine. He indwells all believers no matter how far they drift. Just as He is in their lives individually, He must be present corporately in the church. If these can be called churches, let us be slow to judge churches that do not measure up to our expectations.

IX. THE UNIVERSAL CHURCH

Although the concept of an invisible or universal church was probably held by many, historically the idea was first articulated by Augustine in *City of God*. Some have said the influence of Plato was evident in this doctrine. It is also called the Triumphant Church, true church, or glorified church. Most theologians have held to some form of a non-local church in their teaching, attempting to deal with the description of the church as a mystery (Eph. 3:1-10) or a body (1 Cor. 12:12-23). Some feel it is made up of true believers in the midst of professing believers. Others feel it is the organic aspect of the local organization. Still others feel it is composed of all true believers regardless of local church membership.

Perhaps the most profound influence of the doctrine grew out of the teaching of J. N. Darby that was basically dispensational in nature and popularized by the *Scofield Reference Bible*. As such, the Universal Church would be defined as follows:

> The Universal Church is that group composed of all true believers in this present dispensation (Pentecost to Rapture), permanently united by the baptism of the Holy Spirit into vital spiritual union with all believers of this age thus forming His mystical body.[36]

The Universal Church emphasizes the unity of believers, perhaps because of the division in Christendom. Also, it emphasizes the positional nature of each believer as he stands perfect in Jesus Christ.

One of the key verses to explain the Universal Church is 1 Corinthians 12:13. "For by one spirit are we all baptized into one body, whether we be Jews or Gentiles, whether we be bond or free; and have been all made to drink into one Spirit." The believer is baptized or "placed" into the body of Christ pictured as the universal church. This spiritual union happens at salvation and is the positional basis by which God deals with him. However, there are five different views of Spirit baptism, each of them giving a different interpretation.

A. THE PENTECOSTAL OR HOLINESS VIEW sees the baptism of the Spirit as a second work of grace that happens after salvation, whereby the Holy Spirit sets a person apart for holy living or makes him able not to sin. Most believe the sin nature is eradicated by Spirit baptism. This is an experience that happens after salvation: the person seeks it by prayer, yieldedness, and self-examination to discover impurity or selfish desires, then repents and tarries in the presence of Christ until he is baptized by the Holy Spirit. Pentecostals believe the verification for this is usually the manifestation of tongues.

B. THE POWER-FOR-SERVICE VIEW, held by J. R. Rice, R. A. Torrey, Jack Hyles and others, sees the baptism of the Holy Spirit as an experience in the believer that endows him for power or sets him apart for service. The Christian can seek this baptism or anointing by meeting certain requirements. This is not just a second experience, but can happen many times in the life of the believer.

C. THE SCOFIELD REFERENCE BIBLE VIEW interprets this as the Holy Spirit taking the believer at the moment of salvation and placing him positionally into the Universal Church. All believers of this dispensation from Pentecost to the rapture are included in this view.

D. THE WATER BAPTISM VIEW says the baptism of the Holy Spirit happens when a believer is placed into a local church by water baptism. This view is held by Arthur Pink, Anglicans, Campbellites, and many Lutherans as well.

E. THE ACTUAL BODY VIEW believes Spirit baptism takes place when believers are placed into Christ's body on Calvary and become partakers of His vicarious, substitutionary death (atonement). The body of 1 Corinthians 12:13 is the actual body of Christ on the cross, so Spirit baptism identifies them with His death, burial, and resurrection (Rom. 6:4,5).

The church is both organic and an organization. We do a disservice to the doctrine of the church when we say the true church or spiritual church is located only in heaven. This implies the local church is unspiritual, less than true, or is less than a living church. The local church is spiritually alive, for it is the body of Christ (1 Cor. 12:27), while at the same time it is an organization that needs administration skills (Acts 6:1-7) and job descriptions for its officers (1 Tim. 3:1-14).

The local church is not just the sum of its parts, meaning it is the gathering of Christians who call themselves a church. The local church is greater than the sum of its parts; it has a spiritual existence, which is Jesus Christ Himself. He is the body of the local assembly (1 Cor. 12:12-27), and He is the light of the church which is called a candlestick (Rev. 2:1, 5). The local church can be called Jesus Christ on earth. Because we are human, we have difficulty understanding the intricacies of how the church is both Christ and a human organization.

On the other hand, the church in heaven relates to its spiritual existence in the heavenlies. The believer is described as being a part of His body or having his existence in Him in the heavenlies. Thus, believers dwell together in Christ. They live in the body who is Jesus Christ and who is at the right hand of God the Father.

Some would construct a platonic church of non-material existence that is located in heaven. This picture of a non-material container, which exists in another world that incorporates the spirits of all believers, presents a dualistic view of the church. Paul continually says the believer is "in Christ." This concept makes the body a spiritual being. Then we can say that the believer has the perfection or righteousness of Jesus Christ, for he positionally exists in Christ's body. The believer was placed (baptized) into Christ at Calvary; the believer arose with him in resurrection and now he is enjoying "the heavenlies in Christ." To be in this concept of the church is to be in the "completion" of the Savior.

There are some abuses connected with the phrase "universal church." Some Christians have been misled to place all their allegiance to the heavenly church, so that they neglect their obligations to a local church. Hence, they damage their spiritual growth and service. To be disobedient to a local church obligation is still disobedience, whether attributed to ignorance or willful rebellion. Equal emphasis must be placed on Jesus Christ in heaven and on the church on earth.

Landmarkism. The concepts of Landmarkism were developed in the 1850's by J. R. Graves, an editor of a Southern Baptist church paper. Leon MacBeth, church historian at Southwestern Theological Seminary in Ft. Worth, has attributed Landmarkism as one of the causes for the rise and strength of the Southern Baptist Convention because it excluded them from outside abuse that would have prohibited them from growth, and produced inclusiveness that made many think they were the only true church, hence, their loyalty and devotion to the cause. The beliefs of Landmarkism have shifted to some in the ranks of the Baptist Bible Fellowship and in the position of the Missionary Baptist Association and the American Baptist

Association. *The Trail of Blood* by B. H. Carroll provides historical verification to those who believe in Landmark theology.

A Landmark theologian believes that Christ established only local Baptist churches and that a person enters the church by water baptism after he believes in Jesus Christ. They believe that a church is only established by existing New Testament churches, and that the only valid New Testament baptism is administered by a representative of a valid New Testament church. Only those who are properly baptized are members of Christ's bride which is the church. Hence, only those who are properly baptized will sit with Christ at the Marriage Feast of the Lamb. From this they are called the Baptist bride. Those who are saved, but improperly baptized, will be guests at the Marriage Feast of the Lamb.

Baptist successionism is a major trait of Landmarkism. In essence, it says that water baptism was given to John the Baptist. Jesus was baptized by John the Baptist, hence beginning a succession of proper baptism that must extend down through history. Since this is true baptism, everyone should be baptized by a person who has been properly baptized. The book, *The Trail of Blood*, is an attempt to trace the history of the true local church and, hence, valid water baptism from John the Baptist to its writing. Baptism under any other name or preacher or church or group is not accepted as valid Christian baptism.

There are refutations to Landmarkism. First, Landmarkers are extremely anti-universal Church in that they deny all reference to the existence of the body of Christ and believers dwelling in Christ in the heavenlies. Second, Landmark theology has created a false past and a false future. They cannot identify or prove a succession of water baptism back to John the Baptist (or Christ), nor can they prove that only those baptized by Baptists will be at the Lamb's Supper. Third, Acts 19:1-6 clearly reveals a difference between John's baptism and Christian baptism. Those who were baptized into John's baptism did not have Christian baptism, nor was it adequate. Finally, a pragmatic danger is implied in Landmarkism. Usually the group is so concerned with the doctrinal purity of their local assembly that they forget its mandate is the Great Commission. (This is a pathology of church growth called koinonites.)

X. THE BEGINNING OF THE CHURCH

There are many views that try to determine when the church began. Each grew out of a system of theology and in some way compliment the ideas which gave it life.

A. THE CHURCH BEGAN WITH THE SAINTS IN THE OLD TESTAMENT. This view is common among covenant or reformed theologians. In this position, some believe the church was established with the giving of the promise to Abraham (cf. Rom. 4).

Others believe the church was established with the promise of the covenant of grace. They generally say that the church originated in the garden of Eden immediately after the fall of man when God promised a Savior and man accepted that promise in faith.

B. THE CHURCH BEGAN WITH THE MINISTRY OF JOHN THE BAPTIST. Under this view it is noted that John's baptism is said to be given from heaven, and since Jesus sought baptism by a Baptist, why should Christians do less? John began baptizing and pointing people to the coming Christ; hence, they hold that John the Baptist was the starting point of the church.

C. THE CHURCH BEGAN WITH THE PUBLIC MINISTRY OF JESUS CHRIST. Those who hold this view interpret Matthew 10, where Jesus called His disciples as the beginning of the church because the word church means to "call together." Also they note the followers of Jesus were called disciples before this point and apostles afterwards. The sending forth of the twelve apostles is the beginning point of the church.

D. THE CHURCH BEGAN SOMEWHERE IN THE BOOK OF ACTS (CHAPTER 8, 13 OR 28). This is the hyper-dispensational view of O'Hare and Bullinger. They teach a Jewish church existed in the book of Acts immediately after the resurrection of Christ and before the gospel was carried to the Gentiles. The test of fellowship in the seventh dispensation (the Jewish church) is water baptism. Thus, water baptism is not required in this age of grace.

E. THE CHURCH BEGAN ON THE DAY OF PENTECOST. This is the view of most dispensationalists. It is represented by Chafer in his *Systematic Theology.*[37] He gives four prerequisites for the starting of the church.

1. *There must be a death.*

2. *There must be a resurrection.*

3. *There must be an ascension.* This would be God's seal on Christ's work.

4. *There must be an advent of the Holy Spirit.* Until these four events take place, a church cannot exist. Therefore, Acts 2 is the beginning of the church.

Peter, though chosen of God to be the chief spokesman at Pentecost, did not understand that Spirit baptism had begun on that day. It was not until some time later, when there was visible evidence of the Spirit baptizing new believers at the house of Cornelius, that he realized that this work of Spirit baptism had actually begun on the day of Pentecost. Notice carefully his words of explanation to the Jewish brethren after his return from Caesarea to Jerusalem: "And as I began to speak, the Holy Ghost fell on them, as on us at the beginning. Then remembered I the word of the Lord, how that he said, John indeed baptized with water; but ye shall be baptized with the Holy Ghost. Forasmuch then God gave them the like gift as he did unto us, who believed on the Lord Jesus Christ; what was I, that I could withstand God?" (Acts 11:15-17).

What happened to Cornelius was the same thing that happened at Pentecost (the beginning). This was the same as the gift of the Spirit. Peter identifies himself with them in the words "as He did unto us," not meaning that he had received the baptism and gift of the Spirit on Pentecost, for that would be contradictory to the words of Jesus in John 14:16 "with you . . . shall be in you." Rather, Peter was identifying himself as one of the group upon whom the Spirit came on the day of Pentecost.

Spirit baptism marks the beginning of the church. In 1 Corinthians 12:12-13 Paul writes that the body of Christ, the church, is formed as the Spirit baptizes individuals into the body, and into union with Christ. This is one of the primary identifications of the church as distinct from the people of God in Old Testament times. Since the church is formed by Spirit baptism, and since Spirit baptism began at Pentecost, the church began at Pentecost.

F. THE CHURCH BEGAN AT CALVARY WHEN CHRIST PROVIDED SALVATION.   Since Calvary is the focal point between the Old and New Testaments and between law and grace, then the church was introduced at the initiation of grace. The church is called His body and since He provided salvation by the death of His body on the cross, the church came into existence then. Also, Christians were placed by Spirit baptism into that body at His death, so that event initiated the church.

Jesus states, "I will [future tense] build my church," (Matt. 16:18), indicating that the church would be established future from that time. Later, the Bible declares (Acts 2:41, 47) that on the day of Pentecost the people were added to the church that was already in existence. Hence, the church must have been established after Matthew 16 and before Acts 2. The obvious event between these points of limitation is the death of Christ.

The church is built upon the apostles and prophets (Eph. 2:20) with Jesus Christ as the Chief Cornerstone. The reference to the Cornerstone is to the work He did on Calvary (1 Cor. 3:11; Eph. 2:20-21).

The church is called a mystery (Eph. 3:1-10) which is the dispensation of the grace of God (v. 2). This mystery was not made known in previous generations. It is now revealed (v. 5). The basis of the mystery is the work of redemption that made Jew and Gentile one (v. 6). Since this was accomplished at Calvary, the church was embryonically conceived then.

The church was first manifested on the day of Pentecost. Some say it actually began here (perhaps this is a problem of word definition). No one can deny that a spectacular event occurred on Pentecost. The church was manifested as a functioning organization (not introduced as a theoretical doctrine). What the church was to become was what it was in its first revealing. As a newborn baby, it was born functioning. The church did not emerge as a gradual dawning of a new day, meaning the church was born with one function (evangelism only) or a seed of what it was to become (only a few saved). The church was born as a live, active, and ministering body.

The church was manifested with new leaders who were ministering, serving, preaching, and winning souls. To see the purpose of the church, look at the Great Commission, then look at its manifestation on Pentecost; It was carrying out the Great Commission.

The church was manifested in a new place of worship. The church was not born in the temple. God was no longer a God of the temple, for the veil was rent from top to bottom. God had direct access to people and they to Him. He was now the God of the streets and the God of the people. The church was manifested outside the temple where the people assembled. The church was now an assembly of people.

The church manifested itself through multiple ministry: teaching, soul winning, breaking of bread, fellowshipping, praying, i.e., new areas of service. What it later was expected to do was the way it was born. Israel had not experienced aggressive evangelistic outreach, but now every believer could be filled with the Spirit and witness for Christ (Acts 1:8).

The church was manifested with empirical signs of authority in Acts 2 and throughout the rest of the book. There were signs of cloven tongues of fire, converts, money, miracles, powerful preaching, and judgmental death (Acts 5).

The Holy Spirit is vitally connected to the beginning of the church by "Spirit baptism" and is vitally present when believers were "filled with the Spirit" (Acts 2:4). John the Baptist had first predicted the Holy Spirit's baptism (Matt. 3:11; Mark 1:8; Luke 3:16; John 1:33). Jesus then promised an outpouring of the Spirit (John 7:37). He instructed His disciples to look for the Comforter (John 14:16) and after the resurrection, He promised the outpouring of the Spirit (Acts 1:4-5). The Holy Spirit was poured out on the day of Pentecost, and the disciples were all filled with the Holy Spirit (Acts 2:4). By way of emphasis, they were not "baptized with/by the Spirit" which is a positional action, but they were "filled with the Spirit" which is an experiential action. This was introduced by the following three signs:

1. *Sound of rushing wind*
2. *Tongues of fire*
3. *Every man hearing in his own language (tongues)*

Not until later did Peter realize that people had been baptized by the Holy Spirit (Acts 11:15-17). The Holy Spirit's coming at Pentecost was first called "the filling of the Spirit" (Acts 2:4), which is an endowment of power for service. The second designation of the Holy Spirit on the day of Pentecost was Spirit baptism, which is identifying people with Christ. Since Christian salvation accompanies Spirit baptism, and since the Spirit manifested Himself on Pentecost (when people began getting saved), it is obvious the church was first manifested on Pentecost.

XI. AUTHORITY AND THE LOCAL CHURCH

What authority does the church possess and how can it exercise it? On one extreme is the Roman Catholic church that claims authority through its exclusive claim as God's institution on earth. It controls salvation, access to God and has in the past claimed authority over its adherents in matters such as diet and birth control methods. At the other end of the spectrum are churches that are the extension and reflection of its members, so that the collective church has little authority over individual believers. God does not exercise authority over these believers through the local church. These churches seem to have no concept of local church authority over its members, yet they teach each believer is under the authority of Christ by being under the authority of Scripture.

In contemporary society, there are three basic expressions of local church authority, i.e., (1) episcopal, (2) representative, and (3) congregational. Most every church governs itself by one of these forms, or at least with a variation or addendum to these expressions. All three forms of church authority appeal to Scripture as the basis for how they operate and all three have some pragmatic strengths that seem to make them creditable.

THREE KINDS OF CHURCH GOVERNMENT			
Kind:	Congregational	Representative	Episcopal
Authority:	People	Board	Man
Strengths:	Church decides together—unity	Stability	Takes fullest advantage of gifted leader
Weaknesses:	Lack of direction	Rationalistic	Poor leadership
Philosophy:	Democratic	Representative, Republic	Monarchy

A. EPISCOPAL CHURCH GOVERNMENT. This form of government recognizes bishops as the primary leaders and human source of authority. Hence, the episcopal form of church government places a high degree of authority in the leaders (whether in the office or in the person who is leading). The title "episcopal" comes from the Greek word *episcopas* translated "bishop." It means to "oversee or to rule;" hence, episcopal church government is characterized by a person who oversees or rules the church. Since the word "bishop" meant "overseer," gradually the position of bishop grew to supervise the elders or pastors in a city or larger area. Hence, episcopal church government today implies the rule of one position over a church or many churches, but it can mean the pastor has oversight over one local church. This position holds that the oversight of churches by bishops in the earlier centuries demonstrates the natural and practical way to administer a church. While some forms of episcopal government allow for considerable voice by local congregations, the administrative authority does not usually rest in the congregation, but in a bishop or superintendent over a group of churches. The Methodist church, adopting its church government from the church of England (similar to the Episcopal church), reflects episcopal government. The Roman Catholic church is the most extreme form with its authoritarian hierarchy of bishops headed by the Pope, who is supposedly Christ's earthly Vicar.

The primary basis for rejecting this form of government, is that the structure of oversight is not found in the New Testament, even though the word bishop is found there. Further, the essential spiritual nature of the local church is developed when the people of the church have the final authority over their lives and beliefs, as they interpret it in Scripture.

1. *Representative Church Government.* This form of government is based upon rule of the church by presbyters, *presbuteros* (elders). It is based on the fact the word "elders" is always used in the plural when referring to church government and leaders. Because of the word "presbuteros," it is called the Presbyterian form of church government. Most of those who hold to this type of government acknowledge some post-New Testament development. They feel administrative authority over the churches resides in the denomination or fellowship of churches. Administrative authority in the local church usually resides in a committee of elders (not in the office of the pastor of the local church, bishop, or with the congregation).

This form of church government is weak because it does not allow for the simple, divinely-given system of independent, self-governing churches reflected in the Bible where the authority of a local congregation is centered in the people.

2. *Congregational Church Government.* This form of church government is based upon the principle that ultimate authority in all matters of faith and practice

resides in the congregation of each local church. Most Baptist and other independent churches believe that this system, as set forth in the New Testament, is the divinely-given system to exercise New Testament authority.

There seems to be two weaknesses found in the congregational form of church authority. First, there seems to be occasions of the bishop exercising authority by leadership in local churches (Acts 12:17; 15:13; 20:28), as well as elders exercising authority (1 Tim. 5:17; Heb. 13:7, 17). These men ministered in the church and had more authority than just preaching the Word of God. A second is a pragmatic weakness; churches that exercise democratic authority seem to lack aggressive systematic progress.

The New Testament seems to evidence all three reflections of authority in its ministry. First, churches seem to have one leader or spokesman, as with James in the Jerusalem church (Acts 12:17; 15:13) or the messenger of each of the seven churches in Revelation 2 and 3 (these seven were not angels, for God does not give his message to angels, but human vessels who preach and teach it to the church). Second, there seems to be a council or group of men who represented the wisdom and the desires of the congregation. These were called deacons (Phil. 1:1; Acts 6:1-7) or elders (Acts 20:17); whatever name, they were a body of leaders that were operative within the church. Third, the congregation seemed to be the final seat of authority which determined who could be received into fellowship (Rom. 14:1), and who would determine those that would be examined and/or rejected (2 Cor. 13:5), and which would determine their leaders (Acts 6:3, 5; Acts 14:23). Their authority came from the indwelling Christ (Matt. 28:18-20), the guidance of the Holy Spirit, and their individual priesthood that gave them access to interpret Scripture. Hence, the ultimate authority of the church flows back to God. The pastor leads the church, the deacons counsel and serve the church, and the congregation is the final seat of authority.

The church is not a building or denomination, it is people assembled with Christ. As such, Christ is the designer, architect, building, foundation, owner, and occupant of the church. The church is also called the "body of Christ." He is both the head and fullness of the body (Eph. 1:23). Church government must allow the Head to govern His own body, and He does it through pastors, deacons, and people, each fulfilling the role given by the Head.

XII. WHY THE CHURCH IS INDEPENDENT AND INDIGENOUS

The phrase "indigenous church" has meant churches that were: (1) self-directing, (2) self-governing, and (3) self-supporting. This phrase implies each church should be independent for its authority and support. Because Christ indwells each individual and He indwells the church, the congregation is dependent upon Him alone for its authority and sustenance. Also, because the Word of God is the only source for doctrine, life and ministry, the congregation depends upon Scripture alone for its direction and support. Because every believer can interpret Scripture, since everyone has the indwelling Holy Spirit to enlighten him, the congregation is the judge and court of appeal to determine the mind of the Lord.

The churches of the New Testament were all independent in governing themselves and supporting themselves. Each church depended upon its spiritual resource for evangelism, teaching, and discipline. The example of the churches in the New Testament suggests that today churches should be independent. But even in these examples, there are some problems that must be analyzed. First, some churches sent financial help to other congregations (Acts 11:29-30; 1 Cor. 16:1-3). However, this was not to sustain another church's ministry, but an expression of Christian grace to help suffering Christians. The Jerusalem Council (Acts 15) is seen by some as the embryonic seed of a denomination. But the resulting conclusions were not binding on all churches; rather, they were simply suggestions of Christian leaders who met from at least two congregations to determine how they would solve a doctrinal problem. Actually, the Jerusalem congregation was trying to give direction to the Antioch congregation. The brethren made suggestions (not directives) how one group would not offend the other. Even in this matter of respect, they appealed to Christian testimony and understanding. It was not a legally binding role whereby one church controlled another, or whereby an alleged "super-body" enforced its conclusions on churches.

After the New Testament was completed and God had established the Scriptures, the principle for the organization and administration of a local church was complete. A group of believers in each area had sufficient wisdom, under the illumination of the Holy Spirit, to establish their own organization, choose their own officers, and conduct their own affairs without outside control. There was no need for successors to the apostles to guide or help local churches. As we examine the New Testament, we do not see anyone taking the place of the apostles, nor do we see anyone taking the control of the church.

A. ARGUMENTS FOR THE INDEPENDENT, INDIGENOUS CHURCH. Historically, Baptists have used the term "autonomous churches" to describe their relationship one to another. Today, they tend to use the term "independent." Perhaps they could use the phrase "independent/dependent churches," implying they were independent from one another, but wholly dependent on God for life and direction.

1. *Since Christ indwells every believer* and He is the head of the church, believers are the channel through whom His authority flows to the church. When a decision "pleased the whole multitude" (majority vote), then the measured judgment of all

believers would most likely reflect the decision that Christ would desire for His church.

2. *Since the Word of God is the authority for doctrine* and practice, and every believer can interpret Scripture, then the congregation has the authority to determine the will of God. In what is called "the individual priesthood of the believer," each has access to read, study, interpret, and apply the Scripture to his life and the life of the church. Hence, the final seat of authority is the congregation, as they reflect themselves in consensus.

3. *Since the New Testament holds the believer responsible for correct doctrine and purity of life within the church*, then the congregation is responsible as the court or judge for a church's final appeal to authority. Paul told the church at Corinth to purify itself, "When ye are gathered together . . . to deliver such a one unto Satan for the destruction of the flesh, that the spirit may be saved in the day of the Lord Jesus" (1 Cor. 5:4-5). His constant appeal was that the church was responsible for itself. He did not appeal to an outside bishop, nor did he appeal to a board of elders to exercise authority in their problems. He appealed to the church as corporate members to set matters right.

4. *Since the churches of the New Testament were independent* (self-supporting, self-propagating, and self-governing), and there is no illustration or command for one church to govern another, or an outside authority to control a congregation, then it can be concluded that a church is its own source and final authority.

5. *The figures and/or analogies in the New Testament reflect an independent church.* The analogy of the body reflects that Jesus Christ, the head, is the only person who can give direction to the body. In Revelation 2-3 Jesus is walking in the midst (Gr. center) of all seven churches, which means each church is of equal distance to one another and of equal distance to Him. Hence, no church is over another church. Revelation 2-3 records a letter written to each church individually. This implies the equal importance and independence of each church. Jesus held all seven stars (pastors) in His hand (Rev. 2:1), indicating that each church had one pastor, and no one pastor had power over the other pastors or churches. Each pastor related directly to Christ for the source of his ministry.

HOW MEMBERS CONTROL
A CHURCH

a. They control the church by vote. This includes those times, which Scripture lays down, when matters are to be taken to the church. Such an example is in Matthew 18.

b. They control the church by fellowship (formal and informal acceptance of new members into fellowship: (Rom. 14:1; 15:7).

c. They control the church by exclusion of a member. The church can break fellowship with individuals for disciplinary reasons 1 Cor. 5:13).

d. The saints control the church by counseling, "In the multitude of counselors, there is wisdom" (Prov. 11:14). This would include talking to Christians, deacons, and pastors regarding the direction of the church.

e. The saints control the church by boycotting. This means leaving the church altogether.

The church should be without dictation from without or from within. A pastor should not be a dictator to his church (1 Pet. 5:2-3), nor should outside dictation be allowed. No church should be bound by counsel or association decisions. In Acts 15, they did not dictate to churches. They suggested guidelines for their practice.

Implied in the term "association" or "fellowship," is the right to disassociate. A church should know the aims or purpose of a fellowship before going into any endeavor. A church should always demand an article of self-purging before it associates with any endeavor. It should know how the process to de-fellowship those who do not walk according to its guidelines. Also, a church should know how, and upon what circumstance, it will discontinue its fellowship. This will keep an institution from becoming entangled in groups that are detrimental to its welfare. The purpose and doctrine for fellowship must be stated clearly. But realize, no human doctrinal statement can safeguard the purity of a group.

B. REASONS FOR COOPERATION OR FELLOWSHIP AMONG CHURCHES. Even though each church should be independent from outside authority and control, churches should cooperate for certain reasons and have fellowship on certain occasions. (In the midst of cooperation and fellowship, no congregation should lose control of its autonomy.) But there are biblical reasons for church cooperation. There may be good activities outside of the local church that fall within the functions of the church, but they themselves are not part of the local church. Christ not only commands the church to perform these activities, but also that these activities be performed in general. Therefore, there is a place for para-church organizations to carry out these functions. But even with this allowance, remember, there is no illustration of individual believers joining in a cooperative effort in Scripture. This is an argument from silence, but silence is what allows this ministry.

1. *Any cooperative effort must always be subservient to the efforts of local churches.* When churches join in a cooperative effort, it should only be when the project has the goals of a New Testament church.

2. *Churches should work together for growth in God's work (Eph. 4:1-16).* The work of God on the earth is a reflection of the heart of God. Churches should fellowship to send out missionaries to foreign lands and they should cooperate for home missions outreach. This is something that perhaps most small, local churches cannot carry out alone. When churches cooperate to carry out the Great Commission, their cooperation must be based on the fundamentals of the faith to have the blessing of God on their endeavors.

3. *Churches should recognize and support one another so that they reflect the unity for which Christ prayed (John 17:21-23) and of which Paul commanded (Eph. 4:3).* Caution should be taken, however, as the end does not justify the means. It is never unity for the sake of unity, but unity to carry out the work of Christ. Schismatics are condemned in the Bible. "Mark them who cause divisions . . ." (Rom. 16:17). However, never sacrifice doctrine (Titus 3:10) or standards of purity (1 Cor. 5:7-9) for a show of unity.

4. *Churches can cooperate for recognition of leaders (1 Cor. 16:10).* Today, when a pastor is ordained, other churches are asked to take part in the examination and ordination of the candidate. This is because leaders minister in different churches, not just the ordaining church. If there are any reasons to reject him from ordination, there is a wide basis for such a decision.

5. *Churches should cooperate in times of trial and persecution.* This encourages loyalty on the part of all to Jesus Christ and reveals love one for another (John 13:35).

6. *Churches should cooperate to increase the vision of all Christians.* Congregations can learn from one another and become more efficient in their ministry the same way pastors can learn from one another; hence, the work of Christ can prosper when churches expand the vision of one another.

7. Churches should fellowship for the sake of identification. During the New Testament times, there was no divergence of doctrine among churches. Each church seemed to recognize one another and accepted members and traveling ministries from one another. However, with the passage of time, churches seemed to have developed different doctrinal patterns, yet remained with the fundamentals of the faith. Today, there are differences that are so inherently contradictory that one church cannot fellowship with another. This does not imply that churches should seek to correct those who differ from them, but it suggests that those with similar beliefs and ministries should fellowship together to mutually support and protect one another.

XIII. DENOMINATIONS

The word "connectionism" is the historical term to describe how churches unite in fellowship or organic unity. The modern word is "denominations." There are over 250 denominations in the United States. Some are large, such as the Southern Baptist Convention with over 15.8 million members in 2001; other denominations are small, such as the Two-Seeds-in-the-Spirit Predestinarian Baptists, with 201 members in 16 churches.

A. DEFINITION. Obviously the word "denomination" does not come from Scripture, nor is the idea of a denomination explicitly taught therein. However, their existence is a fact of Christianity, therefore, how they fit into God's plan must be examined. But to understand them, the term must be defined.

> A denomination is a group of churches with similar doctrinal beliefs, who have similar traditions and backgrounds, who share the same goals in ministry, who desire fellowship to encourage one another, and who have organically bound themselves together to establish corporately what they feel cannot be wrought separately.[38]

The above description of a denomination becomes much more inclusive than some religious bodies are willing to admit. Some who are denominationalists deny that label, while others accept it willingly.

Some denominations are much more centralized, while others appear to be a confederacy or an unorganized fellowship. The longer a denomination exists, the more supervision and control over the church grows within the system, hence becoming a tight denomination. At the same time, newly-emerging denominations have no organic connection, but are held together by fellowship or the fact that their churches have similar purposes. These denominations do not require a yearly report of attendance and budgets, nor do they have officials or a district superintendent to supervise the business of the churches. There is little centralized direction, hence little control over the individual churches. These are called loose denominations.

B. SOURCES OF DENOMINATIONS. Some see the seeds of denominationalism early in the book of Acts. Two great churches evolved, each a little different from the other. First, there was a Jewish church at Jerusalem. Its members met on Solomon's porch, they had all things in common, and they banded together to saturate the Holy City with the Gospel. We read of these Christians, "daily in the temple, and every house, they ceased not to teach and preach Jesus Christ" (Acts 5:42). The Jerusalem church grew and was numbered in the thousands (Acts 2:41; 4:4; 6:1, 7). Next, a great church evolved to the north—a Gentile church at Antioch. Their members were the first to be called "Christians." The church had spiritually-gifted leaders in Barnabas and Paul. We read of this Gentile church, "much people was added unto the Lord" (Acts 11:24). They assembled themselves together and taught many people in Antioch. The Gentile church was more world-mission minded than was the Jewish church, and sent Paul and Barnabas out as the first missionaries (Acts 13:1-3).

The seeds of dissension were inherent in the nature of these two churches and were reflected in controversy at the council at Jerusalem. The first issue to divide Christendom was circumcision, the Jewish church demanding, "Except ye be circumcised after the manner of Moses, ye cannot be saved" (Acts 15:1), whereas Gentile churches held views similar to the conclusion of the council, that circumcision was not necessary.

Peter, Paul, James and other leaders of the churches were called to Jerusalem for a conference. The problem was stated and leaders were given opportunity to state their opinion. After a lengthy discussion, a group consensus was reached: "Then pleased it the apostles and elders, with the whole church" (v. 22). The group had to work out their differences for continued fellowship. "It seemed good unto us, being assembled with one accord" (v. 25). The problem among individual churches was solved, giving a biblical basis for church meetings (councils, committees, or conferences) to solve their problems. The conclusion was, "For it seemed good to the Holy Ghost, and to us, to lay upon you no greater burden than these necessary things; That ye abstain from meats offered to idols, and from blood, and from things strangled, and from fornication: from which if ye keep yourselves, ye shall do well. Fare ye well" (Acts 15:28-29). Even though the churches met for a decision, there was no pressure from an authoritarian head or centralized government. Even the answer was not a command to the lordship over an individual church. At the core of the Jerusalem Council was a recognition of the importance of the local church, rather than a doctrine of denominationalism. Each church was autonomous.

These two great churches were both blessed of God, yet differed in their interpretation of the Christian life. Whereas later denominations differed over minor doctrine, these first two churches differed over major doctrine. After the council, the churches agreed to exist and minister through their separate ways, yet stay in fellowship.

God never intended denominationalism to grow into its present splintered form so that in one city over 100 different denominational churches are found. Even though God's primary purpose was not the establishment of denominational churches, He blessed churches of various denominations if they believed in the fundamentals, practiced a godly life, and attempted to carry out the Great Commission. Even when some church's strengths are greater than its weaknesses, the gospel can have some effect through its ministry, hence, the message can go farther and deeper because churches exist with different emphases and practices.

Later in the book of Acts, the Christians at Jerusalem were going through a famine. Paul took up an offering from the Corinthian Christians to help them in this matter (2 Cor. 8:9). Once again, there was no control or central treasury. One group of churches simply provided help for another (1 Cor. 8:1-5).

The book of Acts ends with a number of individual churches, each having fellowship with the other, yet with no centralized superstructure emerging. Luke wrote the book of Acts, yet it is unfinished, indicating that the church which had begun should continue in its original form. At the apostle's death, the only common denominator among the churches was salvation, predicted in the Old Testament and fulfilled in the Person of Jesus Christ, who was dead, yet is now seated at the right hand of God the Father. Churches seemed to recognize one another, receive gifts from one another, and transfer members from one church to another. An attitude of love characterized Christians as they helped one another in their service to Jesus Christ.

After the post-apostolic age, the church began to express its beliefs and practices on paper. The living fellowship of the church was reflected in creeds and statements of expectation. The *Didache* and other doctrinal creeds inevitably appeared. Intellectual conformity to the emerging creeds was the way a Christian expressed his heart's dedication. The early creed makers fought life-and-death struggles in those early days concerning the essentials of Christianity. Eventually, Christians had to fight theological battles for all major church doctrines. When a person did not conform, he was threatened with excommunication. Personal infidelity was equally rewarded. The church grew within the Greek intellectual milieu. Some of the greatest scholars of this time were located within the church, rather than outside its walls.

During the third century, Christianity was announced as an official religion of the empire. When the hordes of barbarians demolished the outward forms of the already decayed Roman Empire, the only remaining nucleus of social order was the preachers of the Gospel who garbed themselves with simple apparel and proclaimed faith in a living God. Church control over society grew; denominationalism was never considered.

In the decades after the apostles, a centralization of authority began to arise. The office of bishop (elder or pastor) began to grow in authority. Bishops no longer gave leadership to only one church; their authority extended over several churches within a geographical area. Bishops began to ordain men into the ministry and control the financial affairs of the churches. Each city had its own bishop supervising the works of smaller surrounding churches. Usually the greater the city, the greater the bishop's authority. Since Rome was the capital of the civilized world, the bishop in Rome became a leading ecclesiastical figure. As individual cities fell to the invading Huns, their bishops and churches were also destroyed. Rome was the last city to hold out against the invaders, hence Rome was the last city to have an ecclesiastical leader.

However, when the Roman Empire and its civilization fell, the church retreated into monasteries. The church endured. During this time, which some characterize as the Dark Ages, ignorance prevailed throughout the world. The church, which held the lamp of knowledge, saw the light flicker through superstitions, tradition, and the addition of works to the grace which had been preached by the apostles.

The church became a church-state, a political-religious institution, and was the only organization able to compete with the times. There was unity in Christian profession and practice. The individual's life was closely controlled by the church's authority. A Christian's belief was born out of deep conviction to God and duty to his church. The problem of such a structure was that the sins of the clergy were hidden from the public and the weaknesses of the organization were not seen by the laymen. There was no successful criticism that could revive the church. Since all religious organizations created by fallible human beings are destined to destruction, the church began decaying. The church hid the light of the gospel under a bushel and sent the world into a millennium of darkness (A.D. 500-1500).

It was inevitable that the conscience and reason of man should revolt from the intolerable claims of papal absolutism. The reformers personified that revolt and gave rise to the reformation churches, and for the first time in history two widely accepted church systems were evident in the world: Catholicism and Protestantism. (However, during this time there was always a remnant church, without notoriety or political influence.) Because of the Reformation, doctrines which had been undiscovered, forgotten, or ignored, now were discovered, declared, and defended. Man's conscience and reason gave him access to the Word of God. Light prevailed and rebelled against the darkness. Men had no problem with the glare of Truth; it was the shadows that gave them trouble.

These questionable areas were unimportant in the early days of the Reformation; men were glorying in their new-found liberty of the gospel. But divisions were inevitable. Men disagreed on minor points, and the minor doctrines became major.

Sin has always been man's problem. Sin blinds man's understanding (2 Cor. 4:3-4; 1 Cor. 2:14), so that he cannot fully and correctly know God. Sin brings on religious pride which leads to doctrinal arrogance, causing good men to disagree and divide over theological distinctives. Also, sin influences man's motives, so that he will recruit and train disciples to perpetuate his doctrinal beliefs. Usually, what is a doctrinal tangent in the founder of a movement becomes heresy in his spiritual grandchildren. They hold the doctrines more vehemently with less understanding.

Surely God cannot sanction false doctrines; baptism by sprinkling and immersion cannot both be right. Therefore, one must be wrong. Yet God seems to use sincere men on both sides of the issue. God does not always withhold His blessings from a person for some false teaching, but when a church preaches the gospel, God uses them to the extent that they have the truth and seek His blessing on their ministry. At the same time, some churches have the truth but are dead. These churches accomplish little for eternity because they neglect spiritual power and disobey the truth they have.

God works in this doctrinal milieu; therefore, He works through various denominations, although they are not the perfect will of God. He could never plan a church that has some false teaching within its creed, yet it appears God blesses those churches in spite of some false doctrine if they are faithful to the essentials of the faith and seek His blessing on their ministry. Therefore, denominations exist within the permissive will of God. He condescends to use the frail creations of religions organizations.

But there are other causes that brought about the explosive growth of denominations in America. The pluralistic society of America gave rise to denominations like no other nation since Pentecost. A careful study of church history will show five or six church types usually develop within a country. But no nation has spawned the hundreds of denominations like the United States of America. After all is said and done, Christianity can only be divided into five or six major camps, each reflecting a different doctrinal statement and each reflecting its own organization. But the strong individualism found in this new frontier community gave rise to a diversity of denominations. Also, economic freedom of travel and the lack of competition from a "State church" produced an environment where a man could begin a church or start a denomination.

Americans glorify their heroes. The invincible man against overwhelming odds brings an unbelievable victory. Thus, Americans have produced the man of God, with a Bible in hand and faith in his heart; he walks into a town and establishes a church. Americans admire strong biblical individualism and firm convictions. The frontier preacher establishes a church and gathers a congregation around his leadership—the stronger the leader, the larger the following. Thus, great men build great churches. But the movement did not stop there. Strong leaders gather several around their cause, hence building a denomination.

Community stability mitigates against the growth of denominations. When families grow and die in the same community, it is difficult to get them to change church membership, much less establish new churches. Children tend to join the same church as their parents and grandparents. However, when a family moves to a new town, there is a tendency to lose moral restrictions and, with it, to drop church loyalties. Americans attend the church of their choice, which is usually the most convenient in the neighborhood or the one where the pastor's personality appeals to them. Hence, it is possible for aggressive denominations to build new churches and increase membership. Lethargic denominations tend to lose members. Americans want to go "where the action is," therefore they attend the church that has life or aggressive outreach. A mobile nation makes possible the growth of denominations, and since the United States is one of the most mobile nations in history, we can only expect to find the greatest number of denominations in our nation.

XIV. ORGANIZATION OF THE CHURCH

The church is both an organism and an organization. As an organism, it is a reflection of the life and power of the Lord Jesus Christ who indwells it. As an organization, it is the result of believers assembling together to carry out the Great Commission. The foundation for church organization comes out of the term "order," as in "church order."

"The word 'order' occurs four times in connection with the proper direction and control of church affairs . . . (1 Cor 11:34; 14:40; . . . Col 2:5; Titus 1:5). The Greek word for *order* is *taxis*, from the verb *tasso*. It is primarily a military term that was commonly used to express the most precise and exact order. It was commonly used of 'drawing up in rank and file, order or disposition of an army.'. . . This order is to be evidenced in the use of spiritual gifts and in the application of the principles of church government.[39]

No group or people can exist socially for very long without having some basis of agreement. There are those who claim the church is just a fellowship. The local church has fellowship, but there is a greater purpose and a more binding relationship among its members. Some churches are loosely organized with non-technical relationships, without written records, lists of members, or formal choice of officers. These have some form of "order," but organization does not seem essential to them. Other churches are highly organized with leadership rules, committees, and systems of accountability. The question remains, "How much organization is found in the early New Testament church?"

A. WHY ORGANIZE THE NEW TESTAMENT CHURCH? This section is not included to discuss organizational types of church structures, but to examine a more elementary question. Was the New Testament Church organized, and how did it express its organization?

1. *The church had definite stated meetings (Acts 20:7).* Regular meetings require some sort of group understanding concerning purpose and the way individuals will relate to one another. Since the early church met on a regular basis, there was internal agreement/ organization among the members.

2. *There are at least three elections which point toward an elementary organization.*

    a. In Acts 6:5, deacons were chosen. This was by the consensus of the people.

    b. In Acts 1:23, there was a replacement chosen for Judas. The disciples agreed to choose by lot.

    c. In Acts 14:23, there was an ordaining of elders. In the original language, *cheirotonesantes,* is "to designate by stretching forth of the hand." This could be referring to the apostle Paul laying his hands on the men for ordination, or it could refer to the members raising their hands in the church to vote for their leaders. In either case, church authority is recognized as leading to organization.

3. *The church in Philippi had a designation of officers (bishops and deacons, Phil. 1:1).* Hence, there was an indication of leadership.

4. *The church had designations and rules for its leaders (job descriptions).* Their qualifications and duties were clearly outlined.

5. *Authority is given to the leaders (1 Tim. 5:17).* The one who preached doctrine was the one who ruled the church. Those under the authority of the ministers are to submit themselves to them (1 Tim. 3:4; 1 Pet. 5:2; Acts 20:28; Heb. 13:7; 1 Thess. 5:12; 1 Cor. 16:16).

6. *A church has authority to correct church members in discipline (1 Cor. 5:4-5, 13).* This was not done by personal counseling, but by group action. Church discipline could not possibly happen unless the church was an organization

with standards that all understood so that those who deviated from the standards of the church could be judged.

7. *There was organization that resulted in the collection of money.* Romans 15:26, Philippians 4, and Acts 11:29-30 indicate a voluntary collection was received for special needs. 1 Corinthians 16:1 and 2 indicate a regular day upon which members were to give money—the first day of the week.

8. *Organization is revealed by letters of commendation being sent out from one church to another (Acts 18:27 and Rom. 16:1).* In Acts 18:27, "the brethren wrote," which probably indicates their letter represented a group standard and a group decision that the recommended believer had met that standard.

9. *There are clear instructions how a church was to deal with widows.* Their role, who was included, and qualifications are outlined in 1 Tim. 5:9.

10. *There were customs which certain churches in one area followed as a matter of practice.* 1 Corinthians 11:16 states that the other "churches of God" did not have a custom in regards to the difficulties that had brought problems in Corinth. Hence, the absence of regulation in one church as opposed to customs in another church implies each church had some freedom to organize themselves to their own needs without violating clear biblical standards.

11. *The early church clearly practiced the ordinances of the church—baptism and the Lord's Table.* These were practiced routinely, implying the members were associated to some group for the practice of these ordinances.

12. *The church practiced its business in an orderly fashion, implying organization (1 Cor. 14:23-40).*

13. *Acts 11:24-26 indicates there were qualifications for membership at the church in Antioch.* The word "numbered" in Acts 1:15; 4:4; 6:1, 7 may have meant added to a roll. The word "added" may have reference to baptism and/or church membership (Acts 2:41, 47; 5:14; 11:24). This would clearly imply organization.

Strong gives an excellent summary statement that reflects the definite organization of the early church.

That there was such organization is abundantly shown from (*a*) its stated meetings (Acts 20:7), (*b*) elections (Acts 1:23-26), and (*c*) officers (Phil. 1:1); (*d*) from the designations of its ministers (Acts 20:17, 28) together with (*e*) the recognized authority of the minister and of the church (1 Tim. 5:17; 3:4; 1 Pet. 5:2; Heb. 13:7; 1 Thess. 5:17); (*f*) from its discipline (1 Cor. 5:4, 5, 13), (*g*) contributions (1 Cor. 16:1, 2; Rom. 15:26), (*h*) letters of commendation (Acts 18:27; Rom. 16:1), (*i*) registers of widows (1 Tim. 5:9), (*j*) uniform customs (1 Cor. 11:16), and (*k*) ordinances (Acts 2:41), (*l*) from the order enjoined and observed (1 Cor. 14:20), (*m*) the qualifications for membership (Matt. 28:19), (*n*) and the common work of the whole body (Phil. 2:30).[40]

B. THE PATTERN FOR DEVELOPING ORGANIZATION. The Lord did not lay down patterns or principles of organization before the church was manifested on the day of Pentecost. The organization of the church grew out of its preaching and ministry. The apostles simply did what Jesus Christ commanded them and their ministry was the seeds of church organization.

The outgrowth of their preaching of the Word resulted in calling the church together as an assembly. The organization grew out of the believers assembling for evangelism, teaching the word, fellowship, and breaking bread together.

The commission to become an apostle implied a commission to the lay foundation of the church (Eph. 2:20). Implied in the commission were the abilities (gifts) to plant churches. (It appears that an apostle had the sum total of all of the gifts. Hence, they were also church planters.) Little organization was necessary in the early days of the church. Prior to Acts 6, which could be the first organizational problem, the early church faced little need of an organization. However, with the passing of time, the apostles felt the need for simple organization. Hence the principle, "Need leads to organization." A greater need brings about greater organization. The planning and implementation of organization must grow under the guidance of the Holy Spirit. In Acts 6, the Holy Spirit was evident in the choosing of deacons.

The apostles had a two-fold duty in establishing the church. First, they were to establish doctrine—teaching the church—and second, polity—church order and organization. The first-century pattern for church belief and practice is the pattern for today's church. We believe God not only revealed content, but methodology to carry out the Great Commission. Since the day of revelation and inspiration has passed, there can be no additional truth added to Scripture and there can be no additional forms or purposes added to the church.

It is very important that we recognize that church organization was complete before the apostles passed from the earthly scene. The New Testament content was completed in the first century, and so was the form of church government. Further, organizational development should only be allowed within the general framework discernable in the New Testament. Both the doctrine and the organization set forth in the New Testament have proven entirely acceptable and practical for all generations.

All the various modern practices such as Sunday School, training programs, and youth activities are valid only insofar as they promote the purposes and goals of the church as set forth in the New Testament.   They must not violate principles established under apostolic authority and recorded in the New Testament.

C. ORGANIZATIONAL AUTHORITY.   Christ is the head of the church (Col. 1:18; Eph. 1:22-23; 1 Cor. 12).   He has absolute sovereignty over the church including its organization, therefore everything is subject to His control and direction.

The Holy Spirit is the superintendent of the church.   He is the resident administrator.   The Holy Spirit administers this authority through: (1) the inspired Scripture, (2) the indwelling of every individual believer to understand Scripture, and (3) the empowering of every believer to do the will of God.   The congregation is the final seat of authority of the church.   This implies some sort of democratic process in the church.   In all cases, Christ is the Head and the Holy Spirit is the superintendent, and the people (church) are responsible for the direction of the church and are its final authority under Christ.

1. *Although the congregation is the earthly authority,* majority vote in and of itself is not a biblical mandate.   Majority vote would have ruined Moses.   When majority vote goes contrary to Scripture, it is not correct.

2. *The church leaders were given veto power and preferential choice in decision matters of the church.*   In Acts 6 we find the first organizational reference.   There was a biblical necessity for creating and filling certain offices.   The apostles suggested the congregation nominate whom "we may appoint" (Acts 6:3).   This raises the question of whether or not the apostles had veto power.   "They chose" (v. 5) is a reference to leadership selection before laying hands on them (v. 6).   Apparently the leaders had intimate, thus confidential, information on the believers of the church.   Thus they could exercise veto over those who did not fit the qualifications for office.

3. *Democratic vote has at times been absolutely wrong.*   In Acts 21:18-26 the church elders urged Paul to make a vow.   On this occasion they were apparently wrong.

The church is believers who seek to glorify Jesus Christ.   God has given believers in each locality sufficient guidance to establish its own government, choose its own officers, and conduct its own affairs without outside control.   In essence, the foundation is Jesus Christ, the authority is the Holy Spirit, the leader is the pastor, the control of the church comes from the saints, while the deacons serve the church.

XV. CHURCH MEMBERSHIP

The idea of belonging to a church is assumed in the New Testament. Every person who was a Christian was part of the fellowship with other Christians in his locality. No one was left to live or minister independently, nor did they become a rule unto themselves. John Donne said "no man is an island," and that description is true of a Christian. The "Lone Ranger" mentality prevalent among some Christians today is foreign to Scripture.

Saints (disciples) in the New Testament were numbered, which seems to be equivalent to adding to a roll (Acts 1:15; 4:4; 6:1, 7). When people were saved and/or baptized they were added to the church (Acts 2:41, 47; 5:14; 11:27). The result of growth is that the church multiplied (Acts 6:1, 7), which implies that both a count of the total number, plus a means of ascertaining new members was recorded. This gives a biblical base for the practice of keeping a roll of church members.

The apostles had an inclusive number of eleven (Acts 1:26) or twelve in its membership (Acts 2:14). The numbering of the leaders of the church implies a roll and numbering of its members.

Some churches do not keep a formal church roll and traditionally the question is asked, "Is church membership biblical?" Even those who do not keep a membership roll have an unwritten standard. They know who is a part of the group and how the church makes decisions.

Access to church membership is by congregational vote. The final decision is usually not made by the deacons, membership committee, or by the pastor, but by the congregation. The Roman believers were exhorted, "Him that is weak in the faith, receive ye" (Rom. 14:1).

There are four conditions to receive a person into church membership: (1) belief, (2) baptism, (3) doctrine, and (4) morals. The Bible explicitly teaches only two: belief and baptism. Nothing is found in Scripture that new members must meet doctrinal and moral requirements. The question arises, should anyone be allowed into the church upon profession of faith and baptism? For example, should a known prostitute be given church membership the moment she professes salvation? How about a known alcoholic? Should these prove themselves before being accepted into church fellowship?

A. PROFESSION OF FAITH FOR CHURCH MEMBERSHIP. A church should accept only regenerate members. Those who are received into the local body must first be born again before they are accepted into the body of Christ, who died for them. The unregenerate are always welcome in church to visit, listen, or attend, but not to become church members. But it is impossible to humanly assess those who truly possess eternal life. Therefore, the church required a candidate to "confess Jesus

Christ" (Rom. 10:9), which is also called public profession of faith. Those who truly believe in their heart will desire to confess it with their mouth (Rom. 10:9-10). However, the opposite is not always true; some confess with their mouth but do not believe in their hearts.

As a result, some are accepted into church membership and at a later time are found not to be Christians. The problem with profession faced the church even in apostolic times, "examine yourselves, whether ye be in the faith" (2 Cor. 13:5). Hebrews 6:1-9 seems to describe those who profess, but are not really saved. Another passage, 1 John 2:19, describes some who were included in the church upon their profession of faith, however, they left the assembly revealing they were never really saved.

The question is often raised whether a church should accept a new convert into church membership, or whether it should wait to make sure the person will continue in his profession. Since some make professions of faith without actually possessing salvation, a church should withhold membership until a voting Christian has proven himself. Those who hold this position argue that Paul was not given immediate recognition/fellowship by the church in Jerusalem, but was only accepted after Barnabas vouched for him (Acts 9:26-28).

On the other side of the issue, there is strong argument to receive new believers into church membership immediately. Paul told the Romans, "Him that is weak in the faith receive ye" (Rom. 14:1), implying the new believer with weak faith will benefit from church fellowship/membership. Paul argues that if Christ received them unto His body, should not the local church receive them into their body (Rom. 15:7)? Further, it is noted that the purpose of membership is to strengthen Christians through fellowship, not to impose a "trial" period to improve oneself for membership. After all, every Christian is a sinner saved by grace who will be strengthened by fellowship.

B. WATER BAPTISM FOR CHURCH MEMBERSHIP. The Bible implies that believers were accepted into fellowship upon baptism in water after their conversion. In reverse, the Bible has no illustration of a believer who was not connected to a fellowship nor does it give any illustration of believers who were unbaptized. Only one place was baptism deferred and that is the case of the thief on the cross. However, his willingness indicates he would have been baptized if given the opportunity. The Bible gives no example of baptism being withheld so a person could prove himself, or so a church could further examine a candidate. Even though an argument from silence, it suggests water baptism precedes church membership. Just as Spirit baptism identifies us in Christ's body in death, burial, and resurrection, so water baptism identifies us with the local body, which is a New Testament church. This argument of symbolism is a major reason to require water baptism before church membership.

C. DOCTRINAL FELLOWSHIP FOR CHURCH MEMBERSHIP. First, how much doctrine does a person have to know in order to be a church member? And second, with how much of the doctrinal statement shall a person agree before becoming a church member? Can a person disagree in minor areas and still fellowship with a community of believers?

Regarding the first question, if a church accepts new Christians as members who are baptized immediately upon their profession of faith, then they probably have a minimum knowledge of doctrine. Therefore, that church cannot require that new members have complete knowledge of the doctrinal position of the church. The candidate for church membership should know basic doctrines of Christianity which are those surrounding salvation. This would include the authority of Scripture, the deity of Christ, and the death and resurrection of Christ (the gospel). The basis of church membership should be the essentials of Christianity.

After a young convert is accepted into church fellowship, it is the responsibility of a church to see that they are taught doctrine. Doctrine is essential for a balanced life; without it there will be an unbalanced church.

But what about disagreement with some aspect of a church's doctrinal statement. How much conformity is necessary for church membership? Luke suggests, "those things which are most surely believed among us" (Luke 1:1). Christian truth is known in the Scriptures as "sound doctrine." Paul notes, "Holding fast the faithful word as he hath been taught, that he may be able by sound doctrine both to exhort and to convince the gainsayers." Sometimes doctrine is referred to as "the faith." "If ye continue in the faith grounded and settled, and be not moved away from the hope of the gospel, which ye have heard" (Col. 1:23 emphasis added). "Beloved, when I gave all diligence to write unto you of the common salvation, it was needful for me to write unto you, and exhort you that ye should earnestly contend for the faith which was delivered unto the saints" (Jude 3).

The basis of good, sound doctrine was the whole body of revealed truth contained in the Scriptures. Therefore, Paul said that the Scriptures are "profitable for doctrine" (2 Tim. 3:16). But, in the day of Acts 2, the New Testament had not yet been written, and doctrine had to be transmitted orally by the apostles. For this reason it is called the "apostles' doctrine." Those who were "added" to the church (Acts 2:41) continued in the apostles' doctrine (Acts 2:42).

Anyone who denies "the doctrine of Christ," meaning His deity, His Sonship, His virgin birth, His atoning death, and His resurrection is not a Christian. "Whosoever transgresseth, and abideth not in the doctrine of Christ, hath not God. He that abideth in the doctrine of Christ, he hath both the Father and the Son" (2 John 9). "Whosoever denieth the Son, the same hath not the Father: [but] he that acknowledgeth the Son hath the Father also" (1 John 2:23). Therefore, any who deny the fundamental doctrine of Christ are denied church fellowship because they have not met the criteria for being a Christian.

However, if a new convert held a heretical doctrine, that would later be a condition to cast him out of church fellowship. That denial would be a condition to not give him the "right hand of fellowship" in the first place. Note the following exhortation by Paul. "A man that is an heretic after the first and second admonition reject (Titus 3:10). Also, some were put out of the church, "which some having put away concerning faith have made shipwreck: of whom is Hymeneus and Alexander; whom I have delivered unto Satan, that they may learn not to blaspheme" (1 Tim. 19-20). Most new converts are ignorant of some doctrine. They should not be rejected. But if a new convert comes from a cult, that person should demonstrate yieldedness to accept the authority of Scripture in his doctrine and life before being accepted into church fellowship.

When candidates for membership come from another church, the receiving church should secure a letter of recommendation from his former church. A church cannot accept someone who is under the discipline of another church. Therefore, the candidate should be voted into membership pending a letter. Also, there should be a testimony given, insuring the candidate has an intelligent profession of salvation.

D. MORAL STANDARDS FOR CHURCH MEMBERSHIP. The basis for receiving church members is explained in Romans 14:1-4. Paul makes it clear that the church is not a body limited to mature saints only. He opens membership to include, "Him that is weak in the faith . . ." (Rom. 14:1). Paul does not mean just ignorance of the creed (statement of faith), but one who had difficulty trusting God for victory in his life. Paul is not saying to receive the one who is weak in reliance for justification (Rom. 4), for that would be accepting those who doubt their salvation. The weak Christian that Paul wanted to accept into fellowship had a problem with sanctification, or the problem of separation (eating meat). "The eater—let him not despise the non-eater" (Rom. 14:3). (*Auton prose labeto* makes non-eating a condition by which he is received.)

Paul exhorts, "Who art thou that judgest another man's servant?" (Rom. 14:4), or he asks if we have the right to judge the servant of God? "Receive ye" is to welcome into fellowship—not to criticize, but to build up. So the church should accept a person on his profession of faith. We cannot determine a person's spirituality. Again, only Christ is the judge (Rom. 14:10).

Therefore, everyone Christ has received into salvation, we ought to be willing to receive as brothers and church Members. Paul states, "Wherefore receive ye one another, as Christ also received us to the glory of God" (Rom. 15:7).

A new Christian is accepted into church membership upon his Profession of faith, and his profession of repentance. The individual testifies that he has turned from his sin to Jesus Christ. Faith and repentance cannot be separated. This does not assume the young Christian is perfect or that he has cleaned up every habit in his life. Therefore, we can ask, What sin should be purged and what sin should be allowed in the new Christian? With this question we remember that no Christian, no matter how mature, is sinless.

Any sin that is a matter for church discipline would be a sin that would exclude a new Christian from church membership. This alleviates any discipline-prone people from entering the church. As an example, a church would exclude any who are living in open immorality, unmarried couples, or the owner of a porno store.

XVI. The Office Of A Pastor

The man who fills the position of pastor of a church must first be called by God into full-time service; second, he must be given the serving gifts of the Holy Spirit; and third, the church gives him the office to lead the church, which is called the office of elder or bishop.

There are at least seven titles for the man of God who leads the New Testament church: (1) elder, (2) bishop, (3) pastor, (4) preacher, (5) teacher, (6) servant, and (7) messenger. Each title describes a different qualification of the man and leads to a distinct duty. The following sections examine both the nature of his job and how he fulfills his duties.

TITLES FOR THE PASTOR	
1. Elder	5. Teacher
2. Bishop	6. Servant
3. Pastor	7. Messenger
4. Preacher	

A. Elder: A Man of Spiritual Maturity. The Greek word for elder, *presbuteras*, is used of church leaders, first in Acts 11:30, and 22 times in the New Testament thereafter. The personal qualifications of the church leaders are emphasized; he must be a man of spiritual maturity in age and experience. An elder must be of recognized spiritual stature (1 Tim. 3:6), who could command respect from the people of God to lead the church. The elder is the visible leader of the local congregation. Vine defines an elder as,

> An Old Man, an elder, is used (*a*) of age . . . (*b*) of rank or positions of responsibility . . . in the Jewish nation, firstly, those who were the heads or leaders of tribes . . . in the Christian churches, those who, being raised up and qualified by the work of the Holy Spirit, were appointed to have the spiritual care of, and to exercise oversight over the churches.[41]

The first question we must ask is, did the office of elder arise as an organizational solution to the need for leadership in the church after the apostles passed off the scene? Another way to ask the same question is, was the office of elder a position that was appointed by God?

From the earliest days of Israel's existence, elders functioned as a group helping the God-appointed individual leader. Thus, God instructed Moses to take the "elders of Israel" with him in the confrontation with Pharaoh (Ex. 3:16-18). Since there is no recorded procedure on how they were chosen, we must assume that they grew into recognition. Elders became the leaders of Israel because of their chronological age. Remember, Israel was led by its patriarchs (Abraham, Isaac, Jacob) before going into Egypt. Each of the twelve sons of Jacob became a ruler in his family and no one person ruled Israel. Hence, the oldest in the families were the leaders. The rulership of patriarchs collapsed in Egypt, and with servitude the people turned to the oldest and wisest to lead them.

The existence and function of elders can be traced throughout the history of Israel: under Joshua, during the period of the judges; with Samuel, throughout the period of the kingdom; during the captivity and after the return. Some 114 times the "elders of Israel," of the "priests," of the "land," and of the "house," are mentioned. All but 16 of these references are found in the historical books. While there is little information concerning their choice or there official duties, it is obvious that they, at times, constituted a regularly recognized group (cf Num. 11:16; Josh. 8:10; 1 Kgs. 8:1; Ezra 5:9-10). It appears that "they retained their position under all the political changes which the Jews underwent."[42]

There is a contrast between the elder and priest in the Old Testament. The priest had a twofold aspect: it was a hereditary office, and it was a functioning office. The priest was taken out of the tribe of Levi, but not all Levites were priests. A Levite had to be called of God (Heb. 5:4). They fulfilled routine functions of worship and sacrifice. In the day of restoration, the entire nation will serve as God's representatives as a nation of priests (Isa. 61:6). The Levites were keepers of the law and instructors in the law for all Israel (2 Chron. 35:3).

There are some recognizable similarities between the Old Testament priest and the New Testament elder. Both were responsible for being God's representatives before the people of God, and both were responsible for the keeping and teaching of the Word of God. But the contrasts between a New Testament pastor and Old Testament priest are important: (1) the elder/pastor is by personal call, not heredity; (2) every believer is a priest, while Israel had a priestly office; and (3) most importantly, the New Testament elder/pastor does not function in a sacrificial system.

The priesthood was not God's original plan for Israel. "Now therefore, if ye will obey my voice indeed, and keep my covenant, then ye shall be a peculiar treasure unto me above all people: for all the earth is mine: And ye shall be unto me a kingdom of priests, and a holy nation. These are the words which thou shalt speak unto the children of Israel" (Exod. 19:5-6). The priesthood was instituted later because of the sin of Israel. God had intended every man to be his own priest, as in the case of Abraham or Job.

Both elder and prophet received the Word of God and delivered it to the people. The prophet did so by revelation, while the elder took the written message and taught it. The prophet could be young or old while an elder was qualified by his age, experience, and leadership. A prophet had infallible direct revelation; therefore, his message should never have been questioned. The authority of the elder's message was already written. It is significant that Paul lists the "pastors and teachers" separately from apostles and prophets (Eph. 4:11). The office of elder/pastor includes some elements in common with both priest and prophet. But, because of the abolition of the sacrificial system, and because of the completed canon, and because of the change from a geographical temple to a gathering of people in the Church dispensation, the elder/pastor of the church is distinctively different from both priest and prophet.

In the first reference to elders in the New Testament (Acts 11:30), the Antioch Christians are giving money to the elders at Jerusalem. In Acts 15, the elders exercise authority along with the apostles (cf. Acts 12:17). Most apostles were also elders (1 Pet. 5 :1; 2 John 1; 3 John 1).

The Bible teaches a plurality of elders, as seen in Acts 14:23; 20:17; James 5:14; Titus 1:5; and 1 Peter 5:1. There are at least three ways to interpret the multiple elders.

a. Some Brethren churches believe there should be many elders (pastors) in a local church. They tend to share preaching, and together, administer the church. The modern Body Life view of the church holds to plurality of elders.

b. The Presbyterian or Reformed church believes in ruling elders and teaching elders. The ruling elders are plural and they take care of spiritual matters in the church. The teaching elder is the pastor, responsible for preaching.

c. Baptist or Independent churches believe in a multiple staff of pastors such as a senior pastor and his staff, youth pastor, minister of music and others. These all function with the title of pastors in the role of elders.

The pastor has several tasks in the church. When he is described as an elder, his duties relate to his spiritual maturity. Just as the original patriarchs (Abraham, Isaac, and Jacob) gave leadership to all the people in their household, so the elder gives leadership to those in the spiritual household. As such, leadership is given by spiritual example and wise decisions, not by doctrinal decree (1 Pet. 5:1-4), or as Peter describes it, "not lording it over the flock."

The second task of the elder is to rule the church. The word "rule" is a hard word for some to accept, but nevertheless, it is a biblical command. "Let the elders that rule well be counted worthy of double honor, especially they who labor in the word and doctrine" (1 Tim. 5:17). In essence, the one who preaches is to rule. "One that ruleth well his own house, having his children in subjection with all gravity; (For if a man know not how to rule his own house, how shall he take care of the church of God?)" (1 Tim. 3:4-5). This implies an elder (bishop) is to rule his family well as a requirement to lead the flock. Note, "taking care" is not quite as strong as the previous passage, ruling the house of God. "The elders which are among you I exhort, who am also an elder, and a witness of the sufferings of Christ, and also a partaker of the glory that shall be revealed: Feed the flock of God which is among you, taking the oversight thereof, not by constraint, but willingly; not for filthy lucre, but of a ready mind" (1 Pet. 5:1-2). These verses indicate that an elder is to feed and take oversight of the church. "Remember them which have the rule over you, who have spoken unto you the word of God: whose faith follow, considering the end of their conversation. Obey them that have the rule over you, and submit yourselves: for they watch for your souls, as they that must give account, that they may do it with joy, and not with grief: for that is unprofitable for you" (Heb. 13:7, 17). Those who preach the Word are to rule the church. "And we beseech you, brethren, to know them which labor among you, and are over you in the Lord, and admonish you." 1 Thessalonians 5:12 states that those who are over the church are the ones who rule. They are the ones who admonish the church. "That ye submit yourselves unto such, and to every one that helpeth with us, and laboreth" (1 Cor. 16:15). Because of the harshness associated with the modern definition of "rule," the preferred phrase is that the elder/pastor should lead the church.

B. BISHOP: THE OFFICE OF OVERSEEING. The Greek word *episcopos*, "bishop," is used five times in the New Testament. It is translated "bishop" four times (Phil. 1:1; 1 Tim. 3:2; Titus 1:7; 1 Pet. 2:25), and "overseer" once (Acts 20:28). The verb *episcopeo* occurs once in the New Testament in relation to church officers, and is translated "take the oversight" (1 Pet. 5:2). The noun *episcopa* occurs once in regard to the church office, and is translated "office of bishop" (1 Tim. 3:1). The basic meaning seems to be that of "overseer."[43]

Thayer defines a bishop as "a man charged with the duty of seeing that things to be done by others are done rightly, any curator, guardian or superintendent. The head or overseer of any Christian church."[44]

The title of bishop identifies the pastor as involving the chief administrative responsibility in the church. The bishop (or overseer) is responsible for the regulation and general functioning of the church in its life and ministry. Leadership (but not authoritarian dictatorship) is implied. This basic oversight is inherent in the title, as shown by A. R. Fausset. For example, he states that *epicsopos* was "applied to the inspectors sent by Athens to her subject states, to inquire into their state, to rule and defend them."[45]

In 1 Timothy 3:1 the word "office" is attached to the bishop. The title elder or pastor is never related to an office. Most likely "elder" referred to his character, "pastor" refers to calling, and "bishop" refers to office. A man grows into being an elder, be becomes a bishop by vote, and he is called by God to pastor (see Eph. 4:11-12). That implies that some men have grown into elders who may have not yet been recognized by the church and are not yet elected as bishop (pastor).

The titles bishop and elder are used interchangeably in Titus 1:5-7, 1 Peter 5:1-5, and Acts 17, 28. Also, Paul tells the elders at Ephesus (Acts 20:17) that they should do the work of a bishop (Acts 20:28). Since we know there were elders ordained to lead the church (Acts 14:23), and later, bishops identified (Phil. 1:1, cf. 1 Tim. 3:1-14) to lead churches, then we can assume elders and bishops are titles used interchangeably. Different words are used because the same person in the same office had different functions.

The word "bishop" is used in the singular (Titus 1:7; 1 Tim. 3:1) implying there was one bishop who had the oversight of the church. Also, it is implied he was the leader among leaders, or the senior pastor of a staff of pastors. The singular pastor or the leadership of one pastor over a church is implied in the singular messenger to the seven churches in Revelation (Rev. 1:20; 2:1, 8, 12, 18; 3:1, 7, 14). The word *aggeloi* is translated both "angels" and "messengers" in Scripture. It is obviously a messenger for each church. God sent a message to the church leaders who would read it to the congregation.

There is another problem with the singular use of the word "bishop" and/or "messenger." There has been an unscriptural development of the office of bishop. Because "bishop" meant "oversight," and was used in the singular, one bishop became dominant in the church. Then one bishop became dominant over several churches, i.e., began to oversee several churches and pastors. Neve interprets the New Testament pattern.

> We are here reviewing the time when bishop and presbyter meant one and the same thing, and when in each local congregation there was to be found a number of men, appointed or elected, who were called either bishops or presbyters. . . . In Phil. 1:1, Paul addresses himself not to one, but to a number of bishops. According to Acts 20:17, 28 all presbyters of the Ephesian Church were appointed bishops. The post-Apostolic Father, Clement of Rome (cir. 96), knew of no distinction between bishops and

presbyters; and the *Didache* (about the beginning of the second century) speaks of only two classes of officers who were elected by the congregation:—bishops and deacons.[46]

Some churches mistakenly hold that all bishops are elders, but that not all elders are bishops. For example, Lowndes says, "Bishops or overseers were probably certain elders chosen out of the body of local elders."[47]

C. SHEPHERD: THE GIFT OF PASTORING. The term "shepherd/pastor" is descriptive of a gift or spiritual ability to look after the sheep of God. The noun, *poimen*, is used by Paul in Ephesians 4:11 as a descriptive title of church leaders. It is translated in the King James as "pastor." From this reference the title, pastor, has gained wide acceptance. The Greek word could better be translated "shepherd." The work of the shepherd is familiar; he is the leader, guide, feeder (in the sense of leading the sheep into places of adequate forage), helper, and protector of the sheep. Therefore, the word "flock" was used as a descriptive title for the church (Acts 20:28-29, Cf. Matt. 26:31 for the common use: John 10:16 for Israel, and Luke 12:32 for the band of disciples).

The title shepherd/pastor is reflective of the title that Jesus gave of Himself, "I am the good shepherd" (John 10:11). Jesus is also called the Great Shepherd (Heb. 13:20), and the Chief Shepherd (1 Pet. 5:4). In connection with this last reference, the chief shepherd is in contrast to the elder (v. 1) who should not "lord it over the flock" (v. 3), but realize Jesus Christ is the Lord of the flock. The pastor is the "undershepherd" while Jesus Christ is the "Chief Shepherd." The undershepherd has a threefold task:

1. *The shepherd's first job is to lead the flock (Acts 20:28; 1 Pet. 5:2).* First, he does this by example, hence, a shepherd (1 Pet. 5:3) is related to being an elder.

2. *As a pastor or shepherd, his ministry is feeding (Acts 20:28; 1 Pet. 5:2) the flock.* This mainly involves the teaching ministry of the pastor. Paul calls him the "pastor-teacher" (Eph. 4:11).

3. *Tending is another duty of a shepherd.* This involves herding, correcting, or protecting the flock. He does this by counseling, ministering, and supporting, to help those under him to gain full maturity. His job is to make them whole or mature (Eph. 4:12).

The term "shepherd" has to do with the summary phrase, "spiritual watch care." The key Scripture is 1 Peter 5:1-2, which ties all three titles together: shepherd, bishop, and elder. The shepherd is not to be a dictator and not to do his job for money, but he is to do it willingly.

D. PREACHER: A PUBLIC PROCLAIMER. The term "preacher" is found 61 times in the New Testament. The word "preach," *keroso*, means "to herald." Paul tells us the result of preaching is "to edification, and exhortation, and comfort" (1 Cor. 14:3). Thayer defines the word, "a herald, a messenger vested with public authority, in the New Testament, God's ambassador and the herald or proclaimer of the divine Word."[48]

Peter introduced Noah as the first "preacher" (2 Pet. 2:5) to point out the similarity of declaring God's Word, both in the Old Testament and New Testament. "No agency of religion is older than preaching. It is as old as the Bible itself. . . . The agency for the spread of a religion of persuasion must be preaching. . . . One of the marks of the new era beginning with John the Baptist was a revival of prophetic preaching" (Mt 11:9).[49]

The predominant theme of preaching is Jesus Christ. "Then Philip went down to Samaria, and preached Christ unto them" (Acts 8:5). The same theme is repeated often (Acts 8:35, 9:20, 10:36, 1 Cor. 1:23, 2 Cor. 4:5). The next task of the preacher was to bring the message of salvation to men, which is to declare the plan of salvation. "How shall they hear without a preacher" (Rom. 10:14). The preacher brought "glad tidings" (Rom. 10:15) to the lost. Even though "the preaching of the cross is to them that perish foolishness" (1 Cor. 1:18), the man of God is still to preach the gospel (1 Cor. 15:1-3). Next, the preacher must, "Cry aloud, spare not, lift up thy voice like a trumpet, and shew my people their transgression" (Isa 58:1). In the task of preaching, he must denounce sin. Paul told Timothy, "Them that sin rebuke before all, that others also may fear" (1 Tim. 5:20). Again Paul exhorted Titus to be bold in public proclamation (Titus 1:9-13).

> In the NT sense a preacher is a man who has the inner call from the Holy Ghost and the external call from the church, the witnessing body of Christ on earth, and has been duly set apart as an accredited and qualified teacher of the Christian religion. His vocation is that of addressing the popular mind and heart on religious truth, as that truth is set forth in the sacred Scripture, for the spiritual profit of the hearer as its end. The preacher, recognized as such by the church, speaks as a personal witness of God's saving truth, explaining it and applying it as the circumstances of the people and the time may require. The gravity and importance of this vocation, as set forth in the sacred Scriptures, and aptly illustrated in the history of the church, surpasses those of any other calling among men. . . . Luther said, "The devil does not

mind the written word, but he is put to flight whenever it is preached aloud."[50]

E. TEACHER: EXPLAINER OF SCRIPTURE. The pastor is a teacher who must feed the flock. The term, "teacher," comes from *didaskalosi*. The verb, *didasko*, is found some 97 times in the New Testament and is used in a broad way of anyone functioning as a teacher. For example, in Romans 12:7 and Col. 3:16, it is used of believers who teach other Christians. The nouns, *didaskalia* and *didache*, are found 51 times, and are used generally in the sense of "doctrine" or "teaching." The process of teaching leads to the product, which is the student knowing doctrine. From this comes the root word for "apostles' doctrine" and "apostles' teaching," showing that the concept of doctrine was present in the church from the beginning (Acts 2:42).

Instruction in the church was to include more than a single reading of the authoritative Scriptures (1 Tim. 4:13). Teaching was the explanation of that which was believed. Paul instructed Timothy to "continue thou in the things which thou hast learned" (2 Tim. 3:14), because he had "known the holy scriptures" (v. 15).

The Great Commission begins with the idea of teaching, "teach all nations," which is to "make disciples" (Matt. 28:19). Then the task of teaching continues, "teaching them to observe . . ." (Matt. 28:20).

F. SERVANT: A MINISTER TO ALL. Another title for the pastor is "servant." The word "servant" comes from *doulos*, which is usually applied to deacons. But the word "servant" is also applied to pastors (1 Pet. 5:2, NIV; Titus 1:1; c.f. Matt. 20:25-28). Pastors are spiritual servants of the flock of God. A pastor will lose touch with a congregation if he only rules or only gives counsel because he is a bishop. In the role of servant, the pastor ministers to the lowly of the congregation. In the role of bishop/elder, the pastor stands at the front of the church as leader. In the role of servant, he symbolically washes feet. Obviously, there is a tension when both titles are assumed by the pastor. But the tension is created by God, for those who serve Him must walk in dignity as an elder/bishop before the flock of God, yet also submit humbly as the servant of the church.

G. MESSENGER: REARER OF GOD'S REVELATION. On seven occasions, the word "messenger," *aggelo*, is associated with each church mentioned in Revelation 2-3. Some translate this word as "angel" because of the King James reading (Rev. 1:20; 2:1, 8, 12, 18; 3:1, 7, 14). However, the best reading is "messenger," because the person was receiving these messages for the church. Since God usually speaks to His church through the prophetic office, not angels, these were the primary messengers in each of the seven churches involved.

The Dictionary of New Testament Words defines messengers as "the ambassador in human affairs, who speaks and acts in the place of the one who has sent him."[51]

Today, we would consider them the senior pastor: those who preach, but also those who determine the preaching emphasis in a local church. Also, remember, these were actual local churches, and God had a unique, but different message for each church. In application, the senior minister is responsible to lead his church (bishop) understand the true message of God (elder) so that their spiritual needs can be met (pastor) through his role of exhorting (preacher) and instructing (teacher), supported by his ministry (servant). Paul Jackson sums up the task of the pastor.

> His authority in the church, as God's leader, is a moral and spiritual power, not a legal one. He should exercise leadership. He must refuse to compromise Biblical convictions, even though he should be gracious in attitude, and never be stubborn about personal opinions or desires that do not involve Biblical principles. His authority rests to the power of a godly example, as well as in the fact that he is a Biblical officer (1 Pet. 5:3; Eph. 4:11, 12). However, he is not to be a lord "over God's heritage" (1 Pet. 5:1-4). He has no Biblical right to be autocratic, dictatorial or domineering. No man of God filled with the Spirit, will manifest such an attitude.[52]

XVII. ORDINATION

The root meaning of the word "ordain" is "to prepare." Its etymological meaning is "to lay hands on." The dictionary meaning is "to invest with ministerial rank." Ordination is the symbolic laying of hands on the candidate for the ministry after he is examined by the church to verify that he is called by God and equipped into the church's leadership. After this event, he is recognized to lead the church in ministry, to determine its soundness of doctrine, to administer its ordinances, and to educate its adherents.

> Ordination is the setting apart of a person divinely called to a work of special ministration in the church. It does not involve the communication of power,—it is simply a recognition of powers previously conferred by God, and a consequent formal authorization, on the part of the church, to exercise the gifts already bestowed.[53]

In the Old Testament, the concept of anointing a person for a spiritual office could be a forerunner of the concept of ordination (Lev. 8:12, 1 Sam. 16:13, Isa. 61:1, c.f. Luke 4:18). First, it is broadly applied in the New Testament when Jesus said that all Christians are "ordained" to bear fruit (John 15:16).   However, many New Testament Scriptures speak of the laying on of hands as a narrow act (Acts 6:6, 13:1-3, 14:23; 1 Tim. 4:14; 2 Tim. 1:6; 2 Cor. 1:21; 1 Tim. 5:22).

> Ordination is the act of the church, not the act of a privileged class in the church, as the eldership has sometimes wrongly been regarded, nor yet the act of other churches, assembled by their representatives in council.   No ecclesiastical authority higher than that of the local church is recognized in the New Testament.[54]

First, men should be ordained who are called by God.   There are three aspects involved in the calling of God into full-time ministry.   The calling is one of burden (Hab. 1:1, Joel 1:1), desire (Jer. 20:9), and is evidenced by fruit-bearing (John 15:16). Second, men who have the New Testament qualifications to be pastors should be ordained.   This would be according to Titus 1 and Timothy 3.   Third, men who have manifested gifts of leadership should be ordained.   In order to be ordained (or serve in an ordained position) one will have to be ready and qualified to lead the church of God.   And fourth, men who are not sound in doctrine and who have not mastered Bible content should not be ordained.   Finally, men who are willing to separate themselves to the ministry should be ordained.   They must commit their total life and livelihood to the ministry.   That is why a good question for a candidate would be, what would you do if we don't ordain you?   The answer of a man called of God should be, "I'll preach anyway."   Ordination is the recognition of what God has done, not the human endowment for divine service.

The following test should be applied to each candidate who applies for ordination. First, he must be recommended by a church.   Obviously, since ordination is a church function, it should be requested by a New Testament church.   This indicates that Christians, to some degree, have recognized the pastor's call from God, and they feel he should be appointed to lead a flock.   Second, he should be examined by representatives of a church.   This may include deacons, the pastor, and probably other pastors.   There should especially be present anyone who has influenced him greatly, such as his home pastor.

> Since each church is bound to recognize the presence of the Spirit in other rightly constituted churches, and its own decisions, in like manner, are to be recognized by others, it is desirable in ordination, as in all important steps affecting other churches, that advice be taken before the candidate is inducted into office, and that other churches be called to sit with it in council, and if thought best, assist in setting the candidate apart for the ministry.[55]

In the third place, he should give evidence of fruit in his ministry before he is ordained. This reveals the Lord is already working in his life. The examination should be made even if the ones on the council know the candidate and even if they feel he knows the answers to the questions. The ordination council should include questions of doctrine, church policy, and issues of the day, and there should be questions about his personal practices and separation.

The candidate himself must first be persuaded that he is called to preach (1 Cor. 9:16, 1 Tim. 1:12); but, secondly, the church must be persuaded also before he can have authority to minister among them (1 Tim. 3:2-7, 4:14, Titus 1:6-9).[56]

Actual laying on of hands should take place after his ordination. The church should vote to ordain the candidate, recognizing that God has called him into the ministry. The men in the ordination service then lay their hands on the candidate's head either, (1) one at a time, or (2) all at once, while prayer is offered.

There are either one or two sermons preached at an ordination service; one is usually a charge to the candidate, the other a charge to the congregation.

> Insofar as ordination is an act performed by the local church with the advice and assistance of other rightly constituted churches, it is justly regarded as giving formal permission to exercise gifts and administer ordinances within the bounds of such churches.[57]

Before ordination, some men are given a license to preach. Licensure simply commends a man to the churches to preach the gospel. Ordination recognizes him and sets him apart to the work of preaching and administering a church, or in some designated field of labor, as representative of the church.

Licensing is practiced by some churches for the following reasons: (1) it recognizes those who have a desire to preach; (2) it places the person with that desire into a place of learning, practice, or apprenticeship; (3) it bestows the privilege of preaching, but does not guarantee full qualifications into the ministry; and (4) it does not provide a guarantee of ordination, but only places the person on a trial basis to see if the calling and gifts of God are manifested in his life.

XVIII. THE DEACONS IN A CHURCH

The office of deacon is identified with the office of bishop (pastor) by Paul, "To all the saints in Christ Jesus which are at Philippi, with the bishops and deacons" (Phil. 1:1). The word, "office," is attributed to bishop (1 Tim. 3:1) and deacons are identified with them by the word "likewise" (1 Tim. 3:11), giving them the status of an office. Because these are the only two that are identified with the title office, most churches conclude these are the only New Testament offices in the church. Others may properly hold positions (such as Sunday school superintendent, church clerk or treasurer), but there are only two offices in the church.

A. DEFINITION OF DEACONS. The word "deacon" is from the root of *diakonia* which means "servant." The etymology is an "under rower," or "an oarsman," as in a Roman sailing vessel. The *diakonia* is the servant who pulled the oars on a lower level of the ship. The office of deacon is characterized more by silence than by its explicit instruction. Not much is said in Scripture concerning the task of deacons. Actually, more is said about what a deacon is, rather than what a deacon does. Who needs to write a job description for a servant? Basically, a servant or a deacon does what needs to be done.

The Bible does not teach that deacons are in charge of churches. This is contrary to Scripture. The pastor (elder/bishop) leads the church, the deacon serves the church, the people are the final seat of authority, but all are controlled by Christ. The one who fills the office of a deacon should also have the gift of serving or helps (Rom. 12:7). The spiritual gift of ministry or helps comes from the same Greek root as "deacon."

B. QUALIFICATIONS FOR THE OFFICE. From 1 Timothy 3:1-13 it is seen that the qualifications of deacons and bishops are similar. These are listed in the chart on the following page.

Further qualifications for the office of deacon may be seen in Acts 6:1-6, if this is recognized as the beginning of deacons.

Since the title "deacon" is not found in Acts 6, one should not be too dogmatic in identifying the seven men chosen by the Jerusalem church as the first deacons. However, the arguments seem to weigh in favor of this identity. With the apostles serving as elders, this group of seven would constitute the second set of officials in the church as suggested in Philippians 1:1. The apostles serving in ministry of the Word parallel "able to teach" (1 Tim. 3:3), leave the men in Acts 6 in the position of servants, the basic meaning of the title deacon. The table-servers of Acts 6 were definitely subordinate to the apostles in both function and position. Faithful service as a deacon may lead to higher service in proclaiming the truth. This was actually the experience of Stephen (Acts 6:8ff) and Philip (Acts 8:5ff; 21:8). Hence, Acts 6 does contribute directly to our understanding of the office of deacon.

| QUALIFICATIONS |
| Acts 6:1-6 |
| 1. Of good report |
| 2. Full of the Spirit |
| 3. Full of wisdom |
| 4. Full of faith |

BISHOPS	DEACONS
1. Without reproach	1. Blameless
2. Husband of one wife	2. Husband of one wife
3. Sober-minded	3. Grave
4. No brawler or striker	4. Not given to wine
5. No lover of money	5. Not greedy for money
6. Good ruler of his house	6. Good ruler of his house
7. Not a novice	7. Of proven ability as servant
8. Temperate	8. Not double-tongued
9. Orderly	
10. Given to hospitality	
11. Gentle	
12. Not contentious	
13. Of good reputation	
14. Able to teach	

No specific statement is discernible in the New Testament to guide in establishing the ways in which deacons are to serve. Rather, a general pattern is recognizable. First, deacons took responsibility for the routine labors in the church, such as seeing that the poor and the widows had their material needs met. This freed the spiritual leaders at Jerusalem to labor in prayer and ministry of the Word (Acts 6:4). Second, the deacons served to make smooth relationships between groups in the church and between the pastors and people (Acts 6:1, 6). It is, therefore, eminently desirable that deacons serve as a liaison group to keep the pastor(s) aware of changing conditions and needs in the church.

In the third place, teaching is not given as a qualification for deacons. But the deacons are to be spiritually mature, because any service for God must be Spirit-guided, and because deacons, as chosen servants, must have the respect and confidence of those to whom and for whom they serve. Thus, deacons do function as leaders of God's people in the mundane affairs of the church. However, being leaders who are spiritual in character is not the same as being leaders in spiritual matters.

In the fourth place, wise pastors will seek the counsel and cooperation of deacons in guiding the church in its programs of worship, education, and evangelism. Since wisdom was one of the criteria for becoming a deacon, it is only natural to expect that God would use their wisdom to contribute to the smooth administration of the church.

Finally, until sufficient pastoral leadership is available, deacons may have to serve in spiritual leadership. However, church constitutions and policy statements should clearly separate the functions of pastors and deacons. For when deacons attempt to function in an office for which they are not qualified and to which they have not been called, the church will suffer. But deacons, as chosen leaders, have a natural open door for helping to preach the gospel and helping people in their spiritual needs (as with Stephen and Philip). All believers are to bear witness to Christ (Acts 1:8), and all may have a ministry of bringing divine truth to others (Heb. 5:12-14). In fact, the pastor-teachers are responsible to train all the believers so that they may have a part in service that builds up the body of Christ.

There is no problem here except for those who will not be subject to the Head of the church. It is not difficult for a Bible-taught church to be subject to the overseer or pastor that God has sent. Neither is it difficult for a faithful pastor to be sensitive to the will of God's people. What a lovely and delightful relationship exists between pastor, deacons and people when all are subject to Christ the Head.

It is vital that this happy relationship should always be evident in each church. When there is jealousy, bitterness, self-seeking and strife, the testimony of the Lord suffers, saints and sinners are caused to stumble, and the church loses its power to be a blessing because the Holy Spirit is grieved. Pastor and people must both recognize that the honor of the Lord and the welfare of His church must take precedence over personal differences. Let us suffer wrong. Let us "lose face." But the Lord must not be dishonored, His church be divided, or sinners be offended.[58]

XIX. THE EVANGELIST

The title evangelist is usually applied to any who travel from church to church or city to city holding evangelistic crusades. But their function is different from the New Testament role of evangelist. The term "evangelist" is only mentioned three times in the New Testament. The first is in Acts 21:8 where Philip, chosen in Acts 6 to be a deacon, is named an evangelist. Philip was called an evangelist because he was carrying out the Great Commission by preaching the gospel and planting a church in Samaria (Acts 8:4 ff.), and winning the Ethiopian to Christ. The other references are 2 Timothy 4:5, where Timothy is told to do the work of an evangelist, and Ephesians 4:11, where the gift of an evangelist is listed.

The root meaning of the term "evangelist" comes from the word "gospel." He brings good tidings, or gospelizes. The evangelist is tied to the gospel message. He usually goes to areas that have never been evangelized and preaches the gospel. When the gospel is presented as commanded in the Great Commission, he begins with announcing the good news, making disciples, baptizing and finally teaching converts to observe all things Christ commanded (Matt. 28:19-20). This process is the function of the church; hence, evangelists are implied church-planters, which is a description of modern foreign missionaries. Philip, the evangelist, carried out these tasks in both Samaria and with the Ethiopian eunuch in the desert.

In noting the gifts in the church, the evangelist is listed after the apostle and the prophet (Eph. 4:11), but appears before the pastor/teacher. This implies that the evangelist is sent forth by the first group and prepares the way for the second group. He is sent by the apostles and prophets (those who established the church by writing revelation) and he prepares the way for the pastor who shepherds the flock after it has been established. The evangelist uses his gift to plant churches. Today's foreign missionary fulfills the role of an evangelist more than the typical role filled by a city-wide revivalist.

An evangelist is not a church office, although some denominations disagree. Since the title office is never identified with evangelists, most leaders view it as a gift, which implies a function. Therefore, there may be many people with the gift of evangelism, but they do not have the title evangelist. Since spiritual gifts are both qualitative and quantitative, this implies some can win souls more than others.

Philip is the classic example of an evangelist. He was a pioneer who went to unevangelized areas. He preached the gospel in Samaria (Acts 8:5), Gaza (Acts 8:27), and in his new home (Acts 8:40). His ministry was an itinerant one—he went from place to place, even into the desert to talk with one man, the Ethiopian eunuch. Philip moved on when his work was finished and let others pastor those he won to Christ.

XX. BAPTISM

The first step of obedience after salvation for the new Christian is to be baptized in water. Strong, the theologian, describes the act. "Christian Baptism is the immersion of a believer in water, in token of his previous entrance into the communion of Christ's death and resurrection,— or, in other words, in token of his regeneration through union with Christ."[59] To this definition is added that baptism is obedience to the command of Scripture, following the example of Jesus Christ and entering into fellowship with other believers.

Baptism is the initial ordinance for believers. It naturally follows conversion. It is an outward sign of that which has taken place within the heart. It might well be likened to photography. Snap your picture; the image is transferred to the film. This is conversion. When the picture is developed, you see what has taken place. This is baptism.[60]

Of all the doctrines in Scripture, none seems to be abused as much as baptism. Perhaps this doctrine is so abused because it is so visible and has so many implications. Since those who are correct on baptism are correct in most other areas of theology, then wrong expressions of baptism will manifest other problems in a person's life or belief. The first and most obvious problem is that some preach baptismal regeneration, that a person cannot be saved without being baptized in water. Next, some baptize children before the age of accountability. In the third place, others baptize using the wrong symbol, not to portray the death, burial, and resurrection of Christ. A fourth abuse is viewing baptism as a continued symbol of a person's covenant relationship to God. Some theologians say the covenant of Abraham and its symbol, circumcision, is continued in baptism. Hence, the candidate becomes a child of the covenant at sprinkling. The fifth problem is centered in those who consider baptism as a sacrament. That is, baptism is viewed as a means of grace other than a symbol of grace. The sixth abuse is Landmarkism, or the idea of Baptist successionism. An individual must be baptized by the correct person or agent and then he becomes a member of the true church. Since baptism is a church ordinance, non-church baptisms are considered a seventh abuse by some. That is, baptism is practiced, being unrelated to a local church. The last illustration in our discussion is the rejection of baptism altogether by some groups such as hyperdispensationalists. This list is only suggestive of the problems surrounding baptism.

A. INTRODUCTION TO BAPTISM. Baptism by the Essenes at Qumran is suggested by some as being the first type of baptism which is similar to Christian baptism. The Qumran community, a small Jewish separated sect that emphasized purity and a return to original Jewish foundations, (200-150 B.C.) practiced washings or absolutions. They attached their baptism to absolution. The "baptism" took place at the end of a six-month period of instruction. Also, it was a continuing rite, not just initiatory. Every one in the Qumran community practiced their "baptism" on a regular basis. However, John the Baptist did not get his idea of immersion from the Qumran community, but from God.

The first biblical record of baptism was by John the Baptist. His baptism had three elements:

1. *Repentance meant a "turning from sin."*

2. *Confession of sins was necessary.*

3. *There had to be a looking for the kingdom.*

The people who responded to John's preaching were baptized upon their confession of sin, repentance, and looking for the coming king (kingdom), Matthew 4:2. Because of the different symbolism, John's baptism is not the same as Christian baptism. This argues against the church starting with John's baptism.

B. ARGUMENTS FOR IMMERSION IN WATER. There has been continuing argument in the church over whether a candidate should be baptized by immersion or sprinkling. The author was sprinkled as a child in the Eastern Heights Presbyterian Church of Savannah, Georgia. Later he was licensed by the Savannah Presbytery and served as pastor of Westminster Presbyterian Church, Savannah, Georgia (1952-53). Later he was convinced that the Scriptures teach baptism by immersion. He was immersed at Canton Baptist Temple, Canton, Ohio. The following is a summary of the argument, for baptism by immersion.

1. *The word "baptism" comes from the Greek baptizo which means "immerse."* This word means "to dip or plunge an object into water." Sprinkling or pouring is not allowed from the meaning of this term. The command to baptize is a command to immerse the person into water. (a) From the usage of secular Greek writers— including the church Fathers, "baptize" means "to dip or immerse." (b) Every passage where the word occurs in the New Testament, "baptize," either requires or allows the meaning, "immerse." (c) The absence of any use of the subject being baptized in the passive voice with "water" confirms that its meaning is "to immerse." If the candidate were passive, it would mean water could be poured over him. But the candidate is actively dipped in water.

2. *The use of the verb, "baptize," with prepositions implies immersion.* For some, this is the strongest argument for baptism by immersion. Note the following: (a) *Baptiso* with *eis* (Mark 1:9—where water, *iordanon*, is the element into which the person passes in the act of being baptized), demands immersion. (b) Baptism with *en* (Mark 1:5, 8; cf. Matt. 3:11; John 1:26, 31, 33;) implies "baptized in water." In these texts, *en* is to be taken, not instrumentally, but as indicating the element in which the immersion takes place. (c) From circumstances attending the administration of the ordinance (Mark 1:10—*anabainon ek tou udatos*, "coming up out of the water;" John 3:23—*polla*, "much water;" Acts 8:38-39—"They went down both into the water . . . they were come up out of the water").

3. *No church has the right to modify or dispense with this command of Christ.* The church is not a legislative body, meaning it cannot make laws about baptism. The

church is to discover God's laws in Scripture and carry them out. First, besides the local church, there is no other visible authority known in the New Testament. Since the only authority which originally imposed laws can amend or abrogate them, and there is no other authority, then the original command is still valid. If the church could change God's command, it would put itself above the Scriptures and above Christ.

Those who change the command to immerse, or have rationalized the symbol or means of baptism are, in essence, questioning the wisdom of the Lawgiver. Those who change the command to baptize can only do so on the ground that Christ has failed to adapt the ordinance to changing circumstances, and has made obedience to it unnecessarily difficult or humiliating. But the church has no right to change the method of administering the ordinance, because such a change makes the ordinance meaningless.

4. *The symbolism of baptism demands immersion.* Baptism symbolizes the believer's identification into the communion of Christ's death, burial, and resurrection,—or, in other words, it symbolizes regeneration through union with Christ. The heart and core of salvation is the death of Jesus Christ. Christ died as a substitute for sinners (Matt. 20:28). When He died, sinners were identified with Him through His vicarious substitutionary death. A sinner died with Christ, was buried with Him and received new life because he was raised with Christ in resurrection (Rom. 6:4,5). Water baptism by immersion fulfills this symbol because it pictures a watery grave and the believer being raised in identification with Christ.

Baptism is a symbol of the total picture of salvation. Note the following parallels:

a. Identification with the purpose of that death and resurrection—namely, to atone for sin, and to deliver sinners from its penalty and power.

b. Identification of the accomplishment of salvation—the candidate professes his death to sin and enters into eternal life.

c. Identification with the method in which salvation is accomplished—by faith the candidate is united with Christ.

d. Identification with other believers in Christ who have made the same step of obedience.

e. Identification with the completed work of Christ and assures all believers are eternally secure.

C. REASONS FOR BAPTISM. On many of the mission fields of the world, profession of faith is a relatively insignificant event in the life of a candidate until he submits to baptism. Opposition usually begins when he identifies with a Christian church. Despite the problems involved in being baptized, thousands obey the Scriptures and are baptized each month. In contrast, in North America, where religious and personal liberties are protected by law, some are not eager to acknowledge the authority of the Bible in the area of baptism. There are several reasons why every Christian should submit to baptism and identify with a local church.

1. *Baptism is the first step of obedience.* Every Christian should be baptized immediately after he is saved because baptism is not optional; it is commanded. There is no record in the New Testament of an unbaptized believer who, given the chance, refused to follow God's plan. On the day of Pentecost, Peter tied baptism as a natural result of conversion. He cried out, "Repent, and be baptized every one of you in the name of Jesus Christ for the remission of sins, and ye shall receive the gift of the Holy Ghost" (Acts 2:38). Those who believed the gospel had to demonstrate it by the public act of baptism. Baptism did not save because the Scriptures bear out, "Then they that gladly received his word were baptized" (Acts 2:41). Receiving the Word of God was the cause that brought salvation; baptism was a demonstration of their faith. That day 3,000 received the Word of God and were baptized. They did so immediately.

2. *Baptism follows the example of Christ.* The ordeal of God becoming flesh is called the humiliation (Phil. 2:8). Even though Jesus was King, He did not demand royal treatment, but came as a servant (Phil. 2:7). John was baptizing in the river of Jordan for the repentance of sin. Jesus could not repent from sin for he knew no sin. Five times in the New Testament we are told that the Son of God was sinless (John 8:46; 2 Cor. 5:21; Heb. 4:15; 1 Pet. 2:22; 1 John 3:5). John the Baptist was reluctant for he said, "I have need to be baptized of thee, and comest thou to me?" (Matt. 3:14). Yet Jesus was baptized because in God's plan it was necessary. First, He was baptized to identify with the remnant of Israel. These were the ones He came to save. Second, He was baptized to fulfill all righteousness. "And Jesus answering said unto him, Suffer it to be so now: for thus it becometh us to fulfill all righteousness. Then he suffered him" (Matt. 3:15). Here Jesus was revealing Himself as the predicted Messiah in the Old Testament, the One coming to bring righteousness to His people. Next, Jesus was baptized to publicly announce the beginning of His ministry. Up until this time, He had not preached or performed miracles. His baptism launched His ministry. In parallel manner, the Levitical priest was immersed in water at age 30 as a public sign of the beginning of His ministry. Jesus, a priest after the order of Melchizedek, fulfilled the sign by being baptized at age 30 (Luke 3:23).

3. *Baptism follows the example of the early Christians.* Soul winners in the New Testament practiced getting new converts baptized, everyone who accepted Christ was baptized: 3,000 on the Day of Pentecost, Paul, Cornelius and his household, the Ethiopian eunuch, new believers in Samaria, Lydia, the Philippian jailor, and many others. Their examples should motivate every young Christian to be baptized. Since every new convert in the New Testament who could be baptized was baptized, why should any put it off today?

There are no great sermons on baptism in the New Testament; people were just baptized. Neither are there long doctrinal dissertations or many commands to be baptized. Jesus commanded baptism and the early church practiced it. In the book of Romans, Paul explained baptism (6:3-6) because the nature of the book is a systematic coverage of salvation. Baptism was included as a picture of the plan of salvation for the Christian.

4. *Baptism is a testimony to the world that the candidate professes salvation.* All a man has to do to become a Christian is believe and receive Christ. After reading the Word of God, then a man can believe in Jesus Christ and become a child of God. He does not have to he baptized for salvation. He does not have to confess publicly in order to be saved. Therefore, he can be a secret believer—but he should not be. If a man is obedient, he will be baptized. The new Christian will place himself before the church where he will give a testimony to salvation (Rom. 10:9). When he is buried in the water, he tells the world that he has died with Christ. Under the water, he is identified with the burial of Christ. And he is brought up to symbolize his resurrection with Christ. The new Christian is telling the world that he now has the life of Christ (Rom. 6:4-6).

Some churches have maintained that a new Christian ought to "prove himself" before he submits to baptism. These churches conduct communicant classes to prepare the believers for baptism. The thought is to protect the church's purity against those who are baptized too early and later drop out of attendance, embarrassing the local congregation.

In contrast, the public confession of baptism may strengthen a new believer. Therefore, he should be baptized as quickly as possible to strengthen his faith and make him obedient to Scripture. Also, the new convert makes a commitment that he is going to follow Jesus Christ. Now, the unsaved community expects him to live like a Christian, and the Christian community will encourage him. God has strengthened many young Christians because they have honestly obeyed Him through baptism. Many have won spiritual battles sooner than they could have otherwise because they took this first obedient stand for Christ.

5. *Baptism is a good conscience before God.* Baptism is simply obedience to Jesus Christ. The hymn writer concludes, "Trust and obey for there's no other way to be happy in Jesus." The candidate fulfills the requirement of his conscience, that which he knows to do. "The like figure whereunto even baptism doth also now save us (not the putting away of the filth of flesh, but the answer of a good conscience toward God" (1 Pet. 3:21). When the candidate has been baptized, he has done all that God has required. His conscience is at peace. Therefore, to be happy and confident in the Christian life, the candidate should submit to baptism.

6. *Baptism fulfills a symbol of salvation.* The heart and core of salvation is the death of Jesus Christ. Christ died as a substitute for sinners (Matt. 20:28). When He died, He took the punishment of sinners. Because of this, Paul testified, "I am crucified with Christ: nevertheless I live . . ." (Gal. 2:20). You were buried with Him and when you came up out the grave with Christ, you were given a new life (Rom. 6:4-6). Therefore, you ought to be baptized to fulfill the symbol of Christ's death.

The symbol is important to God. When God's children violated His symbols in the Old Testament, they were punished, as in the case of Samson after his hair was cut. His strength was not in his hair; it was only a symbol that his strength was in God. The children of Israel were to look on to the brazen serpent on the pole if they wanted to live (Num. 21:8; cf. John 3:14); those who refused the symbol died. These symbols had no power in themselves, but reflected obedience to God. Since baptism (and also the Lord's supper) is a symbol, we destroy God's meaning when we are not properly baptized or do not properly observe the Lord's supper.

7. *Baptism is entrance into a local church.* When you are baptized, you fellowship with a local church. The Bible describes "the church, which is his body" (Eph. 1:22-23). Just as you were actually placed into Christ on Calvary by Spirit baptism, you fulfill the symbol by being placed into His local body by water baptism.

D. THE CANDIDATE FOR BAPTISM. The gospel is the death, burial, and resurrection of Jesus Christ (1 Cor. 15:1-4), and baptism is its symbol (Rom. 6:3, 5). Faith appropriates the gospel (Eph. 2:8-9); therefore, only a person who has believed this message should be baptized. Salvation is not just repeating a verbal formula. There must first be conviction of sin because the Word of God has been planted in the heart. In this act, the Holy Spirit causes the sinner to see his sin and the Savior. Hence, the Word of God is the instrument of salvation, while the Spirit of God is the agent that brings him to salvation.

But our experience tells us that not everyone who has been baptized has actually been converted. Also, the Scriptures tell us of those who were baptized, but not regenerated (Simon the sorcerer, Acts 8:9-25; twelve disciples of John, Acts 19:1-7).

Therefore, what safeguards can the church use to insure the conversion of a person before he is baptized? Actually, none. The church can only require a profession of faith and believe it accordingly. The believer must give witness to the working of God in his heart. Therefore, the criteria to qualify a person for baptism is his profession of faith.

E. WHO CAN BAPTIZE? B. H. Carroll, founder of Southwestern Baptist Theological Seminary, gave four qualities for proper baptism. They were a proper candidate, proper act, proper motives, and proper administration. This last point implies proper authority to baptize. The historic Baptist position is that the church gives the authority to baptize. The ordinances belong to the church, not the individual or pastor. The authority, therefore, resides in the church. Since the church is people, when they vote to receive a person into membership by baptism, they are exercising this authority.

WHEN TO BAPTIZE

1. After a class or time of instruction.
2. After an interview with pastor/deacons.
3. With a congregational vote after interrogation and/or testimony.

The church usually votes on who should administer its baptism. When a pastor is called to serve a church, he is given the authority to exercise the church's ordinances.

F. THE ASPECTS OF BAPTISM. The candidate is placed backwards into the water as a picture of burying a dead person in a grave. Then he is brought up as a picture of resurrection. This act is repeated once, as a person is buried once. Certain churches baptize forward three times. This identifies the candidate with Christ when He bowed His head at death. They do this three times because of Matthew 28:19-20, the reference to baptism and the Trinity. However, the symbolism does not adequately represent burying a person. A dead person is buried on his back. Matthew 28:19 indicates baptism is in the name (singular), not names; hence, one immersion under the water fulfills the picture. Ephesians 4:6 suggests there is only one water baptism because there is only one Spirit baptism. Therefore, once is considered baptism.

XXI. THE LORD'S TABLE OR COMMUNION

If baptism is the first act of obedience for the Christian, then the Lord's Table is the ultimate expression of his Christianity. It is the symbol that is continually used by the child of God to express his fellowship with Christ and other Christians. He partakes in this experiential ordinance and remembers the death of Christ and his conversions. Then, as he expresses thankfulness for salvation, he looks forward to the return of Christ which will complete his salvation and terminate the ordinance. If a child of God is growing to maturity and is serving Christ effectively, he will properly take the Lord's Table.

The Lord's Table, along with baptism, is the most abused and misinterpreted aspect of doctrine. Actually, if a person has a problem with his theology or has some false views, it will ultimately reflect itself in the person's outward expression of his theology. Since the Lord's Table and baptism are the expressions of ecclesiology, and since ecclesiology is the practical expression of all other theology, it is only natural that wrong theology will come to the surface with the two symbolic expressions of one's faith.

SYMBOLS OF THE LORD'S TABLE

1. Symbolizes the death of Christ to forgive our sins.
2. Symbolizes our personal appropriation of peace and joy that comes from the forgiveness of sin.
3. Symbolizes that through union with Christ Himself we have life.
4. Symbolizes the continuous dependence of the believer upon the once crucified, now living Savior.
5. Symbolizes the sanctification of the Christian based upon identification with the death and resurrection of the Lord.
6. Symbolizes the union of Christians together in Christ.
7. Symbolizes the coming anticipation of going to be with Christ at death or "till he comes."

The following are some of the abuses or questions about the Lord's Table. (1) The whole church is required to drink from one cup as opposed to an individual cup for each partaker. (2) Some insist on using fermented wine. This totally misses the concept of the symbolism (and most likely what was used). Jesus could not have used fermented wine at the Last Supper because of the prohibition against using leaven before the Passover. Leaven, used to make wine, was the Old Testament symbol of sin. (3) In some churches, the elders take the Lord's Table first and pass it to the younger (congregation). (4) In some churches, footwashing accompanies or is part of the communion. (5) There is confusion on how to dispose of the elements. This became a problem because of the Catholic mentality that the wine turns into the actual blood of Christ. (How can one pour the blood of Christ down the sink?)

(6) Some believe that only unleavened bread should be used. Some churches make their own juice and bake their own bread. (7) Some churches practice the love-feast supper before the Lord's Table. (8) Some practice kissing at the Lord's Supper according to 1 Corinthians 16:20, "Greet one another with a holy kiss." (9) Another question is whether one should be served in the pew or have a minister place a wafer on the tongue after going forward to the church altar. (10) Probably the biggest question occurs over how often one should take the Lord's Supper. Some do it every Sunday, some once a month, others once a quarter. (11) Some groups, such as the Salvation Army, reject baptism and the Lord's Table altogether.

A. WHAT IS THE LORD'S TABLE? The Lord's Table is the distinctive ordinance of Christian worship instituted by the Lord on the eve of His death, being a spiritual partaking of the fruit of the vine and bread, which is presented in thankful memorial of Christ's sacrifice and is taken by those in fellowship with the church. The purpose of the Lord's Table is to renew and strengthen the Christian's fellowship with Christ and other believers. Therefore, the believer should partake at regular intervals "till he comes."

Christ appointed this outward symbol to be observed by all Christians in remembrance of his death. It was to be observed after his death; because only then could it completely fulfill its purpose to symbolize the realities of his death to his followers. From the apostolic command (1 Cor. 11:23-34) with regard to its celebration in the church until Christ's second coming, it is implied that every Christian should partake.

> The uniform practice of the N. T. churches, and the celebration of such a rite in subsequent ages by almost all churches professing to be Christian, is best explained upon the supposition that the Lord's Supper is an ordinance established by Christ Himself.[61]

B. THE SACRIFICIAL LANGUAGE OF THE LORD'S TABLE. The terms used to describe the Lord's Table are highly symbolical. They are body, blood, covenant, poured out for many, and for the remission of sins. These point out the solemnity of the Lord's Table. As a result, the Lord's Table points to many applications of the one observance. The believer is strengthened as he understands the truths associated with the Lord's Table.

C. WORDS OR TITLES OF THE LORD'S TABLE. There are several terms used to designate the Lord's Table. Actually, Christians seem to use these titles interchangeably (see above).

TERMS

1. "Eucharist" is a Catholic term which means "to give thanks" (Matt. 26:27). It comes from the Greek term meaning "joy and thanksgiving." The Lord's Table should be a time of rejoicing, however, it is usually a solemn service.
2. Communion (1 Cor. 10:16).
3. The Lord's Table (1 Cor. 10:21).
4. The Lord's Supper (1 Cor. 11:20).
5. Breaking of Bread (Acts 2:42; 20:7).
6. Ordinance (1 Cor. 11:2). This occurs in the King James and is the basis for certain denominations calling it an ordinance. The word is *paradosis*, elsewhere translated "tradition."

D. SPIRITUAL BENEFITS OF THE LORD'S TABLE. The person who takes the Lord's Table obeys Christ's command (Matt. 26:26). This act of obedience will cause him to grow in spirituality. There is nothing in the elements that will produce spirituality in the participant. If he obeys and properly confesses his sin, he will grow closer to Christ. No one can refuse the Lord's Table because they do not feel worthy, for in actuality, no one is worthy. But no one is to accept the elements who has not confessed his sin. God leaves no choice but for the Christian to come. "Take, eat" was the command. Also, "Do this" makes it imperative. But the Christian should never partake with sin in his life. He should "examine himself," then confess, then fellowship with Christ.

A person who takes communion joins in fellowship with other Christians. It is a table of communion—communion with other believers (Acts 2:41-42), or an expression of fellowship. Acts 2:41-47 gives a sequence of events that should be followed that leads up to the Lord's Table.

There should be giving of thanks and praise for salvation at the Lord's Table. The Christian should be most thankful for the forgiveness of sins and eternal life (1 Cor. 10:16). The Lord's Table will provoke hope because it looks forward to the Second Coming of Christ. The Lord's Table should cause believers to submit to church discipline. The "you" of 1 Corinthians 11:17 refers to the church and is also seen in verses 23 and 29. When Christians sinned "not discerning the Lord's body" (1 Cor. 11:29), they were violating the meaning of Calvary, or ignoring the benefits that were accomplished by Christ's actual body on the cross. There is a mystery between the body of Christ that accomplished salvation on Calvary and the indwelling Christ in the believer who is partaking of the communion and the church which is called "His body." At the act of communion, the believer should realize the indwelling Christ in his body, and the indwelling Christ in the local church body. But those who bring rebellion and sin to the Lord's Table do so "not discerning the Lord's body"

(1 Cor. 11:29). It is these who are disciplined by sickness or death (1 Cor. 11:30). The Lord's Table is indirectly a tool of church discipline, but this is only when the Christian will not discipline himself, ask forgiveness of his sins, and seek renewed fellowship with Christ.

SEQUENCE

1. You should receive the Word (2:41).
2. You should be baptized (2:41).
3. You should continue in the apostles' doctrine (2:42).
4. You should have fellowship—a mutual building up (2:42).
5. Then you can take the Lord's Supper, break bread (2:42).

The Lord's Supper is the outward expression of a life in the believer, nourished and sustained by the life of Christ. It cannot, therefore, be partaken of by one who is "dead through . . . trespasses and sins." We give no food to a corpse. The Lord's Supper was never offered by the apostles to unbelievers. On the contrary, the injunction that each communicant "examine himself" implies that faith which will enable the communicant to "discern the Lord's body" is a prerequisite to participation.[62]

E. A CHURCH ORDINANCE. Communion is a church ordinance; therefore, an individual should not administer the Lord's Table to other Christians apart from church authority. The book of Corinthians was written to the church and the reference to "ye" (1 Cor. 11:33) implies he is directing his instruction to the church. Also, communion is for the church to "commune" or "fellowship" with one another and in unity or fellowship with Christ. The exhortation, "When ye come together" (1 Cor. 11:33), excludes individuals partaking of the Lord's Table apart from the fellowship of the church.

If communion is for the church and those who are in fellowship with Christ, then communion is for baptized believers. A person who is not baptized should not take the Lord's Table because he has not met the requirements. There is a question about the unbaptized Christian who is not rebellious, but is only ignorant of Scripture. He might be fellowshipping with a church that does not require baptism by immersion. He might have individual faith, and his faith is the thing that pleases God (Heb. 11:6). But when he comes to a church that knows the correct Scriptural pattern, he should be enlightened concerning God's requirement for him.

Historically, most churches require membership in their church before a person could partake at their table. The crossing over of one denominational church to partake with another at the Lord's Table is a new or ecumenical influence.

At the first celebration (on the night before Christ died), only the eleven disciples were invited to join with Jesus Christ. Communion was served after Judas had left. Therefore, by example, only born-again people are allowed to take the Lord's Supper.

The Scripture commands, "'Drink ye all of it,' implying 'all of you corporately drink of it.' This command implies fellowship. It is to be celebrated by the assembled church. It is not a solitary observance on the part of individuals. No 'showing forth' is possible except in company."[63]

F. WHO SHOULD EAT? There are three basic ways that local churches celebrate communion: (1) open communion, (2) closed communion, and (3) close communion.

1. *Open communion.* Those who hold this position teach all Christians in good fellowship with Christ should have access to the Table of the Lord. They believe it is the Lord's Table, not a denominational table, and since Christ indwells the believer, they should come to His table. They interpret "when ye come together" to mean Christians, so all are invited to participate.

This approach interprets Christianity from an individual basis, rather than institution-centered Christianity.

2. *Closed communion.* Those who hold this position teach that only a member of the church in good standing should have access to the Lord's Table of that church. They teach that the church decides who can participate. Since God will punish the sinning Christian who partakes, the church uses the Lord's Table for disciplinary purposes. Since the church should know who is walking with God or not, the church is responsible to close communion to outsiders and allow only those in fellowship with Christ to partake. They also teach communion is for fellowship among believers in a local church; therefore, they should not break ranks with outsiders because they do not know the spiritual condition of outsiders. Next, they close communion to insure correct baptism and/or correct church testimony. Finally, they believe closed communion brings power to their church. If they obey God and keep their table clean, they feel they will have His blessing in their ministry.

3. *Close communion.* Those who use this term warn Christians of the dangers of wrongly partaking the Lord's Table, yet leave the choice to individuals. They teach the individual should examine himself personally and privately without the church forcing the issue or becoming the examining body. This position teaches that anyone

who is properly baptized and in fellowship with Christ should join in the unity of faith.

Then those who accept the close communion position feel the church should not make laws concerning who should partake, but should explain the laws.

a. The church, as possessing executive but not legislative power, is charged with the duty, not of framing rules for the administering and guarding of the ordinance, but of discovering and applying the rules given it in the New Testament. No church has a right to establish any terms of communion; it is responsible only for making known the terms established by Christ and his apostles.

b. These terms, however, are to be ascertained not only from the injunctions, but also from the precedents, of the New Testament.[64]

The following suggestions by Starr give reason for the closed position on the Lord's Table:

(1.) The ordinance of baptism was instituted and administered long before the Supper. [Jesus submitted to baptism at the hands of John the Baptist]. . . .
(2.) The apostles who first celebrated it had, in all probability, been baptized. . . .
(3.) The command of Christ fixes the place of baptism as first in order after discipleship [Matt. 28:19-20]. . . .
(4.) All the recorded cases show [that new Christians were baptized prior to communion]. . . .
(5.) The symbolism of the ordinances requires that baptism should precede the Lord's Supper. The order of the facts signified must be expressed in the order of the ordinances which signify them; else the world is taught that sanctification may take place without regeneration. . . . As none but the circumcised could eat the passover, so before eating with the Christian family, must come adoption into the Christian family. . . .
(6.) The standards of all evangelical denominations . . . confirm the view that this is the natural interpretation of the Scripture requirements respecting the order of the ordinances. . . .
(7.) The practical results of the opposite view are convincing proof that the order here insisted on is the order of nature as well as Scripture. The admission of unbaptized persons to the communion tends always to, and has frequently resulted in, the disuse of baptism itself, the obscuring of the truth which it symbolizes. . . .[65]

ENDNOTES

1.   A. T. Robertson, *Word Pictures in the New Testament* (New York: R. R. Smith, Inc., 1930), 1:132.

2.   David Watson, *I Believe in The Church* (Grand Rapids: Eerdmans, 1978), 65.

3.   Cf. A. B. Bruce, *The Expositor's Greek Testament* (Grand Rapids: Eerdmans, 1952), 1:225, and A. T. Robertson, 1:133-34.*

4.   Robertson, 1:149.

5.   David J. Hesselgrave, *Planting Churches Cross-Culturally* (Grand Rapids: Baker Book House, 1980), 351.

6.   Hermann Cremer, *Biblico-Theological Lexicon of New Testament Greek* (New York: Charles Scribner's Sons, 1895), 333-334.

7.   Earl D. Radmacher, *What the Church Is All About* (Chicago: Moody Press, 1978), 368.*

8.   Alfred Kuen, *I Will Build My Church*, trans. Ruby Lindblad (Chicago: Moody Press, 1971), 46.

9.   Robert L. Saucy, *The Church in God's Program* (Chicago: Moody Press, 1972), 26-32.

10. Ibid., 26.

11. Ibid., 32.

12. Gary Inrig, *Life in His Body* (Wheaton: Harold Shaw, 1975), 36-37.

13. Saucy, 25, ftnt. 11.

14. Earl D. Radmacher, *The Nature of the Church* (Portland, OR: Western Baptist Press, 1972), 240.

15. Homer A. Kent, Jr., *Ephesians: The Glory of the Church* (Chicago: Moody Press, 1971), 48.

16. Lewis Sperry Chafer, *Systematic Theology*, (Dallas: Dallas Seminary Press, 1948), 4:64.

17. Saucy, 33-34.

18. R. C. H. Lenski, *The Interpretation of St. Paul's First and Second Epistle to the Corinthians* (Columbus, OH: The Wartburg Press, 1937), 455.*

19. James L. Boyer, *For a World Like Ours: Studies in I Corinthians* (Winona Lake, IN: BMH Books, 1971), 50.

20. Gene A. Getz, *Sharpening the Focus of the Church* (Chicago: Moody Press, 1974), 61.

21.   Radmacher, *The Nature of the Church*, 246.

22.   Saucy, *The Church in God's Program*, 46.

23.   Ibid., 50, ftnt. 33.

24.   Radmacher, *The Nature of the Church*, 289.

25.   Donald A. McGavran, *Understanding Church Growth* (Grand Rapids: Eerdmans, 1970), 41.*

26.   Saucy, *The Church in God's Program*, 52.

27.   Ibid., 53.

28.   A. R. Tippett, *Church Growth and the Word of God* (Grand Rapids: Eerdmans, 1970), 13.

29.   Ibid.

30.   C. I. Scofield, ed., *Scofield Reference Bible*, 1136-1137.

31.   Chafer, *Systematic Theology*, 4:60-61.

32.   Saucy, *The Church In God's Program*, 55.

33.   Donald Grey Barnhouse, "Chain of Glory," *Eternity*, Vol. 2, No. 17 (March 1958), quoted in Radmacher, *The Nature of the Church*, 294-295.

34.   Hollis L. Green, *Why Churches Die* (Minneapolis: Bethany Fellowship, 1972), 201-202.

35.   W. E. Vine, *An Expository Dictionary of New Testament Words* (London, England: Oliphants, Ltd., 1940), 9.

36.   This definition reflects a consensus view of modern dispensationalists.

37.   Chafer, *Systematic Theology*, 4:45-46.

38.   Elmer Towns, *Is the Day of the Denomination Dead?* (Nashville: Thomas Nelson, 1973), 49.

39.   Radmacher, *What the Church Is All About*, 351.

40.   A. H. Strong, *Systematic Theology* (Philadelphia: Griffith and Rowland Press, 1907-09), 894-95. This listing is a compilation of two sections of Strong—one giving the statement, and the other listing the applicable texts.

41.   Vine, *Expository Dictionary*, 2:20-21.

42.   John McClintock and James Strong, "Elders," *Cyclopedia of Biblical Theological and Ecclesiastical Literature*, (New York: Harper and Brothers, 1883), 3:116.

43.   William F. Arndt and F. Wilbur Gingrich, *A Greek-English Lexicon of the New Testament* (Chicago: The University of Chicago Press, 1957), 299.

44.   Joseph Henry Thayer, *Greek-English Lexicon of The New Testament* (Grand Rapids: Zondervan, 1972), 243.*

45.   A. R. Fausset, *Bible Encyclopedia and Dictionary* (Grand Rapids: Zondervan, n.d.), 96.

46.   J. L. Neve, *A History of Christian Thought* (Philadelphia: The Muhlenberg Press. 1946), 1:71.

47.   Arthur Lowndes, "Bishop," *International Standard Bible Encyclopedia* (Grand Rapids: Eerdmans, 1939), 1:480.

48.   Thayer, *Greek-English Lexicon*, 346.*

49.   David H. Bauslin, "Preacher," *International Standard Bible Encyclopedia*, 4:2434.

50.   Ibid., 4:2333.

51.   Hans Bietenhard, "Messenger," Colin Brown, ed. *Dictionary of New Testament Theology* Grand Rapids: Zondervan, 1975) 1:101.*

52.   Paul R. Jackson, *The Doctrine and Administration of the Church*, rev. ed. (Schaumburg, IL: Regular Baptist Press, 1980), 42.

53.   A. H. Strong, *Systematic Theology*, 918.

54.   Ibid., 920

55.   Ibid.

56.   Ibid., 919.

57.   Ibid., 922.

58.   Jackson, *The Doctrine and Administration of the Church*, 43.

59.   Strong, 931.

60.   Timothy Starr, *Church Planting—Always in Season* (Canada: Timothy Starr, 1978), 15.*

61.   Strong, 959-60.

62.   Ibid., 971.

63.   Ibid., 961.

64.   Ibid., 970.

65.   Ibid., 971-72.

* Denotes page number(s) could not be verified.

CHAPTER XIII – ESCHATOLOGY

The Doctrine of Last Things

I. INTRODUCTION

The final area of study in systematic theology is Eschatology, which means the study of last things. However, the underlying theme of eschatology, like the underlying theme of all doctrine is Jesus Christ. The first verse of the book of Revelation sets the perspective: "The Revelation of Jesus Christ, which God gave unto him, to shew unto his servants things which must shortly come to pass" (Rev. 1:1). Eschatology is not a study of just prophecy, although it includes that. Christ is the unifying theme around which all events are analyzed as they move toward the final consummation in the rapture, the Tribulation, the glorious appearing, the Millennium, the Great White Throne judgment and into the New Heaven and the New Earth. Because Christ is the Alpha and Omega, He gives a revelation of that "which is, and which was, and which is to come" (Rev. 1:4). Eschatology is not just concerned with future events, for the credibility of that which is to come is rooted in the past covenants, dispensations, and what has been fulfilled.

Biblical eschatology deals with end things in two specific areas. First, it involves the future of the physical world and all that it includes as it moves toward the Second Coming of Christ. The second area deals with the future of man and is reflected in the question of Job, "If a man die, shall he live again?" (Job 14:14). The fate of both the saved and the lost after experiencing physical death properly belongs to the study of eschatology. While there are two subjects, the solution is one, for all things come together in Christ.

During the first few centuries in church history, theology often addressed apocalyptic themes. Aside from that period, and perhaps the last 100 years, theologians have been reluctant to examine this subject in depth. Perhaps it would be more accurate to suggest the study of prophecy has actually been discouraged and opposed. Rauschenbush taught, "Eschatology is usually loved in inverse proportion to the square of the mental diameter of those who do the loving."[1] More recently, R. S. Beal lamented,

> It is hard to understand why so many preachers and professing Christians exhibit such a strong prejudice against anything that has to do with prophecy. The mention of the word itself seems to arouse no little antagonism. Many times have I heard it said

that the preaching of this subject produces faddists, cranks, and nuisances. It is often dismissed as being merely "a Jewish conception," or an "oriental garb," or poetic imagery, never to be taken seriously and certainly not literally. Many cannot see any practical value in preaching on prophetic themes, feeling this line of teaching has nothing to do with life as we find it all around us. We are told such preaching removes the Bible far from the issues with which men have to do in their daily living. I am constrained to believe that all this adverse feeling grows out of a misunderstanding of what prophecy really is.[2]

This opposition to the study of prophecy is not completely without cause. Abuses and unusual theories proclaimed as though they were biblical in origin have provided critics with evidence to support their charge. There are various reasons why individuals oppose the study of prophecy, but these can be summarized under a few major headings. According to Thiessen,

Four things have helped along this attitude: First, the setting of dates. . . . This practice has brought the whole doctrine into disrepute in many circles. Secondly, the fanciful and unscriptural doctrines that have often been held by those who teach the truth of Christ's return have given this doctrine a bad reputation. . . . Thirdly, preconceived notions and prejudices have kept many from accepting this doctrine. . . . But chief among the oppositions is the unregenerated heart.[3]

II. WHY STUDY PROPHECY?

In light of the fact that some are opposed to the study of prophecy, it would be wise to ask why this subject should be studied at all. The many personal benefits of such a study are themselves reason enough to induce one to this study, but there are other reasons also. Prophecy is a major part of the Scriptures and serves as an indisputable apologetic for its integrity and authority. Further, an eschatological hope has been the means whereby many have been saved and motivated to live for Christ.

A. PROMINENCE IN SCRIPTURE. Much of the Bible was prophetic when it was originally written. Of course, some has been fulfilled, but there is still much to be fulfilled. To ignore the prophetic Scriptures is to ignore a major portion of the Word of God. Chafer notes,

In all ages it has pleased God to pre-announce certain things He proposed to do. Those announcements are termed prophecies. All prophecy is history pre-written and it is as credible as any word God hath spoken (2 Tim. 3:16). While prophecy is found in almost every book of the Bible, sixteen books of the Old Testament and one book of the New Testament are wholly prophetic in character. In all, clearly one-fourth of the Bible was predictive when it was written.[4]

Concerning the prominence of prophecy in the New Testament, Howitt observes,

If we accept every type and figure as well as reference, then we may say that there is not a single book in the New Testament that does not speak of the Lord's coming. It may be said truthfully also that every writer there speaks of the Lord's coming. It receives more attention than any other doctrine. You read there far more about it than you do about faith; you read there far more about it than you do about the blood of Jesus Christ, that cleanseth from all sin; although both faith and the blood are absolute essentials. You read more about it than you do about even the great doctrine of love, "without which all our doings are as nothing worth."[5]

B. FULFILLED PROPHECY. The fact that God keeps His word is an undisputed fact to the serious student of prophecy. Many contemporary prophets and prophetesses are often wrong in their predictions. They could never be compared to the Old Testament prophets who could never be wrong. The divinely ordained punishment of the false prophet was death by stoning (Deut. 18:20). With that in mind, to speak on behalf of God was a solemn responsibility, and to make predictions in the name of God carried a death penalty when the prediction did not come to pass.

Because fulfilled prophecy is such a strong apologetic for the authority and integrity of Scripture, some have suggested that only prophecy already fulfilled should be studied. This, of course, is contrary in nature to the spirit and specific instructions of 2 Peter 1:19. As Trotter and Smith explain,

> That fulfilled prophecy has the use affirmed, one would not, of course, think of denying. Fulfilled prophecy has this use undoubtedly. But, to say of unfulfilled prophecy that its chief use is after the event, is to go directly in the face of the plainest declarations of God's word. See 2 Pet. i. 19: "We have also a more sure word of prophecy, whereunto ye do well that ye take heed." When? When the events have been accomplished, and the light thus shed upon the prophecy makes plain the truth? Is that the time? No: "whereunto ye do well that ye take heed, *as unto a light that shineth in a dark place*, UNTIL the day dawn, and the day star arise in your hearts." The use of prophecy is that of a lamp, to light the traveller's feet along the dark and dreary path. It is not intended for a candle to be held up to the sun, to make it manifest that the sun shines at noonday.[6]

Because of the fact of fulfilled prophecy, the student can have great confidence in the prophecy which is not yet fulfilled. Every prophecy concerning the first advent of Christ was fulfilled literally as the prophets had promised. It is, therefore, reasonable to expect every unfulfilled prophecy concerning the second advent of Christ to be also fulfilled literally. The fact of fulfilled prophecy makes the study of unfulfilled prophecy a reasonable discipline in which one may engage.

C. REVEALED BY GOD. The source of prophecy is yet another reason the Christian should be engaged in its study. Though written by holy men of God, it was written only as they were moved by the Spirit of God (2 Pet. 1:21). Further, the prophets themselves constantly affirmed that they were speaking the very word of God (cf. Hag. 1:13). As such, prophecy is part of that "all scripture" declared by Paul to be profitable (2 Tim. 3:16-17). Explaining the importance of the study of prophecy, Scofield suggests,

1. Prophecy came to us "by the will of God" (2 Pet. 1:20, 21) for both our instruction and blessing (Rev. 1:3).
2. We are to "rightly divide the Word of truth." This we cannot do unless we search and study the Scriptures, dividing it as to past, present and future (1 Tim. 2:15).
3. Peter speaks of it as "a more sure word of prophecy whereunto ye do well that ye take heed, as unto a light that shineth in a dark place, until the day dawn, etc." (2 Pet. 1:19). . . .
4. As witnesses of Christ, we are giving an imperfect and incomplete testimony if we withhold that concerning Christ's return and earthly reign, which must take place if God would be vindicated as to all the promises of temporal prosperity concerning Israel, and concerning Jesus Himself. Therefore if we close our eyes to that upon which the Author of the book has laid so much importance, and thereby darken the light which He has given to shine in a dark place (2 Pet. 1:19) and which we should hold up as the Christian's "blessed hope," especially in these last days when the apostasy is making such rapid strides, and the spirit of antichrist so manifest—we shall be unfaithful in our testimony.[7]

The neglect of prophecy as part of the revelation of God has not been without its negative consequences. Eschatology is discussed in such a major way in the Scriptures that one can obtain only a limited understanding of many important non-eschatological doctrines when prophecy is neglected. When this is true, it is also neglected in the pulpit. When the pulpits are silent concerning things to come, the world must anticipate and prepare for a future without benefit of the light of God's Word. The results, according to Ayer, are devastating.

> The professing Church has long neglected prophetic truth, and as a result has failed to carry out God's revealed program, not only for herself, but has also failed to tell the world of God's plan for the nations. The Church has failed to keep divine objectives in view because she has neglected the prophetic message on the Word of God. This neglect involves something deeper and more pertinent than the mere ignoring of one phase of truth. Tragedy, universal tragedy, basic tragedy, which is responsible in no small way for the tragedy of our modern world, has come as a result of this neglect.
>
> As a result of the Church's departure from the prophetic message, the race has been left without a social program of authority, and through the centuries men and nations have been experimenting with their own social, national and international ideas, endeavoring to bring about a world-righteousness which is not of God and therefore is not obtainable, but results in a periodical national collapse and world-wide calamity.[8]

D. ABUSES OF PROPHECY. A fourth reason Christians should engage in the study of prophecy is that of the existence of various abuses in this area. Sometimes, the abuses of prophecy will discourage any serious study in this field, but if a Christian will try the spirits (1 John 4:1), there will be some understanding so he can determine if the statements of a contemporary prophetic teacher are accurate and his conclusions rational. The growth of movements and theories essentially heretical in the area of eschatology is evidence that Christians have not prepared themselves in this important area. As Trotter and Smith note,

> We are not to study prophecy, we are told, because fanatical, misguided men have made bad use of it. But if the abuse of any good thing be a sound argument against the use of it, it is not from prophetic Scripture alone that we must turn aside, but from the whole Word of God. What Scripture is there that has not been perverted by misguided men, or wilful deceivers, to purposes of evil? Then, besides, all or nearly all those who are held up as beacons to warn us against the study of prophecy pretended to have received new revelations themselves.[9]

E. PERSONAL BENEFITS. The study of prophecy has direct benefits to the life of the student. It is portrayed in the Scriptures as major incentive to Christian character, duty and ministry. Pettingill argued, "There is nothing like the hope of our Lord's return to quicken the believer and make him fruitful in the service of God. It is God's appointed means by which to separate His people unto Himself and to wean them from the world and its empty allurements."[10] Commenting on Titus 2:2-13, Hunter observes that a correct understanding of Christ's coming produces sound doctrine and sound living.

> This passage of scripture begins with sound doctrine and ends with a sound hope; the coming of our Lord Jesus Christ, for His Church as the blessed hope and expectation of the believer, and His glorious appearing, as the great God, and our Saviour Jesus Christ. Between these two sound things, we find sound living. Here we have a trinity of sound things: sound doctrine, sound living and a sound hope. Take any one away and you have an incomplete picture. Remove the last and you have a train going out from its starting point but having no destination.[11]

Bible doctrine was not taught by the apostles and prophets without personal application. Sometimes, these applications referred to the affairs of the nation, but they also applied to the people. Hope, comfort, peace, soul winning, holy living, and other areas of interest are taught in prophetic Scriptures. As W. B. Riley observed,

> There is one thing that will not be denied, even our opponents themselves being the witnesses, namely, that the men that held this hope, have so far discharged their obligation to God as to have promoted the interests of His church by personal service, by money sacrifice, by missionary zeal, by intelligent counsel, by tireless work, so as not to have been surpassed by any people that have ever named His name, or joined their fortunes to His cause.[12]

The following list of thirty-one benefits come from studying prophecy. When this list is honestly faced, a person must include a study of prophecy in his study of Scripture if he is going to be a well-rounded servant who is obedient to the Lord.

F. THE PRACTICAL AND MOTIVATING NATURE OF PROPHECY

1. *In the Area of Christian Character*
    a. Incentive to Godliness   Titus 2:12-13
    b. Incentive to Holiness   2 Pet. 3:11
    c. Incentive to Joyfulness   1 Pet. 1:8
    d. Incentive to Patience   Jas. 5:8
    e. Incentive to Purity   1 John 3:3
    f. Incentive to Faith   John 14:1-3
    g. Incentive to Sobriety   1 Pet. 1:13
    h. Incentive to Moderation   Phil. 4:5
    i. Incentive to Sincerity   Phil. 1:9-11
    j. Incentive to Faithfulness   Rev. 2:25; 3:11
    k. Incentive to Discernment   1 Cor. 4:5
    l. Incentive to Accountability   Matt. 25:19
    m. Incentive to Righteousness   Titus 2:12

2. *In the Area of Christian Duties*
    a. Incentive to Obedience   1 Tim. 6:13, 14
    b. Incentive to Repentance   Rev. 3:3
    c. Incentive to Watchfulness   1 Thess. 5:6
    d. Incentive to Abiding in Christ   1 John 2:28
    e. Incentive to Brotherly love   1 Thess. 3:12
    f. Incentive to Discipleship   Luke 9:26
    g. Incentive to Readiness   1 Pet. 1:13
    h. Incentive to Mortification   Col. 3:4-5
    i. Incentive to Personal Separation   1 Thess. 5:22, 23
    j. Incentive to Bearing Persecution   1 Pet. 4:13
    k. Incentive to Enduring the Trial of Faith   1 Pet. 1:7
    l. Incentive to Every Good Work   2 Thess. 2:12
    m. Incentive to Faithful Church Attendance   Heb. 10:25

3. *In the Area of Christian Ministry*
    a. Incentive to Preaching Ministry   2 Tim. 4:1-2
    b. Incentive to Pastoral Ministry   1 Pet. 5:2-4
    c. Incentive to Comforting Ministry   1 Thess. 4:18

d. Incentive to Teaching Ministry   Matt. 28:20
e. Incentive to Evangelistic Ministry   1 Thess. 2:19-20

III. DANGERS OF PROPHETIC STUDY

As important as the study of Bible prophecy is, the student of the Scriptures must be cautious not to fall into certain common traps. Some have gone off on a tangent by always seeking new truth. Others have become proud or exploitative with their newfound knowledge of prophetic truth. Others have a tendency to speak on areas where the Bible is silent. Some Bible scholars have made the mistake of fixing dates or identifying personalities, such as the Antichrist, and they have been proven wrong. Sometimes minor differences of opinion in this area of Bible prophecy have become a major source of irritation, leading to a break in Christian fellowship. An additional danger of prophetic studies is that some are so consumed with future events that they exclude the central focus of Scripture, Christ. The divinely inspired title of the final book of the New Testament, "The Revelation of Jesus Christ" (Rev. 1:1), is a good guideline to all prophecy. Ultimately, all prophecy concerns Jesus Christ. As Walter Scott so clearly stated,

> The Revelation is embodied in the visions beheld by the Seer of Patmos. The word "Revelation" gives unity to the many and diversified communications, whether in word or vision, contained in the book. Revelations there were, but these form one compact whole, and this belongs to Jesus Christ. Not only, however, is the Revelation Jesus Christ's as given Him by God, but He is the central object in these as in all prophecy. The rays of the prophetic lamp are directed onward to the millennial glory of Christ, no matter whether the lamp be held in the hands of Isaiah the Grand or John the Beloved.[13]

Beyond these dangers, there are other reasons that people end up with wrong views of prophecy. We need to make sure our motives and presuppositions are correct. Sometimes people have been wrong in their study of prophecy because they do not have all the data. The apostle Paul observed, "For we know in part, and we prophesy in part" (1 Cor. 13:9). Sometimes people have been mistaken because they only study prophecy to prove a point, which leads to pulling verses out of context to find the truth. The presence of sin in the life of the student will also hinder the study of the prophetic Scriptures, as it hinders the study of every part of the Bible.

IV. MAJOR SCHOOLS OF PROPHECY

Many of the theological controversies of this present century have involved the discussion of prophecy. Prophecy, which should be the basis of comfort (1 Thess. 4:18), has in many churches, schools and denominations become a battlefield. There are three historic schools of thought in this area of theology based upon one's view of the thousand-year reign of Christ, i.e., the Millennium: (1) Amillennial, (2) Postmillennial, and (3) Premillennial. Although the term Millennium does not itself occur in Scripture, it comes from the idea of a thousand-year period of time that characterizes the reign of Christ. The phrase "1,000 years" is mentioned six times in Revelation 20.

A. AMILLENNIAL. The Amillennial school of interpretation does not believe in a literal or actual future kingdom of peace and prosperity here on earth that will last one thousand years. They hold that the Old Testament predictions of the kingdom were fulfilled in a non-literal way, either in the present church age or in the experience of the church in heaven. As a result, they tend to interpret prophetic Scriptures more figuratively than literally. Most amillennial Bible students do not recognize a distinction between Israel and the church, but rather argue that Israel was the church of the Old Testament and the church is the Israel of the New Testament. Perhaps it is best to let someone who believes the position explain it. In his exposition of Revelation 20, Hendricksen explains the amillennial interpretation of the kingdom.

> Hence, in close harmony with all these Scripture passages—and our exegesis must always be based on the analogy of Scripture!—we conclude that also here in Rev. 20:1-3 the binding of Satan and the fact that he is hurled into the abyss to remain there for a thousand years indicates that throughout this present Gospel Age, which begins with Christ's first coming and extends nearly to the second coming, the devil's influence on earth is curtailed so that he is tenable to prevent the extension of the church among nations by means of an active missionary program. During this entire period he is prevented from causing the nations—the world in general—to destroy the church as a mighty, missionary institution. . . . Only the individual who lacks the historic sense and is, therefore, unable to see the present in the light of conditions which prevailed throughout the world before Christ's ascension, can fail to appreciate the glories of the millennial age in which we are now living. Truly, the prophecy found in Ps. 72 is being fulfilled before our very eyes.[14]

B. POSTMILLENNIAL. At the beginning of the twentieth century, the most prevalent view of Bible prophecy was probably the postmillennial view. Those who held this view believed that the world from the time of Christ's coming was getting better and better and assumed that a millennial kingdom would be established on earth as the world lived in peace. They interpreted the return of Christ as coming toward the end or just after this reign of peace. The existence of two major international conflicts of the century, WWI and WWII, and scores of other smaller wars have shattered the hopes of most postmillennialists for a man-made perfect world.

Two proponents of this postmillennial view in the nineteenth century were Strong and Hodge. Each of these men interpreted the Millennium as that which came prior to the second advent of Christ. Outlining his position on this issue, Strong wrote,

> Through the preaching of the gospel in all the world, the kingdom of Christ is steadily to enlarge its boundaries, until Jews and Gentiles alike become possessed of

its blessings, and a millennial period is introduced in which Christianity generally prevails throughout the earth. . . .

. . . .

There will be a corresponding development of evil, either extensive or intensive, whose true character shall be manifest not only in deceiving many professed followers of Christ and in persecuting true believers, but in constituting a personal Antichrist as its representative and object of worship. This rapid growth shall continue until the Millennium, during which evil, in the person of its chief, shall be temporarily restrained. . . .

. . . .

At the close of this millennial period, evil will again be permitted to exert its utmost power in a final conflict with righteousness. This spiritual struggle, moreover, will be accompanied and symbolized by political convulsions, and by fearful indications of desolation in the natural world. . . .

. . . .

The Scripture foretells a period, called in the language of prophecy "a thousand years," when Satan shall be restrained and the saints shall reign with Christ on the earth. A comparison of the passages bearing on this subject leads us to the conclusion that this millennial blessedness and dominion is prior to the second advent.[15]

Hodge, who would also agree with this postmillennial view of prophecy, identifies what he calls "the Scriptural doctrine concerning the Millennium.

1st. The Scriptures, both of the Old and New Testament, clearly reveal that the gospel is to exercise an influence over all branches of the human family, immeasurably more extensive and more thoroughly transforming than any it has ever realized in time past. This end is to be gradually attained through the spiritual presence of Christ in the ordinary dispensation of Providence, and ministrations of his church—Matt. xiii. 31, 32; xxviii. 19, 20; Ps. ii. 7, 8; xxii. 27, 29; lxxii. 8-11; Is. ii. 2, 3; xi. 6-9; lx. 12; lxvi. 23; Dan. ii. 35, 44; Zech. ix. 10; xiv. 9; Rev. xi. 15.

2d. The period of this general prevalence of the gospel will continue a thousand years, and is hence designated the Millennium—Rev. xx. 2-7.

3d. The Jews are to be converted to Christianity either at the commencement or during the continuance of this period. Zech. xii. 10; xiii. 1; Rom. xi. 26-29; 2 Cor. iii. 15, 16.

4th. At the end of these thousand years, and before the coming of Christ, there will be a comparatively short season of apostasy and violent conflict between the kingdoms of light and darkness—Luke xvii. 26-30; 2 Pet. iii. 3, 4; Rev. xx. 7-9.

5th. Christ's advent, the general resurrection and judgment, will be simultaneous, and immediately succeeded by the burning of the old, and the revelation of the new earth and heavens.[16]

C. PREMILLENNIAL. The view of prophecy which became increasingly popular in the last half of the twentieth century has been the premillennial position. Essentially it recognizes a distinction between Israel and the church (1 Cor. 10:32), and accepts a literal interpretation of key passages such as Revelation 20:1-10 that call for a future 1,000 years of peace and prosperity. The premillennialist emphasis of the literal interpretation of prophetic passages is recognized by their opponents. Postmillennialist Strong is forced to recognize this, observing, "One passage only seems at first sight to teach the contrary, *viz.*: Rev. 20:4-10. But this supports the theory of a premillennial advent only when the passage is interpreted with the barest literalness."[17]

The premillennial position teaches that Christ will return to the earth and set up a literal kingdom as He promised. With the establishment of Israel as a political state in 1948 and the declaration of Jerusalem as her capital in 1980, this school of interpretation has been gaining credibility in recent years. Most of the popular films and books on Bible prophecy are premillennial, as are many Bible colleges and missionary agencies. Over the years, the premillennial position has been promoted by various institutions, but the ministry of Dallas Theological Seminary has been one of the primary sources. The doctrinal statement of Dallas Theological Seminary says in part,

> We believe that the period of Great Tribulation in the earth will be climaxed by the return of the Lord Jesus Christ to the earth as he went, in person on the clouds of heaven, and with power and great glory to introduce the millennial age, to bind Satan and place him in the abyss, to lift the curse which now rests upon the whole creation, to restore Israel to her own land and to give her the realization of God's covenant promises, and to bring the whole world to the knowledge of God. (Deut. 30:1-10; 1 Sa. 11:9; Ezek. 37:21-28; Matt. 24:15-25; 46; Acts 15:16-17; Rom. 8:19-23; 11:25-27; 1 Tim. 4:1-3; 2 Tim. 3:1-5; Rev. 20:1-3).[18]

Distinguishing between the premillennial and postmillennial views of prophecy, Rogers suggests,

> The only points of difference concern the manner and time of His coming. The premillennialists say He will come suddenly and personally, before the millennium, to usher it in and to set up His kingdom. The postmillennialists say He will come after the Millennium has been effected by the efforts of men.
>
> If he comes after the Millennium then He will come to a world prepared for Him by the genius of man. Such an opinion would compel me to reach the conclusion that His return is far more remote than a century ago, for now the world is characterized by the worst destruction of life and property ever known to mankind.[19]

V. INTERPRETING REVELATION

One of the key books of Scripture dealing with prophetic subjects is the book of The Revelation. Its many symbols and apocalyptic style have caused many writers to develop creative interpretations of its contents. These various interpretations and expositions can be summarized under four major methods. Jensen has presented these four positions in the following chart.[20]

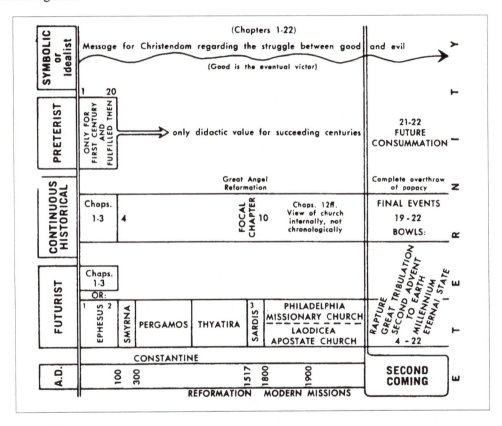

THE FOUR MAIN SCHOOLS OF INTERPRETATION OF REVELATION Chart C

A. PRETERIST. The preterist school believes the book of Revelation speaks entirely of first-century events which had already taken place at the time of writing. The name of this view is derived from the Latin word meaning "past." According to Tenney,

> The Preterist school holds that the symbolism of Revelation relates only to the events of the day in which it was written. All the imagery of the seven seals and trumpets and vials has no bearing upon the future. The writer was simply expressing

his moral indignation concerning the abuses of his own day when he spoke of future judgment. This is the view of the majority of liberal scholars, such as R. H. Charles and C. C. Torrey. It has the advantage of connecting Revelation with the thought and historical events of the day in which it was written, but it makes no allowance for any element of predictive prophecy.[21]

B. IDEALISTIC. The idealistic school holds that the book is nothing more than a series of symbols portraying the general idea of the victory of Christ or the ultimate triumph of good over evil. Those holding this view generally make no attempt to connect its contents with history of any kind. Typical of this interpretive approach to Revelation, Calkins writes,

> We understand now what the word "revelation" means. It does not mean a revelation of the future mysteries of the end of the world, the millennium or the Day of Judgment. Neither does it mean primarily a revelation of all the glories of Heaven or the blessedness of the redeemed. Rather it means a revelation of the infinite God, mighty to save; an uncovering for the consolation and inspiration of God's people of the all-conquering power of an omnipotent Savior.[22]

C. HISTORICAL. A third approach to interpreting Revelation is the historical view. This school holds that the book surveys and presents a history of the Christian church during the past two thousand years. This view was particularly prominent during the Reformation. One of the major problems in identifying this school is that the proponents of this view rarely agree as to which symbol represents which historical event. Concerning this school, Kroll writes,

> Thus, Revelation is symbolic of the continuing struggles of the church against evil. There were earlier proponents, but Joachim, a Roman Catholic scholar, is greatly responsible for the popularization of this view.
>
> According to the historical approach to Revelation, we are today living somewhere in the account of Revelation. This view was especially attractive to the reformers, e.g. Luther, Wycliffe, Newton, etc., for it easily identified opponents of the Reformation with the wicked in Revelation. It is this view which gives rise to a belief in postmillennialism, as well as many cockeyed identifications of present personalities with those of the Apocalypse. Nevertheless, a revival of this view has taken place in the past few years.[23]

D. FUTURIST. The futurist school holds that almost all of the book, especially chapter 4 through the end, is yet future. This is the view held by the early church and by modern dispensationalists. Although many truly born-again Christians subscribe to one of the three previously stated views, this writer believes their understanding of the Word of God is seriously hampered thereby. Though much of the book is symbolic and metaphorical in character, the only wise rule of interpretation is to adhere to the literal interpretation of Scripture, i.e., to determine what was the literal meaning in the mind of the author. This is the basis of the futurist approach. Concerning this school, Thiessen notes,

This view maintains that the book relates mainly to things which are yet to come; more particularly, that from chs. 4-22 practically all is still future. It connects these chapters with the second coming of Christ and the millennium. The beast is an empire that is yet to arise and that will be headed by a great monster; the scarlet-colored woman is the false ecclesiasticism of the last days. It is impossible to cite the early church in favor of this view; but it seems to us they must have held it. They believed in the imminence of the Lord's return; they believed in an earthly millennium; and they believed that there would be a period of tribulation that would introduce the kingdom.[24]

VI. THE INTERPRETATION OF PROPHECY

The major difference between the various millennial positions in the prophetic debate and the differing approaches to interpreting the book of Revelation is a difference in hermeneutical approach. Ramm recognizes this in his discussion on the interpretation of prophecy, noting, "The real issue in prophetic interpretation among evangelicals is this: *can prophetic literature be interpreted by the general method of grammatical exegesis, or is some special principle necessary?*"[25] Similarly, Allis, an amillennialist, acknowledges this as a fundamental issue relating to the difference between his views and those of premillennial teachers.

> One of the most marked features of Premillennialism in all its forms is the emphasis which it places on the literal interpretation of Scripture. It is the insistent claim of its advocates that only when interpreted literally is the Bible interpreted truly; and they denounce as "spiritualizers" or "allegorizers" those who do not interpret the Bible with the same degree of literalness as they do. None have made this charge more pointedly than the Dispensationalist. The question of literal verses figurative interpretation is, therefore, one which has to be faced at the very outset.[26]

In the field of prophecy, the two basic approaches to interpreting Scripture are identified as the literal or historical-grammatical approach and the allegorical or mystical or spiritual approach. Concerning this latter approach, Ramm suggests,

> Allegorical interpretation believes that beneath the letter (*rhētē*) or the obvious (*phanera*) is the real meaning (*hyponoia*) of the passage. Allegory is defined by some as an extended metaphor. There is a literary allegory which is intentionally constructed by the author to tell a message under historical form. . . . But if we presume that the document has a secret meaning (*hyponoia*) and there are no cues concerning the hidden meaning interpretation is difficult. In fact, the basic problem is to determine if the passage has such a meaning at all. The further problem arises whether the secret meaning was in the mind of the original writer or something found there by the interpreter. If there are no cues, hints, connections, or other associations

which indicate that the record is an allegory, and what the allegory intends to teach, we are on very uncertain grounds.[27]

Concerning the other approach to the interpretation of prophecy, Pentecost writes,

> The literal method of interpretation is that method that gives to each word the same exact basic meaning it would have in normal, ordinary, customary usage, whether employed in writing, speaking or thinking. It is called the grammatical-historical method to emphasize the fact that the meaning is to be determined by both grammatical and historical considerations.[28]

It has been well stated, "The Bible is 21, it can speak for itself." The tendency of allegorical interpretation is to try to make the Bible say something that it may or may not otherwise state. Many conservative Bible scholars will interpret the Scriptures literally until they come to a prophetic passage. Then they begin to interpret it allegorically, giving undue consideration to names, numbers, and hidden meanings of symbols. These are important considerations as God will sometimes use these to teach important truth, but we should not allow this emphasis to destroy the use of a consistent, literal interpretation of Bible prophecy. This literal approach to interpreting prophecy is the basis of the premillennial interpretation. According to amillennial writer Hamilton,

> Now we must frankly admit that a literal interpretation of the Old Testament prophecies gives us just such a picture of an earthly reign of the Messiah as the premillennialist pictures. That was the kind of a Messianic kingdom that the Jews of the time of Christ were looking for, on the basis of a literal interpretation of the Old Testament promises. That was the kind of kingdom that the Sadducees were talking about when they ridiculed the idea of the resurrection of the body, drawing from our Lord the clearest statement of the characteristics of the future age, that we have in the New Testament, when He told them that they erred "not knowing the Scriptures nor the power of God" (Matt. 22:29) . . . the Jews were looking for just such a kingdom as that expected by those premillennialists who speak of the Jews holding a preeminent place in an earthly Jewish kingdom to be set up by the Messiah in Jerusalem.[29]

The Bible was revealed, inspired and written by the ordinary use of words and thoughts that were expressed in the language of the day. Therefore, it is expected that Scripture will be interpreted by the same method it was given. Most contemporary Bible students follow the advice of Cooper in his "golden rule of interpretation."

> When the plain sense of Scripture makes common sense, seek no other sense; therefore, take every word at its primary, ordinary, usual, literal meaning unless the facts of the immediate context, studied in the light of related passages and axiomatic and fundamental truths context, indicate clearly otherwise.[30]

This statement is popular and will usually guide the Bible student into a correct understanding of Scripture. However, be careful of the crack in the door that allows for some other form of interpretation when the student gets stuck on a difficult passage. If we allow even one verse to be interpreted in an unwarranted non-literal manner, the whole argument breaks down. When we come to metaphors, symbols and figures of speech, we must be consistent in applying the literal method of interpretation. We must interpret according to the literal meaning in the mind of the author and never seek to read any other meaning into a passage. This is more than an attitude or philosophy, it is a principle of interpretation. Stevens calls it a law.

> It is reasonable to suppose that there is a method of interpreting God's Word that makes the Bible harmonious and produces unity the world over among those who read and believe the same Book. There are certain laws peculiar to various fields of operation. Unless these laws are adhered to, no knowledge can be gained.
> The Bible has its own laws set forth clear and unmistakable. To follow these laws is to behold the unsullied light of the truth of God. When we interpret the Bible in the light of itself, we recognize its sufficiency; we discover its divinity; we become acquainted with its mighty power.[31]

The literal method of interpretation is an attempt to give the same meaning to a word as the author who wrote the passage. This means we do not try to "think up" an interpretation for the book of Daniel, but to seek the author's meaning of words and passages. By "literal interpretation" we mean the normal meaning of words and terms. Obviously, when Jesus is called a Lamb in the Bible, the writer does not mean Jesus had four legs and was covered with wool. Lamb in this case is a figure of speech and must be interpreted with the meaning John the Baptist had in mind when he said, "Behold the Lamb of God" (John 1:29, 36). John the Baptist meant that Jesus was the fulfillment of the typical paschal lamb in the Passover supper. This literal approach is the most secure method of determining what God intended to say. It simply asks, "In the light of the historical context of this passage and the basic rules of grammar as we understand them, what was the writer saying?" But since all Scripture has dual authorship (God and man) we must seek the mind of both authors in interpreting Scripture.

Symbols are an important part of the prophetic Scriptures, but the Christian does not have to rely upon his imagination to interpret them. The Bible often reveals the meaning of a symbol within the context of the same passage. This is illustrated in the first chapter of Revelation. The symbols of stars and candlesticks are used, but they are identified as the churches and messengers of the seven churches in Asia (Rev. 1:20). Sometimes a parallel passage can be used to determine the divine interpretation of a symbol otherwise not understood. This can be illustrated by comparing parallel accounts of the same discussion between Jesus and the Pharisees concerning the casting out of demons. According to Luke, Jesus spoke of casting out demons "with the finger of God" (Luke 11:20). Comparing Matthew's record of the same discussion, it becomes obvious that the finger of God is a title of the Holy Spirit (Matt. 12:28).

One of the implications of literal interpretation is that the author has a literal meaning in his mind and that he can have only one meaning for a word or passage (otherwise we assume mental derangement). However, there is one place where it seems the writer has a double meaning. This is when a prophecy has a double fulfillment. The author, by control of the Holy Spirit, makes a prediction that has two fulfillments.

When Isaiah predicted the Messiah would be born of a virgin (Isa. 7:14), he spoke to an immediate setting (Isa. 7:1-14), but he also predicted the birth of Christ (Matt. 1:21, 22). This is not speculation because Matthew identifies it as such. The double fulfillment is also seen when Joel predicted, "I will pour out my spirit upon all flesh" (Joel 2:28). This applies to the outpouring of the Holy Spirit on the day of Pentecost (Acts 2:16-21) and to the end times. The problem of double fulfillment is answered in that the author had one meaning in his mind, which was to communicate that one prophecy could have two literal fulfillments. He was not being double-minded, but was further revealing the supernatural nature of Scripture. It does not question the literal method of interpretation, but supports it.

VII. PROPHECY AND THE CHURCH

One of the distinctives between amillennialists and premillennialists is their view of the church. Failing to understand the distinctive nature of the church and the biblical difference between Israel and the church (Cf. 1 Cor. 10:32), amillennialists tend to see in the church a spiritual fulfillment of the covenant blessings promised Israel in the Old Testament. It cannot be disputed there exist many similarities between Israel and the church and their respective relationships with God. Still, the only way the church could be recognized as spiritual Israel is to demonstrate God is through with the nation and has transferred His affection exclusively to the church.

In an attempt to demonstrate that God is through with Israel, amillennial writers have taken negative designations of the nation in Scripture and interpreted them in line with their basic presupposition. For example, Hendricksen, commenting on Rev. 2:9 where a group of Jews are identified as "the synagogue of Satan writes,

These so-called Jews might consider themselves to be "the synagogue of God"; in reality they constituted "the synagogue of Satan," the chief accuser of the brethren. How anyone can say that the Jews today are still, in a very special and glorious and preeminent sense, God's people, is more than we can understand. God himself calls those who reject the Saviour and persecute the true believers "the synagogue of Satan." They are no longer his people.[32]

Hendricksen fails to mention the context in which this statement is made. The Jews in question are not those who are or who might be considered typical of all Jews in that day, but rather those who were actually involved in the worship of Satan as expressed through the worship of Caesar. One should not confuse God's acknowledging of one's religious loyalties with His abandoning of the covenant promises. The Scriptures clearly teach God still intends to redeem Israel and fulfill these covenant blessings.

Óne of the several statements concerning God's yet future plan and purpose for Israel is Paul's statement, "All Israel shall be saved" (Rom. 11:26). Whatever else may be true of this statement, its context is such that there can be no question, but that the physical nation or race is meant. Godet makes this point.

> We have already said that there can be no question here of applying the term *Israel* to the spiritual Israel in the sense of Gal. vi. 16. It is no less impossible to limit its application, with Bengel and Olshausen, to *the elect portion* of Israel, which would lead to a tautology with the verb *shall be saved*, and would suppose, besides, the resurrection of all the Israelites who had died before . . . He speaks of a collective movement which shall take hold of *the nation in general*, and bring them as such to the feet of their Messiah.[33]

Commenting on the same text, Murray argues,

> The interpretation by which "all Israel" is taken to mean the elect of Israel, the true Israel in contrast with Israel after the flesh, in accord with the distinction drawn in 9:6, is not tenable for several reasons. (1) While it is true that all the elect of Israel, the true Israel, will be saved, this is so necessary and patent a truth that to assert the same here would have no particular relevance to what is the apostle's governing interest in this section of the epistle . . . (2) The salvation of all the elect of Israel affirms or implies no more than the salvation of a remnant of Israel in all generations. . . . (3) Verse 26 is in close sequence with verse 25. The main thesis of verse 25 is that the hardening of Israel is to terminate and that Israel is to be restored . . . . To regard the climactic statement, "all Israel shall be saved", as having reference to anything else than this precise datum would be exegetical violence.[34]

The second emphasis of the amillennialist is the denial of a distinction between Israel and the church by attempting to demonstrate that in Scripture the church is called Israel and Israel is called the church. Two particular texts are significant in this area. Before the Sanhedrin, Stephen made reference to "the church in the wilderness" (Acts 7:38). Probably, the use of *ecclesia* here should be understood in its non-technical sense of a gathering or group. From this occurrence of *ecclesia*, the amillennialist argues that Israel was the Old Testament church that was replaced by the New Testament church. However, they fail to continue their line of reasoning to its most natural conclusion. The same word, *ecclesia*, is twice used later by Luke to identify a group in Ephesus advocating the worship of Diana (Acts 19:32, 41). Would therefore the amillennialist have us believe the New Testament church has been replaced by the church of Diana? No! The answer is that the word *ecclesia* is used in a non-theological way to refer to an assembly in the Old Testament and to an assembly in Ephesus.

A second text cited by amillennialists in support of their contention that the New Testament recognizes Israel and the church as one and the same is Galatians 6:16. Commenting on the phrase "the Israel of God" in that verse, Matthew Henry suggests,

These, he declares, shall be the portion of *all the Israel of God*, by whom he means all sincere Christians, whether Jews or Gentiles, all who are Israelites indeed, who, though they may not be the natural, yet are become the spiritual seed of Abraham; these, being heirs of his faith, are also heirs together with him of the same promise, and consequently entitled to the peace and mercy here spoken of.[35]

It should be noted that if the church is here called Israel, it is the only place in the New Testament where this is so. But not all commentators and expositors would agree with Henry's interpretation. Kelly, for example, suggests,

"Israel of God" seems to be used here not as a general phrase for every saint, but for the believing ones in Israel—those Jews who had repudiated their own works and found shelter only in Christ Jesus. Two parties are spoken of, and not one only. "As many as walk according to this rule" are rather the Gentile believers; and the "Israel of God" are the Jewish saints, not the mere literal Israel, but the "Israel *of* God"; the Israelites indeed, whom grace made willing to receive the Saviour.[36]

The confusing of the church and Israel is in part due to a misunderstanding of the Pauline concept of mystery. Paul uses the term *musterion* twenty times in his epistles to describe revealed truth previously hidden from common knowledge, but now revealed by God and discernible only with the aid of the Holy Spirit. According to Walvoord,

Mysteries, a word used of secret rites of various religious cults, refers to truth that was not revealed in the Old Testament but is revealed in the New Testament. More than a dozen such truths are revealed in the New Testament, all following the basic definition of Colossians 1:26, which defines a mystery as that "which hath been hid from ages and from generations, but now is made manifest to his saints." A mystery truth, accordingly, has two elements. First, it has to be hidden in the Old Testament and not revealed there. Second, it has to be revealed in the New Testament. It is not necessarily a reference to the truth difficult to understand, but rather to truths that can be understood only on the basis of divine revelation.[37]

This current dispensation of grace and many of its distinctives are described in the New Testament in terms of a mystery. This includes the blindness of Israel, the body of Christ, the indwelling of Christ and salvation itself. Because these are described as "mystery doctrines," one should not be surprised if they are not fully revealed in the Old Testament. The following chart identifies some of the different aspects of the mystery.

VIII. DISPENSATIONALISM

There are vast numbers of Christians in conservative circles who interpret the Bible dispensationally. They teach that salvation is by grace through faith in every dispensation, but that God relates to man in different ways in each dispensation. Dispensationalists are usually found among many denominations and are evident in both the fundamentalist and evangelical camps. Many of these identify with the *Scofield Reference Bible* and interpret Scriptures to some extent in keeping with the notes and outlines found in its pages. On the other hand, there are other Christians ignorant of dispensationalism or anti-dispensational. Speaking of the

DIFFERENT ASPECTS OF THE MYSTERY	
1. The Body of Christ	Col. 1:24-26
2. The Indwelling of Christ	Col. 1:27
3. The Blindness of Israel	Rom. 11:25
4. The Incarnation	1 Tim. 3:16
5. Program of Evil in this Age	2 Thess. 2:7
6. Rise of False Religion	Rev. 17:5-7
7. Christ and His Church	Eph. 5:32
8. The Rapture of the Saints	1 Cor. 15:51
9. All of Salvation	1 Cor. 2:7

Scofield Bible, one writer has suggested, "This book represents perhaps the most dangerous heresy currently to be found within Christian circles."[38] Another has suggested,

> Indeed, the time is fully ripe for a thorough examination and frank exposure of this new and subtle form of *modernism* that has been spreading itself among those who have adopted the name "fundamentalists." For Evangelical Christianity must purge itself of this leaven of *dispensationalism* ere it can display its former power and exert its former influence. . . .
>
> . . . .
>
> The entire system of "dispensational teaching" is *modernistic* in the strictest sense.[39]

In one sense Chafer was right when he suggests "any person is a dispensationalist who trusts in the blood of Christ rather than bringing an animal sacrifice" and "any person is a dispensationalist who observes the first day of the week rather than the seventh."[40] Most students of Scripture would have to admit dispensationalism in this broad sense as they distinguish between the features of the Old and New Testaments. Summarizing the essential nature of dispensationalism, Ryrie suggests,

> Dispensationalism views the world as a household run by God. In this household-world God is dispensing or administering its affairs according to His own will and in various stages of revelation in the process of time. These stages mark off the distinguishably different economies in the outworking of His total purpose, and these economies are the dispensations. The understanding of God's differing economies is essential to a proper interpretation of His revelation within those various economies.[41]

Some critics of dispensationalism tend toward the view that it came about as the result of the creative impulse of C. I. Scofield or his predecessor, J. N. Darby. While these men were important leaders in dispensational circles, it would be wrong to identify them as the first dispensationalists. Published works in this field thoroughly explaining a dispensational approach to the Scriptures are known as early as the seventeenth century.[42] Further statements made by several church fathers are in apparent harmony with the basic tenets of dispensationalism.[43] The following is a summary comparison of some of the early dispensational schemes.[44]

A person must see the relationship between a dispensation and a covenant if he is to understand the plan and objective of God throughout the ages. A dispensation is a temporary period of time based on a conditional test to determine if man will be faithful to the conditions of God. Scofield defined a "dispensation" as "a period of time during which man is tested in respect of obedience to some *specific* revelation of the will of God."[45] According to Ryrie, "A dispensation is a distinguishable economy in the outworking of God's purpose. If one were describing a dispensation he would include other things, such as the ideas of distinctive revelation, testing, failure and judgment."[46] Since man has failed these various testings, each dispensation ends in judgment.

A covenant is an eternal agreement made by God with man, revealing what God will do for man individually or collectively. God made seven covenants with men throughout history. Each covenant reveals principles in embryonic form by which God will relate to man. Man has the free will to reject the covenant or principles of God, and when he violates the covenant, he suffers the consequences.

A. EDENIC COVENANT—FIRST DISPENSATION. The first covenant involved man's physical existence on earth. Remember Adam had no history, hence no knowledge of how to care for his physical needs. These were the first priority. God did not leave man to experiment with ways to provide for his necessities. The goodness of God motivated Him to reveal to Adam how to care for his human needs. In essence, how Adam satisfied his physical necessities is no different from the way twenty-first-century man cares for himself.

When God created Adam sinless in the garden, there were certain principles for him to follow. If Adam kept these principles, he would prosper. These were: (1) to replenish the earth with children (Gen. 1:28); (2) to use nature (subdue the earth) for his needs to provide food, shelter, and clothing (Gen. 1:28); (3) to have dominion over animal life (Gen. 1:28); (4) to eat fruit and vegetables (Gen. 1:29); (5) to work for his sustenance (Gen. 2:15); (6) to obey God (the test involving simple obedience to abstain from eating of the tree that God prohibited).

Tied to the Edenic Covenant is the first dispensation of innocence, whereby God tested man to see if he would live by the conditions imposed upon him. Man was told he could not eat of the fruit of the Tree of Knowledge of Good and Evil (Gen. 2:17). The dispensation ended in man's failure. Eve was deceived (1 Tim. 2:14) and Adam deliberately disobeyed. As a result the first man had personal and experiential knowledge of good and evil. What seemed like a simple, limited act of eating fruit, ended in a broad, conscious knowledge of right and wrong.   In the next dispensation, the descendants of Adam were responsible for their new awareness of sin.

CHART OF REPRESENTATIVE DISPENSATIONAL SCHEMES						
Pierre Poiret 1646-1719	John Edwards 1639-1716	Isaac Watts 1674-1748	J. N. Darby 1800-1882	James H. Brookes 1830-1897 (Pub. 1901)	James M. Gray 1851-1935 (Pub. 1901)	C. I. Scofield 1843-1921 (Pub. 1909)
Creation to the Deluge (Infancy)	Innocency	Innocency	Paradisiacal state (to the Flood)	Eden	Edenic	Innocency
	Adam fallen Antediluvian	Adamical (after the Fall)		Antediluvian	Antediluvian	Conscience
Deluge to Moses (Childhood)	Noahical	Noahical	Noah	Patriarchal	Patriarchal	Human Government
	Abrahamical	Abrahamical	Abraham			Promise
Moses to Prophets (Adolescence)	Mosaical	Mosaical	Israel -under law -under priesthood -under kings	Mosaic	Mosaic	Law
Prophets to Christ (Youth)						
Manhood and Old Age	Christian	Christian	Gentiles	Messianic	Church	Grace
			Spirit	Holy Ghost		
Renovation of All Things			Millennium	Millennial	Millennial	Kingdom
					Fullness of times	
					Eternity	

Because Adam could not keep the conditions of the first dispensation, he was judged by God. The judgment was expulsion from the garden (the perfect environment provided by God). The first dispensation, like all to follow, reveals that, natural man is incapable of obeying God or pleasing God. Man lost the benefit of Eden, i.e. the perfect environment. But the covenantal principle would continue, i.e. that man was responsible to provide for his needs. The dispensation ended in failure; man was not able to keep one simple command while living in a perfect environment. As a result, cherubims were placed at the entrance to the garden to keep man from returning (Gen. 3:24).

B. ADAMIC COVENANT—SECOND DISPENSATION. The second covenant grew out of the failure of the first dispensation. The Adamic Covenant not only promised redemption for man, it promised judgment for the one who was responsible for the first sin. The promises of the Adamic covenant are: (1) the serpent, Satan's tool, was cursed and reduced from a beautiful creature to a hated reptile; (2) destruction was promised for Satan in a future head blow (Gen. 3:15); (3) from the seed of the woman, a Redeemer for man, was promised who would destroy Satan (Gen. 3:15); (4) physical work for the physical necessities of life would be hard and despised (Gen. 3:19); (5) nature (creation) was cursed so that it will reluctantly give its fruit for man's necessities and its beauty was veiled (Gen. 3:17-18); (6) woman would have multiplied sorrow in childbirth and be in submission to her husband (Gen. 3:16); (7) physical death for the human race (Rom. 5:12).

Because man failed to live up to the test of the first dispensation of Innocence, he was given a second dispensational test. Since mankind could not go back, he went forward to his next test. As he entered a hostile environment outside the garden, he was given a second set of conditions by which to live. Called the dispensation of Conscience, this era is based on the limited knowledge of right and wrong that Adam experientially accumulated. The Adamic Covenant was introduced by God at the beginning of this period of time.

Man and woman are expelled from the garden (a perfect environment) into a hostile world that did not automatically provide for their needs, so man is given the mandate to work by the sweat of the brow for his sustenance. But a greater test than a command of physical work was the obligation to obey his inner knowledge of good and evil. Experientially man should have remembered the positive results of obedience and the consequences of disobedience. Out of the garden of Eden, he possessed a knowledgeable conscience that he should have applied to every situation. He had the general responsibility to abstain from all known evil and the responsibility to perform all knowable good. Man lived by an awakened conscience. (A conscience is an extension of the general moral laws of God into the inner knowledge of man.)

During the dispensation of Conscience, man enjoyed long life, but man was not able to follow his conscience. Man failed the test and revealed that be could not keep the general principle of good. Instead, "every imagination of the thoughts of his heart was only evil continually" (Gen. 6:5), and "It repented the LORD that he had made man" (Gen. 6:6). The dispensation of Conscience ended in the judgment of the flood.

C. THE NOAHIC COVENANT—THE THIRD DISPENSATION. After the Flood terminated society and left only eight people alive, God introduced a new covenant with new promises. But also there was a new dispensation with new testings. The principles of the first and second covenant continue (i.e., to provide for himself and live by his conscience), but now man no longer lives as a private individual responsible only for himself. The Noahic Covenant involves the institution of human government. Man is responsible to live in a corporate society. Prior to this, man lived in an extended family ruled by a family head. But as society became larger, man was responsible to live by corporate government.

After the Flood God made a covenant with Noah, then gave the rainbow: "This is the token of the covenant which I make between me and you" (Gen. 9:12). Tied to the Noahic Covenant is the third period of time called "the dispensation of Human Government." God no longer allows the conscience of individuals to be the sole basis of human life. The universal flood punished individuals because God had dealt with individuals through the period of conscience. Since all men failed, then all were punished. However, in the covenant of Human Government, God confirms elements of the previous covenants: God told Noah: (1) man was to subdue the earth and provided for his necessities (Gen. 9:13); (2) the physical laws of the universe will remain ordered (Gen. 8:22); and (3) the earth will never have another universal flood (Gen. 9:15).

There are two aspects of the Noahic Covenant that seem temporary in nature, but have eternal implications. The covenant with Noah involved the principle of government(s) which would apply to a larger group of people than just one extended family. The core of the Noahic Covenant was the judicial taking of life (Gen. 9:6), which is the ultimate expression of government. Since that is the ultimate exercise of justice, all other laws of government lead up to that judicial decision and find their credibility in the death penalty. Noah's three sons were to go their separate ways. When Noah made pronouncements on his sons, he noted: (1) Ham's descendants (Canaan) would be a servant, (2) Shem's descendants would have a peculiar relationship to Jehovah, and (3) Japheth's descendants would be enlarged (science, art, government, and so forth).

Implied in their separate blessings was their separate existence as families enlarged into nations. God was making a covenant for man to live together in social groups under laws and government. Yet man had difficulty keeping the Noahic Covenant, hence he failed the test of Human Government.

The test of the dispensation of Human Government was that man would divide into nations or societies and govern themselves. The Bible says very little about this dispensation and how man lived under its test. Most of written history records the generations of the different sons of Noah, hence Gen. 10:1-32 is only representative of this lengthy, but unknown period of time. However, the judgment that ends this era is well known.

The failure of man is evident from the divine judgment at the Tower of Babel. "The LORD came down to see the city and the tower, which the children of men builded" (Gen. 11:5). God did not like what He saw, "Behold, the people is one, and they have all one language; and this they begin to do: and now nothing will be restrained from them, which they have imagined to do" (Gen. 11:6). Apparently because they were not divided into smaller groups, God judged and forced them to divide. "Let us go down, and there confound their language that they may not understand one another's speech. So the LORD scattered them abroad from thence upon the face of all the earth" (Gen. 11:7-8).

Even though the dispensation of Government failed, God did not dissolve the covenant principle given to Noah. The principle of government, plus the other principles inherent in the first two covenants, continue throughout the next dispensations.

D. THE ABRAHAMIC COVENANT—THE FOURTH DISPENSATION. When God called Abraham, it was a dramatic turning point in the history of man. Up to this point, God has been dealing with all humanity in different dispensations, as though there is one vast river of mankind. But with Abraham, God chose one man and planned to make from him a single nation as the center of His work. Through this single purified stream, God planned to communicate with the vast river—the world.

Through Abraham, God promised to bring blessing to the entire world. The Abrahamic Covenant involved: (1) to make out of him a great nation, meaning that nation would be influential upon the other nations, a nation that would continue when others disappeared, (2) to bless this nation with financial and spiritual prosperity (Gen. 12:2), (3) to make the name of Abraham universal and enduring, (4) to be a blessing to Abraham (Gal. 3:13-14), (5) to bless the nations that bless the seed of Abraham, (7) to bless all the families of the earth through Abraham's seed, the Christ (Gen. 12:3), (8) that God would first show Abraham the land (Gen. 12:1), then when he obeyed the command, God promised to give him the land (Gen. 12:1), hence it is the Promised Land.

The most important aspect of God's covenant to Abraham is its inherent promise. Called the dispensation of Promise, this fourth period of testing involved the spiritual responsibility of accepting and living in light of the promise of God. They were to live in the Promised Land and trust God for the promised seed.

When Abraham disobeyed by going to Egypt, he did not abrogate the promise of the land, but he lost the blessings attached to obeying God and dwelling in the land.

Since each dispensation reveals a testing, so the fourth dispensation reflects man's inability to live by the Promise of God. Remember this dispensation relates only to the descendants of Abraham, not all mankind. But the seed of Abraham refused to live in the land by faith, so they migrated to Egypt. The final testing and failure of Israel in this era of Promise is when God attempted to bring them out of Egypt into the Promised Land. When they refused in unbelief at Kadesh-Barnea, God judged them. Israel wandered forty years in the wilderness. Everyone who did not accept the promise of God died in the wilderness; only those of faith (Joshua and Caleb) entered the Promised Land.

E. THE MOSAIC COVENANT—THE FIFTH DISPENSATION. The covenant that God gave on Mount Sinai was the Mosaic Covenant as reflected in the giving of the law. Among the many purposes of the law was that it revealed to man that he is a personal sinner before God. During the previous dispensations man was a sinner, even when he did not have knowledge of the law. Paul tells us, "Death reigned from Adam to Moses, even over them that had not sinned after the similitude of Adam's transgression" (Rom. 5:14).

The Mosaic Covenant was not given as a means of life or death (it only revealed death): (1) the law reflected the holiness of a personal God, (2) it instructed them in God's discipline,

(3) it reminded them of God's salvation (through its priests and sacrifices), and (4) it was a *pedagogue*, a schoolmaster, to take them to Christ (Gal. 3:24).

The Mosaic Covenant was expressed in three divisions: (1) the commandments expressing the righteous will of God, (2) the judgments expressing the social life of Israel, and (3) the ordinances directing the religions life of Israel. Jesus called all these "the law" (Matt. 5:17) and they were a "ministry of condemnation" (2 Cor. 3:7-9). No one was ever saved by keeping the law, it was simply God's testing for Israel. The nation's failure to keep the law ended in judgment, as did all other dispensational periods of time.

The fourth dispensation of the Law ended in the cross-judgment of Christ. He perfectly kept the law (Matt. 5:17), then nailed the law to the cross (Col. 2:14), and "abolished in his flesh the enmity, even the law of the commandments contained in ordinances" (Eph. 2:15). Just as the principles of the previous covenants continue into the next dispensations, so the principles of the law continue past the cross-judgment of Christ. He did not take the law away, only the penalties of the law.

F. THE NEW COVENANT—THE SIXTH DISPENSATION. The New Covenant was predicted in the Old Testament, "Behold, the days come, saith the LORD, that I will make a new covenant with the house of Israel, and with the house of Judah" (Jer. 31:31). The New Covenant, also called the New Testament, was accomplished at the death of Jesus Christ. It is also called the Second Covenant, in contrast to the Mosaic Covenant of the law: "For if that first covenant had been faultless, then should no place have been sought for the second" (Heb. 8:7).

The New Covenant is "better": (1) because it is unconditional "I will make [a covenant] with the house of Israel" and "I will be to them a God" (Heb. 8:10); (2) because God guarantees that men will keep its conditions "I will put my laws into their mind, and write them in their hearts" (Heb. 8:10); (3) because it would extend to all, "for all shall know me, from the least to the greatest" (Heb. 8:11); (4) because it will completely eradicate sins, "their sins and their iniquities will I remember no more" (Heb. 8:12); and (5) because it rests upon the sacrifice of Christ, the better Mediator, and assures eternal blessedness for those who accept.

Christ predicted the New Covenant on the night of His death, when He instituted the Lord's Supper: "This is my blood of the new testament [covenant] which is shed for many for the remission of sins" (Matt. 26:28). The results of the New Covenant apply primarily to the dispensation of Grace, but just as other covenants have eternal applications in future dispensations, so the results apply to the kingdom age when "all Israel shall be saved" (Rom. 11:26), and "all will know the Lord" (Jer. 31:34).

This era begins with the cross-judgment of Jesus Christ that marked the end of the dispensation of Law. Under the law, God demanded righteousness from man, but now under grace, God gives to the sinner the righteousness of His Son, Jesus Christ. Whereas the law demanded that man live by a perfect standard, under grace, God saves the disobedient by imputing the perfection of Jesus Christ to man.

The test in the dispensation of Grace is no longer legal obedience, but rather, "What will a person do with Jesus Christ?" The condition of this dispensation is for a person to accept Jesus Christ and live by grace. The predicted end to the dispensation of grace will happen when the professing church rejects grace and slides into apostasy. The resulting apocalypse is God's judgment that ends the era of Grace.

G. THE DAVIDIC COVENANT—THE DISPENSATION OF THE KINGDOM. The covenant with David is unique in that there was a period of time between God's revealing it to David and its future accomplishment. The Davidic Covenant had immediate implications for Israel, but was the basis for the future dispensation known as the Kingdom Age—the Millennium—when David's son will sit on the throne of Israel and rule from Jerusalem.

Previously, God had promised a Redeemer-seed through Eve (Gen. 3:15), then later He narrowed the promise to Shem (Gen. 9:26), then still narrower to the seed of Abraham (Gen. 12:3), finally to the tribe of Judah (Gen. 49:10). Now the Redeemer-seed is promised to come from the descendants of David.

The Davidic Covenant (Psa. 89:20-37) is unconditional, hence based on the nature of God. Whereas God established His nation through the Abrahamic Covenant, and laws for His nation through the Mosaic Covenant, God established a ruler over His people in the Davidic Covenant.

The Davidic Covenant has a fourfold promise: (1) that God would establish David's throne (2 Sam. 7:13) i.e., a family line; (2) that God would establish a throne (2 Sam. 7:13) i.e., authority from God to rule over His people; (3) that God would establish His Kingdom (2 Sam. 7:13), i.e., a sphere of rule; and (4) that God would recognize David's reign in perpetuity (2 Sam. 7:13).

This was a perpetual and unconditional covenant: "My covenant will I not break . . . once I have sworn by my holiness that I will not lie to David"

INNOCENCY	CONSCIENCE	HUMAN GOV'T	PROMISE	LAW	GRACE	KINGDOM
Man created in innocence, placed in perfect environment subjected to simple test of obedience and warned of consequences.	By disobedience man came to a personal understanding of good and evil. Approach to God through sacrifice.	A government of man by man. Man was responsible to govern the world for God.	Abraham and his descendants became the heir of the unconditional promise.	Israel was given the law at Mount Sinai.	Characterized as the time of the Gentiles when Christ is gathering believers in the body which is the church. God relates to man by grace.	The coming kingdom is based on the throne of David.
Failure Woman fell by pride, Man fell deliberately	**Failure** Man did only that which was evil.	**Failure** Tower of Babel	**Failure** Left the Land.	**Failure** Long record of disobedience	**Failure** The apostate church	**Failure** Final Rebellion

Result	Result	Result	Result	Result	Result	Result
Expulsion from Garden	Flood judgment	Confusion of tongues	Bondage in Egypt	Judgment to Israel in the captivity and the cross judgment ended the dispensation	Judgment—the tribulation	Judgment—Hell
EDENIC COVENANT	ADAMIC COVENANT	NOAHIC COVENANT	ABRAHAMIC COVENANT	MOSAIC COVENANT	NEW COVENANT	DAVIDIC COVENANT
1. Replenish the earth 2. Subdue the earth 3. Have dominion over animals 4. Eat herbs and fruits 5. Abstain eating from the tree of good and evil 6. Penalty was death	1. Serpent cursed 2. First promise 3. Changed state of woman a. Multiplied conception b. Motherhood sorrow 4. Earth cursed 5. Inevitable sorrow of life 6. Burdensome labor 7. Physical death	1. Relation-ship of man to earth confirmed 2. Order of nature confirmed 3. Human gov't. established 4. No more universal flood – judg-ment by water	1. Make Israel a great nation 2. Bless the seed 3. Great name 4. Be a blessing 5. Bless them that bless you 6. Curse him that curses you 7. In Israel all the families of the earth will be blessed 8. Promised land	1. Given to Israel 2. Three parts, a. Command-ments reveal the righteou-sness of God b. Judgments reveal social requirements c. Ordinances reveal religious life 3. Revealed death	1. Better promises 2. Receive a willing mind and heart 3. Personal relationship with Christ 4. Obliteration of sins 5. Based on accomplished redemption 6. Secures for Israel a. Perpetuity b. National conversion c. Blessing of God	1. Davidic house, prosperity of family 2. Throne - a royal authority 3. Davidic kingdom - a rule 4. In perpetuity - forever 5. Christ will sit on the throne of David

(Psa. 89:34-35). When Israel disobeyed, God did not abrogate the covenant, He only chastised His people for disobedience. The chastisement came when the kingdom was divided under Rehoboam. Later the Davidic Covenant that was confirmed by an oath of the Lord (Psa. 89), was confirmed to the Virgin Mary (Luke 1:31-33) and repeated by Peter on Pentecost (Acts 2:29-32). It will be fulfilled in the future kingdom.

This seventh and last era of time to govern man's life on earth grows out of the apocalyptic judgment at the end of the Church Age. Man will fail to please God, even though he is given just about every opportunity and every circumstance. In this last dispensation man will live in a perfect environment. He will be ruled by Jesus Christ and the curse on nature will be lifted. Even when tested in ideal circumstances, man will fall to live pleasing to God.

The "Dispensation of the Fullness of Time" (Eph. 1:10), is the same as the future kingdom when David's son will rule (2 Sam. 7:8-17, Zech. 12:8, Luke 1:31-33). The conditions for this era are: (1) Christ will take control of the kingdom (Isa. 11:3-4) and put to an end all anarchy and misrule; (2) men will be rewarded and given rest (2 Thess. 1:6-7); (3) those who have suffered will be glorified (Rom. 8:17-18); (4) all Israel will be saved (Rom. 11:26); her blindness will be cured (2 Cor. 3:14-17), and she will be restored (Ezek. 39:25-29); (5) the times of the Gentiles will cease; (6) the curse on creation will be lifted and nature will be magnified (Gen. 3:17, Isa. 11:6-8; 65:20-25; Rom. 8:19-21).

Even this last dispensation of ideal circumstances will end in judgment. The test will be to submit to David's son, Christ, who rules with a rod of iron, which means He is the absolute Ruler who will guide mankind according to justice and equity. Yet at the end of 1,000 years, a group will gather in rebellion against the King (Rev. 20:7-9). They will be judged along with Satan (Rev. 20:10). Then the final judgment of the ages (dispensations) will result in those who rejected God being cast into the lake of fire (Rev. 20:11-15).

Thus God will have demonstrated that in every age (dispensation) under every circumstance or test man could not, or would not, live according to the principles expressed in the covenants and keep the requirements of the dispensations.

Those who live with God throughout eternity will be there because of the grace of God. God will have demonstrated that nothing man has done can merit salvation. Those who suffer eternal separation will realize that God gave mankind varied circumstances and different tests to demonstrate their faith in Him. And in every dispensation, man failed. Hence no man can say throughout the future ages that God was unfair or unmerciful.

IX. THE COURSE OF THIS PRESENT AGE

The age in which we presently live is the sixth of the seventh dispensations, the Age of Grace. In the Old Testament, God was concerned with Israel, His Chosen People, and through them He related to the world. In this age, however, God is dealing not with the nation Israel, but with the Gentile nations and is using His church to carry out His Great Commission (Matt. 28:18-20). During this age, then, God is gathering a people for Himself through individual conversions (Titus 2:14). At the same time, the mystery of the church is being unfolded (Col. 1:24-29; Eph. 2:11-6; 3:3-10).

Sometimes this dispensation is referred to as the Age of the Holy Spirit because of the unique ministry of the third Person of the Trinity during this period, both in the world and in the believer. This does not, however, mean this age is perfect in any sense. The Scriptures describe it as an evil age (Gal. 1:4; 2 Cor. 4:4; Eph. 2:2), an age of darkness (Eph. 6:2), an age marked by ungodliness (Titus 2:12; Eph. 2:1-3) and an age of apostasy (1 Tim. 4:1-3; 2 Tim. 3:1-14; 4:3-4; 2 Pet. 2:1-3, 12-22; Jude 4, 8, 10). It is an age professing not an affirmation of the things of God but rather a denial of the same. Commenting on conditions at the end of this age, Pentecost suggests,

These conditions center around a system of denials. There is a denial of God (Luke 17:26; 2 Tim. 3:4-5), a denial of Christ (1 John 2:18; 4:3; 2 Pet. 2:6), a denial of

Christ's return (2 Pet. 3:3-4), a denial of the faith (1 Tim. 4:1-2; Jude 3), a denial of sound doctrine (2 Tim. 4:3-4), a denial of the separated life (2 Tim. 3:1-7), a denial of Christian liberty (1 Tim. 4:3-4), a denial of morals (2 Tim. 3:1-8, 13; Jude 18), a denial of authority (2 Tim. 3:4). This condition at the close of the age is seen to coincide with the state within the Laodicean Church, before which Christ must stand to seek admission. In view of its close it is not surprising that the age is called an "evil age" in Scripture.[47]

Two passages of Scripture are generally held to present a prophetic history of the major trends of this age. When Jesus gave His "kingdom parables," some commentators believe he was chronologically outlining the characteristics of this present age. Later, as Jesus evaluated the seven churches of Asia, He may have also presented a second clue concerning the future history of this Church Age.

A. KINGDOM PARABLES. Much of the ministry of Jesus during his earthly life was devoted to teaching His disciples. Parables were among His favorite techniques. They enabled Him to address a large group, but speak specifically to a smaller group who would understand the real message of the parable. Matthew 13 records seven such parables in which Jesus sought to teach His disciples "the mysteries of the kingdom of heaven" (Matt. 13:11). Here, Jesus outlined the progress of this current age. Concerning these parables, Walvoord writes,

> The Old Testament reveals, in clear terms, the earthly reign of Christ when he comes as King to reign on the throne of David (which truths are not mysteries). Matthew 13 introduces a different form of the kingdom, namely the present spiritual reign of the King during the period He is physically absent from the earth, prior to His second coming. The mysteries of the kingdom, accordingly, deal with the period between the first and second advent of Christ and not the millennial kingdom which will follow the second coming.[48]

The entire chapter records seven parables of the mysteries of the kingdom and has been outlined in various ways by different expositors. One such interpretive outline sees verse 52, where Jesus speaks of "things new and old" as the key to interpreting the chapter. According to Scroggie,

> It appears to me that the key to the interpretation of these parables is in ver. 52 of this chapter: "Every scribe which is instructed unto the kingdom of heaven is like unto a man that is an householder, which bringeth forth out of his treasure things new and old." These words are spoken of the things which precede, and surely speak of the parables as some *new* and some *old*. But which are the old and which are the new? In ver. 1, we read that our Lord "went out of the house, and sat by the seaside" and taught; and in ver. 36 "then Jesus sent the multitude away, and went into the house" and taught. Thus the parables are divided into four spoken in public, and three spoken in private; and the evidence goes to show (if ver. 52 is the key) that the first

four are the *new* treasures of truth, and the last three are the *old*—that is, truths revealed before. Assuming this, the present Age is presented to our view in a series of seven progressive pictures, describing the course of the kingdom in mystery.

THE NEW THINGS

1. *The Seed and the Soils*: the Proclamation of the Kingdom.
2. *The Wheat and the Darnel*: false Imitation in the Kingdom.
3. *The Mustard Tree*: wide, visible Extension of the Kingdom.
4. *The Leaven in the Meal*: insidious Corruption, of the Kingdom.

THE OLD THINGS

5. *The Treasure*: the Israelitish Nation.
6. *The Pearl*: the Jewish Remnant during the Tribulation.
7. *The Drag-net*: the Judgment of the Nations at the end of the Tribulation.[49]

In the Gospel of Matthew, there is a distinction made between the kingdom of God and the kingdom of heaven. These two expressions indicate different aspects of the rule of God. Neither of these should be confused with the church. This is sometimes a difficult distinction to maintain because, whereas the church is not equal to the kingdom of Heaven, the church certainly does fall under the broader kingdom of heaven. This distinction is emphasized by Gaebelein.

The mercy and grace offered to Israel is to go forth to the Gentiles, the nations, while the King Himself is absent. This is indicated in the first parable where the sower *went out*, which stands for the fact of His going forth into the field, which is the world. So that which is extended to the Gentiles and that in which the name of Christ is confessed is now the kingdom of the heavens, and of this development of what He the Lord from heaven brought and left in the earth, our Lord speaks in these parables. In one word "the kingdom of the heavens" in Matthew is equivalent with "*Christendom*." It includes the whole sphere of Christian profession saved and unsaved, so-called Romanists and Protestants, all who are naming the name of Christ. Therefore, the church is not the kingdom of the heavens, though the church is in the kingdom of the heavens.[50]

When studied in this light, perhaps the seven parables prophetically describe the course of this age. From our perspective closer to the end of the age, the accuracy of these predictions is apparently reflected in the record of church history. The following chart summarizes the course of this age as seen in the kingdom parables of Matthew 13.

THE COURSE OF THE AGE IN MATTHEW 13		
	vv.	
Parable of the Sower	1-23	There will be a sowing of the gospel throughout the world.
Parable of the Tares	24-30	There will be a counter-sowing by Satan.
Parable of the Mustard Seed	31,32	There will be an outward growth of Christendom, but not necessarily the church.
Parable of the Leaven	33-35	There will be a permeation of the gospel into all areas of life.
Parable of the Hidden Treasure Parable of the Pearl of Great Price	44 45,46	God will gather to Himself a peculiar people.
Parable of the Drag-net	47-51	God will end the age in judgment.

B. CHURCH EPISTLES. When Jesus appeared to John on the Isle of Patmos, the first part of his revelation was to dictate seven letters to the messengers of seven specific named churches in Asia (Rev. 2-3). There were far more than seven churches in that region, but only seven were chosen by Christ to receive messages. The order in which the messages are presented is also unusual. It is not the normal order in which these churches would be visited by a traveler. Some conservative scholars believe Christ selected these seven churches in this particular order to prophetically suggest the major

trends in church history. While not all dispensationalists hold to this view, many of the early dispensational writers of this century have. Summarizing this view of the seven churches as representing the seven ages of the church, Scott writes,

Ecclesiastical pretension and departure from first love characterized the close of the apostolic period—*Ephesus* (chap. 2. 1-7). Next succeeded the martyr period, which brings us down to the close of the tenth and last persecution, under Diocletian—*Smyrna* (chap. 2. 8-11). Decreasing spirituality and increasing worldliness went hand in hand from the accession of Constantine and his public patronage of Christianity on to the seventh century—*Pergamos* (chap. 2. 12-17). The Papal Church, which is Satan's masterpiece on earth, is witnessed in the assumption of universal authority and cruel persecution of the saints of God. Its evil reign covers "the Middle Ages," the moral characteristics of which have been well termed "dark."

Popery blights everything it touches—*Thyatira* (chap. 2. 18-29). The Reformation was God's intervention in grace and power to cripple papal authority, and introduce into Europe the light which for 300 years has been burning with more or less brilliancy. Protestantism, with its divisions and deadness, shows clearly enough how far short it comes of God's ideal of the Church and Christianity—*Sardis* (chap. 3. 1-6). Another Reformation, equally the work of God, characterized the beginning of last century—*Philadelphia* (chap. 3. 7-13). The present general state of the professing Church, which is one of lukewarmness, is the most hateful and nauseous of any yet described. We may well term this last phase of Church history on the eve of judgment the Christless period—*Laodicea* (chap. 3. 14-22).

Note, that the history of the first three churches is consecutive, whereas the history of the remaining four overlaps, and then practically runs on concurrently to the end, the Coming of the Lord. One other consideration of interest, and we bring these remarks to a close. The *divine* element, signified by the numeral three, is the predominant thought in the first group of churches, whereas the *human* enters more largely into the second group signified by the number four.[51]

As both the kingdom parables and church epistles describe the course of this present age, it is reasonable to investigate the relationship between these two sections of Scripture. Both were recorded by disciples of Christ, one as the New Testament was first being written and the other as the canon was coming to a close. Contrasting these two passages, Gaebelein suggests the following outline.

1. *The parable of the sower—Ephesus.* The apostolic age. The beginning with failure—leaving the first love.

2. *The parable of the evil seed—Smyrna*, meaning bitterness. The enemy revealed.

3. *The parable of the mustard seed—Pergamos*—meaning high tower and twice married. The professing church becomes big, a state institution under Constantine the Great. The big tree and the unclean birds (nations) find shelter there.

4. *The parable of the leaven—Thyatira*—the one who sacrifices. Rome and her abomination. The woman Jezebel, the harlot, corresponds to the woman in the parable of the leaven.

5. *The parable of the treasure hid—Sardis*—the reformation age—having a name to live, but being dead and a remnant there. Israel, dead but belonging to Him who has purchased the field.

6. *The parable of the Pearl—Philadelphia.* The church, the *one pearl*. The one body of Christ and the removal of the church to be with Him.

7. *The parable of the dragnet—Laodicea—*Judgment. I will spue thee out of my mouth.[52]

THE SEVEN CHURCHES WHICH ARE IN ASIA - REVELATION 2-3							
	2:1-7	2:8-11	2:12-17	2:18-29	3:1-6	3:7-13	3:14-22
City	Ephesus	Smyrna	Pergamum	Thyatira	Sardis	Philadelphia	Laodicea
Meaning of name of city	Let go desirable	Death Myrrh	Tower Marriage	Never Tiring of Sacrifice	Escaping One's Remnant	Brotherly Love	People's Rights
Title	Patient Church	Persecuted Church	Polluted Church	Paganized Church	Peculiar Church	Pure Church	Passive Church
Church Age	First Century	A.D. 100-316	316-500	500-1500	1500-1750	1750-1910	1910-Date
Description of Church	Holds 7 Stars Walks in midst 7 Lampstands	First & Last Was dead and is alive	Has Sharp Sword with 2 Edges	Son of God Eyes like fire Feet like Bronze	Has 7 Spirits of God and 7 Stars	Holy, True Has Key David, Opens & Closes	Amen, Faithful & True Witness Beginning of the Creation of God
Positive	Works Toll Patience	Tribulation Apparent Poverty True Wealth	Hold Fast Name of Christ Did not Deny Faith	Love, Faith Ministry Patience	Reputation of Being Alive	Set Before Thee an Open Door	
Negative	Left first Love		Teaching of Balaam Fornication Nicolatians	Jezebel	But really Dead		Lukewarm, wretched, miserable, poor, blind, naked
Instructions to Church	Remember, repent, do the First Works	Be Faithful Unto Death	Repent or I will come quickly & make war	To judge Jezebel	Be watchful strengthen what remains, remember, hold fast, repent	Hold fast	Be zealous, repent, allow Christ in
Promise	Eat of Tree of Life	Not hurt in 2nd Death	Hidden manna, white stone	Power over nations, Morning Star	White Raiment Confessed before Father	Pillar in Temple, New Names	Right to reign

Similarly, Dwight Pentecost also sees a relationship between the seven churches and seven kingdom parables. In both cases he sees a similar development of evil as reflected in the following chart.[53]

Matt. 13	Rev. 2-3	Meaning of the name	Approximate dates	Characteristics
Sower	Ephesus	Desired	Pentecost to 100 A.D.	Time of sowing, organization, and evangelism
Wheat and Tares	Smyrna	Myrrh	Nero to 300 A.D.	Persecution. Enemy revealed
Mustard Seed	Pergamos	Thoroughly Married	300 to 800 A.D.	Worldly alliance. Great external growth
Leaven	Thyatira	Continual sacrifice	800 to 1517	Papal domination. Doctrinal corruption
Treasure Hid	Sardis	Those escaping	Reformation	Empty profession. Rise of the state church
Pearl	Philadelphia	Brotherly love	The last days	True church of the last days
Dragnet	Laodicea	People ruling	Last days	Apostasy

In both cases, one could argue that some parables or epistles may overlap, but the major theme illustrates the course of this present age. As one surveys the history of these last two millennia, it is possible to see how these prophetic allusions may have been fulfilled. One sign of Christ's soon return is the fact that we are at the end of the age according to these two passages. God's final judgment is all that remains to be fulfilled in this age.

C. ISRAEL AND PROPHECY. The energy that keeps God's prophetic clock running on schedule is the Jewish nation. God's character demands that He honor His covenant with Abraham

(Gen. 12:1-6). Since God promised to give the land of Israel to the seed of Abraham, it is only natural to interpret the return of the Jews to the land as an indication that God's timetable is still on schedule. With the establishment and struggles of the State of Israel since 1948, Bible prophecy has been fulfilled in the eyes of the world. The gathering of the Jews to a Palestinian homeland is setting the stage for Christ's return.

The New Testament writers were careful not to confuse the church with Israel, recognizing each existed as two similar yet distinct groups (1 Cor. 10:32). Israel holds a special place in the heart of God. According to Feinberg,

> Israel means much to God, for He has purposed to use them to witness to the unity of His Person; to show the blessedness of serving Him; to receive, preserve, and transmit the Scriptures; to show the sustaining power of the Scriptures throughout the centuries; to be the channel of the Messiah's incarnation; to show His longsuffering in dealing with sinful man; to reveal to the world the futility of seeking to gain acceptance with Him by works of the flesh; to manifest His faithfulness to His promises; to use them as world-wide missionaries; and to spread abroad the glory and knowledge of Himself in the millennium.[54]

There are some who do not recognize the presence of Israel in the land as an indication the end of the age is near. This is in part due to the fact that the Scriptures describe a believing Israel in the land, whereas, to a large extent today, Israel has returned to the land in unbelief. A closer examination of the Scriptures reveals two aspects of Israel in the land.

1. *Restoration.* God told Ezekiel He would bring His people back into the land (Ezek. 37:11-14). That promise included both the restoration of the Jews to the land God gave Abraham, and the regeneration of that people in the land. During the past century, we have seen maps drawn outlining the boundaries of David's kingdom (following World War I) and that kingdom in part given to the Jews (1948). During the Six-Day War of 1967, Jerusalem and other parts of the Jewish homeland were conquered and became part of the national geography of Israel. When Israel declared Jerusalem her capital during the summer of 1980, yet another step had been taken toward the ultimate fulfillment of those prophecies concerning the restoration of the Jews in Israel.

There are several aspects of Israel's return to the land taught in the Scriptures. In an attempt to summarize chronologically the order of events relating to both the restoration and regeneration of Israel, Trotter and Smith note,

> It remains for us to take a hasty glance at the light shed by Scripture on the order in which Israel's restoration, and the events connected with it, are to take place. . . .
>
> First, it is clear, from several passages, that many of the Jews will return to their own land in unbelief. . . .
>
> Secondly, the whole of those that return to their own land in unbelief will not be involved in these abominations, and in the judgments consequent upon them. . . .

But, thirdly, the restoration of the ten tribes seems to be in a different manner. We have just seen how the Jews pass through the last *tribulation in the land*; the wicked being thus purged from amongst them. . . . The ten tribes, having gone into captivity long before the first coming of Christ, have not to suffer for the sin of crucifying him, and so are not involved in these final troubles *in the land*. The wicked are purged from amongst *them* before they reach the land. . . .

Finally, there are several passages which appear to foretell a still further process of restoration. We have noticed the return of many of the Jews in unbelief, with their sin and judgment, and the preservation from both of a remnant amongst them, who are delivered out of their extreme distress by the coming of the Lord with all his saints. We have seen this remnant joined by the multitude of the ten tribes brought back by the hand of God, who has purged out all the rebels from among them ere they arrive at the land of Israel. But it would seem, that, besides all this, messengers will be dispatched from the place where the Lord has appeared in glory, and destroyed the enemies of his people, to bring back any Israelites who may yet be found among the nations.[55]

2. Regeneration. The second part of Ezekiel's prophecy concerns the spiritual rebirth of the Jews. God committed himself to restore the people to their land and said, "[I] shall put my spirit in you, and ye shall live, and I shall place you in your own land; then shall ye know that I the LORD, have spoken it, and performed it, saith the LORD" (Ezek. 37:14). Even though some Jews have returned to the land today, most are there in unbelief (Deut. 30:1-3). Many Jews could not be considered good practicing Jews and most are certainly not Christians.

The apostle Paul also recognized a future time when "all Israel shall be saved" (Rom. 11:26). While some Jews are always being saved throughout the age (Rom. 11:5), most are still in spiritual blindness (Rom. 11:25). When Jesus returns, the Bible describes a national turning to God. This national regeneration will be the fulfillment of the second part of Ezekiel's promise. According to Pietsch, "a great deal of the faithful, missionary work that is now being done in the evangelizing of the Jew will bear its largest fruitage after the rapture."[56] Similarly, Cohn taught this regeneration of the nation would occur during the Great Tribulation. Commenting on Romans 11:26, he writes,

But the reference is to that black hour of history to come, sometimes known as the great tribulation, sometimes, as the Armageddon battle, and sometimes, and more correctly so, as "the time of Jacob's trouble." When that time comes, the Church will be no longer here, having been caught up to be with the Lord. Only the devil reigns supreme on the earth then. And Israel will undergo the greatest torment and agony of all her tragic history of suffering. God promises, "He (Jacob) shall be saved (delivered) out of it." (Jer. 30:7) This is what Romans 11:26 has in perspective.[57]

The student of Bible prophecy must always find his authority in the Scriptures, not current events. When Bible teachers such as H. A. Ironside and C. I. Scofield taught the restoration of Israel to the land at the beginning of this century, their critics could show them maps which did not even have boundaries, let alone Jews, in the place they claimed a nation would someday be reestablished. Fifty years later the tables were turned and the teaching of Ironside and Scofield has been vindicated. Yet, the critics still reject the clear teaching of Scripture. Present day "anti-missionary" laws in Israel should not discourage the student of prophetic Scripture from believing in a future revival sweeping the land of Israel.

D. THE "SABBATH TYPE" ARGUMENT. A fourth indication that the end of the age may be approaching is found in the typical fulfillment of the sabbath. The argument is that the kingdom of the future is the fulfillment of the rest pictured in the sabbath type (cf. Heb. 4:9). This argument was begun by some rabbis who taught a view of Jewish eschatology which stated that just as God created the world in seven days, so man would dwell on this earth seven "days"—i.e., Millennium (cf. Psa. 90:4) upon the earth, the last of these days (millenniums) being the restoration of David's kingdom. This view has also been adopted by some dispensational writers. Ritchie suggests,

> Possibly these seven ages of time may be prefigured by the seven creative days of Genesis 1 and 2 ending as they do with the Sabbath rest of God. The words of Hebrews 4. 9 will then have a literal fulfillment: "There remaineth therefore a Sabbath-keeping for the people of God." With the dawning of Eternity, ages and dispensations cease to be. Thus it is evident that "the purpose of the ages" is moving forward to a definite consummation, which no opposition or failure on the part of man can thwart.[58]

In an apparent endorsement of this typical interpretation of the sabbath, Ironside notes,

> A millennium, then, is a time-period. It does not necessarily carry with it any thought of perfection or happiness, nor of an era of manifested divine government. Six millenniums have almost elapsed since God put man upon this globe, and there is another millennium and a fraction yet to run ere the course of time is finished. That last thousand years is the period with which we are now to be occupied, and I trust to show that it is the predicted kingdom-age of the prophets, and the "dispensation of the fullness of times" of the New Testament.[59]

This interpretation of the sabbath type may be questioned. First, one would have to accept the general dates of Usher, i.e., that the world was created approximately 4000 B.C. Next, this is arguing from types, and a theologian illustrates from types, never bases an argument on them. One should not depend upon this or any other to set a date to determine the time of the end of the age. This argument should, however, impress upon the Christian the need to watch and pray (Matt. 24:42).

E. GROWTH OF INTERNATIONALISM. We are living in a global community where national borders do not appear as significant in the minds of people as they were even a generation or two ago. Immigration to the Western hemisphere from around the world has produced international cities in our land. The television, airplane, and media have greatly contributed to the cosmopolitan spirit of our day. Our society is being prepared to accept the possibility of an international government and ecumenical "state church."

1. *World Government.* Daniel described the progress of world history in terms of four beasts representing kingdoms. "Thus he said, The fourth beast shall be the fourth kingdom upon the earth, which shall be diverse from all kingdoms, and shall devour the whole earth, and shall tread it down, and break it in pieces" (Dan. 7:23). The beast that he predicted was the Roman Empire, and it will be revived before Christ returns. This revived empire appears to be a world government that will have international control and influence. According to Sale-Harrison,

> If it is the same fourth kingdom, it must be a ten-kingdom one. The Roman Empire never was a confederation of kings, so this indicates the Roman in a revived form, not as a unit under one Caesar, but as a federation. Rome always conquered and assimilated the territory into her one empire; therefore, the past cannot be referred to here.[60]

John also described the ruler of that kingdom, observing, "It was given unto him to make war with the saints, and to overcome them: and power was given him over all kindreds, and tongues, and nations" (Rev. 13:7). Both Daniel and John expected a world leader who would establish a world government. Summarizing the biblical teaching concerning this government Thiessen suggests,

> In Dan. 2:31-43 we have a picture of "the times of the Gentiles" (Luke 21:24), and in the following two verses of the millennial kingdom. After Babylon, Medo-Persia, Greece, and Rome, we have the final form of the Roman empire with its ten cooperating kings. In Dan. 7:1-28 we have this same prediction under the figure of four beasts. The last one with its ten horns represents the final form of the Roman empire with its ten kings. In Rev. 13:1-10 we have this same prophecy as seen by John, except that the horns now have crowns, i.e., the time of their power has come. In Rev. 17:1-18 we see this same beast dominated by the adulterous woman, the false bride of Christ, who has passed into the Tribulation period. In Rev. 19:17-21 we see the end of this empire.[61]

Today, our society appears to be moving toward a place where such a world government would be acceptable. With many major and minor crises that have confronted world leaders in recent years, they have adopted an internationalist view of world politics. Some have cited organizations such as the United Nations and the European Common Market as possible patterns for an international government. It is generally agreed that such a government would demand a strong leader. Since a world government will arise after the return of Christ, many see present trends toward it as setting the stage for His return.

2. *World religion.* Certain religious leaders around the world today are eagerly hoping to establish a greater ecumenical attitude among their followers even to establish a unified church which could include all the various sects of Christianity. Some have even suggested this church should be tolerant of, and include members of, Hindu, Islamic, Jewish and other non-Christian sects.

While cooperation between churches is good and a spirit of unity among Christian leaders is a biblical goal, the current religious ecumenical movement does not fit the biblical pattern for the church of Jesus Christ. The ecumenical church is only biblical in that it is the fulfillment of prophetic Scriptures. John calls it a "harlot church" in his vision on the Isle of Patmos (Rev. 17:1). She was a harlot in that she prostituted her doctrine and standards of purity by compromising with the world. The harlot church is actually guilty of opposing and aggressively seeking to destroy the true followers of Christ, those who practice biblical Christianity. According to Sale-Harrison,

> The City of Rome will be the natural center, and Revelation 17 certainly suggests that the Vatican will ride the beast, even if she does not guide him. The ever increasing power of the Roman Church will make it necessary for the political head—for a time at least—to use her influence for his own ends.[62]

The coming church will probably carry on the ancient pagan custom of interrelating the church and state into a single institution. Presumably, an international state church could be the official religion of the world and the chief religious leader would also be the chief political leader. He would be the Antichrist. Except in a few Islamic republics, the union of the political and religious government is not practiced today as in the past. But as many things come full cycle, this future harlot church would be the state religion of the international state.

F. SIGNS OF HIS COMING. There is much controversy in conservative theological circles concerning the validity of signs before the rapture. Pentecost observes, "Since the church is given the hope of an imminent return of Christ there can be no signs given to her as to when this event will take place."[63] With all the fanaticism related to watching for the return of Christ, one might wonder if there are "signs of the times" that do give some warning that Christ might soon be appearing. Jesus said, "Now learn a parable of the fig tree; When his branch is yet tender, and putteth forth leaves, ye know that summer is nigh: So likewise ye, when ye shall see all these things, know that it is near, even at the doors" (Matt. 24:32-33). Later Jesus stated two words every serious student of Bible prophecy should heed: "Watch therefore" (Matt. 24:42). As Chafer explains,

> The figure of a budding fig tree is introduced here, not to liken Israel to a fig tree, which may be true, but to indicate that as the things which have been announced begin to come to pass, they may know that Christ's return in power and glory and for Israel's deliverance is not to be expected until the events which prepare for it are in evidence.[64]

No one will ever know the date of Jesus' return until they see him coming in the clouds. Still, certain things happening in our world today suggest the day of His return may be very close. We must be careful to obey the Scriptures and accurately interpret the evidences of Christ's return without abusing the Scriptures in an attempt to somehow date His return.

Certain conditions exist in the world today that could end civilization or destroy life as we know it. The threat of atomic annihilation is a possibility, as well as the threat of polluting ourselves out of existence, or populating ourselves into mass starvation. Of course, these will not happen because, as the Bible teaches, Christ will end this age. He will not allow man to destroy himself. But the rapid acceleration of these dangers implies that Christ will return before they run their natural course.

Other conditions in Scripture imply the return of Christ. However, it is difficult to give an objective identification to them, so we are not sure they are "signs." Paul noted, "In the last days perilous times shall come. For men shall be lovers of their own selves, covetous, boasters, proud, blasphemers, disobedient to parents, unthankful, unholy, without natural affection, trucebreakers, false accusers, incontinent, fierce, despisers of those that are good, traitors, heady, highminded, lovers of pleasures more than lovers of God; having a form of godliness, but denying the power thereof" (2 Tim. 3:1-5). Some of these conditions have been true in every age, as they were in Timothy's day. Also, this list is subjective in that there have always been wars and rumors of war. Since these have always been true to some extent, can they be considered objective signs? The following list is only included for illustration and should not be considered as an objective list of signs. Their appearance in Scripture, and/or, mentioned by some prophetic teaching, meant they could not be ignored.

SIGNS OF THE LAST DAYS

Nation shall rise against nation, and kingdom against kingdom .... Matt. 24:7

Earthquakes, famines, and pestilences .... Matt. 24:7

Men shall run to and fro .... Dan. 12:4

Knowledge shall be increased .... Dan. 12:4

Wars and rumors of wars .... Matt. 24:6

Evil men...shall wax worse and worse .... 2 Tim. 3:13

False Christs .... Matt. 24:5; Mark 13:22

Falling away from faith .... 1 Tim. 4:1-2

Will not endure sound doctrine .... 2 Tim. 4:2-4

Scoffers who don't care to hear of the Second Coming of Christ .... 2 Pet. 3:3-14

They shall say, Peace and safety .... 1 Thess. 5:1-3

Men walking after their own lusts .... Jude 16-18

Heaping treasures for last days .... James 5:3-6

False preachers .... Matt. 24:11

Perilous times .... 2 Tim. 3:1

disobedient to parents .... 2 Tim. 3:2

Lovers of pleasures more than lovers of God;

Having a form of godliness, but denying the power thereof .... 2 Tim. 3:4-5

X. THE RAPTURE OF THE CHURCH

One of the most unusual events to occur in this world is yet to happen. The Bible talks about a rapture of every Christian alive when the Lord Jesus Christ returns in the air. These Christians will be caught up in the air to meet Him and, instantaneously, they will receive glorified bodies and go to heaven to be with the Lord. To the Christian, this is a wonderful hope.

Only two men, as far as we know, have entered the presence of God in a similar way (without dying), Enoch and Elijah. In both cases the experience of these men typically represents the experience of all Christians living at the time of the rapture. Enoch was "translated" into the presence of God as a result of his relationship with God, a relationship that had been established by faith (Heb. 11:5). So those included in the coming rapture are also included because of their faith in God. In the same way, the coming of Christ to meet his saints in the air will be an indisputable act of God.

A. THE NATURE OF THE RAPTURE. The word "rapture" does not occur in the English Bible but the idea is described specifically in two key passages. The word itself comes from the Latin term *rapere*, meaning "to be caught up." The apostle Paul taught this doctrine in 1 Corinthians 15 and 1 Thessalonians 4. In these chapters he described a day when the dead in Christ will be raised and all who are living and know Jesus Christ as their personal Savior will be changed and will meet Christ in the air. This will mark the close of the present dispensation.

The rapture is a future event in which Christ returns for His own, for He promised, "I will come again" (John 14:1-3). The rapture is not His coming at death to take Christians to Heaven. Rather, Christ will descend toward earth. "Then we which are alive and remain shall be caught up together with them in the clouds, to meet the Lord in the air" (1 Thess. 4:17). At this meeting in the air, we will be transformed and given glorified bodies. Paul describes this event: "We shall all be changed, in a moment, in the twinkling of an eye" (1 Cor. 15:51-52). All the dead in Christ will be resurrected just prior to the time of the rapture (1 Thess. 4:16). They, too, will receive glorified and incorruptible bodies (1 Cor. 15:52).

Not all Christians are completely agreed concerning the details of the rapture. Differences in views generally relate to the number, nature and time of the rapture. While most agree there is only one rapture, some suggest perhaps a series of raptures. Also, Christians disagree as to who is included in the rapture and when the rapture will occur in relation to the Great Tribulation. According to Pentecost,

> The present age, in respect to the true church, terminates with the translation of the church into the Lord's presence. The doctrine of the translation of the church is one of the major considerations of the Eschatology of the New Testament (John 14:1-3; 2 Thess. 2:1; 1 Thess. 4:13-18; 1 Cor. 1:8; 15:51-52; Phil. 3:20-31; 2 Cor. 5:1-9). It is one of the questions on which Bible students are most in disagreement at the present time. Interpreters of the premillennial school are divided into such camps as the partial rapturist, who raises the issues of the subjects of the rapture, and the

pretribulationist, midtribulationist and posttribulationist, who raise the issue of the time of the rapture in relation to the tribulation period.[65]

1. *Partial rapture.* Every indication is that the rapture could occur at any moment and will include every believer. While our faithfulness to Christ and obedience to His Word are very definitely issues which affect the reward we will or will not receive, it is never indicated that backslidden Christians would be in danger of losing any part of their salvation (1 Cor. 3:15). Some groups teach a partial rapture theory that only some Christians will be taken; while sinning or unbaptized Christians are left behind. The reason some accept the partial rapture theory is their belief that sin or disobedience in the Christian's life makes them unfit to go with Christ, or they must be punished in the Tribulation period. Explaining this view, Waugh wrote,

> But there are not a few—some of them deep and prayerful students of the Scriptures—who believe that only a prepared and *expectant section* of believers will then be translated. They believe that a clear inference from Luke xxi. 36 is that those Christians who do *not* "watch" will *not* "escape all these things that shall come to pass," and will *not* be accounted worthy "to stand before the Son of Man." They gather from such passages as Phil. Iii. 20, Titus ii. 13; 2 Tim. Iv. 8, Heb. Ix. 28, that those only will be taken who "wait," "look for," and "have loved His appearing."[66]

One of the chief problems with this view is that it necessarily denies part of the value in the death of Christ. According to the partial rapturist, good works of a Christian give him a standing before God. But the proper meaning of redemption is that Christ has paid the complete price for every sin. Since every sin has been punished, God cannot legally punish sinning Christians again by omitting them in the rapture. If a person is in Christ, he will be caught up with Christ in the air.

In addition to the above-noted Scriptures, partial rapturists appeal to other passages to prove their view (Matt. 25:1-13; Eph. 2:21-22; 5:27, 30; 1 Cor. 15:23). However, when these Scriptures are understood in their context, it is difficult to recognize a partial rapture. After studying the principle proof texts of the partial rapturist, Dawson concluded, "These Scriptures (and many others might be cited in addition) clearly show that every member of the Church, which is His Body, every truly born again person, will be raptured at our Lord's return."[67]

Gundry summarizes the major arguments against a partial rapture view.

> (1) Exhortations to watch, which contrast true believers and false professors, are made to refer instead to mature and immature believers. But "watching" in the NT perspective characterizes *all* true Christians. (2) Partial rapturism rests on legalism by regarding the rapture as a reward rather than the inheritance by faith of all true believers. (3) The distinction between children in their minority and adult sons (Gal. 3:23-4:7) contrasts saints under the old covenant and saints under the new covenant, not immature and mature saints of the present age. (4) By dividing the body of Christ, partial rapturism does not take account of the "we all" in 1 Corinthians 15:51, "the

dead in Christ" of 1 Thessalonians 4:16, or the identity of those translated with those who "believe that Jesus died and rose again" (1 Thess. 4:14). (5) in viewing the tribulation period as a time of purgation for living believers who failed to qualify for the rapture, partial rapturism logically demands a purgatory for deceased believers who died in a state of Christian immaturity.[68]

Pentecost, like Gundry, opposes the partial rapture, but adds additional arguments. Pentecost notes the partial rapture position rests on the following "misunderstandings of the doctrine of the Word."

1. The partial rapturist position is based on a misunderstanding of the value of the death of Christ as it frees the sinner from condemnation and renders him acceptable to God. . . .
2. The partial rapturist must deny the New Testament teaching on the unity of the body of Christ. . . .
3. The partial rapturist must deny the completeness of the resurrection of the believers at the translation. . . .
4. The partial rapturist confuses the Scriptural teaching on rewards. . . .
5. The partial rapturist confuses the distinction between law and grace. . . .
6. The partial rapturist must deny the distinction between Israel and the church. . . .
7. The partial rapturist must place a portion of the believing church in the tribulation period. This is impossible.[69]

2. *Multiple raptures.* One variation of the partial rapture theory is that all Christians will be raptured at different times in one of several anticipated raptures. Normally it is held that one's degree of spirituality will minimize the duration of one's stay in the Tribulation. This view makes a Protestant purgatory out of the Tribulation. They believe if a person is forced to go through the Tribulation, he will be a better Christian. This view of the Tribulation differs significantly from that taught in the Scriptures. Also, all of the arguments against a partial rapture deny the possibility of a series of partial raptures.

3. *Children at the rapture.* Many of the contemporary films, novels, and fictional accounts concerning the pretribulation rapture suggest not only Christians but also young children will be included in the rapture. The Scriptures, however, speak only specifically concerning those "in Christ" being caught up at the rapture (including both living and dead). The argument that children will be included is based on the silence of Scripture and reasoning concerning the age of accountability. Explaining his view that children are probably included in the rapture, Ritchie writes,

I know of no Scripture in which it is *definitely stated* that little ones will be caught up when the Lord comes, but indirectly there is clear and cumulative evidence that they will be. Matthew 18. 10 reads: "Take heed that ye despise not one of these little ones; for I say unto you that in heaven their angels (spirits—for such I believe to be the correct word here) do always behold the face of My Father which is in heaven." The reason is given in the following verse: "For the Son of Man is come to save that which was lost." You will observe it does not say, as in Luke 19. 10, "The Son of Man is come to *seek and to save* that which was lost." Little children do not require seeking, for they have not actively strayed, but *they require saving*, and this is accomplished by the atoning work of the cross. As a result there is the very definite assurance from our Lord Himself, "Even so, it is not the will of your Father in heaven that one of these little ones should perish" (Ver. 14). The words of King David regarding his dead child in 2 Samuel 12. 23: "I shall go to him, but he shall not return to me" are conclusive, that David confidently expected to be where his child was. I believe therefore that all children of irresponsible years are saved on account of Christ's sacrificial work and as part of "they that are Christ's," will be raised at the first resurrection (1 Cor. 15. 23).[70]

B. The Time of the Rapture. Good men have studied the prophetic Scriptures and arrived at different conclusions concerning when the rapture occurs in relation to the Great Tribulation. Some claim the rapture occurs after the Tribulation is over because the church is promised tribulation on earth (John 16:1-2; Rev. 12:12). This view is known as post-tribulationalism, although it is also sometimes referred to as covenant or historic premillennialism. Others claim that Christians will pass through the first half of the Tribulation, but be raptured prior to the last three and a half years. This view is known as midtribulationalism. A third view holds to a pretribulation rapture, claiming that there are several biblical arguments suggesting the rapture comes just before the beginning of the Great Tribulation.

Most of the debate over the rapture in premillennial circles today exists between the posttribulation and pretribulation positions. (Unfortunately, this debate has often degenerated into a series of unjustified and sometimes slanderous charges against the other side.) All three positions propose several arguments to justify their position and question the conclusions of the other views. Contrasting the basic statements of the pretribulation and posttribulation views, Ryrie has prepared the following chart.[71]

1. *Pos-tribulation rapture.* Posttribulationism is that view which anticipates the church will endure the Great Tribulation and be raptured at its conclusion. The rapture and Second Coming of Christ are viewed as one and the same. According to Reese,

The Church of Christ will not be removed from the earth until the Advent of Christ at the very end of the present Age: the Rapture and the Appearing take place at the same crisis; hence Christians of that generation will be exposed to the final affliction under Antichrist.[72]

	Pretribulationism			Posttribulationism
1.	Rapture occurs before the Tribulation.		1.	Rapture occurs after the Tribulation.
2.	Church experiences Revelation 3:10 before the Tribulation.		2.	Church experiences Revelation 3:10 at the end of Tribulation.
3.	Day of the Lord begins with the Tribulation.		3.	Day of the Lord begins at the close of Tribulation.
4.	1 Thessalonians 5:2-3 occurs at beginning of the Tribulation.		4.	1 Thessalonians 5:2-3 occurs near end of Tribulation.
5.	144,000 redeemed at start of Tribulation.		5.	144,000 redeemed at conclusion of Tribulation.
6.	Rapture and second coming separated by 7 years.		6.	Rapture and second coming are a single event.
7.	Living Israelites judged at second coming.		7.	No such judgment.
8.	Living Gentiles judged at second coming.		8.	Living Gentiles judged after millennium.
9.	Parents of Millennial population come from survivors of judgments on living Jews and Gentiles.		9.	Parents of Millennial population come from 144,000 Jews.
10.	Believers of church age judged in heaven between rapture and second coming.		10.	Believers of church age judged after second coming or at conclusion of Millennium.

Posttribulation writers suggest several "proofs" for their theory. It should be noted that not every writer holding this view would necessarily hold all the arguments listed below, but the following list identifies the major arguments by leading spokesmen in this theological camp.

a. Historical Argument. One argument advanced by posttribulation writers is that the early church held their view. For this reason they sometimes refer to themselves as historic premillennialists. This argument has both a positive and negative emphasis. The positive argument is stated by Gundry.

Until Augustine in the fourth century, the early Church generally held to the premillenarian understanding of Biblical eschatology. This chiliasm entailed a futuristic interpretation of Daniel's seventieth week, the abomination of desolation, and the personal Antichrist. And it was posttribulational. Neither mentioned nor considered, the possibility of a pretribulational rapture seems never to have occurred to anyone in the early church.[73]

The above quotation implies that pretribulationism was conceived at a late date and was the idea of some individual, rather than that which the apostles handed the early church. MacPherson, an advocate of this position, attributes the Pretribulation position to a young girl in Scotland.

> What I'm about to say may come as a shock, but I have to say it. The common doctrine in certain church circles of a Pre-Trib Rapture is something that was never heard of or held by any group of Christians before the year 1830!
> In my earlier book *The Unbelievable Pre-Trib Origin*, I presented a lot of new evidence I found, while researching in Scotland and England in 1972, that Pre-Trib Rapture teaching began in a personal revelation of a young Scottish lassie had in the spring of 1830.[74]

There are three points that need to be observed in relation to the above criticisms of the pretribulational position. First, it is questionable if anyone can demonstrate that there was a finely developed eschatological position taught by the early church. This means the early church was not clearly pretribulational nor posttribulational. Addressing this subject, Ryrie suggests,

> The early church believed in tribulation, the imminent coming of Christ, and a Millennium to follow. The early church was clearly premillennial but not clearly pretribulational, nor was it clearly posttribulational when measured against today's developed pre- or posttribulation teachings.[75]

Second, the time of the rapture was not an issue with early church fathers. They knew Christ was coming imminently. It was not until a hundred years ago that the rapture became an issue. Someone has said that each generation fights its own theological battles. By this they mean that the church does not deal extensively with an issue until a need arises that demands its attention. Then the issue is debated until it becomes systematically formulated. It seems that at different periods in church history different doctrines have been the central issue. In the two centuries following Christ's appearance on earth, the issue was Christology at the end of the Dark Ages the doctrine of justification was emphasized by Martin Luther; during the eighteenth century sanctification was emphasized by John Wesley. This past century the doctrine of eschatology was one of the focal points of theological discussion, hence it is only natural that the timing of the events has been closely analyzed. Pentecost supports this conclusion,

> It should be observed that each era of church history has been occupied with a particular doctrinal controversy, which has become the object of discussion, revision,

and formulation, until there was general acceptance of what Scripture taught. The entire field of theology was thus formulated through the age. It was not until the last century that the field of Eschatology became a matter to which the mind of the church was turned.[76]

In the third place, the statement that "the common doctrine of a Pre-Trib Rapture began in a personal revelation of a young Scottish lassie" cannot stand unchallenged. If MacPherson was half the historian he claims to be, he would have known better than to make what he apparently knew was an inaccurate statement. In his earlier book he devoted 123 pages (including appendix, notes and bibliography) that maintained that Darby was converted to pretribulationalism from posttribulationalism through a Miss Margaret MacDonald of Port Glasgow, Scotland. He attempts to prove she first discovered "the common doctrine of a Pre-Trib Rapture" through a pentecostal-like trance in 1830 in which "the truth" concerning the rapture was revealed to her. He concludes his argument,

> In light of the evidence I have prayerfully and carefully given in this book relative to the Pre-Trib origin (which origin has been hidden for a long time), I hereby ask all Bible teachers to declare a moratorium on such teaching—at least until they can check this out for themselves. If I am wrong, I ask your forgiveness. And if you are wrong, I have already forgiven you. This then is the story of the unbelievable—yet true—Pre-trib origin.[77]

One does not have to go far to "check this out for themselves." MacPherson includes the record of Miss MacDonald's own testimony of the vision. She speaks of "the fiery trial" of the Christian under "THE WICKED" (i.e., Antichrist) and of "the awful sight of a false Christ" which she apparently later identified as an early Communist leader living at the time. Then MacPherson is forced to admit in the final footnote of his book, "Margaret was actually a Partial Rapturist; she saw a select group caught up before the man of sin of 2 Thessalonians 2 is revealed, with the rest of the believers passing through and being purified in the Great Tribulation."[78] It is sad that many who oppose the pretribulational rapture use this argument. Commenting on Miss MacDonald's statements concerning her vision, Ryrie suggests,

> As for the very young and chronically ill Margaret Macdonald, we can only truthfully label her as a "confused rapturist," with elements of partial rapturism, posttribulationism, perhaps midtribulationism, but never pretribulationism.
> By Darby's own testimony, he claimed his ideas came from the Bible, particularly his understanding of the distinctiveness of the church (in 1826-28), that he believed the rapture would be a considerable time before the second coming (in 1830), and that there would be a parenthesis between the sixty-ninth and seventieth weeks of Daniel (no later than 1833). He seemed to be unsettled about the secret aspect of the rapture as late as the 1840s.[79]

b. Argument against imminency. One cannot read the New Testament and conclude the writers believed in other than an imminent return of Christ. Christ can return at any moment. Christians are exhorted to keep watching for His return (1 Thess. 5:1-8; 2 Pet. 3:8-10) and wait for it (1 Cor. 1:7; 1 Thess. 1:9-10; Titus 2:13). These commands were as meaningful and applicable to the first century as they are today. Even if there are "implied" signs concerning the end time, that does not preclude the belief in the imminent return of Christ. Signs are not absolute measurements of time concerning Christ's return, but relate to general conditions on earth when Christ returns. Imminency means He can come at any time.

Posttribulation writers argue that the early church did not believe in, nor do the Scriptures teach the doctrine of imminency. They claim the biblical injunctions to watch for the return of Christ do not necessarily mean it should be anticipated immediately. Stating this conclusion, Gundry writes,

> The full force of the exhortations to watch for Jesus' return, then, does not require imminence of the Parousia. A tribulational interval no more destroys expectancy than did necessary delays during the apostolic age. A number of exhortations to watch, including the fullest, appear in the immediate context of the posttribulational advent and include the observation of precursive signs during the tribulation. Such signs do not enervate expectancy, they stimulate it. Self-purification in the light of the second coming rests, not on the fear of sudden exposure, but on the certainty of the event and on the knowledge that the conduct of our whole Christian life will be revealed in the light of the divine presence. Concerning NT exhortations to watch, we are led to the conclusion: until tribulational events have taken place, New Testament expectancy does not mean to look for the return of the Lord as a present possibility, but to look forward to His return after the events of the tribulation.[80]

The argument against the imminent return of Christ is normally based on a number of signs which had to be accomplished before Christ could return. It is also argued that certain events such as the fall of Jerusalem, or the death of Peter had to happen before Jesus could return; therefore, He could not have returned before these things happened and was not expected by the church prior to these events. Also, the need to accomplish the Great Commission is presented as an argument against imminency. MacPherson lists the following twelve:

1. The Great Commission fulfillment implies a long period of time.
2. Seed growth in Matthew 13 a time-consuming process.
3. Paul expecting death, not Rapture, in II Timothy 4:6-8.
4. Jesus predicted Peter's martyrdom in John 21:18-19.
5. Matthew 24 signs must come first.
6. Big interval between Christ's ascension and return: Jewish dispersion into "all nations" (Luke 21); "man travelling into a far country," "after a long time the lord of those servants cometh" (Matt. 25).
7. Apostasy of last days takes time to develop.

8. Bridegroom tarried in parable of virgins.
9. Pastoral epistles teach Church's continuing ministry, which involves time.
10. Paul says Christ's coming is not imminent (II Thess. 2:1-3), for apostasy and Antichrist must come first.
11. View of seven phases of Church history (seven churches of Revelation) involves big lapse of time and imminence difficulties for Pre-Tribs; could Christ have come before the last phase?
   Exhortations to watch and be ready tied so-called second stage in Matthew 24 and 25, I Corinthians 1:7, Colossians 3:4, I Thessalonians 3:13, II Thessalonians 1:7-10, I Peter 1:13, I Peter 4:13, and I John 2:28.[81]

At first glance, the arguments appear conclusive, but in light of the biblical teaching on imminence, they require closer evaluation. When this is done, the above list reveals at least seven fundamental errors in interpretation. First, MacPherson fails to interpret the Scriptures in the context of revelation. Conservative scholars are generally agreed the prophecy concerning Peter's martyrdom was recorded by John perhaps as much as thirty years after Peter was killed. How this could discourage the early Christians who first read this Gospel from believing in the imminent return of Christ is difficult to comprehend. The context in which this prophecy exists suggests some readers may have believed Christ would return even before the death of the aging apostle John (John 21:23).

A second hermeneutical problem apparent in the above list is evident in the failure to interpret a verse within its biblical context. This is particularly evident in the claim that Paul anticipated death, not rapture. It was Paul who most fully developed the doctrine of an imminent rapture of the church (1 Cor. 15; 1 Thess. 4). If toward the end of his life, he spoke of death as a very real possibility, it does not necessarily mean he was denying the doctrine of imminency. Perhaps he was merely recognizing the reality of the situation he faced at that time. Commenting on the statement in question, Stott notes,

> The apostle uses two vivid figures of speech to portray his coming death, one taken from the language of sacrifice and the other (probably) of boats. First, 'I am already on the point of being sacrificed.' Or 'Already my life is being poured out on the altar' (NEB). He likens his life to a libation or drink offering. So imminent does he believe his martyrdom to be that he speaks of the sacrifice as having already begun. He goes on: 'the time of my departure has come.' 'Departure' (*analysis*) seems to have become a regular word for death, but we need not necessarily conclude from this that its metaphorical origin had been entirely forgotten. It means 'loosing' and could be used either of striking a tent (which Lock favours, because of the soldier's 'I have fought a good fight' in the following verse) or of 'release from shackles' (which Simpson mentions), or of untying a boat from its moorings. The last is certainly the most picturesque of the three possibilities. The two images then to some extent correspond, for the end of this life (outpoured as a libation) is the beginning of another (putting out to sea). Already the anchor is weighed, the ropes are slipped, and the boat is about to set sail for another shore.[82]

Thirdly, MacPherson assumes certain conclusions, that the early church would not have assumed. The fulfillment of the Great Commission does not necessarily imply a long time. Within their generation the early Christians were accused of having turned the world upside down (Acts 17:8). Paul himself claimed the gospel had been preached "in all the world" during his lifetime (Col. 1:5-6). While MacPherson might believe apostasy takes time to develop, that was neither the experience or conviction of the early church. Even before the gospel was preached outside the city limits of Jerusalem, the church had to deal with the problem of deterioration (Acts 5:1-11). The whole emphasis of the biblical teaching concerning apostasy is that its growth is rapid (cf. 2 John 8; Jude; Gal. 3:1-5).

A fourth problem with the above list is its dependence upon parables. MacPherson makes parables teach more than what they may have been intended to teach. Jesus did not teach the parables of the ten virgins to convince His listeners that the bridegroom intends to be late arriving, but to watch because he might come at any moment. Also, Jesus did not teach the parable of the sower to discuss the time it takes for germination, but to teach the certainty of the harvest or judgment. Commenting on the interpretation of parables, Ramm suggests,

> *Determine the one central truth the parable is attempting to teach.* This might be called the golden rule of parabolic interpretation for practically all writers on the subject mention it with stress. "The typical parable presents one single point of comparison," writes Dodd. "The details are not intended to have independent significance." Others have put the rule this way: *Don't make a parable walk on all fours.*[83]

Posttribulationalists tend to ignore the distinction between the rapture and Second Coming. This is evident in arguments 5, 10 and 12 in the above list. As the biblical distinction between the rapture and revelation of Christ is a major argument for the pretribulational view, this distinction will be examined more closely at that point.

A sixth evident error in MacPherson's list is his misunderstanding of the doctrine of imminency and its application to the Christian life. There can be no question that imminency was taught in Scripture and believed by the early church. But no one who properly understood that Christ could return at any moment ever went to the mountains dressed in white sheets to wait for the rapture. Rather, Christians were urged to work hard that they might be found working when he returned. As Pentecost rightly observes,

> The doctrine of imminency is taught in Scripture in such passages as John 14:2-3; 1 Corinthians 1:7; Philippians 3:20-21; 1 Thessalonians 1:9-10; 4:16-17; 5:5-9; Titus 2:13; James 5:8-9; Revelation 3:10; 22:17-22. . . . the early church held to the doctrine of imminency.[84]

When properly understood, none of the objections listed by MacPherson are effective, except his eleventh argument involving the typical interpretation of the seven churches. However, this is not an argument, but an illustration and a weak foundation upon which to erect a denial of a clearly taught biblical doctrine. This typical interpretation regarding Revelation 2-3 has become popular only within this century and not many theologians would dream of building a theology or any part of it upon an illustration.

c. Church in Tribulation. Another argument of the post-tribulationalist is that the church will endure the Great Tribulation. Verses are cited such as Job 15:17-19; John 16:1-2, 33; Acts 8:1-4; Romans 12:12 noting that tribulation is promised to the Christian, not escape from tribulation. Those holding this position argue that this tribulation is simply the trials experienced over the years by Christians, so they equate suffering with "the Great Tribulation." Others agree there is a coming tribulation and that Christians will suffer during this period, but they are not subject to the wrath of God. This appears to be the majority belief of contemporary posttribulational teachers. Gundry states,

> It is not a point of disagreement whether the Church will ever suffer God's retributive wrath. She will not (John 3:36; 5:24: Rom. 5:9; 8:1; Eph. 2:3; 5:6; 1 Thess. 1:10; 5:9). And there are clear indications in the book of Revelation that the bowls of divine wrath will not touch saints, indications in addition to the theological necessity that God's wrath not touch a saved person. . . .
>
> . . . .
>
> As now, the Church will suffer persecution during the tribulation, but no saint can suffer divine wrath.[85]

Similarly, Harold Ockenga argues the church will endure the Tribulation. Further, he recognizes the nature of this argument must deny the identification of the Tribulation with the wrath of God, noting,

> The church will endure the wrath of men, but will not suffer the wrath of God. This distinction which has been of great help to me is generally overlooked by pretribulationalists. . . . Pretribulation rapturists identify the tribulation with the wrath of God. If this cannot be disproven, we must believe that the church will be taken out of the world before the tribulation, for there is no condemnation to them which are in Christ Jesus.[86]

This line of argumentation fails to recognize at least three distinctions between the use and interpretation of the word "tribulation" and "the Great Tribulation" as described in Scripture. First is the argument of intention and fulfillment. When the Great Tribulation and the suffering of saints is confused, it logically demands that every generation experience its own great tribulation. Commenting on John 16:33, Mauro notes, "If the Lord meant that the *Great Tribulation* was the portion of His saints, then there would needs be about three "great tribulations" every century—upwards of fifty to the present time—in order to meet the requirements of the case."[87] The second argument deals with the use of the word "tribulation" in Scripture. Pentecost explains,

Further, it must be noticed that the term *tribulation* is used in several different ways in Scripture. It is used in a non-technical, non-eschatological sense in reference to any time of suffering or testing into which one goes. It is so used in Matthew 13:2; Mark 4:17; John 16:33; Romans 5:3; 12:12; 2 Corinthians 1:4; 2 Thessalonians 1:4; Revelation 1:9. It is used in its technical or eschatological sense in reference to the whole period of the seven years of tribulation, as in Revelation 2:22 or Matthew 24:29. It is also used in reference to the last half of this seven year period, as in Matthew 24:21. When the word *tribulation* is used in reference to the church, as in John 16:33, it is used in a non-technical sense, in which the church is promised an age-long opposition from the god of this age, but it is not teaching that the church will be brought into the period technically known as the tribulation. Otherwise one would have to teach that the tribulation has already existed for over nineteen hundred years.[88]

The third argument notes that the Great Tribulation is everywhere in Scripture discussed as largely Jewish in character and characterized not by the wrath of men so much as by the wrath of God. According to Ironside,

> It will help a great deal if we see at the very beginning that the Great Tribulation is the time of Jacob's trouble, not the time of the Church's trouble. It cannot begin until after that parenthetic period that comes in between Daniel's sixty-ninth and seventieth weeks, for during all this age God makes no distinction between Jew and Gentile. It will be after the Church is taken out of this scene that He will recognize Israel again as a nation in special covenant relationship with Himself. Then their time of final trial will begin.[89]

Further summarizing the character of the Great Tribulation, Thiessen notes,

> We know, of course, that believers must through "much tribulation enter into the kingdom of God" (Acts 14:22, A.V.); but there is besides this common experience of Christians a future *period* of tribulation. In Dan. 12:1 it is spoken of as "A time of trouble, such as never was since there was a nation even to that time"; in Matt. 24:21-29 it is described as a "great tribulation"; Luke 21:34-36 refers to it as "that day," depicted in the preceding part of the chapter; Rev. 3:10 speaks of it as "the hour of trial, that hour which is come upon the whole world, to try them that dwell upon the earth;" and in Rev. 7:14 we read of a great multitude who had come "out of the great tribulation." In the Old Testament it is referred to as the "day of Jacob's trouble" (Jer. 30:4-7) and the time of God's indignation with the inhabitants of the earth (Isa. 24:17-21; 26:20, 21; 31:1-3; Zech. 14:1-3). That the Tribulation period will come between the two phases of Christ's coming appears from a study of the whole program of the future. Note particularly that Matt. 24:29 declares that it will close with Christ's return in glory, i.e., with His Revelation.[90]

d. Daniel. 9:24-27. Some post-tribulationalists hold to an historic fulfillment of Daniel 9:24-27 including the seventieth week of that prophecy. They believe the seventy weeks are a continuous, successive, unbroken period of years that ends with the death of Stephen or the destruction of Jerusalem. Typical of this interpretation, Rose writes,

> If there were "gaps" and "intermissions" the prophecy would be vague, misleading, and deceptive. . . . The "62 weeks" joined immediately onto the "7 weeks", and their combined "69 weeks" reached "UNTO MESSIAH". Beyond His birth, but not to his "triumphal entry;" only "UNTO" His public anointing and introduction. There was no "gap" between the "69th, and the 70" weeks." Adam Clarke ably remarks: "The 'one week' of the prophetic 'seventy weeks' began with John the Baptist; from his first public preaching the kingdom of God, the gospel dispensation commenced. These seven years, added to the 483 years, completes the 490 years . . . so that the whole of the prophecy from the times and corresponding events, has been fulfilled to the very letter. . . .

> . . . .
> All the evidence of the New Testament, and of Christian experience agree with the greatest teachers of the Christian church that the seventieth week of Daniel's prophecy has all been fulfilled more than 1900 years ago. This leaves no future seventieth seek yet to be fulfilled in "the great tribulation after the rapture.[91]

It should be here noted that not all posttribulationalists hold to an historic fulfillment of Daniel's seventieth week. In a rebuttal of the posttribulationism of J. Barton Payne, Gundry emphasizes the futurity of the seventieth week, noting in part,

> We cannot spiritualize the phrase "your people" (v. 24) into a spiritual Israel inclusive of the Gentiles without doing violence to the plain sense of the passage. For example, the destruction of Jerusalem, spoken of prominently in the prophecy, deals with Israel the *nation*. And yet, since in the seventy weeks the goals listed in verse twenty-four were to be accomplished, the seventy weeks cannot have entirely elapsed, for the finishing of Israel's transgression, the purging of her iniquity, and the bringing in of her everlasting righteousness have not reached completion. Paul writes of these as still in the future for Israel (Rom. 11:25-27).[92]

There are five major schools of interpretation surrounding the issue of Daniel's seventieth week. Pretribulationalists are futurists in interpreting this passage. Walvoord summarizes the other views.

> In opposition to the futuristic interpretation, at least four other views have been advanced: (1) the liberal view that the seventieth seven is fulfilled in events following the Maccabean persecution just as the preceding sixty-nine sevens were; (2) the view of Jewish scholars that the seventieth week is fulfilled in the destruction of Jerusalem in A.D. 70; (3) the view that the seventieth week of Daniel is an indefinite period

beginning with Christ but extending to the end, often held by amillennarians such as Young and Leupold; (4) that the seventieth seven is seven literal years beginning with the public ministry of Christ and ending about three and a half years after His death.[93]

The futurist interpretation views a gap of some time between the sixty-ninth and seventieth week. It is during the gap that this present dispensation exists. At some future point, that seventieth week will begin. Most futurists hold that the nature of the Tribulation (focused on regathered Israel) demands that the seventieth week not begin prior to the rapture of the church. Gundry summarizes the view of the futurists.

> Although the lack of certainty regarding the exact dates of our Lord's ministry demands some reserve, the futuristic view rests on a more exact chronology, best and fully set forth in Sir Robert Anderson's *The Coming Prince*. Very briefly, it is common ground that the seventy sevens are weeks of years. Anderson reckons a year at 360 days from the equation of 1,260 days with forty-two months (Rev. 12:6, 7, 13, 14; 13:4-7), from the equation of five months with 150 days (Gen. 7:11; 8:4; 7:24; 8:3), and from other evidence of unequal value. By calculating from the only known decree to rebuild the *city* of Jerusalem (Neh. 1:1-11; 2:1-8) sixty-nine weeks of seven 360-day years, we are brought to Palm Sunday, the only time Jesus was publicly acclaimed King, Prince, and Messiah and shortly after which He was cut off . . . .
>
> The accuracy is so remarkable that the objections seem paltry by comparison. The best answer to the objections is the failure of the historical view to provide an exact and accurate chronology and the resultant substitution of chronologies dealing in wide approximations, with the result that the seventy weeks of years become half-literal and half-symbolic. The futuristic view can be established apart from Anderson's calculations, but they endow the futurist view with a chronology far superior to chronologies under the historical view.[94]

e. The Doctrine of Resurrection. Probably the strongest argument presented by posttribulationalists is the doctrine of resurrection. According to this argument, the rapture must be posttribulational because the resurrection occurs after the Tribulation. The importance of this argument is seen in various statements made by posttribulation writers. According to MacPherson,

> Clearly the resurrection of the holy dead takes place at the rapture of the Church (1 Thes. 4:16). Therefore, "wheresoever the resurrection is, there will be the Rapture also." Upon examination of passages that speak of the resurrection of the holy dead, which is the first resurrection (Rev. 20:5-6), we find that this first resurrection is associated with the coming of the Lord (Isa. 26:19), the conversion of Israel (Rom. 11:15), the inauguration of the Kingdom (Luke 14:14-15; Rev. 20:4-6), the giving of rewards (Rev. 11:15-16), the Great Tribulation coming before it (Dan. 12:1-3).[95]

Ladd views this argument as the only one based upon an explicit statement of Scripture, explaining,

> With the exception of one passage, the author will grant that the Scripture nowhere explicitly states that the Church will go through the Great Tribulation. God's people are seen in the Tribulation, but they are not called the Church but the elect or the saints. Nor does the Word explicitly place the Rapture at the end of the Tribulation. Most of the references to these final events lack chronological indications. . . . However, in one passage, Revelation 20, the Resurrection is placed at the return of Christ in Glory. This is more than an inference.[96]

Similarly, Gundry also stresses the importance of this argument.

> The resurrection of the dead in Christ will immediately precede the rapture (1 Thess. 4:16-18). Therefore, if Scripture places the resurrection of saints in general after the tribulation and does not specifically put the resurrection of deceased members of the Church before the tribulation, it is natural to understand that the deceased of the Church will be raised after the tribulation. Such a resurrection would of course draw the translation of living members of the Church and the rapture of the whole Church into a posttribulational orbit.[97]

This argument is based on the conclusion that the resurrection of Revelation 20:5-6, which is there called "the first resurrection," is the same resurrection referred to in 1 Thessalonians 4:16. Probably the most systematic of the presentations of this argument is that of Reese. Summarizing this position, Stanton writes,

> Reese's argument takes on the form of a syllogism, the major premises being (1) that the Old Testament Scriptures prove that the resurrection of Old Testament saints is at the revelation of Christ, just prior to the millennial kingdom; the minor premise being (2) that all Darbyists agree that the resurrection of the Church synchronizes with the resurrection of Israel; hence, the conclusion is drawn that (3) the resurrection of the Church sets the time of the rapture as posttribulational.[98]

The major weakness of this argument is the equating of "the first resurrection" (Rev. 20:5-6) or the resurrection of the Old Testament saints with that resurrection occurring at the rapture. The Scriptures identify at least four distinct resurrections, the first chronologically being the resurrection of Christ (Matt. 28:1-7). The expression "first resurrection" can therefore be understood only within the immediate context of the passage since Christ's resurrection was first. The resurrection there mentioned is "first" in that it comes one thousand years prior to the fourth and final resurrection, but it is also "third" in that it follows the resurrection of Christ and the resurrection of saints that accompany the rapture. Walvoord, for instance, suggests,

The Old Testament saints are never described by the phrase "in Christ." The fact that the "voice of the archangel"—Israel's defender— is heard at the rapture is not conclusive proof that Israel is raised at that time. The tendency of followers of Darby to spiritualize the resurrection of Daniel 12:1-2 as merely the restoration of Israel, thereby refuting its posttribulationism, is to forsake literal interpretation to gain a point, a rather costly concession for premillenarians who build upon literal interpretation of prophecy. The best answer to Reese and Ladd is to concede the point that the resurrection of Old Testament saints is after the Tribulation, but to divorce it completely from the translation and resurrection of the church. Reese's carefully built argument then proves only that Darby was hasty in claiming the resurrection of the Old Testament saints at the time of the translation of the church. If the translation of the church is a different event entirely, Reese proves nothing by his argument.[99]

Finally, perhaps the word "first" did not mean "first in time" but "first in kind," i.e., the resurrection was of God's people (whether before or after the Tribulation). The "second of a different kind," involved the unsaved.

f. Parable of the wheat and the tares. An additional argument based upon the parable of the wheat and the tares is sometimes used to defend the posttribulational cause. They suggest that Christ spoke of the wheat and the tares together "until the harvest" (Matt. 13:30) and suggest a general judgment at the end of the age. Commenting on this text, Brown writes,

> The harvest is the end of the world . . . the period of Christ's second coming, and of the judicial separation of the righteous and the wicked. Till then, no attempt is to be made to effect such separation. But to stretch this so far as to justify allowing openly scandalous persons to remain in the communion of the Church, is to wrest the teaching of this parable to other than its proper design, and to go in the teeth of apostolic injunctions (1 Cor. v).[100]

It must be remembered, however, that the purpose of the kingdom parables in Matthew 13 is not to record the history of the church, but rather the history of the kingdom in mystery form, i.e., Christendom. Wiersbe emphasizes this point.

> In this series of parables, Jesus explained the course of the Gospel in the world. If Israel had received Him as King, the blessings would have flowed out from Jerusalem to the ends of the earth. But the nation rejected Him, and God had to institute a new program on earth. During this present age, "the kingdom of heaven" is a mixture of true and false, good and bad, as pictured in these parables. It is "Christendom," professing allegiance to the King, and yet containing much that is contrary to the principles of the King.[101]

g. Fruit. Perhaps the weakest argument for any theological position is that based upon fruit, i.e., the apparent results of a doctrinal teaching. MacPherson makes extensive use of this argument suggesting those holding a pretribulational view of the rapture were at least in part responsible for the deaths of "tens of thousands, maybe millions, of Chinese Christians," the persecution of other Christians, church splits, raising funds under false pretenses, and other items.[102]   One has a great deal of difficulty recognizing a direct relationship between eschatology and some of the above-mentioned results. Further, in cases where a relationship might exist, it is difficult to believe that only those holding to a pretribulation rapture are capable of criticizing (or, as MacPherson suggests, "persecuting") other Christians, splitting churches or raising money under false pretenses. The real weakness of this argument is seen in W. B. Riley's observations concerning pretribulational Christian workers.

> There is one thing that will be denied, even our opponents themselves being witnesses, namely, that the men that held this hope, have so far discharged their obligations to God as to have promoted the interests of His church by personal service, by money sacrificed, by missionary zeal, by intelligent counsel, by tireless work, so as not to have been surpassed by any people that have ever named His name, or joined their fortunes to His cause.[103]

2. *Midtribulation rapture.* A second position known as midtribulationalism teaches that the rapture occurs about halfway through the Tribulation. They tend to argue that only the last half of that seven-year period is characterized by the wrath of God and, therefore, sometimes speak of the pretribulational (i.e., before the last half of the Tribulation, day of wrath) rapture. Gundry summarizes this position.

> Midtribulationists place the rapture at the halfway mark in Daniel's seventieth week. To them the tribulation comprises only the latter three and one-half years. The seventh trumpet will sound in the middle of the week. This will be the "last trumpet," at which our translation and the resurrection of the dead in Christ will take place. At that time "the mystery of God" (Rev. 10:7), which is taken to be the Church, will reach completion.   The resurrection and matching up of the two witnesses in Revelation 11 become symbolic of the rapture.[104]

Midtribulationalism tends to be the middle ground in the rapture debate. As a result, dissatisfied posttribulationalists and pretribulationalists tend to drift toward this position. As Walvoord observes,

> Midtribulationalism is, therefore, a mediate view between post-tribulationism and pretribulationism. . . . It has also provided a place for certain prophecies to be fulfilled before the translation of the church instead of afterward, and at the same time is able to claim the promises of comfort and blessing which seem to be denied by the posttribulationists who take the church through the entire period.[105]

While midtribulationalists cite several arguments to support this position, its conclusions rest primarily on two unique interpretations. First, they tend to distinguish between the two halves of the Tribulation limiting the wrath of God to the latter half. Secondly, they tend to identify the trumpet which is to sound at the rapture with the seventh trumpet sounded by an angel in Revelation 11:15.

a. Tribulation and wrath. The argument that only half of Daniel's seventieth week is a day of wrath or time of Great Tribulation is based in part upon the division of that week into two equal parts (Dan. 9:27) and their belief that the latter half of that week was what Jesus referred to as "great tribulation" (Matt. 24:21). Expressing the perceived differing natures of these two parts, Harrison writes,

> The first half of the week, or period of seven years, was a " sweet" anticipation to John, as it is to them; under treaty protection, they will be "sitting pretty," as we say. But the second half—"bitter" indeed: the treaty is broken; the storm breaks; they experience the wrath of the Antichrist on the one hand and of God on the other. This is their "day of trouble." It is the Great Tribulation.[106]

Harrison's description that the first half of the tribulation is "sweet" is difficult to believe in light of biblical revelation concerning this period. While admittedly the latter half will be worse than the former, the first three and a half years are also times in which the earth is subjected to wrath. Commenting on the full seven years, Pentecost notes,

> When this period is anticipated in the Scriptures, it is always dealt with as a unit, as far as its character is concerned, even though divided as to time elements and the degree of the intensity of wrath poured out. The unity of the seventieth week of Daniel in the program for Israel prevents us from dividing it into two separate parts. It is hard to understand how a writer can hold that all the events poured out under the seals and trumpets will be viewed as "sweet" to anyone undergoing those rigorous judgments. Only by spiritualization can this view be held.[107]

b. The last trumpet. It is imperative that the midtribulationist trumpet be sounded by an angel in Revelation 11:15. Harrison adheres so strongly to this interpretation that he suggests it alone is consistent with biblical revelation. Commenting on the idea of a rapture at Revelation 4:1, he writes,

> To place the rapture here is to disprove the unity of Scripture. St. Paul, by inspiration of the Spirit, definitely places the Resurrection and the Rapture of the saints through the coming of Christ "at the last trumpet" (1 Cor. 15:51, 52). This is a specific locating of the event. Unquestionably the Holy Spirit revealed the fact and inspired the recording of it. How dare we locate it otherwise?
> We do well to challenge ourselves as expositors of the Holy Writ: Can we postulate the Rapture at any other place than that given by and through the Apostle Paul and claim to maintain the integrity of God's Word?

Assuredly not. Granted this, the only question is one of interpretation: What is meant by "the last trumpet"? "Last" can mean but one of two things: last in point of time, or last in point of sequence.[108]

Contrary to Harrison's conclusions, to agree that the word "last" refers to the last of a sequence does not necessarily mean that trumpet must be that of Revelation 11:15. In fact, the interpretation proposed by the midtribulationalists is only one of the possible "last trumpets." According to Strombeck,

> From the above it is certain that "the last trump" is the trump of God and that the Lord Himself descends from heaven with it. In the search for "the last trump" one must, then, be guided by the fact that it is God's own trumpet, sounded by the Lord Himself. In view of this one would hardly be willing to contend that the last trumpet of God is the last of a series of trumpets blown by the priests of the Aaronic priesthood. They were not in a class with the trumpet of God. Remembering that the angels are only a little higher than man, it is just as contrary to the laws of logic to say that "the last trump," which is God's own trumpet, is the last of a series of trumpets blown by angels. Both men and angels are creatures of God. They cannot sound the trumpet of the Creator. No, the Lord Himself shall descend from heaven with the trump of God.[109]

Some interpreters equate this last trumpet with the final trumpet in a series blown by the priests in the wilderness. This is apparently the view of English and Armerding. Commenting on the last trump of 1 Corinthians 15:52, English writes,

> The significance of the term, "the last trump," in 1 Corinthians 15:52, inasmuch as this sounding is not one of a series of trumpetings, may possibly be that of a rallying call, or an alarm. In Numbers 10 we read of the sounding of trumpets for calling an assembly of the people and for their journeyings. There were specific calls for each of the camps of the Israelites and special calls for the whole congregation. In connection with this, Dr. Carl Armerding has an interesting comment: "The *last trump* would signify that the whole congregation was finally on the move. In a way this may illustrate what we find in 1 Corinthians 15:23, 'Every man in his own order [or rank—*tagmati*]: Christ the firstfruits; afterward they that are Christ's at His coming.' These last are certainly divided into at least two groups: those who have 'fallen asleep,' and those 'who are alive and remain.'

> "'In a moment' and 'in the twinkling of an eye' are expressions," continues Dr. Armerding, "which are used the world around to indicate suddenness and rapidity. The fact that the third phrase 'at the last trump,' is so understood in the same way. If so, it will begin the nature of an alarm, which is the very word used in Numbers 10:5,6 in connection with the 'journeying of the camps.' The quickening and assembling already accomplished (the former by the voice of the Lord, and the latter

by the voice of the archangel - 1 Thes. 4:16) . . . there is only one more thing necessary to set all in motion. It is 'the last trump.' That will be the final note struck on that momentous occasion.[110]

Ironside interprets the concept of the last trumpet within the context of a Roman army coming to a conclusion similar to that of English and Armerding. In his exposition of 1 Corinthians 15, he explains,

> When a Roman camp was about to be broken up, whether in the middle of the night or in the day, a trumpet was sounded. The first blast meant, "Strike tents and prepare to depart." The second meant, "Fall into line," and when what was called "the last trump" sounded it meant, "March away."[111]

3. *Pretribulation Rapture.* The third view of the time of the rapture is that known as pretribulationalism. According to this view, all those who have died "in Christ" will be resurrected and those who are alive and saved at the time of the rapture, will be "caught up" to be with Christ prior to any part of the seventieth week of Daniel. The author believes this to be the correct view in the light of the biblical teaching on the subject. The above-mentioned seven arguments used by posttribulationalists and two arguments used by midtribulationalists have been answered. When properly analyzed these nine arguments point to a pretribulation rapture. Further, there are eight additional arguments suggesting the rapture comes just before the beginning of the Great Tribulation.

a. Hermeneutics. Fundamentally, a pretribulation rapture of the church is consistent with a literal (i.e., historical-grammatical) interpretation of the Scriptures. Emphasizing this point, Pentecost writes,

> Pretribulation rapturism rests essentially on one major premise—the literal method of interpretation of the Scriptures. As a necessary adjunct to this, the pretribulationist believes in a dispensational interpretation of the Word of God. The church and Israel are two distinct groups with whom God has a divine plan. The church is a mystery, unrevealed in the Old Testament. This present mystery age intervenes within the program of God for Israel because of Israel's rejection of the Messiah at His first advent. This mystery program must be completed before God can resume His program with Israel and bring it to completion. These considerations all arise from the literal method of interpretation.[112]

The difference between the hermeneutics of amillennialism and premillennialism is similar to the distinguishing features of a pretribulationalist and post-tribulationalist hermeneutic. Walvoord argues that post-tribulationalists at some point must abandon a literal interpretation to defend their system.

The choice of a weakened tribulation is not an accident, however, but logically necessary to their position. Only by this device can passages picturing the hope of the Lord's return as a comfort and joy be sustained. It is difficult to harmonize a literal interpretation of the tribulation with posttribulationism, though Ladd attempts it. It would weaken not only the promises of comfort but also the imminency and practical application of the doctrine of the Lord's coming. The controversy between pretribulationists and posttribulationists is, in miniature, a replica of the larger controversy of premillennialism and amillennialism as far as principles of interpretation are concerned. This is brought out more in detail in the scriptural revelation of the tribulation itself.[113]

b. Contrast of Rapture and Revelation. The Scriptures appear to make a distinction between the rapture of the church and the revelation of Christ. Admittedly, there are a large

TWO DISTINCT EVENTS	
The Rapture of the Church	The Revelation of Christ
Called *Parousia* (presence)	Called *Epiphaneia* (unveiling)
New Testament Mystery	Old Testament Prophecy
Meeting in the Air (1 Thess. 4:17)	Standing on the Mount of Olives
Comes to His Church	(Zech. 14:4, 9)
Comes as a Bridegroom	Comes to Israel
Involves Translation of the Church	Comes as a King
Comes prior to Day of Wrath (Rev. 3:10)	Involves Establishment of the Kingdom
Lower Creation Unchanged	Appears after the Vials of Wrath
Christ Returns to Heaven Believers Judged	All nature is Changed (Matt. 24:29-30)
(2 Cor. 5:10)	Christ Remains on Earth unbelievers Judged
Message of Comfort (1 Thess. 4:18)	(1 Thess. 5:4)
Church Listens for Sound (Phil. 4:5)	Message of Judgment (1 Thess. 5:4-9)
Hope of the Church	Israel Looks for Signs
Symbolized by the Morning Star Symbolized	Hope of Israel
as a Thief	Symbolized by the Rising Star
i.e. without warning	Symbolized as Thunder and Lightning
Day of Christ	Day of the Lord
Blessed Hope (Tit. 2:15)	Glorious Appearing (Titus 2:15)

number of similarities in these two events that make it easy to confuse them. Both the rapture and the revelation include a resurrection, both feature Christ's coming, and both indicate that believers are gathered by Christ. Still, that which is different is so significant "as to make any harmony of these two events an impossibility."[114] The rapture could occur at any moment

(1 Thess. 4:16), whereas the revelation of Christ will be preceded by various events, some of which are still unfulfilled. At the rapture, Christians will meet Christ in the air (1 Thess. 4:13), but the revelation occurs with Christ descending to the Mount of Olives just outside Jerusalem (Zech. 14:4,9). The changes in nature described at the revelation of Christ (Matt. 25:28-30; 2 Pet. 3:10) are unknown at the rapture of the church. Some of these distinctions are contrasted in the previous chart.

c. The Necessity of an Interval. A careful study of the events the Great Tribulation reveals the necessity of an interval of time to accomplish the things done both in heaven and on earth between the rapture and the revelation of Christ. This argument, while acknowledging the necessity of some interval, does not state specifically how long that interval will be, except that it will be long enough. In an attempt to harmonize the doctrine of imminence with the existence of unfulfilled prophecy, Trotter and Smith suggest,

> Suppose then, my brethren, that there should be an interval between the coming of Christ into the air, where he receives the saints to himself, and his coming onwards to the earth, attended by his saints, to execute judgment; suppose there should be an interval long enough for the accomplishment of all these prophetic events which must be fulfilled ere he does thus come in judgment; suppose that the Jews should return to their own land, the Gentiles be gathered together against them, the Antichrist arise, the great tribulation takes place, the apocalyptic seals be opened, trumpets sounded, and vials poured out; suppose all this should occur *between the taking away of the Church, and the coming of Christ to execute judgment on his congregated foes.* . . .
> . . . .
> But I believe we are not left to the thought of what may be. There are several considerations which satisfy my own soul, not only that there *may be*, but also that there *will be*, such an interval.[115]

Sometimes the idea of an interval is opposed on the basis of the perceived meaning of "to meet" (*apantēsis*) in 1 Thessalonians 4:17. Pentecost addresses this issue,

> The word *apantēsis* (to meet) is used in Acts 28:15 with the idea of "to meet to return with." It is often argued that that same word used in 1 Thessalonians 4:17 has the same idea and therefore the church must be raptured to return instantly and immediately with the Lord to the earth, denying and making impossible any interval between the rapture and the return. Not only does the Greek word not require such an interpretation, but certain events predicted for the church after her translation make such an interpretation impossible. These events are: (1) the judgment seat of Christ, (2) the presentation of the church to Christ, and (3) the marriage of the Lamb.[116]

d. The Restrainer. A major ministry of the Holy Spirit in the world today is that of restraint. Throughout this dispensation, His presence prevents the complete corruption of the world. The work of the Restrainer is minimized to some degree during the Great Tribulation

(2 Thess. 2). The church cannot find themselves in Daniel's seventieth week until the man of sin is revealed. The man of sin cannot be revealed until the Restrainer "be taken out of the way" (2 Thess. 2:7). Because the body of a Christian is the temple of the Holy Spirit during this dispensation (1 Cor. 6:19-20), this implies the prior removal of Christians. While others have suggested the Restrainer may be someone other than the Holy Spirit, Strombeck is right when he concludes,

> As the Holy Spirit is the only member of the Godhead that has been residentially active on earth during these nineteen hundred years He must be the One who restrains and will continue to restrain until He be taken out of the way. Shortly before Jesus left this earth He promised to send the Comforter, i.e., the Holy Spirit, to the earth (John 16:7).
>
> God's Word clearly teaches that the Holy Spirit is the One who counteracts the influence of Satan during the Church age. It is said that "the God of this world [Satan] hath blinded the minds of them which believe not" (2 Cor. 4:4). The Holy Spirit reproves the world of sin, of righteousness, and of judgment (John 16:8). Through this convicting work of the Spirit, men and women are taken out of darkness and brought into the Church.
>
> The Holy Spirit works in and through the Church of Christ. He guides the Church into all truth (John 16:13). He empowers the Church to witness (Acts 1:8). It is through Him that victory is won over spiritual darkness and wickedness. . . . The offensive weapons of this warfare against Satan's rule are "the sword of the Spirit, which is the Word of God," and "praying. . . .
>
> . . . .
>
> The spirit of antichrist, which is by Satan, is overcome by the Holy Spirit in the children of God."[117]

Because of His present ministry in the world, the Holy Spirit and the church must both be removed prior to the Great Tribulation as the man of sin appears very early during that period. Pentecost concludes,

> Thus, this ministry of the Restrainer, which will continue as long as His temple is on the earth and which must cease before the lawless one can be revealed, requires the pretribulation rapture of the church, for Daniel 9:27 reveals that the lawless one will be manifested at the beginning of the week.[118]

Over the years various Christians have identified the restrainer as Satan's own self-restraint, the idea of law and order, the Roman empire, the Apostle Paul, the church at Jerusalem and the succession of Roman emperors. The conclusion that the Restrainer is the Holy Spirit is based not only on a sound exegesis of the text, but also wider theological considerations.

The ultimate decision on the reference to the restrainer goes back to the larger question of who after all is capable of restraining sin to such an extent that the man of sin cannot be revealed until the restraint is removed.   The doctrine of divine providence, the evidence of Scripture that the Spirit characteristically restrains and strives against sin (Gen. 6:3), and the teaching of Scripture that the Spirit is resident in the world and indwelling the church in a special sense in this age combine to point to the Spirit of God as the only adequate answer to the problem of identification of the restrainer. The failure to identify the restrainer as the Holy Spirit is another indication of the inadequate understanding of the doctrine of the Holy Spirit in general and His work in relation to the larger providential movements of God in human history.[119]

e. Uniqueness of the church.   Another key argument for the pretribulation rapture of the church is the biblical distinction of Israel and the church. The church was not announced until after the rejection of the Messiah by Israel.   This does not mean the church was an afterthought, but rather it is a mystery, previously kept hidden from others until this present age (Eph. 3:1-2). God will not renew His program of salvation with Israel again until He has completed His objective with the church. As Pentecost observes,

> The church is manifestly an interruption of God's program for Israel, which was not brought into being until Israel's rejection of the offer of the Kingdom. It must logically follow that this mystery program must itself be brought to a conclusion before God can resume His dealing with the nation Israel, as has been shown previously He will do. The mystery program, which was so distinct in its inception, will certainly be separate at its conclusion. This program must be concluded before God resumes and culminates His program for Israel. This mystery concept of the church makes a pretribulation rapture a necessity.[120]

Israel and the church represent two distinct and separate programs. The rapture is part of God's program for the church, while the revelation of Himself to the nations is part of God's program for Israel. These are different groups and should not be confused (1 Cor. 10:32). While the two may have several similarities, there are, according to Chafer at least twenty-four differences.[121]

THE DIFFERENCES BETWEEN ISRAEL AND THE CHURCH			
		ISRAEL	CHURCH
1.	Extent of Biblical Revelation:	4/5 of the Bible	1/5 of the Bible
2.	Divine Purpose:	Earthly promises in covenants	Heavenly promises in Gospel

		ISRAEL	CHURCH
	THE DIFFERENCES BETWEEN ISRAEL AND THE CHURCH		
		ISRAEL	CHURCH
3.	Seed of Abraham:	Physical seed	Spiritual seed
4.	Birth:	Physical birth that produces relationship	Spiritual birth that produces relationship
5.	Headship:	Abraham	Christ
6.	Covenants:	Abrahamic and all the following covenants	Indirectly related to the Abrahamic and New covenants
7.	Nationality:	One nation	From all nations
8.	Divine Dealing:	National and individual	Individual only
9.	Dispensations:	Seen in all from Abraham	Only in Present dispensation
10.	Ministry:	No missionary activity, no Gospel to preach	A Commission to fulfill
11.	Death of Christ:	Guilty nationally, to be saved by it	Perfectly saved now
12.	The Father:	God was Father to the nation	God is heavenly Father
13.	Christ:	Messiah, Immanuel, King	Savior, Lord, Bridegroom, Head
14.	The Holy Spirit:	Came upon some temporarily	Indwells all
15.	A Governing Principle:	Mosaic law system	Grace system
16.	Divine Enablement:	None	Indwelling Holy Spirit
17.	Two Farewell Discourses:	Olivet Discourse	Upper room Discourse
18.	The Promise of Christ's Return:	In power and glory for judgment	To receive us to Himself
19.	Position:	A servant	Members of a family

THE DIFFERENCES BETWEEN ISRAEL AND THE CHURCH			
		ISRAEL	CHURCH
20.	Christ's Earthly Reign:	Subjects	Co-reigners
21.	Priesthood:	Had a priesthood	Is a priesthood
22.	Marriage:	Unfaithful wife	Bride
23.	Judgments:	Must face judgment	Delivered from all judgment
24.	Position in Eternity:	Spirits of just men made perfect in the New Earth	Church of the first born in the heavens

If we say the church enters the Great Tribulation, we have difficulty harmonizing that idea with the unique relationship that exists between Christ and the church. Christ and His church are vitally and intricately united together. If the church goes through wrath—i.e., the Great Tribulation—then Christ must also pass through wrath a second time. This conclusion minimizes the accomplishments of Christ in His work at Calvary. Pentecost emphasizes this,

Since the church is the body, of which Christ is the Head (Eph. 1:22, 5:23; Col. 1:18), the bride, of which He is the Bridegroom (1 Cor. 11:2; Eph. 5:23), the object of His love (Eph. 5:25), the branch of which He is the Root and Stem (John 15:5), the building, of which He is the Foundation and Cornerstone (1 Cor. 3:9; Eph. 2:19-22), there exists between the believer and the Lord a union and unity. The believer is no longer separated from Him, but is brought into the closest oneness with Him. If the church is in the seventieth week, she is subjected to the wrath, judgment, and indignation which characterizes the period, and because of her oneness with Christ, He, likewise, would be subjected to that same visitation. This is impossible according to 1 John 4:17, for He can not be brought into judgment again. Inasmuch as the church has been perfected and delivered from all judgment (Rom. 8:1; John 5:24; 1 John 4:17), if she is subjected to judgment again the promises of God would be of none effect and the death of Christ would be ineffectual. Who would dare to assert that the death of Christ could fail to accomplish its purpose? While the members may be experimentally imperfect and need experimental cleansing, yet the church, which is His body, has a perfect standing in Christ and could not need such cleansing. The nature of the testing in the seventieth week, as stated in Revelation 3:10, is not to bring the individual to cleansing, but to reveal the degradation and need of the unregenerate heart. The nature of the church prevents such a testing.[122]

f. Promises to the church. A number of biblical promises to the church seem to insure the rapture of the church prior to the Tribulation. Jesus promised the church at Philadelphia that they would not have to endure the Tribulation (Rev. 3:10). Commenting on this promise, Scott writes,

> The wording of the promise is as precise as it is gracious, and effectually disposes of the theory advanced by some, and that to the fear and dread of believers, that the Church or a part thereof shall have to pass through the coming Tribulation to purge itself from its unfaithfulness. No, the guarantee is, "I also will keep *thee* out of the hour of trial," not brought *through* it, or kept *in* it, but entire exemption *from* it. No portion of the Church shall be in the Tribulation.[123]

Similar promises were made to the church at Thessalonica. In his first epistle to that church, Paul spoke of "Jesus, which delivered us from the wrath to come" (1 Thess. 1:10). Commenting on this phrase, Morris suggests,

> *Delivered, rhuomenon,* is really in the present, being as Frame says, a 'timeless participle.' The word means something like 'rescue,' rather than 'redeem' (which is more specific, and signifies 'deliver by the payment of a price'), and puts the emphasis on the greatness of the peril, and the power of Him who delivers. The completeness of the deliverance is underlined by the use of the preposition *ek*: we are delivered right 'out of' the wrath.[124]

This promised rescue is further clarified by Paul in Thessalonians 5:9. According to Walvoord,

> In this passage he is expressly saying that our appointment is to be caught up to be with Christ; the appointment of the world is for the Day of the Lord, the day of wrath. One cannot keep both of these appointments. . . .
>
> . . . .
>
> But you and I who have trusted Him, who have believed in Christ as our personal Savior, are not appointed to that day of wrath. We are appointed unto the day of grace to meet Christ in the air and to be forever with the Lord. This passage of Scripture teaches that Christ is coming for His church *before* the Day of the Lord begins, *before* the day of trouble pictured in Revelation and all through the Bible overtakes world. We are not appointed to wrath, but to salvation.[125]

g. Typology. The argument from typology does not prove a pretribulational rapture, but rather illustrates and perhaps confirms to some the possibility of a so-called "two-stage" return of Christ. Summarizing a typical illustration of the same, Thiessen writes,

> There are some interesting analogies to these two aspects of His coming in the Bible. One is David's return from the other side of Jordan after Absalom and his followers had been defeated, the going forth of Judah to meet him, and their return together to Jerusalem (2 Sam. 19:10-15, 40; 20:1-3). Another is the private revelation

of Joash to the captains and the Carites, and his public revelation to the people a little later (2 Kings 11:4-12). A third is Jesus' walking on the water, Peter's coming to Him, and their return together to the boat (Matt. 14:22-34). And still another is Paul's approach to Rome, the coming of the brethren from Rome to meet him, and their return together to the capital city (Acts 28:15, 16). These incidents do not prove the theory, but they illustrate the two-fold character of Christ's return.[126]

H. THE ABSENCE OF THE CHURCH IN REVELATION 4-18. A final argument sometimes advocated by pretribulational writers is the argument of silence. This argument alone would be meaningless; however, when viewed in the light of the above arguments, it serves to confirm a pretribulation rapture. Summarizing the pretribulation position, Ryrie writes,

> Pretribulationists consider it a significant support to their view that the church is not mentioned once by that designation in Revelation 4-18, chapters that describe the Tribulation on earth. By contrast, the word *church* occurs 19 times in chapters 1, 2, and 3, once in chapter 22, and the phrase "wife of the lamb" once in chapter 21. Yet in chapters 4-18 there is a silence that pretribulationists say indicates that the church will not be present on the earth during the Tribulation years.[127]

This line of argumentation is followed by Strombeck,

> In reading the record of the tribulation, beginning at the sixth chapter of Revelation and closing with the nineteenth, one cannot fail to be impressed with the fact that there is no mention made of the Church being on earth during that time. The record is not only silent about the presence of the Church on earth, it is also silent concerning any cause, or reason, why the Church should then be on the earth. There is complete silence respecting any purpose to be fulfilled thereby. There is also silence regarding any protection for the Church against the torment of those years. This silence, while not in itself a conclusive argument for the pre-tribulation rapture of the Church, adds great weight to the direct arguments already presented. When, however, the Bible supplies irrefutable reasons for this silence, then this silence does become important evidence in favor of the view that the Church will not be on the earth during that time.[128]

XI. THE GREAT TRIBULATION

In no other period of time in the past or future history of the world will there be so much suffering and universal destruction as in the last half of the seven years called the Great Tribulation. This period of time will unleash more torture and misery than occurred during the Second World War that ended with an atomic holocaust. Most of the final book of the New Testament is devoted to recounting the events of those years. Portions of Daniel, Isaiah, Jeremiah, and Ezekiel also speak to the events. Among Christians, even non-Christians, great interest exists in what will happen to the world during the Great Tribulation. Tim LaHaye and Jerry Jenkins' *Left Behind* series of novels witnesses to this fact.

God still has a future for Israel. There is coming a period of about seven years when Israel will once again be the chief focus of God's activity (Dan. 9:27). Unfortunately, much of that "week" will be devoted to judgment and the world will be in a continual state of chaos. As one sees the gathering thunderclouds of a coming storm, the Great Tribulation period is coming. It is certain as the promise of God (Dan. 9:24-27). The Great Tribulation is as certain as the return of Christ Himself (2 Thess. 2:2-4).

A. THE CHARACTER OF THE TRIBULATION. If the Christian did not realize he would be taken out of the world before the Tribulation begins, he could become discouraged if he felt he had to endure those years. They will be characterized by distress, judgment, darkness, suffering, and sorrow. There is no way to brighten the picture that the Bible paints concerning life in those years. Understanding what lies ahead for unbelievers who are alive at the time of the rapture has caused many people to reconsider the claims of Christ on their lives. The character of this period is revealed in the various expressions used to describe it.

BIBLICAL NAMES FOR DANIEL'S SEVENTIETH WEEK	
Day of the Lord	Isa. 2:12; Ezek. 13:5; Obad. 15; et.
The Great Day of His Wrath	Rev. 6:17; Zeph. 1:15
Time of Jacob's Trouble	Jer. 30:7
The Indignation of the Lord	Isa. 34:2
The Great Tribulation	Rev. 7:14; Matt. 24:21
Day of Trouble	Zeph. 1:15
Day of Wasteness	Zeph. 1:15
Day of Desolation	Zeph. 1:15
Day of Darkness	Amos 5:18; Zeph. 1:15
Day of Gloominess	Zeph. 1:15
Day of Clouds	Zeph. 1:15
Day of Thick Darkness	Amos 5:20; Zeph. 1:15
Day of the Trumpet	Zeph. 1:16
Day of Alarm	Zeph. 1:16
Day of Judgment	Matt. 10:15; 2 Pet. 3:7; Rom. 2:16
Day of Visitation	Isa. 10:3
Hour of Temptation	Rev. 3:10
Hour of His Judgment	Rev. 14:7

Not all of the above titles of the Tribulation would be applied exclusively to that period. The Old Testament term "The day of the Lord" is a primary term for the Tribulation, but it also has a broader meaning. For instance, Scofield suggests,

> The day of Jehovah (called, also, "that day," and "the great day") is that lengthened period of time beginning with the return of the Lord in glory, and ending with the purgation of the heavens and the earth by fire preparatory to the new heavens and the new earth (Isa. 65:17-19; 66:22; 2 Pet. 3:13; Rev. 21:1).[129]

Commenting on the use of this expression in the Old Testament, Dosker writes,

> It denotes the consummation of the kingdom of God and the absolute cessation of all attacks upon it (Isa 2 12; 13 6. 9; 34 8; Ezk 13 5; 30 3; Joel 1 15; 2 11; Am 5 18; Zeph 1 14; Zec 14 1). It is a "day of visitation" (Isa 10 3), a day "of wrath of Jeh" (Ezk 7 19), a "great day of Jeh" (Zeph 1 14). The entire conception in the OT is dark and foreboding.[130]

Writing seven centuries before the birth of Christ, the prophet Zephaniah vividly described the character of the Great Tribulation. "That day is a day of wrath, a day of trouble and distress, a day of wasteness and desolation, a day of darkness and gloominess, a day of clouds and thick darkness" (Zeph. 1:15). What Zephaniah described of Judah during the invasion of Nebuchadnezzar will be multiplied in all the world during the Great Tribulation.

Judgment characterizes much of the Great Tribulation (Rev. 14:7). The judgments of God upon the world that are manifested during this period will be a message to the world to repent and worship God (Rev. 15:4). Those who will not recognize the claims of Christ before the rapture will continually witness the power of God manifest in judgment throughout the Tribulation.

Amos described this period as a time of "darkness, and not light" (Amos 5:18, 20). Darkness is often used in the Bible to portray the state of unregenerated man, lost in the darkness of his sin until the light of the gospel shines through. As the Tribulation begins with the departure of the church (a candlestick—Rev. 1:20), the world will be placed in even greater spiritual darkness than now exists.

While this period of tribulation will affect all "earth-dwellers" (Rev. 8:13), it will include an especially trying time for the Jews. Antisemitism will rise to unprecedented intensity as men attempt to destroy Israel. While many will die, the nation will survive. Commenting on "the time of Jacob's trouble," Ironside advises,

> Observe that this is not the time of the Church's trouble; it has nothing whatsoever to do with the Church. It is the time of Jacob's trouble. What must be the result? That Jacob is scattered and broken and practically destroyed? No, the very opposite! He is saved out of it. The Great Tribulation will end with the deliverance rather than the scattering of Israel. That does not fit in at all with what took place in the land of

Palestine in A.D. 70 and the years that followed. Instead of being saved out of it, Jacob was scattered throughout the entire world as a result of it.[131]

The scriptural representation of the Great Tribulation is wholly negative and makes no attempt at all to minimize the severity of human suffering during that time. Pentecost well summarizes the biblical teaching.

From these Scriptures it is inescapable that the nature or character of this period is that of *wrath* (Zeph. 1:15, 18; 1 Thess. 1:10; 5:9; Rev. 6:16-17; 11:18; 14:10, 19; 15:1, 7; 16:1, 19), *judgment* (Rev. 14:7; 15:4; 16:5, 7; 19:2), *indignation* (Isa. 26:20-21; 34:1-3), *trial* (Rev. 3:10), *trouble* (Jer. 30:7; Zeph. 1:14-15; Dan. 12:1), *destruction* (Joel 1:15; 1 Thess. 5:3), *darkness* (Joel 2:2; Amos 5:18; Zeph. 1:14-18), *desolation* (Dan. 9:27; Zeph. 1:14-15), *overturning* (Isa. 24:1-4, 19-21), *punishment* (Isa. 24:20-21). No passage can be found to alleviate to any degree whatsoever the severity of this time that shall come upon the earth.[132]

During the Great Tribulation when sin is no longer restrained, pain and suffering will be greatly multiplied. Jesus, speaking of this period, said, "For then shall be great tribulation, such as was not since the beginning of the world to this time, no, nor ever shall be" (Matt. 24:21). Those living in the midst of this chaos will call for the rocks to fall on them and destroy them, "For the great day of his wrath is come; and who shall be able to stand?" (Rev. 6:17). Jesus accurately described this period as "the beginning of sorrows" (Matt. 24:8).

B. THE SEQUENCE OF EVENTS IN THE TRIBULATION. The Tribulation will begin with the rapture of the church and the revelation of the man of sin. A covenant will be made between the beast (AntiChrist) and Israel (Dan. 9:27) that will promise peace and security to Israel. Anti-Semitism will be minimal. The peace that is promised by Antichrist will not last. The world begins to experience three series of judgments of God. A gigantic universal state church will be in control as the dominant religious movement. Israel is in the Promised Land, yet is not regenerate.

1. *Seals.* The first of three series of judgments described in Revelation accompanies the breaking of the seals. As each seal on a scroll is broken, a specific judgment takes place on earth. With the breaking of the first seal, a white horseman goes forth to conquer, meaning war (Rev. 6:1-2). The second seal brings a rider on a red horse taking peace from the earth (Rev. 6:3-4). A black horse representing famine accompanies the third seal (Rev. 6:5-6) and a final pale horse takes the life of a fourth of the world's population as the fourth seal is broken (Rev. 6:7-8). The fifth seal is broken, revealing martyred saints in heaven praying for vengeance (Rev. 6:9-11). With the breaking of the sixth seal, various natural phenomena occur, creating great fear in the people who remain (Rev. 6:12-17). The final seal is broken, bringing about an awesome silence in heaven for about half an hour while seven angels prepare to blow their trumpets.

2. *The 144,000.* The appearance of 144,000 Jews occurs early in the seventieth week. These are especially marked by God for the special task of world evangelization (Rev. 7:1-8). As a result of their commitment and effectiveness in accomplishing this task, the Bible identifies an innumerable group of persons from every social, ethnic, and linguistic group who are saved during the Great Tribulation (Rev. 7:9-17).

SEVEN SEALS OF JUDGMENT	
1. White Horse conquering	Rev. 6:1-2
2. Red horse taking peace	Rev. 6:3-4
3. Black horse bringing famine	Rev. 6:5-6
4. Pale horse bringing death	Rev. 6:7-8
5. Martyred saints praying	Rev. 6:9-11
6. Heavenly phenomena	Rev. 6:12-17
7. Silence	Rev. 8:1

3. *Two witnesses.* During the first half of the Tribulation, two special witnesses begin to preach. Although they are not clearly identified, they do have the power of God to perform miracles similar to those of Moses and Elijah (Rev. 11:6). Some have speculated that these witnesses may be Enoch and Elijah as they have not yet died and every man has an appointment with death (Heb. 9:27). These men are killed by the beast, and their bodies are left lying in the streets of Jerusalem (Rev. 11:7). Their bodies will be on the streets while the world celebrates their deaths. Then they will be resurrected and raptured into heaven (Rev. 11:8-12). Despite the evangelistic efforts of these witnesses and the 144,000 Jews, the world will continue in its sin. Many will be saved, but apparently many more will choose to follow the beast.

4. *Trumpets.* As seven angels blow their trumpets in heaven to announce the transfer of ownership of the world to Christ, additional plagues occur on earth. At the blowing of the first trumpet, a third of nature is destroyed (Rev. 8:1-7). The second trumpet marks the destruction of a third of the sea (Rev. 8:8-9). The next plague is the pollution of one third of all the earth's fresh water (Rev. 8:10-11). This is followed by a fourth trumpet, causing the destruction of one-third of the heavens (stars, etc., Rev. 8:12-13). The fifth trumpet is accompanied by a locust-scorpion-like creature bringing with it pain (Rev. 9:1-12). One third of the remaining population of the world is destroyed at the blowing of the sixth trumpet (Rev. 9:13-21). The great announcement is made at the blowing of the seventh trumpet, but is not yet realized. "The kingdoms of this world are become the kingdoms of our Lord and of his Christ; and he shall reign forever and ever" (Rev. 11:15).

SEVEN TRUMPETS	
1. Nature smitten	Rev. 8:1-7
2. Sea turned to blood	Rev. 8:8-9
3. Pollution of fresh water	Rev. 8:10-11
4. Destruction in heavens	Rev. 8:12-13
5. Locusts/scorpions	Rev. 9:1-12
6. 1/3 population destroyed	Rev. 9:13-21
7. Great announcement	Rev. 10:15-19

5. *Battle of Gog and Magog.* During the latter half of the Tribulation, an alliance between Gog and his allies will invade Israel from the north. These nations will fail in great confusion in their attempt to destroy Israel. It will take seven months to bury the dead (Ezek. 38:1-19, 25). The geographic regions included in Ezekiel's vision of the allies is today occupied by the Russian and the former Soviet-bloc countries in eastern Europe. This battle may be fought when an additional nation joins the battle, attacking from the east (Rev. 16:12-16). Today, mainland China is the nation that could fulfill this prophecy.

6. *Bowl judgments.* A final series of judgments precedes the Battle of Armageddon. These are pictured as angels pouring out bowls or vials of judgment upon the world. As the first angel acts, people are covered with boils and sores (Rev. 16:1-2). The destruction of all remaining sea life is contained in the second bowl (Rev. 16:5). The third bowl will turn all fresh water to blood (Rev. 16:4-7). The fourth angel will intensify the sun's heat to unbearable proportions (Rev. 16:8-9). This will be followed with darkness and pain, perhaps as a result of sunburn and other complications of the former judgment (Rev. 16:10-11). The sixth act here performed will effect the drying up of the Euphrates River (Rev. 16:12-16). The final bowl of judgment includes destruction caused by huge hailstones (Rev. 16:17-21).

SEVEN BOWLS OF JUDGMENT	
1. Sores	Rev. 16:1-2
2. Sea life destroyed	Rev. 16:3
3. Fresh water to blood	Rev. 16:4-7
4. Sun's heat intensified	Rev. 16:8-9
5. Darkness and pain	Rev. 16:10-11
6. Drying of Euphrates River	Rev. 16:12-16
7. Hailstones	Rev. 16:17-21

7. *Battle of Armageddon.* The world will be unable to handle the problems caused by these judgments. Many other minor events will take place in these years as anti-Semitism continues to grow. Finally, demons will influence world leaders that assemble for their final battle in an attempt to destroy Israel and God (Rev. 16:14-16). While demons are identified as a source inspiring this battle, the Bible clearly identifies these leaders as responsible for their decision to organize for this battle (Rev. 19:19). Even in this great anti-God struggle, God is in control (Rev. 19:11-16). The Battle of Armageddon and the triumphant return of Christ mark the conclusion of the Great Tribulation.

C. THE ANTICHRIST. Satan has always had his agents, people whom he completely dominated and through whom he did his work. However, there is one coming who will exceed them all. He will be the very embodiment of sin. His coming is declared in 2 Thessalonians 2:3-10 as well as many other passages. Just, as there are today many "antichrists" or false messiahs, so there is coming one Antichrist (1 John 2:18). Though usually referred to as the Antichrist in popular books and articles, in Scripture he is identified by some thirty titles.[133]

NAMES AND TITLES OF THE ANTICHRIST

The bloody and deceitful man .... Psa. 5:6
The wicked one .... Psa. 10:2-4
The man of the earth............................Psa. 10:1.8
The mighty man..................................Psa. 52:1
The enemy..Psa. 55:3
The adversary....................................Psa. 74:8-10
The head of many countries ....Psa. 111:6
The violent man..................................Psa. 140:1
The Assyrian ....Isa. 10:5-12
The King of Babylon..............................Isa. 14:2
The son of the morning ....Isa. 14:12
The spoiler .... Isa. 16:4-5; Jer. 6:26
The nail..Isa. 22:25
The branch of the terrible ones..................Isa. 25:5
The wicked prince of Israel.............Ezek. 21:25-27
The little horn...................................Dan. 7:8
The prince that shall come ....Dan. 9:26
The vile person..................................Dan. 11:21
The willful king.................................Dan. 11:36
The idol shepherd..........................Zech. 11:16-17
The man of sin....................................2 Thes. 2:3
The son of perdition..............................2 Thes. 2:3
The lawless one ....2 Thes. 2:8
The Antichrist .... 1 John 2:22
The angel of the bottomless pit ....Rev. 9:11
The beast.. Rev. 11:7; 13:1
The one coming In his own name..............John 5:43
The king of fierce countenance.................Dan. 8:23
The abomination of desolation ....Matt. 24:15
The desolator...Dan. 9:27

The title "antichrist" can be interpreted two ways. First, it can refer to one who stands in the place of Christ, or a substitute Christ. Second, it means one who opposes Christ. Both interpretations can be justified by the grammar used, so one must decide the meaning of the term based upon usage. This term is used in the New Testament five times and only by John. In his study of the terms antichrist and false-christ, Trench suggests both of the above may to some extent be true of the Antichrist.

To me St. John's words seem decisive that resistance to Christ, and defiance of Him, this, and not any treacherous assumption of his character and offices, is the essential mark of the Antichrist; is that which, therefore, we should expect to find embodied in his name: thus see I John ii. 22; 2 John 7; and in the parallel passage, 2 Thess. ii. 4, he is ὁ ἀντικίμενος 'the opposers;' and in this sense, if not all, yet many of the Fathers have understood the word.[134]

The Antichrist is portrayed predominantly in the Scriptures as a political leader of immense power. He is apparently the head of the revived Roman Empire. Summarizing the major political events of the Tribulation years, Thiessen concludes,

From all this we gather that during the Tribulation period there will be a federated political world, developed chiefly from the old Roman Empire, within which will be ten cooperating kingdoms. This rule will be autocratic and blasphemous. At first the "church" of those days will dominate the government; but after a time the ten kings will destroy it, and then great persecutions will be introduced against the believers of that time. But the emperor and his associates will be destroyed at the return of Christ, and their kingdom will give way to the kingdom which Christ will set up.[135]

D. THE FALSE PROPHET. The chief religious figure in the world during the tribulation years is identified in Scripture as the false prophet. In the absence of a true church, there is a counterfeit religion, headed by an unholy trinity, i.e., Satan, Antichrist and the false prophet. Just as their religious system is designed to take the place of Christianity, so the unholy triad desire to take the place of the Trinity. While twice called the false prophet in the Revelation (Rev. 19:20; 20:10), he is most fully described in that passage where he is simply referred to as "the second beast" (Rev. 13:11-17). From this passage, a number of things can be determined concerning his identity.

(1) This individual is evidently a Jew, since he arises out of the earth, or land, that is Palestine (13:11); (2) he is influential in religions affairs (13:11, "two horns like a lamb"); (3) he is motivated by Satan as the first beast is (13:11); (4) he has a delegated authority (13:12, "the power of the first beast"); (5) he promotes the worship of the first beast and compels the earth to worship the first beast as God (13:12); (6) his ministry is authenticated by the signs and miracles which he does, evidently proving that he is Elijah that was to come (13:13-4); (7) he is successful in deceiving the unbelieving world (13:14); (8) the worship promoted is an idolatrous worship (13:14-15); (9) he has the power of death to compel men to worship the beast (13:15); (10) he has authority in the economic realm to control all commerce (13:16-17); (11) he has a mark that will establish his identity for those who live in that day (13:18).[136]

As the Father sent the Son, so Satan sends the Antichrist. As the Son sends the Holy Spirit to accomplish His purpose, so the false prophet carries out the purpose of the Antichrist. According to Thiessen,

We have already indicated that in Rev. 17:1-6 the false church is seen riding the beast. This shows that the church of this period will be a federation of all the apostates who will pass into the Tribulation. The present effort to unite all the churches into one great Church, will at length succeed; but it will be the union of unbelievers. As we have said, at the beginning of this period, the church will dominate the government. When in the midst of it the emperor breaks his covenant with the Jews and forbids the offering of sacrifices (Dan. 9:27), the ten kings will hate the harlot, cast her off, and destroy her (Rev. 17:16-17). From that time on all will be required to worship the "beast" (Rev. 13:4, 6-8), and the second beast will set out to force the world to do so (Rev. 13:11-17). He will use deception and lying wonders (Rev. 13:13; 2 Thes. 2:9-12), force (Rev. 13:7, 15; cf. 6:9-11; 20:4), persecution of those who will not worship the beast, and boycott (Rev. 13:16, 17). He will require all to take the mark of the beast, and will not allow any to buy or sell unless they take this mark. It is clear that in those days multitudes will be slain for the Word of God and the testimony which they hold. But with the coming of Christ and the destruction of the leaders and their armies, the whole religious system of the end-time will come to nought.[137]

XII. THE SECOND COMING OF CHRIST

Although there is general agreement among biblical scholars concerning the fact of a Second Coming, there is not always agreement on what is meant by the term. Even those who do not believe in a physical return of Christ do hold to a belief in the second coming, but have redefined the expression to mean something different. Thiessen is correct when he observes,

> All who believe that the Bible is the Word of God believe also in the second coming of Christ; but there is a vast difference of opinion as to what is meant by the Lord's return. It is necessary, therefore, to examine this question in the light of the Scriptures. Many today oppose the truth we are considering because they have never gone to the trouble to examine the evidence for themselves. Since the Scriptures have so much to say upon this subject it will not be hard to set forth the nature of Christ's coming.[138]

There are those, generally liberal theologians, who identify the return of Christ in terms other than a personal, bodily return of Christ to this earth. They see the prophecies of a "second coming" fulfilled in the spiritual presence of Christ in His people. Summarizing this view, Walvoord writes,

> A common modern view of the Lord's return is the so-called spiritual view which identifies the coming of Christ as a perpetual advance of Christ in the church that includes many particular events. William Newton Clarke, for instance, held that the promises of the second coming are fulfilled by "his spiritual presence with his people," which is introduced by the coming of the Holy Spirit at Pentecost.[139]

In an apparent attempt to harmonize the liberal and conservative views of the second advent of Christ, Strong suggests,

> While the Scriptures represent great events in the history of the individual Christian, like death, and great events in the history of the church, like the outpouring of the Spirit at Pentecost and the destruction of Jerusalem, as comings of Christ for deliverance or judgment, they also declare that these partial and typical comings shall be concluded by a final, triumphant return of Christ, to punish the wicked and to complete the salvation of his people.[140]

The Scriptures teach a literal, physical or bodily return of Christ to this earth to establish His kingdom and rule for a thousand years. While certain events and experiences in the lives of individuals and nations may result in a deepening of one's relationship with the Lord, this is not properly the return of Christ. The term "Second Coming" should be reserved for the final revelation of Christ at the end of the Tribulation. According to Chafer,

> This the greatest theme of all prophecy was the subject of the first prediction by man (Jude 1:14, 15), and is the last message of the Bible (Rev. 22:20). It is the dominant feature of all Old Testament prophecy concerning the Day of the Lord and, likewise, is the major theme of New Testament prophecy. Beginning with the first evidence of Israel's rejection of His Messianic claims, this great event was continually upon the lips of Christ (Matt. 23:37 to 25:46; Mark 13:1-37; Luke 21:5-38). Again, it is emphasized by the Apostle Paul (Rom. 11:26; 1 Thess. 3:13; 5:1-4; 2 Thess. 1:7 to 2:12), by James (5:1-8), by Peter (2 Pet. 2:1 to 3:17), by Jude (1:14, 15), and by John throughout the Revelation.[141]

XIII. THE RESURRECTION

The idea of resurrection is both fundamental and almost unique to Christianity. While the Old Testament does not deny the doctrine, neither does it greatly emphasize it. Apart from a few clear statements, personal eschatology was largely ignored in the Old Testament. Summarizing the teaching of the Old Testament concerning the resurrection, Pentecost writes,

> The Old Testament associated the hope of resurrection with the Messianic hope of the Day of the Lord. In Daniel the resurrection (12:2) is seen to be an event subsequent to the time of trouble under the Desolater (12:1). In Isaiah the resurrection (26:19) is spoken of in reference to "the indignation" (26:20-21).[142]

In the New Testament, however, the emphasis is completely reversed. The preaching of the apostles tended to be characterized by constant reference to the physical resurrection of Christ. That resurrection became the type and assurance of their personal resurrection. Commenting on this emphasis in apostolic preaching, Morris asserts,

> The most startling characteristic of the first Christian preaching is its emphasis on the resurrection. The first preachers were sure that Christ had risen, and sure, in consequence, that believers would in due course rise also. This set them off from all other teachers of the ancient world. There are resurrections elsewhere, but none of them is like that of Christ. They are mostly mythological tales connected with the change of the season and the annual miracle of spring. The Gospels tell of an individual who truly died but overcame death by rising again. And if it is true that Christ's resurrection bears no resemblance to anything in paganism it is also true that the attitude of believers to their own resurrection, the corollary of their Lord's, is radically different from anything in the heathen world. Nothing is more characteristic of even the best thought of the day than its hopelessness in the face of death. Clearly the resurrection is of the very first importance for the Christian faith.[143]

By resurrection we mean the giving or imparting of heavenly life to that which
has experienced physical death. The resurrection of Christ involved much more than
reviving the physical body of Jesus. Note the following aspects of the resurrection of
Christ. First, the body and spirit that had separated at death were reunited; second,
Jesus was now subjecting to Himself the powers of death, based upon the authority of
the Cross; third, before His death, He was subjected to the limitations of humanity, but
now He enjoyed unlimited deity; fourth, in His resurrected body He again enjoyed
access to heaven, and fifth, He was now glorified. Understanding the nature of Jesus'
resurrection appears to be the key to understanding the nature of our resurrection.
This seems to be the emphasis of the New Testament. As Morris observes,

> Of the nature of the resurrection body Scripture says little. Paul can speak of it as
> 'a spiritual body' (1 Cor. xv. 44), which appears to mean a body which meets the
> needs of the spirit. . . .
> Perhaps we gain some help by thinking of the resurrection body of Christ, for
> John tells us that 'we shall be like him' (1 John iii. 2), and Paul that 'our vile body' is
> to be fashioned 'like unto his glorious body' (Phil. iii. 21).[144]

Believers will have a new body and that body will be somehow related to our present body.
According to Thiessen,

> In general it may be said that the resurrection body will not be an entirely new
> creation. If that were the case, it would not be the present body, but another body.
> This view is sustained by 1 Cor. 15:43, 44, 53, 54. Nor, on the other hand, will the
> resurrection body necessarily be in every detail composed of the identical particles
> contained in this body (1 Cor. 15:37, 38). All that the Scriptures warrant us in saying,
> is that the resurrection body will sustain a similar relation to the present body as the
> wheat in the stalk sustains to the wheat in the ground out of which it grew.[145]

Perhaps the relationship that exists can be seen by contrasting an acorn and an oak. Both
are the same in that the oak is the product of an acorn and vise versa. No distinction can be
made in terms of essence. Yet as the acorn dies and is buried, it springs to life as an oak.
While the body is essentially the same before and after the resurrection, certain distinctives are
noticeable as demonstrated in the following chart,

THE BELIEVER'S RESURRECTION BODY (1 Cor. 15:42-44)			
Sown		Raised	
1.	in corruption	1.	in incorruption
2.	in dishonor	2.	in glory
3.	in weakness	3.	in power
4.	a natural body	4.	a spiritual body

XIV. THE JUDGMENTS

Throughout the Scriptures, God is portrayed in terms of a Judge. In the Old Testament, God raised up judges to lead the nation, and one way they did so was to determine righteousness. They were the earthly representatives of God the Judge. In the New Testament, judgment is committed to Jesus, and He is portrayed as a Judge in the midst of the seven churches. While there are similarities between the work of judges and the work of God as Judge, the judgment of God is unique. Because He is omniscient and omnipresent, nothing is overlooked in rendering a fair and equitable judgment in His court. Comparing the judgment of God with that of earthly courts, Thiessen writes,

> The whole philosophy of the future judgments rests upon the sovereign right of God to punish disobedience and the personal right of the individual to plead his case in court. Though God is sovereign, as Judge of all the earth He will do right (Gen. 18:25). He will do this, not in order to submit to an external law, but as an expression of His innermost character.[146]

That there are coming judgments cannot be denied, but the idea of a single general judgment at the end of time is inconsistent with biblical revelation. Van Gorder observes, "The popular belief that there will be one final judgment in which all humanity will stand is a concept that is foreign to the teaching of the Word of God. Coming judgment? Certainly! A general judgment? Absolutely not!"[147] Throughout the Old Testament, the judgment of God is associated with the Flood, the destruction of Sodom and the falls of various nations, including both Israel and Judah. In the New Testament, judgment is rendered in eight areas. Pentecost repeats the view that there are eight judgments.

The subject of judgments is a large one in the Word of God and encompasses such judgments as the judgment of the cross (John 5:24; Rom. 5:9, 8:1; 2 Cor. 5:21; Gal. 3:13; Heb. 9:26-28; 10:10,14-17), the judgment on the believer in chastening (1 Cor. 11:31-32; Heb. 12:5-11), the self judgment of the believer (1 John 1:9; 1 Cor. 11:31; Ps. 32; 51), the judgment of the believer's works at the judgment seat of Christ (Rom. 14:10; 1 Cor. 3:11-15, 4:5; 2 Cor. 5:10). With the exception of the last mentioned judgment, which has already been considered, these judgments are not related to the eschatological program of God. It is necessary to consider four judgments that have eschatological implications: the judgment on the nation Israel (Ezek. 20:37-38; Zech. 13:8-9), the judgment of the nations (Matt. 25:31-46; Isa. 34:1-2; Joel 3:11-16), the judgment on fallen angels (Jude 6) and the judgment of the great white throne (Rev. 20:11-15).[148]

The chart accompanying this section surveys these eight judgments. The fundamental principles relevant to all the judgments of God are set forth by Paul in Romans 2:1-16. Summarizing these principles, the editors of the *New Scofield Reference Bible* give the principles by which God will render judgment.

The basic principles of divine judgment are set forth in vv. 1-16 as follows: it will be according to (1) truth (v. 2), i.e. , an objective standard of conduct; (2) deeds (v. 6); (3) the light enjoyed (vv. 11-15); and (4) the Gospel by which the secret thoughts and motives of men are judged (v. 16).[149]

A. THE CROSS. On Calvary, Jesus experienced the judgment of God upon the sins of the world. He died in the sinner's place as a substitute. "Christ hath redeemed us from the curse of the law, being made a curse for us: for it is written, Cursed is every one that hangeth on a tree" (Gal. 3:13). The Cross was a judgment by God upon the sins of the world.

The judicial charge that brought about the judgment by God was sin. Every man is a sinner for a threefold reason: First, because of Adam's transgression everyone has been born with a sin nature (Psa. 51:2). Second, all have committed personal sins against God. "For all have sinned and come short of the glory of God" (Rom. 3:23). In the third place, all have had sin imputed to their account (Rom. 5:19). Since man is a sinner, God is his enemy (Eph. 2:3). This is strong language, but sin is a violation of the nature of God. The crime of sin was so great that it brought about the judgment of Calvary.

B. SELF-JUDGMENT. Before God judges Christians for sin in their lives, He first gives them the opportunity to deal with the problem. In explaining the reasoning for the sickness and death among church members in Corinth, Paul pointed to the judgment of God upon sin (1 Cor. 11:30). He then explained "For if we would judge ourselves, we should not be judged" (1 Cor. 11:31).

The chief purpose for self-evaluation (self-judgment) is to prevent oneself from becoming ineffective in the Lord's service. "When we are judged, we are chastened of the Lord, that we should not be condemned with the world" (1 Cor. 11:32). When a believer examines himself he accomplishes the same purpose without having to experience the judgment of God. The apostle Paul, always fearful of becoming ineffective in the service of Christ, constantly disciplined himself. "But I keep under my body, and bring it into subjection: lest that by any means, when I have preached to others, I myself should be a castaway" (1 Cor. 9:27).

C. CHASTISEMENT. While problems, including physical sickness or adversity, in the believer are not always the result of sin in his life, they sometimes are. The Scriptures speak of these events as God's chastising of His sons (Heb. 12:5-11). This judgment can be avoided in the life of the believer through the practice of self-judgment.

D. THE JUDGMENT SEAT OF CHRIST. This is sometimes called the Bema Judgment Seat from the Greek word, *bema*. "For we must all appear before the judgment seat of Christ; that every one may receive the things done in his body, according to that he hath done, whether it be good or bad" (2 Cor. 5:10). The believer's works are judged at the Bema, not his sins. His sins have been completely atoned for and remembered no more forever (Heb. 10:17). At the Bema, every work will be evaluated both for faithfulness and results. Since God is just, He cannot overlook good works, nor evil. The Judgment Seat of Christ is often discussed as the doctrine of rewards for Christians. This is not a judgment to determine if Christians will enter into heaven, but to determine the quality and quantity of our past service on this earth. As a result of faithfulness to Christ, Christians will receive a reward.

Not everyone will obtain the same reward, and faithful service will be tested by God to determine the extent of the reward. Some may have very little with which to enter heaven except their salvation (1 Cor. 3:12-15). The Bible also teaches it is possible to lose part of our reward that had previously accrued. Therefore, it is important that a believer continue faithful in his service for Christ even after he has earned a prize (2 John 8). These rewards are sometimes identified as "crowns" in the Bible.

THE BELIEVER'S REWARDS

1. Incorruptible crown.................... 1 Cor. 9:25
2. Crown of righteousness.............. 2 Tim. 4:8
3. Crown of life................................Rev. 2:10
4. Crown of glory............................ 1 Pet. 5:4
5. Crown of rejoicing ....1 Thes. 2:19

---

1. *Incorruptible crown.* The incorruptible crown was awarded for self-discipline. Just as an athlete will discipline himself and his lifestyle to win a race and trophy, so a Christian should discipline himself in his service for Christ. In the early Olympic Games, the prize won by the victor was a crown of olive leaves. Naturally, with the heat of the day, the crown withered. The apostle Paul contrasts that incident with our Christian life. "Now they do it to obtain a corruptible crown; but we an incorruptible" (1 Cor. 9:25).

2. *Crown of righteousness.* The crown of righteousness will be given to those who are faithful in light of Christ's return. Writing his final epistle to Timothy and expecting his death, Paul was looking forward to the coming of Christ, and if that did not happen in his lifetime, he expected to see the Lord in death. "Henceforth there is laid up for me a crown of righteousness, which the Lord, the righteous judge, shall give me at that day: and not to me

only, but unto all them also that love his appearing" (2 Tim. 4:8). This was probably what Dwight L. Moody was thinking of when on his deathbed, as he passed into eternity he said, "This is my coronation day."

3. *Crown of life.* The crown of life is for those whose service cost them their lives. This is also called the martyr's crown. Speaking to the church that was going through severe persecution, Jesus said, "Be thou faithful unto death, and I will give thee a crown of life" (Rev. 2:10). This reward is also given to those who are victorious in enduring temptation (James 1:12). James may have been thinking of the temptation to Christians to compromise their witness rather than to endure persecution at the cost of their lives.

4. *Crown of glory.* God also has a special reward for those who serve Him in full-time vocational service. Peter spoke to pastors: "And when the chief Shepherd shall appear, ye shall receive a crown of glory that fadeth not away" (1 Pet. 5:4).

5. *Crown of rejoicing.* Every Christian should receive the crown of rejoicing (1 Thess. 2:19). This is the reward given for faithful witnessing and fruitbearing. Many Christians never experience the joy of leading a person to Christ and fulfilling the command to "bear fruit" (John 15:16).

Often the Judgment Seat of Christ is pictured as a place of tears and remorse for some believers because of their unfaithfulness and because of sin in their lives. However, even those who are "saved only" will rejoice. Paul reminds us to "judge nothing before the time, until the Lord come," because then all believers will rejoice because, "then shall every man shall have praise of God" (1 Cor. 4:5).

E. GENTILE NATIONS. At Christ's second coming, all the nations of the world will pass before Him to be judged (Matt. 25:32). This scene is described in terms of a separation of sheep and goats. The basis of their judgment is in relation to their treatment of those identified by Christ as "these my brethren" (Matt. 25:40, 45). These brethren may be (1) Israel, (2) the Church, or (3) the oppressed.

1. *Israel.* Some believe Jesus was referring to the treatment of the Jews as the basis of His judgment. If that is the case, people of those nations which have sought to protect the Jews will be sheep.

The others who have sought to harm the Jews or simply ignore their plight will be goats. This interpretation is in keeping with the promise of blessing in the Abrahamic Covenant to those who blessed the seed of Abraham (Gen. 12:1-3; 15:1-3).

2. *Church.* Some commentators argue that the brethren of Jesus are really the church. Jesus said, "For whosoever shall do the will of my Father which is in heaven, the same is my

brother, and sister, and mother" (Matt. 12:50). In this case, the treatment of churches and Christians in those churches will be the basis of the judgment.

3. *Oppressed.* Throughout the Bible, God is portrayed as a defender of those who cannot defend themselves. Some have suggested God will judge the nations based upon their protection of the oppressed and defenseless members of their society. This would include the very young and very old, the poor and the unborn.

F. TRIBULATION. During the Great Tribulation, God will release three major judgments upon the world (seals, trumpets, and bowls). The first of these accompanies the breaking of the seven seals on a scroll which may be the title deed of the world. The second judgment accompanies the sounding of seven trumpets, while the final series of judgments occurs as seven angels empty vials of the wrath of God upon the world. These judgments will last for seven years.

G. THE GREAT WHITE THRONE JUDGMENT. At the end of the millennial reign of Christ, the unsaved dead will have to stand before the throne of God to be judged. "And I saw the dead, small and great, stand before God; and the books were opened: and another book was opened, which is the book of life: and the dead were judged out of those things which were written in the books, according to their works (Rev. 20:12). This judgment does not suggest these people may enter into heaven or hell on the basis of their works. All those who are judged at the Great White Throne are consigned to hell because they have rejected God. (The saved have already been resurrected and enjoying fellowship with Christ.) The Great White Throne Judgment will determine the degree of punishment the rejecters will endure, based upon the nature of their evil work. When the book of works is opened (Rev. 20:12), a sentence of the severity of their punishment will be determined. All those sentenced will be consigned "into the lake of fire" (Rev. 20:14), where they will suffer according to their personally assigned sentences.

H. ANGELS. The Bible also teaches that fallen angels will be judged. Paul asked the Corinthians, "Know ye not that we shall judge angels?" (1 Cor. 6:3). Toward the end of the age, Christians will represent God in the role of Judge. It may be that during the Tribulation, the millennial kingdom, or eternity to follow, Christians will serve as judges similar to the judges who ruled before Israel's first king.

THE JUDGMENTS									
Judgment	Judge(s)	Subjects of Judgment	Motive of Judgment	Time of Judgment	Place of Judgment	Basis of Judgment	Purposes of Judgment	Penalty	Benefits of Judgment

The Cross	The Father	Christ and those "in Christ"	God's love for Sinners	About 30 A.D. Passover 9 a.m. - Noon	Golgotha	Holiness of God	To provide an Atonement for man's sins & thereby make Possible Reconciliation	Death	Salvation to those who believe
Self-judgment	Individual Christian	Individual Christian	Christian's desire to partake in Lord's Supper	Often in the Christian experience	At the Lord's Table	The Scriptures	To avoid partaking unworthily	Sickness & death	Renewed fellowship
Chastisement	The Father	Individual Christian	God's love for sons	During Christian life when needed	In body or experience of Christian	Sin in the life of the Christian	To demonstrate the existence of a relationship & develop a closer fellowship	Grievous at the time	Yields peaceable fruit of righteousness
Bema-seat of Christ	The Lord Jesus	Individual Christian	The Awarding of Crowns	Soon after Rapture	Heaven, perhaps in the Throne room	Quality of stewardship	To evaluate the works of Christians & award rewards	Loss of some rewards	Purification of some rewards

Tribula-tion	God	"Earth-dwellers"	Prayers of the martyred saints	Between the Rapture and Revelation of Christ	Judged in Heaven, penalty inflicted on Earth	Vengeance of God particularly directed toward those who oppose His work	To release the wrath of God on wickedness & bring about the repentance of some	Sufferings accompanying the 7 seals, 7 trumpets & 7 vials of wrath	Repentance of some
Gentile nations	The Lord Jesus	Gentile nations	The Lord's identification with "My brethren"	At the revelation of Christ in His glory	Before the throne of His glory	The Gentile nations concern or lack thereof for "My brethren"	To effect a separation of sheep & goat nations	Everlasting fire	Inheritance of a Kingdom
Great White Throne	God through the Son	Those not recorded in the Book of Life	Harmony of the love and holiness of God	End of Millennial reign of Christ	Before the throne of God	Individual responses to Christ & their works, i.e., the degree of their opposition	To insure punishment for sin & determine the degree of that eternal punishment	Lake of Fire, Second Death	Lesser degree of eternal suffering for some
Angels	Christians, probably as a group with Christ	Angels, especially fallen Angels	Rebellion of some angels under the leadership of Satan	Sometime after the Rapture of the Church, probably toward the end of the Millennium	Probably Heaven	Sovereignty of God	To evaluate the Angels	Everlasting fire	Marks the end of evil

XV. THE MILLENNIUM

The Scriptures teach that Christ will return and establish a theocratic kingdom on earth. Since Christ will be ruling the earth, His kingdom will be characterized by harmony, not only among men but also within nature. This reign of peace will last one thousand years and Christ Himself will sit on the throne as King. Willmington gives the following list to characterize the Millennium.

NATURE OF THE MILLENNIUM

The Temple to be rebuilt. Ez. 40:48; Isa. 2:2; Hag. 2:7-9; Zech. 6:12,13; Joel 3:18.

Israel to be regathered.   Isa. 43:5,6; Jer. 24:6; 29:14;   Ez.   11:17; 36:24,25,28; Jer. 31:6-9; Amos 9:14,15; Zech. 8:6-8; Matt. 24:31.

Israel to recognize her Messiah. Zech. 12:10-12; Rev. 1:7; Isa 25:9; 8:17; 26:8.

Israel to be cleansed. Jer. 33:8; Zech. 13:1.

Israel to be regenerated. Jer. 31:31-34; 32:39; Ez. 11:19-20; 36:26.

Israel to once again be related to God by marriage. Isa. 54:1-7; 62:2-5; Hos. 2:14-23.

Israel to be exalted above the Gentiles. Isa. 14:1,2; 49:22,23; 60:14-17; 61:6-7.

Israel to become God's witnesses. Isa. 44:8; 61:6; 66:21; Mic. 5:7; Zeph. 3:20; Zech. 4:1-7; 8:3.

Christ to rule from Jerusalem with a rod of Iron. Ps. 2:6-8,11; Isa. 2:3; 11:4.

David to aid in this rule as vice-regent. Jer. 30:9; Isa. 55:3-4; Ez. 34:23; 37:24; Hos. 3:5.

All sickness to be removed. Isa. 33:24; Jer. 30:17; Ez. 34:16.

The heavenly, suspended city (New Jerusalem) to be 1500 by 1500 by 1500 miles. Rev. 21:10,16.

The earthly city to be six miles in circumference. Ez. 48:35.

The wilderness and deserts to bloom. Isa. 35:1,2.

God's glory to be seen by all nations. Isa. 60:1-3; Ez. 39-21; Mic. 4:1-5; Hab. 2:14.

Longevity of man to be restored. Isa. 65:20.

Universal peace. Isa. 2:4; 32:18.

Universal holiness. Zech. 13:20-21.

Solar and lunar light to increase. Isa. 4:5; 30:26; 60:19-20; Zech. 2:5.

Palestine to become greatly enlarged and changed. Isa. 26:15; Obad. 1:17-21.

A river to flow east-west from the Mount of Olives into both the Mediterranean and Dead Seas. Zech. 14:4,8,10; Joel 3:18; Ez. 47:8,9,12.

Jerusalem to become known as Jehovah **Sidkenu** (the Lord, our Righteousness), and Jehovah **Shammah** (the Lord is there). Jer. 33:16; Ez. 48:35.

Jerusalem to become the worship center of the world. Mic. 4:1; Is. 2:2,3.

Jerusalem's streets to be filled with happy boys and girls playing. Zech. 8:5. (Born to those saved Gentiles and Jews who survived the Tribulation).

A unified language. Zeph. 3:9.

The original curse (Gen. 3:17-19) upon Creation to be neutralized.   Isa. 11:6-9; 35:9; 65:25; Joel 3:18; Amos 9:13-15.

The wolf, lamb, calf, and lion to lie down together in peace. Isa. 11:6-7; 65:25.

A little child to safely play with once poisonous serpents and spiders. Isa. 11:8.

Physical death to be swallowed up in victory. Isa. 25:8.

All tears to be dried. Isa. 25:8; 30:19.

The deaf to hear, the blind to see, and the lame to walk. Isa. 29:18; 35:5,6; 61:1-2; Jer. 31:8.

Man's knowledge about God to be vastly increased. Isa. 41:19-20; 54:13; Hab. 2:14.

No social, political or religious oppression. Isa. 14:3-6; 42:6-7; 49:8-9; Zech. 9:11-12.

Full ministry of the Holy Spirit. Isa. 32:15; 59:21; Joel 2:28,29; Ez. 36:27; 37:14.

Christ Himself to be the Good, Great, and Chief Shepherd. Isa. 40:11; 49:10; 58:11; Ez. 34:11-16.

A time of universal singing. Isa. 52:9; 35:6; 54:1; 55:12; Jer. 33:11.

A time of universal praying. Isa. 56:7; 65:24; Zech. 8:22.

The city to occupy an elevated site. Zech. 14:10.[150]

Some claim the Millennium chiefly relates to a particular interpretation of only ten verses in Scripture (Rev. 20:1-10). Therefore, they deny there is a Millennium. In light of the controversy among Bible scholars, some would minimize the doctrine of the Millennium. But, in a somewhat inconsistent manner, the same people would argue the importance of defending the virgin birth, which is mentioned in fewer verses of Scripture. Actually, the importance of any doctrine is not determined by how many verses discuss it. If God said it once, it is enough. The importance of a doctrine is determined by its message and the meaning that God gives to it. Actually, the doctrine of the Millennium has more biblical support than ten verses in Revelation 20. It is the chief theme of the prophets of Israel and Judah. Jonah stands alone in the canonical writings of the prophets as having no reference to the millennial kingdom of God. Both John the Baptist and Jesus preached on this subject. The apostles continued teaching the people concerning the kingdom of God.

A. VIEWS OF THE KINGDOM. Essentially, there are three fundamentally different interpretations of the kingdom of God. Postmillennialists tend to equate the kingdom with the christianizing of society, or the improvement of world conditions by the influence of the gospel, so that the kingdom of God is brought to earth. Explaining this view, Boettner states,

> The Millennium to which the Postmillennialist looks forward is thus a golden age of spiritual prosperity during this present dispensation, that is, during the Church Age, and is to be brought about through forces now active in the world. It is an indefinitely long period of time, perhaps much longer than a literal one thousand years. The changed character of individuals will be reflected in an uplifted social, economic, political and cultural life of mankind. The world at large will then enjoy a state of righteousness such as at the present time has been seen only in relatively small and isolated groups, as for example in some family circles, some local church groups and kindred organizations.
>
> This does not mean that there ever will be a time on this earth when every person will be a Christian, or that all sin will be abolished. But it does mean that evil in all its many forms eventually will be reduced to negligible proportions, that Christian principles will be the rule, not the exception, and that Christ will return to a truly Christianized world.[151]

A second view of the millennial kingdom is that of the amillennialist and amounts to an essential denial of any future kingdom period on the earth. There are two basic views of the amillennialist. First, some believe the Old Testament promises of a kingdom are being fulfilled now in heaven where Christ rules. Second, some believe the kingdom is being fulfilled in a spiritual manifestation through the church. Amillennialism is based on a nonliteral interpretation of those passages dealing with the kingdom. In an attempt to justify this approach, Hamilton suggests,

> The more one studies the complexities and details of the theories which seek to reconcile all the literal interpretations of the Old Testament prophecies with the literal interpretations of the words of Christ and the apostles in the New Testament, the greater is one's belief when one turns to the simple teachings of the Word of God. If one follows the New Testament leadings as to the interpretation of the Old Testament prophecies, the whole picture of the "last things" as taught in the Word of God seems so simple and easy to understand, that one is amazed at the complex theories of many modern commentators. The Bible plainly teaches that Christ is coming again, in the words of the Apostles creed, "to judge the quick and the dead" (II Tim. 4:1). Praise God when one becomes a Christian; that is the end of distinctions of race, and when we are raptured to meet our blessed Saviour, we won't be asked whether we are Jews or Gentiles, for in the words of the Apostle Paul, "There can be neither Jew nor Greek . . . . for ye are one in Christ Jesus!"[152]

The third view of the Millennium is that of the premillennialist. Premillennialism is based upon a consistent literal interpretation of the Scriptures dealing with eschatological themes. It teaches that there is coming a future kingdom on this earth of 1,000 years where Christ will rule and fulfill the promises made to God's people in the Old Testament. This does not deny the spiritual realities of the kingdom. Neither does it deny its literal nature. As Ladd explains,

> We must conclude therefore that there is no *single* interpretation in the study of prophecy, either literal or spiritual. The same laws of hermeneutics and exegesis are to be employed which are used elsewhere. Unless there is some reason intrinsic within the text itself which requires a symbolic interpretation, or unless there are other Scriptures which interpret a parallel prophecy in a symbolic sense, we are required to employ a natural, literal interpretation. The future kingdom will indeed be "spiritual" in that it will be the application of the supernatural power of God to the world and to human society, but such a spiritual interpretation does not empty future events of their literal reality.[153]

B. THE NATURE OF THE MILLENNIUM. The word does not appear in the Bible but is derived from two Latin words meaning "thousand years." That expression is used six times in Revelation 20. The millennial reign of Christ is the thousand-year period when Christ personally sits on the throne of David and reigns over the earth from Jerusalem. The

Millennium is more than an era in history. It will be characterized by the restraining of Satan and the universal recognition of Christ. The land of Palestine will in that day be the focal point of attention, particularly Jerusalem as its political capital. Nature will be released from the bondage it has experienced since the fall of man. Righteousness will influence (and control) all society. By anyone's definition, this kingdom will be desirable for its joys and comforts.

1. *Restraint of Satan.* Today, Satan has the liberty to work in this world, even though certain restraints are placed upon him by God (2 Cor. 4:3-4). During the Millennium complete restraint will be placed on Satan. John saw an angel leave heaven, "And he laid hold on the dragon, that old serpent, which is the Devil and Satan, and bound him a thousand years" (Rev. 20:2). While the specific details of that binding are uncertain, it is clear that Satan will be prevented from exerting evil influence until the end of the Millennium. Hence, there will be no temptation, no deception or counterfeit religion. No one will teach heresy and everyone will recognize the deity and rule of Jesus Christ.

2. *Universal King.* The millennium has been called the "theocratic kingdom" because it is a kingdom ruled directly by God in the person of Christ. Before the first advent of Christ, Isaiah wrote, "For unto us a child is born, unto us a son is given: and the government shall be upon his shoulder: and his name shall be called Wonderful, Counsellor, The mighty God, The everlasting Father, The Prince of Peace" (Isa. 9:6). This Prince of Peace was prophesied to reign on the throne of David in an unending kingdom (Isa. 9:7). Hence, Christ will be "King of kings" (Rev. 19:1-6).

3. *Palestine.* God chose the land of Palestine to be the focal point of His concern in the history of the world. The Jews are God's chosen people and He promised that land to them. This is why it is called the Promised Land. Throughout the years, the Jews have spent comparatively little time in the Land, and much of the time they lived there was filled with uncertainty. Concerning the future, God has promised, "And they shall dwell in the land that I have given unto Jacob my servant, wherein your fathers have dwelt; and they shall dwell therein, even they, and their children, and their children's children for ever: and my servant David shall be their prince forever" (Ezek. 37:25). This land will be the Jewish homeland during the Millennium.

4. *Jerusalem.* The thousand-year reign of Christ will be from Jerusalem. "And it shall come to pass, that every one that is left of all the nations which came against Jerusalem shall even go up from year to year to worship the King, the LORD of hosts, and to keep the feast of tabernacles" (Zech. 14:16). Jerusalem will be a truly international city. The vast numbers of tourists in that city today is nothing in comparison with the crowds that will converge on the city during the reign of Christ. The city of Jerusalem will be the universal capital of the theocratic kingdom.

5. *Nature*. An additional blessing of this golden era will be deliverance of nature from the curse placed upon it at the fall of man (Gen. 3:17-19; Rom. 8:19-22). The apostle Paul talked of a future day when "the creature itself also shall be delivered from the bondage of corruption into the glorious liberty of the children of God" (Rom. 8:21). At the Fall, even the creation which God had perfectly created was made subject to the bondage of sin. At the return of Christ, deliverance from that bondage will be a part of the blessing that Christ brings. Life in the Millennium is pictured in terms of "the wolf also shall dwell with the lamb, and the leopard shall lie down with the kid; and the calf and the young lion and the fatling together; and a little child shall lead them" (Isa. 11:6). There will be no destructive vengeance in nature. There will not be "Survival of the fittest," but survival of all. And children will enjoy all nature with no threat of danger to them.

6. *Righteousness*. Righteousness will be characteristic of the Millennium. "In his days shall the righteous flourish" (Psa. 72:7). God has promised, "For Zion's sake will I not hold my peace, and for Jerusalem's sake I will not rest, until the righteousness thereof go forth as brightness, and the salvation thereof as a lamp that burneth" (Isa. 62:1). Much is being said today concerning morality in legislation. During Christ's reign on earth, all legislation will reflect His righteous character.

7. *Desirable*. The Millennium will fulfill all the biblical desires that have been expressed toward it (Heb. 11:10). That which brings joy and fulfillment to life will be included in the kingdom. Those things which produce sorrow or discomfort in life will be excluded from the kingdom of God. The following chart identifies some of the specific elements of that world.

A KINGDOM TO BE DESIRED (Hebrews 11:10)	
Joy	Isa. 9:3-4
Glory	Isa. 24:23
Comfort	Isa. 12:1-2
Full knowledge	Isa. 11:1-2
No sickness	Isa. 33:24

C. THE GOVERNMENT OF THE MILLENNIUM. Any society, except anarchy, is reflective of some form of government. The Millennium is best designated as a theocracy. In an attempt to define a theocracy in contrast to a monarchy and republic, Peters notes,

While it is not a monarchy in the sense adverted to by Samuel, viz.: of purely human origin, yet it is a monarchy in the highest sense. It is not a Republic, for the legislative, executive, and judicial power is *not potentially* lodged in the people, but *in God the King*; and yet it embraces in itself the elements both of a Monarchy and of a Republic;—a Monarchy in that *the absolute Sovereignty* is lodged in the person of *the One great King*, to which all the rest are subordinated, but Republican in this, that it embraces a Republican element in preserving *the rights of every individual*, from the lowest to the highest. . . . In other words, by a happy combination, Monarchy under divine direction, hence infallible, brings in the blessings that would result from a well-directed ideally Republican form of government, but which the latter can never fully, of itself, realize, owing to the depravity and diversity of man.[154]

Although Christ will reign as Sovereign in the kingdom, there is some question as to whether He is the only one on the throne. There are a number of passages that seem to suggest a reign of David in the Millennium (Isa. 55:3-4; Jer. 30:9; Ezek. 34:23-24; 37:24-25; Hos. 3:5; Amos 9:11). While premillennialists all agree that Christ will reign as "the Son of David" (Matt. 1:1), there are at least two views concerning the meaning of these passages suggesting a regency of David. Ironside sees this use of the name David typically when he says,

I do not understand this to mean David himself will be raised and caused to dwell on the earth as king. . . . The implication is that He who was David's Son, the Lord Jesus Christ Himself, is to be King, and thus David's throne will be reestablished."[155]

The second view suggests a literal reign of the historic David during the Kingdom Age. Newell suggests,

We must not confuse in our minds this situation. We must believe the plain words of God. David is not the Son of David. Christ, as Son of David, will be King; and David, His father after the flesh, will be *prince*, during the Millennium.[156]

Pentecost seems to favor this second interpretation.

There are several considerations which support this interpretation. (1) It is most consistent with the literal principle of interpretation. (2) David alone could sit as regent in the millennium without violating the prophecies concerning David's reign. (3) Resurrected saints are to have positions of responsibility in the millennium as a reward (Matt. 19:28; Luke 19:12-27). David might well be appointed to this responsibility since he was "a man after God's own heart."[157]

The Scriptures also suggest the presence of many other lesser rulers. One of the millennial titles of Christ is "King of kings, an Lord of lords" (Rev. 19:16) suggesting the presence of lesser kings and lords. The twelve disciples will apparently serve as the principal judges of the twelve tribes of Israel (Matt. 19:28). Also, it appears that some individuals may have responsibilities over groups of cities (Luke 19:12-28). The Millennium will probably see a reinstitution the judiciary established when Israel settled in the land (Isa. 1:26). Although the Scriptures are not specific on the political constitution of the kingdom, the following chart is consistent with the biblical references relevant to the government of the kingdom.

THE GOVERNMENT OF THE KINGDOM

Jesus Christ
(King of kings, Lord of lords)

David
(Perhaps Regent of Palestine)
(Other Geographic Regions
may have similar Leaders)

Christ's Twelve Disciples
(Principal Leaders of the Tribes of Israel)

Divinely Appointed Judges

Regional Lords over Groups of Cities

D. WORSHIP IN THE MILLENNIUM. During the millennial age, worship will again be centralized in the appointed place of God's choosing (cf. Deut. 12:14). Most premillennialists believe the temple will be built in or near Jerusalem and will serve as the central place of worship. Much of Ezekiel's prophecy dealt with this millennial temple (Ez. 40:1-46:24). Not all Christians agree that this temple is a literal temple to he used in the Kingdom Age. As a result, several alternative views have been proposed. Summarizing these views, Gray writes,

There are five interpretations of these chapters:
(1)   Some think they describe the temple at Jerusalem prior to the Babylonian captivity, and are designed to preserve a memorial of it. But the objection is that such a memorial is unnecessary because of the records in Kings and Chronicles; while the description is untrue because in many particulars it does not agree with that in the books named.

(2) Some think these chapters describe the temple in Jerusalem after the return from the seventy years in Babylon, but this can not be, because there are more marks of contrast than likeness between the temple here described and that.

(3) Some think they describe the ideal temple which the Jews should have built after the seventy years' return, and which they never realized. But this lowers the character of the divine Word. Why should this prophecy in Ezekiel have been given if it was never to be fulfilled?

(4) Some think this temple in Ezekiel symbolizes the spiritual blessings of the church in the present age. But this appears unlikely, because even those who hold the theory cannot explain the symbolism of which they speak. Moreover, even as symbolism it leaves out several important features of Christianity, such as the atonement and intercession of the high priest.

(5) The last view is that in the preceding comments, that we have here a prediction of the temple that shall be built in the millennial age. This appears a fitting and intelligent sequel to the preceding prophecies.[158]

One might question the need for a temple during the millennium in light of the fact that Israel has not had a temple since A.D. 70. Also, the Scriptures indicate much of the typical significance in both the temple building and service has already found its fulfillment in Christ. Addressing this issue, Unger suggests five purposes realized in the millennial temple.

(1) *To Demonstrate God's Holiness*
(2) *To provide a Dwelling-Place for the Divine Glory*
(3) *To Perpetuate the Memorial of Sacrifice*
(4) *To Provide the Centre for the Divine Government*
(5) *To Provide Victory over the Curse* (47:1-12)[159]

The third of these purposes, relating to the practice of sacrifice in the temple, is one debated among conservative theologians. Allis considers a literal interpretation of these sacrifices necessarily means a renouncing of the gospel and a return to the Mosaic economy.

Its literalistic and Old Testament emphasis leads almost inevitably, if not inevitably, to a doctrine of the millennium which makes it definitely Jewish and represents a turning back from the glory of the gospel to those typical rites and ceremonies which have prepared the way for it, and having served that necessary purpose have lost for ever their validity and propriety.[160]

Kelly seems to justify the conclusion of Allis when he emphasizes a Jewish worship in the kingdom apparently distinct from that Christians. Commenting on these sacrifices, he writes,

Israel shall yet return to the land, and be converted indeed, and blessed, under Jehovah their God, but as Israel, not as *Christians*, which all believers do become meanwhile, whether Jews or Gentiles. They belong to Christ in heaven, where such differences are unknown, and therefore one of the great characteristics of Christianity is that such distinctions disappear while Christ is head on high, and His body is being formed on earth by the Holy Ghost sent down from heaven. When Ezekiel's visions shall be accomplished, it will be the reign of Jehovah-Jesus on earth, and the distinction of Israel from the Gentiles will again be resumed, though for blessing under the new covenant, not as of old for curse under the law. . . . The heavenly people rest upon one sacrifice, and draw near into the holiest of all, where Christ is at the right hand of God. But the earthly people will have a sanctuary as well as land suited to them, and such are all the ordinances of their worship.[161]

A better explanation of these sacrifices during the Millennium emphasizes their memorial nature for all in the kingdom. A similar situation might be seen in the ordinance of the Lord's Supper. When instituted before Jesus died on the cross, the symbolic elements were typically pointing forward to his death. When later practiced by the church, these elements were memorial. At no time was the Supper atoning, although the message of the atonement is undeniably central in its meaning. Similarly, the sacrifices under the law were typical of the only atoning sacrifice, that of Christ. Their reinstitution in the Millennium will emphasize their nature as memorial. Concerning the purpose of the sacrifices in the kingdom, Pentecost concludes,

1. It is to be observed, in the first place, that the millennial sacrifices *will have no relation to the question of expiation.* They will not be expiatory for it is nowhere stated that they are offered with a view to salvation from sin.
. . . .
2. In the second place, the sacrifices *will be memorial* in character. There is general agreement among premillennialists as to the purpose of the sacrificial system as inaugurated in the millennial age. Interpreted in the light of the New Testament, with its teaching on the value of the death of Christ, they must be memorials of that death.
. . . .
3. It is concluded, then, that these sacrifices are not expiatory, for no sacrifice ever accomplished the complete removal of sin, but are memorials of the perfect *sacrifice* of the One typified by all sacrifice, the Lamb of God that taketh away the sin of the world.[162]

E. THE PURPOSE OF THE MILLENNIUM. Since God is wise and omniscient, he does not accomplish acts without reason. God has several purposes to fulfill by ushering in a thousand years of peace in the world. This period of time gives God the opportunity to reward the saints of all time. The reign will come in answer to the prayer "Thy kingdom come." God will redeem creation and rebuild the temple of David. He will finish what was previously began. God will fulfill three important Old Testament covenants during the rule on earth (the Abrahamic, the Davidic, and the New Covenant). The Millennium will also serve to complete the ministry of Christ. But most important, God will fulfill His promise to Abraham and give him the land.

1. *Rewards.* The doctrine of rewards is one of the chief motivational doctrines in Scripture. Isaiah taught concerning rewards, "Behold, the LORD God will come with strong hand, and his arm shall rule for him: behold, his reward is with him, and his work before him" (Isa. 40:10). Jesus said, "For the Son of man shall come in the glory of his Father with his angels; and then he shall reward every man according to his works" (Matt. 16:27). The apostle Paul looked forward to his "crown of righteousness, which the Lord, the righteous judge, shall give me at that day: and not to me only, but unto all them also that love his appearing" (2 Tim. 4:8). The giving of promised rewards is one of the purposes of Christ's reign on earth.

2. *Prayer.* God will keep His promise to hear and answer prayer. When His disciples wanted to know how to pray, Jesus provided a model which has become known as "The Lord's Prayer" (Matt. 6:9-13; Luke 11:1-4). When Christians pray, "Thy kingdom come," they are expressing a twofold desire. First, they seek the rule of God in their lives and in the world today. That is why we pray, "Thy will be done on earth as it is in heaven." A second desire expressed is for the actual, literal reign of Christ on the earth. God will answer both requests in the Millennium.

3. *Redeem creation.* God created a harmonious and perfect world described as "very good" (Gen. 1:31). With the entrance of sin into the world, that creation was placed under the bondage of sin. At the return of Christ to establish His kingdom, the natural world will be delivered from that bondage. Peter described this time as "the times of restitution of all things, which God hath spoken by the mouth of all his holy prophets since the world began" (Acts 3:21). The curse will be lifted. Thorns and thistles that make work torturous will disappear. The earth will yield its strength and man will enjoy the fruit and beauty of nature.

4. *Rebuilding of the temple.* One of the things done in the Millennium will be the rebuilding of the temple. The Old Testament prophets wrote, "After this I will return, and will build again the tabernacle of David, which is fallen down; and I will build again the ruins thereof, and I will set it up" (Acts 15:16). Several chapters in Ezekiel deal specifically with the rebuilding of the millennial temple and conducting of memorial sacrifices (Ezek. 40-48).

5. *Covenants.* The Lord is a covenant-keeping God and on several occasions made covenants with Israel. Three important covenants will be fulfilled in the Millennium: the Abrahamic Covenant (Gen. 12:1-3) promised that Israel would be a great nation and possess the Promised Land. The Davidic Covenant (2 Chron. 13:5; 2 Sam. 7:12-16) promised the seed of David (Christ) would rule forever on the throne of David. The New Covenant (Jer. 31:31-34) promised a spiritual rebirth for the nation Israel. These things will be accomplished in the thousand-year reign of Christ. If a person denies the existence of the Millennium, he attempts to tie the hands of God so He cannot keep his promises in a literal way.

6. *Ministry of Christ.* Peter described the ministry of Christ in terms of "the sufferings of Christ, and the glory that should follow" (1 Pet. 1:11). Much of His earthly ministry would be

included in the first part of that description, but His glory will be revealed in the Millennium. The following chart contrasts these two aspects of Christ's ministry.

"THE SUFFERINGS OF CHRIST, AND THE GLORY THAT SHOULD FOLLOW" (1 Pet. 1:11)	
The Sufferings	The Glory
A baby in humble clothes. Luke 2:12	A king, dressed in majestic apparel. Psa. 93:1
He was weary. John 4:6	He will be untiring. Isa. 40:28-29
He had nowhere to lay His head. Luke. 9:58	He will own all things. Heb. 1:2
He was rejected by His own. John 1:11	He will be recognized by all nations. Isa. 9:6
He was acquainted with grief. Isa. 53:3	He is the Mighty God. Heb. 1:9
His royal robe was mocked. Luke 23:11	He will be clothed with a vesture dipped in the blood of His enemies, Rev. 19:13
He was smitten with a reed. Matt. 27:30	He will rule with a rod of iron. Rev. 19:15
Soldiers bowed their knee and mocked Him. Mark 15:19	Every knee shall bow and acknowledge Him. Phil. 2:10
He wore the crown of thorns. John 19:5	He will wear the crown of gold. Rev. 14:14
His hands were pierced with nails. John 20:25	His hands will carry a sharp sickle. Rev. 14:14
His feet were pierced with nails. Psa. 22:16	His feet will stand on the Mount of Olives. Zech. 14:4
He had no form or beauty. Isa. 53:2	He will be the fairest of ten thousand. Psa. 27:4
He was laid in the tomb. Matt. 27:59-60	He will sit on His throne. Heb. 8:1

XVI. The Eternal Abode Of The Unsaved

No one really wants to talk about hell, but it exists as a definite part of the eternal plan of God. Hell is not the devil's playground, nor is it someone's punishment on earth. God created hell, a real place where real people will suffer real punishment for a real eternity. One of the primary dangers of false religions is their denial of this place. They tend to define it merely as an ancient superstition, yet its existence is so well documented in the Word of God that to deny hell is to deny the authority of the Bible. Hell has rightfully been called the most sobering doctrine in all Scripture. As Braun has noted,

> When it comes right down to it, in the English language, *hell* is the strongest expletive available that carries the idea of ultimate deprivation, devastation, fear, torment, punishment, suffering, and loss. Whether or not the user of the term *hell* believes in an actual, literal hell is of little or no consequence. There is an inbuilt, inarticulated, yet understood bite in the very word itself.[163]

While some apparently would prefer to remove this doctrine from their theological system, the nature of God and the existence of His law demand the existence of such a place. God could scarcely be considered holy, just or righteous if disobedience to His law is tolerated or unchallenged. Law would be nonexistent if God should refuse to invoke a penalty upon those who violate it. In his essay on the subject of hell, Kuehner argues,

> In a world created and governed by a sovereign and holy God, there must be judgment, or else the very fabric of the spiritual universe is torn to shreds. But Scripture calls it God's "strange work" (Isa. 28:21 KJV); he takes no delight in it, and in the fullest way possible he extends his mercy that it may triumph over judgment.[164]

Just as God is holy (Lev. 11:44-45; 19:2; 20:7, 26), so God is also love (1 John 4:8). Neither of these two, nor any of the other attributes of God, may deny or contradict each other. The harmony of the holiness and love of God is perhaps nowhere better illustrated than in the attitude of God toward hell. Chafer notes,

> If eternal punishment cannot be comprehended, it should be remembered that infinite holiness and the sin by which infinite holiness is outraged are equally unmeasurable by the human mind. God is not revealed as one who causes good people to suffer in hell; but He is revealed as one who at infinite cost has wrought to the end that sinners, believing in Christ, may not perish, but have everlasting life.[165]

Most who would be inclined to deny or minimize this doctrine fail to realize its relationship to other dearly held beliefs. To deny hell ultimately must include a denial of Christ's redemptive work and ultimately a denial of heaven itself. Braun emphasizes the relationship between the atonement and the existence of hell.

The atonement Christ made is infinite, because it was God who suffered and died in Christ. An infinite atonement was necessary because man's sin, being against the most Holy God, is an infinite offense. The enormity of that offense is demonstrated by the fact that it deserves eternal punishment. Moreover, the scriptural and traditional teaching on the redemption simply assumes the validity of retributive punishment on the part of God. If we lose sight of the fact that the wicked deserve punishment, the redemption is utterly pointless and nonexistent.[166]

Munsey observed the relationship between heaven and hell.

In fact, if there is no future punishment for the wicked, there is no future reward for the righteous. If there is no eternal future punishment for the wicked, there is no eternal future reward for the righteous. The Bible unites the two, and uses the same language to express the time when both are entered into, and their continuation.[167]

One might well ask why God revealed this doctrine in Scriptures. Pieper suggests, "The purpose of this shocking doctrine of eternal damnation is to warn against unbelief and carnal security and thus to save from eternal damnation."[168] Certainly the preaching of this doctrine has been with an evangelistic end in mind. But this doctrine has also served as a motivating force in the lives of great Christian leaders. General William Booth, founder of the Salvation Army, vowed he would close his training schools if he could send his workers to hell for five minutes. One of America's leading pastors, Dr. Jack Hyles, often says he works hard winning souls because he believes that his father went to hell. It would be impossible to identify all the missionaries who have chosen to spend their lives in a foreign culture because they believed that lost people will spend eternity in hell if they do not believe the gospel. Chafer observes the emphasis on evangelism in Scripture as it relates to the unsaved.

As to the destiny of the heathen to whom no knowledge of the Gospel has come, Scripture again is silent, except that it teaches that all men are lost who do not believe on Christ. Two features characterize this age: (1) the Gospel is to be preached to every creature, and (2) those to whom it is preached are to be judged according to their reception of it. The woeful failure of the children of God to take the Gospel to every creature has created a condition for which Scripture does not and could not provide a revelation. However, it is to be concluded that the heathen are eternally lost apart from the knowledge of divine grace, since the importance of preaching the gospel to them is stressed by Christ beyond any other issue in this age.[169]

A. HISTORICAL ATTITUDES TOWARD THE DOCTRINE OF HELL

1. *Jewish Theology.* Even before the existence of the church, the people of God have believed in a literal place of punishment or retribution for the unsaved. Although the Old Testament tends not to emphasize the after-life, neither does it completely ignore the subject. The term "sheol" is used in the Old Testament to describe the after-death home of both the

saved and unsaved; but even before the teaching of Christ on this subject, Jewish literature had refined the doctrine of sheol to include a separate place for the wicked. Kuehner summarizes both the biblical and extrabiblical understanding of this term.

> Sheol, the place to which both godly and ungodly are said to go after death, is depicted as an abode of shadowy, limited existence, but existence nonetheless. Later, in noncanonical Jewish literature, we meet with the ideas of compartments within sheol, areas designed separately for the wicked and the righteous, in which each experiences a foretaste of his final destiny (Enoch xxii.).[170]

This compartmentalization of sheol in post-canonical Jewish literature is perhaps implied in the canonical writings. Although there is no direct statement concerning a division in sheol, it is implied in the Old Testament statements concerning a place of blessing for the righteous. Buis argues,

> The Old Testament clearly teaches a life after death, commonly in the favor of an existence in Sheol, where good and evil alike share a similar dreary fate. However, there are also passages of inspired hope in a life after death for the believer, a life of glorious fellowship with his God. Although there is in these passages no direct teaching with regard to the eternal punishment of the unbeliever, there is the beginning of a differentiation between the lot of the unbeliever and that of the believer.[171]

2. *Teaching of Jesus.* Though Jesus is not usually characterized as a "hellfire and brimstone preacher," the doctrine of hell was a major tenet in His theology. Shedd suggests the teaching of Christ is the strongest argument for the existence of hell.

> The strongest support of the doctrine of Endless Punishment is the teaching of Christ, the Redeemer of man. . . .
> . . . .
> The mere perusal of Christ's words when he was upon earth, without note or comment upon them, will convince the unprejudiced that the Redeemer of sinners knew and believed, that for impenitent men and devils there is an endless punishment.[172]

The teaching of Christ concerning hell is perhaps the most severe in all Scripture. Summarizing the essence of Jesus' doctrine, Kuehner suggests,

> Never were there words as solemn and as searching as those in which Jesus warned of the judgment to come. In twelve of thirty-six of his parables he depicts men as judged, condemned, and punished for their sins. . . . Some of Jesus' sternest teaching on divine retribution appears in the Sermon on the Mount. . . . Elsewhere in the Gospels, Jesus' teaching sounds the same deep note of judgment. The terms he

employs to warn of that impending crisis are, to be sure, graphic, symbolic, figurative; but they are nonetheless terribly real. He speaks of unquenchable fire, of outer darkness, of the undying worm, of the weeping and gnashing of teeth, of the resurrection of judgment, of the judgment of hell, of perdition, of many stripes.[173]

So extensive is the teaching of Christ on hell that even some of those who would themselves deny the biblical doctrine do not deny that it is a doctrine taught by Christ. Commenting on Christ's use of gehenna (Matt. 10:28; Luke 12:5), Manson observes, "In this passage Gehenna means the place of torment for those who are condemned in the final judgment."[174]   Bultmann confesses concerning the teaching of Christ, "He expects the resurrection of the dead (Mk. 12:18-27) and the judgment (Luke 11:71ff). He shares the idea of a fiery hell into which the damned are to be cast (Mk. 9:43-48; Matt. 10:28)."[175]   Any survey of the teaching of Christ must conclude, in the words of Baird, "Despite its attractiveness, Universalism has many inherent weaknesses that make its tenability as a Christian doctrine extremely dubious and as the teaching of Jesus, impossible."[176]

3. *Early Church and Fathers.* The apostles and church fathers did not alter the view of Christ concerning eternal punishment. The writer of the Hebrews cited "eternal judgment" as one of the seven fundamentals of the early church (Heb. 6:1-2). Though not emphasized to the degree found in the teaching of Christ, no apostle neglects a mention of hell. This will be examined more carefully in the next section.

Concerning the attitude of the fathers, Fisher suggests, "In the ancient period—the patristic period—embracing the first six centuries—the doctrine of endless punishment was the prevalent opinion."[177]   With the notable exception of Origen, who was specifically condemned and opposed by his bishop, three Fourth Century Councils, the Fifth Ecumenical Council, the Seventh Ecumenical Council, Jerome, Epiphanius, Augustine, et. al., the major church fathers were uniform in their insistence upon a doctrine of endless punishment for the wicked. Tertullian taught,

> Therefore after this there is neither death nor repeated resurrections, but we shall be the same that we are now, and still unchanged—the servants of God, ever with God, clothed upon with the proper substance of eternity; but the profane, and all who are not true worshippers of God, in like manner shall be consigned to the punishment of everlasting fire—that which from its very nature indeed directly ministers to their incorruptibility.[178]

Hippolytus of Rome argued,

> The fire which is unquenchable and without end awaits these latter, and a certain fiery worm which dieth not, and which does not waste the body, but continues bursting forth from the body with unending pain. No sleep will give them rest; no night soothe them, no death will deliver them from punishment, nor shall any voice of interceding friends profit them.[179]

According to Cyprian of Carthage,

> An ever-burning Gehenna will burn up the condemned, and a punishment devouring
> with living flames; nor will there be any time whence they may have either rest or end
> to their torments. The pain of punishment will be without the fruit of penitence;
> weeping will be useless, and prayers ineffectual. Too late they will believe in eternal
> punishment who do not believe in eternal life.[180]

Another of the fathers, John Chrysostom, believed,

> It is necessary that those who have sinned shall put on immortality, not, however, for
> any honour to themselves, but in order that the path of that punishment may survive
> increasingly. . . . Neither will any severity of torment destroy the soul, nor will the
> body be able, in that time, to be consumed by burnings, but distressed it will survive
> with the soul, nor will there be any end.[181]

4. *Middle Ages.* Throughout the Middle Ages, a proper theology of hell tended to be
neglected, but not completely ignored. Unfortunately, most of the pressing theological issues
and debates of the day were in the area of speculative theology: i.e., how many angels could
dance on the head of a pin? Still, despite the absence of serious study in the field of
eschatology, the church remained firm in her belief of hell. The popular view of hell during
that era is probably best represented in the words inscribed over the gates of hell as recorded in
Dante's *Inferno*.

> I am the way into the city of woe.
> I am the way to a forsaken people.
> I am the way into eternal sorrow.
>
> Sacred Justice moved my architect.
> I was raised here by divine omnipotence,
> Primordial love and ultimate intellect.
>
> Only those elements time cannot wear
> Were made before me, and beyond time I stand.
> Abandon all hope ye who enter here.[182]

The discussions of hell in the Middle Ages were not left exclusively to the poets and
literary artists of the day. Hell was preached in the pulpits, taught in the catechisms and, on
the rare occasion when serious theological discussions occurred, discussed among the
theologians. Typical of the preaching on hell in that era is the following extract from a sermon
preached in the winter of 829-830.

Yet one must know that, as "in the Father's house are many rooms" for diversity and worth, so dissimilarity of offense subjects the damned in the fires of Gehenna to different punishments. This Gehenna by no means burns all with one and the same quality, although there is only one Gehenna. These punishments torture beyond strength the ones plunged into it; and even while extinguishing in them the bulwark of life the punishments keep them alive that the end may punish life, seeing that one may live forever without cessation of torment, for one hastens through tortures toward an end, but failing he endures without end, a ceaseless cessation, since death lives, the end ever begins, and cessation knows not how to cease.[183]

Perhaps two of the greater thinkers of the Middle Ages were Thomas Aquinas and Anselm of Canterbury. Though writing in different contexts and with differing perspectives on various theological topics, both taught the existence of a place of eternal retribution. According to Anselm,

Nothing can be more sure to follow more consistently, and nothing ought to be believed more assuredly, than that man's soul was created in such a way that if it despises loving the Supreme Being it will suffer eternal wretchedness. Consequently, just as the loving soul will rejoice in an eternal reward, so the despising soul will grieve in eternal punishment. And as the former will experience immutable sufficiency, so the latter will experience inconsolable need.[184]

Similarly, Aquinas taught,

It must also be known that the condition of the damned will be the exact contrary to that of the blessed. Theirs is the state of eternal punishment, which has a fourfold evil condition. The bodies of the damned will not be brilliant; "Their countenances shall be as faces burnt" (Isa. 13:18). Likewise they shall be passable, because they shall never deteriorate and, although burning eternally with fire, they shall never be consumed: "Their worm shall not die and their fire shall not be quenched." They will be weighed down, and the soul of the damned be as it were chained therein." To bind their kings with fetters, and their nobles with manacles of iron." Finally, they will be in a certain manner fleshly in both soul and body: "The beasts have rotted in their dung."[185]

5. *Post-Reformation.* Although the Reformation resulted in diversity in almost every area of dogmatic theology, belief in the existence of a place of everlasting punishment has since characterized both the Reformed and Catholic church. As Hunt observed over a hundred years ago,

If there be any doctrine ever taught in the name of Christianity which can claim to be really catholic, it is the doctrine of never-ending punishment. This has been believed by the majority of Christians in all ages, in all Churches, and, with very insignificant exceptions, in all sects. Fathers, schoolmen, and Reformers, zealous Roman Catholics and ardent Protestants, have agreed that this is an undeniable portion of the Catholic faith.[186]

The universally held doctrine of endless punishment does not prove its orthodoxy, but demonstrates something of the consistency with which the Holy Spirit has illuminated the same truth to various individuals in different cultures at different times. Charles Hodge summarizes the essence of what has been believed,

> The common doctrine is, that the conscious existence of the soul after the death of the body is unending; that there is no repentance or reformation in the future world; that those who depart this life unreconciled with God, remain forever in this state of alienation, and are therefore forever sinful and miserable. This is the doctrine of the whole Christian Church, of the Greeks, of the Latins and of all the great historical Protestant bodies.[187]

Since the Reformation, there has been a broader range of interpretation and systematizing of this doctrine, although there has continued to be an emphasis on the biblical images of hell. Thus Edwards preached hell in New England.

> The wrath of God burns against them, their damnation does not slumber; the pit is prepared, the fire is made ready, the furnace is now hot, ready to receive them; the flames do now rage and glow. The glittering sword is whet, and held over them, and the pit hath opened its mouth under them.[188]

Likewise, Tractarian leader E. B. Pusey declared,

> Remember the parching flame, the never-dying worm, the ever-lasting fire, the gnashing of teeth, "the smoke of torment" which "goeth up for ever and ever"; where they have no rest day nor night. Set heaven and hell before your eyes, so you may escape hell, and by God's mercy attain heaven.[189]

But since the Reformation there has also been a tendency toward an allegorical interpretation of the biblical images of hell, even by otherwise conservative theologians. Berkhof declares, "A great deal of the language concerning heaven and hell must be understood figuratively."[190] His declaration is little more than a summary of Charles Hodge, who seventy-five years earlier wrote,

> There seems to be no more reason for supposing that the fire spoken of in Scripture is to be literal fire, than that the worm that never dies is literally a worm. The devil and his angels who are to suffer the vengeance of eternal fire, and which doom the finally impenitent are to share, have no material bodies to be acted upon by elemental fire.[191]

This is a real danger among conservative Christians when they deviate from a literal approach to interpreting Scripture. It is generally conceded that Origen, the father of allegorical interpretation, was the same Origen whose eschatology was consistently condemned during his lifetime and centuries later. One might well ask how such a view differs, apart from the degree of consistency with which it is held, from that of John A. T. Robinson, who declares,

> To express convictions going beyond sight and touch, the Bible, like all ancient literature, projects pictures (not, of course, intended to be taken literally) of "another world" to which people "go" when they die. Subsequent Christian tradition has elaborated these — and often distorted them.[192]

If the Scriptures fail to give a complete revelation of hell, it is no doubt due to the limitations of human intelligence to comprehend the incredible horror of such a place. This does not mean the biblical images are not real. They are not only real, they represent merely the tip of the iceberg. The popular allegorical approach to interpreting the biblical images of hell accomplishes little more than convey the impression hell is really not as bad as it could be. Braun observes,

> There is a large contingent of moderns who have the unsettling suspicion that there is a hell in the hereafter. But, no worry, "it couldn't be all that bad." Certainly, it isn't as good a place as heaven, but it isn't bad enough to make it worth giving up the sinful things in this life just to avoid going there.
> Those with this view see the difference between heaven and hell as one only of degrees of something basically good.[193]

B. BIBLICAL TEACHING CONCERNING THE CHARACTER OF HELL. The biblical doctrine of hell is revealed by the use of many words and figures in both the Old and New Testaments. Each of these contributes something to the complete revelation concerning hell. Even with these many descriptions, our knowledge of such a place necessarily remains limited. The creator of mankind understands there is a psychological limit to man's ability to comprehend horror. Still, as Strong observes,

> The final state of the wicked is described under the figures of eternal fire (Matt. 25:41); the pit of the abyss (Rev. 9:2, 11); outer darkness (Mat. 8:12); torment (Rev. 14:10, 11); eternal punishment (Matt. 25:46); wrath of God (Rom. 2:5); second death (Rev. 21:8); eternal destruction from the face of the Lord (2 Thess. 1:9); eternal sin (Mark 3:29).[194]

The fact that these and other descriptions of hell are graphic does not mean they are necessarily unreal. While they may also represent other truths, there is no biblical reason for disputing a literal interpretation of the same. Commenting on the terms used in Scripture to describe hell, Alexander Hodge notes,

The terms in Scripture to describe these sufferings . . . certainly establish the following points. These sufferings will consist—1st. In the loss of all good, whether natural, as granted through Adam, or gracious, as offered through Christ. 2d. In all the natural consequences of unrestrained sin, judicial abandonment, utter alienation from God, and the awful society of lost men and devils—2 Thess. i:9. 3d. In the positive infliction of torment, God's wrath and curse descending upon both the moral and physical nature of its objects. The Scriptures also establish the fact that these sufferings must be—1st. Inconceivably dreadful in degree. 2d. Endless in duration. 3d. Various in degree, proportionate to the deserts of the subject.—Matt. x. 15; Luke xii. 48.[195]

1. *Sheol*. The derivation of the Hebrew term *sheol* is disputed among linguists and it is impossible to be dogmatic on linguistic evidence alone. Having summarized the three major views, Orr concludes,

> The etymology of the word is uncertain. A favorite derivation is from *shā'al*, "to ask" (cf Prov **1** 12; **27** 20; **30** 15.16; Isa **5** 14; Hab **2** 5); others prefer the √*sha'al*, "to be hollow." The Babylonians are said to have a similar word *Sualu*, though this is questioned by some.[196]

The Babylonian equivalent to sheol was not *saulu* but *aralu* and different from the Hebrew idea in that it was governed exclusively by its own gods. Sheol, however, is ruled by Jehovah in the Old Testament (cf. Psa. 139:8; Deut. 32:22; Job 26:6). Concerning the second of the above views, Innes suggests,

> The second main theory is that *še'ōl* is derived from the root *s-'-l*, from which come the words for a hollow hand (Is. xl. 12) and a hollow way (between vineyards, Nu. xxii.. 24). In post-biblical Hebrew *ša'al* means the 'deep' of the sea. If this derivation is correct, the original sense will be the hollow, or more probably deep, place.[197]

Some of the confusion over the meaning of "sheol" is due to the fact that it often appears merely to refer to the grave and at other times an existence, either positive or negative, after death. This is in part due to theological rather than grammatical assumptions on the part of the biblical writers. Shedd suggests, "Sheol signifies the 'grave,' to which all men, the good and evil alike, go down. That Sheol should have the two significations of hell and the grave. is explained by the connection between physical death and eternal retribution."[198] Summarizing the biblical usage of this term, Pentecost notes,

> The first is *Sheol*, which is used sixty-five times in the Old Testament, translated "hell" thirty-one times (cf. Deut. 32:22; Ps. 9:17; 18:5; Isa. 14:9), "grave" thirty-one times (cf. 1 Sam. 2:6; Job 7:9; 14:13), and "pit," three times (cf. Num. 16:30, 33; Job

17:16). This was the Old Testament word for the abode of the dead. It was presented, not just as a state of existence, but as a place of conscious existence (Deut. 18:11; 1 Sam. 28:11-15; Isa. 14:9). God was sovereign over it (Deut. 32:22; Job 26:6). It was regarded as temporary and the righteous anticipated the resurrection out of it into the millennial age (Job 14:13-14; 19:25, 27; Ps. 16:9-11; 17:15; 49:15; 73:24).[199]

In later non-canonical Jewish literature, sheol was compartmentalized, with specific areas for the righteous and the wicked (cf. Enoch 17:1-14). Though this was not necessarily a part of the biblical use of the word, there are several indications that at least part of sheol was understood in expressly negative terms. To descend into sheol was apparently a penalty for sin (Psa. 55:15; Prov. 9:18). It is described as destruction (Job 31:12; 26:6; 28:22; Psa. 88:11; Prov. 15:11, 27:20), the pit (Psa. 30:3; Ezek. 31:14) and corruption (Job 33:24; Psa. 16:10; Ezek. 28:8). It was further described as "naked before God" (Job 26:6) and the place where the wrath of God burns (Deut. 32:22). At times sheol appears to be the home of the wicked only. (Psa. 55:15). Summarizing this negative emphasis on sheol in the Old Testament, Braun suggests the concept of hell held by Old Testament saints was that of "a final, forever devouring, silent, purposeless, most distant place from God's heaven, shining with darkness and gloom, seeking all it may devour."[200]

2. *Hades.* When the LXX was translated the translators generally used the Greek word *hades* when translating *sheol*. Hades was also the designation of the underworld in Greek thought. Concerning the relation between these two words, Innes notes, "The Gk. *haidēs* represents the underworld, or realm of the dead, in the classics. In the LXX it almost always renders *še'ōl*, and in the New Testament the Pesh. renders it *seyol*."[201] Braun adds to this the exclusively negative emphasis of hades in the New Testament.

Hades is used ten or eleven times in the New Testament, and without doubt it refers to the exact same place as *Sheol* does in the Old Testament. There is one interesting difference, however. In the New Testament, *Hades* is never used to mean simply a sod grave; its only use is to describe the place of retribution for the wicked.[202]

The key passage in the New Testament describing hades is Luke 16:19-31, yet there is some dispute as to the nature of that passage. Some interpreters consider it little more than another of the parables of Jesus. According to Vos,

In further estimating its bearing upon the problem of the local conditions of the disembodied life after death, the parabolic character of the representation must be taken into account. The parable is certainly not intended to give us topographical information about the realm of the dead, although it presupposes that there is a distinct place of abode for the righteous and wicked respectively.[203]

In contrast with this parable view of the passage, dispensationalists generally argue that the passage is not a parable, but a real account. Commenting on this passage, Ironside writes,

Once more, as on other occasions recorded in this Gospel, Jesus uses the expression, "There was a certain rich man." Was there, or was there not? He definitely declared that there was. He did not introduce the story by saying, "Hear a parable," as on some other occasions; neither did He say, "The kingdom is as if there were a certain rich man and a poor beggar," or some similar language. But in the clearest, most definite way He declared, "There was a certain rich man." If any of His hearers had inquired the name of the man and of the town in which he lived, dare we doubt our Lord's ability to have answered both questions definitely? He knew this man; He knew how he had lived; He knew what took place after he died. We do not know his name and never shall know it until he stands before the great white throne. Ordinarily we call him Dives, but Dives is not a name; it is simply the Latin equivalent of the Greek for "rich man." Yet this unnamed man stands out on the pages of Holy Scripture as a distinct personality, the representative of many others who live for self and ignore the two great commandments which inculcate love to God and love to man.[204]

The rich man went to hades at death and was tormented in flames (Luke 16:24). The punishment of hades is (1) burning, (2) separation/loneliness, (3) conviction by memory, (4) thirst, (5) falling, and (6) stench. The rich man could look across "a great gulf fixed" (Luke 16:20) and see where the saved were located. However, the Scripture is silent as to whether the saved could see the torment of the unsaved. The one thing the rich man could not do was escape his torment. He could not even send a warning to his family.

The presence of the beggar in the relative proximity of the rich man suggests that originally both hades and paradise, or Abraham's bosom were in the same place. At His death, Christ descended "into the lower parts of the earth" and "led captivity captive" then He later ascended from that place (Eph. 4:8-10). Many commentators believe paradise was at that time released from the regions of hades and taken to a place known as the third heaven. Explaining this view, Scofield wrote,

> But when our Lord ascended into heaven, He took with Him those in paradise, and though paradise still exists as the abode of the blessed dead pending the resurrection, it is now in the third heaven, or the very place of our Lord's own presence. This appears from Ephesians 4:8, R.V., and 2 Corinthians 12:2-4. Christ ascending led a multitude of captives; and Paul, caught up into the third heaven, found himself in paradise.[205]

The word hades occurs eleven times in the New Testament although in one place, 1 Corinthians 15:55, the word is replaced with *thanatos* in many texts. Summarizing the use of this term in the New Testament, Bullinger suggests,

> If now the eleven occurrences of Hades in the New Testament be carefully examined, the following conclusions will be reached: (a) Hades is invariably connected with death; but never with life; always with dead people; but never with the living. All in Hades will "NOT LIVE

AGAIN," until they are raised from the dead (Rev. 20:5). If they do not "live again" until after they are raised, it is perfectly clear that they cannot be alive now. Otherwise we do away with the doctrine of the resurrection altogether. (b) That the English word "hell" by no means represents the Greek Hades; as we have seen that it does not give a correct idea of its Hebrew equivalent, Sheol. (c) That Hades can mean only and exactly what Sheol means, viz., the place where "corruption" is seen (Acts 2:31; compare 13:34-37); and from which resurrection is the only exit.[206]

3. *Tartaros.* Another biblical term describing hell is tartaros. It occurs only once in Scripture and even there it is technically a related verb rather than the noun itself. Peter uses the verb *tartarosas,* translated "cast them down to hell" (2 Pet. 2:4). Most agreed the verb is based on a Greek noun describing the lowest of the nine levels of hell in Greek thought. However, there is some disagreement among theologians concerning its relation to human experience. According to Braun,

Tarturtus is another Greek expression almost identical in meaning to Hades. Tarturus was, in fact, the lowest spot in the Greek Hades. Peter wanted an expression that would show the degree of judgment passed by God on angels who sinned. Translated into modern English, he said. "God cast them to the very bottom of hell." The meaning can hardly be mistaken.[207]

Part of the dispute over tartaros relates to its inhabitants. The word occurs in a context with gehenna in Enoch 20:2 suggesting, at least in Jewish theology, that only fallen angels were present there, whereas apostate Jews dwelt in the latter place. Some Christians suggest this "very bottom of hell" is reserved for individuals such as the Judas Iscariots and Adolf Hitlers of history. Others, ignoring the doctrine of degrees of punishment, argue the use of tartaros here shows the Christian view of hell is far worse than even the most horrible place conceived of outside of biblical revelation. More likely, tartaros should be seen as a place of judgment. or incarceration prior to judgment, of fallen angels. Bullinger argues that Tartaros,

. . . is not Sheol or Hades . . . where all men go in death. Nor is it where the wicked are to be consumed and destroyed, which is Gehenna. . . . Not the abode of *men* in any condition. It is used only here, and here only of "the angels that sinned" (see Jude 6). It denotes the bounds or verge of this material world. . . . not only the bounds of this material creation, but is so called from its coldness."[208]

A second part of this dispute relates to its location. As noted above, Bullinger appears to teach tartaros is a part of human experience, at least indirectly, in that it exists within the material creation, presumably within the higher atmosphere. In contrast, Barnes argues tartaros must exist in another place because this world was apparently not made as a prison of fallen angels. Commenting on the use of tartaros as in 2 Peter 2:4, he notes,

The word here used occurs nowhere else in the New Testament, though it is common in the classical writers. It is a verb formed from . . . *Tartarus,* which in Greek mythology was the lower part, or abyss, of hades where the shades of the wicked were supposed to be imprisoned and tormented, and answered to the Jewish word . . . *Gehenna*. It was regarded, commonly, as beneath the earth; as entered through the grave; as dark, dismal, gloomy; and as a place of punishment. Comp. Notes, Job x. 21, 22, and Matt. v. 22. The word here is one that properly refers to a place of punishment, since the whole argument relates to that, and since it cannot be pretended that the 'angels that sinned' were removed to a place of happiness on account of their transgression. It must also refer to punishment in some other world than this, for there is no evidence that *this* world is made a place of punishment for fallen angels.[209]

In his use of the verb *tartarosas*, Peter drew to some degree on both the Greek and Jewish ideas surrounding tartaros. In his context he appears to be in agreement with Enoch in distinguishing a hell for angels as distinct to some degree at least from that of men. Yet his emphasis on the severity of this judgment apparently borrows from the Greek idea of hades in which tartaros is the lowest level. It is difficult to be dogmatic in the denial of any relationship between tartaros and either hades or gehenna. This is particularly so in that Peter's verb really has the idea of being cast into "the lowest part" of hell and could be an emphasis on the most severe of various degrees of punishment in both hades and gehenna.

4. *Gehenna.* A fourth biblical term translated "hell" is gehenna. This is the most severe word for hell in Scripture and one used almost exclusively by Jesus. Because of the severity of some of the statements and images concerning gehenna, those who argue against the existence of a literal hell are most likely to dispute the meaning of this term. For instance, the official position of the Watchtower Bible and Tract Society is that, "In all places where hell is translated from the Greek word *Gehenna* it means everlasting destruction."[210] Of course, there is no suggestion of annihilation at all in any of the biblical statements relating to this word or in the etymological background of the term itself. Concerning gehenna, Pettingill notes,

Hell, properly translated, comes from the word Gehenna, which was a name applied to a place in the valley of Hinnom where in older times human sacrifices were offered (2 Chron. 33:6; Jer. 7:31). It is the name in Scripture for the lake of fire, the final and eternal abode of the lost (Rev. 19:20; 20:10,14,15).

It is a fact of solemn significance that while the word Gehenna, meaning "hell or lake of fire," occurs twelve times in the New Testament, in every instance, with one exception (Jas. 3:6), it came from the lips of our Lord Jesus Christ Himself (see Matt. 5:22,29,30; 10:28; 18:9; 23:15,33; Mark 9:43,45,47; Luke 12:5).[211]

The use of gehenna in the New Testament makes it clear that the word does not refer merely to a historical valley outside of Jerusalem, a garbage dump in that day. This term is associated with fire, punishment, torment and eternity. After identifying the dozen occurrences of this word in the New Testament, Vos explains,

In all of these it designates the place of eternal punishment of the wicked, generally in connection with the final judgment. It is associated with fire as the source of torment. Both body and soul are cast into it. This is not to be explained on the principle that the NT speaks metaphorically of the state after death in terms of the body; it presupposes the resurrection.[212]

When gehenna was first used by Jesus to describe hell, the Jews who heard him were familiar with the term. While associated with the Valley of the Son of Hinnom outside of Jerusalem, this term had previously been used in rabbinic literature as the place of eternal punishment. Summarizing the Jewish background of this term, Innes notes,

> Its original derivation is obscure. Some have regarded it as coming from an obsolete Aramaic root meaning 'wailing', but most authorities now regard this as improbable. Hinnom is almost certainly the name of a person. In later Jewish writings *Gehenna* came to have the sense of the place of punishment for sinners (*Assumption of Moses* x. 10; 2 Esdras vii. 36). The rabbinic literature contains various opinions as to who would suffer eternal punishment. The ideas were widespread that the suffering of some would be terminated by annihilation, or that the fires of *Gehenna* were in some cases purgatorial. But those who held these doctrines also taught the reality of eternal punishment for certain classes of sinners (A. Edersheim, *The Life and Times of Jesus the Messiah*, 1894, ii. 440, 791ff). Both this literature and the Apocryphal books affirm belief in an eternal retribution (*cf.* Judith xvi. 17, *Psalms of Solomon* iii. 13). The teaching of the New Testament endorses this belief.[213]

In using the term "gehenna" to describe hell, Jesus was using a word which would necessarily stir up revulsion in His hearers directed toward that place. That place had been the scene of human sacrifices during some of Israel's darkest hours and had been specifically cursed by God. Even for those unfamiliar with this background, the place was at that time used for the refuse of Jerusalem. Commenting on Jesus' use of hell, Vos suggests,

> That "the Valley of Hinnom" became the technical designation for the place of final punishment was due to two causes. In the first place the valley had been the seat of the idolatrous worship of Molech, to whom children were immolated by fire (2 Ch 28 3; 33 6). Secondly, on account of these practices the place was defiled by King Josiah (2 K 23 10), and became in consequence associated in prophecy with the judgment to be visited upon the people (Jer 7 32). The fact, also, that the city's offal was collected there may have helped to render the name synonymous with extreme defilement.[214]

Gehenna is the place of eternal retribution, the final abode of the unsaved. All of the descriptions emphasizing the repulsiveness of hell, i.e. the worm, fire, and gnashing of teeth are descriptions of gehenna. It is this writer's belief that the horror of gehenna is not completely described in Scripture because of man's inability psychologically, mentally and spiritually to comprehend such a place. Summarizing the biblical description of gehenna, Braun writes,

It defies the imagination to think of a place worse than Gehenna. Any Jew who had seen it, even without knowing its historical background, would have no difficulty understanding why Jesus would use the word to refer to the most loathsome place in all existence.

Understandably then, Gehenna, in its secondary sense, is hell. It is *the* place of retributive suffering, the place of fire and brimstone, the lake of fire, the place of the eternal torment of those condemned because of unrighteousness. It is the everlasting abode of the devil, his angels, and those whose names are "not found written in the Lamb's book of life."[215]

5. *Retribution.* Though the term "retribution" is absent in the Scripture, the idea of retribution is fundamental to our understanding of God. The biblical ideas of punishment, vengeance and wrath all suggest retribution as part of the judgment on sin. M'Caig identifies several terms implying this aspect of hell,

The word as applied to the Divine administration is not used in Scripture, but undoubtedly the idea is commonly enough expressed. The words which come nearest to it are ὀργή, orgē, and θυμός, thumos, wrath attributed to God; ἐκδικέω, ekdikéō, ἐκδίκησις, ekdikasis, giving ideas of vengeance; κόλασις, kolasis, and τιμωρία, timoria "punishment"; besides κρίνω, krinō and its derivatives, words expressive of judgment.[216]

When discussing the punishment of the wicked in a biblical context, "retribution" is the preferred word because of the connotations of each term. As Chafer explains,

In attempting to write a comprehensive statement of the most solemn doctrine of the Bible, the term retribution is chosen in the place of the more familiar word punishment since the latter implies discipline and amendment, which idea is wholly absent from the body of truth which discloses the final divine dealing with those who are eternally lost. It is recognized that, in its earlier and broader meaning, the term retribute was used for any reward, good or evil. The word is used . . . of the doctrine of hell only as reference is made to the eternal perdition of the lost.[217]

Retribution in hell exists for two reasons. First, the natural consequence of sin is necessarily destruction (cf. Prov. 14:12; 16:25; Matt. 7:13; Rom. 5:12). The corrupting nature of sin is such that it necessarily destroys all that it contacts. This does not minimize in any way the concept of divine wrath, but rather identifies another of the sources of retribution. In one sense, hell is hell because it is the place where sin is unrestrained in its destructive passion. According to M'Caig,

Another conclusion we may draw from the general Scriptural representation is that the future retribution is one aspect of the natural consequence of sin, yet it is also in another aspect the positive infliction of Divine wrath. It is shown to be the natural outcome of sin in such passages as "Whatsoever a man soweth, that shall he also reap" (Gal 6 7); "He that soweth unto his own flesh shall of the flesh reap corruption" (Gal 6 8). It is not without suggestiveness that the Hebrew word *āwōn* means both iniquity and punishment, and when Cain said "My punishment is greater than I can bear"; (Gen 4 13), he really said "My iniquity is greater than I can bear"; his iniquity became his punishment. A due consideration of this thought goes a long way toward meeting many of the objections brought against the doctrine of future punishment.[218]

While sin itself affects the character of hell, it must not be forgotten that hell also involves the infliction of the wrath of God. This aspect is particularly emphasized by Paul when he speaks of "the day of wrath and revelation of the righteous judgment of God; who will render to every man according to his deeds" (Rom. 2:5-6). Commenting on these verses, Stifler notes,

> After this solemn appeal under the first principle of the judgment, Paul brings in the second, "to every man according to his deeds." This really constitutes the closing sentence in the appeal, and thus shows that a judgment according to truth and a judgment according to works or "deeds" are practically the same thing. The former is abstract; the measure applied in judgment will be reality. This (v. 6) is concrete. That which is measured will be what is done, "deeds." The judgment will embrace "every one." That there is to be a judgment was not denied by the Jew; it cannot be denied by any sober man; and therefore Paul brings no proof in evidence. In that judgment, sure to come, God will render to every man according to his deeds.[219]

This aspect of the doctrine of retribution is emphasized repeatedly in the Scriptures by the very vocabulary of the Word of God. M'Caig explains.

> The terms in Scripture applied to the doom of sinners all imply Divine displeasure, punitive action, retribution. The two outstanding Gr words for "wrath," *orgē* and *thumos*, are both freely applied to God. *Orgē* indicates settled displeasure, whereas *thumos* is rather the blazing out of the anger. The former is, as we should expect, more frequently applied to God, and, of course, all that is capricious and reprehensible in human wrath must be eliminated from the word as used of God. It indicates the settled opposition of His holy nature against sin . . . . Thus the Divine wrath on account of sin is the dark background of the gospel message. Had there been no such just wrath upon men, there had been no need for the Divine salvation.[220]

Sometimes the character of God is raised in argument against the doctrine of retribution. But it is the character of God which, in fact, demands the judgment of sin. Law, being an extension of the person and nature of God, assumes a penalty for crimes committed. Thus, there could be no moral government of God here on earth or in heaven if this basic principle is denied. Drawing parallels between civil government and the moral government of God, Munsey explains the necessity of retribution.

> There must be a state of future punishment for the wicked, because the amount of the criminality of their sins cannot be estimated during time. There is no government without law. Law is a nullity without a penalty. In fact, as law is a necessity to government, so penalty is a necessity to law. Punishment for the violation of law lies at the very foundation of all government. Upon the certainty with which the penalty of the violation of law is inflicted, depends the existence and rectitude of the government. Government has no power unless its laws have a commensurate penalty, and unless it is well known by the subjects of the government, that the penalty will be enforced.[221]

The conclusion is inescapable. Belief in any positive aspect of the moral government of God (i.e., sovereignty, providence, heaven) necessarily and logically implies the existence of retribution upon those who violate the law of that government. In the Scriptures that place of retribution is identified as hell.

6. *Prison.* On two occasions the Scriptures use the word "prison" in an apparent reference to hell (1 Pet. 3:19; Rev. 20:7). Under Jewish law, imprisonment was not part of the penal code except when a prisoner found guilty was held until the execution of his sentence. This background may be applied to hell as a prison. Apparently, spirits in prison are awaiting a later execution of sentence. Prison, therefore, should be properly applied to hades rather than gehenna. Orr apparently agrees with this conclusion when commenting on the expression "spirits in prison" found in 1 Peter 3:19.

> It is plain that in this context "the spirits in prison" (τοῖς ἐν φυλακῇ πνεύμασιν, *tois en phulake pneumasin*) denote the generation who were disobedient in the days of Noah, while the words "spirits" and "in prison" refer to their present disembodied condition in a place of judgment in the unseen world (cf 2 Pet **2** 4-9).[222]

Concerning the meaning implied in the use of the term *phulaka* (prison) Barnes suggests,

> The word rendered prison, (φυλακῇ) means properly *watch, guard*—the act of keeping watch, or the guard itself; then watchpost, or station; then a place where any one is watched or guarded, as a prison; then a watch in the sense of a division of the night, as the morning watch. . . . The allusion, in the passage before us, is undoubtedly to confinement or imprisonment in the invisible world; and perhaps to those who are reserved there with reference to some future arrangement—for this idea enters commonly into the use of the word prison. There is, however, no specification

of the *place* where this is; no intimation that it is *purgatory*—a place where the departed are supposed to undergo purification; no intimation that their condition can be affected by anything that we can do; no intimation that those particularly referred to differ in any sense from the others who are confined in that world; no hint that they can be released by any prayers or sacrifices of ours.[223]

7. *Chains.* The image of chains is yet another biblical description of hell. In a popular view of eschatology, Charles Dickens portrayed the ghost of Jacob Marley as bound in chains; but in the Scriptures, chains appear to be reserved for angelic beings (2 Pet. 2:4; Jude 6; Rev. 20:1). In two of these three references, the word "chain" is associated with darkness and may not refer to a literal chain as one normally uses the noun. Barnes suggests,

> The meaning seems to be, that they are confined in that dark prison-house *as if* by chains. We are not to suppose that spirits are literally bound; but it was common to bind or fetter prisoners who were in dungeons, and the representation here is taken from that fact. This representation that the mass of fallen angels are confined in *Tartarus*, or in hell, is not inconsistent with the representations which elsewhere occur that their leader is permitted to roam the earth, and that even many of those spirits are allowed to tempt men. It may be still true that the mass are confined within the limits of their dark abode; and it may even be true also that Satan and those who are permitted to roam the earth are under bondage, and are permitted to range only within certain bounds and that they are so secured that they will be brought to trial at the last day.[224]

Concerning the third reference to chains and hell, various commentators are not agreed concerning the meaning of the chain with which Satan is bound during the Millennium. Scott appears to be satisfied with an exclusively symbolic interpretation.

> The angel has the key of the abyss and a great chain in his hand. One need scarcely insist upon the symbolic character of the scene, for *that* seems evident on the surface. The figures, however, of the key and chain surely denote that God is supreme even over the satanic region of the abyss. Thus instrumentally, by angelic agency, He locks (the *key*) up Satan and binds him (the *chain*) secure in the abyss for a thousand years. His liberty is curtailed and his sphere of operation narrowed. He is effectually curbed and restrained from doing further mischief on the earth until his prison door is unlocked (v. 7).[225]

Another premillennialist, however, argues that John saw Satan bound with a literal, an actual, chain. Admittedly, a physical chain that could bind a spiritual being is unique. Lindsey argues,

> I said that the key and chain were unusual, and they would have to be in order to hold a creature such as Satan, who has such enormous power of his own. I don't really

have any problem believing that God could make such a key and chain, since Satan has never really been free anyway. He's only been able to do what God has permitted. God has had him on a long leash, and now the time has come to pull it in![226]

8. *Stripes.* Emphasizing the idea of degrees of punishment in hell, Jesus used the image of "stripes" to describe the judgment to come (Luke 12:48). Not everybody agrees this reference necessarily refers to hell. Rice argues it is a reference to judgments that Christians will receive for disobedience. Commenting on these verses he wrote,

> But verses 47 and 48 teach us Christians that one who knew the Lord's will and did it not would be beaten with many stripes, and one who had more opportunity, had more responsibility, would suffer more when he meets Christ if he is not faithful. And one who had less information, had less place of opportunity, would be punished less if he fails.
> Oh how seriously we should take every open door of service![227]

Most commentators, however, would agree with Brown in applying these words to the unsaved. Commenting on Luke 12:48, he notes,

> So that there will be degrees of future punishment, proportioned to the light enjoyed— the knowledge sinned against. Even heathens are not without knowledge enough for future judgment (see on Rom. ii. 12-16); but the reference here is not to such. It is a solemn truth, and though *general*, like all other revelations of the future world, discloses a tangible and momentous principle in its awards.[228]

Scourging was a common form of punishment even unto recent times. Under the law, the number of stripes a man could receive was limited to forty, though in practice, thirty-nine stripes tended to be the maximum (Deut. 25:1-3). The Romans were not as humane. Dosker describes a Roman scourging,

> The victim was tied to a post (Acts **22** 25) and the blows were applied to the back and loins, sometimes even, in the wanton cruelty of the executioner, to the face and the bowels. In the tense position of the body, the effect can easily be imagined. So hideous was the punishment that the victim usually fainted and not rarely died under it. . . . As among the Russians today, the number of blows was not usually fixed, the severity of the punishment depending entirely on the commanding officer.[229]

Whatever else may be implied by Jesus' reference to stripes with reference to hell, it is certain He intended to emphasize the existence of degrees of punishment in hell. As not all sinners have equal light, nor have they engaged in their sin with equal intensity, it is also true that the degree of suffering will differ in hell. This does not in any way minimize the reality of suffering in hell. It will be of little comfort to one experiencing "few stripes" to know that somewhere else in hell, another is receiving "many stripes." Still, concerning this aspect of the doctrine of hell, Broadus rightly notes,

> This teaching has been in many cases grievously overlooked. Taking images literally, men have found that the 'Gehenna of fire' (Matt. 5:22) will be the same place and the same degree of punishment for all. But the above passage and many others show that there will be differences. The degrees of punishment must be as remote as the east is from the west. All inherited proclivities, 'taints of blood,' all differences of environment, every privilege and every disadvantage, will be taken into account. It is the Divine Judge that will apportion punishment, with perfect knowledge and perfect justice and perfect goodness. This great fact, that there will be *degrees* in future punishment—as well as future rewards—ought to be more prominent in religious instruction.[230]

9. *Weeping and gnashing of teeth.* On several occasions Jesus used the expression "weeping and gnashing of teeth" to describe the personal anguish of individuals in hell (Matt. 8:12; 13:42, 50; 22:13; 24:51; 25:30; Luke 13:28). The word "gnashing" "is used of grinding or striking together the teeth in rage, pain or misery of disappointment. In the OT it . . . represents for the most part rage, anger, hatred."[231] When Jesus used this expression, He was probably thinking of Psalm 112:10. Commenting on the gnashing of the wicked in that place, Spurgeon notes, "Being very wrathful, and exceedingly envious, he would fain grind the righteous between his teeth: but as he cannot do that, he grinds his teeth against each other."[232]

When describing hell in these terms, the language of Christ was vivid. Commenting on Matthew 13:42, Brown concludes,

> What terrific strength of language—the "casting" or "flinging" expressive of indignation, abhorrence, contempt (cf. Ps. ix. 17; Dan. xii. 2); "the furnace of fire" denoting the fierceness of the torment; the "wailing" signifying the anguish this causes; while the "gnashing of teeth" is a graphic way of expressing the despair in which its remedilessness issues.[233]

This expression seems to suggest the sorrow in hell will be caused by a sense of both loss and anger directed toward the righteous. There is some indication that the wicked in hell may have a view of the righteous in heaven, although the reverse is never suggested in Scripture (cf. Luke 16:23). Matthew Henry explains,

> 1. In hell there will be great grief, floods of tears shed to no purpose; anguish of spirit preying eternally upon the vitals, in the sense of the wrath of God, is the torment of the damned. 2. Great indignation: damned sinners will *gnash their teeth* for spite and vexation, *full of the fury of the Lord*; seeing with envy the happiness of others, and reflecting with horror upon the former possibility of their own being happy, which is now past.[234]

10. *Pit of the abyss or bottomless pit.* Seven times in the final book of the Bible, John describes hell as a "bottomless pit" (9:1-2,11; 11:7; 17:8; 20:1, 3). In each case the pit is closely associated with demons and they are generally being released from or confined to the pit. In the Old Testament, the image of a pit is also used of the abode of the wicked dead. In a note on the word "abyss" translated "bottomless" in the Revelation, Scott suggests,

> Abyss signifies *deep* (Luke 8.31) or *bottomless*. The word occurs nine times in the New Testament, seven of these in the Apocalypse, one in Luke as we have seen, and the other in Romans 10.7. *Out* of it the Beast ascends, and *into* it Satan is cast (Rev. 17.8; 20.3). The abyss is a place, but the locality is undetermined.[235]

On the phrase *tou phreatos tes abusson* (bottomless pit; Rev. 9:1), Robertson says,

> *Abussos* is an old adjective (alpha privitive and *buthos*, depth, without depth), but *hē abussos* (supply *chōra* place), the bottomless place. It occurs in Rom. 10:7 for the common receptacle of the dead for Hades (*Sheol*), but in Luke 8:31 a lower depth is sounded (Swete), for the abode of demons, and in this sense it occurs in Rev. 9:1, 2, 11; 11:17; 17:8; 20:1, 3. *Phrear* is an old word for well or cistern (Luke 14:5; John 4:11f.) and it occurs in Rev. 9:1f. for the mouth of the abyss which is pictured as a cistern with a narrow orifice at the entrance and this fifth angel holds the key to it.[236]

Paul, who makes direct reference to the pit of the abyss only once in his writings (Rom. 10:7), appears to use it in the same sense as sheol in the Old Testament. According to Godet, "The *abyss* frequently denotes the abode of the dead and of fallen angels (Luke viii. 31). For as the azure of the sky represents perfect salvation, so the depth of the sea is a natural figure for the abode of the death and the state of condemnation."[237] In apparent agreement, Murray suggests,

> The abyss in this instance may most suitably be taken as the synonym of *sheol* and the latter is frequently in the Old Testament "the grave". As in Matt. 11:23; Luke 10:15 heaven is contrasted with *hades*, so here heaven is contrasted with the abyss and, since it is in reference to Jesus' resurrection that the question is asked, the abyss can most conveniently denote what *sheol* and *hades* frequently denote in the Old Testament. In the LXX ἄβυσσος is very frequently the rendering of the Hebrew תהום the "deep" and in the singular and plural applied to the depths of the sea. In LXX Psalm 70:20 we have "the depths of the earth."[238]

The bottomless pit is portrayed as both the abode of demons and the unsaved. This figure of hell may also imply the idea of imprisonment as pits were most often used as prisons in ancient cultures. The idea of darkness may also be implied in John's use of this expression.

Further he seems to recognize it as a place of suffering (cf. Rev. 9:1-12). In his summary of the use of the abyss in Scripture, Douglas writes,

> It is used to describe the abode of demons (Lk. viii. 31), the place of the dead (Rom. x. 7), and in the Apocalypse as the place of torment (ix. 1, *etc.*). LXX renders Heb. *tehôm*, deep place, as 'abyss' (Gn. i. 2, *etc.*), with reference to the primitive idea of a vast mass of water on which the world floated, or to the underworld (Ps. lxxi. 20).[239]

11. *Outer darkness.* Another image of hell used by Christ was that of darkness. In the eschatology of the New Testament, heaven is portrayed as a bright, well-lighted place. To be exiled from heaven was to be placed in outer darkness. Jesus' use of the word *skotia* to describe this place suggests extreme darkness as opposed to that of a cloudy or foggy day, i.e., gloominess. Commenting on the expression "into the outer darkness" in Matthew 8:12, Robertson states,

> Comparative adjective like our "further out," the darkness outside the limits of the lighted palace, one of the figures for hell or punishment (Matt. 23:13; 25:30). The repeated article makes it bolder and more impressive, "the darkness the outside," there where the wailing and gnashing of teeth is heard in the thick backness of night.[240]

That this contrast between light and darkness should exist in New Testament eschatology is consistent with the use of light and darkness throughout the Scriptures. In Palestine, there is a noticeable contrast between the brightness of day and darkness of night. There is usually less than a single hour between day and night. It is only natural that this contrast, which was a part of the lives of those living in Palestine, should come to be used comparatively to teach theological truth. As Joy explains,

> In the Bible the main use of darkness is in contrast to light. Light is a symbol of God's purity, wisdom and glory. Darkness is the opposite . . . .
> The fig. uses of darkness are many and various. It is used as a symbol (a) of moral depravity and its punishment. The wicked walk and work in darkness (Ps 82 5; Prov 2 13; Jn 3 19; Rom 13 12), and their reward is to "sit in darkness" (Ps 107 10); or to be "cast forth into the outer darkness" (Mt 8 12); (b) of things mysterious or inexplicable (1 K 8 12; Ps 97 2); (c) of trouble and affliction (2 S 22 9; Job 5 14; Prov 20 20; Is 9:2; cf Gen 15 12); (d) of punishment (Lam 3 2; Ezk 32 8; Zeph 1 15); (e) of death (1 S 2 9; Job 10 21 f; Eccl 11 8); (f) of nothingness (Job 3 4-6); (g) of human ignorance (Job 19 8; 1 Jn 2 11).[241]

When Jesus used darkness to describe hell, He was emphasizing the dual nature of suffering in that place. First, the victim would be cut off from the light, the place of blessing and fulfillment. They would be victimized by darkness and all that it implies negatively.

The expression is emphatic—'The darkness which is outside.' To be 'outside' at all—or, in the language of Rev. xxii. 15, to be 'without' the heavenly city [ἔξω,], excluded from its joyous nuptials and gladsome festivities—is sad enough of itself, without anything else. But to find themselves not only excluded from the brightness and glory and joy and felicity of the kingdom above, but thrust into a region of "darkness," with all its horrors, this is the dismal retribution here announced, that awaits the unworthy at the great day.[242]

12. Destruction. On one occasion Paul used the expression "eternal destruction from the presence of the Lord" (2 Thess. 1:9) to describe hell. Although "destroyer" is one of the many titles of Satan (cf. Rev. 9:11), Paul alone of all biblical writers specifically identifies hell as the place of destruction. The idea was not foreign to Jewish thought and was believed to be the lot of the wicked. Paul in this context suggests it is the destiny of "them that know not God, and that obey not the gospel of our Lord Jesus Christ" (1 Thess. 1:8). Commenting on these verses, Morris explains,

> The thought of this verse is not of an unreasoning infliction of vindictive punishment, but of the meting out of merited desert. The penalty is given in some detail. *Destruction* is not to be understood in the sense of 'annihilation', but of complete ruin. It is the loss of all that makes life worth living. Coupled with the adjective *eternal* it is the opposite of eternal life. The exact expression occurs again in 4 Macc. x. 15 (and there only in the Greek Bible), where it is the lot of the wicked tyrant, and is set over against 'the happy death' of the martyr. It is exclusion from the *presence* (literally 'face') of God in accordance with the typical Scriptural position that the real sting of sin is that it separates from fellowship with the Lord.[243]

13. Torments. A further expression describing the suffering of the lost is that it is a place of torment (Luke 16:23, 28). Of the various words for suffering in the New Testament, this one may be the most severe. Barnes explains,

> The word torment means pain, anguish (Mat. iv. 24), particularly the pain inflicted by the ancients in order to induce men to make confession of their crimes. These torments or tortures were the keenest that they could inflict, such as the rack, or scourging, or burning, and the use of the word here denotes that the suffering of the wicked can be represented only by the extremist forms of human suffering.[244]

The rich man described hades as "a place of torments" (Luke 16:28). That torment is the result of several aspects of the suffering endured in that place. The first torment a person encounters in that place is the torment of burning. The rich man acknowledged, "I am tormented in this flame" (Luke 16:24). While it is wrong to say all the torture in hell comes from the flame, it would be also wrong to explain away the literal flames of hell. A second aspect of the torment of hell is sight. Jesus suggested men in hell could see the blessed state of the righteous (Luke 16:23). The Scriptures never mention people in heaven viewing the suffering of the lost because there is pain even in viewing the suffering of others. Those in hell suffer, however, more severely from the constant sight of what might have been, and what is. Commenting on Luke 16:23, Matthew Henry notes,

> The misery of his state is aggravated by his knowledge of the happiness of Lazarus. . . . It is the soul that is *in torment*, and they are the eyes of the mind that are lifted up. He now began to consider what was become of Lazarus. He does not find him where he himself is, nay, he plainly sees him, and with as such assurance as if he had seen him with his bodily eyes, afar off in the bosom of Abraham. This same aggravation of the miseries of the damned we had before (*ch*. xiii. 28).[245]

Third, the inhabitants of hades will also be tormented by one of the most painful sensations known by man, thirst. The Bible portrays the rich man pleading for a single drop of water and being refused (Luke 16:24). But they will also suffer a greater torment than the physical sufferings mentioned above. For eternity, the memories of lost people will function perfectly. They will remember all their injustices and sins. They will remember every instance when they rejected the convicting of the Holy Spirit. And that memory will increase the suffering of the place of torment.

A further suffering in the place of torment is that of hopelessness. Sooner or later, the lost will realize there will be no escape from their eternal fate (Luke 16:26). Without hope, life is not worth living. In hell, men will exist eternally without hope.

14. *Worm.* The image of an undying worm was used by both Isaiah and Jesus in their descriptions of the fate of the wicked (Isa 14:11; 66:24; Mark 9:44, 46, 48). The worm properly belongs to the description of gehenna rather than hades. Robertson notes,

> The Valley of Hinnom had been desecrated by the sacrifice of the children to Moloch so that as an accursed place it was used for the city garbage where worms gnawed and fires burned. It is thus a vivid picture of eternal punishment. . . .
> . . . .
> "The worm, i.e. that preys upon the inhabitants of this dread realm" (Gould). Two bold figures of Gehenna combined (the gnawing worm, the burning flame). No figures of Gehenna can equal the dread reality which is here described.[246]

The specific worm to which Jesus referred was probably one of two common worms in the near east. If His reference to the worm is based on the context of His discussion of gehenna, He was probably making reference to the maggot, so common in places of decay and putrification. If, however, His use of this expression is based on Isaiah's use of the same, He may have been referring to the scarlet worm, a parasite which attaches itself to oak trees and from which a red dye was prepared by various groups in the Near East. Concerning the use of the term "worms" in the Old Testament, Day suggests,

Besides the numerous passages, mostly in Ex referring to the tabernacle, where *tolaàth*, with *shānī* is tr^d "scarlet," there are eight passages in which it is tr^d translated "worm." These denote worms which occur in decaying organic matter or in sores (Ex 20; Isa 14 11; 66 24); or which are destructive to plants (Dt 28 39; Jon 4 7); or the word is used as a term of contempt or depreciation (Job 25 6; Ps 22 6; Isa 41 14).[247]

The image of the worm in gehenna would have been understood by Jesus' listeners as a horrifying picture of the judgment of God. This is the subject of the last verse of Isaiah (Isa. 66:24). Because the picture prompted such an emotion, it was the common practice of the rabbi reading the scroll to complete the reading by repeating the previous verse. It was held that the reading of the Scripture could not end on such a negative description.

15. *Fire.* Probably the best-known popular image of hell is that of fire. The rich man is described as tormented by the flame (Luke 16:24), and men are salted with fire (Mark 9:49), cast into the lake of fire (Rev. 20:15) and cast into a furnace of fire (Matt. 13:42). Further, fire and brimstone (Rev. 21:8) and the unquenchable flame (Mark 9:43, 45-46, 48) are used to describe hell. The use of fire to describe hell is not only descriptive, but also emphasizes the continuous suffering of the lost. Vos explains,

The "lake of fire" can be called "the second death" only with reference to the lost among men (ver 15), not with reference to death and hades (ver 14). In all the above references "the lake of fire" appears as a place of punishment, of perpetual torment, not of annihilation (20 10) . . . . The Scriptural source for the conception of "the lake of fire" lies in Gen 19 24, where already the fire and brimstone occur together, while the locality of the catastrophe described is the neighborhood of the Dead Sea. The association of the Dead Sea with this fearful judgment of God, together with the desolate appearance of the place, rendered it a striking figure for the scene of eschatological retribution.[248]

Orr also emphasizes the fact that this fire does not result in the annihilation of the wicked.

The language is obviously highly metaphorical, conveying the idea of an awful and abiding judgment, but is not to be pressed as teaching a destruction in the sense of annihilation of the wicked. An unquenchable fire is not needed for a momentary act of destruction. Even in the view of Rev. Edward White the wicked survive the period of judgment to which these terms relate.[249]

The past tense of the word ἑτοι μασμένον in Matthew 25:41 is emphasizing the fire "has been prepared" prior to the judgment of the nations. The Bible does not specifically state how long prior to this judgment the fire is prepared, but there are some who argue the fire is already prepared and is known to man today. C. T. Schwarze suggests that what is known as midget or white dwarf stars are remarkably similar to that which is stated concerning the lake of fire. While falling short of identifying these stars as the actual eternal abode of the unsaved, he demonstrates by their existence the possibility of the existence of yet another "lake of fire." "We find, first, an eternal fire which cannot burn out . . . of a liquid consistency it is, secondly, a lake of fire."[250]

16. *Second death.* The eternal abode of the lost is, as noted above, also designated as the second death, in contrast to physical death. Those who teach a view of annihilation or soul-sleep often redefine this term to refer to a state of nonexistence or unconscious existence. Death, however, never refers to the cessation of life in Scripture, but rather to the separation of something from that to which it belongs. The Scriptures identify a body without the spirit and faith without its evident works as dead (Jas. 2:26). In the same way, the expression second death emphasizes the separation of a man from God. The consciousness of man is emphasized in the description of the second death at the final judgment. Chafer explains,

> Having been judged, this unnumbered throng are dismissed into the lake of fire, which is the second death, and the word *death* here, as in all the Scriptures, does not mean a cessation of existence. Physical death is a separation of soul and spirit from the body, while spiritual death is a separation of soul and spirit from God. The second death means continued and conscious existence from God in what is termed a "lake of fire." It is implied that the Beast and the False Prophet who are living men are alive and conscious in this "lake of fire," though they were cast therein a thousand years before (Rev. 19:20; 20:10).[251]

17. *Wrath of God.* Hell is also described in Scripture in terms of the wrath of God. As an expression of His holiness, truth and justice, God must punish sin. As sin is an offense against God personally, it should not, therefore, be surprising that God is offended and is therefore angry. To deny the existence of this anger is to reject the necessity of Christ's reconciling work on the cross. According to Paul, the wrath of God is revealed in nature, this is outside the Scriptures (Rom. 1:18). That wrath which is today revealed in part against sin, will some day be expressed completely in hell. Concerning this wrath, Murray suggests,

> It is unnecessary, and it weakens the biblical concept of the wrath of God, to deprive it of its emotional and affective character. Wrath in God must not be conceived of in terms of the fitful passion with which anger is frequently associated in us. But to construe God's wrath as consisting simply in his purpose to punish sin or to secure the connection between sin and misery is to equate wrath with its effects and virtually eliminate wrath as a movement within the mind of God. Wrath is the holy revulsion of God's being against that which is the contradiction of his holiness. The reality of God's wrath in this specific character is shown by the fact that it is "revealed from heaven against all ungodliness and unrighteousness of men". The same dynamic feature of the term "revealed", as it appears in verse 17, will have to be understood in this case also. The wrath of God is dynamically, effectively operative in the world of men and it is as proceeding from heaven, the throne of God, that it is thus active. We

must regard the penal inflictions, therefore, as due to the exercise of God's wrath upon the ungodly. There is a positive outgoing of the divine displeasure.[252]

The wrath of God is given greater emphasis in the Old Testament than in the New Testament. Because of this, some minimize this expression of wrath. The thought implied, if not stated, is that God was somehow converted from wrath to love between the Testaments. This, of course, is inconsistent with God's immutability. Also, because the New Testament speaks of wrath less often, does not mean that it in any way attempts to minimize the doctrine. According to Evans,

> Nevertheless, it must not be thought that the element of wrath, as a quality of the Divine nature, is by any means overlooked in the NT because of the prominent place there given to love. On the contrary, the wrath of God is intensified because of the more wonderful manifestation of His grace, mercy and love in the gift of His Son Jesus Christ as the Saviour of the world. God is not love only: He is also righteous . . . . No effeminate, sentimental view of the Fatherhood of God or of His mercy and loving-kindness can exclude the manifestation of His just, righteous and holy anger against sin and the sinner because of his transgression (1 Pet 1 17; Heb 10 29.[253]

18. *Eternity*. The above adjectives applied to hell give it a degree of suffering that is beyond the realm of human comprehension. Then add the word "eternity" to all the words that describe suffering, hell is compounded far beyond human understanding. It is one thing to be the object of God's wrath. It is another wholly different thing to be the object of that wrath for eternity. It is one thing to be in torment. It is something else to be eternally tormented. If hell were in any sense tolerable for its inhabitants, the concept of eternity makes it completely intolerable.

The concept of eternity when applied to the future punishment of the lost does not fit well into the eschatological philosophies of some. As a result, those who choose to deny the existence of bell as described in the Scriptures often do so by seeking to redefine the concept of eternity. Fudge objects to the translation of *aionios* as "eternal" or "everlasting" and suggests, "a better translation would probably be the transliteration of '*aionic*,' or 'new age.' *Aiōnios* designates a quality of the Age to Come."[254] Brunner concludes,

> Hence the expressions by which the New Testament emphasizes apparently the finality of the last judgment and of the damnation of the reprobate are so interpreted as to impart to judgment the character of a transitional stage, of a pedagogic cleansing process. *Aionios* does not mean eternal, but only eschatological; the inextinguishable fire, the worm that dieth not, the *apoleia*, the destruction, the second death, etc., all these unequivocal expressions are subjected to such a protracted process of exegetical chemistry that they lose the definiteness of their ultimate character.[255]

The chief problem with the definition proposed by Fudge, Brunner and others is that it is simply not what the word means. Kuehner addresses this issue specifically.

But will the New Testament words for "forever" and "eternal" accommodate these interpretations? Does not the use of these terms for the eternity of God mean that they cannot be taken to imply a limited duration? God is said to be "the King of the ages, immortal, invisible, the only God" (I Tim. 1:17); glory is ascribed to him "forever" (Rom. 11:36); and be is blessed "forever" (II Cor. 11:31). Moreover, their frequent use in the New Testament in reference to the never-ending "age to come" and to "eternal life" indicates that *aion* and *aionios* must have the significance of unlimited time. Thus, James Barr can say in his *Biblical Words for Time*: "The cases of *aionios* refer fairly uniformly to the being of God or to plans and realities which, once established by him are perpetual or unchanging." . . . Fifty-one times it [*aionios*] describes the happiness of the righteous, and seven times the punishment of the wicked. No wonder W. R. Inge declared in *What is Hell?*, "No sound Greek scholar can pretend that *aionios* means anything less than eternal."[256]

The two Greek words *aion* and *aionios* are the terms used to express time without end, i.e. eternity. The use of these terms in the New Testament is not limited only to discussions of hell. If they do not mean "eternal" when applied to hell, they cannot mean "eternal" when applied to God, nor to the estate of God's people after death. As Stuart explains,

In regard to all the cases which have a relation to future times, it is quite plain and certain that they designate an endless period, an unlimited duration. . . . If they have not the meaning which has just been stated, then the Scriptures do not declare that God is eternal, nor that the happiness of the righteous is without end, nor that His covenant of grace will always remain; a conclusion which would forever blast the hopes of Christians and shroud in more than midnight darkness all the glories of the gospel.[257]

But the concept of hell as eternal does not rest on the meaning of these two words alone. The concept of eternity is expressed in the Old Testament by the word *olam*. Also, the language used to describe the punishment of the lost at times implies its eternal duration though not specifically stating it. Munsey argues,

And this future punishment is eternal. 1. Every word in the Hebrew and Greek languages meaning duration without an end is applied to it, and if olam, aion and their various constructions, as applied to the future punishment of the wicked, do not mean duration without end, there is no word in either language which does, and they never had the idea—which is absurd. 2. If not eternal, God is not, and the reward of the righteous is not. 3. This punishment is put after the final resurrection. 4. Some sins were not to be forgiven in this life, or the life to come. 5. The duration of the punishment of the wicked is to be the same with that of the Devil and his angels.[258]

A. A. Hodge would apparently agree that the eternity of hell is not dependent only on the translation of two Greek words. Many of the expressions describing the fate of the lost imply endless punishment. He summarizes his reasoning under two points.

> 1st. There is nothing in Scripture which even, by the most remote implication, suggests that the sufferings of the lost shall ever end.
>
> 2nd. The constant application to the subject of such figurative language as, "fire that shall not be quenched," "fire unquenchable," "the worm that never dies," "bottomless pit," the necessity of paying the "uttermost farthing," "the smoke of their torment arising forever and ever," Luke iii. 17; Mark ix. 45, 56; Rev. xiv. 10, 11, is consistent only with the conviction God wills us to believe on his authority that future punishments are literally endless. It is said of those who commit the unpardonable sin that they shall never be forgiven, "neither in this world nor in that which is to come."—Matt. xii. 32.[259]

C. ALTERNATIVE THEORIES CONCERNING THE STATE OF THE UNSAVED DEAD. In light of the above-stated teaching of Scripture, it is difficult to understand how any objective student who accepts the authority of Scriptures could doubt the existence of a place of torments without end which will serve as the final abode of the lost. Yet this area of eschatology is rarely discussed without deep emotional feelings. Some have rightly observed that many have received slanted teaching about hell from funeral sermons. Too often, even among otherwise conservative ministers of the gospel, the sermon at a funeral service seems to have a single object, to console those who are grieving, suggesting that the deceased went to heaven, whether he did or not. Despite one's feelings for lost friends and relatives who have died without Christ, the teaching of Scripture does not allow anyone to minimize the reality of hell. As Kuehner notes,

> In the light of scriptural testimony we dare not reduce hell to the status of "a remedial, terminable retribution" (Farrar). Nor can we conceive of it as a Roman Catholic purgatory, "a pedagogic cleansing process" (Brunner). Nor may we imagine it to be, of all things, "a means of grace," a place of a second (and successful) chance (Ferré). Hell, in Scripture, is never viewed in temporary terms; it is an ultimate and eternal place of punishment.[260]

Notwithstanding, alternate theories concerning the state of the unsaved dead have been proposed over the years. While these theories find their origin in pagan religious philosophies, they have at times been taught by those who to some degree, identify with Christendom. The reason these alternative theories must be rejected is found in the positive teaching of the Scriptures concerning the character of hell. Eight of the more popular alternative theories are identified below.

1. *Annihilation.* The theory of annihilation briefly stated suggests that hell is a form of instantaneous destruction, if it exists at all. This is a common view among cults like the Jehovah's Witnesses and the followers of Herbert W. Armstrong. It is taught to the followers of these and other cults largely through redefining biblical terms. Concerning gehenna, Jehovah's Witnesses teach, "In all places where hell is translated from the Greek word *Gehenna* it means everlasting destruction."[261] Similarly, part of Armstrong's denial of hell involves a redefinition of death as "the cessation of life" rather than the separation of body and soul that is emphasized in Scripture (Jms. 2:26). In one of their publications, they write, "The Bible, which is God's message and instruction to mankind, nowhere teaches any such thing as the pagan doctrine of an 'immortal soul' going to heaven at death. It teaches that the soul is mortal, and shall die (Ezekiel 18:4, 20)."[262]

2. *Reincarnation.* The theory of reincarnation denies the existence of hell by confining people to earth during various lifetimes, a process to insure all would eventually reach a state of heavenly bliss often referred to as karma. Though this idea is popular in eastern religions, the teachings of Edgar Cayce have probably done more than any other single influence to give this doctrine a sense of "respectability" in western civilization. According to Cayce, the first person to be perfected through this process was Jesus Christ, whom Cayce claims had been reincarnated thirty times before achieving this success. One of the fundamental tenets of Cayce's theology states, "We are all part of God and God is part of us. There is no conflict, no punishment, merely opportunities to develop."[263] Summarizing the teaching of Cayce in this area, Swihart notes,

> In summary, according to the Cayce readings the Bible is neither accurate nor authoritative. Jesus of Nazareth was only one manifestation of Christ; there were many others. Jesus Christ was only one of thirty reincarnations of that soul, and he became the Christ in this particular lifetime. Jesus Christ was not God incarnate but an entity as are you and I. All of us sin and all of us will eventually achieve perfection by repaying our Karmic debt. This requires many lifetimes in which we work our way back toward an eventual reunion with God. There is no eternal judgment, for God does not judge.[264]

3. *Purgatory.* Advocated primarily by the Roman Catholic church, the doctrine of purgatory suggests the existence of a place in many ways similar to hell, but differing in two important areas. First, one's term of stay in purgatory, though sometimes conceived of as a long period of time, is never viewed as eternal. Secondly, the purpose of purgatory is not punitive or retributive, but rather cleansing. The fundamental concept behind purgatory is that all will be saved in the eternal plan of God. Brunner explains,

> That is the revealed Will of God and the plan for the world which He discloses, a plan of universal salvation, of gathering all things into Christ (24). We hear not one word in the Bible of a dual plan, a plan of salvation and its polar opposites. The Will of God had but one point, it is unambiguous and positive. It has one aim, not two.[265]

The strongest argument against the existence of purgatory is the argument of silence. Not one verse in the Old or New Testaments even hints at the existence of such a place. A survey of the history of the Roman Catholic church suggests the reason for its popular development may be other than eschatology. For many years the sale of indulgences was a principle means of financing church projects. It was an abuse of this practice that gave rise to the conditions which resulted in the Protestant Reformation.

4. *Universalism.* Few liberal theologians are prepared to recognize the relationship between the existence of heaven and the existence of hell (Matt. 25:46). Universalism is that view which holds there is a heaven and a hell, but God would not let anyone go to hell. The view was first taught by Origen and repeatedly condemned by the church. More recently it has been revised and is popular in liberal theology. The argument for universalism is normally based on a defective view of the love of God. According to one advocate of this theory,

> Christ, in Origen's old words, remains on the Cross as long as one sinner remains in hell. That is not a speculation; it is a statement grounded in the very necessity of God's nature. In a universe of love there can be no heaven which tolerates a chamber of horrors, no hell for any which does not at the same time make it hell for God. He cannot endure that—for *that* would be the final mockery of His nature—and He will not.[266]

5. *Humanism.* Like the universalist, the humanist believes the concept of men in hell is inconsistent with what the humanist perceives as character of Christ. Though humanists tend not to address theological and eschatological issues directly, by implication they deny the existence of hell. For them, belief in hell takes away from the otherwise positive teaching of the Bible. Mill writes,

> I say nothing of the moral difficulties and perversions involved in revelation itself; though even in the Christianity of the Gospels, at least in its ordinary interpretation, there are some of so flagrant a character as almost to outweigh all the beauty and benignity and moral greatness which so eminently distinguishes the sayings and character of Christ. The recognition, for example, of the highest object of worship, in a being who could make a Hell' and who could create countless generations of human beings with the certain foreknowledge that he was creating them for this fate. Is there any moral enormity which might be justified by imitation of such a Deity?[267]

The humanists' denial of hell is based on the humanist denial of God as revealed in Scripture. Braun, summarizes the humanist position and its major problem.

> The humanists have evolved a God who is nothing more than a tired old man who would need an eternal supply of Kleenex to daub His everlasting eyes should one of these God-denying, humanity-hating, blaspheming, self-centered, self-seeking,

murderous, rebellious man-creatures remain outside the realm of the blessedness of His heaven. Fortunately, for all of us, most human judges, even the worst of them, aren't that irresponsible, and indulgent. Could it be that the humanist has created a God in his own image and to his own liking in order to hedge his bet against the whole idea of any divine retribution? If so, he will have to work harder to thoroughly persuade himself—let alone the rest of a God-conscious world.[268]

6. *Popular Thanatology.* Another subtle denial of the existence of hell is being proposed today by those engaged in the study of thanatology. Thanatology is the study of death and dying, based to a large extent on actual case studies of terminal patients and those who have been declared clinically dead, and later revived. Testimonies of this latter group have often been the subject of sensational articles and books on the subject of life after death. To a large extent, these reports agree that there exists a life after death, normally described as a positive experience and often pictured in a golden setting. Occasionally these reports have included religious symbolism, usually in the form of Jesus, the virgin Mary or an angel welcoming the deceased across a bridge into paradise. The problem with thanatology, however, is that it is based upon unverifiable reports of information presumably gained under extremely unusual conditions, i.e., the brain has been declared to have ceased functioning in some cases. Rawlings has questioned the accuracy of these reports.

> I am convinced that all the cases published by Dr. Raymond Moody and Dr. Kubler-Ross, and subsequently by Dr. Kalis Osis and Enderdur Haroldsson in their excellent collection *At the Hour of Death*, are completely accurately reported by the authors but not always completely recalled or reported by the patients. I have found that most of the bad experiences are soon suppressed deeply into the patient's subliminal or subconscious mind. . . . After many interrogations of patients, I have personally resuscitated, I was amazed by the discovery that many have had bad experiences.[269]

7. *Alternate World.* Another suggestion concerning the state of both the saved and unsaved dead views them as living in another world and able to relate to individuals both in that world and this. This view is the basis of the occult practices of communicating with disincarnate spirits, a practice specifically condemned and forbidden in Scripture. Despite the clear teaching of Scripture concerning this practice, some apologists have pointed to the ability of the witch of Endor to call Samuel from the dead as biblical evidence supporting this view. Commenting on this event, Dawson questions the success of the witch of Endor.

> But while not dogmatising about the matter, it does not seem in the least probable that the real Samuel appeared. The woman was asked to bring up Samuel; A "man appeared" to her; she naturally concluded it was Samuel, and this one that counterfeited Samuel is spoken of as Samuel. Saul did not see him; the woman described the visitor at Saul's request and from the description Saul concluded it was he.

1. God did not answer Saul when he sought Him by proper means, why then should He send Samuel to him at the request of a witch, since He abhorred witchcraft? (Deut. 18:9-14).

2. The Spirit of Jehovah had left Saul and an evil spirit had taken hold of him (1 Sam. 16:14). Is it not probable that Satan or that spirit now impersonated Samuel and appeared in his guise?

3. The prediction was not exactly fulfilled as it would have been if God has sent Samuel with a message for Saul. "Tomorrow shalt thou and thy sons be with me," i.e. dead. The battle does not seem to have taken place on the morrow, when the following chapters are read, and especially the statement in 2 Samuel 1:1, 2. Again, Amoni, Mephibosheth (2 Sam. 21:9), and Ishbosheth, three of Saul's sons, were not slain in that battle, though Jonathan, Abinadab, and Melchishua the other three were.

4. Saul was cut off for disobeying God concerning Amelek (1 Sam. 16:18), and for asking counsel from one that had a familiar spirit (1 Chron. 10:13). It seems impossible that Samuel should be sent by the Lord at the request of a witch, and thus seeming sanction be given to a sin for which Saul was slain.

5. Saul paid the visitor religious worship. "He stooped with his face to the ground, and bowed himself."

6. The visitor said, "Why hast thou disquieted me, to bring Me up?" If these were Samuel's words, would they not indicate that dead saints are at the mercy of living and wicked men?[270]

8. *Second Chance.* A final popular view concerning the state of the unsaved dead suggests some at least will have an additional chance to receive or reject Christ. The obvious implication is that most, if not all, given that option will make the correct choice. The argument is usually based on the mistaken notion that some could not have made a choice for Christ because they did not know about Him or have enough light to be saved (cf. Titus 2:10). MacNeill argues,

> Again, we think of the millions of the heathen who have never heard of Him. No man can surely be condemned because in heathen darkness he did not accept Christ of whom he never heard, and of whom he never had the chance to hear. How God will deal with the heathen who have never yet had their first chance with Christ, we do not know. There is much within the New Testament to indicate that they will be judged according to the moral light they had and, in any case, we may be sure that the Judge of all the earth will certainly do right.[271]

One of the biblical passages sometimes appealed to in defending this position is 1 Peter 3:19 which speaks of Christ preaching "unto the spirits in prison." But, as Barnes notes, if this is a reference to be interpreted in the light of a second-chance theology, it creates other problems.

If the meaning be that he went and preached *after* his death, it seems difficult to know why the reference is to those only who 'had been disobedient in the days of Noah.' Why were *they* alone selected for this message? Are they separate from others? Were they the only ones who could be beneficially affected by his preaching? On the other method of interpretation, we can suggest a reason why they were particularly specified. But how can we on this?[272]

D. THE NECESSITY OF HELL. The existence of hell in the light of what is known or perceived concerning the ability and nature of God creates for some an intellectual conflict. This is normally expressed by those who understand to some degree the severity of the punishment in hell implied by the biblical teaching, yet at the same time fail to understand why sin must be punished so severely. Normally these thoughts are accompanied by a knowledge of a particular individual who had died without Christ. The fact that this person may have lived a "moral life" and that his/her personality has now become a part of the discussion only serves to complicate the matter further. Often the answer one receives to this question is a vague generalization, "I'm sure we'll understand better in heaven." Innes discusses this problem.

> The fact that, on the one hand, God is omnipotent and God is love, and, on the other, eternal retribution is plainly taught in Scripture, raises problems for our minds that in all probability we cannot fully solve. It is easy in such cases to produce a logical answer at the cost of one side of biblical truth, and this has often been done. E. Brunner, on the other hand, invokes the conception of necessary paradox in God's revelation, saying that the Word of God is not intended to teach us objective facts about the hereafter, but merely to challenge us to action (*Eternal Hope*, 1954, 177ff). While not holding this doctrine, we must admit that the counsels of God are past the understanding of our finite minds. The reality and eternity of suffering in Gehenna is an element of biblical truth that an honest exegesis cannot evade.[273]

Perhaps the necessity of hell can be understood at least in part by understanding the very nature of sin. Among other things that are true about sin, is its natural tendency toward destruction. The corrupting influence of sin does not cease at a certain point, but rather continually seeks out the destruction of that which it touches. As energy can neither be created nor destroyed, energy expended in the practice of sin is endless. Therefore, if a man dies in his sins, he is dying in a condition that, if left to himself, would itself develop its own hell. The fact that the Scriptures emphasize degrees of punishment, something which would probably not be characteristic of the destructive influence of sin itself, suggests a man may actually be "better off" suffering the vindictive wrath of God which, despite its severity is still governed by the nature of God than to simply be ignored and allowed to continue along the broad road to destruction. Commenting on objections to hell, Thiessen notes,

> The strongest objection is thought to be the idea that a God of love could not punish His creatures eternally. But this is to forget the fact that at death character is fixed, and that the law of congruity requires that the living be separated from the dead. It is

not a question of God's love, but of the soul's life. But having said all this, we repeat, that there will be degrees of punishment (Luke 12:47, 48; Rom. 2:5, 6; Matt. 11:24; Rev. 20:12,13), according to God's justice.[274]

XVII. THE ETERNAL HOME OF THE SAVED

Most people in this world, even those who deny the existence of hell, talk about the existence of some form of paradise after death. The song over a hundred years ago proclaimed, "Everybody talkin' 'bout heaven ain't goin' there." One of the first references to heaven noted Abraham "looked for a city." Just as a family moving into a new home will want to know every detail about the house, the neighborhood, area churches, schools, bus lines, and shopping centers, so those going there should want to know every detail about their future Home. Jesus said, "I go to prepare a place for you" (John 14:2). Of all areas of theological study, this is perhaps the one most interesting to many Christians. As Chafer correctly noted, "Probably no Bible theme is more agreeable to the mind of man than that of heaven. This is especially true of those who through advancing years of physical limitations are drawing near to the end of the realities of earth."[275]

Although heaven is an area of interest, it is also an area in which man's understanding is necessarily limited. There are two reasons for this limitation. First, the glory of the eternal home is such that human language cannot adequately describe it. According to Pettingill, "Human language is inadequate to describe the state and surroundings of the saved of God in heaven. Paul was caught up to that place, and such was 'the abundance of the revelations' vouchsafed to him that he had to endure for the rest of his earthly ministry a thorn in the flesh, lest he should be exalted above measure (2 Cor. 12:2-9).[276]

A second reason for man's limited understanding of heaven relates to the Scripture's limited revelation of it. Jesus spoke more of hell than He did of heaven. The emphasis of the epistles dealt primarily with church concerns of this age and, to some extent, the coming judgment upon the world. Concerning the Old Testament, Ottman suggests, "The Millennium is the theme, indeed, of the prophecies in the Old Testament, and beyond the Millennium these prophecies rarely go. There are only two passages—and both of them in Isaiah—that give but a brief glance at what lies beyond the Millennial reign of Christ."[277] Pettingill suggests the reason for this relative silence of the Scriptures concerning heaven is due to a state of "homesickness" one would experience if he knew more.

May I suggest a reason for this mystery? It is probably because if we knew all about that celestial place to which we are bound, it would make us so eager to get there, so homesick for heaven, that it would ruin us for our life here before we go hence. Paul got a glimpse of Heaven, and ever afterward he was "in a strait betwixt two, having a desire to depart, and to be with Christ, which is far better" (Phil. 1:23). So great were the revelations that he was given a thorn in the flesh to buffet him, lest he should be exalted above measure (2 Cor. 12:7). It seems that God cannot trust us with such wonderful knowledge of our Heavenly home: it would be more than we could bear.[278]

Over the years, our interests and attitudes toward heaven are bound to change. The older we become and the closer we get to moving into heaven, the more we are concerned with knowing every detail about the biblical doctrine of heaven than when we were younger. Actually, everyone who has received Christ as personal Savior has become a child of God (John 1:12) and now possesses eternal life (John 5:24). Everyone who is saved will go to heaven. But in the final analysis, the destination is not as important as the fact that we will live with God.

A. THE LOCATION OF HEAVEN. The Bible seems to teach there are four heavens. The fact that "Jesus passed through the heavens" (Heb. 4:14) indicates there is more than one heaven. Also, Jesus "ascended up far above all heavens" (Eph. 4:10) means one heaven is above another. Paul taught there were at least three heavens when he testified of being "caught up to the third heaven" (2 Cor. 12:1-4). Apparently, these heavens (three) shall pass away and be replaced with a fourth heaven described as "a new heaven" (2 Pet. 3:10; Rev. 21:1).

The first heaven is the atmosphere. This term is used in Scripture to refer to the air and atmosphere that surrounds humans and all created life upon earth (Matt. 6:26; Jas. 5:18). The second heaven is the stellar spaces or outer space (Matt. 24:29; Gen. 15:5). The third heaven is described as the dwelling place of God. While there is much which is unknown about this heaven, it is the place where God is located (Rev. 3:12; 20:9).

While it is popular in some circles to limit one's definition of heaven to a state of bliss, it is difficult to harmonize this with the biblical teaching and inference of a localized place called heaven. Strong argues that heaven is a place because the body of Christ must be located.

Is heaven a place, as well as a state? We answer that this is probable, for the reason that the presence of Christ's human body is essential to heaven, and that this body must be confined to a place. Since deity and humanity are indissolubly united in Christ's single person, we cannot regard Christ's human soul as limited to a place without vacating his person of its divinity. But we cannot conceive of his human body as thus omnipresent. As the new bodies of the saints are confined to place, so, it would seem, must be the body of their Lord. But, though heaven be the place where Christ manifests his glory through the human body which he assumed in the incarnation, our ruling conception of heaven must be something higher even this, namely, that of a state of holy communion with God.[279]

Similarly, A. A. Hodge declares,

All the Scriptural representations of heaven involve the idea of a definite place, as well as of a state of blessedness. Of that place, however, nothing more is revealed than that it is defined by the local presence of Christ's finite soul and body, and that it is the scene of the pre-eminent manifestation of God's glory. John xvii. 24; 2 Cor. v. 9; Rev. v. 6.[280]

No one is certain as to the exact location of heaven. Several biblical passages give vague hints concerning its direction, but do not identify it specifically. According to Isaiah 14:12-14, heaven appears in this reference to be "above the stars of God," in the, "sides of the north," and "above the heights of the clouds." Psalm 75:6 also seems to imply that the judgment of God comes from the north. Based on these and other similar biblical statements, some early fundamentalists tended to identify an apparently empty area in the northern sky as the site of heaven.[281]

The fourth heaven is described in greater detail in Scripture than the present location of God. It is said to come into existence when "the first heaven and the first earth were passed away" (Rev. 21:1). There is some debate over the relationship between the present heaven and that which is to come. DeHaan addresses this issue.

Some Bible students insist that the new heavens and the new earth will be a completely new creation, having no connection whatsoever with the material which makes up our present universe. Others, pointing out that the Greek word translated "new" may mean new in character rather than in substance, believe that the material of this present will not be annihilated, but transformed. (The same word is used of the regenerated believer: he becomes a "new creature" according to 2 Corinthians 5:17). This latter use seems a bit more likely because "God does not forsake the work of His hands.[282]

This view of a transformation of the elements of both heaven and earth tends to be more harmonious with other biblical statements concerning the continual abiding place of both (cf. Eccl. 1:4; Psa. 104:5; 119:90). As Seiss explains,

In those passages which speak of the *passing away* of the earth and heavens (see Matt. 5:18, 24, 34, 35; Mark 13:30, 31; Luke 16:17, 21, 33; 2 Pet. 3:10; Rev. 21:1), The original word is never one which signifies termination of existence, but παρερχομαι which is a verb of very wide and general meaning, such as *to go* or *come* to a person, place, or point; *to pass*, as a man through a bath, or a ship through the sea; to pass from one place or condition to another, to arrive at, to go through; to go into, to come forward as if to speak or serve. As to time, it means going into the past, as events in a state of things. That is implies great changes when applied to the earth and heavens is very evident, but that it ever means annihilation, or the passing of things *out of being*, there is no clear instance either in the Scripture or in classic Greek to prove. The main idea is *transition* not extinction.[283]

There are some who define heaven in terms of a good life on earth. Sometimes this conclusion is due to a confusion between heaven and the kingdom of God, i.e., the Millennium.

The Scripture seems to indicate the saints will have access to "a new earth" in eternity. Strong discusses the relationship between heaven and earth.

> Is this earth to be the heaven of the saints? We answer: First,—that the earth is to be purified by fire, and perhaps prepared to be the abode of the saints,—although this last is not rendered certain by the Scriptures. . . .
>
> . . . .
>
> Secondly, that this fitting-up of the earth for man's abode, even if it were declared in Scripture, would not render it certain that the saints are to be confined to these narrow limits (John 14:2). It seems rather to be intimated that the effect of Christ's work will be to bring the redeemed into union and intercourse with other orders of intelligence, from communion with whom they are now shut out by sin (Eph. 1:20; Col. 1:20).[284]

B. THE DESCRIPTION OF HEAVEN. The splendor and beauty of heaven far outshines anything the human mind can comprehend. It will be impossible to completely comprehend heaven until we arrive on location, but the Scriptures do reveal heaven as a huge and colorful city. Beyond that, the biblical description of heaven reads like a list of superlatives. According to Chafer,

> In attempting to portray to the mind of man the glories of the celestial sphere, language has been strained to its limits; yet we may believe that no considerable portion of that wondrous glory has ever been revealed. Who can comprehend the blessedness that will be experienced by the redeemed in Heaven, or that has already come to human hearts in anticipation of that wonderful place! It is characterized as a place of abundant life (1 Tim. 4:8), of rest (Rev. 14:13), of knowledge (1 Cor. 13:8-10), of holiness (Rev. 21:27), of service (Rev. 22:3), of worship (Rev. 19:1), of fellowship with God (Rev. 21:3), of fellowship with other believers (1 Thess. 4:8), and of glory (2 Cor. 4:17).[285]

The most complete description of heaven is that of the bride city in the final two chapters of Revelation. Some would argue that it is wrong to describe heaven in specific terms, claiming that these are only heavenly symbols to represent the idea that the presence of God is beautiful. MacNeill, for instance, writes,

> Hidden in every wall and stone and gate and street is the deeper message of the soul. The city is the emblem of a community, for no life is perfect without fellowship. The walls of the city indicate security and separation. The open gates suggest the sympathy and generosity of the perfect soul. The pure river clear as crystal is the emblem of the pure and flowing joy of the holy life. The white robes are the emblems of stainless purity. The crowns and palms are the emblems of victory. The gold and jasper and pearls are emblems of spiritual wealth. The songs and harps and feasting

are the emblems of abounding happiness and fervent thanksgiving for all the goodness of God.[286]

While on the surface this sounds logical, it is also a subtle undermining of the authority of God. God could have made heaven without streets of gold or He could have used other symbols to describe His home, but the fact is that God did not choose to do that. Since He has told us there will be streets of gold in heaven, why should we not expect it to be as He described it? If language is inadequate to describe heaven, why did not God create words that approximated heaven? Also, if God chose, He could have created us with an understanding that could have comprehended heaven. Perhaps a better approach to the biblical description of heaven is that of DeHaan.

The new Jerusalem will be magnificent beyond delineation. John literally described for us what he was shown regarding the heavenly city. The gold, the precious stones, the tree of life, and the crystal river must all be looked upon as real. However, every Christian must also be aware that the materials in Heaven will exceed in purity and appearance their counterparts of earth.[287]

The bride city described by John will be the largest city ever built (Rev. 21:16). This description of heaven suggests that it will be a gigantic cube, or pyramid (foursquare). According to our present measurements, 12,000 furlongs would be equivalent to 1,500 miles or 2,400 kilometers. If placed in America, this city would reach from New York City to Denver, Colorado, and from the Canadian border to Florida. If the New Jerusalem takes the form of a sphere, it will be slightly larger than the moon which presently circles our globe. Despite its immense size, Thiessen describes several of the finer details of the city.

We read that its foundations are garnished with "all manner of precious stone" (Rev. 21:10, 20). Twelve of these are named. It has twelve gates, bearing the names of the twelve tribes of Israel (Rev. 21:12, 13); and the twelve foundations bear the names of the twelve apostles (Rev. 21:14; cf. Eph. 2:20). The wall is of jasper and the city is of pure gold (Rev. 21:18). Every gate is a pearl (Rev. 21:21). We are told that the gates are never closed (Rev. 21:25); but that twelve angels stand before them (Rev. 21:12). Its street is of pure gold (Rev. 21:21). There is in it the river of life and the tree of life (Rev. 22:1,2). It has no need of sun or moon; "for the glory of God did lighten it, and the lamp thereof is the Lamb" (Rev. 21:23) All these things indicate that this is a literal city.[288]

Heaven will be the most beautiful city ever built. The city wall will stand some 216 feet high (Rev. 21:17) and will be built of jasper. It will be as beautiful as a crystal-clear diamond, as bright as a transparent icicle in the sunshine (Rev. 21:18). DeHaan notes,

Present-day scholars cannot determine the exact nature of the stone to which John referred. In ancient days there were many varieties of jasper, with differing shades of color. All of them, however, were either transparent or translucent, allowing the light to pass through. These jasper walls, therefore, will sparkle brilliantly and radiate light over the whole earth.[289]

In addition to adding to the beauty of the eternal state, Ritchie sees the walls as also emphasizing the security of the city.

> The "wall great and high" (verse 12) speaks of security, but though secure from all human or Satanic molestation, the city is not like Jericho of old—"straitly shut up," for its gates (twelve in number) tell of ingress and egress. These gates will not be shut by day (verse 25), and as there is "no night there," they will be open perpetually. A great city like London never has its gates shut, for through them come from every quarter of the land, and at all hours, the supplies she needs. The gates of the Bride-city are open always, not for supplies to come in, but for *supplies to go out to the earth.*[290]

This wall rests upon an unusual foundation inlaid with, or consisting of, various precious stones. These colorful elements will form a cavalcade of beauty as the pure light of the Lamb shines through them.

> Many Bible students believe that these jewels will reflect all the colors of the rainbow, even though we cannot speak with certainty regarding the precise characteristics of each stone. Beginning at the ground level, the jasper stone may have been a light green or yellow; the sapphire, a sky-blue azure; the chalcedony, containing a combination of colors, was mostly green and blue; the emerald, bright green; the sardonyx, red and white; the sardius, reddish in color; chrysolite, golden yellow; beryl, sea-green; topaz, yellow-green and transparent; chrysoprasus, golden-green; jacinth, violet; and amethyst, either rose-red or purple. The brilliant light of the city, shining out through the jasper wall and blazing through the open gates, will reflect from these precious stones in a spectrum of brilliant color. The beauty of the city to the observer from the outside will be dazzling indeed.[291]

Within the wall of this city will be twelve gates, each made from a single pearl and inscribed with the names of the twelve tribes of Israel. DeHaan sees these gates as emblems of salvation.

> The gates are of pearl, which itself is an emblem of salvation by grace. A wound to the shellfish results in the formation of a valuable pearl. So also the pearly gates of Heaven are made possible through the crowning sin of mankind, the crucifixion of Christ. Men rejected the Son of God and crucified Him, but through the injury thus inflicted upon a member of the Godhead, salvation has been poured out to all the world.

The gates are open at all times and in every direction, for salvation is offered to all. . . .

In the gates are inscribed the names of the tribes of Israel, for salvation is of the Jews.[292]

Each gate is guarded by an angel. As angels are servants of God, some writers see their presence and the repetition of the number twelve as an indication of God's authority. Commenting on this, Ritchie writes,

You will observe the frequency of the number "twelve" in the chapter. It is the number associated in Scripture with governmental perfection according to the mind of God. The angels act as the heavenly porters and messengers, going about the business of the King.[293]

From the earliest pages of the Bible, two natural elements are described, which find their ultimate existence in heaven. Both the river (Gen. 2:10; Rev. 22:1) and the tree of life (Gen. 2:9; Rev. 22:2) were part of the original creation of God. They were placed in the original garden and now are in the paradise of God as constant symbolic reminders that God Himself is the source of life. In the midst of the confusion and chaos of his circumstances, David received strength from the eternal presence of God as represented by "a river" (Psa. 46:4). According to DeHaan,

A river running through a city has always been of great value. In ancient times, during a seige, a flowing stream and its channels would bring water, which is essential for both cleanliness and the preservation of life, to every part of the city. Even today a river continues to be an emblem of fruitfulness, freshness, and abundance, its waters being fed by melting snows from mountain ranges and refreshing springs, and being constantly purified as they tumble downward. Our Saviour very fittingly used the term "rivers of living water" to indicate the outflow of blessing from the life of the believer through the work of the Holy Spirit.

In the New Jerusalem the crystal-clear river will forever flow, reminding all of God's gracious and abundant provision for every human need.[294]

The tree of life, though not mentioned after the fall of man until the final chapters of Scripture, is pictured holding a place of prominence and providing for the growth of the people by its fruit (Rev. 22:2). John uses the term "healing" meaning "nurture or growth," speaking of the effect of the leaves of the tree. There will be growth in heaven; Christians will not be static nor frozen into the state in which they enter their eternal home.

Perhaps the most remembered part of the city are the streets of transparent gold (Rev. 21:21). This pure gold will also serve as the basic construction material of the city itself (Rev. 21:18). Concerning the significance of transparent gold, Ritchie writes,

Gold is the well-known symbol in Scripture of Divine righteousness; this we are familiar with in the typology of tabernacle and temple. But "pure gold, like transparent glass" is something new and altogether unique. So far as I am aware, we have never seen or heard of gold so pure as to be transparent. *In the Bride-city everything and everyone is so agreeable to the eye of God, that there is nothing to hide.* Even "the street," which suggests the walk and ways of the saints, shews no defilement but reflects the sinless perfection of all their activities.[295]

The Bible tells us what is not in heaven to help us appreciate what is there. John saw no temple in the new heaven (Rev. 21:22). The temple was a symbol of the presence of God. Since the centralized presence of God is there, there is no need of a temple. In the Old Testament, the presence of the glory of God was evident through the bright cloud resting over the holy of holies. In the bride city, there are no lamps because the brightness of "the Lamb is the light thereof" (Rev. 21:23). Death and sorrow are also absent from heaven. Sin, the reason that God originally cursed the earth with both death and sorrow, is also absent in heaven (Rev. 22:3-4).

WHAT IS MISSING FROM HEAVEN			
Tears	Rev. 12:1	Defilement	Rev. 21:27
Death	Rev. 21:4	Abomination	Rev. 21:27
Sorrow	Rev. 21:4	Curse	Rev. 22:3
Crying	Rev. 21:4	Liars	Rev. 21:27
Pain	Rev. 21:4	Sun	Rev. 21:23
Night	Rev. 21:25	Moon	Rev. 21:23

Heaven is also a place of memory. The question is often asked, "Will we know one another in heaven?" The answer is yes! David said that he would know his son (2 Sam. 12:22-23). Moses and Elijah, who had died long ago, were recognized by Peter, James and John (Mark 9:4-5). Also, it appears we will recognize Abraham, Isaac and Jacob (Matt. 8:11). Paul talked of a time when he would be known and know others also (1 Cor. 13:12).

C. THE INHABITANTS OF HEAVEN. Heaven is more than the eternal home of the saved. Many others will forever live with us there. These include God, His angels and special creations. Both saved Jews and Gentiles will live in perfect harmony. Citizens of every linguistic group and race will live in heaven for eternity. It will be the ultimate international community. The following will inhabit heaven.

1. *Angels.* John "heard the voice of many angels about the throne in heaven" (Rev. 5:11). These include several kinds of angels. The seraphim, a special kind of angel who deals with God's altar will be present in heaven (Isa. 6:1-7). Another special angelic group who deals

with God's throne, the cherubim, will also be there (Psa. 99:1). And of course, Gabriel and Michael will be there too.

2. *Elders.* The Bible identifies twenty-four elders around the throne of God in heaven (Rev. 4:4). Much has been speculated concerning the identity of this group. One suggestion is that these men are twelve tribal leaders of Israel and the twelve apostles of Jesus. Another is that they represent the saved from both Jews and Gentiles.

3. *Saved Israel.* Hebrews 11 lists a number of individuals and groups who practiced faith in the Old Testament. Concerning them, it is said "they desire a better country" (Heb. 11:6). These who have experienced saving faith have an eternal place in heaven.

4. *Church.* One of the first events after the rapture will be the marriage supper of the Lamb. This is when the church, the Bride of Christ, will be presented to her Groom, the Lord Jesus Christ. The New Jerusalem has been described as "the wedding ring of the church."

5. *Nations.* Many Bible scholars believe Christians in heaven will retain some of their ethnic distinctives and perhaps even be organized as nations. Twice the Scriptures use the plural term "peoples" describing the citizens of heaven (Zeph. 3:20; Rev. 21:3). Also, John recognized the ethnic distinctives of some of the redeemed in heaven (Rev. 7:9). However in heaven, there will be perfect acceptance by all of everyone there. The unity of its inhabitants not its diversity will be the dominant characteristic.

6. *The Triune God.* Heaven is, of course, the eternal home of each member of the Trinity of God. The Father sits upon the throne in heaven (Rev. 4:2-3). John saw Jesus standing in heaven (Rev. 5:6). Though not as prominent, the Holy Spirit also lives in heaven and is thrice quoted in John's account of his experience there (Rev. 3:13; 14:13; 22:17).

As one grows older, his attitude toward heaven often changes. He no longer thinks so much of the geography of that land, as of individuals known and loved who have died and gone on before. When preaching on heaven, D. L. Moody often related the following story:

When I was a boy, I thought of heaven as a great, shining city, with vast walls and domes and spires, and with nobody in it except white-robed angels, who were strangers to me. By and by my little brother died; and I thought of a great city with walls and domes and spires, and a flock of cold, unknown angels, and one little fellow that I was acquainted with. He was the only one I knew at the time. Then another brother died; and there were two that I knew. Then my acquaintances began to die; and the flock continually grew. But it was not until I had sent one of my little children to his Heavenly Parent—God—that I began to think I had a little in there myself. A second went, a third went; a fourth went; and by this time I had so many acquaintances in heaven, that I did not see any more walls and domes and spires. I began to think of the residents of the celestial city as my friends. And now so many of my acquaintances have gone there, that it sometimes seems to me that I know more people in heaven than I do on earth.[296]

D. THE ACTIVITIES OF HEAVEN. Heaven is often thought of in terms of angels sitting on clouds with harps and singing in choirs. At best, this imbalanced view is a small part of heaven. Though described as the eternal rest of the believer, heaven will be a very, active place.

```
┌─────────────────────────────────────────────┐
│                                               │
│           WHAT TO DO IN HEAVEN                │
│                                               │
│   1.  Learning .......................... 1 Cor. 13:9-10  │
│   2.  Singing ..................................Rev. 15:3  │
│   3.  Worship.................................Rev. 5:9    │
│   4.  Serving ...................................Rev. 22:3 │
│   5.  Leading.................2 Tim. 2:12; Rev. 22:5      │
│   6.  Fellowship with others ..............Matt. 16:3    │
│   7.  Eating....................................Rev. 2:17 │
│                                               │
└─────────────────────────────────────────────┘
```

1. *A life of fellowship.* We will enjoy communion with the Lord Jesus Christ for all eternity. "They shall see his face" (Rev. 22:4). Christ predicts our future unity with His: "I will come again, and receive you unto myself; that where I am, there ye may be also." (John 14:3). When man is in perfect fellowship with God, that will also affect his relationship with society. As DeHaan has correctly observed,

In the new heavens and new earth man will realize a perfect society of righteousness and harmony, something he has never been able to achieve. The problems of individual freedom and social responsibility have not yet been solved, either by capitalism with its emphasis upon the individual, or communism with its stress upon the right of the community. In our eternal home the perfect society will become a reality, for individual identity on one hand, and harmonious variety on the other, will finally be achieved.[297]

2. *A life of rest.* One of the results of sin was the curse of toil and sweat in a life of work. When we arrive in heaven, we will continue to work, but the agony of labor will be gone. "Blessed are the dead which die in the Lord from henceforth: Yes, saith the Spirit, that they may rest from their labours" (Rev. 14:13).

3. *A life of service.* We will work in heaven, but rather than dread the thought of labor and suffer the physical pain from grueling drudgery, we will enjoy our work. The curse will be gone. "And his servants shall serve him" (Rev. 22:3). As Moody states,

There is not such a great difference between grace and glory after all. Grace is the bud, and glory the blossom. Grace is glory begun, and glory is grace perfected. It will not come hard to people who are serving God down here to do it when they go up yonder. They will change places, but they will not change employments.[298]

4. *A life of growth.* We will not "instantaneously" know everything when we arrive at heaven. We will spend a lifetime growing in knowledge and maturity. Christians will learn

facts about God and His plan. We will grow in love. Also, we will learn how to serve Him and grow in ability to serve Him. "The leaves of the trees were for the healing of the nations" (Rev. 22:2). The word "healing" also means growth, implying the advancement of its inhabitants.

7. *A life of worship.* Jesus said at the beginning of his ministry, "The Father seeketh such to worship him" (John 4:23). Since the Father wanted people to worship Him while they were on earth, it will not change when they get to heaven. "And after these things I heard a great voice of much people in heaven saying, Alleluia; Salvation, and glory, and honour, and power, unto the Lord our God" (Rev. 19:1).

E. DYING WORDS OF SAINTS CONCERNING HEAVEN.

It's all right up there. — Jerry McAuley (1884)

I am sweeping through the gates, washed in the blood of the Lamb. — Alfred Cookman (1871)

You are fighting for an earthly crown; I am going to receive a heavenly one. — James Gardiner (1745)

Christ Jesus the Saviour of sinners and life of the dead. I am going, going to Glory! Farewell, sin! Farewell, death! Praise the Lord! — Richard Newton (1753)

There is another and a better world. — John Palmer (1798)

O Paradise! O Paradise! At last comes to me the grand consolation. My prisons disappear; the great of earth pass away; all before me is rest. — Silvio Pellico (1854)

Blessed be God, though I change my place, I shall not change my company; for I have walked with God while living, and now I go to rest with God. — John Preston (1628)

No mortal man can live after the glories which God has manifested to my soul. — Augustus Montague Toplady

I now draw near to the harbor of death—that harbor that will rescue me from all the future storms and waves of this restless world. I praise God, I am willing to leave it, and expect a better—that world wherein dwelleth righteousness, and I long for It. — Sir Henry Walton

I see earth receding; heaven is opening. God is calling. I must go. If this it death, it is sweet. This is my coronation day. — Dwight Lyman Moody

I didn't know it was so beautiful. — Hulda Reese
THE END

ENDNOTES

1. Walter Rauschenbush, *A Theology for the Social Gospel*, (NY: Abingdon, 1917), 209.

2. R. S. Beal, "The Place of Prophecy in Preaching" in *Light for the World's Darkness*, ed. John W. Bradbury (New York: Loizeaux Brothers, Publishers, 1944), 143.

3. Henry Clarence Thiessen, *Introductory Lectures In Systematic Theology* (Grand Rapids: Eerdmans, 1949), 441.

4. Lewis Sperry Chafer, *Major Bible Themes* (Chicago: Moody Press, 1926), 265.

5. F. E. Howitt, "The Lord's Coming the Key to the Scriptures" in *The Coming and Kingdom of Christ* ed. James M. Gray (Chicago: Bible Institute Colportage Association, 1914), 31.

6. W. Trotter and T. Smith, *Eight Lectures on Prophecy from Short-Hand Notes* (New York: Loizeaux Brothers, n.d.), 34-35.

7. Ella E. Pohle, *Dr. C. I. Scofield's Question Box* (Chicago: Moody Press, 1917), 119-120. Points 4 and 5 are left out because they are covered elsewhere.

8. William Ward Ayer, "What It Has Cost the Church to Neglect the Bible's Prophetic Message" *The Sure Word of Prophecy*, ed. John W. Bradbury (New York: Fleming H. Revell Company, 1943), 37.

9. Trotter and Smith, *Eight Lectures on Prophecy*, 31-32.

10. William L. Pettingill, *The Christian Fundamentals* (Findlay, OH: Fundamental Truth Publishers, 1941), 57.

11. Adam B. Hunter, "Effect of the Doctrine of Our Lord's Return," *The Sure Word of Prophecy*, ed. John W. Bradbury (New York: Fleming H. Revell Company, 1943), 300-301.

12. William B. Riley, *The Evolution of the Kingdom*, revised ed. (New York: The Book Stall, 1913), 208.

13. Walter Scott, *Exposition of the Revelation of Jesus Christ and Prophetic Outlines* (London: Pickering & Inglis, n.d.), 18.

14. W. Hendricksen, *More Than Conquerors: An Interpretation of the Book of Revelation* (Grand Rapids: Baker Book House, 1947), 226-227.*

15. Augustus Hopkins Strong, *Systematic Theology: A Compendium Designed for the Use of Theological Students* (Philadelphia: Judson Press, 1907), 1008-1011.

16. Archibald Alexander Hodge, *Outlines of Theology* (London: Thomas Nelson and Sons, 1883), 568-569.

17. Strong, *Systematic Theology*, 1011.

18. Doctrinal Statement of Dallas Theological Seminary, Article XX.*

19.   W. H. Rogers, "The Second Coming of Christ—Personal and Premillennial" *Light for the World's Darkness*, ed. John W. Bradbury (New York: Loizeaux Brothers, Publishers, 1944), 35.

20.   Chart prepared by Irving L. Jensen, *Revelation: A Self-Study Guide* (Chicago: Moody Press, 1971), 19.*

21.   Merrill C. Tenney, *New Testament Survey* (Grand Rapids: Eerdmans, 1961), 387.

22.   Raymond Calkins, *The Social Message of the Book of Revelation* (New York: The Womans Press, 1920), 13.

23.   Woodrow Michael Kroll, "The Revelation" *Liberty Commentary on the New Testament*, ed. Edward E. Hindson and Woodrow Michael Kroll (Lynchburg, Virginia: Liberty Press, 1978), 745.

24.   Henry Clarence Thiessen, *Introduction to the New Testament* (Grand Rapids: Eerdmans, 1943), 326.

25.   Bernard Ramm, *Protestant Biblical Interpretation: A Textbook in Hermeneutics*, 3rd rev. ed. (Grand Rapids: Baker Book House, 1970), 244.

26.   Oswald T. Allis, *Prophecy and the Church* (Philadelphia: Presbyterian and Reformed Publishing Company, 1945).*

27.   Ramm, *Protestant Biblical Interpretation*, 24.

28.   J. Dwight Pentecost, *Things to Come: A Study in Biblical Eschatology* (Grand Rapids: Zondervan, 1958), 9.

29.   Floyd E. Hamilton, *The Basis of Millennial Faith* (Grand Rapids: Eerdmans, 1942), 38-39.

30.   David L. Cooper, *Messiah: His Historical Appearance* (Los Angeles: Biblical Research Society, 1958), 19.

31.   Charles H. Stevens, "How Shall We Interpret the Bible?" *The Sure Word of Prophecy*, ed. John W. Bradbury (New York: Fleming H. Revell Company, 1943), 33-34.

32.   Hendricksen, *More Than Conquerors*, 81.*

33.   F. Godet, *St. Paul's Epistle to the Romans* (Edinburgh: T. & T. Clark, 1890), 2:256.

34.   John Murray, *The Epistle to the Romans: The English Text with Introduction, Exposition and Notes* (Grand Rapids: Eerdmans, 1965), 2:97.

35.   Matthew Henry, *Commentary on the Whole Bible* (Old Tappan, NJ: Fleming H. Revell Company, n.d.), 6:684.

36.   William Kelly, *Lectures on the Galatians*, cited by Howard W. Ferrin, "Is the Church Ever Called Israel?" *The Sure Word of Prophecy*, ed. John W. Bradbury (New York: Fleming H. Revell Company, 1943), 153.

37.   John F. Walvoord, *Matthew: Thy Kingdom Come* (Chicago: Moody Press, 1974), 97.

38. John Wick Bowman, "The Bible and Modern Religions: II. Dispensationalism," *Interpretation* 10 (April, 1956), 172.

39. Philip Mauro, *The Gospel of the Kingdom* (Boston: Hamilton Brothers, 1928), 8.

40. Lewis Sperry Chafer, *Dispensationalism* (Dallas: Dallas Seminary Press, 1936), 9.*

41. Charles Caldwell Ryrie, *Dispensationalism Today* (Chicago: Moody Press, 1965), 31.

42. Pierre Poiret, *L'Oeconomie Divine* (Amsterdam, 1687). English trans. published in London, 1713.*

43. Ryrie, *Dispensationalism Today*, 68-70.

44. Ibid., 84.

45. *The Scofield Reference Bible* (1917), 5.

46. Ryrie, *Dispensationalism Today*, 29.

47. Pentecost, *Things to Come*, 155.

48. Walvoord, *Matthew: Thy Kingdom Come*, 97.

49. W. Graham Scroggie, *Prophecy and History* (London: Morgan & Scott, 1915), 113-115.

50. A. C. Gaebelein, *The Gospel of Matthew: An Exposition* (New York: Publication Office, Our Hope, 1910), 1:263-264.

51. Walter Scott, *Exposition of the Revelation of Jesus Christ and Prophetic Outlines* (London: Pickering & Inglis, n.d.), 55-56.

52. Gaebelein, *The Gospel of Matthew*, 1:265-266.

53. Pentecost, *Things to Come*, 153.

54. Charles Lee Feinberg, "What Israel Means to God" *The Sure Word of Prophecy*, ed. John W. Bradbury (New York: Fleming H. Revell Company, 1943), 255.

55. Trotter and Smith, *Eight Lectures on Prophecy*, 125-134.

56. W. E. Pietsch, "The Jew After the Rapture" *The Sure Word of Prophecy*, ed. John W. Bradbury (New York: Fleming H. Revell Company, 1943), 264.

57. Joseph Hoffman Cohn, "Is God Through with the Jews?" *The Sure Word of Prophecy*, ed. John W. Bradbury (New York: Fleming H. Revell Company, 1943), 223.

58. John Ritchie, *Impending Great Events*, 2nd ed. (London: Pickering & Inglis Ltd., 1939), 11.

59. Harry A. Ironside, *Lectures on the Book of Revelation* (New York: Loizeaux Brothers, 1920), 334.

60. L. Sale-Harrison, "The Future Confederation of the Ten-Nation Empire" *The Sure Word of Prophecy*, ed. John W. Bradbury (New York: Fleming H. Revell Company, 1943), 79.

61. Thiessen, *Lectures In Systematic Theology*, 465.

62. Sale-Harrison, "The Future Confederation of the Ten-Nation Empire," 83.

63.   Pentecost, *Things to Come*, 155.
64.   Lewis Sperry Chafer, "The Olivet Discourse" *Light for the World's Darkness*, ed. John W. Bradbury (New York: Loizeaux Brothers, 1944), 107-108.
65.   Pentecost, *Things to Come*, 156.
66.   Thomas Waugh, *When Jesus Comes* (London: Charles H. Kelly, 1901), 108.
67.   J. E. M. Dawson, *Present-Day Problems* (London: Pickering & Inglis, 1940), 46.*
68.   Robert H. Gundry, *The Church and the Tribulation* (Grand Rapids: Zondervan, 1973), 201.
69.   Pentecost, *Things to Come*, 158-161.
70.   Ritchie, *Impending Great Events*, 177-178.
71.   Charles C. Ryrie, *What You Should Know About the Rapture* (Chicago: Moody Press, 1981), 38-39.
72.   Alexander Reese, *The Approaching Advent of Christ* (London: Marshall, Morgan & Scott, 1937), 18.
73.   Gundry, *The Church and the Tribulation*, 173.
74.   Dave MacPherson, *The Late Great Pre-Trib Rapture* (Kansas City, MO: Heart of America Bible Society, 1974), 12.
75.   Ryrie, *What You Should Know About the Rapture*, 68.
76.   Pentecost, *Things to Come*, 166.
77.   McPherson, 104.*
78.   Ibid., 118.*
79.   Ryrie, 72.
80.   Gundry, *The Church and the Tribulation*, 43.
81.   MacPherson, *The Late Great Pre-Trib Rapture*, 23.
82.   John R.W. Stott, *Guard the Gospel: The Message of 2 Timothy* (London: InterVarsity Press, 1973), 113.
83.   Ramm, *Protestant Biblical Interpretation*, 283.
84.   Pentecost, *Things to Come*, 168.
85.   Gundry, *The Church and the Tribulation*, 46, 62.
86.   Harold J. Ockenga, "Will the Church Go Through the Tribulation? Yes" *Christian Life*, February 1955, 22.*
87.   Philip Mauro, *Looking for the Savior* (London: Samuel E. Roberts, Publishers, n.d.), 37.
88.   Pentecost, *Things to Come*, 170.
89.   Harry A. Ironside, "Why the Church Will Not Go Through the Great Tribulation" *The Sure Word of Prophecy*, ed. John W. Bradbury (New York: Fleming H. Revell Company, 1943), 127.
90.   Thiessen, *Lectures in Systematic Theology*, 464.

91.   George L. Rose, *Tribulation Till Translation* (Glendale, CA: Rose Publishing
        Company, 1943), 46-47, 62.
92.   Gundry, *The Church and the Tribulation*, 189.
93.   John F. Walvoord, *Daniel: The Key to Prophetic Revelation* (Chicago: Moody
        Press, 1971), 232.
94.   Gundry, *The Church and the Tribulation*, 192-193.
95.   Norman S. MacPherson, *Triumph Through Tribulation* (Otego, NY: Published by
        the Author, 1944), 41.*
96.   George E. Ladd, *The Blessed Hope* (Grand Rapids: Eerdmans, 1956), 165.*
97.   Gundry, *The Church and the Tribulation*, 146.
98.   Gerald B. Stanton, *Kept from the Hour* (Grand Rapids: Zondervan, 1956), 227.
99.   John F. Walvoord, *The Rapture Question* (Grand Rapids: Dunham, 1957), 154.
100.   David Brown, *The Four Gospels* (London: Banner of Truth Trust, 1969), 79.
101.   Warren W. Wiersbe, *Meet Your King* (Wheaton, IL: Victor Books, 1980), 82-83.
102.   MacPherson, *The Late Great Pre-Trib Rapture*, pp. 16-17, 67-80, and *The
        Unbelievable Pre-Trib Origin*, 15.
103.   William B. Riley, *The Evolution of the Kingdom*, rev. ed. (New York: The Book
        Stall, 1913), 167.*
104.   Gundry, *The Church and the Tribulation*, 200.
105.   Walvoord, *The Rapture Question*, 171.
106.   Norman B. Harrison, *The End: Re-Thinking the Revelation* (Minneapolis:
        Harrison Service, 1941), 111.
107.   Pentecost, *Things to Come*, 185.
108.   Harrison, *The End*, 74-75.
109.   J. F. Strombeck, *First the Rapture* (Moline, IL: Strombeck Agency, 1950), 109.
110.   Eugene Schuyler English, *Re-Thinking the Rapture* (Neptune, NJ: Loizeaux
        Brothers, 1954), 109.
111.   Henry A. Ironside, *Addresses on the First Epistle to the Corinthians* (New York:
        Loizeaux Brothers, 1938), 529.
112.   Pentecost, *Things to Come*, 193.
113.   Walvoord, *The Rapture Question*, 60.
114.   Ibid., 101.
115.   Trotter and Smith, *Eight Lectures on Prophecy*, 327, 330.
116.   Pentecost, *Things to Come*, 205.
117.   Strombeck, *First the Rapture*, 100-101.
118.   Pentecost, *Things to Come*, 205.
119.   Walvoord, *The Rapture Question*, 86-87.
120.   Pentecost, *Things to Come*, 201.
121.   Lewis Sperry Chafer, *Systematic Theology*. 4:47-53.
122.   Pentecost, *Things to Come*, 200.

123.   Scott, *Exposition of the Revelation*, 105.

124.   Leon Morris, *The Epistles of Paul to the Thessalonians: An Introduction and Commentary* (Grand Rapids: Eerdmans, 1956), 41-42.

125.   John F. Walvoord, *The Thessalonian Epistles* (Grand Rapids: Dunham, 1967), 85-86.

126.   Thiessen, *Lectures In Systematic Theology*, 450.

127.   Ryrie, *What You Should Know About the Rapture*, 59.

128.   Strombeck, *First the Rapture*, 117.

129.   C. I. Scofield, *Scofield Reference Bible*, 1349.

130.   Henry E. Dosker, "Day of the Lord" *The International Standard Bible Encyclopedia*, ed. James Orr (Grand Rapids: Eerdmans, 1939), 799.

131.   H. A. Ironside, "The Tribulation" *Brief Outline of Things to Come*, comp. Theodore H. Epp (Chicago: Moody Press, 1952), 41.*

132.   Pentecost, *Things to Come*, 235.

133.   Arthur W. Pink, *The Antichrist* (Swengel, PA: Bible Truth Depot, 1923), pp. 59-75 and Pentecost, *Things to Come*, 334.*

134.   Richard Chevevix Trench, *Synonyms of the New Testament* (Grand Rapids: Eerdmans, 1953; reprint of 1880 ninth ed.), 107-109.*

135.   Thiessen, *Lectures in Systematic Theology*, 466.

136.   Pentecost, *Things to Come*, 336-337.

137.   Thiessen, *Lectures In Systematic Theology*, 466.

138.   Ibid., 445.

139.   John F. Walvoord, "The Millennial Issue in Modern Theology" *Bibliotheca Sacra*, 106 (January, 1948), 44.*

140.   Strong, *Systematic Theology*, 1003.

141.   Chafer, *Major Bible Themes*, 280-281.

142.   Pentecost, *Things to Come*, 395.

143.   Leon Morris, "Resurrection" *The New Bible Dictionary*, ed. J. D. Douglas (Grand Rapids: Eerdmans, 1962), 1086.

144.   Morris, "Resurrection," 1088.

145.   Thiessen, *Lectures in Systematic Theology*, 492.

146.   Thiessen, *Lectures in Systematic Theology*, 496.

147.   Paul R. VanGorder, *The Judgments of God* (Grand Rapids: Radio Bible Class, 1972), 1.

148.   Pentecost, *Things to Come*, 412.

149.   *The New Scofield Reference Bible*, 1212.

150.   Harold Willmington, *Class Notes* (Lynchburg, VA: Liberty Bible Institute, n.d.).*

151.   Loraine Boettner, *The Millennium* (Philadelphia, PA: Presbyterian and Reformed Publishing Company, 1957), 14.

152. Floyd E. Hamilton, *The Basis of Millennial Faith* (Grand Rapids: Eerdmans, 1942), 139.

153. George Eldon Ladd, *Crucial Questions About the Kingdom of God* (Grand Rapids: Eerdmans, 1952), 141.

154. George N. H. Peters, *The Theocractic Kingdom* (New York: Funk & Wagnalls, 1884), 1:221.

155. H. A. Ironside, *Ezekiel the Prophet* (New York: Loizeaux Brothers, n.d.), 262.*

156. William R. Newell, *The Book of Revelation* (Chicago: Moody Press, 1935), 323.

157. Pentecost, *Things to Come*, 500.

158. James M. Gray, *Christian Worker's Commentary* (New York: Fleming H. Revell, 1915), 265-266.

159. Merrill F. Unger, "The Temple Vision of Ezekiel," *Bibliotheca Sacra* 106 (January, 1949): 57-64.

160. Allis, *Prophecy and the Church*, 248.

161. William Kelly, *Notes on Ezekiel* (London: G. Morrish), 236-237.

162. Pentecost, *Things to Come*, 524-527. Temple Drawing: G. R. Beasley-Murray, "Ezekiel" *The New Bible Commentary* Revised (London: InterVarsity Press, 1972), 683.

163. Jon E. Braun, *Whatever Happened to Hell?* (New York: Thomas Nelson Publishers, 1979), 11.

164. Fred Carl Kuehner, *Heaven or Hell?* (Washington, D. C.: *Christianity Today*, XII:19 (June 21, 1968), 24f.

165. Lewis Sperry Chafer, *Major Bible Themes*, 299.

166. Braun, 25.

167. William Elbert Munsey, *Eternal Retribution* (Wheaton, IL: Sword of the Lord Publishers, 1951), 55.

168. Francis Pieper, *Christian Dogmatics* (St. Louis: Concordia Publishing House, 1953), 3:548.

169. Chafer, *Major Bible Themes*, 297.

170. Kuehner, *Heaven or Hell?*.*

171. Harry Buis, *The Doctrine of Eternal Punishment* (Grand Rapids: Baker Book House, 1957), 12.

172. William G. T. Shedd, *The Doctrine of Endless Punishment* (New York: Charles Scribners Sons, 1887), 12. To prove his point, Shedd lists the following statements of Christ, and many others, "without note or comment upon them": Matthew 7:22-23; 10:28; 11:23; Mark 9:43-48; Luke 9:25; 12:9-10, 46; 16:22-23; John 5:28-29; 8:21.

173. Kuehner, *Heaven or Hell?*, 24D-24E.*

174. Thomas Walter Manson, *The Sayings of Jesus* (London: SCM Press, 1949), 107.

175.   Rudolph Bultmann, *Theology of the New Testament* (New York: Scribner, 1951-1955), 1:11.*

176.   J. Arthur Baird, *The Justice of God in the Teaching of Jesus* (Philadelphia: Westminster Press, 1963), 230.

177.   George P. Fisher, *Discourses In History and Theology* (New York: Scribners, 1880), 410.*

178.   Tertullian, *Apology*, 48.*

179.   Hippolytus of Rome, *On the Universe, Against the Greeks and Plato.**

180.   Cyprian of Carthage, *To Demetrianus*, 24.*

181.   John Chrysostom, *To Theodore after his Fall*, 1:10.*

182.   Dante Alighieri (1265-1321), *The Inferno.**

183.   Agobard of Lyons cited in *Early Medieval Theology*, trans. and ed. by George E. McCraken (Philadelphia: Westminster Press, 1951), 354.*

184.   Anselm of Canterbury, *Monolegion* 71, from Anselm of Canterbury, ed. and trans. by Jasper Hopkins and Herbert Richardson (Toronto: The Edwin Nellen Press, 1974), 80-81.*

185.   Thomas Aquinas, *The Catechetical Instruction of St. Thomas Aquinas*, trans. and commentary, Rev. Joseph B. Colling (New York: Joseph T. Wagner, 1939), 62.*

186.   John Hunt, *Contemporary Review* (April 1878).*

187.   Charles Hodge, *Systematic Theology* (New York: Scribners, Armstrong, and Co., 1872), 3:869.

188.   Jonathan Edwards, *Edward's Works* (New York: Burt Foundation, 1968), 6:452.*

189.   Cited by Braun, 128.

190.   Louis Berkhof, *Systematic Theology* (Grand Rapids: Eerdmans, 1941), 736.

191.   Hodge, *Systematic Theology*, 3:868.

192.   John A. T. Robinson, *But I Can't Believe*, 67-68.*

193.   Braun, 13.

194.   Augustus Hopkins Strong, *Systematic Theology*, 1033.

195.   Archibald Alexander Hodge, *Outlines of Theology* (London: Thomas Nelson and Sons, 1883), 580-81.

196.   James Orr, "Sheol" *The International Standard Bible Encyclopedia*, ed. James Orr (Grand Rapids: Eerdmans, 1939), 2761.

197.   D. K. Innes, "Hell" *The New Bible Dictionary*, ed. J. D. Douglas (Grand Rapids: Eerdmans, 1962), 518.

198.   Shedd, *Endless Punishment*, 34.

199.   Pentecost, *Things to Come*, 556.

200.   Braun, 141.

201.   Innes, "Hell," 518.

202.   Braun, 148.

203.   Geerhardus Vos, "Hades" *The International Standard Bible Encyclopedia*, ed. James Orr (Grand Rapids: Eerdmans, 1939), 1315.

204.   H. A. Ironside, *Addresses on the Gospel of Luke* (New York: Loizeaux Brothers, 1947), 510.

205.   Pohle, *Dr. C. I. Scofield's Question Box*, 43-44.

206.   Ethelbert W. Bullinger, *A Critical Lexicon and Concordance to the English and Greek New Testament* (London: Longmans, Green, & Company, 1924), 369.*

207.   Braun, 152.

208.   Bullinger, *Critical Lexicon and Concordance*, 370.

209.   Albert Barnes, *Notes on the New Testament Explanatory and Practical: James, Peter, John and Jude* (Grand Rapids: Baker Book House, 1949), 240.

210.   *Let God Be True*, rev. ed. (New York: Watchtower Bible and Tract Society, 1952), 96.

211.   William L. Pettingill, *The Christian Fundamentals* (Findlay, OH: Fundamental Truth Publishers, 1941), 63-64.*

212.   Geerhardus Vos, "Gehenna" *The International Standard Bible Encyclopedia*, ed. James Orr (Grand Rapids: Eerdmans, 1939), 1183.

213.   Innes, "Hell," 518.

214.   Vos, "Gehenna," 1183.

215.   Braun, 154.

216.   Archibald M'Caig, "Retribution" *The International Standard Bible Encyclopedia*, ed. James Orr (Grand Rapids: Eerdmans, 1939), 2570.

217.   Chafer, *Systematic Theology*, 4:429.

218.   M'Caig, "Retribution," 2570.

219.   James M. Stifler, *The Epistle to the Romans: A Commentary Logical and Historical* (Chicago: Moody Press, 1960), 38-39.

220.   M'Caig, "Retribution," 2571.

221.   William Elbert Munsey, *Eternal Retribution* (Murfreesboro, TN: Sword of the Lord Publishers, 1951), 66.

222.   James Orr, "Spirits in Prison" *The International Standard Bible Encyclopedia*, ed. James Orr (Grand Rapids: Eerdmans, 1939), 2457.

223.   Barnes, *Notes on the New Testament*, 179.

224.   Ibid., 240.

225.   Scott, *Exposition of the Revelation*, 396.

226.   Hal Lindsey, *There's a New World Coming: 'A Prophetic Odyssey'* (Santa Ana, CA: Vision House Publishers, 1973), 271.

227.   John R. Rice, *The Son of Man: A Verse-by-Verse Commentary on the Gospel According to Luke* (Murfreesboro, TN: Sword of the Lord Publishers, 1971), 316.

228.   David Brown, *The Four Gospels*, 277.

229. Henry E. Dosker, "Scourge, Scourging" *The International Standard Bible Encyclopedia*, ed. James Orr (Grand Rapids: Eerdmans, 1939), 2704.

230. Cited by Thomas Theodore Martin, *God's Plan with Men* (Fincastle, VA: Scripture Truth, n.d.), 30.

231. W. L. Walker, "Gnash" *The International Standard Bible Encyclopedia*, ed. James Orr (Grand Rapids: Eerdmans, 1939), 1239.

232. Charles Haddon Spurgeon, *The Treasury of David* (Lynchburg, VA: The Old-Time Gospel Hour, 1984), 5:19.*

233. Brown, *The Four Gospels*, 79.

234. Matthew Henry, *Commentary on the Whole Bible* (Old Tappan, NJ: Fleming H. Revell, n.d.), 5:105.

235. Scott, *Exposition of the Revelation*, 396, fnte.

236. Archibald Thomas Robertson, *Word Pictures in the New Testament* (New York: Harper & Brothers Publishers, 1933), 6:361.

237. F. Godet, *St. Paul's Epistle to the Romans* (New York: Funk & Wagnalls, 1883), 381.

238. John Murray, *The Epistle to the Romans: The English Text with Introduction, Exposition and Notes* (Grand Rapids: Eerdmans, 1965), 2:53, fnte 10.

239. J. D. Douglas, "Abyss" *The New Bible Dictionary*, ed. J. D. Douglas (Grand Rapids: Eerdmans, 1962), 8.

240. Robertson, *Word Pictures*, 1:65.

241. Alfred H. Joy, "Dark, Darkness" *The International Standard Bible Encyclopedia*, ed. James Orr (Grand Rapids: Eerdmans, 1939), 789.

242. Brown, *The Four Gospels*, 107.

243. Leon Morris, *The Epistles of Paul to the Thessalonians: An Introduction and Commentary* (Grand Rapids: Eerdmans, 1976), 119.*

244. Barnes, *Notes on the New Testament*, 2:118-119.*

245. Henry, *Commentary*, 5:760.

246. Robertson, *Word Pictures*, 1:346-347.

247. Alfred Ely Day, "Worm, Scarlet-Worm" *The International Standard Bible Encyclopedia*, ed. James Orr (Grand Rapids: Eerdmans, 1939), 3109.

248. Geerhardus Vos, "Lake of Fire" *The International Standard Bible Encyclopedia*, ed. James Orr (Grand Rapids: Eerdmans, 1939), 1822.

249. James Orr, "Unquenchable Fire" *The International Standard Bible Encyclopedia*, ed. James Orr (Grand Rapids: Eerdmans, 1939), 3038.

250. C. T. Schwarze, "The Bible and Science on the Everlasting Fire" *Bibliotheca Sacra*, 95 (January, 1938): 116.

251. Chafer, *Major Bible Themes*, 296.

252. Murray, *The Epistle to the Romans*, 1:35-36.

253.   William Evans, "Wrath" *The International Standard Bible Encyclopedia*, ed. James Orr (Grand Rapids: Eerdmans, 1939), 3113.

254.   Edward Fudge, "Putting Hell In Its Place" *Christianity Today* (6 August, 1976), 15.

255.   Emil Brunner, *Eternal Hope,* trans. By Harold Knight (Philadelphia: Westminster Press, 1954), 183.

256.   Kuehner, *Heaven or Hell?,* 24-h – 24-i.

257.   Moses Stuart, *Future Punishment,* 67.*

258.   Munsey, *Eternal Retribution,* 69-70.

259.   Archibald Alexander Hodge, *Outlines of Theology* (London: Thomas Nelson and Sons, 1883), 582.

260.   Kuehner, *Heaven or Hell?,* 24-m.

261.   *Let God Be True* (New York: Watchtower Bible and Tract Society), 77.

262.   *Just What Do You Mean, Born Again?* (Pasadena, CA: Ambassador College), 13-14.*

263.   Jess Stern, *The Sleeping Prophet* (Garden City, NY: Doubleday, 1967), 243.*

264.   Phillip J. Swihart, *Reincarnation, Edgar Cayce & The Bible* (Downers Grove, IL: InterVarsity Press, 1975), 19-20.

265.   Brunner, *Eternal Hope,* 182.

266.   John A. T. Robinson, "Universalism—Is It Heretical?" *Scottish Journal of Theology* 2:2 (June, 1949), 155.

267.   John Stuart Mill, *Three Essays on Religion,* 3rd ed. (London: Longmans, 1874), 113-114.

268.   Braun, *Whatever Happened to Hell?,* 37.

269.   Maurice Rawlings, *Beyond Death's Door* (Nashville: Thomas Nelson, 1978), 65-66.*

270.   J. E. M. Dawson, *Present-Day Problems* (London: Pickering and Inglis, 1940), 70-71.*

271.   John MacNeill, *Many Mansions: Sermons on the Future Life* (Toronto: McClelland and Stewart Publishers, 1926), 159.

272.   Barnes, *Notes on the New Testament: James to Jude,* 179.

273.   Innes, "Hell," 519.

274.   Thiessen, *Lectures in Systematic Theology,* 504-505.

275.   Lewis Sperry Chafer, *Major Bible Themes,* 301.

276.   William L. Pettingill, *The Christian Fundamentals* (Findlay, OH: Fundamental Truth Publishers, 1941), 61.*

277.   Ford C. Ottman, *The Unfolding of the Ages* (New York: Baker and Taylor, 1905), 458.

278.   William L. Pettingill, *Bible Doctrine Primer* (Findlay, OH: Fundamental Truth Publishers, 1941), 56.*

279. Augustus Hopkins Strong, *Systematic Theology*, 1032.
280. Archibald Alexander Hodge, *Outlines of Theology* (London: Thomas Nelson and Sons, 1883), 578.
281. Pettingill, *Bible Doctrine Primer*, pp. 59-61, *Is Heaven a Place?*, 8-11.*
282. Richard W. DeHaan, *The Heavenly Home* (Grand Rapids: Radio Bible Class, 1968), 16-17.
283. J. A. Seiss, *Lectures on the Apocalypse* (Philadelphia: Philadelphia School of the Bible, 1865), 3:371.
284. Strong, *Systematic Theology*, 1032-1033.
285. Chafer, *Major Bible Themes*, 304.
286. John MacNeill, *Many Mansions* (New York: Richard R. Smith, 1930), 197.
287. DeHaan, *The Heavenly Home*, 19.
288. Thiessen, *Lectures in Systematic Theology*, 517.
289. DeHaan, *The Heavenly Home*, 20.
290. John Ritchie, *Impending Great Events*, 110.
291. DeHaan, *The Heavenly Home*, 20-21.
292. Ibid., 21-22.
293. Ritchie, Impending Great Events, 111.
294. DeHaan, The Heavenly Home, 23.
295. Ritchie, Impending Great Events, 112.
296. D. L. Moody, Heaven (New York: Fleming H. Revell Company, 1887), 3-4, 30-31.*
297. DeHaan, The Heavenly Home, 25.
298. Moody, Heaven, 57.*
* Denotes page number(s) could not be verified.

BIBLIOGRAPHY

Adams, Jay E. *Competent to Counsel* (Grand Rapids: Baker Book House, 1979).

Agobard of Lyons cited in *Early Medieval Theology*, trans. and ed. by George E. McCraken (Philadelphia: Westminster Press, 1951).

Alighieri, Dante. (1265-1321), *The Inferno.*

Allen, Clifton J. *The Broadman Bible Commentary* Vol. 1 revised (Nashville, TN: Broadman Press, 1969).

Allis, Oswald T. *Prophecy and the Church* (Philadelphia: Presbyterian and Reformed Publishing Co., 1945).

Andrew. Jukes, *The Names of God in Holy Scripture* (Grand Rapids: Kregel Publications, 1967; reprint of 1888 edition).

Anselm of Canterbury, *Monolegion* 71, from Anselm of Canterbury, ed. and trans. by Jasper Hopkins and Herbert Richardson (Toronto: The Edwin Nellen Press, 1974).

Aquinas, Thomas. *The Catechetical Instruction of St. Thomas Aquinas*, trans. and commentary, Rev. Joseph B. Colling (New York: Joseph T. Wagner, 1939).

Arndt, William F. and F. Wilbur Gingrich. *A Greek-English Lexicon of the New Testament* (Chicago: The University of Chicago Press, 1957).

Augustine. *City of God*, Book XII.

Ayer, William Ward. "What It Has Cost the Church to Neglect the Bible's Prophetic Message" *The Sure Word of Prophecy*, ed. John W. Bradbury (New York: Fleming H. Revell Company, 1943).

Baillie, John. *The Idea of Revelation and Recent Thought* (New York: Columbia University Press, 1956).

Baird, J. Arthur. *The Justice of God in the Teaching of Jesus* (Philadelphia: Westminster Press, 1963).

Baker, Charles F. *A Dispensational Theology* (Grand Rapids: Grace Bible College Publications, 1972).

Bancroft, Emery H. *Elemental Theology: Doctrinal and Conservative* (Grand Rapids: Zondervan, 1960).

Barclay, William. *The Gospel of John* (Philadelphia: Westminster Press, 1956).

Barnes, Albert. *Notes on the New Testament, Matthew - Mark* (Grand Rapids: Baker Book House, 1949).

_____. *Notes on the New Testament Explanatory and Practical: James, Peter, John and Jude* (Grand Rapids: Baker Book House, 1949).

_____. *Notes on the New Testament,* 1 Corinthians, (Grand Rapids: Baker Book House, 1949).

Barnes, Charles Randall. *The People's Bible Encyclopedia* (Chicago: People's Publication Society, 1913).

Barnhouse, Donald Grey. "Chain of Glory," *Eternity*, Vol. 2, No. 17 (March 1958).

Barrett, C. K. *The Holy Spirit and the Gospel Tradition* (London: The Society for Promoting Christian Knowledge, 1947).

Barth, Karl *The Doctrine of the Word of God* (New York: 1936).

Bass, Clarence B. *Backgrounds to Dispensationalism: Its Historical Genesis and Ecclesiastical Implications* (Grand Rapids: Baker, 1978).

Bauer, Walter. *A Greek-English Lexicon of the New Testament*, trans. by William F. Arndt and F. Wilbur Gingrich (Chicago: The University of Chicago Press, 1957).

_____. *Orthodoxy and Heresy in Earliest Christianity*, ed. By Robert A. Kraft and Gerhard Krodel (Philadelphia: Fortress, 1934).

Bauslin, David H. "Preacher," *International Standard Bible Encyclopedia*.

Beal, R. S. "The Place of Prophecy in Preaching" in *Light for the World's Darkness*, ed. John W. Bradbury (New York: Loizeaux Brothers, Publishers, 1944).

Benjamin B. Warfield, "Revelation," *The International Standard Bible Encyclopedia*, ed. by James Orr (Grand Rapids: Eerdmans, 1939).

Berkhof, Hendrikus. "The Doctrine of the Holy Spirit," *The Annie Kinkead Warfield Lectures*, 1963-1964 (Richmond, Virginia: John Knox Press, 1964).

Berkhof, Louis. *Systematic Theology* (Grand Rapids: Eerdmans, 1932).

_____. *Systematic Theology* (Grand Rapids: Eerdmans, 1939).

_____. *Systematic Theology* (Grand Rapids: Eerdmans, 1941).

_____. *Systematic Theology* (Grand Rapids: Baker, 1951).

_____. *Systematic Theology* (Grand Rapids: Eerdmans, 1972).

_____. *Systematic Theology* (Grand Rapids: Eerdmans, 1976).

_____. *Systematic Theology* (Grand Rapids: Eerdmans, 1981).

Berkouwer, Gerri. Cornelius. *The Person of Christ* (Grand Rapids: Eerdmans, 1954).

_____. *Sin* (Grand Rapids: Eerdmans, 1971).

Bevan, L. D. "Offices of Christ," *The International Standard Bible Encyclopedia*.

Bietenhard, Hans. "Messenger," Colin Brown, ed. *Dictionary of New Testament Theology* Grand Rapids: Zondervan, 1975).

Blackwood, Andrew Watterson. *Doctrinal Preaching for Today: Case Studies of Bible Teachings* (New York: Abingdon Press, 1956).

Boettner, Loraine. *Studies in Theology* (Philadelphia: Presbyterian and Reformed, 1970).

_____. *The Millennium* (Philadelphia, PA: Presbyterian and Reformed Publishing Company, 1957).

_____. *The Reformed Doctrine of Predestination* (Grand Rapids: Eerdmans, 1932).

Boice, James Montgomery *Does Inerrancy Matter?* (Wheaton, IL: Tyndale, 1979).

Booth, John Nicholls. *The Quest for Preaching Power* (New York: MacMillan, 1943).

Borland, James A. *Christ in the Old Testament* (Chicago: Ross-shire: Christian Focus, 1999).

Bowman, John Wick. "The Bible and Modern Religions: II. Dispensationalism," *Interpretation* 10 (April, 1956).

Boyce, James Petigru. *Abstract of Systematic Theology* (Philadelphia: American Baptist Publication Society, 1887).

Boyer, James L. *For a World Like Ours: Studies in I Corinthians* (Winona Lake, IN: BMH Books, 1971).

Boys-Smith, E. P. "Mental Characteristics," *A Dictionary of Christ and the Gospels*, ed James Hastings (New York: Charles Scribner & Sons, 1906).

Bratcher, Robert. "Biblical Authority for the Church Today," *Christianity Today*, (May 29, 1981).

Braun, Jon E. *Whatever Happened to Hell?* (New York: Thomas Nelson Publishers, 1979).

Brooks, Phillips. *Lectures on Preaching* (Grand Rapids: Zondervan, n.d.).

Broomall John Wick, "The Bible and Modern Religions: II, Dispensationalism" *Interpretation* 10 (April, 1956).

Brown, David. *The Four Gospels: A Commentary, Critical, Experimental and Practical* (London: Banner of Truth Trust, 1969).

Brown, Francis S. R. Driver, and Charles A. Briggs. *A Hebrew and English Lexicon of the Old Testament* (Oxford: Clarendon Press, 1977).

Bruce, Alex. B. *The Expositor's Greek Testament* (Grand Rapids: Eerdmans, 1952).

_____. *The Humiliation of Christ* (Grand Rapids: Eerdmans, 1955).

Bruce, F. F. *The Books and the Parchments*, Third Rev. ed. (Westwood, NJ: Revell Co., 1963).

_____. *The Epistle of Paul to the Romans* (Grand Rapids: Eerdmans, 1963).

_____. *The Epistle to the Ephesians: A Verse-by-Verse Exposition* (Old Tappan, New Jersey: Fleming H. Revell Company, 1974).

Brunner, Emil. *Eternal Hope,* trans. By Harold Knight (Philadelphia: Westminster Press, 1954).

Büchsel, Friedrich. *Theological Dictionary of the New Testament* (Grand Rapids: Eerdmans, 1972).

_____. "*Theology Dictionary of the New Testament*, ed. G. Kittel (Grand Rapids: Eerdmans, 1974).

Buis, Harry. *The Doctrine of Eternal Punishment* (Grand Rapids: Baker Book House, 1957).

Bullinger, Ethelbert. W. *A Critical Lexicon and Concordance to the English and Greek New Testament* (London: Longmans, Green, & Company, 1924).

Bultmann, Rudolph. *Existence and Faith: Shorter Writings of Rudolf Bultmann*, ed. And trans. by Schubert M. Ogden (New York: Meridan Books, 1960).

_____. *Kerygma and Myth: A Theological Debate* (London: S.P.C.K., 1953).

_____. *Theology of the New Testament* (New York: Scribner, 1951-1955).

Bush, L. Russ and Tom J. Nettles. *Baptists and the Bible* (Chicago: Moody Press, 1980).

Buswell, J. Oliver. *A Systematic Theology of The Christian Religion* (Grand Rapids: Zondervan, 1962).

_____. *A Systematic Theology of the Christian Religion* (Grand Rapids: Zondervan, 1963).

_____. *A Systematic Theology of the Christian Religion* (Grand Rapids: Zondervan, 1969).

Byrum, Russell R. *Christian Theology* (Anderson, Indiana: Warner Press, 1976).

Calkins, Raymond. *The Social Message of the Book of Revelation* (New York: The Womans Press, 1920).

Calvin, John. *Commentary on a Harmony of the Evangelists Matthew, Mark, and Luke* (Calvin Translation Society, 1845).

_____. *Sermons on the Epistle to the Ephesians*, trans. Arthur Golding (Edinburgh: Banner of Truth Trust, 1973).

Chafer, Lewis Sperry. *Systematic Theology*, (Dallas: Dallas Seminary Press, 1948).

_____. "For Whom Did Christ Die?" *Bibliotheca Sacra* 137:548 (October-December 1980).

_____. *Systematic Theology* (Dallas: Dallas Seminary Press, 1962).

_____. "Inventing Heretics Through Misunderstanding," *Bibliotheca Sacra*, 102 (January, 1945).

_____. "The Olivet Discourse" *Light for the World's Darkness*, ed. John W. Bradbury (New York: Loizeaux Brothers, 1944).

_____. *Dispensationalism* (Dallas: Dallas Seminary Press, 1936).

_____. *Major Bible Themes* (Chicago: Moody Press, 1926).

_____. *Systematic Theology* (Dallas: Dallas Seminary Press, 1947).

_____. *Systematic Theology* (Dallas: Dallas Seminary Press, 1948).

_____. *Systematic Theology* (Dallas: Dallas Seminary Press, 1957).

_____. *Systematic Theology* (Dallas: Dallas Theological Seminary Press, 1975).

_____. *Salvation* (New York: Charles C. Cook, 1917).

Chambers, Oswald. *Biblical Psychology* (London: Simpkin Marshall Ltd., 1912).

Charnock, Stephen. *The Existence and Attributes of God* (Minneapolis, MN: Klock & Klock, 1977).

Chrysostom, John *To Theodore after his Fall*

Clark, Sterling. *The Unpardonable Sin - What Is it?* (Waterford, Ontario: The Fundamental Baptist Mission, 1978).

Clarke, William Newton. *An Outline of Christian Theology* (New York: Charles Scribner's Sons, 1898).

Cohn, Joseph Hoffman. "Is God Through with the Jews?" *The Sure Word of Prophecy*, ed. John W. Bradbury (New York: Fleming H. Revell Company, 1943).

Cooper David L., *Messiah: His Historical Appearance* (Los Angeles: Biblical Research Society, 1958).

Cremer, Herman. *Biblico-Theological Lexicon of New Testament Greek*, trans. Wm. Urwick (Edinburgh: T. & T. Clark, 1895).

_____. *Biblico-Theological Lexicon of New Testament Greek* (New York: Charles Scribner's Sons, 1895).

Curtis, Olin Alfred. *The Christian Faith* (Grand Rapids: Kregel Publishing Company, 1905, reprinted 1971).

Cyprian of Carthage, *To Demetrianus*

_____. *Morality*

Dabney, Robert L. *Lectures in Systematic Theology* (Grand Rapids: Zondervan, 1975).

Dana, H. E. and Julius R. Mantey. *A Manual Grammar of the Greek New Testament* (Toronto: The Macmillan Company, 1955).

Danielou, Jean. *The Angels and Their Mission: According to the Fathers of the Church* (New York: Newman Press, 1976).

Dawson, J. E. M. *Present-Day Problems* (London: Pickering & Inglis, 1940).

Day, Alfred Ely. "Worm, Scarlet-Worm" *The International Standard Bible Encyclopedia*, ed. James Orr (Grand Rapids: Eerdmans, 1939).

DeHaan, Richard W. *The Heavenly Home* (Grand Rapids: Radio Bible Class, 1968).

Delling, Gerhard. *Theological Dictionary of the New Testament*, ed. G. Friedrich (Grand Rapids: Eerdmans, 1975).

DeMent, Byron. "Repentance" *The International Standard Bible Encyclopedia*, ed. James Orr (Grand Rapids: Eerdmans, 1939).

Denney, James. *Jesus and the Gospel* (London: Hodder and Stoughton, 1908).

Dick, John. *Lectures on Theology* (New York: Robert Carter and Brothers, 1878).

Dickason, C. Fred. *Angels, Elect and Evil* (Chicago: Moody Press, 1975).

Dickson, William P. *St. Paul's Use of the Terms Flesh and Spirit* (Glasgow: James Maclehose & Sons, 1883).

Doctrinal Statement of Dallas Theological Seminary, Article XX.*

Dosker, Henry E. "Day of the Lord" *The International Standard Bible Encyclopedia*, ed. James Orr (Grand Rapids: Eerdmans, 1939).

_____. "Scourge, Scourging" *The International Standard Bible Encyclopedia*, ed. James Orr (Grand Rapids: Eerdmans, 1939).

Douglas, J. D. "Abyss" *The New Bible Dictionary*, ed. J. D. Douglas (Grand Rapids: Eerdmans, 1962).

Earle, Ralph. *How We Got Our Bible* (Grand Rapids: Baker).

Easton, Burton Scott "Grace" *The International Standard Bible Encyclopedia*, ed. James Orr (Grand Rapids: Eerdmans, 1939).

_____. "Kenosis," *The International Standard Bible Encyclopedia* (Grand Rapids: Eerdmans, 1939).

_____. "Salvation" *The International Standard Bible Encyclopedia*, ed. James Orr (Grand Rapids: Eerdmans, 1974).

Edwards, Jonathan. *Edward's Works* (New York: Burt Foundation, 1968).

Ella E. Pohle, *Dr. C. I. Scofield's Question Box* (Chicago: Moody Press, 1917).

Emerson, Wallace. *Outline of Psychology* (Wheaton: Van Kampen Press, 1953).

English, Eugene Schuyler. *Re-Thinking the Rapture* (Neptune, NJ: Loizeaux Brothers, 1954).

Erickson, Millard J. *Christian Theology* (Grand Rapids: Baker Book House, 1984).

_____. *Salvation: God's Amazing Plan* (Wheaton, IL: Victor Books, 1978).

Evans, Christopher F. *Resurrection and the New Testament* (Naperville: Allenson, 1970).

Evans, William. "Wrath" *The International Standard Bible Encyclopedia*, ed. James Orr (Grand Rapids: Eerdmans, 1939).

_____. *The Great Doctrines of the Bible* (Chicago, Moody Press, 1912).

Faulkner, John Alfred. "Justification" *The International Standard Bible Encyclopedia*, ed. James Orr (Grand Rapids: Eerdmans, 1939, 1783.

Fausset, A. R. *Bible Encyclopedia and Dictionary* (Grand Rapids: Zondervan, n.d.).

Feinberg, Charles Lee. "What Israel Means to God" *The Sure Word of Prophecy*, ed. John W. Bradbury (New York: Fleming H. Revell Company, 1943).

Feinberg, John S. *Theology of Man, Sin, and Angels* THEO 625 (class lecture, Liberty Baptist Seminary, Spring 1983).

Felder, Hilarin. *Christ and the Critics*, trans. by John L. Stoddard (London: Burns Oates and Washburn Ltd., 1924).

Finney, Charles Grandison *Oberlin Evangelist*, 2:1.

_____. *Lectures on Revivals of Religion* (Old Tappan, NJ: Fleming H. Revell Company, n.d.).

_____. *Finney's Systematic Theology*, ed. And abridged by J. H. Fairchild (Minneapolis, MN: Bethany Fellowship, Inc. 1976).

Fisher, George P. *Discourses In History and Theology* (New York: Scribners, 1880).

Fitch, William. *The Ministry of the Holy Spirit* (Grand Rapids: Zondervan, 1974).

Fitzwater, P. B. *Christian Theology: A Systematic Presentation* (Grand Rapids: Eerdmans, 1948).

_____. *Christian Theology: A Systematic Presentation* (Grand Rapids: Eerdmans, 1956), 19.

Fletcher, M. Scott. *The Psychology of the New Testament* (London: Hodder and Stoughton, 1912).

Flint, Robert. *Anti-Theistic Theories*, 4th ed. (Edinburgh and London: Wm. Blackwood and Sons, 1899).

Flynn, Leslie B. *19 Gifts of the Spirit* (Wheaton: Victor Books, 1974).

Franz Delitzsch, *A System of Biblical Psychology* (Edinburgh: T. & T. Clark & Sons, 1879).

Fudge, Edward. "Putting Hell In Its Place" *Christianity Today* (6 August, 1976).

Fuller, Reginald H. *The Formation of the Resurrection Narratives* (New York: Macmillan and Co., 1971).

Furness, Malcolm. *Vital Doctrines of the Faith* (Grand Rapids: Eerdmans, 1974).

Gaebelein, A. C. *The Gospel of Matthew: An Exposition* (New York: Publication Office, Our Hope, 1910).

_____. *The Angels of God* (Grand Rapids: Baker Book House, 1969).

Gaussen, L. *Theopneustia: The Plenary Inspiration of the Holy Scriptures.* Rev. ed. trans. By David Scott (Chicago: Bible Institute Colportage Ass'n., n.d.).

Geisler, Norman L. *Christ: The Theme of the Bible* (Chicago: Moody Press, 1969).

_____. and William E. Nix. *A General Introduction to the Bible* (Chicago: Moody Press, 1968).

Getz, Gene A. *Sharpening the Focus of the Church* (Chicago: Moody Press, 1974).

Gill, John. *A Body of Divinity* (Grand Rapids: Sovereign Grace Publishers, 1971).

Godet, Frederick Louis. *St. Paul's Epistle to the Romans* (Edinburgh: T. & T. Clark, 1890).

_____. *St. Paul's Epistle to the Romans* (New York: Funk & Wagnalls, 1883).

_____. *Commentary on the Gospel of John with an Historical and Critical Introduction*, trans. Timothy Dwight (New York: Funk and Wagnalls Company, 1886).

Gordon, Adoniram J. *Ministry of the Spirit* (Valley Forge, PA: Judson Press, 1949).

Gordon, M. R. "Regeneration" *The New Bible Dictionary*, ed. J. D. Douglas (Grand Rapids: Eerdmans, 1962).

Gray, James M. *Christian Worker's Commentary* (New York: Fleming H. Revell, 1915).

_____. "Doubt," in *The International Standard Bible Encyclopedia*, James Orr, general editor, (Grand Rapids: Eerdmans, 1939).

Green, Hollis L. *Why Churches Die* (Minneapolis: Bethany Fellowship, 1972).

Green, Michael. *I Believe In the Holy Spirit* (London: Hodder and Stoughton, 1980).

Green, W. H. *Pentateuch Vindicated*, cited by A. A. Hodge, *Outlines of Theology* (London: Thomas Nelson, 1879).

Gundry, Robert H. *The Church and the Tribulation* (Grand Rapids: Zondervan, 1973).

Hamilton, Floyd E. *The Basis of Millennial Faith* (Grand Rapids: Eerdmans, 1942).

Hanson, George. *The Resurrection and the Life* (New York: Fleming H. Revell, 1911).

Harrison, Everett F. *The Christian Doctrine of the Resurrection*, unpublished manuscript, p. 56, cited by L. S. Chafer, *Systematic Theology*.

Harrison, Norman B. *The End: Re-Thinking the Revelation* (Minneapolis: Harrison Service, 1941).

Hendricksen, W. *More Than Conquerors: An Interpretation of the Book of Revelation* (Grand Rapids: Baker Book House, 1947).

Hendry, George S. *The Holy Spirit In Christian Theology* (Philadelphia: The Westminster Press, 1956).

Henry Clarence Thiessen. *Introductory Lectures In Systematic Theology* (Grand Rapids: Eerdmans, 1949).

Henry, Matthew. *Commentary on the Whole Bible* (Old Tappan, NJ: Fleming H. Revell, n.d.).

Heppe, Heinrich. *Reformed Dogmatics: Set Out and Illustrated from the Sources*, trans. G. T. Thomson (London: George Allen and Uwin, 1950).

Hesselgrave, David J. *Planting Churches Cross-Culturally* (Grand Rapids: Baker Book House, 1980).

Hippolytus of Rome, *On the Universe, Against the Greeks and Plato*.

Hoch, Jr., Carl B. "The Significance of the *Syn*-Compounds for Jew-Gentile Relationships in the Body of Christ," *Journal of the Evangelical Theological Society*, 25:2 (June, 1982).

Hodge, Archibald Alexander. *Outlines of Theology* (New York: Robert Carter and Brothers, 1867).

_____. *Outlines of Theology* (London: Thomas Nelson and Sons, 1883).

_____. *Outlines of Theology* (London: Thomas Nelson, 1896).

_____. *Outlines of Theology*, Rev. ed. (Grand Rapids: Zondervan; reprint of 1879 edition).

Hodge, Charles. *Systematic Theology* (New York: Scribners, Armstrong, and Co., 1872).

_____. *Systematic Theology* (New York: Scribner, Armstrong, and Co., 1874).

_____. *Systematic Theology* (Grand Rapids: Eerdmans, 1975).

_____. *A Commentary on Romans* (London: The Banner of Truth Trust, 1972).

_____. *Systematic Theology* (Grand Rapids: Eerdmans, 1972).

_____. *Systematic Theology* (Grand Rapids: Eerdmans, 1975).

_____. *Systematic Theology* (Grand Rapids: Eerdmans, 1975).

Hoekema, Anthony A. *Holy Spirit Baptism* (Grand Rapids: Eerdmans, 1972).

Hoeksema, Herman. *Reformed Dogmatics* (Grand Rapids: Reformed Free Pub. Assoc., 1966).

Horton, T. C. and Charles E. Hurlburt *The Wonderful Names of Our Wonderful Lord* (Los Angeles: Grant Publishing House, 1925).

Howard, Clinton N. "Jesus—Son of Joseph or Son of God?" *The Sword of the Lord* 48 (December 25, 1981).

Howitt, F. E. "The Lord's Coming the Key to the Scriptures" in *The Coming and Kingdom of Christ* ed. James M. Gray (Chicago: Bible Institute Colportage Association, 1914).

Hull, William E. "Shall We Call the Bible Infallible?" *The Baptist Program* (December 1970).

Hunt, John *Contemporary Review* (April 1878).

Hunter, Adam B. "Effect of the Doctrine of Our Lord's Return," *The Sure Word of Prophecy*, ed. John W. Bradbury (New York: Fleming H. Revell Company, 1943).

Idem. *The Christian's Handbook of Manuscript Evidence* (Pensacola, FL: Pensacola Bible Institute, 1976).

Innes, D. K. "Hell" *The New Bible Dictionary*, ed. J. D. Douglas (Grand Rapids: Eerdmans, 1962).

Inrig, Gary *Life in His Body* (Wheaton: Harold Shaw, 1975).

Ironside, Harry A. "The Tribulation" *Brief Outline of Things to Come*, comp. Theodore H. Epp (Chicago: Moody Press, 1952).

_____. *Addresses on the Gospel of Luke* (New York: Loizeaux Brothers, 1947).

_____. *Ezekiel the Prophet* (New York: Loizeaux Brothers, n.d.).

_____. *Holiness: The False and the True* (New York: Loizeaux Brothers, Publishers, n.d.).

_____. *Praying in the Holy Spirit* (New York: Loizeaux Brothers, 1946).

_____. "Why the Church Will Not Go Through the Great Tribulation" *The Sure Word of Prophecy*, ed. John W. Bradbury (New York: Fleming H. Revell Company, 1943).

_____. *Lectures on the Book of Revelation* (New York: Loizeaux Brothers, 1920).

_____. *Addresses on the First Epistle to the Corinthians* (New York: Loizeaux Brothers, 1938).

Jackson, Paul R. *The Doctrine and Administration of the Church*, rev. ed. (Schaumburg, IL: Regular Baptist Press, 1980).

James Oliver Buswell, *A Systematic Theology of Christian Religion* (Grand Rapids: Zondervan, 1962).

Jastrow Jr., Morris. *The Study of Religion* (London: Walter Scott, Ltd., 1902).

Jennings, F. C. *Satan: His Person, Work, Place and Destiny* (Neptune, NJ: Loizeaux Brothers, 1975).

Jensen, Irving L. *Revelation: A Self-Study Guide* (Chicago: Moody Press, 1971).

Jewett, Paul K. "Kenosis," *Wycliffe Bible Encyclopedia* (Chicago: Moody 1975).

Johnson, Jr., Samuel Lewis. "A Survey of Biblical Psychology in the Epistle to the Romans" (unpublished Doctoral dissertation, Dallas Theological Seminary, Dallas, Texas, 1949).

Jones, E. Stanley. *The Way* (Nashville: Abingdon Press, 1946).

Jones, William. *Is God A White Racist?* (Garden City, NJ: Anchor/Doubleday Books, 1973).

Josephus, Flavius. *Wars of the Jews* (Massachusetts: Harvard University Press, 1976).

Josh McDowell, *Evidence That Demands a Verdict* (San Bernardino, CA: Campus Crusade for Christ International, 1972).

Joy, Alfred H. "Dark, Darkness" *The International Standard Bible Encyclopedia*, ed. James Orr (Grand Rapids: Eerdmans, 1939).

Just What Do You Mean, Born Again? (Pasadena, CA: Ambassador College).

Keil, C. F. and F. Delitzsch. *Biblical Commentary on the Old Testament*, trans. James Martin (Grand Rapids: Eerdmans, 1951).

_____. *Commentary on the Old Testament* (Grand Rapids: Eerdmans, 1975).

Kelly, William. *Lectures on the Galatians*, cited by Howard W. Ferrin, "Is the Church Ever Called Israel?" *The Sure Word of Prophecy*, ed. John W. Bradbury (New York: Fleming H. Revell Company, 1943).

_____. *Notes on Ezekiel* (London: G. Morrish).

Kent, Jr., Homer A. *Ephesians: The Glory of the Church* (Chicago: Moody Press, 1971).

Kroll, Woodrow Michael. "The Revelation" *Liberty Commentary on the New Testament*, ed. Edward E. Hindson and Woodrow Michael Kroll (Lynchburg, Virginia: Liberty Press, 1978).

Kuehner, Fred Carl. *Heaven or Hell?* (Washington, D. C.: *Christianity Today*, XII:19 (June 21, 1968).

Kuen, Alfred. *I Will Build My Church*, trans. Ruby Lindblad (Chicago: Moody Press, 1971).

Kunneth, Walter. *The Theology of the Resurrection* (London: S.C.M., 1965).

Kuyper, Abraham. *The Work of the Holy Spirit*, trans, Henri DeVries (New York: Funk & Wagnalls Company, 1900).

L. Harold De Wolf, *Present Trends in Christian Thought* (New York: Association Press, 1960).

Ladd, George E. *The Blessed Hope* (Grand Rapids: Eerdmans, 1956).

_____. *Crucial Questions About the Kingdom of God* (Grand Rapids: Eerdmans, 1952).

_____. *The New Testament and Criticism* (Grand Rapids: Eerdmans, 1967).

Laidlaw, J. "Heart," *A Dictionary of the Bible*, ed. James Hastings (NY: Charles Scribner's Sons, 1909).

Lake, Kirsopp. *The Resurrection of Jesus Christ* (London: Williams and Norgate, 1912).

Lanser Catechism Westminster (Confession of faith of the Presbyterian Church in the United States, 1965).

Larkin, Clarence. *The Spirit World* (Philadelphia: Clarence Larkin Estate, 1921).

Lawlor, George Lawrence. *Almah—Virgin or Young Woman?* (Des Planes, Illinois: Regular Baptist Press, 1973).

_____. *The Epistle of Jude* (United States: Presbyterian and Reformed, 1972).

Leen, Edward. *The Holy Ghost and His Work in Souls* (New York: Sheed & Ward, 1937).

Leisegang, H. "Pneuma Hagion," *Studies in Early Christianity*, ed. S. J. Case.

Lenski, R. C. H. *The Interpretation of St. Matthew's Gospel* (Ohio: Wartburg Press, 1943)

_____. *The Interpretation of St. Paul's First and Second Epistle to the Corinthians* (Columbus, OH: The Wartburg Press, 1937).

_____. *The Interpretation of The Epistles of St. Peter, St. John, and St. Jude* (Minneapolis: Augsburg, 1968).

Let God Be True. rev. ed. (New York: Watchtower Bible and Tract Society, 1952).

Lewis, C. S. *Mere Christianity* (New York: MacMillan Company, 1952).

Lewis, Gordon R. *Decide for Yourself: A Theological Workbook* (Downers Grove, IL: InterVarsity, 1970).

Liddon, H. P. *Explanatory Analysis of St. Paul's Epistle to the Romans* (Minneapolis: James & Klock, 1899, reprinted 1977).

Lightfoot, J. B. *St. Paul's Epistle to the Philippians* (London: Macmillan and Co., 1869).

Lindsell, Harold *God's Incomparable Word* (Wheaton, IL: Victor Books, 1977).

_____. *The Battle for the Bible* (Grand Rapids: Zondervan, 1976).

Lindsey, Hal. *Satan Is Alive and Well on Planet Earth* (Grand Rapids: Zondervan, 1972).

_____. *There's a New World Coming: 'A Prophetic Odyssey'* (Santa Ana, CA: Vision House Publishers, 1973).

Lloyd M. Perry, *Biblical Preaching for Today's World* (Chicago: Moody Press, 1973).

Lloyd-Jones, D. Martyn. *Conversions Psychological and Spiritual* (London: InterVarsity Press, 1959).

Lockyer, Herbert *The Mystery and Ministry of Angels* (Grand Rapids: Eerdmans, 1958).

Lowndes, Arthur. "Bishop," *International Standard Bible Encyclopedia* (Grand Rapids: Eerdmans, 1939).

M'Caig, Archibald. "Retribution" *The International Standard Bible Encyclopedia*, ed. James Orr (Grand Rapids: Eerdmans, 1939).

MacBeth, John. *Notes on The Thirty-Nine Articles, Historical and Explanatory* (Dublin: Wm. McGee, 1894).

_____. *Notes on the Thirty-Nine Articles*. Historical and Explanatory (Dublin: The Association for Promoting Christian Knowledge, 1906).

MacNeill, John. *Many Mansions: Sermons on the Future Life* (Toronto: McClelland and Stewart Publishers, 1926).

_____. *Many Mansions* (New York: Richard R. Smith, 1930).

MacPherson, Dave. *The Late Great Pre-Trib Rapture* (Kansas City, MO: Heart of America Bible Society, 1974).

_____. *Triumph Through Tribulation* (Otego, NY: Published by the Author, 1944).

_____. *The Late Great Pre-Trib Rapture*, pp. 16-17, 67-80, and *The Unbelievable Pre-Trib Origin*.

Manson, Thomas Walter. *The Sayings of Jesus* (London: SCM Press, 1949).

Manton, Thomas. *An Exposition of Jude* (Delaware: Sovereign Grace Publishers, 1972).

Marais, J. I. "Soul," in *The International Standard Bible Encyclopedia* (Grand Rapids: Eerdmans, 1939).

Marsh, F. E. *Emblems of the Holy Spirit* (London: Pickering & Inglis, 1923).

Martin, Thomas Theodore. *God's Plan with Men* (Fincastle, VA: Scripture Truth, n.d.).

Matthew Henry, *Commentary on the Whole Bible* (Old Tappan, NJ: Fleming H. Revell Company, n.d.).

Mauro, Philip. *Looking for the Savior* (London: Samuel E. Roberts, Publishers, n.d.).

_____. *The Gospel of the Kingdom* (Boston: Hamilton Brothers, 1928).

McClintock John, and James Strong, "Elders," *Cyclopedia of Biblical Theological and Ecclesiastical Literature*, (New York: Harper and Brothers, 1883).

McConkey, James H. *The Three-fold Secret of the Holy Spirit* (Chicago: Moody Press, 1897).

McGavran, Donald A. *Understanding Church Growth* (Grand Rapids: Eerdmans, 1970).

McLuhan, Marshall. *The Medium is the Message* (New York:: Bantam Books, 1967).

Metzger, Bruce M. *The Test of the New Testament*, Second Edition (New York: Oxford University Press, 1968).

Mill, John Stuart. *Three Essays on Religion*, 3rd ed. (London: Longmans, 1874).

Montefiore, C. F. *The Synoptic Gospels* (London: MacMillan and Co., Ltd., 1909).

Moody, Barry M. *Repent and Believe: The Baptist Experience in Maritime Canada* (Hantsport, N.S.: Lancelot Press Limited, 1980).

Moody, D. L. Heaven (New York: Fleming H. Revell Company, 1887).

Moody, William R. *The Life of Dwight L. Moody*, (Murfreesboro, TN: Sword of the Lord Publishers; reprinted from 1900 edition).

Moorehead, William G. "Type," *The International Standard Bible Encyclopedia*, ed. by James Orr (Grand Rapids: Eerdmans, 1939).

Morris, Leon L. "Faith" *The New Bible Dictionary*, ed. J. D. Douglas (Grand Rapids: Eerdmans, 1962).

_____. "Propitiation," *Baker's Dictionary of Theology*, ed. Everett F. Harrison (Grand Rapids: Baker Book House).

_____. *The Epistles of Paul to the Thessalonians: An Introduction and Commentary* (Grand Rapids: Eerdmans, 1956).

_____. *The Epistles of Paul to the Thessalonians: An Introduction and Commentary* (Grand Rapids: Eerdmans, 1976).

_____. *The Gospel According to John*, ed. F. F. Bruce, *The New International Commentary on the New Testament* (Grand Rapids: Eerdmans, 1971).

_____. "Resurrection" *The New Bible Dictionary*, ed. J. D. Douglas (Grand Rapids: Eerdmans, 1962).

Moulton, James Hope and George Milligan. *The Vocabulary of the Greek Testament* (Grand Rapids: Eerdmans, 1972).

Mullins, Edgar Young "Holy Spirit" *The International Standard Bible Encyclopedia*, ed. James Orr (Grand Rapids: Eerdmans, 1939).

_____. *Why Is Christianity True?* (Chicago: Christian Culture Press, 1905).

_____. *The Christian Religion in Its Doctrinal Expression* (Philadelphia: Roger Williams Press, 1917).

Munsey, William Elbert. *Eternal Retribution* (Murfreesboro, TN: Sword of the Lord Publishers, 1951).

Murray, Andrew. *Absolute Surrender* (London: Marshall, Morgan & Scott, Ltd., n.d.).

Murray, John. *Redemption Accomplished and Applied* (Grand Rapids: Eerdmans, 1951).

_____. *Redemption Accomplished and Applied* (Grand Rapids: Eerdmans, 1982).

_____. *The Epistle to the Romans: The English Text with Introduction, Exposition and Notes* (Grand Rapids: Eerdmans, 1965).

_____. *The Epistle to the Romans: The English Text with Introduction, Exposition and Notes* (Grand Rapids: Eerdmans, 1965).

Murray, John. *The Epistles to the Romans*, in *The New International Commentary on the New Testament* (Grand Rapids: Eerdmans, 1973).

_____. *The Normal Christian Life* (Fort Washington, PA: Christian Literature Crusade, 1973).

Neve, J. L. *A History of Christian Thought* (Philadelphia: The Muhlenberg Press, 1946).

Nevius, John *Demon Possession* (Grand Rapids: Kregel, 1973).

Newell, William R. *The Book of Revelation* (Chicago: Moody Press, 1935).

Nicholas of Cusa. *The Vision of God*, trans. by Emma G. Salter (New York: E. P. Dutton & Sons, 1928).

Niebuhr, Reinhold. *Nature and Destiny of Man* (New York: Charles Scribner's Sons, 1943).

Ockenga, Harold J. "Will the Church Go Through the Tribulation? Yes" *Christian Life*, February 1955.

Orr, James. "Sheol" *The International Standard Bible Encyclopedia*, ed. James Orr (Grand Rapids: Eerdmans, 1939).

_____. "Spirits in Prison" *The International Standard Bible Encyclopedia*, ed. James Orr (Grand Rapids: Eerdmans, 1939).

_____. "Unquenchable Fire" *The International Standard Bible Encyclopedia*, ed. James Orr (Grand Rapids: Eerdmans, 1939).

Ottman, Ford C. *The Unfolding of the Ages* (New York: Baker and Taylor, 1905).

Pache, René. *The Inspiration and Authority of Scripture* (Chicago: Moody, 1976).

_____. *The Person and Work of the Holy Spirit*, trans. J. D. Emerson (Chicago: Moody Press, 1954).

Packer, J. I. "Justification" *The New Bible Dictionary*, ed. J. D. Douglas (Grand Rapids: Eerdmans, 1962).

Palmer, Edwin H. *The Holy Spirit* (Grand Rapids: Baker Book House, 1958).

Palmer, F. H. "Adoption" *The New Bible Dictionary*, ed. J. D. Douglas (Grand Rapids: Eerdmans, 1962).

Patrick, George T. W. *Introduction to Philosophy*, Revised ed. (New York: Houghton Mifflin, 1952).

Payne, J. Barton. *The Theology of the Older Testament* (Grand Rapids: Zondervan, 1962).

Pember, G. H. *Earth's Earliest Ages* (Grand Rapids: Kregel Publishers, 1975).

Pentecost, J. Dwight. *Things to Come*, 524-527. Temple Drawing: G. R. Beasley-Murray, "Ezekiel" *The New Bible Commentary* Revised (London: InterVarsity Press, 1972).

_____. *Things to Come: A Study in Biblical Eschatology* (Grand Rapids: Zondervan, 1958).

Peters, George N. H. *The Theocractic Kingdom* (New York: Funk & Wagnalls, 1884).

Peters, John Leland. *Christian Perfection and American Methodism* (New York: Abingdon Press, 1956).

Pettingill, William L. *Bible Doctrine Primer* (Findlay, OH: Fundamental Truth Publishers, 1941).

_____. *Bible Questions Answered* (Findlay, OH: Fundamental Truth Publishers, n.d.).

_____. *The Christian Fundamentals* (Findlay, OH: Fundamental Truth Publishers, 1941).

Phillips, J. B. *Letters to Young Churches* (London: MacMillan Company, n.d.).

_____. *Your God Is Too Small* (New York: The MacMillan Company, 1972).

Pick, Bernard. "Theophany," *Cyclopedia of Biblical, Theological, and Ecclesiastical Literature*, ed. John McClintock and James Strong (Grand Rapids: Baker Book House, 1970).

Pieper, Francis. *Christian Dogmatics* (St. Louis: Concordia Publishing House, 1953).

Pietsch, W. E. "The Jew After the Rapture" *The Sure Word of Prophecy*, ed. John W. Bradbury (New York: Fleming H. Revell Company, 1943).

Pink, Arthur Walkington. *The Antichrist* (Swengel, PA: Bible Truth Depot, 1923), pp. 59-75 and Pentecost, *Things to Come*.

_____. *Exposition of the Gospel of John* (Grand Rapids: Zondervan, 1974).

_____. *The Divine Inspiration of the Bible* (Grand Rapids: Guardian Press, 1976).

Pinnock, Clark. "On the Third Day," in *Jesus of Nazareth: Savior and Lord*, ed. by C. F. Henry (Grand Rapids: Eerdmans, 1966).

Pohle, Ella E. comp., *Dr. C. I. Scofield's Question Box* (Chicago: Moody Press, n.d.).

Poiret, Pierre. *L'Oeconomie Divine* (Amsterdam, 1687). English trans. published in London.

Pratt, Dwight M. "Old Man," in *The International Standard Bible Encyclopedia*

Prophecy, ed. John W. Bradbury (New York: Fleming H. Revell Company, 1943).Pusey, Edward Bouverie. *What Is of Faith as to Everlasting Punishment?* 2nd Ed., (Oxford: J. Parker, 1880).

Radmacher, Earl D. *The Nature of the Church* (Portland, OR: Western Baptist Press, 1972).

_____. *What the Church Is All About* (Chicago: Moody Press, 1978).

Ramm, Bernard *Protestant Biblical Interpretation: A Textbook in Hermeneutics*, 3rd rev. ed. (Grand Rapids: Baker Book House, 1970).

_____. *The Witness of the Spirit: An Essay on the Contemporary Relevance of the Internal Witness of the Holy Spirit* (Grand Rapids: Eerdmans, 1959).

Rauschenbush, Walter. *A Theology for the Social Gospel*, (NY: Abingdon, 1917).

Rawlings, Maurice. *Beyond Death's Door* (Nashville: Thomas Nelson, 1978).

Rayan, Samuel. *Breath of Fire: The Holy Spirit: The Heart of the Christian Gospel* (London: Geoffrey Chapman, 1979).

Rees, Thomas. "Adoption" *The International Standard Bible Encyclopedia*, ed. James Orr (Grand Rapids: Eerdmans, 1939).

_____. "Dogma," *The International Standard Bible Encyclopedia* (Grand Rapids: Eerdmans, 1974).

_____. "God", in *The International Standard Bible Encyclopedia* (Grand Rapids: Eerdmans, 1974).

Reese, Alexander. *The Approaching Advent of Christ* (London: Marshall, Morgan & Scott, 1937).

Reimarus, Herman Samuel. *The Goal of Jesus and His Disciples*, trans. by G. W. Buchanan (Leiden: Brill, 1970).

Rice, John R. *Our God-breathed Book—the Bible* (Murfreesboro, TN: Sword of the Lord Publishers, 1969).

_____. *The Son of Man: A Verse-by-Verse Commentary on the Gospel According to Luke* (Murfreesboro, TN: Sword of the Lord Publishers, 1971).

Riley, William B. *The Evolution of the Kingdom*, rev. ed. (New York: The Book Stall, 1913).

Riss, Richard. *The Evidence for the Resurrection of Jesus Christ* (Minnesota: Bethany Fellowship, 1977).

Ritchie, John. *Impending Great Events*, 2nd ed. (London: Pickering & Inglis Ltd., 1939).

Robertson, Archibald Thomas. T. *Word Pictures in the New Testament* (New York: R. R. Smith, Inc., 1930).

_____. and W. Davis. *A New Short Grammar of the Greek Testament* (New York: Harper and Brothers, 1933).

_____. *Word Pictures in the New Testament* (New York: Harper & Brothers Publishers, 1933).

Robinson, John A. T. "Universalism—Is It Heretical?" *Scottish Journal of Theology* 2:2 (June, 1949).

Robinson, William. *Our Lord* (Grand Rapids: Eerdmans, 1949).

Rogers, W. H. "The Second Coming of Christ—Personal and Premillennial" *Light for the World's Darkness*, ed. John W. Bradbury (New York: Loizeaux Brothers, Publishers, 1944).

Rose, George L. *Tribulation Till Translation* (Glendale, CA: Rose Publishing Company, 1943).

Ruckman, Peter S. "Using 'Original' Greek to Prevent Young People From Learning Bible Truth," *Bible Believers' Bulletin* 4 (March 1982).

Ryrie, Charles Caldwell. *Biblical Theology of the New Testament* (Chicago: Moody Press, 1959).

_____. *Dispensationalism Today* (Chicago: Moody Press, 1965).

_____. *What You Should Know About the Rapture* (Chicago: Moody Press, 1981).

_____. *The Basis of the Premillennial Faith* (New Jersey: Loizeaux Brothers, 1981).

S. S. Smalley, "Conscience," *New Bible Dictionary Revised*, ed. by J. D. Douglas (London: Lute Varsity Press, 1973).

Sale-Harrison, L. "The Future Confederation of the Ten-Nation Empire" *The Sure Word of*

Samuel Ridout, *The Person and Work of the Holy Spirit* (New York: Loizeaux Brothers, Bible Truth Depot, 1945), 30.

Sanders, J. Oswald *Satan Is No Myth* (Chicago: Moody Press, 1975).

Sargant, William. *Battle for the Mind*, revised (Baltimore: Penguin, 1961).

Saucy, Robert L. *The Bible: Breathed from God* (Wheaton, IL: Victor Books), 1978).

_____. *The Church in God's Program* (Chicago: Moody Press, 1972).

Scanlan, Michael & Randall J. Cirner. *Deliverance from Evil Spirits: A Weapon for Spiritual Warfare* (Ann Arbor: Servant Book Publications, 1980).

Schaff, Philip. *Creeds of Christendom*, (New York: Harper & Row, 1919)

_____. *Creeds of Christendom*, 3 Volumes (Grand Rapids: Baker, 1977).

Scheffrahn, Karl and Henry Kreyssler. *Jesus of Nazareth: Who Did He Claim to Be?* (Dallas: Pat Booth, 1968).

Schonfield, Hugh. *The Passover Plot* (New York: Bernard Gels, 1965).

Schultz, Thomas. "The Doctrine of the Person of Christ with an Emphasis upon the Hypostatic Union" (Dallas: Dallas Theological Seminary, May 1962).

Schwarze, C. T. "The Bible and Science on the Everlasting Fire" *Bibliotheca Sacra*, 95 (January, 1938).

Scofield, C. I. *The Scofield Reference Bible* (New York: Oxford University Press, 1945).

_____. *The New Scofield Reference Bible* (New York: Oxford, 1967).

Scott, Walter. *Exposition of the Revelation of Jesus Christ and Prophetic Outlines* (London: Pickering & Inglis, n.d.).

_____. *Exposition of the Revelation of Jesus Christ and Prophetic Outlines* (London: Pickering & Inglis, n.d.).

Scougal, Henry. *The Life of God in the Soul of Man* (Philadelphia: Westminster Press, 1948).

Scroggie, W. Graham. *Prophecy and History* (London: Morgan & Scott, 1915).

Seiss, J. A. *Lectures on the Apocalypse* (Philadelphia: Philadelphia School of the Bible, 1865).

Shedd, William G. T. *A History of Christian Doctrine*, 2 vols. (New York: Charles Scribner & Co., 1868).

_____. *Dogmatic Theology* (Nashville: Thomas Nelson, 1980).

_____. *Dogmatic Theology*, 3 vols. (Nashville: Thomas Nelson, 1980).

_____. *The Doctrine of Endless Punishment* (New York: Charles Scribners Sons, 1887).

_____. *A History of Christian Doctrine* (New York: Charles Scribner's Sons, 1889).

Simpson, A. B. *The Holy Spirit or Power from on High: An Unfolding of the Doctrine of the Holy Spirit in the Old and New Testament* (Harrisburg, Pennsylvania: Christian Publications Inc., n.d.).

Smith, Oswald J. *The Enduement of Power* (London: Marshall, Morgan & Scott, 1974).

Smith, Wilbur. *The Incomparable Book* (Minneapolis: Beacon Publications, 1961).

Snyder, Howard A. *The Problem of Wine Skins*: Church Structure in a Technological Age (Downers Grove: InterVarsity Press, 1976).

Spencer, Duane Edward. *TULIP: The Five Points of Calvinism in the Light of Scripture* (Grand Rapids: Baker, 1979).

Spurgeon, Charles Haddon. *Baptismal Regeneration* (Pasadena, Texas: Pilgrim Publications, n.d.).

_____. *The Treasury of David* (Lynchburg, VA: The Old-Time Gospel Hour, 1984).

_____. *Twelve Sermons on the Holy Spirit,* (London: Marshall, Morgan & Scott, Ltd., n.d.).

Stalker, James. "Conscience," *The International Standard Bible Encyclopedia*, ed. James Orr (Grand Rapids: Eerdmans, 1939).

Stanton, Gerald B. *Kept from the Hour* (Grand Rapids: Zondervan, 1956).

Starr, Timothy. *Church Planting—Always in Season* (Canada: Timothy Starr, 1978).

Stern, Jess. *The Sleeping Prophet* (Garden City, NY: Doubleday, 1967).

Stevens, Charles H. "How Shall We Interpret the Bible?" *The Sure Word of Prophecy*, ed. John W. Bradbury (New York: Fleming H. Revell Company, 1943).

Stevens, William Wilson. *Doctrines of the Christian Religion* (Grand Rapids: Eerdmans, 1967).

_____. *Doctrines of the Christian Religion* (Grand Rapids: Eerdmans, 1972).

Stevenson, Herbert F. *Titles of the Triune God* (Westwood, NJ: Fleming H. Revell Co., 1956).

Stifler, James M. *The Epistle to the Romans: A Commentary Logical and Historical* (Chicago: Moody Press, 1960).

Scott, John R. W. *Baptism and Fullness* (Downers Grove: InterVarsity Press, 1964).

_____. *Guard the Gospel: The Message of 2 Timothy* (London: InterVarsity Press, 1973).

Stringer, J. H. "Grace" *The New Bible Dictionary*, ed. J. D. Douglas (Grand Rapids: Eerdmans, 1977), 491.

Strombeck, J. F. *First the Rapture* (Moline, IL: Strombeck Agency, 1950).

Strong, Augustus H. *Systematic Theology* (New Jersey: Fleming H. Revell Co., 1907).

_____. *Systematic Theology* (Valley Forge, PA: Judson Press, 1907).

_____. *Systematic Theology: A Compendium Designed for the Use of Theological Students* (Old Tappan, NJ: Revell, 1976).

Strong, Augustus. *Systematic Theology* (New Jersey: Fleming H. Revell Co., 1907).

_____. *Systematic Theology: A Compendium Designed for the Use of Theological Students* (Old Tappan, NJ: Fleming H. Revell Company, 1970).

_____. *Systematic Theology* (New Jersey: Fleming Revell Co., 1975).

Sunday, William Ashley. *Wonderful And Other Sermons* (Grand Rapids: Zondervan, n.d.).

Surburg, Raymond F. *How Dependable Is the Bible?* (New York: Lippincott Company, 1972).

Sweet, Louis Matthews. "Virgin Birth of Jesus Christ," *The International Standard Bible Encyclopedia.*

Swete, Henry Barclay. *The Holy Spirit in the New Testament: A Study of Primitive Christian Teaching* (London: MacMillan and Co., Limited, 1910).

Swihart, Phillip J. *Reincarnation, Edgar Cayce & The Bible* (Downers Grove, IL: InterVarsity Press, 1975).

Tasker, R. V. G. *The Gospel According to St. John*, ed. R. V. G. Tasker, *The Tyndale New Testament Commentaries* (Grand Rapids: Eerdmans, 1960).

Tenney, Merrill C. *John: The Gospel of Belief* (Grand Rapids: Eerdmans, 1948).

_____. *New Testament Survey* (Grand Rapids: Eerdmans, 1961).

Thayer, Joseph Henry *Greek-English Lexicon of The New Testament* (Grand Rapids: Zondervan, 1972).

_____. *A Greek-English Lexicon of the New Testament*, translated, revised and Enlarged (New York: American Book Co., 1889), s.v., *charisma*; Colin Brown, *The New International Dictionary of New Testament Theology*, 3 vol. (Exeter, U.K.: Paternoster Press, Ltd., 1978).

The Statement of Fundamental Truths of the Assemblies of God, Article 8.

Thiessen, Henry Clarence. *Introduction to the New Testament* (Grand Rapids: Eerdmans, 1943).

_____. *Introductory Lectures in Systematic Theology* (Grand Rapids: Eerdmans, 1949).

_____. *Introductory Lectures in Systematic Theology* (Grand Rapids: Eerdmans, 1951).

_____. *Lectures in Systematic Theology* (Grand Rapids: Eerdmans, 1947).

_____. *Lectures in Systematic Theology* (Grand Rapids: Eerdmans, 1951).

_____. *Lectures in Systematic Theology*, rev. Vernon D. Doerksen (Grand Rapids: Eerdmans, 1979).

Thomson, Alexander. *Did Jesus Rise From the Dead?* (Grand Rapids: Zondervan, 1940).

Tippett, A. R. *Church Growth and the Word of God* (Grand Rapids: Eerdmans, 1970).

Torrey, R. A. *What the Bible Teaches* (New York: Revell Publishing Company, 1898).

_____. *What the Bible Teaches* (New York: Fleming H. Revell, 1933).

Towns, Elmer L. *Is the Day of the Denomination Dead?* (Nashville: Thomas Nelson, 1973)

_____. *The Successful Sunday School and Teachers Guidebook* (Carol Stream, Illinois: Creation House, 1980).

_____. *What the Faith Is All About* (Wheaton, IL: Tyndale House Publishers, 1983).

_____. and Roberta L. Groff. *Successful Ministry to the Mentally Retarded* (Moody: Chicago, 1972).

_____. and Jerry Falwell. *Church Aflame* (Nashville: Impact Books, 1971).

Tozer, A. W. *The Divine Conquest* (Old Tappan, New Jersey: Fleming H. Revell Company, 1950).

_____. *The Knowledge of the Holy: The Attributes of God: Their Meaning in the Christian Life* (San Francisco: Harper & Row, 1961).

_____. *The Root of the Righteous* (Harrisburg, PA: Christian Publications, 1955).

Trench, Richard Chevevix. *Synonyms of the New Testament* (Grand Rapids: Eerdmans, 1953; reprint of 1880 ninth ed.).

Trotter W. and T. Smith. *Eight Lectures on Prophecy from Short-Hand Notes* (New York: Loizeaux Brothers, n.d.).

Tylor, Edward Burnett. *Religion in Primitive Culture* (New York: Putnam, 1920).

Unger, Merrill E. *Biblical Demonology* (Illinois: Scripture Press, 1963).

_____. *Demons in the World Today* (Wheaton: Tyndale House, 1971).

Unger, Merrill F. "The Temple Vision of Ezekiel," *Bibliotheca Sacra* 106 (January, 1949).

VanGorder, Paul R. *The Judgments of God* (Grand Rapids: Radio Bible Class, 1972).

Vaughan, W. Curtis. *The Letter of the Ephesians* (Nashville, TN: Convention Press, 1963).

Vincent, Marvin R. *Word Studies in the New Testament*, 3 vols. (Grand Rapids: Eerdmans, 1946).

_____. *Word Studies in the New Testament* (Grand Rapids: Eerdmans, 1973).

Vincent, Marvin. *Word Studies in the New Testament* (New York: Charles Scribner's Sons, 1907).

Vine, W. E. *An Expository Dictionary of New Testament Words* (London, England: Oliphants, Ltd., 1940).

Vos, Geerhardus. *Biblical Theology: Old and New Testaments* (Grand Rapids: Eerdmans, 1948).

_____. "Gehenna" *The International Standard Bible Encyclopedia*, ed. James Orr (Grand Rapids: Eerdmans, 1939).

_____. "Hades" *The International Standard Bible Encyclopedia*, ed. James Orr (Grand Rapids: Eerdmans, 1939).

_____. "Lake of Fire" *The International Standard Bible Encyclopedia*, ed. James Orr (Grand Rapids: Eerdmans, 1939).

Walker, W. L. "Gnash" *The International Standard Bible Encyclopedia*, ed. James Orr (Grand Rapids: Eerdmans, 1939).

Walters, G. "Holy Spirit," *The New Bible Dictionary Revised*, ed. J. D. Douglas, et. al. (Grand Rapids: Eerdmans, 1977).

_____. "Salvation" *The New Bible Dictionary*, ed. J. D. Douglas (Grand Rapids: Eerdmans, 1977).

Walvoord, John F. "The Millennial Issue in Modern Theology" *Bibliotheca Sacra*, 106 (January, 1948).

_____. *Daniel: The Key to Prophetic Revelation* (Chicago: Moody Press, 1971).

_____. *Jesus Christ Our Lord* (Chicago: Moody, 1969).

_____. *Matthew: Thy Kingdom Come* (Chicago: Moody Press, 1974).

_____. *The Holy Spirit* (Wheaton: Van Kampen Press, 1954).

_____. *The Holy Spirit at Work Today* (Lincoln, Nebraska: Back to the Bible Broadcast, 1973).

_____. *The Holy Spirit: A Comprehensive Study of the Person and Work of the Holy Spirit* (Wheaton: Van Kampen Press, Inc., 1954).

_____. *The Rapture Question* (Grand Rapids: Dunham, 1957).

_____. *The Thessalonian Epistles* (Grand Rapids: Dunham, 1967).

Warfield, Benjamin B. *Limited Inspiration* (Grand Rapids: Baker Book House, 1961).

_____. *Studies in Theology* (New York: Oxford University Press, 1932).

Watson, David. *I Believe in The Church* (Grand Rapids: Eerdmans, 1978).

Watson, Richard. *Theological Institutes*, II, 14-1115, cited by Lewis Sperry Chafer, *Systematic Theology* (Dallas: Dallas Seminary Press, 1975).

Waugh, Thomas. *When Jesus Comes* (London: Charles H. Kelly, 1901).

Wemp, C. Sumner. *Teaching from the Tabernacle* (Chicago: Moody Press, 1976).

Wesley, John. *A Plain Account of Christian Perfectionism*, ed. Thomas S. Kepler (NY: World Publishing, 1954).

Westcott, Brooke Foss and Fenton John Anthony Hort. *The New Testament in The Original Greek* (Cambridge and London: MacMillan, 1889).

Westminster Confession of Faith, cited by William Cutson Stevens, *Doctrines of the Christian Religion* (Grand Rapids: Eerdmans, 1972).

Westminster Larger Catechism, Question 67 (Richmond, VA: John Knox Press, n.d.).

Wiersbe, Warren W. *Meet Your King* (Wheaton, IL: Victor Books, 1980).

Willmington, Harold L. *Class Notes* (Lynchburg, VA: Liberty Bible Institute, n.d.).

_____. *The Doctrine of the Father* (Lynchburg, VA: By the author, 1977).

_____. *Willmington's Guide to the Bible* (Wheaton: 1981).

Young, E. J. *Thy Word Is Truth* (Grand Rapids: Eerdmans, 1957).

GLOSSARY

The number(s) at the end of each Glossary entry indicate(s) the page(s) on which the subject is introduced and/or discussed.

-A-

Conversion – Human side of regeneration. – Man's response to the message
of the Gospel whereby he understands the nature of Christ's atonement,
he feels guilt from conviction and love to God, and his will responds to
the offer of salvation so that God converts him and gives him eternal life . 447

Conscience – The inner agent that makes a person aware of the morality of 597,
his desires or actions... 604

Conviction – The Holy Spirit works in a sinner's heart to make him aware of
his sin, that Jesus is God's standard of righteousness, and that Christ's
death on the cross paid the judgment for sin 292

-D-

Deacon – An office in the church (Lit. servant) 691

Death – First death is at the end of physical life on earth, or separation of a
person's body and spirit. Second death includes eternal separation from 503,
God (began at the fall of Adam) 713

Decree of God – God's plan by which He created, controls, sustains, and
takes responsibility for His creation and His creatures, including their
salvation, nurturing, rewarding and/or punishing within the
predetermined limits of His nature 136

Demons – Fallen angels who rebelled against God and were cast out of the
presence of God. – Beings who are the emissaries of Satan to carry out
his diabolical plans. – They possess tremendous intellectual ability, and
are reprobate, evil having no opportunity of repentance or salvation........ 389

Demon Possession – (Lit. demonizing). – Occurs when God permits demons
to embody a person and control his mind or body – is the culmination of
a volitional rejection of God and a volitional yielding to Satan and his
demons 407

Depravity – (See Total Depravity)

Dichotomy – The basic composition of man, a two-part being (Body and
soul) 595

Doctrinal Faith – A statement of faith or a written confession of what a
person believes concerning the person of God and His words 667

-E-

Elder – (Lit. aged man). – A technical term for a pastor of a local church –
describing especially his qualification of maturity 681

Eternality – God is not limited by time (the sequence of events), has no
beginning, and will have no end (contrary to or other than "time").......... 149

Evangelism – The communication of the Gospel in an understandable manner
and motivating him to respond 695

-F-

Faith – Accepting what God has promised in the Bible and acting upon it 454

Faith (Doctrine) – (See Doctrinal Faith)..

Faith (Gift of) – Spiritual gift the Holy Spirit bestows on men for service
whereby the recipient exercises faith to overcome a problem and/or
accomplish a task for God... 317

Faith (Saving) – An experiential encounter with Jesus Christ whereby the
person exercises his intellect to know the Gospel, his emotions are stirred
by conviction of sin and love to God, and his will responds in belief 454

Paradise – A modern day general reference to heaven. – A biblical reference to the place of departed dead in the Old Testament. – A synonym of Abraham's bosom 819

Pastor – (Lit. shepherd). – A technical expression for the human leader of a church. – (Synonym: bishop or elder).. 681

Personal Sin – That which is committed by a person (as opposed to the sin nature and imputed sin) - and may be an act or attitude, a sin of commission or of omission.. 532, 546

Postmillennial – The belief-system that presupposes the continual moral improvement of society under the influence of the church until a millennial kingdom would be established on earth as the world lives in peace. – Christ returns at the end of this millennium 720

Preacher – One who publicly proclaims the Gospel............................... 687

Premillennial – The belief-system that holds that Christ will return to earth and set up a literal, earthly kingdom as promised 722

Predestinate – (Lit. to mark off or choose). – God chooses those who will participate in His plan of salvation and extends it to all to respond in faith 428

Propitiation – Christ satisfied the demands of God's offended holiness by His death 220

Priesthood of Believers – Every Christian has direct access to God through Jesus Christ 648, 664

Priest – A divinely chosen appointed person to transact with God on man's behalf 648

Prophecy – A representation of God to people, 1) for telling and communicating God's message, 2) foretelling, predicting the future, and 3) forth-telling, announcing judgment on sin 725

Preexistence – Jesus Christ existed before His virgin birth at a point of history.. 179

-R-

Rapture – (Lit. to be caught up). – The bodily return of Jesus Christ at the end of the Church Age for the saved; both dead and alive; to take them to heaven, translate them into resurrected bodies, and give them a heavenly home 753

Reconciliation – The results of the death of Christ that makes man savable because God looks favorably on him because the wrath of God has been propitiated... 222

Redemption – (Lit. to purchase). – The work of the Holy Spirit whereby believers are given God's life and God's nature and made a part of the family of God. – Occurring at the moment of conversion, it lasts for eternity – making the person capable of doing the "righteous things" required by God. – Makes possible his sanctification 217

Religion – Commonly refers to a set of beliefs, attitudes, and practices expressed in worship of God.. 7

Repentance – (Lit. change one's mind). – A change of mind relation to one's actions or attitudes, rather than a change of character or nature. It may reflect itself in sorrow or remorse 451

Special Revelation – The self-revelation of God through Scripture, finalized
in Jesus Christ, and relates to God's plan of salvation for men 31, 34
Spirit – The life-principle within man that give an incorporeal aspect to his
nature and is related to man's heavenly life 587
Spiritual Gift – An ability given to a Christian by the Holy Spirit to serve
God. – A person receives spiritual gifts at salvation which he must
develop for better service.. 306
Systematic Theology – The collecting, arranging, comparing, exhibiting, and
defending of all facts from any and every source, concerning God and
His works, especially as focused in the Scriptures 15

-T-

Temptation – Solicitation to evil 207,
404

Testimony– Christians verbally sharing what they have seen, heard, and
experienced in Jesus Christ; their lives reflecting the inner reality of their
faith.. 235
Theology – (Lit. the study of God). – The study or belief of God and His
relationship to the world and man 1
Total Depravity – Sin has influenced every aspect of man and there is 427,
nothing a person can do to save himself or gain merit before the Lord...... 501
Transgression – Overstepping or breaking the law............................... 539
Tribulation – Seven years of unparalleled trouble at the end of the Church
Age directed at Israel, the physical earth, and those living during this
period. – Characterized by the wrath of God and the presence of Satan.
– The last three and one half years are an intense time of suffering and is
called the Great Tribulation.. 755
Trichotomy – The belief that man is a three-part being (body, soul, and spirit) 589
Trinity – While God is only one divine nature, there are three persons called
Father, Son, and Holy Ghost, who are equal in nature, distinct in person
and subordinate in duties 144
Tritheism – The belief in the existence of three gods. – Not the same as
"Trinity".. 109

-U-

Universalism – Claims that all men are born the children of God, hence
denies the necessity of Christ dying for sin. – Also, believes there is no
eternal punishment for sin, hence there is no need for salvation.............. 150

-V-

Virgin Birth – Begins with the supernatural conception of Jesus Christ in the
womb of Mary without the seed of man. – The miraculous birth was
verified by the statement that she was a virgin, had not had sexual
relations with a man 184

-W-

Word of God – The record of God's self-revelation to man and the
communication of Good News to people at their point of need, as such, it
is rational and logical. – The inspired Word of God is the ultimate
revelation of Jesus Christ in the incarnate Word of God...................... 45
Work of God – (See Decree of God)

PERSON INDEX

SCRIPTURE INDEX

NEW TESTAMENT